W9-BVB-079

EMPIRE CITY

New York Through the Centuries

EMPIRE CITY

New York Through the Centuries

Edited by Kenneth T. Jackson and David S. Dunbar

COLUMBIA UNIVERSITY PRESS | NEW YORK

A Giniger Book

Columbia University Press gratefully acknowledges assistance from Furthermore Grants in Publishing, a program of the J. M. Kaplan Fund, in the publication of this book.

COLUMBIA UNIVERSITY PRESS
Publishers Since 1893
New York   Chichester, West Sussex

Library of Congress Cataloging-in-Publication Data
Empire city : New York through the centuries / edited by Kenneth T. Jackson and David S. Dunbar.
p. cm.
Includes index.
ISBN 0–231–10908–3 (cloth)
1. New York (N.Y.)—History—Sources. 2. New York (N.Y.)—Description and travel—Sources. 3. New York (N.Y.)—Literature collections. 4. American literature—New York (State)—New York. I. Jackson, Kenneth T. II. Dunbar, David S.

F128 .E47 2002
974.7′1—dc21   2002067463

This book is copublished by the K. S. Giniger Company, Inc.,
250 W. 57th St., Suite 414, New York, NY 10107.

Today, I should say—defiant of cynics and pessimists, and with full knowledge of all their exceptions—an appreciative and perceptive study of the current humanity of New York gives the directest proof yet of successful democracy, and of the solution of that paradox, the eligibility of the free and fully developed individual with the paramount aggregate.

—Walt Whitman, *Specimen Days* (1882)

For Barbara

and

For Doug, Walker, and Nicki

CONTENTS

PART 4. WORLD CITY (1898–1948) 397

PREFACE

New York is a city of immigrants and migrants, and as a result, one's arrival takes on a special significance. Everyone remembers the moment when they saw New York City for the first time; the excitement of the arrival is palpable. Whether it was pulling into the dingy bus station at Port Authority off Times Square; circling the majestic island before landing at La Guardia or JFK (or, as it was previously known, Idlewild); emerging into the magnificent caverns of the old Penn Station or Grand Central Terminal; or driving across the shimmering steel of the George Washington Bridge from the west, the city of superlatives is startling and arresting. Part of that arrival is the anticipation of the unexpected and the possible. It is what Nick Carraway feels when he drives over the Queensboro (59th Street) Bridge with Gatsby from Long Island, the feeling that "anything can happen now that we've slid over this bridge." One's arrival is like looking through a window into a new land where you see things you have never seen before. But the eyes of the city are focused firmly on its future, not on its history, and as a result, it subscribes to what the economist Joseph Schumpeter has called "creative destruction." New York is constantly remaking and reinventing itself, both in its physical structures and in its population.

However, longtime residents of the city engage in the experience of repeatedly coming to see the city from a new perspective as well. That can be the literal disequilibrium of turning a corner onto a street one has never walked on before or of emerging from a different subway exit in a familiar place such as Union Square in Manhattan or Grand Army Plaza in Brooklyn to encounter that moment of spatial disorientation that allows the resident to see the familiar scene from a new angle.

The dynamism of New York demands that you see yourself from a new angle as well. In that case, the city acts not as a window but as a mirror. The city is constantly testing its inhabitants to see what they are made of with the promise that, as Frank Sinatra crooned, "if I can make it there, I can make it anywhere." New York always holds out the possibility of the reinvention of the self to achieve one's aspirations; it allows you to plumb the depths of your most authentic being, to see both the city itself and your own self in new and original ways. Because New York acts as both a window onto the new and a mirror into the once familiar, it is the most exciting city in the world.

Gotham is also a vast and varied city. It encompasses no fewer than five hundred distinct neighborhoods; two hundred separate ethnic groups; and many thousands of schools, churches, and private businesses. In this book we have aimed to capture four centuries of the city's history through political documents, poetry, short stories, regional reports, public speeches, memoirs, and excerpts from novels. The task of searching through so much material was both thrilling and daunting, and we ultimately pulled together sufficient potential entries to produce a four-volume anthology. We avoided the temptation to be exhaustive, however, knowing that we could never be comprehensive, and we eliminated dozens of pieces that we wanted to include.

Although we undertook this project with humility, we wound up exercising a substantial editorial voice. The general introduction attempts to enumerate the characteristics that make New York distinctive, and it also explores the ways in which those characteristics have combined to produce the dynamism that is life in Gotham. Similarly, the five section introductions supply overviews of important or, in some cases, overlooked events and people that helped to define the city in each historical era. Finally, the headnotes for each of the 158 individual entries attempt not only to give interesting background information about the author but also to explore themes mentioned in the document that follows. In short, we make a claim about what makes New York City the special place it has always been.

Cities can be like individual people in their unique psychological makeup and history, as one can infer in New York's case from the simple observation of its founding as a Dutch outpost designed to make money and its preeminence as the world financial capital since 1917. And that makeup can best be explored by listening to the city's voices in all of their forms. A great story speaks not only to its audience but to itself as well, and Gotham's own greatness results in part because of its willingness to engage in this kind of discourse. Therefore, *Empire City* is designed to be read not only as an account of the city as it has presented itself to the world but also as the record of a city in dialogue with itself. We believe this is the best way to capture the dynamism of the world's most exciting metropolis.

To accomplish the first goal, we have arranged the selections chronologically. But to accomplish the second, the reader must be alert to the fact that the selections are consciously chosen to speak to one another. Some of those conversations are more obvious than others and are even alluded to in the headnotes that precede each selection. For example, Cynthia Ozick's "The Synthetic Sublime" can be read as her half-century-later answer to E. B. White's classic 1948 essay, *Here Is New York*. Less obvious to most readers will be the juxtaposition of Charles Dickens's account of his journey through the Five Points section of Lower Manhattan in the 1840s and Jack Newfield's description of the Bedford-Stuyvesant section of 1960s Brooklyn in his homage to Robert Kennedy. Finally, the original frame for this book was the account of the first sighting by the explorer Henry Hudson, a white man, of the Upper Bay, the river that came to bear his name, and the island of Manhattan, and that of Junot Diaz as a Dominican boy arriving at John F. Kennedy Airport and seeing New York for the first time. The expectations of what New York might be for each of them in the future speaks volumes about the power of the city to attract people for a myriad of motives. Although the events of September 11, 2001, necessitated a new ending to this volume, John Avlon's essay "The Resilient City" simply refocused our framing on another aspect of New York's approach to the future.

Empire City can be read with attention to particular themes as well. For example, one of the preeminent features of life in New York is its extremism, most particularly, the gap between wealth and poverty that runs as a thread throughout the city's history. Readers might compare the accounts of the "high life" in the late nineteenth century depicted in Edith Wharton's *Age of Innocence* and Ward McAllister's "A Glimpse of High Society" with former homeless crack addict Lee Stringer's drugged "Walking Tour" of a very different Upper East Side than the one in which Wharton and McAllister lived. Stringer's tour, of course, would have taken him almost directly past the building where Leonard Bernstein was hosting a cocktail party for the Black Panthers as glimpsed through Tom Wolfe's hilarious "Radical Chic." Or perhaps they might wonder what nighttime "vice-buster" Anthony Comstock might have made of the nocturnal "low life" journeys of Jack Kerouac in the 1960s and Jay McInerney in the 1980s. Yet if one chose to read Comstock's account of policing New York's streets at night in comparison to Marcus Laffey's "The Midnight Tour: Working the Edgar Allen Poe Beat in the Bronx," one might come to equally interesting but vastly different observations. The combinations, comparisons, and juxtapositions of the different selections are endless, like the city itself.

Part of the delight and joy of putting this anthology together has been to see it as a jigsaw puzzle that does not yield a single definitive picture at the end. One could think of it as an older person's "choose your own adventure" book or a CD-ROM that leads you toward one conclusion if you make one choice but toward a different and equally valid end if you make a different choice. Nothing would seem to capture the visitor's or the resident's experience of New York City better than the act of creating infinite pathways through the city's text. Our hope is that the reader's experience of returning again and again to the text in different combinations will match the pleasure we had in collecting and selecting the entries.

Because this volume does not fit into established academic disciplines and is interdisciplinary in nature, we were able to select entries that captured prominent New York City icons and to see them through a variety of different lenses. For example, the Brooklyn Bridge is revealed in startlingly different lights in Lewis Mumford's essay chronicling his transcendent experience of walking across the bridge in a March twilight, John Dos Passos's fictional account from *Manhattan Transfer,* John Tierney's contemporary understanding of the bridge and its effects on the consolidation of Brooklyn and Manhattan in 1898 from his *New York Times* piece, and the only surviving first-hand account of a "sandhog" working on the construction of the bridge from Frank Harris's autobiography. And the space that the bridge occupies, arguably a part of the effect of the bridge itself, is memorably captured in Walt Whitman's poem "Crossing Brooklyn Ferry."

But if putting this anthology together was in part like creating a fluid jigsaw puzzle, at times it also resembled a treasure hunt. One visit to the New York City archives on a blustery January day yielded the discovery, tucked away in an unlabeled manila folder, of Robert Moses's "Remarks on the Groundbreaking at Lincoln Center" in 1959. To choose only one entry to capture the essence of this author was a daunting task in itself, but that short speech, with its use of the totalitarian phrase "you cannot make an omelet without breaking eggs," seemed to capture an important aspect of Moses with his own words. Yet another visit to the same archives in the heat of summer produced a typewritten document tucked away in the back of a book: "Ten Misconceptions of New York," a promotional piece by Fiorello La Guardia, the "Little Flower," encouraging people to attend the 1939 World's Fair that captured his love of the city.

And there were other surprises as well. Some authors, upon hearing of this project, generously volunteered pieces that they thought might be helpful. Others graciously consented to write pieces specifically for this volume that helped us address areas where we were unable to find documents that fitted our exact needs. Finally, although this had not been our intent, our selection process had produced intriguing and compelling studies of particular decades in New York's history: the scope of the selections for the 1960s, for example, seemed particularly full-bodied.

No one could undertake such a project as this one without all of the work that had gone before. Over the past thirty-four years, literally thousands of students at Columbia University have added their own particular energy and insights to the perspective of Professor Jackson about the Hudson River metropolis. Similarly, twenty miles north of Manhattan in the suburb of Dobbs Ferry in Westchester County, Pam Clarke and David Grant in 1996 brought into being CITYterm at The Masters School, an experience-based, interdisciplinary program devoted entirely to the study of New York City. Maureen Fonseca, the present head of the Masters School, and Susan Morris, the head of its board of trustees, have continued to generously support that endeavor. All the faculty from that program, but especially Rachel Stettler, Kate Knopp, John Barrengos, Pier and Dana Kooistra, David Jacoby, and Joel Lipsitch, have been a large part of this book through their conversations and their teaching. The adjunct faculty, lecturers, authors, and friends of CITY-term, experts on New York City all of them, have shaped this book as well. And the students of CITYterm over the past six years have been willing explorers of much of the material between these covers and have had more of a say than they realize as to what was included and what was not. Several people, among them Barbara Bruce Jackson, Rick Melvoin, Michael Lance, Sandy Stott, Cynde Moore, Stephanie Levy Lipkowitz, Don and Dot Dunbar, and Michael Thomas, read the introductions and supplied valuable commentary that improved the quality of those sections. Jennifer Crewe at Columbia University Press and Mary Boss at Impressions Book and Journal Services have both been patiently forceful and supportive of meeting the deadlines for production, and their enthusiasm for the project was invigorating. Finally, books like this take years of work; Nicki Weiss and Doug and Walker Dunbar have added countless suggestions that improved the quality of the book in profound and subtle ways, and they have done so with great humor, patience, and grace. And Barbara Bruce Jackson not only gave us a place to work but also shared with us her wide reading, her special insights, and her good judgment.

We did the work for this book and chose its title before terrorists hijacked two huge airliners, each filled with thousands of gallons of jet fuel, and intentionally smashed them into the Twin Towers of the World Trade Center on the morning of September 11, 2001. The human costs of that tragedy are incalculable, and it is not yet clear exactly how the city will rebuild, reinvent, and reimagine Lower Manhattan. The editors believe, however, that just as New York managed to overcome the devastating fires of 1776, 1778, and 1835; the horrendous riots of 1849, 1863, 1935, and 1943; and the cataclysmic epidemics of 1833, 1849, and 1866, so also will it manage to overcome this latest challenge to its existence. For almost four hundred years, a little settlement set up by the Dutch in 1624 has offered hope, opportunity, freedom, challenge, and exhilaration—as well as despair, cruelty, and squalor—to millions of newcomers to the United States. We expect that it will continue to do so, certainly for a few more decades and probably for a few more centuries.

Kenneth T. Jackson
David S. Dunbar
May 1, 2002

EMPIRE CITY

New York Through the Centuries

INTRODUCTION

Where else does the ball drop on New Year's Eve but in Times Square? What is the national paper of record other than *The New York Times?* There is only one bridge that anyone would ever try to sell you, and it connects Brooklyn with Lower Manhattan over the East River. Skyscrapers are synonymous with the Empire State Building and the Chrysler Building. Grand Central Terminal defines frenzied activity. Amusement parks everywhere are related to Coney Island. Immigration is embodied forever in Ellis Island. Central Park is the nation's most famous urban open space. In New York City the streets are as much concepts as thoroughfares—Fifth Avenue (fashion), Broadway (theater), The Bowery (skid row), Wall Street (finance), Park Avenue (wealth), and Madison Avenue (advertising)—and neighborhoods have become code words for ideas—Greenwich Village (bohemia), Harlem (ghetto), and the Lower East Side (Jewish culture). Quite simply, New York City is larger than life, and its effect on the American imagination has been profound. As William Dean Howells wrote in *A Hazard of New Fortunes,* New York is "the only city that belongs to the entire country." What is it that makes New York so special, so different from other places? Any list would be necessarily incomplete, but ten factors are clearly important.

First, there is tempo. New Yorkers walk faster, work longer, eat later, and compete harder than most other Americans. These behavioral patterns have deep roots. In 1624, when the Dutch first set up a trading post on Manhattan, their goal was not to convert the Indians or to practice a special religion but to make money. Visiting Manhattan in 1774 from Puritan Boston, John Adams expressed disdain: "I have not seen one real gentleman, one well-bred man, since I came to town. They talk very loud, very fast, and altogether. If they ask you a question, before you can utter three words of your answer, they will break out on you again and talk away." Poor breeding? Perhaps. But New Yorkers established the first chamber of commerce in the Western Hemisphere in 1768, developed the first regularly scheduled shipping service in 1818, built the Erie Canal by 1825, and established the nation's dominant stock exchange by the 1840s.

Second, New York has always been incredibly diverse. In recent decades, every important city has become multicultural, multiracial, and multireligious. But New York has never been anything else. As early as the 1640s, eighteen different languages were already being spoken in tiny New Amsterdam, whose fewer than a thousand residents already represented an ethnic stew. Ever since, Gotham has been the most polyglot place on earth. In 1880, for example, most of its workers were foreign born, and it had the world's largest immigrant labor force; it still does. Travelers often described walking for blocks in New York without hearing or seeing a word of English. As Jacob Riis noted in his 1890 classic, *How the Other Half Lives:* "A map of the city, colored to designate nationalities, would show more stripes than on the skin of a zebra, and more colors than any rainbow." In 1947, when New York became the headquarters of the United Nations, it was already a united nations in miniature. As E. B. White wrote that year, "The collision and intermingling of these millions of foreign-born people representing so many races and creeds make New York a permanent exhibit of the phenomenon of one world." Fifty years later, the only thing that has changed is the source of the newcomers. In 1999, more than eleven of every twenty New Yorkers are immigrants or the children of immigrants, and the metropolitan region has more Jews than Tel Aviv, more Italians than Florence, more Dominicans than Santo Domingo, and more Irish than Dublin. Here the peoples of the world have come. As a result, every important racial, ethnic, religious, and national group on earth has a substantial presence in New York.

Third, there is its reputation for tolerance. Diversity has led to a grudging acceptance of difference. Although tragic incidents in Howard Beach, Crown Heights, and a dozen other places have reminded us that New Yorkers can be as mean spirited, violent, and narrow minded as anyone else, the city's circumstances force residents to control and even to subdue their prejudices. Otherwise, as White wrote, "it would explode in a radioactive cloud of hate and rancor and bigotry." Again, the Dutch set the standard. In the early seventeenth century, when Puritan Boston was banishing Anne Hutchinson from the city because of doctrinal disagreements, the West India Company, fearing that bigotry might threaten trade and discourage immigration, was welcoming Lutherans, Quakers, Anabaptists, Catholics, and even Jews to Manhattan. The tradition was set 375 years ago, and ever since New York has been a haven for outcasts, sinners, revolutionaries, anarchists, dissidents, and people fed up with their hometowns. Is it a coincidence that the American Communist Party, the National Association for the Advancement of Colored People (NAACP), and the gay rights movement all started in the city? Or that Pakistanis and Indians, Arabs and Jews, Bosnians and Serbs, and Irish Protestants and Catholics manage to coexist here in peace?

Fourth, New York is dense. Relative to other American cities, New York has been overcrowded ever since the Dutch settlers huddled together below Wall Street for protection. A century ago, the average population density on the Lower East Side exceeded 260,000 per square mile, and in certain precincts, 600,000 per square mile, a total never matched at any other time or in any other place. At the turn of the millennium, New York still stands apart. The population density of San Francisco is 16,000 per square mile; of Chicago, 12,000; of Boston, 11,000; of Los Angeles, 7,500; of Houston, 3,000; of Memphis, 2,000; and of Jacksonville, 800. The comparable figure for the five boroughs, where most residents are apartment renters rather than homeowners and where yards are both rare and dwarfishly small, is 25,000 per square mile, and for Manhattan, 65,000 per square mile.

New York has also differed from other places in the number, size, and typicality of its tall buildings. Chicago may have given birth to the skyscraper, but Manhattan became its home, and a century ago it was already assuming the tower form that has distinguished it ever since. The Singer, Metropolitan Life, Woolworth, Chrysler, and Empire State buildings were successively the tallest buildings anywhere, as was the World Trade Center. As late as 1974, New York contained as many giants of sixty or more stories as all other cities combined, and even today, after high-rise buildings have sprouted from Los Angeles to São Paulo to Hong Kong, the skyline of Manhattan is impossible to confuse with any other.

Population density in Gotham is also unusual because it has remained stable over the course of the twentieth century and increased since 1980. Elsewhere, Americans have abandoned their cities. Since 1950, for example, the population of Chicago has dropped 25 percent; Baltimore, 28 percent; Philadelphia, 29 percent; Washington, 32 percent; Cleveland, 43 percent; Pittsburgh, 45 percent; Detroit, 46 percent; and St. Louis, 54 percent. New York and San Francisco are the exceptions. Each is down only about 5 percent from its peak and has been growing for the past 15 years. Houston, San Diego, Phoenix, San Antonio, Dallas, and many other cities have made huge gains recently, but they have done so through annexing surrounding territory, even their overall population density. Thus, in the American context, what makes New York exceptional is not that people have left the city, as they have, but that others have always been ready to take their place.

Fifth, New York is oriented toward public transportation. A century ago, the United States had the best and most extensive public transportation system in the world. Berlin, which then had the preeminent system in Europe, would have ranked no higher than twenty-second in the Western Hemisphere. Since that time, Americans have ripped up their streetcar tracks, starved their bus systems, built superhighways everywhere, and joyously sped away in their automobiles. New York is the exception. Its proportion of the nation's transit riders has doubled in the twentieth century, and still it has far and away the nation's most extensive and heavily used subway, bus, and commuter train systems. And in contrast to the larger American pattern, public transit ridership is higher now in New York than it was a quarter century ago.

Sixth, New York's central business district primacy dominates the region. Since 1945, the American exodus to subdivisions, shopping malls, office parks, and highway strip developments has left the typical downtown desolate and forlorn, especially after dark. Great cities have become like doughnuts, with their vitality and excitement concentrated on the urban edges. The once bustling department stores that were the signature institution of every city are now only memories. New York again is an exception. Even without Gimbels, B. Altman, Stern's, and Bonwit Teller, the sidewalks of Manhattan remain crowded, and grand emporiums such as Macy's, Lord and Taylor, Bloomingdale's, Sak's Fifth Avenue, Brooks Brothers, Bergdorf-Goodman, and a dozen others continue to beckon window shoppers. Together, they give the city a vitality that no mall can match. Thus, tourists flock to New York because it reminds them of the lost city centers and downtowns of their youth.

Seventh, New York has retained a substantial middle and upper class. The North American residential pattern is for the rich to live on the edges and the poor to reside in the middle. New Yorkers, of course, have followed and even led this trend. They pioneered the suburban movement, first in Brooklyn Heights and later in Westchester County, Long Island, and New Jersey. Moreover, the region has seen extremes of wealth and poverty since the seventeenth century. But, comparatively speaking, the middle class has not abandoned New York. Neighborhoods throughout the city continue to be filled with the kinds of people who elsewhere would live in the suburbs. The very affluent are conspicuous as well, so much so that Manhattan is the richest county in the nation on a per capita basis, the wealthiest zip code in America is 10021, and the highest residential real estate values in the United States are along Fifth Avenue, Park Avenue, and Central Park West.

Eighth, New York is environmentally sustainable. When one thinks of pristine nature and of clean air and water, the mind conjures up images of wood-burning Vermonters, campers in California, or cowboys in Montana, not cliff dwellers in Manhattan. But New Yorkers, for all their visible garbage and litter, tred lightly on the land because their energy consumption is low by American standards. This is so because they use fewer fossil fuels to get from place to place and to heat and cool their residences. By any measure, apartments are more efficient than houses, and walking and using public transit are more efficient than moving a ton and a half of metal to run to the grocer.

Ninth, New York's public housing is a success. In 1937, the passage of the United States Housing Act meant that for the first time the federal government was accepting responsibility for the provision of decent, low-cost homes for the needy. The idea was exemplary, and by the end of 1962, more than two million Americans had such shelter. But in 2002, more than sixty years after President Franklin D. Roosevelt signed the legislation with such optimism, public housing, especially the high-rise variety, is considered a failure. Many projects are crime ridden, and their hallways, elevators, and public spaces have been taken over by gangs, prostitutes, and drug dealers. Thousands of units have been abandoned because even the poor refuse to live in such miserable environments. As a result, cities across the nation have bulldozed and blown up entire complexes. But New York again is the exception. In Gotham, tens of thousands of hopeful families are on the waiting list, and the projects themselves are in remarkably good order, especially considering the reduction in federal subsidies over the past fifteen years.

Finally, New York is a safe environment. The image of the city, fed by movies and television, is oftentimes scary, and newcomers have always felt a twinge of fear as they contemplated its perils and snares. But the reality is that New York has never statistically been among the nation's most dangerous cities. In part, this is a result of a homicide rate that only rarely has been in America's top ten and recently has plunged so that Gotham no longer ranks in the top 100 most violent American cities.

But the unusual freedom from sudden death that New Yorkers have enjoyed over the past century is related to the transportation system and to population density, not criminals. Quite simply, New Yorkers, whether they live in the outer boroughs or Manhattan, are less likely to die prematurely than other Americans because of a low automobile fatality rate. This happy circumstance is not the result of careful and courteous driving. Instead, because New Yorkers literally live on top of each other, their stores and workplaces are convenient, and they walk to many destinations. Short trips, even in taxis, are the norm. Elsewhere in the country, where the population is more widely dispersed, automobiles are necessary for virtually all journeys. By reducing distance traveled, New Yorkers remain out of the street and thus out of harm's way. And because of short blocks and frequent stoplights, cars that do crash are typically moving too slowly to kill. In other words, the city is safe because of its density and its subways, not in spite of them.

The causes that have characterized New York's difference from other American cities have produced effects that are equally unique. New York is overwhelmingly a city that embodies tension. The lunchtime crowds on Fifth and Madison, the subway at rush hour, Rockefeller Center in December, and Times Square anytime are examples of what is a dominant daily New York reality. Where else can you buy a book that will identify fifty (is that a lot or a few?) "quiet" places in a city? As Ed Koch noted, New Yorkers "talk faster, walk faster and think faster than other Americans." Scientific studies have, in fact, demonstrated at least the first two of those characteristics. Visitors, as a result, find themselves exhausted and ready to return to a more manageable pace of life. Some residents, who are already "back where they came from," as A. J. Liebling put it, simply flee to Long Island, New England, or upstate. But the literal tension is simply the outer manifestation and result of a set of figurative tensions that are deeply embedded in the structure of New York. There are three tensions that are the effects of New York's history—those between commerce and culture, assimilation and diversity, public and private. What makes New York different is that other cities eliminate one of the terms of the figurative tension and thereby resolve the conflict that New York steadfastly holds onto. The willingness of residents to live out the implication of these tensions and to refuse to resolve them by walling them off from one another fuels New York's greatness.

The commercial origins of New York have already been touched upon. When the Dutch sailed into the Upper Bay, they did not see a hill upon which to create a utopian city but a magnificent harbor in which to do business. Ambrose Bierce put it most succinctly when he defined "Mammon" in his *Devil's Dictionary* as "The god of the world's leading religion. His chief temple is the holy city of New York." Indeed, the primary motivation for the grid plan that was adopted in 1811 was to exploit real estate. The present effects of that commercial spirit are visible today in the skyscrapers that tower over the metropolis or from the viewing gallery above the floor of the Stock Exchange. And the curious effects of that spirit on our humanity were what Melville explored in *Bartleby, the Scrivener.*

New York replaced London as the financial capital of the world during World War I. But, as F. Scott Fitzgerald so aptly noted to Edmund Wilson, "Culture follows money." The resulting tension between culture and commerce has a long and storied history. Thomas Bender chronicled this changing relationship in *New York Intellect*, but it has its modern-day battleground in the city today. The current outcry over the "Disneyfication" of Times

Square has generated newspaper articles, editorials, and books. However, because New York lays claim to being a cultural capital as well as a commercial one, that tension fuels the terms of the debate and the types of solutions being proposed.

The ongoing conflict on Forty-second Street is primarily about whether the commercial ventures that have been at work creating "The *New* Times Square" will have the effect of destroying the culture of the old Times Square. In short, will commerce, symbolized by the Disney Corporation, create a homogenized mall out of what was once a distinctive, diverse culture? The crux of the issue is not only the social debate but also the value of the real estate. Condé Nast recently finished new headquarters on Forty-second Street and Seventh Avenue, and Tishman is constructing hotels and office buildings on the corner of Forty-second Street and Eighth Avenue. Every evening busloads of small children empty out at the restored New Amsterdam Theater to view *The Lion King.* Ratso Rizzo and Joe Buck are no longer to be seen wandering the streets. But those poles of the spectrum are false dichotomies; that either–or choice is not a real one. What is being played out in Times Square is the tension between commerce and culture. No other city in America has a place like Times Square; every city in America possesses a gargantuan, numbingly identical, indoor–outdoor mall. But New York City allows no lapses into total familiarity for anyone, and if it is true to its history, the diversity of the culture of Times Square will not become synonymous with commerce.

The Lion King itself provides another example of the tension between commerce and culture in the theater world of Times Square. This time, however, the issue is the financial feasibility of Broadway productions, and the tension is between what is commercially profitable and what is culturally challenging. Broadway theaters behave, in some ways, like apartment buildings. The seats are like individual apartments, and the object is to have your building completely rented out; the production then succeeds. As a creative director of one Broadway theater company joked recently, "I doubt that *Phantom of the Opera* will close in my lifetime." The prolonged runs of *Cats* and *Les Miserables* would argue that he might be correct. Will *The Lion King* recoup its investment? The question is almost irrelevant in traditional theatrical terms. It will probably move out of town after a successful Broadway run and tour other cities. Then, it will reopen for a new generation of New Yorkers in a decade. It will become the Disney theater equivalent of *Snow White, Sleeping Beauty,* and *Fantasia.* By comparison, the highly regarded

Angels in America recouped its investment only through out-of-town performances four years after it had closed on Broadway. The debate is not whether one show is more artistic than the other but whether commercial pressure will force the cutting back of culturally challenging material in the name of monetary profit. The recent Broadway Initiative—the exchange of commercial air rights for the development of dramatic theater venues—and the choice of the former head of the Municipal Arts Society to run the Times Square Business Improvement District show the recent vibrancy of the cultural side of the tension. New York has always been about both–and solutions rather than either–or choices.

Nowhere has this inclusiveness been more apparent than in a second major tension that New Yorkers live with every day—that between assimilation and diversity. The tension between assimilating to a dominant cultural paradigm and maintaining a particular racial, religious, ethnic, or cultural identity has confounded the entire nation, but it is confronted and addressed every day in New York in a way that is significantly different from how other major cities deal with it. Since the end of the Second World War, the automobile has defined the patterns of behavior in the United States. Most people who live in a typical urban environment really only inhabit five or six places within a fairly small radius of their home. Furthermore, they drive to these destinations—school, work, church, the mall, the movie theater, and the grocery store. One of the effects of this pattern, however, is the comfort of the known; one has little fear of being misinterpreted or having to negotiate one's distinct difference from other people.

To find oneself confronted by difference is the norm of daily life in New York. A typical subway car in New York might include a Chinese security guard, a middle-aged Indian man, a white male professional with tie loosened, two young Dominican men reading *The Village Voice,* a pair of white teenage girls with eyebrows pierced, two white boys with headphones curled around their necks, an Arabic man with eyes closed and head back, a turbaned Sikh, and two black teenagers arguing about a possible Mets versus Yankees "subway series." At every stop along the line, the doors would open and a new clientele, just as varied, might exchange places with this one.

That scene, however, has been part of New York from the city's beginning. At the very time that Winthrop's covenanted community was banishing Quakers to the Caribbean for speaking in public, observers in New York City were documenting almost a score of different languages being spoken. In fact, Peter Stuyvesant's attempts to prohibit Quaker worship in what is now

Queens was met with the Flushing Remonstrance of 1657, articulating the displeasure of local residents with his actions. Obviously, tension between differences has not always been so quietly resolved. The Draft Riots of 1863, the bloodiest civil disturbance in American history, were a conflict of race, class, and ethnicity. There were five riots in Harlem between 1935 and 1977. In the summer of 1969, homosexuals stood up to consistent police harassment in a riot at the Stonewall Inn in Greenwich Village that marked the beginning of a confrontational gay rights movement. Most recently, in 1991, several days and nights of rioting were the result of a conflict between Hasidic Jews and blacks in the Crown Heights section of Brooklyn. It is in the public life of the subway and in the parks and the streets that one negotiates between a common civic culture and one's particular difference. This was precisely the negotiation that New York's poet laureate, Walt Whitman, tried and ultimately failed to transcend. Despite his enormous empathic lyricism in *Leaves of Grass,* Whitman did not realize that it is New York's destiny not to resolve the tension between assimilation and diversity but to live it out in daily life.

If Whitman's trope for transcendence, the resolution of the tension, was encapsulated in "Crossing Brooklyn Ferry," Frederick Law Olmsted's metaphor was even grander—Central Park. One of the two authors of the Greensward Plan for the development of the park, Olmsted saw it as a place where "the rich and the poor, the cultivated and well bred and the sturdy and self-made shall be attracted together and encouraged to assimilate." Calvert Vaux, Olmsted's partner in the plan, saw a huge public park as a place to "translate Democratic ideas into Trees and Dirt." As Whitman heard the "blab of the pave" of New York City streets as fostering democratic spirit, Olmsted and Vaux turned to the creation of a massive public green space in what would eventually become the middle of the city. These desires highlight a third tension that has come to be a hallmark of New York—the tension between public and private.

E. B. White saw the relationship between the individual and the crowd in New York City as clearly as any commentator. "New York," he observed, "blends the gift of privacy with the excitement of participation, and better than most dense communities it succeeds in insulating the individual (if he wants it, and almost everybody wants or needs it) against all enormous and violent and wonderful events that are taking place every minute." Hundreds of thousands of people, the size of entire other major cities, can gather to hear Minister Farrakhan on the steps of the United Nations or to march down Fifth Avenue in the annual Gay Pride or St. Patrick's Day parades, and any pedestrian can walk through Times Square at the same time, oblivious to the throng gathered only a few blocks away.

But sheer distance or proximity is not the only issue in describing the relationship between public and private space and time in New York. Gotham is a verbal city; people are always talking. And they do not make the usual separations between public and private conversation. Intermission at the Metropolitan Opera seems to be almost designed to reveal scores of individuals' relationship with their therapist. Every visitor to New York can remember being engaged in a conversation while walking down the street and suddenly being given advice or comment by the stranger walking past him or her. White called this distance "the eighteen inches" that are "both the connection and the separation that New York provides for its inhabitants." Public and private space and time are not separated the way they are in most cities. New York blurs the boundaries between them in the subway, in parks, in restaurants, in the streets, and even through the walls of the apartments.

The streets of New York are the places where separation and connection play out their comedies and dramas most fully. Part of the tension between public and private has to do with limited space, but it is also a function of pace. Vivian Gornick describes the feeling that results from the bustle of the city streets: "The street keeps moving, and you've got to love the moment. You've got to find the composition of the rhythm, lift the story from the motion, understand and not regret that all is dependent on the swiftness with which we come into view and pass out again. The pleasure and the reassurance lie precisely in the speed with which the connection is established and then let go of. No need to clutch. The connection is generic not specific." However, just because the connection is fleeting and general does not mean that it is of no consequence. People often remark that the first rule of thumb on New York City streets is not to look anyone in the eyes. Yet, the pace and dynamism of the human flow around you force you to be unusually aware of both your own thoughts and those of others around you simultaneously.

In New York City, the strange and the familiar are both vital ingredients to the proper functioning of the street. Jane Jacobs, in *The Death and Life of Great American Cities,* tries to explain to a generation of urban planners what New York residents already implicitly feel around them. Streets are safe precisely when they achieve "a marvel of balance between its people's determination to have essential privacy and their simultaneous wishes for differing degrees of contact, enjoyment or help from the people around." An individual's safety is most at risk when there is no one else around. Safe streets, therefore, depend upon strangers in order to function properly. Jacobs writes that once "a street is well equipped to handle strangers . . . and has a basic supply of activity and eyes," it can be both healthy and safe.

This combination of neighbors and strangers also provides a dimension of difference that speaks to precisely why this final tension between public and private may be the most important for the future of cities. In New York, safety can only in part be institutionalized in the form of a large police force; it is also something that must be created by understanding how public and private lives are held in tension. Jacobs concluded that "great differences among neighbors—differences that often go far deeper than differences of color—which are possible and normal in intensely urban life, but which are so foreign to suburbs and pseudo-suburbs, are possible and normal only when streets of great cities have built-in equipment allowing strangers to dwell in peace together." This necessity of difference as normal and beneficial is precisely what the Puritan and Jeffersonian visions were unable to admit. As we become a nation increasingly concerned about the recognition of private difference in tension with public culture, we would be well advised to examine New York, which has been living that tension for four centuries.

The tension between public and private roles applies not only to individuals but also to institutions. Central Park is, ostensibly, a public open space. But the fiscal crisis of the 1970s prompted then Mayor Ed Koch to announce that a group of private individuals, the newly formed Central Park Conservancy, would have a major say in how the park was managed. Although originally strictly a fund-raising body, the conservancy currently provides close to half of the park's operating budget. The relationship between the City Parks Department and the conservancy serves as a perfect example of the way in which the tension between public and private is held in the institutional life of New York City.

This public–private relationship raises questions about spending and access. In a 1987 advertisement, Donald Trump proudly announced, "Central Park. It's not just a view. It's your front yard." But it is not the front yard just for people on Fifty-ninth Street, and there have been questions raised for the past decade about fully democratic access to the park. In 1988, when Parks Commissioner Henry Stern issued a set of tightened regulations regarding loitering, he was met with protest from groups supporting the rights of the homeless; he subsequently backed down. Surveys have shown that black and Hispanic patrons used the park less during the late 1980s. Finally, questions have been raised about the amount of money spent below Eighty-sixth Street as opposed to that spent on the upper section of the park. These kinds of public–private partnerships—not only in Central Park but also in low-income housing and other fundamental arenas—serve to illustrate what will probably be the future, not only for New York City but for other major American cities as well.

If these are the tensions that Gotham refuses to resolve, what are the implications for the role of New York in American life? The most immediate effect of the lack of resolution is seen in the speed, the pace, the dynamism, the excess, and the frenetic quality of life in New York. As Edna St. Vincent Millay wrote from her Greenwich Village apartment, "My candle burns at both ends; / It will not last the night; / But ah, my foes, and oh my friends — / It gives a lovely light." The term *New Yorker* is as much a verb as a noun. Unlike most places that demand a certain elapsed time period before one is considered a native, New York is democratic. If you can talk the talk and walk the walk, you are a New Yorker. More important, New York asks its residents and visitors alike to reside in a daily state of transition—switching back and forth over essential issues of identity. New York doesn't really celebrate difference as much as it demands a constant questioning and remaking across lines of class, race, ethnicity, religion, and sexual orientation. That process is both exhausting and exhilarating.

Unlike most cities on navigable water, New York faces inward toward Central Park and the mainland as much as it faces outward to the harbor and the rest of the world. This simultaneous facing inward and outward is true of its citizens as well. The process of reshaping the familiar is what makes New York City, for the rest of America, the understandable coupled with the unimaginable and the inexplicable. The appropriate human response to such a creative phenomenon is, ironically, a religious one—awe and wonder. As Gatsby drives Nick to the city from Long Island, Nick exclaims that the "'city seen from the Queensboro Bridge is always the city seen for the first time, in all its wild promise of all the mystery and beauty in the world. . . . Anything can happen now that we've slid over this bridge.' I thought: 'anything at all. . . .' Even Gatsby could happen, without any particular wonder." Gatsby's goal was to "re-create the past," but he picked the wrong city. E. B. White's "changeless and changing" New York is, as A. J. Liebling described, constantly "renewing itself until the past is perennially forgotten." The city gives us the future much more than it does a history. More than any other city, New York is about the promise and possibility of what the particular American destiny might be.

The real beauty of New York, however, is that it has also kept alive a part of the national mythology. Individualism, the land of the free, rags to riches, and the melting pot were all characteristics that demanded a frontier stage to enact their dramas. But the days of Daniel Boone moving west as soon as he could see smoke from his neighbor's chimney were doomed with the advent of the railroad, and it has been more than a hundred years since Frederick Jackson Turner proclaimed the demise of the frontier. The twenty-first century will likely be about people living together in cities, not on the land. If we are to look to a city that most realistically maintains and yet questions fundamental American traits and provides an arena where those can be honestly confronted and questioned, it is New York.

The United States has always been a nation that embodied the tension between commerce and culture. New York's special role is to be the place where the tension between assimilation and diversity—in all its manifestations of race, ethnicity, class, gender, religion, and sexual orientation—will be lived to its truest possible conclusion. The tension between public and private may well be the most confrontational of all tensions in the coming century. New York City has much to teach America about how to live with these tensions in a productive and realistic manner. If learning is the coupling of the previously unexperienced to the examination and reinvention of one's assumptions, there is no better place to pursue an education than in New York. This book is an attempt to chronicle part of the story of one city in hope that it might serve as an example for the rest of America. There is no simple lesson; rather, the story of New York is one that reads us even as we read it.

PART 1
Colonial Period (1624–1783)

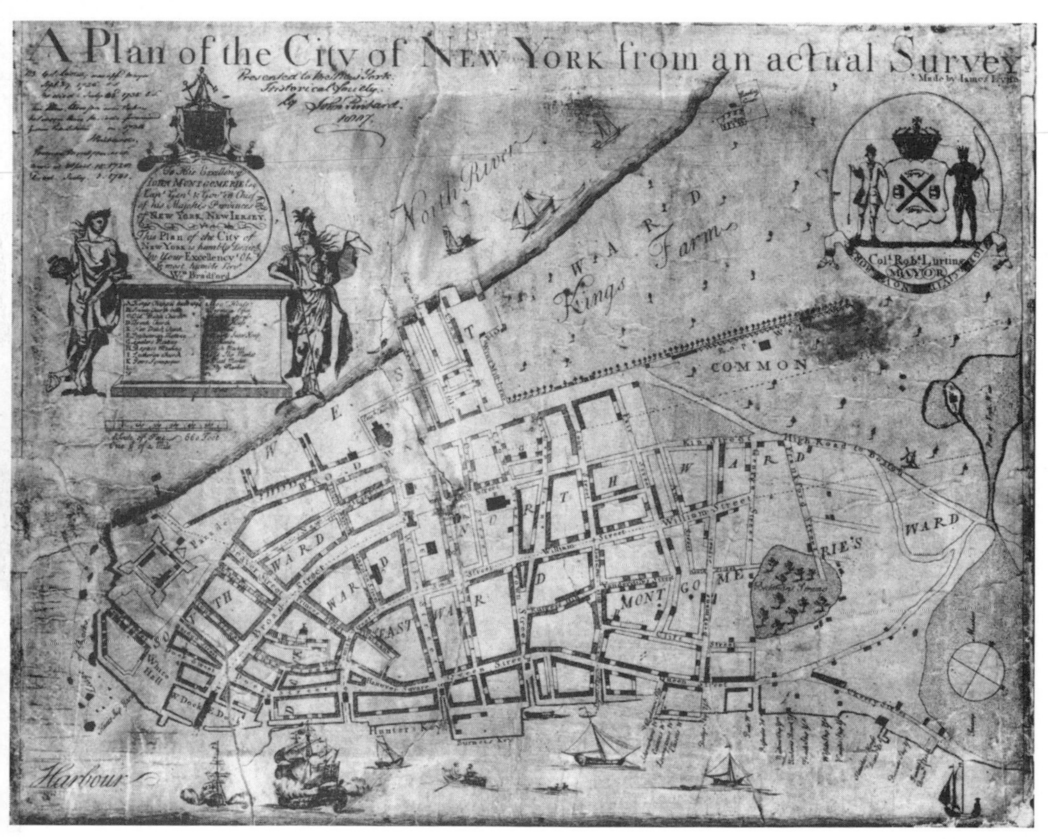

Before 1524, when Giovanni da Verrazano, an Italian in the employ of France, became the first known white man to sail into the great harbor where the Hudson River flows into the Atlantic Ocean, the place that would come to be known as New York City had already been inhabited for centuries by Indians of the Algonquin language group. The Algonquins themselves were divided into hundreds of virtually autonomous bands along the East Coast from roughly North Carolina to Canada. New York was the home base of at least eighteen of these subgroups, including the Canarsees, who were especially prominent in what is now Brooklyn. Several thousand in number, they had settlements in present-day Gowanus, Sheepshead Bay, Flatlands, and Canarsie, as well as the Rockaways, Governors Island, and Staten Island.

None of these northeastern Indian tribes was as advanced as the Mayas, the Incas, or the Aztecs, who lived thousands of miles to the south and once erected great cities as testimony to the strength of their civilization. But the Algonquins, who may have seemed primitive in the eyes of Europeans, did plant wheat, maize, beans, and squash, and they constructed long bark houses of substantial size, replete with thatched domes. Indeed, many twenty-first-century roads, such as Flatbush Avenue and Kings Highway, follow the route of Indian paths that connected their various villages.

Verrazano's arrival did not lead to white settlement, however. That accomplishment remained for Henry Hudson, an Englishman working for the Dutch East India Company. In 1609, he was searching for a northwest passage from Europe to the fabled riches of Asia and the Orient. He failed in that quest, but when he guided his blunt-bowed, seventy-four-foot ship, the *Half Moon,* into New York harbor on September 3 of that year, he began to realize two things that would become even more significant; first that the vast region between French Canada and British Virginia was unfortified and unclaimed, and second, that the Indians who lived at the mouth of what would become the Hudson River were friendly and would happily trade furs for European goods. When he returned to Amsterdam with those pieces of good news, Dutch merchants became excited about the commercial potential of Manhattan Island, which was in the midst of a vast harbor that might be ice-free in all seasons. They made preparations to send other expeditions to the region.

The Dutch established the first permanent white settlement in what is now New York City in 1624, when about eight or ten French-speaking, Protestant Walloons remained behind on Governors Island in the harbor while most of the group proceeded up the river to Fort Orange (now Albany). In

1625, the community was shifted to the southern tip of Manhattan Island, and in 1626, according to legend, Peter Minuit purchased the entire island from the Canarsees for sixty guilders (approximately $24) in trinkets and other goods.

New Amsterdam, as it was soon called, was a sort of company town for the Dutch West India Company. The settlement was only moderately successful and never as profitable as its Amsterdam owners had hoped. But in 1653 it became an independent city according to Dutch law. More importantly, during the administration of the last of the four Dutch governors, Peter Stuyvesant (1647–1664), the little seaport developed the characteristics of religious tolerance and population heterogeneity that would set it apart from other American cities. In fact, at least eighteen different languages could be heard on the streets as early as 1644.

The Dutch period ended in 1664, by which time overseas rivalry with the English had become intense. When a fleet of four English warships and many hundreds of soldiers arrived in the harbor on August 18, Stuyvesant wanted to fight, and he prepared Fort Amsterdam for battle. But the citizens of the town lacked both the stomach and the resources for a contest with the powerful guns of the Royal Navy, and they implored their leader to accept the generous terms offered by the English commander. On September 8, realizing the hopelessness of his position, and with drums beating and flags flying, Stuyvesant surrendered the fort. Thereafter, the English renamed the city to honor the Duke of York. And the city itself then gave its name to the entire colony, which after independence became the Empire State, as George Washington had foreseen.

Except for brief periods from 1673 to 1674 and 1689 to 1691, the entire century between 1664 and 1776 was a time of uninterrupted British rule. Triangular trade became the basis for New York's economy, as agricultural goods were exchanged for manufactured goods in England, for rum and coffee in the West Indies, and for slaves in Africa. The prosperous town always ranked among the top five cities in the New World in both size and importance, but it did not dominate the colonies. In fact, Boston was the largest city along the Atlantic coast until 1740. At that time, Philadelphia, which was not founded until 1682, took over as North America's most important city.

Although New York in the eighteenth century was heterogeneous and, in the context of the times, relatively tolerant, it was not paradise. In 1703, for example, the richest 10 percent of the taxpayers owned 47 percent of the assessed resources; the bottom half of the citizenry controlled less than 20 percent of the wealth. (Note: three centuries later the rich–poor gap is even wider in Gotham.) Similarly, political power was concentrated in the hands of the few. Although most free white men could vote, the city government largely concentrated on maintaining the status quo, and voting had the function of providing constitutional and symbolic affirmations of the authority of the elite.

New York's heterogeneity was racial as well as ethnic, and throughout the eighteenth century it was the largest center of slave population in the northern colonies. Of the approximately 25,000 residents of the city in 1776, for example, about 17 percent were black. Philadelphia, which had about 40,000 residents at the time of the Revolution, had fewer African Americans than Gotham, as did Boston, which had about 16,000 citizens at the same time.

Although New York's population of 25,000 in 1775 is not impressive by twenty-first-century standards, it was a considerable number at the time. Indeed, the number of inhabitants on Manhattan Island was then about the same as other important regional centers of the British Empire, such as Bristol, Manchester, Birmingham, and Liverpool. London, Paris, and Edo (Tokyo) were then in a class by themselves, and each had more than a half million inhabitants.

At the end of the colonial period, New York City extended only about one mile north from the southern tip of Manhattan, and Greenwich Village was a tiny community separated from the seaport by more than a mile of open land. The most developed section of the city was along the East River from the Battery to the current location of the Brooklyn Bridge. Here were the houses of the wealthy, who by 1776 were more English than Dutch in character. And the backbone of the city's economy remained at the water's edge. Commerce was the community's lifeblood, and in 1772, for example, an average of two vessels per day entered the great harbor.

During the American Revolution, New York City played a crucial but little understood role in the ultimate victory of the Continental Army. The larger contest, of course, was between the foremost military power on earth and a small and disorganized group of colonies that had no army, no navy, and no established methods of supply, transport, or training. But King George III also had major problems. He needed to win the war quickly so that his old enemies, France and Spain, would not be tempted to come in on the other side. And he needed to defeat the revolutionaries cheaply so that his own countrymen would not begin to groan under the weight of new taxes.

In 1776, British military leaders studied the map of North America and concluded that New York City was the pivotal spot on the Atlantic coast.

First, it was almost equidistant between the two dominant colonies, Massachusetts and Virginia. Second, it had a magnificent harbor that would be ideal for sheltering the warships and transports of the Royal Navy. Finally, it controlled the mouth of the Hudson River, which itself offered the opportunity of splitting the rebellion in half. So, they chose New York rather than Boston as their base of operations, and in the early summer two brothers, General William Howe and Admiral Richard Howe, began concentrating their forces to take Manhattan.

Unfortunately, they did not reach New York harbor until after the Declaration of Independence had been adopted and after an angry mob had pulled down an equestrian lead statue of the king to be melted into bullets. Moreover, General George Washington had already deduced that the redcoats were heading for Manhattan, and he had already moved the bulk of the American army, such as it was, to New York City.

Advance units of the British fleet arrived in the lower bay on June 29, 1776. The main fleet, which included thirty ships of the line, 400 transport ships, and more than 40,000 soldiers and sailors, arrived on August 12. The vast armada easily surpassed anything ever previously seen in the new world. It was so powerful and so overwhelming that at their leisure the Howe brothers set up a huge encampment on Staten Island. Ten days later, on August 22, their vessels began transferring 20,000 soldiers to Gravesend Bay in what is now Brooklyn. The British were obviously about to attack.

What could General Washington do to defend New York City? If he did not move his forces to Brooklyn and especially the heights overlooking lower Manhattan, the Royal Navy would simply sail into the East River, and, using the powerful guns of their men-of-war, simply blow the city to bits. On the other hand, if he attempted to hold Brooklyn, and if he failed, his soldiers would be backed up against the East River and trapped between the British army and navy. The revolution would be over, and the leadership would be hanged.

The story of the American disaster in Brooklyn on August 27, 1776, has been told elsewhere and need not concern us here. Suffice to say that the Continental Army was defeated all along the line and but for the gallant sacrifice of a Maryland battalion might have been totally destroyed that day. Even so, the retreating Americans faced a perilous situation. They were backed up against the East River, and the redcoats and their Hessian mercenaries were obviously preparing to attack yet again. At this point, George Washington ordered his army to evacuate from Long Island. Incredibly, they succeeded, and the Howe brothers lost a golden opportunity to end the war then and there.

But the American situation remained grave. By taking Brooklyn, the British had exposed Manhattan, and their occupation, in addition to their powerful warships, now made New York untenable for Washington. He continued to retreat, barely escaping a British pincer movement on September 15. Then he divided his forces, leaving some behind at Fort Washington (in Manhattan near what would now be about 183rd Street and Fort Washington Avenue) and taking others with him to Westchester County. On October 28, 1776, at the Battle of White Plains, the result was a draw, but the British then turned south to deal with the Americans left behind in Manhattan. That battle came on November 16, 1776, and it resulted in an utter and complete defeat for the American forces. In hindsight, we now know that Colonel Robert Magaw should not have tried to hold Fort Washington after the Royal Navy had passed all the obstacles on the Hudson River. Almost three thousand Americans passed into British captivity, and many of them would later perish in British prisons or on board the notorious prison ships.

After also losing Fort Lee on the New Jersey side of the river, George Washington began a long and sad retreat. At that point, in late November 1776, the British had more American prisoners than Washington had American soldiers. And the Continental Army commander had learned, painfully, that his men could not stand up against the professional warriors of the powerful European nations.

So why were the battles around New York so significant if they were so disastrous for the American side? Quite simply, George Washington was a wise and crafty military strategist, and he developed new tactics as a result of his failures in Gotham. Knowing that his army was no match for its opponents, he determined to protect his soldiers rather than any particular piece of real estate. Essentially, he determined that if he kept a force in the field and refused to offer the British battle except under extraordinarily favorable terms, as at Saratoga or Yorktown, the stronger side would ultimately weary of the struggle and return home. Two hundred years later, this would be precisely the strategy adopted by Ho Chi Minh and the North Vietnamese in their war with the United States. Hopelessly outgunned and with no chance of victory in any major battle, the communist forces simply kept the war going until the American public tired of the human and financial sacrifice. Essentially, they were following the lead of George Washington, who had followed the same recipe for the ultimate defeat of King George III in the American Revolution.

Account of Henry Hudson's Voyage in 1609, Emanuel Van Meteren (1611)

A native of England who dedicated his life to finding a passage to China through North America, Captain Henry Hudson made two unsuccessful voyages to the New World before the 1609 attempt that made him famous. On September 2, with backing from the Dutch East India Company, he sailed with a crew of eighteen on the *Half Moon* into the lower bay of what became New York harbor. He explored the area for ten days and then sailed up the Hudson River (which he named) to the site of what later became Albany. When Hudson returned to Amsterdam with news of the protected harbor, the numerous resources, and the friendly Indians, his Dutch employers soon decided to place an outpost on the southern tip of Manhattan Island. Meanwhile, Hudson himself made his tragic last voyage in 1611, when his crew mutinied in what is now known as Hudson's Bay and cast him adrift. He was never seen or heard from again.

This excerpt is the account of the Dutch historian Emanuel Van Meteren, and it was written in 1611, the same year that Hudson disappeared forever.

THE account occurs in the thirtieth book, folio 827, of the edition of 1611, and is as follows:

We have said in the preceding book that the Directors of the East India Company in Holland had sent, in the month of March last past, in order to seek a passage to China by the Northwest or Northeast, a brave English pilot named Henry Hudson, with a Vlie-boat, and about eighteen or twenty men, part English and part Dutch, well provided. This Henry Hudson sailed from Texel on the 6th of April, 1609, and doubled the Cape of Norway on the 5th of May; he laid his course toward Nova Zembia, along the northern coast, but found the sea as full of ice there as he had found it the preceding year, so that he was compelled to abandon all hope for that year; whereupon, owing to the cold which some who had been in the East Indies could not support, the English and Dutch fell into disputes among themselves. Whereupon the Master, Hudson, gave them their choice between two things, the first was, to go to the coast of America in the fortieth degree of latitude, mostly incited to this by letters and maps which a certain Captain Smith had sent him from Virginia, and on which he showed him a sea wherein he might circumnavigate their Southern Colony from the North, and from thence pass into a Western sea. If this had been true (which experience up to the present time has shown to the contrary), it would have been very advantageous, and a short route to sail to the Indies. The other proposition was, to search for the passage by Davis' Straits, to which at last they generally agreed; and on the fourteenth they set sail, and, with favorable winds, arrived the last of May at the isle of Faro, where they stopped only twenty-four hours to take in fresh water. Leaving there, they reached, on the eighteenth of July, the coast of New-France in latitude forty-four, where they were obliged to make a stay to replace their *foremast* which they had lost, and where they obtained and rigged one. They found this a good place for catching codfish, and also for carrying on a traffic for good skins and furs, which they could obtain for mere trifles; but the sailors behaved very badly toward the people of the country, taking things by force, which was the cause of a strife between them. *The English,* thinking they would be overpowered and worsted, were afraid to enter further into the country; so they sailed from there on the twenty-sixth of July, and continued at sea until the third of August, when they approached the land in latitude forty-two. From thence they sailed again until the twelfth of August, when they again approached the land at latitude thirty-seven and three-quarters, and kept their course thence along it until they reached the latitude of forty degrees and three-quarters, where they found a good entrance between two headlands. Here they entered on the twelfth of September, and discovered as beautiful a river as could be found, very large and deep, with good anchorage on both shores. They ascended it with their large vessel as high as latitude forty-two degrees and forty minutes, and went still higher up with the ship's boat. At the entrance of the river they had found the natives brave and warlike; but inside, and up to the highest point of the river, they found them friendly and civil, having an abundance of skins and furs, such as martens and foxes, and many other commodities, birds, fruits and even white and blue grapes. They treated these people very civilly, and brought away a little of whatever they found among them. After they had gone about fifty leagues up the river, they returned on the fourth of October, and again put to sea. More could have been accomplished there if there had been a good feeling among the sailors, and had not the want of provisions prevented them.

At sea there was a consultation held at which there was a diversity of opinion. *The mate, who was a Dutchman, thought* that they ought to go and winter in Newfoundland, and seek for the Northwest passage through Davis' Straits. The master, Hudson, was opposed to this; *he feared his crew would mutiny,* because at times they had boldly menaced him, and also because they would be entirely overcome by the cold of winter, and be, after all, obliged to return with many of the crew weak and sickly. No one, however, spoke of returning home to Holland, *which gave cause of further suspicion to the master.* Consequently, he proposed that they should go and winter in Ireland, to which they all agreed, and at length arrived, November 7th, at Dartmouth in England. From this place they sent an account of their voyage to their masters in Holland, proposing to go in search of a passage to the Northwest if they were furnished with fifteen hundred guilders in money to buy provisions, in addition to their wages and what they had in the ship. He wished to have some six or seven of his crew changed, making the number up to twenty men, etc., and to sail from Dartmouth about the first of March, in order to be at the Northwest by the end of that month, and there pass the month of April and half of May in killing whales and other animals in the neighborhood of the isle of Panar; from there to go toward the Northwest and remain there till the middle of September, and afterward to return, by the northeast of Scotland, again to Holland. Thus was the voyage finished; but before the Directors could be informed of their arrival in England, a long time elapsed by reason of contrary winds, when at last they sent orders for the ship and crew to return at once to Holland. And when this was about to be done, the master, Henry Hudson, was ordered by the authorities there, not to depart, but remain and do service for his own country, which was also required of the other Englishmen in the ship. Many, however, thought it very strange that *the Masters,* who had been sent out for the common benefit of all kinds of navigation, should not be permitted to return in order to render an account and make a report of their doings and affairs to their employers. This took place in January, 1610. It was supposed that the English wished to send the same persons with some vessels to Virginia to explore further the before-mentioned river.

New Amsterdam, Frontier Trading Post, from Historisch Verhael, *Nicolaes van Wassenaer (1626)*

Nicolaes van Wassenaer was a Dutch scholar and physician who published his news journals twice a year during the 1620s. Van Wassenaer never visited New Amsterdam, and it appears that his account is based on information culled from sailors of the vessel *Arms of Amsterdam* that returned from the New World that year.

Unlike Boston, which was founded as a kind of religious experiment, New Amsterdam was founded for the purpose of making money. This graphic portrait of the trading post in 1626 reveals that even at that early date, the countinghouse, not the church, was the most important building in town.

Earlier, in 1624, van Wassenaer noted the adverse effects of the Dutch settlement on the native Lenape Indians' leaders. There was at least one Lenape sachem, van Wassenaer reported, "who comes forward to beg a draught of brandy with the rest."

THE colony is now established on the Manhates, where a fort has been staked out by Master Kryn Frederycks, an engineer. It is planned to be of large dimensions. The ship which has returned home this month [November] brings samples of all sorts of produce growing there. . . .

The counting-house there is kept in a stone building, thatched with reed; the other houses are of the bark of trees. Each has his own house. The Director and *Koopman* [commercial agent] live together; there are thirty ordinary houses on the east side of the river, which runs nearly north and south. The Honorable Pieter Minuit is Director there at present; Jan Lempou *schout* [sheriff]; Sebastiaen Jansz. Crol and Jan Huych, comforters of the sick, who, whilst awaiting a clergyman, read to the commonalty there, on Sundays, texts of Scripture and the commentaries. François Molemaecker is busy building a horse-mill, over which shall be constructed a spacious room sufficient to accommodate a large congregation, and then a tower is to be erected where the bells brought from Porto Rico will be hung.

The council there administers justice in criminal matters as far as imposing fines, but not as far as corporal punishment. Should it happen that anyone deserves that, he must be sent to Holland with his sentence. . . . Men work there as in Holland; one trades, upwards, southwards and northwards; another builds houses, the third farms. Each farmer has his farmstead on the land purchased by the Company [through the efforts of Peter Minuit, who purchased Manhattan Island from the Indians for sixty guilders, or about $24], which also owns the cows; but the milk remains to the profit of the farmer; he sells it to those of the people who receive their wages for work every week. The houses of the Hollanders now stand outside the fort, but when that is completed, they will all repair within, so as to garrison it and be secure from sudden attack.*

Those of the South River will abandon their fort [Fort Nassau], and come hither. At Fort Orange, the most northerly point at which the Hollanders traded, no more than fifteen or sixteen men will remain; the remainder will come down [to the Manhates]. . . .

When the fort, staked out at the Manhates, will be completed, it is to be named Amsterdam.

*It apparently never became necessary to concentrate all the residents within the fort, if indeed the enclosure was ever either large enough or secure enough to make this advisable. According to the *Historisch Verhael,* under the date of October 1628, the population numbered 270. "They remained as yet without the fort, in no fear, as the natives live peaceably with them. . . . These strangers for the most part occupy their farms. Whatever they require is supplied by the Directors. . . . The cattle sent thither have thriven well, and everything promises increase, as soon as the land is improved, which is full of weeds and poor."

Letter of the Eight Men to the States-General of the United Netherlands Provinces Regarding the Fear in New Amsterdam of the Indians During the Wars of 1643–1645 (1643)

Initially, the relations between the Dutch and the natives already resident on Manhattan Island were friendly. But white Europeans introduced alcohol and disease to the original inhabitants, as well as the strange concept of individual ownership of land. The Indians believed that land was like the sun and the stars, the wind and the rain, inasmuch as they could be used and enjoyed but not possessed. Increasingly, Dutch settlers came to view the most prominent local tribe, the Munsees, as unwanted and unwelcome neighbors. War finally broke out in 1640, and hostilities continued for almost five years. Among those killed in 1643 were Boston exile Anne Hutchinson and her followers. Both sides were guilty of ruthless atrocities, but the Indians clearly suffered the greater losses, especially in 1644.

The excerpt reprinted below ironically casts the Dutch as the victims and the Indians as the heartless and powerful aggressors, as the New Amsterdam colonists desperately appeal to the Estates General in Amsterdam for military assistance against the "savages."

THIS appeal sets forth that

we poor inhabitants of New Netherland were here in the spring pursued by these wild Heathen and barbarous Savages with fire and sword. Daily in our houses and fields have they cruelly murdered men and women, and with hatchets and tomahawks struck little children dead in their parents' arms, or before their doors, or carried them away into bondage. The houses and grain barracks are burnt with the produce; cattle of all description are slain and destroyed, and such as remain must perish this approaching winter for the want of fodder. Almost every place is abandoned. We, wretched people, must skulk with wives and little ones that still survive in poverty together in and around the fort at the Manahates where we are not safe even for an hour; whilst the Indians daily threaten to overwhelm us with it. Very little can be planted this autumn and much less in the spring; so that it will come to pass that all of us who will yet save our lives must of necessity perish next year of hunger and sorrow with our wives and children unless our God have pity on us.

We are all here, from the smallest to the greatest, devoid of counsel and means, wholly powerless. The enemy meets with scarce any resistance. The garrison consists of but fifty to sixty soldiers unprovided with ammunition. Fort Amsterdam, utterly defenceless, stands open to the enemy day and night.

The Company have few or no effects here (as the Director has informed us). Were it not for this, there would have been still time to receive assistance from the English at the East ere all had gone to ruin; and we wretched settlers, whilst we must abandon all our substance are exceedingly poor.

These heathens are strong in might. They have formed an alliance with seven other Nations, are well provided with guns, powder and lead, which they purchased for beaver from the private traders who have had for a long time free range here; the rest they take from our fellow-countrymen, whom they murder. In fine, we experience the greatest misery, which must astonish a Christian heart to see or to hear.

The Representation of New Netherland, 1650, Adriaen Van Der Donck

From its earliest establishment as an outpost of the Dutch West India Company, the future city of New York exhibited some of the same problems that were to confound its citizens for the next three and a half centuries. For example, the following excerpt by Adriaen Van Der Donck in 1650 demonstrates that New Amsterdam was a city founded on trade, that bad government was a persistent issue, and that racism against both the native Indians and the enslaved blacks was a problem from the beginning of settlement. However, Van Der Donck was also willing to blame the outpost's troubles on native women whom he found "utterly unchaste and shamefully promiscuous."

As we shall speak of the reasons and causes which have brought New Netherlands into the ruinous condition in which it is now found to be, we deem it necessary to state the very first difficulties and for this purpose, regard it as we see and find it in our daily experience. As far as our understanding goes, to describe it in one word (and none other better presents itself), it is *bad government,* with its attendants and consequences, that is the true and only *foundation stone* of the decay and ruin of New Netherlands. . . .

Trade, without which, when it is legitimate, no country is prosperous, is by their acts so decayed that it is like nowhere else. It is more suited for slaves than freemen, in consequences of the restrictions upon it and the annoyances which accompany the exercise of the right of inspection. . . .

In the meantime, the Christians are treated almost like Indians in the purchase of the necessaries with which they cannot dispense. This causes great complaint, distress, and poverty; as, for example, the merchants sell those goods which are liable to little depreciation at 100 percent and more profit, when there is no particular demand or scarcity of them. . . .

There are, also, various other Negroes in this country, some of whom have been made free for their long service, but their children have remained slaves, though it is contrary to the laws of every people that anyone born of a Christian mother should be a slave and be compelled to remain in servitude.

Exclusion of Jews from Military Service in New Amsterdam, The Burgher Council (1655)

The first Jews in New York arrived from Brazil in 1654 and immediately established Shearith Israel, the first Jewish congregation in what became the United States. By the middle of the nineteenth century, New York City was already the home of fifteen different synagogues and of one third of the total Jewish population in the entire country. And soon thereafter, Gotham became the largest Jewish city in the world.

Jews came to New York in large part because of the city's reputation for diversity and religious freedom. But many local citizens never accepted their Hebrew neighbors as equals. Governor Peter Stuyvesant in 1654 objected to "the obstinate and immovable Jews" who "have no other God than the Mammon of unrighteousness, and no other aim than to get possession of Christian property." The next year, as the following document indicates, the Burgher Council successfully excluded Jews from military service and then, showing great chutzpah, taxed them for their inability to serve.

THE captains and officers of the trainbands of this city, having asked the director general and Council whether the Jewish people who reside in this city should also train and mount guard with the citizens' bands, this was taken in consideration and deliberated upon. First, the disgust and unwillingness of these trainbands to be fellow soldiers with the aforesaid nation and to be on guard with them in the same guardhouse, and, on the other side, that the said nation was not admitted or counted among the citizens, as regards trainbands or common citizens' guards, neither in the illustrious city of Amsterdam nor (to our knowledge) in any city in Netherland. But in order that the said nation may honestly be taxed for their freedom in that respect, it is directed by the director general and Council, to prevent further discontent, that the aforesaid nation shall, according to the usages of the renowned city of Amsterdam, remain exempt from the general training and guard duty, on condition that each male person over sixteen and under sixty years contribute for the aforesaid freedom toward the relief of the general municipal taxes sixty-five stivers [one stiver equals two cents] every month. And the military council of the citizens is hereby authorized and charged to carry this into effect until our further orders, and to collect, pursuant to the above, the aforesaid contribution once in every month, and, in case of refusal, to collect it by legal process. Thus done in Council at Fort Amsterdam.

Remonstrance of the Inhabitants of the Town of Flushing (1657)

Although New Yorkers may not be more tolerant than citizens of other cities, the tradition in Gotham is of religious freedom. Whereas in Boston, Anne Hutchinson was expelled from the Massachusetts Bay Colony for expressing views about Puritanism that were at odds with the ruling orthodoxy, in New Amsterdam the colonists were guaranteed freedom of religion almost from the beginning of settlement. No document was more important in this regard than the Flushing Remonstrance.

Governor Peter Stuyvesant had issued a proclamation banning Quakers from New Netherlands and threatening fines for anyone convicted of "harboring" a Quaker. The Remonstrance echoed the sentiment of the Dutch West India Company directors, who in 1654 had chastised Stuyvesant for attempting to turn away twenty-three Sephardic Jews from Recife, Brazil. In their statement of policy they wrote, "The conscience of men ought to be free and unshackled, so long as they continue moderate, peaceable, inoffensive and not hostile to government. Such have been the maxims of . . . toleration by which . . . this city has been governed; and the result has been, that the oppressed and persecuted from every country have among us an asylum from distress. Follow in the same steps and you will be blessed."

Stuyvesant dismissed the Remonstrance as a "seditious, mutinous and detestable letter of defiance" and ordered the town's officials arrested.

To Governor Stuyvesant

DECEMBER 27, 1657

Right Honorable,

YOU have been pleased to send up unto us a certain prohibition or command that we should not receive or entertain any of those people called *Quakers* because they are supposed to be by some, seducers of the people.

For our part we cannot condemn them in this case, neither can we stretch out our hands against them, to punish, banish or persecute them for out of Christ God is a consuming fire, and it is a fearful thing to fall into the hands of the living God.

We desire therefore in this case not to judge lest we be judged, neither to condemn least we be condemned, but rather let every man stand and fall to his own Master. Wee are bounde by the Law to Doe good unto all men, especially to those of the household of faith. And though for the present we seem to be unsensible of the law and the Law giver, yet when death and the Law assault us, if we have our advocate to seeke, who shall plead for us in this case of conscience betwixt God and our own souls; the powers of this world can neither attack us, neither excuse us, for if God justifye who can condemn and if God condemn there is none can justify.

And for those jealousies and suspicions which some have of them, that they are destructive unto Magistracy and Minssereye, that can not bee, for the magistrate hath the sword in his hand and the minister hath the sword in his hand, as witnesse those two great examples which all magistrates and ministers are to follow, Moses and Christ, whom God raised up maintained and defended against all the enemies both of flesh and spirit; and therefore that which is of God will stand, and that which is of man will come to nothing. And as the Lord hath taught Moses or the civil power to give an outward liberty in the state by the law written in his heart designed for the good of all, and can truly judge who is good, who is civil, who is true and who is false, and can pass definite sentence of life or death against that man which rises up against the fundamental law of the States General; soe he hath made his ministers a savor of life unto life, and a savor of death unto death.

The law of love, peace and liberty in the states extending to *Jews, Turks,* and *Egyptians,* as they are considered the sonnes of Adam, which is the glory of the outward state of *Holland,* soe love, peace and liberty, extending to all in Christ Jesus, condemns hatred, war and bondage. And because our Saviour saith it is impossible but that offenses will come, but woe unto him by whom they cometh, our desire is not to offend one of his little ones, in whatsoever form, name or title he appears in, whether Presbyterian, Independent, Baptist or Quaker, but shall be glad to see anything of God in any of them, desiring to doe unto all men as we desire all men should doe unto us, which is the true law both of Church and State; for our Savior saith this is the law and the prophets.

Therefore, if any of these said persons come in love unto us, wee cannot in conscience lay violent hands upon them, but give them free egresse and regresse unto our Town, and houses, as God shall persuade our consciences. And in this we are true subjects both of Church and State, for we are bounde by the law of God and man to doe good unto all men and evil to noe man. And this is according to the patent and charter of our Towne, given unto us in the name of the States General, which we are not willing to infringe, and violate, but shall houlde to our patent and shall remaine, your humble subjects, the inhabitants of *Vlishing.*

Written this 27th day of December, in the year 1657, by mee
Edward Hart, *Clericus*

Description of the Towne of Mannadens, Anonymous (1661)

The last and most important of the four Dutch governors of New Amsterdam, Peter Stuyvesant, arrived in Manhattan in 1647 and remained in power until an English fleet captured the city in 1664 and renamed it New York. Stuyvesant was not altogether attractive as a person. For example, he forbade all religious observances except those of the Dutch Reformed Church, and he tried to prevent Jews from entering the colony. But he was an effective and progressive administrator. Stuyvesant built the first pier on the East River, helped establish the first Latin School, created the first night watch (police) and poorhouse, rebuilt Broad Street, erected the first hospital, opened the first post office, improved relations with English colonists, and allowed the formation of municipal government for New Amsterdam. The following description of the town in 1661 gives some of the flavor of his achievements.

Also of note is that the settlement is referred to as Mannadens (or Manhattan). The unclear origin of the name derives from Munsee words meaning "place of general inebriation," or "place where timber is procured for bows and arrows," or simply "hilly island."

THE Easter-side of the Towne is from the North-East gate [at the eastern extremity of the wall] unto the point, whereon the Governors new house stands, and it contains 490 yards. . . . On this side of the towne there is a gutte [canal], whereby at high water boats goe into the towne. Also on this side stands the Stat-house [originally the town tavern], before w[hi]ch is built a half moon of stone, where are mounted 3 smal bras guns. . . .

The Souther-side or roundhead of the Town [now the Battery] is bounded with the arm of the Sea. . . . Nearest the westerside of this head is a plot of ground, on w[hi]ch stands a windmill; and a Fort foursquare, 100 yards on each side, at each corner flanked out 26 yards. . . . In this Fort is the Church, the Governors house, and houses for soldiers, ammunition, etc.

The wester-side of the towne is from the windmill unto the Northwest corner [the westernmost point of the wall] 480 yards. . . . The land side of the towne is from the Northwest corner unto the North E. gate 520 yards and lyeth neer N. W. and S. E. having six flankers [bastions] at equal distance, in four of w[hi]ch are mounted 8 guns. . . .

Within the towne, in the midway between the N. W. corner and N. E. gate, the ground hath a smal descent on each side much alike, and so continues through the town unto the arme of the water on the Easter-side of the Towne: by the help of this descent they have made a gut almost through the towne [Broad Street canal], keyed it on both sides with timber and boards as far in as the 3 small bridges; and near the coming into the gut they have built two firme timber bridges with railes on each side. At low water the gut is dry, at high water boats come into it, passing under the 2 bridges, and go as far as the 3 small bridges. . . .

The town . . . hath good air, and is healthy, inhabited with severall sorts of trades men and marchants and mariners.

Mercantilist Ideas, from England's Treasure by Forraign Trade, *Thomas Mun (1664)*

On August 27, 1664, an English fleet, sent by James, the Duke of York (the future King James II), arrived in New Amsterdam's great harbor with decidedly unfriendly intentions. Governor Stuyvesant of course sounded the alarm and repaired to the fort, determined to resist until the end. "I would rather be carried to my grave than surrender," he declared. But his fellow citizens were not so brave, especially when they considered the power of the warships arrayed against them, and they implored Stuyvesant to accept the generous surrender terms. The governor knew what the English cannons could do against his largely wooden city, and so, with drums beating and flags flying, the Dutch militia marched out of the fort two days later. The next day, businesses opened at their customary hours as if nothing had happened.

The British were tolerant of Dutch practices and eager to continue to improve New York's mercantile position. In this selection, Thomas Mun (1571–1641), a seventeenth-century English economist, offers a summary of prevailing mercantile views of the time.

1. FIRST, although this Realm be already exceedingly rich by nature, yet might it be much increased by laying the waste grounds (which are infinite) into such employments as should no way hinder the present revenues of other manured [cultivated] lands, but hereby to supply our selves and prevent the importations of Hemp, Flax, Cordage, Tobacco, and divers other things which now we fetch from strangers to our great impoverishing.
2. We may likewise diminish our importations, if we would soberly refrain from excessive consumption of forraign wares in our diet and rayment, . . . which vices at this present are more notorious amongst us than in former ages. Yet might they easily be amended by enforcing the observation of such good laws as are strictly practiced in other Countries

against the said excesses; where likewise by commanding their own manufactures to be used, they prevent the coming in of others. . . .

4. The value of our exportations likewise may be much advanced when we perform it ourselves in our own Ships, for then we get only not the price of our wares as they are worth here, but also the Merchants gains, the charges of insurance, and freight to carry them beyond the seas. . . .

Prosperity in New York, from A Brief Description of New York, *Daniel Denton (1670)*

The first printed description in English of the city of New York was written by Daniel Denton and published in London in 1670. Denton's father, Reverend Richard Denton, was the first minister of Hempstead, Long Island, and a member of the General Assembly of Deputies, which in 1665 drew up the English laws for the new colony of New York.

The attitude of the Lenape Indians toward the potential "inheritances of lands and possessions" to be had through labor startled Denton, however, when he observed that "one having nothing to spare, but he freely imparts it to his friends, and whatsoever they get by gaming or any other way, they share with one another, leaving themselves commonly the least share."

I MAY say, & say truly, that if there be any terrestrial happiness to be had by people of all ranks, especially of an inferior rank, it must certainly be here: here any one may furnish himself with land, & live rent-free, yea, with such a quantity of Land, that he may weary himself with walking over his fields of Corn, and all sorts of Grain: & let his stock of Cattel amount to some hundreds, he needs not fear their want of pasture in the Summer or Fodder in the Winter, the Woods affording sufficient supply. For the *Summer* season, where you have grass as high as a man's knees, nay, as high as his waste, interlaced with Pea-vines and other weeds that Cattel much delight in, as much as a man can press through; and these woods also every mile or half-mile are furnished with fresh ponds, books or rivers, where all sorts of Cattel, during the heat of the day, do quench their thirst and cool themselves. . . . Here those which Fortune hath frown'd upon in *England*, to deny them an inheritance amongst their Brethren, or such as by their utmost labors can scarcely procure a living, I say such may procure here inheritances of lands & possessions, stock themselves with all sorts of Cattel, enjoy the benefit of them whilst they live, & leave them to the benefit of their children when they die.

What shall I say more? you shall scarce see a house, but the South side is begirt with Hives of Bees, which increase after an incredible manner: That I must needs say, that if there be any terrestrial *Canaans*, 'tis surely here, where all the Land floweth with milk & Honey. The inhabitants are blest with Peace & plenty, blessed in their Countrey, blessed in their Fields, blessed in the Fruit of their bodies, in the fruit of their grounds, in the increase of their Cattel, Horses and Sheep, blessed in their Basket, & in their store; In a word, blessed in whatsoever they take in hand, or go about, the Earth yielding plentiful increases to all their painful labours.

True Copy of Articles Whereupon . . . The New Netherlands Were Surrendered (January 1674)

The Dutch briefly recaptured New Netherlands in July 1673; led by Admiral Cornelis Evertsen, the Dutch landed six hundred marines and amongst "demonstrations of joy" on the part of the Dutch population renamed the city New Orange after Prince William. But the Dutch had no interest in defending the colony, and it was returned to England in a formal peace treaty in February 1674.

One early source of tension in the colony had been the "patroon" system that the Dutch West India Company had put in place to promote settlement. In the Charter of Liberties in 1629 the company had awarded large tracts of lands to patroons who agreed to buy the land from the Indians and finance the passage of settlers to the new land. The articles of 1674 took care to allow owners to retain their right to those lands. Although Rensselaerswyck, the property of Kiliaen van Rensselaer, was the only one of these left by the 1640s, the Duke of York had given equally large amounts of land to his supporters. By the early 1700s five families held almost 1.75 million acres in the area of New York City; those families continued to exert profound influence over the city well into the nineteenth century.

We consent that the States General, or the West India Company shall freely enjoy all Farms & Houses (except such as are in the forts) and that within six months they shall have free liberty to transport all such arms and ammunition as do belong to them, or else they shall be paid for them.

2. All publick Houses shall continue for the uses, which now they are for.
3. All people shall continue free Denizens and enjoy their Lands, Houses, Goods, Ships wherever they are within this Country, and dispose of them as they please.

4. If any Inhabitants have a mind to remove himself he shall have a year and six weeks from this day to remove himself, wife, children, serv[an]ts, goods. . . .
5. If any officer of State or public Minister of State have a mind to go for England they shall be transported freight free in His Ma[jesty']s frigates when the frigate shall return thither.
6. It is consented to that any people may freely come from the Netherlands and plant in this Country. . . .
7. All Ships from the Netherlands or any other places, and goods therein, shall be received here and sent hence after the manner which formerly they were before our coming hither for six months. . . .
8. The Dutch here shall enjoy their Liberty of their Consciences in Divine worship and Church Discipline.
9. No Dutchman here or Dutch ship here shall upon any occasion be forced to serve in war against any Nation whatsoever.
10. That . . . Manhattan shall not have any Soldiers quartered among them without being . . . payd for them, by their officers. . . .
11. The Dutch here shall enjoy their own Customs concerning their Inheritances. . . .

The Demand for English Liberties in New York: The Charter of Liberties and Privileges (October 30, 1683)

Although the new English rulers were generally permissive, the Duke of York for fifteen years refused to grant self-government to New York and insisted upon his "full and absolute authority." But citizens of Long Island increasingly refused to pay taxes levied without their consent, and by 1681 they were joined by important New York City merchants. In order to quell this incipient revolt, the duke in 1683 authorized Governor Thomas Dongan to call a representative assembly. The new group met on October 17, 1683, and promptly passed a Charter of Liberties and Privileges.

"Dongan's Charter" made New York a self-governing corporation and although there was some consternation over baronial land grants and feudal powers granted to families such as the van Rensselaers, the van Cortlandts, and the Livingstons, Dongan remained in power until Sir Edmund Andros arrived in August 1688 to incorporate New York as part of the Dominion of New England.

ffOR The better Establishing the Government of this province of New Yorke and that Justice and Right may be Equally done to all persons within the same.

BEE It Enacted by the Governour Councell and Representatives now in Generall Assembly mett and assembled and by the authority of the same.

THAT The Supreme Legislative Authority under his Majesty and Royall Highnesse James Duke of Yorke Albany &c Lord proprietor of the said province shall forever be and reside in a Governour, Councell, and the people mett in General Assembly.

THAT The Exercise of the Cheife Magistracy and Administration of the Government over the said province shall bee in the said Governour assisted by a Councell with whose advice and Consent or with at least four of them he is to rule and Governe the same according to the Lawes thereof.

THAT in Case the Governour shall dye or be absent out of the province and that there be noe person within the said province Comissionated by his Royal Highnesse his heires or Successours to be Governour or Comander in Cheife there That then the Councell for the time being or Soe many of them as are in the Said province doe take upon them the Administration of the Governour and Execution of the Lawes thereof and powers and authorityes belonging to the Governour and Councell the first in nomination in which Councell is to preside untill the said Governour shall returne and arrive in the said province againe, or the pleasure of his Royall Highnesse his heires or Successours Shall be further knowne.

THAT According to the usage Custome and practice of the Realme of England a session of a Generall Assembly be held in this province once in three yeares at least.

THAT Every ffreeholder within this province and ffreeman in any Corporation Shall have his free Choise and Vote in the Electing of the Representatives without any manner of constraint or Imposition. And that in all Elections the Majority of Voices shall carry itt and by freeholders is understood every one who is Soe understood according to the Lawes of England.

THAT the persons to be Elected to sitt as representatives in the Generall Assembly from time to time for the severall Cittyes townes Countyes Shires or Divisions of this province and all places within the same shall be according to the proportion and number hereafter Expressed that is to say for the Citty, and County of New Yorke four, for the County of Suffolke two, for Queens County two, for Kings County two, for the County of Richmond two for the County of West Chester two.

FOR the County of Ulster two for the County of Albany two and for Schenectade within the said County one for Dukes County two, for the County of Cornwall two and as many more as his Royall Highnesse shall think fitt to Establish.

THAT All persons Chosen and Assembled in manner aforesaid or the Major part of them shall be deemed and accounted the Representatives of this province which said Representatives together with the Governour and his Councell Shall forever be the Supreame and only Legislative power under his Royall Highnesse of the said province.

THAT The said Representatives may appoint their owne Times of meeting dureing their sessions and may adjourne their house from time to time to such time as to them shall seeme meet and convenient.

THAT The said Representatives are the sole Judges of the Qualifications of their owne members, and likewise of all undue Elections and may from time to time purge their house as they shall see occasion dureing the said sessions.

THAT noe member of the general Assembly or their servants dureing the time of their Sessions and whilest they shall be goeing to and returning from the said Assembly shall be arrested sued imprisoned or any wayes molested or troubled nor be compelled to make answere to any suite, Bill, plaint, Declaration or otherwise, (Cases of High Treason and felony only Excepted) provided the number of the said servants shall not Exceed three.

THAT All bills agreed upon by the said Representatives or the Major part of them shall be presented unto the Governour and his Councell for their Approbation and Consent All and Every which Said Bills soe approved of Consented to by the Governour and his Councell shall be Esteemed and accounted the Lawes of the province, Which said Lawes shall continue and remaine of force untill they shall be repealed by the authority aforesaid that is to say the Governour Councell and Representatives in General Assembly by and with the Approbation of his Royal Highnesse or Expire by their owne Limittations.

THAT In all Cases of death or removall of any of the said Representatives The Governour shall issue out Sumons by Writt to the Respective Townes Cittyes Shires Countryes or Divisions for which he or they soe removed or deceased were Chosen willing and requireing the ffreeholders of the Same to Elect others in their place and stead.

THAT Noe freeman shall be taken and imprisoned or be disseized of his ffreehold or Libertye or ffree Customes or be outlawed or Exiled or any other wayes destroyed nor shall be passed upon adjudged or condemned But by the Lawfull Judgment of his peers and by the Law of this province. Justice nor Right shall be neither sold denyed or deferred to any man within this province.

THAT Noe aid, Tax, Tallage, Assessment, Custome, Loane, Benevolence or Imposition whatsoever shall be layed assessed imposed or levyed on any of his Majestyes Subjects within this province or their Estates upon any manner of Colour or pretence but by the act and Consent of the Governour Councell and Representatives of the people in Generall Assembly mett and Assembled.

THAT Noe man of what Estate or Condition soever shall be putt out of his Lands or Tenements, nor taken, nor imprisoned, nor disherited, nor banished nor any wayes distroyed without being brought to Answere by due Course of Law.

THAT A ffreeman Shall not be amerced for a small fault, but after the manner of his fault and for a great fault after the Greatnesse thereof Saveing to him his freehold, And a husbandman saveing to him his Wain-age and a merchant likewise saveing to him his merchandize And none of the said Amerciaments shall be assessed but by the oath of twelve honest and Lawfull men of the Vicinage provided the faults and misdemeanours be not in Contempt of Courts of Judicature.

ALL Tryalls shall be by the verdict of twelve men, and as neer as may be peers or Equalls And of the neighbourhood and in the County Shire or Division where the fact Shall arise or grow Whether the Same be by Indictment Information Declaration or otherwise against the person Offender or Defendant.

THAT In all Cases Capitall or Criminall there shall be a grand Inquest who shall first present the offence and then twelve men of the neighbourhood to try the Offender who after his plea to the Indictment shall be allowed his reasonable Challenges.

THAT In all Cases whatsoever Bayle by sufficient Suretyes Shall be allowed and taken unlesse for treason or felony plainly and specially Expressed and menconed in the Warrant of Committment provided Alwayes that nothing herein contained shall Extend to discharge out of prison upon bayle any person taken in Execution for debts or otherwise legally sentenced by the Judgment of any of the Courts of Record within the province.

THAT Noe ffreeman shall be compelled to receive any Marriners or Souldiers into his house and there suffer them to Sojourne, against their willes provided Alwayes it be not in time of Actuall Warr within this province.

THAT Noe Commissions for proceeding by Marshall Law against any of his Majestyes Subjects within this province shall issue forth to any person or persons whatsoever Least by Colour of them any of his Majestyes Subjects bee destroyed or putt to death Except all such officers persons and Soldiers in pay throughout the Government.

THAT from hence forward Noe Lands Within this province shall be Esteemed or accounted a Chattle or personall Estate but an Estate of Inheritance according to the Custome and practice of his Majesties Realme of England.

THAT Noe Court or Courts within this province have or at any time hereafter Shall have any Jurisdiction power or authority to grant out any Execution or other writt whereby any mans Land may be sold or any other way disposed off without the owners Consent provided Alwayes That the issues or meane proffitts of any mans Lands shall or may be Extended by Execution or otherwise to satisfye just debts Any thing to the Contrary hereof in any wise Notwithstanding.

THAT Noe Estate of a feme Covert shall be sold or conveyed But by Deed acknowledged by her in Some Court of Record the Woman being secretly Examined if She doth it freely without threats or Compulsion of her husband.

THAT All Wills in writeing attested by two Credible Witnesses shall be of the same force to convey Lands as other Conveyances being registered in the Secretaryes Office within forty dayes after the testators death.

THAT A Widdow after the death of her husband shall have her Dower And shall and may tarry in the Cheife house of her husband forty dayes after the death of her husband within which forty dayes her Dower shall be assigned her And for her Dower shall be assigned unto her the third part of all the Lands of her husband dureing Coverture, Except shee were Endowed of Lesse before Marriage.

THAT All Lands and Heritages within this province and Dependencyes shall be free from all fines and Lycences upon Alienations, and from all Herriotts Ward Shipps Liveryes primer Seizins yeare day and Wast Escheats and forfeitures upon the death of parents and Ancestors naturall unaturall casuall or Judiciall, and that forever; Cases of High treason only Excepted.

THAT Noe person or persons which professe ffaith in God by Jesus Christ Shall at any time be any wayes molested punished disquieted or called in Question for any Difference in opinion or Matter of Religious Concernment, who doe not actually disturb the Civill peace of the province, But that all and Every such person or persons may from time to time and at all times freely have and fully enjoy his or their Judgments or Consciencyes in matters of Religion throughout all the province, they behaveing themselves peaceably and quietly and not useing this Liberty to Lycentiousnesse nor to the civill Injury or outward disturbance of others provided Alwayes that this liberty or any thing contained therein to the Contrary shall never be Construed or improved to make void the Settlement of any publique Minister on Long Island Whether Such Settlement be by two thirds of the voices in any Towne thereon which shall alwayes include the Minor part Or by Subscriptions of perticuler Inhabitants in Said Townes provided they are the two thirds thereon Butt that all such agreements Covenants and Subscriptions that are there already made and had Or that hereafter shall bee in this Manner Consented to agreed and Subscribed shall at all time and times hereafter be firme and Stable And in Confirmation hereof It is Enacted by the Governour Councell and Representatives; That all Such Sumes of money soe agreed on Consented to or Subscribed as aforesaid for maintenance of said publick Ministers by the two thirds of any Towne on Long Island Shall alwayes include the Minor part who shall be regulated thereby And also Such Subscriptions and agreements as are before mentioned are and Shall be alwayes ratified performed and paid, And if any Towne on said Island in their publick Capacity of agreement with any Such minister or any perticuler persons by their private Subscriptions as aforesaid Shall make default deny or withdraw from Such payment Soe Covenanted to agreed upon and Subscribed That in Such Case upon Complaint of any Collector appointed and Chosen by two thirds of Such Towne upon Long Island unto any Justice of that County Upon his hearing the Same he is here by authorized impowered and required to issue out his warrant unto the Constable or his Deputy or any other person appointed for the Collection of Said Rates or agreement to Levy upon the goods and Chattles of the Said Delinquent or Defaulter all such Sumes of money Soe covenanted and agreed to be paid by distresse with Costs and Charges without any further Suite in Law Any Lawe Custome or usage to the Contrary in any wise Notwithstanding.

PROVIDED Alwayes the said sume or sumes be under forty shillings otherwise to be recovered as the Law directs.

AND WHEREAS All the Respective Christian Churches now in practice within the City of New Yorke and the other places of this province doe appeare to be priviledged Churches and have beene Soe Established and Confirmed by the former authority of this Government BEE it hereby Enacted by this Generall Assembly and by the authority thereof That all the Said Respective Christian Churches be hereby Confirmed therein And that they and Every of them Shall from henceforth forever be held and reputed as priviledged Churches and Enjoy all their former freedomes of their Religion in Divine Worshipp and Church Discipline And that all former Contracts made and agreed upon for the maintenances of the severall ministers of the Said Churches shall stand and continue in full force and virtue And that all Contracts for the future to be made Shall bee of the same power And all persons that are unwilling to performe their part of the said Contract Shall be Constrained thereunto by a warrant from any Justice of the peace provided it be under forty Shillings Or otherwise as this Law directs provided allsoe that all Christian Churches that Shall hereafter come and settle within this province shall have the Same priviledges.

Leisler's Rebellion: Benjamin Blagge's Memorial, from The Documentary History of the State of New-York, *Benjamin Blagge (1689)*

During the Glorious Revolution in England (1689–1691), when the Catholic King James II was overthrown by the Protestant William and Mary, a young captain of the militia in New York took over the fort and made himself the chief military commander of the city. Jacob Leisler (1640–1691) also assumed the title of lieutenant governor of the province and planned a military and naval expedition against Canada. When a contingent of English regular troops arrived in the city in 1691, they arrested Leisler and tried him for treason. He and his chief assistant, Jacob Milborne, were executed on May 16, 1691. Even then the split between Leislerians and anti-Leislerians would dominate New York politics for decades to come.

A Memoriall of What Has Occurred in Their Majesties Province of New York since the News of Their Majesties Happy Arrivall in England

SETTING forth the necessity of removing Capt. Fran: Nicholson (late Lieut. Govr. of the said Province) and putting the command thereof into [the] hands of such persons, of whose fidelity and good Inclination to their present Majesties the aforesaid Province is well assured.

The said Capt. Nicholson (in imitation of his Predecessor Coll Dungan) wholly neglected to repair the Fort and Fortifications of the city, and that not without a vehement suspicion, thereby the more easily to betray the same into the enemies hands, of which he gave the said Province sufficient grounds of apprehensions by discovering both by words and actions, his disaffection to the happy Revolution in England, and also to the inhabitants of the City by threatening to fire the same about their ears.

Whereupon the Inhabitants in order to secure the said Fort and City for their Majesties use and to repair and fortify the same & to place the government of the Province in the hands of some of undoubted loyalty and affection to their present Majesties Did remove the said Capt: Nicholson, and made choice of Capt: Jacob Leisler with a Committee (who were also chosen by the people) to take into their hands the Care and Charge of the Government until Their Majesties Pleasure should be further known.

Shortly after arrived their Majesties Proclamation to Proclaim them King and Queen of England, France and Ireland, notice whereof was given to those of the former Councill, and to the Mayor and Aldrmen of the City to assist in proclaiming thereof with the proper ceremonies for that solemnity, who desired an hours time to consider of it, which time being expired and no complyance yielded, but on the contrary an aversion discovered thereto, The said Capt. Leisler accompanyed with the Committee & most part of the Inhabitants, did with all the Demonstrations of Joy and affection they were capable of celebrate the same.

Whereupon the Mayor and Aldermen were suspended and some persons confined, who were the most eminent in opposing Their Majesties Interest and this Revolution, and some short time after this Their Majesties Letter arrived Directed to Capt Francis Nicholson Esqr Lieut. Governor of Their Majesties Province of New York and in his absence, to such as for the time being do take care for the preservation of their Majesties Peace, and Administring the Laws in that Their Majesties Province, Ordering such to take upon them the Place of Lieut Governor and Commander in Chief of the said Province, and to proclaim King William & Queen Mary King & Queen of England Scotland France and Ireland and Supreme Lord and Lady of the Province of New York, if not already done, which was accordingly performed.

The Inhabitants of the said City and Province conceiving that by vertue of Their Majesties said Letter, the said Capt Leisler was sufficiently Impowered to Receive the same and to act accordingly It gave them a generall satisfaction, whereupon the said Committee were immediately dismissed and a Councill chosen by whose assistance Capt Leisler acts in the said Government pursuant to His Majesties Order.

The members of the former Government notwithstanding gave all the opposition they could to this Reformation & have created a ffaction in the said Province to the endangering the loss thereof, since it happens at a time that we are under continuall alarms from the frequent attacks the French make upon our Frontiers, so that without the care and precaution aforesaid this Their Majesties Province was in apparent hazard of being delivered up to the Canada Forces belonging to the French King, whereby Their present Majesties most loyall protestant subjects of this Province would have been rendered miserable, equall to their fears, and this Province became a Colony of the French.

And to that height of insolence was that disaffected Party growne, that in a riotous manner in the day time they besett and surrounded the Capt. Leisler our Lievt. Govr. in the street treating him will ill Language & threats & had undoubtedly done violence to his person, had they not been apprehensive of danger to themselves from the people, who immediately gathered together and rescued the Governor out of their hands, seizing some of the principall actors and Ringleaders in that Ryott and committing them to prison, and their ffriends and confederates sending them provisions to the prison in a superabundant and extraordinary manner, designedly to affront and insult the Government: thereupon it was thought fit to order, that no provisions should be permitted to be brought them, and they should only be allowed Bread and water, but that severity was continued towards them only for two daies, and afterwards they had the Liberty to have what Provisions they pleased.

This riotous Action of the Male-Contents occasioned a further Tumult of ill consequence to themselves for the Country people upon a rumour that the Government was in danger by the Rising of the disaffected party, flockt into the City armed in great numbers, and notwithstanding the endeavours of the Magistrates to appease them, they took the liberty (as is too usuall with an enraged multitude) to perpetrate revenge on those which were the occasion of their coming, Quartering themselves in their houses for two daies and committing divers Insolences upon them, much to the dissatisfaction of the Magistrates till they could persuade them to return in quiet to their houses, however it was thought requisite by the Government for the preventing such disorders for the future and to secure the publick peace, to detein severall of the disaffected in Prison for a time, some whereof were since fined, but all ordered to be discharged from Prison upon paying their Fines and entering into Recognizance to be of good Behaviour for the future.

The Fort and City are therefore now in a good posture wanting only Ammunition.

The Commissions are called in from those of the former Militia, who acted under Coll Dungan and Sir Edmond Andros, and other Commissions granted in the name of their present Majesties to such as are well affected to their Majesties Interest.

Upon these our actings for the Securing Their Majesties Interest in this Province and conserving the publick Peace our enemys have endeavoured all they can to misrepresent us and load us with Reproach, by terming our aforesaid proceedings a *Dutch Plott,* because indeed three quarter parts of the Inhabitants are descended from the Dutch & speak that language, and they also threaten our ruine, if ever the Government come into their hands again.

Which that it may not doe, and Their Majesties most loyal and dutiful subjects in this province may reap the benefit and blessing of this most happy Revolution, and not be made a Prey to most implacable and Insulting enemies on our Borders, who are ready to enter and devour us—humbly Submitting ourselves to your Majesties most Royall Will and Pleasure.

Contract of an Indentured Apprentice (October 2, 1718)

Travel was expensive in the colonial period, and many persons bound for the New World essentially promised their services for a stated number of years in return for the money for passage. In New York, as in other colonies, this practice of binding someone by a contract, or indenture, was common. Typically, it also involved on-the-job training in a particular skill. In the best circumstances, apprenticeship could be a means of acquiring a useful vocation, and in many cases, the master was in fact legally obligated to teach his trade to an apprentice in return for his labor. The following excerpt is from a contract of October 2, 1718, in which the obligations of the two parties are made explicit.

THIS indenture witnesses that I, William Mathews, son of Marrat of the city of New York, a widow . . . does voluntarily and of his own free will and accord and by the consent of his said mother put himself as an apprentice cordwainer to Thomas Windover of the city aforesaid.

He will live and (after the manner of an apprentice) serve from August 15, 1718, until the full term of seven years be completed and ended. During all of this term, the said apprentice shall faithfully serve his said master, shall faithfully keep his secrets, and gladly obey his lawful commands everywhere. He shall do no damage to his said master, nor see any done by others without giving notice to his said master. He shall not waste his said master's goods nor lend them unlawfully to any. He shall not commit fornication nor contract matrimony within the said term.

At cards, dice, or any other unlawful game, he shall not play (whereby his said master may have damage) with his own goods or the goods of others. Without a license from his master he shall neither buy nor sell during the said term. He shall not absent himself day or night from his master's service without his leave, nor haunt alehouses, but in all things he shall behave himself as a faithful apprentice toward his master all during his said term.

The said master, during the said term, shall, by the best means or methods, teach or cause the said apprentice to be taught the art or mystery of a cordwainer. He shall find and provide unto the said apprentice sufficient meat, drink, apparel, lodging, and washing fit for an apprentice. During the said term, every night in winter he shall give the apprentice one quarter of schooling. At the expiration of the said term he shall provide him with a sufficient new suit of apparel, four shirts, and two necklets.

From the New York Weekly Journal *(March 11, 1733)*

Most historians trace the origins of the American notion of freedom of the press to an obscure German immigrant who arrived in New York City in 1710 and then worked as an apprentice in a printing shop at 81 Pearl Street. After his stint as a journeyman, John Peter Zenger set up shop as a printer. In the early 1730s, he began criticizing the colonial government, and in 1734 he was arrested for seditious libel and imprisoned for almost a year in City Hall. Ultimately, he was found not guilty, and he resumed his printing business. Thus did John Peter Zenger become known as the father of freedom of the press in the United States.

The following piece from the *New York Weekly Journal,* which might seem rather innocuous to the modern reader, was one of the essays that led to Zenger's arrest.

Mr. Zenger,

PRAY insert the following sentiments of Cato, and you'll oblige Yours, &c.

Considering what sort of a Creature Man is, it is scarce possible to put him under too many restraints, when he is possessed of great Power: He may possibly use it well; but they act most prudently, who supposing that he would use it ill enclose him within certain Bounds and make it terrible to him to exceed them.

It is nothing strange, that Men, who think themselves unaccountable, should act unaccountably, and that all Men would be unaccountable if they could . . . ; and no Man cares to be at the entire Mercy of another. Hence it is that if every Man had his Will, all Men would exercise Dominion, and no Man would suffer it. It is therefore owing more to the Necessities of Men, than to their Inclinations, that they have put themselves under the Restraint of Laws, and appointed certain persons, called Magistrates, to execute them;

otherwise they would never be executed, scarce any Man having such a Degree of Virtue as unwillingly to execute the Laws upon himself. . . .

Hence grew the Necessity of Government, which was the mutual Contract of a Number of Men, agreeing upon certain Terms of Union and Society, and putting themselves under Penalties if they violated these terms, which were called Laws, and put into the Hands of one or more Men to execute. And thus men quitted Part of their natural Liberty to acquire civil Security. But frequently the Remedy prov'd worse than the Disease; and humane Society had often no enemies so great as their own Magistrates; who, wherever they were trusted with too much Power, always abused it, and grew mischievous to those who made them what they were. Rome, while she was free, (that is, while she kept her Magistrates within due bounds) could defend herself against all the world, and conquer it; but being enslaved (that is her Magistrates having broke their Bounds) she could not defend her self against her own single Tyrants; nor could they defend her against her foreign Foes and Invaders: For by their Madness and Cruelties they had destroyed her Virtue and Spirit, and exhausted her Strength. . . .

The common People generally think that great Men have great Minds, and scorn base Actions; which Judgment is so false, that the basest and worst of all Actions have been done by great Men; perhaps they have not picked private Pockets, but they have done worse, they have often disturbed, deceived and pillaged the World: And he who is capable of the highest Mischiefs, is capable of the Meanest. He who plunders a Country of Millions of Money, would in suitable Circumstances steal a Silver Spoon; and a Conqueror, who steals and pillages a Kingdom, would in an humbler Fortune rifle a Portmanteau or rob an Orchard.

Political Jealousy, therefore, in the people is a necessary and laudable Passion. But in a Chief Magistrate, a Jealousy of his People is not so justifiable, their Ambition being only to preserve themselves; whereas it is natural for Power to be striving to enlarge itself, and to be encroaching upon those that have none. . . . Now because Liberty chastises and shortens Power, therefore Power would extinguish Liberty; and consequently Liberty has too much cause to be exceeding jealous and always upon her Defence. Power has many Advantages over her; it has generally numerous Guards, many Creatures, and much Treasure; besides it has more Craft and Experience, and less Honesty and Innocence: And whereas Power can, and for the most Part does subsist where Liberty is not, Liberty cannot subsist without Power; so that she has, as it were, the Enemy always at her Gates.

To Conclude: Power without Control appertains to God alone; and no Man ought to be trusted with what no Man is equal to. In Truth, there are so many passions and Inconsistencies, and so much Selfishness, belonging to humane Nature, that we can scarce be too much upon our Guard against each other. The only Security we have that men will be Honest, is to make it their Interest to be Honest; and the best Defence we can have against their being Knaves, is to make it terrible to them to be Knaves. As there are many Men, wicked in some Stations, who would be innocent in others; the best way is to make Wickedness unsafe in any Station.

Andrew Hamilton's Defense, from A Brief Narrative of Case and Trial of John Peter Zenger *(1736)*

Andrew Hamilton, one of the most famous lawyers in the colonies, led Zenger's defense. This excerpt chronicles Hamilton's argument that for an essay to be libelous the words themselves must be "false, scandalous, and seditious." English law decreed that truth or falsity of a charge was irrelevant; Hamilton argued, through an appeal to natural rights, that the veracity of a charge could and must be applied as a defense. Hamilton concluded, "it is not the cause of a poor printer, nor of New York alone, which you are now trying. No! It may in its consequences affect every freeman that lives under a British government on the main of America. It is the best cause. It is the cause of liberty." The principle that Hamilton argued about the definition of libel was finally incorporated into the New York State Constitution in 1821.

But to proceed. I beg leave to insist that the right of complaining or remonstrating is natural; and the restraint upon this natural right is the law only, and those restraints can only extend to what is false; for as it is truth alone which can excuse or justify any man for complaining of a bad administration, I as frankly agree that nothing ought to excuse a man who raises a false charge or accusation, even against a private person, and that no manner of allowance ought to be made to him who does so against a public magistrate. *Truth* ought to govern the whole affair of libels, and yet the party accused runs risk enough even then; for if he fails of proving every tittle of what he has written, and to the satisfaction of the Court and jury too, he may find to his cost that when the prosecution is set on foot by men in power, it seldom wants friends to favor it. And from thence (it is said) has arisen the great diversity of opinions among judges about what words were or were not scandalous or libelous.

I believe it will be granted that there is not greater uncertainty in any part of the law than about words of scandal; it would be misspending of the Court's time to mention the cases; they may be said to be numberless; and therefore the utmost care ought to be taken in following precedents; and the times when the judgments were given which are quoted for authorities in the case of libels are much to be regarded. I think it will be agreed that ever since the time of the Star Chamber, where the most arbitrary and destructive judgments and opinions were given that ever an Englishmen heard of, at least in his own country—I say prosecutions for libels since the time of that arbitrary Court, and until the Glorious Revolution, have generally been set on foot at the instance of the Crown or its ministers. And it is no small reproach to the law that these prosecutions were too often and too much countenanced by the judges, who held their places at pleasure (a disagreeable tenure to any officer, but a dangerous one in the case of a judge). To say more to this point may not be proper. And yet I cannot think it unwarrantable to show the unhappy influence that a sovereign has sometimes had, not only upon judges but even upon Parliaments themselves. It has already been shown how the judges differed in their opinions about the nature of a libel in the case of the seven bishops. . . .

If then, upon the whole, there is so great an uncertainty among judges (learned and great men) in matters of this kind; if power has had so great an influence on judges, how cautious ought we to be in determining by their judgments, especially in the plantations and in the case of libels? There is heresy in law as well as in religion, and both have changed very much. And we well know that it is not two centuries ago that a man would have been burned as a heretic for owning such opinions in matters of religion as are publicly written and printed at this day. They were fallible men, it seems, and we take the liberty not only to differ from them in religious opinions but to condemn them and their opinions too. And I must presume that in taking these freedoms in thinking and speaking about matters of faith or religion, we are in the right; for, though it is said there are very great liberties of this kind taken in New York, yet I have heard of no information preferred by Mr. Attorney for any offenses of this sort. From which I think it is pretty clear that in New York a man may make very free with his God, but he must take special care what he says of his governor.

It is agreed upon by all men that this is a reign of liberty, and while men keep within the bounds of truth, I hope they may with safety both speak and write their sentiments of the conduct of men in power. I mean of that part of their conduct only which affects the liberty or property of the people under their administration. Were this to be denied, then the next step may make them slaves; for what notions can be entertained of slavery beyond that of suffering the greatest injuries and oppressions without the liberty of complaining; or if they do, to be destroyed, body and estate, for so doing?

It is said and insisted on by Mr. Attorney that government is a sacred thing; that it is to be supported and reverenced; it is government that protects our persons and estates; that prevents treasons, murders, robberies, riots, and all the train of evils that overturns kingdoms and states and ruins particular persons; and if those in the administration, especially the supreme magistrate, must have all their conduct censured by private men, government cannot subsist. This is called a licentiousness not to be tolerated. It is said that it brings the rulers of the people into contempt, and their authority not to be regarded, and so in the end, the laws cannot be put in execution. These I say, and such as these, are the general topics insisted upon by men in power and their advocates. But I wish it might be considered at the same time how often it has happened that the abuse of power has been the primary cause of these evils, and that it was the injustice and oppression of these great men which has commonly brought them into contempt with the people. The craft and art of such men is great, and who that is the least acquainted with history or law can be ignorant of the specious pretenses which have often been made use of by men in power to introduce arbitrary rule and destroy the liberties of a free people. . . .

If a libel is understood in the large and unlimited sense urged by Mr. Attorney, there is scarce a writing I know that may not be called a libel, or scarce any person safe from being called to an account as a libeler; for Moses, meek as he was, libeled Cain; and who is it that has not libeled the devil? For according to Mr. Attorney, it is no justification to say one has a bad name. Echard has libeled our good King William; Burnet has libeled among many others King Charles and King James; and Rapin has libeled them all. How must a man speak or write, or what must he hear, read, or sing? Or when must he laugh, so as to be secure from being taken up as a libeler?

I sincerely believe that were some persons to go through the streets of New York nowadays and read a part of the Bible, if it was not known to be such, Mr. Attorney, with the help of his innuendoes, would easily turn it into a libel. As for instance, Isa. 9:16; "The leaders of the people cause them to err, and they that are led by them are destroyed." But should Mr. Attorney go about to make this a libel, he would read it thus; "The leaders of the people" [innuendo, the Governor and Council of New York] "cause them" [innuendo, the people of this Province] "to err, and they" [the people of this Province meaning] "that are led by them" [the Governor and Council meaning] "are destroyed" [innuendo, are deceived into the loss of their liberty], which is the worst kind of destruction. Or if some persons should publicly repeat, in a manner not pleasing to his betters, the 10th and 11th verses of Chapter 56 of the same book, there Mr. Attorney would have a large field to display his skill in the artful application of his innuendoes. The words are; "His watchmen are all blind, they are ignorant, etc. Yea, they are greedy dogs, that can never have enough." But to make them a libel, there is, according to Mr. Attorney's doctrine, no more wanting but the aid of his skill in the right adapting his innuendoes. As for instance; "His watchmen" [innuendo, the Governor's Council and Assembly] "are all blind, they are ignorant" [innuendo, will not see the dangerous designs of His Excellency]. "Yea, they" [the Governor and Council meaning] "are greedy dogs, which can never have enough" [innuendo, enough of riches and power].

Such an instance as this is seems only fit to be laughed at; but I may appeal to Mr. Attorney himself whether these are not at least equally proper to be applied to His Excellency and his ministers as some of the inferences and innuendoes in his information against my client. Then if Mr. Attorney is at liberty to come into court, and file an information in the King's name without leave, who is secure whom he is pleased to prosecute as a libeler? And as the Crown law is contended for in bad times, there is no remedy for the greatest oppression of this sort, even though the party prosecuted is acquitted with honor. And give me leave to say as great men as any in Britain have boldly asserted that the mode of prosecuting by information (when a Grand Jury will not find *billa vera* [a true bill]) is a national grievance, and greatly inconsistent with that freedom which the subjects of England enjoy in most other cases. But if we are so unhappy as not to be able to ward off this stroke of power directly, yet let us take care not to be cheated out of our liberties by forms and appearances; let us always be sure that the charge in the information is made out clearly even beyond a doubt; for though matters in the information may be called form upon trial, yet they may be and often have been found to be matters of substance upon giving judgment.

Gentlemen, the danger is great in proportion to the mischief that may happen through our too great credulity. A proper confidence in a court is commendable; but as the verdict (whatever it is) will be yours, you ought to refer no part of your duty to the discretion of other persons. If you should be of opinion that there is no falsehood in Mr. Zenger's papers, you will, nay (pardon me for the expression), you ought to say so; because you don't know whether others (I mean the Court) may be of that opinion. It is your right to do so, and there is much depending upon your resolution as well as upon your integrity.

The loss of liberty to a generous mind is worse than death; and yet we know there have been those in all ages who for the sake of preferment or some imaginary honor have freely lent a helping hand to oppress, nay, to destroy their country. . . .

Power may justly be compared to a great river, while kept within its due bounds, is both beautiful and useful; but when it overflows its banks, it is then too impetuous to be stemmed, it bears down all before it and brings destruction and desolation wherever it comes. If then this is the nature of power, let us at least do our duty, and, like wise men (who value freedom), use our utmost care to support liberty, the only bulwark against lawless power, which in all ages has sacrificed to its wild lust and boundless ambition the blood of the best men that ever lived.

I hope to be pardoned, sir, for my zeal upon this occasion; it is an old and wise caution that when our neighbor's house is on fire, we ought to take care of our own. For though blessed be God, I live in a government where liberty is well understood and freely enjoyed; yet experience has shown us all (I'm sure it has to me) that a bad precedent in one government is soon set up for an authority in another; and therefore I cannot but think it mine and every honest man's duty that, while we pay all due obedience to men in authority, we ought at the same time to be upon our guard against power wherever we apprehend that it may affect ourselves or our fellow subjects.

I am truly very unequal to such an undertaking on many accounts. And you see I labor under the weight of many years, and am borne down with great infirmities of body; yet old and weak as I am, I should think it my duty, if required, to go to the utmost part of the land where my service could be of any use in assisting to quench the flame of prosecutions upon informations set on foot by the government to deprive a people of the right of remonstrating (and complaining too) of the arbitrary attempts of men in power—men who injure and oppress the people under their administration, provoke them to cry out and complain; and then make that very complaint the foundation for new oppressions and prosecutions. I wish I could say there were no instances of this kind.

But to conclude. The question before the Court and you gentlemen of the jury is not of small or private concern; it is not the cause of a poor printer, nor of New York alone, which you are now trying. No! It may in its consequence affect every freeman that lives under a British government on the main of America. It is the best cause. It is the cause of liberty; and I make no doubt but your upright conduct this day will not only entitle you to the love and esteem of your fellow citizens, but every man who prefers freedom to a life of slavery will bless and honor you as men who have baffled the attempt of tyranny; and by an impartial and uncorrupt verdict, have laid a noble foundation for securing to ourselves, our posterity, and our neighbors that to which nature and the laws of our country have given us a right—the liberty—both of exposing and opposing arbitrary power (in these parts of the world, at least) by speaking and writing truth.

The Great Negro Plot of 1741, from The New York Conspiracy, *Daniel Horsmanden (1741)*

During the eighteenth century, New York City housed more black slaves than any other northern city. Relations between the races were never easy, but they became particularly tense following several major fires in the winter of 1740–1741, when a large number of African Americans and a small number of whites were put on trial for conspiring to burn New York and massacre its citizens. Based upon the testimony of a teenaged servant girl, local authorities suspected an interracial theft ring and illegal interracial meetings. Some of the implicated slaves were Spanish-speaking, which caused particular concern at a time when public attention was focused on the Anglo-Spanish War. Ultimately, the provincial supreme court indicted more than 170 persons for conspiracy. Four white persons, including the tavern keepers John Hughson and his wife as well as Peggy Cary, a white prostitute, along with seventeen blacks were hanged. Another seventy African Americans and seven whites were banished from the city.

We will never know whether or not the alleged plot was real. But the hysterical response to the charges, which were based on nothing more than hearsay and circumstantial evidence, reveals that New York City was a community living in fear and that relations between the races and the classes were tense. This excerpt is a gruesome and grotesque description of the execution of Hughson and three slaves.

THEN the jury were charged, and a constable was sworn to attend them as usual; and they withdrew; and being soon returned, found the prisoners guilty of both indictments.

The prisoners were asked, what they had to offer in arrest of judgment, why they should not receive sentence of death? and they offered nothing but repetitions of protestations of their innocence; the third justice proceeded to sentence, as followeth.

Quack and Cuffee, the criminals at the bar,

You both now stand convicted of one of the most horrid and detestable pieces of villainy, that ever satan instilled into the heart of human creatures to put in practice: ye, and the rest of your colour, though you are called slaves in this country; yet are you all far, very far, from the condition of other slaves in other countries; nay, your lot is superior to that of thousands of white people. You are furnished with all the necessaries of life, meat, drink, and clothing, without care, in a much better manner than you could provide for yourselves, were you at liberty; as the miserable condition of many free people here of your complexion might abundantly convince you. What then could prompt you to undertake so vile, so wicked, so monstrous, so execrable and hellish a scheme, as to murder and destroy your own masters and benefactors? nay, to destroy root and branch, all the white people of this place, and to lay the whole town in ashes.

I know not which is the more astonishing, the extreme folly, or wickedness, of so base and shocking a conspiracy; for as to any view of liberty or government you could propose to yourselves, upon the success of burning the city, robbing, butchering and destroying the inhabitants; what could it be expected to end in, in the account of any rational and considerate person among you, but your own destruction? And as the wickedness of it, you might well have reflected, you that have sense, that there is a God above, who has always a clear view of all your actions, who sees into the most secret recesses of the heart, and knoweth all your thoughts; shall he not, do ye think, for all this bring you into judgment, at that final and great day of account, the day of judgment, when the most secret treachery will be disclosed, and laid open to the view, and every one will be rewarded according to their deeds, and their use of that degree of reason which God Almighty has entrusted them with?

Here ye must have justice, for the justice of human laws has at length overtaken ye, and we ought to be very thankful, and esteem it a most merciful and wondrous act of Providence, that your treacheries and villainies have been discovered; that your plot and contrivances, your hidden works of darkness have been brought to light, and stopped in their career; that in the same net which you have hid so privily for others your own feet are taken; that the same mischief which you have contrived for others, and have in part executed, is at length fallen upon your own pates, whereby the sentence which I am now to pronounce will be justified against ye; which is,

> That you and each of you be carried from hence to the place from whence you came, and from thence to the place of execution, where you and each of you shall be chained to a stake, and burnt to death; and the lord have mercy upon your poor, wretched souls.

May 30, 1741. This day Quack and Cuffee were executed at the stake according to sentence. The spectators at this execution were very numerous; about three o'clock the criminals were brought to the stake, surrounded with piles of wood ready for setting fire to, which the people were very impatient to have done, their resentment being raised to the utmost pitch against them, and no wonder. The criminals shewed great terror in their countenances, and looked as if they would gladly have discovered all they knew of this accursed scheme, could they have had any encouragement to hope for a reprieve. But as the case was, they might flatter themselves with hopes: They both seemed inclinable to make some confession; the only difficulty between them at last being, who should speak first.

After the confessions were minuted down (which were taken in the midst of great noise and confusion) Mr. Moore desired the sheriff to delay the execution until the governor be acquainted therewith, and his pleasure known touching their reprieve; which, could it have been effected, it was thought might have been a means of producing great discoveries; but from the disposition observed in the spectators, it was much to be apprehended, there would have been great difficulty, if not danger in an attempt to take the criminals back. All this was represented to his honour [the governor]; and before Mr. Moore could return from him to the place of execution, he met the sheriff upon the common, who declared his opinion, that the carrying the negroes back would be impracticable; and if that was his honour's order it could not be attempted without a strong guard, which could not be got time enough; and his honour's directions for the reprieve being conditional and discretionary, for these reasons the execution proceeded.

July 3, 1741. This day Duane's Prince, Latham's Tony, Shurmur's Cato, Kip's Harry, and Marschalk's York, negroes, were executed at the gallows, according to sentence; and the body of York was afterwards hung in chains, upon the same gibbet with John Hughson.

Some few days after this the town was amused with a rumour, that Hughson was turned negro, and Vaarck's Caesar a white; and when they came to put up York in chains by Hughson (who was hung upon the gibbet three weeks before) so much of him as was visible, viz. face, hands, neck, and feet, were of a deep shining black, rather blacker than the negro placed by him, who was one of the darkest hue of his kind; and the hair of Hughson's beard and neck (his head could not be seen for he had a cap on) was curling like the wool of a negro's beard and head, and the features of his face were of the symmetry of a negro beauty; the nose broad and flat, the nostrils open and extended, the mouth wide, lips full and thick, his body (which when living was tall, by the view upwards of six feet, but very meagre) swelled to a gigantic size; and as to Caesar (who, though executed for a robbery, was also one of the head negro conspirators, had been hung up in chains a month before Hughson, and was also of the darkest complexion) his face was at the same time somewhat bleached or turned whitish, insomuch that it occasioned a remark, that Hughson and he had changed colours. The beholders were amazed at these appearances; the report of them engaged the attention of many, and drew numbers of all ranks, who had curiosity, to the gibbets, for several days running, in order to be convinced by their own eyes, of the reality of things so confidently reported to be, at least wondrous phenomenons, and upon the view they were found to be such as have been described; many of the spectators were ready to resolve them into miracles; however, others not so hasty, though surprized at the sights, were willing to account for them in a natural way, so that they administered matter for much speculation.

The sun at this time had great power, and the season as usual very hot, that Hughson's body dripped and distilled very much, as it needs must, from the great fermentation and abundance of matter within him, as could not but be supposed at that time, from the extraordinary bulk of his body; though considering the force of the sun, and the natural meagreness of his corpse, one would have been apt to imagine that long ere this it would have been disencumbered of all its juices. At length, about ten days or a fortnight after Hughson's mate, York, was hung by him, Hughson's corpse, unable longer to contain its load, burst and discharged pail fulls of blood and corruption; this was testified by those who were near by, fishing upon the beach when the irruption happened, to whom the stench of it was very offensive.

The Trial of John Ury, from The New York Conspiracy, *Daniel Horsmanden (1741)*

Daniel Horsmanden, the city's recorder and a justice on the supreme court of the province, was the chief interrogator for all the trials relating to "The Great Negro Plot." Horsmanden decided upon John Ury, a private tutor and schoolmaster recently arrived in the city, as the likely candidate for the ringleader of the rebelling slaves. Ury taught Latin (making him a prime candidate for a Catholic plot), which along with a message from James Oglethorpe, Governor of Georgia, that warned of "Spanish agents (disguised as physicians, dancing masters and the like) preparing to burn all the magazines and considerable towns in English North America" made him a hopelessly convenient candidate for Horsmanden's theory. Ury was hanged at the end of August 1741.

MR. Smith summed up the evidence for the king, and addressing himself to the court and jury, proceeded as followeth.

Though this work of darkness, in the contrivance of a horrible plot, to burn and destroy this city, has manifested itself in many blazing effects, to the terror and amazement of us all; yet the secret springs of this mischief lay long concealed: this destructive scene has opened by slow degrees: but now, gentlemen, we have at length great reason to conclude, that it took its rise from a foreign influence; and that it originally depended upon causes that we ourselves little thought of, and which, perhaps, very few of the inferior and subordinate agents were intimately acquainted with.

The monstrous wickedness of this plot would probably among strangers impeach its credit; but if it be considered as the contrivance of the public enemy, and the inhuman dictate of a bloody religion, the wonder ceases.

What more cruel and unnatural can be conceived, than what Rome has contrived; yea what more savage and barbarous, than what popery has attempted, and sometimes executed, for the extirpation of that which the papists call heresy? We need not go so far from home as the vallies of Piedmont, nor rake into the ashes of the ancient Waldenses and Albigenses, for tragical instances of popish cruelty. We need not remind you of the massacre at Paris, nor the later desolations in France, nor mention the horrible slaughters of the duke d'Alva, in the Low Countries. We need not recount the many millions of lives, that in remote countries, and different ages, have been sacrificed to the Roman idol; nor measure out to you that ocean of foreign blood with which the scarlet whore hath made herself perpetually drunk.

No, gentlemen, the histories of our native country will give us a formidable idea of popery; and inform us of the detestable principles of that religion. . . which, in order to promote its interests, never boggles at the vilest means, can sanctify the most execrable villainies; and to encourage its votaries, will canonize for saints a Guy Faux and others, some of the greatest monsters of iniquity that ever trod upon the face of the earth!

Gentlemen, if the evidence you have heard is sufficient to produce a general conviction that the late fires in this city, and the murderous design against its inhabitants, are the effects of a Spanish and popish plot, then the mystery of this iniquity, which has so much puzzled us, is unveiled, and our admiration [wonder] ceases: all the mischiefs we have suffered or been threatened with, are but a sprout from that evil root, a small stream from that overflowing fountain of destruction, that has often deluged the earth with slaughter and blood, and spread ruin and desolation far and wide.

We need not wonder to see a popish priest at this bar, as a prime incendiary; nor think it strange that an Englishman of that religion and character should be concerned in so detestable a design. What can be expected from those that profess a religion that is at war with God and man; not only with the truths of the Holy Scriptures, but also with common sense and reason; and is destructive of all the kind and tender sensations of human nature? When a man, contrary to the evidence of his senses, can believe the absurd doctrine of transubstantiation; can give up his reason to a blind obedience and an implicit faith; can be persuaded to believe that the most unnatural crimes, such as treason and murder, when done in obedience to the pope, or for the service of the holy church, by rooting out what they call heresy, will merit heaven: I say, when a man has imbibed such principles as these, he can easily divest himself of every thing that is human but his shape; he is capable of any villainy, even as bad as that which is charged on the prisoner at the bar.

Description of New York City in 1748, from Travels into America, *Peter Kalm (1748)*

Peter Kalm was a Swedish botanist who visited North America to make a survey of natural history between 1748 and 1751. He was a professor of economics at the University of Abo, in Swedish Finland, and a member of the Swedish Royal Academy of Science, which had sponsored his trip. Kalm had been a student of Carl Linnaeus, "the Father of Taxonomy," whose system of classification is still in use today. Kalm's volume *Travels in North America,* published in England in 1770, was one of the most reliable and astute accounts of not only the natural history but also the political and social customs of eighteenth-century America.

During his residence in New York City, Kalm observed and commented on a variety of topics including not only the natural setting of the port but the religious customs of Jews, the effects of disease, and the machinations of the colonial government.

BESIDES the different sects of Christians, there are many Jews settled in New York, who possess great privileges. They have a synagogue and houses, and great country seats of their own property, and are allowed to keep shops in town. They have likewise several ships, which they freight and send out with their own goods. In fine, they enjoy all the privileges common to the other inhabitants of this town and province.

During my residence at New York, this time and in the two next years, I was frequently in company with Jews. I was informed among other things that these people never boiled any meat for themselves on Saturday, but that they always did it the day before; and that in winter they kept a fire during the whole Saturday. They commonly eat no pork; yet I have been told by several men of credit that many of them (especially among the young Jews) when traveling did not make the least difficulty about eating this or any other meat that was put before them; even though they were in company with Christians.

I was in their synagogue last evening for the first time, and this day at noon I visited it again, and each time I was put into a particular seat which was set apart for strangers or Christians. A young rabbi read the divine service, which was partly in Hebrew and partly in the rabbinical dialect. Both men and women were dressed entirely in the English fashion; the former had all of them their hats on, and did not once take them off during service. The galleries, I observed, were appropriated to the ladies, while the men sat below. During prayers, the men spread a white cloth over their heads; which perhaps is to represent sackcloth. But I observed that the wealthier sort of people had a much richer cloth than the poorer ones. Many of the men had Hebrew books, in which they sang and read alternately. The rabbi stood in the middle of the synagogue, and read with his face turned toward the east; he spoke, however, so fast, as to make it almost impossible for anyone to understand what he said.

New York, the capital of a province of the same name, is situated under 40°40′ north latitude and 47°4′ western longitude from London; and is about ninety-seven English miles distant from Philadelphia. The situation of it is extremely advantageous for trade; for the town stands upon a point which is formed by two bays, into one of which the River Hudson discharges itself, not far from the town. New York is therefore on three sides surrounded with water. The ground it is built on is level in some parts, and hilly in others; the place is generally reckoned very wholesome. . . .

The port is a good one; ships of the greatest burden can lie in it, quite close up to the bridge; but its water is very salty, as the sea continually comes in upon it, and therefore is never frozen, except in extraordinary cold weather. This is of great advantage to the city and its commerce; for many ships either come in or go out of the port at any time of the year, unless the winds be contrary. . . . It is secured from all violent hurricanes from the southeast by Long Island, which is situated just before the town; therefore only the storms from the southwest are dangerous to the ships which ride at anchor here. . . .

The entrance, however, has its faults; one of them is that no men-of-war can pass through it; for though the water is pretty deep, yet it is not sufficiently so for great ships. Sometimes even merchant ships of a large size have, by the rolling of the waves and by sinking down between them, slightly touched the bottom, though without any bad consequences. Besides this, the canal is narrow; and for this reason many ships have been lost here, because they may be easily cast upon a sand, if the ship is not well piloted. Some old people, who had constantly been upon this canal, assured me that it was neither deeper nor shallower at present than in their youth.

The common difference between high and low water at New York amounts to about six feet, English measure. But at a certain time in every month, when the tide flows more than commonly, the difference in the height of the water is seven feet.

New York probably carries on a more extensive commerce than any town in the English North American provinces; at least it may be said to equal them. Boston and Philadelphia, however, come very near up to it. The trade of New York extends to many places, and it is said they send more ships from thence to London than they do from Philadelphia. They export to that capital all the various sorts of skins which they buy of the Indians; sugar, logwood, and other dying woods, rum, mahogany, and many other goods which are the produce of the West Indies; together with all the specie which they get in the course of trade.

Every year they build several ships here, which are sent to London, and there sold; and of late years they have shipped a quantity of iron to England. In return for these, they import from London stuffs and every other article of English growth or manufacture, together with all sorts of foreign goods. England, and especially London, profits immensely by its trade with the American colonies; for not only New York but likewise all the other English towns on the continent, import so many articles from England that all their specie, together with the goods which they get in other countries, must altogether go to Old England, in order to pay the amount to which they are however insufficient. From hence it appears how much a well-regulated colony contributes to the increase and welfare of its mother country. . . .

The goods with which the province of New York trades are not very numerous. They chiefly export the skins of animals, which are bought of the Indians about Oswego; great quantities of boards, coming for the most part from Albany; timber and ready-made lumber, from that part of the country which lies about the River Hudson; and, lastly, wheat, flour, barley, oats, and other kinds of corn, which are brought from New Jersey and the cultivated parts of this province. I have seen yachts from New Brunswick, laden with wheat which lay loose on board, and with flour packed up into tuns; and also with great quantities of linseed. New York likewise exports some flesh and other provisions out of its own province, but they are very few; nor is the quantity of peas which the people about Albany bring much greater. Iron, however, may be had more plentifully, as it is found in several parts of this province, and is of a considerable goodness; but all the other products of this country are of little account.

Most of the wine, which is drank here and in the other colonies, is brought from the Isle of Madeira, and is very strong and fiery.

No manufactures of note have as yet been established here; at present they get all manufactured goods, such as woolen and linen cloth, etc., from England, and especially from London.

The River Hudson is very convenient for the commerce of this city, as it is navigable for near 150 English miles up the country, and falls into the bay not far from the town, on its western side. During eight months of the year this river is full of yachts, and other greater and lesser vessels, either going to New York or returning from thence, laden either with inland or foreign goods.

I cannot make a just estimate of the ships that annually come to this town or sail from it. But I have found by the Pennsylvania gazettes that from the 1st of December in 1729 to the 5th of December in the next year, 211 ships entered the port of New York, and 222 cleared it; and since that time there has been a great increase of trade here.

The country people come to market in New York twice a week, much in the same manner as they do at Philadelphia; with this difference, that the markets are here kept in several places.

The governor of the province of New York resides here, and has a palace in the fort. . . .

An assembly of deputies from all the particular districts of the province of New York is held at New York once or twice every year. It may be looked upon as a parliament or diet in miniature. Everything relating to the good of the province is here debated. The governor calls the assembly, and dissolves it at pleasure. This is a power which he ought only to make use of, either when no further debates are necessary, or when the members are not so unanimous in the service of their King and country as is their duty. It frequently however happens, that, led aside by caprice or by interested views, he exerts it to the prejudice of the province.

The colony has sometimes had a governor whose quarrels with the inhabitants have induced their representatives, or the members of the assembly, through a spirit of revenge, to oppose indifferently everything he proposed, whether it was beneficial to the country or not. In such cases the governor has made use of his power, dissolving the assembly, and calling another soon after, which however he again dissolved upon the least mark of their ill humor. By this means he so much tired them, by the many expenses which they were forced to bear in so short a time, that they were at last glad to unite with him in his endeavors for the good of the province. But there have likewise been governors who have called assemblies and dissolved them soon after merely because the representatives did not act according to their whims, or would not give their assent to proposals which were perhaps dangerous or hurtful to the common welfare.

The King appoints the governor according to his royal pleasure; but the inhabitants of the province make up His Excellency's salary. Therefore, a man entrusted with this place has greater or lesser revenues according as he knows how to gain the confidence of the inhabitants. There are examples of governors in this and other provinces of North America who, by their dissensions with the inhabitants of their respective governments, have lost their whole salary, His Majesty having no power to make them pay it. If a governor had no other resource in these circumstances, he would be obliged either to resign his office, or to be content with an income too small for his dignity; or else to conform himself in everything to the inclinations of the inhabitants. . . .

No disease is more common here than that which the English call fever and ague, which is sometimes quotidian, tertian, or quartan. But it often happens that a person who has had a tertian ague, after losing it for a week or two, gets a quotidian ague in its stead, which after a while changes into a tertian. The fever commonly attacks the people at the end of August or beginning of September, and commonly continues during autumn and winter till toward spring, when it ceases entirely.

Strangers who arrive here commonly are attacked by the sickness the first or second year after their arrival; and it is more violent upon them than upon the natives, so that they sometimes die of it, but if they escape the first time, they have the advantage of not being visited again the next year, or perhaps never any more. It is commonly said here that strangers get the fever to accustom them to the climate. The natives of European offspring have annual fits of this ague in some parts of the country; some, however, are soon delivered from it; with others on the contrary it continues for six months together; and others are afflicted with it till they die. The Indians also suffer it, but not so violently as the Europeans. No age is secured against it. In those places where it rages annually, you see old men and women attacked with it; and even children in the cradle, sometimes not above three weeks old. It is likewise quotidian, tertian, or quartan with them.

This autumn the ague was more violent here than it commonly used to be. People who are afflicted with it look as pale as death, and are greatly weakened, but in general are not prevented from doing their work in the intervals. It is remarkable that every year there are great parts of the country where this fever rages, and others where scarce a single person has been taken ill. It likewise is worth notice that there are places where the people cannot remember that it formerly prevailed in their country, though at present it begins to grow more common; yet there was no other visible difference between the several places.

All the old Swedes, Englishmen, Germans, etc., unanimously asserted that the fever had never been so violent and of such continuance when they were boys as it is at present. They were likewise generally of the opinion that about the year 1680 there were not so many people afflicted with it as about this time. However, others, equally old, were of opinion that the fever was proportionably as common formerly as it is at present; but that it could not at that time be so sensibly perceived on account of the scarcity of inhabitants, and the great distance of their settlements from each other. It is therefore probable that the effects of the fever have at all times been equal. . . .

Opposition to a Sectarian College, from The Independent Reflector, *William Livingston (1753)*

The oldest, richest, and most famous of New York's educational institutions began as King's College in the vestry room of Trinity Church. King George II granted the school a charter in 1754 with Samuel Johnson as its first president. By the time the colonies broke with England in 1776, the college had already attracted such revolutionary luminaries as Alexander Hamilton, John Jay, Robert Livingston, and Gouverneur Morris. The institution suspended instruction during the war, when its facilities were used as a military hospital, and it was rechartered by New York State in 1784 as Columbia College. The following excerpt established the precedent that the university should be open, catholic, and free in its orientation.

THE design of erecting a college in this province is a matter of such grand and general importance that I have frequently made it the topic of my serious meditation. . . .

To imagine that our legislature, by raising the present fund for the college, intended barely to have our children instructed in Greek and Latin, or the art of making exercises and verses, or disputing in mood and figure, were a supposition absurd and defamatory. For these branches of literature, however useful as preparatory to real and substantial knowledge, are in themselves perfectly idle and insignificant. The true use of education is to qualify men for the different employments of life to which it may please God to call them. It is to improve their hearts and understandings; to infuse a public spirit and love of their country; to inspire them with the principles of honor and probity, with a fervent zeal for liberty, and a diffusive benevolence for mankind; and, in a word, to make them the more extensively serviceable to the Commonwealth. . . .

This, therefore, I will venture to lay down for a capital maxim—that unless the education we propose be calculated to render our youth better members of society and useful to the public in proportion to its expense, we had better be without it. As the natural consequence of this proposition, it follows that the plan of education the most conducive to that end is to be chosen, and whatever has a tendency to obstruct or impede it ought carefully to be avoided. . . . I shall now proceed to offer a few arguments which I submit to the consideration of my countrymen to evince the necessity and importance of constituting *our* college upon a basis of the most catholic, generous, and free.

It is, in the first place, observable that, unless its constitution and government be such as will admit persons of all Protestant denominations upon a perfect parity as to privileges, it will itself be greatly prejudiced and prove a nursery of animosity, dissension, and disorder. The sincere men of all sects imagine their own profession, on the whole, more eligible and scriptural than any other. It is, therefore, very natural to suppose they will exert themselves to weaken and diminish all other divisions, the better to strengthen and enlarge their own. To this cause must in a great measure be ascribed that heat and opposition which animate the breasts of many men of religious distinctions, whose intemperate and misapplied zeal is the only blemish that can be thrown upon their characters.

Should our college, therefore, unhappily, through our own bad policy fall into the hands of any one religious sect in the province; should that sect, which is more than probable, establish its religion in the college, show favor to its votaries, and cast contempt upon others, it is easy to foresee that Christians of all other denominations among us, instead of encouraging its prosperity, will, from the same principles, rather conspire to oppose and oppress it. Besides English and Dutch Presbyterians, which perhaps exceed all our other religious professions put together, we have Episcopalians, Anabaptists, Lutherans, Quakers, and a growing church of Moravians, all equally zealous for their discriminating tenets. Whichsoever of these has the sole government of the college will kindle the jealousy of the rest, not only against the persuasion so preferred but the college itself. Nor can anything less be expected than a general discontent and tumult; which, affecting all ranks of people, will naturally tend to disturb the tranquillity and peace of the province. . . .

Another argument against so pernicious a scheme is that it will be dangerous to society. . . . And have we not reason to fear the worst effects of it where none but the principles of one persuasion are taught and all others depressed and discountenanced—where, instead of reason and argument of which the minds of the youth are not capable, they are early imbued with the doctrines of a party, enforced by the authority of a professor's chair and the combining aids of the president and all the other officers of the college?

That religious worship should be constantly maintained there, I am so far from opposing that I strongly recommend it, and do not believe any such kind of society can be kept under a regular and due discipline without it. But instructing the youth in any particular systems of divinity, or recommending and establishing any single method of worship or church government, I am convinced would be both useless and hurtful. Useless, because not one in a hundred of the pupils is capable of making a just examination and reasonable choice. Hurtful, because receiving impressions blindly on authority will corrupt their understandings and fetter them with prejudices which may everlastingly prevent a judicious freedom of thought and infect them all their lives with a contracted turn of mind.

A party college, in less than half a century, will put a new face upon the religion and, in consequence thereof, affect the politics of the country. Let us suppose what may, if the college should be entirely managed by one sect, probably be supposed. Would not all possible care be bestowed in tincturing the minds of the students with the doctrines and sentiments of that sect? Would not the students of the college, after the course of their education, exclusive of any others, fill all the offices of the government? Is it not highly reasonable to think that, in the execution of those offices, the spirit of the college would have a most prevailing influence, especially as that party would perpetually receive new strength, become more fashionable and numerous?

Can it be imagined that all other Christians would continue peaceable under, and unenvious of, the power of that church which was rising to so exalted a preeminence above them? Would they not, on the contrary, like all other parties, reflect upon, reluct at, and vilify such an odious ascendancy? Would not the church which had that ascendancy be thereby irritated to repeated acts of domination, and stretch their ecclesiastical rule to unwarrantable and unreasonable lengths?

Whatever others may, in their lethargy and supineness, think of the project of a party college, I am convinced that under the management of any particular persuasion it will necessarily prove destructive to the civil and religious rights of the people. And should any future House of Representatives become generally infected with the maxims of the college, nothing less can be expected than an establishment of one denomination above all others, who may, perhaps, at the good pleasure of their superiors, be most graciously favored with a bare liberty of conscience while they faithfully continue their annual contributions, their tithes, and their Peter's pence.

A third argument against suffering the college to fall into the hands of a party may be deduced from the design of its erection and support by the public.

The legislature to whom it owes its origin, and under whose care the affair has hitherto been conducted, could never have intended it as an engine to be exercised for the purposes of a party. Such an insinuation would be false and scandalous. It would, therefore, be the height of insolence in any to pervert it to such mean, partial, and little designs. No, it was set on foot and, I hope, will be constituted for general use, for the public benefit, for the education of all who can afford such education. And to suppose it intended for any other less public-spirited uses is ungratefully to reflect upon all who have hitherto had any agency in an undertaking so glorious to the province, so necessary, so important and beneficial.

At present it is but in embryo, yet the money hitherto collected is public money; and, till it is able to support itself, the aids given to it will be public aids. When the community is taxed, it ought to be for the defense or emolument of the whole. Can it, therefore, be supposed that all shall contribute for the uses, the ignominious uses, of a few—nay, what is worse, to that which will be prejudicial to a vast majority? Shall the whole province be made to support what will raise and spread desperate feuds, discontent, and ill blood through the greatest part of the province? Shall the government of the college be delivered out of the hands of the public to a party?

They who wish it are enemies to their country; they who ask it have, besides this antipatriotism, a degree of impudence, arrogance, and assurance unparalleled. And all such as are active in so iniquitous a scheme deserve to be stigmatized with marks of everlasting ignominy and disgrace.

Let it, therefore, ever remain where it is—I mean under the power of the legislature. The influence, whether good or bad, we shall all of us feel and are, therefore, interested in it. It is, for that reason, highly fit that the people should always share in the power to enlarge or restrain it—that power they will have by their representatives in assembly. And no man who is a friend to liberty, his country, and religion will ever rejoice to see it wrested from them. . . .

Add to all this that, in a new country as ours, it is inconsistent with good policy to give any religious profession the ascendancy over others. The rising prosperity of Pennsylvania is the admiration of the continent; and, though disagreeing from them, I should always, for political reasons, exclude Papists from the common and equal benefits of society. Yet, I leave it to the reflections of my judicious readers whether the impartial aspect of their laws upon all professions has not, in a great degree, conduced to their vast importation of religious refugees, to their strength and their riches; and whether a like liberty among us, to all Protestants whatsoever, without any marks of distinction, would not be more commendable, advantageous, and politic.

State of the Province of New York, Cadwallader Colden (1765)

Cadwallader Colden was born in Scotland in 1688 and came to New York City in 1718 to become surveyor general. He was a distinguished scientist and historian who wrote papers on cancer, gravitation, and astronomy in addition to publishing a volume entitled *The History of the Five Indian Nations Depending on the Province of New York.* He was appointed lieutenant governor in 1761 and served fourteen years. His stance on the Stamp Act drew the ire of a mob, however, who burned him in effigy in 1765, speeding the removal of his political appointment.

THE People of New York are properly Distinguished into different Ranks.

1st The Proprietors of the large Tracts of Land, who include within their claims from 100,000 acres to above one Million of acres under one Grant. Some of these remain in one single Family. Others are, by Devises & Purchases claim'd in common by considerable numbers of Persons.

2nd The Gentlemen of the Law make the second class in which properly are included both the Bench & the Bar. Both of them act on the same Principles, & are of the most distinguished Rank in the Policy of the Province.

3rd The Merchants make the third class. Many of them have rose suddenly from the lowest Rank of the People to considerable Fortunes, & chiefly by illicit Trade in the last War. They abhor every limitation of Trade and Duty on it, & therefore gladly go into every Measure whereby they hope to have Trade free.

4thly—In the last Rank may be placed the Farmers and Mechanics. Tho' the Farmers hold their Lands in fee simple, they are as to condition of Life in no way superior to the common Farmers in England; and the Mechanics such only as are necessary in Domestic Life. This last Rank comprehends the bulk of the People, & in them consists the strength of the Provie. They are the most usefull and the most Morall. . . .

From A Tour Through Part of the North Provinces of America, *Patrick M'Robert (1774)*

In the year before the gunfire at Lexington and Concord led to armed conflict between the colonies and the mother country, New York ranked (after Philadelphia) as the second largest city in what would soon become the United States. Gotham's population remained more heterogeneous than any other American metropolis, and it already had a reputation for entrepreneurial hustle and bustle. For example, in 1768, Manhattan merchants created the first chamber of commerce in the New World. Moreover, the finest natural harbor on the East Coast was already attracting hundreds of ships each year, and the mechanics and artisans of the city were more numerous and prosperous than ever before.

Perhaps the best snapshot of New York City on the eve of the Revolution comes from the firsthand observations of Patrick M'Robert, a wealthy Scotsman who visited Manhattan in 1774 and 1775. Writing to a friend in Great Britain, M'Robert demonstrates in these letters that the vigor and variety that characterized New York City centuries later was already present before the United States even came to be.

THE city is large, and contains a great many neat buildings. The publick buildings, and places of worship, are generally very neat, and well finished, if not elegant. The college [King's College, now Columbia], tho' only one third of the plan is compleat, makes a fine appearance, on one of the finest situations perhaps of any college in the world. Here are taught divinity, mathematicks, the practice and theory of medicine, chymistry, surgery, and materia medica. One circumstance I think is a little unlucky, the enterance to this college is thro' one of the streets where the most noted prostitutes live. This is certainly a temptation to the youth that have occasion to pass so often that way.

The new hospital tho' not quite finished is another fine building upon the same plan as the Royal Infirmary at Edinburgh. . . .

They have three English churchs, three Presbyterian, two Dutch Lutherian, two Dutch Calvenists, all neat and well finished buildings, besides a French church, an Anabaptist, a Methodist, a Quaker meeting, a Moravian church, and a Jews synagogue. There are many other fine buildings belonging to private gentlemen and merchants; but the streets are in general ill paved, irregular, and too narrow. There are four market places, all well supplied with all kinds of provisions.

They are pretty well supplied with fresh water from pumps sunk at convenient distances in the streets. Their tea water they get at present brought in carts thro' the streets from the suburbs of the city; but they are now erecting a fire [steam] engine for raising the spring into a reservoir, from whence, by pipes, they can convey it to any part of the city. They are pretty well guarded against accidents from fire, by obliging every citizen to register their house, and for one shilling a vent yearly, to have them swept once a month. They have also a number of engines kept at convenient distances: to each of these is appointed a captain, and a certain number of men. And when a fire happens, a premium is always allowed to the captain and his men who can first make their engines play upon the fire. By this precaution fire seldom happens, and by the proper disposition of the engines, when it does happen, it is seldom allowed to spread farther than the house it brakes out in. . . .

Near the fort is an equestrian statue of king George the III. upon an elegant pedestial in the middle of a fine green rail'd in with iron. At the crossing of two public streets, stands at full length a marble statue of lord Chatham erected by the citizens in gratitude for his strenuous opposition to the stamp act in 1766. They have several large roperies, distilleries, breweries, and a large iron work carried on here. They have plenty of mechanicks of all kinds, by whom almost every thing that is made with you in Britain is made to as great perfection here. The inhabitants are in general brisk and lively, kind to strangers, dress very gay; the fair sex are in general handsome, and said to be very obliging. Above 500 ladies of pleasure keep lodgings contiguous within the consecreated liberties of St. Paul's. This part of the city belongs to the church, and has thence obtained the name of the *Holy Ground.* Here all the prostitutes reside, among whom are many fine well dressed women, and it is remarkable that they live in much greater cordiality one with another than any nests of that kind do in Britain or Ireland.

It rather hurts an Europian eye to see so many negro slaves upon the streets, tho' they are said to deminish yearly here. The city is governed by a mayor, and divided into seven different wards, over each of which an alderman and an assistant presides. They have generally the same laws and regulations as in England. There are computed between twenty-six and thirty thousand inhabitants in the city; in this number are, I believe, included the slaves, who make at least a fifth part of the number. . . .

Labourers have their three and four shillings a-day about New York; but at present they seem rather overstocked, owing to the arrival of so many adventurers from Britain and Ireland. . . .

All necessaries of life are plenty, and reasonable; For example, beef at four and five pence the pound; good mutton the same; a good hen at a shilling, and pork and veal in proportion; butter sixteen pence the pound; the best flower, seventeen shillings the hundred weight; West India rum from three shillings and six pence, and three and nine pence the gallon. Rum distilled here, at two and six pence the gallon; beer, and all sorts of wine, about the same prices that you have them at; cyder, four pence the bottle. The only dear drink is London porter, which is two shillings the bottle. Observe, that in all the above rates and prices, I speak of the currency of the country, which is in proportion as seven pence sterling to a shilling.

From Diary of Pastor Schaukirk, *Ewald G. Schaukirk (1775)*

Unlike Boston and Philadelphia, New York was a royalist stronghold during the American Revolution. It was also the only important place that remained under British control for the entire war. Thus, it was a garrison town, with thousands of redcoats and Hessians in residence and with Royal Navy warships constantly in the harbor. On two occasions, in 1776 and again in 1778, the city very nearly burned to the ground, but for the most part Manhattan passed through the conflict without great loss of life. And after the revolution, Gotham was poised to become the greatest city in the Western Hemisphere.

The excerpt that follows comes from the diary of the Reverend Ewald G. Schaukirk, a minister who served the Moravian congregation of New York between 1775 and 1784. Sympathetic to the king and to England, he was nevertheless critical of soldiers sent by the empire to defend the rebellious colonies.

April 29th. [1775] Saturday. The past week has been one of commotion and confusion.... Fear and panic seized many of the people, who prepared to move into the country....

August 28th. [1775] Monday. Moving out of the city continues, and some of the Streets look plague-stricken, so many houses are closed. The dividing of all men between 16 and 50 years into Ward companies, increases the movement.

September 18th. [1775] Monday. The Minute men paraded today, with their baggage and provisions. It was thought they were going on an expedition, but they marched but five miles out of the city and returned in the evening. Many of them got drunk, fought together where they had halted, and on their return the Doctors and Surgeons were kept busy. May the Lord have mercy on this poor City!

January 20th. [1777] Monday. It appears from the newspapers, that another attempt to destroy the city by fire would be made. The city watch was regulated anew, by which eighty men watched every night in the different wards; and the Light Horse patrol the streets. Today a beginning was made with the inhabitants to take the oath of allegiance to the King. Every day two wards are taken—the Governor, Mayor, and other officers being present.

November 29th. [1777] Saturday. A plot was discovered that many here (it is said there has been prepared a list of 300 to be arrested) had been enlisted for the rebel service, and intended to fall on the city within or set it on fire, when an attack was made on the island by the rebels. Several were arrested, one Mott and wife, in the Bowery; a shoemaker; a saddler; a milkman; and Skimmey, a tailor, who made his escape. . . .

August 19th. [1779] Thursday . . . the military gentlemen amuse themselves with trifles and diversions. Recently the walk by the ruins of Trinity Church and its grave-yard has been railed in and painted green; benches placed there and many lamps fixed in the trees, for gentlemen and ladies to walk and sit there in the evening. A band plays while the commander is present, and a sentry is placed there, that none of the common people may intrude. A paltry affair! . . .

September 22d. [1780] Friday. It being the anniversary of His Majesty's, our dear Kings Coronation-Day, great rejoicing were made. Besides the usual firing at noon from the Battery, and 1 o'clock from the ships in the river, and at the Watering Place, in the afternoon all the City Militia, to a very great number, the volunteer companies, and a part of the regulars marched with flying colors out of town, and drew up in line from the East river to the North river, and in the evening a *Feu de Joie* was fired in respect to the day and in celebration of the brilliant victory obtained by Earl Cornwallis near Camden, in South Carolina. . . .

December 16th. [1780] Saturday. The year is near ended and nothing has been done by the troops here . . . thro' idleness [they] fall into all manner of the worst of vices, contract illnesses, which take off many. Thus they dwindle away by that means, and by small excursions which answer no real purposes. . . . The general language even of the common soldiers is, that the war might and would have been ended long before now, if it was not for the great men, who only want to fill their purses; and indeed it is too apparent that this has been and is the ruling principle in all departments, only to seek their own private interest, and to make hay while the Sun shineth, and when they have got enough then to retreat or go home—let become of America what will! . . .

December 11th. [1781] Tuesday. Weather very cold; great distress for want of wood. . . .

February 1st. [1782] The rents of houses are again raised to extravagant figures. . . .

April 8th. [1783] Tuesday. At noon the King's Proclamation of the cessation of hostilities, was read at the City Hall, which had previously been done on board of the men-of-war and to the troops.

May 3d. [1783] Saturday. Many of those persons who left the city when the troubles began are returning. . . .

November 25th. [1783] Tuesday. Today all the British left New York, and General Washington with his troops marched in and took possession of the city. . . .

Journal of Lieutenant Isaac Bangs (1776)

Isaac Bangs was a twenty-four-year-old medical student, a graduate of Harvard, and a native of Harwich, Massachusetts, when he joined the Revolutionary Army. Bangs arrived in New York City with his troops on April 17, 1776, and kept a journal until July 29.

New York's Provincial Congress gave its assent to the *Declaration of Independence* on July 9, and the document was read to the troops, including Isaac Bangs, on the Common at six o'clock that evening. The crowd then marched down to Bowling Green where they pulled down the statue of George III that had been erected there in 1770. George's "head" was put on a spike and displayed in front of the Blue Bell Tavern near Fort Washington in Washington Heights.

[APRIL] 19th. I spent the greatest part of my Time in viewing the City, which I found vastly surpassing my Expectations. The City is nearly as populous as the Town of Boston; the Publick Edifices greater in number, yet not in general so grand & Magnificent as those of Boston. . . . On the South west part of the Town, which is a Point between the two Rivers, is a very strong & costly Fort built by the Kings Troops & many masons men for the Protection of the City from the Enemy.

On the outside of the Fort at the Edge of the wall was a Battery, erected at a vast Expence to the King, built of hewn stone, the outside about ten feet high, the inside filled up to form a plane that [at] the Wall was not more than a foot and a half high. Our people were busily employed in making a Turf Wall upon the stone Wall, & when we arrived had almost finished as compleat a Battery as ever I saw. Several other Fortifications were erected in this Town, which made it tolerably strong & safe against any attacks of the Enemy. From the above-mentioned Fort a spacious street runing east northerly in a right line, reached without the Town about 1 Mile. In this, near the Fort, is the Equestrian Statue of King George 3d. . . . The design was in imitation of one of the Roman Emperors on Horseback. . . .

June 4. I tarried in the Camp all Day. This Day is the Kings Birth Day. No Festivity, Joy, or Mirth were discovered on this Occasion. . . .

June 12. I mounted Guard at the N[orth] River in the City with the Hair Caps, i.e., York Tories who tho they have & are deserving of a Bad Character, yet they behaved very well by being kept in good Subjection. . . . There are very many in the City of York who have behaved in an inimical Manner to America, a large Mob this Day visited many of them, & treated them very inhumanly by carrying them on a Rail through the Streets, stripping them, &c. Many of the Officers endeavoured to suppress them [the mob], but were able only to disperse them for a little time. Towards Night they [the mob] came nigh our Guard, & I desired the Capn. to turn out the Guard and disperse them, but he was unwilling; however, they did no Violence to the two Tories whom they were in pursuit of, but brought them to us & desired us to keep them, which we did out of compassion to the poor Men, but as no Crime was sent in against them, we dismissed them at relieving of the Guard. They were unwilling to quit the Guard House, which they thought a safe Asylum, & we left them but not as Prisoners. . . .

July 6. Have the News of the United Colonies being Declared free & independent States by the Congress; may they be able to support themselves free & Independent, and never again be brought under the Yoke of Bondage by Cunning & designing Men.

The whole Choir of our Officers, together with Col. Baldwin & the chief of his Officers, went to a Publick House to testify our Joy at the happy news of Independence. We spent the afternoon merily in playing at Bowles for Wine. . . .

July 9. This afternoon the Declaration of the Independence of the 13 American States was read to the Several Brigades. It was received with Joy, which they severally testified by three Cheers.

July 12. [Enemy fire from the harbor prompted a return from the Patriots, in which six Americans were killed from their own cannon fire.] It is said that several of the Company out of which they were killed were drunk, & neglected to Spunge, Worm, & stop the Vent, and the Cartridges took fire while they were raming them down.

The Cannon from the City did but very little execution, as not more than half the Number of the Men belonging to them were present. The others were at their Cups & at their usual place of abode, Viz., on the Holy Ground. . . .

Sunday [July] 14. Almost the whole Regt. are sick with the Camp Distemper. . . .

[July] 23d. . . . Saw the infamous Proclamation issued by Lord Howe & now made publick by order of the Congress, offering Pardon to those in any of the Colonies who will return to their Duty & acknowledge the Supremacy of Parliament. . . . But will Americans tamely submit to those merciless Tyrants who have already done their utmost to reduce them to a state of abject slavery? and will they acknowledge? What can they acknowledge? but that they have bravely stood forth in defence of those Rights & Priviledges which the God of Nature hath bestowed upon them, & which they may not give up (unless unable to support them) without affronting that being who delights in the Liberty & prosperity of all his Creatures?

Hessian Views of New York City, Anonymous (1777, 1780)

The military actuality of the American Revolution arrived in New York City with astonishing force as the British, under the leadership of General William Howe and Admiral Richard Howe, sailed 500 vessels carrying 13,000 sailors and 32,000 soldiers into the bay in August 1776. One American soldier was reported to have thought "that all London was afloat." Indeed, it was the largest British expeditionary force in the country's history and would not be matched again until the invasion of Normandy in World War II. However, opposition to military recruiting for the war in England had led the British to hire 9,000 soldiers from the Landgrave of Hesse in Germany.

After the British easily defeated the Americans in the disastrous Battle of Brooklyn, General George Washington engineered a bold and remarkable nighttime retreat of his remaining 9,500 troops over the East River to Manhattan in late August. But by November, Washington had been forced to retreat westward across New Jersey, and he would not return to Gotham for almost seven years.

What he returned to in November 1783 was a city in ruins. Unlike Boston or Philadelphia, which had received only minimal damage, New York was a blackened ruin, much of which was the result of a fire of unknown origin that destroyed almost a third of the city as the American forces retreated in 1776. Even the majestic spire of Trinity Church was simply a charred skeleton, and the entire main building was destroyed. For the rest of the war, the city would suffer the abuse and neglect of a British garrison town.

FROM a Hessian in Rhode Island to his brother, June 24, 1777.

New York . . . is one of the prettiest, pleasantest harbor towns I have ever seen. For the houses are not only built fine and regular in English style, most of them like palaces, but they are all papered and most extensively furnished. For that reason it is too bad that this land, which is also very fertile, is inhabited by such people, who from luxury and sensuous pleasure didn't know what to do and so owe their fall to naught but their pride. Everyone at home who takes their part and thinks they had good cause for rebellion ought in punishment to spend some time among them and learn how things are here (for the meanest man here can, if he will only do something, live like the richest among us). . . . For though the majority are descended from runaway vagabonds expelled from other places, yet they are so stuck up and make such display, especially in New York, as perhaps nowhere else on earth. . . . The worst thing about it is that at the king's express command the troops must treat these folk most handsomely—though at heart they are all rebels. . . .

Letter from a German Officer in New York, September 11, 1780.

The sums which the army consumes here are incredible. . . . The price of foodstuffs, wages for labor and personal services, and all merchant's wares is dearer than in the East and West Indies, which used to be the most expensive places. You will not believe, I presume, that a wood-chopper earns daily six florin, Rhenish money, and more? or that a good coachman will not serve for less than four hundred florins, good board, and clothing? Perhaps you would like the chimney sweep's profession? There is a royal chimney-sweep here, who has to look after the quarters belonging to the army. He keeps a half-dozen negroes, each of whom can sweep at least twenty chimneys a day, and often must clean more; and for each chimney his master, who sits quietly at home, is paid two shillings York money (twenty-eight coppers). The negroes get nothing out of it save coarse food and rags.

The Forgotten Saga of the Prison Ships, Kenneth T. Jackson (1990)

Kenneth T. Jackson is the author of *Crabgrass Frontier: The Suburbanization of the United States,* which won both the Francis Parkman and Bancroft Prizes in 1985, and the editor of *The Encyclopedia of New York City,* the first such volume of its kind about the city.

In this essay, Jackson recounts the relatively unknown tale of the seamier side of the fate of American prisoners of war aboard the prison ships in the East River after the fall of New York City in 1776.

PAUL Revere, George Washington, John Paul Jones, Valley Forge, Yorktown. The words are familiar to us all. Much less well known is the saga of the prison ships, the ghastly vessels which lay at anchor in New York harbor for virtually the entire war and which caused more deaths than all the battles and campaigns, on land and on sea, in all the years of the Revolution, combined. The 6,824 American fatalities in actual combat represented only about 29 percent of total deaths on the United States side. Most of the other 18,500 persons lost their lives in captivity, more than half of them in New York. Because careful records were probably never kept, and in any case have never been found, exact numbers will never be known. Enough bones later washed up in the muddy flats of Wallabout Bay, however, to indicate that 11,000 Americans died. More conservative estimates conclude that 4,000 lives were lost. Whatever the figure, it was a human tragedy of massive, and unappreciated proportions.

The initial battles and campaigns of the American Revolution took place near Boston in 1775. They were inconclusive, and neither side took many prisoners. In 1776, however, when the primary focus of the fighting shifted toward New York City and its massive, ice-free harbor, the tale was rather different. The August 26–31 Battle of Long Island, for example, was a disaster for George Washington's forces and resulted in a huge total of at least 1300 captives. Indeed, contemporaries suggested that the rout was so complete that even British camp followers took prisoners. Similarly, the ill-fated American decision to defend Fort Washington (near present day 183rd Street in Manhattan), which was ringed on one side by Royal Navy men-of-war, and on the others by Hessian mercenaries and British professional soldiers caused another 2800 members of the Revolutionary forces to fall into the hands of the redcoats on November 16. In fact, as the 3,000 demoralized remnants of the Continental Army retreated across New Jersey later that month, General Howe had more American prisoners than General Washington had American soldiers. It looked to be a short and unsuccessful rebellion.

Where would the British put the thousands of armed rebels who had fallen into their hands? New York City was the obvious choice because it was securely under control, because it was easily accessible to the Royal Navy, and because most American prisoners were already being held in the area. Indeed, the captive ranks continually swelled as British cruisers swept the seas of American vessels and brought the captured seamen back to the Hudson River port. Unfortunately, Gotham could not even provide enough shelter for the victorious British, let alone the vanquished colonials. Thus, the British commandeered barns, sugar houses, churches, and even private residences as temporary stockades. But these spaces proved insufficient for the task and, in any case, two great fires in the fall of 1776 destroyed one third of the city and vastly reduced the number of habitable structures. As winter approached, the British urgently sought an appropriate facility for their captives.

The solution was to convert broken down transports and obsolete warships into floating prisons. Usually anchored in and around Wallabout Bay (an area that was later dredged and rearranged into the Brooklyn Navy Yard), and occasionally in the Hudson River as well, these vessels presented grim silhouettes, with their rigging, spars, masts, and rudders removed, and with iron bars placed across the lower portholes. The first such conversion was the *Whitby,* which became a prison ship on October 20, 1776, and which burned the following October. She was later joined by the *John, Glasgow, Preston, Good Intent, Good Hope, Prince of Wales, Grovnor, Falmouth, Stromboli, Lord Dunlace, Scorpion, Judith, Myrtle, Felicity, Chatham, Kitty, Frederick, Woodlands, Scheldt, Clyde, Hunter, Perserverence,* and *Bristol Packet.*

The most notorious of the species, however, was the *Jersey,* a once-proud 74-gun veteran of wars with the French that was little more than a rotting hulk, with a broken bowsprit and flagstaff, when she became a prison ship late in 1776. For seven years, she sat in the mud flats of the East River, and for seven years she was a floating hell. Indeed, no other similarly-sized space in all of American history (the Confederate prison at Andersonville, Georgia, for example, was much larger) has witnessed as much death and misery as the *Jersey.* She remained in the Wallabout for many years after the war, and portions of her timbers could still be seen well into the nineteenth century.

The routine on the *Jersey,* as for the other prison ships, varied according to the whims of the captors. Sometimes the prisoners were kept below from sunrise to sunset. After dark, one or two captives at a time were occasionally allowed to stretch their legs on deck. Otherwise, the only light they saw came from the twenty inch square openings along the hull. The scene was ghastly, with as many as a thousand men below deck, "some swearing and blaspheming, some crying, praying and wringing their hands, and stalking about like ghosts and apparitions; others delirious, raving and storming; some groaning and dying—all panting for breath."

Fresh air was in short supply because overcrowding was so intense. This gave rise to contagious diseases, especially yellow fever, typhus, dysentery, scurvy, and smallpox, as well as to ordinary maladies like influenza, which became especially dangerous in the absence of decent sanitation or adequate medical care. The *Scorpion, Stromboli,* and *Hunter* were supposedly hospital ships, but the physicians assigned to them were "both lazy and incompetent," and in any case "the ruthless pestilence would have laughed at their efforts to arrest it."

Mealtime, which should have provided a rare opportunity for pleasure, instead was a source of horror. Officially, the diet consisted of peas, oatmeal, beef, and pork; actually, it could not be identified and was often simply the refuse from the English ships of war which also rested in the harbor. A fortunate few prisoners, those who had friends or money or both on shore, could purchase edible provisions from the private boats which often came alongside for this purpose. For the typical "Jack Tar" prisoner, however, as for the unlettered farmer who had volunteered for Continental Army service and found himself suddenly in the bowels of a dark and dingy ship, the slime they were served was the slime they ate.

The poor quality of the rations may have been partially due to the love and illicit passion between General Sir William Howe, who commanded British forces in the area, and a certain Mrs. Loring, who was married to the British army's sole "vendue-master and auctioneer." In other words, as historian Will Brownell tells us, the general was having an affair with the wife of the man who had the responsibility of providing the prisoners with life's necessities. According to Brownell, Mr. Loring was able to pillage the commissary, to sell food officially intended for the prisoners to the public at profitable rates, and to purchase rotten provisions for the prisoner consumption. This cozy arrangement allowed Mr. Loring free reign over foodstuffs in return for allowing General Howe to have free reign with Mrs. Loring. Some observers went so far as to contend that ultimate British military failure derived from Howe's obsession with his mistress and his inattention to his duties. For example, Tory sympathizer Judge Thomas Jones wrote that Mrs. Loring was "the illustrious courtesan" who lost for Sir William "the honor, the laurels and the glory of putting an end to one of the most obstinate rebellions that ever existed."

Whatever the cause of their misery and disease, American prisoners died by the hundreds and then the thousands aboard the rotting ships in New York harbor. The *Jersey* alone typically gave up six or eight corpses every day. Every morning, a gang of prisoners known as the "working party" went from ship to ship collecting bodies. They then rowed to the beach, dug an appropriate trench, deposited the dead, and covered the opening. Eventually, more than a mile of the shore was dotted with graves. As J. Alexander Patten noted in 1856: "Thus, they lived, surrounded by maddening horrors, and thus they were laid in the soil for which they died; no falling tear moistened their resting place; no sculptured marble has yet made their history immortal."

The suffering of the prisoners might have ended had they been swapped for the British and Hessian soldiers who had fallen in American hands. But the King's emissaries did not wish to deal with rebels, for fear that the very act of negotiation would constitute a kind of official recognition. Similarly, George Washington was not anxious to trade the well-trained professional troops in his stockades for the undisciplined and ill-trained members of the Continental forces who languished aboard the stationary ships.

Three points remain to be made. The first is that the redcoats who were captured by the Continental forces fared little better than the patriot captives of the British. Indeed, General Thomas Gage complained that the Americans were mistreating prisoners, forcing them to labor "like slaves to gain their daily sustenance." For his part, George Washington insisted to the British that, "I shall regulate all my conduct towards those gentlemen who are or may be in our possession, exactly by the rule you observe towards those of ours now in your custody."

Secondly, land prisons were not much better than the prison ships. Thomas Stone, for example, was transferred from a ship to the infamous Sugar House prison in New York City in 1778. "We left the floating hell with joy, but alas, our joy was of short duration," Stone recalled. "Not a pane of glass, not even a board to a single window in the house, and no fire but once in three days to cook our small allowance of provision. Old shoes were bought and eaten with as much relish as a pig or a turkey."

"In the spring our misery increased; frozen feet began to mortify; by the first of April death took from our numbers, and I hope from their misery, from seven to ten a day and by the first of May out of 69 taken with me only 15 were alive."

Finally, there was an easy way out for the Americans. All they had to do was to renounce the Revolutionary cause and to enlist in the English forces. Almost all of them refused freedom at such a price.

Forgotten even during their own time, the prisoners of the American Revolution have now been all but obliterated from the historical past. Because their narrative is less one of stained fields and waving banners than of famine, cruelty, and shame, their memory has not been celebrated by the nation they helped create. It is true that in 1907, after a public subscription, a Martyr's Monument was put up in the Fort Greene section of Brooklyn to house their remains. But the monument had deteriorated even before World War II, and a 1940s improvement effort by Robert Moses came to little. Now, in 1990, the monument remains forlorn and forgotten at the center of Fort Greene Park.

PART 2

Rise to National Dominance (1783–1860)

Between the American Revolution and the Civil War, New York surged to urban greatness. But who could have predicted that result in 1783? In the year that the British Army finally left Manhattan, Gotham's population was already decimated, as thousands of Loyalist families, who had supported King George III throughout the conflict, had sailed either for Great Britain or Nova Scotia. The houses they left were in a state of ill repair, and some had not been rebuilt after the fires of 1776 and 1778. Moreover, New York's remaining citizens seemed desperate and forlorn, especially as compared with confident Philadelphians and Bostonians.

As noted elsewhere, the Massachusetts capital had been the most important of colonial cities between 1630 and 1750, when Philadelphia had moved ahead in population and economic significance. The City of Brotherly Love remained the largest American city until 1800. Indeed, throughout the colonial period, the volume of commerce through the port of New York never exceeded that of its two rivals.

After 1783, however, Gotham's population burgeoned. By 1830 it was in a class by itself in the United States, and by the time of the Civil War, it was twice the size of its nearest rival and on its way to world dominance. One measure of its importance could be seen in the harbor. By 1860 the port of New York ranked as the world's busiest, and the value of its trade regularly exceeded that of Boston and Philadelphia combined. Newcomers were awed by the vast traffic of sailing vessels. Docks and piers loomed mile after mile up the East River, as well as along the New Jersey and Brooklyn shores. And behind the docks were acres of warehouses, sugar mills, dry docks, and ship chandlers. How do we account for Gotham's victory over its American rivals in the years between 1783 and 1830?

There were essentially six reasons for this result. First, some New York merchants and many British soldiers kept up their British contacts throughout the seven years of redcoat occupation. When the war ended, they were in a better position than their rivals in Boston and Philadelphia to establish relationships with English manufacturers and wholesalers.

Second, New Yorkers placed less importance on family pedigree and more emphasis on innovation and risk taking than did their rivals elsewhere. And the Dutch heritage of tolerance with regard to ethnicity, religion, race, and class meant that energetic persons could rise to the top more easily than in other cities. Not surprisingly, in 1768 New Yorkers organized the first chamber of commerce in the Western Hemisphere, and in 1818 they introduced to the United States the then novel idea of regularly scheduled shipping service. Previously, ship captains had sailed when they had rounded up a crew or when their cargo holds were full or when the weather was favorable. After the Black Ball Line began to follow a precise regimen, Gotham's merchants had an important advantage over their rivals.

Third, New York had a potential all-water, low-level route to the Great Lakes and the interior of the continent. This potential was realized in 1817 when Governor DeWitt Clinton persuaded the state to finance the Erie Canal. This little ditch, never more than forty feet wide, opened in 1825 and promptly revolutionized transportation. The price of shipment from Buffalo to New York City fell by more than 90 percent in 1825 compared with a decade earlier. By most measures, the Erie Canal, which ran for 325 miles between Albany and Buffalo, benefited New York more than anyplace else and ranks as the most ambitious and successful public works project in the nation before the passage of the Interstate Highway Act of 1956.

Fourth, at the end of the War of 1812, British merchants and manufacturers chose New York as the site for well-publicized auctions to dispose of the large quantities of goods that had accumulated on British docks during the wartime embargo. This circumstance gave Manhattan businessmen an important advantage over Boston and Philadelphia in recovering from the earlier naval blockade.

Fifth, because of its central location between the intensely developed and heavily populated New England and Chesapeake regions and because of its thriving port, by 1800 New York had become pivotal to the circulation of commercial information in North America. Local entrepreneurs took advantage of the availability of business news before their competitors elsewhere, and by 1850 they had developed the largest American collection of firms capable of providing technical and professional information and services.

Finally, and perhaps most important, the Empire City profited from its association with the Empire State. At the time of the American Revolution, Virginia and Massachusetts had ranked as the most important of the colonies. Soon after independence was won in 1783, however, New York State burst forward to become the largest, most populous, and most industrial of American states. And before the twentieth century, there was less of the upstate–downstate dichotomy than would develop after 1900.

Not only economic forces were at work to complete the transformation of New York City from, as Mike Wallace and Ted Burrows have put it, "the capital city to the city of capital." The visions and inventions of individual

New Yorkers in the early nineteenth century would also bring about a radical metamorphosis to the ever-expanding metropolis. On Thursday, April 30, 1789, George Washington stood on the balcony of Federal Hall on Wall Street to be sworn in as the first president of the United States. New York, roughly halfway between Massachusetts and Virginia, appeared to be the logical choice for the new nation's capital. Another logical choice was that of Alexander Hamilton as the first secretary of the treasury. Hamilton was, in many ways, the early immigrant success story. He was born out of wedlock in the British West Indies in 1755 and came to New York at the age of seventeen to study at King's College (now Columbia University). He married into one of the state's powerful families, was a delegate to both the Continental Congress in 1782 and the Constitutional Convention in 1787, and was a primary author of the *Federalist Papers* endorsing ratification. Perhaps as important, he had been a lieutenant colonel on Washington's staff during the revolution and was one of the finest economic minds in the nation.

Not everyone thought New York the best location for the new capital, however, and Thomas Jefferson, the new secretary of state, was foremost among those. The two men dined together on June 20, 1790, a year after Washington's inauguration, and worked out a compromise whereby Jefferson would support Hamilton's plan for federal assumption of the state debts incurred during the revolution in exchange for moving the nation's capital to a swampy area along the Potomac River that would come to be named for the nation's first president. Although this was the end of New York's reign as the country's political capital, it was the beginning of its economic supremacy. As a result of the renewed confidence in federal bonds issued by Hamilton, money began to flood into the city almost immediately. Two years later on May 17, 1792, in response to a financial panic, twenty-four brokers met under a buttonwood tree on Wall Street and created what would become the most powerful securities trading system in the world, the New York Stock Exchange.

In the next half century, a legion of speculators and visionaries would use Gotham's monetary might to give shape to the city and in some cases, the entire country. Along with DeWitt Clinton, whose advocacy and imaginative financing of the Erie Canal has already been mentioned, others also recognized that New York's location on the water provided ways to make money. After a maiden voyage in 1807, by 1812 Robert Fulton had six steamboats keeping scheduled service in the North River. Eventually, Fulton's invention would come to dominate the nation's largest river, the Mississippi. Cornelius Vanderbilt made his mark with the steamboat by running blockades during the War of 1812, and by the 1830s the "Commodore" was worth more than half a million dollars and was on his way to running the largest shipping empire in the world.

John Jacob Astor speculated that if there was profit to be made by water, there was even more money to be made by land. In fact, among Astor's final words were, "Could I begin life again, knowing what I now know, and had money to invest, I would buy every foot of land on the island of Manhattan." From 1810 on, Astor engaged in long-term real estate speculation all the way up the island, including most of the Lower East Side and Times Square. His properties increased tenfold during his lifetime, and when he died in 1848, he was the wealthiest man in the country, with real estate holdings worth more than $20 million.

An exhibition in the newly built Crystal Palace in 1853 showed that there was money to be made not only by land and sea but in the air as well. The Crystal Palace was a cast-iron and glass structure that stood just west of the new Croton water distributing reservoir on the land presently occupied by Bryant Park. The building was designed in direct competition with a similar edifice in London that had housed The Great Exhibition of 1851. Two years later, the first World's Fair in the United States, The Exhibition of the Industry of All Nations, opened on July 14. Perhaps the most thrilling and certainly the most significant demonstration at the exhibition was performed by a young inventor, Elisha Graves Otis, who had developed the first safety elevator. After having himself lifted above the heads of the crowd, he ceremoniously sliced the cable that held the elevator, only to reveal that hidden safety catches would not allow the lift to fall. The sky was now the limit for the height that buildings could attain. With the advent of new building materials and architectural design, the silhouette of Manhattan would soon be altered forever.

Loafing through the exhibition's opening-day crowds was a middle-aged poet, Walt Whitman, whose objective was not to make money but to try to unite all of Gotham's denizens in an appreciation of the city he referred to as "the great place, . . . the heart, the brain, the focus." Whitman's haunts, however, were not Astor's hotel on Broadway or Vanderbilt's town house on Washington Square but the bars and taverns and boardinghouses of the city's lower classes. Most of these people were Irish and German immigrants who flooded into the city from 1820 to 1860. Between 1820 and 1840, almost seven hundred thousand immigrants entered the United States, and between 1840 and 1860 there were more than four million arrivals. Though only a small minority remained in New York, it was enough to almost triple the city's population and to push the total number of residents over the one million mark by 1860.

Whitman gazed past the violent eruptions between Irish and black residents of the world's worst slum, the notorious Five Points Area, past the class antagonism and anti-English sentiment that created the Astor Place riots in 1849, and past the brutality of rival gangs of Protestants and Catholics that roamed the Lower East Side in the 1850s and terrorized the middle class. His ultimate goal was both salvific and celebratory: he would bring together the city—rich and poor, black and white, immigrant and native—by merging them into his very being. In the summer of 1855, he self-published what would become his life's work, a slight volume entitled *Leaves of Grass*. The book, he declared in the preface, "arose out of my life in Brooklyn and New York, absorbing a million people, for fifteen years, with an intimacy, an eagerness, an abandon, probably never equaled." Whitman loved the city with a passion not seen before or since, and he traveled its streets and thoroughfares so relentlessly that more than one hundred years later the urban planner Lewis Mumford would remark, "Wherever one goes in New York, whether one knows it or not, one walks in the steps of Walt Whitman."

The era had begun with the successful establishment of a new nation; it ended with the nation's most intense challenge to its own viability. In between the American Revolution and the Civil War, New York had established itself as the largest, richest, and most dynamic of the country's cities.

From An Excursion to the United States of North America in the Summer of 1794, *Henry Wansey (1794)*

Henry Wansey was a retired clothier who journeyed to the United States in 1794 for both business and personal reasons. In *An Excursion to the United States of North America in the Summer of 1794,* he noted the similarity between Liverpool and New York and admired the patriotic willingness of New Yorkers to give a day's work "gratis" to the new fortifications on Governors Island.

WE moored our vessel at Burling slip at four in the morning, and after a little refreshment I landed, and enquired about the Tontine coffee-house. New York is much more like a city than Boston, having broad footways paved, with a curb to separate them from the road. The streets are wider, and the houses in a better style. Boston is the Bristol, New York the Liverpool, and Philadelphia the London, of America. The Tontine tavern and coffee-house is a handsome large brick building; you ascend six or eight steps under a portico, into a large public room which is the Stock Exchange of New York, where all bargains are made. Here are two books kept, as at Lloyd's, of every ship's arrival and clearing out. This house was built for the accommodation of the merchants, by Tontine shares of two hundred pounds each. It is kept by Mr. Hyde, formerly a woollen-draper in London. You can lodge and board there at a common tale, and you pay ten shillings currency a day, whether you dine out or not. No appearance of shop windows as in London; only stores, which make no shew till you enter the houses. House rent is very dear, a hundred pounds sterling a year is a very usual price for a common storekeeper. . . .

May 19, 1794. Dined with Mr. Jay [the ambassador's brother], and in the evening went to the theatre. . . . Mrs. Cowley's play, *A Bold Stroke for a Husband,* with the farce of *Hob in the Well;* the actors mostly from England: price of admittance to the boxes, one dollar. A very bad theatre; a new one is going to be built by subscription, under the direction of Hodgkinson, the present manager. Mrs. Wrighten, who used to sing at Vauxhall twenty years ago, and was afterwards an actress at Bristol, is one of their principal female performers; her voice is as clear and shrill as ever. I think them altogether far inferior to the Boston company. . . .

May 24, 1794. As I was getting up in the morning, I heard drums beating and fifes playing. I ran to the window, and saw a large body of people on the other side of the Governor's House, with flags flying, and marching two and two towards the water-side. . . . [I]t was a procession of young tradesmen going in boats to Governor's Island, to give the state a day's work. Fortifications are there erecting for strengthening the entrance to New York harbour; it is a patriotic and general resolution of the inhabitants of this city, to work a day gratis, without any distinction of rank or condition, for the public advantage, on these fortifications. Today, the whole trade of carpenters and joiners; yesterday, the body of masons; before this, the grocers, school-masters, coopers, and barbers; next Monday, all the attorneys and men concerned in the law, handle the mattock and shovel, the whole day, and carry their provisions with them. How noble is this! How it cherishes unanimity and love for their country! How much does it tend to unite all ranks of people, and render the social compact firm and united. . . .

You cannot board in any good boarding house, for less than seven or eight dollars a week, finding your own wine. . . . New York is as healthy and pleasant a place to live in, as any city I ever saw. The price of provisions fluctuates here exceedingly, like Bath; and persons who know how to take opportunities, may furnish themselves very cheap; after refusing to buy at their prices, I was soon after asked by the same persons, *what would I give?*

From Travels, *Duke of La Rochefoucauld-Liancourt (1799)*

In the summer of 1789, news of the French Revolution reached New York City. By 1792 Louis XVI had been guillotined for treason, and a flood of political refugees arrived in New York harbor. Observers noted that the "French seemed a considerable part of the population." One of those émigrés who had sided with the monarchy was the duke of La Rochefoucauld-Liancourt. The duke chronicled his journey through Canada and the United States in his *Travels* (1799), noting there with admiration that "there is not in any city in the world a finer street than Broadway. . . . It is naturally the place of residence of the most opulent inhabitants."

NEW York is, next to Philadelphia, the largest and best town in the United States. These two cities rival each other in almost every respect. Philadelphia has hitherto had the advantage, but from the fine situation of New York there is reason to expect that sooner or later it will gain the superiority.

It is calculated that this city contains at present upwards of fifty thousand inhabitants. There have been no less than four hundred and fifty new houses built here in this present year. It is increased and beautified with unheard of quickness; a circumstance owing, no doubt, in a great measure, to the immense benefit its trade has derived for these two or three years from the present state of Europe. But if peace diminish, as it certainly will, their excessive profits, the extension of the cultivated lands and settlements in this vast territory, the produce of which will find, directly or indirectly, a vent by Hudson's River, will insure a solid foundation, independently of all foreign circumstances, for the increasing prosperity of the trade of New York. To all these advantages New York adds that of lying more to the eastward, and nearer to the sea than any port in America, except Boston; and it is never choaked up with ice. . . .

The town had formerly been built without any regular plan, whence every where almost, except what has been rebuilt in consequence of the fire, the streets are small and crooked; the foot-paths, where there are any, narrow, and interrupted by the stairs from the houses, which makes the walking on them extremely inconvenient. Some good brick houses are situated in these narrow streets; but in general the houses are mean, small, and low, built of wood, and a great many of them yet bear the marks of Dutch taste. The new part of the city built adjoining to Hudson's River, and parallel with its course, is infinitely more handsome; the streets there being generally straight, broad, intersecting with each other at right angles, and the houses much better built. There is not in any city in the world a finer street than Broadway; it is near a mile in length, and is meant to be still farther extended: it is more than a hundred feet wide from one end to the other. Most part of the houses are of brick, and a number of them extremely handsome. From its elevated situation, its position on the river, and the elegance of the buildings, it is naturally the place of residence of the most opulent inhabitants.

From Travels Through Canada, and the United States of North America in the Years 1806, 1807, 1808, *John Lambert*

John Lambert appears to have been a professional traveler who, with the approval of the Board of Trade, journeyed to Canada and the United States between 1806 and 1808. Lambert's chronicle of his travels was immensely popular and went through three editions.

By November 1807, when he first arrived, New York was, by Lambert's account, "the first city in the United States for wealth, commerce, and population." Over a dozen wharves had sprung up on the Hudson River side of the island, half as many as were already operational on the East River. Lambert also noted that Bowling Green was "as much crowded as the Bond Street in London." But the effects of Jefferson's Embargo Act of 1808 were evident upon Lambert's return to New York in April of that year, as he noted the "melancholy dejection that was painted upon the countenances of the people."

Lambert's observations were not just commercial, however. He observed both the racial and religious diversity of the inhabitants, noting in particular that "there are several rich and respectable families of Jews in New York; and as they have equal rights with every other citizen in the United States, they suffer no invidious distinctions."

About ten o'clock at night we arrived at New York; it was very dark, and as we sailed by the town, lighted lamps and windows sparkled everywhere, amidst the houses, in the streets, and along the water-side. The wharfs were crowded with shipping, whose tall masts mingled with the buildings, and together with the spires and cupolas of the churches, gave the city an appearance of magnificence, which the gloomy obscurity of the night served to increase. . . .

New York is the first city in the United States for wealth, commerce, and population; as it also is the finest for its situation and buildings. . . . New

York has rapidly improved within the last twenty years; and land which then sold in that city for fifty dollars is now worth 1,500.

The Broadway and the Bowery Road are the two finest avenues in the city. . . . The houses in the Broadway are lofty and well built. . . . In the vicinity of the Battery, and for some distance up the Broadway, they are nearly all private houses, and occupied by the principal merchants and gentry of New York; after which the Broadway is lined with large commodious shops of every description. . . . There are several extensive book stores, print-shops, music-shops, jewellers, and silversmiths; hatters, linen-drapers, milliners, pastry-cooks, coachmakers, hotels, and coffee-houses. The street is well paved, and the foot-paths are chiefly bricked. . . .

The City Hotel is the most extensive building of that description in New York; and nearly resembles, in size and style of architecture, the London Tavern in Bishopsgate-street. The ground-floor of the hotel at New York is, however, converted into shops, which have a very handsome appearance in the Broadway. . . . There are three churches in the Broadway: one of them called Grace Church, is a plain brick building, recently erected: the other two are St. Paul's and Trinity; both handsome structures, built with an intermixture of white and brown stone. The adjoining churchyards, which occupy a large space of ground, railed in from the street, and crowded with tombstones, are far from being agreeable spectacles in such a populous city. . . .

The Park, though not remarkable for its size, is, however, of service, by displaying the surrounding buildings to greater advantage; and is also a relief to the confined appearance of the streets in general. It consists of about four acres planted with elms, planes, willows, and catalpas; and the surrounding foot-walk is encompassed by rows of poplars: the whole is enclosed by a wooden paling. . . .

The Theatre is on the south-east side of the Park, and is a large commodious building. The outside is in an unfinished state; but the interior is handsomely decorated, and fitted up in as good style as the London theatres, upon a scale suitable to the population of the city. It contains a large coffee-room, and good sized lobbies, and is reckoned to hold about 1,200 persons. The scenes are well painted and numerous; and the machinery, dresses, and decorations, are elegant, and appropriate to the performances, which consist of all the new pieces that come out on the London boards, and several of Shakespeare's best plays. The only fault is, that they are too much curtailed, by which they often lose their effect; and the performances are sometimes over by half past ten, though they do not begin at an earlier hour than in

London. The drama had been a favourite in New York before the Revolution. . . .

New York has its Vauxhall and Ranelagh; but they are poor imitations of those near London. They are, however, pleasant places of recreation for the inhabitants. The Vauxhall garden is situated in the Bowery Road about two miles from the City Hall. It is a neat plantation, with gravel walks adorned with shrubs, trees, busts, and statues. In the centre is a large equestrian statue of General Washington. Light musical pieces, interludes, etc. are performed in a small theatre situate in one corner of the gardens: the audience sit in what are called the pit and boxes, in the open air. The orchestra is built among the trees, and a large apparatus is constructed for the display of fireworks. The theatrical corps of New York is chiefly engaged at Vauxhall during summer. . . .

Every day, except Sunday, is a market-day in New York. Meat is cut up and sold by the joint or in pieces, by the licensed butchers only, their agents, or servants. Each of these must sell at his own stall, and conclude his sales by one o'clock in the afternoon, between the 1st of May and the 1st of November, and [by] two [o'clock] between the 1st of November and the 1st of May. Butchers are licensed by the mayor, who is clerk of the market. He receives for every quarter of beef sold in the market six cents; for every hog, shoat, or pig above 14 lbs. weight, six cents; and for each calf, sheep, or lamb, four cents; to be paid by the butchers and other persons selling the same. To prevent engrossing, and to favour housekeepers, it is declared unlawful for persons to purchase articles to sell again in any market or other part of the city before noon of each day, except flour and meal, which must not be bought to be sold again until four in the afternoon: hucksters in the market are restricted to the sale of vegetables, with the exception of fruits. The sale of unwholesome and stale articles of provision; of blown and stuffed meat, and of measly pork, is expressly forbidden. Butter must be sold by the pound, and not by the roll or tub. Persons who are not licensed butchers, selling butchers' meat on commission, pay triple fees to the clerk of the market. . . .

The manufactures of America are yet in an infant state; but in New York there are several excellent cabinet-makers, coach-makers, &c. who not only supply the country with household furniture and carriages, but also export very largely to the West-Indies, and to foreign possessions on the continent of America. Their workmanship would be considered elegant and modern in London; and they have the advantage of procuring mahogany and other wood much cheaper than we. . . .

There are upwards of twenty news-papers published in New York, nearly half of which are daily papers; besides several weekly and monthly magazines or essays. . . .

The booksellers and printers of New York are numerous, and in general men of property. . . .

A public library is established at New York, which consists of about ten thousand volumes, many of them rare and valuable books. The building which contains them is situated in Nassau-street, and the trustees are incorporated by an act of the legislature. There are also three or four public reading-rooms, and circulating libraries, which are supported by some of the principal booksellers, from the annual subscriptions of the inhabitants. There is a museum of natural curiosities in New York, but it contains nothing worthy of particular notice. . . .

Much has been said of the deficiency of the polite and liberal accomplishments among both sexes in the United States. Whatever truth there may have formerly been in this statement, I do not think there is any foundation for it at present, at least in New York, where there appears to be a great thirst after knowledge. The riches that have flowed into that city, for the last twenty years, have brought with them a taste for the refinements of polished society; and though the inhabitants cannot yet boast of having reached the standard of European perfection, they are not wanting in the solid and rational parts of education; nor in many of those accomplishments which ornament and embellish private life. It has become the fashion in New York to attend lectures on moral philosophy, chemistry, mineralogy, botany, mechanics, &c.; and the ladies in particular have made considerable progress in those studies. . . .

Dancing is an amusement that the New York ladies are passionately fond of, and they are said to excel those of every other city in the Union. I visited the *City Assembly,* which is held at the City Hotel in the Broadway, and considered as the best in New York. It was the first night of the season, and there were not more than one hundred and fifty persons present. I did not perceive any thing different from an English assembly, except the cotillons, which were danced in an admirable manner, alternately with the country dances. Several French gentlemen were present, and figured away in the cotillons with considerable taste and agility. The subscription is two dollars and a half for each night, and includes tea, coffee, and a cold collation. None but the first class of society can become subscribers to this assembly. Another has, however, been recently established, in which the genteel part of the second class are admitted, who were shut out from the City Assembly. A spirit of jealousy and pride has caused the subscribers of the *new assembly* to make their subscription three dollars, and to have their balls also at the City Hotel. It was so well conducted, that many of the subscribers of the City Assembly seceded, and joined the opposition one, or subscribed to both. . . .

The style of living in New York is fashionable and splendid; many of the principal merchants and people of property have elegant equipages, and those who have none of their own may be accommodated with handsome carriages and horses at the livery stables; for there are no coach stands. . . .

New York abounds with religious sects of various denominations; but the episcopalians and presbyterians seem to be the most numerous, at least they have more places of worship than any of the others. The quakers form but a small community in this city, and even that is decreasing; for the young people do not appear much inclined to follow up the strict ceremonials of their parents in point of dress and manners. . . .

There are several rich and respectable families of Jews in New York; and as they have equal rights with every other citizen in the United States, they suffer under no invidious distinctions. . . .

There are about 4,000 negroes and people of colour in New York, 1,700 of whom are slaves. These people are mostly of the Methodist persuasion, and have a chapel or two of their own with preachers of their colour; though some attend other places of worship according to their inclination.

Remarks of the Commissioners for Laying Out Streets and Roads in the City of New York (1811)

The "grid plan" that was finally approved by the state legislature in 1811 had begun four years earlier, when the assembly charged the Streets Commission, comprised of Gouverneur Morris, Simeon De Witt, and John Rutherfurd, with the task of dividing the remaining land above Fourteenth Street and into Washington Heights "as to unite regularity and order with the Public convenience and benefit, and in particular to promote the health of the city."

The resulting rectangular grid valued real estate property lines over topography with a ruthless efficiency. Twelve numbered avenues and 155 cross streets created move than two thousand long, narrow blocks. The system of "circles and ovals" used by Pierre Charles L'Enfant in his plan for Washington was chided as violating the principles of economy. There were no exceptions to the commissioners' plan; even Peter Stuyvesant's Bowery farmland was cut up. The family was only able to save the diagonal thoroughfare between Second and Third Avenues now known as Stuyvesant Street.

The commissioners also noted, with no apparent sense of irony, that they had stopped at 155th Street because "it is improbable that (for centuries to come) the grounds north of Harlem Flat will be covered with houses, . . . and to have gone further might have furnished materials to the pernicious spirit of speculation."

THE Commissioners of Streets and Roads in the City of New York appointed in and by an act relative to improvement touching the laying out of streets and roads in the city of New York, and for other purposes, passed the third day of April, in the year of our Lord one thousand eight hundred and seven, according to the form and effect of the said act, remark on the map hereunto annexed:

That as soon as they could meet and take the oath prescribed they entered on the duties of their office, and employed persons to make surveys of Manhattan island, which they personally reconnoitered, so as to acquire the general information needful to the correct prosecution of their work, which has been much delayed by the difficulty of procuring competent persons on those economical terms which they prescribed to themselves, and by reasons peculiarly unfavorable.

That one of the first objects which claimed their attention was the form and manner in which the business should be conducted; that is to say, whether they should confine themselves to rectilinear and rectangular streets, or whether they should adopt some of those supposed improvements by circles, ovals, and stars, which certainly embellish a plan, whatever may be their effect as to convenience and utility. In considering that subject they could not but bear in mind that a city is to be composed principally of the habitations of men, and that straight-sided and right-angled houses are the most cheap to build and the most convenient to live in. The effect of these plain and simple reflections was decisive.

Having determined, therefore, that the work in general should be rectangular, a second, and, in their opinion, an important consideration was so to amalgamate it with the plans already adopted by individuals as not to make any important changes in their dispositions.

This, if it could have been effected consistently with the public interest, was desirable, not only as it might render the work more generally acceptable, but also as it might be the means of avoiding expense. It was therefore a favorite object with the Commissioners, and pursued until after various unsuccessful attempts had proved the extreme difficulty, nor was it abandoned at last but from necessity. To show the obstacles which frustrated every effort can be of no use. It will perhaps be more satisfactory to each person who may feel aggrieved to ask himself whether his sensations would not have been still more unpleasant had his favorite plans been sacrificed to preserve those of a more fortunate neighbor. If it should be asked why was the present plan adopted in preference to any other, the answer is, because, after taking all circumstances into consideration, it appeared to be the best; or, in other and more proper terms, attended with the least inconvenience.

It may to many be a matter of surprise that so few vacant spaces have been left, and those so small, for the benefit of fresh air and consequent preservation of health. Certainly if the city of New York was destined to stand on the side of a small stream such as the Seine or the Thames, a great number of ample places might be needful. But those large arms of the sea which embrace Manhattan island render its situation, in regard to health and pleasure as well as to the convenience of commerce, peculiarly felicitous.

When, therefore, from the same causes the prices of land are so uncommonly great, it seems proper to admit the principles of economy to greater influence than might, under circumstances of a different kind, have consisted with the dictates of prudence and the sense of duty. It appears proper, nevertheless, to select and set apart on an elevated position a space sufficient for a large reservoir when it shall be found needful to furnish the city, by means of aqueducts or by the aid of hydraulic machinery, with a copious supply of pure and wholesome water. In the meantime, and indeed afterwards, the same space may be consecrated to the purposes of science when the public spirit shall dictate the building of an observatory. It did not appear proper, only it was felt to be indispensable, that a much larger space should be set aside for military exercise, as also to assemble, in the case of need, the force destined to defend the city. The question, therefore, was not and could not be whether there should be a grand parade but where it should be placed and what should be its size; and here, again, it is to be lamented that in this late day the parade could not be brought further south and made larger than it is without incurring a frightful expense. The spot nearest to that part of the city already built which could be selected with any regard to economy is at the foot of those heights called Inklingberg, in the vicinity of Kip's Bay. That it is too remote and too small shall not be denied; but it is presumed that those who may be inclined to criticism on that score may feel somewhat mollified when the collector shall call for their proportion of the large and immediate tax which even this small and remote parade shall require.

Another large space, almost as necessary as the last, is that which, at no distant period, will be required for a public market. The city of New York contains a population already sufficient to place it in the rank of cities of the second order, and is rapidly advancing towards a level with the first. It is, perhaps, no unreasonable conjecture that in half a century it will be closely built up to the northern boundary of the parade and contain four hundred thousand souls. The controlling power of necessity will long before that period have taught its inhabitants the advantage of deriving their supplies of butcher's meat, poultry, fish, game, vegetables, and fruit from shops in the neighborhood. The dealers in those articles will also find it convenient, and so will those from whom they purchase, to meet at one general mart. This has a tendency to fix and equalize prices over the whole city. The carcass butcher, gardener, farmer, &c., will be able to calculate with tolerable accuracy on the rate at which the supplies he furnishes can be rendered; and the reasonable profit of the retailer being added will give a price for the consumer varying rather by the quality of the articles than by any other circumstance.

It is no trifling consideration that by this mode of supplying the wants of large cities there is a great saving of time and of the articles consumed. To a person engaged in profitable business one hour spent in market is frequently worth more than the whole of what he purchases; and he is sometimes obliged to purchase a larger quantity than he has occasion to use, so that the surplus is wasted. Moreover, the time spent by those who bring articles of small value from the country in retailing them out bears such great proportion to the articles themselves as to increase the price beyond what it ought to be.

In short, experience having demonstrated to every great aggregation of mankind the expedience of such arrangement, it is reasonable to conclude that it will be adopted hereafter, and there fore it is proper to provide for it now. Neither is it wholly unworthy of consideration that the establishment of a general mart will leave open the spaces now appropriated to that object in parts of the city more closely built than is perfectly consistent with cleanliness and health.

The place selected for this purpose is a salt marsh, and, from that circumstance, of inferior price—though in regard to its destination of greater value—than other soil. The matter dug from a large canal through the middle, for the admission of market-boats, will give a due elevation and solidity to the side; and in a space of more than three thousand feet long and upward of eight hundred wide there will, it is presumed, after deducting what is needful for the canal and markets, be sufficient room for carts and wagons without incommoding those whose business or curiosity may induce them to attend it.

To some it may be a matter of surprise that the whole island has not been laid out as a city. To others it may be a subject of merriment that the Commissioners have provided space for a greater population than is collected at any spot on this side of China. They have in this respect been governed by the shape of the ground. It is not improbable that considerable numbers may be collected at Harlem before the high hills to the southward of it shall be built upon as a city; and it is improbable that (for centuries to come) the grounds north of Harlem Flat will be covered with houses. To have come short of the extent laid out might therefore have defeated just expectations; and to have gone further might have furnished materials to the pernicious spirit of speculation.

To the better understanding of the map, it will be proper to recollect, in examining it, that the term avenue is applied to all those streets which run in a northerly direction parallel to each other. These are one hundred feet wide, and such of them as can be extended as far north as the village of Harlem are numbered (beginning with the most eastern, which passes from the west of Bellevue Hospital to the east of Harlem Church) 1, 2, 3, 4, 5, 6, 7, 8, 9, 10, 11, and 12. This last runs from the wharf at Manhattanville nearly along the shore of the Hudson river, in which it is finally lost, as appears by the map. The avenues to the eastward of number one are marked A, B, C, and D. The space between the First and Second avenues is six hundred and fifty feet; from the Second to the Third avenue is six hundred and ten feet. The spaces from the Third to the Fourth, from the Fourth to the Fifth (which is the Manhattanville avenue or Middle road), and from the Fifth to the Sixth avenue, are each nine hundred and twenty feet. The spaces west of number six are each of them eight hundred feet. The westerly side of the Avenue A begins at the intersection of the northerly side of North street by the westerly side of Essex street. The northerly side of Avenue B begins at the intersection of the northerly side of North street by the westerly side of Trundle street. The westerly side of Avenue C begins at the intersection of the northerly side of North street by the westerly side of Pitt street; and the westerly side of Avenue D begins at the intersection of the northerly side of North street by the westerly side of Columbia street. Those passages which run at right angles to the avenues are termed streets, and are numbered consecutively from one to one hundred and fifty-five. The northerly side of number one begins at the southern end of Avenue B and terminates in the Bower lane; number one hundred and fifty-five runs from Bussing's Point to Hudson river, and is the most northern of those which it was thought at all needful to lay out as part of the city of New York, excepting the Tenth avenue, which is continued to Harlem river and strikes it near Kingsbridge. These streets are all sixty feet wide except fifteen, which are one hundred feet wide, viz.: Numbers fourteen, twenty-three, thirty-four, forty-two, fifty-seven, seventy-two, seventy-nine, eighty-six, ninety-six, one hundred and six, one hundred and sixteen, one hundred and twenty-five, one hundred and thirty-five, one hundred and forty-five, and one hundred and fifty-five—the block or space between them being in general about two hundred feet.

The southern side of the Third street touches the northeastern corner of the house occupied by Mangle Winthorn, opposite the southerly side of Jones street; and the blocks between the First and Third streets are of equal width. The northern side of Fifth street touches the northerly side of Monument No. 5 and the blocks between Third and Fifth streets are of equal breadth. The northerly side of Sixth street touches the southerly side of Monument No. 6.

The northerly side of Seventh street touches the southern side of Monument No. 7, and most the streets from the first to the seventh, inclusive, extend beyond the Bowery, and near the eastern side of which Monuments Nos. 5, 6, and 7 are placed.

The northerly side of Eighth street touches the southwestern corner of a house built on the northerly side of Stuyvesant street, heretofore so called, and easterly side of the Bowery. The northerly side of Ninth street touches the southerly side of Monument No. 9. The northerly side of Tenth street touches the southerly side of Monument No. 10, and after crossing the Sixth Avenue becomes the southerly side of the same Tenth street. The northerly side of Eleventh street touches the northerly side of Monument No. 11. The three last-mentioned monuments are placed near the easterly side of the Bowery road; and the Eighth, Ninth, Tenth, and Eleventh streets extend westwardly to Greenwich lane. The southerly side of Sixteenth street touches the southerly side of Monument No. 16, placed near the western side of the Bloomingdale road. The blocks between Eleventh and Sixteenth streets are of equal breadth, and the Twelfth and Thirteenth streets extend westward to Hudson river, being interrupted, nevertheless, by a northeasterly angle of Greenwich lane. All the streets except First and Second streets (which run into North street) extend eastwardly to the Sound, or East river; and all the streets from Thirteenth street northward extend from river to river, saving where they are interrupted by public places or squares. The southern side of Twenty-first street touches the northern side of Monument No. 21, placed near the western side of the Bloomingdale road; and the blocks between Sixteenth and Twenty-first streets are of the same width. The northern side of Forty-second street touches the southern side of Monuments Nos. 1 and 42, placed four-tenths of a foot eastward of the westerly side of the First avenue; and the blocks between the Twenty-first and Forty-second streets are of equal width. The northern side of the Seventy-first street touches the southern side of Monuments Nos. 5 and 71, whose westerly side is placed on the eastwardly side of the Fifth avenue; and the blocks between the Forty-second and Seventy-first streets are of the same width. The northwardly side of Eighty-sixth street touches the northwardly side of Monuments Nos. 5 and 86, whose westerly side is placed on the eastwardly side of the Fifth avenue; and the blocks between the Seventy-first and Eighty-sixth streets are of the same width. The northwardly side of Ninety-sixth street touches the southwardly side of Monuments Nos. 5 and 96, whose westerly side is placed on the eastwardly side of the Fifth avenue; and the blocks between the Eighty-sixth and Ninety-sixth street are of the same width. The northwardly side of the One hundred and Twenty-fifth street touches the southwardly side of Monuments marked 1 and M, whose eastwardly side is four-tenths of a foot between the westerly side of the First avenue; and the blocks between the Ninety-sixth and One Hundred and Twenty-fifth streets are of the same width. The southerly side of the One Hundred and Fifty-third street touches the northern side of the ten-mile stone on the Kingsbridge road, at the surface of the earth, and all the blocks northward of the One Hundred and Twenty-fifth street are of the same width. All the avenues extend southward to the boundary marked out by the statute, except the Fourth, which stops at the Fifteenth street, being there lost in Union place. This place is irregular trapezium, bounded (as appears on the map) westwardly by Bloomingdale road, southwardly by Tenth street, eastwardly and northwardly by the Bowery road, Broadway (which is continued out to the Parade), Fifteenth street, the Fourth avenue, and Sixteenth street. This place becomes necessary, from various considerations. Its central position requires an opening for the benefit of fresh air; the union of so many large roads demands space for security and convenience, and the morsels into which it would be cut by continuing across it the several streets and avenues would be of little use of value.

There are sundry small places equally the children of necessity, viz.: One bounded northerly by Second street, southwardly by North street, and westwardly by the Avenue C; another bounded northwardly by First street, southwardly by Ninth street, and westwardly by the First avenue; and a third being the space south of Seventh street and west of the Third avenue.

The market-place already mentioned is bounded northwardly by Tenth street, southwardly by Seventh street, eastwardly by the East river, and westwardly by the First avenue. The Parade is bounded northwardly by Thirty-second and Thirty-fourth streets, southwardly by Twenty-third street, eastwardly by the Third avenue from Twenty-third to Thirty-second street, and by the Eastern Post road from the Thirty-second to the Thirty-fourth street, and westwardly by the Seventh avenue; being in its greatest length from east to west little more than 1,350 yards, and in its breadth from north to south not quite 1,000. Bloomingdale square is bounded northwardly by Fifty-seventh street, southwardly by Fifty-third street; eastwardly by the Eighth and westwardly by the Ninth avenues. Hamilton square is bounded southwardly by Sixty-eighth street, southwardly by Sixty-sixth street, eastwardly by the Third and westwardly by the Fifth avenues. Manhattan square is bounded northwardly by Eighty-first street, southwardly by Seventy-seventh street, eastwardly by the Eighth and westwardly by the Ninth avenues. Observatory place, or square for reservoirs, is bounded northwardly by Ninety-fourth street, southwardly by Eighty-ninth street, eastwardly by the Fourth, and westwardly by the Fifth avenues. Harlem Marsh is bounded northwardly by the Hundred and Ninth street, southwardly by the Hundred and Sixth street, eastwardly by the Sound, and westwardly by the Fifth avenue. Finally, Harlem square is bounded northwardly by the Hundred and Twenty-first street; southwardly by the Hundred and Seventeenth street, eastwardly by the Sixth and westwardly by the Seventh avenues.

The position of all the monuments will be seen on the map, and also the several elevations taken above high-water mark.

In witness whereof the said Commissioners have hereunto set their hands and seal the twenty-second day of March, in the year of our Lord one thousand eight hundred and eleven.

GOUV. MORRIS

SIMEON DE WITT

JOHN RUTHERFURD

Free Schools, DeWitt Clinton (1809)

Although he is best known for his leadership in the construction of the Erie Canal between 1816 and 1825, DeWitt Clinton envisioned New York City as a cultural as well as a commercial capital of the new nation. Born in Little Britain, New York, in 1769, he was the son of the Revolutionary War general James Clinton and graduated first in his class in the first class to graduate from Columbia College in 1786. By 1790 he held the "second most powerful position in the executive branch of the state government," secretary to his uncle, Governor George Clinton. From that time until his death in 1828, Clinton was a dominant force in New York politics.

At the heart of Clinton's vision for the city was an active role for government, and he was responsible for countless initiatives to aid education and cultural institutions. Clinton was appointed mayor virtually every year between 1803 and 1815, during which time he spearheaded the founding of the New-York Historical Society, the Literary and Philosophical Society, the American Bible Society, the African Free School, the New York Institution for the Deaf and Dumb, and the Orphan Asylum.

Clinton's view of the government's role was founded on a belief in education for the entire population. In 1805 the New York Free School Society was founded; its president, from its inception until his death, was DeWitt Clinton. Educating only the wealthy was, in Clinton's eyes, "the fundamental error of Europe," and he believed that the mixing of rich and poor in public schools would be "a strong incentive for the display of talents and a felicitous accommodation to the genius of republican government." The creation of one of the best school systems in the country set New York in excellent position to take advantage of the coming market revolution of the next half century.

In casting a view over the civilized world, we find an universal accordance in opinion on the benefits of education; but the practical exposition of this opinion exhibits a deplorable contrast. While magnificent Colleges and

Universities are erected, and endowed, and dedicated to literature, we behold few liberal appropriations for diffusing the blessings of knowledge among all descriptions of people. The fundamental error of Europe has been to confine the light of knowledge to the wealthy and great, while the humble and the depressed have been as sedulously excluded from its participation as the wretched criminal, immured in a dungeon, is from the light of Heaven. This cardinal mistake is not only to be found in the institutions of the old world and in the condition of its inhabitants, but it is to be seen in most of the books which have been written on the subject of education. The celebrated Locke, whose treatises on government and the human understanding have covered him with immortal glory, devoted the powers of his mighty intellect, to the elucidation of education—but in the very threshold of his book, we discover this radical error—his treatise is professedly intended for the children of gentlemen. "If those of that rank (says he), are by their education once set right, they will quickly bring all the rest in order;" and he appears to consider the education of other children as of little importance. The consequence of this monstrous heresy has been, that ignorance, the prolific parent of every crime and vice, has predominated over the great body of the people, and a corresponding moral debasement has prevailed. "Man differs more from man, than man from beast," says a writer, once celebrated. This remark, however generally false, will certainly apply with great force to a man in a state of high mental cultivation, and man in a state of extreme ignorance.

This view of human nature is indeed calculated to excite the most painful feelings; and it entirely originates from a consideration of the predominating error which I have exposed. To this source must the crimes and calamities of the old world be principally imputed. Ignorance is the cause as well as the effect of bad governments, and without the cultivation of our rational powers, we can entertain no just ideas of the obligations of morality or the excellencies of religion. Although England is justly renowned for its cultivation of the arts and sciences, and although the poor rates of that country exceed five millions sterling per annum, yet (I adopt the words of an eminent British writer), "there is no Protestant country where the education of the poor has been so grossly and infamously neglected as in England." If one-tenth part of that sum had been applied to the education of the poor, the blessings of order, knowledge, and innocence would have been diffused among them, the evil would have been attacked on the fountain head, and a total revolution would have taken place in the habits and lives of the people, favorable to the cause of industry, good morals, good order, and rational religion.

More just and rational views have been entertained on this subject in the United States. Here, no privileged orders—no factitious distinctions in society—no hereditary nobility—no royal prerogatives exist, to interpose barriers between the people, and to create distinct classifications in society. All men being considered as enjoying an equality of rights, the propriety and necessity of dispensing, without distinction, the blessings of education, followed of course. In New England the greatest attention has been invariably given to this important object. In Connecticut, particularly, the schools are supported at least three-fourths of the year by the interest of a very large fund created for that purpose, and a small tax on the people; the whole amounting to seventy-eight thousand dollars per annum. The result of this beneficial arrangement is obvious and striking. Our Eastern brethren are a well-informed and moral people. In those States it is as uncommon to find a poor man who cannot read and write, as it is rare to see one in Europe who can.

Pennsylvania has followed the noble example of New England. On the fourth of April last, a law was passed in that State, entitled "An act to provide for the education of the poor, gratis." The expense of educating them is made a county charge, and the county commissioners are directed to carry the law into execution.

New York has proceeded in the same career, but on a different, and perhaps more eligible plan. For a few years back, a fund has been accumulating with great celerity, solemnly appropriated to the support of common schools. This fund consists at present of near four hundred thousand dollars in bank stock, mortgages, and bonds; and produces an annual interest of upwards of twenty-four thousand dollars. The capital will be augmented by the accumulating interest and the sale of three hundred and thirty-six thousand acres of land. When the interest on the whole amounts to fifty thousand dollars, it will be in a state of distribution. It is highly probable that the whole fund will, in a few years, amount to twelve hundred and fifty thousand dollars, yielding a yearly income of seventy-five thousand dollars. If population is taken as the ratio of distribution, the quota of this city will amount to seven thousand, five hundred dollars, a sum amply sufficient on the plan of our establishment, if judiciously applied, to accommodate all our poor with a gratuitous education. . . .

A number of benevolent persons had seen, with concern, the increasing vices of this city, arising in a great degree from the neglected education of the poor. Great cities are at all times the nurseries and hotbeds of crime. Bad men from all quarters repair to them, in order to obtain the benefit of concealment, and to enjoy in a superior degree the advantages of rapine and fraud. And the dreadful examples of vice, which are presented to youth, and the alluring forms in which it is arrayed, connected with a spirit of extravagance and luxury, the never-failing attendant of great wealth and extensive business, cannot fail of augmenting the mass of moral depravity. "In London, says a distinguished writer on its police, above twenty thousand individuals rise every morning, without knowing how, or by what means they are to be supported through the passing day, and in many instances even where they are to lodge on the ensuing night." There can be no doubt that hundreds are in the same situation in this city, prowling about our streets for prey, the victims of intemperance, the slaves of idleness, and ready to fall into any vice, rather than to cultivate industry and good order. How can it be expected that persons so careless of themselves, will pay any attention to their children? The mendicant parent bequeaths his squalid poverty to his offspring, and the hardened thief transmits a legacy of infamy to his unfortunate and depraved descendants. Instances have occurred of little children, arraigned at the bar of our criminal courts, who have been derelict and abandoned, without a hand to protect, or a voice to guide them through life. When interrogated as to their connections, they have replied, that they were without home and without friends. In this state of turpitude and idleness, leading lives of roving mendicancy and petty depredation, they existed a burden and a disgrace to the community.

True it is, that Charity Schools, entitled to eminent praise, were established in this city, but they were attached to particular sects, and did not embrace children of different persuasions. Add to this that some denominations were not provided with those establishments, and that children, the most in want of instruction, were necessarily excluded, by the irreligion of their parents, from the benefit of education.

After a full view of the case, those persons of whom I have spoken, agreed that the evil must be corrected at its source, and that education was the sovereign prescription. Under this impression, they petitioned the Legislature, who, agreeably to their application, passed a law on the 9th of April, 1805, entitled "An Act to incorporate the Society instituted in the city of New York for the Establishment of a Free School, for the education of poor children, who do not belong to, or not provided for, by any religious society." —Thirteen Trustees were elected under this Act, on the first Monday of the ensuing May, with power to manage the affairs of the Corporation. On convening together, they found that they had undertaken a great task, and encountered an important responsibility; without funds, without teachers, without a house in which to instruct, and without a system of instruction; and that their only reliance must be on their own industry, on the liberality of the public, on the bounty of the constituted authorities, and on the smiles of the Almighty Dispenser of all good.

In the year 1798, an obscure man of the name of Joseph Lancaster, possessed of an original genius and a most sagacious mind, and animated by a sublime benevolence, devoted himself to the education of the poor of Great Britain. Wherever he turned his eyes, he saw the deplorable state to which they were reduced by the prevalence of ignorance and vice. He first planted his standard of charity in the city of London, where it was calculated that forty thousand children were left as destitute of instruction as the savages of the desert. And he proceeded by degrees to form and perfect a system, which is in education what the most finished machines for abridging labor and expense are in the mechanic arts.

It comprehends reading, writing, arithmetic, and the knowledge of the Holy Scriptures. It arrives at its object with the least possible trouble and at the least possible expense. Its distinguishing characters are economy, facility, and expedition, and its peculiar improvements are cheapness, activity, order and emulation. It is impossible on this occasion to give a detailed view of the system. For this I refer you to a publication entitled, "Improvements in Education, &c., by Joseph Lancaster," and for its practical exposition, I beg you to look at the operations of this seminary. Reading in all its processes, from the alphabet upwards, is taught at the same time with writing, commencing with sand, proceeding to the slate, and from thence to the copybook. And to borrow a most just and striking remark, "The beauty of the system is, that nothing is trusted to the boy himself—he does not only *repeat* the lesson before a superior, but he *learns* before a superior." Solitary study does not exist in the establishment. The children are taught in companies. Constant habits of attention and vigilance are formed, and an ardent spirit of emulation kept continually alive. Instruction is performed through the instrumentality of the scholars. The school is divided into classes of ten, and a chief, denominated a Monitor, is appointed over each class, who exercises a didactic and supervisional authority. The discipline of the school is enforced by shame, rather than by the infliction of pain. The punishments are varied with circumstances; and a judicious distribution of rewards, calculated to engage the infant mind in the discharge of its duty, forms the keystone which binds together the whole edifice.

Upon this system, Lancaster superintended in person a school of one thousand scholars, at an annual expense of three hundred pounds sterling.

In 1806, he proposed, by establishing twenty or thirty schools in different parts of the kingdom, to educate ten thousand poor children, at four shillings per annum each. This proposition has been carried into effect, and he has succeeded in establishing twenty schools in different parts of the kingdom, all of which are under the care of teachers, educated by him, few of whom are more than eighteen years old. Several of the schools have each about three hundred scholars—that at Manchester has four hundred—his great school in Borough-Road, London, flourishes very much—it has sometimes eleven hundred scholars—seldom less than one thousand.

When I perceive that many boys in our school have been taught to read and write in two months, who did not before know the Alphabet, and that even one has accomplished it in three weeks—when I view all the bearings and tendencies of this system—when I contemplate the habits of order which it forms, the spirit of emulation which it excites—the rapid improvement which it produces—the purity of morals which it inculcates—when I behold the extraordinary union of celerity in instruction, and economy of expense—and when I perceive one great assembly of a thousand children, under the eye of a single teacher, marching with unexampled rapidity, and with perfect discipline, to the goal of knowledge, I confess that I recognize in Lancaster, the benefactor of the human race—I consider his system as creating a new era in education, as a blessing sent down from Heaven to redeem the poor and distressed of this world from the power and dominion of ignorance. . . .

The trustees of this institution, after due deliberation, did not hesitate to adopt the system of Lancaster, and in carrying it into effect, they derived essential aid from one of their body, who had seen it practised in England, and who had had personal communication with its author. A teacher was also selected who has fully answered every reasonable expectation. He has generally followed the prescribed plan. Wherever he has deviated, he has improved. A more numerous, a better governed school, affording equal facilities to improvement, is not to be found in the United States.

Provided thus with an excellent system and an able teacher, the school was opened on the 6th of May, 1806, in a small apartment in Bancker street. This was the first scion of the Lancaster stock engrafted in the United States; and from this humble beginning, in the course of little more than three years, you all observe the rapidity with which we have ascended.

One great desideratum still remained to be supplied. Without sufficient funds, nothing could be efficiently done. Animated appeals were made to the bounty of our citizens, and five thousand six hundred and forty-eight dollars were collected by subscription. Application was also made to the Legislature of this State for assistance, and on the 27th of February, 1807, a law was passed, appropriating four thousand dollars, for the "purpose of erecting a suitable building, or buildings, for the purpose of promoting the benevolent objects of the Society." The preamble of this liberal act contains a legislative declaration of the excellence of the Lancaster system, in the following words:—"Whereas the trustees of the Society for establishing a Free School in the city of New York, for the education of such poor children as do not belong to, or are not provided for, by any religious society, have, by their memorial, solicited the aid of the Legislature; and whereas their plan of extending the benefits of education to poor children, and the excellent mode of instruction adopted by them, are highly deserving of the encouragement of Government."

Application was also made to the Corporation of the city for assistance, and the tenement in Bancker-street, being in all respects inadequate to the accommodation of the increasing establishment, that body appropriated a building adjacent to the Alms-house, for the temporary accommodation of the school, and the sum of five hundred dollars towards putting it in repair; the Society agreeing to receive and educate fifty children from the Alms-house. To this place the school was removed on the 1st of May, 1807, where it has continued until to-day.

The Corporation also presented the ground of this edifice, on which was an arsenal, to the Society, on condition of their educating the children of the Alms-house gratuitously; and also the sum of fifteen hundred dollars, to aid in the completion of this building. The value of this lot, and the old building, may be fairly estimated at ten thousand dollars; and the Society have expended above thirteen thousand dollars in the erection and completion of this edifice and the adjacent buildings. The income of the school, and its expense did not much differ from that sum. This room will contain near six hundred scholars, and below there are apartments for the family of the teacher, for the meeting of the trustees, and for a female school, which may contain one hundred scholars, and may be considered as an useful adjunct to this institution. This seminary was established about twelve years ago, by a number of young women belonging to, or professing with, the Society of Friends; who have, with meritorious zeal and exemplary industry, devoted much of their personal attention, and all their influence, to the education of poor girls in the elementary parts of education and needle-work. The signal success which attended this free-school animated the trustees with a desire to extend its usefulness, and to render it co-extensive with the wants of the community, and commensurate with the objects of public bounty. A statute was accordingly passed, on their application, on the 1st of April, 1808, altering the style of this corporation, denominating it "The Free School Society of New York," and extending its powers to all children who are the proper objects of gratuitous education.

Accounts and Recollections of the War of 1812 from the popular press (1814, 1846)

New Yorkers were of conflicted minds about the War of 1812; the tension was between commerce and patriotism. On the one hand, New York businessmen and traders found it increasingly easier to deal with the British than to support the war effort. And by the end of 1813, the British blockade of the entire New England coast down to Long Island Sound made it impossible for ships to get in and out of the harbor. On the other hand, Manhattan shipbuilders lent their expertise to the building of the gunboats that allowed Captain Oliver Hazard Perry to defeat the British in September 1813. Perry was then honored in New York, being given the keys to the city and having a street named after him.

After the British burned Washington in August 1814, however, New Yorkers rallied behind the words of Mayor DeWitt Clinton, who proclaimed he would rather "die in a ditch than tamely and cowardly surrender this delightful city." Some twenty-three thousand volunteers joined local militia, the women of Brooklyn Heights, and "the free people of color" in digging trenches and erecting barricades. But the Treaty of Ghent ended the war in December 1814 with the city never having been attacked.

From *The Columbian*, August 27, 1814

YOUR capital is taken! 13,000 British troops may have marched for Baltimore, and before this hour it may have fallen. Six days ago the people at Washington were in perfect security. In six days the same enemy may be at the Hook, and if they assail your city with a powerful force by land and by water, what will be your fate? Arise from your slumbers! Let every citizen arise and enroll himself instantly and prepare to defend our city to the last extremity! This is no time to talk! We must act, and act with vigor, or we are lost.

From *New York Evening Post,* August 20, 1814

NOTICE FROM "A CITIZEN OF COLOUR"

The committee of defence have assigned next Monday for the people of colour to contribute their services to work on the fortifications. On this occasion it becomes the duty of every coloured man, resident in this city, to volunteer. The state of New York has evinced a disposition to do us justice. . . . Under the protection of her laws we dwell in safety and pursue our honest callings, none daring to molest us, whatever his complexion or circumstances. And such has been the solicitude in our behalf, manifested from time to time by our legislature, that there is a fair prospect of a period not far distant, when this state will not contain a slave. Our country is now in danger. . . . We have now an opportunity of shewing that we are not ungrateful . . . but are willing to exert ourselves . . . for the protection of our beloved state.—Let no man of colour, who is able to go, stay at home on Monday next; but let every one assemble at 5 o'clock, A.M. in the Park, to join with their brethren in their patriotic effort.

From *Journal of Commerce,* 1846

The evening of February 11, 1815, . . . [the *Gazette*] office was about being closed, when a pilot rushed in and stood for a moment, so entirely exhausted as to be unable to speak. . . . Presently the pilot, gasping for breath, whispered intelligibly, "Peace! peace! . . . An English sloop-of-war is below with news of a treaty of peace. . . . "

All hands rushed into Hanover Square, crying—"Peace! *Peace!* PEACE!" The windows flew up. . . . No sooner were the inmates sure of the sweet sound of peace than the windows began to glow with brilliant illuminations. The cry of "Peace! *Peace!* PEACE!" spread through the city at the top of all voices. No one stopped to inquire about "free trade and sailors' rights." No one inquired whether even the national honor had been preserved. The matters by which politicians had irritated the nation into the war had lost all their importance.—It was enough that the ruinous war was over. . . . Never was there such joy in the city. A few evenings after, there was a general illumination, and although the snow was a foot deep and soaked with rain, yet the streets were crowded with men and women, eager to see and partake of everything which had in it the sight or taste of peace.

From A History of New York, *Diedrich Knickerbocker (Washington Irving) (1819)*

Born in New York City in 1783, Washington Irving spent his childhood at 128 William Street. He never attended secondary school but at sixteen went to work in a law office. After traveling Europe from 1804 to 1806, Irving returned to become one of a literary group known as the Lads of Kilkenny. In 1807 Irving, his brother William, and William's brother-in-law James Kirke Paulding produced a collection of essays entitled *Salmagundi,* in which the trio dubbed New York City "Gotham," after an English nursery rhyme about a village whose inhabitants had pretended to be fools in order to avoid punishment.

On November 28, 1809, after an elaborate and successful publicity hoax in the *Evening Post,* Irving, under the pseudonym Diedrich Knickerbocker, published *A History of New York from the Beginning of the World to the End of the Dutch Dynasty.* Irving's book accomplished two things. First, it was the first American book widely praised in Europe; continental literary luminaries such as Sir Walter Scott, Charles Dickens, and Samuel Coleridge were wildly enthusiastic in their praise of the work. Second, as "Diedrich Knickerbocker" wrote, "Cities of themselves are nothing without an historian." Irving gave the city, which knew little of its Dutch past, a sense of history and of place. He would do the same thing in his fiction by producing stories such as "The Legend of Sleepy Hollow" and "Rip Van Winkle" before retiring to his home, Sunnyside, on the banks of the Hudson. Irving died at his estate in Tarrytown in 1859.

On the Founding and Naming of the New City; of the City Arms; and of the Direful Feud Between Ten Breeches and Tough Breeches

THE land being thus fairly purchased of the Indians, a circumstance very unusual in the history of colonization, and strongly illustrative of the honesty of our Dutch progenitors, a stockade fort and trading-house were forthwith erected on an eminence in front of the place where the good St. Nicholas had appeared in a vision to Oloffe the Dreamer, and which, as has already been observed, was the identical place at present known as the Bowling Green.

Around this fort a progeny of little Dutch-built houses, with tiled roofs and weathercocks, soon sprang up, nestling themselves under its walls for protection, as a brood of half-fledged chickens nestle under the wings of the mother hen. The whole was surrounded by an enclosure of strong palisadoes, to guard against any sudden irruption of the savages. Outside of these extended the cornfields and cabbage-gardens of the community, with here and there an attempt at a tobacco-plantation; all covering these tracts of country at present called Broadway, Wall Street, William Street, and Pearl Street.

I must not omit to mention, that, in portioning out the land, a goodly "bowerie," or farm, was allotted to the sage Oloffe in consideration of the service he had rendered to the public by his talent at dreaming; and the site of his "bowerie" is known by the name of Kortlandt (or Cortlandt) Street to the present day.

And now the infant settlement having advanced in age and stature, it was thought high time it should receive an honest Christian name. Hitherto it had gone by the original Indian name Manna-hata, or, as some will have it, "The Manhattoes"; but this was now decried as savage and heathenish, and as tending to keep up the memory of the pagan brood that originally possessed it. Many were the consultations held upon the subject, without coming to a conclusion, for though everybody condemned the old name, nobody could invent a new one. At length, when the council was almost in despair, a burgher, remarkable for the size and squareness of his head proposed that they should call it New Amsterdam. The proposition took everybody by surprise; it was so striking, so apposite, so ingenious. The name was adopted by acclamation, and New Amsterdam the metropolis was thenceforth called. Still, however, the early authors of the province continued to call it by the general appellation of "The Manhattoes," and the poets fondly clung to the euphonious name of Manna-hata; but those are a kind of folk whose tastes and notions should go for nothing in matters of this kind.

Having thus provided the embryo city with a name, the next was to give it an armorial bearing or device, as some cities have a rampant lion, others a soaring eagle,—emblematical, no doubt, of the valiant and high-flying qualities of the inhabitants; so, after mature deliberation, a sleek beaver was emblazoned on the city standard, as indicative of the amphibious origin, and patient, persevering habits of the New Amsterdammers.

The thriving state of the settlement and the rapid increase of houses soon made it necessary to arrange some plan upon which the city should be built; but at the very first consultation held on the subject, a violent discussion arose; and I mention it with much sorrowing as being the first altercation on record in the councils of New Amsterdam. It was, in fact, a breaking forth of the grudge and heart-burning that had existed between those two eminent burghers, Mynheers Ten Broeck and Harden Broeck, ever since their unhappy dispute on the coast of Bellevue. The great Harden Broeck had waxed very wealthy and powerful, from his domains, which embraced the whole chain of Apulean mountains that stretched along the gulf of Kip's Bay, and from part of which his descendants have been expelled in latter ages by the powerful clans of the Joneses and the Schermerhornes.

An ingenious plan for the city was offered by Mynheer Harden Broeck, who proposed that it should be cut up and intersected by canals, after the manner of the most admired cities in Holland. To this Mynheer Ten Broeck was diametrically opposed, suggesting, in place thereof, that they should run out docks and wharves, by means of piles driven into the bottom of the river, on which the towns should be built. "By these means," said he triumphantly, "shall we rescue a considerable space of territory from these immense rivers, and build a city that shall rival Amsterdam, Venice, or any amphibious city in Europe." To this proposition, Harden Broeck (or Tough Breeches) replied, with a look of as much scorn as he could possibly assume. He cast the utmost censure upon the plan of his antagonist, as being preposterous and against the very order of things, as he would leave to every true Hollander. "For what," said he, "is a town without canals?—it is like a body without veins and arteries, and must perish for want of a free circulation of the vital fluid." Ten Breeches, on the contrary, retorted with a sarcasm upon his antagonist, who was somewhat of an arid, dry-boned habit: he remarked, that as to the circulation of the blood being necessary to existence, Mynheer Tough Breeches was a living contradiction to his own assertion: for everybody knew there had not a drop of blood circulated through his wind-dried carcase for good ten years, and yet there was not a greater busy-body in the whole colony. Personalities have seldom much effect in making converts in argument; nor have I ever seen a man convinced of error by being convicted of deformity. At least, such was not the case at present. If Ten Breeches was very happy in sarcasm, Tough Breeches, who was a sturdy little man, and never gave up the last word, rejoined with increasing spirit; Ten Breeches had the advantage of the greatest volubility, but Tough Breeches had that invaluable coat of mail in argument, called obstinacy. Ten Breeches had, therefore, the most mettle, but Tough Breeches the best bottom; so that though Ten Breeches made a dreadful clattering about his ears, and battered and belabored him with hard words and sound arguments, yet Tough Breeches hung on most resolutely to the last. They parted, therefore, as is usual in all arguments where both parties are in the right, without coming to any conclusion;—but they hated each other most heartily forever after, and a similar breech with that between the houses of Capulet and Montague did ensue between the families of Ten Breeches and Tough Breeches.

I would not fatigue my reader with these dull matters of fact, but that my duty as a faithful historian requires that I should be particular; and in truth, as I am now treating of the critical period when our city, like a young twig, first received the twists and turns which have since contributed to give it its present picturesque irregularity, I cannot be too minute in detailing their first causes.

After the unhappy altercation I have just mentioned, I do not find that anything further was said on the subject worthy of being recorded. The council, consisting of the largest and oldest heads in the community, met regularly once a week, to ponder on this momentous subject; but, either they were deterred by the war of words they had witnessed, or they were naturally averse to the exercise of the tongue, and the subsequent exercise of the brains,—certain it is, the most profound silence was maintained,—the question as usual lay on the table,—the members quietly smoked their pipes, making but few laws, without ever enforcing any,—and in the meantime the affairs of the settlement went on—as it pleased God.

As most of the council were but little skilled in the mystery of combining pot-hooks and hangers, they determined most judiciously not to puzzle either themselves or posterity with voluminous records. The secretary, however, kept the minutes of the council, with tolerable precision, in a large vellum folio, fastened with massy brass clasps; the journal of each meeting consisted but of two lines, stating in Dutch, that "the council sat this day, and smoked twelve pipes, on the affairs of the colony." By which it appears that the first settlers did not regulate their time by hours, but pipes, in the same manner as they measure distances in Holland at this very time: an admirably exact measurement, as a pipe in the mouth of a true-born Dutchman is never liable to those accidents and irregularities that are continually putting our clocks out of order.

In this manner did the profound council of New Amsterdam smoke, and doze, and ponder, from week to week, month to month, and year to year, in what manner they should construct their infant settlement;—meanwhile, the town took care of itself, and like a sturdy brat which is suffered to run about wild, unshackled by clouts and bandages, and other abominations by which your notable nurses and sage old women cripple and disfigure the children of men, increased so rapidly in strength and magnitude, that before the honest burgomasters had determined upon a plan, it was too late to put it in execution,—whereupon they wisely abandoned the subject altogether.

Containing Peter Stuyvesant's Voyage up the Hudson, and the Wonders and Delights of That Renowned River

Now did the soft breezes of the south steal sweetly over the genial face of nature, tempering the panting heats of summer into genial and prolific warmth; when that miracle of hardihood and chivalric virtue, the dauntless Peter Stuyvesant, spread his canvas to the wind, and departed from the fair island of Manna-hata. The galley in which he embarked was sumptuously adorned with pendants and streamers of gorgeous dyes, which fluttered gayly in the wind, or drooped their ends into the bosom of the stream. The bow and poop of this majestic vessel were gallantly bedight, after the rarest Dutch fashion, with figures of little pursy Cupids with periwigs on their heads, and bearing in their hands garlands of flowers, the like of which are not to be found in any book of botany; being the matchless flowers which flourished in the golden age, and exist no longer, unless it be in the imaginations of ingenious carvers of wood and discolorers of canvas.

Thus rarely decorated, in style befitting the puissant potentate of the Manhattoes, did the galley of Peter Stuyvesant launch forth upon the bosom of the lordly Hudson, which, as it rolled its broad waves to the ocean, seemed to pause for a while and swell with pride, as if conscious of the illustrious burthen it sustained.

But trust me, gentlefolk, far other was the scene presented to the contemplation of the crew from that which may be witnessed at this degenerate day. Wildness and savage majesty reigned on the borders of this mighty river—the hand of cultivation had not as yet laid low the dark forest, and tamed the features of the landscape—nor had the frequent sail of commerce broken in upon the profound and awful solitude of ages. Here and there might be seen a rude wig-wam perched among the cliffs of the mountains with its curling column of smoke mounting in the transparent atmosphere—but so loftily situated that the whoopings of the savage children, gamboling on the margin of the dizzy heights, fell almost as faintly on the ear as do the notes of the lark, when lost in the azure vault of heaven. Now and then, from the beetling brow of some precipice, the wild deer would look timidly down upon the splendid pageant as it passed below; and then, tossing his antlers in the air, would bound away into the thickets of the forest.

Through such scenes did the stately vessel of Peter Stuyvesant pass. Now did they skirt the bases of the rocky heights of Jersey, which spring up like everlasting walls, reaching from the waves unto the heavens, and were fashioned, if tradition may be believed, in times long past, by the mighty Manetho, to protect his favorite abodes from the unhallowed eyes of mortals. Now did they career it gayly across the vast expanse of Tappan Bay, whose wide-extended shores present a variety of delectable scenery—here the bold promontory, crowned with embowering tress, advancing into the bay—there the long woodland slope, sweeping up from the shore in rich luxuriance, and terminating in the upland precipice—while at a distance a long waving line of rocky heights threw their gigantic shades across the water. Now would they pass where some modest little interval, opening among these stupendous scenes, yet retreating as it were for protection into the embraces of the neighboring mountains, displayed a rural paradise, fraught with sweet and pastoral beauties; the velvet tufted lawn—the bushy copse—the tinkling rivulet, stealing through the fresh and vivid verdure—on whose banks was situated some little Indian village, or, peradventure, the rude cabin of some solitary hunter.

The different periods of the revolving day seemed each, with cunning magic, to diffuse a different charm over the scene. Now would the jovial sun break gloriously from the east, blazing from the summits of the hills, and sparkling the landscape with a thousand dewy gems; while along the borders of the river were seen heavy masses of mist, which, like midnight caitiffs, disturbed at his approach, made a sluggish retreat, rolling in sullen reluctance up the mountains. At such times all was brightness, and life, and gayety—the atmosphere was of an indescribable pureness and transparency—the birds broke forth in wanton madrigals, and the freshening breezes wafted the vessel merrily on her course. But when the sun sank amid a flood of glory in the west, mantling the leaves and the earth with a thousand gorgeous dyes—then all was calm, and silent, and magnificent. The late swelling sail hung lifelessly against the mast—the seaman, with folded arms, leaned against the shrouds, lost in that involuntary musing which the sober grandeur of nature commands in the rudest of her children. The vast bosom of the Hudson was like an unruffled mirror, reflecting the golden splendor of the heavens excepting that now and then a bark canoe would steal across its surface, filled with painted savages, whose gay feathers glared brightly, as perchance a lingering ray of the setting sun gleamed upon them from the western mountains.

But when the hour of twilight spread its majestic mists around, then did the face of nature assume a thousand fugitive charms, which to the worthy heart that seeks enjoyment in the glorious works of its Maker are inexpressibly captivating. The mellow dubious light that prevailed just served to tinge with illusive colors the softened features of the scenery. The deceived but delighted eye sought vainly to discern in the broad masses of shade, the separating line between the land and water; or to distinguish the fading objects that seemed sinking into chaos. Now did the busy fancy supply the feebleness of vision, producing with industrious craft a fairy creation of her own. Under her plastic wand the barren rocks frowned upon the watery waste, in the semblance of lofty towers, and high embattled castles—trees assumed the direful forms of mighty giants, and the inaccessible summits of the mountains seemed peopled with a thousand shadowy beings.

Now broke forth from the shores the notes of an innumerable variety of insects, which filled the air with a strange but not inharmonious concert—while ever and anon was heard the melancholy plaint of the Whip-poor-will, who, perched on some lone tree, wearied the ear of night with his incessant moanings. The mind, soothed into a hallowed melancholy, listened with pensive stillness to catch and distinguish each sound that vaguely echoed from the shore—now and then startled perchance by the whoop of some straggling savage, or by the dreary howl of a wolf, stealing forth upon his nightly prowlings.

Thus happily did they pursue their course, until they entered upon those awful defiles denominated THE HIGHLANDS, where it would seem that the gigantic Titans had erst waged their impious war with heaven, piling up cliffs on cliffs, and hurling vast masses of rock in wild confusion. But in sooth very different is the history of these cloud-capt mountains.—These in ancient days, before the Hudson poured its waters from the lakes, formed one vast prison, within whose rocky bosom the omnipotent Manetho confined the rebellious spirits who repined at his control. Here, bound in adamantine chains, or jammed in rifted pines, or crushed by ponderous rocks, they groaned for many an age.—At length the conquering Hudson, in its career towards the ocean, burst open their prison-house, rolling its tide triumphantly through the stupendous ruins.

Still, however, do many of them lurk about their old abodes, and these it is, according to venerable legends, that cause the echoes which resound throughout these awful solitudes; which are nothing but their angry clamors when any noise disturbs the profoundness of their repose.—For when the elements are agitated by tempest, when the winds are up and the thunder rolls, then horrible is the yelling and howling of these troubled spirits, making the mountains to rebellow with their hideous uproar; for at such times it is said that they think the great Manetho is returning once more to plunge them in gloomy caverns, and renew their intolerable captivity.

But all these fair and glorious scenes were lost upon the gallant Stuyvesant; naught occupied his mind but thoughts of iron war, and proud anticipations of hardy deeds of arms. Neither did his honest crew trouble their heads with any romantic speculations of the kind. The pilot at the helm quietly smoked his pipe, thinking of nothing either past, present, or to come—those of his comrades who were not industriously smoking under the hatches were listening with open mouths to Antony Van Corlear; who, seated on the windlass, was relating to them the marvelous history of those myriads of fireflies, that sparkled like gems and spangles upon the dusky robe of night. These, according to tradition, were originally a race of pestilent sempiternous beldames, who peopled these parts long before the memory of man; being of that abominated race emphatically called *brimstones;* and who, for their innumerable sins against the children of men, and to furnish an awful warning to the beauteous sex, were doomed to infest the earth in the shape of these threatening and terrible little bugs; enduring the internal torments of that fire, which they formerly carried in their hearts and breathed forth in their words; but now are sentenced to bear about for ever—in their tails!

And now I am going to tell a fact, which I doubt much my readers will hesitate to believe; but if they do, they are welcome not to believe a word in this whole history—for nothing which it contains is more true. It must be known then that the nose of Antony the Trumpeter was a very lusty size, strutting boldly from his countenance like a mountain of Golconda; being sumptuously bedecked with rubies and other precious stones—the true regalia of a king of good fellows, which jolly Bacchus grants to all who bouse it heartily at the flagon. Now thus it happened, that bright and early in the morning, the good Antony, having washed his burly visage, was leaning over the quarter railing of the galley, contemplating it in the glassy wave below. —Just at this moment the illustrious sun, breaking in all his splendor from behind a high bluff of the highlands, did dart one of his most potent beams full upon the refulgent nose of the sounder of brass—the reflection of which shot straightway down, hissing hot, into the water, and killed a mighty sturgeon that was sporting beside the vessel! This huge monster being with infinite labor hoisted on board, furnished a luxurious repast to all the crew, being accounted of excellent flavor, excepting about the wound, where it smacked a little of brimstone—and this, on my veracity, was the first time that ever sturgeon was eaten in these parts by Christian people.

When this astonishing miracle came to be made known to Peter Stuyvesant, and that he tasted of the unknown fish, he, as may well be supposed, marveled exceedingly; and as a monument thereof, he gave the name of *Antony's Nose* to a stout promontory in the neighborhood—and it has continued to be called Antony's Nose ever since that time.

But hold: whither am I wandering? By the mass, if I attempt to accompany the good Peter Stuyvesant on this voyage, I shall never make an end; for never was there a voyage so fraught with marvelous incidents, nor a river so abounding with transcendant beauties, worthy of being severally recorded. Even now I have it on the point of my pen to relate how his crew were most horribly frightened, on going on shore above the highlands, by a gang of merry roistering devils, frisking and curveting on a flat rock, which projected into the river—and which is called the *Duyvel's Dans-Kamer* to this very day.—But no! Diedrich Knickerbocker—it becomes thee not to idle thus in thy historic wayfaring.

Recollect that while dwelling with the fond garrulity of age over these fairy scenes, endeared to thee by the recollections of thy youth, and the charms of a thousand legendary tales, which beguiled the simple ear of thy childhood; recollect that thou art trifling with those fleeting moments which should be devoted to loftier themes.—Is not Time—relentless Time! shaking, with palsied hand, his almost exhausted hour-glass before thee?—hasten then to pursue thy weary task, lest the last sands be run ere thou hast finished thy history of the Manhattoes.

Let us, then, commit the dauntless Peter, his brave galley, and his loyal crew, to the protection of the blessed St. Nicholas; who, I have no doubt, will prosper him in his voyage, while we await his return at the great city of New-Amsterdam.

From Travels Through North America, *Karl Bernhard, Duke of Saxe-Weimar-Eisenach (1825)*

Karl Bernhard journeyed through the United States and Canada in 1825 and 1826 and recorded his findings in his *Travels Through North America.* Bernhard took particular interest in the Erie Canal and even stayed with Thomas Jefferson at Monticello while visiting the University of Virginia in November 1825. During his time in New York earlier in 1825, he paid particular attention to the attitudes of slaves.

Slavery had existed in New York since the Dutch introduced it in 1626. The end of slavery in New York began with an act in 1799 that "declared free the children of slaves born on or after July 4, granted freedom to slaves born before that date at the age of twenty-four for women and twenty-eight for men." In 1809 marriages between slaves were legalized, and the forced separation of slave families was prohibited. The celebration that Bernhard describes in this section of his *Travels* regards the agreement in 1817 between the state legislature and Governor Daniel Tompkins to abolish slavery on July 4, 1827. Abolition, however, was not finally achieved until 1841.

On returning home at night, I observed that the streets were not well lighted. I was afterwards informed, that the corporation of the city was just engaged in a quarrel with the gas-company relative to the lamps; this quarrel protracted the inconvenience, though it was somewhat lessened by the numerous stores, which are kept open till a late hour, and are very splendidly lighted with gas. The gas-lights burn in handsome figures; at a music-store, I saw one in form of a harp. . . .

The servants are generally negroes and mulattos; most of the white servants are Irish; the Americans have a great abhorrence of servitude. Liveries are not to be seen; the male servants wear frock coats. All the families complain of bad servants and their impudence, because the latter consider themselves on an equality with their employers. Of this insolence of servants I saw daily examples. Negroes and mulattos are abundant here, but they generally rank low, and are labourers. There are but a few slaves in the state of New York, and even these are to be freed in the year 1827, according to a law passed by the senate of the state. There are public schools established for the instruction of coloured children and . . . there are several churches belonging to the coloured population; most of them are Methodists, some Episcopalians. A black minister, who was educated in an Episcopalian seminary, is said to be a good preacher. . . .

On the afternoon of the third of October, there was a great procession of negroes, some of them well dressed, parading through the streets, two by two, preceded by music and a flag. An African club, called the Wilberforce Society, thus celebrated the anniversary of the abolition of slavery in New York, and concluded the day by a dinner and ball. The coloured people of New York, belonging to this society, have a fund of their own, raised by weekly subscription, which is employed in assisting sick and unfortunate blacks. This fund, contained in a sky-blue box, was carried in the procession; the treasurer holding in his hand a large gilt key; the rest of the officers wore ribands of several colours, and badges like the officers of free masons; marshals with long staves walked outside of the procession. During a quarter of an hour, scarcely any but black faces were to be seen in Broadway.

From Notions of the Americans *and* New York, *James Fenimore Cooper (1828, 1851)*

James Fenimore Cooper was born in Burlington, New Jersey, in 1789 and educated in the village school in the town his father had founded, Cooperstown. Cooper was expelled from Yale in his junior year for a series of pranks, which reportedly included blowing up a fellow student's door and training a donkey to sit in a professor's chair. After his father's death, Cooper became financially independent, married Susan DeLancey (who was descended from one of the early governors of the colony), and settled in Westchester as a gentleman farmer. Family legend has it that he took up writing as a challenge from his wife to "write a better book than the one he was presently reading." Cooper went on to produce some of the most memorable books of the nineteenth century, including *The Last of the Mohicans* (1826) and *The Deerslayer* (1841).

Cooper's attitude toward New York City vacillated as the city itself developed in the second quarter of the nineteenth century. He came to the city in 1821 in order to pursue the publication of his first novel; the following year he founded a literary club called Bread and Cheese, whose member included the poets William Cullen Bryant and Fitz-Greene Halleck. His volume *Notions of the Americans* (1828) was written while he was abroad but was intended largely as a defense of American society against foreign critics; in it Cooper predicts New York's "growing prosperity, and its probable grandeur." By the late 1830s, however, Cooper noted the "greedy rapacity for money, and the vulgar and indiscriminate expenditure" of New York's commercial elite. Cooper's last work before his death in 1851, however, was a history of New York City which he never completed, *The Towns of Manhattan.* In that piece, he argued that "New York is essentially national in interest, positions, pursuits. No one thinks of the place as belonging to a particular state, but to the United States."

Notions of the Americans (1828)

In construction, New York embraces every variety of house, between that of the second-rate English town residence, and those temporary wooden tenements that are seen in the skirts of most large cities. I do not think, however, that those absolutely miserable, filthy abodes which are often seen in Europe, abound here. The houses of the poor are not indeed large, like those in which families on the continent are piled on one another for six or seven stories, but they are rarely old and tottering; for the growth of the place . . . forces them out of existence before they have had time to decay. I have been told, and I think it probable, that there are not five hundred buildings in New York, that can date further back than the peace of '83. A few old Dutch dwellings yet remain. . . .

In outward appearance, New York, but for two things, would resemble a part of London that should include fair proportions of Westminster (without the great houses and recent improvements), the city, and Wapping. The points of difference are owing to the fact that, probably without an exception, the exterior of all the houses are painted, and that there is scarce a street in the place which is not more or less lined with trees. . . . The common practice is to deepen the colour of the bricks by a red paint, and then to interline them with white. . . . But, in many instances, I saw dwellings of a lively cream colour; and there are also several varieties of stone that seem to be getting much in use latterly. . . .

I have elsewhere said that the city of New York is composed of inhabitants from all the countries of Christendom. Beyond a doubt a very large majority, perhaps nine-tenths, are natives of the United States; but it is not probable that one-third who live here first saw the light on the island of Manhattan. It is computed that one in three are either natives of New England, or are descendants of those who have emigrated from that portion of the country. To these must be added the successors of the Dutch, the English, the French, the Scotch and the Irish, and not a few who came in their proper persons from the countries occupied by these several nations. In the midst of such a mélange of customs and people, it is exceedingly difficult to extract anything like a definite general character. . . .

As might be expected, the general society of New York bears a strong impression of its commercial character. In consequence of the rapid growth of the city, the number of families that may be properly classed among those which have long been distinguished in its history for their wealth and importance, bears a much smaller proportion to its entire population than that of most other places. . . . Still, a much larger class of what in Europe forms the *élite* of society exists here, than strangers commonly suppose. . . .

It strikes me that both a higher and a lower order of men mingle in commerce here, than is seen elsewhere, if, perhaps, the better sort of English merchants be excepted. Their intimate relations on "'Change" bring them all, more or less, together in the saloons; nor can the associations well be avoided, until the place shall attain a size, which must leave every one the perfect master of his own manner of living. That hour is fast approaching for New York, and with it, I think, must come a corresponding change in the marshalling of its coteries. . . .

But it is not difficult to see that society in New York, in consequence of its extraordinary increase, is rather in a state of effervescence than settled, and, where that is the case, I presume you will not be surprised to know, that the lees sometimes get nearer to the surface than is desirable.

New York (1851)

The increase of the towns of Manhattan, as, for the sake of convenience, we shall term New York and her adjuncts, in all that contributes to the importance of a great commercial mart, renders them one of the most remarkable places of the present age. Within the distinct recollections of living men, they have grown from a city of the fifth or sixth class to be near the head of all the purely trading places of the known world. That there are sufficient causes for this unparalleled prosperity, will appear in the analysis of the natural advantages of the port, in its position, security, accessories, and scale. . . .

If the Manhattan towns, or Manhattan, as we shall not scruple to term the several places that compose the prosperous sisterhood at the mouth of the Hudson—a name that is more ancient and better adapted to the history, associations, and convenience of the place than any other—continue to prosper as they have done, ere the close of the present century they will take their station among the capitals of the first rank. It may require a longer period to collect the accessories of a first-class place, for these are the products of time and cultivation; though the facilities of intercourse, the spirit of the age, and the equalizing sentiment that marks the civilization of the epoch, will greatly hasten everything in the shape of improvement. . . .

It will be in their trade, their resources, their activity, and their influence on the rest of the world, as well as in their population, that the towns of

Manhattan will be first entitled to rank with the larger capitals of Europe. So obvious, rapid, and natural has been the advance of all the places, that it is not easy for the mind to regard anything belonging to them as extraordinary, or out of rule. There is not a port in the whole country that is less indebted to art and the fostering hand of Government than this. It is true, certain forts, most of them of very doubtful necessity, have been constructed for defence; but no attack having ever been contemplated, or, if contemplated, attempted, they have been dead letters in the history of its progress. We are not aware that Government has ever expended one cent in the waters of Manhattan, except for the surveys, construction of the aforesaid military works, and the erection of the lighthouses, that form a part of the general provision for the safe navigation of the entire coast. Some money has been expended for the improvement of the shallow waters of the Hudson; but it has been as much, or more, for the advantage of the upper towns, and the trade coastwise, generally, than for the special benefit of New York.

The immense natural advantages of the bays and islands at the mouth of the Hudson have, in a great degree, superseded the necessity of such assistance. Nature has made every material provision for a mart of the first importance: and perhaps it has been fortunate that the towns have been left, like healthful and vigorous children, managed by prudent parents, to take the inclination and growth pointed out to them by this safest and best of guides. . . .

New York is nearer to a state of nature, probably, as regards all its customs and associations, than any other well-established place that could be named. With six hundred thousand souls, collected from all parts of Christendom —with no upper class recognized by, or in any manner connected with, the institutions, it would seem that the circles might enact their own laws, and the popular principle be brought to bear socially on the usages of the town —referring fashion and opinion altogether to a sort of popular will. The result is not exactly what might be expected under the circumstances, the past being intermingled with the present time, in spite of theories and various opposing interests; and, in many instances, caprice is found to be stronger than reason.

We have no desire to exaggerate, or to color beyond their claims, the importance of the towns of Manhattan. No one can better understand the vast chasm which still exists between London and New York, and how much the latter has to achieve before she can lay claim to be the counterpart of that metropolis of Christendom. It is not so much our intention to dilate on existing facts, as to offer a general picture, including the past, the present, and the future, that may aid the mind in forming something like a just estimate of the real importance and probable destinies of this emporium of the New World.

It is now just three-and-twenty years since, that, in another work, we ventured to predict the great fortunes that were in reserve for this American mart, giving some of the reasons that then occurred to us that had a tendency to produce such a result. These predictions drew down upon us sneers, not to say derision, in certain quarters, where nothing that shadows forth the growing power of this republic is ever received with favor. The intervening period has more than fulfilled our expectations. In this short interval, the population of the Manhattan towns has more than trebled, while their wealth and importance have probably increased in a greatly magnified proportion. Should the next quarter of a century see this ratio in growth continued, London would be very closely approached in its leading element of superiority—numbers. We have little doubt that the present century will bring about changes that will place the emporium of the Old World and that of the New nearly on a level. This opinion is given with a perfect knowledge of the vast increase of the English capital itself, and with a due allowance for its continuance. We propose, in the body of this work, to furnish the reasons justifying these anticipations.

Seventeen years since, the writer returned home from a long residence in Europe, during which he had dwelt for years in many of the largest towns of that quarter of the world. At a convivial party in one of the most considerable dwellings in Broadway, the conversation turned on the great improvements that had then been made in the town, with sundry allusions that were intended to draw out the opinions of a traveller on a subject that justly ever has an interest with the Manhattanese. In that conversation the writer—his memory impressed with the objects with which he had been familiar in London and Paris, and Rome, Venice, Naples, etc., and feeling how very provincial was the place where he was, as well as its great need of change to raise it to the level of European improvement—ventured to say that, in his opinion, speaking of Broadway, "There was not a building in the whole street, a few special cases excepted, that would probably be standing thirty years hence." The writer has reason to know that this opinion was deemed extravagant, and was regarded as a consequence of European rather than of American reasoning. If the same opinion were uttered to-day, it would meet with more respect. Buildings now stand in Broadway that may go down to another century, for they are on a level with the wants and tastes of a capital; but none such, with a single exception, existed at the time of which we are writing. . . .

As to the notion of there arising any rival ports, south, to compete with New York, it strikes us as a chimera. New Orleans will always maintain a qualified competition with every place not washed by the waters of the great valley; but New Orleans is nothing but a local port, after all—of great wealth and importance, beyond a doubt, but not the mart of America.

New York is essentially national in interests, position, and pursuits. No one thinks of the place as belonging to a particular State, but to the United States. The revenue paid into the treasury, at this point, comes in reality, from the pockets of the whole country, and belongs to the whole country. The same is true of her sales and their proceeds. Indeed, there is very little political sympathy between the places at the mouth of the Hudson, and the interior—the vulgar prejudice of envy, and the jealousy of the power of collected capital, causing the country to distrust the town.

We are aware that the governing motive of commerce, all over the world, is the love of gain. It differs from the love of gain in its lower aspects, merely in its greater importance and its greater activity. These cause it to be more engrossing among merchants than among the tillers of the soil: still, facts prove that this state of things has many relieving shades. The man who is accustomed to deal in large sums is usually raised above the more sordid vices of covetousness and avarice in detail. There are rich misers, certainly, but they are exceptions. We do not believe that the merchant is one tittle more mercenary than the husbandman in his motives, while he is certainly much more liberal of his gains. One deals in thousands, the other in tens and twenties. It is seldom, however, that a failing market, or a sterile season, drives the owner of the plough to desperation, and his principles, if he have any, may be preserved; while the losses or risks of an investment involving more than the merchant really owns, suspend him for a time on the tenter-hooks of commercial doubt. The man thus placed must have more than a common share of integrity, to reason right when interest tempts him to do wrong.

Notwithstanding the generally fallacious character of the governing motive of all commercial communities, there is much to mitigate its selfishness. The habit of regarding the entire country and its interests with a friendly eye, and of associating themselves with its fortunes, liberalizes its mind and wishes, and confers a catholic spirit that the capital of a mere province does not possess. Boston, for instance, is leagued with Lowell, and Lawrence, and Cambridge, and seldom acts collectively without betraying its provincial mood; while New York receives her goods and her boasted learning by large tran [s] shipments, without any special consciousness of the transactions. This habit of generalizing in interests encourages the catholic spirit mentioned, and will account for the nationality of the great mart of a great and much extended country. The feeling would be apt to endure through many changes, and keep alive the connection of commerce even after that of the political relations may have ceased. New York, at this moment, contributes her full share to the prosperity of London, though she owes no allegiance to St. James. . . .

All large commercial towns are, in their nature, national in feeling. The diversity and magnitude of their interests are certain to keep them so; and, as we have already said, New York forms no exception to the rule. She belongs already more to the country than she does to the State, and every day has a tendency to increase this catholic disposition among the votaries of commerce.

From Travels in North America in the Years 1827 and 1828, *Basil Hall*

Basil Hall was one of a string of Europeans, primarily British, who visited America in the 1820s and 1830s and described in great detail the daily lives of the American working class. Born in 1788, Hall was a British naval officer who commanded vessels on scientific voyages of exploration from 1802 until 1823. From that time until his death in 1844, he traveled throughout the world and wrote extensively about Borneo, India, and Chile, among other places. He visited American cities such as New York, Boston, Philadelphia, Charleston, and Cincinnati and published his observations in *Travels in North America in the Years 1827 and 1828.*

Many Americans felt that Hall had excoriated the manners and customs of the American people, and his volume elicited outrage in the popular press. In appendix C of his *Life on the Mississippi,* Mark Twain registered his shock at the "moral earthquake" Hall had registered and the "war-whoop" that "was sent forth." Twain himself thought that Hall had let Americans off "with a degree of tenderness which may be quite suitable for him to exercise, however little merited; while, at the same time, he has most industriously magnified their merits, whenever he could possibly find anything favorable."

As we passed along, many things recalled the seaports of England to my thoughts, although abundant indications of another country lay on all hands. The signs over the shop doors were written in English; but the language we heard spoken was different in tone from what we had been accustomed to. Still it was English. Yet there was more or less of a foreign air in all we saw, especially about the dress and gait of the men. Negroes and negresses also were seen in abundance on the wharfs. The form of most of the wheeled carriages was novel; and we encountered several covered vehicles, on which was written in large characters, ICE. . . .

At two o'clock in the morning . . . I was awakened by loud cries of Fire! fire! . . . In a few minutes the deep rumbling sound of the engines was heard, mingling in a most alarming way with the cheers of the firemen, the loud rapping of the watchmen at the doors and window-shutters of the sleeping citizens, and various other symptoms of momentous danger, and the necessity of hot haste. . . . A second and far more furious alarm brought all the world to the windows. The church bells were clanging violently on all hands. . . .

On the top of the City Hall, . . . a firewarden or watchman is constantly stationed, whose duty when the alarm is given, is to hoist a lantern at the extremity of a long arm attached to the steeple, and to direct it towards the fire, as a sort of beacon, to instruct the engines what course to steer. There was something singularly striking in this contrivance, which looked as if a great giant, with a blood-red finger, had been posted in the midst of the city, to warn the citizens of their danger.

I succeeded by quick running in getting abreast of a fire engine; but although it was a very ponderous affair, it was dragged along so smartly by its crew of some six-and-twenty men, aided by a whole legion of boys, all bawling as loud as they could, that I found it difficult to keep up with them. On reaching the focus of attraction, the crowd of curious persons like myself began to thicken, while the engines came dashing in amongst us from every avenue, in the most gallant and business-like style.

Four houses, built entirely of wood, were on fire from top to bottom, and sending up a flame that would have defied a thousand engines. But nothing could exceed the dauntless spirit with which the attempt was made. In the midst of a prodigious noise and confusion, the engines were placed along the streets in a line, at the distance of about two hundred feet from one another, and reaching to the bank of the East River, as that inland sea is called, which lies between Long Island and the main. The suction hose of the last engine in the line, or that next the stream, being plunged into the river, the water was drawn up, and then forced along a leathern hose or pipe to the next engine, and so on, till at the tenth link in this curious chain, it came within range of the fire. As more engines arrived, they were marshalled by the superintendent into a new string; and in about five minutes after the first stream of water had been brought to bear on the flames, another was sucked along in like manner, and found its way, leap by leap, to the seat of the mischief. . . .

The chief things to find fault with on this occasion, were the needless shouts and other uproarious noises, which obviously helped to exhaust the men at the engines, and the needless forwardness, or it may be called foolhardiness, with which they entered houses on fire, or climbed upon them by means of ladders, when it must have been apparent to the least skilful person, that their exertions were utterly hopeless. A small amount of discipline, of which, by the way, there was not a particle, might have corrected the noise; and the other evil, I think, might have been removed, by a machine recently invented in Edinburgh, and found to be efficacious on like occasions. . . . I lost no time in writing home for a model of the whole apparatus, which I received just before leaving America, and left with a friend, to be presented to the Fire Department of New York. I hope they may find it useful in that city, which seems to be more plagued with fires than any town in the world. . . .

On the 21st of May, I accompanied two gentlemen, about three o'clock, to a curious place called the Plate House, in the very centre of the business part of the busy town of New York.

We entered a long, narrow, and rather dark room, or gallery, fitted up like a coffeehouse, with a row of boxes on each side made just large enough to hold four persons, and divided into that number by fixed arms limiting the seats. Along the passage, or avenue, between the rows of boxes, which was not above four feet wide, were stationed sundry little boys, and two waiters, with their jackets off—and good need too, as will be seen. At the time we entered, all the compartments were filled except one, of which we took possession. There was an amazing clatter of knives and forks; but not a word audible to us was spoken by any of the guests. The silence, however, on the part of the company, was amply made up for by the rapid vociferations of the attendants, especially of the boys, who were gliding up and down, and across the passage, inclining their heads for an instant, first to one box, then to another, and receiving the whispered wishes of the company, which they straightway bawled out in a loud voice, to give notice of what fare was wanted. It quite baffled my comprehension to imagine how the people at the upper end of the room, by whom a communication was kept up in some magical way with the kitchen, could contrive to distinguish between one order and the other. . . .

We had been told by old stagers of the excellence of the corned beef, and said to the boy we should all three take that dish. Off the gnome glanced from us like a shot, to attend to the beck of another set of guests, on the opposite side of the room; but, in flying across the passage, turned his face towards the upper end of the apartment and called out, "Three beef, 8!" the last word of his sentence referring to the number of our box. In a trice we saw the waiters gliding down the avenue to us, with three sets of little covered dishes, each containing a plate, on which lay a large, piping hot slice of beef.

Another plate was at the same time given, with a moderate proportion of mashed potatoes on it, together with a knife, and a fork on which was stuck a piece of bread. As the waiters passed along, they took occasion to incline their ears to the right and to the left, to receive fresh orders, and also to snatch up empty tumblers, plates, and knives and forks. The multiplicity and rapidity of these orders and movements made me giddy. Had there been one set to receive and forward the orders, and another to put them in execution, we might have seen better through the confusion; but all hands, little and big together, were screaming out with equal loudness and quickness—"Half plate beef, 4!"—"One potato, 5!"—"Two apple pie, one plum pudding, 8!" and so on.

There could not be, I should think, fewer than a dozen boxes, with four people in each; and as everyone seemed to be eating as fast as he could, the extraordinary bustle may be conceived. We were not in the house above twenty minutes, but we sat out two sets of company, at least. . . .

On the first day of every month throughout the year, a number of packet ships sail from this grand focus of American commerce, to various parts of the world; and as they all start about the same hour, no small bustle is the necessary consequence. Exactly as the clock strikes ten, a steam-boat with the passengers for the different packets, leaves the wharf, close to a beautiful public promenade called the Battery. We resolved to take a trip in this boat on the morning in question, as if we had been embarking for a voyage, but merely to see how things were managed. The crowd on the shore was immense. Troops of friends, assembled to take leave, were jostled by tradesmen, hotel keepers, and hackney coachmen, urging the payment of their accounts, and by newsmen disposing of papers wet from the printing press, squeezing amongst carts, waggons, and wheelbarrows, filled with luggage. Through this crowd of idle and busy folks, we elbowed our way, with some difficulty, and at last found ourselves on the deck of the steamer. Here a new description of confusion presented itself. There were no fewer, the captain assured us, than one hundred and sixty persons on board his boat at that moment, destined for the different packets; . . . the crush, therefore, may be imagined!

From The Domestic Manners of the Americans, *Frances Trollope (1832)*

Frances Trollope was born in Hampshire, England, in 1780. The daughter of a clergyman, she was educated at home, where she read the classics and taught herself French and Italian. She married a prominent lawyer and had six children, but her husband's business faltered when she was fifty-two, and they immigrated to Cincinnati to open a business selling luxury imported goods.

She wrote in *Domestic Manners of the Americans* of her impressions upon arriving in New York harbor, declaring, "I have never seen the bay of Naples, I can therefore make no comparison, but my imagination is incapable of conceiving anything of the kind more beautiful than the harbour of New York. . . . New York, indeed, appeared to us, even when we saw it by a soberer light, a lovely and a noble city, . . . as much superior to every other in the Union (Philadelphia not excepted), as London to Liverpool."

Trollope's charming description of America, however, did not apply to the manners of its inhabitants. Elsewhere in her best-selling work she wrote, "I do not like them, I do not like their principles, I do not like their manners, I do not like their opinions." While she was less critical of New Yorkers than of the rest of the American populace, whom she found boorish, coarse, and intemperate, she deeply regretted that "during my whole stay in the country, [I rarely] heard a sentence elegantly turned and correctly pronounced from the lips of a single American."

By the time of her death in 1863, Francis Trollope had written more than forty books. Her son Anthony Trollope was also a successful novelist, who examined English politics and society.

NEW York . . . appeared to us . . . a lovely and a noble city. To us who had been so long travelling through half-cleared forests, and sojourning among an "I'm-as-good-as-you" population, it seemed, perhaps, more beautiful, more splendid, and more refined than it might have done, had we arrived there directly from London; but making every allowance for this, I must still declare that I think New York one of the finest cities I ever saw, and as much superior to every other in the Union (Philadelphia not excepted), as London to Liverpool, or Paris to Rouen. . . .

I think it covers nearly as much ground as Paris, but is much less thickly peopled. The extreme point is fortified towards the sea by a battery, and forms an admirable point of defence; but in these piping days of peace, it is converted into a public promenade, and one more beautiful, I should suppose, no city could boast. From hence commences the splendid Broadway, as the fine avenue is called, which runs through the whole city. This noble street may vie with any I ever saw, for its length and breadth, its handsome shops, neat awnings, excellent *trottoir,* and well-dressed pedestrians. . . . [W]ere it not so very far from all the old-world things which cling about the heart of an European, I should say that I never saw a city more desirable as a residence.

The dwelling houses of the higher classes are extremely handsome, and very richly furnished. Silk or satin furniture is as often, or oftener, seen than chintz; the mirrors are as handsome as in London; the cheffoniers, slabs, and marble tables as elegant. . . . Every part of their houses is well carpeted, and the exterior finishings, such as steps, railings, and door frames, are very superior. Almost every house has handsome green blinds on the outside. . . . I saw many rooms decorated within, exactly like those of an European *petite maîtresse*. . . .

The great defect in the houses is their extreme uniformity. . . . Mixed dinner parties of ladies and gentlemen . . . are very rare.

. . . [W]e saw enough to convince us that there is society to be met with in New York, which would be deemed delightful any where. Cards are very seldom used; and music, from their having very little professional aid at their parties, is seldom, I believe, as good as what is heard at private concerts in London. . . .

If it were not for the peculiar manner of walking, which distinguishes all American women, Broadway might be taken for a French street, where it was the fashion for very smart ladies to promenade. The dress is entirely French; not an article (except perhaps the cotton stockings) must be English, on pain of being stigmatised as out of the fashion. Everything English is decidedly *mauvais ton;* English materials, English fashions, English accent, English manner, are all terms of reproach; and to say that an unfortunate looks like an English woman, is the cruellest satire which can be uttered. . . .

The hackney coaches are the best in the world, but abominably dear, and it is necessary to be on the *qui vive* in making your bargain with the driver; if you do not, he has the power of charging immoderately. On my first experiment I neglected this, and was asked two dollars and a half for an excursion of twenty minutes. When I referred to the waiter of the hotel, he asked if I had made a bargain. "No." "Then I expect" (with the usual look of triumph) "that the Yankee has been too smart for you."

The private carriages of New York are infinitely handsomer and better appointed than any I saw elsewhere; the want of smart liveries destroys much of the gay effect; but, on the whole, a New York summer equipage, with the pretty women and beautiful children it contains, looks extremely well in Broadway, and would not be much amiss anywhere.

. . . [A]gain we enjoyed the elegant hospitality of New York. . . . In truth, were all America like this fair city, and all, no, only a small proportion of its population like the friends we left there, I should say, that the land was the fairest in the world.

From America and the Americans, *James Boardman (1833)*

James Boardman described himself as an "independent businessman" when he arrived in New York in June of 1829; he remained there until May 1, 1831. He wrote *America and the Americans* (1833) in order to better inform fellow Englishmen "as to the actual state of society among our trans-Atlantic descendents." Before his travels in America, Boardman had shared his countrymen's prejudices concerning American customs, but in his descriptions he tried to show "a nation so much further advanced in all the useful arts, as well as the elegancies of life, than I, in common with the great majority of Englishmen, were willing to believe."

Boardman was particularly stunned by the New York custom of Moving Day. The British custom of celebrating May Day had led New Yorkers to the practice of signing their apartment leases on May 1. From the beginning of the nineteenth century, however, the lack of housing had led to the chaos of increasing numbers of people moving on that day in hopes of improving their situation. Businesses were traditionally closed as horse carts clogged the streets with traffic; Frances Trollope thought that it looked as though the residents were "flying from the plague."

My first impressions, on landing in New York,—and they were subsequently confirmed,—were the high character and appearance of the working classes. . . .

The carters, workmen, and others, who earn their bread by the sweat of their brow, appeared extremely well clothed; were intelligent; and, if addressed civilly, were civil in return; yet without any doffing, or even touching the hat, or making the slightest approaches to servility to those who, according to English phraseology, would be styled their betters.

All exhibited an independence of feeling not observable in the same classes of society in England; and yet nothing like insolent vulgarity was apparent. . . .

The boarding-houses of those numerous classes, the smaller shopkeepers and merchants' clerks, are in general miserably furnished. . . .

It is by no means uncommon to see four, or even five or six beds in the same room, and these are of the meanest description, without furniture even in the depth of winter: a chest of drawers is, indeed, a rara avis; each boarder making a general depository of his trunk or portmanteau, as poor Jack does of his chest in the forecastle of a ship. . . .

Oyster cellars abound; and immense quantities of these luxuries are likewise vended from small waggons in the streets; at which locomotive shops, the pedestrian may be supplied with biscuits, pepper, and ginger beer; in short, for a few pence, the carter or mechanic has a whet which might satisfy even a gourmand. . . .

July 4 celebration, 1830. Although the more intellectual part of the population, as the members of literary and scientific institutions, and the ministers of religion, might be content to celebrate the occasion by delivering patriotic odes and addresses, the joyful feelings of the bulk were expressed in a manner more congenial to their tastes; and a review of some thousand militia, cavalry, infantry, and artillery, with marchings and counter-marchings in close order, open order, and, perchance, disorder, together with a liberal expenditure of gunpowder, formed the grand attraction of the day. . . .

A military command is the acme of the ambition of an American storekeeper, and a hundred Major Sturgeons forgot their counters in the delights of pie-bald chargers, leopard-skin housings, and gay uniforms; each of whom, either by his apparent knowledge of tactics, or, what seemed to have more influence, his knowledge of holiday display, endeavoured to win a smile from the delighted fair who crowded the windows, or attract the admiration of the countless thousands who filled the streets. . . .

"The moment night with dusky mantle covered the skies," hundreds of illuminated booths, skirting the more open quarters of the city, displayed their attractions to the moving multitude, in the shape of fringed hams, pickled oysters, garnished lobsters, and roasted pigs, with lemons in their mouths; . . . all which good things might be washed down with Philadelphia porter, ginger beer, foaming mead, or other beverages, more exhilarating perhaps, but less innocent.

Although these places are the resort of the working population, a little excess in whom, at this joyous moment, might be forgiven, I did not, in a perambulation of several hours, witness a single instance of what could be termed disorderly conduct.

During the whole of this festival, every street and alley re-echoed with the reports of petty fireworks, of which quantities are brought from China, no less to the profit of the dealers than to the delight of all the boys, whose little savings banks are drained upon the occasion. . . .

In spite of the declaration of the venerable Franklin, . . . that "three removes are as bad as a fire," the inhabitants of New York are the most locomotive people on the face of the earth. This movable propensity appears to be partly caused by a progressive state of prosperity; for, as the value of property in this city has always been steadily increasing, the owners are unwilling to grant leases, hoping each successive year to add materially to their rent rolls.

In consequence of this encouraging state of things, an annual valuation takes place of every rented building in the city, and one day is appropriated to the letting of tenements and another for removals. These important seasons are the first of February and the first of May. On the former, the landlords, which term, curious enough, is still preserved by the republicans, visit their tenants; and unless arrangements have been previously entered upon, they state the rents they expect to receive for the ensuing year. If the occupier of a building assents to the proposals, the affair is ended; but if the reply is in the negative, the owner placards the walls with the words, "To Let," to which is sometimes added the rent demanded; and on the evening of this day it is common to see at least one third of the houses and stores thus ticketed, and these remain until tenants are found. At last comes the all-important first of May, which, to a stranger just arriving, presents the most singular and ludicrous spectacle imaginable,—nothing less than a whole city turned topsy-turvy, thousands of persons being in the act of removal, the streets filled with carts laden with furniture, porters, servants, children, all carrying their respective movables, from the candelabra of the drawing-room to the fish-kettle of the "foolish fat scullion," and the gingerbread wares of the nursery.

As the operations of entering upon and quitting the houses are simultaneous, the confusion within doors is in perfect keeping with the scene displayed in the streets, the whole affording no bad illustration of chaos.

To an Englishman, with his strong local attachments, this system of change would be an intolerable nuisance; but the New Yorker, no doubt from habit, not only looks upon it as a matter of course, but seems to feel an elevation of spirits at the anticipation of this agreeable variety in his social existence; and it is no uncommon circumstance to meet with individuals who have resided in a dozen different houses in as many years; and yet who speak of their wish to try the advantages of another quarter of the city when the proper season arrives.

Letter, March 1, 1833, John Pintard

John Pintard was born in 1759 and worked as both a city inspector and as clerk of the Common Council in New York City. Pintard, who was seventy-two at the time the following letter to his daughter was written, may well have been aghast at the rate of change in ground transportation in New York.

The first person to operate a horse-drawn omnibus in New York was Abraham Brower, who opened his business in 1831. There were 80 such vehicles in service by 1833, and 108 by 1837. But the drive of the city to expand northward toward Harlem led to the creation of the New York and Harlem Railroad in 1832, which had horses pulling coaches on railroad tracks up Fourth Avenue to Twenty-seventh Street. However, a city ordinance allowed only horse-drawn cars below Twenty-seventh Street (the site of present-day Baruch College), where the horses were unhitched and stabled and a steam engine was hooked up to take passengers up the rest of the island.

[ONE] has only to step to the corner wh[ich] the B[roa]dway caravans pass every 5 minutes. From 8 to 10, they are crammed with business men, after 10 there is space eno[ugh]. Ladies going below or coming up at noon, take a seat in these accommodating vehicles, walk up for exercise & ride back or vice versa. 6 Tickets for 50 c[en]ts from Wall St. to the upper part of B[roa]dway, 8 c[en]ts the ride. Indeed in the Greenwich carriages one may go a distance above 2 miles at the same rate. Take all these stages, West, No[rth] & East & they exceed 70, & from the cheapness of the Fare are always filled. These accommod[ation]s for intercourse have raised the value of Lots in the upper districts of our city & the number will increase with its growth. B[roa]dway is such a thoro'fare as to render it hazardous crossing the streets, to avoid wh[ich] I usually take a side st[reet] where I feel safe.

Workies, from Men and Manners in America, *Thomas Hamilton (1833)*

Thomas Hamilton was an established novelist and Sir Walter Scott's neighbor when he visited America late in 1831. His goal was to write the definitive account of American society for his British countrymen; he published *Men and Manners in America* in 1833.

Ironically, Hamilton's largest effect may have been on the thought of Karl Marx. Marx's notebooks show that he read Hamilton's book with care and that he believed Hamilton's descriptions of the rise of a class-conscious movement in the form of the Workingman's Party—what Marx termed "the first story of an organized political party of labor in the world's history." Hamilton's overestimation of the radicalism of the Workingman's Party appears to have been a basis for Marx's belief that American workers would rise up and abolish capitalism.

The Workingman's Party was short-lived (1829–1831), but it did garner almost a third of the votes in the 1829 elections. Their platform called for state-supported mass education (and even advocated that all children be required to attend public boarding school from the age of six), direct election of the mayor, smaller electoral districts, the abolition of privileged monopolies, and the end of government intervention in the economy. By 1831, torn by internal disagreement and much of their platform co-opted by the Tammany Democrats, the Workingman's Party disbanded.

THE operative class have already formed themselves into a society, under the name of "*The Workies,*" in direct opposition to those who, more favoured by nature or fortune, enjoy the luxuries of life without the necessity of manual labour. These people make no secret of their demands, which to do them justice are few and emphatic. They are published in the newspapers, and may be read on half the walls of New York. Their first postulate is "EQUAL AND UNIVERSAL EDUCATION." . . . They solemnly declare that they will not rest satisfied, till every citizen in the United States shall receive the same degree of education, and start fair in the competition for the honours and offices of the state. . . . There are others who go still further, and boldly advocate the introduction of an AGRARIAN LAW, and a periodical division of property. These unquestionably constitute the *extrême gauche* of the Worky Parliament, but still they only follow out the principles of their less violent neighbours, and eloquently dilate on the justice and propriety of every individual being equally supplied with food and clothing; on the monstrous iniquity of one man riding in his carriage while another walks on foot, and after his drive discussing [over] a bottle of Champagne, while many of his neighbours are shamefully compelled to be content with the pure element. Only equalize property, they say, and neither would drink Champagne or water, but both would have brandy, a consummation worthy of centuries of struggle to attain.

All this is nonsense undoubtedly, nor do I say that this party, though strong in New York, is yet so numerous or so widely diffused as to create immediate alarm. In the elections, however, for the civic offices of the city, their influence is strongly felt; and there can be no doubt that as population becomes more dense, and the supply of labour shall equal, or exceed the demand for it, the strength of this party must be enormously augmented. . . . It is nothing to say, that the immense extent of fertile territory yet to be occupied by an unborn population will delay the day of ruin. It will delay, but it cannot prevent it.

Diary: 1835, 1847, 1849, Philip Hone

Born in New York City in 1780, Philip Hone was the son of a German immigrant and entered the auction business at sixteen. Hone made a small fortune in that business and as an insurance executive before retiring to a life of public service and charitable work in 1821. He was a governor of New York Hospital, trustee of Columbia College, vice president of the New York Historical Society, founder and governor of the Union Club, member of the vestry of Trinity Church, and a supporter of the New York Eye and Ear Infirmary.

Hone was a one-term mayor of New York City starting in 1825, from which position he oversaw the opening of the Erie Canal. He was also president of the Delaware and Hudson Canal Company, for which he received the honor of having a town in Pennsylvania—Honesdale—named after him.

In 1826 Hone began a diary that he kept faithfully until his death in 1851. This document, never published in its entirety, chronicles the daily events of the city but also the life of a man who, as Louis Auchincloss suggested, "may have been the last man able to know personally everyone of importance in the United States. Presidents, congressmen, governors, mayors, writers, merchants, educators, scientists, actors, doctors and lawyers." Hone's diary also records, from his patrician stance, his horror at the deterioration brought by immigrant populations, particularly the Irish.

December 17, 1835, The Great Fire

How shall I record the events of last night, or how attempt to describe the most awful calamity which has ever visited these United States? The greatest loss by fire that has ever been known, with the exception perhaps of the conflagration of Moscow, and that was an incidental concomitant of war. I am fatigued in body, disturbed in mind, and my fancy filled with images of horror which my pen is inadequate to describe. Nearly one half of the first ward is in ashes; 500 to 700 stores, which with their contents are valued at $20,000,000 to $40,000,000, are now lying in an indistinguishable mass of ruins. There is not perhaps in the world the same space of ground covered by so great an amount of real and personal property as the scene of this dreadful conflagration. The fire broke out at nine o'clock last evening. I was waiting in the library when the alarm was given and went immediately down. The night was intensely cold, which was one cause of the precedented progress of the flames, for the water froze in the hydrants, and the engines and their hose could not be worked without great difficulty. The firemen, too, had been on duty all last night, and were almost incapable of performing their usual services.

The fire originated in the store of Comstock & Adams in Merchant Street, a narrow crooked street, filled with high stores lately erected and occupied by dry goods and hardware merchants, which led from Hanover to Pearl Street. When I arrived at the spot the scene exceeded all description; the progress of the flames, like flashes of lightning, communicated in every direction, and a few minutes sufficed to level the lofty edifices on every side. It had crossed the block to Pearl Street. I perceived that the store of my son John (Brown & Hone) was in danger, and made the best of my way by Front Street around the Old Slip to the spot. We succeeded in getting out the stock of valuable dry goods, but they were put in the square, and in the course of the night our labors were rendered unavailing, for the fire reached and destroyed them, with a great part of all which were saved from the neighboring stores; this part of Pearl Street consisted of dry goods stores, with stocks of immense value of which little or nothing was saved. At this period the flames were unmanageable, and the crowd, including the firemen, appeared to look on with the apathy of despair, and the destruction continued until it reached Coenties Slip, in that direction, and Wall Street down to the river, including all South Street and Water Street; while to the west, Exchange Street, including all Post's stores, Lord's beautiful row, William Street, Beaver and Stone Streets, were destroyed. The splendid edifice erected a few years since by the liberality of the merchants, known as the Merchants' Exchange, and one of the ornaments of the city, took fire in the rear, and is now a heap of ruins. The façade and magnificent marble columns fronting on Wall Street are all that remains of this noble building, and resemble the ruins of an ancient temple rather than the new and beautiful resort of the merchants. When the dome of this edifice fell in, the sight was awfully grand. In its fall it demolished the statue of Hamilton executed by Ball Hughes, which was erected in the rotunda only eight months ago by the public spirit of the merchants.

I have been alarmed by some of the signs of the times which this calamity has brought forth: the miserable wretches who prowled about the ruins, and became beastly drunk on the champagne and other wines and liquors with which the streets and wharves were lined, seemed to exult in the misfortune, and such expressions were heard as "Ah! They'll make no more five per cent dividends!" and "This will make the aristocracy haul in their horns!" Poor deluded wretches, little do they know that their own horns "live and move and have their being" in these very horns of the aristocracy, as their instigators teach them to call it. This cant is the very text from which their leaders teach their deluded followers. It forms part of the warfare of the poor against the rich; a warfare which is destined, I fear, to break the hearts of some of the politicians of Tammany Hall, who have used these men to answer a temporary purpose, and find now that the dogs they have taught to bark will bite them as soon as their political opponents.

These remarks are not so much the result of what I have heard of the conduct and conversation of the rabble at the fire as of what I witnessed this afternoon at the Bank for Savings. There was an evident run upon the bank by a gang of low Irishmen, who demanded their money in a peremptory and threatening manner. At this season there is usually a great preponderance of deposits over the drafts, the first of January being the day on which the balances are made up for the semi-annual dividend. All the sums now drawn lose nearly six months interest, which the bank gains. These Irishmen, however, insisted upon having their money, and when they received it were evidently disappointed and would fain have put it back again. This class of men are the most ignorant, and consequently the most obstinate white men in the world, and I have seen enough to satisfy me that, with few exceptions, ignorance and vice go together. These men, rejoicing in the calamity which has ruined so many institutions and individuals, thought it a fine opportunity to use the power which their dirty money gave them, to add to the general distress, and sought to embarrass this excellent institution, which has been established for the sole benefit of the poor. . . . These Irishmen, strangers among us, without a feeling of patriotism or affection in common with American citizens, decide the elections in the city of New York. They make Presidents and Governors, and they send men to represent us in the councils of the nation, and what is worse than all, their importance in these matters is derived from the use which is made of them by political demagogues, who despise the tools they work with. Let them look to it; the time may not be very distant when the same brogue which they have instructed to shout "Hurrah for Jackson!" shall be used to impart additional horror to the cry of "Down with the natives!"

January 29, 1847, Immigration

Our good city of New York has already arrived at the state of society to be found in the large cities of Europe; overburdened with population, and where the two extremes of costly luxury in living, expensive establishments, and improvident waste are presented in daily and hourly contrast with squalid misery and hopeless destitution. This state of things has been hastened in our case by the constant stream of European paupers arriving upon the shores of this land of promise. Alas! how often does it prove to the deluded emigrant a land of broken promise and blasted hope! If we had none but our own poor to take care of, we should get along tolerably well; we could find employment for them, and individual charity, aiding the public institutions, might save us from the sights of woe with which we are assailed in the streets, and the pressing applications which beset us in the retirement of our own houses. Nineteen out of twenty of these mendicants are foreigners cast upon our shores, indigent and helpless, having expended the last shilling in paying their passage-money, deceived by the misrepresentations of unscrupulous agents, and left to starve amongst strangers, who, finding it impossible to extend relief to all, are deterred from assisting any. These reflections upon the extremes of lavish expenditure and absolute destitution are forced upon me by my own recent experience. I partook yesterday of a most expensive dinner, where every article of costly food which the market affords was spread before the guests, and fine wines drunk in abundance, some of which might command eight or ten dollars a bottle; and from this scene of expensive hospitality I was conveyed to another more splendid and expensive entertainment, where the sparkling of diamonds, the reflection of splendid mirrors, the luster of silks and satins, the rich gilding of tasteful furniture were flashed, by the aid of innumerable lights, upon the dazzled eyes of a thousand guests. Now this is all right enough; in both these cases our entertainers could well afford the expense which attended the display of their hospitality, nor is it within the scope of the most remote probability that the money of any others than themselves can be involved in the outlay of their entertainments.

May 10, 1849, Astor Place Riots

The riot at the Opera-House on Monday night was children's play compared with the disgraceful scenes which were enacted in our part of this devoted city this evening, and the melancholy loss of life to which the outrageous proceedings of the mob naturally led.

An appeal to Mr. Macready had been made by many highly respectable citizens, and published in the papers, inviting him to finish his engagement at the Opera-House, with an implied pledge that they would stand by him against the ferocious mob of Mr. Forrest's friends, who had determined that Macready should not be allowed to play, whilst at the same time their oracle was strutting, unmolested, his "hour upon the stage" of the Broadway theater. This announcement served as a firebrand in the mass of combustibles left smoldering from the riot of the former occasion. The *Forresters* perceived that their previous triumph was incomplete, and a new conspiracy was formed to accomplish effectually their nefarious designs. Inflammatory notices were posted in the upper ward, meetings were regularly organized, and bands of ruffians, gratuitously supplied with tickets by richer rascals, were sent to take possession of the theater. The police, however, were beforehand with them, and a large body of their force was posted in different parts of the house.

When Mr. Macready appeared he was assailed in the same manner as on the former occasion; but he continued on the stage and performed his part with firmness, amidst the yells and hisses of the mob. The strength of the police, and their good conduct, as well as that of the Mayor, Recorder, and other public functionaries, succeeded in preventing any serious injury to the property within doors, and many arrests were made; but the war raged with frightful violence in the adjacent streets. The mob—a dreadful one in numbers and ferocity—assailed the extension of the building, broke in the windows, and demolished some of the doors. I walked up to the corner of Astor Place, but was glad to make my escape. On my way down, opposite the New York Hotel, I met a detachment of troops, consisting of about sixty cavalry and three hundred infantry, fine-looking fellows, well armed, who marched steadily to the field of action. Another detachment went by the way of Lafayette Place. On their arrival they were assailed by the mob, pelted with stones and brickbats, and several were carried off severely wounded.

Under this provocation, with the sanction of the civil authorities, orders were given to fire. Three or four volleys were discharged; about twenty persons were killed and a large number wounded. It is to be lamented that in the number were several innocent persons, as is always the case in such affairs. A large proportion of the mob being lookers-on, who, putting no faith in the declaration of the magistrates that the fatal order was about to be given, refused to retire, and shared the fate of the rioters. What is to be the issue of this unhappy affair cannot be surmised; the end is not yet.

July 28, 1849, Cholera

Poor New York has become a charnel house; people die daily of cholera to the number of two or three hundred—that is, of cholera and other cognate diseases. But this mortality is principally among the emigrants in the eastern and western extremities of the city, where hundreds are crowded into a few wretched hovels, amidst filth and bad air, suffering from personal neglect and poisoned by eating garbage which a well-bred hog on a Westchester farm would turn up his snout at.

August 3, 1849, Day of Prayer

This is a day of fasting, humiliation, and prayer, ordered by the President of the United States. May the voice of a nation punished for the sins of the people be heard by the Almighty and serve to avert the dreadful infliction under which we are suffering. It is a sublime and solemn subject of reflection. Millions of people in this vast country, of different sexes, all ages, ranks and professions, and religions and political opinions, simultaneously offering their penitential appeals to heaven for pardon and forgiveness of their sins and a removal of the chastening hand which lies heavy on the nation.

From Cinco meses en los Estados-Unidos de la América del Norte desde el 20 de abril al 23 de setiembre de 1835 (Five Months in the United States of North America from April 20 to September 23, 1835)
Ramon de la Sagra

Ramon de la Sagra was returning to his native Spain from a twelve-year tenure in Cuba as the director of the botanical garden and professor of botany at the University of Havana when he visited New York in the fall of 1835.

The commercial upswing that de la Sagra saw everywhere in his wandering throughout the city would come crashing down less than eighteen months later with the Panic of 1837. New York's economy was intricately tied to the international economy; as Philip Hone succinctly lamented, the Bank of England "was the arbiter of the fate of the American merchant." When the Bank of England raised its discount rate in the summer of 1836, the value of New York landowners' real estate depreciated more than $40 million in half a year. In contrast to de la Sagra's description, Philip Hone noted in May 1837 that "a deadly calm pervades this city. No goods are selling, no business stirring. . . . The grass has begun to grow upon the wharves."

WE arrived on Sunday the 19th. In spite of the bad weather, the docks were crowded with people; elegant and commodious vehicles were stationed at the foot of streets bordered with sidewalks and unusually neat. Broadway is magnificent, especially at night, when gas light brightens its fine stores. . . .

But what pleases me most here is neither the appearance of the city, the width of the streets, the neatness of the dwellings, nor other externals; it is instead the tremendous commercial activity that I see, the continual pursuit of industry, the progress of the population, the general affluence and a certain air of well being which prevails among all classes. Since my arrival, I have spent my time surveying the city, and I have been astonished at the extraordinary development which it is experiencing at the moment. Everywhere they are building houses, repairing whole sections, constructing superb hotels, opening large squares, and as if to second this activity, laying out new streets and embankments. If, turning away from the city, one observes the dock area, the picture is not less vigorous. The whole length of the wharves, there rises up a forest of masts belonging to the vessels of many nations, and steamships engaged in trade among the various states of the Union. On the North River, the bay and its eastern arm, magnificent steamboats cross and recross without ceasing, coming and going at all hours of the day and night, laden with passengers, merchandise, and raw materials. With these ships, which furrow the water in all directions, mingle many little craft.

The Dans Kamer: A Revery in the Highlands, *Andrew Jackson Downing (1835)*

Andrew Jackson Downing was born in Newburgh, New York, just after his namesake's victory in the Battle of New Orleans in 1815, and began his career as an advocate of rural living to combat the "too great bustle and excitement of our commercial cities." He established himself as the authority on landscaping with his work *A Treatise in the Theory and Practice of Landscape Gardening* in 1841. After the European revolutions of 1848, Downing turned his attention to promoting large green spaces where people from various economic classes could mingle in a healthful environment. In the August 1851 issue of his magazine, *Horticulturist,* Downing called for the creation of a large, centrally located park in New York City that he felt would become "the lungs of the city."

Downing's call was hotly debated, and after his death in a freak steamboat accident on the Hudson River in 1852, it fell to his disciple, Calvert Vaux, to pick up the challenge. Vaux had run the architectural side of Downing's practice since 1850 and carried on the business after his mentor's death until moving to New York City in 1856. A year later Vaux and Frederick Law Olmsted began work on their Greensward Plan, which would eventually become the design for Central Park.

Downing also promoted cemeteries as a place where nineteenth-century New Yorkers could commune with nature; Brooklyn's Greenwood Cemetery became a popular tourist attraction, with as many as sixty thousand people a year visiting in the 1840s. Downing's only work in New York City is the Cemetery of the Evergreens on the border between Brooklyn and Queens.

MANY blessings on thee, Diedrich Knickerbocker! First among historians! Thy memory shall rest in our heart, embalmed in the mellowed and never-fading light of immortality. Are we not indebted to thee for all that remains of our calm and peace-loving ancestors of Communipau and

Mannahatta? Nay, did not thy pen, with its mellifluous descriptions, clear away the obscurity that hung like a thick fog of a summer's morning over thy beloved colony, and exhibit to the world in their true brilliancy the illustrious achievements of our worthy Dutch ancestors? And who but thou has saved from shipwreck the rich old legends and antiquarian scraps swimming, as they were, upon the "deep, deep flood" of oblivion? Bear witness *Spijt den duyvel* creek, how he has preserved the tragick story, and unravelled the deep mystery that hung round thy startling name. And thou, Anthony's Nose, speak from thy bed in the Highlands, in lusty glorification of the mighty nasal promontory of thy namesake, Anthony the trumpeter, of whose bodily qualifications thou to this day standest forth the monument! Yes, thanks to thee, Deidrich! the huge moss-covered and cedar-tufted rock on which we repose, bids us return thanks to thee! for preserving in thy immortal pages, the grievous fright which the wild and demon-like dancers (who oft assembled upon thy rocky floor, and made thee the scene of their war dances) gave the goodly Peter Stuyvesant, when sailing past for the first time in his gallant bark, he fancied, from the wild creatures that revelled on thy surface, that thou wert indeed as he called thee, and as thou art to this day called, the *Duyvel's Dans Kamer.*

The Dans Kamer! It awakens thought in our mind and stirs the imagination, like the gazing upon some old and storied moss-gray ruin. Doubtless it had been a favorite meeting ground of the Indians. Their council-fires had gleamed upon its surface, and the red lights had there streamed up to heaven, and shone like the Aurora Borealis to their brother tribes, whose wigwams curled up their blue smoke to the skies, far away among the shadowy glens and dense-timbered shores of the bay of the Highlands. Its situation, creeping tortoise-like out from the hills around it, and the ease with which the Indians could reach it from both sides of the Hudson, all pointed it out as the very spot for a rendezvous. Perhaps even the place where we reclined, had often rebounded to the footsteps of the Indian in his war dance. The wild yell of the savage sounding the warwhoop had often been re-echoed by the neighbouring hills. Here they had often held their hunting-feasts. Here they had sung the exploits of the living warriour and chanted the renown of the dead; the tomahawk had often flashed here in the sunbeams; the bow twanged, and the arrow whizzed a thousand times through the air. A myriad wandering thoughts like these flitted like shadowy dreams through our mind, until in our imagination the old Point was peopled again with its ancient inhabitants; and we almost feared to look around us, lest we should be asked whence we came, and why we had intruded unbidden upon their festivities.

A sudden dashing of the waves at our feet, like the rushing of a tempest, roused us from the revery into which the stillness of the scene seemed to have plunged us. We raised our eyes—they rested upon a steamboat. That object was the representative of another age—it carried our thoughts in a moment through a wide lapse of time. The canoe and the paddle have disappeared; they have given place to the tall-sparred vessel, whose white sails glided along as if borne upon the wings of the breeze; and to the gay and gallant steamer, moving like magick through the foaming waters. Rich, green fields smile along those river glades, where once the winds moaned through the tall forest-trees. The wild yell of the savage re-echoes no more among the hills, but breaking upon the ear come the clear-toned bells, swinging to and fro in the spires that lift their summits out of the deep foliage, and calling with sweet and mellow sound the inhabitants of the neighboring villages to places of instruction and devotion. The wigwam is gone, and in its place are a thousand cheerful houses gleaming in the sunshine. And the Indians, where are them? *Echo answers, where!* Their footsteps are for ever silent. They have disappeared with the wolf and the panther. Their bows and their arrows have decayed like their memories. A nation of warriors, unyielding in battle, crafty and subtle as the serpent, mighty and powerful as the tempest, and courageous as lions, who claimed for their hunting-grounds from the St. Lawrence to the Mississippi, have disappeared from the earth, and their lands are the possessions of others.

There is a set of philanthropists, who live at the present day, and who with a sickly sentimentality, bemoan the extermination of the Indians, and take every opportunity, now that they are securely established in their own comforts and luxuries, to lament the cruelties of their forefathers (whose perils they shared not) to the aborigines of the soil. The "poor Indians," say they, with uplifted hands, "we shall have to answer for them." Look carefully and calmly through the many teinted pages of the history of the continent, that have been written down since the whites and the Indians met, and we doubt not that you will, like us, rest silent in the conviction, that the same Providence has guided their footsteps toward the setting sun, that has watched over and fostered the increase of the whites in this blessed land which the red men have left behind them.

We, who have long forgotten, or who have never heard the savage yell of the Indian, are prone to think of his character only in such lights as the poet and the writer of fiction have depicted him. Courage and fortitude, and valour, shed such a glow around some few of their chieftains, that is apt to cast into the shadow the even and malignant passions which form the groundwork of the Indian character. It was been well remarked by a modern writer of celebrity, that the character of the American Indian forms one of the extremes of human nature. The more acute and tender sensibilities, which soften the heart and keep open the floodgates of sympathy in the bosom of almost all the other races of men, were the special objects of despisal and contempt among them. Their unshaken fortitude and endurance of suffering, have been pointed to as proofs of a mental superiority, but we are inclined to doubt, whether they are anything more than an insensibility to physical suffering, inuring of the body through successive generations. Gloomy and reserved and melancholy, peace seems to have been an unnatural state for them—the only excitements they allowed to disturb their silent moodiness, and to cause an exhibition of the passions that swell in the human heart, where the bloody conflicts of the battle, when their greatest satisfaction seems to have been the gratification of their infuriated revenge. Sanguinary by nature, their highest pleasure seems to have been the cruel scalping of their prisoners—their supremest delight, the writhings of their victims at the stake, under the most demoniacal tortures.

We are aware that this appears to be a harsh picture. We many of us love to fancy to ourselves the Indians passing their days innocently in hunting, and their nights calmly and peacefully in slumber. But the facts bear heavily against us. It is unquestionable, that when this country was discovered, the natives spent the majority of their time in contests, each petty tribe dipping their arrows in the blood of their neighbors. Nay, looking around over the vast monuments found scattered over our western prairies—the lengthy and wide-stretched mounds—the bones of another race, differing widely from the Indians which they cover—the implements and utensils bespeaking the work of a more civilized race of beings found in their neighbourhood—all these facts incline us to believe with those antiquarians who have thought more deeply on the subject, that the Indians were the conquerors and destroyers of a former race far more advanced in the arts and conveniences of life than themselves, and over whose territory, after getting possession, they have scattered themselves, without the spirit of union or peace; their lives a tissue of laziness and indolence, broken in upon by intervals of the most savage and bloody warfare. When the whites landed upon their shores, too indolent to adopt the customs of civilized life, too powerless to resist them, seeking new hunting-grounds farther and farther into the depths of the forest; and as those wild beasts, whose untameable nature prompts them to shun the face of civilized beings, have disappeared with the deep wilderness that once sheltered them, so also have the Indians perished from the east of the Alleghanies, and the memory of their deeds is fast sinking into forgetfulness and oblivion.

Such were our thoughts—a mingled stream of joy and sadness—inspired by the Dans Kamer, its reminiscences, and the beautiful and picturesque scene which surrounds it:—of joy, for the bright face of nature, the hum and murmur and joyousness of life which met our senses on every side of the wild landscape, irresistibly stirred those chords in the heart—of sadness, when we mused on the extinction of the thousand tribes of our fellow-beings who were once the sole masters from the rising to the setting sun, and over whose character, however their total and gradual disappearance may be reconciled with the decrees of Providence, there is a deep spring of humanity in the heart, that prompts us to pause and reflect tenderly and forgivingly, now that they are mingled with the dust of their native hills, and their *dancing grounds are silent forever.*

From Democracy in America, *Alexis de Tocqueville (1835)*

In 1828 the state of New York closed Newgate prison (located off Greenwich Street near the Hudson River) and moved all of its prisoners upstate to Sing Sing. The new prison drew such notoriety that Alexis de Tocqueville (and his traveling companion, Beaumont) journeyed to America in the spring of 1831 to study the workings of the facility. Tocqueville sailed into New York harbor on May 11, 1831, and "uttered cries of admiration on glimpsing the environs of the city. Picture yourself an attractively varied shoreline, the slopes covered by lawns and trees in bloom right down to the water, and more than all that, an unbelievable multitude of country houses, big as boxes of candy, but showing careful workmanship."

Tocqueville stayed approximately seven weeks during the next two years. After his initial enthrallment with the city, he found that "to a Frenchman the aspect of the city is bizarre and not very agreeable. One sees neither dome, nor bell tower, nor great edifice, with the result that one has the constant impression of being in a suburb. In its center the city is built of brick, which gives it a most monotonous appearance." The customs and manners of American culture, as well as its prisons, however, intrigued Tocqueville, and he published his findings in two volumes called *Democracy in America* (1835, 1840). On February 19, 1832, the New York gentry gave Tocqueville a farewell banquet. His final meal in New York was not a highlight, however; he found that it "represented the infancy of art: the vegetables and fish before the meat, the oysters for dessert. In a word, complete barbarism."

WHEN I arrived for the first time at New York, by that part of the Atlantic Ocean which is called the East River, I was surprised to perceive along the shore, at some distance from the city, a number of little palaces of white marble, several of which were of classic architecture. When I went the next day to inspect more closely one which had particularly attracted my notice, I found that its walls were of whitewashed brick, and its columns of painted wood. All the edifices that I had admired the night before were of the same kind.

The social condition and the institutions of democracy impart, moreover, certain peculiar tendencies to all the imitative arts, which it is easy to point out. They frequently withdraw them from the delineation of the soul to fix them exclusively on that of the body, and they substitute the representation of motion and sensation for that of sentiment and thought; in a word, they put the real in the place of the ideal.

Letters from New York, *Lydia Maria Child (September 23, 1841; October 21, 1841; May 1, 1843)*

In 1829 William Lloyd Garrison called Lydia Maria Child, then only twenty-seven years old, "the first woman in the Republic." Child was a leading abolitionist and feminist who worked tirelessly for the rights of the underprivileged for all of her seventy-eight years. Her first novel, *Hobomok,* published when she was only twenty-two, was the story of interracial love between an Indian man and a white woman. Reviewers called it "revolting . . . to every feeling of delicacy in man or woman."

Child's most influential work, *An Appeal in Favor of That Class of Americans Called Africans* (1833), described the history of slavery in America and advocated racial intermarriage as a means to a multiracial nation, but the popular reaction to it forced her to fold her successful journal *Juvenile Miscellany* the following year. Child already had a successful career as a children's writer and publisher; among her works was the famous Thanksgiving Day poem "Over the River and Through the Woods." Undaunted, Child edited and helped publish Harriet Jacobs's classic memoir *Incidents in the Life of a Slave Girl* (1861), which detailed what Child called the "peculiar phase of slavery [that] has generally been kept veiled."

In May 1841 Child took up a nine-year residence in New York, where she detailed life there for a Boston newspaper and published the columns as *Letters from New York* (1843, 1845). As she remarked in this work, she realized that in New York, "the loneliness of the soul is deeper, and far more restless, than the solitude of the mighty forest." She died at her home in Wayland, Massachusetts, in 1880.

September 23, 1841

LAST week, a new synagogue was consecrated in Attorney-street; making, I believe, five Jewish Synagogues in this city, comprising in all about ten thousand of this ancient people. The congregation of the new synagogue are

German emigrants, driven from Bavaria, the Duchy of Baden, &c., by oppressive laws. One of these laws forbade Jews to marry; and among the emigrants were many betrothed couples, who married as soon as they landed on our shores; trusting their future support to the God of Jacob. If not as "rich as Jews," they are now most of them doing well in the world; and one of the first proofs they gave of prosperity, was the erection of a place of worship.

The oldest congregation of Jews in New-York, were called *Shewith Israel.* The Dutch governors would not allow them to build a place of worship; but after the English conquered the colony, they erected a small wooden synagogue, in Mill-street, near which a creek ran up from the East River, where the Jewish women performed their ablutions. In the course of improvement this was sold; and they erected the handsome stone building in Crosby-street, which I visited. It is not particularly striking or magnificent, either in its exterior or interior; nor would it be in good keeping, for a people gone into captivity to have garments like those of Aaron, "for glory and for beauty;" or an "ark overlaid with pure gold, within and without, and a crown of gold to it round about."

There is something deeply impressive in this remnant of a scattered people, coming down to us in continuous links through the long vista of recorded time; preserving themselves carefully unmixed by intermarriage with people of other nations and other faith, and keeping up the ceremonial forms of Abraham, Isaac, and Jacob, through all the manifold changes of revolving generations. Moreover, our religions are connected, though separated; they are shadow and substance, type and fulfilment. To the Jews only, with all their blindness and waywardness, was given the idea of one God, spiritual and invisible; and, therefore, among them only could such a one as Jesus have appeared. To us they have been the medium of glorious truths; and if the murky shadow of their Old dispensation rests too heavily on the mild beauty of the New, it is because the Present can never quite unmoor itself from the Past; and well for the world's safety that it is so.

Quakers were mixed with the congregation of Jews; thus oddly brought together, were the representatives of the extreme of conservatism, and the extreme of innovation!

I was disappointed to see so large a proportion of this peculiar people fair-skinned and blue-eyed. As no one who marries a Gentile is allowed to remain in their synagogues, one would naturally expect to see a decided predominance of the dark eyes, jetty locks, and olive complexions of Palestine. But the Jews furnish incontrovertible evidence that colour is the effect of climate. In the mountains of Bavaria they are light-haired and fair-skinned: in Italy and Spain they are dark: in Hindostan swarthy. The *Black* Jews of Hindostan are said to have been originally African and Hindoo slaves, who received their freedom as soon as they became converted to Judaism, and had fulfilled the rites prescribed by the ceremonial law; for the Jews, unlike Christians, deem it unlawful to hold any one of their own religious faith in slavery. In another respect they put us to shame; for they held a Jubilee of Freedom once in fifty years, and on that occasion emancipated all, even of their heathen slaves.

Whether the Black Jews, now a pretty large class in Hindostan, intermarry with other Jews we are not informed. Moses, their great lawgiver, married an Ethiopian. Miriam and Aaron were shocked at it, as they would have been at any intermarriage with the heathen tribes, of whatever colour. Whether the Ethiopian woman had adopted the faith of Israel is not mentioned; but we are told that the anger of the Lord was kindled against Aaron and his sister for their conduct on this occasion.

The anniversary meetings of the New-York Hebrew Benevolent Society present a singular combination. There meet together pilgrims from the Holy Land, merchants from the Pacific Ocean and the East Indies, exiles from the banks of the Vistula, the Danube, and the Dneiper, bankers from Vienna and Paris, and dwellers on the shores of the Hudson and the Susquehannah. Suspended in their dining hall, between the American and English flags, may be seen the Banner of Judah, with Hebrew inscriptions in golden letters. How this stirs the sea of memory! That national banner has not been unfurled for eighteen hundred years. The last time it floated to the breeze was over the walls of Jerusalem, besieged by Titus Vespasianus. Then, *our* stars and stripes were not foreseen, even in dim shadow, by the vision of a prophet; and here they are intertwined together over this congress of nations!

In New-York, as elsewhere, the vending of "old clo' " is a prominent occupation among the Jews; a fact in which those who look for spiritual correspondences can perceive significance; though singularly enough Sartor Resartus makes no allusion to it, in his "Philosophy of Clothes." When I hear Christian ministers apologizing for slavery by the example of Abraham, defending war, because the Lord commanded Samuel to hew Agag in pieces, and sustaining capital punishment by the retaliatory code of Moses, it seems to me it would be most appropriate to have Jewish criers at the doors of our theological schools, proclaiming at the top of their lungs, "Old Clothes! Old Clothes! Old Clothes all the way from Judea!"

October 21, 1841

In a great metropolis like this, nothing is more observable than the infinite varieties of character. Almost without effort, one may happen to find himself, in the course of a few days, beside the Catholic kneeling before the Cross, the Mohammedan bowing to the East, the Jew veiled before the ark of the testimony, the Baptist walking into the water, the Quaker keeping his head covered in the presence of dignitaries and solemnities of all sorts, and the Mormon quoting from the Golden Book which he has never seen.

More, perhaps, than any other city, except Paris or New Orleans, this is a place of rapid fluctuation, and never-ceasing change. A large portion of the population are like mute actors, who tramp across the stage in pantomime or pageant, and are seen no more. The enterprising, the curious, the reckless, and the criminal, flock hither from all quarters of the world, as to a common centre, whence they can diverge at pleasure. Where men are little known, they are imperfectly restrained; therefore, great numbers here live with somewhat of that wild license which prevails in times of pestilence. Life is a reckless game, and death is a business transaction. Warehouses of ready-made coffins, stand beside warehouses of ready-made clothing, and the shroud is sold with spangled opera-dresses. Nay, you may chance to see exposed at sheriffs' sales, in public squares, piles of coffins, like nests of boxes, one within another, with a hole bored in the topmost lid to sustain the red flag of the auctioneer, who stands by, describing their conveniences and merits, with all the exaggerating eloquence of his tricky trade.

There is something impressive, even to painfulness, in this dense crowding of human existence, this mercantile familiarity with death. It has sometimes forced upon me, for a few moments, an appalling night-mare sensation of vanishing identity; as if I were but an unknown, unnoticed, and unseparated drop in the great ocean of human existence; as if the uncomfortable old theory were true, and we were but portions of a Great Mundane Soul, to which we ultimately return, to be swallowed up in its infinity. But such ideas I expel at once, like phantasms of evil, which indeed they are. Unprofitable to all, they have a peculiarly bewildering and oppressive power over a mind constituted like my own; so prone to eager questioning of the infinite, and curious search into the invisible. I find it wiser to forbear inflating this balloon of thought, lest it roll me away through unlimited space, until I become like the absent man, who put his clothes in bed, and hung himself over the chair; or like his twin-brother, who laid his candle on the pillow and blew himself out.

You will, at least, my dear friend, give these letters the credit of being utterly unpremeditated; for Flibbertigibbet himself never moved with more unexpected and incoherent variety. I have wandered almost as far from my starting point, as Saturn's ring is from Mercury; but I will return to the varieties in New-York. Among them I often meet a tall Scotsman, with sandy hair and high cheek-bones—a regular Sawney, with tartan plaid and bag-pipe. And where do you guess he most frequently plies his poetic trade? Why, in the slaughter-houses! of which a hundred or more send forth their polluted breath into the atmosphere of this swarming city hive! There, if you are curious to witness incongruities, you may almost any day see grunting pigs or bleating lambs, with throats cut to the tune of Highland Mary, or Bonny Doon, or Lochaber No More.

May 1, 1843

May-day in New-York is the saddest thing, to one who has been used to hunting mosses by the brook, and paddling in its waters. Brick walls, instead of budding trees, and rattling wheels in lieu of singing birds, are bad enough; but to make the matter worse, all New-York *moves* on the first of May; not only moves about, as usual, in the everlasting hurry-scurry of business, but one house empties itself into another, all over the city. The streets are full of loaded drays, on which tables are dancing, and carpets rolling to and fro. Small chairs, which bring up such pretty, cozy images of rolly-pooly mannikens and maidens, eating supper from tilted porringers, and spilling the milk on their night-gowns—these go ricketting along on the tops of beds and bureaus, and not unfrequently pitch into the street, and so fall asunder. Children are driving hither and yon, one with a flower-pot in his hand, another with work-box, band-box, or oil-canakin; each so intent upon his important mission, that all the world seems to him (as it does to many a theologian), safely locked up within the little walls *he* carries. Luckily, both boy and bigot are mistaken, or mankind would be in a bad box, sure enough. The dogs seem bewildered with this universal transmigration of bodies; and as for the cats, they sit on the door-steps, mewing piteously, that they were not born in the middle ages, or at least, in the quiet old portion of the world. And I, who have almost as strong a love of localities as poor puss, turn away from the windows, with a suppressed anathema on the nineteenth century, with its perpetual changes. Do you want an appropriate emblem of this country, and this age? Then stand on the side-walks of New-York, and watch the universal transit on the first of May. The facility and speed with which our people change politics, and move from sect to sect, and from theory to theory, is comparatively slow and moss-grown; unless, indeed, one excepts the Rev. O. A. Brownson, who seems to stay in any spiritual habitation a much shorter time than the New-Yorkers do in their houses. It is the custom here, for those who move out to leave the accumulated dust and dirt of the year, for them who enter to clear up. I apprehend it is somewhat so with all the ecclesiastical and civil establishments, which have so long been let out to tenants in rotation. Those who enter them, must make a great sweeping and scrubbing, if they would have a clean residence.

That people should move so *often* in this city, is generally a matter of their own volition. Aspirations after the infinite, lead them to perpetual change, in the restless hope of finding something better and better still. But they would not raise the price of drays, and subject themselves to great inconvenience, by moving *all on one day*, were it not that the law compels everybody who intends to move at all, to quit his premises before twelve o'clock, on May morning. Failing to do this, the police will put him and his goods into the street, where they will fare much like a boy beside an upset hornet's nest. The object of this regulation is to have the Directory for the year arranged with accuracy. For, as theologians, and some reformers, can perceive no higher mission for human souls than to arrange themselves rank and file in sectarian platoons, so the civil authorities do not apprehend that a citizen has any more important object for living, just at this season, than to have his name set in a well-ordered Directory.

However, human beings are such creatures of habit and imitation, that what is necessity soon becomes fashion, and each one wishes to do what everybody else is doing. A lady in the neighbourhood closed all her blinds and shutters, on May-day; being asked by her acquaintance whether she had been in the country, she answered, "I was *ashamed* not to be moving on the first of May; and so I shut up the house that the neighbours might not know it." One could not well imagine a fact more characteristic of the despotic sway of custom and public opinion, in the United States, and the nineteenth century. Elias Hicks' remark, that it takes "*live* fish to swim *up* stream," is emphatically true of this age and country, in which liberty-caps abound, but no one is allowed to wear them.

From American Notes for General Circulation, *Charles Dickens (1842)*

Charles Dickens visited New York twice, once from January to June in 1842 and a second time from December 1867 to April 1868; he recorded the first journey in his *American Notes,* published October 1842. He was in ill health throughout much of his second visit and died, after suffering a stroke, in June 1870.

Dickens was enthusiastically received by the literati of New York in 1842, especially Washington Irving and William Cullen Bryant, and on February 14 the "Boz Ball" (named for Dickens's moniker) was attended by more than three thousand people. Philip Hone called it "the greatest affair of modern times."

Although Dickens echoed New Yorkers' enthusiasm in his description of Broadway (minus his warning about the pigs—"city scavengers"—he encountered crossing the street), he also found the Five Points section worse than the slums of Liverpool and comprised of "all that is loathsome, drooping, and decayed." He concluded that New York was a place where "a vast amount of good and evil is intermixed and jumbled up together."

Despite his criticism, New Yorkers welcomed Dickens back for scores of readings in 1867 and 1868 in Steinway Hall on Broadway and in Henry Ward Beecher's Plymouth Congregational Church in Brooklyn. Dickens delighted in the farewell banquet held in his honor at Delmonico's on April 18, 1868, and proclaimed, "I have now read in New York City to 40,000 people, and am quite as well known in the streets as I am in London."

New York

THE beautiful metropolis of America is by no means so clean a city as Boston, but many of its streets have the same characteristics; except that the houses are not quite so fresh-coloured, the sign-boards are not quite so gaudy, the gilded letters not quite so golden, the bricks not quite so red, the stone not quite so white, the blinds and area railings not quite so green, the knobs and plates upon the street doors not quite so bright and twinkling. There are many by-streets, almost as neutral in clean colours, and positive in dirty ones, as by-streets in London; and there is one quarter, commonly called the Five Points, which, in respect of filth and wretchedness, may be safely backed against Seven Dials, or any other part of famed St. Giles's.

The great promenade and thoroughfare, as most people know, is Broadway; a wide and bustling street, which, from the Battery Gardens to its opposite termination in a country road, may be four miles long. Shall we sit down in an upper floor of the Carlton House Hotel (situated in the best part of this main artery of New York), and when we are tired of looking down upon the life below, sally forth arm-in-arm, and mingle with the stream? . . .

This narrow thoroughfare, baking and blistering in the sun, is Wall Street: the Stock Exchange and Lombard Street of New York. Many a rapid fortune has been made in this street, and many a no less rapid ruin. Some of these very merchants whom you see hanging about here now, have locked up money in their strong-boxes, like the man in the Arabian Nights, and opening them again, have found but withered leaves. Below, here by the waterside, where the bowsprits of ships stretch across the footway, and almost thrust themselves into the windows, lie the noble American vessels which having made their Packet Service the finest in the world. They have brought hither the foreigners who abound in all the streets: not, perhaps, that there are more here, than in other commercial cities; but elsewhere, they have particular haunts, and you must find them out; here, they pervade the town.

We must cross Broadway again; gaining some refreshment from the heat, in the sight of the great blocks of clean ice which are being carried into shops and bar-rooms; and the pine-apples and water-melons profusely displayed for sale. Fine streets of spacious houses here, you see!—Wall Street has furnished and dismantled many of them very often—and here a deep green leafy square. Be sure that is a hospitable house with inmates to be affectionately remembered always, where they have the open door and pretty show of plants within, and where the child with laughing eyes is peeping out of window at the little dog below. You wonder what may be the use of this tall flagstaff in the by-street, with something like Liberty's head-dress on its top: so do I. But there is a passion for tall flagstaffs hereabout, and you may see its twin brother in five minutes, if you have a mind.

Again across Broadway, and so—passing from the many-coloured crowd and glittering shops—into another long main street, the Bowery. A railroad yonder, see, where two stout horses trot along, drawing a score or two of people and a great wooden ark, with ease. The stores are poorer here; the passengers less gay. Clothes ready-made, and meat ready-cooked, are to be bought in these parts; and the lively whirl of carriages is exchanged for the deep rumble of carts and waggons. These signs which are so plentiful, in shape like river buoys, or small balloons, hoisted by cords to poles, and dangling there, announce, as you may see by looking up, "oysters in every style." They tempt the hungry most at night, for then dull candles glimmering inside, illuminate these dainty words, and make the mouths of idlers water, as they read and linger.

What is this dismal-fronted pile of bastard Egyptian, like an enchanter's palace in a melodrama!—a famous prison, called The Tombs. Shall we go in?

So. A long, narrow, lofty building, stove-heated as usual, with four galleries, one above the other, going round it, and communicating by stairs. Between the two sides of each gallery, and in its centre, a bridge, for the greater convenience of crossing. On each of these bridges sits a man: dozing or reading, or talking to an idle companion. On each tier, are two opposite rows of small iron doors. They look like furnace-doors, but are cold and black, as though the fires within had all gone out. Some two or three are open, and women, with drooping heads bent down, are talking to the inmates. The whole is lighted by a skylight, but it is fast closed; and from the roof there dangle, limp and drooping, two useless windsails.

A man with keys appears, to show us round. A good-looking fellow, and, in his way, civil and obliging. . . .

The prison-yard in which he pauses now, has been the scene of terrible performances. Into this narrow, grave-like place, men are brought out to die. The wretched creature stands beneath the gibbet on the ground; the rope about his neck; and when the sign is given, a weight at its other end comes running down, and swings him up into the air—a corpse.

The law requires that there be present at this dismal spectacle, the judge, the jury, and citizens to the amount of twenty-five. From the community it is hidden. To the dissolute and bad, the thing remains a frightful mystery. Between the criminal and them, the prison-wall is interposed as a thick gloomy veil. It is the curtain to his bed of death, his winding-sheet, and grave. From him it shuts out life, and all the motives to unrepenting hardihood in that last hour, which its mere sight and presence is often all-sufficient to sustain. There are no bold eyes to make him bold; no ruffians to uphold a ruffian's name before. All beyond the pitiless stone wall, is unknown space.

Let us go forth again into the cheerful streets.

Once more in Broadway! Here are the same ladies in bright colours, walking to and fro, in pairs and singly; yonder the very same light blue parasol which passed and repassed the hotel-window twenty times while we were sitting there. We are going to cross here. Take care of the pigs. Two portly sows are trotting up behind this carriage, and a select party of half-a-dozen gentlemen hogs have just now turned the corner.

Here is a solitary swine lounging homeward by himself. He has only one ear; having parted with the other to vagrant-dogs in the course of his city rambles. But he gets on very well without it; and leads a roving, gentlemanly, vagabond kind of life, somewhat answering to that of our club-men at home. He leaves his lodgings every morning at a certain hour, throws himself upon the town, gets through his day in some manner quite satisfactory to himself, and regularly appears at the door of his own house again at night, like the mysterious master of Gil Blas. He is a free-and-easy, careless, indifferent kind of pig, having a very large acquaintance among other pigs of the same character, whom he rather knows by sight than conversation, as he seldom troubles himself to stop and exchange civilities, but goes grunting down the kennel, turning up the news and small-talk of the city in the shape of cabbage-stalks and offal, and bearing no tails but his own: which is a very short one, for his old enemies, the dogs, have been at that too, and have left him hardly enough to swear by. He is in every respect a republican pig, going wherever he pleases, and mingling with the best society, on an equal, if not superior footing, for every one makes way when he appears, and the haughtiest give him the wall, if he prefer it. He is a great philosopher, and seldom moved, unless by the dogs before mentioned. Sometimes, indeed, you may see his small eye twinkling on a slaughtered friend, whose carcase garnishes a butcher's door-post, but he grunts out "Such is life: all flesh is pork!" buries his nose in the mire again, and waddles down the gutter: comforting himself with the reflection that there is one snout the less to anticipate stray cabbage-stalks, at any rate.

They are the city scavengers, these pigs. Ugly brutes they are; having, for the most part, scanty brown backs, like the lids of old horsehair trunks: spotted with unwholesome black blotches. They have long, gaunt legs, too, and such peaked snouts, that if one of them could be persuaded to sit for his profile, nobody would recognise it for a pig's likeness. They are never attended upon, or fed, or driven, or caught, but are thrown upon their own resources in early life, and become preternaturally knowing in consequence. Every pig knows where he lives, much better than anybody could tell him.

At this hour, just as evening is closing in, you will see them roaming towards bed by scores, eating their way to the last. Occasionally, some youth among them who has over-eaten himself, or has been worried by dogs, trots shrinkingly homeward, like a prodigal son: but this is a rare case: perfect self-possession and self-reliance, and immovable composure, being their foremost attributes. . . .

Let us go on again; and passing this wilderness of an hotel with stores about its base, like some Continental theatre, or the London Opera House shorn of its colonnade, plunge into the Five Points. But it is needful, first, that we take as our escort these two heads of the police, whom you would know for sharp and well-trained officers if you met them in the Great Desert. So true it is, that certain pursuits, wherever carried on, will stamp men with the same character. These two might have been begotten, born, and bred, in Bow Street.

We have seen no beggars in the streets by night or day; but of other kinds of strollers, plenty. Poverty, wretchedness, and vice, are rife enough where we are going now.

This is the place: these narrow ways, diverging to the right and left, and reeking everywhere with dirt and filth. Such lives as are led here, bear the same fruits here as elsewhere. The coarse and bloated faces at the doors, have counterparts at home, and all the wide world over. Debauchery has made the very houses prematurely old. See how the rotten beams are tumbling down, and how the patched and broken windows seem to scowl dimly, like eyes that have been hurt in drunken frays. Many of those pigs live here. Do they ever wonder why their masters walk upright in lieu of going on all-fours? and why they talk instead of grunting?

So far, nearly every house is a low tavern; and on the bar-room walls, are coloured prints of Washington, and Queen Victoria of England, and the American Eagle. Among the pigeon-holes that hold the bottles, are pieces of plate-glass and coloured paper, for there is, in some sort, a taste for decoration, even here. And as seamen frequent these haunts, there are maritime pictures by the dozen: of partings between sailors and their lady-loves, portraits of William, of the ballad, and his Black-Eyed Susan; of Will Watch, the Bold Smuggler; of Paul Jones the Pirate, and the like: on which the painted eyes of Queen Victoria, and of Washington to boot, rest in as strange companionship, as on most of the scenes that are enacted in their wondering presence.

What place is this, to which the squalid street conducts us? A kind of square of leprous houses, some of which are attainable only by crazy wooden stairs without. What lies beyond this tottering flight of steps, that creak beneath our tread?—a miserable room, lighted by one dim candle, and destitute of all comfort, save that which may be hidden in a wretched bed. Beside it, sits a man: his elbows on his knees: his forehead hidden in his hands. "What ails that man?" asks the foremost officer. "Fever," he sullenly replies, without looking up. Conceive the fancies of a feverish brain, in such a place as this!

Ascend these pitch-dark stairs, heedful of a false footing on the trembling boards, and grope your way with me into this wolfish den, where neither ray of light nor breath of air, appears to come. A negro lad, startled from his sleep by the officer's voice—he knows it well—but comforted by his assurance that he has not come on business, officiously bestirs himself to light a candle. The match flickers for a moment, and shows great mounds of dusty rags upon the ground; then dies away and leaves a denser darkness than before, if there can be degrees in such extremes. He stumbles down the stairs and presently comes back, shading a flaring taper with his hand. Then the mounds of rags are seen to be astir, and rise slowly up, and the floor is covered with heaps of negro women, waking from their sleep: their white teeth chattering, and their bright eyes glistening and winking on all sides with surprise and fear, like the countless repetition of one astonished African face in some strange mirror.

Mount up these other stairs with no less caution (there are traps and pitfalls here, for those who are not so well escorted as ourselves) into the housetop; where the bare beams and rafters meet overhead, and calm night looks down through the crevices in the roof. Open the door of one of these cramped hutches full of sleeping negroes. Pah! They have a charcoal fire within; there is a smell of singeing clothes, or flesh, so close they gather round the brazier; and vapours issue forth that blind and suffocate. From every corner, as you glance about you in these dark retreats, some figure crawls half-awakened, as if the judgment-hour were near at hand, and every obscene grave were giving up its dead. Where dogs would howl to lie, women, and men, and boys slink off to sleep, forcing the dislodged rats to move away in quest of better lodgings.

Here too are lanes and alleys, paved with mud knee-deep, underground chambers, where they dance and game; the walls bedecked with rough designs of ships, and forts, and flags, and American eagles out of number: ruined houses, open to the street, whence, through wide gaps in the walls, other ruins loom upon the eye, as though the world of vice and misery had nothing else to show: hideous tenements which take their name from robbery and murder: all that is loathsome, drooping, and decayed is here.

Our leader has his hand upon the latch of "Almack's," and calls to us from the bottom of the steps; for the assembly-room of the Five Point fashionables is approached by a descent. Shall we go in? It is but a moment.

Heyday! the landlady of Almack's thrives! A buxom fat mulatto woman, with sparkling eyes, whose head is daintily ornamented with a handkerchief of many colours. Nor is the landlord much behind her in his finery, being attired in a smart blue jacket, like a ship's steward, with a thick gold ring upon his little finger, and round his neck a gleaming golden watch-guard. How glad he is to see us! What will we please to call for? A dance? It shall be done directly, sir: "a regular break-down."

The corpulent black fiddler, and his friend who plays the tambourine, stamp upon the boarding of the small raised orchestra in which they sit, and play a lively measure. Five or six couples come upon the floor, marshalled by a lively young negro, who is the wit of the assembly, and the greatest dancer known. He never leaves off making queer faces, and is the delight of all the rest, who grin from ear to ear incessantly. Among the dancers are two young mulatto girls, with large, black, drooping eyes, and head-gear after the fashion of the hostess, who are as shy, or feign to be, as though they never danced before, and so look down before the visitors, that their partners can see nothing but the long fringed lashes.

But the dance commences. Every gentleman sets as long as he likes to the opposite lady, and the opposite lady to him, and all are so long about it that the sport begins to languish, when suddenly the lively hero dashes in to the rescue. Instantly the fiddler grins, and goes at it tooth and nail; there is new energy in the tambourine; new laughter in the dancers; new smiles in the landlady; new confidence in the landlord; new brightness in the very candles.

Single shuffle, double shuffle, cut and cross-cut; snapping his fingers, rolling his eyes, turning in his knees, presenting the backs of his legs in front, spinning about on his toes and heels like nothing but the man's fingers on the tambourine; dancing with two left legs, two right legs, two wooden legs, two wire legs, two spring legs—all sorts of legs and no legs—what is this to him? And in what walk of life, or dance of life, does man ever get such stimulating applause as thunders about him, when, having danced his partner off her feet, and himself too, he finishes by leaping gloriously on the bar-counter, and calling for something to drink, with the chuckle of a million of counterfeit Jim Crows, in one inimitable sound!

The air, even in these distempered parts, is fresh after the stifling atmosphere of the houses; and now, as we emerge into a broader street, it blows upon us with a purer breath, and the stars look bright again. Here are The

Tombs once more. The city watch-house is a part of the building. It follows naturally on the sights we have just left. Let us see that, and then to bed. . . .

What is this intolerable tolling of great bells, and crashing of wheels, and shouting in the distance? A fire. And what that deep red light in the opposite direction? Another fire. And what these charred and blackened walls we stand before? A dwelling where a fire has been. It was more than hinted, in an official report, not long ago, that some of these conflagrations were not wholly accidental, and that speculation and enterprise found a field of exertion, even in flames: but be this as it may, there was a fire last night, there are two to-night, and you may lay an even wager there will be at least one, tomorrow. So, carrying that with us for our comfort, let us say, Good night, and climb up-stairs to bed. . . .

At a short distance from this building is another called the Alms House, that is to say, the workhouse of New York. This is a large Institution also: lodging, I believe, when I was there, nearly a thousand poor. It was badly ventilated, and badly lighted; was not too clean;—and impressed me, on the whole, very uncomfortably. But it must be remembered that New York, as a great emporium of commerce, and as a place of general resort, not only from all parts of the States, but from most parts of the world, has always a large pauper population to provide for; and labours, therefore, under peculiar difficulties in this respect. Nor must it be forgotten that New York is a large town, and that in all large towns a vast amount of good and evil is intermixed and jumbled up together.

In the same neighbourhood is the Farm, where young orphans are nursed and bred. I did not see it, but I believe it is well conducted; and I can the more easily credit it, from knowing how mindful they usually are, in America, of that beautiful passage in the Litany which remembers all sick persons and young children.

I was taken to these Institutions by water, in a boat belonging to the Island jail, and rowed by a crew of prisoners, who were dressed in a striped uniform of black and buff, in which they looked like faded tigers. They took me, by the same conveyance, to the jail itself.

It is an old prison, and quite a pioneer establishment, on the plan I have already described. I was glad to hear this, for it is unquestionably a very indifferent one. The most is made, however, of the means it possesses, and it is as well regulated as such a place can be. . . .

In addition to these establishments, there are in New York, excellent hospitals and schools, literary institutions and libraries; an admirable fire department (as indeed it should be, having constant practice), and charities of every sort and kind. In the suburbs there is a spacious cemetery: unfinished yet, but every day improving. The saddest tomb I saw there was "The Strangers' Grave. Dedicated to the different hotels in this city."

There are three principal theatres. Two of them, the Park and the Bowery, are large, elegant, and handsome buildings, and are, I grieve to write it, generally deserted. The third, the Olympic, is a tiny show-box for vaudevilles and burlesques. It is singularly well conducted by Mr. Mitchell, a comic actor of great quiet humour and originality, who is well remembered and esteemed by London playgoers. I am happy to report of this deserving gentleman, that his benches are usually well filled, and that his theatre rings with merriment every night. I had almost forgotten a small summer theatre, called Niblo's, with gardens and open air amusements attached; but I believe it is not exempt from the general depression under which Theatrical Property, or what is humorously called by that name, unfortunately labours. . . .

The tone of the best society in this city, is like that of Boston; here and there, it may be, with a greater infusion of the mercantile spirit, but generally polished and refined, and always most hospitable. The houses and tables are elegant; the hours later and more rakish; and there is, perhaps, a greater spirit of contention in reference to appearances, and the display of wealth and costly living. The ladies are singularly beautiful.

Two Worlds, from Journal, *Richard Henry Dana (1843)*

Richard Henry Dana was born in 1815 into a family of prominent jurists. In his junior year at Harvard, however, he contracted measles, which affected his eyesight. In the hope that the sea would improve his condition, Dana shipped out in 1834 as a seaman on the brig *Pilgrim.* He returned to graduate from Harvard in 1837 and went on to study law. Three years later he published the classic sea tale *Two Years Before the Mast.*

Dana was one of the founding members of the Free Soil Party, and while not an abolitionist, he defended, pro bono, several fugitive slaves whom federal authorities were trying to return under the Fugitive Slave Act of 1850. Dana later considered this to be the "one great act" of his life.

In January 1843 Dana arrived in New York to visit Julia Ward Howe and William Cullen Bryant and recorded the following incident in his diary. Dana's observations concerning the polarization of New York society reflected a recurring theme in the literature of the 1830s and 1840s; Lydia Maria Child commented on the penchant for dichotomy and the "vituperative alliterations such as magnificence and mud, finery and filth, diamonds and dirt, bullion and brass-tape, etc. etc."

PASSING down Broadway, the name of Anthony street, struck me, & I had a sudden desire to see that sink of iniquity & filth, the "Five Points." Following Anthony street down, I came upon the neighborhood. It was about half past ten, & the night was cloudy. The buildings were ruinous for the most part, as well as I could judge, & the streets & sidewalks muddy & ill lighted. Several of [the] houses had wooden shutters well closed & in almost [each] such case I found by stopping & listening, that there were many voices in the rooms & sometimes the sound of music & dancing. On the opposite side of [the] way I saw a door opened suddenly & a woman thrust into the street with great resistance & most foul language on her part. She seemed to be very drunk & threatened the life of one woman who was in the house, calling upon them to turn her out too, & saying "I'll watch for you." Her oaths were dreadful, & her drunken screeches & curses were so loud that they could be heard several squares off. As I passed on I still heard them behind me. Next there passed me a man holding up under his arm a woman who was so drunk that she could not walk alone & was muttering senseless words to herself. Men & women were passing on each side of the street, sometimes in numbers together, & once or twice a company of half a dozen mere girls ran rapidly, laughed & talking loud, from one house into another. These I gradually found were dancing houses. Grog shops, oyster cellars & close, obscure & suspicious looking places of every description abounded.

Passing out of Anthony street, at the corner of one next to it, a girl who was going into a small shop with a shawl drawn over her head stopped & spoke to me. She asked me where I was going. I stopped & answered that I was only walking about a little, to look round. She said "I am only doing the same," & came down from the doorstep towards me. I hastened my pace & passed on. Turning round, I found she had followed me a few steps & then gone back to the shop.

The night was not cold, & some women were sitting in the door-ways or standing on the sidewalks. From them I received many invitations to walk in & see them, just to sit down a minute, &c., followed usually by laughter & jeers when they saw me pass on without noticing them. At one door, removed from sight & in an obscure place, where no one seemed in sight, two women were sitting, one apparently old, probably the "mother" of the house, & the other rather young, as well as I could judge from her voice & face. They invited me to walk in & just say a word to them. I had a strong inclination to see the interior of such a house as they must live in, & finding that the room was lighted & seeing no men there & no signs of noise or company, I stopped in almost before I knew what I was doing. The room had but little furniture, a sanded floor, one lamp, & a small bar on which were a few glasses, a decanter & behind the bar were two half barrels. The old woman did not speak, but kept her seat in the door way. The younger one, after letting me look round a moment, asked me in a whisper & a very insinuating air, putting on as winning a smile as she could raise, & with the affectation of a simple childish way, to "just step into the bed room: it was only the next room." Here I had a strong desire to see the whole of the establishment, yet some fear of treachery or fouled play. I had more than $50 in my pocket, a gold watch, gold pencil case, gold double eye glass, & other things of value & being well dressed, I might be looked upon as an object for plunder. I had, too, no weapon; not even a cane. When adventure is uppermost, however, we seldom weigh chances. The house I perceived was very small & it being comparatively early & people passing in the street I had little fear, & went in. The bed room was very small, being a mere closet, with one bed & one chair in it, the door through which we came & a window. There was no light in it, but it was dimly lighted by a single pane of glass over the door through which the light came from the adjoining room, in which we had been. The bed stead was a wretched truck, & the bed was of straw, judging from the sound it made when the woman sat upon it. Taking for granted that I wished to use her for the purposes of her calling she asked me how much I would give. I said "What do you ask?" She hesitated a moment, & then answered hesitatingly, & evidently ready to lower her price if necessary, "half a dollar?" I was astonished at the mere pittance for which she would sell her wretched, worn out, prostituted body. I can hardly tell the disgust & pity I felt. I told her at once that I had no object but curiosity in coming into the house, yet gave her the money from fear lest, getting nothing, she might make a difficulty or try to have me plundered. She took the money & thanked me, but expressed no surprise at my curiosity or strangeness. Perhaps they are used to having the visits of persons like myself from abroad & who wish to see the insides of such places. I thought of asking her how she came into such a place & trying to drop a word of warning as to her horrible end; but it was getting late, I had no more time to waste, & I felt a little uneasy at my situation. The thought crossed my mind, if anything should happen to me, if a row should take place in the neighborhood, a descent made by the police & I taken up among others, or I should meet injury or an accident which should render me helpless, I could ill account for my being found in such a place. I therefore left the room, & passing through the front room, & by the old woman who still sat at the door, was at once in the street. Looking round I saw the girl speak to the old woman & heard them laugh. My outside coat had been buttoned tight all the time I was in the house, yet I instinctively felt in my pockets & about my person to see if all my property [was] safe.

From these dark, filthy, violent & degraded regions, I passed into Broadway, where were lighted carriages with footmen, numerous well dressed passers by, cheerful light coming from behind curtained parlor windows, where were happy, affectionate & virtuous people connected by the ties of blood & friendship & enjoying the charities & honors of life. What mighty differences, what awful separations, wide as that of the great gulf & lasting for eternity, do what seem to be the merest chances place between human beings, of the same flesh & blood.

Doings in Gotham, *Letters III and V*, *Edgar Allan Poe (1844)*

Edgar Allan Poe was born in Boston, Massachusetts, in January 1809. Orphaned at age two after his father mysteriously disappeared and his mother died, he subsequently became a foster child of a wealthy Richmond, Virginia, tobacco merchant, John Allan. In 1826 Poe attended the University of Virginia, leaving for a two-year stint in the army. Upon his discharge he secured a commission from West Point but was dismissed for direct disobedience to orders. In 1836 he married his thirteen-year-old cousin Virginia Clemm.

Poe worked as an editor and reviewer for various journals and magazines in Richmond and Philadelphia before establishing a permanent residence with his wife and mother-in-law in New York in 1844. Poe had struggled to make a name for himself until he wrote "The Raven" while living at 85 West Third Street and had it published in the *New York Evening Mirror* on January 29, 1845.

Poe defined the short story as an art form, perfected the psychological thriller and murder mystery, contributed some of the finest literary theory of his generation, and invented the detective story. Unfortunately, he is sometimes more notably remembered for having died, violently inebriated, of "acute congestion of the brain" in a Baltimore gutter in October 1849. Poe's last New York residence, where his wife had died from pneumonia two years before he did, is a landmark cottage at 2640 Grand Concourse in the Bronx.

Letter III

NEW YORK, MAY 27, 1844

THE city is brimful of all kinds of *legitimate* liveliness—the life of money-making, and the life of pleasure;—but political excitement seems, for the moment, to pause—I presume by way of getting breath, and new vigor, for the approaching Presidential contest; while all apprehension of danger from the mob-disorder which so lately beset Philadelphia, is fairly at an end. A crisis, however, was very nearly at hand, and was averted principally, I think, by the firmness and prudence of the new authorities.

You may remember the futile attempt made a short time since, in the city of Brotherly Love, to close the Rum Palaces, and Rum Hovels, on the Sabbath. The point has been carried here by Mr. Harper—at least so far as a point of this character *can* be carried at all. As to the direct benefits accruing to the community at large, by the closing of these hot-houses of iniquity on Sunday—or at all times, indeed—as to this, I say, no one can entertain a doubt. But it appears to me that municipal, or any other regulations for the purpose, are in palpable violation of the Constitution. To declare a thing immoral, and therefore inexpedient, at *all* times, is one thing—to declare it immoral on Sunday, and therefore to forbid it on that particular day, is quite another. Why not equally forbid it on Saturday, which is the Sabbath of the Jew? In particularizing Sunday, we legislate for the protection and convenience of a sect; and although this sect are the majority, this fact can by no means justify the violation of a great principle—the perfect freedom of conscience—the entire separation of Church and State. Were every individual in America known to be in favor of any "Sunday" enactment, even Congress would have no authority to enact it, and it might be violated with impunity. Nothing short of a change in the Constitution could effect what even the *whole people,* in the case I have supposed, should desire.

When you visit Gotham, you should ride out the Fifth Avenue, as far as the distributing reservoir, near Forty-third Street, I believe. The prospect from the walk around the reservoir is particularly beautiful. You can see, from this elevation, the north reservoir at Yorkville; the whole city to the Battery; with a large portion of the harbor, and long reaches of the Hudson and East rivers. Perhaps even a finer view, however, is to be obtained from the summit of the white, light-house-looking shot-tower which stands on the East river, at Fifty-fifth Street, or thereabouts.

A day or two since I procured a light skiff, and with the aid of a pair of *sculls* (as they here term short oars, or paddles) made my way around Blackwell's Island, on a voyage of discovery and exploration. The chief interest of the adventure lay in the scenery of the Manhattan shore, which is here particularly picturesque. The houses are, without exception, *frame,* and antique. Nothing very modern has been attempted—a necessary result of the subdivision of the whole island into streets and town-lots. I could not look on the magnificent cliffs, and stately trees, which at every moment met my view, without a sigh for their inevitable doom—inevitable and swift. In twenty years, or thirty at farthest, we shall see here nothing more romantic than shipping, warehouses, and wharves.

Trinity Church is making rapid strides to completion. When finished, it will be unequalled in America, for richness, elegance, and general beauty. I suppose you know that the property of this Church is some fifteen millions, but that, at present, its income is narrow (about seventy thousand dollars, I believe) on account of the long leases at which most of its estates are held. They are now, however, generally expiring. . . .

The Gothamites, not yet having made sufficient fools of themselves in their fete-ing and festival-ing of Dickens, are already on the *qui vive* to receive Bulwer in a similar manner. If I mistake not, however, the author of "The Last Days of Pompeii" will not be willing "to play Punch and Judy" for the amusement of an American rabble. His character, apart from his book-reputation, is little understood in this country, where he is regarded very much in the light of a mere dandy, a *roue,* and a misanthrope. He has many high qualities—among which generosity and indomitable energy are conspicuous. It is much in his favor that, although born to independence, he has not suffered his talents to be buried in indolence, or pleasure. *He* never went to any public school;—this is not generally known. He graduated at Cambridge; but owes his education chiefly to himself. He once made the tour of England and Scotland, on foot, and of France on horseback; these things smack little of the dandy. His first publication was a poem, at three and twenty.

When I spoke of Bulwer's probably refusing to do, what Dickens made no scruple of doing, I by no means intended a disparagement of the latter. Dickens is a man of *far higher genius* than Bulwer. Bulwer is thoughtful, analytic, industrious, artistical; and therefore will write the better book upon the whole; but Dickens, at times, rises to an unpremeditated elevation altogether beyond the flight—beyond the ability—perhaps even beyond the appreciation, of his contemporary. Dickens, with care and education, might have written "The Last of the Barons"; but nothing short of a miracle could have galvanized Bulwer into the conception of the concluding portion of the "Curiosity Shop." P.

Letter V

NEW YORK, JUNE 12, 1844

Brooklyn has been increasing with great rapidity of late years. This is owing, partly, to the salubrity of its situation; but chiefly to its vicinity to the business portion of the city; the low price of ferriage (two cents); the facility of access, which can be obtained at all hours, except two in the morning; and, especially, to the high rents of New York. Brooklyn, you know, is much admired by the Gothamites; and, in fact, much has been done by Nature for the place. But this much the New Yorkers have contrived very thoroughly to spoil. I know few towns which inspire me with so great disgust and contempt. It puts me often in mind of a city of silvered-gingerbread; no doubt you have seen this article of confectionery in some of the Dutch boroughs of Pennsylvania. Brooklyn, on the immediate shore of the Sound, has, it is true, some tolerable residences; but the majority, throughout, are several steps beyond the preposterous. What can be more sillily and pitiably absurd than palaces of painted white pine, fifteen feet by twenty?—and of such is this boasted "city of villas." You see nowhere a cottage—everywhere a temple which "might have been Grecian had it not been Dutch"—which might have been tasteful had it not been Gothamite—a square box, with Doric or Corinthian pillars, supporting a frieze of unseasoned timber, roughly planed, and daubed with, at best, a couple of coats of whitey-brown paint. This "pavilion" has, usually, a flat roof, covered with red zinc, and surrounded by a balustrade; if not surmounted by something nondescript, intended for a cupola, but wavering in character, between a pigeon-house, a sentry-box, and a pig-sty. The steps, at the front-door, are many, and bright yellow, and from their foot a straight alley of tan-bark, arranged between box-hedges, conducts the tenant, in glory, to the front-gate—which, with the wall of the whole, is of tall white pine boards, painted sky-blue. If we add to this a fountain, giving out a pint of real water per hour, through the mouth of a leaden cat-fish standing upon the tip-end of his tail, and surrounded by a circle of admiring "conchs" (as they here call the strombuses), we have a quite perfect picture of a Brooklynite "villa." In point of downright iniquity—of absolute atrocity—such sin, I mean, as would consign a man, inevitably, to the regions of Pluto—I really can see little difference between the putting up such a house as this, and blowing up a House of Parliament, or cutting the throat of one's grandfather.

Diary: 1857, 1859, 1863, 1869, George Templeton Strong

Born in New York in 1820, George Templeton Strong graduated from Columbia with high honors in 1838 and began practicing law. His diary, which he began while a student at Columbia, coupled with that of Philip Hone, spanned the years 1826–1875 and chronicled the daily life of the city as it went from two hundred thousand to over one million inhabitants. Strong recorded not only his observations of the social, intellectual, and political life of New York but also the musical affairs of the city. Part of Strong's interest was the physical movement of the population up the island of Manhattan. "How this city marches northward," he exulted in his diary in 1850. "Streets are springing up, whole strata of sandstone have transferred themselves from their ancient resting-places to look down on bustling thoroughfares for long years to come. Wealth is rushing in upon us like a freshet." But he brought the people themselves under scrutiny as well, noting how "the diverse races of men seem tending toward development into a living organic unit with railroads and steam-packets for a circulating system, telegraph wires for nerves and the *London Times* and *New York Herald* for a brain."

In 1864 Strong paid a "big Dutch boy of about twenty" $1,100 to be his alter ego in the Civil War. But Strong is probably best remembered for his work as treasurer of the Sanitary Commission, charged with improving military hygiene and inspecting army camps during the war. In 1875 he retired from the law firm his father had started but died within six months at his home in Gramercy Park and was buried in Trinity Churchyard.

New York Riot

JULY 5, 1857

THERE was a riot yesterday afternoon in the Sixth Ward, and several persons killed. This afternoon and evening it has been renewed. The Seventh and other regiments are out with ball cartridge. Some of the downtown streets are made impassable by cordons of police, others, I am told, by barricades. A crowd is gathered round the hospital gates in Broadway; many cases of gunshot wounds have been passed in. We're in a "state of siege," and if half the stories one hears be true, in something like a state of anarchy. Rumors of hard fighting round Tompkins Square, in the Second Avenue, in Franklin Square, of houses sacked in the Fifth Avenue near Twenty-eighth Street. Probably lies and gross exaggerations. But the Old Police being disbanded and the New Police as yet inexperienced and imperfectly organized, we are in an insecure and unsettled state at present. I've just returned from prowling cautiously and at a very respectful distance round the seat of war; but I don't know what the disturbance is or has been about. It seems to have been a battle between Irish Blackguardism and Native Bowery Blackguardism, the belligerents afterwards making common cause against the police and uniting to resist their common enemy.

JULY 7, 1857

Since Sunday night the city has been peaceable. The "Dead Rabbits" and "Bowery Boys" repose on their respective laurels.

Central Park

JUNE 11, 1859

Improved the day by leaving Wall Street early and set off with George Anthon and Johnny to explore the Central Park, which will be a feature of the city within five years and a lovely place in A.D. 1900, when its trees will have acquired dignity and appreciable diameters. Perhaps the city itself will perish before then, by growing too big to live under faulty institutions corruptly administered. Reached the park a little before four, just as the red flag was hoisted—the signal for the blasts of the day. They were all around us for some twenty minutes, now booming far off to the north, now quite near, now distant again, like a desultory "affair" between advanced posts of two great armies. We entered the park at Seventy-first Street, on its east side, and made for "The Ramble," a patch just below the upper reservoir. Its footpaths and plantations are finished, more or less, and it is the first section of the ground that has been polished off and made presentable. It promises very well. So does all the lower park, though now in most ragged condition: long lines of incomplete macadamization, "lakes" without water, mounds of compost, piles of blasted stone, acres of what may be greensward hereafter but is now mere brown earth; groves of slender young transplanted maples and locusts, undecided between life and death, with here and there an arboricultural experiment that has failed utterly and is a mere broomstick with ramifications. Celts, caravans of dirt carts, derricks, steam engines, are the elements out of which our future Pleasaunce is rapidly developing. The work seems pushed with vigor and system, and as far as it has gone, looks thorough and substantial. A small army of Hibernians is distributed over the ground. Narrowness is its chief drawback. One sees quite across this *Rus in Urbe* at many points. This will be less felt as the trees grow. The tract seems to have been judiciously laid out. Roads and paths twist about in curves of artistic tortuosity. A broad avenue, exceptionally straight (at the lower end of the park) with a quadruple row of elms, will look Versailles-y by A.D. 1950. On the Fifth Avenue side, the hideous State Arsenal building stares at students of the picturesque, an eyesore that no landscape gardening can alleviate. Let us hope it will soon be destroyed by an accidental fire. From the summit of the rock mount in which "The Ramble" culminates, and from the little wooden framework of an observatory or signal flag tower thereon erected, the upper reservoir (lying on the north) is an agreeable object, notwithstanding the formalism of its straight lines. Johnny was delighted with his walk. . . .

Draft Riots

JULY 19, 1863

Have been out seeking information and getting none that is to be trusted. Colonel Frank Howe talks darkly and predicts an outbreak on the east side of the town tonight, but that's his way. I think this Celtic beast with many heads is driven back to his hole for the present. When government begins enforcing the draft, we shall have more trouble, but not till then.

Not half the history of this memorable week has been written. I could put down pages of incidents that the newspapers have omitted, any one of which would in ordinary times be the town's talk. Men and ladies attacked and plundered by daylight in the streets; private houses suddenly invaded by gangs of a dozen ruffians and sacked, while the women and children run off for their lives. Then there is the unspeakable infamy of the nigger persecution. They are the most peaceable, sober, and inoffensive of our poor, and the outrages they have suffered during this last week are less excusable—are founded on worse pretext and less provocation—than St. Bartholomew's or the Jew-hunting of the Middle Ages. This is a nice town to call itself a centre of civilization! Life and personal property less safe than in Tipperary, and the "people" (as the *Herald* calls them) burning orphan asylums and conducting a massacre. How this infernal slavery system has corrupted our blood, North as well as South! There should be terrible vengeance for these atrocities, but McCunn, Barnard & Co. are our judges and the disgrace will rest upon us without atonement.

I am sorry to find that England is right about the lower class of Irish. They are brutal, base, cruel, cowards, and as insolent as base. Choate (at the Union League Club) tells me he heard this proposition put forth by one of their political philosophers in conversation with a knot of his brethren last Monday: "Sure and if them dam Dutch would jine us we'd drive the dam Yankees out of New York entirely!" These caitiffs have a trick, I hear, of posting themselves at the window of a tenement house with a musket, while a woman with a baby in her arms squats at their feet. Paddy fires on the police and instantly squats to reload, while Mrs. Paddy rises and looks out. Of course, one can't fire at a window where there is a woman with a child!! But how is one to deal with women who assemble around the lamp-post to which a Negro had been hanged and cut off certain parts of his body to keep as souvenirs? Have they any womanly privilege, immunity, or sanctity?

No wonder St. Patrick drove all the venomous vermin out of Ireland! Its biped mammalia supply that island its full average share of creatures that crawl and eat dirt and poison every community they infest. Vipers were superfluous. But my own theory is that St. Patrick's campaign against the snakes is a Popish delusion. They perished of biting the Irish people.

Women in Law School

OCTOBER 9, 1869

Application from three infatuated young women for admission to Law School. No woman shall degrade herself by practising law, in New York especially, if I can save her. Our committee will probably have to pass on the application, *pro forma,* but I think the clack of these possible Portias will never be heard at Dwight's moot courts. "Women's-Rights Women" are uncommonly loud and offensive of late. I loathe the lot. The first effect of their success would be the introduction into society of a third sex, without the grace of woman or the vigor of man; and then woman, being physically the weaker vessel and having thrown away the protection of her present honors and immunities, would become what the squaw is to the male of her species—a drudge and domestic animal.

Murray Hill Reservoir, November 25, 1849, Walt Whitman (1849)

One of nine children in a family of farmers, Walt Whitman was born in West Hills, Long Island in 1819. He moved to Brooklyn while still a boy and worked initially as an editor and a printer. In 1846 he became the editor of the *Brooklyn Daily Eagle,* and he remained in the New York area most of his life.

Whitman is usually recognized as the poet of New York's city streets who reveled in what he called "the blab of the pave." He was notorious for careening around the city, hanging off of the omnibuses driven by his friends, and democratically reciting, or yelling, his verse aloud for all the citizens of New York to hear. For this reason Lewis Mumford wrote, a century after Whitman's *Leaves of Grass* was published in 1855, "Wherever one goes in New York, whether one knows it or not, one walks in the steps of Walt Whitman."

But Whitman loved the "wilds" of the city as well and particularly the Murray Hill Reservoir (located on the current site of the New York Public Library and Bryant Park at Forty-second Street). This reservoir was part of the Croton Aqueduct system that had been designed by John B. Jervis in 1835. The mountain water would travel from upstate over the High Bridge across the Harlem River to a receiving reservoir between Seventy-ninth and Eighty-sixth Streets in what is now Central Park, and from there to Murray Hill. The aqueduct opened to huge celebration on July 4, 1842, when a fountain at City Hall Park sent skyward the first water from the system. George Templeton Strong happily noted in his diary a week later that he had "led rather an amphibious life for the last week . . . paddling in the bathing tub every night and constantly making new discoveries in the art and mystery of ablution. Taking a shower bath upside down is the last novelty." There is no doubt that New York could not exist with its present population without the more than fifteen hundred million gallons of water that pours through the system every day.

It is a delightful little jaunt to go out, (if on foot, so much the better,) and see the sunset, from the broad walk on the top of this reservoir. A hundred years hence, I often imagine, what an appearance that walk will present, on a fine summer afternoon! You and I, reader, and quite all the people who are now alive, won't be much thought of then; but the world will be just as jolly, and the sun will shine as bright, and the rivers off there—the Hudson on one side and the East on the other—will slap along their green waves, precisely as now; and other eyes will look upon them about the same as we do.

The walks on the battlements of the Croton Reservoir, a hundred years hence! *Then* these immense stretches of vacant ground below, will be covered with houses; the paved streets will clatter with innumerable carts and resound to deafening cries; and the promenaders here will look down upon them, perhaps, and away "up town," toward the quieter and more fashionable quarters, and see great changes—but off to the rivers and shores their eyes will go oftenest, and see not much difference from what we see now. *Then* New York will be more populous than London or Paris, and, it is to be hoped, as *great* a city as either of them—great in treasures of art and science, I mean, and in educational and charitable establishments. Even now, however, as one sweeps his glance from the top of the Reservoir, he can see some seven or eight splendid charities, wholly or partially under the umbrage of the State. Let them prosper and increase, say I. If the moneys of the people only go plentifully for the great purposes of Benevolence and Education, no matter how heavy the taxes or how large the loans. They will be like bread cast upon the waters, and we shall indeed find it again after many days.

Ages after ages, these Croton works will last, for they are more substantial than the old Roman aqueducts, which were mostly built on the surface of the ground. And crowds of busy feet will patter over this flagging, years hence, and here will be melancholy musings, and popping the question, and perhaps bargains and sales, long long after we of the present time are under the sod.

Coming down the hollow-echoing stone stairway, one stops a minute to read the large marble tablet, on which are inscribed the names of the Croton functionaries and contractors and master operatives. You learn that,

"The Aqueduct commences at the Croton river, five miles from the Hudson river, in Westchester county. The dam is 250 feet long, 70 feet wide at bottom, 7 at top, and 40 feet high, and built of stone and cement.

It creates a pond five miles long, covering an extent of 400 acres, and contains 500,000,000 gallons of water. From the dam the Aqueduct proceeds, sometimes tunnelling through solid rocks, crossing valleys by embankments and brooks by culverts, until it reaches Harlem river, a distance of thirty-three miles. It is built of stone, brick and cement, arched over and under, 6 feet 9 inches wide at bottom, 7 feet 8 inches at top of the side walls, and 8 feet 5 inches high; it has a descent of 13 1/2 inches per mile, and will discharge 60,000,000 of gallons every twenty-four hours. It crosses the Harlem river on a magnificent bridge of stone, 1,450 feet in length, with 14 piers, 7 of them bearing arches of 80 feet span, and 7 others of 50 feet span, 114 feet above tide water at the top. The receiving reservoir at Eighty-sixth street, 38 miles from the Croton dam, covers 35 acres, and holds 150,000,000 of gallons. The distributing reservoir on Murray's Hill, in Fortieth street, covers 4 acres, and is constructed of stone and cement, 45 feet high above the street, and holds 20,000,000 of gallons. Thence the water is distributed over the city in iron pipes, laid sufficiently deep under ground to protect them from frost. The whole cost of the work has been about $13,000,000. The water is of the purest kind of river water. There are laid below the distributing reservoir in Fortieth street more than 170 miles of pipe, from 6 to 36 inches in diameter."

The elevated and stony grounds about here will cost their owners dearly to get them graded and paved in the monotonous style required by most of our American cities. I always think it a pity that greater favor is not given to the natural hills and slopes of the ground on the upper part of Manhattan Island. Our perpetual dead flat, and streets cutting each other at right angles, are certainly the last things in the world consistent with beauty of situation.

From Travels in the United States . . . during 1849 and 1850, *Lady Emmelin Stuart-Wortley*

Accompanied by her thirteen-year-old daughter, Victoria, Lady Emmeline Stuart-Wortley spent two years traveling in the United States, Mexico, and Central and South America. The descriptions of their adventures were published in 1852 in *Travels in the United States . . . during 1849 and 1850.* Lady Emmeline was already an accomplished poet when she undertook this trip, and her language and imagery captured some of the turbulence of New York society at midcentury.

Lady Emmeline was struck by the state of flux in New York and saw it as "unlike every city ever beheld before." Antebellum New York seemed to her to be a mix of "heterogeneous compounds and kaleidescopical varieties presented at every turn." With these phrases, she captured one of the enduring features of New York: the tensions between variety and cohesion and between assimilation and diversity. But there was good reason for this to be one of those landmark turbulent times—the population had grown fivefold in the twenty years between 1830 and 1850. Furthermore, fully 40 percent of New Yorkers had been born abroad and 55 percent had been born out of state if not out of the country. Lady Emmeline also recognized one of the concomitant characteristics of that flux—pace—remarking that "nothing and nobody seemed to stand still for half a moment in New York."

New York is certainly altogether the most bustling, cheerful, lifeful, restless city I have yet seen in the United States. Nothing and nobody seem to stand still for half a moment in New York; the multitudinous omnibuses, which drive like insane vehicles from morning till night, appear not to pause to take up their passengers, or it is so short a pause, you have hardly time to see the stoppage, like the instantaneousness of a flash of lightning. How on earth the people get in and out of them, I do not know: the man behind surely must sometimes shut a person half in and half out, and cut them in two, but neither he nor they have time to notice such trifles. . . .

From the cupola that surmounts the [City Hall], a view of the whole vast city is commanded; . . . and there is also an apartment constantly occupied, night and day, by a watchman, whose office it is to keep a perpetual look out for fires, and to give the alarm, by striking an enormous bell which hangs in a belfry in the rear of the cupola, and which is exclusively used for this purpose. . . . The sound can be heard from one end of the city to the other, and is almost instantaneously responded to by a hundred others in every direction. The number of strokes indicates the particular ward. . . .

The French appear to muster numerically stronger than any other people, but this arises from the fact, that nearly all the New Yorkers are accoutred in Parisian costume. Their very hair is cut and combed, and their beards trimmed and clipped strictly *à la Française,* which does not in general improve their personal appearance. Looking merely to the people, you might often fancy yourself in the Boulevards, instead of in Broadway. *Au reste,* Germans, Swedes, Poles, Italians, and hosts of others meet you at every turn. There are but few Russian visitors here it seems; but I am very much struck by the apparent *entente cordiale* that exists between Russia and the United States. There seems an inexplicable instinct of sympathy, some mysterious magnetism at work, which is drawing by degrees these two mighty nations into closer contact. Napoleon, we know, prophesied that the world, ere long, would be either Cossack or Republican. It seems as if it would first be pretty equally shared between these two giant powers. . . .

There are a great number of military companies in New York, and some of them are really very martial-looking indeed. I am told there is a company of Highlanders, formed by the sons of fa[i]r Caledonia; and there are German, French, Italian companies, &c. There are a number of target companies, each known by some particular name—usually, I believe, that of a favourite leader who is locally popular among them. Others take their appellation from some celebrated historical character, and others from anything that happens to occur to them, it would seem.

A few of them are "The Washington Market Chowder Guard" (chowder is a famous dish in the United States), "Bony Fusileers," "Peanut Guard," "Sweet's Epicurean Guard" (surely these must be confectioners), "George R. Jackson and Company's Guard," "Nobody's Guard," "Oregon Blues," "Tenth Ward Light Guard," "Carpenter Guard," "First Ward Magnetizers," "Tompkins' Butcher Association Guard," "Mustache Fusileers," "Henry Rose Light Guard," "Atlantic Light Guard," "Junior Independence Guard," and multitudes of others.

The militia numbers about one hundred companies, which comprise six thousand men. The Target Companies are said not to fall short of ten thousand men. . . .

I hear that some of the best and finest of their organizations are formed out of the fire companies, who thus take upon themselves a twofold responsibility. . . .

Often the lieutenants and captains of the Target Companies are artisans, labourers, clerks, and mechanics. The companies elect their officers, and constantly without the least favour . . . shown "to class, or rank, or wealth." The man who is most distinguished by these advantages, frequently shoulders his musket as a private; and yet he may most largely subscribe to the company's expenses for yearly "excursions," and other contingencies and needs.

The Points at Midnight, George G. Foster (1850)

In 1849 George (Gaslight) Foster, one of the city's first professional city reporters and flaneurs, noted that "a great city is the highest result of human civilization" where people are "excited to their highest state of activity by constant contact with countless other souls." He collected the results of his wanderings through the "untold and underground" city in a sensationalist and extraordinarily popular "travel" book, *New York by Gas-Light,* a compilation of his "New York in Slices" articles written for the *New York Tribune* under the direction of Horace Greeley.

Foster defined the "sunshine and shadow" metaphor as a way of seeing the vast dichotomies of wealth and power in the city. But what was unusual about Foster was that he invited and implored his readers to join him and "do any and everything you please—stay as long as you like, go when it suits you, at any hour of the day or night, and no questions asked nor observations made." Foster's motive was explicit; he believed that "the duty of the present age is to discover the real facts of the actual condition of the wicked and wretched classes—so that Philanthropy and Justice may plant their blow aright."

Five Points was perhaps the section of the city most in need of "righting." The area was named for the intersection of five streets: Mulberry, Anthony (now Worth), Cross (now Park), Orange (now Baxter), and Little Water Street (now defunct). Five Points was a respectable neighborhood until the landfill of what had been the Collect pond (now Foley Square) began to smell and the buildings began to sink in the 1820s. By the time Foster was investigating, the area was notorious as the home of some of New York's toughest gangs—the Dead Rabbits, the Plug Uglies, and the Roach Guards.

THOMAS Carlyle, the great Scotsman, looked up to the starry midnight and exclaimed with a groan, "Tis a sad sight!" What would have been his exclamation had he stood, reader, where you and I now stand—in the very center of the "Five Points,"—knowing the moral geography of the place,—and with that same midnight streaming its glories down upon his head! This is, indeed, a sad, an awful sight—a sight to make the blood slowly congeal and the heart to grow fearful and cease its beatings. Here, whence these streets diverge in dark and endless paths, whose steps take hold on hell—here is the very type and physical semblance, in fact, of hell itself. Moralists no longer entertain a doubt that the monster vice of humanity is licentiousness—the vice teeming with destruction and annihilation to the race itself—pervading all classes,—inextinguishable either by repressive laws or by considerations of personal safety.

The question how to recombine the elements of society so as to do away with this frightful evil, and thus at one blow abolish half the crime and horror of life, is not to be discussed in these pages—nor perhaps has the time yet arrived for discussing it at all. At any rate, before it is or can be profitably debated, we must be fully in possession of all the facts evolved from the present social relations, and must be enabled to view licentiousness and prostitution in all their aspects. It is mainly for this purpose that the present book is written: and to avoid the dryness of mere statistic or the tedious pomposity of a parliamentary report, we have chosen to throw the result of our observations into a series of pen and ink pictures, which will interest while they instruct.

So, then, we are standing at midnight in the center of the Five Points. Over our heads is a large gas-lamp, which throws a strong light for some distance around, over the scene where once complete darkness furnished almost absolute security and escape to the pursued thief and felon, familiar with every step and knowing the exits and entrances to every house. In those days an officer, even with the best intentions, was often baffled at the very moment when he thought he had his victim most secure. Some unexpected cellar-door, or some silent-sliding panel, would suddenly receive the fugitive and thwart the keenest pursuit. Now, however, the large lamp is kept constantly lighted, and a policeman stands ever sentinel to see that it is not extinguished. The existence of this single lamp has greatly improved the character of the whole location and increased the safety of going through the Points at night. Those, however, whose purposes are honest, had better walk a mile round the spot, on their way home, than cross through.

Opposite the lamp, eastwardly, is the "Old Brewery"—a building so often described that it has become as familiar as the Points themselves—in print. We will not, therefore, attempt another description of that which has already been so well depicted. The building was originally, previous to the city being built up so far, used as a brewery. But when the population increased and buildings, streets and squares grew up and spread all around it, the owner —shrewd man, and very respectable church deacon—found that he might make a much larger income from his brewery than by retaining it for the manufacture of malt liquor. It was accordingly floored and partitioned off into small apartments, and rented to persons of disreputable character and vile habits, who had found their inevitable way gradually from the "Golden Gate of Hell," through all the intermediate haunts of prostitution and drunkenness, down to this hell-like den—little less dark, gloomy and terrible than the grave itself, to which it is the prelude. Every room in every story has its separate family or occupant, renting by the week or month and paying in advance. In this one room, the cooking, eating and sleeping of the whole family, and their visitors, are performed. Yes—and their visitors: for it is no unusual thing for a mother and her two or three daughters—all of course prostitutes—to receive their "men" at the same time and in the same room—passing in and out and going through all the transactions of their hellish intercourse, with a sang froid at which devils would stand aghast and struck with horror.

All the houses in this vicinity, and for some considerable distance round —yes, every one—are of the same character, and are filled in precisely the same manner. The lower stories are usually occupied as drinking and dancing rooms; and here, soon as evening sets in, the inmates of the house, dressed in the most shocking immodesty, gather. The bar sends forth its poisonous stream—the door is flung wide open, if the weather will permit it; and the women, bare-headed, bare-armed and bare-bosomed, stand in the doorway or on the side-walk, inviting passers-by, indiscriminately, to enter, or exchanging oaths and obscenity with the inmates of the next house, similarly employed. The walkers in these haunts are mostly sailors, negroes and the worst of loafers and vagabonds, who are enticed and perhaps even dragged in by the painted Jezebels, made to "treat" and then invited to the dance—every room being provided with its fiddler, ready to tune up his villainous squeaking for sixpence a piece and a treat at the end of the figure. The liquor is of course of the most abominable description, poison and fire; and by the time the first dance is concluded, the visitor feels his blood on fire—all his brutal appetites are aroused, and he is ready for any thing. The first object is to produce stupefying intoxication. More drinking is proposed—then more dancing—then drink, and so on, until the poor victim loses what little human sense and precaution he is endowed withal, and hurries his partner off in a paroxysm of drunken lust. Of course if he has any money or valuables on his person he is completely robbed. If his clothes are decent they are stripped off him and a pair of tattered trousers put on, when he is kicked into the street by a back door, and found by the policemen just in time for the loafer's reveille at the Tombs, at day-light. Sometimes the victim is not quite so drunk as is supposed, and doesn't submit quietly to the touching operation. Another glass—or if he refuses, a good "punch" on the head—settles the question for him, with speediest logic, and the problem is solved at once.

In the cellars of these houses are the "oyster saloons," &c. &c. for the accommodation of thieves, burglars, low gamblers and vagabonds in general, who haunt these quarters, and whose "pals" are upstairs carrying on the game of prostitution. They are usually kept open nearly all night, because the population forming the principal class of their customers burrow in their secret holes and dens all day, and only venture out at night. Indeed, this is mostly true of all the inhabitants in this region. They are the obscene night birds who flit and howl and hoot by night, and whose crimes and abominations make them shun the light of day—not merely because they fear detection, but because day is hateful to them. Dropping in from their expeditions of the night—some from picking pockets at the theatres, some from general prowling after what they can pick up about town, and others from more important and regularly-ordered expeditions of robbery or burglary or arson,—they recognize each other with a sullen nod or gather in noisy riot, as the humor takes them. If a stranger enter, they immediately reconnoiter, and if they conclude that he is worth picking, they immediately commence their game. The most usual one is to get up a pretending dispute and call upon the stranger to decide. Often card-tricks or thimbles are introduced, and the conspirators bet carelessly and largely against each other—pulling out and showing pocket-books well crammed with counterfeit or worthless bills. If the stranger is not fully aware of the character of those among whom he has fallen, he is a "goner." If none of the ordinary tricks will answer, as a last resource they get up a sham row and fight, in the course of which general scramble the pigeon is pretty sure of being plucked to the last feather, and most likely left bleeding and senseless in the street.

Leading off easterly from the big gas-lamp we have mentioned, is a little three-cornered piece of ground about the size of a village potato-patch, enclosed in whitewashed palings, containing half-a-dozen stunted trees. This is the "Regent's Park" of that neighborhood, and the walk by which it is surrounded is continually crowded in pleasant evenings by couples chaffering and carrying on their infamous bargains—reminding one of the reversal of rural life with all its innocent blandishments and moonlight love-walks beneath the whispering trees. Indeed throughout the entire realm of metropolitan degradation one is incessantly struck with the ghastly resemblances to the forms of virtue and purity, everywhere starting out before him. There is no virtue nor innocence of a beauteous life which is not reflected in the dark sea of licentiousness and dissipation—though in an inverted position, like the images of green shores and pleasant trees in the turbid waters of the wild-rolling river.

A few steps from the Points is a little alley terminating in a blind court or cul-de-sac, into which is constantly pouring a stream of mephitic air which never finds an outlet nor an escape, save into the lungs of those who inhale it. This alley is called "Cow Bay," and is chiefly celebrated in profane history as being the battle-field of the negroes and police. Of course the negroes form a large and rather controlling portion of the population of the Points, as they bear brutalization better than the whites, (probably from having been so long used to it!) and retain more consistency and force of character; amid all their filth and degradation. They manage, many of them, to become house-keepers and landlords, and in one way and another scrape together a good deal of money. They associate upon at least equal terms with the men and women of the parish, and many of them are regarded as desirable companions and lovers by the "girls." They most of them have either white wives or white mistresses, and sometimes both; and their influence in the community is commanding. But they are savage, sullen, reckless dogs, and are continually promoting some "muss" or other, which not unfrequently leads to absolute riot. Two memorable occasions, at least, have recently occurred in which "Cow Bay" was rendered classic ground by the set fights which took place within its purlieus between the police and the fighting-men among the Ethiopian tribes. Both commenced at dusk and lasted for over an hour,—giving occasion for the display of individual prowess and feats of arms before which the Chronicles of the veracious Froissart sink into insignificance. But as we do not aspire to the historian's bays, we must leave the details to the imagination of our readers, in the good old-fashioned way of those who attempt a description to which their powers are unequal. It is related, however, that the police were for a long time unable to make headway against the furious onslaught of the blacks, who received the official clubs so liberally rattled about their heads, without flinching, and returned the charge with stones and brickbats, so gallantly that several of the protectors of the city had already knocked under, and the whole body began actually to give way—when the renowned Captain Smith bethought him that Cuffee's tender point was not the head, but the SHIN. Passing the word in a whisper to his men to strike low, he himself aimed at the understandings of a gigantic negro who led the assault upon his wing, and brought him instantly, with a terrific yell of agony, to the ground. A shout of triumph, and a simultaneous movement of the police, as if they were mowing, soon decided the contest, and covered the shores and gutters of "Cow Bay" with the sprawling forms of the tender-shinned Africans. Once afterward the very same thing happened, with precisely similar results: and since, the woolly-heads are kept in tolerable subjection. If they ever become troublesome let but a policeman grasp his club tightly and take aim at the shins, and the ground is cleared in a twinkling.

Another peculiar and description-worthy feature of the Five Points are the "fences," or shops for the reception and purchase of stolen goods. These shops are of course kept entirely by Jews, and are situated in a row, in Orange street, near the Points. One who has never seen the squalid undercrust of a fine city would be at a loss to derive any adequate idea, even from the most graphic description, of the sort of building in which the great business of living and trafficking can be carried on. If the reader is a farmer, however, we shall succeed tolerably well in conveying some notion of what we mean. Let him imagine forty or fifty cow-sheds got together in line, furnished with dismal-looking little windows, half broken in and patched up with old newspapers—let him imagine half a hundred of these establishments, we say, standing in a row, with a dark paved street and an uneven narrow brick sidewalk in front, and he will not be far behind the reality of the place where we now stand.

These beggarly little shanties all have pretensions to being considered shops, and in each the front window is heaped up with an indiscriminate indescribableness of wares. Here is a drug-store, with a big bottle of scarlet water in the window, throwing a lurid glare out into the dark. The next is a clothing-store, another hardware, another gentlemen's furnishings, &c. &c. They are all, however, devoted to the one branch of trade, in all its varieties—the purchase of stolen goods. Whatever may be the sign in the window, the thief who has grabbed a watch, prigged a handkerchief or robbed a store, brings his booty confidently in and receives his money for it. Perhaps not at a very high figure—but then, you know "de peoplesh ish very poor in dis neighborhood, and we can't kif much—and besides we don't really want 'em at all." The felon, of course, anxious to have them off his hands, sells them at any price. Whatever may be the article purchased, the first care is naturally to destroy its identity, rub out its ear-marks, and thus prepare it against being claimed by the owner and the purchase of stolen goods fastened upon the "fence." If it is a coat or garment of any kind, the seams are carefully ripped open, the facings, linings, &c. &c. changed, and the whole hastily stitched together again and disposed to the best advantage on the shelves or in the window. If the article purchased is jewelry, it is immediately melted, and converted into bullion,—the precious stones, if there be any, carefully put aside. The most troublesome and dangerous articles are watches—and these the "fence" generally hesitates to have anything to do with, recommending his customer to the pawn-broker, who usually is not much less a rascal than himself. From particular customers, however, whose delicate organizations and long experience render them peculiarly successful in the watch business, the "fence" is willing to receive these dainty wares—although at a terrible sacrifice, and even then never keeping them on hand longer than is necessary to get safely to the pawn-broker's.

In the rear of each of these squalid shops is a wretched apartment or two, combining the various uses of sleeping, eating, cooking and living, with the other performances necessary for carrying on the operations of the front shop. They are generally densely inhabited—the descendants of Israel being as celebrated for fecundity as cats or Irish women. And here it is proper to state one of the most remarkable facts we have encountered in the course of our metropolitan investigations. However low the grade or wretched the habitation—and the latter are generally filthy to abomination—of the Jew, the race always retains the peculiar physical conformation constituting that peculiar style of beauty for which his tribe has been celebrated from remotest antiquity. The roundness and suppleness of limb, the elasticity of flesh, the glittering eye-sparkle—are as inevitable in Jew and Jewess, in whatever rank of existence, as the hook of the nose which betrays the Israelite as the human kite, formed to be feared, hated, and despised, yet to prey upon mankind.

We could not expect to convey any tolerable idea of the Five-Points were we to omit all attempt at describing one of their most remarkable and characteristic features—the great wholesale and retail establishment of Mr. Crown, situated on the corner opposite "Cow Bay." A visit of exploration through this place we regard as one of our most noteworthy experiences in life. The building itself is low and mean in appearance, although covering a good deal of ground. It contains three low stories—the upper one being devoted to the same species of life and traffic as all the other houses in the neighborhood. It is with the two lower stories, however, that we have at present to do—these being occupied as the store. The entrance is on both streets; and, although entirely unobstructed by any thing but the posts that sustain the walls above, it is not without difficulty that we effect an entrance, through the baskets, barrels, boxes, Irish women and sluttish house-keepers, white, black, yellow and brown, thickly crowding the walk, up to the very threshold—as if the store were too full of its commodities and customers, and some of them had tumbled and rolled out-doors. On either hand piles of cabbages, potatoes, squashes, egg-plants, tomatoes, turnips, eggs, dried apples, chestnuts and beans rise like miniature mountains round you. At the left hand as you enter is a row of little boxes, containing anthracite and charcoal, nails, plug-tobacco, &c. &c. which are dealt out in any quantity, from a bushel or a dollar to a cent's-worth. On a shelf near by is a pile of firewood, seven sticks for sixpence, or a cent apiece, and kindling-wood three sticks for two cents. Along the walls are ranged upright casks containing lamp-oil, molasses, rum, whiskey, brandy, and all sorts of cordials, (carefully manufactured in the back room, where a kettle and furnace, with all the necessary instruments for spiritual devilment, are provided for the purpose). The cross-beams that support the ceiling are thickly hung with hams, tongues, sausages, strings of onions, and other light and airy articles, and at every step you tumble over a butter-firkin or a meal-bin. Across one end of the room runs a "long, low, black" counter, armed at either end with bottles of poisoned fire-water, doled out at three cents a glass to the loafers and bloated women who frequent the place—while the shelves behind are filled with an uncatalogueable jumble of candles, allspice, crackers, sugar and tea, pickles, ginger, mustard, and other kitchen necessaries. In the opposite corner is a shorter counter filled with three-cent pies, mince, apple, pumpkin and custard—all kept smoking hot—where you can get a cup of coffee with plenty of milk and sugar, for the same price, and buy a hat-full of "Americans with Spanish wrappers" for a penny.

Groping our way through the back room where the furnace and other machineries are kept—and which may be appropriately termed the laboratory of the concern—we mount a short ladder, and squeeze our way amid piles of drying tobacco, cigar-boxes, tubs, buckets, bales and bundles, of all imaginable shapes and uses, into a little room, similarly filled, but in a corner of which room has been dug for a single cot, upon which lie a heap of rags that evidently have never been washed nor disturbed since they were first slept under, save by the nightly crawlings in and out of the clerk of the premises, and the other inhabitants. Here too is a diminutive iron safe, containing the archives and valuables of the establishment—perhaps silver spoons, rings, watches, and other similar properties—who knows?

One thing is at least certain—the proprietor of this store has amassed a large fortune in a few years, by the immense per centage of profit realized on his minute sales. His customers, living literally from hand to mouth, buy the food they eat and even the fire and whisky that warms them, not only from day to day, but literally from hour to hour. Of many commodities a large proportion sticks to the measure, and on others the profit is incredible—often reaching as high as five or six hundred per cent. No credit—not for a moment—is given to any one, and everything is bought for cash and at the cheapest rates and commonest places.

Well—it is nearly dawn, and we might still prolong our stay upon the Points, there being no lack of subjects well worth our investigation and study. But this is enough for once. To-morrow night—should the fancy take us, for we bind ourselves to nothing—we will return and look in at some of the regular dance-houses and public places in this neighborhood—especially the well known "Dickens' Place," kept by Pete Williams, which, like other more aristocratic establishments, was shut up during the summer, "on account of the cholera." Before we leave this dreadful place—at once the nucleus and consummation of prostitution—we will state a fact or two and make a few reflections bearing generally on the subject. The great source whence the ranks of prostitution are replenished is young women from the country, who, seduced and in the way of becoming mothers, fly from home to escape infamy, and rush to the city with anguish and desperation in their hearts. Either murdering their infants as soon as born, or abandoning them upon a doorstep, they are henceforth ready for any course of crime that will procure them a living,—or, if they still have struggling scruples, necessity soon overcomes them. As an instance of this we were recently informed of a case where thirteen unmarried mothers came from Canada to New York a few weeks before their confinement, and were all sent to the Asylum. Of the thirteen poor, deserted, heart-broken creatures, eleven are now inhabitants of the Five Points or the immediate neighborhood. How has society punished the respectable seducers and destroyers of these women?

Another fact is that those who once enter into this diabolical traffic are seldom saved. The poison is active as lightning, and produces a kind of moral insanity, during which the victim is pleased with ruin and rejects the hand outstretched to save her. We have avoided no pains nor labor in our researches on this subject, and we wish all virtuous and benevolent men and women to mark well our words:—After a woman once enters a house of prostitution and leads the life of all who dwell there, it is too late. The woman is transformed to a devil and there is no hope for her. There may be, and doubtless are, exceptions to this rule, but we are convinced they must be rare. When a woman has once nerved herself to make the fatal plunge, a change comes over her whole character; and sustained by outraged love transmuted to hate, by miscalculating yet indomitable pride, by revenge, and by a reckless abandonment to the unnatural stimulus and excitement of her new profession, her fate is fixed. Take heed, then, philanthropists, and fathers and mothers, and husbands, whose wives and daughters have drank deeply of that damning draught of ambition for dress and display, that makes so many prostitutes! Expend all your watchfulness and tenderness and care upon your charges before they fall. Lay open to them with a bold and faithful hand the horrors of the career which lies before them, unless they learn to unlearn vanity and to learn content. For one whose hair is gray, and whose heart has often bled for grief at sight of so many beautiful creatures wrecked and cast away forever, in the wild pursuit after admiration, tells you that vanity and a love for social distinction are the rocks upon which these noble vessels, freighted with the wealth of immortal souls, have foundered. Strive, oh young woman! whose heart pants with envy at the gay equipages and fine dresses of the more fortunate or more guilty sisters who glitter by you—strive to win to your bosoms the sweet and gentle goddess Content. So shall memory and hope embalm your life and time shall crown you alone with blessings.

From Moby-Dick, *Herman Melville (1851)*

Herman Melville was born in New York in 1819 into a merchant family—his grandfather had been one of the "Indians" who had dumped the tea into Boston harbor in 1773—that rose economically and socially until his father's business failed in 1830 and the family was forced to relocate to Albany. Melville's (the aristocratic last "e" was added later by his mother) story, however, was one of literary underappreciation and neglect, and he died, not unlike one of his most famous characters, Bartleby, in poverty and virtual obscurity in 1891.

After his family had been financially wiped out in the Panic of 1837, Melville set to sea for four years, returning to publish his most popular work, *Typee: A Peep at Polynesian Life,* in 1846. Over the next dozen years, Melville worked at his farm, Arrowhead, in the Berkshire Mountains of western Massachusetts and produced eight novels, among them his most famous work, *Moby-Dick* (1850).

The popular reception of that opus, however, was tepid at best; he wrote his friend Nathaniel Hawthorne that "dollars damn me. What I feel most moved to write, that is banned,—it will not pay." By 1866 Melville was reduced to taking a job as a customs inspector at the piers at Gansevoort Street for four dollars a day, six days a week; he held this job until 1885. Ironically, that street had the same name as Melville's mother, who had come from a family of original Hudson Valley aristocrats.

Chapter I: Loomings

CALL me Ishmael. Some years ago—never mind how long precisely—having little or no money in my purse, and nothing particular to interest me on shore, I thought I would sail about a little and see the watery part of the world. It is a way I have of driving off the spleen, and regulating the circulation. Whenever I find myself growing grim about the mouth; whenever it is a damp, drizzly November in my soul; whenever I find myself involuntarily pausing before coffin warehouses, and bringing up the rear of every funeral I meet; and especially whenever my hypos get such an upper hand of me, that it requires a strong moral principle to prevent me from deliberately stepping into the street, and methodically knocking people's hats off—then, I account it high time to get to sea as soon as I can. This is my substitute for pistol and ball. With a philosophical flourish Cato throws himself upon his sword; I quietly take to the ship. There is nothing surprising in this. If they but knew it, almost all men in their degree, some time or other, cherish very nearly the same feelings towards the ocean with me.

There now is your insular city of the Manhattoes, belted round by wharves as Indian isles by coral reefs—commerce surrounds it with her surf. Right and left, the streets take you waterward. Its extreme down-town is the battery, where that noble mole is washed by waves, and cooled by breezes, which a few hours previous were out of sight of land. Look at the crowds of water-gazers there.

Circumambulate the city of a dreamy Sabbath afternoon. Go from Corlears Hook to Coenties Slip, and from thence, by White-hall, northward. What do you see?—Posted like silent sentinels all around the town, stand thousands upon thousands of mortal men fixed in ocean reveries. Some leaning against the spiles; some seated upon the pier-heads; some looking over the bulwarks of ships from China; some high aloft in the rigging, as if striving to get a still better seaward peep. But these are all landsmen; of week days pent up in lath and plaster—tied to counters, nailed to benches, clinched to desks. How then is this? Are the green fields gone? What do they here?

But look! here come more crowds, pacing straight for the water, and seemingly bound for a dive. Strange! Nothing will content them but the extremest limit of the land; loitering under the shady lee of yonder warehouses will not suffice. No. They must get just as nigh the water as they possibly can without falling in. And there they stand—miles of them—leagues. Inlanders all, they come from lanes and alleys, streets and avenues—north, east, south, and west. Yet here they all unite. Tell me, does the magnetic virtue of the needles of the compasses of all those ships attract them thither?

From Things as They Are in America, *William Chambers (1853)*

William Chambers, along with his brother Robert, was a prominent Edinburgh publisher best known for publishing *Chambers's Edinburgh Journal* (begun in 1832) and the ten-volume *Chambers's Encyclopedia* (1859–1868). His interest in public improvement led him to become the lord provost for Edinburgh from 1865 to 1869. Chambers arrived in New York in late 1853 as part of a journey to North America that he recorded in *Things as They Are in America.* Concerning New York, his final judgment in this work was that "as a great emporium of commerce, growing in size and importance, New York offers employment in a variety of pursuits to the skillful, the steady, and the industrious."

Chambers lodged at the Astor House, where he saw the beginnings of two landmark New York institutions. A public library was erected in Astor Place in 1854 after John Jacob Astor had provided a bequest of $400,000 fifteen years before. That noncirculating library was the forerunner of what would become the New York Public Library, whose main branch is presently on Forty-second Street and Fifth Avenue (the site of the old Murray Hill Reservoir).

Peter Cooper, who had built "Tom Thumb," the nation's first functional steam engine, and had profited greatly from that invention, contributed about $500,000 to create a private, tuition-free college open to men and women of the working class. Cooper Union opened in 1859, also at Astor Place, and was the scene of Abraham Lincoln's famous address in 1860 and of meetings that led to the formation of the International Ladies' Garment Worker' Union, the National Women's Suffrage Association, and the National Association for the Advancement of Colored People. At the time of Cooper's gift, however, the patrician George Templeton Strong called it a "$500,000 waste of money."

At the first look, we see that New York very much resembles the more densely-built parts of London. The houses, tall, and principally of brick, are crowded into narrow streets, such as are seen in the neighbourhood of

Cheapside, with the single difference, that many of the buildings are occupied in floors by different branches of business, with a profusion of large sign-boards in front. For the most part, the houses have sunk floors, accessible by a flight of steps from the foot-pavement; and these cellar-dwellings are very commonly used for some kind of small business, or as "oyster saloons," or "retreats"—the names considerately employed to signify taverns and groggeries. Wherever any of these older brick edifices have been removed, their place has been supplied by tenements built of brown sandstone; and it may be said that at present New York is in process of being renewed by this species of structure. . . . The more narrow thoroughfares are at the same time widened and paved according to modern taste. The more ancient, though much changed part of the city in which the throng of business chiefly prevails, is confined to the southern division, stretching from the Battery a mile northwards. . . .

Hampered as to space, New York has no room for villas; and in this respect there is a marked difference between it and our English cities. Those among the more affluent orders who dislike living in streets, require to proceed by ferry-steamers across either of the two bounding waters, and on the opposite shore find spots for ruralising. . . .

Interest is centered in Broadway, and mainly towards its southern extremity. Hereabouts are the handsomest public buildings, the finest stores, some of the largest hotels, and the greatest throng of passengers. At about half a mile from the Battery, we have on the line of Broadway an opening called the Park, which though only a railed-in patch of ground, with a few trees and footpaths through it, is a very acceptable breathing spot in the midst of everlasting bustle.

Some traveller speaks of the buildings of Broadway as being a mixture of poor wooden structures and splendid edifices. There may be a few houses of an antiquated class, but any such general description is totally inadmissible in the present day. We see for the greater part of its length, a series of high and handsome buildings, of brown sandstone or brick, with several of white marble and granite. Some of the stores and hotels astonish by their size and grandeur. . . .

Without a court, and not even the seat of the state legislature, New York cannot be described as the place of residence of a leisurely or a numerous literary class. Its more opulent inhabitants, connected some way or other with business, form, nevertheless, an aristocracy with refined tastes, and ample means for their gratification. Advancing northwards from the more busy parts of the town, the elegance and regularity of the houses become more conspicuous, and at last we find ourselves in the quietude and splendour of a Belgravia. Here the edifices are entirely of brown sandstone, and of a richly decorated style of street architecture. . . . The furnishings and interior ornaments of these dwellings, particularly those in Fifth Avenue, are of a superb kind; no expense being apparently spared as regards either comfort or elegance. . . .

Standing on the steps of the Astor House, we have the thoroughfare of Broadway right and left, with the Park in front—Barnum's theatre, covered with great gaudy paintings, across the way—and can here perhaps better than anywhere else, observe the concourse of passengers and vehicles. . . . That which appears most novel, is the running to and fro of railway-cars on East Broadway. . . . Permitted, for some mysterious reason, by the civic authorities, lines of rail are laid along several prominent thoroughfares. . . . The cars on these street-railways are hung low, seated like an omnibus, and will stop at any point to take up or set down passengers. The ordinary omnibuses of New York have no cad behind. The door is held close by a cord or belt from the hand of the driver, who relaxes it to allow the entry or exit of the passengers. I was amused with the manner in which the fare is taken in these vehicles. The passenger who wishes to be set down, hands his money through a hole in the roof to the driver, who forthwith relaxes the cord, and the door flies open. As there appeared to be no check on two or more departing when only one had paid, I suppose the practice of shirking fares is not very common. . . . The drivers are . . . unconscionable in their reception of extra passengers, particularly if the applicants be ladies. In such cases, the gentlemen either stand, or take the ladies on their knee. . . .

The necessity for seeking vehicular conveyance arises not more from the extreme length of the city, than the condition of the principal thoroughfares. I am indeed sorry to hint that New York is, or at least *was* during my visit, not so cleanly as it might be. Statists assure us that it possesses 1500 dirt-carts, and in 1853 cost the sum of 250,000 dollars for cleaning. Where these carts were, and where all this money was expended, I cannot imagine. The mire was ankle-deep in Broadway, and the more narrow business streets were barely passable. The thing was really droll. All along the foot-pavements there stood, night and day, as if fixtures, boxes, buckets, lidless flour-barrels, baskets, decayed tea-chests, rusty iron pans, and earthenware jars full of coal-ashes. There they rested, some close to the houses, some leaning over into the gutter, some on the doorsteps, some knocked over and spilt, and to get forward you required to take constant care not to fall over them. . . . Passing up Broadway . . . and looking into a side-street, the scene of confused débris was of a kind not to be easily forgotten-ashes, vegetable refuse, old hats without crowns, worn-out shoes, and other household wreck, lay scattered about as a field of agreeable inquiry for a number of long-legged and industrious pigs. . . .

It was a delicate subject to touch upon, but I did venture to inquire into the cause of these phenomena. One uniform answer—maladministration in civic affairs; jobbing of members of the corporation into each other's hands. . . . You could not take up a newspaper without seeing accounts of unchecked disorders, or reading sarcasms on official delinquencies. . . .

As a great emporium of commerce, growing in size and importance, New York offers employment in a variety of pursuits to the skilful, the steady, and industrious, and on such terms of remuneration as leaves little room for complaint. It would, however, be a prodigious mistake to suppose that amidst this field for well-doing, poverty and wretchedness are unknown. In New York, there is a place called the Five Points, a kind of St. Giles's; and here, as in some other quarters of this great city, you see and hear of a sink of vice and misery resembling the more squalid and dissolute parts of Liverpool or Glasgow. . . .

In New York, the means of social improvement, through the agency of public libraries, lectures, and reading-rooms, are exceedingly conspicuous. One of the most munificent of these institutions, is the recently opened Astor Library, founded by an endowment of the late John Jacob Astor, who bequeathed a fund of 400,000 dollars to erect a handsome building and store it with books for the free use of the public. I went to see this library, and found that it consisted of a splendid collection of 100,000 volumes, a large proportion of which were works in the best European editions, properly classified, with every suitable accommodation for literary study. The New York Mercantile Library, and the Apprentices' Library, are institutions conducted with great spirit, and of much value to the community. A large and handsome building was in process of erection at a cost of 300,000 dollars, by a benevolent citizen, Mr. P. Cooper, for the purpose of a free reading-room and lectures.

From A Few Months in America: Containing Remarks on Some of Its Industrial and Commercial Interests, *James Robertson (1854)*

James Robertson was a businessman who visited America in 1853–1854 in order to gather information on "the material interests of the country," which he published in *A Few Months in America: Containing Remarks on Some of Its Industrial and Commercial Interests.*

Robertson recognized the "great natural advantages" that New York City held as a result of its "magnificent harbor," but he also adroitly identified the opening of the Erie Canal in 1825 as the preeminent influence in creating an avenue of commercial traffic that linked the city with the American West and spurred the "unprecedented" rise of New York as the city of capital. In 1811 DeWitt Clinton put forth the plan to dig a canal through the only natural gap in the Appalachian Mountains, rightly claiming that it would make New York "the greatest commercial emporium in the world."

Work on the canal began on July 4, 1817, and finished on October 26, 1825—on budget and three years ahead of schedule. Clinton's Tammany opponents had mocked "The Big Ditch" relentlessly, but Clinton had devised an imaginative financing plan, and within a few years double the amount of freight was going to New York than was going down the Mississippi to New Orleans. The trade axis for the entire nation had shifted, and New York had become "the granary of the world, . . . the seat of manufactures, the focus of moneyed operations, and the concentrating point of vast . . . capitals," as Clinton had predicted when he poured a bucket of Lake Erie water into New York harbor on November 4, 1825, at a celebration attended by nearly two thirds of the city's population.

THE sudden rise, and wonderful progress of the commerce of New York, have been unprecedented. At the end of the last century, its foreign trade was surpassed by that of Philadelphia; and at no very distant date, it was of no great magnitude; but within the last few years it has advanced with rapid strides.

... [T]here is a wide difference between the value of the exports and imports. This arises from the largest portion of the exports of the States being sent abroad from the southern ports; while of the imports, the largest portion is received at New York. The imports seem to have gradually increased with the wealth and population of the country; but the exports from this and the other northern ports, received a new impulse by the relaxation of the commercial restrictions of Great Britain, and since 1847 have more rapidly increased.

The imports consist of dry goods, or manufactured articles of cotton, wool, silk, and flax; of iron, raw and manufactured; and of sugar, tea, coffee, fruits, &c. From this point they are distributed to other parts of the States, either directly, or through other cities of the seaboard.

The exports are composed of gold, breadstuffs, provision, &c., by far the greater portion of which is sent to Great Britain....

The shipping belonging to the port has increased as rapidly as its commerce, and bears a larger proportion to the value of that commerce than in any other mercantile city of any magnitude. That arises from two causes. First, because the exports from New York are principally of raw produce, therefore bulky, and requiring a large amount of tonnage for their conveyance to foreign markets. Secondly, because much of the shipping that is employed in the southern ports, to convey their cotton and other produce to foreign markets, is owned by New York merchants.

The tonnage belonging to the city ... amounts to more than a fourth part of the entire shipping of the States, and is more, I believe, than that belonging to any other port in the world....

The proud position now occupied by New York as the first commercial city of the New World, insures it a still more rapid progress, and a yet higher pre-eminence. At an early period of its history, it had much to fear from the competition of its rivals, Boston and Philadelphia. Indeed, as I have already remarked, the latter surpassed it in the extent of its foreign commerce, at the end of the last century, and till 1810, was a-head of it in population. With a much richer State, and as convenient access to the west, it might, had its inhabitants been possessed of enterprise, have striven to maintain its superiority. But the favourable opportunity was allowed to slip, and never again presented itself. New York had taken the start, and has now so entirely outstripped it in population, wealth, enterprise, and foreign intercourse, that it can never hereafter fear any rival on the east coast.

That pre-eminence which New York now enjoys, it owes to several favourable circumstances,—to great natural advantages, and to those which it has derived from the enterprise of its inhabitants. It has a most magnificent harbour, twenty-five miles in circumference, and capable of containing the whole navies of the world. It lies close upon the sea; and by the Hudson river, it has convenient access to some distance in the interior. Those natural advantages alone, would have made it a port of much consequence, but they did not satisfy the inhabitants. A new world was opening up in the north and west, and with those regions it was desirable that New York should be brought into communication. In 1825 the Erie Canal was opened, connecting Lake Erie with the Hudson river. By this means New York was brought into communication, not only with the fertile valleys of the western part of the state, but also with the whole coast of the western lakes; an inland navigation of hundreds of miles was opened up for the enterprise of its merchants, and the whole produce of the west was directed to its harbour for distribution to the markets of the world. The cost of transportation from Buffalo to New York previous to the opening of the canal, was about $100 per ton, and the length of passage was twenty days. Now the cost of carriage is from $2 to $3 per ton, and even that is being diminished.

The success which attended the opening of the Erie Canal led to the construction of that to Lake Champlain, and of branches from the former to points on Lake Ontario. . . .

Satisfactory as were those results, the New York people expected they could improve on them by other enterprises, and by the construction of railways to connect their harbour still farther with the north and west. The traffic on the canals was enormous in quantity, the time occupied in transmitting produce was considerable, much of the merchandise going westward could be sent conveniently by railway, and from the severity of an American winter, the navigation of the canal was obstructed at the very time when farmers and others could most conveniently send their produce to market, and when it was most wanted for consumption. Influenced by these and other considerations, stupendous lines of railways have been constructed or are in progress, to join New York to Lakes Erie and Ontario, and the regions bordering on those lakes in the north and west. One of these lines, the Erie railway, spreads out into a number of lines at each end, forming at each terminus a sort of delta, to accommodate its large business. At the city end it has three outlets, and I believe it touches the western lakes at seven separate points.

From those points on the lakes, bordering on the state of New York, communications are carried on westward to all the other lakes, and thence by rivers, and by canals and railways in course of construction, to various points of the interior. By those channels, the foreign imports into the harbour of New York, and the manufactures of the eastern states reach the consumers of the west; and in return, the latter send by the same routes to the east coast their agricultural and forest productions.

By some of those new enterprises, the valleys of the Mississippi and the Ohio have been approached from New York; and produce, which a very few years ago found its natural outlet to the sea, by the Gulf of Mexico, is now diverted to the east coast by this newly-opened inland navigation. In this way, the Indian corn of the state of Missouri above St. Louis, reaches Chicago, by the Illinois river and Chicago canal, and thence by lake and canal finds its way to New York; and by the Ohio river and canal, through Cleveland, the provisions from the regions on the Ohio above Louisville, are carried forward to the same destination. It has been even attempted to divert the cotton of Tennessee into this channel, and several cargoes have been brought to the east coast through those new inland routes.

But those advantages, natural and acquired, which New York now enjoys, have secured to it others which will contribute yet further to its prosperity.

It is now the largest—indeed *the* money market of the States; and, therefore, offers facilities to merchants in the transaction of their business, which cannot be afforded by any other city. It is the largest general market in the Union, and therefore commands a preference from buyers and sellers. The extent of its foreign trade ensures a speedy shipment of produce to any part of the world, and average rates of freight; and from its being the point of communication between Europe and America, it affords to merchants at all times, the fullest and latest information upon every subject affecting the commerce of the country.

The future of New York no one can even imagine, far less venture to predict. The position to which it has now attained, seems to have prepared it only for more gigantic strides. Not only is it now in direct communication with many of the most important points in the interior of the country, but it is daily striving to enlarge those communications, and to reduce their cost. The west, as it advances in population and wealth, will almost in the same degree administer to its greatness; for nearly all the surplus produce of those immense regions, will find its natural outlet to the markets of the world, through the ports on the east coast, and through none so readily as New York; and through the same channel will be distributed to the interior, the merchandise which is imported into the Union from all parts of the world. . . .

Undoubtedly most of the trade of the port is carried on by merchants resident there, but as New York offers the best point for shipment of home produce, and for the distribution to the interior of foreign commodities, merchants of the other cities . . . transact much of their business through this city, finding it to afford them the largest, and frequently the most advantageous market.

From The Englishwoman in America, *Isabella Bird (1854)*

Isabella Bird was one of the most storied and admired travelers of the nineteenth century. Born into a clerical family in 1831, she suffered from ill health; after being diagnosed with a fibrous tumor in her spine at eighteen, she began what became a lifetime of travel to every continent in the world. In 1854, with only one hundred pounds of currency, she traveled to Canada and the United States, covering six thousand miles, and returned to publish *An Englishwoman in America* in 1856. After her parents' death, Bird undertook a life of travel and writing (producing eight volumes) that made her one of the most respected travel writers of her generation. Her documentation of customs in the Middle East and Asia gained her international recognition, and she was the first woman to be elected to the Royal Geographical Society. Bird was more in the mold of Sir Richard Burton than of her dilettante contemporaries who undertook the Grand Tour. She died in Edinburgh in 1904 after completing her final trip, a thousand-mile horseback tour of North Africa.

In New York Bird was particularly struck by the distinctive and revolutionary P. T. Barnum's American Museum, located at the intersection of Broadway and Ann Street. As she recounted in *An Englishwoman in America,* she was shocked by "the collection of horrors and monstrosities attached, which appears to fascinate the vulgar gaze; a dog with two legs, a cow with four horns, and a calf with six legs." But Barnum's museum was more than just the twenty-five-inch midget General Tom Thumb or the much-advertised appearance of the "Swedish Nightingale," Jenny Lind, in 1850. Barnum knew that the real draw was the reaction of the audience itself, and he delighted in exhibiting hoaxes; as the master showman rightly observed, "the public appears disposed to be amused even when they are conscious of being deceived."

WE had steamed down Tenth Avenue for two or three miles, when we came to a standstill where several streets met. The train was taken to pieces, and to each car four horses or mules were attached, which took us for some distance into the very heart of the town, racing apparently with omnibuses and carriages, till at last we were deposited in Chambers Street, not in a station, or even under cover, be it observed. My baggage, or "plunder" as it is termed, had been previously disposed of, but, while waiting with my head disagreeably near to a horse's nose, I saw people making distracted attempts, and futile ones, as it appeared, to preserve their effects from the clutches of numerous porters, many of them probably thieves. . . .

New York deserves the name applied to Washington, "the city of magnificent distances." I drove in a hack for three miles to my destination, along crowded, handsome streets, but I believe that I only traversed a third part of the city. . . .

Broadway is well paved. . . . Its immense length necessitates an enormous number of conveyances; and in order to obviate the obstruction to traffic which would have been caused by providing omnibus accommodation equal to the demand, the authorities have consented to a most alarming inroad upon several of the principal streets. The stranger sees with surprise that double lines of rails are laid along the roadways; and while driving quietly in a carriage, he hears the sound of a warning bell, and presently a railway-car, holding thirty persons, and drawn by two or four horses, comes thundering down the street. These rail-cars run every few minutes, and the fares are very low. For very sufficient reasons, Broadway is not thus encroached upon; and a journey from one end to the other of this marvellous street is a work of time and difficulty. Pack the traffic of the Strand and Cheapside into Oxford Street, and still you will not have an idea of the crush in Broadway. There are streams of scarlet and yellow omnibuses racing in the more open parts, and locking each other's wheels in the narrower—there are helpless females deposited in the middle of a sea of slippery mud, condemned to run a gauntlet between cart-wheels and horses' hoofs—there are loaded stages hastening to and from the huge hotels—carts and waggons laden with merchandise—and "Young Americans" driving fast-trotting horses, edging in and out among the crowd—wheels are locked, horses tumble down, and persons pressed for time are distracted. Occasionally, the whole traffic of the street comes to a dead-lock, in consequence of some obstruction or crowd, there being no policeman at hand with his incessant command, "Move on!" . . .

Strangers frequently doubt whether New York possesses a police; the doubt is very justifiable, for these guardians of the public peace are seldom forthcoming when they are wanted. They are accessible to bribes, and will investigate into crime when liberally rewarded; but probably in no city in the civilised world is life so fearfully insecure. The practice of carrying concealed arms, in the shape of stilettoes for attack, and swordsticks for defence, if illegal, is perfectly common; desperate reprobates, called "Rowdies," infest the lower part of the town; and terrible outrages and murderous assaults are matters of such nightly occurrence as to be thought hardly worthy of notice. . . .

The principal stores are situated in Broadway; and although they attempt very little in the way of window display, the interiors are spacious, and arranged with the greatest taste. An American store is generally a very extensive apartment, handsomely decorated, the roof frequently supported on marble pillars. The owner or clerk is seen seated by his goods, absorbed in the morning paper—probably balancing himself on one leg of his chair, with a spittoon by his side. He deigns to answer your inquiries, but, in place of the pertinacious perseverance with which an English shopman displays his wares, it seems a matter of perfect indifference to the American whether you purchase or no. . . .

One of the sights with which the New York people astonish English visitors is Stewart's dry-goods store in Broadway, an immense square building of white marble, six stories high, with a frontage of 300 feet. The business done in it is stated to be above 1,500,000£ per annum. There are 400 people employed at this establishment, which has even a telegraph office on the premises, where a clerk is for ever flashing dollars and cents along the trembling wires. There were lace collars 40 guineas each, and flounces of Valenciennes lace, half a yard deep, at 120 guineas a flounce. The damasks and brocades for curtains and chairs were at almost fabulous prices. Few gentlemen, the clerk observed, give less than 3£ per yard for these articles. The most costly are purchased by the hotels. I saw some brocade embroidered in gold to the thickness of half an inch, some of which had been supplied to the St. Nicholas Hotel at 9£ per yard! There were stockings from a penny to a guinea a pair, and carpetings from 1s.8d. to 22s. a yard! Besides six stories above ground, there were large light rooms under the building and under Broadway itself, echoing with the roll of its 10,000 vehicles.

The hotels are among the sights in New York. The principal are the Astor House (which has a world-wide reputation), the Metropolitan, and the St. Nicholas, all in Broadway. Prescott House and Irving House also afford accommodation on a very large scale. The entrances to these hotels invariably attract the eye of the stranger. Groups of extraordinary-looking human beings are always lounging on the door-steps, smoking, whittling, and reading newspapers. There are southerners sighing for their sunny homes, smoking

Havana cigars; western men, with that dashing free-and-easy air which renders them unmistakeable; Englishmen, shrouded in exclusiveness, who look on all their neighbours as so many barbarian intruders on their privacy; and people of all nations, whom business has drawn to the American metropolis. . . .

If there are schools, emigrant hospitals, orphan asylums, and nursing institutions, to mark the good sense and philanthropy of the people of New York, so their love of amusement and recreation is strongly evidenced by the numerous places where both may be procured. There is perhaps as much pleasure-seeking as in Paris; the search after amusement is characterised by the same restless energy which marks the pursuit after wealth; . . . Broadway and its neighbourhood contain more places of amusement than perhaps any district of equal size in the world. These present variety sufficient to embrace the tastes of the very heterogeneous population of New York.

There are three large theatres; an opera house of gigantic proportions, which is annually graced by the highest vocal talent of Europe; Wood's minstrels, and Christy's minstrels, where blacks perform in unexceptionable style to unwearied audiences; and comic operas. There are *al fresco* entertainments, masquerades, concerts, restaurants, and oyster saloons. Besides all these, and many more, New York contained in 1853 the amazing number of 5980 taverns. The number of places where amusement is combined with intellectual improvement is small, when compared with other cities of the same population. There are however some very magnificent reading-rooms and libraries.

The amount of oysters eaten in New York surprised me, although there was an idea at the time of my visit that they produced the cholera, which rather checked any extraordinary excesses in this curious fish. In the business streets of New York the eyes are greeted continually with the words "Oyster Saloon," painted in large letters on the basement story. If the stranger's curiosity is sufficient to induce him to dive down a flight of steps into a subterranean abode, at the first glance rather suggestive of robbery, one favourite amusement of the people may be seen in perfection. There is a counter at one side, where two or three persons, frequently blacks, are busily engaged in opening oysters for their customers, who swallow them with astonishing relish and rapidity. In a room beyond, brightly lighted by gas, family groups are to be seen, seated at round tables, and larger parties of friends enjoying basins of stewed oysters; while from some mysterious recess the process of cookery makes itself distinctly audible. Some of these saloons are highly respectable, while many are just the reverse. But the consumption of oysters is by no means confined to the saloons; in private families an oyster supper is frequently a nightly occurrence; the oysters are dressed in the parlour by an ingenious and not inelegant apparatus. So great is the passion for this luxury, that the consumption of it during the season is estimated at 3500£-a-day. . . .

It was almost impossible for a stranger to leave New York without visiting the American museum, the property of Phineas Taylor Barnum. . . . His museum is situated in Broadway, near to the City Hall, and is a gaudy building, denoted by huge paintings, multitudes of flags, and a very noisy band. The museum contains many objects of real interest, particularly to the naturalist and geologist, intermingled with a great deal that is spurious and contemptible. . . . There is a collection of horrors or monstrosities attached, which appears to fascinate the vulgar gaze. The principal objects of attraction at this time were a dog with two legs, a cow with four horns, and a calf with six legs—disgusting specimens of deformity, which ought to have been destroyed, rather than preserved to gratify a morbid taste for the horrible and erratic in nature. . . .

The magnificence of the private dwellings of New York must not escape mention. . . . The squares, and many of the numbered streets, contain very superb houses of a most pleasing uniformity of style. . . . These houses are six stories high, and usually contain three reception-rooms; a dining-room, small, and not striking in appearance in any way, as dinner-parties are seldom given in New York; a small, elegantly furnished drawing-room, used as a family sitting-room, and for the reception of morning visitors; and a magnificent reception-room, furnished in the height of taste and elegance, for dancing, music, and evening parties.

In London the bedrooms are generally inconvenient and uncomfortable, being sacrificed to the reception-rooms; in New York this is not the case. The bedrooms are large, lofty, and airy; and are furnished with all the appurtenances which modern luxury has been able to devise. The profusion of marble gives a very handsome and chaste appearance to these apartments. There are bath-rooms generally on three floors, and hot and cold water are laid on in every story. The houses are warmed by air heated from a furnace at the basement; and though in addition open fires are sometimes adopted, they are made of anthracite coal, which emits no smoke. . . .

Having given a brief description of the style of the ordinary dwellings of the affluent, I will just glance at those of the very wealthy, of which there are several in Fifth Avenue, and some of the squares, surpassing anything I had hitherto witnessed in royal or ducal palaces at home. The externals of some of these mansions in Fifth Avenue are like Apsley House, and Stafford House, St. James's; being substantially built of stone. . . .

The best society in New York would not suffer by comparison in any way with the best society in England. It is not in the upper classes of any nation that we must look for national characteristics or peculiarities. Society throughout the civilized world is, to a certain extent, cast in the same mould. . . . Therefore, it is most probable that balls and dinner-parties are in New York exactly the same as in other places, except that the latter are less numerous, and are principally confined to gentlemen. It is not, in fact, convenient to give dinner parties in New York; there are not sufficient domestics to bear the pressure of an emergency, and the pleasure is not considered worth the trouble. . . .

A great many of these immigrants were evidently from country districts, and some from Ireland; there were a few Germans among them, and these appeared the least affected by the discomforts of the voyage, and by the novel and rather bewildering position in which they found themselves. They probably would feel more at home on first landing in New York than any of the others, for the lower part of the city is to a great extent inhabited by Germans, and at that time there were about 2000 houses where their favourite beverage, *lager-beer,* could be procured.

The goods and chattels of the Irish appeared to consist principally of numerous red-haired, unruly children, and ragged-looking bundles tied round with rope. The Germans were generally ruddy and stout, and took as much care of their substantial-looking, well-corded, heavy chests as though they contained gold. The English appeared pale and debilitated, and sat helpless and weary-looking on their large blue boxes. Here they found themselves in the chaotic confusion of this million-peopled city, not knowing whither to betake themselves, and bewildered by cries of "Cheap hacks!" "All aboard!" "Come to the cheapest house in all the world!" and invitations of a similar description. There were lodging-touters of every grade of dishonesty, and men with large placards were hurrying among the crowd, offering "palace" steamboats and "lightning express" trains, to whirl them at nominal rates to the Elysian Fields of the Far West. . . .

New York, with its novel, varied, and ever-changing features, is calculated to leave a very marked impression on a stranger's mind. In one part one can suppose it to be a negro town; in another, a German city; while a strange dreamy resemblance to Liverpool pervades the whole. In it there is little repose for the mind, and less for the eye, except on the Sabbath-day, which is very well observed, considering the widely-differing creeds and nationalities of the inhabitants. The streets are alive with business, retail and wholesale, and present an aspect of universal bustle. Flags are to be seen in every direction, the tall masts of ships appear above the houses; large square pieces of calico, with names in scarlet or black letters upon them, hang across the streets, to denote the whereabouts of some popular candidate or "puffing" storekeeper; and hosts of omnibuses, hacks, drays, and railway cars at full speed, ringing bells, terrify unaccustomed foot-passengers. There are stores of the magnitude of bazaars, "daguerrean galleries" by hundreds, crowded groggeries and subterranean oyster-saloons, huge hotels, coffee-houses, and places of amusement; while the pavements present men of every land and colour, red, black, yellow, and white, in every variety of costume and beard, and ladies, beautiful and ugly, richly dressed. Then there are mud huts, and palatial residences, and streets of stately dwelling-houses, shaded by avenues of ilanthus-trees; waggons discharging goods across the pavements; shops above and cellars below; railway whistles and steamboat bells, telegraph-wires, eight and ten to a post, all converging towards Wall Street—the Lombard Street of New York; militia regiments in many-coloured uniforms, marching in and out of the city all day; groups of emigrants bewildered and amazed, emaciated with dysentery and sea-sickness, looking in at the shop-windows; representatives of every nation under heaven, speaking in all earth's Babel languages; and as if to render this ceaseless pageant of business, gaiety, and change, as far removed from monotony as possible, the quick toll of the fire alarm-bells may be daily heard, and the huge engines, with their burnished equipments and well-trained companies, may be seen to dash at full speed along the streets to the scene of some brilliant conflagration. New York is calculated to present as imposing an appearance to an Englishman as its antiquated namesake does to an American, with its age, silence, stateliness, and decay.

From Land und Leute in Amerika: Skizzen aus dem Amerikanischen Leben (Land and People in America: Sketches of American Life), *Karl Theodor Griesinger (1857)*

Karl Theodor Griesinger came to America in 1852 after his release from prison for editing a radical newspaper in Baden, Germany. As another group of radicals departing Baden explained, "since Capital so commands Labor in the Fatherland," they sought a country "where the reverse relationship prevails." Griesinger stayed in New York for five years and published his observations in *Land und Leute in Amerika* in 1863.

In 1840 there were twenty-four thousand Germans in New York; in the following twenty years, their number grew to two hundred thousand. This number was fully one quarter of the city's total population, and Manhattan's Germans alone would have constituted the fourth-largest city in the United States; only Berlin and Vienna had larger German populations in the world. Approximately half of the newcomers settled in "Kleindeutschland," an area that stretched from the Bowery to the East River and as far north as Fourteenth Street.

Never before had a foreign-speaking immigrant group banded together so tightly in one area, leading Griesinger to almost casually remark that "life in Kleindeutschland is almost the same as in the Old Country." The "foreignness" of the language, cuisine, and customs of the new immigrants meant that New Yorkers simply grouped them under one label; in reality, the fragmenting of Germany in the nineteenth century and the religious variety of German immigrants produced a Kleindeutschland that was divided up into smaller neighborhoods of Swabians, Bavarians, Hessians, and Prussians who in turn could be Catholics, Protestants, or Jews.

THE traveller who passes up Broadway, through Chatham Street, into the Bowery, up Houston Street, and thence right to First Avenue will find himself in a section which has very little in common with the other parts of

New York. The arrangement of the streets and the monotony of the brownstone dwellings are similar, but the height and detail of the houses, the inhabitants, and their language and customs differ greatly from those of the rest of New York. This is "Kleindeutschland," or "Deutschländle," as the Germans call this part of the city. . . .

The first floor of the houses along these avenues serves as a grocery or shoemaker's shop, or even an inn; but the upper floors still house from five to 24 families, in some buildings as many as 48. . . . On each floor of such buildings there are eight apartments, four on the street side and four on the back. Naturally the apartments are very small: a living room with two windows and a bedroom with no windows—that is all. The room with the two windows is 10 feet by 10 feet, and such apartments rent for five to six dollars a month. Apartments on the back cost four dollars or less monthly. Apartments in buildings where only ten or twelve families reside rent for eight to nine dollars. These apartments contain a comfortable living room, with three windows, and two bedrooms. According to the standards of the German workingman, one can live like a prince for ten to fourteen dollars a month. Apartments at this price contain two bedrooms, two living rooms, one of which is used for a kitchen, and sufficient room for storing coal and wood.

That's how the Germans live in *Kleindeutschland.* But they are satisfied—happy, contented, and, most significantly, among their own people. . . . *Deutschländle* certainly deserves its name, because 15,000 German families, comprising seventy to seventy-five thousand people live here. New York has about 120,000 German-born inhabitants. Two-thirds of these live in *Kleindeutschland.* They come from every part of Germany, although those from northern Germany are rarer than those from the southern part, and Hessians, people from Baden, Wuertembergers, and Rhenish Bavarians are most numerous.

Naturally the Germans were not forced by the authorities, or by law, to settle in this specific area. It just happened. But the location was favorable because of its proximity to the downtown business district where the Germans are employed. Moreover, the Germans like to live together; this permits them to speak their own language and live according to their own customs. The cheapness of the apartments also prompted their concentration. As the first Germans came into *Kleindeutschland,* the Irish began to move and the Americans followed because they were ashamed to live among immigrants.

Life in *Kleindeutschland* is almost the same as in the Old Country. Bakers, butchers, druggists—all are Germans. There is not a single business which is not run by Germans. Not only the shoemakers, tailors, barbers, physicians, grocers, and innkeepers are German, but the pastors and priests as well.

There is even a German lending library where one can get all kinds of German books. The resident of *Kleindeutschland* need not even know English in order to make a living, which is a considerable attraction to the immigrant.

The shabby apartments are the only reminder that one is in America. Tailors or shoemakers use their living rooms as workshops, and there is scarcely space to move about. The smell in the house is not too pleasant, either, because the bedrooms have no windows, and there is a penetrating odor of sauerkraut. But the Germans do not care. They look forward to the time when they can afford a three-room apartment; and they would never willingly leave their beloved *Kleindeutschland.* The Americans who own all these buildings know this. That's why they do not consider improving the housing conditions. They like the Germans as tenants because they pay their rent, punctually, in advance, and keep the buildings neat and clean. The landlords are interested in keeping the German tenants crowded together because such buildings bring more profit than one-story houses. . . .

There are more inns in *Kleindeutschland* than in Germany. Every fourth house is an inn, and there is one for every 200 people. To the stranger, coming for the first time into the section, it would appear that there was nothing but beer saloons. Actually an immense quantity of beer is consumed. Since the German does not care for brandy there is not a single hard liquor saloon in *Kleindeutschland.* Wine is too expensive, so the resident has to be content with beer.

One who has not seen the *Deutschländle* on a Sunday, does not know it at all. What a contrast it presents to the American sections, where the shutters are closed, and the quiet of a cemetery prevails! On Sundays the . . . churches are full, but there is nevertheless general happiness and good cheer. The Protestant Germans do not indulge in much religious observance. They profess to be freethinkers, and do not go to church very often. On the other hand, the Catholic church on Third Street is always overcrowded. It was built from the voluntary contributions of the German workingmen. Saving the money out of their weekly pay, they have built the second largest, and the most beautiful, church in New York City. It has a big tower and three bells, and nearby is a school which the German children attend and where classes are conducted in German. All this has been accomplished through the monthly contributions of the German workingmen, who take great pride in their school and their church.

On Sunday the movement in the streets is like that in a dovecote. People go from the inn to the church and back to the inn again. Everybody wears his Sunday clothes and is in high spirits. In the afternoon, on days when the weather is good, almost everybody leaves town and goes on a picnic. On Sunday night there is still more merriment in *Kleindeutschland.* The inns are crowded, even with women. There is music, in spite of the laws against making noise on Sunday.

The Germans have a *Volkstheater,* although the name theatre can hardly be applied to this long hall where the consumption of beer and cheese is a major activity. At the end of the hall is a small stage; and the performances are not real plays as much as entertainment by comedians whom the proprietor hires to amuse his customers. Their ribald songs receive the enthusiastic applause of the audience. The people enjoy themselves immensely; the entertainment costs only ten cents, and one gets a free beer now and then. Such is the way Sunday is celebrated in *Kleindeutschland.*

From Life and Liberty in America, *Charles Mackay (1859)*

Charles Mackay was born in Scotland in 1814. He was a poet and journalist who worked for several newspapers—the *London Morning Chronicle,* the *Glasgow Argus,* and the *Illustrated London News*—before becoming a special correspondent for the *London Times* covering the American Civil War from New York City in 1862. Mackay also published a classic study of crowd psychology in 1841 called *Extraordinary Popular Delusions.* In December 1857, he was in New York City; he described a parade of fire departments in his *Life and Liberty in America,* published in 1859.

From the 1830s and into the 1860s, fire departments were largely local volunteer companies. While some people were primarily interested in public service, others joined as a means to political advancement. William M. Tweed, who later became the first boss of Tammany Hall, got his start as the foreman of Americus Engine Company No. 33 in 1848. The insignia of his fire company, the tiger, later became the Tammany symbol. Fire companies created songs, slogans, and poems, and as the companies became affiliated with different ethnic or religious groups, rivalries grew to a point where fires would become the occasion for pitched battles between companies. As local gangs allied themselves with fire companies, sabotage of equipment and harassment of rivals were regular features of the job. It was not until 1870 that the Fire Department of New York (the FDNY, or "New York's Bravest") was created, and really not until 1884, with the introduction of civil service examinations, that professionalism replaced politics in New York's firefighting forces.

EACH company had its favourite engine, of which it is as fond as a captain is of his ship, gaily ornamented with ribbons, flags, streamers, and flowers, and preceded by a band of music. Each engine was dragged along the streets by the firemen in their peculiar costume—dark pantaloons, with leathern belt around the waist, large boots, a thick red shirt, with no coat or vest, and the ordinary fireman's helmet. Each man held the rope of the engine in one hand, and a blazing torch in the other. The sight was peculiarly impressive and picturesque. I counted no less than twenty different companies, twenty engines, and twenty bands of music—the whole procession taking upwards of an hour to pass the point at which I stood. The occasion of the gathering was to receive a fire company on its return from a complimentary visit to another fire company in the adjoining Commonwealth of Rhode Island, a hundred miles off. Such interchanges of civility and courtesy are common among the "boys," who incur very considerable expense in making them, the various companies presenting each other with testimonials of regard and esteem, in the shape of silver claret-jugs, candelabra, tea services, etc. But the peculiarities of the firemen, the constitution of their companies, the life they lead, and their influence in the local politics and government of the great cities of the Union, are quite a feature in American civic life, totally different from anything we have in England. . . .

The firemen are mostly youths engaged during the day in various handicrafts and mechanical trades, with a sprinkling of clerks and shopmen. In New York, each candidate for admission into the force must be balloted for, like a member of the London clubs. If elected, he has to serve for five years, during which he is exempt from jury and militia duty. The firemen elect their own superintendents and other officers, by ballot, as they were themselves elected; and are divided into engine companies, hook and ladder companies, and hose companies. The engine and accessories are provided by the municipality; but the firemen are seldom contented with them in the useful but unadorned state in which they receive them, but lavish upon them an amount of ornament, in the shape of painted panels, silver plating, and other finery, more than sufficient to prove their liberality, and the pride they take in their business. The service is entirely voluntary and gratuitous, having no advantages to recommend it but those of exemption from the jury and the militia, and leads those who devote themselves to it not only into great hardship and imminent danger, but into an amount of expenditure which is not the least surprising part of the "institution." The men—or "boys," as they are more commonly called—not only buy their own costume and accoutrements, and spend large sums in the ornamentation of their favourite engines, or hydrants, as already mentioned, but in the furnishing of their bunk-rooms and parlours at the fire-stations. The bunk or sleeping rooms, in which the unmarried, and sometimes the married, members pass the night, to be ready for duty on the first alarm of fire, are plainly and comfortably furnished; but the parlours are fitted up with a degree of luxury equal to that of the public rooms of the most celebrated hotels. At one of the central stations, which I visited in company with an editor of a New York journal, the walls were hung with portraits of Washington, Franklin, Jefferson, Mason, and other founders of the Republic; the floor was covered with velvet-pile carpeting, a noble chandelier hung from the centre, the crimson curtains were rich and heavy, while the sideboard was spread with silver claret-jugs and pieces of plate, presented by citizens whose houses and property had been preserved from fire by the exertions of the brigade; or by the fire companies of other cities.

Crossing Brooklyn Ferry and Mannahatta, Walt Whitman (1856, 1860)

Devoting much of his work to the city, which he called "the great place of the Western continent, the heart, the brain, the focus, the main spring, the pinnacle, the extremity, the no more beyond of the western world," Walt Whitman was one of the first people in the world to write about the experience of commuting, in this case from the suburb of Brooklyn Heights to the bustling city across the East River.

Whitman loved the city so much that he incorporated it into his very being. "When million-footed Manhattan unpent descends to her pavements," he gushed, "I too arising, answering, descend to the pavements, merge with the crowd, and gaze with them." Whitman fused immanence with transcendence or, as Charles Eliot Norton put it, "Yankee transcendentalism with New York rowdyism."

Crossing Brooklyn Ferry

1

Flood-tide below me! I see you face to face!
Clouds of the west—sun there half an hour high—I see you also face to face.
Crowds of men and women attired in the usual costumes, how curious you are to me!
On the ferry-boats the hundreds and hundreds that cross, returning home, are more curious to me than you suppose,
And you that shall cross from shore to shore years hence are more to me, and more in my meditations, than you might suppose.

2

The impalpable sustenance of me from all things at all hours of the day,

The simple, compact, well-join'd scheme, myself disintegrated, every one disintegrated yet part of the scheme,
The similitudes of the past and those of the future,
The glories strung like beads on my smallest sights and hearings, on the walk in the street and the passage over the river,
The current rushing so swiftly and swimming with me far away,
The others that are to follow me, the ties between me and them,
The certainty of others, the life, love, sight, hearing of others.

Others will enter the gates of the ferry and cross from shore to shore,
Others will watch the run of the flood-tide,
Others will see the shipping of Manhattan north and west, and the heights of Brooklyn to the south and east,
Others will see the islands large and small;
Fifty years hence, others will see them as they cross, the sun half an hour high,
A hundred years hence, or ever so many hundred years hence, others will see them,
Will enjoy the sunset, the pouring-in of the flood-tide, the falling-back to the sea of the ebb-tide.

3

It avails not, time nor place—distance avails not,
I am with you, you men and women of a generation, or ever so many generations hence,
Just as you feel when you look on the river and sky, so I felt,
Just as any of you is one of a living crowd, I was one of a crowd,
Just as you are refresh'd by the gladness of the river and the bright flow, I was refresh'd,
Just as you stand and lean on the rail, yet hurry with the swift current, I stood yet was hurried,
Just as you look on the numberless masts of ships and the thick-stemm'd pipes of steamboats, I look'd.

I too many and many a time cross'd the river of old,
Watched the Twelfth-month sea-gulls, saw them high in the air floating with motionless wings, oscillating their bodies,
Saw how the glistening yellow lit up parts of their bodies and left the rest in strong shadow,

Saw the slow-wheeling circles and the gradual edging toward
the south,
Saw the reflection of the summer sky in the water,
Had my eyes dazzled by the shimmering track of beams,
Look'd at the fine centrifugal spokes of light round the shape
of my head in the sunlit water,
Look'd on the haze on the hills southward and south-westward,
Look'd on the vapor as it flew in fleeces tinged with violet,
Look'd toward the lower bay to notice the vessels arriving,
Saw their approach, saw aboard those that were near me,
Saw the white sails of schooners and sloops, saw the ships
at anchor,
The sailors at work in the rigging or out astride the spars,
The round masts, the swinging motion of the hulls, the slender
serpentine pennants,
The large and small steamers in motion, the pilots in their
pilot-houses,
The white wake left by the passage, the quick tremulous whirl
of the wheels,
The flags of all nations, the falling of them at sunset,
The scallop-edged waves in the twilight, the ladled cups, the frolicsome
crests and glistening,
The stretch afar growing dimmer and dimmer, the gray walls of the
granite storehouses by the docks,
On the river the shadowy group, the big steam-tug closely flank'd on
each side by the barges, the hay-boat, the belated lighter,
On the neighboring shore the fires from the foundry chimneys burning
high and glaringly into the night,
Casting their flicker of black contrasted with wild red and yellow light
over the tops of houses, and down into the clefts of streets.

4

These and all else were to me the same as they are to you,
I loved well those cities, loved well the stately and rapid river,
The men and women I saw were all near to me,
Others the same—others who look back on me because I look'd
forward to them,
(The time will come, though I stop here to-day, and to-night.)

5

What is it then between us?
What is the count of the scores or hundreds of years between us?

Whatever it is, it avails not—distance avails not, and place avails not,
I too lived, Brooklyn of ample hills was mine,
I too walk'd the streets of Manhattan island, and bathed in the waters around it,
I too felt the curious abrupt questionings stir within me.
In the day among crowds of people sometimes they came upon me,
In my walks home late at night or as I lay in my bed they came upon me,
I too had been struck from the float forever held in solution,
I too had receiv'd identity by my body,
That I was I knew was of my body, and what I should be I knew I should be of my body.

6

It is not upon you alone the dark patches fall,
The dark threw its patches down upon me also,
The best I had done seem'd to me blank and suspicious,
My great thoughts as I supposed them, were they not in reality meagre?
Nor is it you alone who know what it is to be evil,
I am he who knew what it was to be evil,
I too knitted the old knot of contrariety,
Blabb'd, blush'd, resented, lied, stole, grudg'd,
Had guile, anger, lust, hot wishes I dared not speak,
Was wayward, vain, greedy, shallow, sly, cowardly, malignant,
The wolf, the snake, the hog, not wanting in me,
The cheating look, the frivolous word, the adulterous wish, not wanting,
Refusals, hates, postponements, meanness, laziness, none of these wanting,
Was one with the rest, the days and haps of the rest,
Was call'd by my nighest name by clear loud voices of young men as they saw me approaching or passing,
Felt their arms on my neck as I stood, or the negligent leaning of their flesh against me as I sat,
Saw many I loved in the street or ferry-boat or public assembly, yet

never told them a word,
Lived the same life with the rest, the same old laughing, gnawing, sleeping,
Play'd the part that still looks back on the actor or actress,
The same old role, the role that is what we make it, as great as we like,
Or as small as we like, or both great and small.

7

Closer yet I approach you,
What thought you have of me now, I had as much of you—I laid in my stores in advance,
I consider'd long and seriously of you before you were born.

Who was to know what should come home to me?
Who knows but I am enjoying this?
Who knows, for all the distance, but I am as good as looking at you now, for all you cannot see me?

8

Ah, what can ever be more stately and admirable to me than mast-hemm'd Manhattan?
River and sunset and scallop-edg'd waves of flood-tide?

The sea-gulls oscillating their bodies, the hay-boat in the twilight, and the belated lighter?

What gods can exceed these that clasp me by the hand, and with voices I love call me promptly and loudly by my nighest name as I approach?

What is more subtle than this which ties me to the woman or man that looks in my face?
Which fuses me into you now, and pours my meaning into you?

We understand then do we not?
What I promis'd without mentioning it, have you not accepted?
What the study could not teach—what the preaching could not accomplish is accomplish'd, is it not?

9

Flow on, river! flow with the flood-tide, and ebb with the ebb-tide!
Frolic on, crested and scallop-edg'd waves!

Gorgeous clouds of the sunset! drench with your splendor me,
or the men and women generations after me!
Cross from shore to shore, countless crowds of passengers!
Stand up, tall masts of Mannahatta! stand up, beautiful hills
of Brooklyn!
Throb, baffled and curious brain! throw out questions and answers!
Suspend here and everywhere, eternal float of solution!
Gaze, loving and thirsting eyes, in the house or street or public assembly!
Sound out, voices of young men! loudly and musically call me by my
nighest name!
Live, old life! play the part that looks back on the actor or actress!
Play the old role, the role that is great or small according as one
makes it!
Consider, you who peruse me, whether I may not in unknown ways be
looking upon you;
Be firm, rail over the river, to support those who lean idly, yet haste with
the hasting current;
Fly on, sea-birds! fly sideways, or wheel in large circles high in the air;
Receive the summer sky, you water, and faithfully hold it till all downcast
eyes have time to take it from you!
Diverge, fine spokes of light, from the shape of my head, or any one's head,
in the sunlit water!
Come on, ships from the lower bay! pass up or down, white-sail'd
schooners, sloops, lighters!
Flaunt away, flags of all nations! be duly lower'd at sunset!
Burn high your fires, foundry chimneys! cast black shadows at nightfall!
cast red and yellow light over the tops of the houses!
Appearances, now or henceforth, indicate what you are,
You necessary film, continue to envelop the soul,
About my body for me, and your body for you, be hung our divinest
aromas,
Thrive, cities—bring your freight, bring your shows, ample and sufficient
rivers,
Expand, being than which none else is perhaps more spiritual,
Keep your places, objects than which none else is more lasting.

You have waited, you always wait, you dumb, beautiful ministers,
We receive you with free sense at last, and are insatiate henceforward,
Not you any more shall be able to foil us, or withhold yourselves from us,

We use you, and do not cast you aside—we plant you permanently within us,
We fathom you not—we love you—there is perfection in you also,
You furnish your parts toward eternity,
Great or small, you furnish your parts toward the soul.

Mannahatta

I was asking for something specific and perfect for my city,
Whereupon lo! upsprang the aboriginal name.

Now I see what there is in a name, a word, liquid, sane, unruly, musical, self-sufficient,
I see that the word of my city is that word from of old,
Because I see that word nested in nests of water-bays, superb,
Rich, hemm'd thick all around with sailships and steamships, an island sixteen miles long, solid-founded,
Numberless crowded streets, high growths of iron, slender, strong, light, splendidly uprising toward clear skies,
Tides swift and ample, well-loved by me, toward sundown,
The flowing sea-currents, the little islands, larger adjoining islands, the heights, the villas,
The countless masts, the white shore-steamers, the lighters, the ferry-boats, the black sea-steamers well-model'd,
The down-town streets, the jobbers' houses of business, the houses of business of the ship-merchants and money-brokers, the river-streets,
Immigrants arriving, fifteen or twenty thousand in a week,
The carts hauling goods, the manly race of drivers of horses, the brown-faced sailors,
The summer air, the bright sun shining, and the sailing clouds aloft,
The winter snows, the sleigh-bells, the broken ice in the river, passing along up or down with the flood-tide or ebb-tide,
The mechanics of the city, the masters, well-form'd, beautiful-faced, looking you straight in the eyes,
Trottoirs throng'd, vehicles, Broadway, the women, the shops and shows,
A million people—manners free and superb—open voices—hospitality—the most courageous and friendly young men,
City of hurried and sparkling waters! city of spires and masts!
City nested in bays! my city!

PART 3

Industrial Metropolis (1860–1898)

New York City, including the adjacent suburb of Brooklyn, had more than a million inhabitants by 1860. Forty years later, following the consolidation of Manhattan with Queens, Staten Island, Brooklyn, and the Bronx into one enormous city of more than three hundred square miles and three million residents, Gotham had grown to become the second-largest metropolis on earth, after London, as well as the richest. A new class of "robber barons," led by John D. Rockefeller, Andrew Carnegie, and John Pierpont Morgan, came to dominate the economy and moved their company headquarters to the headquarters city of North America. Great mansions marched up Fifth Avenue, commuter trains by the dozen began to pour into Grand Central Terminal, huge department stores opened, new ways of living in high-rise apartment buildings came to be fashionable, and nightclubs and organized sports began to flourish.

J. P. Morgan was not the richest of those robber barons who made New York the financial capital of the world in the late nineteenth century. In fact, at the time of Morgan's death, in 1913, Rockefeller (whose own wealth was already over $1 billion) was supposed to have remarked when *The New York Times* reported Morgan's net worth at $80 million, "And to think he wasn't even a rich man." But in the 1880s and 1890s, when Rockefeller relocated his corporation from Cleveland, Huntington moved from California, Carnegie came from Pittsburgh, and Armour arrived from Chicago, it was due partially to the financial acumen of the banking world of which Morgan was the acknowledged master. Morgan did not believe so much in the almighty dollar as he did in the system of capitalism, and on at least two occasions, in 1895 and again in 1907, he almost single-handedly rescued the American economy. As important, companies that have become bywords in American life—General Electric, International Harvester, U.S. Steel, and American Telephone and Telegraph—were all originally financed by the "House of Morgan." By the end of the century, Morgan had helped make Gotham a magnet for wealth.

The great city attracted the poor as much as the rich, however, especially from rural areas. Why did the sturdy yeoman barter, in Lewis Mumford's words, "all his glorious heritage for gaslight and paved streets and starched collars and skyscrapers"? The answer of course was complex, but it often came down to economic and social opportunity. For example, a *Harper's New Monthly Magazine* inquiry into continuing migration to New York in 1882 concluded: "A great city always exercises a strange, well-nigh inexplicable fascination on the multitude, not less than on individuals. The former like it for its bigness, its bustle, its movement, its variety, its fluctuations. Where there is so much of everything, they are likely, they believe, to get their share. At any rate, they want to be in the tumble and the tide. Having no inward resources, they hunger for tumultuous externals."

New York was the lodestar of European immigrants even more than of native-born farmers. By 1890, even as the sources of immigration underwent a drastic shift, Gotham not only had more Germans than Hamburg, more Jews than Warsaw, and more Irishmen than Dublin but contained more foreign-born residents than any other city on earth. As Jacob Riis wrote that year: "A map of the city, colored to designate nationalities, would show more stripes than on the skin of a zebra, and more colors than any rainbow."

"Kleindeutschland" had existed in the wards of the Lower East Side since the 1840s, and second-generation Irishmen had already created the infamous Tammany Hall regime and its succession of ten Irish-American sachems in a row in the 1860s. But even though Germany and Ireland continued to be main suppliers of immigrants in the late nineteenth century (New Yorkers of Irish or German extraction constituted 75 percent of the city's population in the mid-1880s), the newest wave of immigrants came from eastern Europe, the Mediterranean, and China. They would add to the New York mix startlingly new customs, traditions, and ways of living together.

The combination of intense overcrowding, the emancipation of serfs in 1863, and the pogroms following the assassination of Czar Alexander in 1881 precipitated a massive exodus of Jews from the shtetls of Russia. Between 1870 and 1900, the number of Jews in New York grew by five times to almost three hundred thousand. The differences between the new arrivals and the already-established German Jews were significant, however; the *Hebrew Standard* proclaimed that the "thoroughly acclimated American Jew is closer to the Christian sentiment around him than to the Judaism of these miserable darkened Hebrews." The demeaning epithet *kike* was first used, in fact, by "Occidental" Jews in reference to the number of Eastern newcomers whose names ended in "ki." But while the "shtetl Jews" were regarded as unhygienic, oddly dressed, and unlearned, they were also a tremendous source of labor for the more than six thousand sweatshops in operation in the city's clothing trade, which was overwhelmingly dominated by Jews.

The rates of Italian immigration were even greater than from eastern Europe. In 1850 there were 833 Italians in the city; by 1900 there were almost a quarter of a million. Unlike the eastern Europeans, Italian immigrants tended to be rural, bachelors, and Catholic. Like the newly arrived Jews, however, they came into conflict with already-established coreligionists, the Irish Catholics. To the Irish, Italian Catholicism ignored church attendance except on major occasions and incorporated too many elements of folk religion from the old country. As a result, they often relegated Italians to the basement for church services and placed their children in the back of mixed parochial schoolrooms. This disdain came on top of dealings that Italian day laborers had with what were often Irish foremen. Italian immigrants, many of whom were single men who came to the United States primarily to make money and then return to the mother country, came to dominate the economic niche of day laborers to the extent that by 1890, upwards of 90 percent of the people employed by the Department of Public Works were Italian. Those Italians who stayed tended to settle together based on which village or town they had come from, and they preserved customs and dialects from those areas. By the turn of the century, Italian neighborhoods were firmly in place along Mulberry, Hester, and Prince Streets between Canal and Houston and in East Harlem (what would later become Fiorello LaGuardia's district), where they had come as strikebreakers for the newly constructed First Avenue trolley.

Although rates of Chinese immigration never matched those of Italians or Jews (there were less than two thousand Chinese residents in 1880), the beginnings of a Chinatown in New York were evident along Pell, Mott, Bayard, and Canal Streets as early as 1870. Many of these people were not immigrants but migrants who had worked on the building of the transcontinental railroad during the 1860s, suffered discrimination after that job was completed, and fled east. After a New Jersey–based steam laundry dismissed three hundred Chinese workers it had initially recruited and employed, hundreds of hand laundries emerged in Manhattan by the early 1880s. A new economic niche had been created by yet another immigrant nationality. Although small in actual numbers, much of the Chinese population in Lower Manhattan was housed dormitory style, with tiers of bunks each occupied by two or three customers at a time. The influx of eastern European Jews, Italians, and Chinese confirmed that New York would now become a city for all the world, and in numbers on a scale unheard of in history.

With such density and size came great problems. One of the most difficult was the lack of public open space. As Manhattan's population pushed northward, people began to wonder if anything would remain of the island's former beauty. In built-up neighborhoods, the average density was well over one hundred thousand residents per square mile; in the poorer quarters, the congestion exceeded a half million per square mile. By 1890 the Tenth Ward had topped Bombay and Calcutta as the most densely packed population in the world, and more than two thirds of the city's 1.5 million residents occupied buildings labeled tenements. In such circumstances, even the infamous "dumbbell tenement" was viewed as an improvement over the miserable, windowless apartments that were built before 1879. Disease, of course, was a frequent visitor. The mournful cry was "Luft, gib mir luft"—"Air, give me air."

One response was to create public open space available to everyone. Boston, Philadelphia, and Savannah, for example, provided their citizens with public parks and squares from the moment of their founding. But those were small spaces. Until 1857, when Frederick Law Olmsted and Calvert Vaux won a contest to design Central Park, no American city had provided a significant area for people to play, partly because the poor conceived of parks as aristocratic preserves and partly because the rich thought of parks as too tempting to idlers and hobos. But the need for open space was nevertheless desperate, especially in Manhattan. Olmsted and Vaux conceived as a remedy a democratic park, a "park for all the people."

Olmsted and Vaux's design for Central Park was an enormous success. Twenty years under construction, the park required the labor of thirty-eight hundred men to dig out its lakes and ponds and to build up its hills and paths. But it was visited by ten million people even before it was completed, and its form—the south end was given over to formal functions like fountains and statues, while the north end was made as rugged and wild as possible—influenced cities and towns throughout the country. Indeed, after Central Park opened and created an increased demand for land around its edges, no city anywhere that thought well of itself and its future prospects could choose not to build a grand open space toward the center.

By 1898, at the moment of consolidation, New York was poised to become the capital of the twentieth century and the capital of capitalism. It had not as yet solved even a fraction of its many problems, but its residents were dealing with their various crises with confidence and hope. As Harry Golden later said of Gotham's Jews: "The second generation came along and soon the sons took the old folks away, out of Brooklyn, or up to the Bronx, and thus they made room for new immigrants. America gave them all life and hope, and they repaid America. There has never been a more even trade."

Selected Writings of African Americans in Brooklyn (1849–1928)

The following documents are part of a permanent exhibition to be opened at the Brooklyn Historical Society in the fall of 2003, entitled *Brooklyn Works: 400 Years of Making a Living in Brooklyn.* Founded in 1863, the Brooklyn Historical Society is a nationally renowned urban history center dedicated to encouraging the exploration and appreciation of Brooklyn's diverse peoples, both past and present. The society's library predates the Brooklyn Public Library and was one of only a handful of cultural organizations in Brooklyn in the mid-nineteenth century. Much more than a museum and library, the society is a place that brings people together and promotes understanding and acceptance. In 1998 the society's national landmark building, built in 1881, closed temporarily for extensive renovation and modernization; it is tentatively scheduled to reopen in 2003.

The first set of documents selected by the exhibition's curator, Dr. Ann Meyerson, focuses on the "work life" of African Americans in Brooklyn in the mid-nineteenth century. In 1626, "a parcel of eleven African males" arrived in New Amsterdam, but by 1644, Africans were suffering from hereditary servitude as their children were deemed property of the Dutch West India Company. However, shortly after the abolition of slavery in New York State in 1827, the communities of Carrville and Weeksville were founded in west central Brooklyn by free black farmers, laborers, and craftsmen. The words of Willis Hodges and Maritcha Lyons provide a description of some of the jobs that African Americans in Brooklyn engaged in around the time of the Civil War.

The second set of documents, "The Draft Riots of 1863," describes the bloodiest urban riot in United States history. Stores were ransacked, the Colored Orphan Asylum was set on fire, gangs of thugs randomly attacked African Americans in the streets, and the newspaper offices of abolitionist Horace Greeley were attacked twice. By the end of the fourth day of rioting at least

105 people were dead. It was only when five regiments of the Union Army were dispatched to Gotham from the battlefield at Gettysburg that order was restored to the city.

In a trend that continued with little change into the twentieth century, jobs in factories or as apprentices to artisans were largely denied to people of African descent in Kings County (and New York), where they made up almost 10 percent of the population in 1820. White racism grew stronger in the 1830s with sharper and more violent opposition to blacks in the trades, housing and transport, churches, schools, and on the streets. One of the most dramatic developments was the supplanting of black women domestics in New York by Irish domestics in the 1840s and 1850s. By 1855 the industrial trades were overwhelmingly Irish. Common occupations for blacks were coachman, barber, cook, farm laborer, seaman, sail maker, horse dealer, grocer, "segar" (cigar) maker, shoemaker, carpenter, "speculator," preacher, and teacher. At the same time, African Americans in Brooklyn forged a community in which many educators, religious leaders, political activists, journalists, etc., flourished and created important institutions.

Work Life

THE first impression New York made upon my mind was unfavorable (1836). My brother William went with me around the city and showed me the different occupations of the people of color, and where they were located. Here my expectations were again disappointed beyond description. I found the majority of them working as servants of some sort and few (very few) carried on business of their own. I had expected to find the people of color in free New York far better off than those in Virginia. In the latter state, both bond and free had trades, that is, many of them, and all the skilled work was done by men of color. In New York I found none, or only one here and there. In fact, many tradesmen I knew from the South were now cooks and waiters. I did not like New York any way it could be placed before me.

I engaged board at my sister's at one dollar and fifty cents per week (supper and lodging was the board), my washing was paid for extra, the price being sixpence a piece for each article. The first job of work I got was as a laborer on the docks, cleaning away ice, mud and snow, so a gentleman could go across to his ship. I did not get much work the first month, only odd jobs here and there, with small pay, because of which I was low spirited and discontented and began to wish I had never left Virginia.

The foreman of the *cartmen* told the gentleman I was a smart young man [looking] for work, and we all worked until night. The gentleman did not allow the men as much as they actually worked (myself included) and they got in a rage and demanded their money, and swore that they would no longer work for him. I had nothing to say, but took what little was coming to me and went home. . . . The next morning early I was on hand but none of the rest. The gentleman then told me to go and get men to do the work and to see that they did it well. I got men and became the boss of the job. My employer was so well pleased with my work that he did not take any time off when I went to my dinner. It was Tuesday when I commenced to work on this job and I worked until Saturday night, at two shillings per hour, and was paid that night $12.50, which was as much again as any man who had worked upon the ship had made from the job. . . . After that the gloom which had darkened my pathway and sky began to clear away and success opened to my view. I had no difficulty in obtaining work, and in a short time was able to go to a tailor's and get fitted out with first-class new fashionable clothes.

I saved up my money and in one year's time bought a lot on S. Seventh Street, Williamsburg, L.I., within a few minutes walk of Peck's Slip ferry. . . . I went into business for myself, (that is, brother William and I opened a grocery store together in his house, corner South Eighth and Fourth streets). I kept the store and William worked for Messrs. Hulbert & Co. . . . One Sunday as I was walking on the north side of the village, I saw several colored persons going as if they were on their way to church, so I followed them. I was soon agreeably surprised to find myself in a church filled with people of color. . . . I gave as my opinion that the people of color had to leave the crowded cities and towns of New York, Brooklyn, Syracuse, Albany, Troy, Utica and the rest and move into the country and small growing villages like Williamsburg, and grow up with the small town. I believe in that way they would overcome much of the prejudice against them, for, as a rule, there is a fraternal feeling between the people of small towns or places (even in the South) that is unknown in the large cities.

Later (1846), . . . finding I could not get work, I borrowed a little money from a friend and opened a stall in Catherine market, where I sold eggs, butter, ducks, chickens, etc. I made quite a respectable living and was soon out of debt. . . . Now white washing was a good business. . . . So I put a nephew in charge of the stall in the market and worked at the white washing business every day except Sundays, when I would stay and sell in the market.

Willis Hodges, 1849

I OFTEN listened to the older folks narrate about the Jim Crow horse cars which traveled on 6th Avenue; these cars had a sign on their sides to inform the public such were for "colored people." My mother's complexion was sufficiently fair to easily mistake her for a white person at a quick glance and she often related her experiences with the various drivers who learned in time that she was not a white woman and would not stop when signaled.

By my thirteenth birthday (1861) going to school involved a journey of several miles every day. At that time a stage route traversed the length of Broadway, but, riding, for colored folks, depended upon the whims of respective stage drivers. Once in awhile one would respond to my signal, but oftener I was ignored or jeered at.

Before the influx of immigrants, work was always in waiting for any and everyone who wanted it. Tasks were undertaken and completed leisurely and small steady gains were satisfactory. These times saw in New York City colored jewellers, carpenters, undertakers, printers, shoemakers, tinsmiths, crockery and china ware dealers.

When hustling and competition arrived to stay, a gradual economic revolution followed by which new methods supplanted old ways. So long as cookery, cake making, pie baking, ice cream manufacturing and the preparation of made dishes were carried on in separate establishments, colored persons in such kinds of business flourished financially; but when the omnibus caterer announced he was prepared to supply everything required for festivities, the isolated [supplier] met rivals with whom they found themselves unable to cope. In other forms of activity, washing was transformed into laundry service, white washing into kalsomining, clothes cleaning into valeting. Such radical changes drove many original workers out of business. The day for making money with limited capital and by slow degrees vanished.

While it lasted, many of our people acquired real estate, accumulated and invested savings and enjoyed a genuine, if not an extensive prosperity. But opportunities for getting a livelihood having become restricted, many of our people were compelled to accept less congenial employment and lower compensation.

Maritcha Lyons, 1928

The Draft Riots of 1863

The Draft Riots of July 1863 were the largest and most heinous in a series of battles between blacks and a white population that was sympathetic to the southern cause during the Civil War and jealous of African Americans in the workforce. Assaults on black workers had occurred in Brooklyn the preceding September (1862), in March along the waterfront, and on May 29, when some Irish longshoremen attacked African Americans at Pier 9. These assaults occurred within a context of intense racial antagonism dating back to the riots of 1834.

In 1860 economic conditions were deteriorating badly for everyone. Having undermined blacks in several occupations, many Irish laborers seemed determined to drive out black competition. Many also had little interest in fighting a war for black emancipation. One New Yorker explained that the Irish were angry at the draft because they believed that the abolition of slavery would cause them to be replaced by "good, faithful, colored servants." She felt sorry for the "cruelties" inflicted upon the blacks during the Draft Riots but hoped that they would "give the Negro a lesson, for since the [Civil] war commenced, they have been so insolent as to be unbearable."

Ironically, it was African Americans who had been displaced by white immigrants in the workforce during this period, not the other way around. And yet the animosity expressed toward black New Yorkers and black Brooklynites during the Draft Riots was so extreme and so brutal as to leave its mark for many decades to come.

BEFORE my graduation from the New York school, the Civil War was raging with intense bitterness on both sides. A draft precipitated the riots of 1863, [which] convulsed the city, spread havoc, and were especially disastrous to many of our colored people.

One July afternoon, a rabble attacked our house breaking window panes, smashing shutters, and practically demolishing the main front door. Lights having been extinguished, a lonely vigil of hours passed in mingled darkness, indignation, uncertainty, and dread. Just after midnight, a yell announced that a second mob was gathering to attempt assault. As one of the foremost of the rioters attempted to ascend the front steps, father advanced into the doorway and fired point blank into the crowd. Not knowing what might be concealed in the darkened interior, the fickle mob more disorganized than reckless, retreated out of sight hastily and no further demonstration was made that night. At dawn, footsteps of a single person were heard, and a voice cried out: "Don't shoot, Al. It's only me." Officer Kelly of the precinct was the speaker. This kind hearted man sat on our steps and sobbed like a child. He said that rumors of the attack had reached the police station, but of help, there was none during the exigency. The next day a third and successful attempt at entrance was effected. This sent father over the back fence to the Oak Street station, while mother took refuge on the premises of a neighbor. This was a friendly German who in the morning had loosened boards of intervening fences in anticipation of an emergency. This charitable man, some weeks after, was waylaid and severely beaten by "parties unknown." In one short hour the police had cleared the premises and both parents were at home after the ravages. What a home! Its interior was dismantled, furniture was missing or broken. From basement to attic evidences of the worst vandalism prevailed. A fire, kindled in one of the upper rooms was discovered in time to prevent a conflagration.

The dismayed parents had to submit to the indignity of taking refuge in the police station house. A three day's reign of terror disgraced a city unable to protect its inhabitants. During this state of anarchy, many were rendered homeless, maltreated, outraged, even put to death by hanging, burning, and similar barbarous acts.

Under the cover of darkness the police conveyed our parents to the Williamsburg ferry; there steamboats were kept in readiness to either transport fugitives or to outwit rioters by pulling out into midstream. To such humiliations, to such outrages, were law abiding citizens exposed and that in a city where they domiciled tax payers. Is it any wonder that for them New York was never after to be considered home.

Maritcha Lyons, 1928

MANY men were killed and thrown into the rivers, a great number hung to trees and lampposts, numbers shot down; no black person could show their heads but what they were hunted like wolves. These scenes continued for four days. Over three thousand are today homeless and destitute, without means of support for their families.

In Brooklyn, we have not had any great trouble, but many of our people have been compelled to leave their houses and flee for refuge. . . . In Weeksville and Flatbush, the colored men who had manhood in them armed themselves, determined to die defending their homes. Hundreds fled there from New York.

The Christian Recorder, July 1863

A RESIDENT of the Eastern part of Brooklyn, who yesterday and the day previous visited the settlement of the colored people in the Ninth Ward of that city, has given us some interesting details of the condition of things in that quarter. There are now known to be about two hundred persons who have sought shelter from their demoniac persecutors in New York, in the wild briars, buslies and low woods which cover the ridge bordering the city. There may, and probably are others who have not yet made themselves known. There were men, women and children found among them, some of them in utter destitution. Husbands driven away without the means of knowing what has become of their wives and children, and families burned out and compelled to flee, ignorant if their natural protector is alive or not.

In some instances separated families have accidentally been united. The permanent residents of the district, though themselves cut off from their ordinary employments and threatened with outrage, are active in succoring the refugees, mostly strangers to them and liberally share their shelter with them so far as able. Many have, however, slept outdoors ever since the riots began, suffering not only from exposure but the effects of terror, such as can hardly be realized. . . . [T]hey are determined and prepared to defend themselves and families against any assailants; and though peaceably disposed, say that if they must die it shall not be while running away.

Anglo African, July 25, 1863

The Republic of New-York from Debow's Review, *George Fitzhugh (1861)*

George Fitzhugh was born in 1806 to an aristocratic southern family in Prince William County, Virginia. Although he received only a sketchy early education, he studied law and began to practice in 1829. Fitzhugh is most remembered for his argument that slavery was a "positive good," which he put forth in two volumes entitled *Sociology for the South* (1854) and *Cannibals All!* (1857). However, Fitzhugh's main fear was socialism, which he saw as the major threat to northern capitalism. Free labor, for Fitzhugh, spelled class warfare and anarchy, which led him to defend the southern slave system as a superior one. Fitzhugh subscribed to the philosophy of "free trade, . . . the philosophy adapted to promote the interests of the strong, the wealthy and the wise." As a result, in an article in *Debow's Review* in February 1861, Fitzhugh called on New York to secede and form its own city-nation.

There was some precedent for this sentiment; a month earlier, Mayor Fernando Wood had proposed to the Common Council that if the South seceded the city should take up the words of the Dongan Charter and "from henceforth forever hereafter . . . be and remain, a free city itself." However, although Wood's idea was discussed among New York businessmen, Abraham Lincoln lampooned the idea, remarking that it would be "some time before the front door sets up house-keeping on its own account."

THE proposition to make the city of New-York, with a few adjoining counties, a free port and an independent nation, is the most brilliant that these eventful times have given birth to. It is practicable and feasible, as it is classical. History, and hundreds of living and speaking traditions, thousands of years older than history, concur in proving that it is the city constitutes the nation. Throughout the torrid and milder temperate zones, the ruins of ancient cities—that were ruins long ere the Man of History began to record the doings of human kind—belt the globe. These cities were such great, wealthy, and highly-civilized nations, blooming like the rose in the desert, in the midst of surrounding barrenness and barbarism. They are ever-living traditions that teach with mute eloquence that the city is the human hive, the natural and the best residence of man. . . .

New-York city, and the country immediately around it, is healthful, easily defended, and admirably situated for trade with the whole world. It is already by far the greatest centre of trade in America, probably the greatest in the world. Its population is more enterprising than that of any European city; for enterprise and invention are never weighed down and suppressed by the cankered prejudices and aversion to innovation, which sit like an incubus on all old societies. It is not only the American centre of trade, but also of intellect; especially of practical active intellect; and there is more of such intellect in America than in the rest of the world. The literary talent of the Union, though not largely native to that city, is greatly attracted to it, on account of the learned associations that may be there enjoyed; because its libraries and other means and facilities of acquiring knowledge and obtaining information are the best in the country; and further, because it is the best point for the publication and sale of books. Its lawyers, doctors, and clergymen, are the best paid in the country, and consequently the ablest. Its mechanics, its manufacturers, and its artists, possess most of genius and of skill, for genius and skill are there most in demand.

Its merchants deal with the whole world, and are well informed about the wants, productions, tastes, laws, institutions, and other affairs of the whole world. They are both enterprising and wealthy, and comprise within their ranks enough men of general information and business talent to conduct all the governments of christendom much better than they are now conducted. That the population of New-York is superior in general information, professional, mechanical and commercial talent, to any population of like numbers, few will be disposed to deny. It has less of prejudice, less of provincialism, less narrowness of heart and intellect, than any other people; for it is in hourly intercourse with the whole world, and is daily reminded that there is much to admire and approve, as well as some things to condemn, in the laws, institutions, manners and morals of all peoples.

Life, in New-York, is one continued industrial and intellectual struggle, a war of competition, an ever-recurring Olympic game, where the highest prizes of fame, reputation and fortune are every day awarded to the most meritorious. The Olympic games recurred but once in four years; the prizes were not a thousandth part as numerous, or as valuable, as those awarded in New-York, yet those games attracted all that was meritorious, great, or distinguished in Greece. Mediocrity did not engage in the Olympic, nor does mediocrity find a congenial residence, or profitable employment, in such great centres as London, Paris, and New-York.

Their motto is, "*Detur digniori*," and they keep the promise conveyed in their motto. None but the worthy, the skilful, the industrious, the gifted, or the talented, will find peculiar advantages in living in New-York. Demand begets supply; and since there is the greatest demand and highest reward of merit in New-York, then, there is most of merit. Why may she not aspire to rival the fame of Athens, of Carthage, or of Venice? She possesses greater advantages of situation, a ten times more extensive commerce, a mercantile marine that in a month she could convert into a powerful navy, a more enterprising spirit, and greater wealth, than either of those cities in their meridian glory.

Looking to all her advantages, we do not hesitate to say: "If we were not a Virginian, we would be a New-Yorker."

When she sets up for herself, her free-trade policy will give offence to none, make friends of all. The great Northwest, the most fertile and productive agricultural region on earth, will continue to find in New-York her natural and best outlet and market. Outlet she will hardly need, for New-York will be ready and able to buy all she has to sell, and to furnish her all she wishes to buy. The South is accustomed to deal in New-York, and although she *can* live independently of her, will feel no disposition to withdraw from a steadfast and a powerful friend, especially, when to do so would only subject her to great temporary privation. For European trade New-York is best situated: she almost now monopolizes it, and will not lose it, unless she comes under Yankee rule, and offends the South. She trades with all the world, and her trade will continue to increase, until she assumes a hostile position towards that part of the world (the South) where are her best customers.

Free trade, carried on by New-York, will have precisely the opposite effect on her wealth, skill, industry, and intellect, that free trade exercises on more agricultural communities.

She has abundance of capital, skill, and cheap labor employed in manufactures; and is the best market for their sale. Merchants from all quarters go there to buy every kind of merchandise; and the immense demand and composition among buyers secures ready sales and fair prices. She is able to compete, without a protective tariff, in the production of all manufactures, because she is unsurpassed in skill, capital; abundance of cheap labor, and in the extent of her market. Each new occupation and each new importation, enhances the profits of all existing pursuits and interests, by giving greater variety to her market, and thereby attracting more customers. With free trade and amicable national relations, business cannot be overdone in New-York. London contains three millions of population, and has not begun to suffer from excess of population. New-York is far better situated for trade and all kinds of business. There is no reason, that we can see, why she and a few adjoining counties might not contain a prosperous and enlightened population of ten millions. Labor is rendered most productive when most associated; and the expenses of education and of living are greatly lessened, when large numbers of men, carrying on various occupations, live contiguous to each other. Half the labor will support a million of men in a city, that will support an equal number sparsely scattered over the country. Besides, sparse populations are extremely ignorant, for want of association and means of observation. City populations become well informed by seeing the productions and the men of all countries, by witnessing the various processes of art and industry, and by intercourse and association with the little world around them.

In an agricultural country, free trade at first depresses and gradually excludes all other pursuits than agriculture. A seaport in such a country is a mere depot or distributing point for foreign merchandise, like Ostea at the mouth of the Tiber, or Havre de Grace at the mouth of the Seine. A little village is all there need be at such a port, with a few agents to receive and send forward packages of goods, by railroads and steamboats, to the towns in the interior. The demand for skill and intellect in a mere farming country, is just enough to carry on agriculture. Educated people become absentees for want of home associations. The crops are sold abroad and spent abroad, and the money is accumulated and invested as capital, in various forms, in such attractive centres as New-York.

Should New-York fail to erect herself into a free port and separate republic; should she remain under the dominion of the corrupt, venal wire-workers of Albany, and of the immoral, infidel, agrarian, free-love democracy of western New-York; should she put herself under the rule of Puritane, the vilest, most selfish, and unprincipled of the human race; should she join a northern confederacy; should she make New-England, western New-York, northern Ohio, northern Indians, or northern Illinois, her masters; should she make enemies of her Southern friends, and deliver herself up to the tender mercies of her Northern enemies, she will sink to rise no more. Better, a thousand times better, to come under the dominion of free negroes or gypsies, than of Yankees or Low Germans, or Canadians. Gypsies and free negroes have many amiable, noble, and generous traits; Yankees, sour krout Germans, and Canadians none. Senator Wade says, and Seward too, that the north will absorb Canada. They are half true; the vile, sensual, animal, brutal, infidel, superstitious democracy of Canada and the Yankee States, will coalesce; and Senator Johnson of Tennessee will join them. But when Canada and western New-York, and New-England, and the whole beastly, puritanic "sour krout," free negro, infidel, superstitious, licentious, democratic population of the North become the masters of New-York—what then? Outside of the city, the State of New-York is Yankee and puritanical; composed of as base, unprincipled, superstitious, licentious, and agrarian and anarchical population as any on earth. Nay, we do not hesitate to say, it is the vilest population on earth. If the city does not secede and erect a separate republic, this population, aided by the ignorant, base, brutal, sensual, German infidels of the Northwest, the stupid democracy of Canada (for Canada will in some way coalesce with the North), and the arrogant and tyrannical people of New-England, will become masters of the destinies of New-York. They hate her for her sympathies with the South, and will so legislate as to divert all her western trade to outlets through Chicago, the Saint Lawrence, Portland, and Boston. She will then be cut off from her trade North and South. In fine, she must set up for herself, as Mr. Sickles advises, or be ruined.

Up Broadway to Madison Square, from Ragged Dick, *Horatio Alger (1868)*

Horatio Alger was born in 1832 in Chelsea (now Revere), Massachusetts. A frail child (he suffered from asthma and nearsightedness) and diminutive (he was rejected for the Union Army three times because he was only five feet tall and weighed only 120 pounds), he did not talk until he was six years old. Alger was a determined student, however, and graduated from both Harvard University and Harvard Divinity School with academic distinction.

Alger's arrival in New York in 1866 was precipitated by charges of pedophilia levied against him by an investigative committee of his parish in Brewster, Massachusetts. He never denied the accusations and did admit to acting "imprudently"; the charges themselves refer only to an "unnatural familiarity with boys." Alger was allowed to resign his ministerial post and set out for New York City to pursue a writing career.

Interestingly, the formula that Alger used in virtually all of his rags-to-riches stories involve a hero who is falsely accused of something but is later exonerated. Alger recast his "strive and succeed" spirit in more than five hundred novels and short stories under various pseudonyms over the next thirty years. His writing seems to have become both his ministry and a means of atonement for his earlier actions. Alger died on July 18, 1899, but the Horatio Alger Jr. Society still exists today to, in the words of its mission statement, "encourage the spirit of Strive and Succeed that for half a century guided Alger's undaunted heroes."

As the boys pursued their way up Broadway, Dick pointed out the prominent hotels and places of amusement. Frank was particularly struck with the imposing fronts of the St. Nicholas and Metropolitan Hotels, the former of white marble, the latter of a subdued brown hue, but not less elegant in its internal appointments. He was not surprised to be informed that each of these splendid structures cost with the furnishing not far from a million dollars.

At Eighth Street Dick turned to the right, and pointed out the Clinton Hall Building now occupied by the Mercantile Library, comprising at that time over fifty thousand volumes.

A little farther on they came to a large building standing by itself just at the opening of Third and Fourth Avenues, and with one side on each.

"What is that building?" asked Frank.

"That's the Cooper Institute," said Dick; "built by Mr. Cooper, a particular friend of mine. Me and Peter Cooper used to go to school together."

"What is there inside?" asked Frank.

"There's a hall for public meetin's and lectures in the basement, and a readin' room and a picture gallery up above," said Dick.

Directly opposite Cooper Institute, Frank saw a very large building of brick, covering about an acre of ground.

"Is that a hotel?" he asked.

"No," said Dick; "that's the Bible House. It's the place where they make Bibles. I was in there once,—saw a big pile of 'em."

"Did you ever read the Bible?" asked Frank, who had some idea of the neglected state of Dick's education.

"No," said Dick; "I've heard it's a good book, but I never read one. I ain't much on readin'. It makes my head ache."

"I suppose you can't read very fast."

"I can read the little words pretty well, but the big ones is what stick me."

"If I lived in the city, you might come every evening to me, and I would teach you."

"Would you take so much trouble about me?" asked Dick, earnestly.

"Certainly; I should like to see you getting on. There isn't much chance of that if you don't know how to read and write."

"You're a good feller," said Dick, gratefully. "I wish you did live in New York. I'd like to know somethin'. Whereabouts do you live?"

"About fifty miles off, in a town on the left bank of the Hudson. I wish you'd come up and see me sometime. I would like to have you come and stop two or three days."

"Honor bright?"

"I don't understand."

"Do you mean it?" asked Dick, incredulously.

"Of course I do. Why shouldn't I?"

"What would your folks say if they knowed you asked a boot-black to visit you?"

"You are none the worse for being a boot-black, Dick."

"I ain't used to genteel society," said Dick. "I shouldn't know how to behave."

"Then I could show you. You won't be a boot-black all your life, you know."

"No," said Dick; "I'm goin' to knock off when I get to be ninety."

"Before that, I hope," said Frank, smiling.

"I really wish I could get somethin' else to do," said Dick, soberly. "I'd like to be a office boy, and learn business, and grow up 'spectable."

"Why don't you try, and see if you can't get a place, Dick?"

"Who'd take Ragged Dick?"

"But you ain't ragged now, Dick."

"No," said Dick; "I look a little better than I did in my Washington coat and Louis Napoleon pants. But if I got in a office, they wouldn't give me more'n three dollars a week, and I couldn't live 'spectable on that."

"No, I suppose not," said Frank, thoughtfully.

"But you would get more at the end of the first year."

"Yes," said Dick; "but by that time I'd be nothin' but skin and bones."

Frank laughed. "That reminds me," he said, "of the story of an Irishman, who, out of economy, thought he would teach his horse to feed on shavings. So he provided the horse with a pair of green spectacles which made the shavings look eatable. But unfortunately, just as the horse got learned, he up and died."

"The hoss must have been a fine specimen of architectur' by the time he got through," remarked Dick.

"Whereabouts are we now?" asked Frank, as they emerged from Fourth Avenue into Union Square.

"That is Union Park," said Dick, pointing to a beautiful enclosure, in the centre of which was a pond, with a fountain playing.

"Is that the statue of General Washington?" asked Frank, pointing to a bronze equestrian statue, on a granite pedestal.

"Yes," said Dick; "he's growed some since he was President. If he'd been as tall as that when he fit in the Revolution, he'd have walloped the Britishers some, I reckon."

Frank looked up at the statue, which is fourteen and a half feet high, and acknowledged the justice of Dick's remark.

"How about the coat, Dick?" he asked. "Would it fit you?"

"Well, it might be rather loose," said Dick, "I ain't much more'n ten feet high with my boots off."

"No, I should think not," said Frank, smiling. "You're a queer boy, Dick."

"Well, I've been brought up queer. Some boys is born with a silver spoon in their mouth. Victoria's boys is born with a gold spoon, set with di'monds; but gold and silver was scarce when I was born, and mine was pewter."

"Perhaps the gold and silver will come by and by, Dick. Did you ever hear of Dick Whittington?"

"Never did. Was he a Ragged Dick?"

"I shouldn't wonder if he was. At any rate he was very poor when he was a boy, but he didn't stay so. Before he died, he became Lord Mayor of London."

"Did he?" asked Dick, looking interested. "How did he do it?"

"Why, you see, a rich merchant took pity on him, and gave him a home in his own house, where he used to stay with the servants, being employed in little errands. One day the merchant noticed Dick picking up pins and needles that had been dropped, and asked him why he did it. Dick told him he was going to sell them when he got enough. The merchant was pleased with his saving disposition, and when soon after, he was going to send a vessel to foreign parts, he told Dick he might send anything he pleased in it, and it should be sold to his advantage. Now Dick had nothing in the world but a kitten which had been given him a short time before."

"How much taxes did he have to pay on it?" asked Dick.

"Not very high, probably. But having only the kitten, he concluded to send it along. After sailing a good many months, during which the kitten grew up to be a strong cat, the ship touched at an island never before known, which happened to be infested with rats and mice to such an extent that they worried everybody's life out, and even ransacked the king's palace. To make a long story short, the captain, seeing how matters stood, brought Dick's cat ashore, and she soon made the rats and mice scatter. The king was highly delighted when he saw what havoc she made among the rats and mice, and resolved to have her at any price. So he offered a great quantity of gold for her, which, of course, the captain was glad to accept. It was faithfully carried back to Dick, and laid the foundation of his fortune. He prospered as he grew up, and in time became a very rich merchant, respected by all, and before he died was elected Lord Mayor of London."

"That's a pretty good story" said Dick; "but I don't believe all the cats in New York will ever make me mayor."

"No, probably not, but you may rise in some other way. A good many distinguished men have once been poor boys. There's hope for you, Dick, if you'll try."

"Nobody ever talked to me so before," said Dick. "They just called me Ragged Dick, and told me I'd grow up to be a vagabone (boys who are better educated need not be surprised at Dick's blunders) and come to the gallows."

"Telling you so won't make it turn out so, Dick. If you'll try to be somebody, and grow up into a respectable member of society, you will. You may not become rich,—it isn't everybody that becomes rich, you know—but you can obtain a good position, and be respected."

"I'll try," said Dick, earnestly. "I needn't have been Ragged Dick so long if I hadn't spent my money in goin' to the theatre, and treatin' boys to oyster-stews, and bettin' money on cards, and such like."

"Have you lost money that way?"

"Lots of it. One time I saved up five dollars to buy me a new rig-out, cos my best suit was all in rags, when Limpy Jim wanted me to play a game with him."

"Limpy Jim?" said Frank, interrogatively.

"Yes, he's lame; that's what makes us call him Limpy Jim."

"I suppose you lost?"

"Yes, I lost every penny, and had to sleep out, cos I hadn't a cent to pay for lodgin'. 'Twas a awful cold night, and I got most froze."

"Wouldn't Jim let you have any of the money he had won to pay for a lodging?"

"No; I axed him for five cents, but he wouldn't let me have it."

"Can you get lodging for five cents?" asked Frank, in surprise.

"Yes," said Dick, "but not at the Fifth Avenue Hotel. That's it right out there."

Selected Writings on Central Park, Frederick Law Olmsted (1858, 1870)

Frederick Law Olmsted was born in Hartford, Connecticut, in 1822 and moved to Staten Island in 1840 with the intent of becoming a "scientific farmer." When that career failed, he traveled in Europe and the American South as a newspaper correspondent.

When the city commissioners of New York laid out the grid system in 1811, there had been no plans for a public park, and there was no real interest in one until William Cullen Bryant, the poet and then editor of the *New York Post,* called for one in 1844. In 1858 Olmsted and Calvert Vaux submitted their Greensward Plan for a Central Park in the middle of Manhattan Island. Olmsted and Vaux's plan won out over several others in a competition, and Olmsted was named superintendent of Central Park.

Olmsted's goal was not simply to create a rural space in the middle of the city; it was to create an organized aesthetic experience for every visitor to the park. Olmsted believed that "landscape moves us in a manner more analogous to music than to anything else." Furthermore, Olmsted's park was intended as a democratic experiment, "a Park for the people." He saw landscape parks as "great places of harmony" where people from all classes of American society could go to stroll, meditate, and intermingle.

Olmsted continued to design landscapes until the 1893 Chicago World's Fair, and his legacy continues in cities all over North America—from Prospect Park in Brooklyn to the Emerald Necklace of Boston to Mont Royal Park in Montreal. Ironically, Olmsted's own sanity gave way to senility, and he was institutionalized on the grounds of McLean Hospital in Waverly, Massachusetts—grounds that he himself had designed—for the last eight years of his life until his death in 1903.

The Plan for the Park (1858)

THE Park throughout is a single work of art, and as such subject to the primary law of every work of art, namely, that it shall be framed upon a single, noble motive, to which the design of all its parts, in some more or less subtle way, shall be confluent and helpful.

To find such a general motive of design for the Central Park, it will be necessary to go back to the beginning and ask, for what worthy purpose could the city be required to take out and keep excluded from the field of ordinary urban improvements, a body of land in what was looked forward to as its very centre, so large as that assigned for the Park? For what such object of great prospective importance would a smaller body of land not have been adequate?

To these questions a sufficient answer can, we believe, be found in the expectation that the whole of the island of New York would, but for such a reservation, before many years be occupied by buildings and paved streets; that millions upon millions of men were to live their lives upon this island, millions more to go out from it, or its immediate densely populated suburbs, only occasionally and at long intervals, and that all its inhabitants would assuredly suffer, in greater or less degree, according to their occupations and the degree of their confinement to it, from influences engendered by these conditions.

Provisions for the improvement of the ground, however, pointed to something more than mere exemption from urban conditions, namely, to the formation of an opposite class of conditions; conditions remedial of the influences of urban conditions.

Two classes of improvements were to be planned for this purpose; one directed to secure pure and wholesome air, to act through the lungs; the other to secure an antithesis of objects of vision to those of the streets and houses, which should act remedially by impressions on the mind and suggestions to the imagination.

It is one great purpose of the Park to supply to the hundreds of thousands of tired workers, who have no opportunity to spend their summers in the country, a specimen of God's handiwork that shall be to them, inexpensively, what a month or two in the White Mountains or the Adirondacks is, at great cost, to those in easier circumstances. The time will come when New York will be built up, when all the grading and filling will be done, and when the picturesquely-varied, rocky formations of the Island will have been converted into formations for rows of monotonous straight streets, and piles of erect buildings. There will be no suggestion left of its present varied surface, with the single exception of the few acres contained in the Park. Then the priceless value of the present picturesque outlines of the ground will be more distinctly perceived, and its adaptability for its purpose more fully recognized. It therefore seems desirable to interfere with its easy, undulating outlines, and picturesque, rocky scenery as little as possible, and, on the other hand, to endeavor rapidly, and by every legitimate means, to increase and judiciously develop these particularly individual and characteristic sources of landscape effects.

Considering that large classes of rural objects and many types of natural scenery are not practicable to be introduced on the site of the Park,—mountain, ocean, desert and prairie scenery for example,—it will be found that the most valuable form that could have been prescribed is that which may be distinguished from all others as pastoral. But the site of the Park having had a very heterogeneous surface, which was largely formed of solid rock, it was not desirable that the attempt should be made to reduce it all to the simplicity of pastoral scenery. What would the central motive of design require of the rest? Clearly that it should be given such a character as, while affording contrast and variety of scene, would as much as possible be confluent to the same end, namely, the constant suggestion to the imagination of an unlimited range of rural conditions.

The question of localizing or adjusting these two classes of landscape elements to the various elements of the natural topography of the Park next occurs, the study of which must begin with the consideration that the Park is to be surrounded by an artificial wall, twice as high as the Great Wall of China, composed of urban buildings. Wherever this should appear across the meadow-view, the imagination would be checked abruptly, at short range. Natural objects were thus required to be interposed, which while excluding the buildings as much as possible from view, would leave an uncertainty as to the occupation of the space beyond, and establish a horizon line, composed, as much as possible, of verdure.

It was, then, first of all, required that such parts of the site as were available and necessary to the purpose should be assigned to the occupation of elements which would compose a wood-side, screening incongruous objects without the Park as much as possible from the view of observers within it.

Secondly, of the remaining ground, it was required to assign as much as was available to the occupation of elements which would compose tranquil, open, pastoral scenes.

Thirdly, it was required to assign all of the yet remaining ground to elements which would tend to form passages of scenery contrasting in depth of obscurity and picturesque character of detail with the softness and simplicity of the open landscape.

By far the most extensive and important of the constructed accommodations of the Central Park are those for convenience of locomotion. How to obtain simply the required amount of room for this purpose, without making this class of its constructions everywhere disagreeably conspicuous, harshly disruptive of all relations of composition between natural landscape elements on their opposite borders, and without the absolute destruction of many valuable topographical features, was the most difficult problem of this design.

Observations of . . . [traffic difficulties] both in our own streets and in European parks, led to the planning of a system of independent ways; 1st for carriages; 2d, for horsemen wishing to gallop; 3d, for footmen; and 4th, for common street traffic requiring to cross the Park. By this means it was made possible, even for the most timid and nervous, to go on foot to any district of the Park designed to be visited, without crossing a line of wheels on the same level, and consequently, without occasion for anxiety or hesitation.

Incidentally, the system provided, in its arched ways, substantial shelters scattered through the Park, which would be rarely seen above the general plane of the landscape, and which would be made as inconspicuous as possible, but to be readily found when required in sudden showers.

Without taking the present occasion to argue the point, we may simply refer to another incidental advantage of the system which, so far as we have observed, has not been publicly recognized, but which, we are confident, may be justly claimed to exist, in the fact that to the visitor, carried by occasional defiles from one field of landscape to another, in which a wholly different series of details is presented, the extent of the Park is practically much greater than it would otherwise be.

Public Parks and the Enlargement of Towns (1870)

It is upon this last point far more than upon any other that the experience of New York is instructive to other communities. I propose, therefore, to occupy your time a little while longer by a narration of those parts of this experience which bear most directly upon this point, and which will also supply certain other information which has been desired of me.

The New York legislature of 1851 passed a bill providing for a park on the east side of the island. Afterwards, the same legislature, precipitately and quite as an after-thought, passed the act under which the city took title to the site of the greater part of the present Central Park.

This final action is said to have been the result of a counter movement, started after the passage of the first bill merely to gratify a private grudge of one of the city aldermen.

When in the formation of the counter project, the question was reached, what land shall be named in the second bill, the originator turned to a map and asked: "*Now where shall I go?*" His comrade, looking over his shoulder, without a moment's reflection, put his finger down and said, "*Go* there;" the point indicated appearing to be about the middle of the island, and therefore, as it occurred to him, one which would least excite local prejudices.

The primary selection of the site was thus made in an off-hand way, by a man who had no special responsibility in the premises, and whose previous studies had not at all led him to be well informed or interested in the purposes of a park.

It would have been difficult to find another body of land of six hundred acres upon the island (unless by taking a long narrow strip upon the precipitous side of a ridge), which possessed less of what we have seen to be the most desirable characteristics of a park, or upon which more time, labor, and expense would be required to establish them.

But besides the topographical objections, when the work of providing suitable facilities for the recreation of the people upon this ground came to be practically and definitely considered, defects of outline were discerned, the incomplete remedy for which has since cost the city more than a million of dollars. The amount which intelligent study would have saved in this way if applied at the outset, might have provided for an amplification of some one of the approaches to the Park, such as, if it were now possible to be gained at a cost of two or three million dollars, I am confident would, if fairly set forth, be ordered by an almost unanimous vote of the tax-payers of the city. Public discussion at the time utterly failed to set this blundering right. Nor was public opinion then clearly dissatisfied with what was done or with those who did it.

During the following six years there was much public and private discussion of park questions; but the progress of public opinion, judged simply by the standard which it has since formed for itself, seems to have been chiefly backward.

This may be, to a considerable degree, accounted for by the fact that many men of wealth and influence—who, through ignorance and lack of mature reflection on this subject, were unable to anticipate any personal advantage from the construction of a park—feared that it would only add to their taxes, and thus were led to form a habit of crying down any hopeful anticipations.

The argument that certain towns of the old country did obtain some advantage from their parks, could not be refuted, but it was easy to say, and it was said, that "our circumstances are very different: surrounded by broad waters on all sides, open to the sea breezes, we need no artificial breathing-places; even if we did, nothing like the parks of the old cities under aristocratic government would be at all practicable here."

This assertion made such an impression as to lead many to believe that little more had better be done than to give the name of park to the ground which it was now too late to avoid taking. A leading citizen suggested that nothing more was necessary than to plough up a strip just within the boundary of the ground and plant it with young trees, and chiefly with cuttings of the poplar, which afterwards, as they came to good size, could be transplanted to the interior, and thus the Park would be furnished economically and quite well enough for the purposes it would be required to serve.

Another of distinguished professional reputation seriously urged through the public press, that the ground should be rented as a sheep-walk. In going to and from their folds the flocks would be sure to form trails which would serve the public perfectly well for foot-paths; nature would in time supply whatever else was essential to form a quite picturesque and perfectly suitable strolling ground for such as would wish to resort to it.

It was frequently alleged, and with truth, that the use made of the existing public grounds was such as to develop riotous and licentious habits. A large park, it was argued, would inevitably present larger opportunities, and would be likely to exhibit an aggravated form of the same tendencies, consequently anything like refinement of treatment would be entirely wasted.

A few passages from a leading article of the "Herald" newspaper, in the seventh year of the enterprise, will indicate what estimate its astute editor had then formed of the prevailing convictions of the public on the subject: —"It is all folly to expect in this country to have parks like those in old aristocratic countries. When we open a public park Sam will air himself in it. He will take his friends whether from church, street, or elsewhere. He will knock down any better dressed man who remonstrates with him. He will talk and sing, and fill his share of the bench, and flirt with the nursery-maids in his own coarse way. Now we ask what chance have William B. Astor and Edward Everett against this fellow-citizen of theirs? Can they and he enjoy the same place? Is it not obvious that he will turn them out, and that the great Central Park will be nothing but a great bear-garden for the lowest denizens of the city, of which we shall yet pray litanies to be delivered.

In the same article it was argued that the effect of the construction of the Park would be unfavorable to the value of property in its neighborhood, except as, to a limited extent, it might be taken up by Irish and German liquor dealers as sites for dram-shops and lager-bier gardens. There were many eminent citizens, who to my personal knowledge, in the sixth, seventh, and eighth year after the passage of the act, entertained similar views to those I have quoted.

I have been asked if I supposed that "gentlemen" would ever resort to the Park, or would allow their wives and daughters to visit it? I heard a renowned lawyer argue that it was preposterous to suppose that a police force would do anything toward preserving order and decency in any broad piece of ground open to the general public of New York. And after the work began, I often heard the conviction expressed that if what was called the reckless, extravagant, inconsiderate policy of those who had the making of the Park in charge, could not be arrested, the weight of taxation and the general disgust which would be aroused among the wealthy classes would drive them from the city, and thus prove a serious injury to its prosperity.

"Why," said one, a man whom you all know by reputation, and many personally, "I should not ask for anything finer in my private grounds for the use of my own family." To whom it was replied that possibly grounds might not unwisely be prepared even more carefully when designed for the use of two hundred thousand families and their guests, than when designed for the use of one.

The constantly growing conviction that it was a rash and ill-considered undertaking, and the apprehension that a great deal would be spent upon it for no good purpose, doubtless had something to do with the choice of men, who in the sixth year were appointed by the Governor of the State, commissioners to manage the work and the very extraordinary powers given them. At all events, it so happened that a majority of them were much better known from their places in the directory of banks, railroads, mining, and manufacturing enterprises, than from their previous services in politics; and their freedom to follow their own judgment and will, in respect to all the interior matters of the Park, was larger than had for a long time been given to any body of men charged with a public duty of similar importance.

I suppose that few of them knew or cared more about the subject of their duties at the time of their appointment, than most other active businessmen. They probably embodied very fairly the average opinion of the public, as to the way in which it was desirable that the work should be managed. If, then, it is asked, how did they come to adopt and resolutely pursue a course so very different from that which the public opinion seemed to expect of them, I think that the answer must be found in the fact that they had not wanted or asked the appointment; that it was made absolutely free from any condition or obligation to serve a party, a faction, or a person; that owing to the extraordinary powers given them, their sense of responsibility in the matter was of an uncommonly simple and direct character, and led them with the trained skill of business men to go straight to the question:—

"Here is a piece of property put into our hands. By what policy can we turn it to the best account for our stockholders?"

It has happened that instead of being turned out about the time they had got to know something about their special business, these commissioners have been allowed to remain in office to this time—a period of twelve years. As to their method of work, it was as like as possible to that of a board of directors of a commercial corporation. They quite set at defiance the ordinary ideas of propriety applied to public servants, by holding their sessions with closed doors, their clerk being directed merely to supply the newspapers with reports of their acts. They spent the whole of the first year on questions simply of policy, organization, and plan, doing no practical work, as it was said, at all.

When the business of construction was taken hold of, they refused to occupy themselves personally with questions of the class which in New York usually take up nine tenths of the time and mind of all public servants, who have it in their power to arrange contracts and determine appointments, promotions, and discharges. All of these they turned over to the heads of the executive operations.

Now, when these deviations from usage were conjoined with the adoption of a policy of construction for which the public was entirely unprepared, and to which the largest tax-payers of the city were strongly opposed, when also those who had a variety of private axes to grind, found themselves and their influence, and their friends' influence, made nothing of by the commissioners, you may be sure that public opinion was manufactured against them at a great rate. The Mayor denounced them in his messages; the Common Council and other departments of the city government refused to cooperate with them, and were frequently induced to put obstructions in their way; they were threatened with impeachment and indictment; some of the city newspapers attacked them for a time in every issue; they were caricatured and lampooned; their session was once broken up by a mob, their business was five times examined (once or twice at great expense, lawyers, accountants, engineers, and other experts being employed for the purpose) by legislative investigating committees. Thus for a time public opinion, through nearly all the channels open to it, apparently set against them like a torrent.

No men less strong, and no men less confident in their strength than these men—by virtue in part of personal character, in part of the extraordinary powers vested in them by the legislature, and in part by the accident of certain anomalous political circumstances—happened to be, could have carried through a policy and a method which commanded so little immediate public favor. As it was, nothing but personal character, the common impression that after all they were honest, saved them. By barely a saber's length they kept ahead of their pursuers, and of this you may still see evidence here and there in the park, chiefly where something left to stop a gap for the time being has been suffered to remain as if a permanence. At one time nearly four thousand laborers were employed; and for a year at one point, work went on night and day in order to put it as quickly as possible beyond the reach of those who were bent on stopping it. Necessarily, under such circumstances, the rule obtains: "Look out for the main chance; we may save the horses, we must save the guns"; and if now you do not find everything in perfect parade order, the guns, at all events, were saved.

To fully understand the significance of the result so far, it must be considered that the Park is to this day, at some points, incomplete; that from the centre of population to the midst of the Park the distance is still four miles; that there is no steam transit; that other means of communication are indirect and excessively uncomfortable, or too expensive. For practical everyday purposes to the great mass of the people, the Park might as well be a hundred miles away. There are hundreds of thousands who have never seen it, more hundreds of thousands who have seen it only on a Sunday or holiday. The children of the city to whom it should be of the greatest use, can only get to it on holidays or in vacations, and then must pay car-fare both ways.

It must be remembered, also, that the Park is not planned for such use as is now made of it, but with regard to the future use, when it will be in the centre of a population of two millions hemmed in by water at a short distance on all sides; and that much of the work done upon it is, for this reason, as yet quite barren of results.

The question of the relative value of what is called off-hand common sense, and of special, deliberate, business-like study, must be settled in the case of the Central Park, by a comparison of benefit with cost. During the last four years over thirty million visits have been made to the Park by actual count, and many have passed uncounted. From fifty to eighty thousand persons on foot, thirty thousand in carriages, and four to five thousand on horseback, have frequently entered it in a day.

Among the frequent visitors, I have found all those who, a few years ago, believed it impossible that there should ever be a park in this republican country,—and especially in New York of all places in this country,—which would be a suitable place of resort for "gentlemen." They, their wives and daughters, frequent the Park more than they do the opera or the church.

There are many men of wealth who resort to the Park habitually and regularly, as much so as business men to their places of business. Of course, there is a reason for it, and a reason based upon their experience.

As to the effect on public health, there is no question that it is already great. The testimony of the older physicians of the city will be found unanimous on this point. Says one: "Where I formerly ordered patients of a certain class to give up their business altogether and go out of town, I now often advise simply moderation, and prescribe a ride in the Park before going to their offices, and again a drive with their families before dinner. By simply adopting this course as a habit, men who have been breaking down frequently recover tone rapidly, and are able to retain an active and controlling influence in an important business, from which they would have otherwise been forced to retire. I direct school-girls, under certain circumstances, to be taken wholly, or in part, from their studies, and sent to spend several hours a day rambling on foot in the Park."

The lives of women and children too poor to be sent to the country, can now be saved in thousands of instances, by making them go to the Park. During a hot day in July last, I counted at one time in the Park eighteen separate groups, consisting of mothers with their children, most of whom were under school-age, taking picnic dinners which they had brought from home with them. The practice is increasing under medical advice, especially when summer complaint is rife.

The much greater rapidity with which patients convalesce, and may be returned with safety to their ordinary occupations after severe illness, when they can be sent to the Park for a few hours a day, is beginning to be understood. The addition thus made to the productive labor of the city is not unimportant.

The Park, moreover, has had a very marked effect in making the city attractive to visitors, and in thus increasing its trade, and causing many who have made fortunes elsewhere to take up their residence and become taxpayers in it,—a much greater effect in this way, beyond all question, than all the colleges, schools, libraries, museums, and art-galleries which the city possesses. It has also induced many foreigners who have grown rich in the country, and who would otherwise have gone to Europe to enjoy their wealth, to settle permanently in the city. And what has become of the great Bugaboo? This is what the "Herald" of later date answers:—

"When one is inclined to despair of the country, let him go to the Central Park on a Saturday, and spend a few hours there in looking at the people, not at those who come in gorgeous carriages, but at those who arrive on foot, or in those exceedingly democratic conveyances, the street-cars; and if, when the sun begins to sink behind the trees, he does not arise and go homeward with a happy swelling heart," and so on, the effusion winding up thus: "We regret to say that the more brilliant becomes the display of vehicles and toilettes, the more shameful is the display of bad manners on the part of the—extremely fine-looking people who ride in carriages and wear the fine dresses. We must add that the pedestrians always behave well."

Here we touch a fact of more value to social science than any other in the history of the Park; but to fully set it before you would take an evening by itself. The difficulty of preventing ruffianism and disorder in a park to be frequented indiscriminately by such a population as that of New York, was from the first regarded as the greatest of all those which the commission had to meet, and the means of overcoming it cost more study than all other things.

It is, perhaps, too soon to judge of the value of the expedients resorted to, but there are as yet a great many parents who are willing to trust their school-girl daughters to ramble without special protection in the Park, as they would almost nowhere else in New York. One is no more likely to see ruffianism or indecencies in the Park than in the churches, and the arrests for offenses of all classes, including the most venial, which arise simply from the ignorance of country people, have amounted to but twenty in the million of the number of visitors, and of these, an exceedingly small proportion have been of that class which was so confidently expected to take possession of the Park and make it a place unsafe and unfit for decent people.

There is a good deal of delicate work on the Park, some of it placed there by private liberality—much that a girl with a parasol, or a boy throwing a pebble, could render valueless in a minute. Except in one or two cases where the ruling policy of the management has been departed from,—cases which prove the rule,—not the slightest injury from wantonness, carelessness, or ruffianism has occurred.

Jeremy Bentham, in treating of "The Means of Preventing Crimes," remarks that any innocent amusement that the human heart can invent is useful under a double point of view: first, for the pleasure itself which results from it; second, from its tendency to weaken the dangerous inclinations which man derives from his nature.

No one who has closely observed the conduct of the people who visit the Park, can doubt that it exercises a distinctly harmonizing and refining influence upon the most unfortunate and most lawless classes of the city,—an influence favorable to courtesy, self-control, and temperance.

At three or four points in the midst of the Park, beer, wine, and cider are sold with other refreshments to visitors, not at bars, but served at tables where men sit in company with women. Whatever harm may have resulted, it has apparently had the good effect of preventing the establishment of drinking-places on the borders of the Park, these not having increased in number since it was opened, as it was originally supposed they would.

I have never seen or heard of a man or woman the worse for liquor taken at the Park, except in a few instances where visitors had brought it with them, and in which it had been drank secretly and unsocially. The present arrangements for refreshments I should say are temporary and imperfect.

Every Sunday in summer from thirty to forty thousand persons, on an average, enter the Park on foot, the number on a very fine day being sometimes nearly a hundred thousand. While most of the grog-shops of the city were effectually closed by the police under the Excise Law on Sunday, the number of visitors to the Park was considerably larger than before. There was no similar increase at the churches.

Shortly after the Park first became attractive, and before any serious attempt was made to interfere with the Sunday liquor trade, the head-keeper told me that he saw among the visitors the proprietor of one of the largest saloons in the city. He accosted him and expressed some surprise; the man replied, "I came to see what the devil you'd got here that took off so many of my Sunday customers."

I believe it may be justly inferred that the Park stands in competition with grog-shops and worse places, and not with the churches and Sunday-schools.

Land immediately about the Park, the frontage on it being seven miles in length, instead of taking the course anticipated by those opposed to the policy of the Commission, has advanced in value at the rate of two hundred per cent. per annum.

The cost of forming the Park, owing to the necessity of overcoming the special difficulties of the locality by extraordinary expedients, has been very great ($5,000,000); but the interest on it would even now be fully met by a toll of three cents on visitors coming on foot, and six cents on all others; and it should be remembered that nearly every visitor in coming from a distance voluntarily pays much more than this for the privilege.

It is universally admitted, however, that the cost, including that of the original off-hand commonsense blunders, has been long since much more than compensated by the additional capital drawn to the city through the influence of the Park.

Finally, to come back to the question of worldly wisdom. As soon as the Park came fairly into use, public opinion began to turn, and in a few months faced square about. The commissioners have long since, by simple persistence in minding their own proper business, come to be by far the most popular men who have had to do with any civic affairs in the time of the present generation. They have been, indeed, almost uncomfortably popular, having had need occasionally to "lobby" off some of the responsibilities which there was an effort to put upon them.

A few facts will show you what the change in public opinion has been. When the commissioners began their work, six hundred acres of ground was thought by many of the friends of the enterprise to be too much, by none too little for all park purposes. Since the Park has come into use, the amount of land laid out and reserved for parks in the two principal cities on the bay of New York has been increased to more than three times that amount, the total reserve for parks alone now being about two thousand acres, and the public demand is now for more, not less. Twelve years ago there was almost no pleasure-driving in New York. There are now, at least, ten thousand horses kept for pleasure-driving. Twelve years ago there were no road-ways adapted to light carriages. There are now fourteen miles of rural drive within the parks complete and in use, and often crowded, and ground has been reserved in the two cities and their suburbs for fifty miles of park-ways, averaging, with their planted borders and inter-spaces, at least one hundred and fifty feet wide.

The land-owners had been trying for years to agree upon a new plan of roads for the upper part of Manhattan Island. A special commission of their own number had been appointed at their solicitation, but had utterly failed to harmonize conflicting interests. A year or two after the Park was opened, they went again to the Legislature and asked that the work might be put upon the Park Commissioners, which was done, giving them absolute control of the matter, and under them it has been arranged in a manner, which appears to be generally satisfactory, and has caused an enormous advance of the property of all those interested.

At the petition of the people of the adjoining counties, the field of the commissioners' operations has been extended over their territory, and their scheme of trunk-ways for pleasure-driving, riding, and walking has thus already been carried far out into what are still perfectly rural districts.

On the west side of the harbor there are other commissioners forming plans for extending a similar system thirty or forty miles back in to the country, and the Legislature of New Jersey has a bill before it for laying out another park of seven hundred acres.

In speaking of parks I have not had in mind the private enterprises, of which there are several. One of the very men who, twelve years ago, thought that any one who pretended that the people of New York wanted a park must be more knave than fool, has himself lately devoted one hundred and fifty acres of his private property to a park designed for public use, and simply as a commercial operation, to improve the adjoining property.

I could enforce the chief lesson of this history from other examples at home and abroad. I could show you that where parks have been laid out and managed in a temporary, off-hand, common-sense way, it has proved a penny-wise pound-foolish way, injurious to the property in their neighborhood. I could show you more particularly how the experience of New York, on the other hand, has been repeated over the river in Brooklyn.

But I have already held you too long. I hope that I have fully satisfied you that this problem of public recreation grounds is one which, from its necessary relation to the larger problem of the future growth of hour honored city, should at once be made a subject of responsibility of a very definite, very exacting, and, consequently, very generous character. In no other way can it be adequately dealt with.

The Life of the Street Rats, from The Dangerous Classes of New York and Twenty Years' Work Among Them, *Charles Loring Brace (1872)*

Charles Loring Brace was born into a prominent Hartford, Connecticut, family in 1826. He graduated from Yale University in 1846 and later attended both Yale Divinity School and Union Theological Seminary in New York City. While in New York, Brace began working with homeless, uneducated street youth and in 1853 was one of the founders of the Children's Aid Society; he remained as its executive officer for the next thirty-seven years. During that time, Brace came to be acknowledged as one of the world's leading experts on child welfare and social reform. He described his efforts in his 1872 book *The Dangerous Classes of New York and Twenty Years' Work Among Them.*

Most significant and controversial among Brace's efforts was his establishment of the "Orphan Trains." Brace argued against the institutionalization of street "Arabs" into orphan asylums and devised a plan whereby agents of the Children's Aid Society would assemble children into groups ranging from 6 to 150 and transport them by rail to the Midwest and South, where they would be taken in by families. These trains left three times a month from 1854 until 1929 and moved an estimated two hundred thousand children off the streets of New York. Critics of Brace pointed to the fact that oftentimes the Catholic children were sent to Protestant homes and that screening of foster parents was substandard. When he died in 1890, Brace was regarded as "the most influential child saver of the nineteenth century."

THE intensity of the American temperament is felt in every fibre of these children of poverty and vice. Their crimes have the unrestrained and sanguinary character of a race accustomed to overcome all obstacles. They rifle a bank, where English thieves pick a pocket; they murder, where European proletaires cudgel or fight with fists; in a riot, they begin what seems about to be the sacking of a city, where English rioters would merely batter policemen, or smash lamps. The "dangerous classes" of New York are mainly American-born, but the children of Irish and German immigrants. . . .

There are thousands on thousands in New York who have no assignable home, and "flirt" from attic to attic, and cellar to cellar; there are other thousands more or less connected with criminal enterprises; and still other tens of thousands, poor, hard-pressed, and depending for daily bread on the day's earnings, swarming in tenement-houses, who behold the gilded rewards of toil all about them, but are never permitted to touch them.

All these great masses of destitute, miserable, and criminal persons believe that for ages the rich have had all the good things of life, while to them have been left the evil things. Capital to them is the tyrant.

Let but Law lift its hand from them for a season, or let the civilizing influences of American life fail to reach them, and, if the opportunity offered, we should see an explosion from this class which might leave this city in ashes and blood.

Seventeen years ago, my attention had been called to the extraordinarily degraded condition of the children in a district lying on the west side of the city, between Seventeenth and Nineteenth Streets, and the Seventh and Tenth Avenues. A certain block, called "Misery Row," in Tenth Avenue, was the main seed-bed of crime and poverty in the quarter, and was also invariably a "fever-nest." Here the poor obtained wretched rooms at a comparatively low rent; these they sublet, and thus, in little, crowded, close tenements, were herded men, women and children of all ages. The parents were invariably given to hard drinking, and the children were sent out to beg or to steal. Besides them, other children, who were orphans, or who had run away from drunkards' homes, or had been working on the canal-boats that discharged on the docks near by, drifted into the quarter, as if attracted by the atmosphere of crime and laziness that prevailed in the neighborhood. These slept around the breweries of the ward, or on the hay-barges, or in the old sheds of Eighteenth and Nineteenth Streets. They were mere children, and kept life together by all sorts of street-jobs—helping the brewery laborers, blackening boots, sweeping sidewalks, "smashing baggages" (as they called it), and the like. Herding together, they soon began to form an unconscious society for vagrancy and idleness. Finding that work brought but poor pay, they tried shorter roads to getting money by petty thefts, in which they were very adroit. Even if they earned a considerable sum by a lucky day's job, they quickly spent it in gambling, or for some folly.

The police soon knew them as "street-rats"; but, like the rats, they were too quick and cunning to be often caught in their petty plunderings, so they gnawed away at the foundations of society undisturbed.

From The Age of Innocence, *Edith Wharton (1920)*

Edith Wharton was born in 1862 into New York high society. She spent most of her adult life chronicling that world in more than forty books, including *The House of Mirth* (1905) and *The Age of Innocence* (1920), for which she was the first female recipient of the Pulitzer Prize. In 1923 she also became the first woman to receive a Doctor of Letters from Yale University. A loveless marriage begun in 1885 (which ended in divorce in 1913) and an aversion to the crass materialism of Gilded Age New York led her to leave the United States in 1907 and take refuge in France. With the exception of two visits in 1913 and 1923, she remained there until her death in 1937.

Wharton's work described the stifling, suffocating atmosphere of social convention that hung over the inhabitants of "old New York" society and the crushing sadness that resulted from adherence to the code of that world. Wharton's life was, in many ways, an attempt to find an exit or a stay from this world. Even her habits of writing reflected an attempt to insulate herself. She wrote daily and produced a volume a year from 1902 on. R. W. B. Lewis noted that her favorite place to write was the bedroom and that "her breakfast was brought to her by Gross, the housekeeper, who almost alone was privy to this innocent secret of the bedchamber. A secretary picked up the pages from the floor for typing." Wharton's friend Henry James noted that "no one fully knows our Edith who hasn't seen her in the act of creating a habitation of herself."

THAT evening, after Mr. Jackson had taken himself away, and the ladies had retired to their chintz-curtained bedroom, Newland Archer mounted thoughtfully to his own study. A vigilant hand had, as usual, kept the fire alive and the lamp trimmed; and the room, with its rows and rows of books, its bronze and steel statuettes of "The Fencers" on the mantelpiece and its many photographs of famous pictures, looked singularly home-like and welcoming.

As he dropped into his armchair near the fire his eyes rested on a large photograph of May Welland, which the young girl had given him in the first days of their romance, and which had now displaced all the other portraits on the table. With a new sense of awe he looked at the frank forehead, serious eyes and gay innocent mouth of the young creature whose soul's custodian he was to be. That terrifying product of the social system he belonged to and believed in, the young girl who knew nothing and expected everything, looked back at him like a stranger through May Welland's familiar features; and once more it was borne in on him that marriage was not the safe anchorage he had been taught to think, but a voyage on uncharted seas.

The case of the Countess Olenska had stirred up old settled convictions and set them drifting dangerously through his mind. His own exclamation: "Women should be free—as free as we are," struck to the root of a problem that it was agreed in his world to regard as nonexistent. "Nice" women, however wronged, would never claim the kind of freedom he meant, and generous-minded men like himself were therefore—in the heat of argument—the more chivalrously ready to concede it to them. Such verbal generosities were in fact only a humbugging disguise of the inexorable conventions that tied things together and bound people down to the old pattern. But here he was pledged to defend, on the part of his betrothed's cousin, conduct that, on his own wife's part, would justify him in calling down on her all the thunders of Church and State. Of course the dilemma was purely hypothetical; since he wasn't a blackguard Polish nobleman, it was absurd to speculate what his wife's rights would be if he *were*. But Newland Archer was too imaginative not to feel that, in his case and May's, the tie might gall for reasons far less gross and palpable. What could he and she really know of each other, since it was his duty, as a "decent" fellow, to conceal his past from her, and hers, as a marriageable girl, to have no past to conceal? What if, for some one of the subtler reasons that would tell with both of them, they should tire of each other, misunderstand or irritate each other? He reviewed his friends' marriages—the supposedly happy ones—and saw none that answered, even remotely, to the passionate and tender comradeship which he pictured as his permanent relation with May Welland. He perceived that such a picture presupposed, on her part, the experience, the versatility, the freedom of judgment, which she had been carefully trained not to possess; and with a shiver of foreboding he saw his marriage becoming what most of the other marriages about him were: a dull association of material and social interests held together by ignorance on the one side and hypocrisy on the other. Lawrence Lefferts occurred to him as the husband who had most completely realised this enviable ideal. As became the high-priest of form, he had formed a wife so completely to his own convenience that, in the most conspicuous moments of his frequent love-affairs with other men's wives, she went about in smiling unconsciousness, saying that "Lawrence was so frightfully strict"; and had been known to blush indignantly, and avert her gaze, when some one alluded in her presence to the fact that Julius Beaufort (as became a "foreigner" of doubtful origin) had what was known in New York as "another establishment."

Archer tried to console himself with the thought that he was not quite such an ass as Larry Lefferts, nor May such a simpleton as poor Gertrude; but the difference was after all one of intelligence and not of standards. In reality they all lived in a kind of hieroglyphic world, where the real thing was never said or done or even thought, but only represented by a set of arbitrary signs; as when Mrs. Welland, who knew exactly why Archer had pressed her to announce her daughter's engagement at the Beaufort ball (and had indeed expected him to do no less), yet felt obliged to simulate reluctance, and the air of having had her hand forced, quite as, in the books on Primitive Man that people of advanced culture were beginning to read, the savage bride is dragged with shrieks from her parents' tent.

The result, of course, was that the young girl who was the centre of this elaborate system of mystification remained the more inscrutable for her very frankness and assurance. She was frank, poor darling, because she had nothing to conceal, assured because she knew of nothing to be on her guard against; and with no better preparation than this, she was to be plunged overnight into what people evasively called "the facts of life."

The young man was sincerely but placidly in love. He delighted in the radiant good looks of his betrothed, in her health, her horsemanship, her grace and quickness at games, and the shy interest in books and ideas that she was beginning to develop under his guidance. (She had advanced far enough to join him in ridiculing the Idyls of the King, but not to feel the beauty of Ulysses and the Lotus Eaters.) She was straightforward, loyal and brave; she had a sense of humour (chiefly proved by her laughing at *his* jokes); and he suspected, in the depths of her innocently-gazing soul, a glow of feeling that it would be a joy to waken. But when he had gone the brief round of her he returned discouraged by the thought that all this frankness and innocence were only an artificial product. Untrained human nature was not frank and innocent; it was full of the twists and defences of an instinctive guile. And he felt himself oppressed by this creation of factitious purity, so cunningly manufactured by a conspiracy of mothers and aunts and grandmothers and long-dead ancestresses, because it was supposed to be what he wanted, what he had a right to, in order that he might exercise his lordly pleasure in smashing it like an image made of snow.

There was a certain triteness in these reflections: they were those habitual to young men on the approach of their wedding day. But they were generally accompanied by a sense of compunction and self-abasement of which Newland Archer felt no trace. He could not deplore (as Thackeray's heroes so often exasperated him by doing) that he had not a blank page to offer his bride in exchange for the unblemished one she was to give to him. He could not get away from the fact that if he had been brought up as she had they would have been no more fit to find their way about than the Babes in the Wood; nor could he, for all his anxious cogitations, see any honest reason (any, that is, unconnected with his own momentary pleasure, and the passion of masculine vanity) why his bride should not have been allowed the same freedom of experience as himself.

Such questions, at such an hour, were bound to drift through his mind; but he was conscious that their uncomfortable persistence and precision were due to the inopportune arrival of the Countess Olenska. Here he was, at the very moment of his betrothal—a moment for pure thoughts and cloudless hopes—pitchforked into a coil of scandal which raised all the special problems he would have preferred to let lie. "Hang Ellen Olenska!" he grumbled, as he covered his fire and began to undress. He could not really see why her fate should have the least bearing on his; yet he dimly felt that he had only just begun to measure the risks of the championship which his engagement had forced upon him.

A few days later the bolt fell.

The Lovell Mingotts had sent out cards for what was known as "a formal dinner" (that is, three extra footmen, two dishes for each course, and a Roman punch in the middle), and had headed their invitations with the words "To meet the Countess Olenska," in accordance with the hospitable American fashion, which treats strangers as if they were royalties, or at least as their ambassadors.

The guests had been selected with a boldness and discrimination in which the initiated recognised the firm hand of Catherine the Great. Associated with such immemorial standbys as the Selfridge Merrys, who were asked everywhere because they always had been, the Beauforts, on whom there was a claim of relationship, and Mr. Sillerton Jackson and his sister Sophy (who went wherever her brother told her to), were some of the most fashionable and yet most irreproachable of the dominant "young married" set; the Lawrence Leffertses, Mrs. Lefferts Rushworth (the lovely widow), the Harry Thorleys, the Reggie Chiverses and young Morris Dagonet and his wife (who was a van der Luyden). The company indeed was perfectly assorted, since all the members belonged to the little inner group of people who, during the long New York season, disported themselves together daily and nightly with apparently undiminished zest.

Forty-eight hours later the unbelievable had happened; every one had refused the Mingotts' invitation except the Beauforts and old Mr. Jackson and his sister. The intended slight was emphasised by the fact that even the Reggie Chiverses, who were of the Mingott clan, were among those inflicting it; and by the uniform wording of the notes, in all of which the writers "regretted that they were unable to accept," without the mitigating plea of a "previous engagement" that ordinary courtesy prescribed.

New York society was, in those days, far too small, and too scant in its resources, for every one in it (including livery-stable-keepers, butlers and cooks) not to know exactly on which evenings people were free; and it was thus possible for the recipients of Mrs. Lovell Mingott's invitations to make cruelly clear their determination not to meet the Countess Olenska.

The blow was unexpected; but the Mingotts, as their way was, met it gallantly. Mrs. Lovell Mingott confided the case to Mrs. Welland, who confided it to Newland Archer; who, aflame at the outrage, appealed passionately and authoritatively to his mother; who, after a painful period of inward resistance and outward temporising, succumbed to his instances (as she always did), and immediately embracing his cause with an energy redoubled by her previous hesitations, put on her grey velvet bonnet and said: "I'll go and see Louisa van der Luyden."

The New York of Newland Archer's day was a small and slippery pyramid, in which, as yet, hardly a fissure had been made or a foothold gained. At its base was a firm foundation of what Mrs. Archer called "plain people"; an honorable but obscure majority of respectable families who (as in the case of the Spicers or the Leffertses or the Jacksons) had been raised above their level by marriage with one of the ruling clans. People, Mrs. Archer always said, were not as particular as they used to be; and with old Catherine Spicer ruling one end of Fifth Avenue, and Julius Beaufort the other, you couldn't expect the old traditions to last much longer.

Firmly narrowing upward from this wealthy but inconspicuous substratum was the compact and dominant group which the Mingotts, Newlands, Chiverses and Mansons so actively represented. Most people imagined them to be the very apex of the pyramid; but they themselves (at least those of

Mrs. Archer's generation) were aware that, in the eyes of the professional genealogist, only a still smaller number of families could lay claim to that eminence.

"Don't tell me," Mrs. Archer would say to her children, "all this modern newspaper rubbish about a New York aristocracy. If there is one, neither the Mingotts nor the Mansons belong to it; no, nor the Newlands or the Chiverses either. Our grandfathers and great-grandfathers were just respectable English or Dutch merchants, who came to the colonies to make their fortune, and stayed here because they did so well. One of your great-grandfathers signed the Declaration, and another was a general on Washington's staff, and received General Burgoyne's sword after the battle of Saratoga. These are things to be proud of, but they have nothing to do with rank or class. New York has always been a commercial community, and there are not more than three families in it who can claim an aristocratic origin in the real sense of the word."

Mrs. Archer and her son and daughter, like every one else in New York, knew who these privileged beings were: the Dagonets of Washington Square, who came of an old English county family allied with the Pitts and Foxes; the Lannings, who had intermarried with the descendants of the first Dutch governor of Manhattan, and related by pre-Revolutionary marriages to several members of the French and British aristocracy.

The Lannings survived only in the person of two very old but lively Miss Lannings, who lived cheerfully and reminiscently among family portraits and Chippendale; the Dagonets were a considerable clan, allied to the best names in Baltimore and Philadelphia; but the van der Luydens, who stood above all of them, had faded into a kind of super-terrestrial twilight, from which only two figures impressively emerged; those of Mr. and Mrs. Henry van der Luyden.

Mrs. Henry van der Luyden had been Louisa Dagonet, and her mother had been the granddaughter of Colonel du Lac, of an old Channel Island family, who had fought under Cornwallis and had settled in Maryland, after the war, with his bride, Lady Angelica Trevenna, fifth daughter of the Earl of St. Austrey. The tie between the Dagonets, the du Lacs of Maryland, and their aristocratic Cornish kinsfolk, the Trevennas, had always remained close and cordial. Mr. and Mrs. van der Luyden had more than once paid long visits to the present head of the house of Trevenna, the Duke of St. Austrey, at his country-seat in Cornwall and at St. Austrey in Gloucestershire; and his Grace had frequently announced his intention of some day returning their visit (without the Duchess, who feared the Atlantic).

Mr. and Mrs. van der Luyden divided their time between Trevenna, their place in Maryland, and Skuytercliff, the great estate on the Hudson which had been one of the colonial grants of the Dutch government to the famous first Governor, and of which Mr. van der Luyden was still "Patroon." Their large solemn house in Madison Avenue was seldom opened, and when they came to town they received in it only their most intimate friends.

"I wish you would go with me, Newland," his mother said, suddenly pausing at the door of the Brown *coupé*. "Louisa is fond of you; and of course it's on account of dear May that I'm taking this step—and also because, if we don't all stand together, there'll be no such thing as Society left."

Sandhog, from My Life and Loves, *Frank Harris (1922)*

Frank Harris's biography reads like a piece of fiction, and his biographers have never been able to sort out the truth from the legend. Even his place of birth (either Brighton, England, or Galway, Ireland) and his name (James or Frank) seem to be in question. "Modesty," Harris claimed, was "the fig leaf of mediocrity." As a result, his recollection, written years later, contains numerous errors but remains one of the few accounts of the men who actually worked on the Brooklyn Bridge.

Harris sailed for America in 1871 when he was only fifteen. He worked as a sandhog on the Brooklyn Bridge, was managing a hotel in Chicago two years later, worked as a cattle rustler across the Rio Grande, and was admitted to the Kansas bar in 1875. He claimed to have shaken Walt Whitman's hand after a lecture and to have visited Emerson in Concord.

Harris joined the Philology Department of Heidelberg University in 1878 but was expelled for "knocking down an insulting student with his fist." In 1884 he gained the editorship of the London *Evening News;* by adapting William Randolph Hearst's yellow journalism techniques, he turned the troubled paper around. In the 1890s he edited both the *Fortnightly Review* and the *Saturday Review* in London. He employed George Bernard Shaw as his drama critic, fostered the career of H. G. Wells, and published Oscar Wilde. He was a man of gargantuan appetite; John Dos Passos reported that "he had taken to using the stomach pump after meals as a substitute for the Roman vomitorium." Harris chronicled all of this in his 1922 memoir, *My Life and Loves.* He died in Nice in 1931 of a heart attack.

The Brooklyn Bridge, the technological marvel of its age, was the inspiration of John Augustus Roebling, who proposed his plan for an "East River Bridge" to *Brooklyn Eagle* publisher William C. Kingsley in 1867. Born in Germany and a favorite student of the philosopher G. W. F. Hegel, Roebling oversaw only the beginning stages of construction before his death in 1869. The task of completion fell to his thirty-two-year-old son, Washington, who became incapacitated with the bends after coming up from inspecting one of the caissons in 1872. Washington Roebling supervised the rest of the construction from his room on Columbia Heights in Brooklyn and relayed instructions to workers through his wife, Emily. The bridge opened to enormous fanfare on May 24, 1883, with Governor Grover Cleveland and President Chester A. Arthur in attendance.

MIKE had a day off, so he came home for dinner at noon and he had great news. They wanted men to work under water in the iron caissons of Brooklyn Bridge and they were giving from five to ten dollars a day.

"Five dollars," cried Mrs. Mulligan. "It must be dangerous or unhealthy or somethin'—sure, you'd never put the child to work like that."

Mike excused himself, but the danger, if danger there was, appealed to me almost as much as the big pay: my only fear was that they'd think me too small or too young. I had told Mrs. Mulligan I was sixteen, for I didn't want to be treated as a child. . . .

Next morning Mike took me to Brooklyn Bridge soon after five o'clock to see the contractor; he wanted to engage Mike at once but shook his head over me. "Give me a trial," I pleaded; "you'll see I'll make good." After a pause, "O.K.," he said; "four shifts have gone down already underhanded: you may try."

In the bare shed where we got ready, the men told me no one could do the work for long without getting the "bends"; the "bends" were a sort of convulsive fit that twisted one's body like a knot and often made you an invalid for life. They soon explained the whole procedure to me. We worked, it appeared, in a huge bell-shaped caisson of iron that went to the bottom of the river and was pumped full of compressed air to keep the water from entering it from below: the top of the caisson is a room called the "material chamber," into which the stuff dug out of the river passes up and is carted away. On the side of the caisson is another room, called the "air-lock," into which we were to go to be "compressed." As the compressed air is admitted, the blood keeps absorbing the gasses of the air till the tension of the gasses in the blood becomes equal to that in the air: When this equilibrium has been reached, men can work in the caisson for hours without serious discomfort, if sufficient pure air is constantly pumped in. It was the foul air that did the harm, it appeared. "If they'd pump in good air, it would be O.K.; but that would cost a little time and trouble, and men's lives are cheaper." I saw that the men wanted to warn me, thinking I was too young, and accordingly I pretended to take little heed.

When we went into the "air-lock" and they turned on one air-lock after another of compressed air, the men put their hands to their ears and I soon imitated them, for the pain was very acute. Indeed, the drums of the ears are often driven in and burst if the compressed air is brought in too quickly. I found that the best way of meeting the pressure was to keep swallowing air and forcing it up into the middle ear, where it acted as an air-pad on the innerside of the drum. . . .

When the air was fully compressed, the door of the air-lock opened at a touch and we all went down to work with pick and shovel on the gravelly bottom. My headache soon became acute. The six of us were working naked to the waist in a small iron chamber with a temperature of about 80° Fahrenheit: in five minutes the sweat was pouring from us, and all the while we were standing in icy water that was only kept from rising by the terrific air pressure. No wonder the headaches were blinding. The men didn't work for more than ten minutes at a time, but I plugged on steadily, resolved to prove myself and get constant employment; only one man, a Swede named Anderson, worked at all as hard.

The amount done each week was estimated, he told me, by an inspector. Anderson was known to the contractor and received half a wage extra as head of our gang. He assured me I could stay as long as I liked, but he advised me to leave at the end of a month: it was too unhealthy: above all, I mustn't drink and should spend all my spare time in the open. He was kindness itself to me, as indeed were all the others. After two hours' work down below we went up into the air-lock room to get gradually "decompressed," the pressure of air in our veins having to be brought down gradually to the usual air pressure. The men began to put on their clothes and passed round a bottle of schnapps; but though I was soon as cold as a wet rat and felt depressed and weak to boot, I would not touch the liquor. In the shed above I took a cupful of hot cocoa with Anderson, which stopped the shivering, and I was soon able to face the afternoon's ordeal.

For three or four days things went fairly well with me, but on the fifth day or sixth we came on a spring of water, or "gusher," and were wet to the waist before the air pressure could be increased to cope with it. As a consequence, a dreadful pain shot through both my ears: I put my hands to them tight and sat still for a little while. Fortunately, the shift was almost over and Anderson came with me to the horse-car. "You'd better knock off," he said. "I've known 'em go deaf from it."

Mrs. Mulligan saw at once something was wrong and made me try her household remedy—a roasted onion cut in two and clapped tight on each ear with a flannel bandage. It acted like magic: in ten minutes I was free of pain; then she poured in a little warm sweet oil and in an hour I was walking in the park as usual. Still, the fear of deafness was on me and I was very glad when Anderson told me he had complained to the boss and we were to get an extra thousand feet of pure air. It would make a great difference, Anderson said, and he was right, but the improvement was not sufficient.

One day, just as the "decompression" of an hour and a half was ending, an Italian named Manfredi fell down and writhed about, knocking his face on the floor till the blood spurted from his nose and mouth. When we got him into the shed, his legs were twisted like plaited hair. The surgeon had him taken to the hospital. I made up my mind that a month would be enough for me.

Selected Writings by Henry George (1879, 1883)

During his lifetime, Henry George may well have been the third most famous man in America, surpassed only by Thomas Edison and Mark Twain. George was born in Philadelphia in 1839 and completed only five months of secondary school before shipping out as a cabin boy when he was fourteen. He ended up in San Francisco in 1866, where he worked as a reporter and typesetter for the *San Francisco Times.*

George burst on the national political and economic scene in 1879 with his masterpiece, *Progress and Poverty;* the book was a worldwide sensation. John Dewey stated that George was "one of a small number of definitely original social philosophers that the world has produced." Albert Einstein lamented that "men like Henry George are rare unfortunately. One cannot imagine a more beautiful combination of intellectual keenness, artistic form, and fervent love of justice." The deluge of interest in George's ideas, especially his notion of a single land tax, led him to move to New York in 1880, from where he launched a national and international speaking tour.

Upon his return, George was urged by labor leaders to enter the mayoral election of 1886. In one of the city's most dramatic elections, and amid widespread claims of fraud, George ran second to the Democratic candidate, Abram Hewitt, but ahead of the Republican candidate, Theodore Roosevelt. George then devoted his time to writing and to forming local "single tax clubs" throughout the country. In 1897, however, already in ill health, George was persuaded to seek the mayoralty again. In an exhausting campaign, George died four days before the election.

His funeral procession drew over one hundred thousand people, the largest since Abraham Lincoln's. On his tombstone in Greenwood Cemetery in Brooklyn are the words, "The truth that I have tried to make clear will not find easy acceptance. If that could be, it would have been accepted long ago. If that could be, it would never have been obscured."

From *Progress and Poverty* (1879)

THE PROBLEM

IN all our investigation we have been advancing to this simple truth: That as land is necessary to the exertion of labor in the production of wealth, to command the land which is necessary to labor, is to command all the fruits of labor save enough to enable labor to exist. We have been advancing as through an enemy's country, in which every step must be secured, every position fortified, and every bypath explored; for this simple truth, in its application to social and political problems, is hid from the great masses of men partly by its very simplicity, and in greater part by widespread fallacies and erroneous habits of thought which lead them to look in every direction but the right one for an explanation of the evils which oppress and threaten the civilized world. And back of these elaborate fallacies and misleading theories is an active, energetic power, a power that in every country, be its political forms what they may, writes laws and molds thought—the power of a vast and dominant pecuniary interest.

But so simple and so clear is this truth, that to see it fully once is always to recognize it. There are pictures which, though looked at again and again, present only a confused labyrinth of lines or scroll work—a landscape, trees, or something of the kind—until once the attention is called to the fact that these things make up a face or a figure. This relation, once recognized, is always afterward clear.

It is so in this case. In the light of this truth all social facts group themselves in an orderly relation, and the most diverse phenomena are seen to spring from one great principle.

It is not in the relations of capital and labor; it is not in the pressure of population against subsistence, that an explanation of the unequal development of our civilization is to be found. The great cause of inequality in the distribution of wealth is inequality in the ownership of land. The ownership of land is the great fundamental fact which ultimately determines the social, the political, and consequently the intellectual and moral condition of a people. And it must be so. For land is the habitation of man, the storehouse upon which he must draw for all his needs, the material to which his labor must be applied for the supply of all his desires; for even the products of the sea cannot be taken, the light of the sun enjoyed, or any of the forces of nature utilized, without the use of land or its products. On the land we are born, from it we live, to it we return again—children of the soil as truly as is the blade of grass or the flower of the field. Take away from man all that belongs to land, and he is but a disembodied spirit. Material progress cannot rid us of our dependence upon land; it can but add to the power of producing wealth from land; and hence, when land is monopolized, it might go on to infinity without increasing wages or improving the condition of those who have but their labor. It can but add to the value of land and the power which its possession gives. Everywhere, in all times, among all peoples, the possession of land is the base of aristocracy, the foundation of great fortunes, the source of power. As said the Brahmins, ages ago—

"To whomsoever the soil at any time belongs, to him belong the fruits of it. White parasols and elephants mad with pride are the flowers of a grant of land."

THE REMEDY

POVERTY deepens as wealth increases, and wages are forced down while productive power grows, because land, which is the source of all wealth and the field of all labor, is monopolized. To extirpate poverty, to make wages what justice commands they should be, the full earnings of the laborer, we must therefore substitute for the individual ownership of land a common ownership.

The right of ownership that springs from labor excludes the possibility of any other right of ownership. If a man be rightfully entitled to the produce of his labor, then no one can be rightfully entitled to the ownership of anything which is not the produce of his labor, or the labor of some one else from whom the right has passed to him. For the right to the produce of labor cannot be enjoyed without the right to the free use of the opportunities offered by nature, and to admit the right of property in these is to deny the right of property in the produce of labor. When non-producers can claim as rent a portion of the wealth created by producers, the right of the producers to the fruits of their labor is to that extent denied.

A house and the lot on which it stands are alike property, as being the subject of ownership, and are alike classed by the lawyers as real estate. Yet in nature and relations they differ widely. The one is produced by human labor and belongs to the class in political economy styled wealth. The other is a part of nature, and belongs to the class in political economy styled land.

The essential character of the one class of things is that they embody labor, are brought into being by human exertion, their existence or non-existence, their increase or diminution, depending on man. The essential character of the other class of things is that they do not embody labor, and exist irrespective of human exertion and irrespective of man; they are the field or environment in which man finds himself; the storehouse from which his needs must be supplied, the raw material upon which, and the forces with which alone his labor can act.

The moment this distinction is realized, that moment is it seen that the sanction which natural justice gives to one species of property is denied to the other.

For as labor cannot produce without the use of land, the denial of the equal right to the use of land is necessarily the denial of the right of labor to its own produce. If one man can command the land upon which others must labor, he can appropriate the produce of their labor as the price of his permission to labor. The fundamental law of nature, that her enjoyment by man shall be consequent upon his exertion, is thus violated. The one receives without producing; the others produce without receiving. The one is unjustly enriched; the others are robbed.

Place one hundred men on an island from which there is no escape, and whether you make one of these men the absolute owner of the other ninety-nine, or the absolute owner of the soil of the island, will make no difference either to him or to them. In the one case, as the other, the one will be the absolute master of the ninety-nine—his power extending even to life and death, for simply to refuse them permission to live upon the island would be to force them into the sea.

Upon a larger scale, and through more complex relations, the same cause must operate in the same way and to the same end—the ultimate result, the enslavement of laborers, becoming apparent just as the pressure increases which compels them to live on and from land which is treated as the exclusive property of others.

Yet, it will be said: As every man has a right to the use and enjoyment of nature, the man who is using land must be permitted the exclusive right to its use in order that he may get the full benefit of his labor. But there is no difficulty in determining where the individual right ends and the common right begins. A delicate and exact test is supplied by *value,* and with its aid there is no difficulty, no matter how dense population may become, in determining and securing the exact rights of each, the equal rights of all.

The *value* of land, as we have seen, is the price of monopoly. It is not the absolute, but the relative, capability of land that determines its value. No matter what may be its intrinsic qualities, land that is no better than other land which may be had for the using can have no value. And the value of land always measures the difference between it and the best land that may be had for the using. Thus, the value of land expresses in exact and tangible form the right of the community in land held by an individual; and rent expresses the exact amount which the individual should pay to the community to satisfy the equal rights of all other members of the community.

Thus, if we concede to priority of possession the undisturbed use of land, taxing rent into the public treasury for the benefit of the community, we reconcile the fixity of tenure which is necessary for improvement with a full and complete recognition of the equal rights of all to the use of land.

Consider what rent is. It does not arise spontaneously from land; it is due to nothing that the land owners have done. It represents a *value created by the whole community.*

Let the land holders have, if you please, all that the possession of the land would give them in the absence of the rest of the community. But rent, the creation of the whole community, necessarily belongs to the whole community.

From *Social Problems* (1883)

SOCIAL PROBLEMS

In a simpler state master and man, neighbor and neighbor, know each other, and there is that touch of the elbow which, in times of danger, enables society to rally. But present tendencies are to the loss of this. In London, dwellers in one house do not know those in the next; the tenants of adjoining rooms are utter strangers to each other. Let civil conflict break or paralyze the authority that preserves order and the vast population would become a terror-stricken mob, without point of rally or principle of cohesion, and your London would be sacked and burned by an army of thieves. London is only the greatest of great cities. What is true of London is true of New York, and in the same measure true of the many cities whose hundreds of thousands are steadily growing toward millions. These vast aggregations of humanity, where he who seeks isolation may find it more truly than in the desert; where wealth and poverty touch and jostle; where one revels and another starves within a few feet of each other, yet separated by as great a gulf as that fixed between Dives in Hell and Lazarus in Abraham's bosom—they are centers and types of our civilization. Let jar or shock dislocate the complex and delicate organization, let the policeman's club be thrown down or wrested from him, and the fountains of the great deep are opened, and quicker than ever before chaos comes again. Strong as it may seem, our civilization is evolving destructive forces. Not desert and forest, but city slums and country roadsides are nursing the barbarians who may be to the new what Hun and Vandal were to the old.

The evils that begin to appear spring from the fact that the application of intelligence to social affairs has not kept pace with the application of intelligence to individual needs and material ends. Natural science strides forward, but political science lags. With all our progress in the arts which produce wealth, we have made no progress in securing its equitable distribution. Knowledge has vastly increased; industry and commerce have been revolutionized; but whether free trade or protection is best for a nation we are not yet agreed. We have brought machinery to a pitch of perfection that, fifty years ago, could not have been imagined; but, in the presence of political corruption, we seem as helpless as idiots. The East River bridge is a crowning triumph of mechanical skill; but to get it built a leading citizen of Brooklyn had to carry to New York sixty thousand dollars in a carpet-bag to bribe New York aldermen. The human soul that thought out the great bridge is prisoned in a crazed and broken body that lies bed-fast, and could only watch it grow by peering through a telescope. Nevertheless, the weight of the immense mass is estimated and adjusted for every inch. But the skill of the engineer could not prevent condemned wire being smuggled into the cable.

The progress of civilization requires that more and more intelligence be devoted to social affairs, and this not the intelligence of the few, but that of the many. We cannot safely leave politics to politicians, or political economy to college professors. The people themselves must think, because the people alone can act.

In a "journal of civilization" a professed teacher declares the saving word for society to be that each shall mind his own business. This is the gospel of selfishness, soothing as soft flutes to those who, having fared well themselves, think everybody should be satisfied. But the salvation of society, the hope for the free, full development of humanity, is in the gospel of brotherhood —the gospel of Christ. Social progress makes the well-being of all more and more the business of each; it binds all closer and closer together in bonds from which none can escape. He who observes the law and the proprieties, and cares for his family, yet takes no interest in the general weal, and gives no thought to those who are trodden under foot, save now and then to bestow alms, is not a true Christian. Nor is he a good citizen. The duty of the citizen is more and harder than this.

The intelligence required for the solving of social problems is not a mere thing of the intellect. It must be animated with the religious sentiment and warm with sympathy for human suffering. It must stretch out beyond self-interest, whether it be the self-interest of the few or the many. It must seek justice. For at the bottom of every social problem we will find a social wrong.

Vice-Buster, from Frauds Exposed, *Anthony Comstock (1880)*

On November 3, 1872, two feminists, Victoria Woodhull (the first woman to run for president of the United States) and Tennessee Claflin, were arrested for publishing a story about the purported affair between Henry Ward Beecher, famous Brooklyn minister, and Elizabeth Tilton, the wife of a parishioner. In 1914 Margaret Sanger was arraigned on eight counts of obscenity for publishing newspaper articles on birth control. These two incidents mark the bookends of the career of Anthony Comstock, who from 1872 to 1915 had ninety-seven people arrested for "advertising or selling abortifacients or indecent rubber articles, including contraceptives" and who seized 202,214 obscene pictures and photographs, 21,150 pounds of books, and 63,819 contraceptive devices and instruments used to enhance sexual pleasure. Comstock gave birth to a new word, *Comstockery*, which George Bernard Shaw defined as the "world's standing joke at the expense of the United States. It confirms the deep-seated conviction of the Old World that America really is a provincial place, and second-rate civilization after all."

Until 1872 Comstock had been a dry goods manager in New York City, but in that year he went to work for the YMCA's Committee for the Suppression of Vice. A year later, he succeeded in lobbying Congress for the passage of the what became known as the Comstock law, which made it a crime to advertise or mail "every . . . publication of indecent character" and also "any information for preventing conception or producing abortion." In 1874 that committee became the New York Society for the Suppression of Vice (NYSSV), with Comstock as its main investigator. Comstock was a federal agent, commissioned as a postal inspector, but drew his salary from the NYSSV, which received its funding from New York's wealthy elite.

Comstock's legacy remains alive and well. The Comstock Act is still on the books (the prohibition on birth control having been deleted in 1971, although the fine for information about abortion was increased in 1994), and the Communications Decency Act, passed overwhelmingly in Congress in 1996, and signed by President Clinton, adopted language from the 1873 Comstock Act to apply to the Internet.

NUMEROUS complaints came to our office against a most disgusting and obscene exhibition that was given by beastly women, to the ruin of hundreds of thoughtless young men. These exhibitions were given almost nightly. At first, I felt such a disgust and abhorrence at the descriptions I received in these complaints, that I was inclined to be cowardly and not act. My conscience, my whole being as a man cried out against this cowardice. I knew well what it would cost me. I humbly and earnestly prayed for grace to do my duty, and then I went forward. The first essential to a successful effort is legal evidence. The momentous question then arose how to get it? There was but one legal way. That was to get it legally. To do it, some one must see this exhibition in order to prove what it was, and identify the parties carrying it on. I could not send young men there; to do that would have been dastardly, after I had been informed of its character. I could not make a strong case without the most positive proof, as it is difficult to conceive of anything more horrible. For two years this place had existed and thrived in the rear of the 15th Precinct Police Station, the yards adjoining. Consequently I could not go there for help. What then? I went to the Mayor's squad and selected six of the truest and best men I knew on the Police force—some of them Christian men. We visited this den, and I saw the party who kept the house, and so doubtful was I of the truth of what I had heard, before anything else I asked if ______ exhibitions were given there? This matron replied, "Oh yes. This has been the headquarters for more than two years. There are six exhibitors, and a regular programme, and the performance lasts about an hour." She further informed us, "that some of the exhibitors were absent, but that it would make no difference, as *the same programme* was always enacted." Here then I had official and reliable information from the mouth of the proprietress of this exhibition, that *it existed*, as it had done for *more than two years* previous, and with a *regular programme*. Here then is a pitfall for the feet of young men! Shall I close it? Here is a hell-trap for the souls of our youth! Shall I allow it to exist? Here is an exhibition given by women that beggars description—so gross that even a reference to it brings a blush.—Shall it continue? No! no! By all that is in us as men, *no!*

There was but one thing left. Close this hell-hole up at once, by all means! you say. Not so fast. The vilest have rights. Whatever an officer of the law does, he must do legally. First get the evidence, and *then* forward. After getting further light from this proprietress, we then did precisely as those frequenters of the vile exhibition formerly known as the "Black Crook," (that sent thousands of youthful souls to perdition,) did; we paid our admission fee, and went into the hall where the performance was nightly given. Here we, sworn officers of the law, remained sufficiently long to secure two things, *and no longer;* to wit:

First.—Legal evidence of an indecent exhibition.

Second.—Proofs that there was a regular programme regularly enacted.

Having obtained these, I immediately went out, and having secured the keeper of this den first (and one thing that delayed was, that she had gone over to one of her other dens of infamy, for she had two or three in this precinct), we arrested the occupants of this hell-hole. The principal was held for trial on a complaint for "keeping a disorderly house." The exhibitors, for an "indecent exhibition."

Now what of the trial . . .

The Assistant District Attorney, of course, had to *nolle prosequi* the indictment against the exhibitors, and then, although the case had closed so far as the testimony went, he asked an adjournment in the case of the principal. He then came into court the next day, and stated he had been informed that it was a conspiracy to injure the Captain of Police of that precinct. I, in open court, declared such a statement false. I had, the previous day, asked him to call some of the officers of that precinct to prove that this was a disorderly house. He said no, that the case was fully made out, and yet the judge granted a motion the next day, made by this officer, to dismiss. The motion was granted, on the ground that the Assistant District Attorney moved it, because, as he said in open court, if this woman is convicted, charges might be preferred against the captain of this precinct and he be dismissed. The court ruled it was the duty of the courts to protect the police, and the case was dismissed.

The New Colossus, Emma Lazarus (1883)

Emma Lazarus wrote "The New Colossus" for an auction in 1883 to raise money for the Statue of Liberty's pedestal. The statue was a gift from France to the United States to commemorate the friendship between the two nations, but financing for the pedestal went so slowly that it provoked the ire of Joseph Pulitzer's *The World,* and he sponsored numerous money-raising ventures.

While Lazarus's poem helped in transforming the Statue of Liberty into a "welcoming beacon" for immigrants fleeing their native countries, she herself came from a wealthy, fourth-generation Jewish family, one of the oldest in the city. Lazarus was privately educated by tutors and had published a book of poems in 1866, when she was only seventeen. These poems caught the attention of Ralph Waldo Emerson, who became a mentor to Lazarus and to whom she dedicated her second book of poems.

In the early 1880s, Lazarus, increasingly aware of the vast number of immigrants fleeing the pogroms in Russia, turned her focus to a wide range of "Jewish issues." She wrote extensively in the *Critic* and the *Century,* bringing attention to the housing needs in the densely packed Lower East Side, encouraging the idea of the resettlement of Jews in Palestine and helping to found the Society for the Improvement and Colonization of East European Jews. Lazarus died at the age of thirty-eight in 1887, probably of cancer, and never saw her words immortalized on the bronze plaque at the base of the Statue of Liberty.

NOT like the brazen giant of Greek fame
With conquering limbs astride from land to land;
Here at our sea-washed, sunset gates shall stand
A mighty woman with a torch, whose flame
Is the imprisoned lightning, and her name
Mother of Exiles. From her beacon-hand
Glows world-wide welcome; her mild eyes command

The air-bridged harbor that twin cities frame,
"Keep, ancient lands, your storied pomp!" cries she
With silent lips. "Give me your tired, your poor,
Your huddled masses yearning to breathe free,
The wretched refuse of your teeming shore,
Send these, the homeless, tempest-tost to me,
I lift my lamp beside the golden door!"

Bathing at Coney Island, from Coney Island Frolics, *Richard K. Fox (1883)*

Richard K. Fox is probably best known as the editor for *The National Police Gazette* from 1877 to 1922. He is also generally credited for the codification of the formula for the "dime-store" novels that were wildly popular at the turn of the twentieth century.

Soon after the Civil War, five separate railroads tied Coney Island to Brooklyn, where tens of thousands of New Yorkers enjoyed hot dogs (introduced in 1870), mixed bathing, and horse racing. Between 1897 and 1904, three enormous amusement parks opened on Surf Avenue: Steeplechase Park at West Seventeenth Street, Luna Park at West Tenth Street, and Dreamland at West Fifth Street. These institutions, the first of their kind in the United States, and the opening of subway lines in 1920 brought millions of visitors to Coney Island on a typical summer's day for the next forty years. In 1923 New York City built the famous boardwalk that stretched four miles from Brighton Beach to Sea Gate.

Dreamland was destroyed by fire in May 1911, Luna Park met the same fate in 1944, and Steeplechase Park, with its now nationally landmarked parachute jump that had been moved from the 1939 World's Fair, closed its doors in 1964. In 2001 the Giuliani administration, trying to bring back the "good old days" of Coney Island, built a baseball park for the New York Mets farm team next to the famed wooden roller coaster The Cyclone, which has been in continuous operation since 1927.

THERE are various ways of bathing at Coney Island. You can go in at the West End, where they give you a tumbledown closet like a sentry box stuck up in the sand, or at the great hotels where more or less approach to genuine comfort is afforded. The pier, too, is fitted up with extensive bathing houses, and altogether no one who wants a dip in the briny and has a quarter to pay for it need to go without it.

If a man is troubled with illusions concerning the female form divine and wishes to be rid of those illusions he should go to Coney Island and closely watch the thousands of women who bathe there every Sunday.

A woman, or at least most women, in bathing undergoes a transformation that is really wonderful. They waltz into the bathing-rooms clad in all the paraphernalia that most gladdens the feminine heart. The hair is gracefully dressed, and appears most abundant; the face is decorated with all that elaborate detail which defies description by one uninitiated in the mysteries of the boudoir; the form is moulded by the milliner to distracting elegance of proportion, and the feet appear aristocratically slender and are arched in French boots.

Thus they appear as they sail past the gaping crowds of men, who make Coney Island a loafing place on Sundays. They seek out their individual dressing-rooms and disappear. Somewhere inside of an hour, they make their appearance ready for the briny surf. If it were not for the men who accompany them it would be impossible to recognize them as the same persons who but a little while ago entered those diminutive rooms. . . .

The broad amphitheatre at Manhattan Beach built at the water's edge is often filled with spectators. Many pay admission fees to witness the feats of swimmers, the clumsiness of beginners and the ludicrous mishaps of the never-absent stout persons. Under the bathinghouse is a sixty horse-power engine. It rinses and washes the suits for the bathers, and its steady puffing is an odd accompaniment to the merry shouts of the bathers and the noise of the shifting crowd ashore. . . .

A person who intends to bathe at Manhattan or Brighton Beach first buys a ticket and deposits it in a box such as is placed in every elevated railroad station. If he carries valuables he may have them deposited without extra charge in a safe that weighs seven tons and has one thousand compartments. He encloses them in an envelope and seals it. Then he writes his name partly on the flap of the envelope and partly on the envelope itself. For this envelope he receives a metal check attached to an elastic string, in order that he might wear it about his neck while bathing. This check has been taken from one of the compartments of the safe which bears the same number as the check. Into the same compartment the sealed envelope is put. When the bather returns from the surf he must return the check and must write his name on a piece of paper. This signature is compared with the one on the envelope. Should the bather report that his check has been lost or stolen his signature is deemed sufficient warrant for the return of the valuables. The safe has double doors in front and behind. Each drawer may be drawn out from either side. When the throng presses six men may be employed at this safe.

The Senate Committee on the Relations Between Labor and Capital, Testimony of Thomas B. McGuire (1883)

On September 5, 1882, the nation's first Labor Day parade marched past the reviewing stand of dignitaries at the northern end of Union Square and continued up Broadway. The parade had been proposed by the recently formed Central Labor Union, which added a dozen different unions a year during its first three years. However, the rise of organized labor had its origin in the previous decade. The Panic of 1873 had sent the country reeling into a depression, and as unemployment rose a rally was called in Tompkins Square on January 13, 1874, "in sympathy with the suffering poor." Samuel Gompers, head of the United Cigarmakers at the time and later head of the American Federation of Labor, described what followed as "an orgy of brutality" as policemen clubbed groups of workers, especially those from the German Tenth Ward Workingman's Association, for hours.

By the fall of 1883, the Senate had convened the Committee on the Relations Between Labor and Capital in New York to gather firsthand reports from "the workingman." The testimony of people like Thomas McGuire had little impact, however; horsecar drivers went on strike to lower their seventeen-hour workdays less than three years later. Although a work stoppage in March 1886 met with some success, the horsecar corporation, owned by Jacob Sharp, was revealed subsequently to have bribed the Board of Aldermen for special privileges and cheated the city of millions of tax dollars.

THOMAS B. McGuire sworn and examined.

BY MR. CALL:

Q. Where do you live?

A. In New York.

Q. What is your occupation?

A. At present I am a truck-driver. I was formerly an expressman.

Q. How long have you been in those respective employments?

A. I have been in the express business about five years. I embarked something like $300 in the business, thinking that I might become something of a capitalist eventually, but I found competition so great that it was impossible for me to do so; I found that the railroad companies had their regular wagons and their collectors on the trains previous to their reaching the city asking for the privilege of carrying the people's baggage, and by that means they were enabled to get any business of that kind that was to be had. I found also that another company had taken the furniture moving into their hands. A case in point: A gentleman in New street asked me one time what I would charge him to bring two truck-loads from a certain station in Jersey. I told him $75. It was 23 miles out there; the truck was a four-horse truck, and I was to handle everything. He went to the Metropolitan Van Company and had the work done for $60. Now, my profit on that job at the price I asked, had I received the work, would have been somewhere in the neighborhood of $20; but that company did the work with better appliances than I could have furnished and made a great deal more money than I could have made out of it. A man in the express business today owning one or two horses and a wagon cannot even eke out an existence from the business. The competition is too great; that is, the competition from these monopolies. For instance, the Adams Express Company and all those other express companies do local express work also, and by that means they prevent people who go into the business in New York City from ever getting any higher up than barely existing—not, living but barely existing. That is my experience. I found that when I lost a horse I was not able to replace him; that is, I could not accumulate enough out of my earnings to do so. I found, moreover, that I was not able to buy feed for my horses even at low prices. Some two years ago I paid $2.10 for 80 pounds of oats, while these corporations could buy the same quantity for $1.60 or $1.80; I paid from $2.50 to $3 a set for horse shoeing, while they had theirs done by contract at a price which would not amount to $1.25 or $1.50 for each horse. So that everything is against a man going into the express business in a small way. . . .

Q. What capital would be required to begin an express business here with a reasonable prospect of success?

A. Ten thousand dollars would give a man a fair opportunity to compete with these large companies, I think.

Q. How was it fifteen or twenty years ago in regard to that?

A. This competition did not exist at that time. Then a man embarking $300 in the business had an excellent chance of becoming a successful expressman and accumulating some money and probably some property.

Q. How is it as to trucking in that respect?

A. Men who embarked in trucking twenty years ago have become wealthy, to my own knowledge, have become the owners of houses and other property, and are doing a vast business, some of them having from fifteen to twenty trucks. They have got employment from different large dry-goods dealers, importers, and others, and they have got into the good graces of some of our custom house officers and got the run of the public stores. Those men who have the custom-house licenses are the only ones that are permitted to do the carting from those public establishments, and in that way they have a monopoly of the business. As a rule you will find them to be active members of one of the "grand old" parties, and of course through that means they have a great deal of influence that other men cannot reach to.

Q. What capital would now be required to begin that business with a fair prospect of success?

A. At the present time, to be able to go into that business with any chance of success, you would have to be somewhat of a ward politician. If you were that, probably with $25,000 you might be able to compete with these other people with a fair chance of success.

Q. You think it would be necessary to be a ward politician and also to have $25,000?

A. Yes, sir. Then also you would have to be able to manage the primaries, and, if it was necessary, to be one of the judges at the primary, so as to make your man "the candidate of the people" at the next election.

Q. Do you mean that that is a sort of a Government position, but that a man must have the money besides?

A. It is not exactly a Government position, but it is a position where bribery is necessary to keep the people under the control of a certain class of politicians. If a man can do those things he will get a good living.

Q. How is it about the hack business?

A. Well, individual ownership of hacks is becoming obsolete. Large stables are taking up the business entirely. Corporations usually take that business to themselves. For instance, a man who can afford to lease a large stable, and can manage to get men at starvation wages, and put them on a hack, and put a livery on them, with a gold band and brass buttons, to show that they are slaves—I beg pardon; I did not intend to use the word slaves;

there are no slaves in this country now—to show that they are merely servants, that class of stable-keepers can secure the patronage of what are called the moneyed classes, who pay a dollar an hour for the use of these cabs, with these men dressed up in that fashion to drive them, and of course they monopolize the business.

Q. What amount of money do you think would be required to engage in that business with a fair prospect of success?

A. Fifty thousand dollars would set up a very nice establishment; or probably if the uniforms could be had cheap a little less might do. A good supply of uniforms is the principal thing.

Q. What else do they give those men besides?

A. They give them permission to exist, and if they own tenement houses they give these men leave to live in them, raising the rent on them every year. They give them enough wages to secure a bare existence, and if the men are found taking 25 cents from a passenger they are immediately discharged and sent adrift to go and compete with somebody else in some other business.

BY MR. GEORGE:

Q. Do you mean if they are found taking a donation from a passenger they are discharged?

A. Yes, sir.

BY MR. CALL:

Q. Why don't those men who are so fond of the gold bands and brass buttons go into some other employment?

A. Well, merely because the unskilled labor market is overstocked, and will be while men work ten hours a day. If the hours of labor were shorter the surplus of labor would disappear, and therefore workingmen could command better wages. . . .

BY MR. CALL:

Q. How does the man who produces nothing get the wealth?

A. Well, let me see—class legislation, national banks, railroad monopolies, telegraph monopolies, Wall street gambling, horse racing, keeping gin-mills, and all the etceteras, and there is one thing more that I had very nearly forgotten, groundrent. . . .

BY MR. GEORGE:

Q. Did you ever know of a bank lending money to a truckman?

A. I was going to mention that, but I was going to put my answer in another way to make it lucid. The banks never lend money to the truckmen or anybody else without collateral, and I never had very much of that. But when this money is loaned, it must be loaned at a rate of interest. Now, when there is only $13 per capita for each individual in the United States, and the interest foots up $20 per capita, where are they going to get the other $7? There is the injustice. The moment the money is loaned; that recognizes the fact that there is a debt, and the moment that debt is there, the man is no longer producing for himself but for the other man, the one who lends the money. . . .

BY MR. CALL:

Q. Why do not "the horny-handed sons of toil" send men of their own choosing to make laws for them?

A. Simply because the entire political system from top to bottom is a system of bribery and corruption.

Q. Then you distrust popular government?

A. I do under the present arrangement. The moment an alderman is elected, some railroad corporation will write to him, saying, "Mr. Reilley, we are glad to see that you have been elected alderman; call upon us immediately, and we will see that you have two or three conductors appointed upon our line."

Q. Are not those very often taken from among the sons of toil?

A. Yes, sir; but the latter is entirely arranged by the idlers who never do any labor. A man who works for his living has to work too long and too hard to be able to find time and opportunity to educate himself in "politics."

Q. You seem to be pretty well educated?

A. Oh, no; I have listened to the politicians somewhat, and being of rather an inquiring turn of mind, I have followed them up a little closer than some of the others do. I heard what they said to the people about election times, and then I tried to see if it would work in practice, but I found it wouldn't.

Q. Don't you think anybody else in the country has done that besides you?

A. Oh, undoubtedly. I am only a drop in the bucket.

Q. Then, how is it that, with so many people looking out for their interests, the workingmen do not get better representative men to make laws for them?

A. Simply because the system of bribery is so complete that it is impossible, and if anybody believes in independent political action and tries to carry it out, he will have the papers of the city of New York hounding him as a "socialist" or a "communist." Whenever a man undertakes to advocate the cause of the working people, the papers come out and denounce what he says as the "ravings of a demagogue," and so on, and for that reason our poor unfortunate, untutored, workingmen are deceived, and are simple enough to believe in the party who promise them that they will do away with the system of convict labor and make the reforms for them.

Q. Do you think you are giving a proper description of the workingmen of this country?

A. I know I am giving a proper description of the workingmen of New York.

Q. What do you call a workingman?

A. Every man that works for a living, every man who produces anything useful. . . .

Q. And you would consider a priest, who worked faithfully to comfort his parishioners, a workingman, I suppose?

A. Yes; provided he had cushioned pews in the front of the church for the working classes, and hard boards for the idlers—

Q. [Interposing.] Oh, well, he might be very superstitious and fanatical and all that, but still, if he came to your family when they were sick and did all he could do to relieve and comfort them, he would be a useful man, no matter what he thought or did about pews. But suppose that the workingmen, according to your definition, that is the men who work with their hands, the cigar-makers, the truck-men, the blacksmiths, the carpenters, and so on, were able to elect a candidate of their own for mayor of this city, would not the probability be that that representative of theirs would not be a corrupt man who might be bought up to betray their interests? I have a better opinion of the workingmen and of humanity generally than you seem to have.

A. Well, I suppose that is because you mingle with the decent classes. I don't.

Q. No; I don't know of any decenter classes than the working people. I have mingled with them all my life, and I do not understand why you should say that the candidate of the workingmen would be corrupt.

A. Well, you put me questions that I would have to know the minds of men in order to answer. I say this, however, if you will take your legislators from the class you belong to, and not from among the whisky class, who produce nothing but headache and delirium tremens—

Q. [Interposing.] Who takes them from that class now?

A. The politicians who control the caucus.

Q. How can that class of politicians control the caucus if you working people attend there and vote?

A. Oh, yes; and if we do attend there they will have three men appointed who won't count our votes.

Q. You need not tell me that the class of men to which you belong will let any three men cheat them out of their votes?
A. Well, I would like to have you ask every witness that comes here and that knows anything about it, whether men are not appointed here in that way to count the votes, and allowed to count them to suit themselves.
Q. Don't you know how to remedy that? Cannot you workingmen vote that the caucus shall not appoint the three men who count the votes, but that the appointment shall be made in public meeting by the people?
A. According to the law we cannot appoint an inspector of election; he has got to be appointed by the dominant party at the police headquarters.
Q. Then your idea is that popular government is a failure?
A. Under these conditions.
Q. Well, according to your theory, we have arrived at the conclusion that the people are not sensible enough to keep themselves from being cheated. Now, what remedy have you to propose for that?
A. In the first place, let me say that I have got no theory. I am speaking of actual facts. In the next place, the only way to remedy this evil is, instead of these party preferences, to let the primary be an open one just the same as our election is, and let an inspector of election be taken from each party, and if there is a third party, as for instance a workingmen's party, let them also be entitled to have one of the inspectors. In that way we would have some chance of having a fair election.
Q. That is what I understand to be the law and the practice now?
A. It is not so in our primaries here. . . .

BY MR. CALL:

Q. I guess you are mistaken.
A. No, I am positive of it. In the city of Brooklyn there is an entirely different law from that which we have in the city of New York; so you see the State does control it. Again, speaking of counting votes, or rather of seeing the ballots deposited, for the primary is one thing and casting the ballot another thing. For instance, if we had a labor party in the field we would have no man present to see the votes being counted.
Q. Why not?
A. Because the recognized parties are the Republicans, the Democrats, the Tammany Hall Democrats, and the Irving Hall Democrats.
Q. If there is any such law as that it is not worth a snap of your finger. It is entirely contrary to the Constitution of the United States.
A. To give you an example of the way these things are done, I went some time ago to get up a meeting at the corner of Fifteenth street and First

avenue. I went to Captain Walling, and he sent me to the captain of the precinct, and the captain of the precinct sent me to the sergeant, and the sergeant sent me to a policeman, and the policeman told me he had no authority.

Q. What did you want permission to do?

A. To go out on the street and talk politics.

Q. You don't mean to tell me that there is any law here that compels you to get permission to go out on the street to talk politics?

A. Yes, I do.

Q. You mean that you must have permission to hold a public meeting on the streets, not permission for an individual to talk politics on the streets?

A. Yes; a public meeting. But, if an individual begins to talk and gathers a crowd around him, then he is violating a corporation ordinance.

Q. Of course every municipal government has control of its streets. Would you change that?

A. No, sir; but I would want that there should be no such thing as class legislation.

Q. That is right; but the city of New York has control of its streets, and it may say where a public meeting shall be held on the streets or where it shall not; now, how would you change that?

A. I would simply ask that the people should be allowed at all times to have the same rights here that they have in Europe under monarchical forms of government.

Q. You ought not to have any city government that would do what you complain of—that would make class legislation.

A. How can we prevent it when these cliques control the whole thing through a system of appointments—I call it bribery. All the appointments, from the street-cleaning department down, are made in that way here.

BY MR. GEORGE:

Q. Do you mean that all those classes you have mentioned who have political influence are required to do certain political work in order to retain their places?

A. That is what I mean. You have got it correctly.

BY MR. CALL:

Q. They do not appoint hackmen, though. What you mean is that that is an incidental effect?

A. I say that wherever a political position is held it is held for the purpose of retaining the party in office, and if I had my way I would prevent any man who held an office in the gift of the people from voting, because he will vote to keep his bread and butter, and his vote will count just as much as mine or any other man's.

BY MR. GEORGE:

Q. That is one practical idea, to prevent any person holding an office under the Government from voting. Is there anything else that you would do?

A. Well, I would also prevent them from having a hand in the primaries.

Q. What else?

A. I guess that after that we could manage our own affairs.

Q. You think that would stop the bribery of which you speak, so that things generally would be improved?

A. Yes, sir; I think that if that was stopped we would have a fair chance of getting representative men from the people instead of from the politicians.

Q. Do you think that would bring about relief in the matter of insufficient wages and competition in the different employments of life?

A. It would prevent class legislation; it would probably make our railroads and our telegraphs the property of the Government the same as the Post-Office is now; and that would do something for us.

Q. But supposing that the fellows who got the Government then should do just as the other fellows do now, and use its patronage for their own friends and for their own party purposes, what would you do?

A. I have stated to you that I would not allow any man in the employ of the Government to vote.

Q. Then you would take the right of suffrage away from all who were connected with the Government?

A. Yes; just the same as you take it away from the soldier.

Q. But supposing you did that, would not those men still be able to use their influence?

A. They might, with money, but we would find a way to deal with that.

Q. Would they not have the same motive to use their influence that they have now?

A. Most undoubtedly; but the man who did it would be a criminal in the eye of the law. Anybody who does anything to subvert the liberties of the people is a criminal.

The CHAIRMAN. I don't care to listen to accusations of this kind much longer. This witness evidently looks upon the legislative bodies of this country as made up of a set of rascals, and he cannot expect anything from a committee which is a part of such a body.

The WITNESS. I did not think that Senator Blair would take the matter that way.

The CHAIRMAN. No, you don't understand me. I feel like this, my friend, that on an average we human beings are all very much alike. I have never known a single instance of bribery in the House of Representatives or in the Senate of the United States; never a single instance of the kind, and I have been there eight years; and I don't believe that either of the other Senators here present have ever known of an instance. There is a very general and wide-spread misconception as to the personal character of the legislators of this country. I don't believe that, man for man, the church in the United States, or any other organization in the United States, averages any better in the matter of personal moral character than do the members of Congress, and you labor under a very serious mistake, and approach the subject from a wrong direction when you come to it with the idea that anybody is here or anybody is there to deal with these great public questions dishonestly. I speak now of the members of Congress generally, and I say that the great majority in either party is composed of honest men. These problems of life are very serious, and I can see how a man in your position, having capacity and ability which, with proper opportunity, would enable you to fill any situation in the country—I can see how you, crowded by circumstances, may come to feel and think as you do, and what I say to you now I do not say reprovingly at all—God knows I do not. But, my friend, you are wrong in your estimate of men. The majority of men are honest men throughout the length and breadth of the world. I do not care to believe in the doctrine of total depravity, for that includes myself, and I don't choose to hold or to admit that I am only fit to be an exemplification hereafter of eternal punishment by fire. I don't believe that men are totally depraved. I believe that men on the whole are good, and that you can safely appeal to their better nature.

The WITNESS. I did not bring out this discussion myself. It was brought out by the questions of a member of the committee.

The CHAIRMAN. That is all true. I am not finding fault with you; I am only speaking of the evident condition of your mind on this subject, and I do wish, if I can, to disabuse you and others who feel and think as you do because life has been hard with them, of the idea that knaves are the rule rather than honest men. It is not so, and you are entirely mistaken and very unjust if you think that the legislators of this country, as a class, are the knaves that you represent them to be.

The WITNESS. Well, if you lived in New York as long as I have lived here, and had lived in the neighborhoods that I have lived in, and if you had looked around you and seen the practices that are going on there among the poorer classes; if you had seen them having to vote themselves slaves every year, I believe you would think as I do. They are trades unionists eleven months in the year and the other month they are worked up by political heat and they go and vote right against their convictions. If you saw these things and if you saw those people send their wives out to scrub other people's floors, and their little children to work as cash-boys and cash-girls in other people's stores, you would have just the same sentiments that I have.

The CHAIRMAN. I have seen some of the things you speak of, and I believe it is because you have seen so much of them that you feel and think as you do, but you are, nevertheless, in error as to the facts.

Experience of a Chinese Journalist, from Puck, *Wong Chin Foo (1885)*

Wong Chin Foo moved to New York City in 1874 while in his early twenties and was a well-known civic leader and newspaperman. In 1882, he started a Chinese newspaper, the *Chinese-American,* which ultimately failed, and started another newspaper in Chicago in 1892. Wong Chin Foo was also a regular lecturer and spoke on various topics including Buddhism, the fallacious reporting of Christian missionaries about life in China, and the reputation of Chinatown in New York City.

Chinatown's reputation had suffered in the late 1870s and early 1880s when sensationalist tabloids depicted the Chinese as opium addicts who were stealing American jobs and corrupting American women. Both fear of economic competition and moral condemnation were, in part, behind the passage of the Chinese Exclusion Act in 1882. This act effectively prohibited most Chinese immigrants from entering the United States. Those that were allowed in were denied citizenship, the right to vote and, therefore, inclusion in licensed professions. Chinatown had been a largely bachelor society of more than two thousand in the 1870s, and the Exclusion Act also guaranteed that would continue as it barred Chinese laborers already here from bringing their wives into the country. In fact, the total Chinese population in New York City remained below 4,000 until after the Second World War. It was not until 1965 that immigration quotas based on national origin were lifted, and the last thirty-five years have witnessed the rapid expansion of the boundaries of Chinatown into Little Italy and the Lower East Side, as well as the creation of Chinese communities in the outer boroughs of Flushing, Sunset Park, Bay Ridge, and Elmhurst.

It is not necessary for me to remark that I was born in the Middle Empire, and that I am now an American citizen; for ever since my advent in this land of the free I have been systematically styled a "pig-tailed renegade," a "moon-eyed leper," a "demon of the Orient," a "gangrened laundryman," a "rat-eating Mongol," etc.

I started life as a lecturer, and, through my connection with a Literary Bureau, was very successful in purveying to the intellectual pleasures of Western Sunday-schools and Southern clubs. That they seldom asked me to come back and lecture again does not invalidate my statement; neither is it inconsistent with popularity when an enthusiastic audience welcomes a speaker with revolvers and shot-guns, and otherwise induces him to depart via a second-story window rather than the stairs. These are incidents in the life of every lecturer.

In an unguarded moment I listened to the voice of the tempter, and fell from my high estate. Persuaded that I was the coming journalist of the Occident and Orient alike, I came to New York City and started the *Chinese American.* I knew nothing of journalism save in a vague way, and went to work accordingly. I took an American partner and a Chinese one, engaged a city editor, a staff, and an artist.

The first issue, after many sleepless nights, appeared. I shall never forget it. It circulated fifty thousand copies, and brought in one thousand five hundred dollars.

That is, it brought in three hundred dollars cash, and one thousand two hundred dollars in notes, bills receivable, and promises. I have a hundred of the latter assorted, which I will sell at one cent on the dollar. I was proud of the issue until I had read the criticisms upon it in my E. C.s. The American E. C.s were contradictory in substance, but unanimous in their drift. The English articles were badly written, poorly thought and wretchedly printed; they were also splendidly written and composed, but displaying signs of some trained journalist, who was posing in my name. The editor, they said, was a Chinese gentleman with more money than brains. He was also a myth and a joke. He was also a Jesuit, a Buddhist missionary, and an Imperial emissary in disguise. Then came the Chinese E. C.s. My native tongue, as I wrote it, was uncouth, illiterate, unintelligent, vapid, hollow, fantastic, bombastic and idiotic. I was a wretch who was endeavoring to ruin the Flowery Kingdom in the eyes of Christendom; I was a renegade, an apostle, and the victim of American gold.

I had written a moral screed against gambling and opium-smoking. The gamblers and joint-keepers invaded my office a week after, and proceeded to flog the associate editor, cashier, and city reporter. The trio did not wait for the end of the performance, but departed for the Empire the same day.

I heard from them at—Panama. They were intact; but the nine hundred and fifty dollars, my entire assets they had carried with them, were not.

I did not come out altogether unscathed. I was "knocked out" twice, arrested four times for criminal libel, once for civil libel, under twenty-five thousand dollars bail, locked up in Ludlow Street jail, and twice poisoned.

I think the paper would have succeeded, if I had had more experience—say a hundred years. But my artist, Jung Fan Tai, became a Bohemian and used too much beer in his designs. Chinese art does not present many differences to the civilized eye; but it does to the Mongolian connaisseur.

Jung's second sacred dragon contained a superfluous cocktail, and was denounced in Chinatown as blasphemy. The luckless draughtsman was thereupon put under the ban of ostracism, and in a fortnight had shaken the dust of Gotham from off his feet. My second cashier was a reporter in bad luck. I do not think he was dishonest; but when you miss your treasurer and treasury, and find the first paralyzed in a neighboring bar-room the next day, and don't find the second at all, it's high time for a head editor to kick. I kicked; but the reporter, with an indescribable oath, swore that no "almond-eyed double blank" could kick him with impunity, and in less time than it takes to tell it had converted me into a ghastly ruin.

My journalistic career culminated recently in the Supreme Court. I had, with the best intentions in the world, allowed an article to appear in my sheet which "showed up" a certain individual in a moderately sensational way.

The style was patented after that employed in many E. C.s, and contained such pleasing epithets as "assassins, cut-throats, viper, scorpion, thief, embezzler, robber, liar, and a member of the Young Men's Christian Association." In short, it was a thoroughly American article. Yet, an imbecile jury gave a verdict for the fellow against me in one thousand dollars. At present there is an order of arrest out for me, and a deputy-sheriff is watching my regular haunts.

It's the old story. I had the capital; now I haven't; but I have the experience. Any paper wishing the services of an experienced editor, who can write in every vein and on every subject, and create libel-suits, can obtain a gem by applying to Wong Chin Foo, *Care of* Puck.

The Two Revelations, from Evolution and Religion, *Henry Ward Beecher (1885)*

Henry Ward Beecher, born in 1813, was the eighth son of the renowned minister Lyman Beecher; one of his sisters was Harriet Beecher Stowe, the author of *Uncle Tom's Cabin,* and another was Catharine Beecher, the author of many books on the joys of domestic living. Henry Ward Beecher attended Amherst College and Lane Theological Seminary before spending a decade in Indiana. In 1847 he was called to Plymouth Congregational Church in Brooklyn, where he spent the rest of his life preaching.

Beecher was the most prominent and popular orator of his day and regularly drew crowds of twenty-five hundred parishioners every Sunday. Beecher's liberalism grew throughout his ministry, and he took a strong stand against slavery and for women's suffrage. His condemnation of the Kansas-Nebraska Bill led him to raise funds to supply weapons for the abolitionist John Brown; these rifles became known as "Beecher Bibles." He gave the main address, entitled "Woman's Duty to Vote," at the Eleventh National Woman's Rights Convention in New York on May 10, 1866. Beecher could be controversial theologically as well as politically; he frequently defended evolution and taught a disbelief in the doctrine of hell.

Beecher's later life was colored by a suit brought against him in 1874 by his friend and successor as the editor of the religious periodical *The Independent,* Theodore Tilton. In one of the most lengthy and scandalous trials of the nineteenth century, Beecher was charged with adultery with Tilton's wife, Elizabeth. While the result of the trial was a hung jury and exoneration from the church council, Beecher's reputation suffered until his death in 1877.

Beecher's final words were, "Now comes the mystery"; he was buried in Greenwood Cemetery.

A VAGUE notion exists with multitudes that science is infidel, and that Evolution in particular is revolutionary—that is, revolutionary of the doctrines of the Church. Men of such views often say, "I know that religion is true. I do not wish to hear anything that threatens to unsettle my faith." But faith that can be unsettled by the access of light and knowledge had better be unsettled. The intensity of such men's faith in their own thoughts is deemed to be safer than a larger view of God's thoughts. Others speak of Evolution as a pseudo-science teaching that man descended from monkeys, or ascended as the case may be. They have no conception of it as the history of the divine process in the building of this world. They dismiss it with jests, mostly ancient jests; or, having a smattering of fragmentary knowledge, they address victorious ridicule to audiences as ignorant as they are themselves.

Now the ascent of man from the anthropoid apes is a mere hypothesis. It has not been proved; and in the broader sense of the word "proved," I see certainly no present means of proving it. It stands in the region of hypothesis, pressed forward by a multitude of probabilities. The probabilities are so many, and the light which this hypothesis throws upon human history and human life and phenomena is such that I quite incline to the supposition that it is, in the order of nature, in analogy with all the rest of God's work, and that in the ascending scale there was a time unknown, and methods not yet discovered, in which man left behind his prior relatives, and came upon the spiritual ground which now distinguishes him from the whole brute creation. Of one thing I am certain, that whatever may have been the origin, it does not change either the destiny or the moral grandeur of man as he stands in the full light of civilization to-day. The theory of the evolution of the human race from an inferior race, not proved and yet probable, throws light upon many obscure points of doctrine and of theology that have most sadly needed light and solution.

First, then, what is Evolution, and what does it reveal? The theory of Evolution teaches that the creation of this earth was not accomplished in six days of twenty-four hours; that the divine method occupied ages and ages of immense duration; that nothing, of all the treasures of the globe as they now stand, was created at first in its present perfectness; that everything has grown through the lapse of ages into its present condition; that the whole earth, with their development in it, was, as it were, an egg, a germ, a seed; that the forests, the fields, the shrubs, the vineyards, all grasses and flowers, all insects, fishes, and birds, all mammals of every gradation, have had a long history, and that they have come to the position in which they now stand through ages and ages of gradual change and unfolding. Also that the earth itself went through a period of long preparation, passing from ether by condensation to a visible cloud form with increasing solidity, to such a condition as now prevails in the sun; that it condensed and became solid; that cold congealed its vapor; that by chemical action and by mechanical grinding of its surface by ice a soil was prepared fit for vegetation, long before it was fit for animal life; that plants simple and coarse came first and developed through all stages of complexity to the present conditions of the vegetable kingdom; that aquatic, invertebrate animals were the earliest of animals, according to the testimony of fossils in the earth. Fishes came next in order, then amphibians, then reptiles. "All these tribes were represented by species before the earliest of the mammals appeared. The existence of birds before the earliest mammal is not proved, though believed by some paleontologists upon probable evidence. The early mammals were marsupial, like the opossum and the kangaroo, and lived in the same era called by Agassiz, the reptilian period. True mammals came into geologic history in the tertiary era. Very long after the appearance of the first bird came man, the last and grandest of the series, it is doubtful whether in the tertiary period or immediately sequent. It is not established whether his bones or relics occur as far back as the tertiary era."

This is a very brief statement, not my own, but that of Professor Dana, of renown. No man is more trusted, more careful, more cautious than he, and this brief history of the unfolding series I have taken bodily from his writings.

Second.—As thus set forth, it may be said that Evolution is accepted as *the method* of creation by the whole scientific world, and that the period of controversy is passed and closed. A few venerable men yet live, with many doubts; but it may be said that ninety-nine per cent.—as has been declared by an eminent physicist—ninety-nine per cent. of scientific men and working scientists of the world are using this theory without any doubt of its validity. While the scientific world is at agreement upon this *order* of occurrence, it has been much divided as to the *causes* which have operated to bring about these results. There is a diversity of opinion still, but with every decade scientific men are drawing together to a common ground of belief.

Third.—The theory of Evolution is the *working* theory of every department of physical science all over the world. Withdraw this theory, and every department of physical research would fall back into heaps of hopelessly dislocated facts, with no more order or reason or philosophical coherence than exists in a basket of marbles, or in the juxtaposition of the multitudinous sands of the seashore. We should go back into chaos if we took out of the laboratories, out of the dissecting-rooms, out of the fields of investigation, this great doctrine of Evolution.

Fourth.—This science of Evolution is taught in all advanced academies, in all colleges and universities, in all medical and surgical schools, and our children are receiving it as they are the elements of astronomy or botany or chemistry. That in another generation Evolution will be regarded as uncontradictable as the Copernican system of astronomy, or the Newtonian doctrine of gravitation, can scarcely be doubted. Each of these passed through the same contradiction by theologians. They were charged by the Church, as is Evolution now, with fostering materialism, infidelity, and atheism. We know what befell Galileo for telling the truth of God's primitive revelation. We know, or do not know, at least, how Newton stood charged with infidelity and with atheism when he announced the doctrine of gravitation. Who doubts the heliocentric theory to-day? Who doubts whether it is the sun which is moving round the earth or the earth round the sun? Who doubts that the law of attraction, as developed by Newton, is God's material law universally? The time is coming when the doctrine of Evolution, or the method of God in the creation of the world, will be just as universally accepted as either of these great physical doctrines. The whole Church fought them; yet they stand, conquerors.

Fifth.—Evolution is substantially held by men of profound Christian faith: by the now venerable and universally honored scientific teacher, Professor Dana of Yale College, a devout Christian and communicant of a Congregational Church; by Professor Le Conte of the University of California, an elder in the Presbyterian Church; by President McCosh of Princeton College, a Presbyterian of the Presbyterians, and a Scotch Presbyterian at that; by Professor Asa Gray of Harvard University, a communicant of the Christian Church; by increasing numbers of Christian preachers in America, by Catholics like Mivart, in England; by Wallace, a Christian not only, but of the spiritualistic school; by the Duke of Argyle of the Scotch Presbyterian Church; by Ground, an ardent admirer of Herbert Spencer and his whole theory, though rejecting his agnosticism—an eminent and leading divine in the Church of England; and finally, among hundreds of other soundly learned and Christian men, by the Bishop of London, Dr. Williams, whose Bampton Lectures for 1884 contain a bold, frank, and judicial estimate of Evolution, and its relations to Christianity.

Sixth.—To the fearful and the timid let me say, that while Evolution is certain to oblige theology to reconstruct its system, it will take nothing away from the grounds of true religion. It will strip off Saul's unmanageable armor from David, to give him greater power of the giant. Simple religion is the unfolding of the best nature of man towards God, and man has been hindered and embittered by the outrageous complexity of unbearable systems of theology that have existed. If you can change theology, you will emancipate religion; yet men are continually confounding the two terms, religion and theology. They are not alike. Religion is the condition of a man's nature as toward God and toward his fellow-men. That is religion—love that breeds truth, love that breeds justice, love that breeds harmonies of intimacy and intercommunication, love that breeds duty, love that breeds conscience, love that carries in its hand the scepter of pain, not to destroy and to torment, but to teach and to save. Religion is that state of mind in which a man is related by his emotions, and through his emotions by his will and conduct, to God and to the proper performance of duty in this world. Theology is the philosophy of God, of divine government, and of human nature. The philosophy of these may be one thing; the reality of them may be another and totally different one. Though intimately connected, they are not all the same. Theology is a science; religion, an art.

Evolution will multiply the motives and facilities of righteousness, which was and is the design of the whole Bible. It will not dull the executive doctrines of religion, that is, the forms of them by which an active and reviving ministry arouses men's consciences, by which they inspire faith, repentance, reformation, spiritual communion with God. Not only will those great truths be unharmed, by which men work zealously for the reformation of their fellow-men, but they will be developed to a breadth and certainty not possible in their present philosophical condition. At present the sword of the spirit is in the sheath of a false theology. Evolution, applied to religion, will influence it only as the hidden temples are restored, by removing the sands which have drifted in from the arid deserts of scholastic and medieval theologies. It will change theology, but only to bring out the simple temple of God in clearer and more beautiful lines and proportions.

Seventh.—In every view of it, I think we are to expect great practical fruit from the application of the truths that flow now from the interpretation of Evolution. It will obliterate the distinction between natural and revealed religion, both of which are the testimony of God; one, God's testimony as to what is best for man in his social and physical relations, and the other, what is best for man in his higher spiritual nature. What is called morality will be no longer dissevered from religion. Morals bear to spirituality the same relation which the root bears to the blossom and the fruit. Hitherto a false and imperfect theology has set them in two different provinces. We have been taught that morality will not avail us, and that spirituality is the only saving element: whereas, there is no spirituality itself without morality; all true spirituality is an outgrowth, it is the blossom and fruit on the stem of morality. It is time that these distinctions were obliterated, as they will be, by the progress and application of the doctrine of Evolution.

In every view, then, it is the duty of the friends of simple and unadulterated Christianity to hail the rising light and to uncover every element of religious teaching to its wholesome beams. Old men may be charitably permitted to die in peace, but young men and men in their prime are by God's providence laid under the most solemn obligation to thus discern the signs of the times, and to make themselves acquainted with the knowledge which science is laying before them. And above all, those zealots of the pulpit—who make faces at a science which they do not understand, and who reason from prejudice to ignorance, who not only will not lead their people, but hold up to scorn those who strive to take off the burden of ignorance from their shoulders—these men are bound to open their eyes and see God's sun shining in the heavens.

From How the Other Half Lives, *Jacob Riis (1890)*

Jacob Riis immigrated to the United States from Denmark in 1870. Unable to find work and one night having no money, he checked into a "police lodging room." In the morning he awoke to find a gold locket—his only memento from home—stolen and his adopted stray dog beaten to death; Riis wrote that "that one night cured him of dreaming." He eventually got a job as a police reporter for the *New York Tribune* from 1877 to 1888. Well known for his vivid descriptions of life in the most densely populated neighborhood in the world—335,000 people per square mile of the Tenth Ward—he left the newspaper in frustration to write *How the Other Half Lives* (1890).

It was not so much Riis's writing that brought him national recognition as the photographs he used to accompany the text. Theodore Roosevelt, then the head of the New York Police Board of Commissioners, stopped by Riis's office one day and left a note that read simply, "I have read your book and I have come to help." Riis's startling documentary photographs of slum life, together with the seven books and countless articles he continued to write, helped in the establishment of the Tenement House Commission, the construction of a multitude of children's playgrounds, and the closing of the police lodging houses. Theodore Roosevelt called him "the most useful citizen of New York and the best American I know."

Christian moralism is evident throughout Riis's work, and he was unable to resist generalizing about entire groups of immigrants. "Italians," he noted, "were happy-go-lucky and content to live in a pig sty." For the Jews, "money is their God," while wherever the Irish "mustered in force the saloon is the gorgeous center of political activity." Nonetheless, Riis's remarkably productive efforts, particularly on behalf of children, occupied most of the rest of his life from his house on 120th Street in Richmond Hill.

The Bend

WHERE Mulberry Street crooks like an elbow within hail of the old depravity of the Five Points is "the Bend," foul core of New York's slums. Long years ago the cows coming home from the pasture trod a path over this hill. Echoes of tinkling bells linger there still, but they do not call up memories of green meadows and summer fields; they proclaim the home-coming of the rag-picker's cart. In the memory of man the old cow-path has never been other than a vast human pig-sty. There is but one "Bend" in the world, and it is enough. The city authorities, moved by the angry protests of ten years of sanitary reform effort, have decided that it is too much and must come down. Another Paradise Park will take its place and let in sunlight and air to work such transformation as at the Five Points, around the corner of the next block. Never was change more urgently needed. Around "the Bend" cluster the bulk of the tenements that are stamped as altogether bad, even by the optimists of the Health Department. Incessant raids cannot keep down the crowds that make them their home. In the scores of back alleys, of stable lanes and hidden byways, of which the rent collector alone can keep track, they share such shelter as the ramshackle structures afford with every kind of abomination rifled from the dumps and ash-barrels of the city. Here, too, shunning the light, skulks the unclean beast of dishonest idleness. "The Bend" is the home of the tramp as well as the rag-picker.

It is not much more than twenty years since a census of "the Bend" district returned only twenty-four of the six hundred and nine tenements as in decent condition. Three-fourths of the population of the "Bloody Sixth" Ward were then Irish. The army of tramps that grew up after the disbandment of the armies in the field, and has kept up its muster-roll, together with the inrush of the Italian tide, have ever since opposed a stubborn barrier to all efforts at permanent improvement. The more that has been done, the less it has seemed to accomplish in the way of real relief, until it has at last become clear that nothing short of entire demolition will ever prove of radical benefit. Corruption could not have chosen ground for its stand with better promise of success. The whole district is a maze of narrow, often unsuspected passageways—necessarily, for there is scarce a lot that has not two, three, or four tenements upon it, swarming with unwholesome crowds. What a birds-eye view of "the Bend" would be like is a matter of bewildering conjecture. Its everyday appearance, as seen from the corner of Bayard Street on a sunny day, is one of the sights of New York.

Bayard Street is the high road to Jewtown across the Bowery, picketed from end to end with the outposts of Israel. Hebrew faces, Hebrew signs, and incessant chatter in the queer lingo that passes for Hebrew on the East Side attend the curious wanderer to the very corner of Mulberry Street. But the moment he turns the corner the scene changes abruptly. Before him lies spread out what might better be the market-place in some town in Southern Italy than a street in New York—all but the houses; they are still the same old tenements of the unromantic type. But for once they do not make the foreground in a slum picture from the American metropolis. The interest centres not in them, but in the crowd they shelter only when the street is not preferable, and that with the Italian is only when it rains or he is sick. When the sun shines the entire population seeks the street, carrying on its household work, its bargaining, its love-making on street or sidewalk, or idling there when it has nothing better to do, with the reverse of the impulse that makes the Polish Jew coop himself up in his den with the thermometer at stewing heat. Along the curb women sit in rows, young and old alike with the odd head-covering, pad or turban, that is their badge of servitude—her's to bear the burden as long as she lives—haggling over baskets of frowsy weeds, some sort of salad probably, stale tomatoes, and oranges not above suspicion. Ash-barrels serve them as counters, and not infrequently does the arrival of the official cart en route for the dump cause a temporary suspension of trade until the barrels have been emptied and restored. Hucksters' and pedlars' carts make two rows of booths in the street itself, and along the houses is still another—a perpetual market doing a very lively trade in its own queer staples, found nowhere on American ground save in "the Bend." Two old hags, camping on the pavement, are dispensing stale bread, baked not in loaves, but in the shape of big wreaths like exaggerated crullers, out of bags of dirty bed-tick. There is no use disguising the fact: they look like and they probably are old mattresses mustered into service under the pressure of a rush of trade. Stale bread was the one article the health officers, after a raid on the market, once reported as "not unwholesome." It was only disgusting. Here is a brawny butcher, sleeves rolled up above the elbows and clay pipe in mouth, skinning a kid that hangs from his hook. They will tell you with a laugh at the Elizabeth Street police station that only a few days ago when a dead goat had been reported lying in Pell Street it was mysteriously missing by the time the offal-cart came to take it away. It turned out that an Italian had carried it off in his sack to a wake or feast of some sort in one of the back alleys.

On either side of the narrow entrance to Bandit's Roost, one of the most notorious of these, is a shop that is a fair sample of the sort of invention necessity is the mother of in "the Bend." It is not enough that trucks and ash-barrels have provided four distinct lines of shops that are not down on the insurance maps, to accommodate the crowds. Here have the very hallways been made into shops. Three feet wide by four deep, they have just room for one, the shop-keeper, who, himself within, does his business outside, his wares displayed on a board hung across what was once the hall door. Back of the rear wall of this unique shop a hole has been punched from the hall into the alley and the tenants go that way. One of the shops is a "tobacco bureau," presided over by an unknown saint, done in yellow and red—there is not a shop, a stand, or an ash-barrel doing duty for a counter, that has not its patron saint—the other is a fish-stand full of slimy, odd-looking creatures, fish that never swam in American waters, or if they did, were never seen on an American fish-stand, and snails. Big, awkward sausages, anything but appetizing, hang in the grocer's doorway, knocking against the customer's head as if to remind him that they are there waiting to be bought. What they are I never had the courage to ask. Down the street comes a file of women carrying enormous bundles of fire-wood on their heads, loads of decaying vegetables from the market wagons in their aprons, and each a baby at the breast supported by a sort of sling that prevents it from tumbling down. The women do all the carrying, all the work one sees going on in "the Bend." The men sit or stand in the streets, on trucks, or in the open doors of the saloons smoking black clay pipes, talking and gesticulating as if forever on the point of coming to blows. Near a particularly boisterous group, a really pretty girl with a string of amber beads twisted artlessly in the knot of her raven hair has been bargaining long and earnestly with an old granny, who presides over a wheel-barrow load of second-hand stockings and faded cotton yarn, industriously darning the biggest holes while she extols the virtues of her stock. One of the rude swains, with patched overalls tucked into his boots, to whom the girl's eyes have strayed more than once, steps up and gallantly offers to pick her out the handsomest pair, whereat she laughs and pushes him away with a gesture which he interprets as an invitation to stay; and he does, evidently to the satisfaction of the beldame, who forthwith raises her prices fifty per cent. without being detected by the girl.

Red bandannas and yellow kerchiefs are everywhere; so is the Italian tongue, infinitely sweeter than the harsh gutturals of the Russian Jew around the corner. So are the "ristorantes" of innumerable Pasquales; half of the people in "the Bend" are christened Pasquale, or get the name in some other way. When the police do not know the name of an escaped murderer, they guess at Pasquale and send the name out on alarm; in nine cases out of ten it fits. So are the "banks" that hang out their shingle as tempting bait on every hand. There are half a dozen in the single block, steamship agencies, employment offices, and savings-banks, all in one. So are the toddling youngsters, bow-legged half of them, and so are no end of mothers, present and prospective, some of them scarce yet in their teens. Those who are not in the street are hanging half way out of the windows, shouting at some one below. All "the Bend" must be, if not altogether, at least half out of doors when the sun shines.

In the street, where the city wields the broom, there is at least an effort at cleaning up. There has to be, or it would be swamped in filth overrunning from the courts and alleys where the rag-pickers live. It requires more than ordinary courage to explore these on a hot day. The undertaker has to do it then, the police always. Right here, in this tenement on the east side of the street, they found little Antonia Candia, victim of fiendish cruelty, "covered," says the account found in the records of the Society for the Prevention of Cruelty to Children, "with sores, and her hair matted with dried blood." Abuse is the normal condition of "the Bend," murder its everyday crop, with the tenants not always the criminals. In this block between Bayard, Park, Mulberry, and Baxter Streets, "the Bend" proper, the late Tenement House Commission counted 155 deaths of children[1] in a specimen year (1882). Their percentage of the total mortality in the block was 68.28, while for the whole city the proportion was only 46.20. The infant mortality in any city or place as compared with the whole number of deaths is justly considered a good barometer of its general sanitary condition. Here, in this tenement, No. 591/2, next to Bandits' Roost, fourteen persons died that year, and eleven of them were children; in No. 61 eleven, and eight of them not yet five years old. According to the records in the Bureau of Vital Statistics only thirty-nine people lived in No. 591/2 in the year 1888, nine of them little children. There were five baby funerals in that house the same year. Out of the alley itself, No. 59, nine dead were carried in 1888, five in baby coffins. Here is the record of the year for the whole block, as furnished by the Registrar of Vital Statistics, Dr. Roger S. Tracy:

1. The term child means in the mortality tables a person under five years of age. Children five years old and over figure in the tables as adults.

DEATHS AND DEATH-RATES IN 1888 IN BAXTER AND MULBERRY STREET, BETWEEN PARK AND BAYARD STREETS

	Population			*Deaths*			*Death-rate*		
	Five years old and over	Under five years	Total	Five years old and over	Under five years	Total	Five years old and over	Under five years	General
Baxter Street	1,918	315	2,233	26	46	72	13.56	146.02	32.24
Mulberry Street	2,788	629	3,417	44	86	130	15.78	136.70	38.05
Total	4,706	944	5,650	70	132	202	14.87	139.83	35.75

The general death-rate for the whole city that year was 26.27.

These figures speak for themselves, when it is shown that in the model tenement across the way at Nos. 48 and 50, where the same class of people live in greater swarms (161, according to the record), but under good management, and in decent quarters, the hearse called that year only twice, once for a baby. The agent of the Christian people who built that tenement will tell you that Italians are good tenants, while the owner of the alley will oppose every order to put his property in repair with the claim that they are the worst of a bad lot. Both are right, from their different stand-points. It is the stand-point that makes the difference—and the tenant.

What if I were to tell you that this alley, and more tenement property in "the Bend," all of it notorious for years as the vilest and worst to be found anywhere, stood associated on the tax-books all through the long struggle to make its owners responsible, which has at last resulted in a qualified victory for the law, with the name of an honored family, one of the "oldest and best," rich in possessions and in influence, and high in the councils of the city's government? It would be but the plain truth. Nor would it be the only instance by very many that stand recorded on the Health Department's books of a kind that has come near to making the name of landlord as odious in New York as it has become in Ireland.

Bottle Alley is around the corner in Baxter Street; but it is a fair specimen of its kind, wherever found. Look into any of these houses, everywhere the same piles of rags, of malodorous bones and musty paper, all of which the sanitary police flatter themselves they have banished to the dumps and the warehouses. Here is a "flat" of "parlor" and two pitch-dark coops called bedrooms. Truly, the bed is all there is room for. The family tea-kettle is on the stove, doing duty for the time being as a wash-boiler. By night it will have returned to its proper use again, a practical illustration of how poverty in "the Bend" makes both ends meet. One, two, three beds are there, if the old boxes and heaps of foul straw can be called by that name; a broken stove with crazy pipe from which the smoke leaks at every joint, a table of rough boards propped up on boxes, piles of rubbish in the corner. The closeness and smell are appalling. How many people sleep here? The woman with the red bandanna shakes her head sullenly, but the bare-legged girl with the bright face counts on her fingers—five, six!

"Six, sir!" Six grown people and five children.

"Only five," she says with a smile, swathing the little one on her lap in its cruel bandage. There is another in the cradle—actually a cradle. And how much the rent?

Nine and a half, and "please, sir! he won't put the paper on."

"He" is the landlord. The "paper" hangs in musty shreds on the wall.

Well do I recollect the visit of a health inspector to one of these tenements on a July day when the thermometer outside was climbing high in the nineties; but inside, in that awful room, with half a dozen persons washing, cooking, and sorting rags, lay the dying baby alongside the stove, where the doctor's thermometer ran up to 115°! Perishing for the want of a breath of fresh air in this city of untold charities! Did not the manager of the Fresh Air Fund write to the pastor of an Italian Church only last year[2] that "no one asked for Italian children," and hence he could not send any to the country?

Half a dozen blocks up Mulberry Street there is a rag-picker's settlement, a sort of overflow from "the Bend," that exists to-day in all its pristine nastiness. Something like forty families are packed into five old two-story and attic houses that were built to hold five, and out in the yards additional crowds are, or were until very recently, accommodated in sheds built of all sorts of old boards and used as drying racks for the Italian tenants' "stock." I found them empty when I visited the settlement while writing this. The last two tenants had just left. Their fate was characteristic. The "old man," who lived in the corner coop, with barely room to crouch beside the stove —there would not have been room for him to sleep had not age crooked his frame to fit his house—had been taken to the "crazy-house," and the woman who was his neighbor and had lived in her shed for years had simply disappeared. The agent and the other tenants "guessed," doubtless correctly, that she might be found on the "island," but she was decrepit anyhow from rheumatism, and "not much good," and no one took the trouble to inquire for her. They had all they could do attending to their own business and raising the rent. No wonder; I found that for one front room and two "bed-

2. See City Mission Report, February, 1890, page 77.

rooms" in the shameful old wrecks of buildings the tenant was paying $10 a month, for the back-room and one bedroom $9, and for the attic rooms, according to size, from $3.75 to $5.50.

There is a standing quarrel between the professional—I mean now the official—sanitarian and the unsalaried agitator for sanitary reform over the question of overcrowded tenements. The one puts the number a little vaguely at four or five hundred, while the other asserts that there are thirty-two thousand, the whole number of houses classed as tenements at the census of two years ago, taking no account of the better kind of flats. It depends on the angle from which one sees it which is right. At best the term overcrowding is a relative one, and the scale of official measurement conveniently sliding. Under the pressure of the Italian influx the standard of breathing space required for an adult by the health officers has been cut down from six to four hundred cubic feet. The "needs of the situation" is their plea, and no more perfect argument could be advanced for the reformer's position.

It is in "the Bend" the sanitary policeman locates the bulk of his four hundred, and the sanitary reformer gives up the task in despair. Of its vast homeless crowds the census takes no account. It is their instinct to shun the light, and they cannot be corralled in one place long enough to be counted. But the houses can, and the last count showed that in "the Bend" district, between Broadway and the Bowery and Canal and Chatham Streets, in a total of four thousand three hundred and sixty-seven "apartments" only nine were for the moment vacant, while in the old "Africa," west of Broadway, that receives the overflow from Mulberry Street and is rapidly changing its character, the notice "standing room only" is up. Not a single vacant room was found there. Nearly a hundred and fifty "lodgers" were driven out of two adjoining Mulberry Street tenements, one of them aptly named "the House of Blazes," during that census. What squalor and degradation inhabit these dens the health officers know. Through the long summer days their carts patrol "the Bend," scattering disinfectants in streets and lanes, in sinks and cellars, and hidden hovels where the tramp burrows. From midnight till far into the small hours of the morning the policeman's thundering rap on closed doors is heard, with his stern command, "*Apri port'!*" on his rounds gathering evidence of illegal overcrowding. The doors are opened unwillingly enough—but the order means business, and the tenant knows it even if he understands no word of English—upon such scenes: In a room not thirteen feet either way slept twelve men and women, two or three in bunks set in a sort of alcove, the rest on the floor. A kerosene lamp burned dimly in the fearful atmosphere, probably to guide other and later arrivals to their "beds," for it was only just past midnight. A baby's fretful wail came from an adjoining hall-room, where, in the semi-darkness, three recumbent figures could be made out. The "apartment" was one of three in two adjoining buildings we had found, within half an hour, similarly crowded. Most of the men were lodgers, who slept there for five cents a spot.

Another room on the top floor, that had been examined a few nights before, was comparatively empty. There were only four persons in it, two men, an old woman, and a young girl. The landlord opened the door with alacrity, and exhibited with a proud sweep of his hand the sacrifice he had made of his personal interests to satisfy the law. Our visit had been anticipated. The policeman's back was probably no sooner turned than the room was reopened for business.

The Color Line in New York

The color line must be drawn through the tenements to give the picture its proper shading. The landlord does the drawing, does it with an absence of pretence, a frankness of despotism, that is nothing if not brutal. The Czar of all the Russias is not more absolute upon his own soil than the New York landlord in his dealings with colored tenants. Where he permits them to live, they go; where he shuts the door, stay out. By his grace they exist at all in certain localities; his ukase banishes them from others. He accepts the responsibility, when laid at his door, with unruffled complacency. It is business, he will tell you. And it is. He makes the prejudice in which he traffics pay him well, and that, as he thinks it quite superfluous to tell you, is what he is there for.

That his pencil does not make quite as black a mark as it did, that the hand that wields it does not bear down as hard as only a short half dozen years ago, is the hopeful sign of an awakening public conscience under the stress of which the line shows signs of wavering. But for this the landlord deserves no credit. It has come, is coming about despite him. The line may not be wholly effaced while the name of the negro, alone among the world's races, is spelled with a small n. Natural selection will have more or less to do beyond a doubt in every age with dividing the races; only so, it may be, can they work out together their highest destiny. But with the despotism that deliberately assigns to the defenceless Black the lowest level for the purpose of robbing him there that has nothing to do. Of such slavery, different only in degree from the other kind that held him as a chattel, to be sold or bartered at the will of his master, this century, if signs fail not, will see the end in New York.

Ever since the war New York has been receiving the overflow of colored population from the Southern cities. In the last decade this migration has grown to such proportions that it is estimated that our Blacks have quite doubled in number since the Tenth Census. Whether the exchange has been of advantage to the negro may well be questioned. Trades of which he had practical control in his Southern home are not open to him here. I know that it may be answered that there is no industrial proscription of color; that it is a matter of choice. Perhaps so. At all events he does not choose then. How many colored carpenters or masons has anyone seen at work in New York? In the South there are enough of them and, if the testimony of the most intelligent of their people is worth anything, plenty of them have come here. As a matter of fact the colored man takes in New York, without a struggle, the lower level of menial service for which his past traditions and natural love of ease perhaps as yet fit him best. Even the colored barber is rapidly getting to be a thing of the past. Along shore, at any unskilled labor, he works unmolested; but he does not appear to prefer the job. His sphere thus defined, he naturally takes his stand among the poor, and in the homes of the poor. Until very recent times—the years since a change was wrought can be counted on the fingers of one hand—he was practically restricted in the choice of a home to a narrow section on the West Side, that nevertheless had a social top and bottom to it—the top in the tenements on the line of Seventh Avenue as far north as Thirty-second Street, where he was allowed to occupy the houses of unsavory reputation which the police had cleared and for which decent white tenants could not be found; the bottom in the vile rookeries of Thompson Street and South Fifth Avenue, the old "Africa" that is now fast becoming a modern Italy. To-day there are black colonies in Yorkville and Morrisania. The encroachment of business and the Italian below, and the swelling of the population above, have been the chief agents in working out his second emancipation, a very real one, for with his cutting loose from the old tenements there has come a distinct and gratifying improvement in the tenant, that argues louder than theories or speeches the influence of vile surroundings in debasing the man. The colored citizen whom this year's census man found in his Ninety-ninth Street "flat" is a very different individual from the "nigger" his predecessor counted in the black-and-tan slums of Thompson and Sullivan Streets. There is no more clean and orderly community in New York than the new settlement of colored people that is growing up on the East Side from Yorkville to Harlem.

Cleanliness is the characteristic of the negro in his new surroundings, as it was his virtue in the old. In this respect he is immensely the superior of the lowest of the whites, the Italians and the Polish Jews, below whom he has been classed in the past in the tenant scale. Nevertheless, he has always had to pay higher rents than even these for the poorest and most stinted rooms. The exceptions I have come across, in which the rents, though high, have seemed more nearly on a level with what was asked for the same number and size of rooms in the average tenement, were in the case of tumble-down rookeries in which no one else would live, and were always coupled with the condition that the landlord should "make no repairs." It can readily be seen that his profits were scarcely curtailed by his "humanity." The reason advanced for this systematic robbery is that white people will not live in the same house with colored tenants, or even in a house recently occupied by negroes, and that consequently its selling value is injured. The prejudice undoubtedly exists, but it is not lessened by the house agents, who have set up the maxim "once a colored house, always a colored house."

There is method in the maxim, as shown by an inquiry made last year by the *Real Estate Record.* It proved agents to be practically unanimous in the endorsement of the negro as a clean, orderly, and "profitable" tenant. Here is the testimony of one of the largest real estate firms in the city: "We would rather have negro tenants in our poorest class of tenements than the lower grades of foreign white people. We find the former cleaner than the latter, and they do not destroy the property so much. We also get higher prices. We have a tenement on Nineteenth Street, where we get $10 for two rooms which we could not get more than $7.50 for from white tenants previously. We have a four-story tenement on our books on Thirty-third Street, between Sixth and Seventh Avenues, with four rooms per floor—a parlor, two bedrooms, and a kitchen. We get $20 for the first floor, $24 for the second, $23 for the third and $20 for the fourth, in all $87 or $1,044 per annum. The size of the building is only 21 + 55." Another firm declared that in a specified instance they had saved fifteen to twenty per cent. on the gross rentals since they changed from white to colored tenants. Still another gave the following case of a front and rear tenement that had formerly been occupied by tenants of a "low European type," who had been turned out on account of filthy habits and poor pay. The negroes proved cleaner, better, and steadier tenants. Instead, however, of having their rents reduced in consequence, [there was] an increased rental of $17 per month, or $204 a year, and an advance of nearly thirteen and one-half per cent. on the gross rental "in favor" of the colored tenant. Profitable, surely! . . .

Poverty, abuse, and injustice alike the negro accepts with imperturbable cheerfulness. His philosophy is of the kind that has no room for repining.

Whether he lives in an Eighth Ward barrack or in a tenement with a brownstone front and pretensions to the title of "flat," he looks at the sunny side of life and enjoys it. He loves fine clothes and good living a good deal more than he does a bank account. The proverbial rainy day it would be rank ingratitude, from his point of view, to look for when the sun shines unclouded in a clear sky. His home surroundings, except when he is utterly depraved, reflect his blithesome temper. The poorest negro housekeeper's room in New York is bright with gaily-colored prints of his beloved "Abe Linkum," General Grant, President Garfield, Mrs. Cleveland, and other national celebrities, and cheery with flowers and singing birds. In the art of putting the best foot foremost, of disguising his poverty by making a little go a long way, our negro has no equal. When a fair share of prosperity is his, he knows how to make life and home very pleasant to those about him. Pianos and parlor furniture abound in the uptown homes of colored tenants and give them a very prosperous air. But even where the wolf howls at the door, he makes a bold and gorgeous front. The amount of "style" displayed on fine Sundays on Sixth and Seventh Avenues by colored holiday-makers would turn a pessimist black with wrath. The negro's great ambition is to rise in the social scale to which his color has made him a stranger and an outsider, and he is quite willing to accept the shadow for the substance where that is the best he can get. The claw-hammer coat and white tie of a waiter in a first-class summer hotel, with the chance of taking his ease in six months of winter, are to him the next best thing to mingling with the white quality he serves, on equal terms. His festive gatherings, pre-eminently his cakewalks, at which a sugared and frosted cake is the proud prize of the couple with the most aristocratic step and carriage, are comic mixtures of elaborate ceremonial and the joyous abandon of the natural man. With all his ludicrous incongruities, his sensuality and his lack of moral accountability, his superstition and other faults that are the effect of temperament and of centuries of slavery, he has his eminently good points. He is loyal to the backbone, proud of being an American and of his new-found citizenship. He is at least as easily moulded for good as for evil. His churches are crowded to the doors on Sunday nights when the colored colony turns out to worship. His people own church property in this city upon which they have paid half a million dollars out of the depth of their poverty, with comparatively little assistance from their white brethren. He is both willing and anxious to learn, and his intellectual status is distinctly improving. If his emotions are not very deeply rooted, they are at least sincere while they last, and until the tempter gets the upper hand again.

Of all the temptations that beset him, the one that troubles him and the police most is his passion for gambling. The game of policy is a kind of unlawful penny lottery specially adapted to his means, but patronized extensively by poor white players as well. It is the meanest of swindles, but reaps for its backers rich fortunes wherever colored people congregate. Between the fortune-teller and the policy shop, closely allied frauds always, the wages of many a hard day's work are wasted by the negro; but the loss causes him few regrets. Penniless, but with undaunted faith in his ultimate "luck," he looks forward to the time when he shall once more be able to take a hand at "beating policy." When periodically the negro's lucky numbers, 4-11-44, come out on the slips of the alleged daily drawings, that are supposed to be held in some far-off Western town, intense excitement reigns in Thompson Street and along the Avenue, where someone is always the winner. An immense impetus is given then to the bogus business that has no existence outside of the cigar stores and candy shops where it hides from the law, save in some cunning Bowery "broker's" back office, where the slips are printed and the "winnings" apportioned daily with due regard to the backer's interests.

It is a question whether "Africa" has been improved by the advent of the Italian, with the tramp from the Mulberry Street Bend in his train. The moral turpitude of Thompson Street has been notorious for years, and the mingling of the three elements does not seem to have wrought any change for the better. The border-land where the white and black races meet in common debauch, the aptly-named black-and-tan saloon, has never been debatable ground from a moral stand-point. It has always been the worst of the desperately bad. Than this commingling of the utterly depraved of both sexes, white and black, on such ground, there can be no greater abomination. Usually it is some foul cellar dive, perhaps run by the political "leader" of the district, who is "in with" the police. In any event it gathers to itself all the lawbreakers and all the human wrecks within reach. When a fight breaks out during the dance a dozen razors are handy in as many boot-legs, and there is always a job for the surgeon and the ambulance. The black "tough" is as handy with the razor in a fight as his peaceably inclined brother is with it in pursuit of his honest trade. As the Chinaman hides his knife in his sleeve and the Italian his stiletto in the bosom, so the negro goes to the ball with a razor in his boot-leg, and on occasion does as much execution with it as both of the others together. More than three-fourths of the business the police have with the colored people in New York arises in the black-and-tan district, now no longer fairly representative of their color.

I have touched briefly upon such facts in the negro's life as may serve to throw light on the social condition of his people in New York. If, when the account is made up between the races, it shall be claimed that he falls short of the result to be expected from twenty-five years of freedom, it may be well to turn to the other side of the ledger and see how much of the blame is borne by the prejudice and greed that have kept him from rising under a burden of responsibility to which he could hardly be equal. And in this view he may be seen to have advanced much farther and faster than before suspected, and to promise, after all, with fair treatment, quite as well as the rest of us, his white-skinned fellow-citizens, had any right to expect.

The Mixed Crowd

When once I asked the agent of a notorious Fourth Ward alley how many people might be living in it I was told: One hundred and forty families, one hundred Irish, thirty-eight Italian, and two that spoke the German tongue. Barring the agent herself, there was not a native-born individual in the court. The answer was characteristic of the cosmopolitan character of lower New York, very nearly so of the whole of it, wherever it runs to alleys and courts. One may find for the asking an Italian, a German, a French, African, Spanish, Bohemian, Russian, Scandinavian, Jewish, and Chinese colony. Even the Arab, who peddles "holy earth" from the Battery as a direct importation from Jerusalem, has his exclusive preserves at the lower end of Washington Street. The one thing you shall vainly ask for in the chief city of America is a distinctively American community. There is none; certainly not among the tenements. Where have they gone to, the old inhabitants? I put the question to one who might fairly be presumed to be of the number, since I had found him sighing for the "good old days" when the legend "no Irish need apply" was familiar in the advertising columns of the newspapers. He looked at me with a puzzled air. "I don't know," he said. "I wish I did. Some went to California in '49, some to the war and never came back. The rest, I expect, have gone to heaven, or somewhere. I don't see them 'round here."

Whatever the merit of the good man's conjectures, his eyes did not deceive him. They are not here. In their place has come this queer conglomerate mass of heterogeneous elements, ever striving and working like whiskey and water in one glass, and with the like result: final union and a prevailing taint of whiskey. The once unwelcome Irishman has been followed in his turn by the Italian, the Russian Jew, and the Chinaman, and has himself taken a hand at opposition, quite as bitter and quite as ineffectual, against these later hordes. Wherever these have gone they have crowded him out, possessing the block, the street, the ward with their denser swarms. But the Irishman's revenge is complete. Victorious in defeat over his recent as over his more ancient foe, the one who opposed his coming no less than the one who drove him out, he dictates to both their politics, and, secure in possession of the offices, returns the native his greeting with interest, while collecting the rents of the Italian whose house he has bought with the profits of his saloon. As a landlord he is picturesquely autocratic. An amusing instance of his methods came under my notice while writing these lines. An inspector of the Health Department found an Italian family paying a man with a Celtic name twenty-five dollars a month for three small rooms in a ramshackle rear tenement—more than twice what they were worth—and expressed his astonishment to the tenant, an ignorant Sicilian laborer. He replied that he had once asked the landlord to reduce the rent, but he would not do it.

"Well! What did he say?" asked the inspector.

"'Damma, man!' he said: 'if you speaka thata way to me, I fira you and your things in the streeta.'" And the frightened Italian paid the rent.

In justice to the Irish landlord it must be said that like an apt pupil he was merely showing forth the result of the schooling he had received, re-enacting, in his own way, the scheme of the tenements. It is only his frankness that shocks. The Irishman does not naturally take kindly to tenement life, though with characteristic versatility he adapts himself to its conditions at once. It does violence, nevertheless, to the best that is in him, and for that very reason of all who come within its sphere soonest corrupts him. The result is a sediment, the product of more than a generation in the city's slums, that, as distinguished from the larger body of his class, justly ranks at the foot of tenement dwellers, the so-called "low Irish."

It is not to be assumed, of course, that the whole body of the population living in the tenements, of which New Yorkers are in the habit of speaking vaguely as "the poor," or even the larger part of it, is to be classed as vicious or as poor in the sense of verging on beggary.

New York's wage-earners have no other place to live, more is the pity. They are truly poor for having no better homes; waxing poorer in purse as the exorbitant rents to which they are tied, as ever was serf to soil, keep rising. The wonder is that they are not all corrupted, and speedily, by their surroundings. If, on the contrary, there be a steady working up, if not out of the slough, the fact is a powerful argument for the optimist's belief that the world is, after all, growing better, not worse, and would go far toward disarming apprehension, were it not for the steadier growth of the sediment of the slums and its constant menace. Such an impulse toward better things there certainly is. The German rag-picker of thirty years ago, quite as low in the scale as his Italian successor, is the thrifty tradesman or prosperous farmer of to-day.[3]

The Italian scavenger of our time is fast graduating into exclusive control of the corner fruit-stands, while his black-eyed boy monopolizes the boot-blacking industry in which a few years ago he was an intruder. The Irish hod-carrier in the second generation has become a bricklayer, if not the Alderman of his ward, while the Chinese coolie is in almost exclusive possession of the laundry business. The reason is obvious. The poorest immigrant comes here with the purpose and ambition to better himself and, given half a chance, might be reasonably expected to make the most of it. To the false plea that he prefers the squalid homes in which his kind are housed there could be no better answer. The truth is, his half chance has too long been wanting, and for the bad result he has been unjustly blamed.

As emigration from east to west follows the latitude, so does the foreign influx in New York distribute itself along certain well-defined lines that waver and break only under the stronger pressure of a more gregarious race or the encroachments of inexorable business. A feeling of dependence upon mutual effort, natural to strangers in a strange land, unacquainted with its language and customs, sufficiently accounts for this.

The Irishman is the true cosmopolitan immigrant. All-pervading, he shares his lodging with perfect impartiality with the Italian, the Greek, and the "Dutchman," yielding only to sheer force of numbers, and objects equally to them all. A map of the city, colored to designate nationalities, would show more stripes than on the skin of a zebra, and more colors than any rainbow. The city on such a map would fall into two great halves, green for the Irish prevailing in the West Side tenement districts, and blue for the Germans on the East Side. But intermingled with these ground colors would be an odd variety of tints that would give the whole the appearance of an extraordinary crazy-quilt. From down in the Sixth Ward, upon the site of the old Collect Pond that in the days of the fathers drained the hills which are no more, the red of the Italian would be seen forcing its way northward along the line of Mulberry Street to the quarter of the French purple on Bleecker Street and South Fifth Avenue, to lose itself and reappear, after a lapse of miles, in the

3. The Sheriff Street Colony of rag-pickers, long since gone, is an instance in point. The thrifty Germans saved up money during years of hard work in squalor and apparently wretched poverty to buy a township in a Western State, and the whole colony moved out there in a body. There need be no doubt about their thriving there.

"Little Italy" of Harlem, east of Second Avenue. Dashes of red, sharply defined, would be seen strung through the Annexed District, northward to the city line. On the West Side the red would be seen overrunning the old Africa of Thompson Street, pushing the black of the negro rapidly uptown, against querulous but unavailing protests, occupying his home, his church, his trade and all, with merciless impartiality. There is a church in Mulberry Street that has stood for two generations as a sort of milestone of these migrations. Built originally for the worship of staid New Yorkers of the "old stock," it was engulfed by the colored tide, when the draft-riots drove the negroes out of reach of Cherry Street and the Five Points. Within the past decade the advance wave of the Italian onset reached it, and to-day the arms of United Italy adorn its front. The negroes have made a stand at several points along Seventh and Eighth Avenues; but their main body, still pursued by the Italian foe, is on the march yet, and the black mark will be found overshadowing to-day many blocks on the East Side, with One Hundredth Street as the center, where colonies of them have settled recently.

Hardly less aggressive than the Italian, the Russian and Polish Jew, having overrun the district between Rivington and Division Streets, east of the Bowery, to the point of suffocation, is filling the tenements of the old Seventh Ward to the river front, and disputing with the Italian every foot of available space in the back alleys of Mulberry Street. The two races, differing hopelessly in much, have this in common: they carry their slums with them wherever they go, if allowed to do it. Little Italy already rivals its parent, the "Bend," in foulness. Other nationalities that begin at the bottom make a fresh start when crowded up the ladder. Happily both are manageable, the one by rabbinical, the other by the civil law. Between the dull gray of the Jew, his favorite color, and the Italian red, would be seen squeezed in on the map a sharp streak of yellow, marking the narrow boundaries of Chinatown. Dovetailed in with the German population, the poor but thrifty Bohemian might be picked out by the sombre hue of his life as of his philosophy, struggling against heavy odds in the big human bee-hives of the East Side. Colonies of his people extend northward, with long lapses of space, from below the Cooper Institute more than three miles. The Bohemian is the only foreigner with any considerable representation in the city who counts no wealthy man of his race, none who has not to work hard for a living, or has got beyond the reach of the tenement.

Down near the Battery the West Side emerald would be soiled by a dirty stain, spreading rapidly like a splash of ink on a sheet of blotting paper, headquarters of the Arab tribe, that in a single year has swelled from the original dozen to twelve hundred, intent, every mother's son, on trade and barter. Dots and dashes of color here and there would show where the Finnish sailors worship their djumala (God), the Greek pedlars the ancient name of their race, and the Swiss the goddess of thrift. And so on to the end of the long register, all toiling together in the galling fetters of the tenement. Were the question raised who makes the most of life thus mortgaged, who resists most stubbornly its levelling tendency—knows how to drag even the barracks upward a part of the way at least toward the ideal plane of the home—the palm must be unhesitatingly awarded the Teuton. The Italian and the poor Jew rise only by compulsion. The Chinaman does not rise at all; here, as at home, he simply remains stationary. The Irishman's genius runs to public affairs rather than domestic life; wherever he is mustered in force the saloon is the gorgeous centre of political activity. The German struggles vainly to learn his trick; his Teutonic wit is too heavy, and the political ladder he raises from his saloon usually too short or too clumsy to reach the desired goal. The best part of his life is lived at home, and he makes himself a home independent of the surroundings, giving the lie to the saying, unhappily become a maxim of social truth, that pauperism and drunkenness naturally grow in the tenements. He makes the most of his tenement, and it should be added that whenever and as soon as he can save up money enough, he gets out and never crosses the threshold of one again.

A Glimpse of High Society, from Society as I Have Found It, *Ward McAllister (1890)*

"A dinner invitation, once accepted, is a sacred obligation. If you die before the dinner takes place, your executor must attend." So wrote Samuel Ward McAllister in his memoir *Society as I Have Found It* (1890). In some ways, McAllister essentially founded New York Society through the formation of the "Four Hundred"—the number of elite members who could fit into Mrs. William Astor's ballroom. The "Four Hundred"—actually 213 families and individuals whose lineage could be traced back at least three generations—was promoted heavily and finally published in *The New York Times* in February 1892. These were the people who controlled the social scene of winters in New York and summers in Newport, Rhode Island, where many of them built million-dollar "cottages."

Ironically, McAllister had been born in Savannah, Georgia, in 1827, made a significant amount of money as a lawyer in San Francisco, married a Georgia millionaire's daughter in 1853, and moved to New York City (with a second residence in Newport). McAllister's rise as social arbiter was actually the result of William Astor's love of yachting. His wife, Caroline Astor, took McAllister as her social escort; together they ruthlessly plotted, planned, and oversaw the "high society" that Edith Wharton described in her novels.

Entering Society

I WOULD now make some suggestions as to the proper way of introducing a young girl into New York society, particularly if she is not well supported by an old family connection. It is cruel to take a girl to a ball where she knows no one,

> *"And to subject her to*
> *The fashionable stare of twenty score*
> *Of well-bred persons, called 'the world.'"*

Had I charged a fee for every consultation with anxious mothers on this subject, I would be a rich man. I well remember a near relative of mine once writing me from Paris, as follows: "I consign my wife and daughter to your care. They will spend the winter in New York; at once give them a ball at Delmonico's, and draw on me for the outlay." I replied, "My dear fellow, how many people do you know in this city whom you could invite to a ball? The funds you send me will be used, but not in giving a ball." The girl being a beauty, all the rest was easy enough. I gave her theatre party after theatre party, followed by charming little suppers, asked to them the *jeunesse dorée* of the day; took her repeatedly to the opera, and saw that she was there always surrounded by admirers; incessantly talked of her fascinations; assured my young friends that she was endowed with a fortune equal to the mines of Ophir, that she danced like a dream, and possessed all the graces, a sunbeam across one's path; then saw to it that she had a prominent place in every cotillion, and a fitting partner; showed her whom to smile upon, and on whom to frown; gave her the *entrée* to all the nice houses; criticised severely her toilet until it became perfect; daily met her on the Avenue with the most charming man in town, who by one pretext or another I turned over to her; made her the constant subject of conversation; insisted upon it that she was to be the belle of the coming winter; advised her parents that she should have her first season at Bar Harbor, where she could learn to flirt to her heart's content, and vie with other girls. Her second summer, when she was older, I suggested her passing at Newport, where she should have a pair of ponies, a pretty trap, with a well-gotten-up groom, and Worth to dress her. Here I hinted that much must depend on her father's purse, as to her wardrobe. As a friend of mine once said to me, "Your pace is charming, but can you keep it up?" I also advised keeping the young girl well in hand and not letting her give offense to the powers that be; to see to it that she was not the first to arrive and the last to leave a ball, and further, that nothing was more winning in a girl than a pleasant bow and a gracious smile given to either young or old. The fashion now for women is to hold themselves erect. The modern manner of shaking hands I do not like, but yet it is adopted. Being interested in the girl's success, I further impressed upon her the importance of making herself agreeable to older people, remembering that much of her enjoyment would be derived from them. If asked to dance a cotillion, let it be conditional that no bouquet be sent her; to be cautious how she refused the first offers of marriage made her, as they were generally the best. . . .

The launching of a beautiful young girl into society is one thing; it is another to place her family on a good, sound social footing. You can launch them into the social sea, but can they float? "Manners maketh man," is an old proverb. These they certainly must possess. There is no society in the world as generous as New York society is; "friend, parent, neighbor, all it will embrace," but once embraced they must have the power of sustaining themselves. The best quality for them to possess is modesty in asserting their claims; letting people seek them rather than attempting to rush too quickly to the front. The Prince of Wales, on a charming American young woman expressing her surprise at the cordial reception given her by London society, replied, "My dear lady, there are certain people who are bound to come to the front and stay there; you are one of them." It requires not only money, but brains, and, above all, infinite tact; possessing the three, your success is assured. If taken by the hand by a person in society you are at once led into the charmed circle, and then your own correct perceptions of what should or should not be done must do the rest. As a philosophical friend once said to me, "A gentleman can always walk, but he cannot afford to have a shabby equipage." Another philosopher soliloquized as follows: "The first evidence of wealth is your equipage." By the way, his definition of aristocracy in America was, the possession of hereditary wealth.

If you want to be fashionable, be always in the company of fashionable people. As an old beau suggested to me, If you see a fossil of a man, shabbily dressed, relying solely on his pedigree, dating back to time immemorial, who has the aspirations of a duke and the fortunes of a footman, do not cut him; it is better to cross the street and avoid meeting him. It is well to be in with the nobs who are born to their position, but the support of the swells is more advantageous, for society is sustained and carried on by the swells, the nobs looking quietly on and accepting the position, feeling they are there by divine right; but they do not make fashionable society, or carry it on. A nob can be a swell if he chooses, i.e. if he will spend the money; but for his social existence this is unnecessary. A nob is like a poet,—*nascitur non fit;* not so a swell,—he creates himself. . . .

Here, all men are more or less in business. We hardly have a class who are not. They are, of necessity, daily brought in contact with all sorts and conditions of men, and in self-defense oftentimes have to acquire and adopt an abrupt, a brusque manner of address, which, as a rule, they generally leave in their offices when they quit them. If they do not, they certainly should. When such rough manners become by practice a second nature, they unfit one to go into society. It pays well for young and old to cultivate politeness and courtesy. Nothing is gained by trying roughly to elbow yourself into society, and push your way through into the inner circle; for when such a one has reached it, he will find its atmosphere uncongenial and be only too glad to escape from it. . . .

I think the great secret of life is to be contented with the position to which it has pleased God to call you. Living myself in a modest, though comfortable little house in Twenty-first Street in this city, a Wall Street banker honored me with a visit, and exclaimed against my surroundings.

"What!" said he, "are you contented to live in this modest little house? Why, man, this will never do! The first thing you must have is a fine house. I will see that you get it. All that you have to do is to let me buy ten thousand shares of stock for you at the opening of the Board; by three I can sell it, and I will then send you a check for the profit of the transaction, which will not be less than ten thousand dollars! Do it for you? Of course I will, with pleasure. You will run no risk; if there is a loss I will bear it."

I thanked my friend, assured him I was wholly and absolutely contented, and must respectfully decline his offer. A similar offer was made to me by my old friend, Commodore Vanderbilt, in his house in Washington Place. I was a great admirer of this grand old man, and he was very fond of me. He had taken me over his stables, and was then showing me his parlors and statuary, and kept all the time calling me "his boy." I turned to him and said, "Commodore, you will be as great a railroad king, as you were once an ocean king, and as you call me your boy, why don't you make my fortune?" He thought a moment, and then said, slapping me on the back, "Mc, sell everything you have and put it in Harlem stock; it is now twenty-four; you will make more money than you will know how to take care of." If I had followed his advice, I would now have been indeed a millionaire.

One word more here about the Commodore. He then turned to me and said, "Mc, look at that bust,"—a bust of himself, by Powers. "What do you think Powers said of that head?"

"What did he say?" I replied.

"He said, 'It is a finer head than Webster's!'"

Success in Entertaining

The first object to be aimed at is to make your dinners so charming and agreeable that invitations to them are eagerly sought for, and to let all feel that it is a great privilege to dine at your house, where they are sure they will meet only those whom they wish to meet. You cannot instruct people by a book how to entertain, though Aristotle is said to have applied *his* talents to a compilation of a code of laws for the table. Success in entertaining is accomplished by magnetism and tact, which combined constitute social genius. It is the ladder to social success. If successfully done, it naturally creates jealousy. I have known a family who for years outdid every one in giving exquisite dinners—(this was when this city was a small community)—driven to Europe and passing the rest of their days there on finding a neighbor outdoing them. I myself once lost a charming friend by giving a better soup than he did. His wife rushed home from my house, and in despair, throwing up her hands to her husband, exclaimed, "Oh! what a soup!" I related this to my cousin, the distinguished *gourmet,* who laughingly said: "Why did you not at once invite them to pork and beans?"

The highest cultivation in social manners enables a person to conceal from the world his real feelings. He can go through any annoyance as if it were a pleasure; go to a rival's house as if to a dear friend's; "Smile and smile, yet murder while he smiles." A great compliment once paid me in Newport was the speech of an old public waiter, who had grown gray in the service, when to a *confrère* he exclaimed: "In this house, my friend, you meet none but quality."

In planning a dinner the question is not to whom you owe dinners, but who is most desirable. The success of the dinner depends as much upon the company as the cook. Discordant elements—people invited alphabetically, or to pay off debts—are fatal. Of course, I speak of ladies' dinners. And here, great tact must be used in bringing together young womanhood and the dowagers. A dinner wholly made up of young people is generally stupid. You require the experienced woman of the world, who has at her fingers' ends the history of past, present, and future. Critical, scandalous, with keen and ready wit, appreciating the dinner and wine at their worth. Ladies in beautiful toilets are necessary to the elegance of a dinner, as a most exquisitely arranged table is only a solemn affair surrounded by black coats. I make it a rule never to attend such dismal feasts, listening to prepared witticisms and "twice-told tales." So much for your guests.

The next step is an interview with your *chef,* if you have one, or *cordon bleu,* whom you must arouse to fever heat by working on his ambition and vanity. You must impress upon him that this particular dinner will give him fame and lead to fortune. My distinguished cousin, who enjoyed the reputation of being one of the most finished *gourmets* in this country, when he reached this point, would bury his head in his hands and (seemingly to the *chef*) rack his brain seeking inspiration, fearing lest the fatal mistake should occur of letting two white or brown sauces follow each other in succession; or truffles appear twice in that dinner. The distress that his countenance wore as he repeatedly looked up at the *chef,* as if for advice and assistance, would have its intended effect on the culinary artist, and *his* brain would at once act in sympathy.

From New York History 1860–1890, *Theodore Roosevelt (1891)*

Theodore Roosevelt was born at 28 East Twentieth Street in 1858 into the sixth generation of a prominent and wealthy New York City family. During the course of his lifetime, Teddy Roosevelt would lead one of the most storied public careers in American history. Roosevelt was the only native of New York City ever to become president of the United States, and his belief in the power of the city as a force was palpable. "In short," Roosevelt wrote in his volume *New York History* (1891), "the most important lesson taught by the history of New York City is the lesson of Americanism—the lesson that he among us who wishes to win honor in our life, and to play honestly and manfully, must be indeed an American in spirit and purpose, in heart and thought and deed."

While Roosevelt hated and feared "the mob" when it arose from the ever-increasing tide of immigrants entering Gotham, he was also equally disdainful of the capitalist greed and bureaucratic corruption he saw going on during the Gilded Age. Roosevelt was elected to three terms to the State Assembly and was responsible for numerous "good government" bills that attacked the spoils system of Tammany Hall patronage as well as fighting in favor of tenement reform legislation.

As president of the Police Commissioners Board from 1895 to 1897, Roosevelt set the standard for the modern New York Police Department by establishing disciplinary rules and opening admission into the department to ethnic minorities and women. As governor of New York from 1899 to 1900, he attacked tax benefits for corporate franchises, upgraded teacher' salaries, passed a bill that outlawed racial discrimination in public schools, and set up an extensive program to preserve the natural landscape of the entire state. He died in Oyster Bay in 1919.

In 1860, New York had over eight hundred thousand inhabitants. During the thirty years that have since passed, its population has nearly doubled. If the city limits were enlarged, like those of London and Chicago, so as to take in the suburbs, the population would amount to some three millions. Recently there has been a great territorial expansion northward, beyond the Haarlem, by the admission of what is known as the Annexed District. The growth of wealth has fully kept pace with the growth of population. The city is one of the two or three greatest commercial and manufacturing centres of the world.

The ten years between 1860 and 1870 form the worst decade in the city's political annals, although the sombre picture is relieved by touches of splendid heroism, martial prowess, and civic devotion. At the outbreak of the Civil War the city was—as it has since continued to be—the stronghold of the Democratic party in the North; and unfortunately, during the Rebellion, while the Democratic party contained many of the loyal, it also contained all of the disloyal, elements. A Democratic victory at the polls, hardly, if at all, less than a Confederate victory in the field, meant a Union defeat. A very large and possibly controlling element in the city Democracy was at heart strongly disunion in sentiment, and showed the feeling whenever it dared.

At the outset of the Civil War there was even an effort made to force the city into active rebellion. The small local Democratic leaders, of the type of Isaiah Rynders, the brutal and turbulent ruffians who led the mob and controlled the politics of the lower wards, openly and defiantly threatened to make common cause with the South, and to forbid the passage of Union troops through the city. The mayor, Fernando Wood, in January, 1861, proclaimed disunion to be "a fixed fact" in a message to the Common Council, and proposed that New York should herself secede and become a free city, with but a nominal duty upon imports. The independent commonwealth was to be named "Tri-Insula," as being composed of three islands—Long, Staten, and Manhattan. The Common Council, a corrupt body as disloyal as Wood himself, received the message enthusiastically, and had it printed and circulated wholesale.

But when Sumter was fired on the whole current changed like magic. There were many more good men than bad in New York; but they had been supine, or selfish, or indifferent, or undecided, and so the bad had had it all their own way. The thunder of Sumter's guns waked the heart of the people to passionate loyalty. The bulk of the Democrats joined with the Republicans to show by word and act their fervent and patriotic devotion to the Union. Huge mass-meetings were held, and regiment after regiment was organized and sent to the front. Shifty Fernando Wood, true to his nature, went with the stream, and was loudest in proclaiming his horror of rebellion. The city, through all her best and bravest men, pledged her faithful and steadfast support to the government at Washington. The Seventh Regiment of the

New York National Guards, by all odds the best regiment in the United States militia, was the first in the whole country to go to the front and reach Washington, securing it against any sudden surprise.

The Union men of New York kept their pledge of loyalty in spirit and letter. Taking advantage of the intensity of the loyal excitement, they even elected a Republican mayor. The New Yorkers of means were those whose part was greatest in sustaining the nation's credit, while almost every high-spirited young man in the city went into the army. The city, from the beginning to the end of the war, sent her sons to the front by scores of thousands. Her troops alone would have formed a large army; and on a hundred battlefields, and throughout the harder trails of the long, dreary campaigns, they bore themselves with high courage and stern, unyielding resolution. Those who by a hard lot were forced to stay at home busied themselves in caring for the men at the front, or for their widows and orphans; and the Sanitary Commission, the Allotment Commission, and other kindred organizations which did incalculable good, originated in New York.

Yet the very energy with which New York sent her citizen soldiery to the front, left her exposed to a terrible danger. Much of the low foreign element, as well as the worst among the native-born roughs, had been hostile to the war all along, and a ferocious outbreak was produced by the enforcement of the draft in July, 1863. The mob, mainly foreign, especially Irish, but reinforced by all the native rascality of the city, broke out for three days in what are known as the draft riots. They committed the most horrible outrages, their hostility being directed especially against the unfortunate negroes, many of whom they hung or beat to death with lingering cruelty; and they attacked various charitable institutions where negroes were cared for. They also showed their hatred to the national government and its defenders in every way, and even set out to burn down a hospital filled with wounded Union soldiers, besides mobbing all government officials. From attacking government property they speedily went to assailing private property as well, burning and plundering the houses of rich and poor alike, and threatened to destroy the whole city in their anarchic fury—the criminal classes, as always in such a movement, taking the control into their own hands. Many of the baser Democratic politicians, in order to curry favor with the mob, sought to prevent effective measures being taken against it; and even the Democratic governor, Seymour, an estimable man of high private character, but utterly unfit to grapple with the times that tried men's souls, took refuge in temporizing, half measures, and concessions. The Roman Catholic archbishop and priests opposed and denounced the rioters with greater or less boldness, according to their individual temperaments.

But the governing authorities, both national and municipal, acted with courage and energy. The American people are good-natured to the point of lax indifference; but once roused, they act with the most straightforward and practical resolution. Much fear had been expressed lest the large contingent of Irish among the police and State troops would be lukewarm or doubtful, but throughout the crisis they showed to the full as much courage and steadfast loyalty as their associates of native origin. One of the most deeply mourned victims of the mob was the gallant Colonel O'Brien of the Eleventh New York Volunteers, who had dispersed a crowd of rioters with considerable slaughter, and was afterward caught by them when alone, and butchered under circumstances of foul and revolting brutality.

Most of the real working men refused to join with the rioters, except when overawed and forced into their ranks; and many of them formed themselves into armed bodies, and assisted to restore order. The city was bare of troops, for they had all been sent to the front to face Lee at Gettysburg; and the police at first could not quell the mob. As regiment after regiment was hurried back to their assistance desperate street-fighting took place. The troops and police were thoroughly aroused, and attacked the rioters with the most wholesome desire to do them harm. In a very short time after the forces of order put forth their strength the outbreak was stamped out, and a lesson inflicted on the lawless and disorderly which they never entirely forgot. Two millions of property had been destroyed, and many valuable lives lost. But over twelve hundred rioters were slain—an admirable object-lesson to the remainder.

It was several years before the next riot occurred. This was of a race or religious character. The different nationalities of New York are in the habit of parading on certain days—a particularly senseless and objectionable custom. The Orangemen on this occasion paraded on the anniversary of the Battle of the Boyne, with the usual array of flags and banners, covered with mottoes especially insulting to the Celtic Irish; the latter threatened to stop the procession, and made the attempt; but the militia had been called out, and after a moment's sharp fighting, in which three of their number and seventy or eighty rioters were slain, the mob was scattered to the four winds. For the last twenty years no serious riots have occurred, and no mob has assembled which the police could not handle without the assistance of the State troops. The outbreaks that have taken place have almost invariably been caused by strikes or other labor troubles. Yet the general order and peacefulness should not blind us to the fact that there exists ever in our midst a slumbering "volcano under the city," as under all other large cities of the civilized world. This danger must continue to exist as long as our rich men look at life from a standpoint of silly frivolity, or else pursue a commercial career in a spirit of ferocious greed and disregard of justice, while the poor feel with sullen anger the pressure of many evils—some of their own making, and some not—and are far more sensible of the wrongs they suffer than of the folly of trying to right them under the lead of ignorant visionaries or criminal demagogues. . . .

Matters reached their climax in the feats of the "Tweed Ring." William M. Tweed was the master spirit among the politicians of his own party, and also secured a hold on a number of the local Republican leaders of the baser sort. He was a coarse, jovial, able man, utterly without scruple of any kind; and he organized all of his political allies and adherents into a gigantic "ring" to plunder the city. Incredible sums of money were stolen, especially in the construction of the new court-house. When the frauds were discovered, Tweed, secure in his power, asked in words that have become proverbial: "What are you going to do about it?" But the end came in 1871. Then the decent citizens, irrespective of party, banded together, urged on by the newspapers, especially the *Times* and *Harper's Weekly*—for the city press deserves the chief credit for the defeat of Tweed. At the fall elections the ring candidates were overwhelmingly defeated; and the chief malefactors were afterward prosecuted, and many of them imprisoned, Tweed himself dying in a felon's cell. The offending judges were impeached, or resigned in time to escape impeachment.

For the last twenty years our politics have been better and purer, though with plenty of corruption and jobbery left still. There are shoals of base, ignorant, vicious "heelers" and "ward workers," who form a solid, well-disciplined army of evil, led on by abler men whose very ability renders them dangerous. Some of these leaders are personally corrupt; others are not, but do almost as much harm as if they were, because they divorce political from private morality. As a prominent politician recently phrased it, they believe that "the purification of politics is an iridescent dream; the decalogue and the golden rule have no place in a political campaign." The cynicism, no less silly than vicious, with which such men regard political life is repaid by the contemptuous anger with which they themselves are regarded by all men who are proud of their country and wish her well. . . .

The character of the immigration to the city is changing. The Irish, who in 1860 formed three-fifths of the foreign-born population, have come in steadily lessening numbers, until the Germans stand well at the head; while increasing multitudes of Italians, Poles, Bohemians, Russian Jews, and Hungarians—both Slavs and Magyars—continually arrive. The English and Scandinavian elements among the immigrants have likewise increased. At the present time four-fifths of New York's population are of foreign birth or parentage; and among them there has been as yet but little race inter-mixture, though the rising generation is as a whole well on the way to complete Americanization. Certainly hardly a tenth of the people are of old Revolutionary American stock. The Catholic Church has continued to grow at a rate faster than the general rate of increase. The Episcopalian and Lutheran are the only Protestant churches whereof the growth has kept pace with that of the population.

The material prosperity of the city has increased steadily. There has been a marked improvement in architecture; and one really great engineering work, the bridge across the East River, was completed in 1883. The stately and beautiful Riverside Drive, skirting the Hudson, along the hills which front the river, from the middle of the island northward, is well worth mention. It is one of the most striking roads or streets of which any city can boast, and the handsome houses that are springing up along it bid fair to make the neighborhood the most attractive portion of New York. Another attractive feature of the city is Central Park, while many other parks are being planned and laid out beyond where the town has as yet been built up. There are large numbers of handsome social clubs, such as the Knickerbocker, Union, and University, and many others of a politico-social character—the most noted of them, alike for its architecture, political influence, and its important past history, being the Union League Club.

There are many public buildings which are extremely interesting as showing the growth of a proper civic spirit, and of a desire for a life with higher possibilities than money-making. There has been an enormous increase in the number of hospitals, many of them admirably equipped and managed; and the numerous Newsboys' Lodging Houses, Night Schools, Working Girls' Clubs and the like, bear witness to the fact that many New Yorkers who have at their disposal time or money are alive to their responsibilities, and are actively striving to help their less fortunate fellows to help themselves. The Cooper Union building, a gift to the city for the use of all its citizens, in the widest sense, keeps alive the memory of old Peter Cooper, a man whose broad generosity and simple kindliness of character, while not rendering him fit for the public life into which he at times sought entrance, yet inspired in New Yorkers of every class a genuine regard such as they felt for no other philanthropist. Indeed, uncharitableness and lack of generosity have never been New York failings; the citizens are keenly sensible to any real, tangible distress or need. A blizzard in Dakota, an earthquake in South Carolina, a flood in Pennsylvania—after any such catastrophe hundreds of thousands of dollars are raised in New York at a day's notice, for the relief of the sufferers; while, on the other hand, it is a difficult matter to raise money for a monument or a work of art.

In science and art, in musical and literary development, much remains to be wished for; yet something has already been done. The building of the Metropolitan Museum of Art, of the American Museum of Natural History, of the Metropolitan Opera House, the gradual change of Columbia College into a University—all show a development which tends to make the city more and more attractive to people of culture; and the growth of literary and dramatic clubs, such as the Century and the Players, is scarcely less significant. The illustrated monthly magazines—the *Century, Scribner's,* and *Harper's*—occupy an entirely original position of a very high order in periodical literature.

Grim dangers confront us in the future, yet there is more ground to believe that we shall succeed than that we shall fail in overcoming them. Taking into account the enormous mass of immigrants, utterly unused to self-government of any kind, who have been thrust into our midst, and are even yet not assimilated, the wonder is not that universal suffrage has worked so badly, but that it has worked so well. We are better, not worse off than we were a generation ago. There is much gross civic corruption and commercial and social selfishness and immorality, upon which we are in honor bound to wage active and relentless war. But honesty and moral cleanliness are the rule; and under the laws order is well preserved, and all men are kept secure in the possession of life, liberty and property. The sons and grandsons of the immigrants of fifty years back have as a whole become good Americans, and have prospered wonderfully, both as regards their moral and material well-being. There is no reason to suppose that the condition of the working classes as a whole has grown worse, though there are enormous bodies of them whose condition is certainly very bad. There are grave social dangers and evils to meet, but there are plenty of earnest men and women who devote their minds and energies to meeting them. With many very serious shortcomings and defects, the average New Yorker yet possesses courage, energy, business capacity, much generosity of a practical sort, and shrewd, humorous common sense. The greedy tyranny of the unscrupulous rich and the anarchic violence of the vicious and ignorant poor are ever-threatening dangers; but though there is every reason why we should realize the gravity of the perils ahead of us, there is none why we should not face them with confident and resolute hope, if only each of us, according to the measure of his capacity, will with manly honesty and good faith do his full share of the all-important duties incident to American citizenship.

From Darkness and Daylight, *Helen Campbell (1892)*

Helen Campbell Stuart was born in Lockport, New York, in 1839. She began writing children's books under the name Helen Stuart Campbell and eventually simply adopted the name change. In the 1880s and 1890s, she was one of the most vocal reformers in creating widespread public awareness about issues of poverty. Her book *The Problem of the Poor* (1882) detailed the inequity in wages given to working-class women; her 1887 exposé *Prisoners of Poverty* documented in vivid detail the conditions of women in the needle trades and in department stores.

In 1891 Campbell, along with Josephine Shaw Lowell and Dr. Mary Putnam Jacobi, organized the New York Consumer's League. The league's most inventive strategy was to draw up a "White List" of stores that treated women employees fairly and, through mailings to the four thousand names on the Social Register and lists placed in the parlors of the city's twenty largest hotels, to encourage New York's wealthiest shoppers to shop only at stores on the list.

Campbell was also a regular contributor to *Arena,* a periodical that addressed issues of poverty in urban settings. The editor of that publication described Campbell's presence as "always an inspiration, her thought well poised and fundamentally sound. . . . Not a few artists, writers, and social workers of eminence rightly look upon her as a kind of foster-mother."

Child Labor

IN one night-school eighty of them [girls] registered as "nurses." Being interpreted, this means that they take care of the baby at home while the mother goes out to "day's work." It is astonishing to see the real motherliness of the little things, who lug about the baby with devotion; and if they feed it on strange diet they are but following in the footsteps of the mothers, who regard the baby at six months old as the sharer of whatever the family bill of fare has to offer. The small German child is early to take his portion of lager; . . . the Irish children have tea or coffee and even a sup of the "craytur. . . ."

I have seen a six-year-old girl scrubbing the floor of the one room in which lived a widowed mother and three children.

"She's a widdy washerwoman," said the dot, a creature with big blue eyes and a thin eager little face. "Yes, ma'am, she's a widdy washerwoman, an' I keep house. That's the baby there, an' he's good all the time, savin' whin his teeth is too big for him. It's teeth that's hard on babies, but I mind him good an' he thinks more o' me than he does of mother. See how beautiful he sucks at the pork."

The small housekeeper pointed with pride to the bed, where the tiny baby lay, a strip of fat pork in his mouth.

"He's weakly like, an' mother gives him the pork to set him up. An' he takes his sup o' tay beautiful too. Whin the summer comes we'll get to have him go to the Children's Home at Bath, maybe, or down to Coney Island or somewhere. I might be a 'Fresh Air' child myself, but I have to keep house you know, an' so mother can't let me go."

This is one phase of child-labor, and the most natural and innocent one, though it is a heavy burden to lay on small shoulders, and premature age and debility are its inevitable results. Far truer is this of the long hours in shop or manufactory. A child of eight—one of a dozen in a shop on Walker Street—stripped feathers, and had for a year earned three dollars a week. In this case the father was dead and the mother sick, and the little thing went home to do such cooking as she could. Like many a worker, she had already learned to take strong tea and to believe that it gave her strength. She was dwarfed in growth from confinement in the air of the workshop, from lack of proper food and no play, and thousands of these little feather-strippers are in like case.

In another workshop in the same neighborhood, children of from eight to ten, and one much younger, cut the feathers from cock-tails. The hours were from eight to six, and so for ten hours daily they bent over the work, which included cutting from the stem, steaming, curling, and packing.

Eight thousand children make envelopes at three and a half cents a thousand. They gum, separate, and sort. The hours are the same, but the rooms are generally lighter and better ventilated than the feather workers' surroundings. Many more burnish china, for, strange as it may seem, the most delicate ware is entrusted to children of ten or twelve. The burnishing instrument is held close against the breast, and this is a fruitful source of sickness, since the constant pressure brings with it various stomach and other troubles, dyspepsia being the chief.

Paper collars employ a host. The youngest bend over them, for even a child of five can do this. One child of twelve counts and boxes twenty thousand a day, and one who pastes the lining on the Buttonholes does five thousand a day. Over ten thousand children make paper boxes. Even in the making of gold-leaf a good many are employed, though chiefly young girls of fifteen and upwards. It is one of the most exhausting of the trades, as no air can be admitted, and the atmosphere is stifling.

Feathers, flowers, and tobacco employ the greatest number. A child of six can strip tobacco or cut feathers. In one great firm, employing over a thousand men, women, and children, a woman of eighty and her grandchild of four sit side by side and strip the leaves. . . . With the exception of matchmaking and one or two other industries there is hardly a trade so deadly in its effects. There are many operations which children are competent to carry on, and the phases of work done at home in the tenement-houses often employ the entire family.

In a report of the State Bureau of Labor it is stated that in one room less than twelve by fourteen feet, whose duplicate can be found at many points, a family of seven worked. Three of these, all girls, were under ten years of age. Tobacco lay in piles on the floor and under the long table at one end where cigars were rolled. Two of the children sat on the floor, stripping the leaves, and another sat on a small stool. A girl of twenty sat near them, and all had sores on lips, cheeks, and hands. Some four thousand women are engaged in this industry, and an equal number of unregistered young children share it with them. As in sewing, a number of women often club together and use one room, and in such cases their babies crawl about in the filth on the wet floors, playing with the damp tobacco and breathing the poison with which the room is saturated.

Skin diseases of many sorts develop in the children who work in this way, and for the women and girls nervous and hysterical complaints are common, the direct result of poisoning by nicotine. . . .

Twine-factories are clean and well ventilated, but they are often as disastrous in their effects. The twisting-room is filled with long spindles, innocent-looking enough, but taking a finger along with the flax as silently and suddenly as the thread forms. . . .

One [child] explained how it happened in her case.

"You see you mustn't talk or look off a minute. They just march right along. My sister was like me. She forgot and talked, and just that minute her finger was off, and she didn't even cry till she picked it up. My little finger always did stick out, and I was trying to twist fast like the girl next to me, and somehow it caught in the flax. I tried to jerk away, but it wasn't any use. It was off just the same as hers, and it took a great while before I could come back. I'm sort of afraid of them, for any minute your whole hand might go and you'd hardly know till it was done."

In a small room on Hester Street a woman at work on overalls—for the making of which she received one dollar a dozen—said:—

"I couldn't do as well if it wasn't for Jinny and Mame there. Mame has learned to sew on buttons first-rate, and Jinny is doing almost as well. I'm alone to-day, but most days three of us sew together here, and Jinny keeps right along. We'll do better yet when Mame gets a bit older."

As she spoke the door opened and a woman with an enormous bundle of overalls entered and sat down on the nearest chair with a gasp.

"Them stairs is killin'," she said. "It's lucky I've not to climb 'em often."

Something crept forward as the bundle slid to the floor, and busied itself with the string that bound it.

"Here you, Jinny," said the woman, "don't you be foolin'. What do you want anyhow?"

The something shook back a mat of thick hair and rose to its feet,—a tiny child who in size seemed scarcely three, but whose countenance indicated the experience of three hundred.

"It's the string I want," the small voice said. "Me and Mame was goin' to play with it."

"There's small time for play," said the mother; "there'll be two pair more in a minute or two, an' you are to see how Mame does one an' do it good, too, or I'll find out why not."

Mame had come forward and stood holding to the one thin garment which but partly covered Jinny's little bones. She, too, looked out from a wild thatch of black hair, and with the same expression of deep experience, the pallid, hungry little faces lighting suddenly as some cheap cakes were produced. Both of them sat down on the floor and ate their portion silently.

"Mame's seven, and Jinny's goin' on six," said the mother," but Jinny's the smartest. She could sew on buttons when she wasn't much over four. I had five, but the Lord took 'em all but these two. I couldn't get on if it wasn't for Mame."

Mame looked up, but said no word, and, as I left the room, settled herself with her back against the wall, Jinny at her side, laying the coveted string near at hand for use if any minute for play arrived.

The Newsboys of New York

Most of us have never bothered ourselves about how the newsboy lives. We know that he exists. We are too apt to regard him only as a necessary evil. What is his daily life? What becomes of him? Does he ever grow up to man's estate, or are his inches never increased?

Though it is by no means true that all newsboys are wanderers, yet most of those seen in New York streets have no homes. Out from the alleys and by-ways of the slums pours this stream of child humanity, an army of happy barbarians, for they are happy in spite of privations that seem enough to crush the spirit of the bravest. Comparatively few in number before the war, they increased manyfold with the demand of that period, and swarm now at every point where a sale is probable. Naturally only the brightest among them prospered. They began as "street rats"—the old name of the police for them,—and pilfered and gnawed at all social foundations with the recklessness and energy of their prototypes. Their life was of the hardest. Driven out from the dens in tenement districts, where most of them were born, to beg or steal as need might be, they slept in boxes, or under stairways, and sometimes in hay barges in coldest nights of winter. Two of them were known to have slept for an entire winter in the iron tube of a bridge, and two others in a burned-out safe in Wall Street. Sometimes they slipped into the cabin of a ferry-boat. Old boilers were a favorite refuge, but first and chief, then and now, came the steam gratings, where at any time of night or day in winter one may find a crowd of shivering urchins warming half-frozen fingers and toes, or curled up in a heap snatching such sleep as is to be had under adverse circumstances.

Watch a group of this nature. Their faces are old from constant exposure as well as from the struggle for existence. Their thin clothes fluttering in the wind afford small protection against winter's cold, and are made up of contributions from all sources, often rescued from the ragpicker and cut down to meet requirements. Shoes are of the same order, but worn only in winter, the toes even then looking stockingless, from gaping holes stopped sometimes by rags wound about the feet. Kicked and cuffed by every ruffian they meet, ordered about by the police, creeping into doorways as winter storms rage, they lose no atom of cheer, and shame the prosperous passer-by who gives them small thought save as a nuisance to be tolerated. They are the pertinacious little chaps who spring up at every crossing, almost at every hour of the day and night, and thrust a paper under your nose. They run to every fire, and are present wherever a horse falls down, or a street car gets into trouble, or a brawl is in progress. They are the boys who play toss-penny in the sun in the City Hall Park, who play baseball by electric light, who rob the push-cart of the Italian banana-seller, who can scent a "copper" a block away, and who always have a plentiful supply of crocodile tears when caught in *flagrante delicto.*

The tiny fellow who flies across your path with a bundle of papers under his arm found out, almost before he ceased to be a baby, that life is very earnest, and he knows that upon his success in disposing of his stock in trade depends his supper and a warm bed for the night. Though so young he has had as many knocks as are crowded into the lives of a good many folk twice his age. He is every inch a philosopher, too, for he accepts bad fortune with stoical indifference.

Homeless boys may be divided into two classes,—the street arab and the gutter-snipe. The newsboy may be found in both these classes. As a street arab he is strong, sturdy, self-reliant, full of fight, always ready to take his own part, as well as that of the gutter-snipe, who naturally looks to him for protection.

Gutter-snipe is the name which has been given to the more weakly street arab, the little fellow who, though scarcely more than a baby, is frequently left by brutalized parents at the mercy of any fate, no matter what. This little chap generally roams around until he finds some courageous street arab, scarcely bigger than himself, perhaps, to fight his battles and put him in the way of making a living, which is generally done by selling papers. In time the gutter-snipe becomes himself a full-fledged arab with a large *clientèle,* two hard and ready fists, and a horde of dependent and grateful snipes.

This is the evolution of the newsboy wherever he be found. Some of them bring up in penal institutions and reformatories, and no wonder. Their mornings are too apt to be spent in pitching pennies or frequenting policy-shops. They are passionately devoted to the theatre, and they will cheerfully give up a prospect of a warm bed for the night for an evening in some cheap playhouse. Their applause is always discriminating. They despise humbug, whether in real life or on the mimic stage. The cheap morality current in Bowery plays, where the villain always meets his just deserts, gives them a certain standard which is as high as can well be when one lives among fighters, stealers, gamblers, and swearers. After squandering his earnings for an evening's entertainment of this sort, a convenient doorway or a sidewalk grating, through whose bars an occasional breath of warm air is wafted from underground furnaces in winter, are often the only places he has to sleep. This is the boy who is the veritable street arab, the newsboy pure and simple.

You can see him early any morning hugging some warm corner or huddled into some dark passage, waiting for the moment when the papers shall be ready for distribution.

Their light-heartedness is a miracle. Merry as clowns, flashing back repartee to any joker, keen and quick to take points, they manage their small affairs with a wisdom one would believe impossible. Their views of life have come from association with "flash-men" of every order, with pugilists, pickpockets, cockfighters, and all the habitués of pot-houses or bucket-shops. . . .

Almost forty years ago these were the conditions for hundreds as they are to-day for thousands, though philanthropy has fought every step of the way, as industrial schools, lodging-houses, and Homes bear witness. Chief among these rank the Newsboys' Lodging-Houses, in many respects the most unique sight to be seen in New York.

A thousand difficulties hedged about the way of those who first sought to make life easier for this class, not the least of which were how not to assail too roughly their established opinions and habits, nor to touch their sturdy independence. They had a terror of Sunday-schools, believing them only a sort of trap to let them suddenly into the House of Refuge or some equally detested place. Even when the right sort of superintendent had been found, and a loft had been secured in the old "Sun" building and fitted up as a lodging-room, the small skeptics regarded the movement with great suspicion and contempt. . . .

In 1869 and 1870 8,835 different boys were entered. Many of them found good homes through the agency of the Children's Aid Society; some found places for themselves; and some drifted away no one knows where, too deeply tainted with the vices of street life for reclamation. In this same year the lads themselves paid $3,349 toward expenses.

What sort of home is it that their money helps to provide? The present one, with its familiar sign, "NEWSBOYS′ LODGING HOUSE," on the corner of Duane and Chambers Street, is planned like the old one on Park Place. The cleanliness is perfect, for in all the years since its founding no case of contagious disease has occurred among the boys. The first story is rented for use as shops. The next has a large dining-room where nearly two hundred boys can sit down at table; a kitchen, laundry, store-room, servant's room, and rooms for the family of the superintendent. The next story is partitioned off into a school-room, gymnasium, and bath and washrooms, all fully supplied with cold and hot water, a steam-boiler below providing both the latter and the means of heating the rooms. The two upper stories are large and roomy dormitories, each furnished with from fifty to one hundred beds or berths, arranged like a ship's bunks, over each other. The beds have spring mattresses of wire and are supplied with white cotton sheets and plenty of comforters. For these beds the boys pay six cents a night each, including supper. For ten cents a boy may hire a "private room," which consists of a square space curtained off from the vulgar gaze and supplied with a bed and locker. The private rooms are always full, no matter what the population of the dormitories may be, showing that the newsboy shares the weakness of his more fortunate brothers.

Up to midnight the little lodgers are welcome to enter the house, but later than that they are not admitted. Once in, he is expected after supper to attend the night school and remain until the end of the session; and once outside the door after the hour of closing he must make the best of a night in the streets.

Confident of his ability to take care of himself, he resents the slightest encroachment upon his freedom. The discipline of the lodging-house, therefore, does not seek to impose any more restraints upon him than those which are absolutely necessary. He goes and comes as he pleases, except that if he accepts the hospitality of the lodging-house he must abide by the rules and regulations.

Supper is served at seven o'clock and is usually well patronized, especially on Mondays and Thursdays, which are pork-and-beans days. Every boy has his bed-number, which corresponds with the number of the locker in which he keeps his clothes. When he is ready to retire he applies to the superintendent's assistant, who sits beside the keyboard. The lodger gives his number and is handed the key of his locker, in which he bestows all his clothing but his shirt and trousers. He then mounts to the dormitory, and after carefully secreting his shirt and trousers under his mattress is ready for the sleep of childhood.

The boys are wakened at different hours. Some of them rise as early as two o'clock and go down town to the newspaper offices for their stock in trade. Others rise between that hour and five o'clock. All hands, however, are routed out at seven. The boys may enjoy instruction in the rudimentary branches every night from half-past seven until nine o'clock, with the exception of Sundays, when devotional services are held and addresses made by well-known citizens.

A large majority of the boys who frequent the lodging-houses are waifs pure and simple. They have never known a mother's or a father's care, and have no sense of identity. Generally they have no name, or if they ever had one have preferred to convert it into something short and practically descriptive. As a rule they are known by nicknames and nothing else, and in speaking of one another they generally do so by these names. As a rule these names indicate some personal peculiarity or characteristic. On a recent visit to a Newsboys' Lodging House pains were taken to learn the names of a group of boys who were holding an animated conversation. It was a representative group. A very thin little fellow was called "Skinny"; another boy with light hair and complexion, being nearly as blonde as an albino, was known only as "Whitey." When "Slobbery Jack" was asked how he came by his name, "Bumlets," who appeared to be chief spokesman of the party, exclaimed, "When he eats he scatters all down himself." "Yaller" was the name given to an Italian boy of soft brown complexion. Near him stood "Kelly the Rake," who owned but one sleeve to his jacket. In newsboy parlance a "rake" is a boy who will appropriate to his own use anything he can lay his hands on. No one could give an explanation of "Snoddy's" name nor what it meant,—it was a thorough mystery to even the savants in newsboy parlance. In the crowd was "The Snitcher,"—"a fellow w'at tattles," said Bumlets, contemptuously, and near by stood the "King of Crapshooters." "A crapshooter," said Bumlets, "is a fellow w'ats fond of playin' toss-penny, throwin' dice, an' goin' to policy shops." The "King of Bums" was a tall and rather good-looking lad, who, no doubt, had come honestly by his name. The "Snipe-Shooter" was guilty of smoking cigar-stubs picked out of the gutter, a habit known among the boys as "snipe-shooting." "Hoppy," a little lame boy; "Dutchy," a German lad; "Smoke," a colored boy; "Pie-eater," a boy very fond of pie; "Sheeney," "Skittery," "Bag of Bones," "One Lung Pete," and "Scotty" were in the same group; and so also was "Jake the Oyster," a tender-hearted boy who was spoken of by the others as "a reg'lar soft puddin'." . . .

Since the foundation of the first Newsboys' Lodging House in 1854, the various homes have sheltered nearly two hundred and fifty thousand different boys at a total expense of about four hundred and fifty thousand dollars. The amount contributed by the lads themselves during these years is nearly one hundred and seventy-five thousand dollars. Multitudes have been sent to good homes in the West.

To awaken the demand for these children, thousands of circulars were sent out, through the city weeklies and the rural newspapers, to the country districts. Hundreds of applications poured in at once from the farmers, especially from the West. At first an effort was made to meet individual applications by sending just the kind of boy wanted. Each applicant wanted a "perfect boy," without any of the taints of earthly depravity. He must be well made, of good stock, never disposed to steal apples or pelt cattle, using language of perfect propriety, fond of making fires at daylight, and delighting in family-worship and prayer-meetings more than in fishing or skating.

The defects of the first plan of emigration were speedily developed, and another and more practicable one inaugurated which has since been followed. Companies of boys are formed, and after thoroughly cleaning and clothing them they are put under a competent agent and distributed among the farmers, the utmost care being taken to select good homes for all. The parties are usually made up from the brightest and most deserving, though often one picked up in the street tells a story so pitiful and so true that he is included. . . .

An average of three thousand a year is sent to the West, many of whom are formally adopted. A volume would not suffice for the letters that come back, or the strange experiences of many a boy who under the new influences grows into an honored citizen. . . .

The stranger in New York can hardly find a more interesting sight than the gymnasium or schoolroom through the week, or the crowded Sunday night meeting, where the singing is always a fascinating part of the programme. Thanksgiving Day, with its dinner, is no less amusing and suggestive. The boys watch all visitors and know by instinct how far they are in sympathy with them. They call loudly for talk from any one whose face appeals to them. Often they make speeches on their own account. Here is a specimen taken down by a stenographer who had been given a dark corner at the end of the room and thus was not suspected by the boys.

Mr. Brace, whose appearance always called out applause, had brought down some friends, and after one or two of them had spoken, he said,

"Boys, I want my friends to see that you have some talkers amongst yourselves. Whom do you choose for your speaker?"

"Paddy, Paddy!" they shouted. "Come out, Paddy, an' show yerself."

Paddy came forward and mounted a stool; a youngster not more than twelve, with little round eyes, a short nose profusely freckled, and a lithe form full of fun.

"Bummers," he began, "Snoozers, and citizens, I've come down here among yer to talk to yer a little. Me an' me friend Brace have come to see how ye're gittin' along an' to advise yer. You fellers w'at stands at the shops with yer noses over the railin', a smellin' of the roast beef an' hash,—you fellers who's got no home,—think of it, how are we to encourage yer. [Derisive laughter, and various ironical kinds of applause.] I say bummers, for ye're all bummers, [in a tone of kind patronage,] I was a bummer once meself. [Great laughter.] I hate to see yer spending yer money for penny ice-creams an' bad cigars. Why don't yer save yer money? You feller without no boots over there, how would you like a new pair, eh? [Laughter from all the boys but the one addressed.] Well, I hope you may get 'em. Raything think you won't. I have hopes for yer all. I want yer to grow up to be rich men, —citizens, gover'ment men, lawyers, ginerals, an' inflooence men. Well, boys, I'll tell yer a story. Me dad was a hard un. One beautiful day he went on a spree, an' he come home an' told me, where's yer mother? an' I axed him I didn't know, an' he clipped me over the head with an iron pot an' knocked me down, an' me mother drapped in on him an' at it they wint. [Hi-hi's and demonstrative applause.] An' at it they wint agin, an' at it they kept; ye should have seen 'em, an' whilst they were a fightin' I slipped meself out o' the back dure an' away I wint like a scart dog. Well, boys, I wint on till I come to a Home; [great laughter among the boys] an' they tuk me in, [renewed laughter] an' thin I ran away, an' here I am. Now, boys, be good, mind yer manners, copy me, an' see what ye'll become."

A boy who wished to advocate the claims of the West, to which he was soon to go with a party sent out from the Children's Aid Society, made a long speech, a paragraph of which will show the sense of humor which seems to be the common property of all.

"Do ye want to be newsboys always, an' shoeblacks, an' timber merchants in a small way sellin' matches? If ye do, ye'll stay in New York; but if ye don't, ye'll go out West an' begin to be farmers, for the beginning of a farmer, me boys, is the makin' of a Congressman an' a President. Do ye want to be rowdies an' loafers an' shoulder-hitters? If ye do, why, thin, ye can keep around these diggins. Do ye want to be gintlemin an' independent citizens? Ye do? Thin make tracks fer the West. If ye want to be snoozers, an' bummers, an' policy-players, an' Peter-Funk min, why ye'll hang up yer caps an' stay round the groggeries; but if ye want to be min to make your mark in the country ye'll get up steam an' go ahead, an' there's lots on the prairies waiting for the likes o' ye. Well, I'll now come off the stump. I'm booked for the West in the next company from the Lodging-House. I hear they have big school-houses there, an' a place for me in the winter time. I've made up me mind to be somebody, an' you'll find me on a farm in the West an' I hope yees will come to see me soon. I thank ye, boys, for yer patient attintion. I can't say no more at present, boys. Good bye."

The newsboys' lodging-houses are like the ancient cities of refuge to these little fellows, and yet there are cases which the lodging-houses never reach.

"Recently," said a gentleman, "I found a tiny fellow playing a solitary game of marbles in a remote corner of the City Hall corridors. His little legs were very thin, and dark circles under his big gray eyes intensified the chalk-like pallor of his cheeks. He looked up when he became aware that some one was watching him, but resumed his game of solitaire as soon as he saw he had nothing to fear from the intruder.

"What are you doing here, my little fellow?" I asked.

The mite hastily gathered up all his marbles and stowed them very carefully away in his capacious trousers pocket. Then he backed up against the wall and surveyed me doubtfully. I repeated my question,—this time more gently, so as to reassure him.

"I'm waitin' fur Jack de Robber," he piped, and then, as he began to gain confidence, seeing no signs of "swipes" about me, he added, "him as brings me de Telies (Dailies) every day."

"And you sell the papers?"

"I sells 'em for Jack," he promptly answered.

I was glad, when I looked at the lad's attire, that he was protected for the time being by the comparative warmth of the corridor. Outdoors it was cold and blustering. Still I resolved to wait and see "Jack de Robber." Shortly after three o'clock a short chunky boy with a shock of black hair hustled through the door and made in the direction of my pale little friend. He was struggling with a big mass of papers and was issuing orders in a rather peremptory tone to his diminutive lieutenant.

"Do you know this little boy?" I asked.

"Jack de Robber" gave me a look which was not reassuring. "Does I naw him? Of corse I naws him. What de—!"

"Why don't you send him home to his mother; he's neither big enough nor strong enough to sell papers?"

At this Jack gave utterance to an oath too utterly original for reproduction; then he said, "Dat ere kid ain't got no mammy; I looks after dat kid meself."

I slipped a coin into Jack's hand and urged him to tell me the whole story. He dropped his heap of papers, tested the coin with his teeth, slid it into his pocket, and began:—

"Blokes is allus axin' 'bout dat ere kid, but you is de fust one what ever raised de ante. Dat ere kid don't naw no more 'bout his mammy'n me. Cause why? Cause he ain't never had no mammy."

Here Jack paused, as if determined to go no further, but another coin gave wings to his words.

"Dat ere kid," he resumed, "ain't got no more sand'n a John Chinee. He'd be kilt ony fur me. He can't come along de Row or up de alley widout gitin' his face broke. So I gives him papers to sell and looks arter him meself."

I asked Jack where the "Kid" and himself slept. "I ain't givin' dat away," said he, "ony taint no lodgin'-house where you has to git up early in the mawnin'. De 'Kid' and me likes to sleep late."

The "Kid," however, was now eager to be off with his papers, and without another word the protector and protégé sped into the street, filling the air with their shrill cries. . . .

Instances of this class of newsboys could be multiplied indefinitely. These are the absolute Bohemians of their kind, who prefer a doorway to a warm bed, and the sights of the streets any time and all the time to the simple restraints imposed by the lodging-houses.

The newsboy's life is filled with the hardest sort of work. His gains are not always in proportion, for he must begin often before light, huddling over the steam gratings at the printing-offices, and waiting for his share of the morning papers. He scurries to work these off before the hour for taking the evening editions, and sometimes cannot with his utmost diligence take in more than fifty cents a day, though it ranges from this to a dollar and a quarter. The period of elections is the harvest-time. A boy has been known to sell six hundred papers in two hours, at a profit of between eleven and twelve dollars.

Among over twenty-one thousand children who in the early years of the work were sent West, but twelve became criminals, and not more than six annually return to New York. No work done for children compares with this in importance, and whoever studies the record of the Children's Aid Society will be amazed at the good already accomplished. Twenty-one industrial schools, twelve night-schools, two free reading-rooms, six lodging-houses for girls and boys, four summer homes, and the Crippled Boy's Brush Shop, are the record plain to all; but who shall count the good that no man has recorded, but which has rescued thousands from the streets and given them the chance which is the right of every human soul.

Minetta Lane, Stephen Crane (1896)

The youngest of fourteen children, Stephen Crane was born in Newark, New Jersey, in 1871. Never a serious academician, Crane left Lafayette College without completing a semester's work and attended Syracuse University for one semester, where he flunked five out six courses but received an A in English literature. His greatest passion there was catching for the college baseball team.

Crane claimed to have written *Maggie: Girl of the Streets* in just two days before Christmas in 1891; he self-published the novella in 1893. By that time, Crane was already at work on his famous Civil War novel, *The Red Badge of Courage,* which became an international best-seller in 1895. The reputation he gained from this work led him to jobs as a war correspondent covering the Greco-Turkish War of 1897 and the Spanish-American War of 1898 for the *New York World* and the *New York Journal.*

While at Syracuse, Crane had been a correspondent for the *New York Tribune;* he moved to East Twenty-third Street in 1891 and set out to become acquainted firsthand with the life of the tenements and saloons of New York. These experiences prompted some of his most compelling sketches, "An Experiment in Misery" and "Three Men in a Storm."

In 1897 Crane settled in England, where he joined a circle of novelists including Henry James, Joseph Conrad, and Ford Madox Ford. After several bouts with tuberculosis, Crane died on June 5, 1900, in a sanatorium in Badenweiler, Germany.

MINETTA Lane is a small and becobbled valley between hills of dingy brick. At night the street lamps, burning dimly, cause the shadows to be important, and in the gloom one sees groups of quietly conversant negroes with occasionally the gleam of a passing growler. Everything is vaguely outlined and of uncertain identity unless indeed it be the flashing buttons and shield of the policeman on post. The Sixth Avenue horse cars jingle past one end of the Lane and, a block eastward, the little thoroughfare ends in the darkness of MacDougal Street.

One wonders how such an insignificant alley could get such an absurdly large reputation, but, as a matter of fact, Minetta Lane, and Minetta Street, which leads from it southward to Bleecker Street, MacDougal Street and nearly all the streets thereabouts were most unmistakably bad, but when the Minettas started out the other streets went away and hid. To gain a reputation in Minetta Lane, in those days, a man was obliged to commit a number of furious crimes, and no celebrity was more important than the man who had a good honest killing to his credit. The inhabitants, for the most part, were negroes, and they represented the very worst elements of their race. The razor habit clung to them with the tenacity of an epidemic, and every night the uneven cobbles felt blood. Minetta Lane was not a public thoroughfare at this period. It was a street set apart, a refuge for criminals. Thieves came here preferably with their gains, and almost any day peculiar sentences passed among the inhabitants. "Big Jim turned a thousand last night." "No-Toe's made another haul." And the worshipful citizens would make haste to be present at the consequent revel.

Not Then a Thoroughfare

As has been said, Minetta Lane was then no thoroughfare. A peaceable citizen chose to make a circuit rather than venture through this place, that swarmed with the most dangerous people in the city. Indeed, the thieves of the district used to say: "Once get in the Lane and you're all right." Even a policeman in chase of a criminal would probably shy away instead of pursuing him into the lane. The odds were too great against a lone officer.

Sailors, and many men who might appear to have money about them, were welcomed with all proper ceremony at the terrible dens of the Lane. At departure, they were fortunate if they still retained their teeth. It was the custom to leave very little else to them. There was every facility for the capture of coin, from trapdoors to plain ordinary knockout drops.

And yet Minetta Lane is built on the grave of Minetta Brook, where, in olden times, lovers walked under the willows of the bank, and Minetta Lane, in later times, was the home of many of the best families of the town.

A negro named Bloodthirsty was perhaps the most luminous figure of Minetta Lane's aggregation of desperadoes. Bloodthirsty, supposedly, is alive now, but he has vanished from the Lane. The police want him for murder. Bloodthirsty is a large negro and very hideous. He has a rolling eye that shows white at the wrong time and his neck, under the jaw, is dreadfully scarred and pitted.

Bloodthirsty was particularly eloquent when drunk, and in the wildness of a spree he would rave so graphically about gore, that even the habituated wool of old timers would stand straight. Bloodthirsty meant most of it, too. That is why his orations were impressive. His remarks were usually followed by the wide lightning sweep of his razor. None cared to exchange epithets with Bloodthirsty. A man in a boiler iron suit would walk down to City Hall and look at the clock before he would ask the time of day from single minded and ingenuous Bloodthirsty.

No Toe Charley

After Bloodthirsty, in combative importance, came No Toe Charley. Singularly enough Charley was called No Toe solely because he did not have a toe to his feet. Charley was a small negro and his manner of amusement was not Bloodthirsty's simple ways. As befitting a smaller man, Charley was more wise, more sly, more roundabout than the other man. The path of his crimes was like a corkscrew, in architecture, and his method led him to make many tunnels. With all his cleverness, however, No Toe was finally induced to pay a visit to the gentlemen in the grim gray building up the river.

Black-Cat was another famous bandit who made the Lane his home. Black-Cat is dead. It is within some months that Jube Tyler has been sent to prison, and after mentioning the recent disappearance of Old Man Spriggs, it may be said that the Lane is now destitute of the men who once crowned it with a glory of crime. It is hardly essential to mention Guinea Johnson. Guinea is not a great figure. Guinea is just an ordinary little crook. Sometimes Guinea pays a visit to his friends, the other little crooks who make homes in the Lane, but he himself does not live there, and with him out of it, there is now no one whose industry in unlawfulness has yet earned him the dignity of a nickname. Indeed, it is difficult to find people now who remember the old gorgeous days, although it is but two years since the Lane shone with sin like a new headlight. But after a search the reporter found three.

Mammy Ross is one of the last relics of the days of slaughter still living there. Her weird history also reaches back to the blossoming of the first members of the Whyo gang in the old Sixth Ward, and her mind is stored with bloody memories. She at one time kept a sailor's boarding house near the Tombs Prison, and accounts of all the festive crimes of that neighborhood in ancient years roll easily from her tongue. They killed a sailor man every day, and the pedestrians went about the streets wearing stoves for fear of the handy knives. At the present day the route to Mammy's home is up a flight of grimy stairs that is pasted on the outside of an old and tottering frame house. Then there is a hall blacker than a wolf's throat, and this hall leads to a little kitchen where Mammy usually sits groaning by the fire. She is, of course, very old, and she is also very fat. She seems always to be in great pain. She says she is suffering from "de very las' dregs of de yaller fever."

A Picture of Suffering

During the first part of a reporter's recent visit old Mammy seemed most dolefully oppressed by her various diseases. Her great body shook and her teeth clicked spasmodically during her long and painful respirations. From time to time she reached her trembling hand and drew a shawl closer about her shoulders. She presented as true a picture of a person undergoing steady, unchangeable, chronic pain as a patent medicine firm could wish to discover for miraculous purposes. She breathed like a fish thrown out on the bank, and her old head continually quivered in the nervous tremors of the extremely aged and debilitated person. Meanwhile her daughter hung over the stove and placidly cooked sausages.

Appeals were made to the old woman's memory. Various personnages who had been sublime figures of crime in the long-gone days were mentioned to her, and presently her eyes began to brighten. Her head no longer quivered. She seemed to lose for a period her sense of pain in the gentle excitement caused by the invocation of the spirits of her memory.

It appears that she had had a historic quarrel with Apple Mag. She first recited the prowess of Apple Mag; how this emphatic lady used to argue with paving stones, carving knives and bricks. Then she told of the quarrel; what Mag said; what she said; what Mag said; what she said: It seems that they cited each other as spectacles of sin and corruption in more fully explanatory terms than are commonly known to be possible. But it was one of Mammy's most gorgeous recollections, and, as she told it, a smile widened over her face.

Finally she explained her celebrated retort to one of the most illustrious thugs that had blessed the city in bygone days. "Ah says to 'im, Ah says: 'You—you'll die in yer boots like Gallopin' Thompson—dat's what you'll do.' [Slug missing from newsprint here.] one chile an' he ain't nuthin' but er cripple, but le'me tel' you, man, dat boy'll live t' pick de feathers f'm de goose dat'll eat de grass dat grows over your grave, man! Dat's what I tol' 'm. But—lan's sake—how I know dat in less'n three day, dat man be lying in de gutter wif a knife stickin' out'n his back. Lawd, no, I sholy never s'pected nothing like dat."

Memories of the Past

These reminiscences, at once maimed and reconstructed, have been treasured by old Mammy as carefully, as tenderly, as if they were the various little tokens of an early love. She applies the same back-handed sentiment to them, and, as she sits groaning by the fire, it is plainly to be seen that there is only one food for her ancient brain, and that is the recollection of the beautiful fights and murders of the past.

On the other side of the Lane, but near Mammy's house, Pop Babcock keeps a restaurant. Pop says it is a restaurant, and so it must be one, but you could pass there ninety times each day and never know that you were passing a restaurant. There is one obscure little window in the basement and if you went close and peered in, you might, after a time, be able to make out a small, dusty sign, lying amid jars on a shelf. This sign reads: "Oysters in every style." If you are of a gambling turn of mind, you will probably stand out in the street and bet yourself black in the face that there isn't an oyster within a hundred yards. But Pop Babcock made that sign and Pop Babcock could not tell an untruth. Pop is a model of all the virtues which an inventive fate has made for us. He says so.

As far as goes the management of Pop's restaurant, it differs from Sherry's. In the first place the door is always kept locked. The wardmen of the Fifteenth Precinct have a way of prowling through the restaurant almost every night, and Pop keeps the door locked in order to keep out the objectionable people that cause the wardmen's visits. He says so. The cooking stove is located in the main room of the restaurant, and it is placed in such a strategic manner that it occupies about all the space that is not already occupied by a table, a bench and two chairs. The table will, on a pinch, furnish room for the plates of two people if they are willing to crowd. Pop says he is the best cook in the world.

"Pop's" View of It

When questioned concerning the present condition of the Lane, Pop said: "Quiet? Quiet? Lo'd save us, maybe it ain't! Quiet? Quiet?" His emphasis was arranged crescendo, until the last word was really a vocal explosion. "Why, disher' Lane ain't nohow like what it useter be—no indeed, it ain't. No, sir! 'Deed it ain't! Why, I kin remember dey was a-cuttin' an' a'slashin' 'long yere all night. 'Deed dey was! My—my, dem times was different! Dat dar Kent, he kep' de place at Green Gate Cou't—down yer ol' Mammy's—an' he was a hard baby—'deed, he was—an' ol' Black-Cat an' ol' Bloodthirsty, dey was a-roamin' round yere a-cuttin' an' a-slashin'. Didn't dar' say boo to a goose in dose days, dat you didn't, less'n you lookin' fer a scrap. No, sir!" Then he gave information concerning his own prowess at that time. Pop is about as tall as a picket on an undersized fence. "But dey didn't have nothin' ter say to me! No, sir! 'Deed, dey didn't! I wouldn't lay down fer none of 'em. No, sir! Dey knew my gait, 'deed, dey did! Man, man, many's de time I buck up agin 'em. Yes, sir!"

At this time Pop had three customers in his place, one asleep on the bench, one asleep on the two chairs, and one asleep on the floor behind the stove.

But there is one man who lends dignity of the real bevel-edged type to Minetta Lane, and that man is Hank Anderson. Hank, of course, does not live in the Lane, but the shadow of his social perfections falls upon it as refreshingly as a morning dew. Hank gives a dance twice in each week, at a hall hard by in MacDougal Street, and the dusky aristocracy of the neighborhood know their guiding beacon. Moreover, Hank holds an annual ball in Forty-fourth Street. Also he gives a picnic each year to the Montezuma Club, when he again appears as a guiding beacon. This picnic is usually held on a barge and the occasion is a very joyous one. Some years ago it required the entire reserve squad of an up-town police precinct to properly control the enthusiasm of the gay picnickers, but that was an exceptional exuberance and no measure of Hank's ability for management.

He is really a great manager. He was Boss Tweed's body-servant in the days when Tweed was a political prince, and anyone who saw Bill Tweed through a spyglass learned the science of leading, pulling, driving and hauling men in a way to keep men ignorant of it. Hank imbibed from this fount of knowledge and he applied his information in Thompson Street. Thompson Street salaamed. Presently he bore a proud title: "The Mayor of Thompson Street." Dignities from the principal political organization of the city adorned his brow and he speedily became illustrious.

Keeping in Touch

Hank knew the Lane well in its direful days. As for the inhabitants, he kept clear of them and yet in touch with them according to a method that he might have learned in the Sixth Ward. The Sixth Ward was a good place in which to learn that trick. Anderson can tell many strange tales and good of the Lane, and he tells them in the graphic way of his class. "Why, they could steal your shirt without moving a wrinkle on it."

The killing of Joe Carey was the last murder that happened in the Minettas. Carey had what might be called a mixed ale difference with a man named Kenny. They went out to the middle of Minetta Street to affably fight it out and determine the justice of the question. In the scrimmage Kenny drew a knife, thrust quickly and Carey fell. Kenny had not gone a hundred feet before he ran into the arms of a policeman.

There is probably no street in New York where the police keep closer watch than they do in Minetta Lane. There was a time when the inhabitants had a profound and reasonable contempt for the public guardians, but they have it no longer apparently. Any citizen can walk through there at any time in perfect safety unless, perhaps, he should happen to get too frivolous. To be strictly accurate, the change began under the reign of Police Captain Chapman. Under Captain Groo, the present commander of the Fifteenth Precinct, the Lane has donned a complete new garb. Its denizens brag now of its peace precisely as they once bragged of its war. It is no more a bloody lane. The song of the razor is seldom heard. There are still toughs and semi-toughs galore in it, but they can't get a chance with the copper looking the other way. Groo has got the poor old Lane by the throat. If a man should insist on becoming a victim of the badger game he could probably succeed upon search in Minetta Lane, as indeed, he could on any of the great avenues; but then Minetta Lane is not supposed to be a pearly street in Paradise.

In the meantime the Italians have begun to dispute possession of the Lane with the negroes. Green Gate Court is filled with them now, and a row of houses near the MacDougal Street corner is occupied entirely by Italian families. None of them seems to be overfond of the old Mulberry Bend fashion of life, and there are no cutting affrays among them worth mentioning. It is the original negro element that makes the trouble when there is trouble.

But they are happy in this condition, are these people. The most extraordinary quality of the negro is his enormous capacity for happiness under most adverse circumstances. Minetta Lane is a place of poverty and sin, but these influences cannot destroy the broad smile of the negro, a vain and simple child but happy. They all smile here, the most evil as well as the poorest. Knowing the negro, one always expects laughter from him, be he ever so poor, but it was a new experience to see a broad grin on the face of the devil. Even old Pop Babcock had a laugh as fine and mellow as would be the sound of falling glass, broken saints from high windows, in the silence of some great cathedral's hollow.

Selected Writings by Colonel George Waring (1897, 1899)

In November 1894, New Yorkers went to polling sites, monitored by more than two thousand representatives from Good Government Clubs, and swept into office a Republican, William Strong, who promised to run the city on purely "business principles" as opposed to the corrupt Tammany Hall rule. Strong appointed a reform police commissioner in Teddy Roosevelt and delegated the job of Department of Street Cleaning to a Civil War veteran, Colonel George Waring.

Waring had been Frederick Law Olmsted's choice as drainage engineer in 1857 and in the 1870s had designed drainage and sewage systems throughout the country, particularly in Memphis, Tennessee. Waring ran his department the way he had his Civil War troops, and he began his administration with a parade of his twenty-seven hundred men down Fifth Avenue. He immediately cut salaries but gave his "troops" employee benefits to undermine Tammany's hold on the workers. He also reduced nepotism and enforced new stringent regulations on personal behavior, carrying them out with personal inspection tours. Most notably, he dressed his "soldiers of the public" in startling white uniforms, and they became known as "Waring White Angels." Waring also introduced a collection system based on recycling that allowed for the end of ocean dumping, which had been drawing complaints from residents near the Riker's Island landfills.

At the end of his term of office, Waring was sent by President William McKinley to Cuba to investigate how to combat the yellow fever epidemic. Unfortunately, Waring contracted the disease himself and died shortly after his return in 1898.

Sanitary Conditions in New York

BEFORE 1895 the streets were almost universally in a filthy state. In wet weather they were covered with slime, and in dry weather the air was filled with dust. Artificial sprinkling in summer converted the dust into mud, and the drying winds changed the mud to powder. Rubbish of all kinds, garbage, and ashes lay neglected in the streets, and in the hot weather the city stank with the emanations of putrefying organic matter. It was not always possible to see the pavement, because of the dirt that covered it. One expert, a former contractor of street-cleaning, told me that West Broadway could not be cleaned, because it was so coated with grease from wagon-axles; it was really coated with slimy mud. The sewer inlets were clogged with refuse. Dirty paper was prevalent everywhere, and black rottenness was seen and smelled on every hand.

The practice of standing unharnessed trucks and wagons in the public streets was well-nigh universal in all except the main thoroughfares and the better residence districts. The Board of Health made an enumeration of vehicles so standing on Sunday, counting twenty-five thousand on a portion of one side of the city; they reached the conclusion that there were in all more than sixty thousand. These trucks not only restricted traffic and made complete street-cleaning practically impossible, but they were harbors of vice and crime. Thieves and highwaymen made them their dens, toughs caroused in them, both sexes resorted to them, and they were used for the vilest purposes, until they became, both figuratively and literally, a stench in the nostrils of the people. In the crowded districts they were a veritable nocturnal hell. Against all this the poor people were powerless to get relief. The highest city officials, after feeble attempts at removal, declared that New York was so peculiarly constructed (having no alleys through which the rear of the lots could be reached) that its commerce could not be carried on unless this privilege were given to its truckmen; in short, the removal of the trucks was "an impossibility." . . .

The condition of the streets, of the force, and of the stock was the fault of no man and of no set of men. It was the fault of the system. The department was throttled by partisan control—so throttled it could neither do good work, command its own respect and that of the public, nor maintain its material in good order. It was run as an adjunct of a political organization. In that capacity it was a marked success. It paid fat tribute; it fed thousands of voters, and it gave power and influence to hundreds of political leaders. It had this appointed function, and it performed it well. . . .

New York is now thoroughly clean in every part, the empty vehicles are gone. . . . "Clean streets" means much more than the casual observer is apt to think. It has justly been said that "cleanliness is catching," and clean streets are leading to clean hallways and stair cases and cleaner living-rooms. . . .

Few realize the many minor ways in which the work of the department has benefited the people at large. For example, there is far less injury from dust to clothing, to furniture, and to goods in shops; mud is not tracked from the streets on to the sidewalks, and thence into the houses; boots require far less cleaning; the wearing of overshoes has been largely abandoned; wet feet and bedraggled skirts are mainly things of the past; and children now make free use of a playground of streets which were formerly impossible to them. "Scratches," a skin disease of horses due to mud and slush, used to entail very serious cost on truckmen and liverymen. It is now almost unknown. Horses used to "pick up a nail" with alarming frequency, and this caused great loss of service, and, like scratches made the bill of the veterinary surgeon a serious matter. There are practically no nails now to be found in the streets.

The great, the almost inestimable, beneficial effect of the work of the department is showing the large reduction of the death-rate and in the less keenly realized but still more important reduction in the sick-rate. As compared with the average death-rate of 26.78 of 1882–94, that of 1895 was 23.10, that of 1896 was 21.52, and that of the first half of 1897 was 19.63. If this latter figure is maintained throughout the year, there will have been fifteen thousand fewer deaths than there would have been had the average rate of the thirteen previous years prevailed. The report of the Board of Health for 1896, basing its calculations on diarrheal diseases July, August, and September, in the filthiest wards, in the most crowded wards, and in the remainder of the city, shows a very marked reduction in all, and the largest reduction in the first two classes.

New York, A.D., 1997: A Prophecy

If the population centering in New York increases during the next hundred years as rapidly as it has during the past fifty years, it will comprise, probably, twenty million souls. It would be futile, of course, to attempt to predict, with even a probability of accuracy, what the character and conditions of life of that community would be.

Judging from the building progress of the past twenty years, Manhattan Island will be covered, aside from its great public buildings and their ornamental and roomy surroundings, and the parks, which are forever dedicated to the use of the people, with architectural monstrosities which the sky scrapers of the present day portend. It is not unlikely that the whole island will be largely abandoned as a place of residence. Staten Island will be given over to shipping, longshoremen and unsavory industries. The shoal western side of the harbor below Jersey City will be filled with docks, warehouses and railroad terminals. The beautiful ridge on the west side of the Hudson and all the northeastern portion of New Jersey, as well as the upper portion of Westchester County and the whole of Long Island, will become one vast residence region, save for the frequent manufacturing centres which will be established in favorable localities.

HOW WILL THE PEOPLE LIVE?

How the people will live it is impossible even to guess, but it is not likely that they will live in the closely huddled habitations of the present day. The indications are these: The tenement house will be unknown, and no man, rich or poor, will live in a house of which every room does not open freely to the outer air. The present tendency to aggregation and conglomeration will yield to Heaven knows what method of free, easy and cheap transportation. He would be a bold man who, recalling the short interval of time between the days of the ubiquitous omnibus and the rapid and pleasant trolley of today, would venture to predict what will be our means of urban travel. A quarter of a century ago no one would have believed that old and young, rich and poor, would be flying about our streets and over our country roads on rubber tired bicycles. It would have been as absurd to predict then what we are now so familiar with as to predict now that there will be some safe and universal method of aerial or subterranean mode of conveyance.

ENGINEERING PROBLEMS—WATER SUPPLY, SEWAGE

The problems of municipal engineering are no less difficult to adjust, in view of the great possible changes of method and arrangement. For example, to supply a population of twenty millions with water, according to our present system and at our present rate, would be practically impossible. It would involve the forcing of rivers of water from Lake Ontario, and the waste water of the great community would foul both shores of Long Island and the entire Hudson. The lower bay would be a cesspool. . . .

NO HORSES OR OTHER DOMESTIC ANIMALS

Domestic animals will cease to be domesticated within the limits of towns. Indeed, I believe that twenty years will not elapse before the horse will be unknown in New York, and that automobile carriages and trucks will entirely supplant the vehicles of to-day. Heavens! What a relief this will be to the Department of Street Cleaning. In fact, there seems to be no end to what one may imagine as to the material changes that are to take place in our modes of life. . . .

PUBLIC EDUCATION

The public schools of New York are marvelous—not so much for the mere book instruction that they are giving to the children of all classes of the people as for the influence that school life is exerting on the children's character. It has been my good fortune to see a great deal of the public schools of this city, and I have never ceased to marvel at the good order, the good training, the cleanly appearance and the individual ambition of children, even of the lowest class, brought in from the streets and subjected to the influence of competition in all matters appealing to their ambition. The value of the reflex action on the character of parents and their pride in sending their children to school in tidy condition cannot be overestimated.

POPULAR WILL SUPPLANT MONARCHICAL SCHOOL GOVERNMENT

The interest shown by the school children of all classes in the organization of the juvenile street cleaning leagues and in the civic organizations established by Mr. Wilson L. Gill, president of the Patriotic League, especially his "School City"; the avidity with which they acquire information as to the minor details of government; the idea that is beginning to prevail among them that government means something more than the policeman to be run away from—as when building bonfires in the street—and the interest that they show in everything affecting public welfare—these alone are enough to give one the most confident hope for the future.

There are two other influences which are working most effectively throughout the whole community. One is the series of public free lectures given in the public schools, under the direction of Dr. Leipziger, where crowds of intelligent, earnest men and women drink in eagerly the information laid before them to their and our lasting good. The other is the formation of fellowship clubs and associations, largely under the direction of the University and College Settlements and kindred organizations. These are gatherings mainly of young men eager to improve their condition, and to secure for themselves and their neighbors the improvement that their united action can effect.

The tendency toward the formation of these associations is extending rapidly, and the indications are that within a very few years every little community—certainly every Assembly district—will have an organization properly guided, but left free for such action as it may desire, looking to the bettering of local conditions and to the exertion of useful influences on those who have the direction of municipal forces.

PEOPLE WILL DO THEIR OWN THINKING

Through these agencies we cannot fail soon to reach a condition where the people of all classes and in all parts of the city will begin to do their own thinking and to act together for the advancement of the best interests of all. It is hardly too much to hope that these organization, rather than the boss-guided primary, will become the source of nominations for municipal offices. When the desire for such a result is generally realized, it will be backed by such a political power as must suffice to exterminate "politics" as we know it, from the control of the business of the city.

Relief, especially in this respect, is not to be secured in a moment, but we may certainly say that the condition is most hopeful.

NOT AFRAID OF TAMMANY

The town is now filled with apprehension as to what may happen if Tammany Hall returns to power, and the fear is far too general that this would mean a return to the worst conditions of the past. I have no such apprehension. I have had occasion, during the past two or three years, to make a familiar acquaintance with many of the most active leaders of the Tammany organization, and I have made the important discovery that they are human beings; that, as a rule, they are actuated by the same aspirations that are felt by others. They seek success in life, and the acme of such success is to secure the approbation and the esteem of the people.

WE SHALL ALWAYS HAVE AS GOOD A GOVERNMENT AS THE PEOPLE AT LARGE APPRECIATE. These Tammany gentlemen are not hankering after public obloquy and disgrace. The voice of the people is the controlling power with them. Some of them make mistakes and some of them do wrong, but the worst man among them will hold his hand before he will knowingly shock public opinion. They still have a greedy hankering after "patronage," and they will make mischief in satisfying it for some years yet, but this tendency will lessen as time goes on.

PUBLIC OPINION

Public opinion is constantly growing more intelligent and more exacting, and it cannot fail to react to our rulers, of whatever party, in leading them to conform to such standards as the people may establish. In the present case the conditions seem very clear. The people have learned what good government is, and they will not give it up for long under any administration.

Long before the great city of the future shall have approached the lines laid down above, ITS PEOPLE WILL BE A DIFFERENT PEOPLE FROM WHAT THEY NOW ARE, AND ITS RULERS WILL BE DIFFERENT RULERS.

PART 4
World City (1898–1948)

In the half century between the consolidation of the five boroughs into one enormous municipality with a single mayor and city council in 1898 and the return of thousands of victorious American troops after the surrender of Hitler's armies in 1945, New York enjoyed a kind of golden age. The world had never before seen such a place. Of course, there had already been great cities for thousands of years—Athens, Rome, Tokyo, London, and Paris. But Gotham was a different kind of city, a place of unimaginable size filled with buildings that seemed to reach to the clouds. By the end of World War II the city contained almost eight million inhabitants, and at least another five million lived in the surrounding suburbs. Moreover, New York had both the largest immigrant labor force and the most densely populated neighborhoods of any place on earth.

But New York's true distinctiveness was less a function of size and more a function of the way its citizens lived. Although it was not the national capital, Gotham assumed a cultural dominance early in the century that equaled its role in finance, commerce, and industry. Once inferior to Boston as an intellectual and publishing center, Manhattan swept past the Massachusetts city late in the nineteenth century to become the center of the book, magazine, and newspaper world. America's foremost writers and artists made their homes in Greenwich Village, while the Metropolitan Museum of Art and the Metropolitan Opera set a standard of excellence matched only in Europe.

New York also built the infrastructure, created the institutions, and celebrated the heterogeneity that would define metropolitan life for decades to come. The city became the home of modernity in the first half of the nineteenth century with five developments in particular: new residential patterns that led to the development both of tall apartment buildings and low-density single-family homes; new types of buildings for both office and retail use; new mass market newspapers and commercial radio networks; new forms of leisure, especially restaurants, amusement parks, and spectator sports; and new forms of transportation, especially a subway system of unprecedented size and complexity.

First, New Yorkers lived in new kinds of dwellings. Two thirds of the residents of New York City in 1900 lived in tenement buildings, often of the "dumbbell" variety. Such structures stood six stories high, contained eighty-four small rooms, and housed approximately 150 persons. So many of Gotham's citizens crowded into those airless and dimly lit dwellings that in 1914, one sixth of the city's total population lived on the teeming Lower East

Side, where the *average* density was more than 250,000 per square mile, the most intense concentration of humanity the planet had ever seen.

In 1901, reformers passed legislation in Albany that prohibited the construction of any more dumbbell units. Commonly called the New Law, the Tenement House Act of 1901 became the most significant municipal housing statute in American history. In effect, it not only improved the quality of low-income housing but also established design controls that were effective and enforceable.

In addition to tenements, Gotham created two other residential types that had more enduring influence. The first—perhaps surprisingly for the nation's most concentrated city—was the suburban house. The ideal of semi-rural living dated back for centuries, but its realization on a large scale took place in the early decades of the twentieth century, as a human tide of huge proportions engulfed thousands of square miles to the north, east, and west of the city. Meanwhile, the row house that was common in the first suburb, Brooklyn Heights, was replaced in the middle-class imagination by the classic single-family house on its own plot of land. This cottage ideal caught on quickly in other cities, but no other city developed such an extensive suburban network as New York.

Despite this suburbanization, the Hudson River metropolis remained both in fact and in the popular imagination a city of renters and of big residential buildings. Although as late as 1870, the guardians of middle-class morality thought it scandalous to place two unrelated families in the same building or even to put a bedroom on the same floor as the parlor, by 1900, the large apartment house was replacing the brownstone as the residence of choice for the Manhattan upper class. And as apartment living became acceptable to the rich, middle-class families began looking with more favor on the multistory buildings that awaited them in ordinary neighborhoods.

Second, new types of buildings—the skyscraper and the department store—made their appearance in Gotham. In 1898, when the Greater City came together as one metropolis, New York was already the home of the greatest concentration of corporate officials, industrial designers, lawyers, bankers, and architects in North America. By that time, the Wall Street law firm was already a national institution, and investment bankers like J. P. Morgan, August Belmont, and Jacob Schiff had become legendary figures. And as the great corporation emerged as the new business form, Gotham became the headquarters city for American industry.

Two kinds of commercial structures—the skyscraper and the grand department store—symbolized the new metropolitan way of life. For example, by the beginning of World War I in 1914, hundreds of thousands of white-collar clerical employees in Manhattan were riding elevators to work in artificially lit rooms where hundreds of other people were engaged in similar routines. In some respects, the office building was a kind of giant filing cabinet, with separate drawers and compartments.

The department store defined the modern city as much as the office skyscraper. This new form of retailing was born in 1846, when Alexander T. Stewart, a Scottish immigrant, opened a huge new emporium at Broadway and Chambers Streets in Lower Manhattan. Previously, a person wishing to buy a dress or a pair of shoes went to specialized establishments, often a dry goods store, to make arrangements for a one-of-a-kind purchase. Stewart changed all this. Dividing his store into departments, guaranteeing customer satisfaction, offering low prices, and advertising his wares on a large scale, he revolutionized retailing.

Between 1890 and 1950, department stores around the nation, and especially in New York, had become a passion of the middle class. By 1900, the term "Ladies' Mile" referred to a stretch along Broadway and Sixth Avenue, roughly from Tenth Street to Twenty-third Street, in which there were more and better stores than anywhere else on earth. The grand structures were important not just for their architecture and their economic liveliness. Rather, they represented the "feminization" of the central business district. By the early decades of the twentieth century, shopping had become almost the exclusive preserve of women. And because of the department store, women found their way into the heart of the city, a district previously dominated by the business activities of men only.

In typical New York fashion, just as the Ladies' Mile was becoming famous, the big retail emporiums followed their customers uptown and moved northward. R. H. Macy was the first to shift uptown. Nathan Straus and his brother Isidor (who went down on the *Titanic* in 1912) relocated the store to a gargantuan structure at Thirty-fourth Street and Broadway in 1902. Soon after, B. Altman began work on a new store on Madison Avenue. Built of French limestone in the Italian Renaissance style, it had broad aisles, high ceilings, crystal chandeliers, and parquet floors, and it was especially well known for its elaborate window displays during the Christmas holidays.

Anchored by Altman's and Macy's, two great new shopping districts, Fifth Avenue and Herald Square, arose in Midtown with new structures for Gimbel's, Arnold Constable, Saks Fifth Avenue, Lord and Taylor, Bonwit Teller, and a dozen others. Taken together, they offered a cornucopia of retailing extravagance unmatched anywhere else on the planet.

Third, New York revitalized old forms of communication and developed new ones as well. New York was the home of the "penny press" and of "yellow journalism." And in the first half of the twentieth century, the metropolis offered its citizens dozens of newspaper choices, including many ethnic or otherwise special publications, such as the *Jewish Daily Forward* (1897) or the Communist *Daily Worker* (1927). The 1920s saw the development of tabloid newspapers, which were characterized by huge headlines, truncated stories, numerous pictures, and huge circulations. The most notable was the *Illustrated Daily News* (1919), soon renamed the *Daily News,* the circulation of which reached almost two million per day by 1930, making it the most widely read newspaper in the world at the time.

The most important newspaper development of the first half of the twentieth century was the emergence of *The New York Times* as the newspaper of record in the United States and as the world's most powerful and prestigious daily publication. Floundering in the 1890s, it was purchased by Adolph S. Ochs in 1896, and it began focusing on the news rather than emphasizing sex and crime. It won critical recognition for its balanced and thorough coverage of notable issues and for its focus on financial news and the growth of the retailing and fashion industries.

When newspapers were threatened by the new science of telecommunications in the 1920s, New York again led the way to a new journalistic paradigm. Wireless telegraphy, the forerunner of radio, was introduced to the United States in 1899, when *New York Herald* owner James Gordon Bennett broadcast an America's Cup yacht race in New York harbor to a Midtown station. Soon, Manhattan was the center of radio programming and management. The first network, the National Broadcasting Company (NBC), led by David Sarnoff, began in Manhattan in 1926. The rival Columbia Broadcasting System (CBS), also headquartered in New York, began operating in 1927, as did the Blue Network, later to be called the American Broadcasting Company (ABC).

Fourth, New York set the standard for how America spent its time away from the workplace. In the nineteenth century, urban life was more a grind than a party, and even the simplest act, like going out to eat, was a rarity. Most New York households, like those elsewhere in the United States, took all their meals at home until the twentieth century, and even then, it was a special treat to be served by someone else. But New York was the place where this shift in living patterns first occurred. Delmonico's on William Street in Lower Manhattan opened in 1831, and by the time of the Civil War it was the nation's most famous restaurant. The trend accelerated after 1900, especially because of the arrival of hundreds of thousands of new immigrants, who introduced new cuisine to the city's expanding elite. By 1925, new restaurants like Barbetta, Mamma Leone's, and Luchow's made New York the undisputed food capital of the nation. And with the growth of the Jewish population, a new-style, combination grocery-restaurant, called a delicatessen, began offering everything from salmon to pickles to cream soda.

After dining out, the next step toward modernity was the creation of the nightclub, a kind of establishment that made New York—as much as Madrid or Barcelona—a stay-up-late kind of town. The new trend began about 1911, the year of the fox-trot and the year the Bustanoby brothers introduced dancing with dinner to their popular restaurant. Other establishments, like Rector's and Reisenweber's, soon followed suit, so that drinking, dining, and dancing were no longer separate endeavors, but essential parts of a sophisticated evening spent in the company of the opposite sex. Prohibition put a temporary crimp in the revelries of New Yorkers, but the city's entrepreneurs soon developed a new phenomenon—the speakeasy—to appeal to the same audience. And after Prohibition ended in 1933, a new set of nightclubs, like El Morocco, the Stork Club, and the Copacabana, set new standards for spectacle and opulence.

If the nightclub was the preserve of the comfortable and the fashionable, the amusement park was the special home of the working classes. And no amusement park anywhere could compare to Coney Island, at the southern edge of Brooklyn. In 1897, Steeplechase Park, featuring a mechanical racetrack, opened. In 1903, Luna Park, which featured Venetian gondoliers, a Japanese garden, and an elevated promenade, began operating. And in 1904 came Dreamland, which lit the night sky with one million lightbulbs. Until Disneyland opened in 1955, Coney Island was the best-known and most heavily patronized amusement park in the world.

New York also provided opportunity for spectator sports. In addition to a variety of racetracks, the metropolis was the nation's most important venue for boxing matches in the first half of the twentieth century. On September 14, 1923, Jack Dempsey's victory over Luis Firpo attracted 82,000 spectators to the Polo Grounds. Meanwhile, Madison Square Garden became the most famous indoor arena in the United States.

But baseball was the New York game, and it became the only city in American history to have had three major league teams within the city limits at the same time—the New York Giants, the Brooklyn Dodgers, and the New York Yankees. Although each of them had a devoted fan base, the Yankees became the most storied franchise in sports, largely because of the ability and personality of one man—George Herman (Babe) Ruth. Nicknamed the Sultan of Swat and the Bambino, he began playing for the Yankees in 1920 and was soon hitting so many home runs that he changed the way baseball was played. He led the "Bronx Bombers" to seven pennants and four world championships, and Yankee Stadium, whose 67,000 seats made it the biggest sports facility in the world at the time, came to be known as "The House That Ruth Built."

Fifth, New York's geography and topography, as well as its size and density, demanded a varied and intricately linked transportation system. New York City is a transportation planner's nightmare. Virtually an archipelago, with only the Bronx attached to the mainland of the United States, New York has more than five hundred miles of shoreline. And its rivers and bays are wide, unlike the small and charming waterways that bisect other world cities like London and Paris. Thus, Gotham's challenge was to find a way to link the islands and to transform the metropolis into an organic whole.

The solution was to build bridges, tunnels, railroads, subways, and highways and to build more of them than any other place. Seventy-six bridges ultimately crossed Gotham's waterways, as well as a spidery web of tunnels. And there were steam railroads, elevated trains, and electric streetcars, all of which gave the region a public transportation system without equal in the world in the first half of the twentieth century, whether measured by route miles, track miles, capital investment, or ridership.

The subway in particular became New York's signature, the physical manifestation of a new kind of city, a place of concentrated human, commercial, and economic activity. Manhattan's first subway did not open until 1904, years after those of London, Budapest, Glasgow, Boston, Paris, and Berlin. But New York's subway was more than twice as large as any other system in the first half of the century, carrying more than seven million passengers per day in the years immediately after World War II.

New York's immense and interconnected transportation system changed the way people lived. Because a ride on the subways, elevated trains, streetcars, and buses cost only five cents until 1948, the city's inhabitants were able to see more than their immediate neighborhood and to experience more than their particular ethnic group. For example, the first subway line was carrying 600,000 passengers *per day* within one year of its opening, and that number doubled by 1914. And in 1925, an incredible 86 percent of New York's population lived in the ninety-seven square miles served by subways or elevated trains. The remaining 14 percent lived on 70 percent of the city's land area.

During the period between 1910 and 1955, New York, the quintessential subway and railroad city, even led the world in the building of expressways. Particularly significant was the bucolic and meandering Bronx River Parkway, which ran sixteen miles from Bruckner Boulevard in the Bronx to White Plains in Westchester County. Begun in 1906 and completed in 1923, it ran through a valley and thus could be bridged without massive earthwork. Within ten years the metropolitan region also witnessed the construction of the Hutchinson River Parkway (1928), the Saw Mill River Parkway (1929), and the Cross County Parkway (1931). And as late as 1950, New York, not Los Angeles, had the largest total of highway miles within its borders.

New York was not the only city to build apartment buildings, subways, or office towers. But it was perhaps the only place in the world where the hand of man shaped the environment as much as the hand of God. The metropolis at the mouth of the Hudson River was not only a big city but a new kind of city a place of commuting, of movement, of crowded sidewalks, of stone, and of glass. Apartment buildings, skyscrapers, department stores, spectator sports, and subway tracks changed the daily experience of ordinary citizens.

In 1929—where else but in New York—the Great Depression began with the collapse of stock market prices on Wall Street. For almost the entire decade that followed, the metropolis suffered. Almost two million people in the city alone were on the relief rolls, and jobs of almost any kind seemed to dry up. Only the election of Fiorello La Guardia as mayor of the city in 1934 seemed to offer a way out of the gloom. He was brash and confident, like the city he served, and he constantly called for "patience and fortitude" even in the worst of the crisis.

By 1938, as the world moved ominously toward war, the local economy began to pick up. And soon it began to surge once again. Employment at the Brooklyn Navy Yard had more than doubled, to 25,000, in the two years before the Japanese attacked Pearl Harbor. And during the war years, the busy navy yard employed more than 70,000 people, who worked in shifts 24 hours per day, 7 days per week. More importantly, New York harbor became a kind of huge marshalling yard for the European Theater of Operations. Half of all the hardware and at least a third of all the American soldiers who crossed the Atlantic Ocean during the conflict did so from New York harbor.

When the war ended in 1945, New York was the largest, richest, and most important city in the world. But would it be able to hold onto its rank in the second half of the century?

Brooklyn Could Have Been a Contender, from The New York Times, *John Tierney (December 28, 1997)*

John Tierney has worked for *The New York Times* for a number of years and presently writes the "City" column for the Metro section of the paper.

The landmass that became Brooklyn was first sighted by the explorer Giovanni da Verrazano in 1524, and it was chartered in the 1640s and 1650s into the towns of Breuckelen (Brooklyn), named for a town just south of Amsterdam, New Amersfoort (Flatlands), Midwout (Flatbush), New Utrecht, Boswick (Bushwick), and Gravesend. It maintained a rural existence until the introduction of Robert Fulton's steam ferry in 1814, which transformed the region into the first commuter suburb. In 1834, the entire region contained only sixteen thousand people, less than one tenth the population of Manhattan, when it was chartered as the City of Brooklyn.

Just after the Civil War, however, City Planner Andrew Haswell Green lobbied various groups for all of the boroughs—Manhattan, Staten Island, Queens, the Bronx, and Brooklyn—to consolidate into one political entity. Green had been president of the Central Park Commission that had overseen the construction of Central Park between 1857 and 1871 and played an important role in the creation of the New York Public Library charter in 1895. In that same year, he used his post as president of the Consolidation Inquiry Committee to help draft the Consolidation Law of 1895, which was passed in 1897 and took effect on January 1, 1898.

On that day the *New York Tribune* boldly announced that, "The sun will rise this morning on the greatest experiment in municipal government that the world has ever known." The road to consolidation had not been smooth, however, and while the other boroughs had voted convincingly for the merger in a nonbinding public referendum four years earlier, Brooklyn itself had passed the measure by only 277 votes out of 129,211. Whether or not Brooklyn benefited from consolidation has been debated for the past century, but the William Randolph Hearst–provided fireworks that morning signaled the creation of a city of over three hundred square miles with a population of almost

3.5 million, the largest city in the world except for London, and one poised to become the "capital of the world" in the twentieth century.

It is a little late to be running a correction, but The New York Times owes one to the people who gathered at Brooklyn's City Hall on New Year's Eve 100 years ago. They met on that miserably cold, rainy night for an "observance"—they specifically refused to call it a celebration—of their city's merger with New York at midnight. Brooklyn's Mayor got a long round of applause for his efforts to prevent New York City, which then consisted of just Manhattan and the southwestern Bronx, from annexing its neighbors to create the boroughs of Brooklyn, Queens, the Bronx and Staten Island. The evening's featured speaker was another leader of the resistance, St. Clair McKelway, the editor of The Brooklyn Daily Eagle. Sharing Manhattan's tax revenues appealed to many Brooklynites (enough, at least, to vote for the merger), but McKelway feared his industrious city would be corrupted by marrying for money.

"Brooklyn has repeatedly shown herself to be the most independent urban community in the world," McKelway told the somber audience. "There need be no apology for the poverty of Brooklyn. It is an honorable poverty."

Across the river, Manhattan's merchants, bankers and publishers celebrated their triumph with fireworks and a parade. The Times could not resist gloating. It ridiculed McKelway's speech in an article pretending to share his concern. "Complete assimilation," The Times warned, "would rob Brooklyn of that treasured jewel, her poverty, by which, it appears, she sets such store." The Times described the "peril" awaiting Brooklyn: thriving new industries, ample tax revenues, less public debt, fine affordable homes for the new workers, improved public utilities, streets that would be "well paved and clean," bustling business and shopping districts. Brooklyn would soon be so "rich and noisy" it would rival Manhattan.

McKelway's paper had tried warning Brooklyn's taxpayers that they couldn't afford New York's profligate style of government, but The Times vowed that consolidation would be a blessing to taxpayers in both cities: "Brooklyn's taxes would fall at once. New York's would not perhaps fall at once, but they would fall certainly." Suggesting that The Eagle's opposition to consolidation was motivated by "selfish reasons" instead of "regard for the public welfare," The Times reassured the Brooklyn paper that it would go on publishing "with undiminished profit and honor in the same city with ourselves."

Today, the latest incarnation of The Brooklyn Daily Eagle—the original shut down in 1955—has a circulation of 20,000, which is approximately 1.7 million less than the circulation of the periodical in your hands. Consolidation has been very good for The New York Times and other Manhattan institutions. The public's welfare is another matter.

Contrary to The Times's prediction, Brooklyn is more of a poor relation today than it was a century ago. While some sections of Manhattan are booming, Brooklyn, with its factories closed and its piers abandoned, has a 10 percent unemployment rate, one of the highest in the country. It is part of a city renowned for decrepit roads and public utilities, high taxes, heavy public debt and a perpetual shortage of affordable housing. In retrospect, consolidation looks an awful lot like what the Brooklynites gathered on New Year's Eve called it: the Great Mistake.

Modern Brooklyn does have some success stories, like the revival of Brooklyn Heights and Park Slope and the new communities of immigrants. Russians have created a thriving Little Odessa in Brighton Beach; Mexican manufacturers have turned empty factories in Bushwick into Tortilla Triangle; other Hispanic, Asian and Caribbean entrepreneurs have reinvigorated neighborhoods and commercial districts. On Flatbush Avenue, Caribbean jitney drivers have created a mass-transit system that is better than the municipal bus lines and actually turns a profit. Large office buildings have recently opened in downtown Brooklyn, the first such development there in half a century—but that's also the bad news. It shouldn't have taken so long.

Brooklyn today is famous mainly for what it has lost: industries, neighborhoods, a baseball team. As Pete Hamill writes of his fellow Brooklynites, "An inner voice always seems to whisper: *There was another place here once and it was better than this.*" The borough has become a convenient symbol for doom in movies like "Last Exit to Brooklyn," a brutal story of hoods and striking workers in Red Hook's industrial wasteland, and "Do the Right Thing," which ends with a riot by despairing blacks in Bedford-Stuyvesant. In the Bay Ridge of "Saturday Night Fever," the grand ennobling dream is to escape across the river to the City.

New York's consolidation was predicated on the philosophy that bigger was better, that a city would prosper under the centralized guidance of experts—rule by the "best men," as the consolidationists put it. In the first few decades of consolidation, Greater New York did thrive, partly because centralization produced some legitimate benefits (like simplifying the building of the subway system) but mainly because the city was already established as a hub of wealth and talent. Eventually, though, the best men's plans became too expensive and stifling, not only in New York but in the other cities that emulated its bureaucracies. New York inspired America's golden age of urban planning, which was marred only by the mass exodus of urbanites to suburban communities offering large houses, uncrowded streets—and smaller governments that were *not* run by those best men.

American cities have finally begun to revive themselves by abandoning the New York model. New York itself has made a comeback by decentralizing. Crime has fallen thanks to police strategies that make local precincts more accountable; parks and neighborhoods have been restored by non-profit groups and local businesses that do jobs neglected by city bureaucracies. New Yorkers are learning to ignore the best men and pay attention to people like Jane Jacobs, the former Greenwich Village resident who fought Robert Moses and criticized centralized planning in her classic 1961 book, "The Death and Life of Great American Cities."

"Brooklyn and the other boroughs would all be better off on their own," says Jacobs, who now lives in Toronto. "The idea behind New York's amalgamation was that taxes would be pooled and the poor would benefit. But look at the results. The richest borough, Manhattan, has received some economic and cultural benefits, and the others have been stultified in their development. Big bureaucracies can't allow for the diversity and the experimentation that are essential to cities. When mistakes are made, they're made everywhere."

Many Brooklynites knew the perils of bigness last century. The merger was approved by a margin of just 277 votes out of more than 129,000 cast in the city of Brooklyn and the small neighboring communities that now make up the borough. What if the vote had gone the other way? What if Brooklyn's resistance had stopped the consolidation process, leaving Brooklyn—not to mention Queens, Staten Island and the northeastern Bronx—independent? Mike Wallace, a professor at John Jay College and co-author of the forthcoming "Gotham," a history of New York City, sees two possibilities.

"One scenario is war between Brooklyn and New York," he says. "To develop independently, Brooklyn needed to expand its tax base and get access to drinking water. If New York refused to sell it water, Brooklyn might have looked on Long Island. It might have expanded its own borders by annexing Queens and Suffolk County, then declared war on New York by turning Jamaica Bay into a rival port. With its larger population and with all the land available to build docks and airports, Brooklyn could conceivably have ended up as an urban powerhouse on its own."

Wallace's other scenario seems more likely: Brooklyn and New York continue as relatively peaceful twin cities, negotiating arrangement for water and transportation. They had already collaborated on the Brooklyn Bridge (financed chiefly by Brooklyn) and the trains that carried commuters across it. The subway system, constructed mainly by private transit companies in Brooklyn and Manhattan, could have been built without merging the cities, perhaps with coordination by a regional agency.

It's also conceivable that something would have gone very wrong between the independent cities. Maybe the political squabbling would have slowed development so much that a competing metropolitan power would have risen across the Hudson River (and today, people in New Jersey would be telling jokes about the yokels in New York). Or maybe Chicago would have displaced New York as America's prominent city. At the time of the merger, Chicago was about to surpass New York in population, which the consolidationists viewed as a terrible threat to the city's pride.

But consolidation, whatever ego gratification it provided to the city's leaders, was not necessary to make New York a great city. In 1897, the unconsolidated city was already firmly established as a capital of trade, finance, commerce, manufacturing, immigration and culture. Relative to the rest of America, it was a far more dominant and dynamic city that it is today.

Nor was consolidation necessary for Brooklyn's survival. In 1897, it was the fourth-largest city in the country, its population and manufacturing output exceeded only by New York, Philadelphia and Chicago. It refined half of the sugar in America and produced hats, clocks, shoes, cigars and books. Two thousand ships a year docked there. Fulton Street was thronged with shoppers. The system of streetcars and elevated trains was one of the most advanced in the world, which was why Brooklynites were called Trolley Dodgers. Developers were building small houses in Brownsville for the working class and elegant brownstones in Bedford-Stuyvesant for merchants. Brooklyn was famous for its parks—many landscape architects still consider Prospect Park superior to its architects' better-known work, Central Park—and its grand hotels on Coney Island. Construction was underway on the Brooklyn Museum's Beaux-Arts palace, which, if all the wings had been completed, would have been bigger than the Metropolitan Museum. And there was, of course, a baseball team named after those Trolley Dodgers.

If it had been left alone in 1898, Brooklyn might still have the Dodgers and a lot more. Today, with 2.2 million people, it could be the third-largest city in America, behind Los Angeles and Chicago. (Manhattan, with 1.5 million people, would rank seventh, below Queens with 1.9 million, Houston and Philadelphia.) An independent Brooklyn would probably never have rivaled Manhattan for power or wealth or glamour. But in its own way, it could have been a contender.

On the Waterfront

Dominick Massa's view of Manhattan is from the Sunset Park neighborhood, looking through the charred, twisted girders covering the abandoned piers of the old Bush Terminal near the Gowanus Expressway. Massa's grandfather was a carpenter in the terminal, a 20-block stretch of docks, warehouses and factories. His mother and father worked nearby, making macaroni and chocolate for A&P stores.

"I used to sneak into this terminal as a kid to watch all the action," recalls Massa, who is 52. "There were thousands of workers, freight cars everywhere, trucks lined up for two blocks to get in. The ships were unloading cocoa, coffee, wine, cheese, oil, everything from soup to nuts." In 1989, Massa leased eight blocks of the terminal from the city, intending to bring in new businesses. By then it was an expanse of rotting piers, abandoned cars and dozens of ramshackle buildings with leaky roofs and thousands of broken windows.

What would have happened to this waterfront if Brooklyn had stayed independent? Massa smiles at the possibility, then dismisses the ugly reality with a wave of his hand.

"Ah, fuhgeddaboudit," he says. "There might be a container port here, or some new factories or offices, or some kind of recreational facility—maybe a marina, a promenade, places where people would come for a walk, go fishing. We never would have let it deteriorate the way it did."

Brooklyn's woes are usually attributed to national trends beyond anyone's control. Shippers and manufacturers headed for places with cheaper labor and land. Federally subsidized highways and mortgages opened up the suburbs. The middle class fled the old industrial cities, leaving behind the unemployed poor and their problems.

But New York, even with all its inherent advantages, has generally fared worse than the other cities. When Massa's grandfather worked here in the 1950's, New York's jobs-per-capita ratio was higher than just about every other major American city's. Today, it is among the lowest, well below most other old industrial centers in the East and Midwest. New York's problem was not simply that industries fled from places like the Brooklyn waterfront. "The problem," Massa says, "was that nothing replaced them."

Brooklyn has the same basic economic assets today that it had in 1897: location, location, location. It still sits across a narrow river from an economic and cultural capital. Like Silicon Valley outside San Francisco and Burbank next to Los Angeles, Brooklyn is endowed with proximity to an expensive city that attracts the ambitious and the creative from around the world. But while the computer industry was being created in Silicon Valley, while television and movie companies from Los Angeles were filling Burbank with sound stages, the chief new economic activities on Brooklyn's waterfront were drug dealing and garbage dumping.

Why didn't computer companies move into those old brick buildings at the Bush Terminal? The office views would have been better than anything in Silicon Valley or on Microsoft's campus outside Seattle, and the companies could have recruited young talent from Polytechnic University in downtown Brooklyn, one of the country's largest graduate engineering schools. Why didn't the television and movie producers who complain about Manhattan's paucity of sound stages establish an outpost called Brooklywood? Why did the white-collar corporations fleeing Manhattan's high rents so rarely settle in downtown Brooklyn? Why didn't someone in Manhattan's publishing world use Brooklyn's empty warehouses to start something like Amazon.com? Why doesn't New York's left bank resemble Paris's? Why doesn't Coney Island's boardwalk resemble Atlantic City's?

"An independent Brooklyn," Hamill says, "would never have mutilated those amazing beaches by putting in high-rise public housing projects as far as possible from any kind of job. Coney Island could have had casinos before Atlantic City: 'Take the train to the game.' There would be a famous symphony orchestra in Brooklyn—they've got one in Cleveland. An independent Brooklyn probably would have built a new stadium for the Dodgers, so today there might be not just baseball but also the only football team on this side of the Hudson."

Under New York's master planners, Brooklyn has lost the nimbleness that helped it adapt before consolidation. Its first commercial waterfront developed near the landing used by Robert Fulton's ferries to Manhattan. That area became obsolete when the Brooklyn Bridge was built high overhead, creating a new commercial center up the hill. But Fulton Landing did not remain a wasteland: Robert Gair promptly built factories there to turn out his innovation, the corrugated cardboard box, conveniently close to his customers across the river. New York's lucrative market stimulated all kinds of development. Ferries took Manhattanites out to Ambrose Park, an amusement park on the waterfront where Dominick Massa now works, and then the amusement park gave way to Irving T. Bush's docks and factories. Starting with one warehouse in 1890, Bush created a 200-acre terminal complete with its own piers, police and fire forces, power plants and railroad, whose cars traveled on barges across the harbor to rail lines in New Jersey.

To keep Brooklyn competitive with other Eastern ports, New York's leaders promised in 1920 to build a rail tunnel under the harbor, giving Brooklyn a direct link to the mainland. The tunnel was supposed to be the first project of the Port Authority of New York and New Jersey. But it never happened. The Port Authority instead moved on to a long series of projects benefiting Manhattan and New Jersey, like the Hudson River crossings, the World Trade Center and the PATH commuter train. It built a port for Newark, capable of handling the large new cargo containers, that took business away from the docks in Brooklyn and Manhattan.

The city's master builder, Robert Moses, concentrated on highways for commuters to Manhattan. The residents of Sunset Park objected to his plan to build the Gowanus highway through their neighborhood. But while Manhattanites managed to prevent Moses from building an expressway across SoHo, Sunset Park residents lacked such clout. Then, after the Gowanus was built, New York's leaders became so preoccupied with social programs that there was no money to properly maintain its roads, so Sunset Park ended up not only with a blighted neighborhood but also a decrepit highway atop it.

When Massa began renovating the waterfront buildings between 42d and 50th Streets, he hoped to fill them with small manufacturers and distributors. His biggest obstacle was the city's commercial occupancy tax, a surcharge on rent of up to 6 percent, which does not exist in other cities. "I was practically on my hands and knees trying to get a tenant in here," he says. "The occupancy tax was the last straw. Once they heard about it, they were off to Jersey."

They did not want to pay a Manhattan premium to be in Brooklyn, the same reason so many other businesses fled from the taxes and union contracts designed for Manhattan. An independent Brooklyn would never have imposed the occupancy tax or the many other only-in-New-York fees. The unincorporated business tax, for instance, was aimed at the partners of Manhattan's law and securities firms, but it also levied a 4 percent surcharge on the income of self-employed professionals in the other boroughs. The lawyers needed to stay in Manhattan, but when a struggling screenwriter in Fort Greene finally sold a script, or when an independent consultant in Manhattan was considering a bigger home in Park Slope, their tax accountant's first advice was to leave New York.

After years of complaints, the city last year finally eliminated the occupancy tax in the outer boroughs and parts of Manhattan. "Now the buildings are filling up," Massa says. "People said the waterfront was finished, but we're close to 90 percent occupancy here and in other parts of Sunset Park. Companies are moving back here from Jersey because they want to be closer to their customers in Manhattan and the labor force in Brooklyn." Massa's waterfront buildings are occupied by small firms that bake bread, roast coffee, silk-screen T-shirts, build wooden cribs, cut marble for kitchen counters and distribute goods ranging from jeans to light bulbs to appliances. The upsurge in business has induced Massa to convert the workers' cafeteria of the old terminal into a restaurant. Above the fireplace, he has dusted off an inscription put there by Mr. Bush.

"Success is not an accident," the inscription reads. "It comes to the man who does his work better than the other fellow."

Brooklynites last century feared that this sort of bourgeois thinking would be endangered by consorting with the hustlers across the river, and they turned out to be right.

"We have no street analogous to your Fifth Avenue," The Eagle's editor told New York a century ago, "but neither have we any resembling those of your tenderloin district. With us are as yet no extremes of wealth or poverty; but the families of moderate means are becoming fewer with you."

The city of homes and churches, as Brooklyn called itself, remained a middle-class bastion through the 1950's, when Jackie Gleason portrayed a bus driver from Bensonhurst in "The Honeymooners." But McElway's fears were eventually realized, as another Brooklynite, Fred Siegel, laments in his new book analyzing urban problems, "The Future Once Happened Here."

"Manhattan's wealth has been a curse to Brooklyn," says Siegel, a professor of history at the Cooper Union. "It's like a rich gravy that covers the failure of the food below. The city's infrastructure was allowed to collapse because Wall Street was doing well and Manhattan thought the city didn't need an old-fashioned industrial base. An independent Brooklyn would have had to develop the economic assets of its citizens, but instead it has become an object of pity—an opportunity for rich Manhattanites to demonstrate their generosity by providing welfare and social programs."

Like the former Bartons chocolate factory on Fulton Street, which now houses tax collectors and social workers, Brooklyn stopped making and started taking. The villains in Siegel's book are the Manhattan politicians and activists who built the nation's first welfare state during the 1960's. It was a time of economic prosperity—unemployment among black males in New York City was only 4 percent—but the welfare rolls tripled to more than a million people as city officials, academics and lawyers crusaded for new "welfare rights." Mitchell I. Ginsberg, the associate dean of Columbia University's social-work school who became Mayor John V. Lindsay's Social Services Commissioner, was dubbed "Come and Get It Ginsberg" by The Daily News when he announced that the city would no longer verify whether applicants actually met the requirements for welfare. Siegel, who lives in Flatbush, sees the results of this philanthropy close to home when he walks by the small apartment buildings that now house welfare recipients instead of working-class families.

"The problem is not that poor people moved into the neighborhood," he says, pausing at a corner that was until recently a 24-hour crack market. "The problem is that they now stay poor. Brooklyn ceased being the seedbed of the middle class. During the biggest economic boom the country had ever seen, Manhattan's elite gave up on the idea of upward mobility, and Brooklyn paid the price."

Brooklyn Agonistes

On Jan. 1, 1898, the best prediction for the consolidated city was unintentionally made by Rabbi Joseph Silverman at Temple Emanu-el in Manhattan. "We need fear no great danger of the misrule of the city," he said, hailing the strength of Greater New York. "Like Samson rising in moral and physical might, it will destroy beneath the temple of injustice and anarchy the men who rob it of its strength and its beauty."

In comparing Greater New York to Samson, Rabbi Silverman overlooked a complication at the end of the biblical story: the temple falls on Samson as well as on the Philistines. This complication has not been overlooked by Brad De Long, an economist at the University of California at Berkeley who has studied the historical fortunes of cities. One of his essays takes its title from the scene in Milton's "Samson Agonistes" in which Samson's father addresses his dead son:

> O lastly overstrong against thyself!
> A dreadful way thou took'st to thy revenge.

De Long's essay, "Overstrong Against Thyself," deals with a central predicament that cities have faced since the first agricultural marketplaces. To protect their wealth, merchants typically shared power and their earnings with princes and priests. The city prospered as long as these authorities maintained social order and were satisfied with a reasonable share of the profits. But as the city grew, it offered increasingly dangerous temptations.

"A large, rich city has the accoutrements of civilization that appeal to the most ambitious princes and priests of the age," says De Long. "Eventually the merchants lose power to an overstrong prince." As the new prince and priests pursue their ambitious projects—places and wars, temples and moral crusades—taxes rise and decrees proliferate. The city stagnates as merchants go elsewhere.

By comparing nine different regions of Western Europe over the past millennium, De Long and a colleague, Andrei Shleifer, found that urban populations shrank during periods when cities were consolidated into larger empires. "City growth," De Long concludes, "has a strong allergy to the presence of strong, centralizing princes."

Why did the Renaissance begin in Northern Italy, which had previously been a relative backwater? In the year 1000, Italy's economy had been dominated by Naples and other city-states in the South, but these cities were subsequently conquered by Robert (the Crafty) d'Hauteville and brought under the control of the Kingdom of Sicily. The Northern city-states remained independent and prospered under the control of merchants like Lorenzo (the Magnificent) Medici in Florence, whose income came chiefly from his family's bank, not taxes. Culture and commerce flourished in the independent Northern cities; but when these cities eventually fell under the sway of foreign warrior princes (from Spain and France), the Renaissance waned along with the merchants' prosperity. New commercial and cultural hubs formed in the independent cities of the Low Countries.

A similar historical progression can be observed today on the two shores facing lower Manhattan: Brooklyn across the East River and Jersey City across the Hudson. The Brooklyn shore is a neighborhood called Dumbo, for Down Under the Manhattan Bridge Overpass. Near the site of Fulton's old ferryboat landing are empty warehouses, former factories and a riverside parking lot with one of the greatest views in the world. Most of the property belongs to David Walentas, a developer who has been trying since 1981 to revive the waterfront by restoring the old buildings and adding a shorefront promenade. He has plans for a marina, stores, movie theaters, apartments, offices and lofts for artists and artisans.

Walentas's project has won the support of the Brooklyn Borough President, Howard Golden, but it has long been stymied by the overstrong princes and priests across the river. During the boom of the 1980's, Walentas got into a feud with the Koch Administration. Then the real-estate market collapsed. Now the market has been revived and City Hall is backing the project, but construction along the waterfront probably won't begin before the millennium. Walentas still must contend with New York's mandarin classes: the bureaucracies and judges who administer the nation's most complex zoning, housing and environmental regulations. Even a project backed by the city, like the Metrotech Center buildings in downtown Brooklyn (which received tax incentives worth more than $300 million), can be held up for years by lawsuits from special-interest groups.

While Walentas was waiting two decades, the developer Sam LeFrak was busy elsewhere. "I would have loved to do something on the Brooklyn waterfront," says LeFrak, whose company once built large projects on Sheepshead Bay and Coney Island. "When Ed Koch was Mayor, I took him on my yacht past the Manhattan Bridge and told him he should develop that great real estate. But the zoning and political straitjacket in New York was impossible. So we took a page from Horace Greeley and went west."

LeFrak set his sights on 600 acres of old docks and railroad yards in Jersey City, just across the Hudson from the World Trade towers. Jersey City officials welcomed the plans he presented in 1983, and within three years construction was under way on a $10 billion project. So far, LeFrak has built two office towers, a marina, a shopping mall, movie theaters, a gigantic international food market and 2,500 apartments, with New York skyline views at half the cost of Manhattan rents. LeFrak refuses even to contemplate how much time and money it would take to build a similar project in Brooklyn.

"Forget it," he says. "Forget it. Even God couldn't do it."

Besides LeFrak's project, Jersey City's booming waterfront has other new office and apartment buildings, stores, warehouses, industrial plants and a new science museum. Since the end of the recession in 1992, Jersey City has gained 12,000 new jobs—about the same number gained in all of Brooklyn, which has 10 times the population and 6 times the area. Jersey City and the old industrial centers nearby still have pockets of poverty, but the unemployment rate in the counties along the west side of the Hudson is significantly lower than New York City's. While Brooklyn and Queens have gained a few big new office buildings, developers in the small towns across the Hudson have recently built the equivalent of a whole new downtown, giving northern New Jersey the fifth-largest concentration of office space in America.

New Yorkers may have a hard time seeing the resemblance between Jersey City and Renaissance Florence. They may sneer that its new developments lack the urban charms of Brooklyn. But Brooklyn's chief advantages over New Jersey—its historic buildings and neighborhoods, its access to Manhattan—were even greater *before* Brooklyn consolidated with New York. In 1897, there was no comparison between the large sophisticated city of Brooklyn and the isolated New Jersey waterfront of rail yards and swampland. Today it's New Jersey that has the active port and the urban status symbols—professional sports teams in the Meadowlands, the science museum in Jersey City, a new performing-arts center in Newark. The Hudson River crossings are not falling apart like the East River bridges. Unconsolidated New Jersey has ended up with the benefits that The Times promised Brooklyn a century ago: well-maintained roads and public utilities, thriving retail and business districts, lower taxes and lower public debt, jobs and affordable homes for workers.

If New Jersey is not a sufficiently inspiring model, consider the Los Angeles area, which today may contain the most dynamic approximation of Renaissance cities: an urban center thriving because of its international combination of traders, merchants, artisans and artists. Unlike New York's economy, dominated by Manhattan's large white-collar corporations, Los Angeles's has been bolstered by a rich assortment of small new businesses and factories, particularly in the independent cities that adjoin Los Angeles.

"The best urban models are the small cities like Glendale and Burbank," says Joel Kotkin, a fellow at the Pepperdine University Institute for Public Policy in Malibu and a Brooklyn native. "They aren't necessarily rich enclaves—some have substantial blue-collar, minority populations—but almost without exception the independent cities are doing better than the adjoining sections of Los Angeles. Small cities can experiment and learn because they have short feedback loops. That's why they've managed to keep the middle class and big cities haven't."

If Brooklyn had remained independent—or, better yet, been broken into even smaller cities—Kotkin says that his family might still be there. "My parents didn't want to leave the city for Long Island. My father hated it out there, but the alternative was becoming too expensive. The only ones in my family who stayed were ones who hit it big and could afford Manhattan. New York became an all-or-nothing city, a place for the rich and the poor and people with special incentives to be there—immigrants, gays, singles. Brooklyn needs to get back middle-class families, and it can't do it playing by Manhattan's rules."

Could New York ever humble itself to emulate Jersey City and Los Angeles? It's hard to imagine the princes in City Hall and Albany ever surrendering their power over Brooklyn, but on this centennial it doesn't hurt to fantasize about deconsolidation.

The best plan is still probably the one put forward by Brooklyn's own Norman Mailer during his 1969 mayoral campaign. He proposed turning

New York City into a separate state and then giving "every opportunity to neighborhoods to vote to become townships, villages, hamlets, sub-boroughs, tracts or small cities." He envisioned autonomous communities in charge of their own municipal services, dedicated to ideologies that "might run from Compulsory Free Love to Mandatory Attendance in Church on Sunday!"

In a deconsolidated New York, the independent local communities could have the option of buying some services, like sanitation or police, from the new state government, the way that independent cities do now from the Los Angeles county government. Transportation and other regional issues could be coordinated by agencies like the Port Authority or the Metropolitan Transportation Authority. A few broad social tasks could be entrusted to the Federal Government, particularly the redistribution of wealth—a well-intentioned goal of New York's best men, but one that is beyond the scope of any city.

The hardest part of any divorce is dividing up the property and figuring how much income the poorer spouse needs to survive. Independent Brooklynites could afford to pay for their own basic services as well as people anywhere else. The per capita expenditures in New York for basic services—schools, public safety, transportation, parks—are about the same as in other cities. What makes New York such a big spender are its singularly costly housing projects, social programs and public debt. Only Manhattan has the tax revenues to support this life style. Since it was Manhattanites who ran up these bills, they could pay off the debt and finance a gradual phase-out of the welfare state in Brooklyn. It's not unreasonable for conquering princes to pay reparations.

In the new State of New York City, Brooklyn might become one city or revert to smaller communities, perhaps towns that once existed, like Bushwick and Flatbush. A deconsolidated New York would not be as socially fragmented and diffuse as Los Angeles—Manhattan's dense core would always provide a common meeting place and spiritual center—but it would feel different than New York does today. A deconsolidated city would be richer and more creative, yet less grandiose, less sweeping in its plans, less obsessed with having the biggest of everything.

Perhaps some Brooklynites would miss being part of the Big Apple. They might agree with the pamphlet circulated a century ago urging Brooklynites to merge with New York for the "increased social prestige and civic pride" of belonging to "the first city of the world." But, as The Daily Eagle pointed out in response, Brooklyn's businesses "do not need 'prestige.' They need solvency." And as its editor told that crowd on New Year's Eve 1897, Brooklyn's citizens could find another source of pride.

"In proportion as we define ourselves, we shall respect ourselves, and in proportion as we respect ourselves will our brethren respect us," McElway said, and then he closed with a line that brought down the house: "Though borough it may be, Brooklyn it is, Brooklyn it remains and Brooklynites are we!"

The Tenement-House Exhibition of 1899, Lawrence Veiller (1901)

Following on the heels of his mentor, Jacob Riis, Lawrence Veiller was already the chief executive officer of the Tenement Housing Committee when he organized a moving exhibition in the winter of 1900 designed to bring to light the housing conditions of people living on the Lower East Side. The Tenement House Department would later conduct a survey that found the Tenth Ward the most densely populated in the city, housing 69,944 people or approximately 665 people per acre. Graphically, Veiller's exhibition of photographs, maps, and charts revealed the poverty, disease, and sanitation horrors that were part of everyday life for the area's denizens. The outcry was so mammoth that within weeks Veiller had drafted the language for a new Tenement House Law that was rushed through the New York state legislature by Teddy Roosevelt and signed into law on April 18, 1900. "The horrible dumbbell tenement is now a thing of the past," Veiller predicted. "In its place is the new-law tenement, with large courts providing adequate light and ventilation for every room. What this one change means to the future welfare of the city cannot be overstated."

Indeed, Veiller's effect was national as well as citywide. He was the founder and director of the National Housing Association (1911–1936), which transformed housing reform from a local to a national project and, in 1921, he helped to draft the Standard Zoning Law for the U.S. Department of Commerce.

It has been reserved for New York city, the modern Rome, to duplicate evils of tenement-house structure known in ancient Rome alone among all the cities of the world. In characteristic fashion, she has not only duplicated these evils, but has intensified them to a degree beyond belief. Since 1846, we have been conscious in New York city of a tenement-house problem. Although numerous efforts have been made to solve the problem at different times, we stand today in a much worse condition in many respects than we did fifty years ago, enjoying the unenviable distinction of having the worst tenement houses in the world, although the highest rents for living accommodations are charged. If one were to try to find the reason for the failure to solve the problem, it would not be hard. Interest in the question, aroused spasmodically every ten years, and then allowed to flag, is not calculated to secure either beneficent results or much progress toward improved conditions.

The latest movement in this direction, however, promises to have greater stability than any former one, and, therefore, holds out greater prospects of definite results. It was started about a year ago, by the formation of the tenement-house committee of the charity organization society of New York city. This committee devoted the first six months of its existence to attempting to secure from the local authorities an improved law relating to the construction of new tenement houses. None of its recommendations were adopted. The committee felt, however, that its six months' labor had been worth while, in that it has directed that attention of the community to what is needed in legislation. Being convinced that no real progress was to be made unless the whole community was aroused to a knowledge of existing condition, the committee then set itself at work to prepare for the public such a statement of tenement-house needs that no one concerned could longer neglect taking action looking toward the amelioration of the living conditions of the working people of New York.

The tenement-house exhibition which has just closed, and which was held in the old Sherry building on Fifth avenue for a period of two weeks, has been viewed by a large number of persons, and has given to many a conception of what the tenement-house problem is that could not have been given in any other way. It has shown, step by step, the different changes that have taken place in New York tenement houses, and by means of 1,000 photographs has illustrated nearly all the evils of the present tenement-house system. Special emphasis has been laid upon the terrible evils of the dark, unventilated airshafts, which are the chief characteristic of the present type of buildings. There are over forty-four thousand tenement houses in the boroughs of Manhattan and the Bronx, and in the year 1899 about two thousand new tenement houses were erected. These, as a rule, are built on lots twenty-five feet wide by one hundred feet deep, and are planned to accommodate four families on a floor. The buildings are six or seven stories high, and each floor generally contains fourteen different rooms.

Only four of these rooms on each floor have direct light and air from the street or the small yard. The other ten open on a narrow "air-shaft," which is a well hole closed at both ends, seldom more than five feet wide, when between two buildings, and often only two feet six inches wide, varying in length from forty to sixty feet, and being generally from sixty to seventy-two feet high.

The first of the accompanying illustrations represent a typical airshaft. As usual, it is closed at both ends. It is two feet ten inches wide, forty-eight feet long, and seventy-two feet high. Forty-two windows open upon it, the sole source of light and air to the rooms. Rents in this building run from $10 a month for three rooms to $17 for four rooms. The baby's bathtub is hung out of the window because the rooms are so small that there is no place to keep it inside. The shaft is only a little wider than the tub.

Another of these well holes is shown. It, too, is closed at both ends. It is two feet four inches wide, forty-two feet long, and sixty feet high. Forty-five windows open on it, the sole source of light and air to the rooms. Rents run from $11 a month for three rooms, two of which open entirely on the shaft, to $17 for four rooms, three of which open entirely on the shaft. The picture shows the tenants utilizing the windows as well as the airshaft for the storage of furniture, on account of the smallness of the rooms. The picture was taken at 11 A.M., in bright sunlight.

The sunlight seldom penetrates below the fifth floor in these shafts. There is never a circulation of air. Bringing up children in such darkness and amidst filthy odors insures its inevitable result: $25,000,000 are annually expended for charity in the state of New York. It is a simple matter to investigate the records of our reformations, hospitals, dispensaries, and institutions of similar kind, to find out what proportion of the patients and inmates come from tenement houses. Here in New York we know that nearly all are tenement-house dwellers. We also know that most of our criminals are young men between the ages of eighteen and twenty-five, and that the majority of them come from large cities, the breeding places of vice and crime.

The tenement-house exhibition has enforced the general opinion that has prevailed for some time as to the conditions causing these evils, by presenting in accurate, scientific form a number of maps showing the entire tenement city of New York. These maps show on a large scale each block in the tenement-house district, indicating which buildings are tenement houses and which are business buildings or used for other purposes; they give the street number of each building, the height in stories, and show exactly the amount of land covered, the shape of the building, and the small amount left vacant for light and air. These maps are arranged in two parallel series, one of poverty maps, and the other of disease maps. Upon the poverty maps are stamped black dots, each of which indicates that five different families from the building marked have applied for charity to one of the large charitable societies of the city within a definite period of years. It seems beyond belief, yet is its a fact, that there is hardly a tenement house in the entire city that does not contain a number of these dots, and many contain as many as fifteen of them, meaning that seventy-five different families have applied for charity from that house. Similarly, on the disease maps, which are placed directly below the poverty maps, district by district, so that a comparative study of them may be made, there are stamped black dots, each indicating that from this house there has been reported to the Board of Health one case of tuberculosis within the last five years. While these dots do not cover the building to the same extent that they are covered in the poverty maps, it is appalling to note the extent of this disease. Nearly every tenement house has one dot on it, many have three or four, and there are some houses in Cherry street that contain as many as twelve. Other colored dots indicate the prevalence of typhoid, diphtheria, etc. The maps also contain, stamped upon each block a statement of the number of people living in that block, so that the student thus has opportunity of weighing all the conditions that help to produce the epidemics of poverty and disease. The maps, as they appear in the exhibition, might well earn for New York city the title of the city of living death. No other words so accurately and graphically describe the real conditions as these.

An accompanying illustration gives the appearance of an actual block on the east side of New York city, as it stood on January 1, 1900. The block is bounded by Chrystie, Forsyth, Canal, and Bayard streets. It includes thirty-nine tenement houses, containing 605 different apartments for 2,781 persons. Of these 2,315 are over five years of age, and 466 under five years. There are 263 two-room, 179 three-room, 105 four-room, and twenty-one five room apartments, making a total of 1,588 rooms, or about two persons to a room day and night. There are only 264 water-closets in the block. There is not one bath in the entire block. Only forty apartments are supplied with hot water. There are 441 dark rooms, having no ventilation to the outer air, and no light or air except that derived from other rooms. There are 635 rooms getting their sole light and air from dark, narrow airshafts. The disease map shows that in the last five years there have been recorded thirty-two cases of tuberculosis, and during the past year thirteen cases of diphtheria from this block, while the poverty map shows that 665 applications have been recorded. The rentals derived from the block amount to $113,964 a year. It has been selected merely as characteristic of the city. There are worse.

The exhibition has been planned and developed to prove to the community the fact that in New York city the workingman is housed worse than in any other city in the civilized world, notwithstanding the fact that he pays more for such accommodations than is paid anywhere else, being compelled to give over one-fourth of his income for rent. To bring this fact home to the minds of the public a very extensive parallel exhibit has been developed, showing the great work accomplished in London and other cities in building model tenements for the accommodation of workingmen. . . .

Believing that the tenement-house problem is at the root of most of our social evils, the committee has given attention to those subordinate problems which are affected by the housing problem, and which in turn deeply affect it. The need of playgrounds, parks, public baths, and libraries is shown in many ways. Probably the most interesting feature of this exhibit is a series of diagrams illustrating sixteen "city wildernesses" in New York. These are proposed as sites of needed parks, play-grounds, and public baths. The actual shape of the buildings on these blocks is shown; the number of people living in them, the character of the soil, whether near an underground stream or not, is stated; and the nearness to public schools, the character of the neighborhood, whether strictly a business neighborhood or one where business is crowding out tenements, is most carefully considered. The parks proposed indicate the minimum needs of the city at the present time. They are what is now absolutely indispensable, not what is desirable or ideal. They indicate what the city must do if it expects to have decent citizens. It is the first time that so definite and positive a program of the kind has been placed before the city authorities, or has been given into the hands of those interested in promoting the welfare of the community. A series of photographs is displayed, showing how some waste places in the city have already been transformed into children's play-grounds, where thousands of children now enjoy themselves. There is no way in which the city can neglect its own welfare more than by neglecting its children. It is its first duty to see that they have an opportunity for play, that they have freedom for physical exercise, and that they are not repressed and hunted by the city authorities at every turn. It would be economical for the city to spend many millions of dollars in providing play places of this kind, thus cutting down its future appropriations for jails, almhouses, hospitals, and dispensaries.

More important than the opportunity for play is the opportunity for cleanliness. That we should have silently endured the reproach cast upon us by the last tenement-house investigation, which, in 1894, found that out of 255,000 persons with whom their investigation had been concerned, only 306 had an opportunity to bathe, is a disgrace, not only to the city of New York, but to the entire state. If the old-fashioned idea that working people did not wish to bathe, and did not wish to be clean, were true, there might be some reason for this state of affairs, but if there was ever an absurd and foolish fallacy, this is it. It has been demonstrated over and over again, that if the working people have an opportunity to bathe, they are only too anxious to take advantage of it. The only public bath house in the city which keeps open all the year round, a small building with small accommodations, bathed over 120,000 persons during the last year, notwithstanding the fact that a fee of five cents was charged for each bath. And yet nothing is done to meet this crying need. The new tenement houses that are being built provide no bathing accommodations, and few public baths are being constructed to meet the needs of dwellers in existing buildings.

The problem of how properly to house single men and women is one that has been a source of annoyance to us in New York for many years. We have at last solved the problem of housing the men, although we have as yet only started our attempt to properly house single women. A very interesting part of the exhibition is that showing the different types of lodging houses in the city of New York, beginning with the indescribably filthy police station lodgings which Commissioner Roosevelt abolished, and working gradually up through the Bowery lodging to the municipal lodging house and the Mills hotel which have supplanted the old buildings.

One way out of the tenement-house problem, a way that has been thought for many years the chief way, but one which seems to the writer to have slight bearing on the question, is to set the drift back to the fields, away from the city. Such movements must be undertaken always, but it must equally be borne in mind that we shall continue to have in our large cities a dense population which must be housed. Let us not deceive ourselves and neglect the housing of this population, with the thought that people "ought to live in the country." The well to do classes do not live in the country, and so long as they live here there will be a large number of persons to do their work, on whom they are dependent for their very lives, "hewers of wood and drawers of water," or their modern equivalent.

Besides the many photographs illustrating how workingmen are housed in European cities, there is an elaborate series showing the worst workingmen's dwelling in every city in the United States having a population of 25,000 or more, so that students may compare the conditions under which workingmen live in New York with the conditions in other American cities. In no city, except Boston and Chicago, do we find the slightest trace of conditions at all similar to those of New York's tenement houses.

So much of the solution of the tenement-house problem lies in the scientific planning of the buildings, that any movement looking toward reform must concern itself primarily with this phase of the subject. Realizing this, the committee has tried to stimulate the interest of architects in the subject by offering a prize for the best type of plans for model tenements. One hundred and seventy different architects submitted drawings in this competition. The plans were for buildings on lots of various sizes—25 feet by 100 feet, 50 feet by 100 feet, 75 feet by 100 feet, and 100 feet by 100 feet. A special jury of award was appointed to adjudge the merits of the different drawings, and, after careful deliberation and study, the first prize was awarded to Mr. R. Thomas Short, a New York architect. A copy of his plan is given on the following page. This plan is designed for a tenement house on a lot 100 feet wide by 100 feet deep. A space 10 feet in width and 100 feet in length is left at the rear of the building for light and air, as required by the New York building laws. The main features of the plan are the large street court, which in its narrowest part is 12 feet wide, and one-half of which is 24 feet wide. This court is 60 feet in total depth, and provides an abundance of light and air for all the rooms. Being open to the street, it permits free circulation of air at all times, and has the additional advantage of giving a number of rooms an outlook upon the street, thus creating a greater number of "front apartments," and materially increasing the rental values of the building. The plan provides accommodations for fourteen families on a floor, having a total of forty-four rooms, and an abundance of closets. The lack of closet space has been one of the serious inconveniences of tenement-house life. Besides this, the plan possesses the further advantage of having a private hall for every set of rooms, thus insuring privacy to the tenants. Every family has its own water-closet entirely within its own control. There is no part of the building more than two rooms deep. This is the secret of the whole tenement-house problem, because it means that there are no dark interior rooms. Besides these many advantages, there are four light staircases and staircase halls provided for the tenants, thus securing greater safety in case of fire, and removing to a considerable extent the social friction that exists in the ordinary tenement house. A large open court also provides a natural play-ground for the children, and does away with the necessity of subjecting them to the influences of the street. Many of the other plans submitted are of unusual merit, and many contain admirable ideas excellently developed. It is gratifying to learn that already several builders are proposing to erect tenement houses upon some of these plans.

The exhibition has demonstrated to the people of New York city, in a way not to be forgotten, the fact that two-thirds of its population lives under conditions that ought not be tolerated by any community, and which can not help but cause poverty, crime, disease, and destitution. What the outcome of the exhibition will be, it is hard to say. It hardly seems possible that we are for another decade to sit idle and permit conditions to grow worse and worse, as they have done for nearly fifty years.

The writer, for one, believes that the time has come for radical measures. We can not expect to solve the problem by spasmodic efforts every ten years. The only way that success can come is through constant and continuous effort.

There are many things to be done. In the first place, legislation must be secured, absolutely prohibiting the erection of tenement houses of the present type. Then it will be necessary to put forth considerable effort to see that such a law is enforced. This will take care of the future, but negative work of this kind alone will not solve the problem. Model tenements must be built by wealthy men as investments, and on a large scale. In the last ten years two such tenements were erected in New York. In the same time nearly 15,000 tenements of a bad type were built by speculative builders. It we are to keep up with conditions, let alone get ahead of them, we must take up this work on a larger scale than has ever before been attempted. There is much that can be done by men and women of means in improving many of the old, bad tenement houses, buying them up, one at a time, altering them to suit the needs of the tenants, and then, by wise management, making them financial successes. Nor is this all that has to be done before it can be felt that New York affords decent living conditions. There is opportunity for nearly every form of social effort. The model tenement is the best kind of a social settlement. There is no other way in which so much personal influence can be exerted as in managing such a tenement.

The Padrone System, from Reports of the Industrial Commission on Immigration and Education *(1901)*

The flood of immigrants from Eastern Europe and the Mediterranean at the turn of the century produced a number of investigations by government agencies, both local and national, into working conditions on the Lower East Side of Manhattan. The federal Industrial Commission on Immigration and Education carried out one such investigation in 1901.

Immigrants of three nationalities—Italian, Austro-Hungarian, and Russian—constituted more than half of all immigrants between the years 1890 and 1900. The Austro-Hungarian and Russian immigrants did not concern the commission because while more than three quarters of all immigrants from these groups landed in New York City, a large proportion of them passed into the interior of the country. In 1899–1900, however, 97 percent of all Italian immigrants landed on Ellis Island, and well over half of those indicated that New York City was their destination. Further, while in 1880 foreign-born residents made up only 12 percent of the population, by 1890, they made up almost 40 percent. The Fourteenth Ward (just below Houston Street) was commonly known as "Little Italy" as early as 1880.

The fears of native New Yorkers are stated in another report of the Industrial Commission, which noted that "a large proportion of these early Italian immigrants were men without families" who crammed together in tenements. The report continued with its main concern that "in all classes the Italian of the first generation is somewhat slower than some other races to take on the habits and customs of the people he has come among. Italians are distrustful of other races and even of those of their own race who are not of their province. Notwithstanding the abuses of the padroni, Italians cannot be induced to accept employment through other means. And in their colonies they gather in provincial groups."

IN the period of industrial recovery following the civil war there was a pressing demand for labor. Special legislation was even invoked to aid in supplying this demand. Thus the act of 1864, for the encouragement of immigration, gave manufacturers and contractors the right to import foreign laborers under contract. Speculation in cheap labor ensued; agents were sent to foreign countries in search for workmen. The unenlightened peasants of Italy were the easiest victims of this speculation. Their coming, in fact, was not of their own accord, as was the case with the people of northern Europe, but they came usually under contract.

This difference between the Italian immigrant and the northern people, and the reason for their having been so easily exploited, is brought out by their illiteracy and ignorance of the English language.

The great bulk of Italian immigration has come from southern Italy, the provinces, Abruzzi, Auelbino, Basilicata, Sicily, Calabria, and Naples. Almost the whole number from these provinces are of the peasant class, accustomed to hard work and meager fare. Their illiteracy is high. In 1899 the illiteracy for all races of immigrants was 22.9 per cent, while for the immigrants from southern Italy it was 57.3 per cent and for northern Italy the illiteracy was only 11.4 per cent, showing clearly the contrast between this ignorant peasant class of unskilled laborers and the skilled workmen from the manufacturing centers of northern Italy. In 1900 the percentage of illiteracy for these immigrants was 54.5 in contrast to 24.2 for all races and 11.8 for the northern Italians. . . .

Some form of contract was then necessary to induce these people to leave their country, for by temperament they were not the self-reliant people of the north who came of their own volition. The dread of change, the fear of coming to a strange and unknown land, had to be counteracted by material inducements. It was thus that they came not in search of work, but under contract for several years, and thus were assured in advance of permanent work at what seemed to them high wages.

At this earliest stage in the Italian immigration the padrone was the agent of the contractor or manufacturer. Laborers were demanded, and he acted simply as the agent in supplying specific demands. The manufacturer or contractor was of another nationality, but in looking for cheap labor he had recourse to an Italian already in this country. This Italian, undertaking to supply the number of laborers called for, went or sent to Italy for the number, who entered upon a contract binding themselves to service for from 1 to 3 years, and in rare instances even for 7 years. At the same time he furnished transportation and took care of them upon landing here until they were sent to the work for which they were contracted. It was thus that the padrone was merely a middleman, the man who stood between the contractor and the men. He was looked upon by the men as their representative, not as their employer, and upon him they depended.

Under this early system there were numerous ways in which the padrone could make money. In the first place, he had a commission from the men as well as from the contractor for furnishing the men, and commission on their passage. Upon getting them here he had a profit from boarding them until they went to work. This was deducted from their prospective earnings. After that the padrone usually furnished food and shelter for them while at work. This privilege was usually given free by the contractor who furnished shelter and for which the padrone charged rent. Then there was also the commission from sending money back to Italy, and finally the commission on the return passage after the contract had been completed.

But the padrone par excellence was not an agent and did not act for the contractor. He acted primarily upon his own initiative and for himself. Instead of waiting for a call for men, he would upon his own responsibility engage Italians to come, and contract for their labor for a certain number of years. After having brought them here he would farm them out to anyone who wanted them. He boarded them, received their wages, and paid them what he saw fit. Sometimes a laborer would receive $40 a year and as often only $40 for 2 years. Under this system the padrone occasionally would buy outright a minor from his or her parents. Men, women, and children were thus brought into the country, the boys to become bootblacks, newsboys, or strolling musicians. In this stage the padrone system most closely resembled the system as it existed in Italy, which meant in general the employment of children, or minors, in the "roving professions," such as strolling musicians, performers on the harp or hand organ, and street acrobats. These persons were under the direction of a master or padrone more or less inhuman, to whom belonged all the earnings of these persons. This system flourished most widely during the decade 1870–1880, and under its influence Italian immigration was stimulated to such an extent that the flow soon equaled the demand. The sphere of the padrone then changed. His work of inducing immigration was no longer necessary: immigrants came without having previously made contracts and governmental action was aimed at preventing the importation of contract labor. Under these two influences—the great increase in immigration and governmental opposition—the character of the padrone has changed.

As a result of this demand for laborers and the activities of the padroni, the Italian immigrants have been largely males, and until recent years have not come by families, as have the other nationalities, notably the German and Scandinavian people. . . .

Under [present] conditions it is probable that the padrone has very little do to with bringing Italians into the country, since it is no longer necessary to have a contract to bring them in, and because it is even unsafe according to Federal statutes. The padrone is now nothing more than an employment agent, and exists only because of the immigrants and their illiteracy and ignorance of American institutions. He procures his subjects at the port, upon their landing, by promising them steady work at high wages. If the immigrant does not get under the control of the padrone by this means, the immigrant need only go to the colony of his race in any of the large cities, where he will readily be picked up by one of the padroni and promised employment. By this means the newcomers are attached to the padrone, who is able to fulfill his promises, because he "stands in" with the contractors, he knows officials and bosses of the railroads and he is thus in a way to furnish employment for his fellow-countrymen who can not speak English and have no other way of finding employment. It may then be said that the padrone system no longer exists, and that the padrone is an employment agency, which collects the labor only after it has already arrived in this country, and makes its profit through commissions and keeping boarders.

As Dr. Egisto Rossi, of the Italian Immigration Bureau, has summed up the situation, "The padrone system, or bossism, can be defined as the forced tribute which the newly arrived pays to those who are already acquainted with the ways and language of the country." . . .

Under this system the padrone is in combination with the Italian banker, who furnishes the money to pay for transportation, for the erection of shanties when they are not provided by the contractor, and to buy provisions. All this money is then deducted from the earnings of the men. The profits derived from the venture are finally shared by the padrone with the banker, who, however, finds his chief source of gain in holding the savings of the laborers, sending their money to Italy, and changing the money from American to Italian, in which process great shrinkage usually takes place.

The padrone has a further hold upon these people as a result of irregular employment. During the winter there is almost no employment at all. This means that during the greater part of 5 months these people are without work. When work is plentiful, the laborer who boards with his boss is said to be fortunate if he can save more than one-half of his earnings. Some of these earnings are sent to Italy or frequently squandered, so that the laborer often finds himself in winter without resources of his own. In such cases he finds it convenient to go to the boarding house of the boss or banker, where he remains until spring, when it is understood that he shall enter the employ of the boss. In New York there are large tenements owned by Italian bankers which serve as winter quarters for these laborers. Here the men are crowded together, a dozen or more in one room, under the worst sanitary conditions. It is frequently said that the padrone encourages the men in extravagance in order to have a firmer hold on their future earnings. The employment is even made irregular by the padrone, who furnishes employment for several weeks at a time and then keeps them idle, claiming that the work is not regular. . . .

The padrone provides transportation for the men. But in the rates he overcharges the men, charging for first-class transportation or regular ticket rates, and securing greatly reduced rates because of the large number. If the work is some distance from the city, the padrone often boards the men, and usually buys the privilege from the contractor at a fixed rate per head per month. In some cases the privilege is given by the contractor free, because the padrone saves him trouble in employing men, and is convenient to have around in managing the men. But usually the contractor sells the privilege of furnishing the laborers with board and lodging and wearing apparel, the cost of which is generally deducted from their wages. In consideration of the many advantages which the padroni have in this transaction, they generally have to pay pretty high prices for the privilege, which naturally comes out of the pockets of the immigrants. If the men board themselves, their food must be bought at the shanty store which is operated by the padrone. Notices are posted to this effect, and fines are imposed for disobedience. Even dismissal is often the penalty. Occasionally a fixed daily amount of purchases is required by the padrone, but only at the padrone store. For example, in 1894 Italian laborers were shipped from New York to Brunswick, Ga., for work on a sewerage contract. Each man paid the padrone $1 for finding the employment. The passage money, $7 per head, was paid by the banker with the understanding that this was to be deducted from their wages. The agent of the banker paid $25 a month rent for 10 huts, but charged each laborer $1 a month, which for 215 men was $215 a month. All supplies had to be bought at the shanty store, the penalty for disobedience being a fine of $5. . . .

As to the kind of labor, it may be said that the padrone undertakes to furnish only unskilled labor in the large cities, though the Immigration Investigation Commission of 1895 reported "that padroni in New York not only guarantee to supply unskilled labor for sewer, railroad, and water-works construction, but also skilled labor for building trades, and will, furthermore, arrange for their transportation to a remote point if a small percentage of the passage money is advanced or guaranteed." . . .

The Italian immigrant, however, does not always limit himself to becoming a common laborer on railroad work and other excavations, but often becomes an artisan. In so far as he becomes an artisan he comes in conflict with American workmen, but the conflict is less sharp than formerly, because the American unions are organizing Italian labor. The Italians themselves are coming to understand the importance of organized labor. This is noticeable especially among the Italian hod carriers, masons, and stone cutters, and where this feeling and sense of organization has developed there is no opportunity for the padrone system.

The Plan of a City, Jean Schopfer (1902)

Jean Schopfer was born in Switzerland in 1868 and was educated at the Sorbonne and the Ecole du Louvre in Paris. Schopfer traveled extensively, with a particular interest in Russia, but for most of his travel books he used a pen name, Claude Anet.

Schopfer wrote three articles for *The Architectural Record* in 1902–1903 in which he presented his views on how cities should be planned. He was unreserved in his harsh review of the commissioners of the 1811 "grid plan," calling them "men devoid of all imagination."

A man of varied experiences, he won the tennis championship of France in 1892, was thrown into a Bolshevik prison during World War I, and wrote a romance novel set in the Cro-Magnon period.

The Rectangular Plan

As everybody knows, the City of New York—with the exception of the downtown districts, which already existed—was planned out by commissioners appointed in the beginning of the nineteenth century to determine the lines which the city should follow in its growth. The New York of to-day is their workmanship to the very letter. It is the triumph of the straight lines. The sight of that endless series of straight streets has inspired a literary friend of ours to compose a ballad in prose which we take the liberty to quote:

"In straight New York, Broadway runs riot."

BROADWAY

On a chess-board, imagine a line cutting the squares it traverses, into obtuse and sharp angles, all equal geometrically to two right angles, doubtless, but in reality, so different: this is Broadway crossing New York.

New York's birth was a natural one: a settlement of houses placed right and left on the extremity of a narrow tongue of land; houses upon houses, streets upon streets, churches upon churches, that had grown according to the increasing necessities of life, in picturesque irregularity. Each street received a name. New York: was formed like every city in the world, and it did not lack charm.

When, on a sombre day, the councils of the city reunited, councils composed of grave men with shaved upper lip and round beard covering the chin. The eldest member arose and spoke:

"Brother citizens, complaints of the disorder and irregularity of our town multiply; the license of our streets is extreme; they cross at all manners of angles, stretch out or stop, according to their good pleasure, and assume fantastic names difficult to remember, whose origin is often obscure and even vulgar. This is contrary to propriety and good policy; There are, moreover; graver faults: wasted grounds, little fields that some call parks, oval and strange shaped places. This scandalous state of affairs must not be allowed to continue.

"I propose that we decide upon a general plan, by which our dearly beloved city may be properly developed, and which should bring order and correction to the scattered flock of our houses.

"Let us divide the land of the peninsula of Manhattan in equal rectangular lots, where the streets will reach from the Hudson to the East River; perpendicularly, throughout the entire length of the city, may be traced avenues. Let us make away with the use of sonorous names; let us number them from south to north; let the avenues be counted from one to ten, the fifth serving to divide the east and the west of the city. In this manner all will become clear and arithmetical, and our children going to school in the morning can measure, by the number of the blocks passed, the number of miles-accomplished; twenty blocks being equal to one mile, or to sixteen hundred and nine of those metres which the French people, who love change, have adopted as measurement."

Having spoken in such wise, he spat on the floor, and held his peace.

Everything was done according to these proposals. Old New York was left as it stood, and lots for the new town were traced on paper up to two hundred and I know not what number. And young New York, from that time on, grew like a child in an orthopaedic corset. There were no places set apart in the plan for sparkling fountains under shady trees; no edifice to interrupt the monotony of eternally straight and parallel lines; and the streets, each with its number like a convict in a prison; and the avenues, all the avenues, stretched onward, onward indefinitely, with the sky for background; and not an inch of land lost: all is geometrically correct and convenient for the little children, who, going to school, measure, by the number of blocks they pass, the number of miles accomplished.

But, in the general regularity, one street emancipates itself[.] Broadway, from the south to the north of the city, traces its diagonal line, makes even a bend—impossible as it may seem—at Grace Church, and, maintains its name and individuality, runs in adventurous manner across the chess-board, making merry upon meeting her little sisters, so well balanced and keeping straight file, saluting such proper ladies as are the avenues; here leaving a strip of land so narrow that it cannot be built upon—a lost space; there mingling tumultuously with the life of another artery, destroying all frightful symmetries and creating all along its course picturesque fantasy.

"In straight New York, Broadway runs riot."

The commissioners who committed New York to the rectangular plan incurred a grave responsibility. They mortgaged the future. Modern New York is their handiwork *ne varietur.* For a task of that sort men of genius were needed—men able to foresee the city's immense growth, and imbued with a strong sense of the beauty which cities ought to have. Unhappily, they were simply engineers—men devoid of all imagination. Their work proves only too clearly that they also lacked intelligence.

Nothing is more tiresome than an infinite number of perfectly straight streets and avenues running on and on until they lose themselves in the sky. One goes along them without ever seeing an edifice closing the vista. There is a terrible monotony about a city each street of which is the counterpart of its neighbors. The ideal for a city to aim at is not that the newly arrived stranger shall be able to dispense with a map and find his road unaided.

The commissioners of 1812—whose names ought to be execrated by every inhabitant of New York—left little space for parks. Let us quote their report:

"It may be a matter of surprise that so few vacant spaces have been left, and those so small, for the benefit of fresh air and consequent preservation of health. Certainly, if the City of New York was destined to stand on the side of a small stream, such as the Seine or Thames, a great number of ample spaces might be needful. But those large arms of the sea which embrace Manhattan Island render its situation, in regard to health and pleasure, as well as to convenience of commerce, peculiarly felicitous. When, therefore, from the same causes, the prices of land are so uncommonly great, it seems proper to admit the principles of economy to greater influence than might, under circumstances of a different kind, have consisted with the dictates of prudence and the sense of duty."

What wise commissioners, and what well-placed economy! In the middle of the century Central Park was opened, and at the end of the century Riverside was planned; but all the rest of the city, as far as One Hundred and Fifty-sixth Street, is practically without parks or gardens, as those wise commissioners wished it to be.

The commissioners, after choosing the abominable rectangular plan, had not even sufficient intelligence to foresee that certain districts of the city would be centers of luxury. Having traced the long avenues and decided that Fifth Avenue should divide the city, they ought to have foreseen that that thoroughfare would, some day or other, become the main avenue of New York—that all the luxury of the city would gravitate thereto, and, in view of this, they should have planned it two or three times as wide as the other avenues. They did nothing of the kind, and now Fifth Avenue is a narrow, treeless, congested avenue, the like of which would not be tolerated by a provincial town at any price.

Suppose, on the contrary, that there existed, between Madison Square and Central Park, an avenue three hundred feet in width, planted with trees on either side of a spacious roadway, with broad sidewalks, and a continuous series of flower beds, clumps of shrubs and patches of well-kept grass—in fact, something similar to the Avenue des Champs-Elysées in Paris; and suppose, further, that this avenue was bordered by the palaces of American millionaires—Silver Kings, Petroleum Kings, and other monarchs. In that case New York would possess a central artery worthy of the city and the renown of which would be world wide.

Let the new cities of the United States profit by New York's experience and take care not to follow her example.

Immigrant Attitudes, a Humorous View, from Observations by Mr. Dooley, *Finley Peter Dunne (1902)*

Martin J. Dooley, a saloon keeper/philosopher, was the creation of Finley Peter Dunne, a Chicago journalist who first put Mr. Dooley in the Saturday edition of the *Chicago Daily Tribune* in 1893. Mr. Dooley dispensed down-to-earth wisdom from behind his bar in Chicago's West Side and had commentary on everything from immigration, the vice presidency, foreign affairs, and women's fashion. He was such an immediate hit that he became nationally syndicated. A couple of Mr. Dooley's aphorisms—"Trust everyone, but cut the cards," and "A fanatic is someone who is doing God's will, if only God knew the facts of the matter"—demonstrate his worldly wit.

Finley Peter Dunne was invited to Europe and toured the Continent entertaining (and educating) crowds with Mr. Dooley's thoughts on the question of Irish independence from England, the Boxer Rebellion, and the Dreyfus affair. After becoming the managing editor of the *Chicago Journal,* Dunne moved to New York City in 1901, where he had an editorial position with Lincoln Steffens on the muckraking *American Magazine.* Mark Twain even invited Dunne to be a member of his "Damned Human Race Lunch Club."

"But they'se wan question that Congress is goin' to take up that you an' me are intherested in. As a pilgrim father that missed th' first boats, I must raise me claryon voice again' th' invasion iv this fair land be th' paupers an' arnychists iv effete Europe. Ye bet I must—because I'm here first. 'Twas diff'rent whin I was dashed high on th' stern an' rockbound coast. In thim days America was th' refuge iv th' oppressed iv all th' wurruld. They cud come over here an' do a good job iv oppressin' thimsilves. As I told ye I came a little late. Th' Rosenfelts an' th' Lodges bate me be at laste a boat lenth, an' be th' time I got here they was stern an' rockbound thimsilves. So I got a gloryous rayciption as soon as I was towed off th' rocks. Th' stars an' sthripes whispered a welcome in th' breeze an' a shovel was thrust into me hand an' I was pushed into a sthreet excyvatin' as though I'd been born here.

Th' pilgrim father who bossed th' job was a fine ol' puritan be th' name iv Doherty, who come over in th' May-flower about th' time iv th' potato rot in Wexford, an' he made me think they was a hole in th' breakwather iv th' haven iv refuge an' some iv th' wash iv th' seas iv opprission had got through. He was a stern an' rockbound la-ad himself, but I was a good hand at loose stones an' wan day—but I'll tell ye about that another time.

"Annyhow, I was rayceived with open arms that sometimes ended in a clinch. I was afraid I wasn't goin' to assimilate with th' airlyer pilgrim fathers an' th' instichoochions iv th' counthry, but I soon found that a long swing iv th' pick made me as good as another man an' it didn't require a gr-reat intellect, or sometimes anny at all, to vote th' dimmycrat ticket, an' before I was here a month, I felt enough like a native born American to burn a witch. Wanst in a while a mob iv intilligint collajeens, whose grandfathers had bate me to th' dock, wud take a shy at me Pathrick's Day procission or burn down wan iv me churches, but they got tired iv that before long; 'twas too much like wurruk.

"But as I tell ye, Hinnissy, 'tis diff'rent now. I don't know why 'tis diff'rent but 'tis diff'rent. 'Tis time we put our back again' th' open dure an' keep out th' savage horde. If that cousin iv ye'ers expects to cross, he'd betther tear f'r th' ship. In a few minyits th' gates 'll be down an' whin th' oppressed wurruld comes hikin' acrost to th' haven iv refuge, they'll do well to put a couplin' pin undher their hats, f'r th' Goddess iv Liberty 'll meet thim at th' dock with an axe in her hand. Congress is goin' to fix it. Me frind Shaughnessy says so. He was in yisterdah an' says he: 'Tis time we done something to make th' immigration laws sthronger,' says he. 'Thrue f'r ye, Miles Standish,' says I; 'but what wud ye do?' 'I'd keep out th' offscourin's iv Europe,' says he. 'Wud ye go back?' says I. 'Have ye'er joke,' says he. 'Tis not so seeryus as it was befure ye come,' says I. 'But what ar-re th' immygrants doin' that's roonous to us?' I says. 'Well,' says he, 'they're arnychists,' he says: 'they don't assymilate with th' counthry,' he says. 'Maybe th' counthry's digestion has gone wrong fr'm too much rich food,' says I; 'perhaps now if we'd lave off thryin' to digest Rockyfellar an' thry a simple diet like Schwartzmeister, we wudden't feel th' effects iv our vittels,' I says. 'Maybe if we'd season th' immygrants a little or cook thim thurly, they'd go down betther,' I says.

"'They're arnychists, like Parsons,' he says. 'He wud've been an immygrant if Texas hadn't been admitted to th' Union,' I says. 'Or Snolgosh,' he says. 'Has Mitchigan seceded?' I says. 'Or Gittoo,' he says. 'Who come fr'm th' effete monarchies iv Chicago, west iv Ashland Av'noo,' I says. 'Or what's-his-name, Wilkes Booth,' he says. 'I don't know what he was—maybe a Boolgharyen,' says I. 'Well, annyhow,' says he, 'they're th' scum iv th' earth.' 'They may be that,' says I; 'but we used to think they was th' cream iv civilization,' I says. 'They're off th' top annyhow. I wanst believed 'twas th' best men iv Europe come here, th' la-ads that was too sthrong and indepindant to be kicked around be a boorgomasther at home an' wanted to dig out f'r a place where they cud get a chanst to make their way to th' money. I see their sons fightin' into politics an' their daughters tachin' young American idee how to shoot too high in th' public school, an' I thought they was all right. But I see I was wrong. Thim boys out there towin' wan heavy foot afther th' other to th' rowlin' mills is all arnychists. There's warrants out f'r all names endin' in 'inski, an' I think I'll board up me windows, f'r,' I says, 'if immygrants is as dangerous to this counthry as ye an' I an' other pilgrim fathers believe they are, they'se enough iv thim sneaked in already to make us aborigines about as infloointial as the prohibition vote in th' Twinty-ninth Ward. They'll dash again' our stern an' rock-bound coast till they bust it,' says I.

"'But I ain't so much afraid as ye ar-re. I'm not afraid iv me father an' I'm not afraid iv mesilf. An' I'm not afraid iv Schwartzmeister's father or Hinnery Cabin Lodge's grandfather. We all come over th' same way, an' if me ancestors were not what Hogan calls rigicides, 'twas not because they were not ready an' willin', on'y a king niver come their way. I don't believe in killin' kings, mesilf. I never wud've sawed th' block off that curly-headed potintate that I see in th' pitchers down town, but, be hivins, Presarved Codfish Shaughnessy, if we'd begun a few years ago shuttin' out folks that wudden't mind handin' a bomb to a king, they wudden't be enough people in Mattsachoosetts to make a quorum f'r th' Anti-Impeeryal S'ciety,' says I. 'But what wud ye do with th' offscourin' iv Europe?' says he. 'I'd scour thim some more,' says I.

"An' so th' meetin' iv th' Plymouth Rock Assocyation come to an end. But if ye wud like to get it together, Deacon Hinnissy, to discuss th' immygration question, I'll sind out a hurry call f'r Schwartzmeister an' Mulcahey an' Ignacio Sbarbaro an' Nels Larsen an' Petrus Gooldvink, an' we 'll gather to-night at Fanneilnoviski Hall at th' corner iv Sheridan an' Sigel sthreets. All th' pilgrim fathers is rayquested f'r to bring interpreters."

"Well," said Mr. Hennessy, "divvle th' bit I care, on'y I'm here first, an' I ought to have th' right to keep th' bus fr'm bein' overcrowded."

"Well," said Mr. Dooley, "as a pilgrim father on me gran' nephew's side, I don't know but ye're right. An' they'se wan sure way to keep thim out."

"What's that?" asked Mr. Hennessy.

"Teach thim all about our instichoochions befure they come," said Mr. Dooley.

New York: Good Government in Danger, from McClure's, *Lincoln Steffens (1903)*

"I have seen the future and it works." Lincoln Steffens's comment while watching the Russian Revolution of 1917 may be his most well-known statement, but regardless of its veracity, it derived from Steffens's lifelong hope in the ability of people to organize and rise up against corrupt government. He saw the same spirit in the rebels of the Mexican Revolution, which he covered in 1910, and even in the popular support of Mussolini in the 1930s, which he saw firsthand while living in Italy.

Lincoln Steffens was a lifelong reformer, a "muckraker" in his friend Teddy Roosevelt's language, and he began his career as a reporter in 1892 for the *New York Evening Post.* He worked with and was a rival of Jacob Riis, author of the exposé on New York City's slums, *How the Other Half Lives.* In 1903 he produced his most famous work, *The Shame of the Cities,* a collection of his investigative essays on big city government corruption culled from *McClure's* magazine and directly intended to influence the New York City mayoral election. But he was disappointed when Seth Low, a reform mayor, failed to win a second term.

Steffens is less known for another quotation, "Power is what men seek and any group that gets it will abuse it."

TAMMANY is bad government; not inefficient, but dishonest; not a party, not a delusion and a snare, hardly known by its party name—Democracy; having little standing in the national councils of the party and caring little for influence outside of the city. Tammany is Tammany, the embodiment of corruption. All the world knows and all the world may know what it is and what it is after. For hypocrisy is not a Tammany vice. Tammany is for Tammany, and the Tammany men say so. Other rings proclaim lies and make pretensions, other rogues talk about the tariff and imperialism. Tammany is honestly dishonest. Time and time again, in private and in public, the leaders, big and little, have said they are out for themselves and their own; not for the public, but for "me and my friends"; not for New York, but for Tammany. Richard Croker said under oath once that he worked for his own pockets all the time, and Tom Grady, the Tammany orator, has brought his crowds to their feet cheering sentiments as primitive, stated with candor as brutal.

The man from Mars would say that such an organization, so self-confessed, could not be very dangerous to an intelligent people. Foreigners marvel at it and at us, and even Americans—Pennsylvanians, for example—cannot understand why we New Yorkers regard Tammany as so formidable. I think I can explain it. Tammany is corruption with consent; it is bad government founded on the suffrages of the people. The Philadelphia machine is more powerful. It rules Philadelphia by fraud and force and does not require the votes of the people. The Philadelphians do not vote for their machines; their machines vote for them. Tammany used to stuff the ballot boxes and intimidate voters; today there is practically none of that. Tammany rules, when it rules, by right of the votes of the people of New York.

Tammany corruption is democratic corruption. That of the Philadelphia ring is rooted in special interests. Tammany, too, is allied with "vested interests"—but Tammany labors under disadvantages not known in Philadelphia. The Philadelphia ring is of the same party that rules the State and the nation, and the local ring forms a living chain with the state and national rings. Tammany is a purely local concern. With a majority only in old New York, it has not only to buy what it wants from the Republican majority in the State, but must trade to get the whole city. Big business everywhere is the chief source of political corruption, and it is one source in New York; but most of the big businesses represented in New York have no plants there. Offices there are, and head offices, of many trusts and railways, for example, but that is all. There are but two railway terminals in the city, and but three railways use them. These have to do more with Albany than New York. So with Wall Street. Philadelphia's stock exchange deals largely in Pennsylvania securities, New York's in those of the whole United States. There is a small Wall Street group that specializes in local corporations, and they are active and give Tammany a Wall Street connection, but the biggest and the majority of our financial leaders, bribers though they may be in other cities and even in New York State, are independent of Tammany Hall and can be honest citizens at home. From this class, indeed, New York can and often does draw some of its reformers. Not so Philadelphia. That bourgeois opposition which has persisted for thirty years in the fight against Tammany corruption, was squelched in Philadelphia after its first great uprising. Matt Quay, through the banks, railways and other business interests, was able to reach it. A large part of his power is negative; there is no opposition. Tammany's power is positive. Tammany cannot reach all the largest interests and its hold is upon the people.

Tammany's democratic corruption rests upon the corruption of the people, the plain people, and there lies its great significance; its grafting system is one in which more individuals share than any I have studied. The people themselves get very little; they come cheap, but they are interested. Divided into districts, the organization subdivides them into precincts or neighborhoods, and their sovereign power, in the form of votes, is bought up by kindness and petty privileges. They are forced to a surrender, when necessary, by intimidation, but the leader and his captains have their hold because they take care of their own. They speak pleasant words, smile friendly smiles, notice the baby, give picnics up the River or the Sound, or a slap on the back; find jobs, most of them at the city's expense, but they have also news-stands, peddling privileges, railroad and other business places to dispense; they permit violations of the law, and, if a man has broken the law without permission, see him through the court. Though a blow in the face is as readily given as a shake of the hand, Tammany kindness is real kindness, and will go far, remember long, and take infinite trouble for a friend.

The power that is gathered up thus cheaply, like garbage, in the districts is concentrated in the district leader who in turn passes it on through a general committee to the boss. This is a form of living government, extra-legal, but very actual, and, though the beginnings of it are purely democratic, it develops at each stage into an autocracy. In Philadelphia the boss appoints a district leader and gives him power. Tammany has done that in two or three notable instances, but never without causing a bitter fight which lasts often for years. In Philadelphia the State boss designates the city boss. In New York, Croker has failed signally to maintain vice-bosses whom he appointed. The boss of Tammany Hall is a growth, and just as Croker grew, so has Charles F. Murphy grown up to Croker's place. Again, whereas in Philadelphia the boss and his ring handle and keep almost all of the graft, leaving little to the district leaders, in New York the district leaders share handsomely in the spoils.

There is more to share in New York. It is impossible to estimate the amount of it, not only for me, but for anybody. No Tammany man knows it all. Police friends of mine say that the Tammany leaders never knew how rich police corruption was till the Lexow committee exposed it, and that the politicians who had been content with small presents, contributions, and influence, "did not butt in" for their share till they saw by the testimony of frightened police grafters that the department was worth from four to five millions a year. The items are so incredible that I hesitate to print them. Devery told a friend once that in one year the police graft was "something over $3,000,000." Afterward the syndicate which divided the graft under Devery took in for thirty-six months $400,000 a month from gambling and poolrooms alone. Saloon bribers, disorderly house blackmail, policy, etc., etc., bring this total up to amazing proportions.

Yet this was but one department, and a department that was overlooked by Tammany for years. The annual budget of the city is about $100,000,000, and though the power that comes of the expenditure of that amount is enormous and the opportunities for rake-offs infinite, this sum is not one-half of the resources of Tammany when it is in power. Her resources are the resources of the city as a business, as a political, as a social power. If Tammany could be incorporated and all its earnings, both legitimate and illegitimate, gathered up and paid over in dividends, the stockholders would get more than the New York Central bond and stockholders, more than the Standard Oil stockholders, and the controlling clique would wield a power equal to that of the United States Steel Company. Tammany, when in control of New York, takes out of the city unbelievable millions of dollars a year.

No wonder the leaders are all rich; no wonder so many more Tammany men are rich than are the leaders in any other town; no wonder Tammany is liberal in its division of the graft. Croker took the best and the safest of it, and he accepted shares in others. He was "in on the Wall Street end," and the Tammany clique of financiers have knocked down and bought up at low prices Manhattan Railway stock by threats of the city's power over the road; they have been let in on Metropolitan deals and on the Third Avenue Railroad grab; the Ice Trust is a Tammany trust; they have banks and trust companies, and through the New York Realty Company are forcing alliances with such financial groups as that of the Standard Oil Company. Croker shared in these deals and businesses. He sold judgeships, taking his pay in the form of contributions to the Tammany campaign fund, of which he was treasurer, and he had the judges take from the regular real estate exchange all the enormous real estate business that passed through the courts, and give it to an exchange connected with the real estate business of his firm, Peter F. Meyer & Co. This alone would maintain a ducal estate in England. But his real estate business was greater than that. It had extraordinary legal facilities, the free advertising of abuse, the prestige of political privilege, all of which brought in trade; and it had advance information and followed with profitable deals, great public improvements.

Though Croker said he worked for his own pockets all the time, and did take the best of the graft, he was not "hoggish." One of the richest graft in the city is in the Department of Buildings. $100,000,000 a year goes into building operations in New York. All of this, from out-houses to skyscrapers, is subject to very precise laws and regulations, most of them wise, some impossible. The Building Department has the enforcement of these; it passes upon all construction, private and public, at all stages from plan-making to actual completion; and can cause not only "unavoidable delay" but can wink at most profitable violations. Architects and builders had to stand in with the department. They called on the right man and they settled on a scale which was not fixed, but which generally was on the basis of the department's estimate of a fair half of the value of the saving in time or bad material. This brought in at least a banker's percentage on one hundred millions a year. Croker, so far as I can make out, took none of this; it was let out to other leaders and was their own graft.

District Attorney William Travers Jerome has looked into the Dock Department, and he knows things which he yet may prove. This is an important investigation for two reasons. It is very large graft and the new Tammany leader, Charlie Murphy, had it. New York wants to know more about Murphy, and it should want to know about the management of its docks, since, just as other cities have their corrupt dealings with railways and their terminals, so New York's great terminal business is with steamships and docks. These docks should pay the city handsomely. Mr. Murphy says they shouldn't; he is wise, as Croker was before he became old and garrulous, and, as Tammany men put it, "keeps his mouth shut," but he did say that the docks should not be run for revenue to the city but for their own improvement. The Dock Board has exclusive and private and secret control of the expenditure of $10,000,000 a year. No wonder Murphy chose it.

It is impossible to follow all New York graft from its source to its final destination. It is impossible to follow here the course of that which is well known to New Yorkers. There are public works for Tammany contractors. There are private works for Tammany contractors, and corporations and individuals find it expedient to let it go to Tammany contractors. Tammany has a very good system of grafting on public works; I mean that it is "good" from the criminal point of view—and so it has for the furnishing of supplies. Low bids and short deliveries, generally speaking (and that is the only way I can speak here), is the method. But the Tammany system, as a whole, is weak.

Tammany men as grafters have a confidence in their methods and system, which, in the light of such perfection as that of Philadelphia, is amusing, and the average New Yorker takes in "the organization" a queer sort of pride, which is ignorant and provincial. Tammany is way behind the times. It is growing; it has improved. In Tweed's day the politicians stole from the city treasury, divided the money on the steps of the City Hall, and, not only the leaders, big and little, but heelers and outsiders; not only Tweed, but ward carpenters robbed the city; not only politicians, but newspapers and citizens were "in on the divvy." New York, not Tammany alone, was corrupt. When the exposure came, and Tweed asked his famous question, "What are you going to do about it?" the ring mayor, A. Oakey Hall, asked another as significant. It was reported that suit was to be brought against the ring to recover stolen funds. "Who is going to sue?" said Mayor Hall, who could not think of anybody of importance sufficiently without sin to throw the first stone. Stealing was stopped and grafting was made more business-like, but still it was too general, and the boodling for the Broadway street railway franchise prompted a still closer grip on the business. The organization since then has been gradually concentrating the control of graft. Croker did not proceed so far along the line as the Philadelphia ring has, as the police scandals showed. After the Lexow exposures, Tammany took over that graft, but still let it go practically by districts, and the police captains still got a third. After the Mazet exposures, Devery became Chief and the police graft was so concentrated that the division was reduced to fourteen parts. Again, later, it was reduced to a syndicate of four or five men, with a dribble of miscellaneous graft for the police. In Philadelphia the police have nothing to do with the police graft; a policeman may collect it, but he acts for a politician, who in turn passes it up to a small ring. That is the drift in New York. Under Devery the police officers got comparatively little, and the rank and file themselves were blackmailed for transfers and promotions, for remittances of fines, and in a dozen other petty ways.

Philadelphia is the end toward which New York under Tammany is driving as fast as the lower intelligence and higher conceit of its leaders will let it. In Philadelphia one very small ring gets everything, dividing the whole as it pleases, and not all those in the inner ring are politicians. Trusting few individuals, they are safe from exposure, more powerful, more deliberate, and they are wise as politicians. When, as in New York, the number of grafters is large, this delicate business is in some hands that are rapacious. The police grafters, for example, in Devery's day, were not content with the amounts collected from the big vices. They cultivated minor vices, like policy, to such an extent that the Policy King was caught and sent to prison, and Devery's wardman, Glennon, was pushed into so tight a hole that there was danger that District Attorney Jerome would get past Glennon to Devery and the syndicate. The murder of a witness the night he was in the Tenderloin police station served to save the day. But, worst of all, Tammany, the "friend of the people," permitted the organization of a band of so-called Cadets, who made a business, under the protection of the police, of ruining the daughters of the tenements and even of catching and imprisoning in disorderly houses the wives of poor men. This horrid traffic never was exposed; it could not and cannot be. Vicious women were "planted" in tenement houses and (I know this personally) the children of decent parents counted the customers, witnessed their transactions with these creatures, and, as a father told with shame and tears, reported totals at the family table.

Tammany leaders are usually the natural leaders of the people in these districts, and they are originally good-natured, kindly men. No one has a more sincere liking than I for some of those common but generous fellows; their charity is real, at first. But they sell out their own people. They do give them coal and help them in their private troubles, but, as they grow rich and powerful, the kindness goes out of the charity and they not only collect at their saloons or in rents—cash for their "goodness"; they not only ruin fathers and sons and cause the troubles they relieve; they sacrifice the children in the schools; let the Health Department neglect the tenements, and, worst of all, plant vice in neighborhood and in the homes of the poor.

This is not only bad; it is bad politics; it has defeated Tammany. Woe to New York when Tammany learns better. Honest fools talk of the reform of Tammany Hall. It is an old hope, this, and twice it has been disappointed, but it is not vain. That is the real danger ahead. The reform of a corrupt ring means, as I have said before, the reform of its system of grafting and a wise consideration of certain features of good government. Croker turned his "best chief of police," William S. Devery, out of Tammany Hall, and, slow and old as he was, Croker learned what clean streets were from Col. Waring, and gave them. Now there is a new boss, a young man, Charles F. Murphy, and unknown to New Yorkers. He looks dense, but he acts with force, decision, and skill. The new mayor will be his man. He may divide with Croker and leave to the "old man" all his accustomed graft, but Charlie Murphy will rule Tammany and, if Tammany is elected, New York also. Lewis Nixon is urging Murphy publicly, as I write, to declare against the police scandals and all the worst practices of Tammany. Lewis Nixon is an honest man, but he was one of the men Croker tried to appoint leader of Tammany Hall. And when he resigned Mr. Nixon said that he found that a man could not keep that leadership and his self-respect. Yet Mr. Nixon is a type of the man who thinks Tammany would be fit to rule New York if the organization would "reform."

As a New Yorker, I fear Murphy will prove sagacious enough to do just that: stop the scandals, put all the graft in the hands of a few tried and true men, and give the city what it would call good government. Murphy says he will nominate for mayor a man so "good" that his goodness will astonish New York. I don't fear a bad Tammany mayor; I dread the election of a good one. For I have been to Philadelphia.

Philadelphia had a bad ring mayor, a man who promoted the graft and caused scandal after scandal. The leaders there, the wisest political grafters in this country, learned a great lesson from that. As one of them said to me:

"The American people don't mind grafting, but they hate scandals. They don't kick so much on a jiggered public contract for a boulevard, but they want the boulevard and no fuss and no dust. We want to give them that. We want to give them what they really want, a quiet Sabbath, safe streets, orderly nights, and homes secure. They let us have the police graft. But this mayor was a hog. You see, he had but one term and he could get a share only on what was made in his term. He not only took a hog's share off what was coming, but he wanted everything to come in his term. So I'm down on grafting mayors and grafting office-holders. I tell you it's good politics to have honest men in office. I mean men that are personally honest."

So they got John Weaver for Mayor, and honest John Weaver is checking corruption, restoring order, and doing a great many good things, which it is "good politics" to do. For he is satisfying the people, soothing their ruffled pride, and reconciling them to machine rule. I have letters from friends of mine there, honest men, who wish me to bear witness to the goodness of Mayor Weaver. I do. And I believe that if the Philadelphia machine leaders are as careful with Mayor Weaver as they have been and let him continue to give to the end as good government as he has given so far, the "Philadelphia plan" of graft will last and Philadelphia will never again be a free American city.

Philadelphia and New York began about the same time, some thirty years ago, to reform their city governments. Philadelphia got "good government"—what the Philadelphians call good—from a corrupt ring and quit, satisfied to be a scandal to the nation and a disgrace to democracy. New

York has gone on fighting, advancing and retreating, for thirty years till now it has achieved the beginnings, under Mayor Low, of a government for the people. Do the New Yorkers know it? Do they care? They are Americans, mixed and typical; do we Americans really want good government? Or, as I said at starting, have they worked for thirty years along the wrong road—crowded with unhappy American cities—the road to Philadelphia and despair?

From The Gospel of Wealth, *Andrew Carnegie (1903)*

Andrew Carnegie was the living example of Horatio Alger's philosophy of America as a land where one could go from "rags to riches." Carnegie was born in Scotland in 1835 and immigrated to Pittsburgh when he was thirteen. He started as a bobbin boy earning $1.25 a week but later sold the Carnegie Steel Company to J. P. Morgan for $480 million; this transaction made Carnegie the richest man in the world.

In 1889 Carnegie published *The Gospel of Wealth* with its famous dictum, "He who dies rich, dies disgraced." By the end of his life he had given away $350 million (fully 90 percent of his fortune) to philanthropic causes, colleges, the building of libraries, and even requests for pipe organs from around the world. In New York City, he donated the $1 million necessary to build what became known as Carnegie Hall, the most famous concert hall in the United States, on the corner of Fifty-seventh Street and Seventh Avenue. In 1911 he endowed the Carnegie Corporation of New York with $135 million dollars to "promote the advancement and diffusion of knowledge and understanding." Carnegie also gives his name to a residential area on Manhattan's Upper East Side, where he built a mansion in 1902 on the corner of Ninety-first Street and Fifth Avenue in what became known as Carnegie Hill.

THIS, then, is held to be the duty of the man of wealth: To set an example of modest, unostentatious living, shunning display or extravagance; to provide moderately for the legitimate wants of those dependent upon him; and, after doing so, to consider all surplus revenues which come to him simply as trust funds, which he is called upon to administer, and strictly bound as a matter of duty to administer in the manner which, in his judgment, is best calculated to produce the most beneficial results for the community—the man of wealth thus becoming the mere trustee and agent for his poorer brethren, bringing to their service his superior wisdom, experience, and ability to administer, doing for them better than they would or could do for themselves.

We are met here with the difficulty of determining what are moderate sums to leave to members of the family; what is modest, unostentatious living; what is the test of extravagance. There must be different standards for different conditions. The answer is that it is as impossible to name exact amounts or actions as it is to define good manners, good taste, or the rules of propriety; but, nevertheless, these are verities, well known, although indefinable. Public sentiment is quick to know and to feel what offends these. So in the case of wealth. The rule in regard to good taste in the dress of men or women applies here. Whatever makes one conspicuous offends the canon. If any family be chiefly known for display, for extravagance in home, table, or equipage, for enormous sums ostentatiously spent in any form upon itself—if these be its chief distinctions, we have no difficulty in estimating its nature or culture. So likewise in regard to the use or abuse of its surplus wealth, or to generous, free-handed cooperation in good public uses, or to unabated efforts to accumulate and hoard to the last, or whether they administer or bequeath. The verdict rests with the best and most enlightened public sentiment. The community will surely judge, and its judgments will not often be wrong.

The best uses to which surplus wealth can be put have already been indicated. Those who would administer wisely must, indeed, be wise; for one of the serious obstacles to the improvement of our race is indiscriminate charity. It were better for mankind that the millions of the rich were thrown into the sea than so spent as to encourage the slothful, the drunken, the unworthy. Of every thousand dollars spent in so-called charity to-day, it is probable that nine hundred and fifty dollars is unwisely spent—so spent, indeed, as to produce the very evils which it hopes to mitigate or cure. A well-known writer of philosophic books admitted the other day that he had given a quarter of a dollar to a man who approached him as he was coming to visit the house of his friend. He knew nothing of the habits of this beggar, knew not the use that would be made of this money, although he had every reason to suspect that it would be spent improperly. This man professed to be a disciple of Herbert Spencer; yet the quarter-dollar given that night will probably work more injury than all the money will do good which its thoughtless donor will ever be able to give in true charity. He only gratified his own feelings, saved himself from annoyance—and this was probably one of the most selfish and very worst actions of his life, for in all respects he is most worthy.

In bestowing charity, the main consideration should be to help those who will help themselves; to provide part of the means by which those who desire to improve may do so; to give those who desire to rise the aids by which they may rise; to assist, but rarely or never to do all. Neither the individual nor the race is improved by almsgiving. Those worthy of assistance, except in rare cases, seldom require assistance. The really valuable men of the race never do, except in case of accident or sudden change. Every one has, of course, cases of individuals brought to his own knowledge where temporary assistance can do genuine good, and these he will not overlook. But the amount which can be wisely given by the individual for individuals is necessarily limited by his lack of knowledge of the circumstances connected with each. He is the only true reformer who is as careful and as anxious not to aid the unworthy as he is to aid the worthy, and, perhaps, even more so, for in almsgiving more injury is probably done by rewarding vice than by relieving virtue.

The rich man is thus almost restricted to following the examples of Peter Cooper, Enoch Pratt of Baltimore, Mr. Pratt of Brooklyn, Senator Stanford, and others, who know that the best means of benefiting the community is to place within its reach the ladders upon which the aspiring can rise—free libraries, parks, and means of recreation, by which men are helped in body and mind; works of art, certain to give pleasure and improve the public taste; and public institutions of various kinds, which will improve the general condition of the people; in this manner returning their surplus wealth to the mass of their fellows in the forms best calculated to do them lasting good.

Thus is the problem of rich and poor to be solved. The laws of accumulation will be left free, the laws of distribution free. Individualism will continue, but the millionaire will be but a trustee for the poor, intrusted for a season with a great part of the increased wealth of the community, but administering it for the community far better than it could or would have done for itself. The best minds will thus have reached a stage in the development of the race in which it is clearly seen that there is no mode of disposing of surplus wealth creditable to thoughtful and earnest men into whose hands it flows, save by using it year by year for the general good. This day already dawns. Men may die without incurring the pity of their fellows, still sharers in great business enterprises from which their capital cannot be or has not been withdrawn, and which is left chiefly at death for public uses; yet the day is not far distant when the man who dies leaving behind him millions of available wealth, which was free for him to administer during life, will pass away "unwept, unhonored, and unsung," no matter to what uses he leaves the dross which he cannot take with him. Of such as these the public verdict will then be: "The man who dies thus rich dies disgraced."

Such, in my opinion, is the true gospel concerning wealth, obedience to which is destined some day to solve the problem of the rich and the poor, and to bring "Peace on earth, among men good will."

No Constantine in Sight, from The Education of Henry Adams, *Henry Adams (1904)*

Henry Adams was a member of what was probably the best-known family in America. His grandfather and great-grandfather had both been president of the United States, and his father was a congressman and minister to Britain. After being secretary to his father in England, Adams returned to take a medieval history teaching position at Harvard University. But following his wife's suicide in December 1886, Adams traveled almost continuously until his death in 1918.

In his most-known work, the autobiographical *The Education of Henry Adams* (1907), he examined the education he received and found it unsatisfactory for the "chaos" that he saw being unleashed in the new technological "nunc age." Nowhere was that "hysteria" more apparent to Adams than in the New York City he visited in 1904. Of course, as he wrote to his niece in 1902, "My idea of paradise is a perfect automobile going thirty miles an hour on a smooth road to a twelfth-century cathedral." *The Education of Henry Adams* won the Pulitzer Prize in 1919 and was selected, in 1999, as the best English-language work of nonfiction in literary history.

NEARLY forty years had passed since the ex-private secretary landed at New York with the ex-Ministers Adams and Motley, when they saw American society as a long caravan stretching out towards the plains. As he came up the bay again, November 5, 1904, an older man than either his father or Motley in 1868, he found the approach more striking than ever—wonderful—unlike anything man had ever seen—and like nothing he had ever much cared to see. The outline of the city became frantic in its effort to explain something that defied meaning. Power seemed to have outgrown its servitude and to have asserted its freedom. The cylinder had exploded, and thrown great masses of stone and steam against the sky. The city had the air and movement of hysteria, and the citizens were crying, in every accent of anger and alarm, that the new forces must at any cost be brought under control. Prosperity never before imagined, power never yet wielded by man, speed never reached by anything but a meteor, had made the world irritable, nervous, querulous, unreasonable and afraid. All New York was demanding new men, and all the new forces, condensed into corporations, were demanding a new type of man—a man with ten times the endurance, energy, will and mind of the old type—for whom they were ready to pay millions at sight. As one jolted over the pavements or read the last week's newspapers, the new man seemed close at hand, for the old one had plainly reached the end of his strength, and his failure had become catastrophic. Every one saw it, and every municipal election shrieked chaos. A traveller in the highways of history looked out of the club window on the turmoil of Fifth Avenue, and felt himself in Rome, under Diocletian, witnessing the anarchy, conscious of the compulsion, eager for the solution, but unable to conceive whence the next impulse was to come or how it was to act. The two-thousand-years' failure of Christianity roared upward from Broadway, and no Constantine the Great was in sight.

Built Like a Bonfire: The General Slocum *Disaster, June 15, 1904, Edward T. O'Donnell (2001)*

Edward T. O'Donnell is associate professor of history at Holy Cross College in Worcester, Massachusetts. He is currently working on a book about the *General Slocum* tragedy.

New York has been relatively free from citywide disasters during the course of its long history, but there have been a number of fires that have caused significant damage and accounted for hundreds of deaths. During the American Revolution, once in September 1776 and again in August 1778 fires destroyed up to one third of the city. The Great Fire of 1835 caused more property damage than any other event in the history of the city until September 11, 2001; the volume of the claims forced twenty-three of the city's twenty-six insurance companies to declare bankruptcy. Both the reorganization of the fire department and an examination of the water supply to the city were outcomes from that conflagration.

Other blazes have been more notorious. The Crystal Palace was a cast-iron and glass exhibition hall completed in 1853 on the site of present-day Bryant Park. The structure was reputed to be fireproof. On October 5, 1858, it was completely destroyed by fire in fifteen minutes. On Coney Island, Dreamland amusement park went up in flames just before opening day 1911. One of its competitors, Luna Park, succumbed to the same fate in 1944. The most recent fire-related tragedy was the March 1990 torching of the Happy Land Social Club located on Southern Avenue in the Bronx. Eighty-seven people died in that intentionally set blaze, the most since the Triangle Shirtwaist fire of March 1911.

O'Donnell examines the events surrounding the single largest loss of life in New York City history, the burning of the steamship *General Slocum* on June 15, 1904.

Ask any New Yorker to name the city's greatest disaster before September 11, 2001 and invariably they offer the same answer: the Triangle Shirtwaist Factory fire of 1911. That tragic event garnered international headlines as 146 young immigrant women lost their lives in an unsafe garment factory. Yet even though it is certainly Gotham's most famous disaster in the twentieth century, it runs a distant second to a much larger catastrophe that occurred only seven years earlier. On June 15, 1904, more than 1,000 people died when their steamship, the *General Slocum,* burst into flames while moving up the East River. It was both the most deadly fire and the most deadly peacetime maritime disaster in American history.

The story of the *General Slocum* tragedy begins in the thriving German neighborhood known as *Kleindeutschland,* or Little Germany. Located on the Lower East Side in what is today called the East Village, *Kleindeutschland* had been home to New York's German immigrant population since they first began arriving in large numbers in the 1840s. With more than 100,000 Germans living there by the 1870s, the neighborhood lived up to its name. German fraternal societies, athletic clubs, theaters, bookshops, and restaurants and beer gardens abounded. So too did synagogues and churches.

One of those churches, St. Mark's Lutheran Church on East 6th Street, held an annual outing to celebrate the end of the Sunday school year. They usually chartered an excursion boat to take them to a nearby recreation spot for a day of swimming, games, and food. On June 15, 1904, more than 2,000 people boarded the *General Slocum* for a day at Locust Grove on Long Island Sound.

Shortly before 10:00 A.M., the crew of the *General Slocum* cast off and the ship pulled away from the pier. It chugged northward up the East River, gradually increasing speed. Hundreds of children jammed the upper deck to take it all in. Like most mornings, the river was full of boats of every description—barges, lighters, tenders, and tugs. The adults talked and listened to a band play German favorites.

Then disaster struck. As the ship passed East 90th Street, smoke started billowing from a forward storage room. A spark, most likely from a carelessly tossed match, had ignited a barrel of straw. Several crewmen tried to put the fire out, but they had never conducted a fire drill or undergone any emergency training. To make matters worse, the ship's rotten fire hoses burst when the water was turned on. By the time they notified Captain William Van Schaick of the emergency—fully ten minutes after discovering the fire—the blaze raged out of control.

The captain looked to the piers along the East River, but feared he might touch off an explosion among the many oil tanks there. Instead, even as onlookers on the Manhattan shore shouted for him to dock the ship, he opted to proceed at top speed to North Brother Island a mile ahead. Several small boats followed the floating inferno as it roared upriver.

The increased speed fanned the flames. Panicked passengers ran about the deck, unsure where to take refuge. Mothers screamed for their children, husbands for their wives. The flames, accelerated by a fresh coat of highly flammable paint, rapidly enveloped the ship, and passengers began to jump overboard. Some clung to the rails as long as they could before jumping into the churning water. A few were rescued by nearby boats, but most did not know how to swim and simply drowned.

The inexperienced crew provided no help. Nor did the 3,000 lifejackets on board. Rotten and filled with disintegrated cork, they had long since lost their buoyancy. Those who put them on sank as soon as they hit the water. Wired in place, none of the lifeboats could be dislodged. Even if they had, they would never have made it safely into the water with the ship chugging along at top speed.

By the time the ship finally beached at North Brother Island, it was almost completely engulfed in fire. Survivors poured over the railings into the water. Some huddled in the few places not yet reached by the flames, too terrified to jump. Nurses and patients at the island's contagious disease hospital rushed to offer assistance. Several of them grabbed ladders being used to renovate the facility and used them to bring the survivors off the ship. Others caught children tossed by distraught parents. Within minutes, all who could be saved, including the captain and several crew, were moved away from the burning hulk.

The *General Slocum* left a grisly wake. The boats that followed seeking to offer assistance plucked a few survivors from the water. But mostly they found only the lifeless bodies of the ship's ill-fated passengers. The fact that most were young children only added to the horror.

Within minutes of the tragedy, reporters from the New York *World* and other major dailies were on the scene. The dispatches they sent back to their newsrooms sickened many a hardened editor. Rescue workers openly wept as the corpses piled up. By the time they were done counting the bodies and tabulating a list of the missing, the death toll stood at 1,021.

With more than 2,000 people on the outing, nearly everyone in the neighborhood knew someone on the ship. As word of the fire spread, it caused panic and confusion. No one seemed to know where to go. Thousands gathered at St. Mark's Church awaiting word about survivors. Thousands more rushed uptown to the East 23rd Street pier designated as a temporary morgue. By midafternoon, those not yet reunited with their family members began to lose hope. Many discovered they had lost a wife or child. Dozens learned they had lost their entire families.

At the morgue, policemen, and Coroner's Department workers labored to lay out the hundreds of corpses as they arrived. Others were dispatched to scour the city for coffins. Wagons arrived laden with tons of ice for the preservation of the bodies. Outside, hundreds of policemen strained to control the swelling crowds of relatives and friends, not to mention curiosity seekers, reporters, and undertakers.

For the next week, thousands paraded past the gruesome lineup of victims resting in open coffins. The better preserved were identified quickly. Some of the burned and disfigured were identified by their clothing or jewelry. The sixty-one that could not be identified—including many of the bodies recovered days after the event—were buried in a common grave. Funerals were held every hour for days on end in the churches of *Kleindeutschland.* These tragic scenes were punctuated by the suicides of several men and women who lost their entire families in the fire.

The story of the *General Slocum* made headlines across the nation and around the globe. World leaders and European royalty sent money and letters of condolence to Mayor George B. McClellan and the people of St. Mark's. Funds poured in from private citizens and charitable groups from Rhode Island to California.

How could a tragedy of such magnitude occur within a few hundred yards of the shores of the nation's most modern city? In the weeks and months that followed the fire, an outraged public searched for answers and culprits. City officials vowed to conduct a thorough investigation and within weeks, Captain Van Schaick, executives of the Knickerbocker Steamship Co., and the Inspector who certified the *General Slocum* as safe only a month before the fire were indicted.

Captain Van Schaick came under the most intense scrutiny. Why had he failed to dock the ship immediately after discovering the fire? Why had he instead raced upriver and allowed the fire to claim more victims? Why was his crew so poorly trained? How was it that *he* survived when so many others perished?

At his trial Van Schaick offered plausible explanations for his actions, but the jury was not convinced. A convenient scapegoat, he was convicted of criminal negligence and manslaughter and sentenced to ten years hard labor in the Sing Sing prison. He served three years before receiving a pardon from President William H. Taft. Van Schaick was free, but broken by the horrible tragedy and subsequent legal crucifixion, he lived out his days in melancholy seclusion.

In contrast, the officials at the Knickerbocker Steamship Company escaped with only a nominal fine. This despite the fact that the trial revealed the company had illegally falsified records to cover up their lack of attention to passenger safety.

The *General Slocum* tragedy left a lasting impact on New York City. First, it caused the rapid dissolution of the German enclave of *Kleindeutschland.* Most survivors and their relatives were unwilling to remain in a neighborhood suffused by tragedy and simply moved. The steady exodus of Germans to Upper Manhattan's Yorkville begun in the 1890s now became a torrent. By the time of the 1910 census, only a handful of German families remained in *Kleindeutschland.* The *Slocum* tragedy not only consumed 1,021 lives but took with it an entire community as well.

Second, the *General Slocum* disaster brought about a major upgrading of steamboat safety regulations and a sweeping reform of the United States Steamboat Inspection Service (USSIS). One week after the fire, President Theodore Roosevelt named a five-man commission to investigate the *Slocum* tragedy and recommend measures that would prevent an event like it from occurring again. The commission held hearings in New York and Washington, D.C. and took testimony from hundreds of witnesses and experts. In October 1904 it issued a scathing report that placed most of the blame at the feet of the USSIS. Dozens were fired and a complete reinspection of steamboats was ordered. Not surprisingly, the new inspections turned up widespread safety problems, from useless lifejackets to rotten fire hoses. The result was a long list of recommended reforms, including requiring new steamboats be equipped with:

- fireproof metal bulkheads to contain fires
- steam pipes extended from the boiler into cargo areas (to act as a sprinkler)
- improved lifejackets (one for each passenger and crew member)
- fire hoses capable of handling 100 pounds of pressure per square inch
- accessible lifeboats

All were subsequently enacted, leading to dramatic improvements in steamboat safety.

Remarkably, the *Slocum* tragedy rapidly faded from public memory, to the point that it was replaced as the city's GREAT fire just seven years later when the Triangle Shirtwaist Factory burned. There were similarities between the two fires—both involved immigrants and mostly female victims and both aroused public wrath. But the Triangle fire's death toll was 15% that of the *Slocum* just seven years earlier. How then did it become the fire of fires in New York's (and the nation's) memory?

Two factors begin to explain this remarkable legacy. First, there was the context. The Triangle Shirtwaist Factory fire occurred at a time of intense labor struggle, especially in the garment trades. Only a year before, the shirtwaist makers had staged a huge strike for better wages, hours, and conditions. Now 146 of them lay dead. There was no question about who was to blame. This conclusion was reinforced when the public learned that the factory owners had locked the exits to keep the women at their machines. Second, the onset of World War I eradicated sympathy for anything German, including the innocent victims of the *General Slocum* fire. By the 1920s, as the Triangle fire became firmly entrenched in the American memory, all that remained of the *General Slocum* fire was an ever-shrinking annual commemoration at the Lutheran cemetery in Middle Village, Queens.

The Desirability of Comprehensive Municipal Planning in Advance of Development, Calvin Tomkins (1905)

Calvin Tomkins was born in 1858 and graduated from Cornell University in 1879. During a career in manufacturing he was president of the Newark Plaster Company, the Tomkins Cove Stone Company, and the Bonner Brick Company. In 1906, he became president of the New York City Municipal Art Society and was later Commissioner of Docks and Ferries for the city.

Tomkins was one of the first proponents of a "comprehensive plan" to guide the development of New York City. His article, "The Desirability of Comprehensive Municipal Planning in Advance of Development" (1905), was a forerunner of the formation of the Regional Plan Association that would produce three Regional Plans during the century.

Tomkins was also influenced by the City Beautiful Movement, an urban planning movement whose goal was to achieve a cultural parity with the cities of Europe and who believed that the creation of "beauty" in a city could inspire civic virtue and moral rectitude in its inhabitants. The architectural idiom that City Beautiful leaders chose was the Beaux-Arts style from Paris that emphasized order, dignity, and harmony in imposing public structures. The U.S. Customs House (1907), the New York Public Library (1911), and Grand Central Terminal (1913) were only three of the buildings completed shortly after Tomkins's article.

THE wonderful growth of New York City and the fact that the City is rapidly assuming the position of the metropolis of the world, creates interest in all plans connected with its development. By the State census of 1905 which has just come out, you will notice that we have a population within the five boroughs of four million one hundred and fifty odd thousand inhabitants. Taking into consideration the four northern counties of New Jersey and the Westchester district, the Connecticut district and Long Island, adjacent to New York, the population of the metropolitan district of New

York is certainly not much under five and one-half million people at the present time. There is only one other city having a larger population—the great city of London, with six and one-half million people contained in its metropolitan district of 700 square miles—and it is to be noted that the rate of growth of New York is very much more rapid annually than that of London. Between 1890 and 1900 the City increased 37% in population, and it is estimated by good judges that during the next ten years, as a consequence of rapid transit facilities and other underlying causes, it is not improbable that the City will increase 45%. When we consider the significance of this and what future possibilities are involved, we understand how important the present planning of this great metropolis is.

The City of New York is a great city on account of its peculiar position. The great city of antiquity was Rome, as a consequence of its position in the Mediterranean basin. The supremacy passed in sequence to Venice and Genoa, and subsequently to Amsterdam and London. Now it is rapidly coming to New York. New York is situated at the mouth of the Hudson River Valley, which is backed by the Mohawk Valley, through which we reach the great waters of the West by railroad now, as formerly we did by the canoe and the canal boat. The only other cities which have any strategic position on the Atlantic seaboard are Montreal on the St. Lawrence and the city of New Orleans on the Gulf of Mexico. The one is interfered with by the cold of winter and the other by the heat of summer. In the case of every other city along the seaboard, the trains coming to it have to climb up over the Allegheny Mountains and down again, and the expense is heavy as compared to the level haul from the West to New York. The situation of the city is such that it already commands the commerce of Europe. New York is situated in the North Atlantic Basin, that vast district bounded by the Ural Mountains on one side and the Rockies on the other—in such a way as to make it the central point of exchange for the great commercial states of modern times. The fact that the transportation of the world is coming to its gates makes New York the city that it is.

It is incumbent on us to arrange our own plan of internal city development so that it shall be commensurate with the destiny which is awaiting us as the result of our situation. The features of New York have actually been too large to have been taken advantage of until the present time. The East River on the one side and the Hudson River on the other have heretofore disadvantageously divided the city. At one time the Harlem did so, but that has been overcome by bridges. The bridges over the East River will similarly do away with the barrier effect of the East River and the tunnels which are now being built under the Hudson River will have the same effect there; so that ultimately we shall see the Long Island section and the New Jersey section connected with the Manhattan section just as conveniently as the Westchester section is at the present time, and we shall then have here a round or square city like Chicago or Paris. The water to the east and west of us will afford facilities for carrying heavy goods, and passenger transportation will no longer be interfered with by the rivers. We are only beginning to organize so as to take advantage of our natural opportunities.

I have referred to the metropolitan district about New York—the section not alone included within the five boroughs, but comprising the four northern counties of New Jersey, Long Island outside of Queens, the Westchester and Connecticut districts, all as much a part of the social and economic City of New York as the five boroughs. . . .

As far as we have had any plan of development, it has been very largely that of private enterprise; enterprising real estate operators, acting in concert with enterprising transportation speculators, have developed the City. Most cities are developed that way. This is not a matter of such relative importance to smaller cities, but with a city such as we have here it is of the greatest importance. Transportation is regarded from the point of view of the greatest immediate results in the way of railroad fares. Street and park systems considered largely as to how they can be made to fit in with little separate schemes for real estate development and the desirability for a comprehensive plan are only beginning to be apparent. One of the most notable events in recognition of this fact was the appointment by Mayor McClellan of the City Improvement Commission. Most of you are doubtless familiar with the report of that Commission, a most admirable report, recommending many improvements, some of which may now be open to criticism in view of the wider experience had, but which, in the main, is as effective and as practical as it is broad in its scope. In recommending to the Board of Aldermen the appointment of such a commission, the Mayor said—and I cannot do better than to quote his language in that matter, because it is very precise: "The great error of the past, both from the material and artistic standpoint, has been that public improvements have been undertaken only to meet the emergency of the moment and without regard for ultimate ends. Public buildings have been scattered far and wide or erected in impossible locations. Streets have been opened, bridges built and money spent at haphazard, according to the fancy or whim of changing administrations, with far more regard for the interest of individuals than for the good of the City as a whole."

Private enterprise has conflicted with public works and the good of the individual has not always been the public good, although the results are unexpectedly better than I think we could have anticipated. A plan such as I have suggested cannot be a hard and fixed plan; it must grow and change with changing conditions. But I think it is important that the desirability for, and the main features of, such a plan should be established in the public mind. My own impression is that such a plan is likely to grow largely as a result of local interest in local affairs in the different boroughs. The different improvements will be brought to the attention of the local boards and then to the attention of the Board of Estimate and Apportionment, and forwarded by a public opinion, first local in character and subsequently general among all the boards as the relation of local improvements to a general scheme becomes apparent. In that way they will finally become so fixed in the public mind that they will perforce be carried through by successive administrations.

The great difficulty has been that one administration succeeds another administration so rapidly, and that private interest is so constantly at work, that it is very hard to maintain a continuous policy. But if we arouse sufficient general public interest in these matters the force of opinion will compel the Board of Estimate and apportionment and changing city administrations to carry through consecutive borough plans.

As regards the practicability of specific improvements, this body of technical men in the City employ is, by criticism and encouragement, more capable of directing public opinion correctly than any other body in the City, and a correspondingly great responsibility rests upon it.

To be more specific: the general idea of a city plan includes the following subsidiary ideas:

The first matter of importance is planning for city streets and parks, first, in the outlying boroughs where the field is open, particularly in Richmond, in The Bronx east of the Bronx River, in Queens, and rearranging streets and parks in the older parts of the City. The park and the street arrangement should go on at the same time. It is impossible to plan a good street and park system unless they are planned together. Changes and rearrangements in the older parts of the City are enormously expensive. The acquisition of small parks, while very necessary, is an exceedingly expensive operation for the City, and widening or changing well-established street lines in the older parts of the City is also extremely expensive. London is feeling the great lack of City planning in this respect. There they are obliged to make important street changes at a heavy expense, and here in the City of New York we have got to do the same thing. This has been effectively done in Paris and in Vienna, and done at a time when the changes could be carried out far better and easier than they could now. In Vienna this was accomplished when they tore down the old fortifications, and in Paris they did the work under the strong hand of Napoleon III. We must widen Fifty-ninth Street when the Blackwell's Island Bridge is carried across to Manhattan. We must extend Sixth and Seventh Avenues downtown. We must make some provision, I think ultimately, for diagonal streets between the bridge terminals of the Williamsburg and Manhattan Bridges and the downtown section and the Cooper Union section, and there are numerous other street changes in addition to the acquisition of small parks. We are now paying for our lack of foresight in these respects. However, in the new boroughs, the opportunity exists and should be taken advantage of, and it will be most unfortunate if it shall be longer neglected.

The next matter is that of bridges and tunnels, including docks, ferries and warehouses. As I have indicated, bridges and tunnels will serve to connect the whole city together and make it a round city instead of a long city. Bridges are virtually sections of continuous streets and ought to be so considered.

In connection with the warehouses I would like to leave one thought with you. Many cities have excellent warehouse systems. In New York, in Manhattan at least, we have no adequate system. The sheds on the piers are virtually the warehouses and the immense rentals that they command for the double purpose of landings and storage makes the docks unavailable for other purposes. Domestic and foreign commerce is suffering as a consequence for lack of good landing facilities and this will continue as long as the docks are used for warehouse purposes, when warehouses should be provided elsewhere.

The opportunity for acquiring parks in Richmond, and seashore parks on Long Island, and an immense park on the submerged lands about Jamaica Bay and in Queens, exists at the present time, and that situation is not going to exist long. Fortunately, the Borough of The Bronx supplied itself with a magnificent system of parks some fifteen years ago, but the same judgment has not characterized the Borough of Brooklyn or the Borough of Queens, or the Borough of Richmond, and in each one of those boroughs there are splendid opportunities for the acquisition of cheap parks at the present time, which should be availed of.

The harbor is under the jurisdiction of the United States Government as regards its commerce and as regards dredging, but the matter of the pollution of the water itself is a matter that has not received the consideration that it should. The sewage from all that section back of the ridge on Long Island is coming into the New York Harbor through cross sewers; the Bronx Valley sewage will be deflected into the Hudson River; the Passaic and Hackensack sewage will be deflected into New York Harbor. The water in the upper harbor now is foul compared to what it was a few years ago, and unless some purification system is provided for the increased drainage which runs into our harbor, the conditions will, before very long, be as bad as they are in the Passaic Valley now. They are unbearable there at present, and the harbor should not be converted into a cesspool.

The matter of the grouping of public buildings and of the development of sections of a city so that there shall be uniformity of character is a matter that should receive attention. Cities are beautiful just about in proportion as their public buildings are effectively grouped about centrally located public squares. That constitutes the great beauty of the City of Paris and Vienna—the two finest cities of the world from an aesthetic standpoint. Many of you remember the wonderful effect that was created at Chicago during the World's Fair by the grouping of buildings. We have neglected this in New York City. I had a map made some time ago showing the public buildings in the City of New York and I was surprised when the map came out to see how dotted it was with the parcels of property belonging to or leased by the City of New York scattered all over the lower part of Manhattan. If those buildings, fire engine houses, school houses, court houses, libraries, department offices, etc., were properly grouped at centrally located points the effect would be very different from what it is now. The important site in connection with this matter now is City Hall Park. If we lose the opportunity of making a civic centre and a beautiful square out of City Hall Park, we shall have lost the greatest aesthetic opportunity in the city. The new Hall of Records on Chambers Street is the key to the situation there; the north side of Chambers Street should be taken by the City and the Hall of Records extended along it to Broadway. The antiquated United States Post Office Building should be taken out of the southern extremity of City Hall Park, where it is now located. Many people do not know that it is standing in the original park enclosure, but such is the fact, and the land was deeded to the United States Government for a nominal consideration. It should be taken out and the ground returned to the City. With that share in front, with an adequate bridge approach at Park Row, City Hall Park would compare favorably with some of the beautiful European squares. It is a matter of convenience to have public buildings grouped in places where they can be conveniently reached. Chicago, Cleveland, St. Louis and Buffalo, and particularly the City of Washington, realized this, and all of them planned elaborately for the future and particularly with reference to this matter of the placement of public buildings effectively and so as to create grand effects. Architects have very properly stated the matter in this way: That two public buildings properly grouped are far more effective than half a dozen separate buildings, although each better possibly in individual design, but scattered. Anybody who has the opportunity of noting the effect at Washington, for instance, or the effect in any European cities, realizes the importance of massed public architecture.

Lastly, and most important of all, there is the question of transit. The transportation of the City, particularly its passenger transportation, constitutes the circulatory system of the City—the very life of the City. The problem in all cities is to provide for expansion without congestion, and that is the problem we have to face here in New York. In the vicinity of Sixtieth Street, on the West Side, and of Hester Street, on the East Side, we are housing a denser population than any city in the world permits. Conditions are uncivilized in those sections. Subway transit will take the people out of New York on a low rate of fare and give them opportunities for sunlight and decency outside of the crowded sections. Cheap rapid transit is the solution of the problem of the slums. Just as the City has grown up by transportation to its gates, so must it look to developing its own transportation if it expects to take advantage of its opportunities. The City will become a civilized city just in proportion as it shall provide adequate transit. In The Bronx it has always seemed to us that the problem of transit consists in continuing the subways right up to the city line so that there shall be only one fare. It would seem unfortunate if the lines should stop after going into The Bronx a short distance only; and is it not a fair criticism to make against the plans as they are at present proposed, that they do so stop and that they are not extended to the north? As regards the Long Island section and the New Jersey section, it seems important that the lines of communication east and west, should be so organized that transfers can be obtained between lines of transportation north and south on Manhattan Island; that the north and south Manhattan lines should be directly under the surface; that the east and west lines to New Jersey and Long Island should be directly under the Manhattan lines, and that a transfer station should be established at each intersecting point, so that any person coming from Brooklyn or the New Jersey section can transfer north or south on any avenue in New York City, mined by a subway, and that any passenger traveling north or south on Manhattan will have a similar opportunity of transferring east or west on the transverse lines. Again, it seems important that these lines of congested traffic, at least in lower Manhattan, should remain under municipal control. I do not know that I can do better than to read a brief extract from the report of the Board of Trade and Transportation of New York, which will indicate what I mean:

"The fundamental mistake has consisted in treating franchise grants as contracts, unalterable without the consent of both parties, like ordinary contracts concerning property. Governments, like individuals, may properly enough enter into contracts relating to property, and such contracts when made should be respected; but governments ought not by contract to divest themselves of governmental functions as they do to an extent when they surrender partial control of the public streets, by giving to private interests definite term structural rights therein. The City can control completely only when it is in a position to terminate at any time the right of use claimed by any person or corporation that may choose to defy the will of the City in any respect. In other words, the grant terminable at the will of the governing authorities is the only kind under which the City can be sure of its ability to dominate the situation at all times."

Private corporations are organized primarily for dividends and, in the nature of things, they cannot provide the service necessary for the growing needs of the City. In order to obtain that service, in order to avoid going back to such conditions as prevailed two years ago on the elevated railroad and on the surface roads, the City must itself keep control of its transit system. We think very properly that the City should not attempt to operate at the present time. The City is not prepared to do this nor are the roads themselves organized sufficiently to be taken over. But in order to provide good service, and more important even than that, in order to provide control so as to be able to take care of extensions and improvements and not find ourselves handicapped by what we want to do in the future on account of what we have permitted in the past—the City must keep itself in continual, constant, effective control of the transit grants it gives out hereafter. These transit lines under the great avenues will control not only the future subway traffic of the City, but they will control the elevated and surface traffic as well. To whatever arrangements are made for conducting those lines, other transportation lines will have to conform. If these franchises are given out so that the City can recover them on the payment of indemnity at any time, it will keep itself in control. If the attempt is made to give them out under contractual provisions for extensions, service, etc., the result will be flat failure as heretofore. You cannot hold a public service corporation to a service contract. The only way you can provide for good service and needed extensions is to place the City in a position to take back what it has given and then the City will be able to exert its authority, otherwise its authority amounts to nothing and vanishes in words and legal contests.

The question of the use of the subways by the steam railroads is a very interesting one and is beginning to attract attention among trolley railroad men and among steam railroad men. There is no reason why the subway system of the City should not be used by the trains of the steam roads. It is desirable that the steam road system of the country should have the same degree of elasticity in collecting and distributing passengers that the trolley system has now, but it is of the greatest importance to the City that if this is permitted the City shall keep control of its transit so that local transit may not be made subordinate to the interests of the steam roads. In the city of London extensive street improvements have been made as a result of the City's taking large areas of adjacent land in addition to the lands actually required for the specific improvement, then making the improvement and selling or renting this excess land after its enhancement in value as a consequence of the improvement and so recouping, in large part, or in whole, for the expenditure incurred. That has been the custom in European cities and I have no doubt we have got to come to it here. The City Improvement Commission have recommended resort to the principle of excess condemnation, and a most opportune occasion can now be found for its application in connection with the acquisition of a court house or other public building site on Chambers Street opposite City Hall Park, the land condemned to include the entire section back of the tall Broadway buildings and between Leonard Street, the Park and Park Row, a section which must soon be reorganized in any event. Why should not the City itself reap the principal benefit of the improvement?

I believe that we will have, at least as regards our transit, to eliminate it from the debt limit-restriction. The City is restricted in the amount of debt that it can incur to 10% on the assessed valuation. Water is excepted, but dock improvements should also be excepted and transit improvements should be excepted as well. I notice such conservative organs as the *Record and Guide* are now beginning to advocate that idea.

In regard to co-operation of officials: In the Art Society we have secured co-operation as far as we could get it, and when we did not get it we did not scold too much. We recognized the fact that city officials are limited in three ways,—their term is short to begin with; they have very little money to spend; and lastly there is a natural and very proper tendency towards conservatism on the part of any prominent city disinclination to try new things.

Then they are hampered by the counterclaims of private interests, which seriously interfere with their ability always to do what the City's interest demands. The Society has found it far more effective to build up a public opinion through the newspapers and through Boards of Trade and local civic associations and by so doing trusting ultimately to overcome opposition.

There are many other things that I could refer to. I should like particularly to go into the recommendations of the City Improvement Commission, but I will not undertake to discuss these here to-night.

The Day's Work of a "New Law" Tenement Inspector, from Charities and the Commons 17, *Lewis E. Palmer (1906–1907)*

Lewis E. Palmer was a tenement inspector who wrote the following article for New York's Charity Organization Society. The society was founded by Josephine Shaw Lowell (whose brother, Robert Gould Shaw, led the first black regiment in the Civil War, died in action with his troops, and was memorialized in Augustus St.-Gauden's statue in Boston Common) in 1882 with the belief that empirical knowledge would be the spur to alleviate the conditions of poverty in the slums of New York City. The society kept extensive records about living conditions, but also sponsored Laurence Veiller's work in drafting the city's Tenement House Law of 1901.

The "scientific" methodology used by the society for investigating poverty was a forerunner for twentieth-century public relief programs. Much of the work of collecting documentation was based on the beliefs of Edward Thomas Devine (1867–1948), who charged that "housing reform would be easier than it is . . . if there were not strong pecuniary interests at stake." Devine eventually joined another children's rights activist, Lillian Weld, a founder of the Henry Street Settlement on the Lower East Side, to promote a federal child welfare bureau.

The "Dumb-bell" Type

THE "dumb-bell" tenement that he had found such a profitable investment was first constructed in New York about 1879, and until the passage of the Tenement House Act in 1901, was the prevailing type of tenement building. For a breeder of ill health and immorality and as a menace to life the "dumb-bell" type cannot be surpassed.

The entrance hallway in the center of the building is a long dark passage three feet or less in width, extending sixty feet to the rear of the tenement.

Each floor above the first is generally divided into four sets of apartments with seven rooms on each side of the hall. Of these fourteen rooms, only four receive direct light and air from the street, or from the small yard back of the building. The five rooms on each side of the house that get no light or ventilation from the street or yard, are supposed to be ventilated by an air shaft about twenty-eight inches wide and fifty to sixty feet in length, running from the top to the bottom of the building. There is no intake at the bottom of the shaft and as a result the ventilation is practically nil. In fact it would often be better if this narrow shaft could be closed up entirely, thus cutting off the foul air that is constantly arising from its semi-dark recesses.

One of the witnesses before the Tenement House Committee in 1900 said that the proper name was "foul air shaft" and others designated it as "a culture tube on a gigantic scale." To quote from the advance sheets of part of the report of the Tenement House Commission:

> Many persons testified that the air from these shafts was so foul and the odors so vile that they had to close the windows opening into them, and in some cases the windows were permanently nailed up for this reason. Moreover, the tenants often use the air shaft as a receptacle for garbage and all sorts of refuse and indescribable filth thrown out of the windows, and this mass of filth is often allowed to remain, rotting at the bottom of the shaft for weeks without being cleaned out.

From other points of view than that of light and air the air shaft stands condemned. It serves as a conveyor of smells and noise and is one of the greatest elements in destroying privacy in the tenement house. Through it one hears the sounds that occur in the rooms of every other family in the building, and often in these narrow shafts the windows of one apartment look directly into the windows of another apartment not more than five feet away. Privacy under such conditions is not only difficult, but impossible.

There is no requirement for the size of living rooms in the old law buildings. The front room, the largest in the apartment, is generally about ten feet, six inches by eleven feet, three inches, while the bedrooms average about seven feet by eight and a half feet. The latter generally get no light or air except from the air shaft.

The fire escapes with their vertical ladders make it practically impossible for any but a strong man to get from a burning building, and the wooden stairs and non-fireproof halls in the buildings as high as five stories, together with the inflammable flues furnished by the air shafts, cut off most of the chances for even a man's escape.

New Law Tenements—A Contrast

And now what has the new law done? Perhaps most important of all, it has abolished the air shafts. In their places are inner courts at least twenty-four feet wide in the center of each building. At the bottom of each court is an intake tunnel through which a fresh supply of air is constantly passing. Every room in the new law tenements is light and well ventilated. At least one of the living rooms for each family must have one hundred and twenty square feet of floor space and seventy square feet is the minimum allowance for any room.

Instead of water closets in the public halls, used by two families, each family has its own closet in its own apartments. The old vertical ladders have been abolished from the fire escapes and in their places are substituted stairs with hand rails. The fire escape balconies, thirty inches wide on the old buildings, must now be at least three feet in width. The stairs and halls are completely fire proof, and the public halls are entirely shut off from the non-fireproof portions of the building.

Safety, sanitation and morality—the three principles that were so largely left out of consideration in the erection of the old buildings—have become with the new law the essentials of construction. And the new law houses are an unqualified success. Most of the builders are endeavoring to comply with the law not only because it is the law, but because in the end it is far more profitable for them to do so. Careful planning at the outset and thorough inspection during construction means in the end a building that will last—and perhaps more important to the builder—apartments that will rent.

In most sections of the city the demand for the new law buildings is growing. Only in a few of the outlying districts where the transit facilities are inadequate is this not true. Plans were filed in 1905 for 5,918 new law tenements. Of these the one-fourth located in Manhattan were to contain when completed 36,311 families. In many cases apartments are rented before the buildings are completed and in some instances rooms have been engaged after a study of the plans alone.

Happily those builders who would return to the old days of "dumb-bell" tenements are rare. From the standpoint of a money investment alone the new law tenement pays.

From The American Scene, *Henry James (1907)*

Henry James was born in New York City at 21 Washington Place in 1843, but he left the city in 1855 and returned only sporadically after that. His visit in 1904–1905 came on the heels of a four-year period where he completed five novels, among them *The Ambassadors* and *The Wings of the Dove.*

James was drawn back to America, and particularly to New York City, in part by nostalgia. What he found when he returned was a "bristling" city engaged in a frenetic dance of destruction and re-creation characterized by two main trends—the transformation of the architectural landscape by the development of the skyscraper and the spectacular rise in immigration from non-English speaking countries. When James left Gotham, Trinity Church was still the tallest structure in the city; when he returned more than a dozen skyscrapers, led by the Flatiron Building, overshadowed it. For James, however, in contrast to photographers Alfred Stieglitz and Edward Steichen, these buildings were not pieces of art but simply "giants of the mere market" and part of the "steel-souled machine room" that New York had become in his eyes.

James, revealing the patrician sensibility of his class, also recoiled at the sight of the masses of immigrants and described the fire escapes of the Lower East Side as "the spaciously organized cage for the nimbler class of animals in some great zoological garden." Still, he found that the lower parts of Manhattan "hummed with the human presence." At Ellis Island, echoing his later short story, "The Jolly Corner," he feels that he has "seen a ghost in his supposedly safe old house," but he is concerned about the effect "such a hotch-potch of racial ingredients will have on the American character."

It is indubitably a "great" bay, a great harbour, but no one item of the romantic, or even of the picturesque, as commonly understood, contributes to its effect. The shores are low and for the most part depressingly furnished and prosaically peopled; the islands, though numerous, have not a grace to exhibit, and one thinks of the other, the real flowers of geography in this order, of Naples, of Capetown, of Sydney, of Seattle, of San Francisco, of Rio, asking how if *they* justify a reputation, New York should seem to justify one. Then, after all, we remember that there are reputations and reputations; we remember above all that the imaginative response to the conditions here presented may just happen to proceed from the intellectual extravagance of the given observer. When this personage is open to corruption by almost any large view of an intensity of life, his vibrations tend to become a matter difficult even for *him* to explain. He may have to confess that the group of evident facts fails to account by itself for the complacency of his appreciation. Therefore it is that I find myself rather backward with a perceived sanction, of an at all proportionate kind, for the fine exhilaration with which, in this free wayfaring relation to them, the wide waters of New York inspire me. There is the beauty of light and air, the great scale of space, and, seen far away to the west, the open gates of the Hudson, majestic in their degree, even at a distance, and announcing still nobler things. But the real appeal, unmistakably, is in that note of vehemence in the local life of which I have spoken, for it is the appeal of a particular type of dauntless power.

The aspect the power wears then is indescribable; it is the power of the most extravagant of cities, rejoicing, as with the voice of the morning, in its might, its fortune, its unsurpassable conditions, and imparting to every object and element, to the motion and expression of every floating, hurrying, panting thing, to the throb of ferries and tugs, to the plash of waves and the play of winds and the glint of lights and the shrill of whistles and the quality and authority of breeze-borne cries—all, practically, a diffused, wasted clamour of *detonations*—something of its sharp free accent and, above all, of its sovereign sense of being "backed" and able to back. The universal *applied* passion struck me as shining unprecedentedly out of the composition; in the bigness and bravery and insolence, especially, of everything that rushed and shrieked; in the air as of a great intricate frenzied dance, half merry, half desperate, or at least half defiant, performed on the huge watery floor. This appearance of the bold lacing-together, across the waters, of the scattered members of the monstrous organism—lacing as by the ceaseless play of an enormous system of steam-shuttles or electric bobbins (I scarce know what to call them), commensurate in form with their infinite work—does perhaps more than anything else to give the pitch of the vision of energy. One has the sense that the monster grows and grows, flinging abroad its loose limbs even as some unmannered young giant at his "larks," and that the binding stitches must for ever fly further and faster and draw harder; the future complexity of the web, all under the sky and over the sea, becoming thus that of some colossal set of clockworks, some steel-souled machine-room of brandished arms and hammering fists and opening and closing jaws. The immeasurable bridges are but as the horizontal sheaths of pistons working at high pressure, day and night, and subject, one apprehends with perhaps inconsistent gloom, to certain, to fantastic, to merciless multiplication. In the light of this apprehension indeed the breezy brightness of the Bay puts on the semblance of the vast white page that awaits beyond any other perhaps the black overscoring of science.

Let me hasten to add that its present whiteness is precisely its charming note, the frankest of the signs you recognize and remember it by. That is the distinction I was just feeling my way to name as the main ground of its doing so well, for effect, without technical scenery. There are great imposing ports—Glasgow and Liverpool and London—that have already their page blackened almost beyond redemption from any such light of the picturesque as can hope to irradiate fog and grime, and there are others, Marseilles and Constantinople say, or, for all I know to the contrary, New Orleans, that contrive to abound before everything else in colour, and so to make a rich and instant and obvious show. But memory and the actual impression keep investing New York with the tone, predominantly, of summer dawns and winter frosts, of sea-foam, of bleached sails and stretched awnings, of blanched hulls, of scoured decks, of new ropes, of polished brasses, of streamers clear in the blue air; and it is by this harmony, doubtless, that the projection of the individual character of the place, of the candour of its avidity and the freshness of its audacity, is most conveyed. The "tall buildings," which have so promptly usurped a glory that affects you as rather surprised, as yet, at itself, the multitudinous sky-scrapers standing up to the view, from the water, like extravagant pins in a cushion already overplanted, and stuck in as in the dark, anywhere and anyhow, have at least the felicity of carrying out the fairness of tone, of taking the sun and the shade in the manner of towers of marble. They are not all of marble, I believe, by any means, even if some may be, but they are impudently new and still more impudently "novel"—this in common with so many other terrible things in America—and they are triumphant payers of dividends; all of which uncontested and unabashed pride, with flash of innumerable windows and flicker of subordinate gilt attributions, is like the flare, up and down their long, narrow faces, of the lamps of some general permanent "celebration."

You see the pin-cushion in profile, so to speak, on passing between Jersey City and Twenty-third Street, but you get it broadside on, this loose nosegay of architectural flowers, if you skirt the Battery, well out, and embrace the whole plantation. Then the "American beauty," the rose of interminable stem, becomes the token of the cluster at large—to that degree that, positively, this is all that is wanted for emphasis of your final impression. Such growths, you feel, have confessedly arisen but to be "picked," in time, with a shears; nipped short off, by waiting fate, as soon as "science," applied to gain, has put upon the table, from far up its sleeve, some more winning card. Crowned not only with no history, but with no credible possibility of time for history, and consecrated by no uses save the commercial at any cost, they are simply the most piercing notes in that concert of the expensively provisional into which your supreme sense of New York resolves itself. They never begin to speak to you, in the manner of the builded majestics of the world as we have heretofore known such—towers or temples or fortresses or palaces—with the authority of things of permanence or even of things of long duration. One story is good only till another is told, and sky-scrapers are the last word of economic ingenuity only till another word be written. This shall be possibly a word of still uglier meaning, but the vocabulary of thrift at any price shows boundless resources, and the consciousness of that truth, the consciousness of the finite, the menaced, the essentially *invented* state, twinkles ever, to my perception, in the thousand glassy eyes of these giants of the mere market. Such a structure as the comparatively windowless bell-tower of Giotto, in Florence, looks supremely serene in its beauty. You don't feel it to have risen by the breath of an interested passion that, restless beyond all passions, is for ever seeking more pliable forms. Beauty has been the object of its creator's idea, and, having found beauty, it has found the form in which it splendidly rests.

Beauty indeed was the aim of the creator of the spire of Trinity Church, so cruelly overtopped and so barely distinguishable, from your train-bearing barge, as you stand off, in its abject helpless humility; and it may of course be asked how much of this superstition finds voice in the actual shrunken presence of that laudable effort. Where, for the eye, is the felicity of simplified Gothic, of noble preeminence, that once made of this highly-pleasing edifice the pride of the town and the feature of Broadway? The answer is, as obviously, that these charming elements are still there, just where they ever were, but that they have been mercilessly deprived of their visibility. It aches and throbs, this smothered visibility, we easily feel, in its caged and dishonoured condition, supported only by the consciousness that the dishonour is no fault of its own. We commune with it, in tenderness and pity, through the encumbered air; our eyes, made, however unwillingly, at home in strange vertiginous upper atmospheres, look down on it as on a poor ineffectual thing, an architectural object addressed, even in its prime aspiration, to the patient pedestrian sense and permitting thereby a relation of intimacy. It was to speak to me audibly enough on two or three other occasions—even through the thick of that frenzy of Broadway just where Broadway receives from Wall Street the fiercest application of the maddening lash; it was to put its tragic case there with irresistible lucidity. "Yes, the wretched figure I am making is as little as you see my fault—it is the fault of the buildings whose very first care is to deprive churches of their visibility. There are but two or three—two or three outward and visible churches—left in New York 'anyway,' as you must have noticed, and even they are hideously threatened: a fact at which no one, indeed, appears to be shocked, from which no one draws the least of the inferences that stick straight out of it, which every one seems in short to take for granted either with remarkable stupidity or with remarkable cynicism." So, at any rate, they may still effectively communicate, ruddy-brown (where not browny-black) old Trinity and any pausing, any attending survivor of the clearer age—and there is yet more of the bitterness of history to be tasted in such a tacit passage, as I shall presently show. . . .

The impression of Ellis Island, in fine, would be—as I was to find throughout that so many of my impressions would be—a chapter by itself; and with a particular page for recognition of the degree in which the liberal hospitality of the eminent Commissioner of this wonderful service, to whom I had been introduced, helped to make the interest of the whole watched drama poignant and unforgettable. It is a drama that goes on, without a pause, day by day and year by year, this visible act of ingurgitation on the part of our body politic and social, and constituting really an appeal to amazement beyond that of any sword-swallowing or fire-swallowing of the circus. The wonder that one couldn't keep down was the thought that these two or three hours of one's own chance vision of the business were but as a tick or two of the mighty clock, the clock that never, never stops—least of all when it strikes, for a sign of so much winding-up, some louder hour of our national fate than usual. I think indeed that the simplest account of the action of Ellis Island on the spirit of any sensitive citizen who may have happened to "look in" is that he comes back from his visit not at all the same person that he went. He has eaten of the tree of knowledge, and the taste will be for ever in his mouth. He had thought he knew before, thought he had the sense of the degree in which it is his American fate to share the sanctity of his American consciousness, the intimacy of his American patriotism, with the inconceivable alien; but the truth had never come home to him with any such force. In the lurid light projected upon it by those courts of dismay it shakes him—or I like at least to imagine it shakes him—to the depths of his being; I like to think of him, I positively *have* to think of him, as going about ever afterwards with a new look, for those who can see it, in his face, the outward sign of the new chill in his heart. So is stamped, for detection, the questionably privileged person who has had an apparition, seen a ghost in his supposedly safe old house. Let not the unwary, therefore, visit Ellis Island.

The after-sense of that acute experience, however, I myself found, was by no means to be brushed away; I felt it grow and grow, on the contrary, wherever I turned: other impressions might come and go, but this affirmed claim of the alien, however immeasurably alien, to share in one's supreme relation was everywhere the fixed element, the reminder not to be dodged. One's supreme relation, as one had always put it, was one's relation to one's country—a conception made up so largely of one's countrymen and one's countrywomen. Thus it was as if, all the while, with such a fond tradition of what these products predominantly were, the idea of the country itself underwent something of that profane overhauling through which it appears to suffer the indignity of change. Is not our instinct in this matter, in general, essentially the safe one—that of keeping the idea simple and strong and continuous, so that it shall be perfectly sound? To touch it overmuch, to pull it about, is to put it in peril of weakening; yet on this free assault upon it, this readjustment of it in *their* monstrous, presumptuous interest, the aliens, in New York, seemed perpetually to insist. The combination there of their quantity and their quality—that loud primary stage of alienism which New York most offers to sight—operates, for the native, as their note of settled possession, something they have nobody to thank for; so that *un*settled possession is what we, on our side, seem reduced to—the implication of which, in its turn, is that, to recover confidence and regain lost ground, we, not they, must make the surrender and accept the orientation. We must go, in other words, *more* than half-way to meet them; which is all the difference, for us, between possession and dispossession. This sense of dispossession, to be brief about it, haunted me so, I was to feel, in the New York streets and in the packed trajectiles to which one clingingly appeals from the streets, just as one tumbles back into the streets in appalled reaction from *them,* that the art of beguiling or duping it became an art to be cultivated—though the fond alternative vision was never long to be obscured, the imagination, exasperated to envy, of the ideal, in the order in question; of the luxury of some such close and sweet and *whole* national consciousness as that of the Switzer and the Scot. . . .

New York really, I think, is all formidable foreground; or, if it be not, there is more than enough of this pressure of the present and the immediate to cut out the close sketcher's work for him. These things are a thick growth all round him, and when I recall the intensity of the material picture in the dense Yiddish quarter, for instance, I wonder at its not having forestalled, on my page, mere musings and, as they will doubtless be called, moonings. There abides with me, ineffaceably, the memory of a summer evening spent there by invitation of a high public functionary domiciled on the spot—to the extreme enhancement of the romantic interest his visitor found him foredoomed to inspire—who was to prove one of the most liberal of hosts and most luminous of guides. I can scarce help it if this brilliant personality, on that occasion the very medium itself through which the whole spectacle showed, so colours my impressions that if I speak, by intention, of the facts that played into them I may really but reflect the rich talk and the general privilege of the hour. That accident moreover must take its place simply as the highest value and the strongest note in the total show—so much did it testify to the quality of appealing, surrounding life. The sense of this quality was already strong in my drive, with a companion, through the long, warm June twilight, from a comparatively conventional neighbourhood; it was the sense, after all, of a great swarming, a swarming that had begun to thicken, infinitely, as soon as we had crossed to the East side and long before we had got to Rutgers Street. There is no swarming like that of Israel when once Israel has got a start, and the scene here bristled, at every step, with the signs and sounds, immitigable, unmistakable, of a Jewry that had burst all bounds. That it has burst all bounds in New York, almost any combination of figures or of objects taken at hazard sufficiently proclaims; but I remember how the rising waters, on this summer night, rose, to the imagination, even above the housetops and seemed to sound their murmur to the pale distant stars. It was as if we had been thus, in the crowded, hustled roadway, where multiplication, multiplication of everything, was the dominant note, at the bottom of some vast sallow aquarium in which innumerable fish, of overdeveloped proboscis, were to bump together, for ever, amid heaped spoils of the sea.

The children swarmed above all—here was multiplication with a vengeance; and the number of very old persons, of either sex, was almost equally remarkable; the very old persons being in equal vague occupation of the doorstep, pavement, curbstone, gutter, roadway, and every one alike using the street for overflow. As overflow, in the whole quarter, is the main fact of life—I was to learn later on that, with the exception of some shy corner of Asia, no district in the world known to the statistician has so many inhabitants to the yard—the scene hummed with the human presence beyond any I had ever faced in quest even of refreshment; producing part of the impression, moreover, no doubt, as a direct consequence of the intensity of the Jewish aspect. This, I think, makes the individual Jew more of a concentrated person, savingly possessed of everything that is in him, than any other human, noted at random—or is it simply, rather, that the unsurpassed strength of the race permits of the chopping into myriads of fine fragments without loss of race-quality? There are small strange animals, known to natural history, snakes or worms, I believe, who, when cut into pieces, wriggle away contentedly and live in the snippet as completely as in the whole. So the denizens of the New York Ghetto, heaped as thick as the splinters on the table of a glass-blower, had each, like the fine glass particle, his or her individual share of the whole hard glitter of Israel. This diffused intensity, as I have called it, causes any array of Jews to resemble (if I may be allowed another image) some long nocturnal street where every window in every house shows a maintained light. The advanced age of so many of the figures, the ubiquity of the children, carried out in fact this analogy; they were all there for race, and not, as it were, for reason: that excess of lurid meaning, in some of the old men's and old women's faces in particular, would have been absurd, in the conditions, as a really directed attention—it could only be the gathered past of Israel mechanically pushing through. The way, at the same time, this chapter of history did, all that evening, seem to push, was a matter that made the "ethnic" apparition again sit like a skeleton at the feast. It was fairly as if I could see the spectre grin while the talk of the hour gave me, across the board, facts and figures, chapter and verse, for the extent of the Hebrew conquest of New York. With a reverence for intellect, one should doubtless have drunk in tribute to an intellectual people; but I remember being at no time more conscious of that merely portentous element, in the aspects of American growth, which reduces to inanity any marked dismay quite as much as any high elation. The portent is one of too many—you always come back, as I have hinted, with your easier gasp, to *that:* it will be time enough to sigh or to shout when the relation of the particular appearance to all the other relations shall have cleared itself up. Phantasmagoric for me, accordingly, in a high degree, are the interesting hours I here glance at content to remain—setting in this respect, I recognize, an excellent example to all the rest of the New York phantasmagoria. Let me speak of the remainder only as phantasmagoric too, so that I may both the more kindly recall it and the sooner have done with it.

I have not done, however, with the impression of that large evening in the Ghetto; there was too much in the vision, and it has left too much the sense of a rare experience. For what did it all really come to but that one had seen with one's eyes the New Jerusalem on earth? What less than that could it all have been, in its far-spreading light and its celestial serenity of multiplication? There it was, there it is, and when I think of the dark, foul, stifling Ghettos of other remembered cities, I shall think by the same stroke of the city of redemption, and evoke in particular the rich Rutgers Street perspective—rich, so peculiarly, for the eye, in that complexity of fire-escapes with which each house-front bristles and which gives the whole vista so modernized and appointed a look. Omnipresent in the "poor" regions, this neat applied machinery has, for the stranger, a common side with the electric light and the telephone, suggests the distance achieved from the old Jerusalem. (These frontal iron ladders and platforms, by the way, so numerous throughout New York, strike more New York notes than can be parenthetically named—and among them perhaps most sharply the note of the ease with which, in the terrible town, on opportunity, "architecture" goes by the board; but the appearance to which they often most conduce is that of the spaciously organized cage for the nimbler class of animals in some great zoological garden. This general analogy is irresistible—it seems to offer, in each district, a little world of bars and perches and swings for human squirrels and monkeys. The very name of architecture perishes, for the fire-escapes look like abashed afterthoughts, staircases and communications forgotten in the construction; but the inhabitants lead, like the squirrels and monkeys, all the merrier life.) It was while I hung over the prospect from the windows of my friend, however, the presiding genius of the district, and it was while, at a later hour, I proceeded in his company, and in that of a trio of contributive fellow-pilgrims, from one "characteristic" place of public entertainment to another: it was during this rich climax, I say, that the city of redemption was least to be taken for anything less than it was. The windows, while we sat at meat, looked out on a swarming little square in which an ant-like population darted to and fro; the square consisted in part of a "district" public garden, or public lounge rather, one of those small backwaters or refuges, artfully economized for rest, here and there, in the very heart of the New York whirlpool, and which spoke louder than anything else of a Jerusalem disinfected. . . .

I must positively get into the gate of the Park, however—even at the risk of appearing to have marched round through Georgia to do so. I found myself, in May and June, getting into it whenever I could, and if I spoke just now of the loud and inexpensive charm (inexpensive in the æsthetic sense) of the precinct of approach to it, that must positively have been because the Park diffuses its grace. One grasped at every pretext for finding it inordinately amiable, and nothing was more noteworthy than that one felt, in doing so, how this was the only way to play the game in fairness. The perception comes quickly, in New York, of the singular and beautiful but almost crushing mission that has been laid, as an effect of time, upon this limited territory, which has risen to the occasion, from the first, so consistently and bravely. It is a case, distinctly, in which appreciation and gratitude for a public function admirably performed are twice the duty, on the visitor's part, that they may be in other such cases. We may even say, putting it simply and strongly, that if he doesn't here, in his thought, keep patting the Park on the back, he is guilty not alone of a failure of natural tenderness, but of a real deviation from social morality. For this mere narrow oblong, much *too* narrow and very much too short, had directly prescribed to it, from its origin, to "do," officially, on behalf of he City, the publicly amiable, and *all* the publicly amiable—all there could be any question of in the conditions: incurring thus a heavier charge, I respectfully submit, than one has ever before seen so gallantly carried. Such places, the municipally-instituted pleasure-grounds of the greater and the smaller cities, about the world and everywhere, no doubt, agreeably enough play their part; but is the part anywhere else as heroically played in proportion to the difficulty? The difficulty in New York, *that* is the point for the restless analyst; conscious as he is that other cities even in spite of themselves lighten the strain and beguile the task—a burden which here on the contrary makes every inch of its weight felt. This means a good deal, for the space comprised in the original New York scheme represents in truth a wonderful economy and intensity of effort. It would go hard with us not to satisfy ourselves, in other quarters (and it is of the political and commercial capitals we speak), of some such amount of "general" outside amenity, of charm in the town at large, as may here and there, even at widely-scattered points, relieve the o'erfraught heart. The sense of the picturesque often finds its account in strange and unlikely matters, but has none the less a way of finding it, and so, in the coming and going, takes the chance. But the New York problem has always resided in the absence of any chance to take, however one might come and go—come and go, that is, before reaching the Park.

To the Park, accordingly, and to the Park only, hitherto, the æsthetic appetite has had to address itself, and the place has therefore borne the brunt of many a preemptory call, acting out year after year the character of the cheerful, capable, bustling, even if overworked, hostess of the one inn, somewhere, who has to take all the travel, who is often at her wits' end to know how to deal with it, but who, none the less, has, for the honour of the house, never once failed of hospitality. That is how we see Central Park, utterly overdone by the "run" on its resources, yet also never having had to make an excuse. When once we have taken in thus its remarkable little history, there is no endearment of appreciation that we are not ready to lay, as a tribute, on its breast; with the interesting effect, besides, of our recognizing in this light how the place has had to be, in detail and feature, exactly what it is. It has had to have something for everybody, since everybody arrives famished; it has had to multiply itself to extravagance, to pathetic little efforts of exaggeration and deception, to be, breathlessly, everywhere and everything at once, and produce on the spot the particular romantic object demanded, lake or river or cataract, wild woodland or teeming garden, boundless vista or bosky nook, noble eminence or smiling valley. It has had to have feature at any price, the clamour of its customers being inevitably *for* feature; which accounts, as we forgivingly see, for the general rather eruptive and agitated effect, the effect of those old quaint prints which give in a single view the classic, gothic and other architectural wonders of the world. That is its sole defect—its being inevitably too self-conscious, being afraid to be just vague and frank and quiet. I should compare her again—and the property is proved by this instinctively feminine pronoun—to an actress in a company destitute, through an epidemic or some other stress, of all other feminine talent; so that she assumes on successive nights the most dissimilar parts and ranges in the course of a week from the tragedy queen to the singing chambermaid. That valour by itself wins the public and brings down the house —it being really a marvel that she should in no part fail of a hit. Which is what I mean, in short, by the sweet *ingratiation* of the Park. You are perfectly aware, as you hang about her in May and June, that you *have*, as a travelled person, beheld more remarkable scenery and communed with nature in ampler or fairer forms; but it is quite equally definite to you that none of those adventures have counted more to you for experience, for stirred sensibility —inasmuch as you can be, at the best, and in the showiest countries, only thrilled by the pastoral or the awful, and as to pass, in New York, from the discipline of the streets to this so different many-smiling presence is to be thrilled at every turn.

From Plunkitt of Tammany Hall, *William Riordon (1905)*

George Washington Plunkitt, known as the "sage of Tammany Hall," was born in a shantytown in New York City in 1842. During his career he was an alderman, a state senator, a Democratic district leader for the West Side of Manhattan, a "sachem" of the Tammany Society, and eventually the Father of the Council.

The Society of St. Tammany or Columbian Order was formed in New York in 1788 as an organization of craftsmen who supported the interests of the workingman. The society gained significant power, influence, and votes by helping immigrants, predominately from Ireland in the 1840s, find work and gain citizenship quickly. Mayor Fernando Wood and Boss William Tweed consolidated political power in the mid-nineteenth century but not without extraordinary graft and scandal. The Tweed Courthouse on Chambers Street was begun in 1858 for a projected $350,000 but was only nearing completion in 1870 at a cost of $13 million. One contractor alone was paid $5.5 million for window shades, carpets, and furniture. The scandal was the undoing of Tweed, who was indicted for grand larceny in 1871, escaped to Spain four years later only to be apprehended with the aid of political cartoons drawn by Thomas Nast, and, in 1878, died penniless in the Ludlow Street jail he had constructed.

In contrast, George Washington Plunkitt was a proponent of a more modest "honest graft," which he summed up in the phrase, "I seen my opportunities and I took 'em." He died a millionaire in 1924.

Honest Graft and Dishonest Graft

"EVERYBODY is talkin' these days about Tammany men growin' rich on graft, but nobody thinks of drawin' the distinction between honest graft and dishonest graft. There's all the difference in the world between the two. Yes, many of our men have grown rich in politics. I have myself. I've made a big fortune out of the game, and I'm gettin' richer every day, but I've not gone in for dishonest graft—blackmailin' gamblers, saloon-keepers, disorderly people, etc.—and neither has any of the men who have made big fortunes in politics.

"There's an honest graft, and I'm an example of how it works. I might sum up the whole thing by sayin': 'I seen my opportunities and I took 'em.'

"Just let me explain by examples. My party's in power in the city, and it's goin' to undertake a lot of public improvements. Well, I'm tipped off, say, that they're going to lay out a new park at a certain place.

"I see my opportunity and I take it. I go to that place and I buy up all the land I can in the neighborhood. Then the board of this or that makes its plan public, and there is a rush to get my land, which nobody cared particular for before.

"Ain't it perfectly honest to charge a good price and make a profit on my investment and foresight? Of course, it is. Well, that's honest graft.

"Or, supposin' it's a new bridge they're goin' to build. I get tipped off and I buy as much property as I can that has to be taken for approaches. I sell at my own price later on and drop some more money in the bank.

"Wouldn't you? It's just like lookin' ahead in Wall Street or in the coffee or cotton market. It's honest graft, and I'm lookin' for it every day in the year. I will tell you frankly that I've got a good lot of it, too.

"I'll tell you of one case. They were goin' to fix up a big park, no matter where. I got on to it, and went lookin' about for land in that neighborhood.

"I could get nothin' at a bargain but a big piece of swamp, but I took it fast enough and held on to it. What turned out was just what I counted on. They couldn't make the park complete without Plunkitt's swamp, and they had to pay a good price for it. Anything dishonest in that?

"Up in the watershed I made some money, too. I bought up several bits of land there some years ago and made a pretty good guess that they would be bought up for water purposes later by the city.

"Somehow, I always guessed about right, and shouldn't I enjoy the profit of my foresight? It was rather amusin' when the condemnation commissioners came along and found piece after piece of the land in the name of George Plunkitt of the Fifteenth Assembly District, New York City. They wondered how I knew just what to buy. The answer is—I seen my opportunity and I took it. I haven't confined myself to land; anything that pays is in my line.

"For instance, the city is repavin' a street and has several hundred thousand old granite blocks to sell. I am on hand to buy, and I know just what they are worth.

"How? Never mind that. I had a sort of monopoly of this business for a while, but once a newspaper tried to do me. It got some outside men to come over from Brooklyn and New Jersey to bid against me.

"Was I done? Not much. I went to each of the men and said: 'How many of these 250,000 stones do you want?' One said 20,000, and another wanted 15,000, and another wanted 10,000. I said: 'All right, let me bid for the lot, and I'll give each of you all you want for nothin'.'

"They agreed, of course. Then the auctioneer yelled: 'How much am I bid for these 250,000 fine pavin' stones?'

"'Two dollars and fifty cents,' says I.

"'Two dollars and fifty cents!' screamed the auctioneer. 'Oh, that's a joke! Give me a real bid.'

"He found the bid was real enough. My rivals stood silent. I got the lot for $2.50 and gave them their share. That's how the attempt to do Plunkitt ended, and that's how all such attempts end.

"I've told you how I got rich by honest graft. Now, let me tell you that most politicians who are accused of robbin' the city get rich the same way.

"They didn't steal a dollar from the city treasury. They just seen their opportunities and took them. That is why, when a reform administration comes in and spends a half million dollars in tryin' to find the public robberies they talked about in the campaign, they don't find them.

"The books are always all right. The money in the city treasury is all right. Everything is all right. All they can show is that the Tammany heads of departments looked after their friends, within the law, and gave them what opportunities they could to make honest graft. Now, let me tell you that's never goin' to hurt Tammany with the people. Every good man looks after his friends, and any man who doesn't isn't likely to be popular. If I have a good thing to hand out in private life, I give it to a friend. Why shouldn't I do the same in public life?

"Another kind of honest graft. Tammany has raised a good many salaries. There was an awful howl by the reformers, but don't you know that Tammany gains ten votes for every one it lost by salary raisin'?

"The Wall Street banker thinks it shameful to raise a department clerk's salary from $1500 to $1800 a year, but every man who draws a salary himself says: 'That's all right. I wish it was me.' And he feels very much like votin' the Tammany ticket on election day, just out of sympathy.

"Tammany was beat in 1901 because the people were deceived into believin' that it worked dishonest graft. They didn't draw a distinction between dishonest and honest graft, but they saw that some Tammany men grew rich, and supposed they had been robbin' the city treasury or levyin' blackmail on disorderly houses, or workin' in with the gamblers and lawbreakers.

"As a matter of policy, if nothing else, why should the Tammany leaders go into such dirty business, when there is so much honest graft lyin' around when they are in power? Did you ever consider that?

"Now, in conclusion, I want to say that I don't own a dishonest dollar. If my worst enemy was given the job of writin' my epitaph when I'm gone, he couldn't do more than write:

"'George W. Plunkitt. He Seen His Opportunities, and He Took 'Em.'". . .

Reformers Only Mornin' Glories

"College professors and philosophers who go up in a balloon to think are always discussin' the question: 'Why Reform Administrations Never Succeed Themselves!' The reason is plain to anybody who has learned the a, b, c of politics.

"I can't tell just how many of these movements I've seen started in New York during my forty years in politics, but I can tell you how many have lasted more than a few years—none. There have been reform committees of fifty, of sixty, of seventy, of one hundred, and all sorts of numbers that started out to do up the regular political organizations. They were mornin' glories—looked lovely in the mornin' and withered up in a short time, while the regular machines went on flourishin' forever, like fine old oaks. Say, that's the first poetry I ever worked off. Ain't it great?

"Just look back a few years. You remember the People's Municipal League that nominated Frank Scott for mayor in 1890? Do you remember the reformers that got up that league? Have you ever heard of them since? I haven't. Scott himself survived because he had always been a first-rate politician, but you'd have to look in the newspaper almanacs of 1891 to find out who made up the People's Municipal League. Oh, yes! I remember one name—Ollie Teall; dear, pretty Ollie and his big dog. They're about all that's left of the League.

"Now take the reform movement of 1894. A lot of good politicians joined in that—the Republicans, the State Democrats, the Stecklerites, and the O'Brienites, and they gave us a lickin', but the real reform part of the affair, the Committee of Seventy that started the thing goin', what's become of those reformers? What's become of Charles Stewart Smith? Where's Bangs? Do you ever hear of Cornell, the iron man, in politics now? Could a search party find R. W. G. Welling? Have you seen the name of Fulton McMahon or McMahon Fulton—I ain't sure which—in the papers lately? Or Preble Tucker? Or—but it's no use to go through the list of the reformers who said they sounded in the death knell of Tammany in 1894. They're gone for good, and Tammany's pretty well, thank you. They did the talkin' and posin', and the politicians in the movement got all the plums. It's always the case.

"The Citizens' Union has lasted a little bit longer than the reform crowd that went before them, but that's because they learned a thing or two from us. They learned how to put up a pretty good bluff—and bluff counts a lot in politics. With only a few thousand members, they had the nerve to run the whole Fusion movement, make the Republicans and other organizations come to their headquarters to select a ticket and dictate what every candidate must do or not do. I love nerve, and I've had a sort of respect for the Citizens' Union lately, but the Union can't last. Its people haven't been trained to politics, and whenever Tammany calls their bluff they lay right down. You'll never hear of the Union again after a year or two.

"And, by the way, what's become of the good government clubs, the political nurseries of a few years ago? Do you ever hear of Good Government Club D and P and Q and Z any more? What's become of the infants who were to grow up and show us how to govern the city? I know what's become of the nursery that was started in my district. You can find pretty much the whole outfit over in my headquarters, Washington Hall.

"The fact is that a reformer can't last in politics. He can make a show for a while, but he always comes down like a rocket. Politics is as much a regular business as the grocery or the dry-goods or the drug business. You've got to be trained up to it or you're sure to fall. Suppose a man who knew nothing about the grocery trade suddenly went into the business and tried to conduct it according to his own ideas. Wouldn't he make a mess of it? He might make a splurge for a while, as long as his money lasted, but his store would soon be empty. It's just the same with a reformer. He hasn't been brought up in the difficult business of politics and he makes a mess of it every time.

"I've been studyin' the political game for forty-five years, and I don't know it all yet. I'm learnin' somethin' all the time. How, then, can you expect what they call 'business men' to turn into politics all at once and make a success of it? It is just as if I went up to Columbia University and started to teach Greek. They usually last about as long in politics as I would last at Columbia.

"You can't begin too early in politics if you want to succeed at the game. I began several years before I could vote, and so did every successful leader in Tammany Hall. When I was twelve years old I made myself useful around the district headquarters and did work at all the polls on election day. Later on, I hustled about gettin' out voters who had jags on or who were too lazy to come to the polls. There's a hundred ways that boys can help, and they get an experience that's the first real step in statesmanship. Show me a boy that hustles for the organization on election day, and I'll show you a comin' statesman.

"That's the a b c of politics. It ain't easy work to get up to y and z. You have to give nearly all your time and attention to it. Of course, you may have some business or occupation on the side, but the great business of your life must be politics if you want to succeed in it. A few years ago Tammany tried to mix politics and business in equal quantities, by havin' two leaders for each district, a politician and a business man. They wouldn't mix. They were like oil and water. The politician looked after the politics of his district; the business man looked after his grocery store or his milk route, and whenever he appeared at an executive meeting, it was only to make trouble. The whole scheme turned out to be a farce and was abandoned mighty quick.

"Do you understand now, why it is that a reformer goes down and out in the first or second round, while a politician answers to the gong every time? It is because the one has gone into the fight without trainin', while the other trains all the time and knows every fine point of the game."...

On "The Shame of the Cities"

"I've been readin' a book by Lincoln Steffens on 'The Shame of the Cities.' Steffens means well but, like all reformers, he don't know how to make distinctions. He can't see no difference between honest graft and dishonest graft and, consequent, he gets things all mixed up. There's the biggest kind of a difference between political looters and politicians who make a fortune out of politics by keepin' their eyes wide open. The looter goes in for himself alone without considerin' his organization or his city. The politician looks after his own interests, the organization's interests, and the city's interests all at the same time. See the distinction? For instance, I ain't no looter. The looter hogs it. I never hogged. I made my pile in politics, but, at the same time, I served the organization and got more big improvements for New York City than any other livin' man. And I never monkeyed with the penal code.

"The difference between a looter and a practical politician is the difference between the Philadelphia Republican gang and Tammany Hall. Steffens seems to think they're both about the same; but he's all wrong. The Philadelphia crowd runs up against the penal code. Tammany don't. The Philadelphians ain't satisfied with robbin' the bank of all its gold and paper money. They stay to pick up the nickels and pennies and the cop comes and nabs them. Tammany ain't no such fool. Why, I remember, about fifteen or twenty years ago, a Republican superintendent of the Philadelphia almshouse stole the zinc roof off the buildin' and sold it for junk. That was carryin' things to excess. There's a limit to everything, and the Philadelphia Republicans go beyond the limit. It seems like they can't be cool and moderate like real politicians. It ain't fair, therefore, to class Tammany men with the Philadelphia gang. Any man who undertakes to write political books should never for a moment lose sight of the distinction between honest graft and dishonest graft, which I explained in full in another talk. If he puts all kinds of graft on the same level, he'll make the fatal mistake that Steffens made and spoil his book.

"A big city like New York or Philadelphia or Chicago might be compared to a sort of Garden of Eden, from a political point of view. It's an orchard full of beautiful apple-trees. One of them has got a big sign on it, marked: 'Penal Code Tree-Poison.' The other trees have lots of apples on them for all. Yet, the fools go to the Penal Code Tree. Why? For the reason, I guess, that a cranky child refuses to eat good food and chews up a box of matches with relish. I never had any temptation to touch the Penal Code Tree. The other apples are good enough for me, and O Lord! how many of them there are in a big city!

"Steffens made one good point in his book. He said he found that Philadelphia, ruled almost entirely by Americans, was more corrupt than New York, where the Irish do almost all the governin'. I could have told him that before he did any investigatin' if he had come to me. The Irish was born to rule, and they're the honestest people in the world. Show me the Irishman who would steal a roof off an almshouse! He don't exist. Of course, if an Irishman had the political pull and the roof was much worn, he might get the city authorities to put on a new one and get the contract for it himself, and buy the old roof at a bargain—but that's honest graft. It's goin' about the thing like a gentleman—and there's more money in it than in tearin' down an old roof and cartin' it to the junkman's—more money and no penal code.

"One reason why the Irishman is more honest in politics than many Sons of the Revolution is that he is grateful to the country and the city that gave him protection and prosperity when he was driven by oppression from the Emerald Isle. Say, that sentence is fine, ain't it? I'm goin' to get some literary feller to work it over into poetry for next St. Patrick's Day dinner.

"Yes, the Irishman is grateful. His one thought is to serve the city which gave him a home. He has this thought even before he lands in New York, for his friends here often have a good place in one of the city departments picked out for him while he is still in the old country. Is it any wonder that he has a tender spot in his heart for old New York when he is on its salary list the mornin' after he lands?

"Now, a few words on the general subject of the so-called shame of cities. I don't believe that the government of our cities is any worse, in proportion to opportunities, than it was fifty years ago. I'll explain what I mean by 'in proportion to opportunities.' A half a century ago, our cities were small and poor. There wasn't many temptations lyin' around for politicians. There was hardly anything to steal, and hardly any opportunities for even honest graft. A city could count its money every night before goin' to bed, and if three cents was missin', all the fire-bells would be rung. What credit was there in bein' honest under them circumstances? It makes me tired to hear of old codgers back in the thirties or forties boastin' that they retired from politics without a dollar except what they earned in their profession or business. If they lived to-day, with all the existin' opportunities, they would be just the same as twentieth century politicians. There ain't any more honest people in the world just now than the convicts in Sing Sing. Not one of them steals anything. Why? Because they can't. See the application?

"Understand, I ain't defendin' politicians of to-day who steal. The politician who steals is worse than a thief. He is a fool. With the grand opportunities all around for the man with a political pull, there's no excuse for stealin' a cent. The point I want to make is that if there is some stealin' in politics, it don't mean that the politicians of 1905 are, as a class, worse than them of 1835. It just means that the old-timers had nothin' to steal, while the politicians now are surrounded by all kinds of temptations and some of them naturally—the fool ones—buck up against the penal code."

Selected Writings of O. Henry (William Sydney Porter) (1862–1910)

Like many other writers, O. Henry (the pen name for William Sydney Porter) came to New York City because he wanted to start a new life and because he was convinced that all the "good magazines" were published there. But, unlike most migrants, when he took the ferry over from New Jersey in the first week of April in 1902, he was coming from three years in prison in Ohio after being convicted of embezzling funds from the First National Bank of Austin, Texas.

While in prison, O. Henry had already begun writing stories and selling them to editors in New York. He was immediately given at job at *Ainslees* magazine, and in less than a year he was writing a story a week for the *New York Sunday World,* while also publishing in other magazines. He became one of the most popular authors of his day, and at one point he was in thirty-four different Sunday supplements across the country.

O. Henry's beloved New York, what he called "Little Old Bagdad on the Subway," was populated by characters from all walks of life, and his second volume of stories, entitled *The Four Million* (1906), was a dig at Lady Caroline Astor's formation of the "four hundred" people in Gotham she thought were worthy dinner companions. A raging alcoholic, who lived primarily in hotels like the Chelsea on Twenty-third Street, he died in the Caledonia Hotel on Twenty-sixth Street in 1910 with nine empty liquor bottles under his bed.

The Duel (1910)

THE gods, lying beside their nectar on 'Lympus and peeping over the edge of the cliff, perceive a difference in cities. Although it would seem that to their vision towns must appear as large or small ant-hills without special characteristics, yet it is not so. Studying the habits of ants from so great a height should be but a mild diversion when coupled with the soft drink that mythology tells us is their only solace. But doubtless they have amused themselves by the comparison of villages and towns; and it will be no news to them (nor, perhaps, to many mortals), that in one particularity New York stands unique among the cities of the world. This shall be the theme of a little story addressed to the man who sits smoking with his Sabbath—slippered feet on another chair, and to the woman who snatches the paper for a moment while boiling greens or a narcotized baby leaves her free. With these I love to sit upon the ground and tell sad stories of the death of Kings.

New York City is inhabited by 4,000,000 mysterious strangers; thus beating Bird Centre by three millions and half a dozen nine's. They came here in various ways and for many reasons—Hendrik Hudson, the art schools, green goods, the stork, the annual dressmakers' convention, the Pennsylvania Railroad, love of money, the stage, cheap excursion rates, brains, personal column ads., heavy walking shoes, ambition, freight trains—all these have had a hand in making up the population.

But every man Jack when he first sets foot on the stones of Manhattan has got to fight. He has got to fight at once until either he or his adversary wins. There is no resting between rounds, for there are no rounds. It is slugging from the first. It is a fight to a finish.

Your opponent is the City. You must do battle with it from the time the ferry-boat lands you on the island until either it is yours or it has conquered you. It is the same whether you have a million in your pocket or only the price of a week's lodging.

The battle is to decide whether you shall become a New Yorker or turn the rankest outlander and Philistine. You must be one or the other. You cannot remain neutral. You must be for or against—lover or enemy—bosom friend or outcast. And, oh, the city is a general in the ring. Not only by blows does it seek to subdue you. It woos you to its heart with the subtlety of a siren. It is a combination of Delilah, green Chartreuse, Beethoven, chloral and John L. in his best days.

In other cities you may wander and abide as a stranger man as long as you please. You may live in Chicago until your hair whitens, and be a citizen and still prate of beans if Boston mothered you, and without rebuke. You may become a civic pillar in any other town but Knickerbocker's, and all the time publicly sneering at its buildings, comparing them with the architecture of Colonel Telfair's residence in Jackson, Miss., whence you hail, and you will not be set upon. But in New York you must be either a New Yorker or an invader of a modern Troy, concealed in the wooden horse of your conceited provincialism. And this dreary preamble is only to introduce to you the unimportant figures of William and Jack.

They came out of the West together, where they had been friends. They came to dig their fortunes out of the big city.

Father Knickerbocker met them at the ferry, giving one a right-hander on the nose and the other an uppercut with his left, just to let them know that the fight was on.

William was for business; Jack was for Art. Both were young and ambitious; so they countered and clinched. I think they were from Nebraska or possibly Missouri or Minnesota. Anyhow, they were out for success and scraps and scads, and they tackled the city like two Lockinvars with brass knucks and a pull at the City Hall.

Four years afterward William and Jack met at luncheon. The business man blew in like a March wind, hurled his silk hat at a waiter, dropped into the chair that was pushed under him, seized the bill of fare, and had ordered as far as cheese before the artist had time to do more than nod. After the nod a humorous smile came into his eyes.

"Billy," he said, "you're done for. The city has gobbled you up. It has taken you and cut you to its pattern and stamped you with its brand. You are so nearly like ten thousand men I have seen to-day that you couldn't be picked out from them if it weren't for your laundry marks."

"Camembert," finished William. "What's that? Oh, you've still got your hammer out for New York, have you? Well, little old Noisyville-on-the-Subway is good enough for me. It's giving me mine. And, say, I used to think the West was the whole round world—only slightly flattened at the poles whenever Bryan ran. I used to yell myself hoarse about the free expanse, and hang my hat on the horizon, and say cutting things in the grocery to little soap drummers from the East. But I'd never seen New York, then, Jack. Me for it from the rathskellers up. Sixth Avenue is the West to me now. Have you heard this fellow Crusoe sing? The desert isle for him, I say, but my wife made me go. Give me May Irwin or E. S. Willard any time."

"Poor Billy," said the artist, delicately fingering a cigarette. "You remember, when we were on our way to the East, how we talked about this great, wonderful city, and how we meant to conquer it and never let it get the best of us? We were going to be just the same fellows we had always been, and never let it master us. It has downed you, old man. You have changed from a maverick into a butterick."

"Don't see exactly what you are driving at," said William. "I don't wear an alpaca coat with blue trousers and a seersucker vest on dress occasions, like I used to do at home. You talk about being cut to a pattern—well, ain't the pattern all right? When you're in Rome you've got to do as the Dagoes do. This town seems to me to have other alleged metropolises skinned to flag stations. According to the railroad schedule I've got in my mind, Chicago and Saint Jo and Paris, France, are asterisk stops—which means you wave a red flag and get on every other Tuesday. I like this little suburb of Tarrytown-on-the Hudson. There's something or somebody doing all the time. I'm clearing $8,000 a year selling automatic pumps, and I'm living like kings-up. Why, yesterday, I was introduced to John W. Gates. I took an auto ride with a wine agent's sister. I saw two men run over by a street car, and I seen Edna May play in the evening. Talk about the West, why, the other night I woke everybody up in the hotel hollering. I dreamed I was walking on a board sidewalk in Oshkosh. What have you got against this town, Jack? There's only one thing in it that I don't care for, and that's a ferry-boat."

The artist gazed dreamily at the cartridge paper on the wall. "This town;" said he, "is a leech. It drains the blood of the country. Whoever comes to it accepts a challenge to a duel. Abandoning the figure of the leech, it is a juggernaut, a Moloch, a monster to which the innocence, the genius, and the beauty of the land must pay tribute. Hand to hand every newcomer must struggle with the leviathan. You've lost, Billy. It shall never conquer me. I hate it as one hates sin or pestilence or—the color work in a ten-cent magazine. I despise its very vastness and power. It has the poorest millionaires, the littlest great men, the haughtiest beggars, the plainest beauties, the lowest skyscrapers, the dolefulest pleasures of any town I ever saw. It has caught you, old man, but I will never run beside its chariot wheels. It glosses itself as the Chinaman glosses his collars. Give me the domestic finish. I could stand a town ruled by wealth or one ruled by an aristocracy; but this is one controlled by its lowest ingredients. Claiming culture, it is the crudest; asseverating its preeminence, it is the basest; denying all outside values and virtue, it is the narrowest. Give me the pure air and the open heart of the West country. I would go back there to-morrow if I could."

"Don't you like this *filet mignon?*"said William. "Shucks, now, what's the use to knock the town! It's the greatest ever. I couldn't sell one automatic pump between Harrisburg and Tommy O'Keefe's saloon, in Sacramento, where I sell twenty here. And have you seen Sara Bernhardt in 'Andrew Mack' yet?"

"The town's got you, Billy," said Jack.

"All right," said William. "I'm going to buy a cottage on Lake Ronkonkoma next summer."

At midnight Jack raised his window and sat close to it. He caught his breath at what he saw, though he had seen and felt it a hundred times.

Far below and around lay the city like a ragged purple dream. The irregular houses were like the broken exteriors of cliffs lining deep gulches and winding streams. Some were mountainous; some lay in long, monotonous rows like the basalt precipices hanging over desert canons. Such was the background of the wonderful, cruel, enchanting, bewildering, fatal, great city. But into this background were cut myriads of brilliant parallelograms and circles and squares through which glowed many colored lights. And out of the violet and purple depths ascended like the city's soul sounds and odors and thrills that make up the civic body. There arose the breath of gaiety unrestrained, of love, of hate, of all the passions that man can know. There below him lay all things, good or bad, that can be brought from the four corners of the earth to instruct, please, thrill, enrich, despoil, elevate, cast down, nurture or kill. Thus the flavor of it came up to him and went into his blood.

There was a knock on his door. A telegram had come for him. It came from the West, and these were its words:

"Come back home and the answer will be yes.

"Dolly."

He kept the boy waiting ten minutes, and then wrote the reply: "Impossible to leave here at present." Then he sat at the window again and let the city put its cup of mandragora to his lips again.

After all it isn't a story; but I wanted to know which one of the heroes won the battle against the city. So I went to a very learned friend and laid the case before him. What he said was: "Please don't bother me; I have Christmas presents to buy."

So there it rests; and you will have to decide for yourself.

The Cop and the Anthem (1904)

On his bench in Madison Square Soapy moved uneasily. When wild geese honk high of nights, and when women without sealskin coats grow kind to their husbands, and when Soapy moves uneasily on his bench in the park, you may know that winter is near at hand.

A dead leaf fell in Soapy's lap. That was Jack Frost's card. Jack is kind to the regular denizens of Madison Square, and gives fair warning of his annual call. At the corners of four streets he hands his pasteboard to the North Wind, footman of the mansion of All Outdoors, so that the inhabitants thereof may make ready.

Soapy's mind became cognizant of the fact that the time had come for him to resolve himself into a singular Committee of Ways and Means to provide against the coming rigor. And therefore he moved uneasily on his bench.

The hibernatorial ambitions of Soapy were not of the highest. In them were no considerations of Mediterranean cruises, of soporific Southern skies or drifting in the Vesuvian Bay. Three months on the Island was what his soul craved. Three months of assured board and bed and congenial company, safe from Boreas and bluecoats, seemed to Soapy the essence of things desirable.

For years the hospitable Blackwell's had been his winter quarters. Just as his more fortunate fellow New Yorkers had bought their tickets to Palm Beach and the Riviera each winter, so Soapy had made his humble arrangements for his annual hegira to the Island. And now the time was come. On the previous night three Sabbath newspapers, distributed beneath his coat, about his ankles and over his lap, had failed to repulse the cold as he slept on his bench near the spurting fountain in the ancient square. So the Island loomed big and timely in Soapy's mind. He scorned the provisions made in the name of charity for the city's dependents. In Soapy's opinion the Law was more benign than Philanthropy. There was an endless round of institutions, municipal and eleemosynary, on which he might set out and receive lodging and food accordant with the simple life. But to one of Soapy's proud spirit the gifts of charity are encumbered. If not in coin you must pay in humiliation of spirit for every benefit received at the hands of philanthropy. As Caesar had his Brutus, every bed of charity must have its toll of a bath, every loaf of bread its compensation of a private and personal inquisition. Wherefore it is better to be a guest of the law, which, though conducted by rules, does not meddle unduly with a gentleman's private affairs.

Soapy, having decided to go to the Island, at once set about accomplishing his desire. There were many easy ways of doing this. The pleasantest was to dine luxuriously at some expensive restaurant; and then, after declaring insolvency, be handed over quietly and without uproar to a policeman. An accommodating magistrate would do the rest. Soapy left his bench and strolled out of the square and across the level sea of asphalt, where Broadway and Fifth Avenue flow together. Up Broadway he turned, and halted at a glittering café, where are gathered together nightly the choicest products of the grape, the silkworm and the protoplasm.

Soapy had confidence in himself from the lowest button of his vest upward. He was shaven, and his coat was decent and his neat black, ready tied four-in-hand had been presented to him by a lady missionary on Thanksgiving Day. If he could reach a table in the restaurant unsuspected success would be his. The portion of him that would show above the table would raise no doubt in the waiter's mind. A roasted mallard duck, thought Soapy, would be about the thing—with a bottle of Chablis, and then Camembert, a demitasse and a cigar. One dollar for the cigar would be enough. The total would not be so high as to call forth any supreme manifestation of revenge from the café management; and yet the meat would leave him filled and happy for the journey to his winter refuge.

But as Soapy set foot inside the restaurant door the headwaiter's eye fell upon his frayed trousers and decadent shoes. Strong and ready hands turned him about and conveyed him in silence and haste to the sidewalk and averted the ignoble fate of the menaced mallard.

Soapy turned off Broadway. It seemed that his route to the coveted Island was not to be an epicurean one. Some other way of entering limbo must be thought of.

At a corner of Sixth Avenue electric lights and cunningly displayed wares behind plate glass made a shopwindow conspicuous. Soapy took a cobblestone and dashed it through the glass. People came running around the corner, a policeman in the lead. Soapy stood still, with his hands in his pockets, and smiled at the sight of brass buttons.

"Where's the man that done that?" inquired the officer, excitedly.

"Don't you figure out that I might have had something to do with it?" said Soapy, not without sarcasm, but friendly, as one greets good fortune.

The policeman's mind refused to accept Soapy even as a clue. Men who smash windows do not remain to parley with the law's minions. They take to their heels. The policeman saw a man halfway down the block running to catch a car. With drawn club he joined in the pursuit. Soapy, with disgust in his heart, loafed along, twice unsuccessful.

On the opposite side of the street was a restaurant of no great pretensions. It catered to large appetites and modest purses. Its crockery and atmosphere were thick; its soup and napery thin. Into this place Soapy took his accusive shoes and telltale trousers without challenge. At a table he sat and consumed beefsteak, flapjacks, doughnuts and pie. And then to the waiter he betrayed the fact that the minutest coin and himself were strangers.

"Now, get busy and call a cop," said Soapy. "And don't keep a gentleman waiting."

"No cop for youse," said the waiter, with a voice like butter cakes and an eye like the cherry in a Manhattan cocktail. "Hey, Con!"

Neatly upon his left ear on the callous pavement two waiters pitched Soapy. He arose joint by joint, as a carpenter's rule opens, and beat the dust from his clothes. Arrest seemed but a rosy dream. The Island seemed very far away. A policeman who stood before a drugstore two doors away laughed and walked down the street.

Five blocks Soapy traveled before his courage permitted him to woo capture again. This time the opportunity presented what he fatuously termed to himself a "cinch." A young woman of a modest and pleasing guise was standing before a show window gazing with sprightly interest at its display of shaving mugs and inkstands, and two yards from the window a large policeman of severe demeanor leaned against a water plug.

It was Soapy's design to assume the role of the despicable and execrated "masher." The refined and elegant appearance of his victim and the contiguity of the conscientious cop encouraged him to believe that he would soon feel the pleasant official clutch upon his arm that would ensure his winter quarters on the right little, tight little isle.

Soapy straightened the lady missionary's ready-made tie, dragged his shrinking cuffs into the open, set his hat at a killing cant and sidled toward the young woman. He made eyes at her, was taken with sudden coughs and "hems," smiled, smirked and went brazenly through the impudent and contemptible litany of the "masher." With half an eye Soapy saw that the policeman was watching him fixedly. The young woman moved away a few steps, and again bestowed her absorbed attention upon the shaving mugs. Soapy followed, boldly stepping to her side, raised his hat and said:

"Ah there, Bedelia! Don't you want to come and play in my yard?"

The policeman was still looking. The persecuted young woman had but to beckon a finger and Soapy would be practically en route for his insular haven. Already he imagined he could feel the cozy warmth of the station house. The young woman faced him and, stretching out a hand, caught Soapy's coat sleeve.

"Sure, Mike," she said, joyfully, "if you'll blow me to a pail of suds. I'd have spoke to you sooner, but the cop was watching."

With the young woman playing the clinging ivy to his oak Soapy walked past the policeman overcome with gloom. He seemed doomed to liberty.

At the next corner he shook off his companion and ran. He halted in the district where by night are found the lightest streets, hearts, vows and librettos. Women in furs and men in greatcoats moved gaily in the wintry air. A sudden fear seized Soapy that some dreadful enchantment had rendered him immune to arrest. The thought brought a little of panic upon it, and when he came upon another policeman lounging grandly in front of a transplendent theater he caught at the immediate straw of "disorderly conduct."

On the sidewalk Soapy began to yell drunken gibberish at the top of his harsh voice. He danced, howled, raved, and otherwise disturbed the welkin. The policeman twirled his club, turned his back to Soapy and remarked to a citizen: "'Tis one of them Yale lads celebratin' the goose egg they give to the Hartford College. Noisy; but no harm. We've instructions to lave them be."

Disconsolate, Soapy ceased his unavailing racket. Would never a policeman lay hands on him? In his fancy the Island seemed an unattainable Arcadia. He buttoned his thin coat against the chilling wind.

In a cigar store he saw a well-dressed man lighting a cigar at a swinging light. His silk umbrella he had set by the door on entering. Soapy stepped inside, secured the umbrella and sauntered off with it slowly. The man at the cigar light followed hastily.

"My umbrella," he said, sternly.

"Oh, is it?" sneered Soapy, adding insult to petit larceny. "Well, why don't you call a policeman? I took it. Your umbrella! Why don't you call a cop? There stands one on the corner."

The umbrella owner slowed his steps. Soapy did likewise, with a presentiment that luck would again run against him. The policeman looked at the two curiously.

"Of course," said the umbrella man—"that is—well, you know how these mistakes occur—I—if it's your umbrella I hope you'll excuse me—I picked it up this morning in a restaurant—If you recognize it as yours, why—I hope you'll—"

"Of course it's mine," said Soapy, viciously.

The ex-umbrella man retreated. The policeman hurried to assist a tall blonde in an opera cloak across the street in front of a streetcar that was approaching two blocks away.

Soapy walked eastward through a street damaged by improvements. He hurled the umbrella wrathfully into an excavation. He muttered against the men who wear helmets and carry clubs. Because he wanted to fall into their clutches, they seemed to regard him as a king who could do no wrong.

At length Soapy reached one of the avenues to the east where the glitter and turmoil was but faint. He set his face down this toward Madison Square, for the homing instinct survives even when the home is a park bench.

But on an unusually quiet corner Soapy came to a standstill. Here was an old church, quaint and rambling and gabled. Through one violet-stained window a soft light glowed, where, no doubt, the organist loitered over the keys, making sure of his mastery of the coming Sabbath anthem. For there drifted out to Soapy's ears sweet music that caught and held him transfixed against the convolutions of the iron fence.

The moon was above, lustrous and serene; vehicles and pedestrians were few; sparrows twittered sleepily in the eaves—for a little while the scene might have been a country churchyard. And the anthem that the organist played cemented Soapy to the iron fence, for he had known it well in the days when his life contained such things as mothers and roses and ambitions and friends and immaculate thoughts and collars.

The conjunction of Soapy's receptive state of mind and the influences about the old church wrought a sudden and wonderful change in his soul. He viewed with swift horror the pit into which he had tumbled, the degraded days, unworthy desires, dead hopes, wrecked faculties and base motives that made up his existence.

And also in a moment his heart responded thrillingly to this novel mood. An instantaneous and strong impulse moved him to battle with his desperate fate. He would pull himself out of the mire; he would make a man of himself again; he would conquer the evil that had taken possession of him. There was time; he was comparatively young yet: he would resurrect his old eager ambitions and pursue them without faltering. Those solemn but sweet organ notes had set up a revolution in him. Tomorrow he would go into the roaring downtown district and find work. A fur importer had once offered him a place as driver. He would find him tomorrow and ask for the position. He would be somebody in the world. He would—

Soapy felt a hand laid on his arm. He looked quickly around into the broad face of a policeman.

"What are you doin' here?" asked the officer.

"Nothin'," said Soapy.

"Then come along," said the policeman.

"Three months on the Island," said the Magistrate in the Police Court the next morning.

The Spirit of the Girl Strikers, from The Outlook, *Miriam Finn Scott (1910)*

By 1909, more than a quarter of a million garment workers in New York City produced almost two thirds of the clothing in the entire United States. Sanitary and safety conditions in the sweatshops that produced that clothing, however, led Frances Perkins (at that time a member of the Consumers' League and later the executive secretary of the New York Commission on Safety) to dub them "fire and death traps."

On November 23, 1910, upwards of twenty thousand garment workers, inspired by a mass meeting in the Great Hall of Cooper Union at Astor Place the night before, joined the Ladies' Garment Workers Union in a general strike. Starting in December, however, they were supported both physically and financially by upper-class women like Anne Morgan (J. P. Morgan's daughter) and Miriam Finn Scott through the auspices of the Women's Trade Union League. Though the strike had ended by the last week of February, it set a precedent for the workers' ability to strike, and it united wealthy reformers and working-class union organizers for the first time.

THE "Grand American Palace" was packed with a strangely unaccustomed crowd. Every night "Professor" Somebody's orchestra (the "professor" and two pasty-faced helpers) dispensed music from the little platform in the corner, and some scores of work-worn immigrant boys and girls, at so much per head, struggled and giggled through the waltz and the two-step. But now, instead of these weary revelers, from gaudy wall to gaudy wall were jammed girls with determined, workaday faces. Strikers they were—a group of shirt-waist makers, whose strike in New York has been the biggest and most bitter strike of women in the history of American labor troubles.

And the faces of this group were fixed on the "Professor's" stage, and on that stage stood a slight, pale girl of perhaps nineteen, her dark eyes flashing.

"Girls, from the bottom of my heart," she cried, "I beg you not to go back to work. We are all poor, many of us are suffering hunger, none of us can afford to lose a day's wages. But only by fighting for our rights, and fighting all together, can we better our miseries; and so let us fight for them to the end!"

The strikers applauded long, and in scores of other East Side dance-halls at the time when the strike was at its height and forty thousand girls were out, just so at this same hour were other speakers applauded by other groups; and by meetings such as this was the spirit kept in the girls for their remarkable fight. When the girl left the platform, I edged my way to her and asked her for her story. She had come from Russia, she told me—come with her parents, who had found life in the land of the Czar no longer endurable.

"Close your eyes and point to any girl in this hall," said the little shirt-waist maker, "and my story will be her story. We are all the same. Why do we strike? I will tell you where we work, how we work; from that perhaps you will understand. My shop is a long and narrow loft on the fifth floor of the building, with the ceiling almost on our heads. In it one hundred electric-power machines are so closely packed together that, unless I am always on the lookout, my clothes or hair or hand is likely to catch in one of the whizzing machines. In the shop it is always night. The windows are only on the narrow ends of the room, so even the few girls who sit near them sew by gas-light most of the time, for the panes are so dirty the weak daylight hardly goes through them. The shop is swept only once a week; the air is so close that sometimes you can hardly breathe. In this place I work from eight to six o'clock six days in the week in the ordinary season; and in the busy season, when we are compelled to work nights and Sundays, I put in what equals eight work-days in the week. Thirty minutes is allowed for lunch, which I must eat in the dressing-room four flights above the shop, on the ninth floor. These stairs I must always climb; the elevator, the boss says, is not for the shop girls.

"I began as a shirt-waist maker in this shop five years ago. For the first three weeks I got nothing, though I had already worked on a machine in Russia. Then the boss paid me three dollars a week. Now, after five years' experience, and I am considered a good worker, I am paid nine. But I never get the nine dollars. There are always 'charges' against me. If I laugh, or cry, or speak to a girl during work hours, I am fined ten cents for each 'crime.' Five cents is taken from my pay every week to pay for benzine which is used to clean waists that have been soiled in the making; and even if I have not soiled a waist in a year, I must pay the five cents just the same. If I lose a little piece of lining, that possibly is worth two cents, I am charged ten cents for the goods and five cents for losing it. If I am one minute late, I am fined one cent, though I get only fifteen cents an hour; and if I am five minutes late, I lose half a day's pay. Each of these things seems small, I know, but when you only earn ninety dimes a week, and are fined for this and fined for that, why, a lot of them are missing when pay day comes, and you know what it means when your money is the only regular money that comes in a family of eight."

She told me other grievances, many of them. And as I went from meeting to meeting talking to the girls, as I walked with them on picket duty, I found that she had spoken truly when she said, "My story is their story."...

There is one very simple explanation for the wretched conditions under which the girls have worked—they have been very easy to exploit. Ninety per cent of the workers are Russian and Italian girls between eighteen and twenty-five. These girls enter the shop almost immediately after landing in America. They come from great poverty and oppression, where they were compelled to accept conditions without complaint. And so, accustomed to fear and obey, these girls have for years suffered their grievances here, and kept silent.

Now and then in the past there have been attempts made by the workers to fight the conditions, but the individual uprisings had no effect. The spirit of discontent among the workers grew, and continued to grow deeper and wider; it set the girls thinking, and finally they realized that the only possible remedy for these conditions was for all of them to stand together and make common demands—to organize a strong union and gain recognition for it. . . .

But to appreciate what sufferings these girls are undergoing for the sake of better conditions in the future, one must know a little of how they live in times when there is no strike. Some of the girls earn but $3 or $4 a week; a few exceptionally clever girls working in exceptionally well run shops, earn as high as $20 and $25.

The story circulated by the bosses that some of the girls get $35 and $40 a week is false, and the evidence by which they seek to substantiate the story amounts to a mere trick of bookkeeping. The average wages for the forty thousand workers is $9, and this is not for fifty-two weeks in the year, but only for the busy season, a period of about three months. During six months of the year the average is from $3 to $5 a week, and during the remaining three months the girls are practically idle. So the average wage is in reality only about $5 a week, and on this amount the girls must feed, clothe, and house themselves. How do they manage to exist in New York, where the cost of living is so high?

This is how. Most of the strikers board with a "missus" who lives in a miserable four-room flat in an East Side tenement. Besides the missus, her husband, and numerous children, the flat is shared by two or three boarders. The charge is $3 a week. This entitles the boarder to a cot in the sitting-room, a breakfast of coffee and bread without butter, and a supper of cheap meat, bread, and tea. The board must provide her own lunch, usually at a cost of from three to six cents. She does her own laundry of nights, makes some of her clothes on Sundays, and does without necessaries most of the time. Such is her life in the fat times of peace.

The period of any strike is always a time of suffering and sacrifice for the workers—for at his greatest prosperity the worker's hand barely reaches his mouth; but this strike of girls has been distinguished by the added suffering, yes, and disgrace, inflicted by the brutality of the police, by the brutality of thugs hired by the bosses and protected by the police, and by the shameless brutality of the police court magistrates. So flagrant has been the harshness of the magistrates that great numbers of prominent New York men and women, people who usually take no interest in labor struggles, have risen in protest—and this very harshness and brutality, whose seeming purpose was to browbeat the girls into submission, has served to gain for them a wider sympathy, and is materially aiding them in winning their long fight. . . .

Of all the wearying duties that have devolved upon the girls, none has been so trying and dangerous as this duty of picketing. It means long and weary hours of walking and waiting, often in bitter cold and rain, often with little food to keep you warm within and too little clothing to protect you from without. It means exposure to the street loafer; it often means abuse and insult from the boss; it has meant, as has been shown, suffering from the lawlessness of police and magistrates for merely performing an act which is a legal right according to the statutes of the State of New York; it has meant being thrown into cells with the most degraded women of the street, and finally, for many, a sentence to five days in the workhouse.

"Why was I sent to the workhouse?" repeated Rose Perr, a little fifteen-year-old girl, with wonderment and pain in her face. "It happened so: Before I go to picket I always read my little piece of paper with the picketing rules printed on it so as not to get arrested. '1. Don't call *Scab*. 2. Don't touch *Scab* while you speak to her. 3. Don't speak to *Scab* when she says "stop." 4. Don't stand with *Scab* on sidewalk; keep on walking.'

"One evening a friend and I were picketing a shop when a great big fat policeman came over to us. Holding out his club as a threat, he told us in a rough way, 'You girls go home and mind your own business!' We did not answer, but walked on.

"Just then a scab came down from the shop, and we quietly told her the usual thing : 'This shop is on strike; won't you please join the union?' While we were speaking a thug came suddenly over and hit my friend right in the chest. She fell down crying. I turned to the policeman, who saw the whole thing, and asked him to arrest the thug. 'All right,' he said, 'but you must come along as a witness.

"I went with him. But at the station-house we were treated as the criminals. We were insulted by everybody; men pulled at our hats and coats and talked to us in a way that is impossible for a decent person to repeat. We were thrown into a cell and kept there six hours with drunken women—oh, the worst kind of women! When our case came up we had no chance to say a word. In the courtroom was the employer with the scab. She was Italian and could not speak English, so the boss spoke for her. He made a complaint against my friend and myself; he said that we hit her; and the judge sent my friend and myself for five days to the workhouse."

Some of the actions of the magistrates seem almost unbelievable, but are only too sadly, too frequently, true. There is one little girl who is always doing something at the union's headquarters—you can distinguish her from the rest because she wears her coat like a cape. There is a reason for that, for her right arm is in a sling. When she arose in her shop to announce to the workers that a strike had been called and asked them to join the union, the boss in his fury threw a pair of scissors at her, which inflicted a deep wound in her forearm. When she applied at court for a warrant for the arrest of her assailant, the magistrate expressed himself as follows:

"You cannot have a warrant. You are a criminal, and you have got no more than your just deserts. God says in the Bible that by the sweat of his brow every man must earn his bread. You are keeping the girls from earning their bread. Your strike is a strike against God."

But despite it all—despite cold, hunger, police brutality, magisterial insult and injustice, the shame and degraded companionship of the workhouse—these girls have kept up their spirit, a spirit that has brought them much sympathetic outside aid, a spirit that is, as I write, bringing toward a successful close the longest, biggest, bitterest struggle for better living conditions ever waged by women in America.

Scenes at the Morgue, from The New York Times *(March 26, 1911)*

In the late afternoon of March 25, 1911, William Shepherd, a reporter for United Press International, "was walking through Washington Square when a puff of smoke issuing from the factory building caught my eye . . . I saw every feature of the tragedy visible from outside the building. I learned a new sound—a more horrible sound than description can picture. It was the thud of a speeding, living body on a stone sidewalk. Thud-dead. Thud-dead. Thud-dead. Sixty-two thud-deads."

The Triangle Shirtwaist Factory fire (in the Asch building on the northwest corner of Washington and Greene Streets) claimed, in less than fifteen minutes, the lives of 146 immigrant garment workers, mostly Jewish and Italian, in the greatest industrial disaster in New York's history. On the ninth floor, just above where the fire started, owners had locked the exit door in order to increase productivity.

William Shepherd concluded, "I looked upon the heap of dead bodies and I remembered these girls were shirtwaist makers. I remembered their great strike of last year in which these same girls had demanded more sanitary conditions and more safety precautions in these shops. These dead bodies were the answer." On April 5, in a heavy rain, more than half a million New Yorkers marched in and watched a mass funeral procession.

A FEW minutes after the first load of fire victims was received at the Bellevue Hospital Morgue the streets were filled with a clamoring throng, which struggled with the reserves stationed about the building in an effort to gain entrance to view the bodies of the dead in the hope of identifying loved ones.

The frantic mob was reinforced as the hospital wagon brought more of the dead to the institution. The sobbing and shrieking mothers and wives, and frantic fathers and husbands of those who had not been accounted for struggled with the police and tried to stop the wagon that was bearing the dead on its trips to the Morgue. Mothers and wives ran frantically through the street in front of the hospital, pulling their hair from their heads and calling the names of their dear ones.

A few of the surging mob who viewed the situation in a calmer manner attempted to calm the excited ones, but in vain. The police were abused because they would not allow the surging mob in the Morgue, and in many instances they were threatened and had to resort to the use of their nightsticks to keep the struggling mass from breaking in.

Police Work Desperately

A hundred policemen, most of them ashen and with trembling lips, worked at the heart-rending task of keeping back, without undue roughness, the maddened thousands.

"For God's sake," one cried to a reporter, who was wedging his way out of the mob, "get me a drink!"

The poor bluecoat needed it.

Every few minutes a patrol wagon or a hastily improvised morgue wagon that had done duty as an auto truck earlier in the day appeared at the head of the mob at First Avenue and Twenty-sixth Street, and the reserves of six precincts had to force open a narrow path through the crowd for it. As soon as the path was opened in front, however, the crowd surged in behind it. At the sight of the bodies the crowd broke into fresh weeping and screaming, each seeming to see in the charred and often unrecognizable remains a loved one.

Twelve patrol wagons from as many stations, besides dozens of hastily impressed dispensary wagons of the Police Department and the Department of Public Charities and a few auto trucks were used in transporting the dead from the fire to the Morgue. The Morgue itself became too crowded, early in the evening, for further storage of bodies, and the Charities Department decided to throw open the long public dock adjoining it. Here, as night settled over the city, the bodies were taken from the wagons and laid out, side by side, in double rows along either side of the long docks.

Besides the thirty attendants regularly at the pier, twenty derelicts who had applied at the Municipal Lodging House in East Twenty-sixth Street for a night's rest, were pressed into service for the ghastly work.

In the narrow lane left between the double rows of the dead on the dark pier, the patrol wagons and rude dead wagons crept slowly to where the lines had freshly ended. They deposited their freight, backed slowly out, and returned to the scene of the fire for more bodies. As fast as the dead were brought to the pier the grimy panhandlers and derelicts were set to work arranging them in rows, and later putting them in the rough wooden boxes that serve as coffins nightly at the Morgue. But the supply of boxes was soon exhausted, and Commissioner Drummond of the Department of Charities was obliged to send over to the storage warehouse on Blackwell's Island for more. Presently there steamed up to the pier from the island a large double-decked launch, bringing stacked up on its deck 100 more boxes.

At 11:30 o'clock, with the mob still storming more and more outside, the police had counted in the Morgue and on the pier 136 bodies—thirteen men and 123 women. Fifty-six of these were burned beyond all but human semblance and may never be identified. The thousands of clamorers outside could not have identified them, even if the police had let them swarm in on the pier.

As the maddened throng swarmed around the ghastly laden patrol wagons and improvised hearses their misery wrung even the hardened habitual handlers of the dead in the Morgue, making them frequently turn away from their work. There were hundreds scantily clad and shivering, despite their raving, in the cold night air. Many of them had no money. Their week's funds were in the pay envelopes, found in dozens, on the scorched and irrecognizable bodies on the pier. One woman, her head charred to a mere twisted blur of black, carried in her stocking $600 in tightly crumpled bills. Dozens of the girls whose bodies were laid out on the pier were found to have carried their scant savings in this way.

Clung Together in Death

Two girls, charred beyond all hope of identification, and found in the smoking ruins with their arms clasped around each other's necks, were conveyed to the pier, still together, and placed in one box.

Horrible cries had burst from the misery stricken mob outside when these two were carried through the narrow lane in the street, and a few of the clamorous throng had forced their way to the wagon and lifted the dark tarpaulin. Everywhere burst anguished cries for sister, mother, and wife, a dozen pet names in Italian and Yiddish rising in shrill agony above the deeper moan of the throng.

Now and then a reporter, the way cleared before him by a broad, white-faced policeman, forced his way to the nearest telephone, to send to his office a report of what was happening there. Each time a hundred faces were turned up to him imploringly, and a hundred anguished voices begged of him tidings of those within. Had he seen a little girl with black hair and dark-brown cheeks? Had he seen a tall, thin man, with stooped shoulders? Could he describe any one of the many he had seen in there? The poor wretches were hunting for a "story," too.

Piteously they pleaded with the policemen to let them—only them—past, so that they might see whether their loved ones were on the pier. They would only look around, one short glance, and come straight out. The policemen, struggling with their own emotions more roughly than with the crowd could only put them off. Presently, they said, in a very little while now, they would let them all in.

"Fifty-six!" muttered Inspector Walsh, turning his face away. They call him "Smiling Dick" Walsh, but his averted face was not smiling. He meant the fifty-six bodies that were burnt or crushed beyond recognition; fifty-six that would certainly be buried in unnamed graves. Dozens of them had every stitch of clothing burned off them. One body—that of a young girl—was headless and burned to a crisp.

Commissioner Drummond realized that when the mad throng was let into the Morgue and on the pier, many of them, already crazed by uncertainty concerning their loved ones, might at the sight of the dead throw themselves into the river. He therefore ordered that every opening in the Morgue building and on the covered pier be boarded up at once, and that no space should be left which would permit of the passage of a body.

At midnight, . . . the door of the Morgue was opened for a brief moment, and the foremost of the surging mob outside, to the number of fifteen, was allowed to enter. The police squad at the doors could hardly keep the rest back, with promises of letting them, too, presently enter in groups of fifteen.

Each group, shivering and clamoring and weeping, was lined up at the door and allowed slowly to file between the rows of boxes. Two policemen accompanied each of them, ready to support them if they should faint. And more than half of them did. They looked around with an air of frightened bewilderment at the ghastly array of dead, and then, one by one, looking down at the nearest box at their feet, where the mangled bodies lay, with heads propped up on boards for the light of the attendant beside the box, they collapsed with cries of terror. Such were carried to one side and revived by physicians from Bellevue, and later warmed with coffee handed to them by attendants and panhandlers at the pier.

Scores of men and women thought they saw in the ghastly bodies propped up in the boxes the relatives they were looking for, but could not identify them positively.

Around several bodies gathered men and women in small knots, each insisting pitifully that what was propped up there belonged to them, and calling the unrecognizable mass with tender pet names.

At 1 A.M. eight bodies had been identified by relatives and set aside in sealed boxes. The relatives filed into the improvised Coroner's office in the morgue and tearfully stood in line for their slips permitting them to have the bodies removed. There was a competitive mob of undertakers with their wagons at the outskirts of the crowd ready to do that.

Abram I. Elkus, Opening Statement, from New York State Factory Investigating Commission *(October 10, 1911)*

A rally held at the Metropolitan Opera House less than a week after the Triangle fire galvanized disparate groups to petition the Albany legislature and led to the formation of the New York State Factory Investigating Commission. Tammany boss "Silent Charlie" Murphy, in part motivated by the desire to garner votes from the new immigrants pouring through Ellis Island, supported the establishment of the commission. Murphy chose two of his deputies, Robert F. Wagner and Alfred E. Smith, to lead it. After calling hundreds of witnesses and collecting thousands of pages of testimony in its first year alone, the commission eventually made sixty recommendations covering all industrial conditions. Through the political savvy of Wagner and Smith, fifty-six of them were adopted, implementing strict fire codes, establishing a limit to the work week, setting standards for lighting, and establishing a board empowered to issue regulations that had the force of law.

The effect of the Triangle Shirtwaist Fire and the subsequent work of the Factory Investigating Commission were monumental and far reaching. Frances Perkins, who as Franklin Roosevelt's Secretary of Labor became the first woman cabinet appointment in American history, maintained that the New Deal itself was born in "that terrible fire, on March 25, 1911."

Minutes of the Hearing of the New York State Factory Investigating Commission Held in the City Hall at 10:30 A.M.

Mr. Elkus: . . . It is unfortunate that the occurrence of a catastrophe is often necessary to awaken a people to its true sense of responsibility. The Triangle Waist Company fire of March, 1911, with its attendant horrors and loss of life shocked both city and State. The loss of one hundred and forty-three lives in one factory fire brought to the attention of the public with terrible force the dangers that daily threaten the lives of hundreds of thousands of employees in manufacturing establishments in the City of New York and elsewhere throughout the State.

Public attention was directed not only to the dangers which threaten employees because of inadequate fire-escape facilities, and because of the lack of precautions against fire, but also to the less obvious but greater menace of unsanitary conditions.

It has become increasingly clear that it is the duty of the State to safeguard the worker, not only against the occasional accidents, but the daily incidents of industry, not only against the accidents which are extraordinary, but against the incidents which are the ordinary occurrences of industrial life.

The problem before the Commission which meets to-day, is the problem of human conservation—the conservation of the lives of the toilers who most need protection at toil on the part of the State, and the destruction of whom by accidents, avoidable or unavoidable, constitutes a deadly injury to the State. This Commission must concern itself with the problem of how to meet the evils that have arisen in the development of industry out of human wastage that has not only been needless but often reckless and wanton.

If it has rightly been said that a man may be killed by a tenement house as truly as by a club or a gun, is it not equally true that a man may be killed by a factory and the unsanitary conditions which obtain therein, as surely as he may be killed by a fire accident. And it is not less true that the slaughter of men and women workers by the slow processes of unsanitary and unhealthful conditions is not only immoral and anti-social, but the state is beginning to declare that it is legally indefensible, and therefore must, through carefully considered legislation, be made virtually impossible.

Apart from the humanitarian aspect of the matter which must appeal strongly to every lover of his kind, to require the establishment and maintenance of safe and hygienic conditions in the places of employment of these hundreds of thousands of operatives so that their industrial efficiency may be unimpaired is of prime economic importance to the state. Sickness due to unwholesome conditions is one of the chief causes of poverty and distress, of the destruction of the lives of men and women whose energy are the sources of the nation's wealth. The economic value of the human life is everywhere being more and more recognized. The proper safeguarding of the health of the employees, the prevention and limitation of industrial or occupational diseases is now one of the most important problems before any industrial community and one which must be solved.

Under the act creating it, the Commission is charged with the duty of inquiring into the following matters:

1. Hazard to life because of fire: covering such matters as fire prevention, inadequate fire-escapes and exits, number of persons employed in factories and lofts, arrangement of machinery, fire drills. etc.
2. Accident prevention; guarding of machinery, proper and adequate inspection of factories and manufacturing establishments.
3. Danger to life and health because of unsanitary conditions: ventilation, lighting, seating arrangement, hours of labor, etc.
4. Occupational diseases: industrial consumption, lead poisoning, bone disease, etc.
5. An examination of the present statutes and ordinances that deal with or relate to the foregoing matters, and of the extent to which the present laws are enforced.

The Commission is to recommend such new legislation as may be found necessary to remedy defects in existing legislation and to provide for conditions now unregulated.

The Commission is directed to present its report to the Legislature before the 12th day of February, 1912.

From The Autobiography of an Ex-Colored Man, *James Weldon Johnson (1912)*

When James Weldon Johnson arrived in New York in 1901, blacks represented only 2 percent of the population. But the combination of a huge migration from the South, the building of Pennsylvania Station in the Tenderloin area inhabited primarily by blacks, and a new subway system that produced rabid overbuilding of residential buildings in Upper Manhattan gave birth to "black Harlem." James Weldon Johnson described it as a "black city, located in the heart of white Manhattan, and containing more Negroes to the square mile than any other spot on earth. It strikes the uninformed observer as a phenomenon, a miracle straight out of the skies."

James Weldon Johnson's parents raised him to be one of what W. E. B. DuBois called the "Talented Tenth"; and he was one of the most noted links between Harlem and downtown white Manhattan. Johnson's talents were virtually endless—songwriter (he wrote "Lift Ev'ry Voice and Sing," what became known as the Negro National Anthem), poet, novelist, attorney (the first black admitted to the bar in Florida), historian, diplomat, and the first black head of the NAACP. In that capacity, Johnson organized more than ten thousand blacks in a silent march down Fifth Avenue on July 28, 1917, to protest the race riots and spate of lynchings that erupted after the First World War. Johnson died in 1938, and he is buried in Greenwood Cemetery in Brooklyn.

VI

WE steamed up into New York Harbor late one afternoon in spring. The last efforts of the sun were being put forth in turning the waters of the bay to glistening gold; the green islands on either side, in spite of their warlike mountings, looked calm and peaceful; the buildings of the town shone out in a reflected light which gave the city an air of enchantment; and, truly, it is an enchanted spot. New York City is the most fatally fascinating thing in America. She sits like a great witch at the gate of the country, showing her alluring white face and hiding her crooked hands and feet under the folds of her wide garments—constantly enticing thousands from far within, and tempting those who come from across the seas to go no farther. And all these become the victims of her caprice. Some she at once crushes beneath her cruel feet; others she condemns to a fate like that of galley slaves; a few she favors and fondles, riding them high on the bubbles of fortune; then with a sudden breath she blows the bubbles out and laughs mockingly as she watches them fall.

Twice I had passed through it, but this was really my first visit to New York; and as I walked about that evening, I began to feel the dread power of the city; the crowds, the lights, the excitement, the gaiety, and all its subtler stimulating influences began to take effect upon me. My blood ran quicker and I felt that I was just beginning to live. To some natures this stimulant of life in a great city becomes a thing as binding and necessary as opium is to one addicted to the habit. It becomes their breath of life; they cannot exist outside of it; rather than be deprived of it they are content to suffer hunger, want, pain, and misery; they would not exchange even a ragged and wretched condition among the great crowd for any degree of comfort away from it.

As soon as we landed, four of us went directly to a lodging house in Twenty-seventh Street, just west of Sixth Avenue. The house was run by a short, stout mulatto man, who was exceedingly talkative and inquisitive. In fifteen minutes he not only knew the history of the past life of each one of us, but had a clearer idea of what we intended to do in the future than we ourselves. He sought this information so much with an air of being very particular as to whom he admitted into his house that we tremblingly answered every question that he asked. When we had become located, we went out and got supper, then walked around until about ten o'clock. At that hour we met a couple of young fellows who lived in New York and were known to one of the members of our party. It was suggested we go to a certain place which was known by the proprietor's name. We turned into one of the cross streets and mounted the stoop of a house in about the middle of a block between Sixth and Seventh Avenues. One of the young men whom we had met rang a bell, and a man on the inside cracked the door a couple of inches; then opened it and let us in. We found ourselves in the hallway of what had once been a residence. The front parlor had been converted into a bar, and a half-dozen or so well-dressed men were in the room. We went in and after a general introduction had several rounds of beer. In the back parlor a crowd was sitting and standing around the walls of the room watching an exciting and noisy game of pool. I walked back and joined this crowd to watch the game, and principally to get away from the drinking party. The game was really interesting, the players being quite expert, and the excitement was heightened by the bets which were being made on the result. At times the antics and remarks of both players and spectators were amusing. When, at a critical point, a player missed a shot, he was deluged, by those financially interested in his making it, with a flood of epithets synonymous with "chump"; while from the others he would be jeered by such remarks as "Nigger, dat cue ain't no hoe-handle." I noticed that among this class of colored men the word "nigger" was freely used in about the same sense as the word "fellow," and sometimes as a term of almost endearment; but I soon learned that its use was positively and absolutely prohibited to white men. . . .

I asked if there was no other place to which we could go; our guides said yes, and suggested that we go to the "Club." We went to Sixth Avenue, walked two blocks, and turned to the west into another street. We stopped in front of a house with three stories and a basement. In the basement was a Chinese chop-suey restaurant. There was a red lantern at the iron gate to the areaway, inside of which the Chinaman's name was printed. We went up the steps of the stoop, rang the bell, and were admitted without any delay. From the outside the house bore a rather gloomy aspect, the windows being absolutely dark, but within, it was a veritable house of mirth. When we had passed through a small vestibule and reached the hallway, we heard mingled sounds of music and laughter, the clink of glasses, and the pop of bottles. We went into the main room and I was little prepared for what I saw. The brilliancy of the place, the display of diamond rings, scarf-pins, ear-rings, and breast-pins, the big rolls of money that were brought into evidence when drinks were paid for, and the air of gaiety that pervaded the place, all completely dazzled and dazed me. I felt positively giddy, and it was several minutes before I was able to make any clear and definite observations.

We at length secured places at a table in a corner of the room and, as soon as we could attract the attention of one of the busy waiters, ordered a round of drinks. When I had somewhat collected my senses, I realized that in a large back room into which the main room opened, there was a young fellow singing a song, accompanied on the piano by a short, thickset, dark man. After each verse he did some dance steps, which brought forth great applause and a shower of small coins at his feet. After the singer had responded to a rousing encore, the stout man at the piano began to run his fingers up and down the keyboard. This he did in a manner which indicated that he was master of a good deal of technique. Then he began to play; and such playing! I stopped talking to listen. It was music of a kind I had never heard before. It was music that demanded physical response, patting of the feet, drumming of the fingers, or nodding of the head in time with the beat. The barbaric harmonies, the audacious resolutions, often consisting of an abrupt jump from one key to another, the intricate rhythms in which the accents fell in the most unexpected places, but in which the beat was never lost, produced a most curious effect. And, too, the player—the dexterity of his left hand in making rapid octave runs and jumps was little short of marvelous; and with his right hand he frequently swept half the keyboard with clean-cut chromatics which he fitted in so nicely as never to fail to arouse in his listeners a sort of pleasant surprise at the accomplishment of the feat.

This was ragtime music, then a novelty in New York, and just growing to be a rage, which has not yet subsided. It was originated in the questionable resorts about Memphis and St. Louis by Negro piano players who knew no more of the theory of music than they did of the theory of the universe, but were guided by natural musical instinct and talent. It made its way to Chicago, where it was popular some time before it reached New York. These players often improvised crude and, at times, vulgar words to fit the melodies. This was the beginning of the ragtime song. Several of these improvisations were taken down by white men, the words slightly altered, and published under the names of the arrangers. They sprang into immediate popularity and earned small fortunes, of which the Negro originators got only a few dollars. But I have learned that since that time a number of colored men, of not only musical talent, but training, are writing out their own melodies and words and reaping the reward of their work. I have learned also that they have a large number of white imitators and adulterators.

American musicians, instead of investigating ragtime, attempt to ignore it, or dismiss it with a contemptuous word. But that has always been the course of scholasticism in every branch of art. Whatever new thing the *people* like is pooh-poohed; whatever is *popular* is spoken of as not worth the while. The fact is, nothing great or enduring, especially in music, has ever sprung full-fledged and unprecedented from the brain of any master; the best that he gives to the world he gathers from the hearts of the people, and runs it through the alembic of his genius. In spite of the bans which musicians and music teachers have placed upon it, the people still demand and enjoy ragtime. One thing cannot be denied; it is music which possesses at least one strong element of greatness: it appeals universally; not only the American, but the English, the French, and even the German people find delight in it. In fact, there is not a corner of the civilized world in which it is not known, and this proves its originality; for if it were an imitation, the people of Europe, anyhow, would not have found it a novelty. Anyone who doubts that there is a peculiar heel-tickling, smile-provoking, joy-awakening charm in ragtime needs only to hear a skillful performer play the genuine article to be convinced. I believe that it has its place as well as the music which draws from us sighs and tears.

I became so interested in both the music and the player that I left the table where I was sitting, and made my way through the hall into the back room, where I could see as well as hear. I talked to the piano player between the musical numbers and found out that he was just a natural musician, never having taken a lesson in his life. Not only could he play almost anything he heard, but he could accompany singers in songs he had never heard. He had, by ear alone, composed some pieces, several of which he played over for me; each of them was properly proportioned and balanced. I began to wonder what this man with such a lavish natural endowment would have done had he been trained. Perhaps he wouldn't have done anything at all; he might have become, at best, a mediocre imitator of the great masters in what they have already done to a finish, or one of the modern innovators who strive after originality by seeing how cleverly they can dodge about through the rules of harmony and at the same time avoid melody. It is certain that he would not have been so delightful as he was in ragtime.

I sat by, watching and listening to this man until I was dragged away by my friends. The place was now almost deserted; only a few stragglers hung on, and they were all the worse for drink. My friends were well up in this class. We passed into the street; the lamps were pale against the sky; day was just breaking. We went home and got into bed. I fell into a fitful sort of sleep, with ragtime music ringing continually in my ears.

VII

I shall take advantage of this pause in my narrative to describe more closely the "Club" spoken of in the latter part of the preceding chapter—to describe it as I afterwards came to know it, as an habitué. I shall do this not only because of the direct influence it had on my life, but also because it was at that time the most famous place of its kind in New York, and was well known to both white and colored people of certain classes. . . .

These notables of the ring, the turf, and the stage, drew to the place crowds of admirers, both white and colored. Whenever one of them came in, there were awe-inspired whispers from those who knew him by sight, in which they enlightened those around them as to his identity, and hinted darkly at their great intimacy with the noted one. Those who were on terms of approach immediately showed their privilege over others less fortunate by gathering around their divinity. I was, at first, among those who dwelt in darkness. Most of these celebrities I had never heard of. This made me an object of pity among many of my new associates. I soon learned, however, to fake a knowledge for the benefit of those who were greener than I; and, finally, I became personally acquainted with the majority of the famous personages who came to the "Club."...

Besides the people I have just been describing, there was at the place almost every night one or two parties of white people, men and women, who were out sight-seeing, or slumming. They generally came in cabs; some of them would stay only for a few minutes, while others sometimes stayed until morning. There was also another set of white people who came frequently; it was made up of variety performers and others who delineated "darky characters"; they came to get their imitations first hand from the Negro entertainers they saw there.

There was still another set of white patrons, composed of women; these were not occasional visitors, but five or six of them were regular habitués. When I first saw them, I was not sure that they were white. In the first place, among the many colored women who came to the "Club" there were several just as fair; and, secondly, I always saw these women in company with colored men. They were all good-looking and well-dressed, and seemed to be women of some education. One of these in particular attracted my attention; she was an exceedingly beautiful woman of perhaps thirty-five; she had glistening copper-colored hair, very white skin, and eyes very much like Du Maurier's conception of Trilby's "twin gray stars." When I came to know her, I found that she was a woman of considerable culture; she had traveled in Europe, spoke French, and played the piano well. She was always dressed elegantly, but in absolute good taste. She always came to the "Club" in a cab, and was soon joined by a well-set-up, very black young fellow. He was always faultlessly dressed; one of the most exclusive tailors in New York made his clothes, and he wore a number of diamonds in about as good taste as they could be worn in by a man. I learned that she paid for his clothes and his diamonds. I learned, too, that he was not the only one of his kind. More that I learned would be better suited to a book on social phenomena than to a narrative of my life.

This woman was known at the "Club" as the rich widow. She went by a very aristocratic-sounding name, which corresponded to her appearance. I shall never forget how hard it was for me to get over my feelings of surprise, perhaps more than surprise, at seeing her with her black companion; somehow I never exactly enjoyed the sight. I have devoted so much time to this pair, the "widow" and her companion, because it was through them that another decided turn was brought about in my life.

Judges in the Gate, from They Who Knock at Our Gates *in* American Magazine, *Mary Antin (1914)*

Mary Antin was born in Polotsk, Russia, in 1881, immigrated to Boston in 1894, and moved to New York in 1901, where she attended Barnard and Columbia Teacher's College. She was a literary prodigy and published her account of her journey to the United States in *From Plotzk to Boston* when she was only eighteen years old. Her autobiographical *The Promised Land* was published in 1912 after being originally serialized in the *Atlantic Monthly.*

Antin's *They Who Knock at Our Gates* (1914) examined immigrant's hopes and experiences but also defended the entire process of immigration and assimilation into a broader American culture. She campaigned aggressively for Teddy Roosevelt in his Bull Moose campaign of 1916 and against congressional legislation in the 1920s that imposed more restrictive quotas on immigrants. For Mary Antin it was best that we remember that "the ghost of the Mayflower pilots every immigrant ship, and Ellis Island is another name for Plymouth Rock."

NEITHER does the immigrant's civic reputation depend entirely on negative evidence. New York City has the largest foreign population in the United States, and precisely in that city the politicians have learned that they cannot count on the foreign vote, because it is not for sale. A student of New York politics speaks of the "uncontrollable and unapproachable vote of the Ghetto." Repeated analyses of the election returns of the Eighth District, which has the largest foreign population of all, show that "politically it is one of the most uncertain sections" in the city. Many generations of campaign managers have discovered to their sorrow that the usual party blandishments are wasted on the East Side masses. Hester Street follows leaders and causes rather than party emblems. Nowhere is the art of splitting a ticket better understood. The only time you can predict the East Side vote is when there is a sharp alignment of the better citizens against the boss-ridden. Then you will find the naturalized citizens in the same camp with men like Jacob Riis and women like Lillian Wald. And the experience of New York is duplicated in Chicago and in Philadelphia and in every center of immigration. Ask the reformers.

How often we demand more civic virtue of the stranger than we ourselves possess! A little more time spent in weeding our own garden will relieve us of the necessity of counting the tin cans in the immigrant's back yard.

As to tin cans, the immigrants are not the only ones who scatter them broadcast. How can we talk about the foreigners defacing public property, when our own bill-boards disfigure every open space that God tries to make beautiful for us? It is true that the East Side crowds litter the parks with papers and fruit-skins and peanut shells, but they would not be able to do so if the park regulations were persistently enforced. And in the mean time the East Side children, in their pageants and dance festivals, make the most beautiful use of the parks that a poet could desire.

There exists a society in the United States the object of which is to protect the natural beauties and historical landmarks of our country. Who are the marauders who have called such a society into being? Who is it that threatens to demolish the Palisades and drain off Niagara? Who are the vulgar folk who scrawl their initials on trees and monuments, who chip off bits from historic tombstones, who profane the holy echoes of the mountains by calling foolish phrases through a megaphone? The officers of the Scenic and Historic Preservation Society are not watching Ellis Island. On the contrary, it was the son of an immigrant whose expert testimony, given before a legislative committee at Albany, helped the Society to save the Falls of the Genesee from devastation by a power company. This same immigrant's son, on another occasion, spent two mortal hours tearing off visiting-cards from poet's grave-cards bearing the names of American vacationists.

Some of the things we say against the immigrants sound very strange from American lips. We speak of the corruption of our children's manners through contact with immigrant children in the public schools, when all the world is scolding us for our children's rude deportment. Finer manners are grown on a tiny farm in Italy than in the roaring subways of New York; and contrast our lunch-counter manners with the table-manners of the Polish ghetto, where bread must not be touched with unwashed hands, where a pause for prayer begins and ends each meal, and on festival occasions parents and children join in folk-songs between courses!

If there is a corruption of manners, it may be that it works in the opposite direction from what we suppose. At any rate, we ourselves admit that the children of foreigners, before they are Americanized, have a greater respect than our children for the Fifth Commandment.

We say that immigrants nowadays come only to exploit our country, because some of them go back after a few years, taking their savings with them. The real exploiters of our country's wealth are not the foreign laborers, but the capitalists who pay them wages. The laborer who returns home with his savings leaves us an equivalent in the products of labor; a day's service rendered for every day's wages. The capitalists take away our forests and watercourses and mineral treasures and give us watered stock in return.

Of the class of aliens who do not come to make their homes here, but only to earn a few hundred dollars to invest in a farm or a cottage in their native village, a greater number than we imagine are brought over by industrial agents in violation of the contract labor law. Put an end to the stimulation of immigration, and we shall see very few of the class who do not come to stay. And even as it is, not all of those who return to Europe do so in order to spend their American fortune. Some go back to recover from ruin encountered at the hands of American land swindlers. Some go back to be buried beside their fathers, having lost their health in unsanitary American factories. And some are helped aboard on crutches, having lost a limb in a mine explosion that could have been prevented. When we watch the procession of cripples hobbling back to their native villages, it looks more as if America is exploiting Europe.

O that the American people would learn where their enemies lurk! Not the immigrant is ruining our country, but the venal politicians who try to make the immigrant the scapegoat for all the sins of untrammeled capitalism—these and their masters. Find me the agent who obstructs the movement for the abolition of child labor, and I will show you who it is that condemns able-bodied men to eat their hearts out in idleness; who brutalizes our mothers and tortures tender babies; who fills the morgues with the emaciated bodies of young girls, and the infirmaries with little white cots; who fastens the shame of illiteracy on our enlightened land, and causes American boys to grow up too ignorant to mark a ballot; who sucks the blood of the nation, fattens on its brains, and throws its heart to the wolves of the money market.

The stench of the slums is nothing to the stench of the child-labor iniquity. If the foreigners are taking the bread out of the mouth of the American workingman, it is by the maimed fingers of their fainting little ones.

And if we want to know whether the immigrant parents are the promoters or the victims of the child labor system, we turn to the cotton mills, where forty thousand native American children between seven and sixteen years of age toil between ten and twelve hours a day, while the fathers rot in the degradation of idleness.

From all this does it follow that we should let down the bars and dispense with the guard at Ellis Island? Only in so far as the policy of restriction is based on the theory that the present immigration is derived from the scum of humanity. But the immigrants may be desirable and immigration undesirable. We sometimes have to deny ourselves to the most congenial friends who knock at our door. At this point, however, we are not trying to answer the question whether immigration is good for us. We are concerned only with the reputation of the immigrant—and incidentally with the reputation of those who have sought to degrade him in our eyes. If statecraft bids us lock the gate, and our national code of ethics ratifies the order, lock it we must, but we need not call names through the keyhole.

Mount guard in the name of the Republic if the health of the Republic requires it, but let no such order be issued until her statesmen and philosophers and patriots have consulted together. Above all, let the voice of prejudice be stilled, let not self-interest chew the cud of envy in full sight of the nation, and let no syllable of willful defamation mar the oracles of state. For those who are excluded when our bars are down are exiles from Egypt, whose feet stumble in the desert of political and social slavery, whose hearts hunger for the bread of freedom. The ghost of the Mayflower pilots every immigrant ship, and Ellis Island is another name for Plymouth Rock.

Compact Between the States of New York and New Jersey, "The Port Authority" (1921)

New York City would not have become the commercial capital that it is if it had not been blessed with the most hospitable and functional harbor on the Atlantic seaboard. When the ice sheets melted approximately 17,000 years ago, the melting left the 100-square-mile Lower Bay with channels that led to easily navigable rivers and 770 miles of waterfront. Furthermore, it had deep water next to shore, shelter from potentially damaging winds, and virtually no ice throughout the winter months. As a result, New York became a leading port from the time Governor Peter Stuyvesant built the first wharf on the East River in 1648. Robert Fulton's invention of the first steam-powered vessel in 1807 and completion of DeWitt Clinton's Erie Canal in 1825 contributed to the port handling more goods and passengers than all other ports in the country by the mid-nineteenth century. By 1900, the Port of New York was the busiest port in the world.

In 1917, the governors of New York and New Jersey appointed a bistate commission to study the coordination of port and harbor development of the two states as well as resolve the disputes about boundaries, marine jurisdiction, and freight rates that had arisen. The result, in 1921, was the creation of the Port of New York Authority (later changed in 1972 to the Port Authority of New York and New Jersey). Since that time the Port Authority, consisting of twelve unsalaried commissioners (six appointed by the governor of each state), has overseen the development of the harbor as well as the construction of the George Washington Bridge, the Lincoln Tunnel, the Port Authority Bus Terminal, the PATH trains, and marine terminals in Newark and Elizabeth, New Jersey.

COMPACT

BETWEEN THE

States of New York and New Jersey

1921

For the Creation of the "Port of New York District" and the Establishment of the "Port of New York Authority" for the Comprehensive Development of the Port of New York

Entered into Pursuant to Chapter 154, Laws of New York, 1921; Chapter 151, Laws of New Jersey, 1921

Whereas, In the year eighteen hundred and thirty-four the states of New York and New Jersey did enter into an agreement fixing and determining the rights and obligations of the two states in and about the waters between the two states, especially in and about the bay of New York and the Hudson river; and

Whereas, Since that time the commerce of the port of New York has greatly developed and increased and the territory in and around the port has become commercially one center or district; and

Whereas, It is confidently believed that a better co-ordination of the terminal, transportation and other facilities of commerce in, about and through the port of New York, will result in great economies, benefiting the nation, as well as the states of New York and New Jersey; and

Whereas, The future development of such terminal, transportation and other facilities of commerce will require the expenditure of large sums of money and the cordial co-operation of the states of New York and New Jersey in the encouragement of the investment of capital, and in the formulation and execution of the necessary physical plans; and

Whereas, Such result can best be accomplished through the co-operation of the two states by and through a joint or common agency.

Now, therefore, The said states of New Jersey and New York do supplement and amend the existing agreement of eighteen hundred and thirty-four in the following respects:

Article I

They agree to and pledge, each to the other, faithful co-operation in the future planning and development of the port of New York, holding in high trust for the benefit of the nation the special blessings and natural advantages thereof.

Article II

To that end the two states do agree that there shall be created and they do hereby create a district to be known as the "Port of New York District" (for brevity hereinafter referred to as "The District") which shall embrace the territory bounded and described as follows: . . .

The boundaries of said district may be changed from time to time by the action of the legislature of either state concurred in by the legislature of the other.

Article III

There is hereby created "The Port of New York Authority" (for brevity hereinafter referred to as the "Port Authority"), which shall be a body corporate and politic, having the powers and jurisdiction hereinafter enumerated, and such other and additional powers as shall be conferred upon it by the legislature of either state concurred in by the legislature of the other, or by act or acts of congress, as hereinafter provided.

Article IV

The port authority shall consist of six commissioners—three resident voters from the state of New York, two of whom shall be resident voters of the city of New York, and three resident voters from the state of New Jersey, two of whom shall be resident voters within the New Jersey portion of the district, the New York members to be chosen by the state of New York and the New Jersey members by the state of New Jersey in the manner and for the terms fixed and determined from time to time by the legislature of each state respectively, except as herein provided.

Each commissioner may be removed or suspended from office as provided by the law of the state for which he shall be appointed.

A Meditation in Broadway, from What I Saw in America, *G. K. Chesterton (1921)*

G. K. Chesterton, the British theologian, philosopher, novelist, and self-described "rollicking journalist," began a three-month tour of America on January 10, 1921. He found New York City to be "a cosmopolitan city; but . . . not a city of cosmopolitans. . . . They are exiles or they are citizens; there is no moment where they are cosmopolitans." Chesterton recognized the heterogeneous nature of New York that had "nationalities at the end of the street that for us (the British) are at the ends of the earth." But he also saw New York as reflecting the fundamental American ideal, citizenship. For Chesterton, Americans "are very patriotic, and wish to make their new citizens patriotic Americans. But it is the idea of making a new nation literally out of any nation that comes along. In a word, what is unique is not America but what is called Americanization."

Chesterton was a prolific author of more than one hundred books and one thousand newspaper articles; he was also of such prodigious size that his coffin could not be carried down the staircase of his house but had to be lowered out of a window.

When I had looked at the lights of Broadway by night, I made to my American friends an innocent remark that seemed for some reason to amuse them. I had looked, not without joy, at that long kaleidoscope of coloured lights arranged in large letters and sprawling trade-marks, advertising everything, from pork to pianos, through the agency of the two most vivid and most mystical of the gifts of God; colour and fire. I said to them, in my simplicity, "What a glorious garden of wonders this would be, to any one who was lucky enough to be unable to read."

Here it is but a text for a further suggestion. But let us suppose that there does walk down this flaming avenue a peasant, of the sort called scornfully an illiterate peasant; by those who think that insisting on people reading and writing is the best way to keep out the spies who read in all languages and the forgers who write in all hands. On this principle indeed, a peasant merely acquainted with things of little practical use to mankind, such as ploughing, cutting wood, or growing vegetables, would very probably be excluded; and it is not for us to criticise from the outside the philosophy of those who would keep out the farmer and let in the forger. But let us suppose, if only for the sake of argument, that the peasant is walking under the artificial suns and stars of this tremendous thoroughfare; that he has escaped to the land of liberty upon some general rumour and romance of the story of its liberation, but without being yet able to understand the arbitrary signs of its alphabet. The soul of such a man would surely soar higher than the skyscrapers, and embrace a brotherhood broader than Broadway. Realising that he had arrived on an evening of exceptional festivity, worthy to be blazoned with all this burning heraldry, he would please himself by guessing what great proclamation or principle of the Republic hung in the sky like a constellation or rippled across the street like a comet. He would be shrewd enough to guess that the three festoons fringed with fiery words of somewhat similar pattern stood for "Government of the People, For the People, By the People"; for it must obviously be that, unless it were "Liberty, Equality, Fraternity." His shrewdness would perhaps be a little shaken if he knew that the triad stood for "Tang Tonic To-day; Tang Tonic To-morrow; Tang Tonic All the Time." He will soon identify a restless ribbon of red lettering, red hot and rebellious, as the saying, "Give me liberty or give me death." He will fail to identify it as the equally famous saying, "Skyoline Has Gout Beaten to a Frazzle." Therefore it was that I desired the peasant to walk down that grove of fiery trees, under all that golden foliage and fruits like monstrous jewels, as innocent as Adam before the Fall. He would see sights almost as fine as the flaming sword or the purple and peacock plumage of the seraphim; so long as he did not go near the Tree of Knowledge.

In other words, if once he went to school it would be all up; and indeed I fear in any case he would soon discover his error. If he stood wildly waving his hat for liberty in the middle of the road as Chunk Chutney picked itself out in ruby stars upon the sky, he would impede the excellent but extremely rigid traffic system of New York. If he fell on his knees before a sapphire splendour, and began saying an Ave Maria under a mistaken association, he would be conducted, kindly but firmly by an Irish policeman to a more authentic shrine. But though the foreign simplicity might not long survive in New York, it is quite a mistake to suppose that such foreign simplicity cannot enter New York. He may be excluded for being illiterate, but he cannot be excluded for being ignorant, nor for being innocent. Least of all can he be excluded for being wiser in his innocence than the world in its knowledge. There is here indeed more than one distinction to be made. New York is a cosmopolitan city; but it is not a city of cosmopolitans. Most of the masses in New York have a nation, whether or no it be the nation to which New York belongs. Those who are Americanised are American, and very patriotically American. Those who are not thus nationalised are not in the least internationalised. They simply continue to be themselves; the Irish are Irish; the Jews are Jewish; and all sorts of other tribes carry on the traditions of remote European valleys almost untouched. In short, there is a sort of slender bridge between their old country and their new, which they either cross or do not cross, but which they seldom simply occupy. They are exiles or they are citizens; there is no moment when they are cosmopolitans. But very often the exiles bring with them not only rooted traditions, but rooted truths. Indeed it is to a great extent the thought of these strange souls in crude American garb that gives a meaning to the masquerade of New York.

From The Color of a Great City *(1923), Theodore Dreiser*

Theodore Dreiser was the leader of the American Naturalist literary movement, a group that counted Stephen Crane and Frank Norris among its members, in turn-of-the-century New York. John Dos Passos felt indebted to Dreiser's novels for being the "battering ram . . . that opened the way through the genteel reticences of American nineteenth century fiction." Dreiser came to New York in 1895 (his brother, the composer Paul Dresser, was already living here) and published *Sister Carrie* five years later. The critical vilification of that novel caused Dreiser to suffer a nervous breakdown, and he found work as an editor of women's magazines following his release from the sanatorium.

Dreiser's Gotham was usually a city of forces that had a life of their own and overwhelmed the residents of the metropolis. But *The Color of a Great City* (1923) was a nostalgic set of vignettes of the city from 1900–1915. New York at that time was "more varied and arresting and, after its fashion, poetic and even idealistic than it is now." The wealth of Fifth Avenue and Wall Street seemed less ostentatious and the poverty of the Lower East Side less severe; as a result, for Dreiser, the city was "duller because less differentiated." Dreiser took the reader on an intimate ramble through the New York that first captivated him with "its romance, its enthusiasm, its illusions, its difficulties"; his hard-bitten realism had been softened by the splendor of what he discovered and remembered.

The City of My Dreams

It was silent, the city of my dreams, marble and serene, due perhaps to the fact that in reality I knew nothing of crowds, poverty, the winds and storms of the inadequate that blow like dust along the paths of life. It was an amazing city, so far-flung, so beautiful, so dead. There were tracks of iron stalking through the air, and streets that were as cañons, and stairways that mounted in vast flights to noble plazas, and steps that led down into deep places where were, strangely enough, underworld silences. And there were parks and flowers and rivers. And then, after twenty years, here it stood, as amazing almost as my dream, save that in the waking the flush of life was over it. It possessed the tang of contests and dreams and enthusiasms and delights and terrors and despairs. Through its ways and cañons and open spaces and underground passages were running, seething, sparkling, darkling, a mass of beings such as my dream-city never knew.

The thing that interested me then as now about New York . . . was the sharp, and at the same time immense, contrast it showed between the dull and the shrewd, the strong and the weak, the rich and the poor, the wise and the ignorant. This, perhaps, was more by reason of numbers and opportunity than anything else, for of course humanity is much the same everywhere. But the number from which to choose was so great here that the strong, or those who ultimately dominated, were so very strong, and the weak so very, very weak—and so very, very many.

I once knew a poor, half-demented, and very much shriveled little seamstress who occupied a tiny hall-bedroom in a side-street rooming-house, cooked her meals on a small alcohol stove set on a bureau, and who had about space enough outside of this to take three good steps either way.

"I would rather live in my hall-bedroom in New York than in any fifteen-room house in the country that I ever saw," she commented once, and her poor little colorless eyes held more of sparkle and snap in them than I ever saw there, before or after. She was wont to add to her sewing income by reading fortunes in cards and tea-leaves and coffee-grounds, telling of love and prosperity to scores as lowly as herself, who would never see either. The color and noise and splendor of the city as a spectacle was sufficient to pay her for all her ills.

And have I not felt the glamour of it myself? And do I not still? Broadway, at Forty-second Street, on those selfsame spring evenings when the city is crowded with an idle, sightseeing cloud of Westerners; when the doors of all shops are open, the windows of nearly all restaurants wide to the gaze of the idlest passer-by. Here is the great city, and it is lush and dreamy. A May or June moon will be hanging like a burnished silver disc between the high walls aloft. A hundred, a thousand electric signs will blink and wink. And the floods of citizens and visitors in summer clothes and with gay hats; the street cars jouncing their endless carloads on indifferent errands; the taxis and private cars fluttering about like jeweled flies. The very gasoline contributes a distinct perfume. Life bubbles, sparkles; chatters gay, incoherent stuff. . . .

I often think of the vast mass of underlings, boys and girls, who, with nothing but their youth and their ambitions to commend them, are daily and hourly setting their faces New Yorkward, reconnoitering the city for what it may hold in the shape of wealth or fame, or, if not that, position and comfort in the future; and what, if anything, they will reap. Ah, their young eyes drinking in its promise! And then, again, I think of all the powerful or semi-powerful men and women throughout the world, toiling at one task or another—a store, a mine, a bank, a profession—somewhere outside of New York, whose one ambition is to reach the place where their wealth will permit them to enter and remain in New York, dominant above the mass, luxuriating in what they consider luxury.

The illusion of it, the hypnosis deep and moving that it is! How the strong and the weak, the wise and the fools, the greedy of heart and of eye, seek the nepenthe, the Lethe, of its something hugeness. I always marvel at those who are willing, seemingly, to pay any price—*the* price, whatever it may be—for one sip of this poison cup. What a stinging, quivering zest they display. How beauty is willing to sell its bloom, virtue its last rag, strength an almost usurious portion of that which it controls, youth its very best years, its hope or dream of fame, fame and power their dignity and presence, age its weary hours, to secure but a minor part of all this, a taste of its vibrating presence and the picture that it makes. Can you not hear them almost, singing its praises?

The City Awakes

Have you ever arisen at dawn or earlier in New York and watched the outpouring in the meaner side-streets or avenues? It is a wondrous thing. It seems to have so little to do with the later, showier, brisker life of the day, and yet it has so very much. It is in the main so drab or shabby-smart at best, poor copies of what you see done more efficiently later in the day. Typewriter girls in almost stage or society costumes entering shabby offices; boys and men made up to look like actors and millionaires turning into the humblest institutions, where they are clerks or managers. These might be called the machinery of the city, after the elevators and street cars and wagons are excluded, the implements by which things are made to go.

Take your place on Williamsburg Bridge some morning, for instance, at say three or four o'clock, and watch the long, the quite unbroken line of Jews trundling pushcarts eastward to the great Wall-about Market over the bridge.

A procession out of Assyria or Egypt or Chaldea, you might suppose, Biblical in quality; or, better yet, a huge chorus in some operatic dawn scene laid in Paris or Petrograd or here. A vast, silent mass it is, marching to the music of necessity. They are so grimy, so mechanistic, so elemental in their movements and needs. And later on you will find them seated or standing, with their little charcoal buckets or braziers to warm their hands and feet, in those gusty, icy streets of the East Side in winter, or coatless and almost shirtless in hot weather, open-mouthed for want of air. And they are New York, too—Bucharest and Lemberg and Odessa come to the Bowery, and adding rich, dark, colorful threads to the rug or tapestry which is New York.

Since these are but a portion, think of those other masses that come from the surrounding territory, north, south, east and west. The ferries—have you ever observed them in the morning? Or the bridges, railway terminals, and every elevated and subway exit?

Already at six and six-thirty in the morning they have begun to trickle small streams of human beings Manhattan or cityward, and by seven and seven-fifteen these streams have become sizable affairs. By seven-thirty and eight they have changed into heavy, turbulent rivers, and by eight-fifteen and eight-thirty and nine they are raging torrents, no less. They overflow all the streets and avenues and every available means of conveyance. They are pouring into all available doorways, shops, factories, office-buildings—those huge affairs towering so significantly above them. Here they stay all day long, causing those great hives and their adjacent streets to flush with a softness of color not indigenous to them, and then at night, between five and six, they are going again, pouring forth over the bridges and through the subways and across the ferries and out on the trains, until the last drop of them appears to have been exuded, and they are pocketed in some outlying side-street or village or metropolitan hall-room—and the great, turbulent night of the city is on once more.

And yet they continue to stream cityward—this cityward. From all parts of the world they are pouring into New York: Greeks from Athens and the realms of Sparta and Macedonia, living six, seven, eight, nine, ten, eleven, twelve, in one room, sleeping on the floors and dressing and eating and entertaining themselves God knows how; Jews from Russia, Poland, Hungary, the Balkans, crowding the East Side and the inlying sections of Brooklyn, and huddling together in thick, gummy streets, singing in street crowds around balladmongers of the woes of their native land, seeking with a kind of divine, poetic flare a modicum of that material comfort which their natures so greatly crave, which their previous condition for at least fifteen hundred years has scarcely warranted; Italians from Sicily and the warmer vales of the South, crowding into great sections of their own, all hungry for a taste of New York; Germans, Hungarians, French, Polish, Swedish, Armenians, all with sections of their own and all alive to the joys of the city, and how eager to live—great gold and scarlet streets throbbing with the thoughts of them!

And last but not least, the illusioned American from the Middle West and the South and the Northwest and the Far West, crowding in and eyeing it all so eagerly, so yearningly, like the others. Ah, the little, shabby, blue-light restaurants! The boarding houses in silent streets! The moral, hungry "homes"—how full they are of them and how hopeless! How the city sings and sings for them, and in spite of them, flaunting ever afresh its lures and beauties—a city as wonderful and fateful and ironic as life itself.

From Manhattan Transfer, *John Dos Passos (1925)*

John Dos Passos was born in 1896 in Chicago, but his parents were married to other people, and Dos Passos did not take his father's name until he was sixteen years old. Much of his early life was spent traveling in Europe with his mother, and he was, as he put it, "a hotel child." After graduating from Harvard in 1916, Dos Passos spent time in the East Village before embarking for France to be a volunteer ambulance driver in the First World War. He described how he had been "going to pacifist meetings and being dispersed by the police. I am getting quite experienced in the cossack tactics of the New York police force. . . . Every day I become more red. My one ambition is to be able to sing the International."

Dos Passos's first novel was *Manhattan Transfer* (1925), but it was after the publication of the trilogy entitled *U.S.A.* in 1938 that Jean Paul Sartre declared, "I regard John Dos Passos as the greatest writer of our time." In the 1920s and 1930s Dos Passos was in the circle of critics of American consumerism that included Sinclair Lewis, Ernest Hemingway, and F. Scott Fitzgerald, but it was his style that showcased his genius. Dos Passos's narratives appear to be fragmented sections or vignettes where the reader isn't given enough background for coherence, but, by the end, the narratives twist and dovetail into magnificent structures that embroider a central theme.

By the 1950s, Dos Passos's politics had taken a sharp right and, in 1962, he accepted an award, alongside Strom Thurmond and John Wayne, from the right-wing Young Americans for Freedom.

I. Ferryslip

Three gulls wheel above the broken boxes, orangerinds, spoiled cabbage heads that heave between the splintered plank walls, the green waves spume under the round bow as the ferry, skidding on the tide, crashes, gulps the broken water, slides, settles slowly into the slip. Handwinches whirl with jingle of chains. Gates fold upwards, feet step out across the crack, men and women press through the manure-smelling wooden tunnel of the ferry-house, crushed and jostling like apples fed down a chute into a press.

THE nurse, holding the basket at arm's length as if it were a bedpan, opened the door to a big dry hot room with greenish distempered walls where in the air tinctured with smells of alcohol and iodoform hung writhing a faint sourish squalling from other baskets along the wall. As she set her basket down she glanced into it with pursed-up lips. The newborn baby squirmed in the cottonwool feebly like a knot of earthworms.

On the ferry there was an old man playing the violin. He had a monkey's face puckered up in one corner and kept time with the toe of a cracked patent-leather shoe. Bud Korpenning sat on the rail watching him, his back to the river. The breeze made the hair stir round the tight line of his cap and dried the sweat on his temples. His feet were blistered, he was leadentired, but when the ferry moved out of the slip, bucking the little slapping scalloped waves of the river he felt something warm and tingling shoot suddenly through all his veins. "Say, friend, how fur is it into the city from where this ferry lands?" he asked a young man in a straw hat wearing a blue and white striped necktie who stood beside him.

The young man's glance moved up from Bud's road-swelled shoes to the red wrist that stuck out from the frayed sleeves of his coat, past the skinny turkey's throat and slid up cockily into the intent eyes under the broken-visored cap.

"That depends where you want to get to."

"How do I get to Broadway? . . . I want to get to the center of things."

"Walk east a block and turn down Broadway and you'll find the center of things if you walk far enough."

"Thank you sir. I'll do that."

The violinist was going through the crowd with his hat held out, the wind ruffling the wisps of gray hair on his shabby bald head. Bud found the face tilted up at him, the crushed eyes like two black pins looking into his. "Nothin," he said gruffly and turned away to look at the expanse of river bright as knifeblades. The plank walls of the slip closed in, cracked as the ferry lurched against them; there was rattling of chains, and Bud was pushed forward among the crowd through the ferryhouse. He walked between two coal wagons and out over a dusty expanse of street towards yellow streetcars. A trembling took hold of his knees. He thrust his hands deep in his pockets.

EAT on a lunchwagon halfway down the block. He slid stiffly onto a revolving stool and looked for a long while at the pricelist.

"Fried eggs and a cup o coffee."

"Want 'em turned over?" asked the redhaired man behind the counter who was wiping off his beefy freckled forearms with his apron. Bud Korpenning sat up with a start.

"What?"

"The eggs? Want em turned over or sunny side up?"

"Oh sure, turn 'em over." Bud slouched over the counter again with his head between his hands.

"You look all in, feller," the man said as he broke the eggs into the sizzling grease of the frying pan.

"Came down from upstate. I walked fifteen miles this mornin."

The man made a whistling sound through his eyeteeth. "Comin to the big city to look for a job, eh?"

Bud nodded. The man flopped the eggs sizzling and netted with brown out onto the plate and pushed it towards Bud with some bread and butter on the edge of it. "I'm goin to slip you a bit of advice, feller, and it won't cost you nutten. You go an git a shave and a haircut and brush the hayseeds out o yer suit a bit before you start lookin. You'll be more likely to git somethin. It's looks that count in this city."

"I kin work all right. I'm a good worker," growled Bud with his mouth full.

"I'm tellin yez, that's all," said the redhaired man and turned back to his stove. . . .

Bud sat on the edge of his cot and stretched out his arms and yawned. From all round through a smell of sweat and sour breath and wet clothes came snores, the sound of men stirring in their sleep, creaking of bedsprings. Far away through the murk burned a single electric light. Bud closed his eyes and let his head fall over on his shoulder. O God I want to go to sleep. Sweet Jesus I want to go to sleep. He pressed his knees together against his clasped hands to keep them from trembling. Our father which art in Heaven I want to go to sleep.

"Wassa matter pardner cant ye sleep?" came a quiet whisper from the next cot.

"Hell, no." "Me neither."

Bud looked at the big head of curly hair held up on an elbow turned towards him.

"This is a hell of a lousy stinking flop," went on the voice evenly. "I'll tell the world . . . Forty cents too! They can take their Hotel Plaza an . . . "

"Been long in the city?"

"Ten years come August."

"Great snakes!"

A voice rasped down the line cots, "Cut de comedy yous guys, what do you tink dis is, a Jewish picnic?"

Bud lowered his voice: "Funny, it's years I been thinkin an wantin to come to the city. . . . I was born an raised on a farm upstate."

"Why dont ye go back?"

"I cant go back." Bud was cold; he wanted to stop trembling. He pulled the blanket up to his chin and rolled over facing the man who was talking. "Every spring I says to myself I'll hit the road again, go out an plant myself among the weeds an the grass an the cows comin home milkin time, but I dont; I juss kinder hangs on."

"What d'ye do all this time in the city?"

"I dunno. . . . I used to set in Union Square most of the time, then I set in Madison Square. I been up in Hoboken an Joisey and Flatbush an now I'm a Bowery bum."

"God I swear I'm goin to git outa here tomorrow. I git sceered here. Too many bulls an detectives in this town."

"You could make a livin in handouts. . . . But take it from me kid you go back to the farm an the ole folks while the goin's good."

Bud jumped out of bed and yanked roughly at the man's shoulder. "Come over here to the light, I want to show ye sumpen." Bud's own voice crinkled queerly in his ears. He strode along the snoring lane of cots. The bum, a shambling man with curly weatherbleached hair and beard and eyes as if hammered into his head, climbed fully dressed out from the blankets and followed him. Under the light Bud unbuttoned the front of his unionsuit and pulled it off his knottymuscled gaunt arms and shoulders. "Look at my back."

"Christ Jesus," whispered the man running a grimy hand with long yellow nails over the mass of white and red deep-gouged scars. "I aint never seen nothin like it."

"That's what the ole man done to me. For twelve years he licked me when he had a mind to. Used to strip me and take a piece of light chain to my back. They said he was my dad but I know he aint. I run away when I was thirteen. That was when he ketched me an began to lick me. I'm twentyfive now."

They went back without speaking to their cots and lay down.

Bud lay staring at the ceiling with the blanket up to his eyes. When he looked down towards the door at the end of the room, he saw standing there a man in a derby hat with a cigar in his mouth. He crushed his lower lip between his teeth to keep from crying out. When he looked again the man was gone. "Say are you awake yet?" he whispered.

The bum grunted. "I was goin to tell yer. I mashed his head in with the grubbinhoe, mashed it in like when you kick a rotten punkin. I told him to lay offn me an he wouldn't. . . . He was a hard godfearin man an he wanted you to be sceered of him. We was grubbin the sumach outa the old pasture to plant pertoters there. . . . I let him lay till night with his head mashed in like a rotten punkin. A bit of scrub along the fence hid him from the road. Then I buried him an went up to the house an made me a pot of coffee. He hadn't never let me drink no coffee. Before light I got up an walked down the road. I was tellin myself in a big city it'd be like lookin for a needle in a haystack to find yer. I knowed where the ole man kep his money; he had a roll as big as your head but I was sceered to take more'en ten dollars. . . . You awake yet?"

The bum grunted. "When I was a kid I kep company with ole man Sackett's girl. Her and me used to keep company in the ole icehouse down in Sackett's woods an we used to talk about how we'd come to New York City an git rich and now I'm here I cant git work an I cant git over bein sceered. There's detectives follow me all round, men in derbyhats with badges under their coats. Last night I wanted to go with a hooker an she saw it in my eyes an throwed me out. . . . She could see it in my eyes." He was sitting on the edge of the cot, leaning over, talking into the other man's face in a hissing whisper. The bum suddenly grabbed him by the wrists.

"Look here kid, you're goin blooy if you keep up like this. . . . Got any mazuma?" Bud nodded. "You better give it to me to keep. I'm an old timer an I'll git yez outa this. You put yer clothes on an take a walk round the block to a hash joint an eat up strong. How much you got?"

"Change from a dollar."

"You give me a quarter an eat all the stuff you kin git offn the rest." Bud pulled on his trousers and handed the man a quarter. "Then you come back here an you'll sleep good an tomorrer me'n you'll go upstate an git that roll of bills. Did ye say it was as big as yer head? Then we'll beat it where they cant ketch us. We'll split fifty fifty. Are you on?"

Bud shook his hand with a wooden jerk, then with the laces flickering round his shoes he shuffled to the door and down the spitmarked stairs.

The rain had stopped, a cool wind that smelled of woods and grass was ruffling the puddles in the cleanwashed streets. In the lunchroom in Chatham Square three men sat asleep with their hats over their eyes. The man behind the counter was reading a pink sportingsheet. Bud waited long for his order. He felt cool, unthinking, happy. When it came he ate the browned corned beef hash, deliberately enjoying every mouthful, mashing the crisp bits of potato against his teeth with his tongue, between sips of heavily sugared coffee. After polishing the plate with a crust of bread he took a toothpick and went out.

Picking his teeth he walked through the grimydark entrance to Brooklyn Bridge. A man in a derby hat was smoking a cigar in the middle of the broad tunnel. Bud brushed past him walking with a tough swagger. I dont care about him; let him follow me. The arching footwalk was empty except for a single policeman who stood yawning, looking up at the sky. It was like walking among the stars. Below in either direction streets tapered into dotted lines of lights between square blackwindowed buildings. The river glimmered underneath like the Milky Way above. Silently smoothly the bunch of lights of a tug slipped through the moist darkness. A car whirred across the bridge making the girders rattle and the spiderwork of cables thrum like a shaken banjo.

When he got to the tangle of girders of the elevated railroads of the Brooklyn side, he turned back along the southern driveway. Dont matter where I go, cant go nowhere now. An edge of the blue night had started to glow behind him the way iron starts to glow in a forge. Beyond black chimneys and lines of roofs faint rosy contours of the downtown buildings were brightening. All the darkness was growing pearly, warming. They're all of em detectives chasin me, all of em, men in derbies, bums on the Bowery, old women in kitchens, barkeeps, streetcar conductors, bulls, hookers, sailors, longshoremen, stiffs in employment agencies. . . . He thought I'd tell him where the ole man's roll was, the lousy bum. . . . One on him. One on all them goddam detectives. The river was smooth, sleek as a bluesteel gunbarrel. Dont matter where I go; cant go nowhere now. The shadows between the wharves and the buildings were powdery like washingblue. Masts fringed the river; smoke, purple chocolatecolor fleshpink climbed into light. Cant go nowhere now.

In a swallowtail suit with a gold watchchain and a red seal ring riding to his wedding beside Maria Sackett, riding in a carriage to City Hall with four white horses to be made an alderman by the mayor; and the light grows behind them brighter brighter, riding in satins and silks to his wedding, riding in pinkplush in a white carriage with Maria Sackett by his side through rows of men waving cigars, bowing, doffing brown derbies, Alderman Bud riding in a carriage full of diamonds with his milliondollar bride. . . . Bud is sitting on the rail of the bridge. The sun has risen behind Brooklyn. The windows of Manhattan have caught fire. He jerks himself forward, slips, dangles by a hand with the sun in his eyes. The yell strangles in his throat as he drops.

Captain McAvoy of the tugboat *Prudence* stood in the pilothouse with one hand on the wheel. In the other he held a piece of biscuit he had just dipped into a cup of coffee that stood on the shelf beside the binnacle. He was a wellset man with bushy eyebrows and a bushy black mustache waxed at the tips. He was about to put the piece of coffeesoaked biscuit into his mouth when something black dropped and hit the water with a thudding splash a few yards off the bow. At the same moment a man leaning out of the engineroom door shouted, "A guy juss jumped offn de bridge."

"God damn it to hell," said Captain McAvoy dropping his piece of biscuit and spinning the wheel. The strong ebbtide whisked the boat round like a straw. Three bells jangled in the engineroom. A negro ran forward to the bow with a boathook.

"Give a hand there Red," shouted Captain McAvoy.

After a tussle they landed a long black limp thing on the deck. One bell. Two bells, Captain McAvoy frowning and haggard spun the tug's nose into the current again.

"Any life in him Red?" he asked hoarsely. The negro's face was green, his teeth were chattering.

"Naw sir," said the redhaired man slowly. "His neck's broke clear off."

Captain McAvoy sucked a good half of his mustache into his mouth. "God damn it to hell," he groaned. "A pretty thing to happen on a man's wedding day."

Arrangement in Black and White, Dorothy Parker (1927)

Dorothy Parker once wrote her own rhymed "Resume." It read, "Razors pain you;/Rivers are damp;/Acids stain you;/And drugs cause cramp;/Guns aren't lawful;/Nooses give;/Gas smells awful;/You might as well live." And while Parker was most known for her wisecracking, cutting wit, the literary critic Edmund Wilson described her in a review of her book of poems, *Enough Rope* (1927), as having emerged as "a distinguished and interesting poet." More tellingly, Wilson concluded that Parker's "unprecedented feat has been to raise to the dignity of poetry the 'wise-cracking' humor of New York; she has thus almost invented a new kind of epigram; she has made the comic anti-climax tragic."

Sadly, that review might be applied to the remaining forty years of Parker's life as well. Parker was born in New Jersey but was raised at 57 West Sixty-eighth Street. After finishing at the Blessed Sacrament Convent School, she worked for *Vogue* magazine, and wrote movie reviews for *Vanity Fair* (before being fired because her reviews were too devastating). She wrote book reviews for *The New Yorker* from 1927 to 1933 when she was also the only female member of the Algonquin Round Table, a group of literati including Robert Benchley, James Thurber, and Ring Lardner. Parker then moved to Hollywood where she worked on film scripts such as *A Star Is Born* and *Saboteur* before returning to New York and living in the Volney, a residence hotel at 23 West Seventy-fourth Street, where she died in 1967. She left her estate to the Reverend Martin Luther King Jr.

THE woman with the pink velvet poppies wreathed round the assisted gold of her hair traversed the crowded room at an interesting gait combining a skip with a sidle, and clutched the lean arm of her host.

"Now I got you!" she said. "Now you can't get away!"

"Why, hello," said her host. "Well. How are you?"

"Oh, I'm finely," she said. "Just simply finely. Listen. I want you to do me the most terrible favor. Will you? Will you please? Pretty please?"

"What is it?" said her host.

"Listen," she said. "I want to meet Walter Williams. Honestly, I'm just simply crazy about that man. Oh, when he sings! When he sings those spirituals! Well, I said to Burton, 'It's a good thing for you Walter Williams is colored,' I said, 'or you'd have lots of reason to be jealous.' I'd really love to meet him. I'd like to tell him I've heard him sing. Will you be an angel and introduce me to him?"

"Why, certainly," said her host. "I thought you'd met him. The party's for him. Where is he, anyway?"

"He's over there by the bookcase," she said. "Let's wait till those people get through talking to him. Well, I think you're simply marvellous, giving this perfectly marvellous party for him, and having him meet all these white people, and all. Isn't he terribly grateful?"

"I hope not," said her host.

"I think it's really terribly nice," she said. "I do. I don't see why on earth it isn't perfectly all right to meet colored people. I haven't any feeling at all about it—not one single bit. Burton—oh, he's just the other way. Well, you know, he comes from Virginia, and you know how they are."

"Did he come tonight?" said her host.

"No, he couldn't," she said. "I'm a regular grass widow tonight. I told him when I left. 'There's no telling what I'll do,' I said. He was just so tired out, he couldn't move. Isn't it a shame?"

"Ah," said her host.

"Wait till I tell him I met Walter Williams!" she said. "He'll just about die. Oh, we have more arguments about colored people. I talk to him like I don't know what, I get so excited. 'Oh, don't be so silly,' I say. But I must say for Burton, he's heaps broader-minded than lots of these Southerners. He's really awfully fond of colored people. Well, he says himself, he wouldn't have white servants. And you know, he had this old colored nurse, this regular old nigger mammy, and he just simply loves her. Why, every time he goes home, he goes out in the kitchen to see her. He does, really, to this day. All he says is, he says he hasn't got a word to say against colored people as long as they keep their place. He's always doing things for them—giving them clothes and I don't know what all. The only thing he says, he says he wouldn't sit down at the table with one for a million dollars. 'Oh,' I say to him, 'you make me sick, talking like that.' I'm just terrible to him. Aren't I terrible?"

"Oh, no, no, no," said her host. "No, no."

"I am," she said. "I know I am. Poor Burton! Now, me, I don't feel that way at all. I haven't the slightest feeling about colored people. Why, I'm just crazy about some of them. They're just like children—just as easy-going, and always singing and laughing and everything. Aren't they the happiest things you ever saw in your life? Honestly, it makes me laugh just to hear them. Oh, I like them. I really do. Well, now, listen. I have this colored laundress, I've had her for years, and I'm devoted to her. She's a real character. And I want to tell you, I think of her as my friend. That's the way I think of her. As I say to Burton. 'Well, for Heaven's sakes, we're all human beings!' Aren't we?"

"Yes," said her host. "Yes, indeed."

"Now this Walter Williams," she said. "I think a man like that's a real artist. I do. I think he deserves an awful lot of credit. Goodness, I'm so crazy about music or anything, I don't care what color he is. I honestly think if a person's an artist, nobody ought to have any feeling at all about meeting them. That's absolutely what I say to Burton. Don't you think I'm right?"

"Yes," said her host. "Oh, yes."

"That's the way I feel," she said. "I just can't understand people being narrow-minded. Why, I absolutely think it's a privilege to meet a man like Walter Williams. Now, I do. I haven't any feeling at all. Well, my goodness, the good Lord made him, just the same as He did any of us. Didn't He?"

"Surely," said her host. "Yes, indeed."

"That's what I say," she said. "Oh, I get so furious when people are narrow-minded about colored people. It's just all I can do not to say something. Of course, I do admit when you get a bad colored man, they're simply terrible. But as I say to Burton, there are some bad white people, too, in this world. Aren't there?"

"I guess there are," said her host.

"Why, I'd really be glad to have a man like Walter Williams come to my house and sing for us, some time," she said. "Of course, I couldn't ask him on account of Burton, but I wouldn't have any feeling about it at all. Oh, can't he sing! Isn't it marvellous, the way they all have music in them? It just seems to be right *in* them. Come on, let's us go on over and talk to him. Listen, what shall I do when I'm introduced? Ought I to shake hands? Or what?"

"Why, do whatever you want," said her host.

"I guess maybe I'd better," she said. "I wouldn't for the world have him think I had any feeling. I think I'd better shake hands, just the way I would with anybody else. That's just exactly what I'll do."

They reached the tall young Negro, standing by the bookcase. The host performed introductions; the Negro bowed.

"How do you do?" he said. "Isn't it a nice party?"

The woman with the pink velvet poppies extended her hand at the length of her arm and held it so, in fine determination, for all the world to see, until the Negro took it, shook it, and gave it back to her.

"Oh, how do you do, Mr. Williams," she said. "Well, how do you do. I've just been saying, I've enjoyed your singing so awfully much. I've been to your concerts, and we have you on the phonograph and everything. Oh, I just enjoy it!"

She spoke with great distinctness, moving her lips meticulously, as if in parlance with the deaf.

"I'm so glad," he said.

"I'm just simply crazy about that 'Water Boy' thing you sing," she said. "Honestly, I can't get it out of my head. I have my husband nearly crazy, the way I go around humming it all the time. Oh, he looks just as black as the ace of—er. Well, tell me, where on earth do you ever get all those songs of yours? How do you ever get hold of them?"

"Why," he said, "there are so many different—"

"I should think you'd love singing them," she said. "It must be more fun. All those darling old spirituals—oh, I just love them! Well, what are you doing, now? Are you still keeping up your singing? Why don't you have another concert, some time?"

"I'm having one the sixteenth of this month," he said.

"Well, I'll be there," she said. "I'll be there, if I possibly can. You can count on me. Goodness, here comes a whole raft of people to talk to you. You're just a regular guest of honor! Oh, who's that girl in white? I've seen her some place."

"That's Katherine Burke," said her host.

"Good Heavens," she said, "is that Katherine Burke? Why, she looks entirely different off the stage. I thought she was much better-looking. I had no idea she was so terribly dark. Why, she looks almost like—Oh, I think she's a wonderful actress! Don't you think she's a wonderful actress, Mr. Williams? Oh, I think she's marvellous. Don't you?"

"Yes, I do," he said.

"Oh, I do, too," she said. "Just wonderful. Well, goodness, we must give some one else a chance to talk to the guest of honor. Now, don't forget, Mr. Williams, I'm going to be at that concert if I possibly can. I'll be there applauding like everything. And if I can't come, I'm going to tell everybody I know to go, anyway. Don't you forget!"

"I won't," he said. "Thank you so much."

The host took her arm and piloted her firmly into the next room.

"Oh, my dear," she said. "I nearly died! Honestly, I give you my word, I nearly passed away. Did you hear that terrible break I made? I was just going to say Katherine Burke looked almost like a nigger. I just caught myself in time. Oh, do you think he noticed?"

"I don't believe so," said her host.

"Well, thank goodness," she said, "because I wouldn't have embarrassed him for anything. Why, he's awfully nice. Just as nice as he can be. Nice manners, and everything. You know, so many colored people, you give them an inch, and they walk all over you. But he doesn't try any of that. Well, he's got more sense, I suppose. He's really nice. Don't you think so?"

"Yes," said her host.

"I liked him," she said. "I haven't any feeling at all because he's a colored man. I felt just as natural as I would with anybody. Talked to him just as naturally, and everything. But honestly, I could hardly keep a straight face. I kept thinking of Burton. Oh, wait till I tell Burton I called him 'Mister'!"

An American Catholic Answers Back, from the Atlantic Monthly, *Alfred E. Smith (1927)*

Al Smith was born on Manhattan's Lower East Side on December 30, 1873, the grandson of Irish immigrants. Today, the Alfred E. Smith Houses sit on the site of his birth at 174 South Street. Smith rose to be a presidential candidate in 1928, the first Catholic to run for that office, and he was known as New York City's "First Citizen." Smith rose through the political ranks as a protégé of Tammany boss "Silent Charlie" Murphy. Between 1903 and 1928, he was a state assemblyman, delegate to the state constitutional convention, New York county sheriff, president of the New York City Board of Aldermen, and three-time governor of New York State.

Smith brought a common touch to politics with his characteristic brown derby hat, Bowery accent, and campaign theme song, "The Sidewalks of New York." More important, his record as governor showed a farsighted progressivism that was echoed later in the New Deal. Smith reorganized the governmental structure, rammed through legislation that covered everything from housing to education to worker's rights, and, through his parks commissioner, Robert Moses, developed a massive public works program. The country, however, voted against both his Catholicism and his New York urbanism in the presidential election of 1928, and Smith retired from politics to live on Fifth Avenue. On "the Avenue," as president of the Empire State Building Corporation, he helped to construct what would become the single most recognizable structure in New York City history, the Empire State Building.

This particular article from the *Atlantic Monthly* was, according to Robert Moses, one of the few ghostwritten pieces that Smith ever put his name to. It was a response to Charles C. Marshall's article outlining what he thought would be the "menace of a Roman Catholic in the White House."

I SUMMARIZE my creed as an American Catholic. I believe in the worship of God according to the faith and practice of the Roman Catholic Church. I recognize no power in the institutions of my Church to interfere with the operations of the Constitution of the United States or the enforcement of the law of the land. I believe in absolute freedom of conscience for all men and in equality of all churches, all sects, and all beliefs before the law as a matter of right and not as a matter of favor. I believe in the absolute separation of Church and State and in the strict enforcement of the provisions of the Constitution that Congress shall make no law respecting an establishment of religion or prohibiting the free exercise thereof. I believe that no tribunal of any church has any power to make any decree of any force in the law of the land, other than to establish the status of its own communicants within its own church.

I believe in the support of the public school as one of the cornerstones of American liberty. I believe in the right of every parent to choose whether his child shall be educated in the public school or in a religious school supported by those of his own faith. I believe in the principle of noninterference by this country in the internal affairs of other nations and that we should stand steadfastly against any such interference by whomsoever it may be urged. And I believe in the common brotherhood of man under the common fatherhood of God.

In this spirit I join with fellow Americans of all creeds in a fervent prayer that never again in this land will any public servant be challenged because of the faith in which he has tried to walk humbly with his God.

General Retrospect and Summary, from The Graphic Regional Plan of 1929

The Graphic Regional Plan was the result of an eight-year study undertaken by many of the most powerful men in New York. The plan was privately funded (by the Russell Sage Foundation) and had no governmental authority. But as committee member Elihu Root pointed out, "Draw all the lines you like for states and counties, but a city is a growth, responding to the inherent atoms that make it up, apart from political or governmental considerations. The force from which that growth comes is the force of industrial enterprise. . . . That is the great force of life and modern civilization, and that is the thing government cannot imitate."

The massive ten-volume report took on a scope that was unprecedented; the plan examined not just New York City but 3 states, 22 counties, and 436 local and municipal governments. The purpose of the plan was to ensure that the region would remain the epicenter of national economic activity and that Manhattan would become the first postindustrial city. In order for that to occur, the Plan proposed an expansive and intricately linked road system. Expressways and bridges—what would later be called the Triborough Bridge, the Verrazano-Narrows Bridge, the Cross-Bronx Expressway, and the Bronx-Whitestone Bridge—would allow for traffic patterns that linked the region while bypassing Manhattan.

The plan was prophetic and visionary and its implementation was assured when the most influential builder of the twentieth century, Robert Moses, unveiled his master transportation plan for the New York region in February 1930 in the Hotel Commodore. Moses's proposal would create the infrastructure the entire city rested upon for the future, and few present failed to see its similarity to the *Graphic Regional Plan of 1929*.

Some Outstanding Developments of Recent Years

In contemplating the picture presented in the Graphic Plan, the first impression given to the reader may be one of amazement at the expected extent of growth and the cost of meeting its needs. Yet when we look back over the less than thirty years which have elapsed in this century we will be amazed also to find how vast the changes have been and what enormous expenditures have been incurred merely to meet the needs caused by these changes and to maintain progress. It is necessary to mention only a few of the new developments in the last twenty-five or thirty years—broken by four years of world war—to show the astounding power of the Region to re-form and re-create itself.

In recalling a few of these outstanding public improvements we are able to get an impression of what may happen after an equal period when the population may have doubled. Thirty or forty years is a short period in the life of a city, and yet it is long enough to witness a complete reformation in its growth. Full realization of what the last twenty-five years have produced, however, can only come to those who, first having intimate knowledge of the Region, can project their memories back for from twenty to thirty years and visualize what has been accomplished, and, still more, what influences have accrued from these accomplishments.

The significance of these changes is more in their effect on growth and distribution of industry and population than in the simple fact that they have occurred.

A complete record of the major enterprises of a quarter of a century within this Region alone would fill a volume. Their cost, if added, would prove almost as startling as any estimate that might now be made as to the cost of carrying out the projects put forward in the Graphic Plan. There follows a brief reference to some of the outstanding developments.

RAIL TRANSPORTATION AND TRANSIT

In the general field of railroad transportation changes in the Region since the beginning of the century have included 351 miles of electrified operation. The Pennsylvania Terminal was opened in 1910 and the new Grand Central Terminal was not completed until 1913.

The first rapid transit subway line in New York City was not opened until 1904, and the Hudson & Manhattan Tubes were opened in 1908. The Manhattan and Queensboro Bridges were both completed in 1909.

HIGHWAYS

The highway improvements prior to 1900 were largely of a primitive character and were few in number compared to those that have since been carried out. Asphaltic and cement surfaces are inventions of this century and so is the development of the motor car which has revolutionized road systems and surfaces. In 1902 there were 1,793 miles of paved streets in the City of New York. At the beginning of the year 1929 there were 2,359 miles paved; yet there were still 1,939 miles of unpaved streets. The extension of Riverside Drive north of 155th Street was approved as recently as 1908. The Grand Boulevard and Concourse in The Bronx was not opened until 1909 and the Bronx Parkway, begun in 1913, was only finished in 1923. The development of the Westchester parkway system is the result of less than ten years of work. In 1911 and later it was possible to close Fifth Avenue on a week-day for a Marathon race without serious interference to traffic.

The Holland vehicular tunnel under the Hudson River has been open only two years and the first new bridge connecting Manhattan and New Jersey was begun in 1927 at 178th Street. Two bridges were completed in 1928 between Staten Island and New Jersey and a third one was started in that same year. The first great highway with separated grades is now being constructed from the Holland Tunnel to beyond Newark.

AIR TRANSPORT

In ten years about 22 landing fields have been constructed in the Region in connection with air transportation. The construction of New York City's first municipal airport, Floyd Bennett Field at Barren Island in Brooklyn, was started in 1928. Mapping of land by aerial photography was only imperfectly developed during the War. Its present standard was achieved only within the last five years.

BUILDINGS

The steel frame structure and the elevator are also twentieth century inventions. Skyscrapers are as modern as the motor car. Their influence has been great but has really only begun to be felt. What effect they have had is small compared to what may be expected. In 1902 there were only 184 buildings of ten stories or more in Manhattan south of 65th Street; by 1925 this number had increased to 935. In all of Manhattan there were in 1924 a total of 1,686 buildings of ten or more stories. Each year since has added many to the number.

PARKS

As recently as 1921 there were only 53,071 acres of parks in the Region as compared with over 90,000 acres today. From 1921 to 1927 the park areas in New York City alone were increased 18 per cent. The Westchester County Park Commission, created in 1922, had by April 30, 1928, approved projects calling for the acquisition of 16,671 acres of land and acquired about 95 per cent of this total. By 1928 county park commissions also existed in Essex, Hudson, Union and Passaic Counties, all but the first of these having been organized within the past twenty-five years.

Summary of Principal Proposals on the Graphic Plan

NUMBER OF PROPOSALS

It is impossible to give the precise number of proposals, as many of them are composite proposals including several parts and others are listed or referred to twice under different headings. The following is an approximate estimate of the projects listed under the various headings, some being of major and others of more or less minor importance:

	Approximate Number of Proposals Involved
1. Trunk line railroads	
Belt lines	10
Connections or waterfront lines	19
Union passenger terminals	13
2. Suburban rapid transit	
First step	5
Completion of ultimate plan	22
3. New railroad crossings of major waterways	11
4. Waterway projects and water areas	7
5. Major regional highways	
Metropolitan loop	3
Inner routes	12
Radial routes	28
Outer circumferential routes	5
Metropolitan by-pass routes	2
Express highways	8
Supplementary routes	29
6. Minor regional highways	107
7. Parkways and boulevards	39
8. Major industrial sites to be developed	14
9. Extensions of residence areas	12
10. Proposed public parks in the environs	
Compact park areas	26
Ribbon parks	29

11.	Proposed public parks in New York City	
	Compact park areas	28
	Ribbon parks	5
12.	Airports and landing facilities	
	Proposed additional landing fields	16
	Seaplane landings, existing and proposed	20
	Total, including a few duplications of proposals	470

PREDOMINANT FEATURES

Before presenting a list of specific projects in their order of importance it is well to reiterate certain points which have been brought out in the preceding description and the survey reports as to the predominance of certain major features over others—a matter which has to be considered in determining what most needs to be done.

Port and Transportation Facilities. The development of the present Port of New York is the matter of greatest importance in the planning of the Region, and the comprehensive plans prepared for its extension should be amplified, adopted and carried out. The Plan includes the proposals for extensions of railroads and rapid transit lines so as to indicate the possibilities in regard to these main features of transportation and thereby to enable proper consideration to be given to the relation of these features to the planning of highways and land uses, and vice versa. A proper solution of the transportation problem should provide for electrification of trunk lines, unification of their management, and the creation and operation of belt lines.

It is essential that suburban rapid transit should be considered independently of trunk railroad facilities, and it is in this connection that there is probably the greatest demand for new facilities. The suburban rapid transit system should be planned in harmony with the other features of a comprehensive plan of physical growth.

One of the main needs of the Region is the construction of a metropolitan railroad, rapid transit and highway loop. Such a loop should be constructed in a form to make it an attractive corridor, providing in some places for adjoining residential and recreational areas, and in others for industry and business.

Highways. Comprehensive treatment of the highway system is necessary because highways come under the direct control of municipal authorities and are involved with all questions connected with utilization of land. An important feature of the Plan is that it includes a great many highway proposals already adopted by official bodies, and greatly adds to the value of these proposals by classifying them and co-ordinating them in a complete system.

The proposals shown for marginal ways along the edges of Manhattan and elsewhere are of primary importance. They will be treated in detail as specific projects in Plan Volume II for the purpose of illustrating the great possibilities of the waterfront areas—particularly of the east waterfront of Manhattan and the Harlem River valley.

The Plan shows certain lines of approach by highway to the 178th Street Hudson River Bridge and to the positions proposed for other new bridges and tunnels. It is urgently necessary that these be dealt with on more comprehensive lines than are now contemplated.

Land Uses. The Graphic Plan, while indicating the adaptability of land for different uses, does not specify precise boundaries and does not deal with the problems of heights, densities and area of occupancy of building. These are matters which do not lend themselves to being placed on a map but are dealt with in Plan Volume II.

It is of vital importance for the future welfare of the communities in the Region that the utmost should be done to promote more spaciousness in all new developments and to conserve as many private open spaces as possible, in the future. In particular it is desirable to discourage conversion of golf courses or large acreage of residential properties into building developments, in those places where there is already other land that is better adaptable for subdivision.

The Plan as a Practical Ideal

The Graphic Plan has been prepared on the basis that administrative as well as economic and physical changes are inevitable, and that there are enormous new developments in prospect for the future which may either create new evils or, by well-conceived planning, both prevent new evils and arrest those with which communities are now confronted.

While the basic plan has been conceived in an endeavor to comprehend future needs, it is conceived also in the belief that the solution of the problems of the present lies in the proper understanding of what these future needs are likely to be. The idea that the problems of today can be solved without study of trends of growth, and planning for the future, underlies much of the inertia of the so-called practical man towards the planning of cities.

Much of the inability to deal with current problems is due to a too prevailing unwillingness to look beyond them to what lies ahead. The policy that needs to be pursued in the interests of posterity is the one that will help most the present generation.

In making the Plan it has not been assumed that the maintenance of present standards of health, safety and convenience will be satisfactory for the increased population in the future. It seems to be inevitable that a population of twenty-one million will need higher average standards of living conditions and of efficiency and economy in the processes of production and government than a population of ten million. So far as new needs and desires are concerned, new measures will no doubt be taken as demands arise to obtain the necessary satisfactions. So far, however, as future demands are occasioned by acceleration of growth and by new inventions as well as by the combined results of increased expansion over wider areas—it will be impossible to introduce measures in the future to adequately overcome the evils that will arise from failure to lay the right foundations now in advance of growth. With the prospects that are in view it may be anticipated that as the population increases the quality of artificial environment of the urban areas must be raised.

The question of what is practical depends as much on what is permissible under the law as it is, or may be made, as it does on what is financially feasible. In a regional plan, however, we are more concerned with what the law ought to permit to meet conditions as they are likely to arise in the future than with what is now authorized by the law. Such a plan should be based on the principles stressed by Edmund Burke on "American Taxation": "It is not what a lawyer tells me I *may,* but what humanity, reason and justice tell me I *ought* to do." In the future the people will determine what law and interpretations of police power are fitted for conditions that will then arise.

At the same time we have to base our expectations of a broader law on the general principles laid down in the existing law and in the best judgments of the courts. As a general principle we may accept as sound the view expressed in a judgment in the courts of Massachusetts, namely, that "the absolute right of the individual must yield to and be modified by corresponding rights of other individuals in the community. The resulting general good of all, or the public welfare, is the foundation upon which the power rests."

On this broad basis we may anticipate that, where needed, the law will be changed so as to secure any reasonable restriction of the rights of private owners or of one part of the public, or to modify the rights of individuals or corporations in their mutual relations so that the general welfare of the whole community will be obtained. The Regional Plan must seek to set up a conception of what is best for the community under conditions as they are likely to be in the future, and leave it to the good sense and sound judgment of future generations to modify the law in accordance with the above principles. Even if the proposals are mistaken in their conception of what is best they should not be circumscribed by considerations of that which is only now practicable.

It is difficult to suggest a program that depends for the support needed to carry it out on a more intelligent public opinion than now exists, and yet is limited in the ideal it seeks to achieve by those practical considerations that must always keep collective effort from achieving a high degree of perfection in artificial growth. Because of this the Plan may fail to satisfy either the practical man who thinks mainly of the immediate present or the idealist who dreams of a perfect future.

Thus the Plan will appear to some to be too idealistic in its conception of what is needed, while to others it will appear to be lacking in true vision.

Generally speaking, planning may be inspired by one of three policies. The two that are easiest to follow in planning for the future are, first, that practical policy which does not extend beyond the concrete and the present, and second, that idealistic policy that is based solely on the abstract and the future. Under the former policy proposals are made to flow with the current created by established habits and vested interests; and under the second they are confined to what ought to be, without regard to the limits imposed by unalterable conditions. The one policy lacks soul, and the other flesh and blood, and those who follow them find planning a simple exercise.

The third, which seeks an ideal based on realities—an ideal shaped by the processes of reason and not by the play of fancy—involves the greater labor but seems to present the only possibility for improving conditions of life and society. Such an ideal in regional or city planning has regard to circumstances as they now are in the city, but also must be alert to seize the openings towards better things that appear on the horizon of the future. An ideal, to be a worthy one, must be capable of being expressed in action; and it must be action based on a study of future trends and possibilities as well as of past events. To make an ideal real, we must believe it is a good thing to do, but also that it can be done. Because of this, a plan may appear to be of the highest quality in the sphere of what is attainable and yet of comparatively poor quality in the sphere of what is desirable in the abstract. Life offers ample scope for achievement within the realms of the practical, and greater satisfaction comes from conceiving the smaller things that can be done than in dreaming of the larger things that cannot be done.

On this basis a plan for an urban region must present a picture of possibilities within the limits of reasonable anticipation of what the collective intelligence of the community will accept and promote. This raises as a final issue the importance of education of the public with regard to their responsibilities in civic affairs.

Selected Writings of Thomas Wolfe (1925–1935, 1935)

For Thomas Wolfe "the city is the place where men are constantly seeking to find their door and where they are doomed to wandering forever. Of no place is this more true than of New York." Wolfe humorously chronicled this sense of dislocation in his short story "Only the Dead Know Brooklyn," but he was also drawn to the "proud and passionate beauty" of places such as Pennsylvania Station. "Here," Wolfe speculated, "as nowhere else on earth, men were brought together for a moment at the beginning or end of their innumerable journeys, here one saw their greetings and farewells, here, in a single instant, one got the entire picture of human destiny. Men came and went, they passed and vanished, all were moving through the moments of their lives . . . but the voice of time remained aloof and unperturbed, a drowsy and eternal murmur below the immense and distant roof."

Wolfe, born in Asheville, North Carolina, in 1900, came to New York in 1923 after taking George Pierce Baker's renowned theater class, 47 Workshop, at Harvard. After failing to get plays such as his *Welcome to Our City,* a prophetic look at race relations in a small southern town, produced, Wolfe turned to teaching at New York University. Wolfe published his masterpiece, *Look Homeward, Angel,* in 1929 with the help of designer Aline Bernstein, who financially supported him during their five-year affair, and Maxwell Perkins, his editor at Scribner's, who tightened Wolfe's gargantuan manuscripts. Wolfe left New York in 1938, after depositing a manuscript literally eight feet high on the desk of his new editor, Edward Aswell, but Wolfe contracted tuberculosis of the brain and died that summer. Aswell turned that stack into three books, including *The Web and the Rock* and *You Can't Go Home Again.*

Enchanted City, from The Web and the Rock *(1925–1935)*

THERE is no truer legend in the world than the one about the country boy, the provincial innocent, in his first contact with the city. Hackneyed by repetition, parodied and burlesqued by the devices of cheap fiction and the slap-stick of vaudeville humor, it is nevertheless one of the most tremendous and vital experiences in the life of a man, and in the life of the nation. It has found inspired and glorious tongues in Tolstoy and in Goethe, in Balzac and in Dickens, in Fielding and Mark Twain. It has found splendid examples in every artery of life, as well in Shakespeare as in the young Napoleon. And day after day the great cities of the world are being fed, enriched, and replenished ceaselessly with the life-blood of the nation, with all the passion, aspiration, eagerness, faith, and high imagining that youth can know, or that the tenement of life can hold.

For one born to the obscure village and brought up within the narrow geography of provincial ways, the city experience is such as no city man himself can ever know. It is conceived in absence and in silence and in youth; it is built up to the cloud-capped pinnacles of a boy's imagining; it is written like a golden legend in the heart of youth with a plume plucked out of an angel's wing; it lives and flames there in his heart and spirit with all the timeless faery of the magic land.

When such a man, therefore, comes first to the great city—but how can we speak of such a man coming first to the great city, when really the great city is within him, encysted in his heart, built up in all the flaming images of his brain: a symbol of his hope, the image of his high desire, the final crown, the citadel of all that he has ever dreamed of or longed for or imagined that life could bring to him? For such a man as this, there really is no coming to the city. He brings the city with him everywhere he goes, and when that final moment comes when he at last breathes in the city's air, feels his foot upon the city street, looks around him at the city's pinnacles, into the dark, unceasing tide of city faces, grips his sinews, feels his flesh, pinches himself to make sure he is really there—for such a man as this, and for such a moment, it will always be a question to be considered in its bewildering ramifications by the subtle soul psychologists to know which city is the real one, which city he has found and seen, which city for this man is really there.

For the city has a million faces, and just as it is said that no two men can really know what each is thinking of, what either sees when he speaks of "red" or "blue," so can no man ever know just what another means when he tells about the city that he sees. For the city that he sees is just the city that he brings with him, that he has within his heart; and even at that immeasurable moment of first perception, when for the first time he sees the city with his naked eye, at that tremendous moment of final apprehension when the great city smites at last upon his living sense, still no man can be certain he has seen the city as it is, because in the hairbreadth of that instant recognition a whole new city is composed, made out of sense but shaped and colored and unalterable from all that he has felt and thought and dreamed about before.

And more than this! There are so many other instant, swift, and accidental things that happen in a moment, that are gone forever, and that shape the city in the heart of youth. It may be a light that comes and goes, a grey day, or a leaf upon a bough; it may be the first image of a city face, a woman's smile, an oath, a half-heard word; it may be sunset, morning, or the crowded traffics of the street, the furious pinnacle of dusty noon; or it may be April, April, and the songs they sang that year. No one can say, except it may be something chance and swift and fleeting, as are all of these, together with the accidents of pine and clay, the weather of one's youth, the place, the structure, and the life from which one came, and all conditioned so, so memoried, built up into the vision of the city that a man first brings there in his heart.

Perhaps it is just here, in the iron-breasted city, that one comes closest to the enigma that haunts and curses the whole land. The city is the place where men are constantly seeking to find their door and where they are doomed to wandering forever. Of no place is this more true than of New York. Hideously ugly for the most part, one yet remembers it as a place of proud and passionate beauty; the place of everlasting hunger, it is also the place where men feel their lives will gloriously be fulfilled and their hunger fed.

In no place in the world can the life of the lonely boy, the countryman who has been drawn northwards to the flame of his lust, be more barren, more drab, more hungry and comfortless. His life is the life of subways, of rebreathed air, of the smell of burned steel, weariness and the exhausted fetidity of a cheap rented room in the apartment of "a nice couple" on 113th Street, or perhaps the triumph of an eighty-dollar apartment in Brooklyn, upper Manhattan, or the Bronx which he rents with three or four other youths. Here they "can do as they please," a romantic aspiration which leads to Saturday night parties, to cheap gin, cheap girls, to a feverish and impotent fumbling, and perhaps to an occasional distressed, drunken, and half-public fornication.

If the youth is of a serious bent, if he has thoughts of "improving" himself, there is the gigantic desolation of the Public Library, a cutrate ticket at Gray's and a seat in the balcony of an art-theatre play that has been highly praised and that all intellectual people will be seeing, or the grey depression of a musical Sunday afternoon at Carnegie Hall, filled with arrogant-looking little musicians with silky mustaches who hiss like vipers in the dark when the works of a hated composer are played; or there is always the Metropolitan Museum.

Again, there is something spurious and unreal in almost all attempts at established life in the city. When one enters the neat little apartment of a young man or a young married couple, and sees there on neat, gaily-painted shelves neat rows of books—the solid little squares of the Every-man, and the Modern Library, the D. H. Lawrence, the *Buddenbrooks,* the Cabell, the art edition of *Penguin Island,* then a few of the paper-backed French books, the Proust and the Gide, and so on—one feels a sense of embarrassment and shame: there is something fraudulent about it. One feels this also in the homes of wealthy people, whether they live in a "charming little house" on Ninth Street which they have rented, or in the massive rooms of a Park Avenue apartment.

No matter what atmosphere of usage, servants, habitude, ease, and solid establishment there may be, one always has this same feeling that the thing is fraudulent, that the effort to achieve permanence in this impermanent and constantly changing life is no more real than the suggested permanence in a theatrical setting: one would not be surprised to return the next morning and find the scene dismantled, the stage bare, and the actors departed. Sometimes even the simplest social acts—the act of visiting one's friends, of talking to them in a room, of sitting around a hearth-fire with them—oh, above all else, of sitting around a hearth-fire in an apartment in the city!—seem naked and pitiful. There is an enormous sadness and wistfulness about these attempts to simulate an established life in a place where the one permanent thing is change itself.

In recent years many people have felt this insistent and constant movement. Some have blamed it on the war, some on the tempo of the time, some have called it "a jazz age" and suggested that men should meet the rhythm of the age and move and live by it; but although this notion has been fashionable, it can hardly recommend itself to men who have been driven by their hunger, who have known loneliness and exile, who have wandered upon the face of the earth and found no doors that they could enter, and who would to God now that they might make an end to all their wandering and loneliness, that they might find one home and heart of all their hunger where they could live abundantly forever. Such men, and they are numbered not by thousands but by millions, are hardly prepared to understand that the agony and loneliness of the human spirit may be assuaged by the jerky automata of jazz.

Perhaps this sense of restlessness, loneliness, and hunger is intensified in the city, but if anyone remembers his own childhood and youth in America he is certain to remember these desires and movements, too. Everywhere people were driven by them. Everyone had a rocking chair, and in the months of good weather everyone was out on his front porch rocking away. People were always eager to "go somewheres," and when the automobile came in, the roads, particularly on Sunday, were choked with cars going into the country, going to another town, going anywhere, no matter how ugly or barren the excursion might be, so long as this terrible restlessness might in some measure be appeased.

In the city, it is appalling to think how much pain and hunger people—and particularly young men—have suffered, because there is no goal whatever for these feverish extravasations. They return, after their day's work to a room which, despite all efforts to trick it out with a neat bed, bright colors, a few painted bookshelves, a few pictures, is obviously only a masked cell. It becomes impossible to use the room for any purpose at all save for sleeping; the act of reading a book in it, of sitting in a chair in it, of staying in it for any period of time whatever when one is in a state of wakefulness, becomes intolerable.

Yet, what are these wretched people to do? Every instant, every deep conviction a man has for a reasonable human comfort is outraged. He knows that every man on earth should have the decency of space—of space enough to extend his limbs and draw in the air without fear or labor; and he knows that his life here in this miserable closet is base, barren, mean, and naked. He knows that men should not defile themselves in this way, so he keeps out of his room as much as possible. But what can he do? Where can he go? In the terrible streets of the city there is neither pause nor repose, there are no turnings and no place where he can detach himself from the incessant tide of the crowd, and sink unto himself in tranquil meditation. He flees from one desolation to another, he escapes by buying a seat "at some show," or snatching at food in a cafeteria, he lashes about the huge streets of the night, and he returns to his cell having found no doors that he could open, no place that he could call his own.

It is therefore astonishing that nowhere in the world can a young man feel greater hope and expectancy than here. The promise of glorious fulfillment, of love, wealth, fame—or unimaginable joy—is always impending in the air. He is torn with a thousand desires and he is unable to articulate one of them, but he is sure that he will grasp joy to his heart, that he will hold love and glory in his arms, that the intangible will be touched, the inarticulate spoken, the inapprehensible apprehended; and that this may happen at any moment.

Perhaps there is some chemistry of air that causes this exuberance and joy, but it also belongs to the enigma of the whole country, which is so rich, and yet where people starve, which is so abundant, exultant, savage, full-blooded, humorous, liquid, and magnificent, and yet where so many people are poor, meager, dry, and baffled. But the richness and depth of the place is visible, it is not an illusion; there is always the feeling that the earth is full of gold, and that who will seek and strive can mine it.

In New York there are certain wonderful seasons in which this feeling grows to a lyrical intensity. One of these are those first tender days of Spring when lovely girls and women seem suddenly to burst out of the pavements like flowers: all at once the street is peopled with them, walking along with a proud, undulant rhythm of breasts and buttocks and a look of passionate tenderness on their faces. Another season is early Autumn, in October, when the city begins to take on a magnificent flash and sparkle: there are swift whippings of bright wind, a flare of bitter leaves, the smell of frost and harvest in the air; after the enervation of Summer, the place awakens to an electric vitality, the beautiful women have come back from Europe or from the summer resorts, and the air is charged with exultancy and joy.

Finally, there is a wonderful, secret thrill of some impending ecstasy on a frozen Winter's night. On one of these nights of frozen silence when the cold is so intense that it numbs one's flesh, and the sky above the city flashes with one deep jewelry of cold stars, the whole city, no matter how ugly its parts may be, becomes a proud, passionate, Northern place: everything about it seems to soar up with an aspirant, vertical, glittering magnificence to meet the stars. One hears the hoarse notes of the great ships in the river, and one remembers suddenly the princely girdle of proud, potent tides that bind the city, and suddenly New York blazes like a magnificent jewel in its fit setting of sea, and earth, and stars.

There is no place like it, no place with an atom of its glory, pride, and exultancy. It lays its hand upon a man's bowels; he grows drunk with ecstasy; he grows young and full of glory, he feels that he can never die.

Only the Dead Know Brooklyn (1935)

DERE'S no guy livin' dat knows Brooklyn t'roo an' t'roo, because it'd take a guy a lifetime just to find his way aroun' duh f—— town.

So like I say, I'm waitin' for my train t' come when I sees dis big guy standin' deh—dis is duh foist I eveh see of him. Well, he's lookin' wild, y'know, an' I can see dat he's had plenty, but still he's holdin' it; he talks good an' is walkin' straight enough. So den, dis big guy steps up to a little guy dat's standin' deh, an' says, "How d'yuh get t' Eighteent' Avenoo an' Sixty-sevent' Street?" he says.

"Jesus! Yuh got me, chief," duh little guy says to him. "I ain't been heah long myself. Where is duh place?" he says. "Out in duh Flatbush section somewhere?"

"Nah," duh big guy says. "It's out in Bensonhoist. But I was neveh deh befoeh. How d'yuh get deh?"

"Jesus," duh little guy says, scratchin' his head, y'know—yuh could see duh little guy didn't know his way about—"yuh got me, chief. I neveh hoid of it. Do any of youse guys know where it is?" he says to me.

"Sure," I says. "It's out in Bensonhoist. Yuh take duh Fourt' Avenoo express, get off at Fifty-nint' Street, change to a Sea Beach local deh, get off at Eighteent' Avenoo an' Sixty-toid, an' den walk down foeh blocks. Dat's all yuh got to do," I says.

"G'wan!" some wise guy dat I neveh seen befoeh pipes up. "Whatcha talkin' about?" he says—oh, he was wise, y'know. "Duh guy is crazy! I tell yuh what yuh do," he says to duh big guy. "Yuh change to duh West End line at Toity-sixt'," he tells him. "Get off at Noo Utrecht an' Sixteent' Avenoo," he says. "Walk two blocks oveh, foeh blocks up," he says, "an' you'll be right deh." Oh, a *wise* guy, y'know.

"Oh yeah?" I says. "Who told *you* so much?" He got me sore because he was so wise about it. "How long you been livin' heah?" I says.

"All my life," he says. "I was bawn in Williamsboig," he says. "An' I can tell you t'ings about dis town you neveh hoid of," he says.

"Yeah?" I says.

"Yeah," he says.

"Well, den, you can tell me t'ings about dis town dat nobody else has eveh hoid of, either. Maybe you make it all up yoehself at night," I says, "befoeh you go to sleep—like cuttin' out papeh dolls, or somp'n."

"Oh, yeah?" he says. "You're pretty wise, ain't yuh?"

"Oh, I don't know," I says. "Duh boids ain't usin' my head for Lincoln's statue yet," I says. "But I'm wise enough to know a phony when I see one."

"Yeah?" he says. "A wise guy, huh? Well, you're so wise dat some one's goin' t'bust yuh one right on duh snoot some day," he says. "Dat's how wise *you* are."

Well my train was comin', or I'da smacked him den and dere, but when I seen duh train was comin', all I said was, "All right, mugg! I'm sorry I can't stay to take keh of you, but I'll be seein' yuh sometime, I hope, out in duh cemetery." So den I says to duh big guy, who'd been standin' deh all duh time, "You come wit me," I says. So when we gets on duh train I says to him, "Where yuh goin' out in Bensonhoist?" I says. "What numbeh are yuh lookin' for?" I says. *You* know—I t'ought if he told me duh address I might be able to help him out.

"Oh," he says, "I'm not lookin' for no one. I don't know no one out deh."

"Then whatcha goin' out deh for?" I says.

"Oh," duh guy says, "I'm just goin' out to see duh place," he says. "I like duh sound of duh name—Bensonhoist, y'know—so I t'ought I'd go out an' have a look at it."

"Whatcha tryin' t'hand me?" I says. "Whatcha tryin' t'do—kid me?" *You* know, I t'ought duh guy was bein' wise wit me.

"No," he says, "I'm tellin' yuh duh troot. I like to go out an' take a look at places wit nice names like dat. I like to go out an' look at all kinds of places," he says.

"How'd yuh know deh was such a place," I says, "if yuh neveh been deh befoeh?"

"Oh," he says, "I got a map."

"A *map?*" I says.

"Sure," he says, "I got a map dat tells me about all dese places. I take it wit me every time I come out heah," he says.

And Jesus! Wit dat, he pulls it out of his pocket, an' so help me, but he's *got* it—he's tellin' duh troot—a big map of duh whole f—— place with all duh different pahts mahked out. You know—Canarsie an' East Noo Yawk an' Flatbush, Bensonhoist, Sout' Brooklyn, duh Heights, Bay Ridge, Greenpernt—duh whole goddam layout, he's got it right deh on duh map.

"You been to any of dose places?" I says.

"Sure," he says, "I been to most of 'em. I was down in Red Hook just last night," he says.

"Jesus! Red Hook!" I says. "Whatcha do down deh?"

"Oh," he says, "nuttin' much. I just walked aroun'. I went into a coupla places an' had a drink," he says, "but most of the time I just walked aroun'."

"Just walked aroun'?" I says.

"Sure," he says, "just lookin' at t'ings, y'know."

"Where'd yuh go?" I asts him.

"Oh," he says, "I don't know duh name of duh place, but I could find it on my map," he says. "One time I was walkin' across some big fields where deh ain't no houses," he says, "but I could see ships oveh deh all lighted up. Dey was loadin'. So I walks across duh fields," he says, "to where duh ships are."

"Sure," I says, "I know where you was. You was down to duh Erie Basin."

"Yeah," he says, "I guess dat was it. Dey had some of dose big elevators an' cranes an' dey was loadin' ships, an' I could see some ships in drydock all lighted up, so I walks across duh fields to where dey are," he says.

"Den what did yuh do?" I says.

"Oh," he says, "nuttin' much. I came on back across duh fields after a while an' went into a coupla places an' had a drink."

"Didn't nuttin' happen while yuh was in dere?" I says.

"No," he says. "Nuttin' much. A coupla guys was drunk in one of duh places an' started a fight, but dey bounced 'em out," he says, "an' den one of duh guys stahted to come back again, but duh bartender gets his baseball bat out from under duh counteh, so duh guy goes on."

"Jesus!" I said. "Red Hook!"

"Sure," he says. "Dat's where it was, all right."

"Well, you keep outa deh," I says. "You stay away from deh."

"Why?" he says. "What's wrong wit it?"

"Oh," I says, "it's a good place to stay away from, dat's all. It's a good place to keep out of."

"Why?" he says. "Why is it?"

Jesus! Whatcha gonna do wit a guy as dumb as dat? I saw it wasn't no use to try to tell him nuttin', he wouldn't know what I was talkin' about, so I just says to him, "Oh, nuttin'. Yuh might get lost down deh, dat's all."

"Lost?" he says. "No, I wouldn't get lost. I got a map," he says.

A map! Red Hook! Jesus!

So den duh guy begins to ast me all kinds of nutty questions: how big was Brooklyn an' could I find my way aroun' in it, an' how long would it take a guy to know duh place.

"Listen!" I says. "You get dat idea outa yoeh head right now," I says. "You ain't neveh gonna get to know Brooklyn," I says. "Not in a hunderd yeahs. I been livin' heah all my life," I says, "an' I don't even know all deh is to know about it, so how do you expect to know duh town," I says, "when you don't even live heah?"

"Yes," he says, "but I got a map to help me find my way about."

"Map or no map," I says, "yuh ain't gonna get to know Brooklyn wit no map," I says.

"Can you swim?" he says, just like dat. Jesus! By dat time, y'know, I begun to see dat duh guy was some kind of nut. He'd had plenty to drink, of course, be he had dat crazy look in his eye I didn't like. "Can you swim?" he says.

"Sure," I says. "Can't you?"

"No," he says. "Not more'n a stroke or two. I neveh loined good."

"Well, it's easy," I says. "All yuh need is a little confidence. Duh way I loined, me older bruddeh pitched me off duh dock one day when I was eight yeahs old, cloes an' all. 'You'll swim,' he says. 'You'll swim all right—or drown.' An', believe me, I *swam*! When yuh know yuh got to, you'll do it. Duh only t'ing yuh need is confidence. An' once you've loined," I says, "you've got nuttin' else to worry about. You'll neveh forget it. It's somp'n dat stays wit yuh as long as yuh live."

"Can yuh swim good?" he says.

"Like a fish," I tells him. "I'm a regulah fish in duh wateh," I says. "I loined to swim right off duh docks wit all duh oddeh kids," I says.

"What would you do if yuh saw a man drownin'?" duh guy says.

"Do?" Why, I'd jump in an' pull him out," I says. "Dat's what I'd do."

"Did yuh eveh see a man drown?" he says.

"Sure," I says. "I see two guys—bot' times at Coney Island. Dey got out too far, an' neider one could swim. Dey drowned befoeh any one could get to 'em."

"What becomes of people after dey've drowned out heah?" he says.

"Drowned out where?" I says.

"Out heah in Brooklyn."

"I don't know whatcha mean," I says. "Neveh hoid of no one drownin' heah in Brooklyn, unless you mean a swimmin' pool. Yuh can't drown in Brooklyn," I says. "Yuh gotta drown somewhere else—in duh ocean, where dere's wateh."

"Drownin'," duh guy says, lookin' at his map. "Drownin'." Jesus! I could see by den he was some kind of nut, he had dat crazy expression in his eyes when he looked at you, an' I didn't know what he might do. So we was comin' to a station, an' it wasn't my stop, but I got off anyway, an' waited for duh next train.

"Well, so long, chief," I says. "Take it easy, now."

"Drownin'," duh guy says, lookin' at his map. "Drownin'."

Jesus! I've t'ought about dat guy a t'ousand times since den an' wondered what eveh happened to 'm goin' out to look at Bensonhoist because he liked duh name! Walkin' aroun' t'roo Red Hook by himself at night an' lookin' at his map! How many people did I see get drowned out heah in Brooklyn! How long would it take a guy wit a good map to know all deh was to know about Brooklyn!

Jesus! What a nut *he* was! I wondeh what eveh happened to 'im, anyway! I wondeh if some one knocked him on duh head, or if he's still wanderin' aroun' in duh subway in duh middle of duh night wit his little map! Duh poor guy! Say, I've got to laugh, at dat, when I t'ink about him! Maybe he's found out by now dat he'll neveh live long enough to know duh whole of Brooklyn. It'd take a guy a lifetime to know Brooklyn t'roo an' t'roo. An' even den, yuh wouldn't know it all.

Harlem Runs Wild, Claude McKay (1935)

In 1925, Alain Locke published an anthology entitled *The New Negro* in which he described the "younger generation" of black Americans as "vibrant with a new psychology based on self-respect and self-dependence." The first major poet of the psychology that would spur the Harlem Renaissance was Claude McKay, and he signaled that most forcefully in his sonnet "If We Must Die." McKay had been working as an itinerant "railroad man" during 1919, a year in which there occurred at least twenty-five riots in major urban areas; the Chicago riot alone killed thirty-eight blacks. McKay's verses, "If we must die, let it not be like hogs/Hunted and penned in an inglorious spot. . . . Like men we'll face the murderous, cowardly pack,/Pressed to the wall, dying, but fighting back!" defined an attitude of defiance and courage that captured the spirit of a multitude of black Americans. However, the poem is never specific about the race of its protagonists, and the poem gained wider notoriety after Winston Churchill used it as a rallying cry against the Nazis during World War II.

Though he was born in 1889 in Jamaica and had already established himself as a poet there, McKay used prize money he received to enroll at Booker T. Washington's Tuskegee Institute in Alabama. Less than two years later, however, he was in Harlem which, he wrote, "is more than the Negro capital of the nation. It is the Negro capital of the world. And as New York is the most glorious experiment on earth of different races of divers groups of humanity struggling and scrambling to live together, so Harlem is the most interesting sample of black humanity marching along with white humanity." McKay compared arriving in Harlem to "entering a paradise of my own people."

Despite this sentiment, between 1922 and 1934 McKay traveled to the Soviet Union, France, and North Africa. His resume reads like that of a later expatriate, James Baldwin, and, like Baldwin, McKay was a political activist who saw his primary responsibility to be an advocate for social change. In fact, McKay's description of his first encounter with racism in the United States, "At first I was horrified; my spirit revolted against the ignoble cruelty and blindness of it all. . . . Then I found myself hating in return, but this feeling could not last long for to hate is to be miserable," could easily have been penned by Baldwin decades later.

DOCILE Harlem went on a rampage last week, smashing stores and looting them and piling up destruction of thousands of dollars worth of goods. But the mass riot in Harlem was not a race riot. A few whites were jostled by colored people in the melee, but there was no manifest hostility between colored and white as such. All night until dawn on the Tuesday of the outbreak white persons, singly and in groups, walked the streets of Harlem without being molested. The action of the police was commendable in the highest degree. The looting was brazen and daring, but the police were restrained. In extreme cases, when they fired, it was into the air. Their restraint saved Harlem from becoming a shambles.

The outbreak was spontaneous. It was directed against the stores exclusively. One Hundred and Twenty-fifth Street is Harlem's main street and the theatrical and shopping center of the colored thousands. Anything that starts there will flash through Harlem as quick as lightning. The alleged beating of a kid caught stealing a trifle in one of the stores merely served to explode the smoldering discontent of the colored people against the Harlem merchants.

It would be too sweeping to assert that radicals incited the Harlem mass to riot and pillage. The Young Liberators seized an opportune moment, but the explosion on Tuesday was not the result of Communist propaganda. There were, indeed, months of propaganda in it. But the propagandists are eager to dissociate themselves from Communists. Proudly they declare that they have agitated only in the American constitutional way for fair play for colored Harlem.

Colored people all over the world are notoriously the most exploitable material, and colored Harlem is no exception. The population is gullible to an extreme. And apparently the people are exploited so flagrantly because they invite and take it. It is their gullibility that gives to Harlem so much of its charm, its air of insouciance and gaiety. But the facade of the Harlem masses' happy-go-lucky and hand-to-mouth existence has been badly broken by the Depression. A considerable part of the population can no longer cling even to the hand-to-mouth margin.

Wherever an ethnologically related group of people is exploited by others, the exploiters often operate on the principle of granting certain concessions as sops. In Harlem the exploiting group is overwhelmingly white. And it gives no sops. And so for the past two years colored agitators have exhorted the colored consumers to organize and demand of the white merchants a new deal: that they should employ Negroes as clerks in the colored community. These agitators are crude men, theoretically. They have little understanding of and little interest in the American labor movement, even from the most conservative trade-union angle. They address their audience mainly on the streets. Their following is not so big as that of the cultists and occultists. But it is far larger than that of the Communists.

One of the agitators is outstanding and picturesque. He dresses in turban and gorgeous robe. He has a bigger following than his rivals. He calls himself Sufi Abdul Hamid. His organization is the Negro Industrial and Clerical Alliance. It was the first to start picketing the stores of Harlem demanding clerical employment for colored persons. Sufi Hamid achieved a little success. A few of the smaller Harlem stores engaged colored clerks. But on 125th Street the merchants steadfastly refused to employ colored clerical help. The time came when the Negro Industrial and Clerical Alliance felt strong enough to picket the big stores on 125th Street. At first the movement got scant sympathy from influential Negroes and the Harlem intelligentsia as a whole. Physically and mentally, Sufi Hamid is a different type. He does not belong. And moreover he used to excoriate the colored newspapers, pointing out that they would not support his demands on the bigger Harlem stores because they were carrying the stores' little ads.

Harlem was excited by the continued picketing and the resultant "incidents." Sufi Hamid won his first big support last spring when one of the most popular young men in Harlem, the Reverend Adam Clayton Powell, Jr., assistant pastor of the Abyssinian Church—the largest in Harlem—went on the picket line on 125th Street. This gesture set all Harlem talking and thinking and made the headlines of the local newspapers. It prompted the formation of a Citizens' League for Fair Play. The league was endorsed and supported by sixty-two organizations, among which were eighteen of the leading churches of Harlem. And at last the local press conceded some support.

One of the big stores capitulated and took on a number of colored clerks. The picketing of other stores was continued. And soon business was not so good as it used to be on 125th Street.

In the midst of the campaign Sufi Hamid was arrested. Sometime before his arrest a committee of Jewish Minute Men had visited the Mayor and complained about an anti-Semitic movement among the colored people and the activities of a black Hitler in Harlem. The *Day* and the *Bulletin,* Jewish newspapers, devoted columns to the Harlem Hitler and anti-Semitism among negroes. The articles were translated and printed in the Harlem newspapers under big headlines denouncing the black Hitler and his work.

On October 13 of last year Sufi Hamid was brought before the courts charged with disorderly conduct and using invective against the Jews. The witnesses against him were the chairman of the Minute Men and other persons more or less connected with the merchants. After hearing the evidence and defense, the judge decided that the evidence was biased and discharged Sufi Hamid. Meanwhile Sufi Hamid had withdrawn from the Citizens' League for Fair Play. He had to move from his headquarters and his immediate following was greatly diminished. An all-white Harlem Merchants' Association came into existence. Dissension divided the Citizens' League; the prominent members denounced Sufi Hamid and his organization.

In an interview last October Sufi Hamid told me that he had never styled himself the black Hitler. He said that once when he visited a store to ask for the employment of colored clerks, the proprietor remarked, "We are fighting Hitler in Germany." Sufi said that he replied, "We are fighting Hitler in Harlem." He went on to say that although he was a Moslem he had never entertained any prejudices against Jews as Jews. He was an Egyptian and in Egypt the relations between Moslem and Jew were happier than in any other country. He was opposed to Hitlerism, for he had read Hitler's book, *Mein Kampf,* and knew Hitler's attitude and ideas about all colored peoples. Sufi Hamid said that the merchants of Harlem spread the rumor of anti-Semitism among the colored people because they did not want to face the issue of giving them a square deal.

The Citizens' League continued picketing, and some stores capitulated. But the Leaguers began quarreling among themselves as to whether the clerks employed should be light-skinned or dark-skinned. Meanwhile the united white Harlem Merchants' Association was fighting back. In November the picketing committee was enjoined from picketing by Supreme Court Justice Samuel Rosenman. The court ruled that the Citizen's League was not a labor organization. It was the first time that such a case had come before the courts of New York. The chairman of the picketing committee remarked that "the decision would make trouble in Harlem."

One by one the colored clerks who had been employed in 125th Street stores lost their places. When inquiries were made as to the cause, the managements gave the excuse of slack business. The clerks had no organization behind them. Of the grapevine intrigue and treachery that contributed to the debacle of the movement, who can give the facts? They are as obscure and inscrutable as the composite mind of the Negro race itself. So the masses of Harlem remain disunited and helpless, while their would-be leaders wrangle and scheme and denounce one another to the whites. Each one is ambitious to wear the piebald mantle of Marcus Garvey.

On Tuesday the crowds went crazy like the remnants of a defeated, abandoned, and hungry army. Their rioting was the gesture of despair of a bewildered, baffled, and disillusioned people.

New York, Marianne Moore (1935)

Marianne Moore was born on November 15, 1887 (the same day as Georgia O'Keeffe), and moved to New York with her mother in 1918. They lived at 14 St. Luke's Place and Moore became part of the bohemian West Village crowd that included Hart Crane, Alfred Stieglitz, William Carlos Williams, and Edna St. Vincent Millay. In a letter to Ezra Pound she once described avant-garde New York as having "too many captains in one boat, but on the whole, the amount of steady cooperation that is to be counted on in the interest of getting things launched, is an amazement to me."

After working in the New York Public Library, Moore became the editor of *The Dial* in 1925. When the magazine folded four years later Moore moved, with her mother, to the Fort Greene section of Brooklyn and devoted the rest of her life to her writing. By the 1950s, Moore had become a nationally recognized poet after winning the Bollingen Prize, the National Book Award, and the Pulitzer Prize. Moore also became a nationally known writer in the pages of *Life, The New York Times,* and even *Sports Illustrated* and, in her trademark black cape and tricornered hat, threw out the first ball to open the Yankees' 1968 baseball season (even though her real love had been the Brooklyn Dodgers).

The level of Moore's national recognition might best be measured by the invitation of the Ford Motor Company in 1955 to assist them in naming their new car. Moore suggested such names as "The Intelligent Whale" and "The Utopian Turtletop," but the company eventually selected the Edsel for its new bubble-topped model. Moore died in Manhattan in 1972 at the age of eighty-five.

THE savage's romance,
accreted where we need the space for commerce—
the centre of the wholesale fur trade,
starred with tepees of ermine and peopled with foxes,

the long guard-hairs waving two inches beyond the body of the pelt;
the ground dotted with deer-skins—white with white spots,
"as satin needlework in a single colour may carry a varied pattern,"
and wilting eagle's-down compacted by the wind;
and picardels of beaver-skin; white ones alert with snow.
It is a far cry from the "queen full of jewels"
and the beau with the muff,
from the gilt coach shaped like a perfume-bottle,
to the conjunction of the Monongahela and the Allegheny,
and the scholastic philosophy of the wilderness
to combat which one must stand outside and laugh
since to go in is to be lost.
It is not the dime-novel exterior,
Niagara Falls, the calico horses and the war-canoe;
it is not that "if the fur is not finer than such as one sees others wear,
one would rather be without it"—
that estimated in raw meat and berries, we could feed the universe;
it is not the atmosphere of ingenuity,
the otter, the beaver, the puma skins
without shooting-irons or dogs;
it is not the plunder,
but "accessibility to experience."

The Man-Moth, Elizabeth Bishop (1935)*

Elizabeth Bishop was born on February 8, 1911, in Worcester, Massachusetts; but her father died before she was a year old, and her mother was committed to a mental institution when Bishop was five. Bishop came to New York in 1935, after meeting Marianne Moore the previous year while a senior at Vassar College. Moore had a profound, lifelong influence on Bishop aesthetically and personally, and one of Bishop's most moving poems is an "invitation" to Moore to "Come like a light in the white mackerel sky,/come like a daytime comet/with a long unnebulous train of words,/from Brooklyn, over the Brooklyn Bridge, on this fine morning,/please come flying." Bishop, however, was only in the city for extended visits and made her home mostly in Key West and in Brazil. Before her death in 1979, Bishop's poetry had been awarded the Pulitzer Prize, the National Book Award, the National Book Critics Award, and the Neustadt Prize for Literature, and she had been the recipient of two Guggenheim fellowships.

"The Man-Moth" explored a revelatory moment that Bishop had after reading a misprint in *The New York Times,* and Bishop's enigmatic, subterranean, surreal tone seems to embody Wallace Stevens's decree that "the poem should resist the intelligence, almost successfully." Bishop herself believed that the moment was "an oracle spoke from the page of *The New York Times,* kindly explaining New York City to me, at least for a moment. One is offered such oracular statements all the time, but often misses them, gets lazy writing them out in detail, or the meaning refuses to stay put. This poem seems to have stayed put fairly well—but as 'Fats' Waller used to say, 'One never knows, do one?'"

HERE, above,
cracks in the buildings are filled with battered moonlight.
The whole shadow of Man is only as big as his hat.
It lies at his feet like a circle for a doll to stand on,

*Newspaper misprint for "mammoth."

and he makes an inverted pin, the point magnetized to the moon.
He does not see the moon; he observes only her vast properties,
feeling the queer light on his hands, neither warm nor cold,
of a temperature impossible to record in thermometers.

But when the Man-Moth
pays his rare, although occasional, visits to the surface,
the moon looks rather different to him. He emerges
from an opening under the edge of one of the sidewalks
and nervously begins to scale the faces of the buildings.
He thinks the moon is a small hole at the top of the sky,
proving the sky quite useless for protection.
He trembles, but must investigate as high as he can climb.

Up the façades,
his shadow dragging like a photographer's cloth behind him,
he climbs fearfully, thinking that this time he will manage
to push his small head through that round clean opening
and be forced through, as from a tube, in black scrolls on the light.
(Man, standing below him, has no such illusions.)
But what the Man-Moth fears most he must do, although
he fails, of course, and falls back scared but quite unhurt.

Then he returns
to the pale subways of cement he calls his home. He flits,
he flutters, and cannot get aboard the silent trains
fast enough to suit him. The doors close swiftly.
The Man-Moth always seats himself facing the wrong way
and the train starts at once at its full, terrible speed,
without a shift in gears or a gradation of any sort.
He cannot tell the rate at which he travels backwards.

Each night he must
be carried through artificial tunnels and dream recurrent dreams.
Just as the ties recur beneath his train, these underlie
his rushing brain. He does not dare look out the window,
for the third rail, the unbroken draught of poison,
runs there beside him. He regards it as a disease
he has inherited the susceptibility to. He has to keep
his hands in his pockets, as others must wear mufflers.

If you catch him,
hold up a flashlight to his eye. It's all dark pupil,
an entire night itself, whose haired horizon tightens
as he stares back, and closes up the eye. Then from the lids
one tear, his only possession, like the bee's sting, slips.
Slyly he palms it, and if you're not paying attention
he'll swallow it. However, if you watch, he'll hand it over,
cool as from underground springs and pure enough to drink.

From Going to the Territory, *Ralph Ellison (1986)*

Ralph Ellison came to New York in the summer of 1936 after his junior year at Tuskegee Institute, where he had been on a music scholarship. He took a room at the YMCA on 135th Street and the next day met Alain Locke and Langston Hughes, who in turn introduced Ellison to Richard Wright. Hughes also took Ellison to his first Broadway show, a dramatization of Erskine Caldwell's novel *Tobacco Road,* and Ellison later noted that he was so excited that he "failed to note the irony of circumstance that would have as my introduction to New York theater a play with a southern setting and characters that were based upon a type and class of whites whom I had spent the last three years trying to avoid."

With Wright's help, Ellison was able to land a job with the Federal Writer's Project in 1939 that allowed him to interview Harlem residents about African American folklore. Ellison's work for the Federal Writer's Project was to come to fruition in 1952, however, with the publication of one of the most extraordinary books in American fiction, *Invisible Man,* which won the National Book Award in 1953. Ellison lived the last decades of his life in an apartment on Riverside Drive until his death in 1994. In one of his last pieces Ellison described how he discovered that "if you acted as you were in fact a New Yorker exercising a routine freedom, chances were that you'd be accepted. Which is to say that in many instances I found my air and attitude could offset the inescapable fact of my color. . . . So, to enjoy the wonders of New York, I assumed a mask which I conceived to be that of a 'New Yorker,' and decided to leave it to those whites who might object to seek out the questioning Tuskegeean who was hidden behind the mask."

It was at Tuskegee Institute during the mid-1930s that I was made aware of the little man behind the stove. At the time I was a trumpeter majoring in music and had aspirations of becoming a classical composer. As such, shortly before the little man came to my attention, I had outraged the faculty members who judged my monthly student's recital by substituting a certain skill of lips and fingers for the intelligent and artistic structuring of emotion that was demanded in performing the music assigned to me. Afterward, still dressed in my hired tuxedo, my ears burning from the harsh negatives of their criticism, I had sought solace in the basement studio of Hazel Harrison, a highly respected concert pianist and teacher. Miss Harrison had been one of Ferruccio Busoni's prize pupils, had lived (until the rise of Hitler had driven her back to a U.S.A. that was not yet ready to recognize her talents) in Busoni's home in Berlin, and was a friend of such masters as Egon Petri, Percy Grainger, and Sergei Prokofiev. It was not the first time that I had appealed to Miss Harrison's generosity of spirit, but today her reaction to my rather adolescent complaint was less than sympathetic.

"But, baby," she said, "in this country you must always prepare yourself to play your very best wherever you are, and on all occasions."

"But everybody tells you that," I said.

"Yes," she said, "but there's more to it than you're usually told. Of course you've always been taught to *do* your best, *look* your best, *be* your best. You've been told such things all your life. But now you're becoming a musician, an artist, and when it comes to performing the classics in this country, there's something more involved."

Watching me closely, she paused.

"Are you ready to listen?"

"Yes, ma'am."

"All right," she said, "you must *always* play your best, even if it's only in the waiting room at Chehaw Station, because in this country there'll always be a little man hidden behind the stove."

"A *what?*"

She nodded. "That's right," she said. "There'll always be the little man whom you don't expect, and he'll know the *music,* and the *tradition,* and the standards of *musicianship* required for whatever you set out to perform!"

Speechless, I stared at her. After the working-over I'd just received from the faculty, I was in no mood for joking. But no, Miss Harrison's face was quite serious. So what did she mean? Chehaw Station was a lonely whistle-stop where swift north- or southbound trains paused with haughty impatience to drop off or take on passengers; the point where, on homecoming weekends, special coaches crowded with festive visitors were cut loose, coupled to a waiting switch engine, and hauled to Tuskegee's railroad siding. I knew it well, and as I stood beside Miss Harrison's piano, visualizing the station, I told myself, *She has GOT to be kidding!*

For, in my view, the atmosphere of Chehaw's claustrophobic little waiting room was enough to discourage even a blind street musician from picking out blues on his guitar, no matter how tedious his wait for a train. Biased toward disaster by bruised feelings, my imagination pictured the vibrations set in motion by the winding of a trumpet within that drab, utilitarian structure: first shattering, then bringing its walls "a-tumbling down"—like Jericho's at the sounding of Joshua's priest-blown ram horns.

True, Tuskegee possessed a rich musical tradition, both classical and folk, and many music lovers and musicians lived or moved through its environs, but—and my regard for Miss Harrison notwithstanding—Chehaw Station was the last place in the area where I would expect to encounter a connoisseur lying in wait to pounce upon some rash, unsuspecting musician. Sure, a connoisseur might hear the haunting, blues-echoing, train-whistle rhapsodies blared by fast express trains as they thundered past—but the classics? Not a chance!

So as Miss Harrison watched to see the effect of her words, I said with a shrug, "Yes, ma'am."

She smiled, her prominent eyes a-twinkle.

"I hope so," she said. "But if you don't just now, you will by the time you become an artist. So remember the little man behind the stove."

With that, seating herself at her piano, she began thumbing through a sheaf of scores—a signal that our discussion was ended.

So, I thought, *you ask for sympathy and you get a riddle.* I would have felt better if she had said, "Sorry, baby, I know how you feel, but after all, I was *there,* I *heard* you; and you treated your audience as though you were some kind of confidence man with a horn. So forget it, because I will not violate my own standards by condoning sterile musicianship." Some such reply, by reaffirming the "sacred principles" of art to which we were both committed, would have done much to supply the emotional catharsis for which I was appealing. By refusing, she forced me to accept full responsibility and thus learn from my offense. The condition of artistic communication is, as the saying goes, hard but fair. . . .

Three years later, after having abandoned my hope of becoming a musician, I had just about forgotten Miss Harrison's mythical little man behind the stove. Then, in faraway New York, concrete evidence of his actual existence arose and blasted me like the heat from an internally combusted ton of coal.

As a member of the New York Writers' Project, I was spending a clammy, late fall afternoon of freedom circulating a petition in support of some now long-forgotten social issue that I regarded as indispensable to the public good. I found myself inside a tenement building in San Juan Hill, a Negro district that disappeared with the coming of Lincoln Center. Starting on the top floor of the building, I had collected an acceptable number of signatures and, having descended from the ground floor to the basement level, was moving along the dimly lit hallway toward a door through which I could hear loud voices. They were male Afro-American voices, raised in violent argument. The language was profane, the style of speech a southern idiomatic vernacular such as was spoken by formally uneducated Afro-American workingmen. Reaching the door, I paused, sounding out the lay of the land before knocking to present my petition.

But my delay led to indecision. Not, however, because of the loud, unmistakable anger sounding within; being myself a slum dweller, I knew that voices in slums are often raised in anger, but that the *rhetoric* of anger, being in itself cathartic, is not necessarily a prelude to physical violence. Rather, it is frequently a form of symbolic action, a verbal equivalent of fisticuffs. No, I hesitated because I realized that behind the door a mystery was unfolding. A mystery so incongruous, outrageous, and surreal that it struck me as a threat to my sense of rational order. It was as though a bizarre practical joke had been staged and its perpetrators were waiting for me, its designated but unknowing scapegoat, to arrive; a joke designed to assault my knowledge of American culture and its hierarchal dispersal. At the very least, it appeared that my pride in my knowledge of my own people was under attack.

For the angry voices behind the door were proclaiming an intimate familiarity with a subject of which, by all the logic of their linguistically projected social status, they should have been oblivious. The subject of their contention confounded all my assumptions regarding the correlation between educational levels, class, race, and the possession of conscious culture. Impossible as it seemed, these foulmouthed black workingmen were locked in verbal combat over which of two celebrated Metropolitan Opera divas was the superior soprano!

I myself attended the opera only when I could raise the funds, and I knew full well that opera going was far from the usual cultural pursuit of men identified with the linguistic style of such voices. And yet, confounding such facile logic, they were voicing (and loudly) a familiarity with the Met far greater than my own. In their graphic, irreverent, and vehement criticism they were describing not only the sopranos' acting abilities but were ridiculing the gestures with which each gave animation to her roles, and they shouted strong opinions as to the ranges of the divas' vocal equipment. Thus, with such a distortion of perspective being imposed upon me, I was challenged either to solve the mystery of their knowledge by entering into their midst or to leave the building with my sense of logic reduced forever to a level of college-trained absurdity.

So challenged, I knocked. I knocked out of curiosity, I knocked out of outrage. I knocked in fear and trembling. I knocked in anticipation of whatever insights—malicious or transcendent, I no longer cared which—I would discover beyond the door.

For a moment there was an abrupt and portentous silence; then came the sound of chair legs thumping dully upon the floor, followed by further silence. I knocked again, loudly, with an authority fired by an impatient and anxious urgency.

Again silence—until a gravel voice boomed an annoyed "Come in!"

Opening the door with an unsteady hand, I looked inside, and was even less prepared for the scene that met my eyes than for the content of their loud-mouthed contention.

In a small, rank-smelling, lamp-lit room, four huge black men sat sprawled around a circular dining-room table, looking toward me with undisguised hostility. The sooty-chimneyed lamp glowed in the center of the bare oak table, casting its yellow light upon four water tumblers and a half-empty pint of whiskey. As the men straightened in their chairs I became aware of a fireplace with a coal fire glowing in its grate, and leaning against the ornate marble facing of its mantelpiece, I saw four enormous coal scoops.

"All right," one of the men said, rising to his feet. "What the hell can we do for *you*?"

"And we ain't buying nothing, buddy," one of the seated men added, his palm slapping the table.

Closing the door, I moved forward, holding my petition like a flag of truce before me, noting that the men wore faded blue overalls and jumper jackets, and becoming aware that while all were of dark complexion, their blackness was accentuated in the dim lamplight by the dust and grime of their profession.

"Come on, man, speak up," the man who had arisen said. "We ain't got all day."

"I'm sorry to interrupt," I said, "but I thought you might be interested in supporting my petition," and began hurriedly to explain.

"Say," one of the men said, "you look like one of them relief investigators. You're not out to jive us, are you?"

"Oh, no, sir," I said. "I happen to work on the Writers' Project. . . ."

The standing man leaned toward me. "You on the Writers' Project?" he said, looking me up and down.

"That's right," I said. "I'm a writer."

"Now is that right?" he said. "How long you been writing?"

I hesitated. "About a year," I said.

He grinned, looking at the others. "Y'all hear that? Ole Home-boy here has done up and jumped on the *gravy* train! Now that's pretty good. Pretty damn good! So what did you do before that?" he said.

"I studied music," I said, "at Tuskegee."

"Hey, now!" the standing man said. "They got a damn good choir down there. Y'all remember back when they opened Radio City? They had that fellow William L. Dawson for a director. Son, let's see that paper."

Relieved, I handed him the petition, watching him stretch it between his hardened hands. After a moment of soundlessly mouthing the words of its appeal, he gave me a skeptical look and turned to the others.

"What the hell," he said, "signing this piece of paper won't do no good, but since Home here's a musician, it won't do us no harm to help him out. Let's go along with him."

Fishing a blunt-pointed pencil from the bib of his overalls, he wrote his name and passed the petition to his friends, who followed suit.

This took some time, and as I watched the petition move from hand to hand, I could barely contain myself or control my need to unravel the mystery that had now become far more important than just getting their signatures on my petition.

"There you go," the last one said, extending the petition toward me. "Having our names on there don't mean a thing, but you got 'em."

"Thank you," I said. "Thank you very much."

They watched me with amused eyes, expecting me to leave, but, clearing my throat nervously, I stood in my tracks, too intrigued to leave and suddenly too embarrassed to ask my question.

"So what'er you waiting for?" one of them said. "You got what you came for. What else do you want?"

And then I blurted it out. "I'd like to ask you just one question," I said.

"Like what?" the standing one said.

"Like where on earth did you gentlemen learn so much about grand opera?"

For a moment he stared at me with parted lips; then, pounding the mantelpiece with his palm, he collapsed with a roar of laughter. As the laughter of the others erupted like a string of giant firecrackers I looked on with growing feelings of embarrassment and insult, trying to grasp the handle to what appeared to be an unfriendly joke. Finally, wiping coal-dust-stained tears from his cheeks, he interrupted his laughter long enough to initiate me into the mystery.

"Hell, son," he laughed, "we learned it down at the Met, that's where . . ."

"You learned it *where*?"

"At the Metropolitan Opera, just like I told you. Strip us fellows down and give us some costumes and we make about the finest damn bunch of Egyptians you ever seen. Hell, we been down there wearing leopard skins and carrying spears or waving things like palm leafs and ostrich-tail fans for *years!*"

Now, purged by the revelation, and with Hazel Harrison's voice echoing in my ears, it was my turn to roar with laughter. With a shock of recognition I joined them in appreciation of the hilarious American joke that centered on the incongruities of race, economic status, and culture. My sense of order restored, my appreciation of the arcane ways of American cultural possibility was vastly extended. The men were products of both past *and* present; were both coal heavers *and* Met extras; were both workingmen *and* opera buffs. Seen in the clear, pluralistic, melting-pot light of American cultural possibility there was no contradiction. The joke, the apparent contradiction, sprang from my attempting to see them by the light of social concepts that cast less illumination than an inert lump of coal. I was delighted, because during a moment when I least expected to encounter the little man behind the stove (Miss Harrison's vernacular music critic, as it were), I had stumbled upon four such men. Not behind the stove, it is true, but even more wondrously, they had materialized at an even more unexpected location: at the depth of the American social hierarchy and, of all possible hiding places, behind a coal pile. Where there's a melting pot there's smoke, and where there's smoke it is not simply optimistic to expect fire, it's imperative to watch for the phoenix's vernacular, but transcendent, rising.

The Fourteenth Ward, from Black Spring, *Henry Miller (1936)*

Henry Miller came into the world the day after Christmas 1891 in the Yorkville section of Manhattan; but his family moved to Williamsburg, Brooklyn, less than a year later. But as Miller saw it, he "was born in the street and raised in the street . . . and to be born in the street means to wander all your life, to be free. It means accident and incident, drama, movement. It means above all dream." One of Miller's other dictums was that people "should not stop to reflect, compare, analyze, possess, but flow on through, endlessly, like music."

Miller's life embodied his dictum. His formal education ended when he left City College in 1909 after only two months, and a year later he began his first love affair with "Pauline Choteau of Phoebus, Virginia, a woman old enough to be my mother." His final marriage was in September 1970 to Hiroko Tokuda, a Japanese jazz singer more than forty years his junior. In between there were four other marriages and countless affairs, the most celebrated being with Anais Nin, the French writer, who simultaneously had an affair with Miller's wife.

Before his death in 1980, however, Miller had made significant contributions to the literary world. His most famous work was *Tropic of Cancer*, which he began in 1930 when he was an expatriate living in Paris. The novel was published in Paris in 1934, but was the topic of an almost thirty-year debate about censorship and obscenity that Miller finally won when Grove Press published the book in the United States in 1961. Although he lived in Big Sur and Pacific Palisades, California, from 1944 on, Miller always regarded himself as "just a Brooklyn boy."

I AM a patriot—of the Fourteenth Ward, Brooklyn, where I was raised. The rest of the United States doesn't exist for me, except as idea, or history, or literature. At ten years of age I was uprooted from my native soil and removed to a cemetery, a *Lutheran* cemetery, where the tombstones were always in order and the wreaths never faded.

But I was born in the street and raised in the street. "The post-mechanical open street where the most beautiful and hallucinating iron vegetation," etc. . . . Born under the sign of Aries which gives a fiery, active, energetic and somewhat restless body. *With Mars in the ninth house!*

To be born in the street means to wander all your life, to be free. It means accident and incident, drama, movement. It means above all dream. A harmony of irrelevant facts which gives to your wandering a metaphysical certitude. In the street you learn what human beings really are; otherwise, or afterwards, you invent them. What is not in the open street is false, derived, that is to say, *literature.* Nothing of what is called "adventure" ever approaches the flavor of the street. It doesn't matter whether you fly to the Pole, whether you sit on the floor of the ocean with a pad in your hand, whether you pull up nine cities one after the other, or whether, like Kurtz, you sail up the river and go mad. No matter how exciting, how intolerable the situation, there are always exits, always ameliorations, comforts, compensations, newspapers, religions. But once there was none of this. Once you were free, wild, murderous. . . .

The boys you worshiped when you first came down into the street remain with you all your life. They are the only real heroes. Napoleon, Lenin, Capone—all fiction. Napoleon is nothing to me in comparison with Eddie Carney, who gave me my first black eye. No man I have ever met seems as princely, as regal, as noble, as Lester Reardon, who, by the mere act of walking down the street, inspired fear and admiration. Jules Verne never led me to the places that Stanley Borowski had up his sleeve when it came dark. Robinson Crusoe lacked imagination in comparison with Johnny Paul. All these boys of the Fourteenth Ward have a flavor about them still. They were not invented or imagined: they were real. Their names ring out like gold coins—Tom Fowler, Jim Buckley, Matt Owen, Rob Ramsay, Harry Martin, Johnny Dunne, to say nothing of Eddie Carney or the great Lester Reardon. Why, even now when I say Johnny Paul the names of the saints leave a bad taste in my mouth. Johnny Paul was the living Odyssey of the Fourteenth Ward; that he later became a truck driver is an irrelevant fact.

Before the great change no one seemed to notice that the streets were ugly or dirty. If the sewer mains were opened you held your nose. If you blew your nose you found snot in your handkerchief and not your nose. There was more of inward peace and contentment. There was the saloon, the race track, bicycles, fast women and trot horses. Life was still moving along leisurely. In the Fourteenth Ward, at least. Sunday mornings no one was dressed. If Mrs. Gorman came down in her wrapper with dirt in her eyes to bow to the priest—"Good morning, Father!" "Good morning, Mrs. Gorman!"—the street was purged of all sin. Pat McCarren carried his handkerchief in the tailflap of his frock coat; it was nice and handy there, like the shamrock in his buttonhole. The foam was on the lager and people stopped to chat with one another.

In my dreams I come back to the Fourteenth Ward as a paranoiac returns to his obsessions. When I think of those steel-gray battleships in the Navy Yard I see them lying there in some astrologic dimension in which I am the gunnersmith, the chemist, the dealer in high explosives, the undertaker, the coroner, the cuckold, the sadist, the lawyer and contender, the scholar, the restless one, the jolt-head, and the brazen-faced.

Where others remember of their youth a beautiful garden, a fond mother, a sojourn at the seashore, I remember, with a vividness as if it were etched in acid, the grim, soot-covered walls and chimneys of the tin factory opposite us and the bright, circular pieces of tin that were strewn in the street, some bright and gleaming, others rusted, dull, copperish, leaving a stain on the fingers; I remember the ironworks where the red furnace glowed and men walked toward the glowing pit with huge shovels in their hands, while outside were the shallow wooden forms like coffins with rods through them on which you scraped your shins or broke your neck. I remember the black hands of the ironmolders, the grit that had sunk so deep into the skin that nothing could remove it, not soap, nor elbow grease, nor money, nor love, nor death. Like a black mark on them! Walking into the furnace like devils with black hands—and later, with flowers over them, cool and rigid in their Sunday suits, not even the rain can wash away the grit. All these beautiful gorillas going up to God with swollen muscles and lumbago and black hands. . . .

For me the whole world was embraced in the confines of the Fourteenth Ward. If anything happened outside it either didn't happen or it was unimportant. If my father went outside that world to fish it was of no interest to me. I remember only his boozy breath when he came home in the evening and opening the big green basket spilled the squirming, goggle-eyed monsters on the floor. If a man went off to the war I remember only that he came back of a Sunday afternoon and standing in front of the minister's house puked up his guts and then wiped it up with his vest. Such was Rob Ramsay, the minister's son. I remember that everybody liked Rob Ramsay—he was the black sheep of the family. They liked him because he was a good-for-nothing and he made no bones about it. Sundays or Wednesdays made no difference to him: you could see him coming down the street under the drooping awnings with his coat over his arm and the sweat rolling down his face; his legs wobbly, with that long, steady roll of a sailor coming ashore after a long cruise; the tobacco juice dribbling from his lips, together with warm, silent curses and some loud and foul ones too. The utter indolence, the insouciance of the man, the obscenities, the sacrilege. Not a man of God, like his father. No, a man who inspired love! His frailties were human frailties and he wore them jauntily, tauntingly, flauntingly, like banderillas. He would come down the warm open street with the gas mains bursting and the air full of sun and shit and oaths and maybe his fly would be open and his suspenders undone, or maybe his vest bright with vomit. Sometimes he came charging down the street, like a bull skidding on all fours, and then the street cleared magically, as if the manholes had opened up and swallowed their offal. Crazy Willy Maine would be standing on the shed over the paint shop, with his pants down, jerking away for dear life. There they stood in the dry electrical crackle of the open street with the gas mains bursting. A tandem that broke the minister's heart.

That was how he was then, Rob Ramsay. A man on a perpetual spree. He came back from the war with medals, and with fire in his guts. He puked up in front of his own door and he wiped up his puke with his own vest. He could clear the street quicker than a machine gun. *Faugh a balla!* That was his way. And a little later, in his warmheartedness, in that fine, careless way he had, he walked off the end of a pier and drowned himself.

I remember him so well and the house he lived in. Because it was on the doorstep of Rob Ramsay's house that we used to congregate in the warm summer evenings and watch the goings-on over the saloon across the street. A coming and going all night long and nobody bothered to pull down the shades. Just a stone's throw away from the little burlesque house called The Bum. All around The Bum were the saloons, and Saturday nights there was a long line outside, milling and pushing and squirming to get at the ticket window. Saturday nights, when the Girl in Blue was in her glory, some wild tar from the Navy Yard would be sure to jump out of his seat and grab off one of Millie de Leon's garters. And a little later that night they'd be sure to come strolling down the street and turn in at the family entrance. And soon they'd be standing in the bedroom over the saloon, pulling off their right pants and the women yanking off their corsets and scratching themselves like monkeys, while down below they were scuttling the suds and biting each other's ears off, and such a wild, shrill laughter all bottled up inside there, like dynamite evaporating. All this from Rob Ramsay's doorstep, the old man upstairs saying his prayers over a kerosene lamp, praying like an obscene nanny goat for an end to come, or when he got tired of praying coming down in his nightshirt, like an old leprechaun, and belaying us with a broom-stick.

From Saturday afternoon on until Monday morning it was a period without end, one thing melting into another. Saturday morning already—how it happened God only knows—you could *feel* the war vessels lying at anchor in the big basin. Saturday mornings my heart was in my mouth. I could see the decks being scrubbed down and the guns polished and the weight of those big sea monsters resting on the dirty glass lake of the basin was a luxurious weight on me. I was already dreaming of running away, of going to far places. But I got only as far as the other side of the river, about as far north as Second Avenue and Twenty-eighth Street, via the Belt Line. There I played the Orange Blossom Waltz and in the entr'actes I washed my eyes at the iron sink. The piano stood in the rear of the saloon. The keys were very yellow and my feet wouldn't reach to the pedals. I wore a velvet suit because velvet was the order of the day.

Everything that passed on the other side of the river was sheer lunacy: the sanded floor, the argand lamps, the mica pictures in which the snow never melted, the crazy Dutchmen with steins in their hands, the iron sink that had grown such a mossy coat of slime, the woman from Hamburg whose ass always hung over the back of the chair, the courtyard choked with sauerkraut. . . . Everything in three-quarter time that goes on forever. I walk between my parents, with one hand in my mother's muff and the other in my father's sleeve. My eyes are shut tight, tight as clams which draw back their lids only to weep.

All the changing tides and weather that passed over the river are in my blood. I can still feel the slipperiness of the big handrail which I leaned against in fog and rain, which sent through my cool forehead the shrill blasts of the ferryboat as she slid out of the slip. I can still see the mossy planks of the ferry slip buckling as the big round prow grazed her sides and the green, juicy water sloshed through the heaving, groaning planks of the slip. And overhead the sea gulls wheeling and diving, making a dirty noise with their dirty beaks, a hoarse, preying sound of inhuman feasting, of mouths fastened down on refuse, of scabby legs skimming the green-churned water.

One passes imperceptibly from one scene, one age, one life to another. Suddenly, walking down a street, be it real or be it a dream, one realizes for the first time that the years have flown, that all this has passed forever and will live on only in memory; and then the memory turns inward with a strange, clutching brilliance and one goes over these scenes and incidents perpetually, in dream and reverie, while walking a street, while lying with a woman, while reading a book, while talking to a stranger . . . suddenly, but always with terrific insistence and always with terrific accuracy, these memories intrude, rise up like ghosts and permeate every fiber of one's being. Henceforward everything moves on shifting levels—our thoughts, our dreams, our actions, our whole life. A parallelogram in which we drop from one platform of our scaffold to another. Henceforward we walk split into myriad fragments, like an insect with a hundred feet, a centipede with soft-stirring feet that drinks in the atmosphere; we walk with sensitive filaments that drink avidly of past and future, and all things melt into music and sorrow; we walk against a united world, asserting our dividedness. All things, as we walk, splitting with us into a myriad of iridescent fragments. The great fragmentation of maturity. The great change. In youth we were whole and the terror and pain of the world penetrated us through and through. There was no sharp separation between joy and sorrow: they fused into one, as our waking life fuses with dream and sleep. We rose one being in the morning and at night we went down into an ocean, drowned out completely, clutching the stars and the fever of the day.

And then comes a time when suddenly all seems to be reversed. We live in the mind, in ideas, in fragments. We no longer drink in the wild outer music of the streets—we *remember* only. Like a monomaniac we relive the drama of youth. Like a spider that picks up the thread over and over and spews it out according to some obsessive, logarithmic pattern. If we are stirred by a fat bust it is the fat bust of a whore who bent over on a rainy night and showed us for the first time the wonder of the great milky globes; if we are stirred by the reflections on a wet pavement it is because at the age of seven we were suddenly speared by a premonition of the life to come as we stared unthinkingly into that bright, liquid mirror of the street. If the sight of a swinging door intrigues us it is the memory of a summer's evening when all the doors were swinging softly and where the light bent down to caress the shadow there were golden calves and lace and glittering parasols and through the chinks in the swinging door, like fine sand sifting through a bed of rubies, there drifted the music and the incense of gorgeous unknown bodies. Perhaps when that door parted to give us a choking glimpse of the world, perhaps then we had the first intimation of the great impact of sin, the first intimation that here over little round tables spinning in the light, our feet idly scraping the sawdust, our hands touching the cold stem of a glass, that here over these little round tables which later we are to look at with such yearning and reverence, that here, I say, we are to feel in the years to come the first iron of love, the first stains of rust, the first black, clawing hands of the pit, the bright circular pieces of tin in the streets, the gaunt soot-colored chimneys, the bare elm tree that lashes out in the summer's lightning and screams and shrieks as the rain beats down, while out of the hot earth the snails scoot away miraculously and all the air turns blue and sulphurous. Here over these tables, at the first call, the first touch of a hand, there is to come the bitter, gnawing pain that gripes at the bowels; the wine turns sour in our bellies and a pain rises from the soles of the feet and the round tabletops whirl with the anguish and the fever in our bones at the soft, burning touch of a hand. Here there is buried legend after legend of youth and melancholy, of savage nights and mysterious bosoms dancing on the wet mirror of the pavement, of women chuckling softly as they scratch themselves, of wild sailors' shouts, of long queues standing in front of the lobby, of boats brushing each other in the fog and tugs snorting furiously against the rush of tide while up on the Brooklyn Bridge a man is standing in agony, waiting to jump, or waiting to write a poem, or waiting for the blood to leave his vessels because if he advances another foot the pain of his love will kill him.

The plasm of the dream is the pain of separation. The dream lives on after the body is buried. We walk the streets with a thousand legs and eyes, with furry antennae picking up the slightest clue and memory of the past. In the aimless to and fro we pause now and then, like long, sticky plants, and we swallow whole the live morsels of the past. We open up soft and yielding to drink in the night and the oceans of blood which drowned the sleep of our youth. We drink and drink with an insatiable thirst. We are never whole again, but living in fragments, and all our parts separated by thinnest membrane. Thus when the fleet maneuvers in the Pacific it is the whole saga of youth flashing before your eyes, the dream of the open street and the sound of gulls wheeling and diving with garbage in their beaks; or it's the sound of the trumpet and flags flying and all the unknown parts of the earth sailing before your eyes without dates or meaning, wheeling like the tabletop in an iridescent sheen of power and glory. Day comes when you stand on the Brooklyn Bridge looking down into black funnels belching smoke and the gun barrels gleam and the buttons gleam and the water divides miraculously under the sharp, cutting prow, and like ice and lace, like a breaking and a smoking, the water churns green and blue with a cold incandescence, with the chill of champagne and burnt gills. And the prow cleaves the waters in an unending metaphor: the heavy body of the vessel moves on, with the prow ever dividing, and the weight of her is the unweighable weight of the world, the sinking down into unknown barometric pressures, into unknown geologic fissures and caverns where the waters roll melodiously and the stars turn over and die and hands reach up and grasp and clutch and never seize nor close but clutch and grasp while the stars die out one by one, myriads of them, myriads and myriads of worlds sinking down into cold incandescence, into fuliginous night of green and blue with broken ice and the burn of champagne and the hoarse cry of gulls, their beaks swollen with barnacles, their foul garbaged mouths stuffed forever under the silent keel of the ship.

One looks down from the Brooklyn Bridge on a spot of foam or a little lake of gasoline or a broken splinter or an empty scow; the world goes by upside down with pain and light devouring the innards, the sides of flesh bursting, the spears pressing in against the cartilage, the very armature of the body floating off into nothingness. Passes through you crazy words from the ancient world, signs and portents, the writing on the wall, the chinks of the saloon door, the cardplayers with their clay pipes, the gaunt tree against the tin factory, the black hands stained even in death. One walks the street at night with the bridge against the sky like a harp and the festered eyes of sleep burn into the shanties, deflower the walls; the stairs collapse in a smudge and the rats scamper across the ceiling; a voice is nailed against the door and long creepy things with furry antennae and thousand legs drop from the pipes like beads of sweat. Glad, murderous ghosts with the shriek of night-wind and the curses of warm-legged men; low, shallow coffins with rods through the body; grief-spit drooling down into the cold, waxen flesh, searing the dead eyes, the hard, chipped lids of dead clams. One walks around in a circular cage on shifting levels, stars and clouds under the escalator, and the walls of the cage revolve and there are no men and women without tails or claws, while over all things are written the letters of the alphabet in iron and permanganate. One walks round and round in a circular cage to the roll of drum-fire; the theater burns and the actors go on mouthing their lines; the bladder bursts, the teeth fall out, but the wailing of the clown is like the noise of dandruff falling. One walks around on moonless nights in the valley of craters, valley of dead fires and whitened skulls, of birds without wings. Round and round one walks, seeking the hub and nodality, but the fires are burned to ash and the sex of things is hidden in the finger of a glove.

And then one day, as if suddenly the flesh came undone and the blood beneath the flesh had coalesced with the air, suddenly the whole world roars again and the very skeleton of the body melts like wax. Such a day it may be when first you encounter Dostoyevski. You remember the smell of the tablecloth on which the book rests; you look at the clock and it is only five minutes from eternity; you count the objects on the mantelpiece because the sound of numbers is a totally new sound in your mouth, because everything new and old, or touched and forgotten, is a fire and a mesmerism. Now every door of the cage is open and whichever way you walk is a straight line toward infinity, a straight, mad line over which the breakers roar and great rocs of marble and indigo swoop to lower their fevered eggs. Out of the waves beating phosphorescent step proud and prancing the enameled horses that marched with Alexander, their tight-proud bellies glowing with calcium, their nostrils dipped in laudanum. Now it is all snow and lice, with the great band of Orion slung around the ocean's crotch.

It was exactly five minutes past seven, at the corner of Broadway and Kosciusko Street, when Dostoyevski first flashed across my horizon. Two men and a woman were dressing a shop window. From the middle of the upper legs down the mannikins were all wire. Empty shoe boxes lay banked against the window like last year's snow. . . .

That is how Dostoyevski's name came in. Unostentatiously. Like an old shoe box. The Jew who pronounced his name for me had thick lips; he could not say Vladivostok, for instance, nor Carpathians—but he could say Dostoyevski divinely. Even now, when I say Dostoyevski, I see again his big, blubbery lips and the thin thread of spittle stretching like a rubber band as he pronounced the word. Between his two front teeth there was a more than usual space; it was exactly in the middle of this cavity that the word Dostoyevski quivered and stretched, a thin, iridescent film of sputum in which all the gold of twilight had collected—for the sun was just going down over Kosciusko Street and the traffic overhead was breaking into a spring thaw, a chewing and grinding noise as if the mannikins in their wire legs were chewing each other alive. A little later, when I came to the land of the Houyhnhnms, I heard the same chewing and grinding overhead and again the spittle in a man's mouth quivered and stretched and shone iridescent in a dying sun. This time it is at the Dragon's Gorge: a man standing over me with a rattan stick and banging away with a wild Arabian smile. Again, as if my brain were a uterus, the walls of the world gave way. The name Swift was like a clear, hard pissing against the tin-plate lid of the world. Overhead the green fire-eater, his delicate intestines wrapped in tarpaulin; two enormous milk-white teeth champing down over a belt of black-greased cogs connecting with the shooting gallery and the Turkish baths; the belt of cogs slipping over a frame of bleached bones. The green dragon of Swift moves over the cogs with an endless pissing sound, grinding down fine and foreshortened the human-sized midgets that are sucked in like macaroni. In and out of the esophagus, up and down and around the scapular bones and the mastoid delta, falling through the bottomless pit of the viscera, gurgitating and exgurgitating, the crotch spreading and slipping, the cogs moving on relentlessly, chewing alive all the fine, foreshortened macaroni hanging by the whiskers from the dragon's red gulch. I look into the milk-white smile of the barker, that fanatical Arabian smile which came out of the Dreamland fire, and then I step quietly into the open belly of the dragon. Between the crazy slats of the skeleton that holds the revolving cogs the land of the Houyhnhnms spreads out before me; that hissing, pissing noise in my ears as if the language of men were made of seltzer water. Up and down over the greasy black belt, over the Turkish baths, through the house of the winds, over the sky-blue waters, between the clay pipes and the silver balls dancing on liquid jets: the infra-human world of fedoras and banjos, of bandannas and black cigars; butterscotch stretching from peg to Winnipeg, beer bottles bursting, spun-glass molasses and hot tamales, surf-roar and griddle sizzle, foam and eucalyptus, dirt, chalk, confetti, a woman's white thigh, a broken oar; the razzle-dazzle of wooden slats, the Meccano puzzle, the smile that never comes off, the wild Arabian smile with spits of fire, the red gulch and the green intestines. . . .

O world, strangled and collapsed, where are the strong white teeth? O world, sinking with the silver balls and the corks and the life-preservers, where are the rosy scalps? O glab and glairy, O glabrous world now chewed to a frazzle, under what dead moon do you lie cold and gleaming?

My Lost City, from The Crack-Up, *F. Scott Fitzgerald (1936)*

In *The Great Gatsby* Fitzgerald wrote that "the city seen from the Queensboro Bridge is always the city seen for the first time, in its first wild promise of all the mystery and beauty in the world." However, the city that Fitzgerald first moved to in 1919, fresh from Princeton and service in the First World War, was a dingy, one-room apartment at 200 Claremont Avenue where he slept after working tedious days in an advertising agency.

However, all that changed when Scribner's published *This Side of Paradise* in 1920. Before he moved to the French Riviera with his wife Zelda, in 1924, the two of them had been thrown out of the best hotels in the city—the Biltmore, the Algonquin, the Commodore, and the Knickerbocker. Fitzgerald captured the Jazz Age as no other writer of his time and he recognized that "America was going on the greatest, gaudiest spree in history and there was going to be plenty to tell about it." Furthermore, he understood that the city adopted him "not as a Middle Westerner, not even as (a) detached observer, but as the archetype of what New York wanted." In the early twenties, that archetype could be found riding on the tops of cabs down Fifth Avenue or dancing in the Pulitzer fountain in front of the Plaza Hotel.

A year after the stock market crash, however, Zelda was institutionalized with schizophrenia, and Fitzgerald had, in his essay "My Lost City," come to see the "crowning error" of New York. This error was the "realization that New York was a city after all and not a universe . . . that the city was not the endless succession of canyons that he had supposed but that *it had limits.*" Fitzgerald died in Hollywood in 1940 after trying to create a career as a screenwriter.

JULY, 1932

THERE was first the ferry boat moving softly from the Jersey shore at dawn—the moment crystallized into my first symbol of New York. Five years later when I was fifteen I went into the city from school to see Ina

Claire in *The Quaker Girl* and Gertrude Bryan in *Little Boy Blue.* Confused by my hopeless and melancholy love for them both, I was unable to choose between them—so they blurred into one lovely entity, the girl. She was my second symbol of New York. The ferry boat stood for triumph, the girl for romance. In time I was to achieve some of both, but there was a third symbol that I have lost somewhere, and lost forever.

I found it on a dark April afternoon after five more years.

"Oh, Bunny," I yelled. "*Bunny!*"

He did not hear me—my taxi lost him, picked him up again half a block down the street. There were black spots of rain on the sidewalk and I saw him walking briskly through the crowd wearing a tan raincoat over his inevitable brown get-up; I noted with a shock that he was carrying a light cane.

"Bunny!" I called again, and stopped. I was still an undergraduate at Princeton while he had become a New Yorker. This was his afternoon walk, this hurry along with his stick through the gathering rain, and as I was not to meet him for an hour it seemed an intrusion to happen upon him engrossed in his private life. But the taxi kept pace with him and as I continued to watch I was impressed: he was no longer the shy little scholar of Holder Court—he walked with confidence, wrapped in his thoughts and looking straight ahead, and it was obvious that his new background was entirely sufficient to him. I knew that he had an apartment where he lived with three other men; released now from all undergraduate taboos, but there was something else that was nourishing him and I got my first impression of that new thing—the Metropolitan spirit.

Up to this time I had seen only the New York that offered itself for inspection—I was Dick Whittington up from the country gaping at the trained bears, or a youth of the Midi dazzled by the boulevards of Paris. I had come only to stare at the show, though the designers of the Woolworth Building and the Chariot Race Sign, the producers of musical comedies and problem plays, could ask for no more appreciative spectator, for I took the style and glitter of New York even above its own valuation. But I had never accepted any of the practically anonymous invitations to debutante balls that turned up in an undergraduate's mail, perhaps because I felt that no actuality could live up to my conception of New York's splendor. Moreover, she to whom I fatuously referred as "my girl" was a Middle Westerner, a fact which kept the warm center of the world out there, so I thought of New York as essentially cynical and heartless—save for one night when she made luminous the Ritz Roof on a brief passage through.

Lately, however, I had definitely lost her and I wanted a man's world, and this sight of Bunny made me see New York as just that. A week before, Monsignor Fay had taken me to the Lafayette where there was spread before us a brilliant flag of food, called an *hors d'oeuvre,* and with it we drank claret that was as brave as Bunny's confident cane—but after all it was a restaurant and afterwards we would drive back over a bridge into the hinterland. The New York of undergraduate dissipation, of Bustanoby's, Shanley's, Jack's, had become a horror and though I returned to it, alas, through many an alcoholic mist, I felt each time a betrayal of a persistent idealism. My participance was prurient rather than licentious and scarcely one pleasant memory of it remains from those days; as Ernest Hemingway once remarked, the sole purpose of the cabaret is for unattached men to find complaisant women. All the rest is a wasting of time in bad air.

But that night, in Bunny's apartment, life was mellow and safe, a finer distillation of all that I had come to love at Princeton. The gentle playing of an oboe mingled with city noises from the street outside, which penetrated into the room with difficulty through great barricades of books; only the crisp tearing open of invitations by one man was a discordant note. I had found a third symbol of New York and I began wondering about the rent of such apartments and casting about for the appropriate friends to share one with me.

Fat chance—for the next two years I had as much control over my own destiny as a convict over the cut of his clothes. When I got back to New York in 1919 I was so entangled in life that a period of mellow monasticism in Washington Square was not to be dreamed of. The thing was to make enough money in the advertising business to rent a stuffy apartment for two in the Bronx. The girl concerned had never seen New York but she was wise enough to be rather reluctant. And in a haze of anxiety and unhappiness I passed the four most impressionable months of my life.

New York had all the iridescence of the beginning of the world. The returning troops marched up Fifth Avenue and girls were instinctively drawn East and North toward them—this was the greatest nation and there was gala in the air. As I hovered ghost-like in the Plaza Red Room of a Saturday afternoon, or went to lush and liquid garden parties in the East Sixties or tippled with Princetonians in the Biltmore Bar I was haunted always by my other life—my drab room in the Bronx, my square foot of the subway, my fixation upon the day's letter from Alabama—would it come and what would it say?—my shabby suits, my poverty, and love. While my friends were launching decently into life I had muscled my inadequate bark into midstream. The gilded youth circling around young Constance Bennett in the Club de Vingt, the classmates in the Yale-Princeton Club whooping up our first after-the-war reunion, the atmosphere of the millionaires' houses that I sometimes frequented—these things were empty for me, though I recognized them as impressive scenery and regretted that I was committed to other romance. The most hilarious luncheon table or the most moony cabaret—it was all the same; from them I returned eagerly to my home on Claremont Avenue—home because there might be a letter waiting outside the door. One by one my great dreams of New York became tainted. The remembered charm of Bunny's apartment faded with the rest when I interviewed a blowsy landlady in Greenwich Village. She told me I could bring girls to the room, and the idea filled me with dismay—why should I want to bring girls to my room?—I had a girl. I wandered through the town of 127th Street, resenting its vibrant life; or else I bought cheap theatre seats at Gray's drugstore and tried to lose myself for a few hours in my old passion for Broadway. I was a failure—mediocre at advertising work and unable to get started as a writer. Hating the city, I got roaring, weeping drunk on my last penny and went home. . . .

Incalculable city. What ensued was only one of a thousand success stories of those gaudy days, but it plays a part in my own movie of New York. When I returned six months later the offices of editors and publishers were open to me, impresarios begged plays, the movies panted for screen material. To my bewilderment, I was adopted, not as a Middle Westerner, not even as a detached observer, but as the archetype of what New York wanted. This statement requires some account of the metropolis in 1920.

There was already the tall white city of today, already the feverish activity of the boom, but there was a general inarticulateness. As much as anyone the columnist F. P. A. guessed the pulse of the individual and the crowd, but shyly, as one watching from a window. Society and the native arts had not mingled—Ellen Mackay was not yet married to Irving Berlin. Many of Peter Arno's people would have been meaningless to the citizen of 1920, and save for F. P. A.'s column there was no forum for metropolitan urbanity.

Then, for just a moment, the "younger generation" idea became a fusion of many elements in New York life. People of fifty might pretend there was still a four hundred or Maxwell Bodenheim might pretend there was a Bohemia worth its paint and pencils—but the blending of the bright, gay, vigorous elements began then and for the first time there appeared a society a little livelier than the solid mahogany dinner parties of Emily Price Post. If this society produced the cocktail party, it also evolved Park Avenue wit and for the first time an educated European could envisage a trip to New

York as something more amusing than a gold-trek into a formalized Australian Bush.

For just a moment, before it was demonstrated that I was unable to play the role, I, who knew less of New York than any reporter of six months standing and less of its society than any hall-room boy in a Ritz stag line, was pushed into the position not only of spokesman for the time but of the typical product of that same moment. I, or rather it was "we" now, did not know exactly what New York expected of us and found it rather confusing. Within a few months after our embarkation on the Metropolitan venture we scarcely knew any more who we were and we hadn't a notion what we were. A dive into a civic fountain, a casual brush with the law, was enough to get us into the gossip columns, and we were quoted on a variety of subjects we knew nothing about. Actually our "contacts" included half a dozen unmarried college friends and a few new literary acquaintances—I remember a lonesome Christmas when we had not one friend in the city, nor one house we could go to. Finding no nucleus to which we could cling, we became a small nucleus ourselves and gradually we fitted our disruptive personalities into the contemporary scene of New York. Or rather New York forgot us and let us stay.

This is not an account of the city's changes but of the changes in this writer's feeling for the city. From the confusion of the year 1920 I remember riding on top of a taxi-cab along deserted Fifth Avenue on a hot Sunday night, and a luncheon in the cool Japanese gardens at the Ritz with the wistful Kay Laurel and George Jean Nathan, and writing all night again and again, and paying too much for minute apartments, and buying magnificent but broken-down cars. The first speakeasies had arrived, the toddle was *passé,* the Montmartre was the smart place to dance and Lillian Tashman's fair hair weaved around the floor among the enliquored college boys. The plays were *Declasée* and *Sacred and Profane Love,* and at the Midnight Frolic you danced elbow to elbow with Marion Davies and perhaps picked out the vivacious Mary Hay in the pony chorus. We thought we were apart from all that; perhaps everyone thinks they are apart from their milieu. We felt like small children in a great bright unexplored barn. Summoned out to Griffith's studio on Long Island, we trembled in the presence of the familiar faces of the *Birth of a Nation;* later I realized that behind much of the entertainment that the city poured forth into the nation there were only a lot of rather lost and lonely people. The world of the picture actors was like our own in that it was in New York and not of it. It had little sense of itself and no center: when I first met Dorothy Gish I had the feeling that we were both standing on the North Pole and it was snowing. Since then they have found home but it was not destined to be New York.

When bored we took our city with a Huysmans-like perversity. An afternoon alone in our "apartment" eating olive sandwiches and drinking a quart of Bushmill's whiskey presented by Zoë Atkins, then out into the freshly bewitched city, through strange doors into strange apartments with intermittent swings along in taxis through the soft nights. At last we were one with New York, pulling it after us through every portal. Even now I go into many flats with the sense that I have been there before or in the one above or below—was it the night I tried to disrobe in the *Scandals*, or the night when (as I read with astonishment in the paper next morning) "Fitzgerald Knocks Officer This Side of Paradise"? Successful scrapping not being among my accomplishments, I tried in vain to reconstruct the sequence of events which led up to this dénouement in Webster Hall. And lastly from that period I remember riding in a taxi one afternoon between very tall buildings under a mauve and rosy sky. I began to bawl because I had everything I wanted and knew I would never be so happy again.

It was typical of our precarious position in New York that when our child was to be born we played safe and went home to St. Paul—it seemed inappropriate to bring a baby into all that glamor and loneliness. But in a year we were back and we began doing the same things over again and not liking them so much. We had run through a lot, though we had retained an almost theatrical innocence by preferring the role of the observed to that of the observer. But innocence is no end in itself and as our minds unwillingly matured we began to see New York whole and try to save some of it for the selves we would inevitably become.

It was too late—or too soon. For us the city was inevitably linked up with Bacchic diversions, mild or fantastic. We could organize ourselves only on our return to Long Island and not always there. We had no incentive to meet the city half way. My first symbol was now a memory, for I knew that triumph is in oneself; my second one had grown commonplace—two of the actresses whom I had worshipped from afar in 1913 had dined in our house. But it filled me with a certain fear that even the third symbol had grown dim—the tranquillity of Bunny's apartment was not to be found in the ever-quickening city. Bunny himself was married, and about to become a father, other friends had gone to Europe, and the bachelors had become cadets of houses larger and more social than ours. By this time we "knew everybody"—which is to say most of those whom Ralph Barton would draw as in the orchestra on an opening night.

But we were no longer important. The flapper, upon whose activities the popularity of my first books was based, had become *passé* by 1923—anyhow in the East. I decided to crash Broadway with a play, but Broadway sent its scouts to Atlantic City and quashed the idea in advance, so I felt that, for the moment, the city and I had little to offer each other. I would take the Long Island atmosphere that I had familiarly breathed and materialize it beneath unfamiliar skies.

It was three years before we saw New York again. As the ship glided up the river, the city burst thunderously upon us in the early dusk—the white glacier of lower New York swooping down like a strand of a bridge to rise into uptown New York, a miracle of foamy light suspended by the stars. A band started to play on deck, but the majesty of the city made the march trivial and tinkling. From that moment I knew that New York, however often I might leave it, was home.

The tempo of the city had changed sharply. The uncertainties of 1920 were drowned in a steady golden roar and many of our friends had grown wealthy. But the restlessness of New York in 1927 approached hysteria. The parties were bigger—those of Condé Nast, for example, rivaled in their way the fabled balls of the nineties; the pace was faster—the catering to dissipation set an example to Paris; the shows were broader, the buildings were higher, the morals were looser and the liquor was cheaper; but all these benefits did not really minister to much delight. Young people wore out early—they were hard and languid at twenty-one and save for Peter Arno none of them contributed anything new; perhaps Peter Arno and his collaborators said everything there was to say about the boom days in New York that couldn't be said by a jazz band. Many people who were not alcoholics were lit up four days out of seven, and frayed nerves were strewn everywhere; groups were held together by a generic nervousness and the hangover became a part of the day as well allowed-for as the Spanish siesta. Most of my friends drank too much—the more they were in tune to the times the more they drank. And as effort *per se* had no dignity against the mere bounty of those days in New York, a depreciatory word was found for it: a successful programme became a racket—I was in the literary racket.

We settled a few hours from New York and I found that every time I came to the city I was caught up into a complication of events that deposited me a few days later in a somewhat exhausted state on the train for Delaware. Whole sections of the city had grown rather poisonous, but invariably I found a moment of utter peace in riding south through Central Park at dark toward where the façade of 59th Street thrusts its lights through the trees. There again was my lost city, wrapped cool in its mystery and promise. But that detachment never lasted long—as the toiler must live in the city's belly, so I was compelled to live in its disordered mind.

Instead there were the speakeasies—the moving from luxurious bars, which advertised in the campus publications of Yale and Princeton, to the beer gardens where the snarling face of the underworld peered through the German good nature of the entertainment, then on to strange and even more sinister localities where one was eyed by granite-faced boys and there was nothing left of joviality but only a brutishness that corrupted the new day into which one presently went out. Back in 1920 I shocked a rising young business man by suggesting a cocktail before lunch. In 1929 there was liquor in half the downtown offices, and a speakeasy in half the large buildings.

One was increasingly conscious of the speakeasy and of Park Avenue. In the past decade Greenwich Village, Washington Square, Murray Hill, the châteaux of Fifth Avenue had somehow disappeared, or become unexpressive of anything. The city was bloated, glutted, stupid with cake and circuses, and a new expression "Oh yeah?" summed up all the enthusiasm evoked by the announcement of the last super-skyscrapers. My barber retired on a half million bet in the market and I was conscious that the head waiters who bowed me, or failed to bow me, to my table were far, far wealthier than I. This was no fun—once again I had enough of New York and it was good to be safe on shipboard where the ceaseless revelry remained in the bar in transport to the fleecing rooms of France.

"What news from New York?"

"Stocks go up. A baby murdered a gangster."

"Nothing more?"

"Nothing. Radios blare in the street."

I once thought that there were no second acts in American lives, but there was certainly to be a second act to New York's boom days. We were somewhere in North Africa when we heard a dull distant crash which echoed to the farthest wastes of the desert.

"What was that?"

"Did you hear it?"

"It was nothing."

"Do you think we ought to go home and see?"

"No—it was nothing."

In the dark autumn of two years later we saw New York again. We passed through curiously polite customs agents, and then with bowed head and hat in hand I walked reverently through the echoing tomb. Among the ruins a few childish wraiths still played to keep up the pretense that they were alive, betraying by their feverish voices and hectic cheeks the thinness of the masquerade. Cocktail parties, a last hollow survival from the days of carnival, echoed to the plaints of the wounded: "Shoot me, for the love of God, someone shoot me!" and the groans and wails of the dying: "Did you see that United States Steel is down three more points?" My barber was back at work in his shop; again the head waiters bowed people to their tables, if there were people to be bowed. From the ruins, lonely and inexplicable as the sphinx, rose the Empire State Building and, just as it had been a tradition of mine to climb to the Plaza Roof to take leave of the beautiful city, extending as far as eyes could reach, so now I went to the roof of the last and most magnificent of towers. Then I understood—everything was explained: I had discovered the crowning error of the city, its Pandora's box. Full of vaunting pride the New Yorker had climbed here and seen with dismay what he had never suspected, that the city was not the endless succession of canyons that he had supposed but that *it had limits*—from the tallest structure he saw for the first time that it faded out into the country on all sides, into an expanse of green and blue that alone was limitless. And with the awful realization that New York was a city after all and not a universe, the whole shining edifice that he had reared in his imagination came crashing to the ground. That was the rash gift of Alfred E. Smith to the citizens of New York.

Thus I take leave of my lost city. Seen from the ferry boat in the early morning, it no longer whispers of fantastic success and eternal youth. The whoopee mamas who prance before its empty parquets do not suggest to me the ineffable beauty of my dream girls of 1914. And Bunny, swinging along confidently with his cane toward his cloister in a carnival, had gone over to Communism and frets about the wrongs of southern mill workers and western farmers whose voices, fifteen years ago, would not have penetrated his study walls.

All is lost save memory, yet sometimes I imagine myself reading, with curious interest, a *Daily News* of the issue of 1945:

MAN OF FIFTY RUNS AMUCK IN NEW YORK

Fitzgerald Feathered Many Love Nests Cutie Avers

Bumped Off By Outraged Gunman

So perhaps I am destined to return some day and find in the city new experiences that so far I have only read about. For the moment I can only cry out that I have lost my splendid mirage. Come back, come back, O glittering and white!

The Fairy Catastrophe, from When the Cathedrals Were White, *Le Corbusier (1936)*

Charles Edouard Jeanneret, better known as Le Corbusier, was an architect, painter, writer, and urban theorist who was the leading spokesman for a modernist school of architecture known as the International movement. As Witold Rybczynski has described, "Le Corbusier loved Manhattan. He loved its newness, he loved its Cartesian regularity, above all he loved its tall buildings." Le Corbusier himself saw New York as the place for the new metropolis: "It gushes up. I cannot forget New York, Vertical city, now that I have had the happiness of seeing it, raised in the sky. (It is) the first place in the world on the scale of the new times, the work yard of our era."

However, in his volume entitled *When the Cathedrals Were White* (1936) Le Corbusier wrote that "a hundred times I have thought: New York is a catastrophe, and fifty times: it is a beautiful catastrophe." For Le Corbusier, the catastrophe could be summed up in his astute quip to the question, "What do you think of New York?" His answer? "The skyscrapers are too small." Still, he thought the George Washington Bridge "blessed" and "the most beautiful bridge in the world" and saw the "fairy catastrophe" that was New York City as "the lever of hope."

Le Corbusier's influence in New York can be seen most clearly in the Kips Bay Apartment complex (East Thirtieth to Thirty-third between First and Second Avenues), in the glassy curtain wall of the Lever House (390 Park Ave.) and, of course, in the façade of the United Nations Headquarters (First Avenue between East Forty-second and Forty-eighth), which he designed with a team of international architects.

But the collaborative effort mellowed Le Corbusier's original vision and, as Rem Koolhaas concluded, "Le Corbusier has after all not swallowed Manhattan. Manhattanism has choked on, but finally digested, Le Corbusier." Koolhaas, the 2000 Pritzker Architecture Prize Laureate, published his first book, *Delirious New York,* in 1978. In that volume he pronounced Manhattan "the 20th century's Rosetta Stone." For Koolhaas, his incredibly imaginative book was a "blueprint for a *Culture of Congestion*" in which he saw Manhattan as "the product of an unformulated theory, *Manhattanism,* whose program —to exist in a world totally fabricated by man, i.e., to live inside fantasy— was so ambitious that to be realized, it could never be openly stated." The island is a "theater of progress . . . the performance can never end or even progress in the conventional sense of dramatic plotting; it can only be the cyclic restatement of a single theme: creation and destruction irrevocable interlocked, endlessly reenacted." Koolhaas, perhaps more than any other architect or artist, understood the stubborn refusal of New York to reconcile the fundamental tensions that underlie the city's energy, dynamism, and character.

Savage and Mystic

1936

A HUNDRED years have been enough to make cities inhuman.

Monday morning, when my ship stopped at Quarantine, I saw a fantastic, almost mystic city rising up in the mist. But the ship moves forward and the apparition is transformed into an image of incredible brutality and savagery. Here is certainly the most prominent manifestation of the power of modern times. This brutality and this savagery do not displease me. It is thus that great enterprises begin: by strength.

In the evening, on the avenues of the city, I began to appreciate the people who, by a law of life which is their own, have been able to create a race: handsome men, very beautiful women.

The world is undergoing one of the great metamorphoses of history. The collective and the individual collide instead of combining. Is a synthesis possible? Yes, in a program on a *human scale* and guided by *human wisdom.*

This is architecture's hour. There can be no new architecture without a new city planning. New cities have always replaced old cities, by periods. But today it is possible for the city of modern times, the happy city, the radiant city, to be born. . . .

Vertical City

New York is a vertical city, under the sign of the new times. It is a catastrophe with which a too hasty destiny has overwhelmed courageous and confident people, though a beautiful and worthy catastrophe. Nothing is lost. Faced with difficulties, New York falters. Still streaming with sweat from its exertions, wiping off its forehead, it sees what it has done and suddenly realizes:

"Well, we didn't get it done properly. Let's start over again!" New York has such courage and enthusiasm that everything can be begun again, sent back to the building yard and made into something still greater, something mastered! These people are not on the point of going to sleep. In reality, the city is hardly more than twenty years old, that is the city which I am talking about, the city which is vertical and on the scale of the new times. . . .

I am not able to bear the thought of millions of people undergoing the diminution of life imposed by devouring distances, the subways filled with uproar, the wastelands on the edges of the city, in the blackened brick streets, hard, implacably soulless streets—tenement streets, streets of hovels that make up the cities of the century of money—the slums of New York or Chicago.

I am offended by this blow at legitimate human hopes. Nevertheless, if I am observant, I discover that my despair is not always shared by the victims themselves. In New York, the people who have come in order to "make money" shake off black thoughts and, looking at the sparkle of the great avenues, the entrances of apartment houses and fine homes, think: "O.K., it will be my turn tomorrow!"

Seven million people are bound in the chains of New York, and that turn will never come unless they learn to adopt drastic measures.

Knowing quite well that the turn cannot come quickly enough for seven million beings, there are moments when I hate the city of today; clearly and coolly I know that a proper plan can make New York the city par excellence of modern times, can actively spread daily happiness for these oppressed families—children, women, men stupefied by work, stunned by the noise of the rails of the subways or elevateds—who sink down each evening, at the end of their appointed tasks, in the impasse of an inhuman hovel.

In sober offices, on the fifty-sixth floor of the newest skyscraper, men carry on business. Big business probably. I do not have a sense of figures and I know from experience that it is often more difficult to make small matters come out right than big ones. In the domain of money, the law is like that of the swing at the fair: at the beginning the effort is normal; everyone can take off and make a start. But at a certain point in the swing, when the acrobat is on the horizontal, it becomes precarious; he is too far away from the gravitational norm, and gravity acts on him. Then it takes an effort of a very particular kind to achieve a vertical position, with head down, and having passed the "meridian" of the swing, to come on around effortlessly from that point. Brute strength is not enough. The repeated attempts require a regular and harmonious progression. Harmonious, that's the word. Harmony is the cause of the success. The most difficult thing—the real difficulty—comes when you are a hair's-breadth from success: at the moment of swinging over. If you manage it, you are thenceforth launched! Many will not succeed in managing it. Those who have passed over this financial hazard owe it to their merits just as they owe it to the combination of circumstances: the things necessary to make the effort profitable, to stimulate it, to support it, were present. It was a happy conjuncture. And now the financial swing moves easily, with no further effort required except a scrupulous supervision.

That is why the skyscrapers were not constructed with a wise and serious intention. They were applauded acrobatic feats. The *skyscraper as proclamation* won. Here the skyscraper is not an element in city planning, but a banner in the sky, a fireworks rocket, an aigrette in the coiffure of a name henceforth listed in the financial Almanach de Gotha.

Beneath the immaculate office on the fifty-sixth floor the vast nocturnal festival of New York spreads out. No one can imagine it who has not seen it. It is a titanic mineral display, a prismatic stratification shot through with an infinite number of lights, from top to bottom, in depth, in a violent silhouette like a fever chart beside a sick bed. A diamond, incalculable diamonds.

The great masters of economic destiny are up there, like eagles, in the silence of their eminences. Seated in their chairs, framed by two plate glass windows which fuse their rooms with the surrounding space, they appear to us made out of the substance of this event which is as strong and violent as a cosmic mutation: New York standing up above Manhattan is like a rose-colored stone in the blue of a maritime sky; New York at night is like a limitless cluster of jewels. . . .

The Skyscrapers Are Too Small

The cardinal question asked of every traveler on his arrival is: "What do you think of New York?" Coolly I replied: "The skyscrapers are too small."

And I explained what I meant.

For a moment my questioners were speechless! So much the worse for them! The reasoning is clear and the supporting proofs abundant, streets full of them, a complete urban disaster.

The skyscraper is not a plume rising from the face of the city. It has been made that, and wrongly. The plume was a poison to the city. The skyscraper is an instrument. A magnificent instrument for the concentration of population, for getting rid of land congestion, for classification, for internal efficiency. A prodigious means of improving the conditions of work, a creator of economies and, through that, a dispenser of wealth. But the skyscraper as plume, multiplied over the area of Manhattan, has disregarded experience. The New York skyscrapers are out of line with the rational skyscraper which I have called: *the Cartesian skyscraper. . . .*

Now we are ready to state the fundamental principle: the skyscraper *is a function of capacity* (the offices) *and of the area of free ground at its base.* A skyscraper which does not fulfill this function harmoniously is a disease. That is the disease of New York.

The Cartesian skyscraper is a miracle in the urbanization of the cities of machine civilization. It makes possible extraordinary concentrations, from three to four thousand persons on each two and one-half acres. It does so while taking up only 8 to 12 per cent of the ground, 92 to 88 per cent being restored, usable, available for the circulation of pedestrians and cars! These immense free areas, this whole ward in the business section, will become a park. The glass skyscrapers will rise up like crystals, clean and transparent in the midst of the foliage of the trees. . . .

The skyscrapers of New York are too small and there are too many of them. They are proof of the new dimensions and the new tools; the proof also that henceforth everything can be carried out on a new general plan, a symphonic plan—extent and height. . . .

A Place of Radiant Grace

The George Washington Bridge over the Hudson is the most beautiful bridge in the world. Made of cables and steel beams, it gleams in the sky like a reversed arch. It is blessed. It is the only seat of grace in the disordered city. It is painted an aluminum color and, between water and sky, you see nothing but the bent cord supported by two steel towers. When your car moves up the ramp the two towers rise so high that it brings you happiness; their structure is so pure, so resolute, so regular that here, finally, steel architecture seems to laugh. The car reaches an unexpectedly wide apron; the second tower is very far away; innumerable vertical cables, gleaming against the sky, are suspended from the magisterial curve which swings down and then up. The rose-colored towers of New York appear, a vision whose harshness is mitigated by distance.

The bridge has a story which almost turned out ridiculously. Mr. Cullman, president of the Port of New York, told me about it. The bridge was constructed under his supervision. The problem required the utmost engineering boldness. Calculation aided by a fortunate hypothesis gave the work the severity of things which are exact. The bridge leaps over the Hudson in a single bound. Two steel-topped concrete piers between the banks and the apron hold the suspension chains. I have mentioned the extraordinary dimensions of the two towers. Constructed of riveted steel they stand up in the sky with a striking nobility. Now the towers were to have been faced with stone molded and sculptured in "Beaux-Arts" style (New York term for the aesthetic ideas current on the quai Voltaire in Paris).

Someone acted before it was too late. Then the whole committee of the Port of New York Authority. Little by little the spirit of modern times makes itself felt: these men said, "Stop! no stone or decoration here. The two towers and the mathematical play of the cables make a splendid unity. It is one. That is the new beauty." They made some calculations; the maintenance of the towers by proper painting would cost an amount equal to the interest on the capital which would have been invested in stone-faced towers. Thus the two proposals were financially equivalent. They were not looking for a means of saving expense. But "in the name of beauty and of the spirit" they dismissed the architect with his decorations. Those men are citizens!

Lesson for Tomorrow

I could never have imagined such a violent, such a decisive, such a simple and also such a diversified arrangement of the ground of a city. The eight or nine longitudinal avenues mark off the character of areas in a quickly changing gamut which runs from the hideous to the luxurious. Manhattan—a kind of sole stretched out on a rock—has value only along its spinal column; the borders are slums. On foot, you can walk across town in twenty minutes and see that spectacle of contrasts. But what satisfaction can rationality find in it? The borders—the East River and the Hudson are inaccessible! The sea is inaccessible, invisible. Looking at the plan of New York or an airplane view, you think: "It is certainly the best organized city in the world." Well, the sea and the vast rivers are invisible and no one gets the benefit of their beauty, their spaciousness, their movement, the splendid play of light on the water! New York, an immense seaport, is as landlocked for its inhabitants as Moscow! And the admirable terrain, seemingly destined to be taken up by immense apartments with windows opening on space, that terrain is desolating: it is filled with slums! A well-managed municipal operation could easily restore the value of those sections and the profit would make it possible to do something about the rest of the city, which is in violent disorder. It astounds a visitor to learn that Manhattan, bristling with skyscrapers, has an average building height of four and one-half stories. Do you realize that: *four and one-half stories?* But it is the imperative and revealing statistical fact which brings hope for the success of a transforming plan capable of establishing order in the city.

Here the skyscraper is negative: it kills the street and the city, it has destroyed circulation. More than that, it is a man-eating monster: it sucks the life out of the neighboring areas; it empties them and ruins them. Once again, saving solutions of the urban problem come to mind. The skyscraper is too small and it destroys everything. Make it larger, true and useful: it will restore an immense area of ground, it will pay for the ruined properties, it will give the city verdure and excellent circulation: all the ground in parks for pedestrians and cars up in the air, on elevated roads, *a few roads* (one-way), permitting a speed of ninety miles an hour and going . . . simply from one skyscraper to another. Collaborative measures are needed to achieve that goal; without them, no salvation is possible! We shall have to think about that someday, through the organization of co-operatives or real-estate syndicates, or through strong and paternal governmental measures (with all the energy of the father who knows what the children should do).

Between the present skyscrapers there are masses of large and small buildings. Most of them small. What are these small houses doing in dramatic Manhattan? I haven't the slightest idea. It is incomprehensible. It is a fact, nothing more, as the debris after an earthquake or bombardment is a fact.

Central Park has a different lesson. Notice how normal and spontaneous it is for the great hotels and large apartment houses to come there and open their windows on the clear space. But Central Park is too large and it is a hole in the midst of buildings. It is a lesson. You go through Central Park as if you were in a no man's land. The verdure, and especially the space, of Central Park should be distributed and multiplied throughout Manhattan. . . .

The Fairy Catastrophe

A hundred times I have thought: New York is a catastrophe, and fifty times: it is a beautiful catastrophe.

One evening about six o'clock I had cocktails with James Johnson Sweeney—a friend who lives in an apartment house east of Central Park, over toward the East River; he is on the top floor, one hundred and sixty feet above the street; after having looked out the windows, we went outside on the balcony, and finally we climbed up on the roof.

The night was dark, the air dry and cold. The whole city was lighted up. If you have not seen it, you cannot know or imagine what it is like. You must have had it sweep over you. Then you begin to understand why Americans have become proud of themselves in the last twenty years and why they raise their voices in the world and why they are impatient when they come to our country. The sky is decked out. It is a Milky Way come down to earth; you are in it. Each window, each person, is a light in the sky. At the same time a perspective is established by the arrangement of the thousand lights of each skyscraper; it forms itself more in your mind than in the darkness perforated by illimitable fires. The stars are part of it also—the real stars—but sparkling quietly in the distance. Splendor, scintillation, promise, proof, act of faith, etc. Feeling comes into play; the action of the heart is released; crescendo, allegro, fortissimo. We are charged with feeling, we are intoxicated; legs strengthened, chests expanded, eager for action, we are filled with confidence.

That is the Manhattan of vehement silhouettes. Those are the verities of technique, which is the springboard of lyricism. The fields of water, the railroads, the planes, the stars, and the vertical city with its unimaginable diamonds. Everything is there, and it is real.

The nineteenth century covered the earth with ugly and soulless works. Bestiality of money. The twentieth century aspires to grace, suppleness. The catastrophe is before us in the darkness, a spectacle young and new. The night effaces a thousand objects of debate and mental reservation. What is here then is true! Then everything is possible. Let the human be written into this by conscious intention, let joy be brought into the city by means of wisely conceived urban machinery and by generous thinking, aware of human misery. Let order reign.

The Fairy Catastrophe! That is the phrase that expresses my emotion and rings within me in the stormy debate which has not stopped tormenting me for fifty days: hate and love.

For me the fairy catastrophe is the lever of hope!

Apology for Breathing, from Back Where I Came From, *A. J. Liebling (1938)*

Abbot Joseph Liebling was born in New York City on October 18, 1904, and was raised in Far Rockaway, Queens. Liebling "went up to Dartmouth in the fall of 1920, lacking a month of being sixteen," but was dismissed after he regularly missed compulsory chapel attendance. After attending Columbia's journalism school, he began his newspaper career as a reporter for the *Providence Evening Bulletin.* Liebling also worked for the *New York World* and the *New York World-Telegram* before becoming an essayist for *The New Yorker* from 1935 until his death in 1963.

While at *The New Yorker,* Liebling forged a lifelong friendship with another noted essayist, Joseph Mitchell. Both Mitchell and Liebling shared a passion for the city's idiosyncratic cast of characters, and they both roamed the uncharted regions of the metropolis chronicling the lives of its more quirky residents. Liebling's own passions were for boxing, horse racing, and eating, and he wrote about each with regularity. Liebling's volume *Back Where I Come From* (1938) captures what he thought was finest about New York City, "that it is like one of those complicated Renaissance clocks where on one level an allegorical marionette pops out to mark the day of the week, on another a skeleton death bangs the quarter hour with his scythe, and on a third the Twelve Apostles do a cakewalk."

PEOPLE I know in New York are incessantly on the point of going back where they came from to write a book, or of staying on and writing a book about back where they came from. Back where they came from, I gather, is the American scene (New York, of course, just isn't America). It is all pretty hard on me because I have no place to go back to. I was born in an apartment house at Ninety-third Street and Lexington Avenue, about three miles from where I now live. Friends often tell me of their excitement when the train on which they are riding passes from Indiana into Illinois, or back again. I am ashamed to admit that when the Jerome Avenue express rolls into Eighty-sixth Street station I have absolutely no reaction.

I always think of back where my friends came from as one place, possessing a homogeneous quality of not being New York. The thought has been well expressed by my literary adviser, Whitey Bimstein, who also trains prize-fighters. I once asked him how he liked the country. He said, "It is a nice spot." I have been to the country myself. I went to a college in New Hampshire. But I seldom mention this, because I would like to be considered quaint and regional, like Jesse Stuart or Kenneth Roberts.

The finest thing about New York City, I think, is that it is like one of those complicated Renaissance clocks where on one level an allegorical marionette pops out to mark the day of the week, on another a skeleton death bangs the quarter hour with his scythe, and on a third the Twelve Apostles do a cakewalk. The variety of the sideshows distracts one's attention from the advance of the hour hand. I know people who say that, as in the clock, all the exhibits depend upon the same movement. This they insist is economic. But they are the sort of people who look at a fine woman and remind you that the human body is composed of one dollar and sixty-two cents worth of chemicals.

I like to think of all the city microcosms so nicely synchronized though unaware of one another: the worlds of the weight-lifters, yodelers, tugboat captains and sideshow barkers, of the book-dutchers, sparring partners, song pluggers, sporting girls and religious painters, of the dealers in rhesus monkeys and the bishops of churches that they establish themselves under the religious corporations law. It strengthens my hold on reality to know when I awake with a brandy headache in my house which is nine blocks due south of the Chrysler Building and four blocks due east of the Empire State, that Eddie Arcaro, the jockey, is galloping a horse around the track at Belmont while Ollie Thomas, a colored clocker of my acquaintance, is holding a watch on him. I can be sure that Kit Coates, at the Aquarium, is worrying over the liverish deportment of a new tropical fish, that presently Whitey will be laying out the gloves and headguards for the fighters he trains at Stillman's gymnasium, while Miss Ira, the Harlem modiste, will be trying to talk a dark-complexioned girl out of buying herself an orange turban and Hymie the Tummler ruminates a plan for opening a new night club. It would be easier to predicate the existence of God on such recurrences than on the cracking of ice in ponds, the peeping of spring peepers in their peeperies and the shy green sprigs of poison ivy so well advertised by writers like Thoreau.

There are New Yorkers so completely submerged in one environment, like the Garment Centre or Jack and Charlie's, that they live and die oblivious of the other worlds around them. Others are instinctively aware of the wonders of New York natural history, but think them hardly worthy of mention. My father was a New Yorker of the latter sort. In separate phases of his business life, he had occasion to retain Monk Eastman, a leading pre-war gangster, and the Rev. Charles Parkhurst, a notorious crusader against vice. This seemed to him no more paradoxical than going to Coward's for his shoes while he bought his hats of Knox. When Father was President of an association of furriers during a strike he hired Eastman to break up a strikers' mass meeting. His employment of Dr. Parkhurst was more subtle. In about 1910 Father bought some real estate in West Twenty-sixth Street on which he purposed to put several loft buildings. He believed that the fur industry was going to move up in that direction from below Twenty-third. But Twenty-sixth Street between Sixth and Seventh Avenues was full of brothels, and there was no hope of getting tenants for the new buildings until the block was made respectable. First Father dispossessed the hock shops from the houses which he had acquired with his building lots. But the watchmen rented the empty rooms to the drabs for fifty cents a night. Then Father made a substantial gift to Dr. Parkhurst's society, enclosing with his check a letter that called attention to the sinful conditions on West Twenty-sixth Street. Dr. Parkhurst raised Hell with the police, who made the girls move on to another block, and then Father put up his buildings. Father always said Monk and Dr. Parkhurst gave him his money's worth, but he never liked either of them. He became labor conscious after he retired from business, and toward the end of his life often said that unions were a fine thing, but that they had doubtless changed a lot since the time he hired Eastman. He died a staunch Roosevelt man.

Even though he made his home during the second part of his life among middle-class enterprisers with horizons slimmer than a gnat's waist, Father lived in other milieus in retrospect. He liked to talk of the lower East Side in the eighties, when the carters left their wagons in the streets of nights and the small boys would roll the wains away and burn them on election day, and of how he, a workingman at ten, boxed with the other furriers' apprentices using beaver muffs for mitts. He would even tell of the gay life of London and Paris and Leipzig in the late nineties when he was a bachelor buyer, although, he always protested, he had finished with that sort of thing when he got married. And he early introduced me to those worlds into which one may escape temporarily for the payment of a fee, the race course and the baseball park. These have their own conflicts that do not follow scenarios pre-determined in Hollywood.

Since this is a regional book about people I met back where I came from,

I should like to say something here about the local language. This is a regional tongue imported from the British Isles, as is the dialect spoken by the retarded inhabitants of the Great Smoky Mountains back where *they* come from. Being spoken by several million people, it has not been considered of any philological importance. Basically, New Yorkese is the common speech of early nineteenth century Cork, transplanted during the mass immigration of the South Irish a hundred years ago. Of this Cork dialect Thomas Crofton Croker in 1839 wrote: "The vernacular of this region may be regarded as the ancient cockneyism of the mixed race who held the old city—Danes, English and Irish. It is a jargon, whose principal characteristic appears in the pronunciation of *th*, as exemplified in *dis, dat, den, dey*—this, that, then, they; and in the dovetailing of words as, 'kum our rish' for 'come of this.'" New York example, "gerradahere" for "get out of here." The neo-Corkonian proved particularly suited to the later immigrants who came here from continental Europe—the *th* sound is equally impossible for French, Germans and Italians. Moreover, it was impressed upon the latecomers because it was the talk of the police and the elementary school teachers, the only Americans who would talk to them at all. Father, who was born in Austria but came here when he was seven years old, spoke New Yorkese perfectly.

It is true that since the diaspora the modern dialects of Cork and New York have diverged slightly like Italian and Provencal, both of which stem from vulgar Latin. Yet Sean O'Faolain's modern story of Cork, "A Born Genius," contains dialogue that might have come out of Eleventh Avenue: "He's after painting two swans on deh kitchen windes. Wan is facin' wan way and d'oder is facin' d'oder way.—So dat so help me God dis day you'd tink deh swans was floatin' in a garden! And deh garden was floatin' in trough deh winda! And dere was no winda!"

There are interesting things about New York besides the language. It is one of the oldest places in the United States, but doesn't live in retrospect like the professionally picturesque provinces. Any city may have one period of magnificence, like Boston or New Orleans or San Francisco, but it takes a real one to keep renewing itself until the past is perennially forgotten. There were plenty of clipper ships out of New York in the old days and privateers before them, but there are better ships out of here today. The Revolution was fought all over town, from Harlem to Red Hook and back again, but that isn't the revolution you will hear New Yorkers discussing now.

Native New Yorkers are the best mannered people in America; they never speak out of turn in saloons, because they have experience in group etiquette. Whenever you hear a drinker let a blat out of him you can be sure he is a recent immigrant from the south or middle west. New Yorkers are modest. It is a distinction for a child in New York to be the brightest on one block; he acquires no exaggerated idea of his own relative intelligence. Prairie geniuses are raced in cheap company when young. They are intoxicated by the feel of being boy wonders in Amarillo, and when they bounce off New York's skin as adults they resent it.

New York women are the most beautiful in the world. They have their teeth straightened in early youth. They get their notions of chic from S. Klein's windows instead of the movies. Really loud and funny New Yorkers, like Bruce Barton, are invariably carpetbaggers. The climate is extremely healthy. The death rate is lower in Queens and the Bronx than in any other large city in the United States, and the average life expectancy is so high that one of our morning newspapers specializes in interviewing people a hundred years old and upward. The average is slightly lowered, however, by the inlanders who come here and insist on eating in Little Southern Tea Roomes on side streets.

The natives put up with a lot back here where I came from. If the inhabitants of Kentucky are distrustful of strangers, that is duly noted as an entertaining local trait. But if a New Yorker says that he doesn't like Kentuckians he is marked a cold churl. It is perennially difficult for the New Yorker who subscribes to a circulating library to understand how the city survived destruction during the Civil War. When he reads about those regional demigods haunted by ancestral daemons and festooned in magnolia blossoms and ghosts who composed practically the whole Confederate Army, he wonders what happened to them en route. I asked Whitey Bimstein what he thought of that one. He said: "Our guys must have slapped their ears down." Whitey does not know that we have been paying a war indemnity ever since in the form of royalties.

From The Mohawks in High Steel, from Up in the Old Hotel, *Joseph Mitchell (1938)*

There have been many chroniclers of New York throughout its history—Washington Irving, Edgar Allan Poe, Herman Melville, Walt Whitman, and Edith Wharton spanning the nineteenth century and F. Scott Fitzgerald in the 1920s. Joseph Mitchell arrived in the city on October 25, 1929, the day after the stock market crash, and there was no better reporter of the "underside" of New York life for the next thirty years. In his first nine years in the city, Mitchell worked for the *Morning World,* the *Herald Tribune* and the *World-Telegram* until, in 1938, he became a feature writer for *The New Yorker,* where he spent the next fifty-eight years. He published a collection of his best newspaper stories in 1938 in his first book, *My Ears Are Bent,* and, in 1992, most of his work at *The New Yorker* was collected in a volume entitled *Up in the Old Hotel.* Mitchell's last piece, "Joe Gould's Secret," was published in 1964; but for the next thirty-two years Mitchell arrived for work every day and never published another word.

Mitchell's New York can only be experienced now through his writings, which are populated not only with gypsies, sea captains, bearded ladies, bartenders, and prostitutes but also with the likes of Huey Long, George Bernard Shaw, and the baseball player-turned-evangelist Billy Sunday. Mitchell's prose—tight, sparse, understated, and both simultaneously sweet and darkly humorous—was inimitable, and Calvin Trillin cited him as "the *New Yorker* reporter who set the standard." Mitchell himself noted his "graveyard humor" in his author's note to his final volume and noted that "it turns up often in the conversations between me and the people I interviewed, or in the parts of conversations that I chose to quote. I was pleased to discover this because graveyard humor is an exemplification of the way I look at the world. It typifies my cast of mind."

THE most footloose Indians in North America are a band of mixed-blood Mohawks whose home, the Caughnawaga Reservation, is on the St. Lawrence River in Quebec. They are generally called the Caughnawagas. In times past, they were called the Christian Mohawks or the Praying Mohawks. There are three thousand of them, at least six hundred and fifty of whom spend more time in cities and towns all over the United States than they do on the reservation. Some are as restless as gypsies. It is not unusual for a family to lock up its house, leave the key with a neighbor, get into an automobile, and go away for years. There are colonies of Caughnawagas in Brooklyn, Buffalo, and Detroit. The biggest colony is in Brooklyn, out in the North Gowanus neighborhood. It was started in the late twenties, there are approximately four hundred men, women, and children in it, it is growing, and it shows signs of permanence. A few families have bought houses. The pastor of one of the churches in the neighborhood, the Cuyler Presbyterian, has learned the Mohawk dialect of the Iroquois language and holds a service in it once a month, and the church has elected a Caughnawaga to its board of deacons. There have been marriages between Caughnawagas and members of other groups in the neighborhood. The Caughnawaga women once had trouble in finding a brand of corn meal (Quaker White Enriched and Degerminated) that they like to use in making *ka-na-ta-rok*, or Indian boiled bread; all the grocery stores in North Gowanus, even the little Italian ones, now carry it. One saloon, the Nevins Bar & Grill, has become a Caughnawaga hangout and is referred to in the neighborhood as the Indian Bank; on weekend nights, two-thirds of its customers are Caughnawagas; to encourage their patronage, it stocks one Montreal ale and two Montreal beers. A saying in the band is that Brooklyn is the downtown of Caughnawaga. . . .

In 1886, the life at Caughnawaga changed abruptly. In the spring of that year, the Dominion Bridge Company began the construction of a cantilever railroad bridge across the St. Lawrence for the Canadian Pacific Railroad, crossing from the French-Canadian village of Lachine on the north shore to a point just below Caughnawaga village on the south shore. The D.B.C. is the biggest erector of iron and steel structures in Canada; it corresponds to the Bethlehem Steel Company in the United States. In obtaining the right to use reservation land for the bridge abutment, the Canadian Pacific and the D.B.C. promised that Caughnawagas would be employed on the job wherever possible.

"The records of the company for this bridge show that it was our understanding that we would employ these Indians as ordinary day laborers unloading materials," an official of the D.B.C. wrote recently in a letter. "They were dissatisfied with this arrangement and would come out on the bridge itself every chance they got. It was quite impossible to keep them off. As the work progressed, it became apparent to all concerned that these Indians were very odd in that they did not have any fear of heights. If not watched, they would climb up into the spans and walk around up there as cool and collected as the toughest of our riveters, most of whom at that period were old sailing-ship men especially picked for their experience in working aloft. These Indians were as agile as goats. They would walk a narrow beam high up in the air with nothing below them but the river, which is rough there and ugly to look down on, and it wouldn't mean any more to them than walking on the solid ground. They seemed immune to the noise of the riveting, which goes right through you and is often enough in itself to make newcomers to construction feel sick and dizzy. They were inquisitive about the riveting and were continually bothering our foremen by requesting that they be allowed to take a crack at it. This happens to be the most dangerous work in all construction, and the highest-paid. Men who want to do it are rare and men who can do it are even rarer, and in good construction years there are sometimes not enough of them to go around. We decided it would be mutually advantageous to see what these Indians could do, so we picked out some and gave them a little training, and it turned out that putting riveting tools in their hands was like putting ham with eggs. In other words, they were natural-born bridgemen. Our records do not show how many we trained on this bridge. There is a tradition in the company that we trained twelve, or enough to form three riveting gangs."

In the erection of steel structures, whether bridge or building, there are three main divisions of workers—raising gangs, fitting-up gangs, and riveting gangs. The steel comes to a job already cut and built up into various kinds of columns and beams and girders; the columns are the perpendicular pieces and the beams and girders are the horizontal ones. Each piece has two or more groups of holes bored through it to receive bolts and rivets, and each piece has a code mark chalked or painted on it, indicating where it should go in the structure. Using a crane or a derrick, the men in the raising gang hoist the pieces up and set them in position and join them by running bolts through a few of the holes in them; these bolts are temporary. Then the men in the fitting-up gang come along; they are divided into plumbers and bolters. The plumbers tighten up the pieces with guy wires and turnbuckles and make sure that they are in plumb. The bolters put in some more temporary bolts. Then the riveting gangs come along; one raising gang and one fitting-up gang will keep several riveting gangs busy. There are four men in a riveting gang—a heater, a sticker-in, a bucker-up, and a riveter. The heater lays some wooden planks across a couple of beams, making a platform for the portable, coal-burning forge in which he heats the rivets. The three other men hang a plank scaffold by ropes from the steel on which they are going to work. There are usually six two-by-ten planks in a scaffold, three on each side of the steel, affording just room enough to work; one false step and it's goodbye Charlie. The three men climb down with their tools and take their positions on the scaffold; most often the sticker-in and the bucker-up stand on one side and the riveter stands or kneels on the other. The heater, on his platform, picks a red-hot rivet off the coals in his forge with tongs and tosses it to the sticker-in, who catches it in a metal can. At this stage, the rivet is shaped like a mushroom; it has a buttonhead and a stem. Meanwhile, the bucker-up has unscrewed and pulled out one of the temporary bolts joining two pieces of steel, leaving the hole empty. The sticker-in picks the rivet out of his can with tongs and sticks it in the hole and pushes it in until the buttonhead is flush with the steel on his side and the stem protrudes from the other side, the riveter's side. The sticker-in steps out of the way. The bucker-up fits a tool called a dolly bar over the buttonhead and holds it there, bracing the rivet. Then the riveter presses the cupped head of his pneumatic hammer against the protruding stem end of the rivet, which is still red-hot and malleable, and turns on the power and forms a buttonhead on it. This operation is repeated until every hole that can be got at from the scaffold is riveted up. Then the scaffold is moved. The heater's platform stays in one place until all the work within a rivet-tossing radius of thirty to forty feet is completed. The men on the scaffold know each other's jobs and are interchangeable; the riveter's job is bone-shaking and nerve-racking, and every so often one of the others swaps with him for a while. In the days before pneumatic hammers, the riveter used two tools, a cupped die and an iron maul; he placed the die over the stem end of the red-hot rivet and beat on it with the maul until he squashed the stem end into a buttonhead.

After the D.B.C. completed the Canadian Pacific Bridge, it began work on a jackknife bridge now known as the Soo Bridge, which crosses two canals and a river and connects the twin cities of Sault Ste. Marie, Ontario, and Sault Ste. Marie, Michigan. This job took two years. Old Mr. Jacobs, the patriarch of the band, says that the Caughnawaga riveting gangs went straight from the Canadian Pacific job to the Soo job and that each gang took along an apprentice. Mr. Jacobs is in his eighties. In his youth, he was a member of a riveting gang; in his middle age, he was, successively, a commercial traveller for a wholesale grocer in Montreal, a schoolteacher on the reservation, and a campaigner for compulsory education for Indians. "The Indian boys turned the Soo Bridge into a college for themselves," he says. "The way they worked it, as soon as one apprentice was trained, they'd send back to the reservation for another one. By and by, there'd be enough men for a new

Indian gang. When the new gang was organized, there'd be a shuffle-up—a couple of men from the old gangs would go into the new gang and a couple of the new men would go into the old gangs; the old would balance the new." This proliferation continued on subsequent jobs, and by 1907 there were over seventy skilled bridgemen in the Caughnawaga band. On August 29, 1907, during the erection of the Quebec Bridge, which crosses the St. Lawrence nine miles above Quebec City, a span collapsed, killing ninety-six men, of whom thirty-five were Caughnawagas. In the band, this is always spoken of as "the disaster."

"People thought the disaster would scare the Indians away from high steel for good," Mr. Jacobs says. "Instead of which, the general effect it had, it made high steel much more interesting to them. It made them take pride in themselves that they could do such dangerous work. Up to then, the majority of them, they didn't consider it any more dangerous than timber-rafting. Also, it made them the most looked-up-to men on the reservation. The little boys in Caughnawaga used to look up to the men that went out with circuses in the summer and danced and war-whooped all over the States and came back to the reservation in the winter and holed up and sat by the stove and drank whiskey and bragged. That's what they wanted to do. Either that, or work on the timber rafts. After the disaster, they changed their minds—they all wanted to go into high steel. The disaster was a terrible blow to the women. The first thing they did, they got together a sum of money for a life-size crucifix to hang over the main altar in St. Francis Xavier's. They did that to show their Christian resignation. The next thing they did, they got in behind the men and made them split up and scatter out. That is, they wouldn't allow all the gangs to work together on one bridge any more, which, if something went wrong, it might widow half the young women on the reservation. A few gangs would go to this bridge and a few would go to that. Pretty soon, there weren't enough bridge jobs, and the gangs began working on all types of high steel—factories, office buildings, department stores, hospitals, hotels, apartment houses, schools, breweries, distilleries, power-houses, piers, railroad stations, grain elevators, anything and everything. In a few years, every steel structure of any size that went up in Canada, there were Indians on it. Then Canada got too small and they began crossing the border. They began going down to Buffalo and Cleveland and Detroit."

Sometime in 1915 or 1916, a Caughnawaga bridgeman named John Diabo came down to New York City and got a job on Hell Gate Bridge. He was a curiosity and was called Indian Joe; two old foremen still remember him. After he had worked for some months as bucker-up in an Irish gang, three other Caughnawagas joined him and they formed a gang of their own. They had worked together only a few weeks when Diabo stepped off a scaffold and dropped into the river and was drowned. He was highly skilled and his misstep was freakish; recently, in trying to explain it, a Caughnawaga said, "It must've been one of those cases, he got in the way of himself." The other Caughnawagas went back to the reservation with his body and did not return. As well as the old men in the band can recollect, no other Caughnawagas worked here until the twenties. In 1926, attracted by the building boom, three or four Caughnawaga gangs came down. The old men say that these gangs worked first on the Fred F. French Building, the Graybar Building, and One Fifth Avenue. In 1928, three more gangs came down. They worked first on the George Washington Bridge. In the thirties, when Rockefeller Center was the biggest steel job in the country, at least seven additional Caughnawaga gangs came down. Upon arriving here, the men in all these gangs enrolled in the Brooklyn local of the high-steel union, the International Association of Bridge, Structural, and Ornamental Iron Workers, American Federation of Labor. Why they enrolled in the Brooklyn instead of the Manhattan local, no one now seems able to remember. The hall of the Brooklyn local is on Atlantic Avenue, in the block between Times Plaza and Third Avenue, and the Caughnawagas got lodgings in furnished-room houses and cheap hotels in the North Gowanus neighborhood, a couple of blocks up Atlantic from the hall. In the early thirties, they began sending for their families and moving into tenements and apartment houses in the same neighborhood. During the war, Caughnawagas continued to come down. Many of these enrolled in the Manhattan local, but all of them settled in North Gowanus.

At present there are eighty-three Caughnawagas in the Brooklyn local and forty-two in the Manhattan local. Less than a third of them work steadily in the city. The others keep their families in North Gowanus and work here intermittently but spend much of their time in other cities. They roam from coast to coast, usually by automobile, seeking rush jobs that offer unlimited overtime work at double pay; in New York City, the steel-erecting companies use as little overtime as possible. A gang may work in half a dozen widely separated cities in a single year. Occasionally, between jobs, they return to Brooklyn to see their families. Now and then, after long jobs, they pick up their families and go up to the reservation for a vacation; some go up every summer. A few men sometimes take their families along on trips to jobs and send them back to Brooklyn by bus or train. Several foremen who have had years of experience with Caughnawagas believe that they roam because they can't help doing so, it is a passion, and that their search for overtime is only an excuse. A veteran foreman for the American Bridge Company says he has seen Caughnawagas leave jobs that offered all the overtime they could handle. When they are making up their minds to move on, he says, they become erratic. "Everything will be going along fine on a job," he says. "Good working conditions. Plenty of overtime. A nice city. Then the news will come over the grapevine about some big new job opening up somewhere; it might be a thousand miles away. That kind of news always causes a lot of talk, what we call water-bucket talk, but the Indians don't talk; they know what's in each other's mind. For a couple of days, they're tensed up and edgy. They look a little wild in the eyes. They've heard the call. Then, all of a sudden, they turn in their tools, and they're gone. Can't wait another minute. They'll quit at lunchtime, in the middle of the week. They won't even wait for their pay. Some other gang will collect their money and hold it until a postcard comes back telling where to send it." George C. Lane, manager of erections in the New York district for the Bethlehem Steel Company, once said that the movements of a Caughnawaga gang are as impossible to foresee as the movements of a flock of sparrows. "In the summer of 1936," Mr. Lane said, "we finished a job here in the city and the very next day we were starting in on a job exactly three blocks away. I heard one of our foremen trying his best to persuade an Indian gang to go on the new job. They had got word about a job in Hartford and wanted to go up there. The foreman told them the rate of pay was the same; there wouldn't be any more overtime up there than here; their families were here; they'd have travelling expenses; they'd have to root around Hartford for lodgings. Oh, no; it was Hartford or nothing. A year or so later I ran into this gang on a job in Newark, and I asked the heater how they made out in Hartford that time. He said they didn't go to Hartford. 'We went to San Francisco, California,' he said. 'We went out and worked on the Golden Gate Bridge.'"

In New York City, the Caughnawagas work mostly for the big companies—Bethlehem, American Bridge, the Lehigh Structural Steel Company, and the Harris Structural Steel Company. Among the structures in and around the city on which they worked in numbers are the R.C.A. Building, the Cities Service Building, the Empire State Building, the Daily News Building, the Chanin Building, the Bank of the Manhattan Company Building, the City Bank Farmers Trust Building, the George Washington Bridge, the Bayonne Bridge, the Passaic River Bridge, the Triborough Bridge, the Henry Hudson Bridge, the Little Hell Gate Bridge, the Bronx-Whitestone Bridge, the Marine Parkway Bridge, the Pulaski Skyway, the West Side Highway, the Waldorf-Astoria, London Terrace, and Knickerbocker Village.

North Gowanus is an old, sleepy, shabby neighborhood that lies between the head of the Gowanus Canal and the Borough Hall shopping district. There are factories in it, and coal tipples and junk yards, but it is primarily residential, and red-brick tenements and brownstone apartment houses are most numerous. The Caughnawagas all live within ten blocks of each other, in an area bounded by Court Street on the west, Schermerhorn Street on the north, Fourth Avenue on the east, and Warren Street on the south. They live in the best houses on the best blocks. As a rule, Caughnawaga women are good housekeepers and keep their apartments Dutch-clean. Most of them decorate a mantel or a wall with heirlooms brought down from the reservation—a drum, a set of rattles, a mask, a cradleboard. Otherwise, their apartments look much the same as those of their white neighbors. A typical family group consists of husband and wife and a couple of children and a female relative or two. After they get through school on the reservation, many Caughnawaga girls come down to North Gowanus and work in factories. Some work for the Fred Goat Company, a metal-stamping factory in the neighborhood, and some work for the Gem Safety Razor Corporation, whose factory is within walking distance. Quite a few of these girls have married whites; several have broken all ties with the band and the reservation. In the last ten years, Caughnawaga girls have married Filipinos, Germans, Italians, Jews, Norwegians, and Puerto Ricans. Many North Gowanus families often have relatives visiting them for long periods; when there is a new baby in a family, a grandmother or an aunt almost always comes down from the reservation and helps out. Caughnawagas are allowed to cross the border freely. However, each is required to carry a card, to which a photograph is attached, certifying that he or she is a member of the band. These cards are issued by the Indian Affairs Branch; the Caughnawagas refer to them as "passports." More than half of the North Gowanus housewives spend their spare time making souvenirs. They make a lot of them. They specialize in dolls, handbags, and belts, which they ornament with colored beads, using variations of ancient Iroquois designs such as the sky dome, the night sun, the day sun, the fern head, the ever-growing tree, the world turtle, and the council fire. Every fall, a few of the most Indian-looking of the men take vacations from structural steel for a month or so and go out with automobile loads of these souvenirs and sell them on the midways of state, county, and community fairs in New York, Connecticut, New Jersey, and Pennsylvania. The men wear buckskins and feathers on these trips and sleep in canvas tepees pitched on fairgrounds. Occasionally, on midways, to attract attention, they let out self-conscious wahoos and do fragments of the Duel Dance, the Dove Dance, the Falseface

Dance, and other old half-forgotten Mohawk dances. The women obtain the raw materials for souvenirs from the Plume Trading & Sales Company, at 155 Lexington Avenue, in Manhattan, a concern that sells beads, deerskin, imitation eagle feathers, and similar merchandise to Indian handicraftsmen all over the United States and Canada. There are approximately fifty children of school age in the colony. Two-thirds go to Public School 47, on Pacific Street, and the others go to parochial schools—St. Paul's, St. Agnes's, and St. Charles Borromeo's. Caughnawaga children read comic books, listen to the radio while doing their homework, sit twice through double features, and play stick ball in vacant lots the same as the other children in the neighborhood; teachers say that they differ from the others mainly in that they are more reserved and polite. They have unusual manual dexterity; by the age of three, most of them are able to tie their shoelaces. The adult Caughnawagas are multilingual; all speak Mohawk, all speak English, and all speak or understand at least a little French. In homes where both parents are Caughnawagas, Mohawk is spoken almost exclusively and the children pick it up. In homes where the mother is non-Indian and the father is away a good deal, a situation that is becoming more and more frequent, the children sometimes fail to learn the language, and this causes much sadness.

The Caughnawagas are churchgoers. The majority of the Catholics go to St. Paul's Church, at Court and Congress streets, and the majority of the Protestants go to Cuyler Presbyterian Church, on Pacific Street. Dr. David Munroe Cory, the pastor at Cuyler, is a man of incongruous interests. He is an amateur wrestler; he is vice-president of the Iceberg Athletic Club, a group that swims in the ocean at Coney Island throughout the winter; he once ran for Borough President of Brooklyn on the Socialist ticket; he is an authority on Faustus Socinus, the sixteenth-century Italian religious thinker; he studies languages for pleasure and knows eight, among them Hebrew, Greek, and Gaelic. A few Caughnawagas started turning up at Cuyler Church in the middle thirties, and Dr. Cory decided to learn Mohawk and see if he could attract more of them. He has not achieved fluency in Mohawk, but Caughnawagas say that he speaks it better than other white men, mostly anthropologists and priests, who have studied it. He holds a complete service in Mohawk the first Sunday evening in each month, after the English service, and twenty or thirty Caughnawagas usually attend. Twenty-five have joined the church. Michael Diabo, a retired riveter, was recently elected a deacon. Steven M. Schmidt, an Austrian-American who is married to Mrs. Josephine Skye Schmidt, a Caughnawaga woman, is an elder. Mr. Schmidt works in the compensation-claim department of an insurance company. Under Dr. Cory's guidance, two Caughnawaga women, Mrs. Schmidt and Mrs. Margaret Lahache, translated a group of hymns into Mohawk and compiled a hymnal, *The Caughnawaga Hymnal*, which is used in Cuyler and in the Protestant church on the reservation. Dr. Cory himself translated the Gospel According to Luke into Mohawk. Dr. Cory is quiet and serious, his sermons are free of cant, he has an intuitive understanding of Indian conversational taboos, and he is the only white person who is liked and trusted by the whole colony. Caughnawagas who are not members of his congregation, even some Catholics and longhouse people, go to him for advice.

Occasionally, in a saloon or at a wedding or a wake, Caughnawagas become vivacious and talkative. Ordinarily, however, they are rather dour and don't talk much. There is only one person in the North Gowanus colony who has a reputation for garrulity. He is a man of fifty-four whose white name is Orvis Diabo and whose Indian name is O-ron-ia-ke-te, or He Carries the Sky. Mr. Diabo is squat and barrel-chested. He has small, sharp eyes and a round, swarthy, double-chinned, piratical face. Unlike most other Caughnawagas, he does not deny or even minimize his white blood. "My mother was half Scotch and half Indian," he says. "My grandmother on my father's side was Scotch-Irish. Somewhere along the line, I forget just where, some French immigrant and some full Irish crept in. If you were to take my blood and strain it, God only knows what you'd find." He was born a Catholic; in young manhood, he became a Presbyterian; he now thinks of himself as "a kind of a free-thinker." Mr. Diabo started working in riveting gangs when he was nineteen and quit a year and a half ago. He had to quit because of crippling attacks of arthritis. He was a heater and worked on bridges and buildings in seventeen states. "I heated a million rivets," he says. "When they talk about the men that built this country, one of the men they mean is me." Mr. Diabo owns a house and thirty-three acres of farmland on the reservation. He inherited the farmland and rents it to a French Canadian. Soon after he quit work, his wife, who had lived in North Gowanus off and on for almost twenty years but had never liked it, went back to the reservation. She tried to get him to go along, but he decided to stay on awhile and rented a room in the apartment of a cousin. "I enjoy New York," he says. "The people are as high-strung as rats and the air is too gritty, but I enjoy it." Mr. Diabo reads a lot. Some years ago, in a Western magazine, he came across an advertisement of the Haldeman-Julius Company, a mail-order publishing house in Girard, Kansas, that puts out over eighteen hundred paperbound books, most of them dealing with religion, health, sex, history, or popular science. They are called Little Blue Books and cost a dime apiece. "I sent away for a dollar's worth of Little Blue Books," Mr. Diabo says, "and they opened my eyes to what an ignorant man I was. Ignorant and superstitious. Didn't know beans from back up. Since then, I've become a great reader. I've read dozens upon dozens of Little Blue Books, and I've improved my mind to the extent that I'm far beyond most of the people I associate with. When you come right down to it, I'm an educated man." Mr. Diabo has five favorite Little Blue Books—*Absurdities of the Bible,* by Clarence Darrow; *Seven Infidel U.S. Presidents,* by Joseph McCabe; *Queer Facts About Lost Civilizations,* by Charles J. Finger; *Why I Do Not Fear Death,* by E. Haldeman-Julius; and *Is Our Civilization Over-Sexed?,* by Theodore Dreiser. He carries them around in his pockets and reads them over and over. Mr. Diabo stays in bed until noon. Then, using a cane, he hobbles over to a neighborhood saloon, the Nevins Bar & Grill, at 75 Nevins Street, and sits in a booth. If there is someone around who will sit still and listen, he talks. If not, he reads a Little Blue Book. The Nevins is the social center of the Caughnawaga colony. The men in the gangs that work in the city customarily stop there for an hour or so on the way home. On weekend nights, they go there with their wives and drink Montreal ale and look at the television. When gangs come in from out-of-town jobs, they go on sprees there. When a Caughnawaga high-steel man is killed on the job, a collection is taken up in the Nevins for the immediate expenses of his family; these collections rarely run less than two hundred dollars; pasted on the bar mirror are several notes of thanks from widows. The Nevins is small and snug and plain and old. It is one of the oldest saloons in Brooklyn. It was opened in 1888, when North Gowanus was an Irishtown, and it was originally called Connelly's Abbey. Irish customers still call it the Abbey. Its present owners are Artie Rose and Bunny Davis. Davis is married to a Caughnawaga girl, the former Mavis Rice.

One afternoon a while back, I sat down with Mr. Diabo in his booth in the Nevins. He almost always drinks ale. This day he was drinking gin.

"I feel very low in my mind," he said. "I've got to go back to the reservation. I've run out of excuses and I can't put it off much longer. I got a letter from my wife today and she's disgusted with me. 'I'm sick and tired of begging you to come home,' she said. 'You can sit in Brooklyn until your tail takes root.' The trouble is, I don't want to go. That is, I do and I don't. I'll try to explain what I mean. An Indian high-steel man, when he first leaves the reservation to work in the States, the homesickness just about kills him. The first few years, he goes back as often as he can. Every time he finishes a job, unless he's thousands of miles away, he goes back. If he's working in

New York, he drives up weekends, and it's a twelve-hour drive. After a while, he gets married and brings his wife down and starts a family, and he doesn't go back so often. Oh, he most likely takes the wife and children up for the summer, but he doesn't stay with them. After three or four days, the reservation gets on his nerves and he highballs it back to the States. He gets used to the States. The years go by. He gets to be my age, maybe a little older, maybe a little younger, and one fine morning he comes to the conclusion he's a little too damned stiff in the joints to be walking a naked beam five hundred feet up in the air. Either that, or some foreman notices he hasn't got a sure step any longer and takes him aside and tells him a few home truths. He gives up high-steel work and he packs his belongings and he takes his money out of the bank or the postal savings, what little he's been able to squirrel away, and he goes on back to the reservation for good. And it's hard on him. He's used to danger, and reservation life is very slow; the biggest thing that ever happens is a funeral. He's used to jumping around from job to job, and reservation life boxes him in. He's used to having a drink, and it's against the law to traffic in liquor on the reservation; he has to buy a bottle in some French-Canadian town across the river and smuggle it in like a high-school boy, and that annoys the hell out of him.

"There's not much he can do to occupy the time. He can sit on the highway and watch the cars go by, or he can sit on the riverbank and fish for eels and watch the boats go by, or he can weed the garden, or he can go to church, or he can congregate in the grocery stores with the other old retired high-steel men and play cards and talk. That is, if he can stand it. You'd think those old men would talk about the cities they worked in, the sprees they went on, the girls that follow construction all over the country that they knew, the skyscrapers and bridges they put up—only they don't. After they been sitting around the reservation five years, six years, seven years, they seem to turn against their high-steel days. Some of them, they get to be as Indian as all hell; they won't even speak English any more; they make out they can't understand it. And some of them, they get to be soreheads, the kind of old men that can chew nails and spit rust. When they do talk, they talk gloomy. They like to talk about family fights. There's families on the reservation that got on the outs with each other generations ago and they're still on the outs; maybe it started with a land dispute, maybe it started with a mixed-marriage dispute, maybe it started when some woman accused another woman of meeting her husband in the bushes in the graveyard. Even down here in Brooklyn, there's certain Indians that won't work in gangs with certain other Indians because of bad blood between their families; their wives, when they meet on Atlantic Avenue, they look right through each other. The old men like to bring up such matters and refresh their recollections on some of the details. Also, they like to talk about religion. A miraculous cure they heard about, something the priest said—they'll harp on it for weeks. They're all amateur priests, or preachers. They've all got some religious notion lurking around in their minds.

"And they like to talk about reservation matters. The last time I was home, I sat down with the bunch in a store and I tried to tell them about something I'd been studying up on that interested me very much—Mongolian spots. They're dark-purple spots that occur on the skin on the backs of Japanese and other Mongolians. Every now and then, a full-blood American Indian is born with them. The old men didn't want to hear about Mongolian spots. They were too busy discussing the matter of street names for Caughnawaga village. The electric-light company that supplies the village had been trying and trying to get the Indians to name the streets and lanes. The meter-readers are always getting balled up, and the company had offered to put up street signs and house numbers free of charge. The old men didn't want street names; they were raising holy hell about it. It wouldn't be Indian. And they were discussing the pros and cons of a waterworks system. They're eternally discussing that. Some want a waterworks, but the majority don't. The majority of them, they'd a whole lot rather get behind a poor old horse that his next step might be his last and cart their water up from the river by the barrel. It's more Indian. Sometimes, the way an Indian reasons, there's no rhyme or reason to it. Electric lights are all right and the biggest second-hand car they can find, and radios that the only time they turn them off is when they're changing the tubes, and seventy-five-dollar baby carriages, and four-hundred-dollar coffins, but street names and tap water—oh, Jesus, no! That's going entirely too damned far.

"On the other hand, there's things I look forward to. I look forward to eating real Indian grub again. Such as *o-nen-sto,* or corn soup. That's the Mohawk national dish. Some of the women make it down here in Brooklyn, but they use Quaker corn meal. The good old women up on the reservation, they make it the hard way, the way the Mohawks were making it five hundred years ago. They shell some corn, and they put it in a pot with a handful of maple ashes and boil it. The lye in the ashes skins the hulls off the kernels, and the kernels swell up into big fat pearls. Then they wash off the lye. Then they put in some red kidney beans. Then they put in a pig's head; in the old days, it was a bear's head. Then they cook it until it's as thick as mud. And when it's cooking, it smells so good. If you were breathing your last, if you had the rattle in your throat, and the wind blew you a faint suggestion of a smell of it, you'd rise and walk. And I look forward to eating some Indian bread that's made with the same kind of corn. Down here, the women always use Quaker meal. Indian bread is boiled; and it's shaped like a hamburger, and it's got kidney beans sprinkled through it. On the reservation, according to an old-time custom, we have steak for breakfast every Sunday morning, whether we can afford it or not, and we pour the steak gravy on the Indian bread.

"And another thing I look forward to, if I can manage it—I want to attend a longhouse festival. If I have to join to do so, I'll join. One night, the last time I was home, the longhousers were having a festival. I decided I'd go up to the Catholic graveyard that's right below the longhouse and hide in the bushes and listen to the music. So I snuck up there and waded through the thistles and the twitch grass and the Queen Anne's lace, and I sat down on a flat stone on the grave of an uncle of mine, Miles Diabo, who was a warwhooper with the Miller Brothers 101 Ranch Wild West Show and died with the pneumonia in Wheeling, West Virginia, in 1916. Uncle Miles was one of the last of the Caughnawaga circus Indians. My mother is in that graveyard, and my father, old Nazareth Diabo that I hardly even knew. They called him Nazzry. He was a pioneer high-steel Indian. He was away from home the majority of the time, and he was killed in the disaster—when the Quebec Bridge went down. There's hundreds of high-steel men buried in there. The ones that were killed on the job, they don't have stones; their graves are marked with lengths of steel girders made into crosses. There's a forest of girder crosses in there. So I was sitting on Uncle Miles's stone, thinking of the way things go in life, and suddenly the people in the longhouse began to sing and dance and drum on their drums. They were singing Mohawk chants that came down from the old, old red-Indian times. I could hear men's voices and women's voices and children's voices. The Mohawk language, when it's sung, it's beautiful to hear. Oh, it takes your breath away. A feeling ran through me that made me tremble; I had to take a deep breath to quiet my heart, it was beating so fast. I felt very sad; at the same time, I felt very peaceful. I thought I was all alone in the graveyard, and then who loomed up out of the dark and sat down beside me but an old high-steel man I had been talking with in a store that afternoon, one of the soreheads, an old man that fights every improvement that's suggested on the reservation, whatever it is, on the grounds it isn't Indian—this isn't Indian, that isn't Indian. So he said to me, 'You're not alone up here. Look over there.' I looked where he pointed, and I saw a white shirt in among the bushes. And he said,

'Look over there,' and I saw a cigarette gleaming in the dark. 'The bushes are full of Catholics and Protestants,' he said. 'Every night there's a longhouse festival, they creep up here and listen to the singing. It draws them like flies.' So I said, 'The longhouse music is beautiful to hear, isn't it?' And he remarked it ought to be, it was the old Indian music. So I said the longhouse religion appealed to me. 'One of these days,' I said, 'I might possibly join.' I asked him how he felt about it. He said he was a Catholic and it was out of the question. 'If I was to join the longhouse,' he said, 'I'd be excommunicated, and I couldn't be buried in holy ground, and I'd burn in Hell.' I said to him, 'Hell isn't Indian.' It was the wrong thing to say. He didn't reply to me. He sat there awhile—I guess he was thinking it over—and then he got up and walked away."

In Dreams Begin Responsibilities, Delmore Schwartz (1938)

Delmore Schwartz was, as Elizabeth Hardwick described him, "irredeemably urban and New York City at that." He was born in Brooklyn, of Romanian descent, on December 8, 1913, but moved to Washington Heights as a teenager and graduated from George Washington High School and New York University. Schwartz burst onto the New York literary scene in the Autumn 1937 issue of the *Partisan Review* with a story entitled "In Dreams Begin Responsibilities." Schwartz, only twenty-four at the time, had actually written the story two years earlier during his junior year at NYU while he was living in an apartment at 813 Greenwich Avenue. The story was hailed as a work of genius and seemed to be the prelude to a distinguished literary career.

However, Schwartz's life was, in many ways, a tragic one, and although he made a living writing poetry, critical essays, and plays while also teaching at Syracuse (where he taught the musician Lou Reed) and Harvard, Schwartz never realized his initial promise. His picture rests atop the bar at the White Horse Tavern (Hudson and West Eleventh Street) in the West Village where he entertained friends throughout the 1950s. His untimely, early death at the age of fifty-three occurred in the dilapidated Hotel Dixie at 250 West 43rd Street, and only a reporter who recognized his name on the morgue list prevented him from a potter's field burial.

Schwartz's friend Saul Bellow re-created him as the title character in his novel *Humboldt's Gift* and John Berryman, in *Dream Song*, wrote of Schwartz "we never learnt why he came, or what he wanted. His mission was obscure. His mission was real, but obscure."

I

I THINK it is the year 1909. I feel as if I were in a motion picture theatre, the long arm of light crossing the darkness and spinning, my eyes fixed on the screen. This is a silent picture as if an old Biograph one, in which the actors are dressed in ridiculously old-fashioned clothes, and one flash succeeds another with sudden jumps. The actors too seem to jump about and walk too fast. The shots themselves are full of dots and rays, as if it were raining when the picture was photographed. The light is bad.

It is Sunday afternoon, June 12th, 1909, and my father is walking down the quiet streets of Brooklyn on his way to visit my mother. His clothes are newly pressed and his tie is too tight in his high collar. He jingles the coins in his pockets, thinking of the witty things he will say. I feel as if I had by now relaxed entirely in the soft darkness of the theatre; the organist peals out the obvious and approximate emotions on which the audience rocks unknowingly. I am anonymous, and I have forgotten myself. It is always so when one goes to the movies, it is, as they say, a drug.

My father walks from street to street of trees, lawns and houses, once in a while coming to an avenue on which a street-car skates and gnaws, slowly progressing. The conductor, who has a handle-bar mustache, helps a young lady wearing a hat like a bowl with feathers on to the car. She lifts her long skirts slightly as she mounts the steps. He leisurely makes change and rings his bell. It is obviously Sunday, for everyone is wearing Sunday clothes, and the street-car's noises emphasize the quiet of the holiday. Is not Brooklyn the City of Churches? The shops are closed and their shades drawn, but for an occasional stationery store or drug-store with great green balls in the window.

My father has chosen to take this long walk because he likes to walk and think. He thinks about himself in the future and so arrives at the place he is to visit in a state of mild exaltation. He pays no attention to the houses he is passing, in which the Sunday dinner is being eaten, nor to the many trees which patrol each street, now coming to their full leafage and the time when they will room the whole street in cool shadow. An occasional carriage passes, the horse's hooves falling like stones in the quiet afternoon, and once in a while an automobile, looking like an enormous upholstered sofa, puffs and passes.

My father thinks of my mother, of how nice it will be to introduce her to his family. But he is not yet sure that he wants to marry her, and once in a while he becomes panicky about the bond already established. He reassures himself by thinking of the big men he admires who are married: William Randolph Hearst, and William Howard Taft, who has just become President of the United States.

My father arrives at my mother's house. He has come too early and so is suddenly embarrassed. My aunt, my mother's sister, answers the loud bell with her napkin in her hand, for the family is still at dinner. As my father enters, my grandfather rises from the table and shakes hands with him. My mother has run upstairs to tidy herself. My grandmother asks my father if he has had dinner, and tells him that Rose will be downstairs soon. My grandfather opens the conversation by remarking on the mild June weather. My father sits uncomfortably near the table, holding his hat in his hand. My grandmother tells my aunt to take my father's hat. My uncle, twelve years old, runs into the house, his hair tousled. He shouts a greeting to my father, who has often given him a nickel, and then runs upstairs. It is evident that the respect in which my father is held in this household is tempered by a good deal of mirth. He is impressive, yet he is very awkward.

II

Finally my mother comes downstairs, all dressed up, and my father being engaged in conversation with my grandfather becomes uneasy, not knowing whether to greet my mother or continue the conversation. He gets up from the chair clumsily and says "hello" gruffly. My grandfather watches, examining their congruence, such as it is, with a critical eye, and meanwhile rubbing his bearded cheek roughly, as he always does when he reflects. He is worried; he is afraid that my father will not make a good husband for his oldest daughter. At this point something happens to the film, just as my father is saying something funny to my mother; I am awakened to myself and my unhappiness just as my interest was rising. The audience begins to clap impatiently. Then the trouble is cared for but the film has been returned to a portion just shown, and once more I see my grandfather rubbing his bearded cheek and pondering my father's character. It is difficult to get back into the picture once more and forget myself, but as my mother giggles at my father's words, the darkness drowns me.

My father and mother depart from the house, my father shaking hands with my mother once more, out of some unknown uneasiness. I stir uneasily also, slouched in the hard chair of the theatre. Where is the older uncle, my mother's older brother? He is studying in his bedroom upstairs, studying for his final examination at the College of the City of New York, having been dead of rapid pneumonia for the last twenty-one years. My mother and father walk down the same quiet streets once more. My mother is holding my father's arm and telling him of the novel which she has been reading; and my father utters judgments of the characters as the plot is made clear to him. This is a habit which he very much enjoys, for he feels the utmost superiority and confidence when he approves and condemns the behavior of other people. At times he feels moved to utter a brief "Ugh"—whenever the story becomes what he would call sugary. This tribute is paid to his manliness. My mother feels satisfied by the interest which she has awakened; she is showing my father how intelligent she is, and how interesting.

They reach the avenue, and the street-car leisurely arrives. They are going to Coney Island this afternoon, although my mother considers that such pleasures are inferior. She has made up her mind to indulge only in a walk on the boardwalk and a pleasant dinner, avoiding the riotous amusements as being beneath the dignity of so dignified a couple.

My father tells my mother how much money he has made in the past week, exaggerating an amount which need not have been exaggerated. But my father has always felt that actualities somehow fall short. Suddenly I begin to weep. The determined old lady who sits next to me in the theatre is annoyed and looks at me with an angry face, and being intimidated, I stop. I drag out my handkerchief and dry my face, licking the drop which has fallen near my lips. Meanwhile I have missed something, for here are my mother and father alighting at the last stop, Coney Island.

III

They walk toward the boardwalk, and my father commands my mother to inhale the pungent air from the sea. They both breathe in deeply, both of them laughing as they do so. They have in common a great interest in health, although my father is strong and husky, my mother frail. Their minds are full of theories of what is good to eat and not good to eat, and sometimes they engage in heated discussions of the subject, the whole matter ending in my father's announcement, made with a scornful bluster, that you have to die sooner or later anyway. On the boardwalk's flagpole, the American flag is pulsing in an intermittent wind from the sea.

My father and mother go to the rail of the boardwalk and look down on the beach where a good many bathers are casually walking about. A few are in the surf. A peanut whistle pierces the air with its pleasant and active whine, and my father goes to buy peanuts. My mother remains at the rail and stares at the ocean. The ocean seems merry to her; it pointedly sparkles and again and again the pony waves are released. She notices the children digging in the wet sand, and the bathing costumes of the girls who are her own age. My father returns with the peanuts. Overhead the sun's lightning strikes and strikes, but neither of them are at all aware of it. The boardwalk is full of people dressed in their Sunday clothes and idly strolling. The tide does not reach as far as the boardwalk, and the strollers would feel no danger if it did. My mother and father lean on the rail of the boardwalk and absently stare at the ocean. The ocean is becoming rough; the waves come in slowly, tugging strength from far back. The moment before they somersault, the moment when they arch their backs so beautifully, showing green and white veins amid the black, that moment is intolerable. They finally crack, dashing fiercely upon the sand, actually driving, full force downward, against the sand, bouncing upward and forward, and at last petering out into a small stream which races up the beach and then is recalled. My parents gaze absentmindedly at the ocean, scarcely interested in its harshness. The sun overhead does not disturb them. But I stare at the terrible sun which breaks up sight, and the fatal, merciless, passionate ocean, I forget my parents. I stare fascinated and finally, shocked by the indifference of my father and mother, I burst out weeping once more. The old lady next to me pats me on the shoulder and says "There, there, all of this is only a movie, young man, only a movie," but I look up once more at the terrifying sun and the terrifying ocean, and being unable to control my tears, I get up and go to the men's room, stumbling over the feet of the other people seated in my row.

IV

When I return, feeling as if I had awakened in the morning sick for lack of sleep, several hours have apparently passed and my parents are riding on the merry-go-round. My father is on a black horse, my mother on a white one, and they seem to be making an eternal circuit for the single purpose of snatching the nickel rings which are attached to the arm of one of the posts. A hand-organ is playing; it is one with the ceaseless circling of the merry-go-round.

For a moment it seems that they will never get off the merry-go-round because it will never stop. I feel like one who looks down on the avenue from the 50th story of a building. But at length they do get off; even the music of the hand-organ has ceased for a moment. My father has acquired ten rings, my mother only two, although it was my mother who really wanted them.

They walk on along the boardwalk as the afternoon descends by imperceptible degrees into the incredible violet of dusk. Everything fades into a relaxed glow, even the ceaseless murmuring from the beach, and the revolutions of the merry-go-round. They look for a place to have dinner. My father suggests the best one on the boardwalk and my mother demurs, in accordance with her principles.

However they do go to the best place, asking for a table near the window, so that they can look out on the boardwalk and the mobile ocean. My father feels omnipotent as he places a quarter in the waiter's hand as he asks for a table. The place is crowded and here too there is music, this time from a kind of string trio. My father orders dinner with a fine confidence.

As the dinner is eaten, my father tells of his plans for the future, and my mother shows with expressive face how interested she is, and how impressed. My father becomes exultant. He is lifted up by the waltz that is being played, and his own future begins to intoxicate him. My father tells my mother that he is going to expand his business, for there is a great deal of money to be made. He wants to settle down. After all, he is twenty-nine, he has lived by himself since he was thirteen, he is making more and more money, and he is envious of his married friends when he visits them in the cozy security of their homes, surrounded, it seems, by the calm domestic pleasures, and by delightful children, and then, as the waltz reaches the moment when all the dancers swing madly, then, then with awful daring, then he asks my mother to marry him, although awkwardly enough and puzzled, even in his excitement, at how he had arrived at the proposal, and she, to make the whole business worse, begins to cry, and my father looks nervously about, not knowing at all what to do now, and my mother says: "It's all I've wanted from the moment I saw you," sobbing, and he finds all of this very difficult, scarcely to his taste, scarcely as he had thought it would be, on his long walks over Brooklyn Bridge in the revery of a fine cigar, and it was then that I stood up in the theatre and shouted: "Don't do it. It's not too late to change your minds, both of you. Nothing good will come of it, only remorse, hatred, scandal, and two children whose characters are monstrous." The whole audience turned to look at me, annoyed, the usher came hurrying down the aisle flashing his searchlight, and the old lady next to me tugged me down into my seat, saying: "Be quiet. You'll be put out, and you paid thirty-five cents to come in." And so I shut my eyes because I could not bear to see what was happening. I sat there quietly.

V

But after awhile I begin to take brief glimpses, and at length I watch again with thirsty interest, like a child who wants to maintain his sulk although offered the bribe of candy. My parents are now having their picture taken in a photographer's booth along the boardwalk. The place is shadowed in the mauve light which is apparently necessary. The camera is set to the side on its tripod and looks like a Martian man. The photographer is instructing my parents in how to pose. My father has his arm over my mother's shoulder, and both of them smile emphatically. The photographer brings my mother a bouquet of flowers to hold in her hand but she holds it at the wrong angle. Then the photographer covers himself with the black cloth which drapes the camera and all that one sees of him is one protruding arm and his hand which clutches the rubber ball which he will squeeze when the picture is finally taken. But he is not satisfied with their appearance. He feels with certainty that somehow there is something wrong in their pose. Again and again he issues from his hidden place with new directions. Each suggestion merely makes matters worse. My father is becoming impatient. They try a seated pose. The photographer explains that he has pride, he is not interested in all of this for the money, he wants to make beautiful pictures. My father says: "Hurry up, will you? We haven't got all night." But the photographer only scurries about apologetically, and issues new directions. The photographer charms me. I approve of him with all my heart, for I know just how he feels, and as he criticizes each revised pose according to some unknown idea of rightness, I become quite hopeful. But then my father says angrily: "Come on, you've had enough time, we're not going to wait any longer." And the photographer, sighing unhappily, goes back under his black covering, holds out his hand, says: "One, two, three, Now!" and the picture is taken, with my father's smile turned to a grimace and my mother's bright and false. It takes a few minutes for the picture to be developed and as my parents sit in the curious light they become quite depressed.

VI

They have passed a fortune-teller's booth, and my mother wishes to go in, but my father does not. They begin to argue about it. My mother becomes stubborn, my father once more impatient, and then they begin to quarrel, and what my father would like to do is walk off and leave my mother there, but he knows that that would never do. My mother refuses to budge. She is near to tears, but she feels an uncontrollable desire to hear what the palm-reader will say. My father consents angrily, and they both go into a booth which is in a way like the photographer's, since it is draped in black cloth and its light is shadowed. The place is too warm, and my father keeps saying this is all nonsense, pointing to the crystal ball on the table. The fortuneteller, a fat, short woman, garbed in what is supposed to be Oriental robes, comes into the room from the back and greets them, speaking with an accent. But suddenly my father feels that the whole thing is intolerable; he tugs at my mother's arm, but my mother refuses to budge. And then, in terrible anger, my father lets go of my mother's arm and strides out, leaving my mother stunned. She moves to go after my father, but the fortune-teller holds her arm tightly and begs her not to do so, and I in my seat am shocked more than can ever be said, for I feel as if I were walking a tight-rope a hundred feet over a circus-audience and suddenly the rope is showing signs of breaking, and I get up from my seat and begin to shout once more the first words I can think of to communicate my terrible fear and once more the usher comes hurrying down the aisle flashing his searchlight, and the old lady pleads with me, and the shocked audience has turned to stare at me, and I keep shouting: "What are they doing? Don't they know what they are doing? Why doesn't my mother go after my father? If she does not do that, what will she do? Doesn't my father know what he is doing?"—But the usher has seized my arm and is dragging me away, and as he does so, he says: "What are *you* doing? Don't you know that you can't do whatever you want to do? Why should a young man like you, with your whole life before you, get hysterical like this? Why don't you *think* of what you're doing? You can't act like this even if other people aren't around! You will be sorry if you do not do what you should do, you can't carry on like this, it is not right, you will find that out soon enough, everything you do matters too much," and he said that dragging me through the lobby of the theatre into the cold light, and I woke up into the bleak winter morning of my 21st birthday, the windowsill shining with its lip of snow, and the morning already begun.

Ten Misconceptions of New York, Fiorello La Guardia (1939)

Fiorello La Guardia was born at 177 Sullivan Street in 1882, the son of an Austrian Jewish mother and an agnostic Italian father, and became the first Italian-American elected to Congress in 1916. By the time he died in 1947, two years after he had served an unprecedented twelve years as mayor of New York, he had transformed the city into what he called "the world's greatest experiment in social and political democracy."

La Guardia possessed the energy—he routinely worked sixteen-hour days seven days a week that exhausted his staff by summoning them with one of six buzzers he had installed beneath his gigantic, thirty-two-foot desk—and a style that made "the Little Flower" the most beloved mayor in the city's history. He regularly turned up at murder scenes, fires, and car accidents to help police and emergency workers; he gave dramatic readings over the radio airways of the comic strip "Dick Tracy" during the newspaper strike of July 1945; and throughout the Depression years of the 1930s he hopped airplanes (in an era where air transportation was a novelty) to the nation's capital to meet with President Franklin Roosevelt only to return to his desk by the end of the day.

It was La Guardia's relationship with the former New York governor that culminated in the most ambitious program of public works the nation had ever seen. La Guardia took office in 1934 in the midst of the nation's most catastrophic economic depression and in the next five years the city received $1.1 billion from federal agencies—fully a sixth of the entire national budget for public works. With his "master builder," Robert Moses, whom he appointed within days of taking office, La Guardia would forever alter the infrastructure of New York into what he called "a gigantic laboratory of civic reconstruction." The legacy of pouring public money into the economy in order to stimulate private investment would be felt in many areas but none more than La Guardia's attack on the slums. In 1934, La Guardia created the New York City Housing Authority, which built the First Houses on First Avenue and Third Street on the Lower East Side, the first public housing project ever built in the United States. As La Guardia himself remarked, "Sometimes I see the City of Tomorrow . . . I see a City with no slums and little poverty. It will be a reality some day." This vision gave birth to a new sense of civic responsibility that would be as lasting a legacy as all of the physical structures created during his time in office.

MANY of the visitors who come to the World's Fair this year will be seeing New York City for the first time, and their joy at visiting the greatest metropolis in the country may be dimmed somewhat by certain misconceptions about the city which have grown into popular belief in some sections of the country.

There are ten principal misconceptions held, for one reason or another, by people living outside New York. Perhaps the most widely held is the notion that the city is a cold, hard place in which to live. As New Yorkers travel, they hear their community condemned with the phrase, "Nice place to visit, but you couldn't pay me to live there."

Far from being cold, New York is a warm-hearted and generous community. Let a great catastrophe happen, and the New Yorker is the first person to grieve about it and offer what help he can.

I wish some of the critics could peep inside our great city hospitals, where the sick and aged get the finest food and the best care we can give them. I wish they could see an entire neighborhood drop its concerns until our police rescue a kitten from a tree. I wish they could realize that we spend $10,000,000 a month to take care of our unemployed; unfortunate persons who, we feel, are without work through no fault of their own. The city's share of this great sum is raised through relief taxes, which are cheerfully paid by those who sympathize with the plight of others less fortunate than themselves. This relief undertaking could not be maintained a month if the typical New Yorker were the cold-hearted person he is credited with being. In size, our relief load is without parallel anywhere in the country.

Having spent my early youth in the small community of Prescott, Arizona, I am able to look at this city through the eyes of a Westerner as well as of a person who lives here. I know well the open-handed friendship of the West, and I also know that the people of my city have just as much friendship to offer.

People who get to know each other get to like each other. The unfortunate type of New Yorker who looks down his nose at the stranger merely shows that he has no understanding of people in other parts of the country. Fortunately, this type is in the minority.

No city in the country does more for the individual than this great city does. New York is the most generous community in the country for the simple reason that throughout its schools, its hospitals and its other public institutions there is less inquiry made about the origin of pupils and patients than in any other city.

Now take Legend No. 2, which is that New York is a city of sweatshops. That impression is due to the horrible working conditions which existed here through the Eighteen Eighties. The pioneering work in wiping them out was started by Jacob Riis, Samuel Gompers, Theodore Roosevelt and other outstanding citizens. Their work was combined with the drive on the slums made by the Charity Organizations Society and similar welfare organizations. The first law against sweatshops covered bakeries and cigar factories. It was enacted to remove sweatshop conditions—and of course it was declared unconstitutional by the courts. Later it was modified and became effective.

Today this city is clean of sweatshops. "Made in New York" is the hallmark of superior merchandise, produced under sanitary and decent working conditions and with decent living wages.

Third, there is a mistaken notion that this city is strictly a money mart, where the first consideration is the making of money. Of course New York is the financial capital of the country, but few realize that funds are held in trust here for industrial enterprises throughout the country.

The person who uses New York as a synonym for Wall Street does not realize that this city has a soul, and that its residents are devoted to the best in music and art. We have spent more than $225,000,000 in the last five years on parks and playgrounds primarily for the use of our children. We maintain some of the finest museums in the world. Any resident or visitor to the city can find free concerts of really good music without difficulty. The young artist with ability finds his greatest encouragement here, the finest opportunities for study, and superior possibilities for advancement in his field.

Take the fourth notion—that New Yorkers are impolite. That's a fallacy also, because actually they are most considerate. The subway—where trains running one minute apart transport up to 6,000,000 passengers a day—makes for a speed and rush which are not necessary in smaller communities. Analysis of New York's rush hour crowds shows that only a most courteous and considerate people could live under such conditions. Without good humor and without good temper the rush-hour crowd would become a disorderly mob.

We train almost 20,000 policemen to be polite in their dealings with citizens and strangers. Every city employee—and there are more than 155,000 of them—is expected to show kindness and consideration in his contacts with the public. I do not believe any city should boast because its public servants are polite, for courtesy should be their habit. I do not expect any praise because New York City's employees are considerate. Outside the city service, the stranger will find cab drivers, waiters and almost any one he comes in contact with eager to help him. The average man on the street is customarily helpful and obliging to those who need his assistance.

Now let us look at the fifth misconception—the idea that the New Yorker looks down upon the small-towner. The complete answer to that is that the typical New Yorker comes from a small town himself, or his parents do. There is not the slightest trace of any such scorn here. A young man may come into New York off the farm and become a policeman, and the policeman born in New York looks with longing toward a small-town existence. That goes up to and includes the Mayor. It's just human nature—and we're intensely human. Persons are drawn from small towns to this city by ambition to further their careers. The process in reverse sends the city dweller into the country. Instead of disdaining the small country place we admire it as a place to live in.

Misconception No. 6 is the idea that New Yorkers lack patriotism, that they are unconcerned with the welfare of the country as a whole. We answer that by the simple statement that in any national emergency the city's contribution will compare favorably with that of any State. We won't even make the comparison with any other city. We'll compare our community with any State, and I think New York will stand out favorably in the comparison.

Seventh, we frequently hear the criticism that New York is an expensive place to live. Comparatively, it is expensive. But that is true only because wages here are the finest in the country. On a weighted comparison which takes all the factors of living into account, the person living in this city gets more of the finer and better things of life than the person living in the small community could possibly get. Again it must be said that New York is a great center of art and culture as well as an outstanding industrial center.

New York has taken the leadership in establishing sanitary standards and high economic standards for its workers. That leadership gives a direct and tangible benefit to the men and women who work here, and it has not yet been paralleled in any other part of the country. New York has indicated that it will not reduce these standards to the low base where exploitation of labor is detrimental to the health of its workers. Through the production of better merchandise and the application of more efficiency, we are going to beat other cities where lower working standards prevail. By so doing we will destroy the theory that cheap, exploited, sub-standard labor pays.

Sometimes we hear people refer to this city as an architectural hodgepodge, and we'll call that the eighth misconception about it. New York is not hodgepodge in its architecture at all. Its ensemble is unique and anything but hodgepodge, as any photograph or distant perspective will prove.

Look at the Manhattan skyline and you will see a smoothly blended city. The beauty of its individual architecture is not surpassed anywhere in the world. Remember that New York is a constantly growing city, and that it has an architectural theme all its own. Rather than concede that it was hodgepodge, I would call it a patchwork of beauty.

Passing on to Notion Nine, we take up the assertion that New York, because of its immense population and crowded districts, is an unhealthful place to live in. That is answered in full by our vital statistics. In the last five years we have shown our lowest mortality and child mortality rates, and the general death rate compares well with that of other cities.

We are constantly building new sewage disposal plants in the interest of public health. And now I can say one thing that I had hoped to be able to say before I went out of office. I'll take 500 school children selected at random and compare them in health with any 500 children from rural districts. That's the answer.

Our water supply system, bringing water from 120 miles away in the Catskill Mountains, is a greater engineering feat than the Panama Canal. We use 990 million gallons of water a day, which speaks well for the cleanliness of our people. And this whole system is self-supporting. The climate here is a matter beyond the control of the city administration—we can't claim credit for it, but we're very happy to have it.

Lastly, we face the idea that our time as a great metropolis has passed. I believe that the future of New York is inextricably interwoven with the future of America. When America declines, New York will go with it. But I have abundant faith in the future of this city, and every one of my predecessors in the Mayor's office has had the same faith.

No city in America has invested more in its future than New York has. This is its tradition, and has always been its tradition. In every period we find public improvements ahead of their time, looking toward the future. As we look ahead I think New York will continue to be the cultural and educational center of the country. I think also that it will be the center for scientific research and the development of science. New York leads the parade of cities in the comfort and safety of its people, public health, education, the arts and sciences. My administration has followed the tradition and has increased the tempo.

We could afford to stop for the next twenty years and still we would be slightly ahead of the procession. But New York just can't stop. It's like flying—the city is sustained by the thrust of its forward momentum and by its speed. When the law of gravity changes, New York will stop progressing. When the Day of Judgment comes, New York will be the model municipality and will have reached its limit.

The Eighty Yard Run, Irwin Shaw (1942)

Irwin Gilbert Shamforoff was born in the Bronx in 1913 to Jewish Russian immigrants. His parents subsequently changed their name to Shaw and moved to Brooklyn. Irwin Shaw graduated from Brooklyn College in 1934, but by that time he had already begun writing radio scripts for episodes of *Dick Tracy.*

Shaw wrote short stories, novels, screenplays, and international best-sellers. He was prolific, producing a piece of work almost every year from 1936 until his death in Davos, Switzerland, in 1984. Commercial highlights of his career included winning an Oscar for best adapted screenplay in 1942 for *The Talk of the Town,* and the novels *Rich Man, Poor Man* (1970) and *Beggar, Thief* (1977), both of which were adapted into blockbuster television miniseries.

But Shaw's short story collections, *Sailor Off the Bremen* (1939) and *Welcome to the City* (1942), contain some of the best short stories of this century and have led critics to compare Shaw to John Cheever and Ernest Hemingway.

THE pass was high and wide and he jumped for it, feeling it slap flatly against his hands, as he shook his hips to throw off the halfback who was diving at him. The center floated by, his hands desperately brushing Darling's knee as Darling picked his feet up high and delicately ran over a blocker and an opposing linesman in a jumble on the ground near the scrimmage line. He had ten yards in the clear and picked up speed, breathing easily, feeling his thigh pads rising and falling against his legs, listening to the sound of cleats behind him, pulling away from them, watching the other backs heading him off toward the sideline, the whole picture, the men closing in on him, the blockers fighting for position, the ground he had to cross, all suddenly clear in his head, for the first time in his life not a meaningless confusion of men, sounds, speed. He smiled a little to himself as he ran, holding the ball lightly in front of him with his two hands, his knees pumping high, his hips twisting in the almost girlish run of a back in a broken field. The first halfback came at him and he fed him his leg, then swung at the last moment, took the shock of the man's shoulder without breaking stride, ran right through him, his cleats biting securely into the turf. There was only the safety man now, coming warily at him, his arms crooked, hands spread. Darling tucked the ball in, spurted at him, driving hard, hurling himself along, all two hundred pounds bunched into controlled attack. He was sure he was going to get past the safety man. Without thought, his arms and legs working beautifully together, he headed right for the safety man, stiff-armed him, feeling blood spurt instantaneously from the man's nose onto his hand, seeing his face go awry, head turned, mouth pulled to one side. He pivoted away, keeping the arm locked, dropping the safety man as he ran easily toward the goal line, with the drumming of cleats diminishing behind him.

How long ago? It was autumn then, and the ground was getting hard because the nights were cold and leaves from the maples around the stadium blew across the practice fields in gusts of wind, and the girls were beginning to put polo coats over their sweaters when they came to watch practice in the afternoons. . . . Fifteen years. Darling walked slowly over the same ground in the spring twilight, in his neat shoes, a man of thirty-five dressed in a double-breasted suit, ten pounds heavier in the fifteen years, but not fat, with the years between 1925 and 1940 showing in his face.

The coach was smiling quietly to himself and the assistant coaches were looking at each other with pleasure the way they always did when one of the second stringers suddenly did something fine, bringing credit to them, making their $2,000 a year a tiny bit more secure.

Darling trotted back, smiling, breathing deeply but easily, feeling wonderful, not tired, though this was the tail end of practice and he'd run eighty yards. The sweat poured off his face and soaked his jersey and he liked the feeling, the warm moistness lubricating his skin like oil. Off in a corner of the field some players were punting and the smack of leather against the ball came pleasantly through the afternoon air. The freshmen were running signals on the next field and the quarterback's sharp voice, the pound of the eleven pairs of cleats, the "Dig, now *dig!*" of the coaches, the laughter of the players all somehow made him feel happy as he trotted back to midfield, listening to the applause and shouts of the students along the sidelines, knowing that after that run the coach would have to start him Saturday against Illinois.

Fifteen years, Darling thought, remembering the shower after the workout, the hot water steaming off his skin and the deep soapsuds and all the young voices singing with the water streaming down and towels going and managers running in and out and the sharp sweet smell of oil of wintergreen and everybody clapping him on the back as he dressed and Packard, the captain, who took being captain very seriously, coming over to him and shaking his hand and saying, "Darling, you're going to go places in the next two years."

The assistant manager fussed over him, wiping a cut on his leg with alcohol and iodine, the little sting making him realize suddenly how fresh and whole and solid his body felt. The manager slapped a piece of adhesive tape over the cut, and Darling noticed the sharp clean white of the tape against the ruddiness of the skin, fresh from the shower.

He dressed slowly, the softness of his shirt and the soft warmth of his wool socks and his flannel trousers a reward against his skin after the harsh pressure of the shoulder harness and thigh and hip pads. He drank three glasses of cold water, the liquid reaching down coldly inside of him, soothing the harsh dry places in his throat and belly left by the sweat and running and shouting of practice.

Fifteen years.

The sun had gone down and the sky was green behind the stadium and he laughed quietly to himself as he looked at the stadium, rearing above the trees, and knew that on Saturday when the 70,000 voices roared as the team came running out onto the field, part of that enormous salute would be for him. He walked slowly, listening to the gravel crunch satisfactorily under his shoes in the still twilight, feeling his clothes swing lightly against his skin, breathing the thin evening air, feeling the wind more softly in his damp hair, wonderfully cool behind his ears and at the nape of his neck.

Louise was waiting for him at the road, in her car. The top was down and he noticed all over again, as he always did when he saw her, how pretty she was, the rough blonde hair and the large, inquiring eyes and the bright mouth, smiling now.

She threw the door open. "Were you good today?" she asked.

"Pretty good," he said, He climbed in, sank luxuriously into the soft leather, stretched his legs far out. He smiled, thinking of the eighty yards. "Pretty damn good."

She looked at him seriously for a moment, then scrambled around, like a little girl, kneeling on the seat next to him, grabbed him, her hands along his ears, and kissed him as he sprawled, head back, on the seat cushion. She let go of him, but kept her head close to his, over his. Darling reached up slowly and rubbed the back of his hand against her cheek, lit softly by a street lamp a hundred feet away. They looked at each other, smiling.

Louise drove down to the lake and they sat there silently, watching the moon rise behind the hills on the other side. Finally he reached over, pulled her gently to him, kissed her. Her lips grew soft, her body sank into his, tears formed slowly in her eyes. He knew, for the first time, that he could do whatever he wanted with her.

"Tonight," he said. "I'll call for you at seven-thirty. Can you get out?"

She looked at him. She was smiling, but the tears were still full in her eyes. "All right," she said. "I'll get out. How about you? Won't the coach raise hell?"

Darling grinned. "I got the coach in the palm of my hand," he said. "Can you wait till seven-thirty?"

She grinned back at him. "No," she said.

They kissed and she started the car and they went back to town for dinner. He sang on the way home.

Christian Darling, thirty-five years old, sat on the frail spring grass, greener now than it ever would be again on the practice field, looked thoughtfully up at the stadium, a deserted ruin in the twilight. He had started on the first team that Saturday and every Saturday after that for the next two years, but it had never been as satisfactory as it should have been. He never had broken away, the longest run he'd ever made was thirty-five yards, and that in a game that was already won, and then that kid had come up from the third team, Diederich, a blank-faced German kid from Wisconsin, who ran like a bull, ripping lines to pieces Saturday after Saturday, plowing through, never getting hurt, never changing his expression, scoring more points, gaining more ground than all the rest of the team put together, making everybody's All-American, carrying the ball three times out of four, keeping everybody else out of the headlines. Darling was a good blocker and he spent his Saturday afternoons working on the big Swedes and Polacks who played tackle and end for Michigan, Illinois, Purdue, hurling into huge pile-ups, bobbing his head wildly to elude the great raw hands swinging like meat-cleavers at him as he went charging in to open up holes for Diederich coming through like a locomotive behind him. Still, it wasn't so bad. Everybody liked him and he did his job and he was pointed out on the campus and boys always felt important when they introduced their girls to him at their proms, and Louise loved him and watched him faithfully in the games, even in the mud, when your own mother wouldn't know you, and drove him around in her car keeping the top down because she was proud of him and wanted to show everybody that she was Christian Darling's girl. She bought him crazy presents because her father was rich, watches, pipes, humidors, an icebox for beer for his room, curtains, wallets, a fifty-dollar dictionary.

"You'll spend every cent your old man owns," Darling protested once when she showed up at his rooms with seven different packages in her arms and tossed them onto the couch.

"Kiss me," Louise said, "and shut up."

"Do you want to break your poor old man?"

"I don't mind. I want to buy you presents."

"Why?"

"It makes me feel good. Kiss me. I don't know why. Did you know that you're an important figure?"

"Yes," Darling said gravely.

"When I was waiting for you at the library yesterday two girls saw you coming and one of them said to the other, 'That's Christian Darling. He's an important figure.' "

"You're a liar."

"I'm in love with an important figure."

"Still, why the hell did you have to give me a forty-pound dictionary?"

"I wanted to make sure," Louise said, "that you had a token of my esteem. I want to smother you in tokens of my esteem."

Fifteen years ago.

They'd married when they got out of college. There'd been other women for him, but all casual and secret, more for curiosity's sake, and vanity, women who'd thrown themselves at him and flattered him, a pretty mother at a summer camp for boys, an old girl from his home town who'd suddenly blossomed into a coquette, a friend of Louise's who had dogged him grimly for six months and had taken advantage of the two weeks that Louise went home when her mother died. Perhaps Louise had known, but she'd kept quiet, loving him completely, filling his rooms with presents, religiously watching him battling with the big Swedes and Polacks on the line of scrimmage on Saturday afternoons, making plans for marrying him and living with him in New York and going with him there to the night clubs, the theaters, the good restaurants, being proud of him in advance, tall, white-teethed, smiling, large, yet moving lightly, with an athlete's grace, dressed in evening clothes, approvingly eyed by magnificently dressed and famous women in theater lobbies, with Louise adoringly at his side.

Her father, who manufactured inks, set up a New York office for Darling to manage and presented him with three hundred accounts, and they lived on Beekman Place with a view of the river with fifteen thousand dollars a year between them, because everybody was buying everything in those days, including ink. They saw all the shows and went to all the speakeasies and spent their fifteen thousand dollars a year and in the afternoons Louise went to the art galleries and the matinees of the more serious plays that Darling didn't like to sit through and Darling slept with a girl who danced in the chorus of *Rosalie* and with the wife of a man who owned three copper mines. Darling played squash three times a week and remained as solid as a stone barn and Louise never took her eyes off him when they were in the same room together, watching him with a secret, miser's smile, with a trick of coming over to him in the middle of a crowded room and saying gravely, in a low voice, "You're the handsomest man I've ever seen in my whole life. Want a drink?"

Nineteen twenty-nine came to Darling and to his wife and father-in-law, the maker of inks, just as it came to everyone else. The father-in-law waited until 1933 and then blew his brains out and when Darling went to Chicago to see what the books of the firm looked like he found out all that was left were debts and three or four gallons of unbought ink.

"Please, Christian," Louise said, sitting in their neat Beekman Place apartment, with a view of the river and prints of paintings by Dufy and Braque and Picasso on the wall, "please, why do you want to start drinking at two o'clock in the afternoon?"

"I have nothing else to do," Darling said, putting down his glass, emptied of its fourth drink. "Please pass the whisky."

Louise filled his glass. "Come take a walk with me," she said. "We'll walk along the river."

"I don't want to walk along the river," Darling said, squinting intensely at the prints of paintings by Dufy, Braque and Picasso.

"We'll walk along Fifth Avenue."

"I don't want to walk along Fifth Avenue."

"Maybe," Louise said gently, "you'd like to come with me to some art galleries. There's an exhibition by a man named Klee. . . . "

"I don't want to go to any art galleries. I want to sit here and drink Scotch whisky," Darling said. "Who the hell hung these goddam pictures up on the wall?"

"I did," Louise said.

"I hate them."

"I'll take them down," Louise said.

"Leave them there. It gives me something to do in the afternoon. I can hate them," Darling took a long swallow. "Is that the way people paint these days?"

"Yes, Christian. Please don't drink any more."

"Do you like painting like that?"

"Yes dear."

"Really?"

"Really."

Darling looked carefully at the prints once more. "Little Louise Tucker. The middle-western beauty. I like pictures with horses in them. Why should you like pictures like that?"

"I just happen to have gone to a lot of galleries in the last few years . . ."

"Is that what you do in the afternoon?"

"That's what I do in the afternoon," Louise said.

"I drink in the afternoon."

Louise kissed him lightly on the top of his head as he sat there squinting at the pictures on the wall, the glass of whisky held firmly in his hand. She put on her coat and went out without saying another word. When she came back in the early evening, she had a job on a woman's fashion magazine.

They moved downtown and Louise went out to work every morning and Darling sat home and drank and Louise paid the bills as they came up. She made believe she was going to quit work as soon as Darling found a job, even though she was taking over more responsibility day by day at the magazine, interviewing authors, picking painters for the illustrations and covers, getting actresses to pose for pictures, going out for drinks with the right people, making a thousand new friends whom she loyally introduced to Darling.

"I don't like your hat," Darling said, once, when she came in in the evening and kissed him, her breath rich with Martinis.

"What's the matter with my hat, Baby?" she asked, running her fingers through his hair. "Everybody says it's very smart."

"It's too damned smart," he said. "It's not for you. It's for a rich, sophisticated woman of thirty-five with admirers."

Louise laughed. "I'm practicing to be a rich, sophisticated woman of thirty-five with admirers," she said. He started soberly at her. "Now, don't look so grim, Baby. It's still the same simple little wife under the hat." She took the hat off, threw it into a corner, sat on his lap. "See? Homebody Number One."

"Your breath could run a train," Darling said, not wanting to be mean, but talking out of boredom, and sudden shock at seeing his wife curiously a stranger in a new hat, with a new expression in her eyes under the little brim, secret, confident, knowing.

Louise tucked her head under his chin so he couldn't smell her breath. "I had to take an author out for cocktails," she said. "He's a boy from the Ozark Mountains and he drinks like a fish. He's a Communist."

"What the hell is a Communist from the Ozarks doing writing for a woman's fashion magazine?"

Louise chuckled. "The magazine business is getting all mixed up these days. The publishers want to have a foot in every camp. And anyway, you can't find an author under seventy these days who isn't a Communist."

"I don't think I like you to associate with all those people, Louise," Darling said. "Drinking with them."

"He's a very nice, gentle boy," Louise said. "He reads Ernest Dowson."

"Who's Ernest Dowson?"

Louise patted his arm, stood up, fixed her hair. "He's an English poet."

Darling felt that somehow he had disappointed her. "Am I supposed to know who Ernest Dowson is?"

"No, dear. I'd better go in and take a bath."

After she had gone, Darling went over to the corner where the hat was lying and picked it up. It was nothing, a scrap of straw, a red flower, a veil, meaningless on his big hand, but on his wife's head a signal of something . . . big city, smart and knowing women drinking and dining with men other than their husbands, conversation about things a normal man wouldn't know much about, Frenchmen who painted as though they used their elbows instead of brushes, composers who wrote whole symphonies without a single melody in them, writers who knew all about politics and women who knew all about writers, the movement of the proletariat, Marx, somehow mixed up with five-dollar dinners and the best-looking women in America and fairies who made them laugh and half-sentences immediately understood and secretly hilarious and wives who called their husbands "Baby." He put the hat down, a scrap of straw and a red flower, and a little veil. He drank some whisky straight and went into the bathroom where his wife was lying deep in her bath, singing to herself and smiling from time to time like a little girl, paddling the water gently with her hands, sending up a slight spicy fragrance from the bath salts she used.

He stood over her, looking down at her. She smiled up at him, her eyes half closed, her body pink and shimmering in the warm, scented water. All over again, with all the old suddenness; he was hit deep inside him with the knowledge of how beautiful she was, how much he needed her.

"I came in here," he said, "to tell you I wish you wouldn't call me 'Baby.' "

She looked up at him from the bath, her eyes quickly full of sorrow, half-understanding what he meant. He knelt and put his arms around her, his sleeves plunged heedlessly in the water, his shirt and jacket soaking wet as he clutched her wordlessly, holding her crazily tight, crushing her breath from her, kissing her desperately, searchingly, regretfully.

He got jobs after that, selling real estate and automobiles, but somehow, although he had a desk with his name on a wooden wedge on it, and he went to the office religiously at nine each morning, he never managed to sell anything and he never made any money.

Louise was made assistant editor, and the house was always full of strange men and women who talked fast and got angry on abstract subjects like mural painting, novelists, labor unions. Negro short-story writers drank Louise's liquor, and a lot of Jews, and big solemn men with scarred faces and knotted hands who talked slowly but clearly about picket lines and battles with guns and leadpipe at mine-shaft-heads and in front of factory gates. And Louise moved among them all, confidently, knowing what they were talking about, with opinions that they listened to and argued about just as though she were a man. She knew everybody, condescended to no one, devoured books that Darling had never heard of, walked along the streets of the city, excited, at home, soaking in all the million tides of New York without fear, with constant wonder.

Her friends liked Darling and sometimes he found a man who wanted to get off in the corner and talk about the new boy who played fullback for Princeton, and the decline of the double wing-back, or even the state of the stock market, but for the most part he sat on the edge of things, solid and quiet in the high storm of words. "The dialectics of the situation . . . The theater has been given over to expert jugglers . . . Picasso? What man has a right to paint old bones and collect ten thousand dollars for them? . . . I stand firmly behind Trotsky . . . Poe was the last American critic. When he died they put lilies on the grave of American criticism. I don't say this because they panned my last book, but . . ."

Once in a while he caught Louise looking soberly and consideringly at him through the cigarette smoke and the noise and he avoided her eyes and found an excuse to get up and go into the kitchen for more ice or to open another bottle.

"Come on," Cathal Flaherty was saying, standing at the door with a girl, "you've got to come down and see this. It's down on Fourteenth Street, in the old Civic Repertory, and you can only see it on Sunday nights and I guarantee you'll come out of the theater singing." Flaherty was a big young Irishman with a broken nose who was the lawyer for a longshoreman's union, and he had been hanging around the house for six months on and off, roaring and shutting everybody else up when he got in an argument. "It's a new play, *Waiting for Lefty;* it's about taxi-drivers."

"Odets," the girl with Flaherty said. "It's by a guy named Odets."

"I never heard of him," Darling said.

"He's a new one," the girl said.

"It's like watching a bombardment," Flaherty said. "I saw it last Sunday night. You've got to see it."

"Come on, Baby," Louise said to Darling, excitement in her eyes already. "We've been sitting in the Sunday *Times* all day, this'll be a great change."

"I see enough taxi-drivers every day," Darling said, not because he meant that, but because he didn't like to be around Flaherty, who said things that made Louise laugh a lot and whose judgment she accepted on almost every subject. "Let's go to the movies."

"You've never seen anything like this before," Flaherty said. "He wrote this play with a baseball bat."

"Come on," Louise coaxed, "I bet it's wonderful."

"He has long hair," the girl with Flaherty said. "Odets, I met him at a party. He's an actor. He didn't say a goddam thing all night."

"I don't feel like going down to Fourteenth Street," Darling said, wishing Flaherty and his girl would get out. "It's gloomy."

"Oh, hell!" Louise said loudly. She looked coolly at Darling, as though she'd just been introduced to him and was making up her mind about him, and not very favorably. He saw her looking at him, knowing there was something new and dangerous in her face and he wanted to say something, but Flaherty was there and his damned girl, and anyway, he didn't know what to say.

"I'm going," Louise said, getting her coat. "I don't think Fourteenth Street is gloomy."

"I'm telling you," Flaherty was saying, helping her on with her coat, "it's the Battle of Gettysburg, in Brooklynese."

"Nobody could get a word out of him," Flaherty's girl was saying as they went through the door. "He just sat there all night."

The door closed. Louise hadn't said good night to him. Darling walked around the room four times, then sprawled out on the sofa, on top of the Sunday *Times*. He lay there for five minutes looking at the ceiling, thinking of Flaherty walking down the street talking in that booming voice, between the girls, holding their arms.

Louise had looked wonderful. She'd washed her hair in the afternoon and it had been very soft and light and clung close to her head as she stood there angrily putting her coat on. Louise was getting prettier every year, partly because she knew by now how pretty she was, and made the most of it.

"Nuts," Darling said, standing up. "Oh, nuts."

He put on his coat and went down to the nearest bar and had five drinks off by himself in a corner before his money ran out.

The years since then had been foggy and downhill. Louise had been nice to him, and in a way, loving and kind, and they'd fought only once, when he said he was going to vote for Landon. ("Oh, Christ," she'd said, "doesn't *anything* happen inside your head? Don't you read the papers? The penniless Republican!") She'd been sorry later and apologized for hurting him, but apologized as she might to a child. He'd tried hard, had gone grimly to the art galleries, the concert halls, the bookshops, trying to gain on the trail of his wife, but it was no use. He was bored, and none of what he saw or heard or dutifully read made much sense to him and finally he gave it up. He had thought, many nights as he ate dinner alone, knowing that Louise would come home late and drop silently into bed without explanation, of getting a divorce, but he knew the loneliness, the hopelessness, of not seeing her again would be too much to take. So he was good, completely devoted, ready at all times to go any place with her, do anything she wanted. He even got a small job, in a broker's office and paid his own way, bought his own liquor.

Then he'd been offered the job of going from college to college as a tailor's representative. "We want a man," Mr. Rosenberg had said, "who as soon as you look at him, you say, 'There's a university man.' " Rosenberg had looked approvingly at Darling's broad shoulders and well-kept waist, at his carefully brushed hair and his honest, wrinkleless face. "Frankly, Mr. Darling, I am willing to make you a proposition. I have inquired about you, you are favorably known on your old campus, I understand you were in the backfield with Alfred Diederich."

Darling nodded. "Whatever happened to him?"

"He is walking around in a cast for seven years now. An iron brace. He played professional football and they broke his neck for him."

Darling smiled. That, at least, had turned out well.

"Our suits are an easy product to sell, Mr. Darling," Rosenberg said. "We have a handsome, custom-made garment. What has Brooks Brothers got that we haven't got? A name. No more."

"I can make fifty-sixty dollars a week," Darling said to Louise that night. "And expenses. I can save some money and then come back to New York and really get started here."

"Yes, Baby," Louise said.

"As it is," Darling said carefully, "I can make it back here once a month, and holidays and the summer. We can see each other often."

"Yes, Baby." He looked at her face, lovelier now at thirty-five than it had ever been before, but fogged over now as it had been for five years with a kind of patient, kindly, remote boredom.

"What do you say?" he asked. "Should I take it?" Deep within him he hoped fiercely, longingly, for her to say, "No, Baby, you stay right here," but she said, as he knew she'd say, "I think you'd better take it."

He nodded. He had to get up and stand with his back to her, looking out the window because there were things plain on his face that she had never seen in the fifteen years she'd known him. "Fifty dollars is a lot of money," he said. "I never thought I'd ever see fifty dollars again." He laughed. Louise laughed, too.

Christian Darling sat on the frail green grass of the practice field. The shadow of the stadium had reached out and covered him. In the distance the lights of the university shone a little mistily in the light haze of evening. Fifteen years. Flaherty even now was calling for his wife, buying her a drink, filling whatever bar they were in with that voice of his and that easy laugh. Darling half-closed his eyes, almost saw the boy fifteen years ago reach for the pass, slip the halfback, go skittering lightly down the field, his knees high and fast and graceful, smiling to himself because he knew he was going to get past the safety man. That was the high point, Darling thought, fifteen years ago, on an autumn afternoon, twenty years old and far from death, with the air coming easily into his lungs, and a deep feeling inside him that he could do anything, knock over anybody, outrun whatever had to be outrun. And the shower after and the three glasses of water and the cool night air on his damp head and Louise sitting hatless in the open car with a smile and the first kiss she ever really meant. The high point, an eighty-yard run in the practice, and a girl's kiss and everything after that a decline. Darling laughed. He had practiced the wrong thing, perhaps. He hadn't practiced for 1929 and New York City and a girl who would turn into a woman. Somewhere, he thought, there must have been a point where she moved up to me, was even with me for a moment, when I could have held her hand, if I'd known, held tight, gone with her. Well, he'd never known. Here he was on a playing field that was fifteen years away and his wife was in another city having dinner with another and better man, speaking with him a different, new language, a language nobody had ever taught him.

Darling stood up, smiled a little, because if he didn't smile he knew the tears would come. He looked around him. This was the spot. O'Connor's pass had come sliding out just to here . . . the high point. Darling put up his hands, felt all over again the flat slap of the ball. He shook his hips to throw off the halfback, cut back inside the center, picked his knees high as he ran gracefully over two men jumbled on the ground at the line of scrimmage, ran easily, gaining speed, for ten yards, holding the ball lightly in his two hands, swung away from the halfback diving at him, ran, swinging his hips in the almost girlish manner of a back in a broken field, tore into the safety man, his shoes drumming heavily on the turf, stiff-armed, elbow locked, pivoted, raced lightly and exultantly for the goal line.

It was only after he had sped over the goal line and slowed to a trot that he saw the boy and girl sitting together on the turf, looking at him wonderingly.

He stopped short, dropping his arms. "I . . ." he said, gasping a little, though his condition was fine and the run hadn't winded him. "I—once I played here."

The boy and the girl said nothing. Darling laughed embarrassedly, looked hard at them sitting there, close to each other, shrugged, turned and went toward his hotel, the sweat breaking out on his face and running down into his collar.

The Making of a New Yorker, John Steinbeck (1943)

John Steinbeck was born in Salinas, California, in 1902 and his most famous writing, the novels *The Grapes of Wrath* and *Of Mice and Men* and the short story "The Red Pony," described the people and landscape of California; but Steinbeck always felt a strong draw to New York City. In his 1943 essay, "The Making of a New Yorker," Steinbeck wrote, "New York is an ugly city, a dirty city. Its climate is a scandal, its politics are used to frighten children, its traffic is madness, its competition is murderous. But there is one thing about it—once you have lived in New York and it has become your home, no place else is good enough."

Steinbeck first arrived in New York in 1925 after attending Stanford University and soon found a place to live in the Fort Greene section of Brooklyn and a job as a construction worker "wheeling cement" at the new Madison Square Garden. He began work on a set of short stories about New York that was never published but left New York in 1926 with the "respect plain unadulterated fear gives."

However, Steinbeck returned as a respected author in 1941, a year after winning the Pulitzer Prize for *The Grapes of Wrath,* and lived on the Upper East Side and Upper West Side until his death in 1968. Steinbeck would travel occasionally, for example, to pick up a Nobel Prize for Literature in 1962, but he always came back "with a 'Thank God I'm home' feeling. For New York is the world with every vice and blemish and beauty and there's privacy thrown in. What more could you ask?"

New York is the only city I have ever lived in. I have lived in the country, in the small town, and in New York. It is true I have had apartments in San Francisco, Mexico City, Los Angeles, Paris, and sometimes stayed for months, but that is a very different thing. This is a matter of feeling.

The transition from small town to New York is a slow and rough process. I am writing it not because I think my experience was unique; quite the contrary. I suspect that millions of New Yorkers who were not born here have had much the same experience—at least parallel experiences. . . .

When I came the first time to New York in 1925 I had never been to a city in my life. I arrived on a boat, tourist, one hundred dollars. It was November. . . .

From a porthole, then, I saw the city, and it horrified me. There was something monstrous about it—the tall buildings looming to the sky and the lights shining through the falling snow. I crept ashore—frightened and cold and with a touch of panic in my stomach. This Dick Whittington didn't even have a cat.

I wasn't really bad off. I had a sister in New York and she had a good job. She had a husband and he had a good job. My brother-in-law got me a job as a laborer and I found a room three flights up in Fort Greene Place in Brooklyn. This is about as alone as you can get. The job was on Madison Square Garden which was being finished in a hurry. There was time and a half and there was double time. I was big and strong. My job was wheeling cement—one of a long line—one barrow behind another, hour after hour. I wasn't that big and strong. It nearly killed me and it probably saved my life. I was too tired to see what went on around me. . . .

My knowledge of the city was blurred—aching, lights and the roar of the subway, climbing three flights to a room with dirty green walls, falling into bed half-washed, beef stew, coffee and sinkers in a coffeepot, a sidewalk that pitched a little as I walked, then the line of barrows again. It's all mixed up like a fever dream. There would be big salamanders of glowing coke to warm our hands and I would warm mine just for the rest, long after I couldn't feel my hands at all. . . .

I don't even remember how long the job went on. It seems interminable and was maybe a month or six weeks. Anyway, the Garden got finished for the six-day bicycle races and Tex Rikard congratulated us all, without respect to race or color. I still get a shiver from the place sometimes.

About that time, my rich and successful uncle came to town from Chicago. He was an advertising man with connections everywhere. He was fabulous. He stayed in a suite at the Commodore, ordered drinks or coffee and sandwiches sent up any time he wanted, sent telegrams even if they weren't important. This last still strikes me as Lucullan. My uncle got me a job on a newspaper—The New York *American* down on William Street. I didn't know the first thing about being a reporter. I think now that the twenty-five dollars a week that they paid me was a total loss. They gave me stories to cover in Queens and Brooklyn and I would get lost and spend hours trying to find my way back. I couldn't learn to steal a picture from a desk when a family refused to be photographed and I invariably got emotionally involved and tried to kill the whole story to save the subject.

But for my uncle, I think they would have fired me the first week. Instead, they gave me Federal courts in the old Park Row Post Office. Why, I will never know. It was a specialist's job. Some of the men there had been on that beat for many years and I knew nothing about courts and didn't learn easily. I wonder if I could ever be as kind to a young punk as those men in the reporters' room at the Park Row Post Office were to me. They pretended that I knew what I was doing, and they did their best to teach me in a roundabout way. I learned to play bridge and where to look for suits and scandals. They informed me which judges were pushovers for publicity and several times they covered for me when I didn't show up. You can't repay that kind of thing. I never got to know them. Didn't know where they lived, what they did, or how they lived when they left the room. . . .

I had a reason for that, a girl. I had known her slightly in California and she was most beautiful. I don't think this was only my memory. For she got a job in the Greenwich Village Follies just walking around—and she got it with no trouble whatever. . . .

Now New York changed for me. My girl lived on Gramercy Park and naturally I moved there. The old Parkwood Hotel had some tiny rooms—six walk-up flights above the street—for seven dollars a week. I had nothing to do with New York. It was a stage set in which this golden romance was taking place. The girl was very kind. Since she made four times as much money as I did, she paid for many little dinners. Every night I waited for her outside the stage door.

We would sit in Italian restaurants—she paid—and drink red wine. I wanted to write fiction-novels. She approved of that in theory, but said I should go into advertising—first, that is. I refused. I was being the poor artist, shielding his integrity.

During all this time, I never once knew or saw one New Yorker as a person. They were all minor characters in this intense personal drama. Then everything happened at once. The girl had more sense than I thought. She married a banker from the Middle West and moved there. And she didn't argue. She simply left a note, and two days later I was fired from *The American.*

And now at last the city moved in on me and scared me to death. I looked for jobs—but good jobs, pleasant jobs. I didn't get them. I wrote short stories and tried to sell them. I applied for work on other papers, which was ridiculous on the face of it. And the city crept in—cold and heartless, I thought. I began to fall behind in my room rent. I always had that one ace in the hole. I could go back to laboring. I had a friend who occasionally loaned me a little money. And finally, I was shocked enough to go for a job as a laborer. But by that time short feeding had taken hold. I could hardly lift a pick. I had trouble climbing the six flights back to my room. My friend loaned me a dollar and I bought two loaves of rye bread and a bag of dried herrings and never left my room for a week. I was afraid to go out on the street—actually afraid of traffic—the noise. Afraid of the landlord and afraid of people. Afraid even of acquaintances.

Then a man who had been in college with me got me a job as a workaway on a ship to San Francisco. And he didn't have to urge me, either. The city had beat the pants off me. Whatever it required to get ahead, I didn't have. I didn't leave the city in disgust—I left it with the respect plain unadulterated fear gives.

My second assault on New York was different but just as ridiculous as the first. I had had a kind of success with a novel after many tries. Three of my preceding novels did not make their advance and the advance was four hundred dollars. The largest amount I ever got for a short story was ninety dollars, for "The Red Pony." When royalties for "Tortilla Flat" went over a thousand dollars, and when Paramount bought the book for $3,000-$2,700 net, I should have been filled with joy but instead I was frightened. During the preceding years I had learned to live comfortably, and contentedly, on an absolute minimum of money—thirty-five to fifty dollars a month. When gigantic sums like $2,700 came over the horizon I was afraid I could not go back to the old simplicity.

Whereas on my first try New York was a dark, hulking frustration, the second time it became the Temptation and I a whistle-stop St. Anthony. As with most St. Anthonys, if I had not been drawn toward luxury and sin, and to me they were the same thing, there would have been no temptation. I reacted without originality: today I see people coming to success doing the same things I did, so I guess I didn't invent it. I pretended and believed my pretense, that I hated the city and all its miles and traps. I longed for the quiet and contemplation of the West Coast. I preferred twenty-nine-cent wine and red beans. And again I didn't even see New York. It had scared me again but this time in another way. So I shut my eyes and drew virtue over my head. I insulted everyone who tried to be kind to me and I fled the

Whore of Babylon with relief and virtuous satisfaction, for I had convinced myself that the city was a great snare set in the path of my artistic simplicity and integrity.

Back to the West I plunged, built a new house, bought a Chevrolet and imperceptibly moved from twenty-nine-cent wine to fifty-nine-cent wine. Now I made a number of business trips to New York and I was so completely in my role of country boy that I didn't look at it because I must have been enjoying my triumph over the snares and pitfalls. I had a successful play but never saw it. I believed I wasn't interested but it is probable that I was afraid to see it. I even built up a pleasant fiction that I hated the theatre. And the various trips to New York were very like the visits of the Salvation Army to a brothel—necessary and fascinating but distasteful.

The very first time I came to the city and settled was engineered by a girl. Looking back from the cool position of middle age I can see that most of my heroic decisions somehow stemmed from a girl. I got an apartment on East 51st Street between First and Second Avenues, but even then I kept contact with my prejudices. My new home consisted of the first and second floors of a three-story house and the living room looked out on a small soot field called a garden. Two triumphant Brooklyn trees called ailanthus not only survived but thumbed their noses at the soft coal dust and nitric acid which passed for air in New York.

I was going to live in New York but I was going to avoid it. I planted a lawn in the garden, bought huge pots and planted tomatoes, pollinating the blossoms with a water-color brush. But I can see now that a conspiracy was going on, of which I was not even aware. I walked miles through the streets for exercise, and began to know the butcher and the newsdealer and the liquor man, not as props or as enemies but as people.

I have talked to many people about this and it seems to be a kind of mystical experience. The preparation is unconscious, the realization happens in a flaming second. It was on Third Avenue. The trains were grinding over my head. The snow was nearly waist-high in the gutters and uncollected garbage was scattered in a dirty mess. The wind was cold, and frozen pieces of paper went scraping along the pavement. I stopped to look in a drug-store window where a latex cooch dancer was undulating by a concealed motor—and something burst in my head, a kind of light and a kind of feeling blended into an emotion which if it had spoken would have said, "My God! I belong here. Isn't this wonderful?"

Everything fell into place. I saw every face I passed. I noticed every doorway and the stairways to apartments. I looked across the street at the windows, lace curtains and potted geraniums through sooty glass. It was beautiful—but most important, I was part of it. I was no longer a stranger. I had become a New Yorker.

Now there may be people who move easily into New York without travail, but most I have talked to about it have had some kind of trial by torture before acceptance. And the acceptance is a double thing. It seems to me that the city finally accepts you just as you finally accept the city.

A young man in a small town, a frog in a small puddle, if he kicks his feet is able to make waves, get mud in his neighbor's eyes—make some impression. He is known. His family is known. People watch him with some interest, whether kindly or maliciously. He comes to New York and no matter what he does, no one is impressed. He challenges the city to fight and it licks him without being aware of him. This is a dreadful blow to a small-town ego. He hates the organism that ignores him. He hates the people who look through him.

And then one day he falls into place, accepts the city and does not fight it any more. It is too huge to notice him and suddenly the fact that it doesn't notice him becomes the most delightful thing in the world. His self-consciousness evaporates. If he is dressed superbly well—there are half a million people dressed equally well. If he is in rags—there are a million ragged people. If he is tall, it is a city of tall people. If he is short the streets are full of dwarfs; if ugly, ten perfect horrors pass him in one block; if beautiful, the competition is overwhelming. If he is talented, talent is a dime a dozen. If he tries to make an impression by wearing a toga—there's a man down the street in a leopard skin. Whatever he does or says or wears or thinks he is not unique. Once accepted this gives him perfect freedom to be himself, but unaccepted it horrifies him.

I don't think New York City is like other cities. It does not have character like Los Angeles or New Orleans. It is all characters—in fact, it is everything. It can destroy a man, but if his eyes are open it cannot bore him.

New York is an ugly city, a dirty city. Its climate is a scandal, its politics are used to frighten children, its traffic is madness, its competition is murderous. But there is one thing about it—once you have lived in New York and it has become your home, no place else is good enough. All of everything is concentrated here, population, theatre, art, writing, publishing, importing, business, murder, mugging, luxury, poverty. It is all of everything. It goes all right. It is tireless and its air is charged with energy. I can work longer and harder without weariness in New York than anyplace else. . . .

I live in a small house on the East Side in the Seventies. It has a pretty little south garden. My neighborhood is my village. I know all of the storekeepers and some of the neighbors. Sometimes I don't go out of my village for weeks at a time. It has every quality of a village except nosiness. No one interferes with our business—no one by chance visits us without first telephoning, certainly a most civilized practice. When we close the front door, the city and the world are shut out and we are more private than any country man below the Arctic Circle has ever been. We have many friends—good friends in the city. Sometimes we don't see them for six or eight months and this in no way interferes with our friendship. Any place else this would be resented as neglect. . . .

Everyone at one time or another tries to explain to himself why he likes New York better than any place else. A man who worked for me liked it because if he couldn't sleep he could go to an all-night movie. That's as good a reason as any.

Every once and a while we go away for several months and we always come back with a "Thank God I'm home" feeling. For New York is the world with every vice and blemish and beauty and there's privacy thrown in. What more could you ask?

Voice, Woody Guthrie (1945)

Woodrow Wilson Guthrie was born on July 14, 1912, in Okfuskee County, Oklahoma. When Oklahoma was transformed into the "Dust Bowl" in 1935, Guthrie rode freight trains and hitchhiked his way to California. His ballads describing that experience and the plight of migrant workers in Southern California were broadcast over KFVD in Los Angeles and brought him to public attention. He arrived in New York City in 1940, and sang in barrooms, pool halls, and union rallies through the early forties until he joined the Merchant Marine during the Second World War.

Guthrie lived throughout the boroughs, but 3520 Mermaid Avenue in Coney Island was where he spent most of the 1940s. During that time, Guthrie recorded his songs, amongst the most famous being *This Land Is Your Land,* for the Library of Congress, performed for CBS radio, and published his memoir *Bound for Glory* (1943).

Tragically, Guthrie suffered from Huntington's chorea, an incurable hereditary illness of the central nervous system that forced him to admit himself to Greystone Hospital in New Jersey in 1954, where he stayed sporadically until his death in 1967.

Guthrie was, in many ways, the national folk poet of America for the twentieth century, and his legacy is heard in the words and music of Bob Dylan, Peter Seeger, Bruce Springsteen, and his son, Arlo Guthrie. In "Voice" he talks of discovering his own voice, and the voice of America, in a delicatessen in Coney Island.

I DON'T know how far I'm going to have to go
To sell my own self or to hear my own voice
I tuned in on the radio and for hours never heard it
And then I went to the moving pictures show
And never heard it there
I put handsful of coins into machines and watched records turn

But the voice there was no voice of mine
I mean it was not my voice
The words not my words that I hear in my own ears
When I walk along and look at your faces
I set here in a Jewish delicatessen, I order a hot pastrami
Sandwich on rye bread and I hear the lady ask me
Would you like to have a portion of cole slaw on the side
And I know when I heard her speak like that
She spoke my voice
And I told her I would take my slaw on a side dish
And would like to have a glass of tea with lemon
And she knew that I was speaking her words
And a fellow sat across at a table near my wall
And spoke while he ate his salami and drank his beer
And somehow I had the feeling
As I heard him speak, and he spoke for a long time,
But not one word was in my personal language,
And I could tell by the deep sound, by the full tone
Of his voice he spoke my language
I suppose you may wonder just how he could speak
In a dialect that I could not savvy nor understand
And yet understand every sound that he made
I learned to do this a long time ago
Walking up and down the side roads and the main stems
Of this land here
I learned to listen this way when I washed dishes on the ships
I had to learn how to do it when I walked ashore in Africa
London, Liverpool, Glasgow, Scot's towns and Anglo's farms,
Irish canals and railroad bridges, Highlander's cows and horses
And here I knew the speech was the same as mine but
But it was the dialect again, nasal, throaty, deep chesty,
From the stomach, lungs, high in the head, pitched up and down,
And here I had to learn again
To say this is my language and part of my voice
Oh but I have not even heard this voice, these voices,
On stages, screens, radios, records, juke boxes,
In magazines nor not in newspapers, seldom in courtrooms,
And more seldom when students and policemen study the faces
Behind the voices

And I thought as I saw a streetwalking man mutter
And spit and curse the wind out of the cafe's plate glass,
That maybe, if I looked close enough, I might hear
Some more of my voice
And I ate as quiet as I could, so as to keep my eyes
And my ears and my feelings wide open
And did hear
Heard all that I came to hear here in Coney Island's Jewish air
Heard reflections, recollections, seen faces in memory,
Heard voices untangle their words before me
And I knew by the feeling I felt that here was my voice.

Beyond, from A Walker in the City, *Alfred Kazin (1946)*

Alfred Kazin was born on June 5, 1915, and died eighty-three years later on the same day in 1998. In the time in between he fused together two forces that make New York unique. On the one hand, he wrote memoirs—*A Walker in the City, Starting Out in the City, New York Jew,* and *A Lifetime in Every Moment*—that evoked the immigrant experience in New York. On the other hand, he wrote the first, and perhaps best, academic, intellectual understanding of the American literature between 1890 and 1940, *On Native Grounds,* published when he was only twenty-seven years old. That volume was the result of five years of writing and research, twelve hours a day five or six days a week, in the main reading room of the Public Library on 42nd Street.

Kazin was the son of Jewish immigrants fleeing Tsarist Russia. His father was a socialist housepainter; his mother was a garment worker; the language of home was Yiddish. He grew up in the Brownsville section of Brooklyn, and graduated from City College in 1935 and Columbia four years later. Later he taught at City University of New York, Hunter College, and New York University. He wrote for virtually every scholarly magazine and journal published in New York and was one of the leaders of the so-called "New York intellectuals" who formed during the 1930s.

Kazin wrote that he "read as if books would fill my every gap, legitimize my strange quest for the American past, remedy my every flaw, let me in at last into the great world that was anything just out of Brownsville." What he accomplished was much greater—Kazin brought a greater understanding of how the immigrant past and the American intellectual past could be absorbed into each other in one man whom the playwright A. R. Gurney called "the quintessential New Yorker."

BEYOND! Beyond! *Beyond* was "the city," connected only by interminable subway lines and some old Brooklyn-Manhattan trolley car rattling across Manhattan Bridge. At night, as the trolley ground its way home in the rain through miles of unknown streets from some meeting in the Jewish Daily *Forward* building on the East Side to which my father had taken me, I saw the flickering light bulbs in the car, the hard yellow benches on which we sat half asleep, the motorman's figure bulging the green curtain he had drawn against the lights in the car, as a rickety cart stumbling through infinite space—the driver taking us where? *Beyond* was the wheeze of an accordion on the Staten Island ferry boat—the music rocking in such unison with the vibration of the engines as the old man walked in and out of the cars on the lower deck squeezing the tunes out of the pleats that never after would I be able to take a ferry from South Ferry, from Christopher Street, from 23rd, from Dyckman, from 125th, without expecting that same man to come round with his silver-backed accordion and his hat in his hand as he jangled a few coins in a metal plate. *Beyond* was the long shivering blast of the ferry starting out from the Battery in sight of the big Colgate ad across the river in Jersey; the depth of peace as the sun warmed the panels of the doors sliding out to the observation deck; the old Italian shoeshine men walking round and round with their boxes between all those suddenly relaxed New Yorkers comfortably staring at each other in the high wind on the top deck; a garbage scow burning in the upper bay just under Liberty's right arm; the minarets on Ellis Island; the old prison walls under the trees of Governor's Island; then, floating back in the cold dusk toward the diamond-lighted wall of Manhattan skyscrapers, the way we huddled in the great wooden varnish-smelling cabin inside as if we were all getting under the same quilt on a cold night.

Beyond was the canvas awnings over an El station in summer. Inside, the florid red windows had curlicues running up and down their borders. I had never seen anything like them in all the gritty I.R.T. stations below. Those windows were richer than all my present. The long march of snails up and down and around the borders of those windows, the cursive scrolls in the middle patch forever turning back on themselves, promised to lead me straight into the old New York of gaslight and police stations I always looked for in the lower city. And of a winter afternoon—the time for which I most lovingly remember the El, for the color of the winter dusk as it fell through those painted windows, and the beauty of the snow on the black cars and iron rails and tar roofs we saw somewhere off Brooklyn Bridge—when the country stove next to the change booth blazed and blazed as some crusty old woman with a pince-nez gave out change, and the heavy turnstiles crashed with a roar inside the wooden shed—then, among the darkly huddled crowds waiting to go out to the train, looking out on Brooklyn Bridge all dark sweeping cable lines under drifts of snow, I pretended those were gaslights I saw in the streets below, that all old New Yorkers were my fathers, and that the train we waited for could finally take me back—back and back to that old New York of wood and brownstones and iron, where Theodore Roosevelt as Police Commissioner had walked every night.

Beyond was anything old and American—the name *Fraunces Tavern* repeated to us on a school excursion; the eighteenth-century muskets and glazed oil paintings on the wall; the very streets, the deeper you got into Brooklyn, named after generals of the Revolutionary War—Putnam, Gates, Kosciusko, DeKalb, Lafayette, Pulaski. *Beyond* was the sound of *Desbrosses* Street that steaming July morning we crossed back on a Jersey ferry, and the smell of the salt air in the rotting planks floating on the green scummy waters of the Hudson. *Beyond* was the watery floor of the Aquarium that smelled of the eternally wet skins of the seals in the great tank; the curve of lower Broadway around Bowling Green Park when you went up to Wall Street; the yellow wicker seats facing each other in the middle of the El car; the dome of the Manhattan Savings Bank over Chinatown at the entrance to Manhattan Bridge, and then in Brooklyn again, after we had traveled from light into dark, dark into light, along the shuddering shadowy criss-cross of the bridge's pillars, the miles and miles of Gentile cemeteries where crosses toppled up and down endless slopes. *Beyond* was that autumn morning in New Haven when I walked up and down two *red* broken paving stones, smelled the leaves burning in the yard, and played with black battered poker chips near the country stove in an aunt's kitchen; it was the speckles on the bananas hanging in the window of the grocery store another aunt owned in the Negro streets just behind Union Station in Washington; the outrageously warm taste of milk fresh from a cow that summer my mother cooked with a dozen others in the same Catskill boarding house; it was the open trolley cars going to Coney Island, the conductor swinging from bar to bar as he came around the ledge collecting fares; it was the *Robert Fulton* going up the Hudson to Indian Point, the ventilators on the upper deck smelling of soup.

Beyond, even in Brownsville, was the summer sound of *flax* when my mother talked of *der heym.* It was the Negroes singing as they passed under our windows late at night on their way back to Livonia Avenue. It was the Children's Library on Stone Avenue, because they had an awning over the front door; in the long peaceful reading room there were storybook tiles over the fireplace and covered deep wooden benches on each side of it where I read my way year after year from every story of King Alfred the Great to *Twenty Thousand Leagues Under the Sea. Beyond* was the burly Jewish truckers from the wholesale fruit markets on Osborne Street sitting in their dark smoky "Odessa" and "Roumanian" tearooms, where each table had its own teapot, and where the men sat over mounds of saucers smoking Turkish cigarettes and beating time to the balalaika. *Beyond* was the way to the other end of Sutter Avenue, past a store I often went into to buy buttons and thread for my mother, and where the light simmered on the thin upturned curves of the pearl buttons in the window. *Beyond* was the roar in the Pennsylvania freight yards on the way to East New York; even the snow houses we built in the backyard of a cousin's house on Herzl Street waiting to ambush those thieves from Bristol Street. It was the knife grinder's horse and wagon when he stopped on our block, and an "American" voice called up to every window, *Sharpen knives! Sharpen knives!*—that man had obviously come from a long way off.

Beyond! Beyond! It was the clean, general store smell of packaged white bread in the A&P that Passover week I could not eat matzoh, and going home, hid the soft squunchy loaf of Ward's bread under my coat so that the neighbors would not see. It was the way past the car barns at the end of Rockaway Avenue, that week my father was painting in New Lots, and I took that route for the first time, bringing him his lunch one summer afternoon. I could not wait to get out on the other side of the dark subway station. I had never seen another part of Brownsville where the going was so strange, where streets looked so empty, where the sun felt so hot. It was as if there were not enough houses there to stand in its way. When the sun fell across the great white pile of the new Telephone Company building, you could smell the stucco burning as you passed; then some liquid sweetness that came to me from deep in the rings of freshly cut lumber stacked in the yards, and the fresh plaster and paint on the brand-new storefronts. Rawness, sunshiny rawness down the end streets of the city, as I thought of them then—the hot ash-laden stink of the refuse dumps in my nostrils and the only sound at noon the resonant metal plunk of a tin can I kicked ahead of me as I went my way. Then two blocks more, and the car barns I loved. The light falling down the hollows in the corrugated tin roof seemed to say *Go over! Go over!*, marked the place from which the stacked trolley cars began all over again their long weary march into the city. I liked to see them stacked against each other, a thin trail of track leading out of the sheds, then another track, then another, until everywhere you could see, the streets were wild with car tracks pointing the way back to the city.

Beyond was that day they took us first to the Botanic Garden next to the

Brooklyn Museum, and after we went through the bamboo gate into the Japanese Garden, crossed over a curved wooden bridge past the stone figure of a heron dreaming in the water, I lay in the grass waiting to eat my lunch out of the shoe box and wondered why water lilies floated half-submerged in the pond and did not sink. They led us into the museum that day, up the big stone steps they had then, through vast empty halls that stung my nose with the prickly smell of new varnish and were lined with the effigies of medieval Japanese warriors—the black stringy hairs on their wigs oppressively unreal, the faces mock-terrible as they glared down at us through their stiffly raised swords, everything in that museum wearisome and empty and smelling of floor polish until they pushed us through a circular room upstairs violently ablaze with John Singer Sargent's watercolors of the Caribbean and into a long room lined with oily dim farmscapes of America in the nineteenth century, and I knew I would come back, that I would have to come back.

Museums and parks were related, both oases to stop in "beyond." But in some way museums and parks were painful, each an explosion of unbearable fullness in my brain. I could never go home from the Brooklyn Museum, a walk around the reservoir in Central Park, or sit in a rowboat Sunday afternoons in Prospect Park—where your voice hallooed against the stone walls of the footbridge as you waited in that sudden cold darkness below, boat against boat, to be pushed on to the boathouse and so end the afternoon—without feeling the same sadness that came after the movies. The day they took us to the Children's Museum—rain was dripping on the porch of that old wooden house, the halls were lined with Audubon prints and were hazel in the thin antique light—I was left with the distinct impression that I had been stirring between my fingers dried earth and fallen leaves that I had found in between the red broken paving stones of some small American town. I seemed to see neighborhood rocks and minerals in the dusty light of the late afternoon slowly stirring behind glass at the back of the village museum. But that same day they took us to Forest Park in Queens, and I saw a clearing filled with stone picnic tables—*nothing* had ever cried out such a welcome as those stone tables in the clearing—saw the trees in their dim green recede in one long moving tide back into dusk, and gasped in pain when the evening rushed upon us before I had a chance to walk that woodland through.

There was never enough time. The morning they led us through the Natural History Museum, under the skeletons of great whales floating dreamlike on wires from the ceiling, I had to wait afterward against the meteor in the entrance yard for my dizziness to pass. Those whales! those whales! But that same morning they took us across Central Park to the Metropolitan, and entering through the back door in from the park, I was flung spinning in a bewilderment of delight from the Greek discus-throwers to the Egyptians to the long rows of medieval knights to the breasts of Venus glistening in my eyes as she sat—some curtain drawn before her hiding the worst of her nakedness—smiling with Mars and surrounded by their children.

The bewilderment eased, a little, when we went up many white steps directly to the American paintings. There was a long, narrow, corridor-looking room lined with the portraits of seventeenth-century merchants and divines—nothing for me there as they coldly stared at me, their faces uninterruptedly rosy in time. But far in the back, in an alcove near the freight elevator, hung so low and the figures so dim in the faint light that I crouched to take them in, were pictures of New York some time after the Civil War—skaters in Central Park, a red muffler flying in the wind; a gay crowd moving round and round Union Square Park; horse cars charging between the brownstones of lower Fifth Avenue at dusk. I could not believe my eyes. Room on room they had painted my city, my country—Winslow Homer's dark oblong of Union soldiers making camp in the rain, tenting tonight, tenting on the old camp ground as I had never thought I *would* get to see them when we sang that song in school; Thomas Eakins's solitary sculler on the Schuylkill, resting to have his picture taken in the yellow light bright with patches of some raw spring in Pennsylvania showing on the other side of him; and most wonderful to me then, John Sloan's picture of a young girl standing in the wind on the deck of a New York ferryboat—surely to Staten Island, and just about the year of my birth?—looking out to water.

PART 5
World Capital (1948–2002)

In his classic 1949 piece *Here Is New York*, the veteran *New Yorker* essayist E. B. White wrote that, "To a New Yorker the city is both changeless and changing." But even White described a city that "has never been so uncomfortable, so crowded, so tense." Some of that tension may well have been a result of the next chapter in Gotham's expansive history, for following the Second World War, New York was poised to become not just the leading city in the United States but the capital of the world. Nothing symbolized that development more fittingly than the construction, begun in 1947, of the United Nations headquarters. White noted that, "Along the East River, from the razed slaughterhouses of Turtle Bay . . . men are carving out the permanent headquarters of the United Nations—the greatest housing project of them all. In its stride, New York takes on one more interior city, to shelter, this time, all governments, and to clear the slum called war. New York is not a capital city—it is not a national capital or a state capital. But it is by way of becoming the capital of the world."

While the United Nations may have symbolized the emergence of New York City as the "capital of the world," it was the urban renewal plans of Robert Moses that would more sharply shape the lives of the people who lived in the city. Moses, true to Fiorello La Guardia's predictions, had accumulated more power than could be checked by any single person, even if that person were the mayor. In 1946, Moses coerced Mayor William O'Dwyer to appoint him to a newly created post—city construction coordinator. Later, in 1948, he would add to that position the job as chairman of the Mayor's Committee on Slum Clearance. Armed with near dictatorial control, and the passage of a federal statute, Title I of the Housing Act of 1949, which allowed for funds (more than a billion dollars was appropriated in 1949 alone) for the government to buy or condemn land, Moses began a campaign of destruction and rebuilding that had New York City spending more than twice what all the cities in the nation put together would spend on urban renewal.

The most obvious effect of that spending was the erection of the so-called "tower in the park" model of public housing. While the corporate architecture of midtown Manhattan in the 1950s reflected the radiant glass and steel of the "International Style" in almost nine hundred new office buildings, most notably in Lever House (1952) and in Mies van der Rohe's Seagram Building (1958), many of the public housing projects were repetitive, numbing red brick towers that imposed a mazelike, soulless anonymity on living conditions for the poor. The housing authority built 75,000 units (40,000 of them in Harlem alone) before Moses resigned his urban renewal directorship in 1960 and, by the end of the decade, it was landlord to more than 500,000 low-income residents.

The Housing Act of 1949 had another provision that would also define the shape of New York City. Title II provided federal financial assistance for buying a house and, coupled with the Interstate Highway Act of 1956 (the largest peacetime construction project in history), provided the motive and the means for New Yorkers to flood to the suburbs. During the twenty years from 1950 to 1970 the suburbs would double in size, eighteen of the country's twenty-five largest cities would lose population, and, in 1960, for the first time, the number of people in New York would be lower than the previous census. Robert Moses would be in the thick of this development as well.

Ironically, Moses, America's foremost champion of the automobile, never learned to drive. But he was the mastermind behind the construction of more than 600 miles of highways, and increasingly in the 1950s of eight-lane expressways, in the New York metropolitan area. Perhaps the most infamous was the seven-mile-long Cross-Bronx Expressway that ran through the middle of the neighborhood of East Tremont in the west central Bronx. Though residents organized a furtive protest, and even mapped out a financially plausible alternative route, Moses was unmoved. "When you operate in an overbuilt metropolis," he intoned, "you have to hack your way with a meat ax." By 1955, nine years after Moses had first proposed his idea, many of the 60,000 residents had been displaced. In 1963, the expressway was finally finished.

There were other signs of destruction and loss as well. Between 1950 and 1970, New York lost its manufacturing base and with it three quarters of its one million industrial jobs. The Port Authority moved most of its shipping operations to the New Jersey side of the Hudson in newly built facilities in Newark and Elizabeth. In 1957, Walter O'Malley moved the Dodgers (named for the skill of Brooklyn residents at avoiding the streetcars of a growing mass transit system) to Los Angeles and its enormous parking lots. And in the same year, the Giants left the Polo Grounds of northern Manhattan for California's other major city, San Francisco. Finally, one of the city's most monumental structures, Pennsylvania Station, designed by McKim, Mead, and White, covering two full blocks bounded by Thirty-third Street, Seventh Avenue, Thirty-first Street, and Eighth Avenue, and completed in 1911, was demolished. The commuter culture of the car had triumphed, and the architectural historian Vincent Scully bemoaned that while through Pennsylvania Station's majestic marble and granite corridors "one entered the city like a god. . . . One scuttles in now like a rat." However, the destruction of Pennsylvania Station revealed a need for preservation in the face of economic demand, and, as a result, the city formed a Landmarks Preservation Commission in 1965 with the intention of preserving historic structures.

The economic value of real estate had long been one of the driving forces behind the creation and destruction of New York City's buildings and neighborhoods. However, in one volume, *The Death and Life of American Cities* (1960), a Greenwich Village woman shifted the terms of the debate from economics to ecology—human ecology. Jane Jacobs's seminal work advocated a new way of looking at neighborhoods and streets that would influence a generation of urban planners. While Le Corbusier had adhered to a maxim that advocated that the city must "kill the street," Jacobs's intimate detailing of the "ballet" of her native Hudson Street demanded that city planners not only preserve existing structures but that they celebrate the unique human interaction that occurred in daily street life. While Robert Moses had declared that "a city without traffic is a ghost town," Jacobs concluded that "expressways . . . eviscerate great cities."

The battleground between the two would be the dilapidated buildings of SoHo (the area south of Houston Street). Moses proposed a Lower Manhattan Expressway to link the Manhattan and Williamsburg bridges over the East River with the Holland Tunnel under the Hudson. Jacobs fought a brilliant grassroots campaign that mobilized the upper- and middle-class residents of Lower Manhattan in a way that lower-class residents of East Tremont could not ten years earlier. The Landmarks Preservation Commission solidified the victory in 1973 when the cast-iron buildings of the South Houston Industrial District (SoHo) were declared a historic district.

The shifting of the human ecology of the city was nowhere more apparent than in the changing demographics of the city in the last half of the century. In 1949, *Time* magazine succinctly summarized the change by declaring simply that, "This immigration is different." The reference, in this case, was to the enormous influx of nonwhite Puerto Ricans entering the city seeking economic opportunity and transforming the Italian East Harlem neighborhood of Fiorello La Guardia into El Barrio. But American blacks from the Deep South also began to pour into the city following World War II in one of the greatest migrations in the nation's history. By the late 1950s the black population had doubled from before the war, and New York had become the first city in the world to count more than a million black residents. Weeksville and Bedford had been major black communities since before the Civil War, but neighboring Bushwick and Crown Heights filled with West Indian immigrants and blacks. Many of these Harlem residents followed Duke Ellington's charge to "Take the A Train," and by 1960 there were nearly half a million blacks living throughout Brooklyn.

Newcomers were greeted with an economy that had lost most of its blue-collar jobs, however, and black unemployment was double the rate for whites. Compounding the problem, in the decade of the 1960s the number of people receiving welfare would climb from 4 percent of the population to 14 percent. Poverty increased social disorder as drug use and vandalism increased and crime rates soared. In July 1964, when a white police lieutenant accidentally killed a black Harlem boy, three days of rioting, looting, and protest resulted in one death, hundreds seriously injured, and 519 arrests. By the sultry summer of 1967, newly elected Mayor John Lindsay was walking the streets of Harlem and other neighborhoods in an effort to show that the city government had not abandoned its poor.

Multinational corporations, however, had no such loyalty, and in the first half of the 1970s sixteen major companies (including Fortune 500 members Pepsico, Shell Oil, and American Tobacco) decided that the increased tax rates and shaky fiscal state were no longer bearable and abandoned the city. Not everything appeared to be plummeting, however. The first of the World Trade Center's Twin Towers opened in 1970, adding new office space the equivalent to the total office space of many major American cities. But in the fall of 1975 the city reached its economic nadir when the massive increases in the budget during the Lindsay years coupled with federal cutbacks under Nixon forced the city to default on its municipal loans. The *Daily News* carried the ominous response of the federal government in its headline on October 30, FORD TO CITY: DROP DEAD. Two years later, during a World Series game, Howard Cosell sounded another death knell as he watched arson fires blazing in gutted housing developments from his booth in Yankee Stadium and intoned over national television, "There it is again, ladies and gentlemen. The Bronx is burning." This remark only confirmed what the rest of America had suspected when they had watched the looting and fires after a July 13, 1977, total blackout in the city: New York City was unsafe, ungovernable, unsustainable.

Mr. Sammler, a character from Saul Bellow's novel *Mr. Sammler's Planet,* had declared that "New York makes one think about the collapse of civilization, about Sodom and Gomorrah, the end of the world." But in the last quarter of the century, New York resurrected itself and emerged once again as the world capital. By 1981, the city had balanced its budget and was paying off the last of its the federal loans. Even weathering a severe economic dip in the late 1980s and the early 1990s (brought on, in part, by the collapse on Black Monday, October 17, 1987, when the stock market lost fully a third of its value), the city enjoyed almost twenty years of economic prosperity. Feisty Mayor Ed Koch brought back a pride in being a New Yorker as he traveled the subways and streets of the city asking residents, "How'm I doing?" David Dinkins, the city's first African American mayor, suffered from unfortunate timing of serving during hard economic times, but even before his successor, Rudy Giuliani, had taken the oath of office in 1993, there had been signs of revitalization.

By the late 1990s New York again regained its status as the financial capital of the world. The stock market, fueled in part by the advent of computer-driven market mechanisms, reached record levels; tourism flourished with almost forty million people visiting the city from all over the globe in 2000; the city budget was showing a record surplus of $2.2 billion; real estate values were soaring, and Broadway was reporting all-time-high box-office receipts of more than $13 million per week in the summer of 2001.

The resurgence of Broadway was due, in part, to the remarkable revitalization of Times Square. In 1969, the film *Midnight Cowboy* earned Academy Award nominations for its two young stars, Dustin Hoffman and Jon Voight, but also earned Times Square the national reputation as the haven of drug pushers, prostitution, and pornographic peep shows. In 1980, a group of city and state officials formed the 42nd Street Development Project. But nothing was really achieved until the formation of the Times Square Business Improvement District (BID) in 1992. The BID, aided by investments from private companies such as Walt Disney, helped lead a resurgence of towering office buildings, renovated theaters, and larger pedestrian areas to accommodate the 1.5 million people who strode the Great White Way each day. While there was criticism that the new Times Square represented the "malling" of New York City, it also symbolically showed that the commercial entrepreneurial spirit of the city was alive and well at the end of the century.

Perhaps nothing showed the health, both material and spiritual, of the city more clearly than the number of people who wanted to be there. The 2000 census revealed a record number of people in New York City, more than eight million. Even though there was a substantial outflow of city residents to other parts of the nation, nearly 1.2 million immigrants were admitted to New York in the 1990s, resulting in an almost 10 percent increase in the city's population. New York City continued to act, as it had for its entire history, like a giant heart pumping citizens out into the rest of the country while simultaneously taking in new immigrants. Perhaps as significant as the sheer numbers, however, was the number of places they came from. Every Asian national subgroup grew by at least 25 percent, some by as much as 80 percent. Every continent on the globe contributed people to the point where there were nearly 180 languages being spoken in the city at the turn of the century. New York embodied globalization like no other city on earth.

Why had they all come? There were sociopolitical push factors and economic pull factors, to be sure, but there were personal reasons as well. Simply put, it was the desire to be what one had always wanted to be, to fully realize one's potential. As the architect Robert A. M. Stern described the process, "You can come here and reinvent yourself or can be born here and reinvent yourself, and you can change yourself. And if you can change your self, presumably, in the process, you are also changing the whole structure of the world that you operate in, in order to make your new fictive reality come alive." New York City has been to the United States what America has been to the rest of the world, the great experiment in multicultural re-creation. And, in the last half of the twentieth century, New York City took on the role that the American West, the frontier, had played in the American imagination in the nineteenth century, the opening of the door to possibility.

A Place (Any Place) to Transcend All Places,
William Carlos Williams (1948)

William Carlos Williams, born to a Puerto Rican mother and a British father reared in the Spanish Caribbean, never lived in New York City, but he did attend the Horace Mann School and interned as a physician at the French Hospital in Hell's Kitchen. New York held a fascination for Williams, however, especially after he attended the famed "Armory Show" at the 69th Regiment Armory at Lexington and 25th Street in 1913. In that same year Alfred Keymborg's magazine *Others* made its first appearance. Williams's association with this magazine led him to lustily partake in the bohemian literary life of Greenwich Village, and there he met John Reed, Marcel Duchamp, Marianne Moore, Hart Crane, and Djuna Barnes.

In Williams's poem "A Place (Any Place) to Transcend All Places," there is a reference to Elsa von Freytag Loringhofen. She was a German baroness, a sculptor and poet who offered once to sleep with Williams so that he could contract syphilis and thus free his true creativity. Despite declining her offer, Williams was an enormous influence on later New York poets such as Frank O'Hara and Allen Ginsberg, for whom he wrote the foreword to the groundbreaking epic poem *Howl.*

IN *New York, it is said,*
they do *meet (if that is*
what is wanted) talk but
nothing is exchanged
unless that guff
can be retranslated: as
to say, that is not
the end, there are channels
above that, draining
places from which New York

is dignified, created (the
deaf are not tuned in).

A church in New Hampshire
built by its pastor
from his own wood lot. One
black (of course, red)
rose; a fat old woman backing
through a screen door. Two,
from the armpits
down, contrasting in bed,
breathless; a letter from
a ship; leaves filling,
making, a tree (but
wait) not just leaves,
leaves of one design that
make a certain design,
no two alike, not like
the locust either, next in line,
nor the Rose of Sharon, in
the pod-stage, near it—a
tree! Imagine it! Pears
philosophically hard. Nor
thought that is from
branches on a root, from
an acid soil, with scant
grass about the bole
where it breaks through.

New York is built of
such grass and weeds; a modern
tuberculin-tested herd
white-faced behind a
white fence, patient and
uniform; a museum of looks
across a breakfast
table; subways of dreams;
towers of divisions
from thin pay envelopes.
What else is it? And what

else can it be? Sweatshops
and railroad yards at dusk
(puffed up by fantasy
to seem real) what else
can they be budded on
to live a little longer?
The eyes by this
far quicker than the mind.
—and we have
:Southern writers, foreign
writers, hugging a dis-
tinction, while perspectived
behind them following
the crisis (at home)
peasant loyalties inspire
the avant-garde. Abstractly?
No: That was for something
else. "Lefutur!" grimly.
New York? That hodge-podge?
The international city
(from the Bosphorus). Poor
Hoboken. Poor sad
Eliot. Poor memory.
—and we have
:the memory of Elsa
von Freytag Loringhofen,
a fixation from the street
door of a Berlin
playhouse; all who "wear
their manner too obviously,"
the adopted English (white)
and many others.
—and we have
:the script writer advising
"every line to be like
a ten word telegram" but
neglecting to add, "to a
child of twelve"—obscene
beyond belief.

Obscene and
abstract as excrement—
that no one wants to own
except the coolie
with a garden of which
the lettuce particularly
depends on it—if you
like lettuce, but
very, very specially, heaped
about the roots for nourishment.

Here Is New York, *E. B. White (1949)*

There may be no more quoted piece of prose about New York City than E. B. White's 1949 essay, *Here Is New York.* White had been commissioned by Roger Angell (who was also White's stepson) to write a piece for *Holiday* magazine, and what he produced captured his love of the city in fairy tale style. "New York is to the nation what the white church is to the village—the visible symbol of aspiration and faith, the white plume saying the way is up," crooned White. But he ended his essay with the ominous threat of destruction that took on new resonance in the wake of the September 11, 2001, terrorist attacks that leveled the World Trade Center. "A single flight of planes no bigger than a wedge of geese," White intoned, "can quickly end this island fantasy, burn the towers, crumble the bridges, turn the underground passages into lethal chambers, cremate millions." White proclaimed that while New York is not a "national capital or a state capital . . . it is by way of becoming a capital of the world."

White was born in 1899 in Mount Vernon, New York, and graduated from Cornell University in 1921, where he was the editor of the student newspaper. He joined *The New Yorker* magazine in 1925 and wrote for the columns "Talk of the Town" and, with his friend James Thurber, "Notes and Comment" from 1926–1938. In 1938, White left the city and moved to his beloved farm in Maine. While he continued to return to the city on a regular basis, it was from his home in North Brooklyn that he wrote two of the most famous children's books of the century, *Stuart Little* (1945) and *Charlotte's Web* (1952). Before his death in 1985, White was awarded a special Pulitzer Prize (1978) and the Presidential Medal of Freedom (1963), and was elected to the American Academy of Arts and Letters (1973).

On any person who desires such queer prizes, New York will bestow the gift of loneliness and the gift of privacy. It is this largess that accounts for the presence within the city's walls of a considerable section of the population; for the residents of Manhattan are to a large extent strangers who have pulled up stakes somewhere and come to town, seeking sanctuary or fulfillment or some greater or lesser grail. The capacity to make such dubious gifts is a mysterious quality of New York. It can destroy an individual, or it can fulfill him, depending a good deal on luck. No one should come to New York to live unless he is willing to be lucky.

New York is the concentrate of art and commerce and sport and religion and entertainment and finance, bringing to a single compact arena the gladiator, the evangelist, the promoter, the actor, the trader and the merchant. It carries on its lapel the unexpungeable odor of the long past, so that no matter where you sit in New York you feel the vibrations of great times and tall deeds, of queer people and events and undertakings. I am sitting at the moment in a stifling hotel room in 90-degree heat, halfway down an air shaft, in midtown. No air moves in or out of the room, yet I am curiously affected by emanations from the immediate surroundings. I am twenty-two blocks from where Rudolph Valentino lay in state, eight blocks from where Nathan Hale was executed, five blocks from the publisher's office where Ernest Hemingway hit Max Eastman on the nose, four miles from where Walt Whitman sat sweating out editorials for the Brooklyn Eagle, thirty-four blocks from the street Willa Cather lived in when she came to New York to write books about Nebraska, one block from where Marceline used to clown on the boards of the Hippodrome, thirty-six blocks from the spot where the historian Joe Gould kicked a radio to pieces in full view of the public, thirteen blocks from where Harry Thaw shot Stanford White, five blocks from where I used to usher at the Metropolitan Opera and only a hundred and twelve blocks from the spot where Clarence Day the Elder was washed of his sins in the Church of the Epiphany (I could continue this list indefinitely); and for that matter I am probably occupying the very room that any number of exalted and some wise memorable characters sat in, some of them on hot, breathless afternoons, lonely and private and full of their own sense of emanations from without.

When I went down to lunch a few minutes ago I noticed that the man sitting next to me (about eighteen inches away along the wall) was Fred Stone. The eighteen inches were both the connection and the separation that New York provides for its inhabitants. My only connection with Fred Stone was that I saw him in *The Wizard of Oz* around the beginning of the century. But our waiter felt the same stimulus from being close to a man from Oz, and after Mr. Stone left the room the waiter told me that when he (the waiter) was a young man just arrived in this country and before he could understand a word of English, he had taken his girl for their first theater date to *The Wizard of Oz.* It was a wonderful show, the waiter recalled—a man of straw, a man of tin. Wonderful! (And still only eighteen inches away.) "Mr. Stone is a very hearty eater," said the waiter thoughtfully, content with this fragile participation in destiny, this link with Oz.

New York blends the gift of privacy with the excitement of participation; and better than most dense communities it succeeds in insulating the individual (if he wants it, and almost everybody wants or needs it) against all enormous and violent and wonderful events that are taking place every minute. Since I have been sitting in this miasmic air shaft, a good many rather splashy events have occurred in town. A man shot and killed his wife in a fit of jealousy. It caused no stir outside his block and got only small mention in the papers. I did not attend. Since my arrival, the greatest air show ever staged in all the world took place in town. I didn't attend and neither did most of the eight million other inhabitants, although they say there was quite a crowd. I didn't even hear any planes except a couple of westbound commercial airliners that habitually use this air shaft to fly over. The biggest ocean-going ships on the North Atlantic arrived and departed. I didn't notice them and neither did most other New Yorkers. I am told this is the greatest seaport in the world, with six hundred and fifty miles of water front, and ships calling here from many exotic lands, but the only boat I've happened to notice since my arrival was a small sloop tacking out of the East River night before last on the ebb tide when I was walking across the Brooklyn Bridge. I heard the *Queen Mary* blow one midnight, though, and the sound carried the whole history of departure and longing and loss. The Lions have been in convention. I've seen not one Lion. A friend of mine saw one and told me about him. (He was lame, and was wearing a bolero.) At the ballgrounds and horse parks the greatest sporting spectacles have been enacted. I saw no ballplayer, no race horse. The governor came to town. I heard the siren scream, but that was all there was to that—an eighteen-inch margin again. A man was killed by a falling cornice. I was not a party to the tragedy, and again the inches counted heavily.

I mention these merely to show that New York is peculiarly constructed to absorb almost anything that comes along (whether a thousand-foot liner out of the East or a twenty-thousand-man convention out of the West) without inflicting the event on its inhabitants; so that every event is, in a sense, optional, and the inhabitant is in the happy position of being able to choose his spectacle and so conserve his soul. In most metropolises, small and large, the choice is often not with the individual at all. He is thrown to the Lions.

The Lions are overwhelming; the event is unavoidable. A cornice falls, and it hits every citizen on the head, every last man in town. I sometimes think that the only event that hits every New Yorker on the head is the annual St. Patrick's Day parade, which is fairly penetrating—the Irish are a hard race to tune out, there are 500,000 of them in residence, and they have the police force right in the family.

The quality in New York that insulates its inhabitants from life may simply weaken them as individuals. Perhaps it is healthier to live in a community where, when a cornice falls, you feel the blow; where, when the governor passes, you see at any rate his hat.

I am not defending New York in this regard. Many of its settlers are probably here merely to escape, not face, reality. But whatever it means, it is a rather rare gift, and I believe it has a positive effect on the creative capacities of New Yorkers—for creation is in part merely the business of forgoing the great and small distractions.

Although New York often imparts a feeling of great forlornness or forsakenness, it seldom seems dead or unresourceful; and you always feel that either by shifting your location ten blocks or by reducing your fortune by five dollars you can experience rejuvenation. Many people who have no real independence of spirit depend on the city's tremendous variety and sources of excitement for spiritual sustenance and maintenance of morale. In the country there are a few chances of sudden rejuvenation—a shift in weather, perhaps, or something arriving in the mail. But in New York the chances are endless. I think that although many persons are here from some excess of spirit (which caused them to break away from their small town), some, too, are here from a deficiency of spirit, who find in New York a protection, or an easy substitution.

There are roughly three New Yorks. There is, first, the New York of the man or woman who was born here, who takes the city for granted and accepts its size and its turbulence as natural and inevitable. Second, there is the New York of the commuter—the city that is devoured by locusts each day and spat out each night. Third, there is the New York of the person who was born somewhere else and came to New York in quest of something. Of these three trembling cities the greatest is the last—the city of final destination, the city that is a goal. It is this third city that accounts for New York's high-strung disposition, its poetical deportment, its dedication to the arts, and its incomparable achievements. Commuters give the city its tidal restlessness; natives give it solidity and continuity; but the settlers give it passion. And whether it is a farmer arriving from Italy to set up a small grocery store in a slum, or a young girl arriving from a small town in Mississippi to escape the indignity of being observed by her neighbors, or a boy arriving from the Corn Belt with a manuscript in his suitcase and a pain in his heart, it makes no difference: each embraces New York with the intense excitement of first love, each absorbs New York with the fresh eyes of an adventurer, each generates heat and light to dwarf the Consolidated Edison Company.

The commuter is the queerest bird of all. The suburb he inhabits has no essential vitality of its own and is a mere roost where he comes at day's end to go to sleep. Except in rare cases, the man who lives in Mamaroneck or Little Neck or Teaneck, and works in New York, discovers nothing much about the city except the time of arrival and departure of trains and buses, and the path to a quick lunch. He is desk-bound, and has never, idly roaming in the gloaming, stumbled suddenly on Belvedere Tower in the Park, seen the ramparts rise sheer from the water of the pond, and the boys along the shore fishing for minnows, girls stretched out negligently on the shelves of the rocks; he has never come suddenly on anything at all in New York as a loiterer, because he has had no time between trains. He has fished in Manhattan's wallet and dug out coins, but has never listened to Manhattan's breathing, never awakened to its morning, never dropped off to sleep in its night. About 400,000 men and women come charging onto the Island each week-day morning, out of the mouths of tubes and tunnels. Not many among them have ever spent a drowsy afternoon in the great rustling oaken silence of the reading room of the Public Library, with the book elevator (like an old water wheel) spewing out books onto the trays. They tend their furnaces in Westchester and in Jersey, but have never seen the furnaces of the Bowery, the fires that burn in oil drums on zero winter nights. They may work in the financial district downtown and never see the extravagant plantings of Rockefeller Center—the daffodils and grape hyacinths and birches and the flags trimmed to the wind on a fine morning in spring. Or they may work in a midtown office and may let a whole year swing round without sighting Governors Island from the sea wall. The commuter dies with tremendous mileage to his credit, but he is no rover. His entrances and exits are more devious than those in a prairie-dog village; and he calmly plays bridge while buried in the mud at the bottom of the East River. The Long Island Rail Road alone carried forty million commuters last year; but many of them were the same fellow retracing his steps.

The terrain of New York is such that a resident sometimes travels farther, in the end, than a commuter. Irving Berlin's journey from Cherry Street in the lower East Side to an apartment uptown was through an alley and was only three or four miles in length; but it was like going three times around the world.

A poem compresses much in a small space and adds music, thus heightening its meaning. The city is like poetry: it compresses all life, all races and breeds, into a small island and adds music and the accompaniment of internal engines. The island of Manhattan is without any doubt the greatest human concentrate on earth, the poem whose magic is comprehensible to millions of permanent residents but whose full meaning will always remain illusive. At the feet of the tallest and plushiest offices lie the crummiest slums. The genteel mysteries housed in the Riverside Church are only a few blocks from the voodoo charms of Harlem. The merchant princes, riding to Wall Street in their limousines down the East River Drive, pass within a few hundred yards of the gypsy kings; but the princes do not know they are passing kings, and the kings are not up yet anyway—they live a more leisurely life than the princes and get drunk more consistently.

New York is nothing like Paris; it is nothing like London; and it is not Spokane multiplied by sixty, or Detroit multiplied by four. It is by all odds the loftiest of cities. It even managed to reach the highest point in the sky at the lowest moment of the depression. The Empire State Building shot twelve hundred and fifty feet into the air when it was madness to put out as much as six inches of new growth. (The building has a mooring mast that no dirigible has ever tied to; it employs a man to flush toilets in slack times; it has been hit by an airplane in a fog, struck countless times by lightning, and been jumped off of by so many unhappy people that pedestrians instinctively quicken step when passing Fifth Avenue and 34th Street.)

Manhattan has been compelled to expand skyward because of the absence of any other direction in which to grow. This, more than any other thing, is responsible for its physical majesty. It is to the nation what the white church spire is to the village—the visible symbol of aspiration and faith, the white plume saying that the way is up. The summer traveler swings in over Hell Gate Bridge and from the window of his sleeping car as it glides above the pigeon lofts and back yards of Queens looks southwest to where the morning light first strikes the steel peaks of midtown, and he sees its upward thrust unmistakable: the great walls and towers rising, the smoke rising, the heat not yet rising, the hopes and ferments of so many awakening millions rising—this vigorous spear that presses heaven hard.

It is a miracle that New York works at all. The whole thing is implausible. Every time the residents brush their teeth, millions of gallons of water must be drawn from the Catskills and the hills of Westchester. When a young man in Manhattan writes a letter to his girl in Brooklyn, the love message gets blown to her through a pneumatic tube—pfft—just like that. The subterranean system of telephone cables, power lines, steam pipes, gas mains and sewer pipes is reason enough to abandon the island to the gods and the weevils. Every time an incision is made in the pavement, the noisy surgeons expose ganglia that are tangled beyond belief. By rights New York should have destroyed itself long ago, from panic or fire or rioting or failure of some vital supply line in its circulatory system or from some deep labyrinthine short circuit. Long ago the city should have experienced an insoluble traffic snarl at some impossible bottleneck. It should have perished of hunger when food lines failed for a few days. It should have been wiped out by a plague starting in its slums or carried in by ships' rats. It should have been overwhelmed by the sea that licks at it on every side. The workers in its myriad cells should have succumbed to nerves, from the fearful pall of smoke-fog that drifts over every few days from Jersey, blotting out all light at noon and leaving the high offices suspended, men groping and depressed, and the sense of world's end. It should have been touched in the head by the August heat and gone off its rocker.

Mass hysteria is a terrible force, yet New Yorkers seem always to escape it by some tiny margin: they sit in stalled subways without claustrophobia, they extricate themselves from panic situations by some lucky wisecrack, they meet confusion and congestion with patience and grit—a sort of perpetual muddling through. Every facility is inadequate—the hospitals and schools and playgrounds are overcrowded, the express highways are feverish, the unimproved highways and bridges are bottlenecks; there is not enough air and not enough light, and there is usually either too much heat or too little. But the city makes up for its hazards and its deficiencies by supplying its citizens with massive doses of a supplementary vitamin—the sense of belonging to something unique, cosmopolitan, mighty and unparalleled.

To an outlander a stay in New York can be and often is a series of small embarrassments and discomforts and disappointments: not understanding the waiter, not being able to distinguish between a sucker joint and a friendly saloon, riding the wrong subway, being slapped down by a bus driver for asking an innocent question, enduring sleepless nights when the street noises fill the bedroom. Tourists make for New York, particularly in summertime

—they swarm all over the Statue of Liberty (where many a resident of the town has never set foot), they invade the Automat, visit radio studios, St. Patrick's Cathedral, and they window shop. Mostly they have a pretty good time. But sometimes in New York you run across the disillusioned—a young couple who are obviously visitors, newlyweds perhaps, for whom the bright dream has vanished. The place has been too much for them; they sit languishing in a cheap restaurant over a speechless meal.

The oft-quoted thumbnail sketch of New York is, of course: "It's a wonderful place, but I'd hate to live there." I have an idea that people from villages and small towns, people accustomed to the convenience and the friendliness of neighborhood over-the-fence living, are unaware that life in New York follows the neighborhood pattern. The city is literally a composite of tens of thousands of tiny neighborhood units. There are, of course, the big districts and big units: Chelsea and Murray Hill and Gramercy (which are residential units), Harlem (a racial unit), Greenwich Village (a unit dedicated to the arts and other matters), and there is Radio City (a commercial development), Peter Cooper Village (a housing unit), the Medical Center (a sickness unit) and many other sections each of which has some distinguishing characteristic. But the curious thing about New York is that each large geographical unit is composed of countless small neighborhoods. Each neighborhood is virtually self-sufficient. Usually it is no more than two or three blocks long and a couple of blocks wide. Each area is a city within a city within a city. Thus, no matter where you live in New York, you will find within a block or two a grocery store, a barbershop, a newsstand and shoeshine shack, an ice-coal-and-wood cellar (where you write your order on a pad outside as you walk by), a dry cleaner, a laundry, a delicatessen (beer and sandwiches delivered at any hour to your door), a flower shop, an undertaker's parlor, a movie house, a radio-repair shop, a stationer, a haberdasher, a tailor, a drugstore, a garage, a tearoom, a saloon, a hardware store, a liquor store, a shoe-repair shop. Every block or two, in most residential sections of New York, is a little main street. A man starts for work in the morning and before he has gone two hundred yards he has completed half a dozen missions: bought a paper, left a pair of shoes to be soled, picked up a pack of cigarettes, ordered a bottle of whiskey to be dispatched in the opposite direction against his home-coming, written a message to the unseen forces of the wood cellar, and notified the dry cleaner that a pair of trousers awaits call. Homeward bound eight hours later, he buys a bunch of pussy willows, a Mazda bulb, a drink, a shine—all between the corner where he steps off the bus and his apartment. So complete is each neighborhood, and so strong the sense of neighborhood, that many a New Yorker spends a lifetime within the confines of an area smaller than a country village. Let him walk two blocks from his corner and he is in a strange land and will feel uneasy till he gets back.

Storekeepers are particularly conscious of neighborhood boundary lines. A woman friend of mine moved recently from one apartment to another, a distance of three blocks. When she turned up, the day after the move, at the same grocer's that she had patronized for years, the proprietor was in ecstasy—almost in tears—at seeing her. "I was afraid," he said, "now that you've moved away I wouldn't be seeing you any more." To him, *away* was three blocks, or about seven hundred and fifty feet.

I am, at the moment of writing this, living not as a neighborhood man in New York but as a transient, or vagrant, in from the country for a few days. Summertime is a good time to re-examine New York and to receive again the gift of privacy, the jewel of loneliness. In summer the city contains (except for tourists) only die-hards and authentic characters. No casual, spotty dwellers are around, only the real article. And the town has a somewhat relaxed air, and one can lie in a loincloth, gasping and remembering things.

I've been remembering what it felt like as a young man to live in the same town with giants. When I first arrived in New York my personal giants were a dozen or so columnists and critics and poets whose names appeared regularly in the papers. I burned with a low steady fever just because I was on the same island with Don Marquis, Heywood Broun, Christopher Morley, Franklin P. Adams, Robert C. Benchley, Frank Sullivan, Dorothy Parker, Alexander Woollcott, Ring Lardner and Stephen Vincent Benét. I would hang around the corner of Chambers Street and Broadway, thinking: "Somewhere in that building is the typewriter that archy the cockroach jumps on at night." New York hardly gave me a living at that period, but it sustained me. I used to walk quickly past the house in West 13th Street between Sixth and Seventh where F. P. A. lived, and the block seemed to tremble under my feet—the way Park Avenue trembles when a train leaves Grand Central. This excitation (nearness of giants) is a continuing thing. The city is always full of young worshipful beginners—young actors, young aspiring poets, ballerinas, painters, reporters, singers—each depending on his own brand of tonic to stay alive, each with his own stable of giants.

New York provides not only a continuing excitation but also a spectacle that is continuing. I wander around, re-examining this spectacle, hoping that

I can put it on paper. It is Saturday, toward the end of the afternoon. I turn through West 48th Street. From the open windows of the drum and saxophone parlors come the listless sounds of musical instruction, monstrous insect noises in the brooding field of summer. The Cort Theater is disgorging its matinee audience. Suddenly the whole block is filled with the mighty voice of a street singer. He approaches, looking for an audience, a large, cheerful Negro with grand-opera contours, strolling with head thrown back, filling the canyon with uninhibited song. He carries a long cane as his sole prop, and is tidily but casually dressed—slacks, seersucker jacket, a book showing in his pocket.

This is perfect artistic timing; the audience from the Cort, where *The Respectful Prostitute* is playing, has just received a lesson in race relations and is in a mood to improve the condition of the black race as speedily as possible. Coins (mostly quarters) rattle to the street, and a few minutes of minstrelsy improves the condition of one Negro by about eight dollars. If he does as well as this at every performance, he has a living right there. New York is the city of opportunity, they say. Even the mounted cop, clumping along on his nag a few minutes later, scans the gutter carefully for dropped silver, like a bird watching for spilt grain.

It is seven o'clock and I re-examine an ex-speakeasy in East 53rd Street, with dinner in mind. A thin crowd, a summer-night buzz of fans interrupted by an occasional drink being shaken at the small bar. It is dark in here (the proprietor sees no reason for boosting his light bill just because liquor laws have changed). How dark, how pleasing; and how miraculously beautiful the murals showing Italian lake scenes—probably executed by a cousin of the owner. The owner himself mixes. The fans intone the prayer for cool salvation. From the next booth drifts the conversation of radio executives; from the green salad comes the little taste of garlic. Behind me (eighteen inches again) a young intellectual is trying to persuade a girl to come live with him and be his love. She has her guard up, but he is extremely reasonable, careful not to overplay his hand. A combination of intellectual companionship and sexuality is what they have to offer each other, he feels. In the mirror over the bar I can see the ritual of the second drink. Then he has to go to the men's room and she has to go to the ladies' room, and when they return, the argument has lost its tone. And the fan takes over again, and the heat and the relaxed air and the memory of so many good little dinners in so many good little illegal places, with the theme of love, the sound of ventilation, the brief medicinal illusion of gin.

Another hot night I stop off at the Goldman Band concert in the Mall in Central Park. The people seated on the benches fanned out in front of the band shell are attentive, appreciative. In the trees the night wind stirs, bringing the leaves to life, endowing them with speech; the electric lights illuminate the green branches from the under side, translating them into a new language. Overhead a plane passes dreamily, its running lights winking. On the bench directly in front of me, a boy sits with his arm around his girl; they are proud of each other and are swathed in music. The cornetist steps forward for a solo, begins, "Drink to me only with thine eyes. . . . " In the wide, warm night the horn is startlingly pure and magical. Then from the North River another horn solo begins—the *Queen Mary* announcing her intentions. She is not on key; she is a half tone off. The trumpeter in the bandstand never flinches. The horns quarrel savagely, but no one minds having the intimation of travel injected into the pledge of love. "I leave," sobs Mary. "And I will pledge with mine," sighs the trumpeter. Along the asphalt paths strollers pass to and fro; they behave considerately, respecting the musical atmosphere. Popsicles are moving well. In the warm grass beyond the fence, forms wriggle in the shadows, and the skirts of the girls approaching on the Mall are ballooned by the breeze, and their bare shoulders catch the lamplight. "Drink to me only with thine eyes." It is a magical occasion, and it's all free.

On week ends in summer the town empties. I visit my office on a Saturday afternoon. No phone rings, no one feeds the hungry in-baskets, no one disturbs the papers; it is a building of the dead, a time of awesome suspension. The whole city is honeycombed with abandoned cells—a jail that has been effectively broken. Occasionally from somewhere in the building a night bell rings, summoning the elevator—a special fire-alarm rings. This is the pit of loneliness, in an office on a summer Saturday. I stand at the window and look down at the batteries and batteries of offices across the way, recalling how the thing looks in winter twilight when everything is going full blast, every cell lighted, and how you can see in pantomime the puppets fumbling with their slips of paper (but you don't hear the rustle), see them pick up their phone (but you don't hear the ring), see the noiseless, ceaseless moving about of so many passers of pieces of paper: New York, the capital of memoranda, in touch with Calcutta, in touch with Reykjavik, and always fooling with something.

In the café of the Lafayette, the regulars sit and talk. It is busy yet peaceful. Nursing a drink, I stare through the west windows at the Manufacturers Trust Company and at the red brick fronts on the north side of Ninth Street, watching the red turning slowly to purple as the light dwindles. Brick buildings have a way of turning color at the end of the day, the way a red rose turns bluish as it wilts. The café is a sanctuary. The waiters are ageless and they change not. Nothing has been modernized. Notre Dame stands guard in its travel poster. The coffee is strong and full of chicory, and good.

Walk the Bowery under the El at night and all you feel is a sort of cold guilt. Touched for a dime, you try to drop the coin and not touch the hand, because the hand is dirty; you try to avoid the glance, because the glance accuses. This is not so much personal menace as universal—the cold menace of unresolved human suffering and poverty and the advanced stages of the disease alcoholism. On a summer night the drunks sleep in the open. The sidewalk is a free bed, and there are no lice. Pedestrians step along and over and around the still forms as though walking on a battlefield among the dead. In doorways, on the steps of the savings bank, the bums lie sleeping it off. Standing sentinel at each sleeper's head is the empty bottle from which he drained his release. Wedged in the crook of his arm is the paper bag containing his things. The glib barker on the sight-seeing bus tells his passengers that this is the "street of lost souls," but the Bowery does not think of itself as lost; it meets its peculiar problem in its own way—plenty of gin mills, plenty of flop-houses, plenty of indifference, and always, at the end of the line, Bellevue.

A block or two east and the atmosphere changes sharply. In the slums are poverty and bad housing, but with them the reassuring sobriety and safety of family life. I head east along Rivington. All is cheerful and filthy and crowded. Small shops overflow onto the side-walk, leaving only half the normal width for passers-by. In the candid light from unshaded bulbs gleam watermelons and lingerie. Families have fled the hot rooms upstairs and have found relief on the pavement. They sit on orange crates, smoking, relaxed, congenial. This is the nightly garden party of the vast Lower East Side—and on the whole they are more agreeable-looking hot-weather groups than some you see in bright canvas deck chairs on green lawns in country circumstances. It is folksy here with the smell of warm flesh and squashed fruit and fly-bitten filth in the gutter, and cooking.

At the corner of Lewis, in the playground behind the wire fence, an open-air dance is going on—some sort of neighborhood affair, probably designed to combat delinquency. Women push baby carriages in and out among the dancers, as though to exhibit what dancing leads to at last. Overhead, like banners decorating a cotillion hall, stream the pants and bras from the pulley lines. The music stops, and a beautiful Italian girl takes a brush from her handbag and stands under the street lamp brushing her long blue-black hair till it shines. The cop in the patrol car watches sullenly.

The Consolidated Edison Company says there are eight million people in the five boroughs of New York, and the company is in a position to know. Of these eight million, two million are Jews—or one person in every four. Among this two million who are Jewish are, of course, a great many nationalities—Russian, German, Polish, Rumanian, Austrian, a long list. The Urban League of Greater New York estimates that the number of Negroes in New York is about 700,000. Of these, about 500,000 live in Harlem, a district that extends northward from 110th Street. The Negro population has increased rapidly in the last few years. There are half again as many Negroes in New York today as there were in 1940. There are about 230,000 Puerto Ricans living in New York. There are half a million Irish, half a million Germans. There are 900,000 Russians, 150,000 English, 400,000 Poles, and there are quantities of Finns and Czechs and Swedes and Danes and Norwegians and Latvians and Belgians and Welsh and Greeks, and even Dutch, who have been here from away back. It is very hard to say how many Chinese there are. Officially there are 12,000, but there are many Chinese who are in New York illegally and who don't like census takers.

The collision and the intermingling of these millions of foreign-born people representing so many races and creeds make New York a permanent exhibit of the phenomenon of one world. The citizens of New York are tolerant not only from disposition but from necessity. The city has to be tolerant, otherwise it would explode in a radioactive cloud of hate and rancor and bigotry. If the people were to depart even briefly from the peace of cosmopolitan intercourse, the town would blow up higher than a kite. In New York smolders every race problem there is, but the noticeable thing is not the problem but the inviolate truce. Harlem is a city in itself, and being a city Harlem symbolizes segregation; yet Negro life in New York lacks the more conspicuous elements of Jim Crowism. Negroes ride subways and buses on terms of equality with whites, but they have not yet found that same equality in hotels and restaurants. Professionally, Negroes get on well in the theater, in music, in art and in literature; but in many fields of employment the going is tough. The Jim Crow principle lives chiefly in the housing rules and customs. Private owners of dwellings legally can, and do, exclude Negroes. Under a recent city ordinance, however, apartment buildings that are financed with public moneys or that receive any tax exemption must accept tenants without regard to race, color or religion.

To a New Yorker the city is both changeless and changing. In many respects it neither looks nor feels the way it did twenty-five years ago. The elevated railways have been pulled down, all but the Third Avenue. An old-timer walking up Sixth past the Jefferson Market jail misses the railroad, misses its sound, its spotted shade, its little aerial stations, and the tremor of the thing. Broadway has changed in aspect. It used to have a discernible bony structure beneath its loud bright surface; but the signs are so enormous now, the buildings and shops and hotels have largely disappeared under the neon lights and letters and the frozen-custard façade. Broadway is a custard street with no frame supporting it. In Greenwich Village the light is thinning: big apartments have come in, bordering the Square, and the bars are mirrored and chromed. But there are still in the Village the lingering traces of poesy, Mexican glass, hammered brass, batik, lamps made of whisky bottles, first novels made of fresh memories—the old Village with its alleys and ratty one-room rents catering to the erratic needs of those whose hearts are young and gay.

Grand Central has become honky-tonk, with its extradimensional advertising displays and its tendency to adopt the tactics of a travel broker. I practically lived in Grand Central Terminal at one period (it has all the conveniences and I had no other place to stay) and the great hall seemed to me one of the more inspiring interiors in New York, until Lastex and Coca-Cola got into the temple.

All over town the great mansions are in decline. Schwab's house facing the Hudson on Riverside is gone. Gould's house on Fifth Avenue is an antique shop. Morgan's house on Madison Avenue is a church administration office. What was once the Fahnestock house is now Random House. Rich men nowadays don't live in houses; they live in the attics of big apartment buildings and plant trees on the setbacks, hundreds of feet above the street.

There are fewer newspapers than there used to be, thanks somewhat to the late Frank Munsey. One misses the *Globe,* the *Mail,* the *Herald;* and to many a New Yorker life has never seemed the same since the *World* took the count.

Police now ride in radio prowl cars instead of gumshoeing around the block swinging their sticks. A ride in the subway costs ten cents, and the seats are apt to be dark green instead of straw yellow. Men go to saloons to gaze at televised events instead of to think long thoughts. It is all very disconcerting. Even parades have changed some. The last triumphal military procession in Manhattan simply filled the city with an ominous and terrible rumble of heavy tanks.

The slums are gradually giving way to the lofty housing projects—high in stature, high in purpose, low in rent. There are a couple of dozens of these new developments scattered around; each is a city in itself (one of them in the Bronx accommodates twelve thousand families), sky acreage hitherto untilled, lifting people far above the street, standardizing their sanitary life, giving them some place to sit other than an orange crate. Federal money, state money, city money and private money have flowed into these projects. Banks and insurance companies are in back of some of them. Architects have turned the buildings slightly on their bases, to catch more light. In some of them, rents are as low as eight dollars a room. Thousands of new units are still needed and will eventually be built, but New York never quite catches up with itself, is never in equilibrium. In flush times the population mushrooms and the new dwellings sprout from the rock. Come bad times and the population scatters and the lofts are abandoned and the landlord withers and dies.

New York has changed in tempo and in temper during the years I have known it. There is greater tension, increased irritability. You encounter it in many places, in many faces. The normal frustrations of modern life are here multiplied and amplified—a single run of a crosstown bus contains, for the driver, enough frustration and annoyance to carry him over the edge of sanity: the light that changes always an instant too soon, the passenger that bangs on the shut door, the truck that blocks the only opening, the coin that slips to the floor, the question asked at the wrong moment. There is greater tension and there is greater speed. Taxis roll faster than they rolled ten years ago—and they were rolling fast then. Hackmen used to drive with verve; now they sometimes seem to drive with desperation, toward the ultimate tip. On the West Side Highway, approaching the city, the motorist is swept along in a trance—a sort of fever of inescapable motion, goaded from behind, hemmed in on either side, a mere chip in a millrace.

The city has never been so uncomfortable, so crowded, so tense. Money has been plentiful and New York has responded. Restaurants are hard to get into; businessmen stand in line for a Schrafft's luncheon as meekly as idle men used to stand in soup lines. (Prosperity creates its bread lines, the same as depression.) The lunch hour in Manhattan has been shoved ahead half an hour, to 12:00 or 12:30, in the hopes of beating the crowd to a table. Everyone is a little emptier at quitting time than he used to be. Apartments are festooned with No Vacancy signs. There is standing-room-only in Fifth Avenue buses, which once reserved a seat for every paying guest. The old double-deckers are disappearing—people don't ride just for the fun of it any more.

At certain hours on certain days it is almost impossible to find an empty taxi and there is a great deal of chasing around after them. You grab a handle and open the door, and find that some other citizen is entering from the other side. Doormen grow rich blowing their whistles for cabs; and some doormen belong to no door at all—merely wander about through the streets, opening cabs for people as they happen to find them. By comparison with other less hectic days, the city is uncomfortable and inconvenient; but New Yorkers temperamentally do not crave comfort and convenience—if they did they would live elsewhere.

The subtlest change in New York is something people don't speak much about but that is in everyone's mind. The city, for the first time in its long history, is destructible. A single flight of planes no bigger than a wedge of geese can quickly end this island fantasy, burn the towers, crumble the bridges, turn the underground passages into lethal chambers, cremate the millions. The intimation of mortality is part of New York now: in the sound of jets overhead, in the black headlines of the latest edition.

All dwellers in cities must live with the stubborn fact of annihilation; in New York the fact is somewhat more concentrated because of the concentration of the city itself, and because, of all targets, New York has a certain clear priority. In the mind of whatever perverted dreamer might loose the lightning, New York must hold a steady, irresistible charm.

It used to be that the Statue of Liberty was the signpost that proclaimed New York and translated it for all the world. Today Liberty shares the role with Death. Along the East River, from the razed slaughterhouses of Turtle Bay, as though in a race with the spectral flight of planes, men are carving out the permanent headquarters of the United Nations—the greatest housing project of them all. In its stride, New York takes on one more interior city, to shelter, this time, all governments, and to clear the slum called war. New York is not a capital city—it is not a national capital or a state capital. But it is by way of becoming the capital of the world. The buildings, as conceived by architects, will be cigar boxes set on end. Traffic will flow in a new tunnel under First Avenue. Forty-seventh Street will be widened (and if my guess is any good, trucks will appear late at night to plant tall trees surreptitiously, their roots to mingle with the intestines of the town). Once again the city will absorb, almost without showing any sign of it, a congress of visitors. It has already shown itself capable of stashing away the United Nations—a great many of the delegates have been around town during the past couple of years, and the citizenry has hardly caught a glimpse of their coattails or their black Homburgs.

This race—this race between the destroying planes and the struggling Parliament of Man—it sticks in all our heads. The city at last perfectly illustrates both the universal dilemma and the general solution, this riddle in steel and stone is at once the perfect target and the perfect demonstration of nonviolence, of racial brotherhood, this lofty target scraping the skies and meeting the destroying planes halfway, home of all people and all nations, capital of everything, housing the deliberations by which the planes are to be stayed and their errand forestalled.

A block or two west of the new City of Man in Turtle Bay there is an old willow tree that presides over an interior garden. It is a battered tree, long suffering and much climbed, held together by strands of wire but beloved of those who know it. In a way it symbolizes the city: life under difficulties, growth against odds, sap-rise in the midst of concrete, and the steady reaching for the sun. Whenever I look at it nowadays, and feel the cold shadow of the planes, I think: "This must be saved, this particular thing, this very tree." If it were to go, all would go—this city, this mischievous and marvelous monument which not to look upon would be like death.

Selected Writings of Langston Hughes

Though he was born in Joplin, Missouri in 1902, Langston Hughes felt that he came alive when he emerged from the subway one fall day in Harlem in 1921. "I exulted at the sight of so many Negroes," he wrote. "I wanted to shake hands with them all." Hughes had arrived in New York to attend Columbia University, but he chose to remain there for only one year. He had already published one of his best-known poems, "The Negro Speaks of Rivers," in the *Crisis* in 1920 and after taking a number of odd jobs around the city, he sailed for Africa and Europe. Harlem, however, was the place he loved most and he eventually bought a three-story brownstone at 20 East 127th Street, where he lived for much of his life.

Hughes was probably the most recognizable, lasting, and prodigious of the writers of the Harlem Renaissance. In 1926, in the *Nation,* he published "The Negro Artist and the Racial Mountain," and sounded the clarion call of the "New Negro" artist when he wrote, "We younger Negro artists who create now intend to express our individual dark-skinned selves without fear or shame. We know we are beautiful. And ugly too." Harlem in the 1920s became what Wallace Thurman called "almost a Negro Greenwich Village," and Hughes was in the center of a group he called, in his autobiography *The Big Sea,* the "Harlem Literati." Hughes maintained often-stormy relationships with such figures as Countee Cullen, Zora Neale Hurston, and Alain Locke. He was also a writer of many genres and his drama, *Mulatto,* was the longest-running play by an African American on Broadway until Lorraine Hansberry's *A Raisin in the Sun,* which took its title from a line in Hughes's poem "Harlem."

Harlem (1951)

What happens to a dream deferred?
Does it dry up
like a raisin in the sun?

Or fester like a sore
And then run?
Does it stink like rotten meat?
Or crust and sugar over
like a syrupy sweet?

Maybe it just sags
like a heavy load.

Or does it explode?

When the Negro Was in Vogue (1940)

The 1920's were the years of Manhattan's black Renaissance. It began with *Shuffle Along, Running Wild,* and the Charleston. Perhaps some people would say even with *The Emperor Jones,* Charles Gilpin, and the tom-toms at the Provincetown. But certainly it was the musical revue, *Shuffle Along,* that gave a scintillating send-off to that Negro vogue in Manhattan, which reached its peak just before the crash of 1929, the crash that sent Negroes, white folks, and all rolling down the hill toward the Works Progress Administration.

Shuffle Along was a honey of a show. Swift, bright, funny, rollicking, and gay, with a dozen danceable, singable tunes. Besides, look who were in it: The now famous choir director, Hall Johnson, and the composer, William Grant Still, were a part of the orchestra. Eubie Blake and Noble Sissle wrote the music and played and acted in the show. Miller and Lyles were the comics. Florence Mills skyrocketed to fame in the second act. Trixie Smith sang "He May Be Your Man But He Comes to See Me Sometimes." And Caterina Jarboro, now a European prima donna, and the internationally celebrated Josephine Baker were merely in the chorus. Everybody was in the audience—including me. People came back to see it innumerable times. It was always packed.

To see *Shuffle Along* was the main reason I wanted to go to Columbia. When I saw it, I was thrilled and delighted. From then on I was in the gallery of the Cort Theatre every time I got a chance. That year, too, I saw Katharine Cornell in *A Bill of Divorcement,* Margaret Wycherly in *The Verge,* Maugham's *The Circle* with Mrs. Leslie Carter, and the Theatre Guild production of Kaiser's *From Morn Till Midnight.* But I remember *Shuffle Along* best of all. It gave just the proper push—a pre-Charleston kick—to that Negro vogue of the 20's, that spread to books, African sculpture, music, and dancing.

Put down the 1920's for the rise of Roland Hayes, who packed Carnegie Hall, the rise of Paul Robeson in New York and London, of Florence Mills over two continents, of Rose McClendon in Broadway parts that never measured up to her, the booming voice of Bessie Smith and the low moan of Clara on thousands of records, and the rise of that grand comedienne of song, Ethel Waters, singing: "Charlie's elected now! He's in right for sure!" Put down the 1920's for Louis Armstrong and Gladys Bentley and Josephine Baker.

White people began to come to Harlem in droves. For several years they packed the expensive Cotton Club on Lenox Avenue. But I was never there, because the Cotton Club was a Jim Crow club for gangsters and monied whites. They were not cordial to Negro patronage, unless you were a celebrity like Bojangles. So Harlem Negroes did not like the Cotton Club and never appreciated its Jim Crow policy in the very heart of their dark community. Nor did ordinary Negroes like the growing influx of whites toward Harlem after sundown, flooding the little cabarets and bars where formerly only colored people laughed and sang, and where now the strangers were given the best ringside tables to sit and stare at the Negro customers—like amusing animals in a zoo.

The Negroes said: "We can't go downtown and sit and stare at you in your clubs. You won't even let us in your clubs." But they didn't say it out loud—for Negroes are practically never rude to white people. So thousands of whites came to Harlem night after night, thinking the Negroes loved to have them there, and firmly believing that all Harlemites left their houses at sundown to sing and dance in cabarets, because most of the whites saw nothing but the cabarets, not the houses.

Some of the owners of Harlem clubs, delighted at the flood of white patronage, made the grievous error of barring their own race, after the manner of the famous Cotton Club. But most of these quickly lost business and folded up, because they failed to realize that a large part of the Harlem attraction for downtown New Yorkers lay in simply watching the colored customers amuse themselves. And the smaller clubs, of course, had no big floor shows or a name band like the Cotton Club, where Duke Ellington usually held forth, so without black patronage, they were not amusing at all.

Some of the small clubs, however, had people like Gladys Bentley, who was something worth discovering in those days, before she got famous, acquired an accompanist, specially written material, and conscious vulgarity. But for two or three amazing years, Miss Bentley sat, and played a big piano all night long, literally all night, without stopping—singing songs like "The

St. James Infirmary," from ten in the evening until dawn, with scarcely a break between the notes, sliding from one song to another, with a powerful and continuous underbeat of jungle rhythm. Miss Bentley was an amazing exhibition of musical energy—a large, dark, masculine lady, whose feet pounded the floor while her fingers pounded the keyboard—a perfect piece of African sculpture, animated by her own rhythm.

But when the place where she played became too well known, she began to sing with an accompanist, became a star, moved to a larger place, then downtown, and is now in Hollywood. The old magic of the woman and the piano and the night and the rhythm being one is gone. But everything goes, one way or another. The '20's are gone and lots of fine things in Harlem night life have disappeared like snow in the sun—since it became utterly commercial, planned for the downtown tourist trade, and therefore dull.

The lindy-hoppers at the Savoy even began to practice acrobatic routines, and to do absurd things for the entertainment of the whites, that probably never would have entered their heads to attempt merely for their own effortless amusement. Some of the lindy-hoppers had cards printed with their names on them and became dance professors teaching the tourists. Then Harlem nights became show nights for the Nordics.

Some critics say that that is what happened to certain Negro writers, too—that they ceased to write to amuse themselves and began to write to amuse and entertain white people, and in so doing distorted and over-colored their material, and left out a great many things they thought would offend their American brothers of a lighter complexion. Maybe—since Negroes have writer-racketeers, as has any other race. But I have known almost all of them, and most of the good ones have tried to be honest, write honestly, and express their world as they saw it.

All of us know that the gay and sparkling life of the so-called Negro Renaissance of the '20's was not so gay and sparkling beneath the surface as it looked. Carl Van Vechten, in the character of Byron in *Nigger Heaven*, captured some of the bitterness and frustration of literary Harlem that Wallace Thurman later so effectively poured into his *Infants of the Spring*—the only novel by a Negro about that fantastic period when Harlem was in vogue.

It was a period when, at almost every Harlem uppercrust dance or party, one would be introduced to various distinguished white celebrities there as guests. It was a period when almost any Harlem Negro of any social importance at all would be likely to say casually: "As I was remarking the other day to Heywood—," meaning Heywood Broun. Or: "As I said to George—," referring to George Gershwin. It was a period when local and visiting royalty were not at all uncommon in Harlem. And when the parties of A'Lelia Walker, the Negro heiress, were filled with guests whose names would turn any Nordic social climber green with envy. It was a period when Harold Jackman, a handsome young Harlem school teacher of modest means, calmly announced one day that he was sailing for the Riviera for a fortnight, to attend Princess Murat's yachting party. It was a period when Charleston preachers opened up shouting churches as sideshows for white tourists. It was a period when at least one charming colored chorus girl, amber enough to pass for a Latin American, was living in a pent house; with all her bills paid by a gentleman whose name was banker's magic on Wall Street. It was a period when every season there was at least one hit play on Broadway acted by a Negro cast. And when books by Negro authors were being published with much greater frequency and much more publicity than ever before or since in history. It was a period when white writers wrote about Negroes more successfully (commercially speaking) than Negroes did about themselves. It was the period (God help us!) when Ethel Barrymore appeared in blackface in *Scarlet Sister Mary!* It was the period when the Negro was in vogue.

I was there. I had a swell time while it lasted. But I thought it wouldn't last long. (I remember the vogue for things Russian, the season the Chauve-Souris first came to town.) For how could a large and enthusiastic number of people be crazy about Negroes forever? But some Harlemites thought the millennium had come. They thought the race problem had at last been solved through Art plus Gladys Bentley. They were sure the New Negro would lead a new life from then on in green pastures of tolerance created by Countee Cullen, Ethel Waters, Claude McKay, Duke Ellington, Bojangles, and Alain Locke.

I don't know what made any Negroes think that—except that they were mostly intellectuals doing the thinking. The ordinary Negroes hadn't heard of the Negro Renaissance. And if they had, it hadn't raised their wages any. As for all those white folks in the speakeasies and night clubs of Harlem—well, maybe a colored man could find *some* place to have a drink that the tourists hadn't yet discovered.

Then it was that house-rent parties began to flourish—and not always to raise the rent either. But, as often as not, to have a get-together of one's own, where you could do the black-bottom with no stranger behind you trying to do it, too. Non-theatrical, non-intellectual Harlem was an unwilling victim of its own vogue. It didn't like to be stared at by white folks. But perhaps the downtowners never knew this—for the cabaret owners, the entertainers, and the speakeasy proprietors treated them fine—as long as they paid.

The Saturday night rent parties that I attended were often more amusing than any night club, in small apartments where God knows who lived—because the guests seldom did—but where the piano would often be augmented by a guitar, or an odd cornet, or somebody with a pair of drums walking in off the street. And where awful bootleg whiskey and good fried fish or steaming chitterling were sold at very low prices. And the dancing and singing and impromptu entertaining went on until dawn came in at the windows.

These parties, often termed whist parties or dances, were usually announced by brightly colored cards stuck in the grille of apartment house elevators. Some of the cards were highly entertaining in themselves:

We got yellow girls, we've got black and tan
Will you have a good time?—YEAH MAN!
A Social Whist Party
—GIVEN BY—
MARY WINSTON
147 West 145th Street Apt. 5
SATURDAY EVE., MARCH 19th, 1932
GOOD MUSIC REFRESHMENTS

HURRAY
COME AND SEE WHAT IS IN STORE FOR YOU AT THE
TEA CUP PARTY
GIVEN BY MRS. VANDERBILT SMITH
at 409 EDGECOMBE AVENUE
NEW YORK CITY
Apartment 10-A
on Thursday evening, January 23rd, 1930
at 8:30 P.M.
ORIENTAL-GYPSY-SOUTHERN MAMMY-
STARLIGHT
and other readers will be present
Music and Talent — Refreshments Served
Ribbons-Maws and Trotters A Specialty

Fall in line, and watch your step, For there'll be
Lots of Browns with plenty of Pep At
A Social Whist Party
Given by
Lucille & Minnie
149 West 117th Street, N. Y. Gr. floor, W,
Saturday Evening, Nov. 2nd 1929
Refreshments Just It   Music Won't Quit

If Sweet Mamma is running wild, and you are looking
for a Do-right child, just come around and
linger awhile at a
SOCIAL WHIST PARTY
GIVEN BY
PINKNEY & EPPS
260 West 129th Street   Apartment 10
SATURDAY EVENING, JUNE 9, 1928
GOOD MUSIC   REFRESHMENTS

Railroad Men's Ball
AT CANDY'S PLACE
FRIDAY, SATURDAY & SUNDAY,
April 29 30, May 1, 1927
Black Wax, says change your mind and say they
do and he will give you a hearing, while MEAT
HOUSE SLIM, laying in the bin
killing all good men.
L. A. VAUGH, *President*

OH BOY   OH JOY
The Eleven Brown Skins
of the
Evening Shadow Social Club
are giving their
Second Annual St. Valentine Dance
Saturday evening, Feb. 18th, 1928
At 129 West 136th Street, New York City
Good Music   Refreshments Served
Subscription   25 Cents

Some wear pajamas, some wear pants, what does it matter
just so you can dance, at
A Social Whist Party
GIVEN BY
Mr. & Mrs. Brown
At 258 W. 115th Street, Apt. 9
SATURDAY EVE., SEPT. 14, 1929
The music is sweet and everything good to eat!

Almost every Saturday night when I was in Harlem I went to a house-rent party. I wrote lots of poems about house-rent parties, and ate thereat many a fried fish and pig's foot—with liquid refreshments on the side. I met ladies' maids and truck drivers, laundry workers and shoe shine boys, seamstresses and porters. I can still hear their laughter in my ears, hear the soft slow music, and feel the floor shaking as the dancers danced.

The King of Harlem, Federico Garcia Lorca (1955)

Federico Garcia Lorca journeyed to New York in 1929 from his native Spain because he thought the city was "a dreadful place, and that's why I am going." Lorca was already a highly respected poet in his native country and a good friend of the surrealist painter Salvador Dali, who would make a celebrated appearance in New York five years later. Lorca was also a devotee of Walt Whitman and discussed poetry with another Whitman admirer, Hart Crane, during his stay.

Lorca's commentary on New York after he returned to Spain was acerbic and dyspeptic. "New York," he wrote, "is something awful, something monstrous. I like to walk the streets, lost, but I recognize that New York is the world's great lie. New York is Senegal with machines. The only things that the United States has given to the world are skyscrapers, jazz, and cocktails. Besides black art, there is only automation and mechanization." Lorca took a room at Columbia University when he arrived and was soon exploring Harlem with Nella Larsen, a well-known Harlem Renaissance writer, as his guide. What he saw was not a renaissance, however, but a loss of cultural identity. His poem, "The King of Harlem," is both a protest and a warning about the effects of a mechanical city engaged in severe racial discrimination. The poem was written in John Jay Hall at Columbia University.

WITH a spoon
he gouged out the crocodile's eyes
and thumped on the monkey-rumps,
with a spoon.
Eternity's spark still slept in the flint
and the scarabs that tippled on anise
had forgotten the moss of the parish.

And that patriarch, covered with mushrooms,
went on to the place where the black men were weeping
while the king's ladle crackled
and the tanks of the pestilent water arrived.

Roses fled on the blades
of the last loops of air
and on hummocks of saffron
the little boys smashed little squirrels
in the flush of a soiled exaltation.

Yes: the bridge must be crossed
and the florid black found
if the perfume we bear in our lungs
is to strike, in its guises of peppery pine,
on our temples.

We must murder the yellow-haired hawkers of brandy
and the comrades of apple and sand;
we must batter with fistblows
the gone little jewesses, in a lather of bubbles:
for the king and his hosts must come singing from Harlem,
the crocodiles sleep in the great enfilades,
in a moon of asbestos,
so that none may discredit the infinite beauty
of the dusters, the graters, the kitchenware coppers and
casseroles.

You Harlem! You Harlem! You Harlem!
No anguish to equal your thwarted vermilions,
your blood-shaken, darkened eclipses,
your garnet ferocity, deaf and dumb in the shadows,
your hobbled, great king in the janitor's suit.

Night opened a fissure: ivory salamanders were mute.
The American girls
carried children and coins in their bellies
and the boys lay inert on the cross of a yawn and stretched muscle.

Take note of them:
They drink silver whiskey within sight of volcanoes
and devour little silvers of heart on the frozen ascents of the bear.

King Harlem that night, with the hardest of spoons,
gouged out the crocodile's eyes
and thumped on the monkey-rumps.
With a spoon.
The black men, befuddled, went wailing,
between gold sun and umbrellas,
the mulattoes pulled rubber, impatient to gain a white torso,
and wind blurred the mirrors
and ruptured the veins of the dancers.

Negroes, Negroes, Negroes, Negroes.

Blood has no doors in your night, lying face to the sky.
Nowhere a blush. But under the skins, blood is raging,
alive in the spine of a dagger and the breast of a landscape,
under the pincers and brackens of Cancer's heavenly moon.

Blood on its thousand pathways seeking powder-meal deaths,
ashes of spikenard,
skies fixed in a slant, where the planets' assemblages
toss on the beach with the castaway things.
Blood that looks long, through a corner of eye,
blood pressed out of matweed, subterranean nectars.
Blood rusting the tracks of the negligent trade wind
and melting the moth on the panes.
Blood flows; and will flow
on the rooftops and sheds everywhere;
to burn off the chlorophyl blondes,
to sob at the foot of the bed by insomniac washbowls
and explode in a low-yellow dawn of tobacco.

Escape, since you must:
escape in the corners, hole up in the uppermost stories,
for a marrow of forests will enter the crevices
and leave in your flesh a tentative trail of eclipse,
mock mourning: the discoloring glove and the chemical rose.

In the shrewdest of silences
go the cooks and the valets, and those who would cleanse with their tongues
the millionaire's wounds,
seeking a king in the streets, or on crossways of nitre.

A wooden south wind, atilt on black slime
spits upon boatwrecks and tacks down its shoulders;
a southerly wind bearing
alphabets, sunflowers, incisors,
a storage-cell powered with a smother of wasps.

Oblivion spoke in three ink-droppings spotting a monocle,
and love, in the lonely, invisible face, on the rind of a rock.
Medullas, corollas, contrived on the cloud
a rose-barren desert of stubble.

To left and to right, southward, northward,
looms up the impassable wall
for the mole and the water-jet.
Black man, never search in its cleft
the immemorial mask.
Seek out the great sun of the center,
be the hum in the cluster.
Sun gliding through groves
with no expectation of dryads,
sun that undoes all the numbers, yet never crossed over a dream,
sun dropping tattooed on the river,
hallooing, with crocodiles after.

Negroes, Negroes, Negroes, Negroes.

Never serpent or zebra or mule
That paled at death's imminence.
Not even the woodcutter knows
when the death of the thunderous tree he brings down is accomplished.
Abide in the vegetal shade of your king
till the hemlock and thistle and thorn rock the furthermost roofs.

Black man: only then, only then, only then
can you kiss out your frenzy on bicycle-wheels
or pair off the microscopes in the caves of the squirrels,
and assuredly dance out the dance while the flower-stems stiffen
and murder our Moses—almost into bulrushes' heaven.

You Harlem in masquerade!
You Harlem, whom torsos of street-clothing menace!
Your murmur has come to me,
your murmur has come over tree trunks and dumb-waiters,
over grey metal-plate
where float all your tooth-covered speed-cars,
across the dead horses and the petty offenses,
past your noble and desperate king
whose beard-lengths go down to the sea.

Translated from the Spanish by Ben Belitt

Angel Levine, Bernard Malamud (1955)

Bernard Malamud was born on April 26, 1914, to Russian Jewish immigrants who operated a small grocery store in Brooklyn. He finished Erasmus High School in 1932 and graduated from City College before doing graduate work at Columbia University. Malamud later taught at his high school alma mater (1940–1948), Harlem High School (1948–1949), and Oregon State (1949–1961) before finishing his teaching career at Bennington College from 1961 until his death from a heart attack in his New York apartment on March 18, 1986. Malamud was one of the most honored writers in the nation, receiving the National Book Award for his short story collection *The Magic Barrel* (1958) and both that award and the Pulitzer Prize for his novel *The Fixer* (1966). He was a member of the American Academy and Institute of Arts and Letters, which in 1983 presented him its Gold Medal in Fiction, and from 1979 to 1981 he was president of the PEN American Center.

Malamud began to be considered, along with Saul Bellow and Philip Roth, one of the leading men in Jewish arts and letters in post–World War II America, but as Malamud himself said, "I was concerned with what Jews stood for, with their getting down to the bare bones of things. I was concerned with their ethicality—how Jews felt they had to live in order to go on living . . . Jewishness is important to me, but I don't consider myself only a Jewish writer. I have interests beyond that, and I feel I'm writing for all men." Malamud is supposed to have remarked cryptically that "all men are Jews," and the story "Angel Levine" confirms the author's definition of a universal Malamud character—"someone who fears his fate, is caught up in it, yet manages to outrun it. He's the subject and object of laughter and pity." Philip Roth summarized Malamud's deepest concern as "what it is to be human, and to be humane."

Malamud is buried in Mount Auburn Cemetery in Cambridge, Massachusetts; on his gravestone are the words, "Art celebrates life and gives us our measure."

MANISCHEVITZ, a tailor, in his fifty-first year suffered many reverses and indignities. Previously a man of comfortable means, he overnight lost all he had when his establishment caught fire, after a metal container of cleaning fluid exploded, and burned to the ground. Although Manischevitz was insured against fire, damage suits by two customers who had been hurt in the flames deprived him of every penny he had saved. At almost the same time, his son, of much promise, was killed in the war, and his daughter, without so much as a word of warning, married a lout and disappeared with him as off the face of the earth. Thereafter Manischevitz was victimized by excruciating backaches and found himself unable to work even as a presser—the only kind of work available to him—for more than an hour or two daily, because beyond that the pain from standing was maddening. His Fanny, a good wife and mother, who had taken in washing and sewing, began before his eyes to waste away. Suffering shortness of breath, she at last became seriously ill and took to her bed. The doctor, a former customer of Manischevitz, who out of pity treated them, at first had difficulty diagnosing her ailment, but later put it down as hardening of the arteries at an advanced stage. He took Manischevitz aside, prescribed complete rest for her, and in whispers gave him to know there was little hope.

Throughout his trials Manischevitz had remained somewhat stoic, almost unbelieving that all this had descended on his head, as if it were happening, let us say, to an acquaintance or some distant relative; it was, in sheer quantity of woe, incomprehensible. It was also ridiculous, unjust, and because he had always been a religious man, an affront to God. Manischevitz believed this in all his suffering. When his burden had grown too crushingly heavy to be borne he prayed in his chair with shut hollow eyes: "My dear God, sweetheart, did I deserve that this should happen to me?" Then recognizing the worthlessness of it, he set aside the complaint and prayed humbly for assistance: "Give Fanny back her health, and to me for myself that I shouldn't feel pain in every step. Help now or tomorrow is too late." And Manischevitz wept.

Manischevitz's flat, which he had moved into after the disastrous fire, was a meager one, furnished with a few sticks of chairs, a table, and bed, in one of the poorer sections of the city. There were three rooms: a small, poorly papered living room; an apology for a kitchen with a wooden icebox; and the comparatively large bedroom where Fanny lay in a sagging secondhand bed, gasping for breath. The bedroom was the warmest room in the house and it was here, after his outburst to God, that Manischevitz, by the light of two small bulbs overhead, sat reading his Jewish newspaper. He was not truly reading because his thoughts were everywhere; however the print offered a convenient resting place for his eyes, and a word or two, when he permitted himself to comprehend them, had the momentary effect of helping him forget his troubles. After a short while he discovered, to his surprise, that he was actively scanning the news, searching for an item of great interest to him. Exactly what he thought he would read he couldn't say—until he realized, with some astonishment, that he was expecting to discover something about himself. Manischevitz put his paper down and looked up with the distinct impression that someone had come into the apartment, though he could not remember having heard the sound of the door opening. He looked around: the room was very still, Fanny sleeping, for once, quietly. Half frightened, he watched her until he was satisfied she wasn't dead; then, still disturbed by the thought of an unannounced visitor, he stumbled into the living room and there had the shock of his life, for at the table sat a black man reading a newspaper he had folded up to fit into one hand.

"What do you want here?" Manischevitz asked in fright.

The Negro put down the paper and glanced up with a gentle expression. "Good evening." He seemed not to be sure of himself, as if he had got into the wrong house. He was a large man, bonily built, with a heavy head covered by a hard derby, which he made no attempt to remove. His eyes seemed sad, but his lips, above which he wore a slight mustache, sought to smile; he was not otherwise prepossessing. The cuffs of his sleeves, Manischevitz noted, were frayed to the lining, and the dark suit was badly fitted. He had very large feet. Recovering from his fright, Manischevitz guessed he had left the door open and was being visited by a case worker from the Welfare Department—some came at night—for he had recently applied for welfare. Therefore he lowered himself into a chair opposite the Negro, trying, before the man's uncertain smile, to feel comfortable. The former tailor sat stiffly but patiently at the table, waiting for the investigator to take out his pad and pencil and begin asking questions; but before long he became convinced the man intended to do nothing of the sort.

"Who are you?" Manischevitz at last asked uneasily.

"If I may, insofar as one is able to, identify myself, I bear the name of Alexander Levine."

In spite of his troubles Manischevitz felt a smile growing on his lips. "You said Levine?" he politely inquired.

The Negro nodded. "That is exactly right."

Carrying the jest further, Manischevitz asked, "You are maybe Jewish?"

"All my life I was, willingly."

The tailor hesitated. He had heard of black Jews but had never met one. It gave an unusual sensation.

Recognizing in afterthought something odd about the tense of Levine's remark, he said doubtfully, "You ain't Jewish anymore?"

Levine at this point removed his hat, revealing a very white part in his black hair, but quickly replaced it. He replied, "I have recently been disincarnated into an angel. As such, I offer you my humble assistance, if to offer is within my province and power—in the best sense." He lowered his eyes in apology. "Which calls for added explanation: I am what I am granted to be, and at present the completion is in the future."

"What kind of angel is this?" Manischevitz gravely asked.

"A bona fide angel of God, within prescribed limitations," answered Levine, "not to be confused with the members of any particular sect, order, or organization here on earth operating under a similar name."

Manischevitz was thoroughly disturbed. He had been expecting something, but not this. What sort of mockery was it—provided that Levine was an angel—of a faithful servant who had from childhood lived in the synagogues, concerned with the word of God?

To test Levine he asked, "Then where are your wings?"

The Negro blushed as well as he could. Manischevitz understood this from his altered expression. "Under certain circumstances we lose privileges and prerogatives upon returning to earth, no matter for what purpose or endeavoring to assist whomsoever."

"So tell me," Manischevitz said triumphantly, "how did you get here?"

"I was translated."

Still troubled, the tailor said, "If you are a Jew, say the blessing for bread."

Levine recited it in sonorous Hebrew.

Although moved by the familiar words Manischevitz still felt doubt he was dealing with an angel.

"If you are an angel," he demanded somewhat angrily, "give me the proof."

Levine wet his lips. "Frankly, I cannot perform either miracles or near-miracles, due to the fact that I am in a condition of probation. How long that will persist or even consist depends on the outcome."

Manischevitz racked his brains for some means of causing Levine positively to reveal his true identity, when the Negro spoke again:

"It was given me to understand that both your wife and you require assistance of a salubrious nature?"

The tailor could not rid himself of the feeling that he was the butt of a jokester. Is this what a Jewish angel looks like? he asked himself. This I am not convinced.

He asked a last question. "So if God sends to me an angel, why a black? Why not a white that there are so many of them?"

"It was my turn to go next," Levine explained.

Manischevitz could not be persuaded. "I think you are a faker."

Levine slowly rose. His eyes indicated disappointment and worry. "Mr. Manischevitz," he said tonelessly, "if you should desire me to be of assistance to you any time in the near future; or possibly before, I can be found"—he glanced at his fingernails—"in Harlem."

He was by then gone.

The next day Manischevitz felt some relief from his backache and was able to work four hours at pressing. The day after, he put in six hours; and the third day four again. Fanny sat up a little and asked for some halvah to suck. But after the fourth day the stabbing, breaking ache afflicted his back, and Fanny again lay supine, breathing with blue-lipped difficulty.

Manischevitz was profoundly disappointed at the return of his active pain and suffering. He had hoped for a longer interval of easement, long enough to have a thought other than of himself and his troubles. Day by day, minute after minute, he lived in pain, pain his only memory, questioning the necessity of it, inveighing, though with affection, against God. Why *so much*, Gottenyu? If He wanted to teach His servant a lesson for some reason, some cause—the nature of His nature—to teach him, say, for reasons of his weakness, his pride, perhaps, during his years of prosperity, his frequent neglect of God—to give him a little lesson, why then any of the tragedies that had happened to him, any *one* would have sufficed to chasten him. But *all together*—the loss of both his children, his means of livelihood, Fanny's health and his—that was too much to ask one frail-boned man to endure. Who, after all, was Manischevitz that he had been given so much to suffer? A tailor. Certainly not a man of talent. Upon him suffering was largely wasted. It went nowhere, into nothing: into more suffering. His pain did not earn him bread, nor fill the cracks in the wall, nor lift, in the middle of the night, the kitchen table; only lay upon him, sleepless, so sharply oppressive that he could many times have cried out yet not heard himself this misery.

In this mood he gave no thought to Mr. Alexander Levine, but at moments when the pain wavered, slightly diminishing, he sometimes wondered if he had been mistaken to dismiss him. A black Jew and angel to boot—very hard to believe, but suppose he *had* been sent to succor him, and he, Manischevitz, was in his blindness too blind to understand? It was this thought that put him on the knife-point of agony.

Therefore the tailor, after much self-questioning and continuing doubt, decided he would seek the self-styled angel in Harlem. Of course he had great difficulty because he had not asked for specific directions, and movement was tedious to him. The subway took him to 116th Street, and from there he wandered in the open dark world. It was vast and its lights lit nothing. Everywhere were shadows, often moving. Manischevitz hobbled along with the aid of a cane and, not knowing where to seek in the blackened tenement buildings, would look fruitlessly through store windows. In the stores he saw people and everybody was black. It was an amazing thing to observe. When he was too tired, too unhappy to go farther, Manischevitz stopped in front of a tailor's shop. Out of familiarity with the appearance of it, with some sadness he entered. The tailor, an old skinny man with a mop of woolly gray hair, was sitting cross-legged on his workbench, sewing a pair of tuxedo pants that had a razor slit all the way down the seat.

"You'll excuse me, please, gentleman," said Manischevitz, admiring the tailor's deft thimbled fingerwork, "but you know maybe somebody by the name Alexander Levine?"

The tailor, who, Manischevitz thought, seemed a little antagonistic to him, scratched his scalp.

"Cain't say I ever heared dat name."

"Alex-ander Lev-ine," Manischevitz repeated it.

The man shook his head. "Cain't say I heared."

Manischevitz remembered to say: "He is an angel, maybe."

"Oh, *him,*" said the tailor, clucking. "He hang out in dat honky-tonk down here a ways." He pointed with his skinny finger and returned to sewing the pants.

Manischevitz crossed the street against a red light and was almost run down by a taxi. On the block after the next, the sixth store from the corner was a cabaret, and the name in sparkling lights was Bella's. Ashamed to go in, Manischevitz gazed through the neon-lit window, and when the dancing couples had parted and drifted away, he discovered at a table on the side, toward the rear, Alexander Levine.

He was sitting alone, a cigarette butt hanging from the corner of his mouth, playing solitaire with a dirty pack of cards, and Manischevitz felt a touch of pity for him, because Levine had deteriorated in appearance. His derby hat was dented and had a gray smudge. His ill-fitting suit was shabbier, as if he had been sleeping in it. His shoes and trouser cuffs were muddy, and his face covered with an impenetrable stubble the color of licorice. Manischevitz, though deeply disappointed, was about to enter, when a big-breasted Negress in a purple evening gown appeared before Levine's table and, with much laughter through many white teeth, broke into a vigorous shimmy. Levine looked at Manischevitz with a haunted expression, but the tailor was too paralyzed to move or acknowledge it. As Bella's gyrations continued Levine rose, his eyes lit in excitement. She embraced him with vigor, both his hands clasped around her restless buttocks, and they tangoed together across the floor, loudly applauded by the customers. She seemed to have lifted Levine off his feet and his large shoes hung limp as they danced. They slid past the windows where Manischevitz, white-faced, stood staring in. Levine winked slyly and the tailor left for home.

Fanny lay at death's door. Through shrunken lips she muttered concerning her childhood, the sorrows of the marriage bed, the loss of her children; yet wept to live. Manischevitz tried not to listen, but even without ears he would have heard. It was not a gift. The doctor panted up the stairs, a broad but bland, unshaven man (it was Sunday), and soon shook his head. A day at most, or two. He left at once to spare himself Manischevitz's multiplied sorrow; the man who never stopped hurting. He would someday get him into a public home.

Manischevitz visited a synagogue and there spoke to God, but God had absented Himself. The tailor searched his heart and found no hope. When she died, he would live dead. He considered taking his life although he knew he wouldn't. Yet it was something to consider. Considering, you existed. He railed against God—Can you love a rock, a broom, an emptiness? Baring his chest, he smote the naked bones, cursing himself for having, beyond belief, believed.

Asleep in a chair that afternoon, he dreamed of Levine. He was standing before a faded mirror, preening small decaying opalescent wings. "This means," mumbled Manischevitz, as he broke out of sleep, "that it is possible he could be an angel." Begging a neighbor lady to look in on Fanny and occasionally wet her lips with water, he drew on his thin coat, gripped his walking stick, exchanged some pennies for a subway token, and rode to Harlem. He knew this act was the last desperate one of his woe: to go seeking a black magician to restore his wife to invalidism. Yet if there was no choice, he did at least what was chosen.

He hobbled to Bella's, but the place seemed to have changed hands. It was now, as he breathed, a synagogue in a store. In the front, toward him, were several rows of empty wooden benches. In the rear stood the Ark, its portals of rough wood covered with rainbows of sequins; under it a long table on which lay the sacred scroll unrolled, illuminated by the dim light from a bulb on a chain overhead. Around the table, as if frozen to it and the scroll, which they all touched with their fingers, sat four Negroes wearing skullcaps. Now as they read the Holy Word, Manischevitz could, through the plate-glass window, hear the singsong chant of their voices. One of them was old, with a gray beard. One was bubble-eyed. One was humpbacked. The fourth was a boy, no older than thirteen. Their heads moved in rhythmic swaying. Touched by this sight from his childhood and youth, Manischevitz entered and stood silent in the rear.

"Neshoma," said bubble eyes, pointing to the word with a stubby finger. "Now what dat mean?"

"That's the word that means soul," said the boy. He wore eyeglasses.

"Let's git on wid de commentary," said the old man.

"Ain't necessary," said the humpback. "Souls is immaterial substance. That's all. The soul is derived in that manner. The immateriality is derived from the substance, and they both, causally an otherwise, derived from the soul. There can be no higher."

"That's the highest."

"Over de top."

"Wait a minute," said bubble eyes. "I don't see what is dat immaterial substance. How come de one gits hitched up to de odder?" He addressed the humpback.

"Ask me somethin hard. Because it is substanceless immateriality. It couldn't be closer together, like all the parts of the body under one skin—closer."

"Hear now," said the old man.

"All you done is switched de words."

"It's the primum mobile, the substanceless substance from which comes all things that were incepted in the idea—you, me, and everything and body else."

"Now how did all dat happen? Make it sound simple."

"It de speerit," said the old man. "On de face of de water moved de speerit. An dat was good. It say so in de Book. From de speerit ariz de man."

"But now listen here. How come it become substance if it all de time a spirit?"

"God alone done dat."

"Holy! Holy! Praise His Name."

"But has dis spirit got some kind of a shade or color?" asked bubble eyes, deadpan.

"Man, of course not. A spirit is a spirit."

"Then how come we is colored?" he said with a triumphant glare.

"Ain't got nothing to do wid dat."

"I still like to know."

"God put the spirit in all things," answered the boy. "He put it in the green leaves and the yellow flowers. He put it with the gold in the fishes and the blue in the sky. That's how come it came to us."

"Amen."

"Praise Lawd and utter loud His speechless Name."

"Blow de bugle till it bust the sky."

They fell silent, intent upon the next word. Manischevitz, with doubt, approached them.

"You'll excuse me," he said. "I am looking for Alexander Levine. You know him maybe?"

"That's the angel," said the boy.

"Oh, *him*," snuffed bubble eyes.

"You'll find him at Bella's. It's the establishment right down the street," the humpback said.

Manischevitz said he was sorry that he could not stay, thanked them, and limped across the street. It was already night. The city was dark and he could barely find his way.

But Bella's was bursting with jazz and the blues. Through the window Manischevitz recognized the dancing crowd and among them sought Levine. He was sitting loose-lipped at Bella's side table. They were tippling from an almost empty whiskey fifth. Levine had shed his old clothes, wore a shiny new checkered suit, pearl-gray derby hat, cigar, and big, two-tone, button shoes. To the tailor's dismay, a drunken look had settled upon his formerly dignified face. He leaned toward Bella, tickled her earlobe with his pinky while whispering words that sent her into gales of raucous laughter. She fondled his knee.

Manischevitz, girding himself, pushed open the door and was not welcomed.

"This place reserved."

"Beat it, pale puss."

"Exit, Yankel, Semitic trash."

But he moved toward the table where Levine sat, the crowd breaking before him as he hobbled forward.

"Mr. Levine," he spoke in a trembly voice. "Is here Manischevitz."

Levine glared blearily. "Speak yo piece, son."

Manischevitz shivered. His back plagued him. Tremors tormented his legs. He looked around, everybody was all ears.

"You'll excuse me. I would like to talk to you in a private place."

"Speak, Ah is a private pusson."

Bella laughed piercingly. "Stop it, boy, you killin me."

Manischevitz, no end disturbed, considered fleeing, but Levine addressed him:

"Kindly state the pu'pose of yo communication with yo's truly."

The tailor wet cracked lips. "You are Jewish. This I am sure."

Levine rose, nostrils flaring. "Anythin else yo got to say?"

Manischevitz's tongue lay like a slab of stone.

"Speak now or fo'ever hold off."

Tears blinded the tailor's eyes. Was ever man so tried? Should he say he believed a half-drunk Negro was an angel?

The silence slowly petrified.

Manischevitz was recalling scenes of his youth as a wheel in his mind whirred: believe, do not, yes, no, yes, no. The pointer pointed to yes, to between yes and no, to no, no it was yes. He sighed. It moved but one still had to make a choice.

"I think you are an angel from God." He said it in a broken voice, thinking, If you said it, it was said. If you believed it, you must say it. If you believed, you believed.

The hush broke. Everybody talked but the music began and they went on dancing. Bella, grown bored, picked up the cards and dealt herself a hand.

Levine burst into tears. "How you have humiliated me."

Manischevitz apologized.

"Wait'll I freshen up." Levine went to the men's room and returned in his old suit.

No one said goodbye as they left.

They rode to the flat via subway. As they walked up the stairs Manischevitz pointed with his cane at his door.

"That's all been taken care of," Levine said. "You go in while I take off."

Disappointed that it was so soon over, but torn by curiosity, Manischevitz followed the angel up three flights to the roof. When he got there the door was already padlocked.

Luckily he could see through a small broken window. He heard an odd noise, as though of a whirring of wings, and, when he strained for a wider view, could have sworn he saw a dark figure borne aloft on a pair of strong black wings.

A feather drifted down. Manischevitz gasped as it turned white, but it was only snowing.

He rushed downstairs. In the flat Fanny wielded a dust mop under the bed, and then upon the cobwebs on the wall.

"A wonderful thing, Fanny," Manischevitz said. "Believe me, there are Jews everywhere."

Remarks on the Groundbreaking at Lincoln Square, Robert Moses (1959)

Robert Moses was a man with a vision. That vision did nothing less than transform the landscape of New York City into the model metropolis of the nation—for better and for worse. Mayor Fiorello La Guardia called him "the greatest engineer in the world" and noted that "no law, no regulation, no budget stops Bob Moses in his appointed task." His effect on urban planning was so great that Lewis Mumford concluded that "in the twentieth century, the influence of Robert Moses on the cities of America was greater than that of any other person." Robert Moses first gained power on April 23, 1924, when he was appointed president of the state parks council by Governor Al Smith, and it took the combined power of the leaders of the most powerful family in the country, Nelson and David Rockefeller, to wrest away his last vestige of power, the Triborough Authority, on March 1, 1968. In the span of those forty-four years Moses through various public agencies built twelve bridges (including the Triborough, the Henry Hudson, the Bronx-Whitestone, the Throgs Neck, and the Verrazano-Narrows), 627 miles of highways (including the Brooklyn-Queens Expressway, the Long Island Expressway, the Major Deegan Expressway, and the East River Drive) and more than 2.5 million acres of parks. Lincoln Center, Shea Stadium, and the United Nations were among countless other Moses creations.

But Moses was not without his critics. As his biographer, Robert Caro, has said, "Robert Moses was an utterly racist man, and his racism was reflected in what he built." He kept the water in public pools deliberately cold because he believed that black people would not swim in them if the temperature was regulated down; he refused to hire black lifeguards and employees at Jones Beach in an effort to discourage black patronage; and out of 255 playgrounds he built in the 1930s alone, exactly one was in Harlem. Urban advocate Jane Jacobs was critical of his disdain for neighborhoods and criticized his attempt to run traffic through Washington Square Park in Greenwich Village and his evisceration of the South Bronx neighborhoods with the construction of the

Cross-Bronx Expressway. Moses, for his part, noted in a speech at the groundbreaking of Lincoln Center that "you cannot make an omelet without breaking eggs."

SOMETHING superlative happens every day in New York, and new adjectives, gaudier circus posters and bolder metaphors must be invented to attract public attention. It is not, however, often that this busy City pauses to mark something as significant as ground breaking at Lincoln Square.

It is no small thing that in establishing the arts among the future recognized objectives of the nation, our Chief Executive, at a time when men's thoughts are on the crudest problems of survival and when he himself is burdened with the most oppressive and immediate cares of state, should come here to give his personal endorsement to this enterprise.

This is indeed our claim to building the boldest and most complex urban slum clearance project in America, substituting for urban rot not only new residence and business but education, culture, the performing arts, the Red Cross and a dozen related services and utilities. Here we rebuild by free cooperation of federal and city agencies, by the use of private risk capital and by the donation of large funds by generous individuals and philanthropic corporations. Here we stake our claim that New York will become the World Center of the Performing Arts as it has already become the World Political Capital.

You cannot rebuild a city without moving people. You cannot make an omelet without breaking eggs. You cannot provide in this program exclusively for tax exempt low or partially tax exempt middle income families and wholly tax exempt educational, charitable and cultural purposes. Some one has to pay the real estate taxes, and that is where the speculative builder who charges higher rentals and pays full taxes comes in. Without him the program envisaged by Title One of the Federal Law would be just rhetoric. It is easy for demagogues to insinuate that only the small income man should be considered in such projects, to sneer about windfalls and handouts for private builders and to play up and exaggerate individual tenant hardship. We do indeed sympathize with tenants and do everything possible to help them, but we cannot give everybody and his lawyer what they want.

I wish I could honestly say that the Opera, the Philharmonic, the Juilliard School, the other theatres and features of the Performing Arts will rise like the walls of Thebes to music and that neither hammer nor axe nor any tool of iron will be heard as in the case of Solomon's Temple. There will be noise, dirt flying and inevitably some disruption of business, and beams and motes will have to be removed from sensitive eyes. Mr. Rockefeller and his associates still have a long way to go to their final magnificent objective, but no one who knows them, their motives, their reputation, their persistence, their pride in this City and their belief in the national and international repercussions of the Performing Arts Center can have the slightest doubt of the outcome.

Speaking for the Slum Clearance Committee, I pledge our full and enthusiastic support to the early and triumphant completion of Lincoln Square.

The Day Lady Died, Frank O'Hara (1959)

Frank O'Hara was born in Baltimore in 1926, graduated from Harvard University in 1950, and arrived in New York City in 1951. From that time until his premature death sixteen years later in a freak jeep accident on Fire Island, O'Hara embraced the New York art and poetry world like few others before him. He worked as a curator at the Museum of Modern Art and cultivated friendships with scores of artists, among them Jackson Pollock and Franz Kline. After his death, the museum published a volume, *In Memory of My Feelings,* in tribute to his work, in which his poems were illustrated by Willem de Kooning and Jasper Johns.

O'Hara was one of the leaders of the so-called "New York School" of poetry that counted Kenneth Koch and John Ashbery among its members. O'Hara championed what he called "the personal poem" and often it was the city itself that was the subject as much as O'Hara's feelings. Helen Vendler noted that O'Hara "follows Walt Whitman and William Carlos Williams in writing urban pastoral, but neither Whitman nor Williams took the pleasure in the city that O'Hara did."

Precisely because of his personal connection to the city he adored, O'Hara captured the New York of the 1950s better than any of his contemporaries. In a *New Yorker* article in 1993, Joan Acocella concluded that, "In one of New York's most splendid moments—some would say its last splendid moment—O'Hara was for many Manhattanites a symbol of the city and a kind of paradigm of the phenomenon that E. B. White has described, the person who becomes himself, or his most interesting self, by moving to New York."

O'Hara's poem "The Day Lady Died" described his reaction to the death of the legendary singer Billie Holiday on July 17, 1959. Holiday had been the most important jazz singer in New York since the 1930s and had been given the moniker "Lady Day" by the saxophonist Lester Young when she was recording with Count Basie's band.

It is 12:20 in New York a Friday
three days after Bastille Day, yes
it is 1959 and I go get a shoeshine
because I will get off the 419 in Easthampton
at 7:15 and then go straight to dinner
and I don't know the people who will feed me

I walk up the muggy street beginning to sun
and have a hamburger and a malted and buy
an ugly NEW WORLD WRITING to see what the poets
in Ghana are doing these days
I go on to the bank
and Miss Stillwagon (first name Linda I once heard)
doesn't even look up my balance for once in her life
and in the GOLDEN GRIFFIN I get a little Verlaine
for Patsy with drawings by Bonnard although I do
think of Hesiold, trans. Richmond Lattimore or
Brendan Behan's new play or Le Balcon *or* Les Negres
of Genet, but I don't, I stink with Verlaine
after practically going to sleep with quandariness

and for Mike I just stroll into the PARK LANE
Liquor Store and ask for a bottle of Strega and
then I go back where I came from to 6th Avenue
and the tobacconist in the Ziegfeld Theatre and
casually ask for a carton of Gauloises and a carton
of Picayunes, and a NEW YORK POST with her face on it

and I am sweating a lot by now and thinking
of leaning on the john door in the FIVE SPOT
while she whispered a song along the keyboard
to Mal Waldron and everyone and I stopped breathing

Fifth Avenue, Uptown, James Baldwin (1960)

The British journalist W. J. Weatherby paid tribute to James Baldwin at his funeral at the Cathedral of St. John the Divine (Amsterdam and West 112th Street) with the following words: "He had departed from Harlem," Weatherby intoned, "when he was eighteen never to return except for brief visits, but as a writer he never left. In book after book, he returned obsessively to the Harlem he had grown up in. . . . He kept the faith—the Harlem test—in all the ways that mattered. For many white Americans even when they gave up listening, he remained the messenger with the bad news right up to the end." James Baldwin was the first major black writer to be born in Harlem, at Harlem Hospital, in August 1924 in the midst of the Harlem Renaissance and, for some, his death was the close of that period.

Beginning with his autobiographical *Go Tell It on the Mountain* and continuing in his short story "Sonny's Blues" and his essay "Notes of a Native Son," Baldwin's literary genius focused on translating the American, and particularly New York, black experience to the white world. In "Fifth Avenue, Uptown: A Letter from Harlem," Baldwin described the psychological effects of living in the black ghetto and how "the pressure within the ghetto causes the ghetto walls to expand, and this expansion is always violent."

The consummate societal "outsider" who saw the "inside" more clearly than those enmeshed in it, Baldwin once responded to a question as to whether he felt disadvantaged by being black, poor, and homosexual with the quip, "No, I rather feel like I have hit the trifecta." Baldwin reveled in late-night conversations where he felt that the truth came forth, and his writing upholds his dictum that "all art is a kind of confession."

A LETTER FROM HARLEM

THERE is a housing project standing now where the house in which we grew up once stood, and one of those stunted city trees is snarling where our doorway used to be. This is on the rehabilitated side of the avenue. The other side of the avenue—for progress takes time—has not been rehabilitated yet and it looks exactly as it looked in the days when we sat with our noses pressed against the windowpane, longing to be allowed to go "across the street." The grocery store which gave us credit is still there, and there can be no doubt that it is still giving credit. The people in the project certainly need it—far more, indeed, than they ever needed the project. The last time I passed by, the Jewish proprietor was still standing among his shelves, looking sadder and heavier but scarcely any older. Farther down the block stands the shoe-repair store in which our shoes were repaired until reparation became impossible and in which, then, we bought all our "new" ones. The Negro proprietor is still in the window, head down, working at the leather.

These two, I imagine, could tell a long tale if they would (perhaps they would be glad to if they could), having watched so many, for so long, struggling in the fishhooks, the barbed wire, of this avenue.

The avenue is elsewhere the renowned and elegant Fifth. The area I am describing, which, in today's gang parlance, would be called "the turf," is bounded by Lenox Avenue on the west, the Harlem River on the east, 135th Street on the north, and 130th Street on the south. We never lived beyond these boundaries; this is where we grew up. Walking along 145th Street, for example, familiar as it is, and similar, does not have the same impact because I do not know any of the people on the block. But when I turn east on 131st Street and Lenox Avenue, there is first a soda-pop joint, then a shoeshine "parlor," then a grocery store, then a dry cleaners', then the houses. All along the street there are people who watched me grow up, people who grew up with me, people I watched grow up along with my brothers and sisters; and, sometimes in my arms, sometimes underfoot, sometimes at my shoulder—or on it—their children, a riot, a forest of children, who include my nieces and nephews.

When we reach the end of this long block, we find ourselves on wide, filthy, hostile Fifth Avenue, facing that project which hangs over the avenue like a monument to the folly, and the cowardice, of good intentions. All along the block, for anyone who knows it, are immense human gaps, like craters. These gaps are not created merely by those who have moved away, inevitably into some other ghetto; or by those who have risen, almost always into a greater capacity for self-loathing and self-delusion; or yet by those who, by whatever means—the Second World War, the Korean war, a policeman's gun or billy, a gang war, a brawl, madness, an overdose of heroin, or, simply, unnatural exhaustion—are dead. I am talking about those who are left, and I am talking principally about the young. What are they doing?

Well, some, a minority, are fanatical churchgoers, members of the more extreme of the Holy Roller sects. Many, many more are "moslems," by affiliation or sympathy, that is to say that they are united by nothing more—and nothing less—than a hatred of the white world and all its works. They are present, for example, at every Buy Black street-corner meeting—meetings in which the speaker urges his hearers to cease trading with white men and establish a separate economy. Neither the speaker nor his hearers can possibly do this, of course, since the Negroes do not own General Motors or RCA or the A&P, nor indeed, do they own more than a wholly insufficient fraction of anything else in Harlem (those who *do* own anything are more interested in their profits than in their fellows). But these meetings nevertheless keep alive in the participators a certain pride of bitterness without which, however futile this bitterness may be, they could scarcely remain alive at all. Many have given up. They stay home and watch the TV screen, living on the earnings of their parents, cousins, brothers, or uncles, and only leave the house to go to the movies or to the nearest bar. "How're you making it?" one may ask, running into them along the block, or in the bar. "Oh, I'm TV-ing it"; with the saddest, sweetest, most shamefaced of smiles, and from a great distance. This distance one is compelled to respect; anyone who has traveled so far will not easily be dragged again into the world. There are further retreats, of course, than the TV screen or the bar. There are those who are simply sitting on their stoops, "stoned," animated for a moment only, and hideously, by the approach of someone who may lend them the money for a "fix." Or by the approach of someone from whom they can purchase it, one of the shrewd ones, on the way to prison or just coming out.

And the others, who have avoided all of these deaths, get up in the morning and go downtown to meet "the man." They work in the white man's world all day and come home in the evening to this fetid block. They struggle to instill in their children some private sense of honor or dignity which will help the child to survive. This means, of course, that they must struggle, stolidly, incessantly, to keep this sense alive in themselves, in spite of the insults, the indifference, and the cruelty they are certain to encounter in their working day. They patiently browbeat the landlord into fixing the heat, the plaster, the plumbing; this demands prodigious patience; nor is patience usually enough. In trying to make their hovels habitable, they are perpetually throwing good money after bad. Such frustration, so long endured, is driving many strong, admirable men and women whose only crime is color to the very gates of paranoia.

One remembers them from another time—playing handball in the playground, going to church, wondering if they were going to be promoted at school. One remembers them going off to war—gladly, to escape this block. One remembers their return. Perhaps one remembers their wedding day. And one sees where the girl is now—vainly looking for salvation from some other embittered, trussed, and struggling boy—and sees the all-but-abandoned children in the streets.

Now I am perfectly aware that there are other slums in which white men are fighting for their lives, and mainly losing. I know that blood is also flowing through those streets and that the human damage there is incalculable. People are continually pointing out to me the wretchedness of white people in order to console me for the wretchedness of blacks. But an itemized account of the American failure does not console me and it should not console anyone else. That hundreds of thousands of white people are living, in effect, no better than the "niggers" is not a fact to be regarded with complacency. The social and moral bankruptcy suggested by this fact is the bitterest, most terrifying kind.

The people, however, who believe that this democratic anguish has some consoling value are always pointing out that So-and-So, white, and So-and-So, black, rose from the slums into the big time. The existence—the public existence—of, say, Frank Sinatra and Sammy Davis, Jr., proves to them that America is still the land of opportunity and that inequalities vanish before the determined will. It proves nothing of the sort. The determined will is rare—at the moment, in this country, it is unspeakably rare—and the inequalities suffered by the many are in no way justified by the rise of a few. A few have always risen—in every country, every era, and in the teeth of regimes which can by no stretch of the imagination be thought of as free. Not all of these people, it is worth remembering, left the world better than they found it. The determined will is rare, but it is not invariably benevolent. Furthermore, the American equation of success with the big times reveals an awful disrespect for human life and human achievement. This equation has placed our cities among the most dangerous in the world and has placed our youth among the most empty and most bewildered. The situation of our youth is not mysterious. Children have never been very good at listening to their elders, but they have never failed to imitate them. They must, they have no other models. That is exactly what our children are doing. They are imitating our immorality, our disrespect for the pain of others.

All other slum dwellers, when the bank account permits it, can move out of the slum and vanish altogether from the eye of persecution. No Negro in this country has ever made that much money and it will be a long time before any Negro does. The Negroes in Harlem, who have no money, spend what they have in such gimcracks as they are sold. These include "wider" TV screens, more "faithful" hi-fi sets, more "powerful" cars, all of which, of course, are obsolete long before they are paid for. Anyone who has ever struggled with poverty knows how extremely expensive it is to be poor; and if one is a member of a captive population, economically speaking, one's feet have simply been placed on the treadmill forever. One is victimized, economically, in a thousand ways—rent, for example, or car insurance. Go shopping one day in Harlem—for anything—and compare Harlem prices and quality with those downtown.

The people who have managed to get off this block have only got as far as a more respectable ghetto. This respectable ghetto does not even have the advantages of the disreputable one—friends, neighbors, a familiar church, and friendly tradesmen; and it is not, moreover, in the nature of any ghetto to remain respectable long. Every Sunday, people who have left the block take the lonely ride back, dragging their increasingly discontented children with them. They spend the day talking, not always with words, about the trouble they've seen and the trouble—one must watch their eyes as they watch their children—they are only too likely to see. For children do not like ghettos. It takes them nearly no time to discover exactly why they are there.

The projects in Harlem are hated. They are hated almost as much as policemen, and this is saying a great deal. And they are hated for the same reason: both reveal, unbearably, the real attitude of the white world, no matter how many liberal speeches are made, no matter how many lofty editorials are written, no matter how many civil-rights commissions are set up.

The projects are hideous, of course, there being a law, apparently respected throughout the world, that popular housing shall be as cheerless as a prison. They are lumped all over Harlem, colorless, bleak, high, and revolting. The wide windows look out on Harlem's invincible and indescribable squalor: the Park Avenue railroad tracks, around which, about forty years ago, the present dark community began; the unrehabilitated houses, bowed down, it would seem, under the great weight of frustration and bitterness they contain; the dark, the ominous school-houses from which the child may emerge maimed, blinded, hooked, or enraged for life; and the churches, churches, block upon block of churches, niched in the walls like cannon in the walls of a fortress. Even if the administration of the projects were not so insanely humiliating (for example: one must report raises in salary to the management, which will then eat up the profit by raising one's rent; the management has the right to know who is staying in your apartment; the management can ask you to leave, at their discretion), the projects would still be hated because they are an insult to the meanest intelligence.

Harlem got its first private project, Riverton*—which is now, naturally, a slum—about twelve years ago because at that time Negroes were not allowed to live in Stuyvesant Town. Harlem watched Riverton go up, therefore, in the most violent bitterness of spirit, and hated it long before the builders arrived. They began hating it at about the time people began moving out of their condemned houses to make room for this additional proof of how thoroughly the white world despised them. And they had scarcely moved in, naturally, before they began smashing windows, defacing walls, urinating in the elevators, and fornicating in the playgrounds. Liberals, both white and black, were appalled at the spectacle. I was appalled by the liberal innocence—or cynicism, which comes out in practice as much the same thing. Other people were delighted to be able to point to proof positive that nothing could be done to better the lot of the colored people. They were, and are, right in one respect: that nothing can be done as long as they are treated like colored people. The people in Harlem know they are living there because white people do not think they are good enough to live anywhere else. No amount of "improvement" can sweeten this fact. Whatever money is now being earmarked to improve this, or any other ghetto, might as well be burnt. A ghetto can be improved in one way only: out of existence.

Similarly, the only way to police a ghetto is to be oppressive. None of the Police Commissioner's men, even with the best will in the world, have any way of understanding the lives led by the people they swagger about in twos and threes controlling. Their very presence is an insult, and it would be, even if they spent their entire day feeding gumdrops to children. They represent the force of the white world, and that world's real intentions are, simply, for that world's criminal profit and ease, to keep the black man corraled up here,

---

*The inhabitants of Riverton were much embittered by this description; they have, apparently, forgotten how their project came into being; and have repeatedly informed me that I cannot possibly be referring to Riverton, but to another housing project which is directly across the street. It is quite clear, I think, that I have no interest in accusing any individuals or families of the depredations herein described: but neither can I deny the evidence of my own eyes. Nor do I blame anyone in Harlem for making the best of a dreadful bargain. But anyone who lives in Harlem and imagines that he has *not* struck this bargain, or that what he takes to be his status (in whose eyes?) protects him against the common pain, demoralization, and danger, is simply self-deluded.

in his place. The badge, the gun in the holster, and the swinging club make vivid what will happen should his rebellion become overt. Rare, indeed, is the Harlem citizen, from the most circumspect church member to the most shiftless adolescent, who does not have a long tale to tell of police incompetence, injustice, or brutality. I myself have witnessed and endured it more than once. The businessmen and racketeers also have a story. And so do the prostitutes. (And this is not, perhaps, the place to discuss Harlem's very complex attitude toward black policemen, nor the reasons, according to Harlem, that they are nearly all downtown.)

It is hard, on the other hand, to blame the policeman, blank, goodnatured, thoughtless, and insuperably innocent, for being such a perfect representative of the people he serves. He, too, believes in good intentions and is astounded and offended when they are not taken for the deed. He has never, himself, done anything for which to be hated—which of us has?—and yet he is facing, daily and nightly, people who would gladly see him dead, and he knows it. There is no way for him not to know it: there are few things under heaven more unnerving than the silent, accumulating contempt and hatred of a people. He moves through Harlem, therefore, like an occupying soldier in a bitterly hostile country; which is precisely what, and where, he is, and is the reason he walks in twos and threes. And he is not the only one who knows why he is always in company: the people who are watching him know why, too. Any street meeting, sacred or secular, which he and his colleagues uneasily cover has as its explicit or implicit burden the cruelty and injustice of the white domination. And these days, of course, in terms increasingly vivid and jubilant, it speaks of the end of that domination. The white policeman standing on a Harlem street corner finds himself at the very center of the revolution now occurring in the world. He is not prepared for it—naturally, nobody is—and, what is possibly much more to the point, he is exposed, as few white people are, to the anguish of the black people around him. Even if he is gifted with the merest mustard grain of imagination, something must seep in. He cannot avoid observing that some of the children, in spite of their color, remind him of children he has known and loved, perhaps even of his own children. He knows that he certainly does not want *his* children living this way. He can retreat from his uneasiness in only one direction: into a callousness which very shortly becomes second nature. He becomes more callous, the population becomes more hostile, the situation grows more tense, and the police force is increased. One day, to everyone's astonishment, someone drops a match in the powder keg and everything blows up. Before the dust has settled or the blood congealed, editorials, speeches, and civil-rights commissions are loud in the land, demanding to know what happened. What happened is that Negroes want to be treated like men.

Negroes want to be treated like men: a perfectly straightforward statement, containing only seven words. People who have mastered Kant, Hegel, Shakespeare, Marx, Freud, and the Bible find this statement utterly impenetrable. The idea seems to threaten profound, barely conscious assumptions. A kind of panic paralyzes their features, as though they found themselves trapped on the edge of a steep place. I once tried to describe to a very well-known American intellectual the conditions among Negroes in the South. My recital disturbed him and made him indignant; and he asked me in perfect innocence, "Why don't all the Negroes in the South move North?" I tried to explain what *has* happened, unfailingly, whenever a significant body of Negroes move North. They do not escape Jim Crow: they merely encounter another, not-less-deadly variety. They do not move to Chicago, they move to the South Side; they do not move to New York, they move to Harlem. The pressure within the ghetto causes the ghetto walls to expand, and this expansion is always violent. White people hold the line as long as they can, and in as many ways as they can, from verbal intimidation to physical violence. But inevitably the border which has divided the ghetto from the rest of the world falls into the hands of the ghetto. The white people fall back bitterly before the black horde; the landlords make a tidy profit by raising the rent, chopping up the rooms, and all but dispensing with the upkeep; and what has once been a neighborhood turns into a "turf." This is precisely what happened when the Puerto Ricans arrived in their thousands—and the bitterness thus caused is, as I write, being fought out all up and down those streets.

Northerners indulge in an extremely dangerous luxury. They seem to feel that because they fought on the right side during the Civil War, and won, they have earned the right merely to deplore what is going on in the South, without taking any responsibility for it; and that they can ignore what is happening in northern cities because what is happening in Little Rock or Birmingham is worse. Well, in the first place, it is not possible for anyone who has not endured both to know which is "worse." I know Negroes who prefer the South and white southerners, because "At least there, you haven't got to play any guessing games." The guessing games referred to have driven more than one Negro into the narcotics ward, the madhouse, or the river. I know another Negro, a man very dear to me, who says, with conviction and with truth, "The spirit of the South is the spirit of America." He was born in the North and did his military training in the South. He did not, as far as I can gather, find the South "worse"; he found it, if anything, all too familiar. In the second place, though, even if Birmingham *is* worse, no doubt Johannesburg, South Africa, beats it by several miles, and Buchenwald was one of the worst things that ever happened in the entire history of the world. The world has never lacked for horrifying examples; but I do not believe that these examples are meant to be used as justification for our own crimes. This perpetual justification empties the heart of all human feeling. The emptier our hearts become, the greater will be our crimes. Thirdly, the South is not merely an embarrassingly backward region, but a part of this country, and what happens there concerns every one of us.

As far as the color problem is concerned, there is but one great difference between the southern white and the northerner: the southerner remembers, historically and in his own psyche, a kind of Eden in which he loved black people and they loved him. Historically, the flaming sword laid across this Eden is the Civil War. Personally, it is the southerner's sexual coming of age, when, without any warning, unbreakable taboos are set up between himself and his past. Everything, thereafter, is permitted him except the love he remembers and has never ceased to need. The resulting, indescribable torment affects every southern mind and is the basis of the southern hysteria.

None of this is true for the northerner. Negroes represent nothing to him personally, except, perhaps, the dangers of carnality. He never sees Negroes. Southerners see them all the time. Northerners never think about them whereas southerners are never really thinking of anything else. Negroes are, therefore, ignored in the North and are under surveillance in the South, and suffer hideously in both places. Neither the southerner nor northerner is able to look on the Negro simply as a man. It seems to be indispensable to the national self-esteem that the Negro be considered either as a kind of ward (in which case we are told how many Negroes, comparatively, bought Cadillacs last year and how few, comparatively, were lynched), or as a victim (in which case we are promised that he will never vote in our assemblies or go to school with our kids). They are two sides of the same coin and the South will not change—*cannot* change—until the North changes. The country will not change until it reexamines itself and discovers what it really means by freedom. In the meantime, generations keep being born, bitterness is increased by incompetence, pride, and folly, and the world shrinks around us.

It is a terrible, an inexorable, law that one cannot deny the humanity of another without diminishing one's own: in the face of one's victim, one sees oneself. Walk through the streets of Harlem and see what we, this nation, have become.

1960

New York Scenes, from Lonesome Traveler, *Jack Kerouac (1960)*

The "Beat Generation"—though the poet Gary Snyder once quipped that "three or four people don't really make up a generation"—began when Jack Kerouac met Lucien Carr (father of another New York novelist, Caleb Carr) in the West End Bar (114th and West End Avenue) when both were students at Columbia. Kerouac had actually arrived at Columbia, from his native Lowell, Massachusetts, as a football recruit after a postgraduate year at the Horace Mann School in the Bronx. But he broke his leg freshman year, read Thomas Wolfe, and "roamed his [Wolfe's] New York on crutches." Carr then introduced Kerouac to Allen Ginsberg and William Burroughs, and that cadre made Times Square, not Greenwich Village, their geographical nexus.

Kerouac's first book, *The Town and the City,* takes place largely in Times Square and is modeled on Wolfe's fiction. Kerouac's method of writing was frenetic, what he called "spontaneous"; he wrote his most famous work, *On the Road,* on a roll of teletype paper in his apartment at 454 West Twentieth Street in three weeks, and his next novel, *The Subterraneans,* was created in only three days of coffee- and Benzedrine-fueled energy.

"New York Scenes" is from one of his last books, *Lonesome Traveler,* and chronicles "the beat night life." In Kerouac's travels through the city at night it is obvious how the "Beats" were, as Alfred Kazin called them, "a family of friends" embracing what Kerouac called "all the mad joy you have" when you come to New York City.

AT this time my mother was living alone in a little apartment in Jamaica Long Island, working in the shoe factory, waiting for me to come home so I could keep her company and escort her to Radio City once a month. She had a tiny bedroom waiting for me, clean linen in the dresser, clean sheets in the bed. It was a relief after all the sleepingbags and bunks and railroad earth. It was another of the many opportunities she's given me all her life to just stay home and write.

I always give her all my leftover pay. I settled down to long sweet sleeps, day-long meditations in the house, writing, and long walks around beloved old Manhattan a half hour subway ride away. I roamed the streets, the bridges, Times Square, cafeterias, the waterfront, I looked up all my poet beatnik friends and roamed with them, I had love affairs with girls in the Village, I did everything with that great mad joy you get when you return to New York City.

I've heard great singing Negroes call it "The Apple!"

"There now is your insular city of the Manhattoes, belted round by wharves," sang Herman Melville.

"Bound round by flashing tides," sang Thomas Wolfe.

Whole panoramas of New York everywhere, from New Jersey, from skyscrapers.—

Even from bars, like a Third Avenue bar—4 P.M. the men are all roaring in clink bonk glass brass-foot barrail "where ya goin" excitement—October's in the air, in the Indian Summer sun of door.—Two Madison Avenue salesmen who been working all day long come in young, well dressed, justsuits, puffing cigars, glad to have the day done and the drink comin in, side by side march in smiling but there's no room at the roaring (Shit!) crowded bar so they stand two deep from it waiting and smiling and talking.—Men do love bars and good bars should be loved.—It's full of businessmen, workmen, Finn MacCools of Time.—Be-overalled oldgray topers dirty and beerswiggin glad.—Nameless truck busdrivers with flashlites slung from hips—old beatfaced beerswallowers sadly upraising purple lips to happy drinking ceilings.—Bartenders are fast, courteous, interested in their work as well as clientele.—Like Dublin at 4:30 P.M. when the work is done, but this is great New York Third Avenue, free lunch, smells of Moody street exhaust river lunch in road of grime bysmashing the door, guitarplaying long sideburned heroes smell out there on wood doorsteps of afternoon drowse.—But it's New York towers rise beyond, voices crash mangle to talk and chew the gossip till Earwicker drops his load—Ah Jack Fitzgerald Mighty Murphy where are you?.—Semi bald blue shirt tattered shovellers in broken end dungarees fisting glasses of glistenglass foam top brown afternoon beer.—The subway rumbles underneath as man in homburg in vest but coatless executive changes from right to left foot on ye brass rail.—Colored man in hat, dignified, young, paper underarm, says goodbye at bar warm and paternal leaning over men—elevator operator around the corner.—And wasnt this where they say Novak the real estator who used to stay up late a-nights linefaced to become right and rich in his little white worm cellule of the night typing up reports and letters wife and kids go mad at home at eleven P.M.—ambitious, worried, in a little office of the Island, right on the street undignified but open to all business and in infancy any business can be small as ambition's big—pushing how many daisies now? and never made his million, never had a drink with So Long Gee Gee and I Love You Too in this late afternoon beer room of men excited shifting stools and footbottom rail scuffle heel soles in New York?—Never called Old Glasses over and offered his rim red nose a drink—never laughed and let the fly his nose use as a landingmark—but ulcerated in the middle of the night to be rich and get his family the best.—So the best American sod's his blanket now, made in upper mills of Hudson Bay Moonface Sassenach and carted down by housepainter in white coveralls (silent) to rim the roam of his once formed flesh, and let worms ram—Rim! So have another beer, topers—Bloody mugglers! Lovers!

My friends and I in New York city have our own special way of having fun without having to spend much money and most important of all without having to be importuned by formalistic bores, such as, say, a swell evening at the mayor's ball.—We dont have to shake hands and we dont have to make appointments and we feel all right.—We sorta wander around like children.—We walk into parties and tell everybody what we've been doing and people think we're showing off.—They say: "Oh look at the beatniks!"

Take, for example, this typical evening you can have:—

Emerging from the Seventh Avenue subway on 42nd Street, you pass the john, which is the beatest john in New York—you never can tell if it's open or not, usually there's a big chain in front of it saying it's out of order, or else it's got some white-haired decaying monster slinking outside, a john which all seven million people in New York City have at one time passed and taken strange notice of—past the new charcoal-fried-hamburger stand, Bible booths, operatic jukeboxes, and a seedy underground used-magazine store next to a peanut-brittle store smelling of subway arcades—here and there a used copy of that old bard Plotinus sneaked in with the remainders of collections of German high-school textbooks—where they sell long ratty-looking hotdogs (no, actually they're quite beautiful, particularly if you havent got 15 cents and are looking for someone in Bickford's Cafeteria who can lay some smash on you) (lend you some change).—

Coming up that stairway, people stand there for hours and hours drooling in the rain, with soaking wet umbrellas—lots of boys in dungarees scared to go into the Army standing halfway up the stairway on the iron steps waiting for God Who knows what, certainly among them some romantic heroes just in from Oklahoma with ambitions to end up yearning in the arms of some unpredictable sexy young blonde in a penthouse on the Empire State Building—some of them probably stand there dreaming of owning the Empire State Building by virtue of a magic spell which they've dreamed up by a creek in the backwoods of a ratty old house on the outskirts of Texarkana.—Ashamed of being seen going into the dirty movie (what's its name?) across the street from the New York *Times*—The lion and the tiger passing, as Tom Wolfe used to say about certain types passing that corner.—

Leaning against that cigar store with a lot of telephone booths on the corner of 42nd and Seventh where you make beautiful telephone calls looking out into the street and it gets real cozy in there when it's raining outside and you like to prolong the conversation, who do you find? Basketball teams? Basketball coaches? All those guys from the rollerskating rink go there? Cats from the Bronx again, looking for some action, really looking for romance? Strange duos of girls coming out of dirty movies? Did you ever see them? Or bemused drunken businessmen with their hats tipped awry on their graying heads staring catatonically upward at the signs floating by on the Times Building, huge sentences about Khrushchev reeling by, the populations of Asia enumerated in flashing lightbulbs, always five hundred periods after each sentence.—Suddenly a psychopathically worried policeman appears on the corner and tells everybody to go away.—This is the center of the greatest city the world has ever known and this is what beatniks do here.—"Standing on the street corner waiting for no one is Power," sayeth poet Gregory Corso.

Instead of going to night clubs—if you're in a position to make the nightclub scene (most beatniks rattle empty pockets passing Birdland)—how strange to stand on the sidewalk and just watch that weird eccentric from Second Avenue looking like Napoleon going by feeling cooky crumbs in his pocket, or a young 15-year-old kid with a bratty face, or suddenly somebody swishing by in a baseball hat (because that's what you see), and finally an old lady dressed in seven hats and a long ratty fur coat in the middle of the July night carrying a huge Russian woolen purse filled with scribbled bits of paper which say "Festival Foundation Inc., 70,000 Germs" and moths flying out of her sleeve—she rushes up and importunes Shriners. And dufflebag soldiers without a war—harmonica players off freight trains.—Of course there are the normal New Yorkers, looking ridiculously out of place and as odd as their own neat oddity, carrying pizzas and *Daily Newses* and headed for brown basements or Pennsylvania trains—W. H. Auden himself may be seen fumbling by in the rain—Paul Bowles, natty in a Dacron suit, passing through on a trip from Morocco, the ghost of Herman Melville himself followed by Bartleby the Wall Street Scrivener and Pierre the ambiguous hipster of 1848 out on a walk—to see what's up in the news flashes of the *Times*—Let's go back to the corner newsstand.—SPACE BLAST . . . POPE WASHES FEET OF POOR . . .

Let's go across the street to Grant's, our favored dining place. For 65 cents you get a huge plate of fried clams, a lot of French fried potatoes, a little portion of cole slaw, some tartar sauce, a little cup of red sauce for fish, a slice of lemon, two slices of fresh rye bread, a pat of butter, another ten cents brings a glass of rare birch beer.—What a ball it is to eat here! Migrations of Spaniards chewing on hotdogs, standing up, leaning against big pots of mustard.—Ten different counters with different specialties.—Ten-cent cheese sandwiches, two liquor bars for the Apocalypse, oh yeah and great indifferent bartenders.—And cops that stand in the back getting free meals—drunken saxophone players on the nod—lonely dignified ragpickers from Hudson Street supping soup without a word to anybody, with black fingers, woe.—Twenty thousand customers a day—fifty thousand on rainy days—one hundred thousand on snowy days.—Operation twenty-four hours a night. Privacy—supreme under a glary red light full of conversation.—Toulouse-Lautrec, with his deformity and cane, sketching in the corner.—You can stay there for five minutes and gobble up your food, or else stay there for hours having insane philosophical conversation with your buddy and wondering about the people.—"Let's have a hotdog before we go to the movie!" and you get so high in there you never get to the movies because it's better than a show about Doris Day on a holiday in the Caribbean.

"But what are we gonna do tonight? Marty would go to a movie but we're going to connect for some junk.—Let's go down to the Automat."

"Just a minute, I've got to shine my shoes on top of a fire hydrant."

"You wanta see yourself in the fun mirror?"

"Wanta take four pictures for a quarter? Because we're on the eternal scene. We can look at the picture and remember it when we're wise old white-haired Thoreaus in cabins."

"Ah, the fun mirrors are gone, they used to have fun mirrors here."

"How about the Laff Movie?"

"That's gone too."

"They got the flea circus."

"They still got donzinggerls?"

"The burlesque is gone millions and millions of years ago."

"Shall we go down by the Automat and watch the old ladies eating beans, or the deaf-mutes that stand in front of the window there and you watch 'em and try to figure the invisible language as it flees across the window from face to face and finger to finger . . . ? Why does Times Square feel like a big room?"

Across the street is Bickford's, right in the middle of the block under the Apollo Theater marquee and right next door to a little bookshop that specializes in Havelock Ellis and Rabelais with thousands of sex fiends leafing at the bins.—Bickford's is the greatest stage on Times Square—many people have hung around there for years man and boy searching God alone knows for what, maybe some angel of Times Square who would make the whole big room home, the old homestead—civilization needs it.—What's Times Square doing there anyway? Might as well enjoy it.—Greatest city the world has ever seen.—Have they got a Times Square on Mars? What would the Blob do on Times Square? Or St. Francis?

A girl gets off a bus in the Port Authority Terminal and goes into Bickford's, Chinese girl, red shoes, sits down with coffee, looking for daddy.

There's a whole floating population around Times Square that has always made Bickford's their headquarters day and night. In the old days of the beat generation some poets used to go in there to meet the famous character "Hunkey" who used to come in and out in an oversized black raincoat and a cigarette holder looking for somebody to lay a pawnticket on—Remington typewriter, portable radio, black raincoat—to score for some toast, (get some money) so he can go uptown and get in trouble with the cops or any of his boys. Also a lot of stupid gangsters from 8th Avenue used to cut in—maybe they still do—the ones from the early days are all in jail or dead. Now the poets just go there and smoke a peace pipe, looking for the ghost of Hunkey or his boys, and dream over the fading cups of tea.

The beatniks make the point that if you went there every night and stayed there you could start a whole Dostoevski season on Times Square by yourself and meet all the midnight newspaper peddlers and their involvements and families and woes—religious fanatics who would take you home and give you long sermons over the kitchen table about the "new apocalypse" and similar ideas:—"My Baptist minister back in Winston-Salem told me the reason that God invented television was that when Christ comes back to earth again they shall crucify Him right on the streets of this here Babylon and they gonna have television cameras pointin' down on that spot and the streets shall run with blood and every eye shall see."

Still hungry, go out down to the Oriental Cafeteria—"favored dining spot" also—some night life—cheap—down in the basement across the street from the Port Authority monolith bus terminal on 40th Street and eat big oily lambs' heads with Greek rice for 90¢.—Oriental zig-zag tunes on the jukebox.

Depends how high you are by now—assuming you've picked up on one of the corners—say 42nd Street and 8th Avenue, near the great Whelan's drug store, another lonely haunt spot where you can meet people—Negro whores, ladies limping in a Benzedrine psychosis.—Across the street you can see the ruins of New York already started—the Globe Hotel being torn down there, an empty tooth hole right on 44th Street—and the green McGraw-Hill building gaping up in the sky, higher than you'd believe—lonely all by itself down towards the Hudson River where freighters wait in the rain for their Montevideo limestone.—

Might as well go on home. It's getting old.—Or: "Let's make the Village or go to the Lower East Side and play Symphony Sid on the radio—or play our Indian records—and eat big dead Puerto Rican steaks—or lung stew—see if Bruno has slashed any more car roofs in Brooklyn—though Bruno's gentled now, maybe he's written a new poem."

Or look at Television. Night life—Oscar Levant talking about his melancholia on the Jack Paar show.

The Five Spot on 5th Street and Bowery sometimes features Thelonious Monk on the piano and you go on there. If you know the proprietor you sit down at the table free with a beer, but if you dont know him you can sneak in and stand by the ventilator and listen. Always crowded weekends. Monk cogitates with deadly abstraction, clonk, and makes a statement, huge foot beating delicately on the floor, head turned to one side listening, entering the piano.

Lester Young played there just before he died and used to sit in the back kitchen between sets. My buddy poet Allen Ginsberg went back and got on his knees and asked him what he would do if an atom bomb fell on New York. Lester said he would break the window in Tiffany's and get some jewels anyway. He also said, "What you doin' on your knees?" not realizing he is a great hero of the beat generation and now enshrined. The Five Spot is darkly lit, has weird waiters, good music always, sometimes John "Train" Coltrane showers his rough notes from his big tenor horn all over the place. On weekends parties of well-dressed uptowners jam-pack the place talking continuously—nobody minds.

O for a couple of hours, though, in the Egyptian Gardens in the lower

West Side Chelsea district of Greek restaurants.—Glasses of ouzo, Greek liqueur, and beautiful girls dancing the belly dance in spangles and beaded bras, the incomparable Zara on the floor and weaving like mystery to the flutes and tingtang beats of Greece—when she's not dancing she sits in the orchestra with the men plapping a drum against her belly, dreams in her eyes.—Huge crowds of what appear to be Suburbia couples sit at the tables clapping to the swaying Oriental idea.—If you're late you have to stand along the wall.

Wanta dance? The Garden Bar on Third Avenue where you can do fantastic sprawling dances in the dim back room to a jukebox, cheap, the waiter doesnt care.

Wanta just talk? The Cedar Bar on University Place where all the painters hang out and a 16-year-old kid who was there one afternoon squirting red wine out of a Spanish wine skin into his friends' mouths and kept missing. . . .

The night clubs of Greenwich Village known as the Half Note, the Village Vanguard, the Café Bohemia, the Village Gate also feature jazz (Lee Konitz, J. J. Johnson, Miles Davis), but you've got to have mucho money and it's not so much that you've got to have mucho money but the sad commercial atmosphere is killing jazz and jazz *is* killing itself there, because jazz belongs to open joyful ten-cent beer joints, as in the beginning.

There's a big party at some painter's loft, wild loud flamenco on the phonograph, the girls suddenly become all hips and heels and people try to dance between their flying hair.—Men go mad and start tackling people, flying wedges hurtle across the room, men grab men around the knees and lift them nine feet from the floor and lose their balance and nobody gets hurt, blonk.—Girls are balanced hands on men's knees, their skirts falling and revealing frills on their thighs.—Finally everybody dresses to go home and the host says dazedly.—"You all look so *respectable.*"

Or somebody just had an opening, or there's a poetry reading at the Living Theater, or at the Gaslight Café, or at the Seven Arts Coffee Gallery, up around Times Square (9th Avenue and 43rd Street, amazing spot) (begins at midnight Fridays), where afterward everybody rushes out to the old wild bar.—Or else a huge party at Leroi Jones's—he's got a new issue of Yugen Magazine which he printed himself on a little cranky machine and everybody's poems are in it, from San Francisco to Gloucester Mass., and costs only 50 cents.—Historic publisher, secret hipster of the trade.—Leroi's getting sick of parties, everyone's always taking off his shirt and dancing, three sentimental girls are crooning over poet Raymond Bremser, my buddy Gregory Corso is arguing with a New York *Post* reporter saying, "But you dont understand Kangaroonian weep! Forsake thy trade! Flee to the Enchenedian Islands!"

Let's get out of here, it's too literary.—Let's go get drunk on the Bowery or eat those long noodles and tea in glasses at Hong Fat's in Chinatown.—What are we always eating for? Let's walk over the Brooklyn Bridge and build up another appetite.—How about some okra on Sands Street?

Shades of Hart Crane!

"Let's go see if we can find Don Joseph!"

"Who's Don Joseph?"

Don Joseph is a terrific cornet player who wanders around the Village with his little mustache and his arms hangin at the sides with the cornet, which creaks when he plays softly, nay whispers, the greatest sweetest cornet since Bix and more.—He stands at the jukebox in the bar and plays with the music for a beer.—He looks like a handsome movie actor.—He's the great super glamorous secret Bobby Hackett of the jazz world.

What about that guy Tony Fruscella who sits crosslegged on the rug and plays Bach on his trumpet, by ear, and later on at night there he is blowing with the guys at a session, modern jazz—

Or George Jones the secret Bowery shroud who plays great tenor in parks at dawn with Charley Mariano, for kicks, because they love jazz, and that time on the waterfront at dawn they played a whole session as the guy beat on the dock with a stick for the beat.

Talkin of Bowery shrouds, what about Charley Mills walkin down the street with bums drinkin his bottle of wine singing in twelve tone scale.

"Let's go see the strange great secret painters of America and discuss their paintings and their visions with them—Iris Brodie with her delicate fawn Byzantine filigree of Virgins—"

"Or Miles Forst and his black bull in the orange cave."

"Or Franz Klein and his spiderwebs."

"His bloody spiderwebs!"

"Or Willem de Kooning and his White."

"Or Robert De Niro."

"Or Dody Muller and her Annunciations in seven feet tall flowers."

"Or Al Leslie and his giant feet canvases."

"Al Leslie's giant is sleeping in the Paramount building."

There's another great painter, his name is Bill Heine, he's a really secret subterranean painter who sits with all those weird new cats in the East Tenth street coffeeshops that dont look coffeeshops at all but like sorta Henry Street basement secondhand clothes stores except you see an African sculpture or maybe a Mary Frank sculpture over the door and inside they play Frescobaldi on the hi fi.

Ah, let's go back to the Village and stand on the corner of Eighth Street and Sixth Avenue and watch the intellectuals go by.—AP reporters lurching home to their basement apartments on Washington Square, lady editorialists with huge German police dogs breaking their chains, lonely dikes melting by, unknown experts on Sherlock Holmes with blue fingernails going up to their rooms to take scopolamine, a muscle-bound young man in a cheap gray German suit explaining something weird to his fat girl friend, great editors leaning politely at the newsstand buying the early edition of the *Times,* great fat furniture movers out of 1910 Charlie Chaplin films coming home with great bags full of chop suey (feeding everybody), Picasso's melancholy harlequin now owner of a print and frame shop musing on his wife and newborn child lifting up his finger for a taxi, rolypoly recording engineers rush in fur hats, girl artists down from Columbia with D. H. Lawrence problems picking up 50-year-old men, old men in the Kettle of Fish, and the melancholy spectre of New York Women's prison that looms high and is folded in silence as the night itself—at sunset their windows look like oranges—poet e. e. cummings buying a package of cough drops in the shade of that monstrosity.—If it's raining you can stand under the awning in front of Howard Johnson's and watch the street from the other side.

Beatnik Angel Peter Orlovsky in the supermarket five doors away buying Uneeda Biscuits (late Friday night), ice cream, caviar, bacon, pretzels, sodapop, *TV Guide,* Vaseline, three toothbrushes, chocolate milk (dreaming of roast suckling pig), buying whole Idaho potatoes, raisin bread, wormy cabbage by mistake, and fresh-felt tomatoes and collecting purple stamps.—Then he goes home broke and dumps it all on the table, takes out a big book of Mayakovsky poems, turns on the 1949 television set to the horror movie, and goes to sleep.

And this is the beat night life of New York.

The Blackout, November 9, 1965, from POPism: The Warhol '60's, *Andy Warhol (1980)*

Andy Warhol was famous for much longer than the allotted "fifteen minutes" that he thought everyone would get at some time in the future. He was born to Czechoslovak immigrant parents in Pittsburgh in 1930, but Warhol's larger-than-life persona demanded a stage as enormous as New York for its playing out. His first work in New York was doing advertisements for the I. Miller Shoe Company. In the early 1960s, however, Warhol became the most famous practitioner of what was called "Pop Art." His ability to hold a creative tension between the commercial entertainment world and the world of "high" art produced silk-screened images of Marilyn Monroe, Elvis Presley, and even Mao. Warhol spent much of his career managing his "Factory," located primarily off Union Square after 1968, where he produced paintings, films, and rock and roll. He also supported and collaborated with young artists such as Keith Haring and Jean-Michel Basquiat.

Warhol's art had a playful political side to it as well. In 1964 Philip Johnson, the architect for the New York State Pavilion at the World's Fair at Flushing Meadows, commissioned an avant-garde piece from Warhol. Warhol attached a giant silk-screen blowup of the police department's *Thirteen Most Wanted Men.* Forced to remove the images, Warhol wanted to replace them with giant images of Robert Moses, the fair's czar.

WE were really laughing hard, and Paul and Gerard were fighting with someone out in the corridor when Edie, who had the TV on, started getting very excited, saying there was a big power blackout in the Northeast over eight states and two Canadian provinces, and we were missing it! We all wanted to get right back up to New York, but we were scheduled to go to a screening and pose for pictures. We checked right out of the hotel, ran over to the theater, did our number there quick, and jumped into a limousine for the return trip.

All the way back to New York, we kept hoping the blackout would still be going on when we got there. We couldn't go through any tunnels—the radio was saying they couldn't ventilate them without electricity—and when we got to the bridge, we couldn't see any lights on the whole Manhattan skyline, just car headlights. The moon was full and it was all like a big party somehow—we drove through the Village and everybody was dancing around, lighting candles. Chock Full o' Nuts looked so elegant all lit by candles. There were no traffic lights on, so of course everything moved very slowly—the buses were just creeping. People in suits and briefcases were sleeping in doorways, because all the hotels were booked solid, and Governor Rockefeller had had to open the armories up.

There were cute National Guard soldiers around helping people up out of the stuck subways and I thought that down there must be the worst place to be—the only thing that could ruin a beautiful idea like this. It was the biggest, most Pop happening of the sixties, really—it involved everybody.

After driving around a little, we went over to Ondine and then on to Le Club where we stayed until the lights started going on around four. Then all around the city things started coming to life like the Sleeping Beauty castle.

The Balloon, Donald Barthelme (1968)

Donald Barthelme was born in Philadelphia but grew up in Houston, Texas. He moved to New York in 1962 to be the managing editor of an art-literary review called *Location*. Barthelme sold his first story to *The New Yorker* the following year and moved to an apartment on West 11th Street in Greenwich Village. He continued to be a regular contributor to various magazines and produced hundreds of short stories, and four novels, as well as fables and children's books, before his death from cancer in 1989.

Barthelme has been called an "existentialist" and a "postmodernist," but he was first and foremost a relentless experimenter and innovator. In his essay "Not-Knowing," Barthelme wrote, "Art is not difficult because it wishes to be difficult, but because it wishes to be art." Later in that same essay he made a remark that he applied to Rauschenberg's famous goat and tire but might equally apply to all of New York City, "What is magical about the object is that it at once invites and resists interpretation. Its artistic worth is measurable by the degree to which it remains, after interpretation, vital—no interpretation or cardiopulmonary push-pull can exhaust or empty it."

THE balloon, beginning at a point on Fourteenth Street, the exact location of which I cannot reveal, expanded northward all one night, while people were sleeping, until it reached the Park. There, I stopped it, at dawn the northernmost edges lay over the Plaza, the free-hanging motion was frivolous and gentle. But experiencing a faint irritation at stopping, even to protect the trees, and seeing no reason the balloon should not be allowed to expand upward, over the parts of the city it was already covering, into the "air space" to be found there, I asked the engineers to see to it. This expansion took place throughout the morning, soft imperceptible sighing of gas through the valves. The balloon then covered forty-five blocks north-south and an irregular area east-west, as many as six crosstown blocks on either side of the Avenue in some places. That was the situation, then.

But it is wrong to speak of "situations," implying sets of circumstances leading to some resolution, some escape of tension, there were no situations, simply the balloon hanging there—muted heavy grays and browns for the most part, contrasting with walnut and soft yellows. A deliberate lack of finish, enhanced by skillful installation, gave the surface a rough, forgotten quality, sliding weights on the inside, carefully adjusted, anchored the great, vari-shaped mass at a number of points. Now we have had a flood of original ideas in all media, works of singular beauty as well as significant milestones in the history of inflation, but at that moment there was only *this balloon,* concrete particular, hanging there.

There were reactions. Some people found the balloon "interesting." As a response this seemed inadequate to the immensity of the balloon, the suddenness of its appearance over the city, on the other hand, in the absence of hysteria or other societally induced anxiety, it must be judged a calm, "mature" one. There was a certain amount of initial argumentation about the "meaning" of the balloon; this subsided, because we have learned not to insist on meanings, and they are rarely even looked for now, except in cases involving the simplest, safest phenomena. It was agreed that since the meaning of the balloon could never be known absolutely, extended discussion was pointless, or at least less purposeful than the activities of those who, for example, hung green and blue paper lanterns from the warm gray underside, in certain streets, or seized the occasion to write messages on the surface, announcing their availability for the performance of unnatural acts, or the availability of acquaintances.

Daring children jumped, especially at those points where the balloon hovered close to a building, so that the gap between balloon and building was a matter of a few inches, or points where the balloon actually made contact, exerting an ever-so-slight pressure against the side of a building, so that balloon and building seemed a unity. The upper surface was so structured that a "landscape" was presented, small valleys as well as slight knolls, or mounds; once atop the balloon, a stroll was possible, or even a trip, from one place to another. There was pleasure in being able to run down an incline, then up the opposing slope, both gently graded, or in making a leap from one side to the other. Bouncing was possible, because of the pneumaticity of the surface, and even falling, if that was your wish. That all these varied motions, as well as others, were within one's possibilities, in experiencing the "up" side of the balloon, was extremely exciting for children, accustomed to the city's flat, hard skin. But the purpose of the balloon was not to amuse children.

Too, the number of people, children and adults, who took advantage of the opportunities described was not so large as it might have been: a certain timidity, lack of trust in the balloon, was seen. There was, furthermore, some hostility. Because we had hidden the pumps, which fed helium to the interior, and because the surface was so vast that the authorities could not determine the point of entry—that is, the point at which the gas was injected—a degree of frustration was evidenced by those city officers into whose province such manifestations normally fell. The apparent purposelessness of the balloon was vexing (as was the fact that it was "there" at all). Had we painted, in great letters, "LABORATORY TESTS PROVE" or "18% MORE EFFECTIVE" on the sides of the balloon, this difficulty would have been circumvented. But I could not bear to do so. On the whole these officers were remarkably tolerant, considering the dimensions of the anomaly, this tolerance being the result of, first, secret tests conducted by night that convinced them that little or nothing could be done in the way of removing or destroying the balloon, and, secondly, a public warmth that arose (not uncolored by touches of the aforementioned hostility) toward the balloon, from ordinary citizens.

As a single balloon must stand for a lifetime of thinking about balloons, so each citizen expressed, in the attitude he chose, a complex of attitudes. One man might consider that the balloon had to do with the notion *sullied,* as in the sentence *The big balloon sullied the otherwise clear and radiant Manhattan sky.* That is, the balloon was, in this man's view, an imposture, something inferior to the sky that had formerly been there, something interposed between the people and their "sky." But in fact it was January, the sky was dark and ugly, it was not a sky you could look up into, lying on your back in the street, with pleasure, unless pleasure, for you, proceeded from having been threatened, from having been misused. And the underside of the balloon was a pleasure to look up into, we had seen to that, muted grays and browns for the most part, contrasted with walnut and soft, forgotten yellows. And so, while this man was thinking *sullied,* still there was an admixture of pleasurable cognition in his thinking, struggling with the original perception.

Another man, on the other hand, might view the balloon as if it were part of a system of unanticipated rewards, as when one's employer walks in and says, "Here, Henry, take this package of money I have wrapped for you, because we have been doing so well in the business here, and I admire the way you bruise the tulips, without which bruising your department would not be a success, or at least not the success that it is." For this man the balloon might be a brilliantly heroic "muscle and pluck" experience, even if an experience poorly understood.

Another man might say, "Without the example of —, it is doubtful that —would exist today in its present form," and find many to agree with him, or to argue with him. Ideas of "bloat" and "float" were introduced, as well as concepts of dream and responsibility. Others engaged in remarkably detailed fantasies having to do with a wish either to lose themselves in the balloon, or to engorge it. The private character of these wishes, of their origins, deeply buried and unknown, was such that they were not much spoken of, yet there is evidence that they were widespread. It was also argued that what was important was what you felt when you stood under the balloon; some people claimed that they felt sheltered, warmed, as never before, while enemies of the balloon felt, or reported feeling, constrained, a "heavy" feeling.

Critical opinion was divided:

> "monstrous pourings"
> "harp"
> XXXXXXX "certain contrasts with darker portions"
> "inner joy"
> "large, square corners"
> "conservative eclecticism that has so far governed modern balloon design"
> ::::::: "abnormal vigor"
> "warm, soft lazy passages"
> "Has unity been sacrificed for a sprawling quality?"
> "*Quelle catastrophe!*"
> "munching"

People began, in a curious way, to locate themselves in relation to aspects of the balloon: "I'll be at that place where it dips down into Forty-seventh Street almost to the sidewalk, near the Alamo Chile House," or, "Why don't we go stand on top, and take the air, and maybe walk about a bit, where it forms a tight, curving line with the façade of the Gallery of Modern Art—" Marginal intersections offered entrances within a given time duration, as well as "warm, soft, lazy passages" in which . . . But it is wrong to speak of "marginal intersections," each intersection was crucial, none could be ignored (as if, walking there, you might not find someone capable of turning your attention, in a flash, from old exercises to new exercises, risks and escalations). Each intersection was crucial, meeting of balloon and building, meeting of balloon and man, meeting of balloon and balloon.

It was suggested that what was admired about the balloon was finally this: that it was not limited, or defined. Sometimes a bulge, blister, or sub-section would carry all the way east to the river on its own initiative, in the manner of an army's movements on a map, as seen in a headquarters remote from the fighting. Then that part would be, as it were, thrown back again, or would withdraw into new dispositions; the next morning, that part would have made another sortie, or disappeared altogether. This ability of the balloon to shift its shape, to change, was very pleasing, especially to people whose lives were rather rigidly patterned, persons to whom change, although desired, was not available. The balloon, for the twenty-two days of its existence, offered the possibility, in its randomness, of mislocation of the self, in contradistinction to the grid of precise, rectangular pathways under our feet. The amount of specialized training currently needed, and the consequent desirability of long-term commitments, has been occasioned by the steadily growing importance of complex machinery, in virtually all kinds of operations, as this tendency increases, more and more people will turn, in bewildered inadequacy, to solutions for which the balloon may stand as a prototype, or "rough draft."

I met you under the balloon, on the occasion of your return from Norway; you asked if it was mine, I said it was. The balloon, I said, is a spontaneous autobiographical disclosure, having to do with the unease I felt at your absence, and with sexual deprivation, but now that your visit to Bergen has been terminated, it is no longer necessary or appropriate. Removal of the balloon was easy, trailer trucks carried away the depleted fabric, which is now stored in West Virginia, awaiting some other time of unhappiness, some time, perhaps, when we are angry with one another.

Introduction and Summary, from The Second Regional Plan *(1968)*

In 1968, one year after devastating race riots throughout the country, the nationally funded Kerner Commission, with then Mayor John Lindsay serving as vice-chairman, released its report that concluded that America was rapidly moving toward becoming "two nations—one black and one white." The *Second Regional Plan*, released in the same year, is most notable for its attention to the problem of racial segregation in the inner cities. Whereas the intention of the *1929 Graphic Regional Plan* had been primarily to "ease congestion and improve productivity," the *Second Regional Plan* cited as its second "public concern that launched the Plan" a "segregated society: the growing separation of rich and poor, Negro and white." The report concluded that the movement "of white, middle- and upper-income families from the older cities to the suburbs" continues.

The plan offers as a solution a reversal of the *1929 Graphic Regional Plan*'s call for decentralization and calls for the creation of "two dozen partially self-contained metropolitan communities within the Region." Finally, in answer to the self-addressed question, "What does the Plan add up to?" the report concludes that "it affirms the city's function: bringing people together. But it accepts the suburban value of a one-family house on its own lot for most families with children." Furthermore, it "sets a goal of increasing participation of Negroes and Puerto Ricans in the full life of the Region." In order to achieve that goal, the plan calls for more affordable housing, job training, and guaranteed public employment.

A Plan for a Region

THIS is a plan for what man will build and reserve unbuilt over the coming generation—homes and apartments, factories and offices, highways and railroads, schools and colleges, stores, museums, theatres, parks.

Where people build, what they build, how they build affect all of the urban problems that fill today's newspapers: opportunities for the poor, relations between Negroes and whites, smog, traffic jams. They also affect the abiding issues that do not make headlines: man's relationship to nature, conditions that promote a good society, the form of a great civilization.

So the plan that begins with buildings also gets into questions of costs and values, taxes and government, welfare and recreation, jobs and health care.

Faced with the daily tensions of urban areas related to poverty and race, The Second Regional Plan is shaped to help resolve them. But recognizing, also, the steep climb in income that this economy could provide for everyone if recent economic trends can be continued and the prosperity widely distributed, the Plan also concentrates on arranging the activities of the Region to best allow people to enjoy their new wealth and leisure and use them to genuinely enrich their lives. In seeking the best arrangement of what is built for the New York Metropolitan Region, the Plan paradoxically addresses both the needs of poverty and the tremendous potential of wealth.

The Region of this Plan consists of New York City and more than 12,000 square miles around it in New Jersey, New York and Connecticut. The area was chosen because its parts are closely related in jobs, housing and transportation. (The outlying parts, not yet closely related, may become so during the Plan's life.)

A firm locating a plant or office first decides to locate it somewhere in the Region and then looks for the best place within the Region. So the Region is almost a single economy.

Similarly, a person moving his family to a job in the Region is likely to look in any of dozens of towns or villages—even several counties—for the right place to live. So it is almost a single housing market as well.

The price of a piece of land, then, is related to the value of land throughout the Region, and major highways are located as part of a regional system. In these and other ways, the Region is a unified place and must be planned as a whole.

In different ways, New York City must be planned as a unit, each county in the Region must plan itself and each municipality. The Second Regional Plan does not replace the plans of any of these areas. It provides a view of what is happening and could happen all around them, allowing each to plan more realistically for itself.

This Plan concentrates, therefore, on those activities that affect more than one local area, issues on which only a wider view can assure solutions that best satisfy the needs of all the people of this Region.

Public Concerns That Launched the Plan

The Second Regional Plan was begun when it became clear that large numbers of people were dissatisfied with the prospects of the New York Metropolitan Region of the future. Through meetings, conversations and a formal public response project involving 5,600 volunteers, Goals for the Region, Regional Plan Association identified eight major concerns:

1. *Uncontrolled urbanization:* the swift spread of building without saving enough green space. A general sense (expressed by a significant minority) of too many people, too crowded together with too many more to come.
2. *A segregated society:* the growing separation of rich and poor, Negro and white. The movement continues of white, middle-and upper-income families from the older cities to the suburbs. Unskilled unemployed—mainly Negroes and Puerto Ricans—fill almost every housing unit left by the fleeing middle class. Newark's Negro-Puerto Rican population is about 60 percent, New York City's about 30 percent and both percentages are growing rapidly. Outside the Core and a handful of older cities beyond it, the percentage of Negroes and Puerto Ricans is only 7 percent and growing very little.
3. *Lengthening work trips:* the growing separation of worker and workplace. Many unskilled jobs are moving out but housing is unavailable outside the older cities for unskilled workers; increasing white-collar jobs are in the center while white-collar workers move farther from the center.
4. *Inadequate shelter:* the tight housing market, low rate of replacement of obsolete housing and limited choice of types of new housing even for middle-income families with children. One cause is the zoning by suburban governments, almost uniformly requiring one-family houses on very large lots. One result is that about 1 million people still live in old-law tenements, declared inadequate in 1901.
5. *Few urban advantages:* the lack of big city advantages for the 10 million people in the Region beyond convenient range of the Region's Core. Most of the future population is likely to live beyond this range, also.

For example, only a small minority outside the Core is served by hospitals large enough to provide a broad range of medical skills. High quality library services, adult education, museums, theatres and professional sports are very limited outside the Core compared to large cities elsewhere in the country with many fewer people. And for almost all trips, there is no alternative to driving.

6. *Low transportation standards:* extremely low standards of transportation in most parts of the Region: subways overcrowded, slow, noisy, uncomfortable, infrequent service off-peak; public transportation non-existent in most places; highways congested, local traffic jams in most of the Region. And now traffic jams in the sky, too.
7. *Lack of community focus* in many parts of the Region.
8. *A general tawdriness* about what is built; a system of development that encourages mediocre design, from the individual building to the regional pattern, and an indifference to natural beauty and functioning of nature.

And on the horizon. These problems already are evident. Without any effort to combat them, they would get worse and they would affect far more people.

They would get worse if present trends continue because:

- Population will be rising by 60 percent between 1965 and 2000 and, with rapidly rising incomes, demand for most regional facilities will rise even faster—automobiles and miles driven will go up by about 85 percent, college places by 260 percent, park use by 175 percent—assuring slipshod response if there is no advance consideration of how the demands should be handled.
- The economy has been making a sharp turn from factory jobs which favor spread development to office and service jobs, which often do better in compact urban centers, but plans for future development have scarcely responded to this change.
- The band of spread city—spread and scattered development—wrapped around the Core and older suburbs would cover more land between 1965 and 2000 for the additional 11 million people expected than all the land now urbanized in the Study Area on which 19 million live.
- The islands of the poor and black would enlarge to continents, diminishing the hope for one society.

The problems would affect more people in two ways:

- There will not be enough room in the cities and older suburbs for the children of those who live there. So the city lover, contemptuously dismissing suburban inadequacies as fitting punishment for those who left the city, will find that those inadequacies are the lot of his children. (If all the children of today's 8 million New York City residents remained to live in the City, the population would be 12½ million by 2000, surely unnecessarily crowded.) Similarly, the Scarsdale or Great Neck, Ridgewood or Tenafly residents who feel they have it made—having both the opportunities of the City and the pleasures of a suburban community, must recognize that the older suburbs have no room for their children either, and the new areas are not being built to that mold.
- Fewer city residents would find it convenient to reach large outlying parks like Great Piece Meadows or Bear Mountain because the added population will have filled in between the cities and the parks. At the same time, smaller percentages of non-city residents would find it convenient to get to Manhattan. And there would be no substitute for either outlying regional parks or for Manhattan's opportunities.

Programs to Overcome These Concerns

To turn the trends now causing these concerns, The Second Regional Plan proposes programs in five areas:

1. *Urban centers and metropolitan communities.* To change the amorphous spread of urbanization into genuine metropolitan communities capable of supporting high-quality services in health, retailing, the arts, entertainment (including professional sports), libraries, and adult education (including job training) and to provide a real community framework for civic and political action, The Second Regional Plan proposes the creation of about two dozen partially self-contained metropolitan communities within the Region. These new metropolitan communities would include Brooklyn and Queens and possibly the Bronx, which would be strengthened as distinct communities within New York City.

   New metropolitan communities would be formed by clustering most of the major metropolitan facilities of those areas in a main center, a modern "downtown" for each metropolis. Typically, the facilities would include 30,000–100,000 office jobs, one or more colleges, a major hospital, several department and specialty stores, theatres, a museum, a concert hall, a central library. Around this center would be a large percentage of the apartments the population of the area will need, primarily for households without children. . . .

Most of these centers would grow up where smaller centers are now. First efforts should go toward increasing the office jobs and modernizing the facilities in Jamaica (Queens), downtown Brooklyn and downtown Newark. They are advantageous sites for offices and relatively cheap to serve with added transportation. Equally important, these centers would improve the opportunities for minority groups living nearby. They also would maintain the interest in the old cities of middle- and upper-income people and keep a strong economic and tax base there.

The Manhattan central business district (south of 59th Street) seems likely to gain about 500,000 more office jobs, 35 percent of the Study Area's prospective increase, if new, faster transportation can be provided beyond present plans to build new subways to handle gross overcrowding.

Areas outside the Core will absorb about half the prospective office growth, 650,000–750,000 jobs.

2. *Housing.* Housing now being built for families with children consists predominantly of one-family houses on lots of half-acre or larger. (As a measure, houses in Levittown, Long Island, have yards of one-seventh acre; one-family-house neighborhoods in Queens and the Bronx have about ten houses to the acre.)

The principal reason that almost all new houses are set on large lots is that local governments require it. They want to limit the number of families, and therefore of school children, who can live within the school district because each school child costs the district more taxes. They also want to increase the cost of each house so families pay more taxes. Some favor the policy because it keeps out lower-middle-income families.

The result is that almost no new housing is being built for families with incomes of under $10,000 a year, except government subsidized housing, which is mostly in the old cities. So these families remain crowded into obsolete housing in the older cities. By far the majority of Negro and Puerto Rican families are among these families, and their segregation from the rest of the Region is growing.

Another result of large-lot zoning policies is that even families with enough money to buy a new house have little choice of lot size or type of neighborhood. A third result is that open land is wasted and urban facilities are inefficiently spread out.

The proposed metropolitan communities should have varied types and prices of housing, including some publicly assisted, so these communities are as balanced economically and ethnically as possible. The new centers throughout the Region would help to change the spread housing pattern because there would be a strong demand to live close to them. (Notice the way Manhattan's jobs and activities create a demand to live near them and therefore a willingness to give up living space to do it.) This prospective demand to be close to the new centers, coupled with a change in local zoning to allow builders to put up houses on small lots, attached houses and garden apartments for families with children, would produce a variety of houses and neighborhoods, including cheaper types of housing than we are now building and possibly a restraint on booming land prices.

3. *Poverty and older cities.* Older cities would be helped by the policy of strengthening their business centers, but that is not enough. They will never be pleasant places to live compared to the newer areas until the cost of poverty-related public services is lifted from them. Nor will the poor ever have the quality of education and other public services needed to raise themselves from poverty as long as the cities must contribute a large share of the costs. They just can't afford the substantial added investment in poverty-related public services that are needed. Poverty is a national problem even though free migration within the country has allowed it to concentrate in cities. It should be counteracted by federal funds, not by city and state funds. Furthermore, states should provide more of the cost of education (apart from special education programs to overcome the effects of poverty). Then, cities will have enough tax money to provide much better education for all children, more parks, better maintenance of public places, better public transportation, policing and waste disposal.

With improved public services and modern, growing business and cultural centers in the cities and with housing outside the older cities for those of all incomes who want to live there, these cities will be in a position to attract a diverse population that really wants to live there. . . .

All of this is essential to keep our Region from completely dividing between black and white, rich and poor: making cities attractive to live in, opening housing for families of all income groups outside the older cities, investing much more in education and other special services for the poor but freeing the cities from their share of the financial burden, and slowing in-migration of Negroes and Puerto Ricans so that the older cities have breathing space to renew themselves at much higher quality for families with children. . . .

4. *Nature and design.* Nature. More attention should be paid to a body of knowledge now widely called ecology, which deals with the life cycle of earth, water, plants and animals. Generally, ecologists warn, man should stop upsetting the balances of nature as much as urbanization now does. There is too much draining of wetlands; too much clearing and building on steep slopes, allowing water that once soaked into the ground to pour into the sea; too little concern for animal, bird and fish habitat; too many wastes in air and water.

In general, advice from ecologists adds up to keeping a larger proportion of the Region in a natural state than present development patterns would allow. Instead of scattering housing, factories and things of the city throughout the countryside, city and country should be more clearly distinguished, with city taking less of the earth's surface than our recent spread-city pattern does.

Parks. Much more public parkland either in or near the Region is needed to meet fast-rising demand for outdoor recreation. About 10,000 square miles of the Appalachian Mountains from Vermont to Virginia should be set aside as a green backdrop and recreation area for the residents of the Atlantic Urban Seaboard. All the remaining open oceanfront and large portions of the major river valleys, bayfronts and wetlands should be set aside for outdoor recreation, conservation and aesthetic enjoyment. . . .

Open-space planning should weigh the cost in time and money of the trip to play, both public costs (i.e., roads) and private. Parks like South Mountain Reservation and Jones Beach, once built with city residents in mind, have become surrounded by suburban dwellings. Central city residents find them hard to reach by highway and crowded when they arrive. Costly as city land is for parks, it may be cheaper than buying parks farther out and cutting additional highways through the suburbs to them. One method that might prove feasible in providing outdoor recreation in cities is to depollute rivers and beautify their banks. Pools can be built on the river's edge if the current is too strong or the water not pure enough for swimming.

Environmental quality. Wastes should be managed more rationally so the air and water in the inner parts of the Region are restored to a more natural state, landscapes are kept free of junk, and most remaining wetlands are protected against filling. Five steps would lead to better waste management:

1. Much more research should be done on the damages to the environment from waste disposal (e.g., air and water pollution) and on improving methods of disposal.
2. Costs of waste handling and of the damages to the environment caused by wastes should be charged to those responsible for the decisions that determine the wastes that are generated. This would encourage people to cut down on wastes and to search for more efficient ways of treating them. For example, if the costs of disposable bottles and cans included the full costs of their disposal, including their negative effects on the land, more efficient ways of reusing the glass and metal or destroying them would be sought.
3. Public waste handling should be organized more efficiently, particularly larger units should manage collections and disposal of solid wastes and sewage.
4. A regional organization is needed for research and monitoring of damages from all three forms of wastes—solid, liquid and gaseous.
5. The costs of various levels of environmental quality should be made clear to people so they can register their choice and see that their governments achieve it. . . .

5. *Transportation.* The recommendations already made have important transportation implications. They *require* certain transportation action to make them work; they *make possible* certain transportation goals if we follow them.

Without metropolitan centers in the outlying areas, there is unlikely to be good public transportation.

On the other hand, large centers will require good public transportation. Centers with more than 10 million square feet of non-residential floor space (offices, factories or stores) in a square mile are too large for everyone to arrive by car. (Ten million square feet would house about 40,000 office workers and 10,000 service workers in restaurants, shops, etc.) Travel corridors in which 15,000 persons or more want to move toward a center in the peak hour also require public transportation. Good public transportation must be available before the center becomes so large that it is essential, or developers may resist locating in the center in fear of growing congestion on approaches and streets.

The Core downtowns of Brooklyn, Newark and Jamaica can tap onto the rail network to Manhattan, but the outlying centers will be served mainly by automobile and bus. Clearly the expressways of each new metropolitan area should be focused on the main center in each area. Buses should have their own right-of-way at least during rush hours. Otherwise they can never compete with the automobile in speed door-to-door, and everyone who can afford to will try to drive, clogging the highways and slowing everyone down.

Metropolitan centers linked to Manhattan by railroad will have a distinct business advantage over downtowns outside of the Region. . . .

In sum, good public transportation and express-ways to each center, good rail service throughout the day from each center to Manhattan, and good circulation within the centers are the transportation requirements of successful metropolitan centers. . . .

But important as public transportation is for the Region, even if all the public transportation proposals in this Plan were implemented, probably about 70 percent of all trips in the Region will be made by car in the year 2000 just as they are today. As incomes, number of automobiles, leisure and population all go up substantially, travel by automobile also will skyrocket, if the trends over many years continue. So highway construction also must be continued at almost the pace of construction of the past two decades.

Because expressways allow twice the speed of other roads with a third to a fifth the accident risk, and because they use only a fourth the space for the number of vehicle miles travelled, they should be available for most relatively long trips by car (at least a few miles). They should be built only where a lot of trips will be made, however, not through sparsely settled areas.

The standard of expressway service we recommend is roughly that existing now in Queens, the Bronx and Westchester (comparing total miles driven with total miles driven on expressways—about 35 percent of vehicle miles travelled in these counties are on expressways). Increasing trips on local streets and roads would make some added expressways necessary there. In New Jersey, enough new expressways should be built to double their share of all miles driven and to provide for increasing car-miles driven.

Since improved highways induce people to drive more, there is no precise total of expressway miles that exactly matches the driving demand. Build more and people will drive more. But would they prefer to drive less and have fewer miles of highway cutting through communities and country-side? That must be decided highway by highway. The totals recommended here are our estimates of a reasonable balance over-all, between easy travel and landscape unspoiled by too much highway.

These recommendations call for a large increase in spending for transportation. Comparing the proposed improvements with other goods and services we might buy with the same amount of money over the next decades, this program probably would be worth the cost to most residents. But if we cannot increase the total expenditure on transportation, this Region would benefit from giving priority in transportation spending to the public transportation proposals. Even motorists would gain more from these programs than they would from many highway projects that would be built if highways continue to receive transportation investment priority. . . .

What Do the Proposals Add up To?

That is the Second Regional Plan in summary.

What does the Plan add up to?

It affirms the city's function: bringing people together. But it accepts the suburban value of a one-family house on its own lot for most families with children.

It proposes that each of the Region's residents have both a small local community and a large, metropolitan-sized community. It demonstrates that these communities, though joined like beads on a string along the Eastern Seaboard, can retain their identity.

It provides for a much wider choice of jobs, housing, goods, services, activities and friends than man has ever had before, particularly enlarging these choices for the poor and minority groups.

It sets a goal of increasing participation of Negroes and Puerto Ricans in the full life of the Region.

And it issues a call for man to live in greater harmony with nature even in a huge urban region and to devote more resources to making the urban setting efficient, pleasant and image-able, to which end it offers some principles and processes.

Goodbye to All That, Joan Didion (1968)

Joan Didion was born on December 5, 1934, in Sacramento, California. In 1956, while an undergraduate at Berkeley, she won an essay competition sponsored by *Vogue* magazine. *Vogue* then hired her, and she lived for eight years in New York, during which time she eventually rose to the position of associate features editor. While Didion has written a number of novels and screenplays, her early reputation was made with the publication of two volumes of essays, *Slouching Towards Bethlehem* (1968) and *The White Album* (1979). Among her many accolades have been nominations for a National Book Award in fiction and an American Book Award in nonfiction. After nearly a quarter century of living in Los Angeles, Didion returned to Manhattan in 1988.

In describing her college career, Didion has written that it was an effort "to buy some temporary visa into the world of ideas, to forge for myself a mind that could deal with the abstract. In short, I tried to think. I failed. My attention veered inexorably back to the specific, to the tangible, to what was generally considered, by everyone I knew then and for that matter have known since, the peripheral." But it is precisely those peripheral details that make her prose so compelling and effective. Didion's understanding of what New York means to many young people who have traveled from somewhere else in the United States is beautifully explored in her essay, "Goodbye to All That," whose title alludes to Robert Graves's powerful autobiography about the trenches of the western front in World War I. The search for home has been a consistent theme in Didion's work, and she has written that "the impulse for much writing is homesickness. You are trying to get back home, and in your writing you are invoking that home, so you are assuaging the homesickness."

How many miles to Babylon?
Three score miles and ten—
Can I get there by candlelight?
Yes, and back again—

If your feet are nimble and light
You can get there by candlelight.

IT is easy to see the beginnings of things, and harder to see the ends. I can remember now, with a clarity that makes the nerves in the back of my neck constrict, when New York began for me, but I cannot lay my finger upon the moment it ended, can never cut through the ambiguities and second starts and broken resolves to the exact place on the page where the heroine is no longer as optimistic as she once was. When I first saw New York I was twenty, and it was summertime, and I got off a DC-7 at the old Idlewild temporary terminal in a new dress which had seemed very smart in Sacramento but seemed less smart already, even in the old Idlewild temporary terminal, and the warm air smelled of mildew and some instinct, programmed by all the movies I had ever seen and all the songs I had ever heard sung and all the stories I had ever read about New York, informed me that it would never be quite the same again. In fact it never was. Some time later there was a song on all the jukeboxes on the upper East Side that went "but where is the schoolgirl who used to be me," and if it was late enough at night I used to wonder that. I know now that almost everyone wonders something like that, sooner or later and no matter what he or she is doing, but one of the mixed blessings of being twenty and twenty-one and even twenty-three is the conviction that nothing like this, all evidence to the contrary notwithstanding, has ever happened to anyone before.

Of course it might have been some other city, had circumstances been different and the time been different and had I been different, might have been Paris or Chicago or even San Francisco, but because I am talking about myself I am talking here about New York. That first night I opened my window on the bus into town and watched for the skyline, but all I could see were the wastes of Queens and the big signs that said MIDTOWN TUNNEL THIS LANE and then a flood of summer rain (even that seemed remarkable and exotic, for I had come out of the West where there was no summer rain), and for the next three days I sat wrapped in blankets in a hotel room air-conditioned to 35° and tried to get over a bad cold and a high fever. It did not occur to me to call a doctor, because I knew none, and although it did occur to me to call the desk and ask that the air conditioner be turned off, I never called, because I did not know how much to tip whoever might come—was anyone ever so young? I am here to tell you that someone was. All I could do during those three days was talk long-distance to the boy I already knew I would never marry in the spring. I would stay in New York, I told him, just six months, and I could see the Brooklyn Bridge from my window. As it turned out the bridge was the Triborough, and I stayed eight years.

In retrospect it seems to me that those days before I knew the names of all the bridges were happier than the ones that came later, but perhaps you will see that as we go along. Part of what I want to tell you is what it is like to be young in New York, how six months can become eight years with the deceptive ease of a film dissolve, for that is how those years appear to me now, in a long sequence of sentimental dissolves and old-fashioned trick shots—the Seagram Building fountains dissolve into snowflakes, I enter a revolving door at twenty and come out a good deal older, and on a different street. But most particularly I want to explain to you, and in the process perhaps to myself, why I no longer live in New York. It is often said that New York is a city for only the rich and the very poor. It is less often said that New York is also, at least for those of us who came there from somewhere else, a city for only the very young.

I remember once, one cold bright December evening in New York, suggesting to a friend who complained of having been around too long that he come with me to a party where there would be, I assured him with the bright resourcefulness of twenty-three, "new faces." He laughed literally until he choked, and I had to roll down the taxi window and hit him on the back. "New faces," he said finally, "don't tell me about *new faces.*" It seemed that the last time he had gone to a party where he had been promised "new faces," there had been fifteen people in the room, and he had already slept with five of the women and owed money to all but two of the men. I laughed with him, but the first snow had just begun to fall and the big Christmas trees glittered yellow and white as far as I could see up Park Avenue and I had a new dress and it would be a long while before I would come to understand the particular moral of the story.

It would be a long while because, quite simply, I was in love with New York. I do not mean "love" in any colloquial way, I mean that I was in love with the city, the way you love the first person who ever touches you and never love anyone quite that way again. I remember walking across Sixty-second Street one twilight that first spring, or the second spring, they were all alike for a while. I was late to meet someone but I stopped at Lexington Avenue and bought a peach and stood on the corner eating it and knew that I had come out of the West and reached the mirage. I could taste the peach and feel the soft air blowing from a subway grating on my legs and I could smell lilac and garbage and expensive perfume and I knew that it would cost something sooner or later—because I did not belong there, did not come from there—but when you are twenty-two or twenty-three, you figure that later you will have a high emotional balance, and be able to pay whatever it costs. I still believed in possibilities then, still had the sense, so peculiar to New York, that something extraordinary would happen any minute, any day, any month. I was making only $65 or $70 a week then ("Put yourself in Hattie Carnegie's hands," I was advised without the slightest trace of irony by an editor of the magazine for which I worked), so little money that some weeks I had to charge food at Bloomingdale's gourmet shop in order to eat, a fact which went unmentioned in the letters I wrote to California. I never told my father that I needed money because then he would have sent it, and I would never know if I could do it by myself. At that time making a living seemed a game to me, with arbitrary but quite inflexible rules. And except on a certain kind of winter evening—six-thirty in the Seventies, say, already dark and bitter with a wind off the river, when I would be walking very fast toward a bus and would look in the bright windows of brownstones and see cooks working in clean kitchens and imagine women lighting candles on the floor above and beautiful children being bathed on the floor above that—except on nights like those, I never felt poor; I had the feeling that if I needed money I could always get it. I could write a syndicated column for teenagers under the name "Debbi Lynn" or I could smuggle gold into India or I could become a $100 call girl, and none of it would matter.

Nothing was irrevocable; everything was within reach. Just around every corner lay something curious and interesting, something I had never before seen or done or known about. I could go to a party and meet someone who called himself Mr. Emotional Appeal and ran The Emotional Appeal Institute or Tina Onassis Blandford or a Florida cracker who was then a regular on what he called "the Big C," the Southampton–El Morocco circuit ("I'm well-connected on the Big C, honey," he would tell me over collard greens on his vast borrowed terrace), or the widow of the celery king of the Harlem market or a piano salesman from Bonne Terre, Missouri, or someone who had already made and lost two fortunes in Midland, Texas. I could make promises to myself and to other people and there would be all the time in the world to keep them. I could stay up all night and make mistakes, and none of it would count.

You see I was in a curious position in New York: it never occurred to me that I was living a real life there. In my imagination I was always there for just another few months, just until Christmas or Easter or the first warm day in May. For that reason I was most comfortable in the company of Southerners. They seemed to be in New York as I was, on some indefinitely extended leave from wherever they belonged, disinclined to consider the future, temporary exiles who always knew when the flights left for New Orleans or Memphis or Richmond or, in my case, California. Someone who lives always with a plane schedule in the drawer lives on a slightly different calendar. Christmas, for example, was a difficult season. Other people could take it in stride, going to Stowe or going abroad or going for the day to their mothers' places in Connecticut; those of us who believed that we lived somewhere else would spend it making and canceling airline reservations, waiting for weatherbound flights as if for the last plane out of Lisbon in 1940, and finally comforting one another, those of us who were left, with the oranges and mementos and smoked-oyster stuffings of childhood, gathering close, colonials in a far country.

Which is precisely what we were. I am not sure that it is possible for anyone brought up in the East to appreciate entirely what New York, the idea of New York, means to those of us who came out of the West and the South. To an Eastern child, particularly a child who has always had an uncle on Wall Street and who has spent several hundred Saturdays first at F. A. O. Schwarz and being fitted for shoes at Best's and then waiting under the Biltmore clock and dancing to Lester Lanin, New York is just a city, albeit *the* city, a plausible place for people to live. But to those of us who came from places where no one had heard of Lester Lanin and Grand Central Station was a Saturday radio program, where Wall Street and Fifth Avenue and Madison Avenue were not places at all but abstractions ("Money," and "High Fashion," and "The Hucksters"), New York was no mere city. It was instead an infinitely romantic notion, the mysterious nexus of all love and money and power, the shining and perishable dream itself. To think of "living" there was to reduce the miraculous to the mundane; one does not "live" at Xanadu.

In fact it was difficult in the extreme for me to understand those young women for whom New York was not simply an ephemeral Estoril but a real place, girls who bought toasters and installed new cabinets in their apartments and committed themselves to some reasonable future. I never bought any furniture in New York. For a year or so I lived in other people's apartments; after that I lived in the Nineties in an apartment furnished entirely with things taken from storage by a friend whose wife had moved away. And when I left the apartment in the Nineties (that was when I was leaving everything, when it was all breaking up) I left everything in it, even my winter clothes and the map of Sacramento County I had hung on the bedroom wall to remind me who I was, and I moved into a monastic four-room floor-through on Seventy-fifth Street. "Monastic" is perhaps misleading here, implying some chic severity; until after I was married and my husband moved some furniture in, there was nothing at all in those four rooms except a cheap double mattress and box springs, ordered by telephone the day I decided to move, and two French garden chairs lent me by a friend who imported them. (It strikes me now that the people I knew in New York all had curious and self-defeating sidelines. They imported garden chairs which did not sell very well at Hammacher Schlemmer or they tried to market hair straighteners in Harlem or they ghosted exposés of Murder Incorporated for Sunday supplements. I think that perhaps none of us was very serious, *engagé* only about our most private lives.)

All I ever did to that apartment was hang fifty yards of yellow theatrical silk across the bedroom windows, because I had some idea that the gold light would make me feel better, but I did not bother to weight the curtains correctly and all that summer the long panels of transparent golden silk would blow out the windows and get tangled and drenched in the afternoon thunderstorms. That was the year, my twenty-eighth, when I was discovering that not all of the promises would be kept, that some things are in fact irrevocable and that it had counted after all, every evasion and every procrastination, every mistake, every word, all of it.

That is what it was all about, wasn't it? Promises? Now when New York comes back to me it comes in hallucinatory flashes, so clinically detailed that I sometimes wish that memory would effect the distortion with which it is commonly credited. For a lot of the time I was in New York I used a perfume called *Fleurs de Rocaille,* and then *L'Air du Temps,* and now the slightest trace of either can short-circuit my connections for the rest of the day. Nor can I smell Henri Bendel jasmine soap without falling back into the past, or the particular mixture of spices used for boiling crabs. There were barrels of crab boil in a Czech place in the Eighties where I once shopped. Smells, of course, are notorious memory stimuli, but there are other things which affect me the same way. Blue-and-white striped sheets. Vermouth cassis. Some faded nightgowns which were new in 1959 or 1960, and some chiffon scarves I bought about the same time.

I suppose that a lot of us who have been young in New York have the same scenes on our home screens. I remember sitting in a lot of apartments with a slight headache about five o'clock in the morning. I had a friend who could not sleep, and he knew a few other people who had the same trouble, and we would watch the sky lighten and have a last drink with no ice and then go home in the early morning light, when the streets were clean and wet (had it rained in the night? we never knew) and the few cruising taxis still had their headlights on and the only color was the red and green of traffic signals. The White Rose bars opened very early in the morning; I recall waiting in one of them to watch an astronaut go into space, waiting so long that at the moment it actually happened I had my eyes not on the television screen but on a cockroach on the tile floor. I liked the bleak branches above Washington Square at dawn, and the monochromatic flatness of Second Avenue, the fire escapes and the grilled storefronts peculiar and empty in their perspective.

It is relatively hard to fight at six-thirty or seven in the morning without any sleep, which was perhaps one reason we stayed up all night, and it seemed to me a pleasant time of day. The windows were shuttered in that apartment in the Nineties and I could sleep a few hours and then go to work. I could work then on two or three hours' sleep and a container of coffee from Chock Full O' Nuts. I liked going to work, liked the soothing and satisfactory rhythm of getting out a magazine, liked the orderly progression of four-color closings and two-color closings and black-and-white closings and then The Product, no abstraction but something which looked effortlessly glossy and could be picked up on a newsstand and weighed in the hand. I liked all the minutiae of proofs and layouts, liked working late on the nights the magazine went to press, sitting and reading *Variety* and waiting for the copy desk to call. From my office I could look across town to the weather signal on the Mutual of New York Building and the lights that alternately spelled out TIME and LIFE above Rockefeller Plaza; that pleased me obscurely, and so did walking uptown in the mauve eight o'clocks of early summer evenings and looking at things, Lowestoft tureens in Fifty-seventh Street windows, people in evening clothes trying to get taxis, the trees just coming into full leaf, the lambent air, all the sweet promises of money and summer.

Some years passed, but I still did not lose that sense of wonder about New York. I began to cherish the loneliness of it, the sense that at any given time no one need know where I was or what I was doing. I liked walking, from the East River over to the Hudson and back on brisk days, down around the Village on warm days. A friend would leave me the key to her apartment in the West Village when she was out of town, and sometimes I would just move down there, because by that time the telephone was beginning to bother me (the canker, you see, was already in the rose) and not many people had that number. I remember one day when someone who did have the West Village number came to pick me up for lunch there, and we both had hangovers, and I cut my finger opening him a beer and burst into tears, and we walked to a Spanish restaurant and drank Bloody Marys and *gazpacho* until we felt better. I was not then guilt-ridden about spending afternoons that way, because I still had all the afternoons in the world.

And even that late in the game I still liked going to parties, all parties, bad parties, Saturday-afternoon parties given by recently married couples who lived in Stuyvesant Town, West Side parties given by unpublished or failed writers who served cheap red wine and talked about going to Guadalajara, Village parties where all the guests worked for advertising agencies and voted for Reform Democrats, press parties at Sardi's, the worst kinds of parties. You will have perceived by now that I was not one to profit by the experience of others, that it was a very long time indeed before I stopped believing in new faces and began to understand the lesson in that story, which was that it is distinctly possible to stay too long at the Fair.

I could not tell you when I began to understand that. All I know is that it was very bad when I was twenty-eight. Everything that was said to me I seemed to have heard before, and I could no longer listen. I could no longer sit in little bars near Grand Central and listen to someone complaining of his wife's inability to cope with the help while he missed another train to Connecticut. I no longer had any interest in hearing about the advances other people had received from their publishers, about plays which were having second-act trouble in Philadelphia, or about people I would like very much if only I would come out and meet them. I had already met them, always. There were certain parts of the city which I had to avoid. I could not bear upper Madison Avenue on weekday mornings (this was a particularly inconvenient aversion, since I then lived just fifty or sixty feet east of Madison), because I would see women walking Yorkshire terriers and shopping at Gristede's, and some Veblenesque gorge would rise in my throat. I could not go to Times Square in the afternoon, or to the New York Public Library for any reason whatsoever. One day I could not go into a Schrafft's; the next day it would be Bonwit Teller.

I hurt the people I cared about, and insulted those I did not. I cut myself off from the one person who was closer to me than any other. I cried until I was not even aware when I was crying and when I was not, cried in elevators and in taxis and in Chinese laundries, and when I went to the doctor he said only that I seemed to be depressed, and should see a "specialist." He wrote down a psychiatrist's name and address for me, but I did not go.

Instead I got married, which as it turned out was a very good thing to do but badly timed, since I still could not walk on upper Madison Avenue in the mornings and still could not talk to people and still cried in Chinese laundries. I had never before understood what "despair" meant, and I am not sure that I understand now, but I understood that year. Of course I could not work. I could not even get dinner with any degree of certainty, and I would sit in the apartment on Seventy-fifth Street paralyzed until my husband would call from his office and say gently that I did not have to get dinner, that I could meet him Michael's Pub or at Toots Shor's or at Sardi's East. And then one morning in April (we had been married in January) he called and told me that he wanted to get out of New York for a while, that he would take a six-month leave of absence, that we would go somewhere.

It was three years ago that he told me that, and we have lived in Los Angeles since. Many of the people we knew in New York think this a curious aberration, and in fact tell us so. There is no possible, no adequate answer to that, and so we give certain stock answers, the answers everyone gives. I talk about how difficult it would be for us to "afford" to live in New York right now, about how much "space" we need. All I mean is that I was very young in New York, and that at some point the golden rhythm was broken, and I am not that young any more. The last time I was in New York was in a cold January, and everyone was ill and tired. Many of the people I used to know there had moved to Dallas or had gone on Antabuse or had bought a farm in New Hampshire. We stayed ten days, and then we took an afternoon flight back to Los Angeles, and on the way home from the airport that night I could see the moon on the Pacific and smell jasmine all around and we both knew that there was no longer any point in keeping the apartment we still kept in New York. There were years when I called Los Angeles "the Coast," but they seem a long time ago.

The Yankees, Bruce Catton (1968)

New York City is the Capital of Baseball. The national pastime was born on sandlots near Murray Hill in the 1840s, and it has continued to flourish in its hometown. More than 100 of the 257 ballplayers currently in the Hall of Fame played all or part of their careers in a New York uniform; among these are legends like Christie Mathewson, Babe Ruth, Lou Gehrig, Jackie Robinson, Mickey Mantle, and Willie Mays.

So it is appropriate that the most successful team in New York history is also the most successful team in American history. Between 1921 and 2001, the New York Yankees brought home twenty-six world championships and captured the American League pennant thirty-eight times. Their habit of winning led some opposing fans to claim that cheering for the Yankees was like rooting for U.S. Steel. But the Yankees' success was never preordained and their victories were not without passion—they were the product of talent and teamwork, of larger-than-life personalities and Yankee pride.

The Yankees have seen frustration as well as success. As their great 1970s pitcher Catfish Hunter once remarked after losing a game, "the sun don't shine on the same dog's ass every day." When Pulitzer Prize–winning Civil War historian Bruce Catton (1899–1978) sat down to write this essay, the Yankees were enduring an exceptionally cold moment in the shade. Catton approached his subject as though he were writing an obituary. At a time when New York City itself seemed to be falling apart and fading into the shadows, Catton says an inevitable good-bye "to the whole Yankee era with its bright razzmatazz and pinstriped arrogance, an era that is gone forever."

History has proven Bruce Catton wrong. But he was right about one thing: the New York Yankees *have* always functioned somewhat like a barometer of the state of their city. When things are looking up for the city—the Roaring Twenties, the postwar years of boom and expansion between 1949 and 1962, or the low-crime renaissance of 1996–2000—the Yankees respond with a string of world championships. But when the city is facing the abyss of social dissolution, financial bankruptcy, and high crime—1969, 1973, and 1990—

the Yankees find themselves stuck in the cellar. However, like New York City itself, the Yankees can't be kept down. The tradition of excellence reasserts itself, as when the team reached unprecedented heights, winning a record 127 games in 1998.

IN their long heyday, the New York Yankees were partly a professional baseball team, partly a state of mind, and partly a national affliction. Their golden age began in 1921 and lasted well into the 1960's, and during this era they won the American League pennant twenty-nine times and won the World Series twenty times. They remodelled the game of baseball and they dominated it; through the years their collective personality changed so much that nothing but the habit of winning remained unaltered, and when at last it went, everything else went with it.

The Yankees began as a set of rugged individualists whose idea of strategy was to take the baseball bats and beat the opposing pitcher's brains out. Then they became an organization, a team whose custom it was to have in each position a man who was just a little better than the men other teams had in such positions. Their beginning testified to the power of money; their continued excellence was a triumph of good management; and their sad decline apparently came because they believed too much in their own legend.

Through most of this time the Yankees perfectly represented what might be called the New York Idea, which held that New York had and was the best of everything. No matter what line of work a man was in—finance, industry, communications, the arts, sports, or fashion—he was not really *in* unless he was in New York. New York made the pace; it led the way, and everybody else had to follow and like it.

There are those who say that it was two New York teams, the Knickerbockers of Murray Hill and the New York Baseball Club, who played the first organized baseball game with hard-and-fast rules. The legendary date is June 19, 1846, and the place was a park called the Elysian Fields across the Hudson in Hoboken, New Jersey.

It is certain that New York had a team—called the Highlanders because its ball park was up on Washington Heights—in the American League practically from the AL's founding around 1900. It was strictly a run-of-the-mill outfit which shuttled in and out of the second division, never winning any pennants and rarely coming close, and was somewhat worn down by the fact that it had to compete with the lustrous Giants for patronage. (Later, sportswriter Mark Roth penned the name Yankees, and it stuck.)

Then, in 1915, the team was touched by the hand of fate; that is to say, the Yankee franchise was bought by two New York businessmen, Colonel Jacob Ruppert, a successful brewer and sometime-congressman, and Colonel Tillinghast L'Hommedieu Huston, an engineer who had made a fortune reconstructing Cuba after the Spanish-American War. (Huston had given names of such surpassing beauty that the writers who covered the Yankees worked him into their stories whenever they could think of a good excuse.)

The two colonels were prepared to spend a great deal of money to develop a pennant-winner, but this is a slow process. During the last half century, a good many wealthy men have bought franchises and have tried to buy enough stars to finish on top, and the attempt never works simply because the men who own stars usually refuse to sell. But Ruppert and Huston, after spending four or five years slowly re-building, got an enormous break. They discovered Harry Frazee, who owned the Boston Red Sox.

Frazee was a theatrical magnate, and the theatre interested him more than baseball did; furthermore, he was a plunger, and he was forever wanting money to launch some new theatrical attraction. His Red Sox team was loaded with topflight performers: chief among them was a left-handed pitcher who was just being changed to an outfielder because he could hit more home runs than anyone else in the game. The burly young athlete born in Baltimore in 1859 was named George Herman Ruth, later universally known as the Babe. In 1920 Babe Ruth was just beginning his great career, and the two colonels learned that Frazee was pressed for cash and was willing to make a deal. They promptly made one. Shortly after New Year's Day of 1920, they bought the Babe for $125,000 plus a loan of $350,000. The Yankees were on their way.

Finding Frazee a good man to do business with, the colonels went back to him on a number of occasions, and over a four-year period they bought more than a dozen of his players, many of them first-magnitude stars. Among others, they got pitchers Carl Mays, Sam Jones, Waite Hoyt, Joe Bush, and a slim left-hander named Herb Pennock, who was probably the most completely graceful pitcher in baseball history, to say nothing of being one of the best. They got catcher Wally Schang; Everett Scott, who was considered the finest shortstop in the game; and third baseman Joe Dugan, who enjoyed a similar ranking in his own position. They also got a number of lesser lights who never quite became famous, but who were very useful men to have on a ball club. When these were added to the established players the Yankees already had—first baseman Wally Pipp, pitcher Bob Shawkey, and left fielder Bob Meusel—the team was ready to go.

Before long it was off and running. It won the American League pennant in 1921 and 1922, losing the World Series to the Giants each time. Then, in 1923, the Yankees won the pennant and polished off the Giants in the Series and became world champions. The Yankee era had begun.

Its take-off point was the home run, which is to say, Babe Ruth. Until Ruth's day, home runs were scarce. An American Leaguer who could hit a dozen of them in a whole year was likely to wind up as the home-run leader. The big slugger of the pre-1920 era was J. Franklin Baker of the Philadelphia Athletics—who, aptly enough, finished out his declining years as a Yankee. He was known as Home Run Baker, and he had led the league in homers three times: in 1911 with nine, in 1912 with ten, and in 1913 with twelve. The home run was very special, somewhat like a straight flush in poker. When you got one, it was remembered.

But now Ruth came along, and they began to play poker with the deuces and the one-eyed jacks wild. Having hit 29 of them in his last year with Boston, Ruth went on to hit 54 for the Yankees in 1920; then, in the next few years, 59, 41, and 46; and after a bad year in 1925, he hit 47 in 1926, and then 60 in 1927. Nobody had ever dreamed of anything like this, and baseball was turned upside down. People came out in fantastic numbers to see this new game of the long ball. The Yankees prospered mightily. In 1923 they pulled out of the Polo Grounds, the field they had shared with the Giants, and constructed a place of their own up in the Bronx, Yankee Stadium—"The house that Ruth built"—which could seat 60,000.

Baseball magnates as a group may not be the brightest of living mortals, but in the early 1920's they could recognize a good thing when they saw it, and they perceived that the public liked to watch men hit home runs. Ruth showed the way, and the magnates quietly doctored up the baseball, making it livelier, so that it would travel farther when a good man hit it. The players, no brighter than the magnates but also able to learn a thing or two, began to realize that there was a new era and started swinging from the hips. Traditional baseball of the scratch single, the stolen base, the sacrifice, and the squeeze play went out of the window. Why work for one run at a time if you had some power boys who could knock the runs across in batches? All that mattered was sheer power, and the Yankees had more power than anyone else. And yet, oddly enough, although the Yankees dominated the decade of the 1920's, they set their greatest records later. From 1920 through 1930 they failed to win the American League pennant five times. Sure, they won it six times, but they won only three World Series, and although the record was very good indeed, it was not quite up to what later became the Yankee standard.

In the 1920's, the Yankees were still a gang rather than a team; a gang of all-stars, most of whom had been bought ready-made, who never felt that they had any special need for a manager. All the manager had to do, as far as they were concerned, was pick his starting pitcher and hand the lineup to the umpire. The sluggers would do the rest.

This made life a burden for Miller J. Huggins, who had become manager in 1918. Huggins was a wispy little man who had never been any great shakes as a player, but who was a managerial genius, of sorts. Perhaps his genius found its fullest expression in the fact that he finally persuaded his troupe of prima donnas that he was the boss and they were part of a machine. He did this by putting the clamps on Babe Ruth.

Ruth was virtually uncontrollable. He had more fame and was making more money than any player who had ever lived, and he was first to recognize his own position as "the Sultan of Swat." He signed a contract for $80,000 a year in the mid-twenties, and when a newspaperman reminded him that this was more money than was paid to President of the United States Calvin Coolidge, Ruth was not impressed. "Yeah," he said airily, "but I had a better year last year than Coolidge had." He saw no reason for giving more than token attention to the orders of any manager, especially a manager who was only half his size and had never commanded anything much higher than a .245 batting average. There was a big showdown in the summer of 1925.

Ruth paid no attention to training rules, and one night when the team was in St. Louis, he went out on the town. He got to bed, after a fashion, late in the morning, arose after noon, and got to the ball park an hour late—only to be met by a wrathful Huggins who told him not to put on his uniform: he was under suspension and, furthermore, he was fined $5,000.

Ruth was outraged. He announced for the world to hear that he was going to go back to New York and talk to Colonel Ruppert, who would unquestionably uphold the star who brought in all those gate receipts rather than the manager who was not especially needed anyhow. (At this time, by the way, Ruppert was sole owner. He had bought out Huston a year or so earlier.)

Back to New York went Ruth—to learn the hard facts of life. Ruppert was a successful businessman who had no time for the employee who considered himself bigger than the organization, and he stood by Huggins. Ruth's suspension was lifted, but the $5,000 fine stuck, and Ruth made a public apology to Huggins . . . and from that time on Huggins was unmistakably in charge. The Yankees were going to be a team.

Their progress in that direction was helped along mightily by business manager Ed Barrow, whom the Yankees had hired away from Frazee just before they bought all of Frazee's best players. Barrow knew that there would never be another Frazee in the Yankees' life. If the team was to retain its eminence, it must start developing stars on its own hook, and Barrow set up the machinery to do this.

Its first fruits were displayed in the year of Ruth's rebellion, when Lou Gehrig—picked off the Columbia University campus—was installed as the regular first baseman. He was a slugger of a power and consistency second only to Ruth himself, and together the two men made a fearfully indigestible lump in the fat part of the Yankee batting order. A year later, the Yankees found Tony Lazzeri, a new second baseman on a minor-league team in Salt Lake City, who quickly became one of the game's leaders. In the years to come, the Yankees would buy a star when and if they could—what team won't?—but by and large, Yankee teams from now on would be homegrown.

The change was visible by 1927, when the Yankees fielded what many people consider their greatest team. Their outfield included Ruth, Meusel, and a brilliant center fielder named Earl Combs; in the infield were Gehrig, Lazzeri, Dugan, and a good shortstop up from the minors, Mark Koenig. Of the lot, only Ruth and Dugan were from the old Red Sox team. This aggregation won the World Series that fall in four straight games, and in 1928 it did the same. And now there began to be heard, in rival major-league cities around the country, the despairing and unavailing cry: "Break up the Yankees!"

The fans need not have worried, because the Yankees ran into trouble. Some of the older players were showing their age, and the team as a whole seemed to have lost fire, almost as if the men had grown jaded from so much winning. Late in the 1929 season, Miller Huggins died, and it was only after his death that those who had played for him began to admit that he had been a superlatively good manager. His place was taken by the veteran pitcher Bob Shawkey, but managing the Yankees is a special sort of job and Shawkey did not quite have the touch. His lot was made no easier by the fact that some of the other American League clubs, notably Philadelphia and Detroit, had been developing first-rate teams. In any case, the Yankees won just one pennant in the next seven years. In 1932 they took the league championship and the World Series—four straight, once more, giving them the unheard-of record of having won three World Series in that fashion. But in the three years before 1932 and the three years after it, the Yankees finished out of first place.

Then, beginning in 1936, the Yankees began a new golden age which was even more dazzling than the one in the 1920's; more dazzling, and yet somehow very different. The Yankees were no longer the gaudy, colorful, roistering crew of old. They had great players, yet they were not just a grab bag full of stars. They were a team, going about their business with a cool, quiet expertise that was as strong on the defense as it was on the offense.

Two things had happened. First, Joe McCarthy was hired as manager. McCarthy was a solid, unemotional sort who had never in his life played in the big leagues. He had been a minor-league player, and then he was a minor-league manager, and at last he was brought to Chicago to manage the Cubs. He did well there, and, after Huggins and Shawkey, when Ruppert and Barrow were looking for a man, McCarthy's name came into the conversation. He was hired, and from then on no Yankee player ever had the least doubt who was boss.

They tell how, in one of his early days as manager, McCarthy came into the club-house and saw a wooden table in a corner of the room. He wanted to know what the table was for, and learned that it was for cards. He immediately had a man come in with an axe and chop it to splinters; then he had the splinters carried out and informed the assembled players that if they wanted to play cards, they could do it somewhere else—the Yankee clubhouse was a place where people thought and talked about baseball and nothing else.

McCarthy detested flamboyance. One spring the team brought up a promising rookie; and on the first road trip McCarthy descended to the hotel lobby, where the players were waiting to go out to the park, and saw the rookie gaily attired in ice-cream pants, a tie-less sport shirt, and a bright blue jacket. He strolled over to the young man, gestured at the flashy clothing, indicated abhorrence in no uncertain words, and said, "Son, you're a Yankee now." Next day, and thereafter, the young player wore a business suit, a white shirt and a necktie, and looked like a promising bond salesman.

The other event was the hiring, at the end of the 1931 season, of George Weiss to run their minor-league team at Newark. Weiss quickly picked up an idea. Out in St. Louis, the Cardinals had acquired a sterling genius named Branch Rickey, who had built up a whole chain of minor-league clubs from which the parent team drew its players. Weiss figured that the Yankees ought to do the same, sold the idea, and built up the famous Yankee farm system. Promising players were picked young and fed into the minor-league chain. They developed their skills, were taught how ballplayers ought to behave, and when the time was ripe, were brought up to become Yankees themselves. There was always a capable replacement coming up when a ballplayer wore out. The stars could come and go; what mattered was that the Yankees, as a team, were almost always one notch better than their competitors simply because they always knew where the promising players were and could lay their hands on them on a moment's notice. They became, for a quarter of a century, almost unbeatable.

In this new era, the Yankees did not look much like the old team. Babe Ruth was gone, worn out at last, and so were most of the others. But there were replacements: the star among them was Joe DiMaggio, a fantastically skillful center fielder brought up from the minor-league team at San Francisco. There were others, and if this team was not quite as good as the fabulous group of 1927 and 1928, it did not miss by very much. In the outfield it had DiMaggio and two capable partners, Jack Powell and George Selkirk, flanking him. The infield was as good as the most demanding purist could ask—Gehrig at first, Lazzeri at second, Frank Crosetti at shortstop, and Red Rolfe at third. Bill Dickey was behind the bat, and the pitching staff included such men as Bump Hadley, Monte Pearson, Red Ruffing, and Vernon Gomez. A point that sometimes went unnoticed (except by opposing managers) was that while this team was almost as powerful, offensively, as the old group in the twenties, it was even stronger on defense. The infield was the kind that turns a fair pitcher into a great one, and the outfield was just about as good. Now the Yankees began to win pennants, not simply by overpowering the opposition, but by outplaying them in almost every position.

In the four years beginning in 1936, McCarthy's Yankees won four league pennants and four world championships. They missed in 1940, came back in 1941 to win three pennants in a row, and then ran into three bad years beginning in 1944, when nobody's system was worth much because the armed services claimed so many men and all organization rules were upset. They came back in 1947 to win the pennant and the Series, missed again in 1948; and then, in 1949, they began the most spectacular success story of all.

There had been changes. Ruppert died in 1939, and in 1945 his heirs sold the club to tinplate magnate Dan Topping, construction mogul Del E. Webb, and former Dodger president Leland Stanford MacPhail. McCarthy retired in 1946 and was followed by a succession of interim managers; Ed Barrow departed; MacPhail sold out to his two partners at the end of 1947; Weiss became general manager. At the beginning of 1949, Charles Dillon Stengel was hired as team manager.

Stengel remained manager for twelve years, and in those years the Yankees won the American League pennant ten times, plus seven world championships. At the heart of this success was the continuation of the old Yankee tradition that there was always a Big Guy in the center of the lineup; there had been Ruth, and then Gehrig, and then DiMaggio—three Hall of Famers—and when DiMaggio at last faded out, there was a fast, powerful young man named Mickey Mantle to take his place—always somebody to strike fear in the opposition and to pull the fans through the turnstiles. Perhaps even more important was the fact that there was always a topflight supporting cast. When Crosetti left, the Yankees came up with Phil Rizzuto; when Lazzeri departed, they found Joe Gordon; they got men like Tommy Henrich, King Kong Keller, and Hank Bauer for the outfield, brought Yogi Berra in when Bill Dickey was finished, and uncovered such pitchers as Whitey Ford, Vic Raschi, and Eddie Lopat. Stengel occasionally made jokes about how smoothly the system functioned. He had managed in the minors, without great success, and he had managed second division clubs in the majors, but when he got to New York he was the all-time winner. He remarked once that it was funny how smart he got as soon as he put on a Yankee uniform.

It looked as if it would go on forever, but it did not. That it did not was due to a combination of circumstances, and chief among these was the advent of television. All across the land, baseball fans began to find that it was in many ways more rewarding to watch a big-league game on the screen than to go out to the park to see a minor-league game; as a result the minor leagues began to die like flies, and the foundation on which a club could build or maintain a far-flung farm system began to crumble. At the same time draft rules were changed, so that a bright young player could no longer be quietly stashed away for four or five years on a minor-league club until he had had the proper seasoning; try that, and somebody else was likely to draft him out from under you. In addition, the Yankees were among the last of all clubs to realize that Negro players constituted a rich vein of talent. They did get Elston Howard, a first-rate catcher, and later they got a few more, but such men as Willie Mays, Roberto Clemente, Hank Aaron—well, you name them—went to other teams.

At the end of 1960, the front office decided that both Stengel and Weiss had outlived their usefulness and let them go. By the early 1960's the team was in deep trouble. It is possible that the Yankees, as an organization, had begun to believe their own press clippings; the quiet, unobtrusive arrogance built up by so many years of success resulted at last in opaque vision. The replacement system was not working the way it had. Stars wore out, as stars always do, but new stars did not come up to replace them. In 1965 the Yankees sank to an ignominious sixth place, and 1966 was even worse—they finished dead last.

On top of everything else, there was a change in ownership. In 1964 the Columbia Broadcasting System bought the Yankees, ratifying the long drift that had been turning big-league baseball into an arm of the television industry. The new ownership reacted to the decline in the team's fortunes in a forthright manner. It began jabbing desperately at the panic button.

It fired two managers, first Yogi Berra and then Johnny Keane. It followed this by firing two television announcers, Mel Allen and after him Red Barber; it also repainted Yankee Stadium, hired a number of usherettes, and gave away thousands of ball bats to Little Leaguers. But even these stern measures failed. The bright stars were fading out, and the new men looked strictly like run-of-the-mill operatives.

Today there is a feeling in New York that the three most famous memorials of baseball, the three monuments that stand in the center field of Yankee Stadium, are not only memorials to Miller Huggins, Lou Gehrig, and the Babe, but that they are, in a symbolic way, memorials to something greater than any one of the three—memorials to the whole Yankee era with its bright razzmatazz and pinstriped arrogance, an era that is gone forever.

Bedford-Stuyvesant: Giving a Damn About Hell, from Robert Kennedy: A Memoir, *Jack Newfield (1969)*

Jack Newfield was raised in Bedford-Stuyvesant, Brooklyn, attended Public School 54, and was one of the last whites to graduate the area's Boys' High School. Born in 1939, he would find Jackie Robinson, who broke baseball's color barrier to play for the Brooklyn Dodgers in 1947, "the first outsider/underdog I identified with." Newfield's first journalistic models were Jimmy Cannon and Murray Kempton, who later became his mentor. I. F. Stone, whom Newfield first discovered in college, provided the momentum for him to become an investigative journalist, and after being a charter member of the Students for Democratic Society at Hunter College in 1960, Newfield began writing pamphlets for the Student Non-Violent Coordinating Committee in 1962.

After working at the *Village Voice* from 1964 to 1988 and for two years at the *Daily News,* Newfield joined the *New York Post* in 1991, but his style harkens back to muckrakers like Lincoln Steffens from the Progressive Era. His admiration of Bobby Kennedy started when he saw him delivering speeches in 1965, and while riding aboard RFK's funeral train from New York to Washington, Newfield observed that "all the way down you could see, literally, blacks on one side of the tracks and whites on the other side of the tracks. That was his coalition coming together one last time, but divided by those railroad tracks."

DISEASED debris rotting under a halo of mosquitoes in a vacant lot. Teenage girls feinting and punching with the fluent fury of grown men. Burned-out houses with families still living behind the boarded-up windows. Roaches so bold they no longer flee from the light. A shabby record store loudspeaker blaring Aretha Franklin singing, "I can't get no satisfaction," while a junkie shoots up with heroin in the doorway. Bedford-Stuyvesant's everyday reality is filled with the surreal imagery of a bad LSD trip.

There is the sour stench of urine that pollutes the Myrtle-Willoughby IND subway station. The bittersweet monologue of the red-wigged prostitute after she has been shaken down by a white cop. The visor of suffocated hatred that comes down across the taut face of every black youth before his thirteenth birthday. And the counterfeit escapes wherever you look. Neon signs promising credit. Bars. Pimps. Churches. Pushers. TV sets on sale. Liquor stores. Pawnshops. More storefront churches. Numbers runners.

Then, the statistics. Eighty percent of the teen-agers are high school dropouts. Thirty-six percent of the families headed by women. Twenty-eight percent with annual incomes of less than $3,000. The highest infant mortality rate in the nation. The highest incidence of lead poisoning in the country.

More than 90 percent of the housing was built before 1920. Almost half of it officially classified as "dilapidated and insufficient." A fifth with hall toilets.

And no one has ever counted all the rats.

Harlem has always been viewed as the universal symbol for the Negro ghetto. It is the place that suffers and swings. It is the place James Baldwin writes about and Billie Holiday sang about. It is where the Federal antipoverty funds go first. It is home for Sugar Ray and Adam Powell. Harlem has its own newspaper, its own mayor, its own identity. It is a community. It had a black Congressman more than twenty-five years before Bedford-Stuyvesant did.

But the unromantically baptized ghetto of Bedford-Stuyvesant (named for the Duke of Bedford and Peter Stuyvesant) is much poorer than Harlem. It is the place where people land when they fall out of Harlem; it is where the Wagner Administration used to dump black people after they were uprooted by the urban renewal bulldozer.

Bedford-Stuyvesant is larger and more diffuse than Harlem. Harlem is compact, limited on three sides by rivers, and on the south by Central Park. But Bedford-Stuyvesant's borders keep growing like an amoeba's. Its exact geographical definition keeps changing, pushing into Crown Heights, East New York, and Brownsville. "Bedford-Stuyvesant is wherever Negroes live," says a local politician. While Harlem lost 50,000 in population between 1950 and 1960, Bedford-Stuyvesant gained about 50,000. It now consists of about 450,000 people jammed into 500 square blocks, or about the same population as Kansas City or Cincinnati. According to a 1967 study compiled by the New York University Graduate School of Social Work:

> Bedford Stuyvesant is more depressed and impaired than Harlem —i.e., fewer unified families, more unemployment, lower incomes, less job history. . . . Furthermore, the Bedford-Stuyvesant youth have (*sic*) a vastly lower degree of self-esteem than does Harlem youth, with much less hope for his future. . . .

At the turn of the century Bedford-Stuyvesant was an elite, white, middle-class community. Sturdy brownstones, numerous churches, and tranquil, tree-lined streets gave the section its character. Employment was plentiful and the crime rate low. In 1907, after the completion of the Williamsburg Bridge, a few working-class Jews and Italians emigrated from the Lower East Side of Manhattan.

During the 1930's, the first wave of black migration from the West Indies and the rural South deposited thousands of Negroes into Brooklyn. Farm mechanization—especially the cotton picker—and the Depression drove millions of jobless Negroes into the spreading black slums of the North. At the same time, the A train—immortalized by Duke Ellington—began to operate, and transport thousands of Negroes from 125th Street in Harlem, to Fulton Street in Brooklyn.

The second wave broke over Bedford-Stuyvesant during World War II. The Brooklyn Navy Yard, only a few minutes away, offered employment, and war economy prosperity was enabling many of the area's older Jewish and Italian residents to move to Queens or Long Island. In 1930 the black population of Bedford-Stuyvesant was 30,000; by 1950 it was 155,000, or about 55 percent. By 1960 it was about 85 percent, and now it is more than 90 percent.*

Bedford-Stuyvesant became a ghetto because real-estate speculators and professional blockbusters, abetted by banks and mortgage companies, were there to exploit it, and pocket millions in panic profits. During the 1950's, many Negro families paid as much as $20,000 for brownstones that speculators had acquired for $12,000 the week before. The remaining white families, mostly elderly, became the targets of wild rumors, staged street brawls between Negroes, and almost daily mimeographed postcards claiming, "We have a buyer for your house."

I was growing up in Bedford-Stuyvesant during the early fifties, and remember white real-estate brokers offering my Negro friends fifty cents an hour to slip circulars under the doors of white-owned houses, saying there was a buyer available. Real-estate speculators easily obtained loans from banks, but the stable, hardworking Negro family next door to my house could not get a bank loan to rehabilitate their dirty, peeling frame house. I remember how one frightened white family two blocks away from me—on Hart Street—became a neighborhood legend by simply walking out of their home one day, leaving all their furniture behind, and never returning. Quite rapidly

*The same pattern created other urban ghettos. Between 1940 and 1960, the black population of Philadelphia doubled, the black populations of Chicago and Detroit tripled, and that of Los Angeles multiplied five times.

the community became segregated. Garbage collection grew less frequent. Bopping youth gangs were organized. Newspapers began to write about the "crime wave" in Bedford-Stuyvesant. Unemployment increased. The hospitals, high schools, and libraries in the community continued to decay, and the city would not build any new ones to replace them. Boys High School was sixty-four years old by the time I was graduated in 1956. The senior class was 90 percent Negro, but 80 percent of those of us who went on to college were white.† And several of the Negroes who went to college were able to do so only because of athletic scholarships. By 1956, the old, white, middle-class Bedford-Stuyvesant was dead, a "For Sale" sign its venal epitaph.

Although few recognized it at the time, the history of race relations in America changed on July 16, 1964. On that day a fifteen-year-old Negro boy named James Powell was shot to death on a Manhattan street by a white, off-duty police lieutenant named Thomas Gilligan. That gunshot signaled the end of the civil rights movement and the beginning of the long, hot summers.

James Powell had been an almost-too-perfect symbol of the new generation of the black youth. The summer before he died, when he was fourteen, he went to Washington to join the biggest civil rights march in history. He was shot while attending a summer school for remedial reading, subsidized by the then new and hopeful war on poverty. Two days after his death, on July 18, a hot, restless Saturday night, rioting broke out in Harlem. Two nights later, as if the trouble itself had taken the A train, violence, looting, and vandalism exploded at the intersection of Fulton Street and Nostrand Avenue, the Times Square of Bedford-Stuyvesant.

Compared with what was to come in following summers, the three nights of rioting in Brooklyn were an abortive skirmish. There were no deaths. No sniping. Almost no fire bombing. The violence was limited to an eight-square-block area. When it was over, the accounting came to 276 arrests, 22 injuries, and 556 incidents of property damage, estimated to total $350,000. The rioters were almost all young Negroes—that revolutionary class between fourteen and twenty-one—that roams the limbo between school, work, and the Army. They were the vanguard of the lost black generation that has grown up in the North—not the South—watching the sit-ins and Freedom Rides on television, and listening to black nationalist orators on the street corners.

On the third night of the riot I was sent to cover it by the *New York Post*. Early in the evening the familiar fugue of the police siren and the burglar

†Kennedy once said to me, "I'm jealous of the fact you grew up in a ghetto. I wish I did. I wish I had that experience."

alarm began to play along Fulton Street. At about 9 P.M. a sound truck manned by officials of the NAACP parked at the corner of Fulton and Nostrand, its loudspeaker shouting:

"Ladies and gentlemen, will you please return to your homes. Help our community. Help save our community. Help us make Bedford-Stuyvesant a safe place again. Please do not destroy our community anymore. *Please get off the streets.*"

A group of teen-agers, with that remarkable *élan* and energy of the streets, began to taunt and jeer the middle-aged ministers inside the truck. Suddenly, a large, buxom black woman of about fifty, with a back bent from washing too many white people's floors, shouted at the truck from the doorway of a looted store. "Sheet, man. *These are our streets.* You fools, *you go home.*"

The dream deferred had dried up and become desperation. And Bedford-Stuyvesant, in July of 1964, was a portent of the next four summers, whose history would be written in the geography of violence: Watts, Newark, Cleveland, Detroit, Chicago, Washington, D.C.

The riot gave Bedford-Stuyvesant national visibility, and there was considerable press release jargon about "crash programs," "task forces" and "target areas." But the sense of urgency quickly passed, and nothing was done. There was no new job program, or new school construction, or rat extermination program. Six months after the violence the only change was that one vacant lot had been blacktopped. The shopkeepers along Fulton Street did not even bother to replace their broken windows; they kept them boarded up with plywood, expecting another outbreak any day.

In November of 1964 Lyndon Johnson was reelected President, Robert Kennedy was elected the new Senator from New York, the first Democrat to win a statewide election for Governor or Senator in ten years, and the well-publicized "unconditional war against poverty" was beginning to build up hopes inside the other America. On November 21, the Central Brooklyn Coordinating Council, a loose federation of over ninety local organizations, sponsored an all-day conference at Pratt Institute, in the heart of Bedford-Stuyvesant. The meeting was called in response to the summer's violence, and 600 civic, religious, and political leaders came to tell each other how desperate the situation was, and how urgently the area needed a coordinated and comprehensive rehabilitation program. The one concrete result of the conference was the decision to commission Pratt's Planning Department to make a six-month survey of the community's problems, as well as its potential for becoming more attractive to the middle class.

The study, directed by Planning Department chairman George Raymond, concentrated on a twelve-block area, more than 95-percent Negro, that contained 2,900 dwelling units occupied by 8,600 persons. The survey found the area at the point of decay. Only 10.5 percent of the buildings were "in a dilapidated condition," but 28.5 percent were "seriously deteriorating," and in need of "immediate attention."

The Pratt study also suggested that the chances of rehabilitation of the area were "greatly enhanced" by the fact that 22.5 percent of the buildings were owner occupied, another 9.7 percent owned by individuals who lived in close proximity, and that homeowners had lived in the area on an average of fifteen years. All this indicated the presence of a stable, middle-class base in the community, able to provide leadership for reform. The report concluded with a plea that the city "mobilize all necessary antipoverty and other social welfare and educational programs" to save the community from imminent violence and deterioration.

But less than a month after the study was released, Bedford-Stuyvesant's city antipoverty agency, Youth-in-Action, reported its budget slashed. Dorothy Orr, the executive director of YIA, had originally requested $5.5 million for summer programs in 1965. Later, she reduced that to $2.6 million. But in the end, YIA was allocated only $440,000. The project had to abandon many of its programs, like prekindergarten classes and college-preparatory courses. YIA received 1,000 more requests for summer jobs than it could fill in 1965.

Late in 1965 Robert Kennedy decided he wanted to make a major address on the themes of race and poverty, and sent Adam Walinsky to work collecting data and talking to experts. Kennedy had been shaken by the Watts riot and felt that the racial crisis had now shifted its focus from the rural South to the urban North. He also felt that support for Negro demands within the white community was declining, and that race relations had reached a historical turning point—that if something were not done quickly to stem the white backlash, then violence and separation would increase.

It developed, however, that Kennedy had so much he wanted to say, the single speech grew into three separate speeches, which were delivered consecutively in Manhattan on January 20, 21, and 22 of 1966. The speeches were not revolutionary in content. For the most part, they were a rehash of New Frontier programs—job training, rent subsidies, student loans for the poor, housing desegregation. But they were well crafted and documented, and they did offer an impressive synthesis of the practical, fueled by Kennedy's insatiable drive for immediate, concrete action.

They also provided the first glimpse of Kennedy's own insights into the problem. Going against the grain of liberal optimism and Great Society rhetoric, he asserted that the plight of the Negro was getting worse, not better, and that some of the accepted liberal formulas like welfare and stricter code enforcement were not working. He placed new emphasis on the need for a sense of community inside the ghettos, on the need for ghetto residents to participate in governmental decision-making, and the need for private industry to enlist in the war on poverty.

The three speeches also dramatized Kennedy's emotional urgency and feelings of frustration. "We are now at the crossroads," he said. "The present pace is unsatisfactory . . . at such a pace we can expect continuing explosions like Watts. . . . We must break down the ghettos . . . we must begin to do so immediately."

A few days after giving the last of the three speeches, Kennedy decided to create his own antislum project. In his typically vague, offhand manner, he told Adam Walinsky, "I want to do something about all this. Some kind of project that goes after some of these problems. Why don't you and Tom [Johnston] see what you can put together."

In mid-February, Kennedy spent a cold, cloudy afternoon touring Bedford-Stuyvesant. He saw what visiting Senators and celebrities have always seen. Unemployed men lounging on street corners, or in bars. Pyramids of uncollected garbage. Children playing in the street without coats in temperatures of thirty degrees. After the tour, Kennedy went to a meeting with community activists arranged for the Bedford-Stuyvesant YMCA. At that point Bedford-Stuyvesant was unable to receive a single urban renewal grant from the Federal Government despite ten years of trying. The community also received almost no antipoverty money; most of it went to Harlem.

The meeting turned out to be reminiscent of the famous confrontation Kennedy had as Attorney General in 1963, with James Baldwin, Harry Belafonte, and other Negro cultural and civil rights leaders. The Brooklyn Negroes, bitter over Federal indifference to the area, despite the 1964 riot, took out their frustrations on the surprised Senator. They insulted and lectured him, insisting he explain the failures of Washington, Albany, and City Hall. At one point, Civil Court Judge Thomas Jones, the highest ranking black politician in the community, who had pointedly refused to accompany Kennedy on his tour, told the Senator: "I'm weary of study, Senator. Weary of speeches, weary of promises that aren't kept. . . . The Negro people are angry, Senator, and judge that I am, I'm angry, too. No one is helping us."

1966 was the year the country began moving to the Right, and Robert Kennedy began moving to the Left. And both these trends contributed to the project in Brooklyn continually expanding in concept during the nine months Kennedy and his staff worked on it. They did, however, start out with two negative premises. One was that because of the Vietnam war the Federal Government was unlikely to appropriate any new funds for antipoverty legislation. Therefore, the private sector—corporations, foundations, universities, banks—must be convinced to pick up the slack. Second, the existing Office of Economic Opportunity programs had suffered from three flaws: an insufficient emphasis on jobs as the critical factor in poverty; not enough community participation in the creation and control of programs; and a piecemeal approach that was inadequately coordinated.

Back in February of 1966 Kennedy declared his independence from the Johnson Administration by directly challenging its Vietnam policy. In May, Kennedy broke with Tammany Hall by actively campaigning in the Democratic primary for a reform candidate for surrogate against the regular organization's choice. In August he badgered Cabinet level officers of the Johnson Administration during committee hearings on the poverty program. In October he went to the Berkeley campus, mecca of student radicalism, to make a speech on "the duty to dissent."

Meanwhile, the Vietnam war continued to escalate and absorb the money and energy of the government. The poverty program began to falter, as some of its best staff quit the agency; an effort by Kennedy and Senator Joseph Clark to increase its budget failed, and its community action program was curtailed. In the November election, forty-seven Democrats—almost all of them supporters of OEO—lost their seats. The civilian review board, despite the backing of Kennedy, Senator Javits, and Mayor Lindsay, was turned down by the voters of New York City in a referendum. And Ronald Reagan, Claude Kirk, and Lester Maddox were elected governors.

Through the violent summer of 1966 Walinsky and Johnston spent almost half their time working on the project. They traveled across the country several times, picking the brains of black militants, university urbanists, Federal administrators, journalists, mayors, foundation executives, millionaires from the banking and business communities. Johnston spent many of his evenings in Bedford-Stuyvesant, talking to the hostile street radicals, and trying to sort out the Byzantine feuds that split the middle-class leadership. Kennedy, meanwhile, realizing that both the Johnson Administration in Washington and the local white Democrats in Brooklyn felt threatened by his experiment, lined up crucial bipartisan support from Republicans Mayor Lindsay and Senator Javits. Then he went to his personal friends in the corporate world like Thomas Watson of IBM; William Paley of CBS; investment banker André Meyer; and Douglas Dillon, the Republican Secretary of the Treasury of his brother's Cabinet. After some sharp jabs to their conscience, they agreed to help. André Meyer, however, had one half-serious condition to his participation—that Kennedy give another speech against the Vietnam war. The only person who rejected Kennedy's invitation to join the corporation board was David Rockefeller. Daniel Moynihan, then a professor at MIT, privately urged Kennedy not to attempt the project at all.

By October, Kennedy, his staff, and the community leaders agreed not to try to rehabilitate a single block, or attack one problem area like health or housing, but attempt a community development project for almost the entire ghetto of Bedford-Stuyvesant.

"We must grab the web whole," Kennedy said in a 1966 speech, and that idea of a holistic, systematic attack on the ghetto itself was at the heart of the Bedford-Stuyvesant project.

The initial plan included coordinated programs for the creation of jobs, housing renovation and rehabilitation, improved health, sanitation and recreation facilities, the construction of two "super blocks," the conversion of an abandoned bottling plant into a town hall and community center, a mortgage consortium to provide low-cost loans for homeowners, the starting of a private work-study community university geared toward dropouts, and a campaign to convince industry to relocate in the community.

"An effort in one problem area," Kennedy said when the project started, "is almost worthless. A program for housing, without simultaneous programs for jobs, education, welfare reform, health, and economic development cannot succeed. The whole community must be involved as a whole."

The October decision to go was made even though the dry bones of failed projects littered many of the nation's urban slums. Martin Luther King had failed in his campaign to "end slums" in Chicago. The Student Nonviolent Coordinating Committee (SNCC) project had folded up in Atlanta. The SDS-initiated Newark Community Union Project (NCUP) was barely surviving. Despite grandiose plans, Walter Reuther's Citizens Crusade Against Poverty (CCAP) had never gotten off the ground. In Bedford-Stuyvesant itself, CORE had failed to grow beyond 60 or 70 dedicated activists. The Mobilization for Youth pilot project on Manhattan's Lower East Side had lost its momentum after a series of red-bating articles published by the *Daily*

News. HARYOU in Harlem had been demoralized by scandals and factionalism. The Saul Alinsky approach to urban organizing had not scored a success since the formation of The Woodlawn Organization (TWO) in Chicago in the early sixties.

A few days before the Bedford-Stuyvesant project was publicly unveiled, Kennedy was saying, "I'm not at all sure this is going to work. But it's going to test some new ideas, some new ways of doing this, that are different from the government's. Even if we fail, we'll have learned something. But more important than that, something has to be done. People like myself just can't go around making nice speeches all the time. We can't just keep raising expectations. We have to do some damn hard work, too."

13-Point Program and Platform, Young Lords Party (1969)

Although there had been Puerto Ricans in New York City from the seventeenth century on, between 1940 and 1970 the Puerto Rican population of the city rose from 61,000, less than 1 percent of the population, to 817,712, more than 10 percent of the total. More than a quarter of a million of the new arrivals were concentrated in one district in Upper Manhattan, El Barrio, from 90th Street to 116th Street between 1st and 5th Avenues, and from 110th Street to 125th Street between 5th Avenue and Manhattan Avenue.

Agricultural depression, brought on in part by Operation Bootstrap (the U.S. government's attempt to industrialize the island), and lack of housing drove many islanders to seek employment in New York City. The Jones Act of 1917 had granted all Puerto Ricans U.S. citizenship, and with ticket prices as low as $40, flights from San Juan landed regularly in Newark and Idlewild airports from 1948 on. But the economic dreams were rarely met, and Puerto Ricans were forced into low-paying service industry jobs as the industrial, manufacturing base of the city's economy shrank.

The Young Lords were formed in New York City in July 1969 with the intention of addressing El Barrio's needs for health care, sanitation, and education. The group gained notoriety when it took over a Methodist church on 111th Street and Lexington Avenue on December 28, 1969, and renamed it the "People's Church." The Young Lords used radical politics and flamboyant protest to call attention to the needs of the Puerto Rican community. Perhaps most important, in the second point of their 13-Point Program, they coined the Spanglish term "Latino," an English word with a Spanish pronunciation, to describe the psychological realities of second-generation Puerto Ricans and other Hispanics demanding full rights in a predominately Anglo-American culture.

THE Young Lords Party is a Revolutionary Political Party Fighting for the Liberation of All Oppressed People

1. We want self-determination for Puerto Ricans—Liberation of the Island and inside the United States.

   For 500 years, first spain and then united states have colonized our country. Billions of dollars in profits leave our country of the united states every year. In every way we are slaves of the gringo. We want liberation and the Power in the hands of the People, not Puerto Rican exploiters.

Que Viva Puerto Rico Libre!

2. We want self-determination for all Latinos.

   Our Latin Brothers and Sisters, inside and outside the united states, are oppressed by amerikkan business. The Chicano people built the Southwest, and we support their right to control their lives and their land. The people of Santo Domingo continue to fight against gringo domination and its puppet generals. The armed liberation struggles in Latin America are part of the war of Latinos against imperialism.

Que Viva La Raza!

3. We want liberation of all third world people.

   Just as Latins first slaved under spain and the yanquis, Black people, Indians, and Asians slaved to build the wealth of this country. For 400 years they have fought for freedom and dignity against racist Babylon (decadent empire). Third World people have led the fight for freedom. All the colored and oppressed peoples of the world are one nation under oppression.

No Puerto Rican Is Free Until All People Are Free!

4. We are revolutionary nationalists and oppose racism.

   The Latin, Black, Indian and Asian people inside the u.s. are colonies fighting for liberation. We know that washington, wall street and city hall will try to make our nationalism into racism; but Puerto Ricans are of all colors and we resist racism. Millions of poor white people are rising up to demand freedom and we support them. These are the ones in the u.s. that are stepped on by the rules and the government. We each organize our people, but our fights are against the same oppression and we will defeat it together.

Power To All Oppressed People!

5. We want community control of our institutions and land.

   We want control of our communities by our people and programs to guarantee that all institutions serve the needs of our people. People's control of police, health services, churches, schools, housing, transportation and welfare are needed. We want an end to attacks on our land by urban removal, highway destruction, universities and corporations.

Land Belongs To All People!

6. We want a true education of our Creole culture and Spanish language.

   We must learn our history of fighting against cultural, as well as economic genocide by the yanqui. Revolutionary culture, culture of the people, is the only true teaching.

7. We oppose capitalists and alliances with traitors.

   Puerto Rican rulers, or puppets of the oppressor, do not help our people. They are paid by the system to lead our people down blind alleys, just like the thousands of poverty pimps who keep our communities peaceful for business, or street workers who keep gangs divided and blowing each other away. We want a society where the people socialistically control their labor.

Venceremos!

8. We oppose the Amerikkan military.

   We demand immediate withdrawal of u.s. military forces and bases from Puerto Rico, Vietnam and all oppressed communities inside and outside the u.s. No Puerto Rican should serve in the u.s. army against his Brothers and Sisters, for the only true army of oppressed people is the people's army to fight all rulers.

U.S. Out Of Vietnam, Free Puerto Rico!

9. We want freedom for all political prisoners.

   We want all Puerto Ricans freed because they have been tried by the racist courts of the colonizers, and not by their own people and peers. We want all freedom fighters released from jail.

Free All Political Prisoners!

10. We want equality for women. Machismo must be revolutionary . . . not oppressive.

    Under Capitalism, our women have been oppressed by both the society and our own men. The doctrine of machismo has been used by our men to take out their frustrations against their wives, sisters, mothers, and children. Our men must support their women in their fight for economic and social equality, and must recognize that our women are equals in every way within the revolutionary ranks.

Forward, Sisters, In The Struggle!

11. We fight anti-communism with international unity.

    Anyone who resists injustice is called a communist by "the man" and condemned. Our people are brainwashed by television, radio, newspapers, schools, and books to oppose people in other countries fighting for their freedom. No longer will our people believe attacks and slanders, because they have learned who the real enemy is and who their real friends are. We will defend our Brothers and Sisters around the world who fight for justice against the rich rulers of this country.

Viva Che!

12. We believe armed self-defense and armed struggle are the only means to liberation.

    We are opposed to violence—the violence of hungry children, illiterate adults, diseased old people, and the violence of poverty and profit. We have asked, petitioned, gone to courts, demonstrated peacefully, and voted for politicians full of empty promises. But we still ain't free. The time has come to defend the lives of our people against repression and for revolutionary war against the businessman, politician, and police. When a government oppresses our people, we have the right to abolish it and create a new one.

Boricua Is Awake! All Pigs Beware!

13. We want a socialist society.

    We want liberation, clothing, free food, education, health care, transportation, utilities, and employment for all. We want a society where the needs of our people come first, and where we give solidarity and aid to the peoples of the world, not oppression and racism.

Hasta La Victoria Siempre!

Ten-Point Health Program of the Young Lords

1. We want total self-determination of all health services in East Harlem (El Barrio) through an incorporated Community-Staff Governing Board for Metropolitan Hospital. (Staff is anyone and everyone working at Metropolitan.)
2. We want immediate replacement of all Lindsay administrators by community and staff appointed people whose practice has demonstrated their commitment to serve our poor community.
3. We demand immediate end to construction of the new emergency room until the Metropolitan Hospital Community-Staff Governing Board inspects and approves them or authorizes new plans.
4. We want employment for our people. All jobs filled in El Barrio must be filled by residents first, using on-the-job training and other educational opportunities as bases for service and promotion.
5. We want free publicly supported health care for treatment and prevention. We want an end to all fees.
6. We want total decentralization—block health officers responsible to the community-staff board should be instituted.
7. We want "door-to-door" preventive health services emphasizing environment and sanitation control, nutrition, drug addiction, maternal and child care, and senior citizen's services.
8. We want education programs for all the people to expose health problems—sanitation, rats, poor housing, malnutrition, police brutality, pollution, and other forms of oppression.
9. We want total control by the Metropolitan hospital community-staff governing board of the budget allocations, medical policy along the above points, hiring, firing, and salaries of employees, construction and health code enforcement.
10. Any community, union, or workers organization must support all the points of this program and work and fight for that or be shown as what they are—enemies of the poor people of East Harlem.

Get the Mafia and the Cops Out of Gay Bars, Anonymous (1969)

The Stonewall Rebellion, called by historian Martin Duberman "the emblematic event in modern lesbian and gay history," began on June 27, 1969. The Stonewall Inn (named for Confederate General "Stonewall" Jackson) was a gay bar at 51–53 Christopher Street in Greenwich Village. On that June night police and agents from the Alcoholic Beverage Control Board were allegedly there to look for violations of the alcohol control laws, but these raids were common on gay bars and the regular routine was for patrons, fearful of having their names publicly associated with such establishments, to either submit to arrest or to quietly vacate the premises.

Whether it was the result of the mourning for the passing of gay icon Judy Garland (her funeral had been that same day and many had been to see her lying in state at a local funeral home the day before) or the built-up frustration of years of harassment by police, the patrons chose not to go passively. After the first paddy wagon had carried off patrons, the mood of the crowd of 300 or more turned defiant and they began throwing rocks, bottles, and coins at the police. Reinforcements were called, but for the next two nights similar acts of confrontation and resistance occurred.

The New York Mattachine Society (the leading homosexual political organization, which had been using legal techniques to combat police harassment) called it "the hairpin drop heard round the world." The event has taken on a mythic proportion and is celebrated every year by a parade held in New York City on the last Sunday in June during Gay Pride Week.

THE nights of Friday, June 27, 1969 and Saturday, June 28, 1969 will go down in history as the first time that thousands of Homosexual men and women went out into the streets to protest the intolerable situation which has existed in New York City for many years—namely, the Mafia (or syndicate) control of this city's Gay bars in collusion with certain elements in the Police Dept. of the City of New York. The demonstrations were triggered by a Police raid on the Stonewall Inn late Friday night, June 27th. The purported reason for the raid was the Stonewall's lack of a liquor license. Who's kidding whom here? Can anybody really believe that an operation as big as the Stonewall could continue for almost three years just a few blocks from the 6th Precinct house without having a liquor license? No! The Police have known about the Stonewall operation all along. What's happened is the presence of new "brass" in 6th Precinct which has vowed to "drive the fags out of the Village."

Many of you have noticed one of the signs which the "management" of the Stonewall has placed outside stating "Legalize Gay bars and lick the problem." Judge Kenneth Keating (a former U.S. Senator) ruled in January, 1968 that even close dancing between Homosexuals is legal. Since that date there has been nothing legal, per se, about a Gay bar. What is illegal about New York City's Gay bars today is the Mafia (or syndicate) stranglehold on them. Legitimate Gay businessmen are afraid to open decent Gay bars with a healthy social atmosphere (as opposed to the hell-hole atmosphere of places typified by the Stonewall) because of fear of pressure from the unholy alliance of the Mafia and elements in the Police Dept. who accept payoffs and protect the Mafia monopoly.

We at the Homophile Youth Movement (HYMN) believe that the only way this monopoly can be broken is through the action of Homosexual men and women themselves. We obviously cannot rely on the various agencies of government who for years have known about this situation but who have refused to do anything about it. Therefore we urge the following:

1. That Gay businessmen step forward and open Gay bars that will be run legally with competitive pricing and a healthy social atmosphere.
2. That Homosexual men and women boycott places like the Stonewall. The only way, it seems, that we can get the criminal elements out of gay bars is simply to make it unprofitable for them.
3. That the Homosexual citizens of New York City, and concerned Heterosexuals, write to mayor Lindsay demanding a thorough investigation and effective action to correct this intolerable situation.

From Radical Chic and Mau-Mauing the Flak Catchers, *Tom Wolfe (1970)*

A native Virginian, Tom Wolfe was born in Richmond on March 2, 1931, and graduated from Washington and Lee University in 1951. After taking a doctorate in American Studies from Yale University in 1957 and turning down a teaching offer there, he embarked on a ten-year newspaper career. In 1962, he became a reporter for the *New York Herald-Tribune* before becoming an editor at *New York Magazine* and *Esquire.* In volumes such as *The Kandy-Kolored Tangerine-Flake Streamline Baby* (1965), *The Pump House Gang* (1968), *The Electric Kool-Aid Acid Test* (1968), and *Radical Chic & Mau-Mauing the Flak Catchers* (1970), he became a leading figure, along with Norman Mailer and Hunter S. Thompson, in what came to be known as the "New Journalism." In 1985, he turned his talents to writing a novel, *The Bonfire of the Vanities.* At the time, Wolfe wrote that, "To me the idea of writing a novel about this astonishing metropolis, a big novel, cramming as much of New York City between covers as you could, was the most tempting, the most challenging, and the most obvious idea an American writer could possible have."

But Wolfe's most prodigious talent has been to capture the spirit of his time in pithy phrases and devastating observation. He popularized such phrases as "good ol' boy," "the right stuff," "The Me Decade," and "radical chic." But as Wolfe himself has said, his real interest is "status, which has to do with how people group themselves, rank themselves. And it's not all about trying to rise to the next level. Many people spend their lives trying to maintain a certain status." He has been a brilliant satirist of that subject in his writings about New York City.

At 2 or 3 or 4 A.M., somewhere along in there, on August 25, 1966, his forty-eighth birthday, in fact, Leonard Bernstein woke up in the dark in a state of wild alarm. That had happened before. It was one of the forms his insomnia took. So he did the usual. He got up and walked around a bit.

He felt groggy. Suddenly he had a vision, an inspiration. He could see himself, Leonard Bernstein, the *egregio maestro*, walking out on stage in white tie and tails in front of a full orchestra. On one side of the conductor's podium is a piano. On the other is a chair with a guitar leaning against it. He sits in the chair and picks up the guitar. A guitar! One of those half-witted instruments, like the accordion, that are made for the Learn-to-Play-in-Eight-Days E-Z-Diagram 110-IQ fourteen-year-olds of Levittown! But there's a reason. He has an anti-war message to deliver to this great starched white-throated audience in the symphony hall. He announces to them: "I love." Just that. The effect is mortifying. All at once a Negro rises up from out of the curve of the grand piano and starts saying things like, "The audience is curiously embarrassed." Lenny tries to start again, plays some quick numbers on the piano, says, "I love. *Amo ergo sum.*" The Negro rises again and says, "The audience thinks he ought to get up and walk out. The audience thinks, 'I am ashamed even to nudge my neighbor.' " Finally, Lenny gets off a heartfelt anti-war speech and exits.

For a moment, sitting there alone in his home in the small hours of the morning, Lenny thought it might just work and he jotted the idea down. Think of the headlines: BERNSTEIN ELECTRIFIES CONCERT AUDIENCE WITH ANTI-WAR APPEAL. But then his enthusiasm collapsed. He lost heart. Who the hell was this Negro rising up from the piano and informing the world what an ass Leonard Bernstein was making of himself? It didn't make sense, this superego Negro by the concert grand.

mmmmmmmmmmmmmmmmm. These are nice. Little Roquefort cheese morsels rolled in crushed nuts. Very tasty. Very subtle. It's the way the dry sackiness of the nuts tiptoes up against the dour savor of the cheese that is so nice, so subtle. Wonder what the Black Panthers eat here on the hors d'oeuvre trail? Do the Panthers like little Roquefort cheese morsels rolled in crushed nuts this way, and asparagus tips in mayonnaise dabs, and *meatballs petites au Coq Hardi*, all of which are at this very moment being offered to them on gadrooned silver platters by maids in black uniforms with hand-ironed white aprons . . . The butler will bring them their drinks . . . Deny it if you wish to, but such are the *pensées méta-physiques* that rush through one's head on these Radical Chic evenings just now in New York. For example, does that huge Black Panther there in the hallway, the one shaking hands with Felicia Bernstein herself, the one with the black leather coat and the dark glasses and the absolutely unbelievable Afro, Fuzzy-Wuzzy-scale, in fact—is he, a Black Panther, going on to pick up a Roquefort cheese morsel rolled in crushed nuts from off the tray, from a maid in uniform, and just pop it down the gullet without so much as missing a beat of Felicia's perfect Mary Astor voice . . .

Felicia is remarkable. She is beautiful, with that rare burnished beauty that lasts through the years. Her hair is pale blond and set just so. She has a voice that is "theatrical," to use a term from her youth. She greets the Black Panthers with the same bend of the wrist, the same tilt of the head, the same perfect Mary Astor voice with which she greets people like Jason, John and D. D., Adolph, Betty, Gian-Carlo, Schuyler, and Goddard, during those *après*-concert suppers she and Lenny are so famous for. What evenings! She lights the candles over the dining-room table, and in the Gotham gloaming the little tremulous tips of flame are reflected in the mirrored surface of the table, a bottomless blackness with a thousand stars, and it is that moment that Lenny loves. There seem to be a thousand stars above and a thousand stars below, a room full of stars, a penthouse duplex full of stars, a Manhattan tower full of stars, with marvelous people drifting through the heavens, Jason Robards, John and D. D. Ryan, Gian-Carlo Menotti, Schuyler Chapin, Goddard Lieberson, Mike Nichols, Lillian Hellman, Larry Rivers, Aaron Copland, Richard Avedon, Milton and Amy Greene, Lukas Foss, Jennie Tourel, Samuel Barber, Jerome Robbins, Steve Sondheim, Adolph and Phyllis Green, Betty Comden, and the Patrick O'Neals . . .

. . . and now, in the season of Radical Chic, the Black Panthers. That huge Panther there, the one Felicia is smiling her tango smile at, is Robert Bay, who just forty-one hours ago was arrested in an altercation with the police, supposedly over a .38-caliber revolver that someone had, in a parked car in Queens at Northern Boulevard and 104th Street or some such unbelievable place, and taken to jail on a most unusual charge called "criminal facilitation." And now he is out on bail and walking into Leonard and Felicia Bernstein's thirteen-room penthouse duplex on Park Avenue. Harassment & Hassles, Guns & Pigs, Jail & Bail—they're *real,* these Black Panthers. The very idea of them, these real revolutionaries, who actually put their lives on the line, runs through Lenny's duplex like a rogue hormone. Everyone casts a glance, or stares, or tries a smile, and then sizes up the house for the somehow delicious counterpoint . . . Deny it if you want to! but one *does* end up making such sweet furtive comparisons in this season of Radical Chic . . . There's Otto Preminger in the library and Jean vanden Heuvel in the hall, and Peter and Cheray Duchin in the living room, and Frank and Domna Stanton, Gail Lumet, Sheldon Harnick, Cynthia Phipps, Burton Lane, Mrs. August Heckscher, Roger Wilkins, Barbara Walters, Bob Silvers, Mrs. Richard

Avedon, Mrs. Arthur Penn, Julie Belafonte, Harold Taylor, and scores more, including Charlotte Curtis, women's news editor of *The New York Times,* America's foremost chronicler of Society, a lean woman in black, with her notebook out, standing near Felicia and big Robert Bay, and talking to Cheray Duchin.

Cheray tells her: "I've never met a Panther—this is a first for me!"... never dreaming that within forty-eight hours her words will be on the desk of the President of the United States . . .

This is a first for me. But she is not alone in her thrill as the Black Panthers come trucking on in, into Lenny's house, Robert Bay, Don Cox the Panthers' Field Marshal from Oakland, Henry Miller the Harlem Panther defense captain, the Panther women—Christ, if the Panthers don't know how to get it all together, as they say, the tight pants, the tight black turtlenecks, the leather coats, Cuban shades, Afros. But real Afros, not the ones that have been shaped and trimmed like a topiary hedge and sprayed until they have a sheen like acrylic wall-to-wall—but like funky, natural, scraggly . . . wild . . .

These are no civil-rights Negroes *wearing gray suits three sizes too big—*

—no more interminable Urban League banquets in hotel ballrooms where they try to alternate the blacks and whites around the tables as if they were stringing Arapaho beads—

—*these are* real men!

Shoot-outs, revolutions, pictures in *Life* magazine of policemen grabbing Black Panthers like they were Vietcong—somehow it all runs together in the head with the whole thing of how *beautiful* they are. *Sharp as a blade.* The Panther women—there are three or four of them on hand, wives of the Panther 21 defendants, and they are so lean, so *lithe,* as they say, with tight pants and Yoruba-style headdresses, almost like turbans, as if they'd stepped out of the pages of *Vogue,* although no doubt *Vogue* got it from them. All at once every woman in the room knows exactly what Amanda Burden meant when she said she was now anti-fashion because "the sophistication of the baby blacks made me rethink my attitudes." God knows the Panther women don't spend thirty minutes in front of the mirror in the morning shoring up their eye holes with contact lenses, eyeliner, eye shadow, eyebrow pencil, occipital rim brush, false eyelashes, mascara, Shadow-Ban for undereye and Eterna Creme for the corners . . . And here they are, right in front of you, trucking on into the Bernsteins' Chinese yellow duplex, amid the sconces, silver bowls full of white and lavender anemones, and uniformed servants serving drinks and Roquefort cheese morsels rolled in crushed nuts—

But it's all right. They're *white* servants, not Claude and Maude, but white

South Americans. Lenny and Felicia are geniuses. After a while, it all comes down to servants. They are the cutting edge in Radical Chic. Obviously, if you are giving a party for the Black Panthers, as Lenny and Felicia are this evening, or as Sidney and Gail Lumet did last week, or as John Simon of Random House and Richard Baron, the publisher, did before that; or for the Chicago Eight, such as the party Jean vanden Heuvel gave; or for the grape workers or Bernadette Devlin, such as the parties Andrew Stein gave; or for the Young Lords, such as the party Ellie Guggenheimer is giving next week in *her* Park Avenue duplex; or for the Indians or the SDS or the G.I. coffee shops or even for the Friends of the Earth—well, then, obviously you can't have a Negro butler and maid, Claude and Maude, in uniform, circulating through the living room, the library, and the main hall serving drinks and canapés. Plenty of people have tried to think it out. They try to picture the Panthers or whoever walking in bristling with electric hair and Cuban shades and leather pieces and the rest of it, and they try to picture Claude and Maude with the black uniforms coming up and saying, "Would you care for a drink, sir?" They close their eyes and try to picture it *some way,* but there *is* no way. One simply cannot see that moment. So the current wave of Radical Chic has touched off the most desperate search for white servants. Carter and Amanda Burden have white servants. Sidney Lumet and his wife Gail, who is Lena Horne's daughter, have three white servants, including a Scottish nurse. Everybody has white servants. And Lenny and Felicia—they had it worked out before Radical Chic even started. Felicia grew up in Chile. Her father, Roy Elwood Cohn, an engineer from San Francisco, worked for the American Smelting and Refining Co. in Santiago. As Felicia Montealegre (her mother's maiden name), she became an actress in New York and won the *Motion Picture Daily* critics' award as the best new television actress of 1949. Anyway, they have a house staff of three white South American servants, including a Chilean cook, plus Lenny's English chauffeur and dresser, who is also white, of course. Can one comprehend how perfect that is, given . . . the times? Well, many of their friends can, and they ring up the Bernsteins and ask them to get South American servants for them, and the Bernsteins are so generous about it, so obliging, that people refer to them, good-naturedly and gratefully, as "the Spic and Span Employment Agency," with an easygoing ethnic humor, of course.

The only other thing to do is what Ellie Guggenheimer is doing next week with her party for the Young Lords in her duplex on Park Avenue at 89th Street, just ten blocks up from Lenny and Felicia. She is giving her party on a Sunday, which is the day off for the maid and the cleaning woman. "Two friends of mine"—she confides on the telephone—"two friends of mine who happen to be . . . not white—that's what I hate about the times we live in, the *terms*—well, they've agreed to be butler and maid . . . and I'm going to be a maid myself!"

Just at this point some well-meaning soul is going to say, Why not do without servants altogether if the matter creates such unbearable tension and one truly believes in equality? Well, even to raise the question is to reveal the most fundamental ignorance of life in the great co-ops and townhouses of the East Side in the age of Radical Chic. Why, my God! servants are not a mere convenience, they're an absolute psychological necessity. Once one is into that life, truly into it, with the morning workout on the velvet swings at Kounovsky's and the late mornings on the telephone, and lunch at the Running Footman, which is now regarded as really better than La Grenouille, Lutèce, Lafayette, La Caravelle, and the rest of the general Frog Pond, less ostentatious, more of the David Hicks feeling, less of the Parish-Hadley look, and then—well, then, the idea of not having servants is unthinkable. But even that does not say it all. It makes it sound like a matter of convenience, when actually it is a sheer and fundamental matter of—*having servants.* Does one comprehend?

God, what a flood of taboo thoughts runs through one's head at these Radical Chic events . . . But it's delicious. It is as if one's nerve endings were on red alert to the most intimate nuances of status. Deny it if you want to! Nevertheless, it runs through every soul here. It is the matter of the marvelous contradictions on all sides. It is like the delicious shudder you get when you try to force the prongs of two horseshoe magnets together . . . *them* and *us* . . .

For example, one's own servants, although white, are generally no problem. A discreet, euphemistic word about what sort of party it is going to be, and they will generally be models of correctness. The euphemisms are not always an easy matter, however. When talking to one's white servants, one doesn't really know whether to refer to blacks as *blacks, Negroes,* or *colored people.* When talking to other . . . well, *cultivated* persons, one says *blacks,* of course. It is the only word, currently, that implicitly shows one's awareness of the dignity of the black race. But somehow when you start to say the word to your own white servants, you hesitate. You can't get it out of your throat. Why? *Counter-guilt!* You realize that you are about to utter one of those touchstone words that divide the cultivated from the uncultivated, the attuned from the unattuned, the *hip* from the dreary. As soon as the word comes out of your mouth—you know it before the first vocable pops on your lips—your own servant is going to size you up as one of those *limousine liberals,* or whatever epithet they use, who are busy pouring white soul all over the black movement, and would you do as much for the white lower class, for the domestics of the East Side, for example, fat chance, sahib. Deny it if you want to! but such are the delicious little agonies of Radical Chic. So one settles for *Negro,* with the hope that the great god Culturatus has laid the ledger aside for the moment. . . . In any case, if one is able to make that small compromise, one's own servants are no real problem. But the elevator man and the doorman—the death rays they begin projecting, the curt responses, as soon as they see it is going to be one of *those* parties! Of course, they're all from Queens, and so forth, and one has to allow for that. For some reason the elevator men tend to be worse about it than the doormen, even; less sense of *politesse,* perhaps.

Or—what does one wear to these parties for the Panthers or the Young Lords or the grape workers? What does a woman wear? Obviously one does not want to wear something frivolously and pompously expensive, such as a Gerard Pipart party dress. On the other hand one does not want to arrive "poor-mouthing it" in some outrageous turtleneck and West Eighth Street bell-jean combination, as if one is "funky" and of "the people." Frankly, Jean vanden Heuvel—that's Jean there in the hallway giving everyone her famous smile, in which her eyes narrow down to f/16—frankly, Jean tends too much toward the funky fallacy. Jean, who is the daughter of Jules Stein, one of the wealthiest men in the country, is wearing some sort of rust-red snap-around suede skirt, the sort that English working girls pick up on Saturday afternoons in those absolutely *berserk* London boutiques like Bus Stop or Biba, where everything looks chic and yet skimpy and raw and vital. Felicia Bernstein seems to understand the whole thing better. Look at Felicia. She is wearing the simplest little black frock imaginable, with absolutely no ornamentation save for a plain gold necklace. It is perfect. It has dignity without any overt class symbolism.

Lenny? Lenny himself has been in the living room all this time, talking to old friends like the Duchins and the Stantons and the Lanes. Lenny is wearing a black turtleneck, navy blazer, Black Watch plaid trousers, and a necklace with a pendant hanging down to his sternum. His tailor comes here to the apartment to take the measurements and do the fittings. Lenny is a short, trim man, and yet he always seems tall. It is his head. He has a noble head, with a face that is at once sensitive and rugged, and a full stand of iron-gray hair, with side-burns, all set off nicely by the Chinese yellow of the room. His success radiates from his eyes and his smile with a charm that illustrates

Lord Jersey's adage that "contrary to what the Methodists tell us, money and success are good for the soul." Lenny may be fifty-one, but he is still the *Wunderkind* of American music. Everyone says so. He is not only one of the world's outstanding conductors, but a more than competent composer and pianist as well. He is the man who more than any other has broken down the wall between elite music and popular tastes, with *West Side Story* and his children's concerts on television. How natural that he should stand here in his own home radiating the charm and grace that make him an easy host for leaders of the oppressed. How ironic that the next hour should prove so shattering for this *egregio maestro!* How curious that the Negro by the piano should emerge tonight!

A bell rang, a dinner-table bell, by the sound of it, the sort one summons the maid out of the kitchen with, and the party shifted from out of the hall and into the living room. Felicia led the way, Felicia and a small gray man, with gray hair, a gray face, a gray suit, and a pair of Groovy but gray sideburns. A little gray man, in short, who would be popping up at key moments . . . to keep the freight train of history on the track, as it were . . .

Felicia was down at the far end of the living room trying to coax everybody in.

"Lenny!" she said. "Tell the fringes to come on in!" Lenny was still in the back of the living room, near the hall. "Fringes!" said Lenny. "Come on in!"

In the living room most of the furniture, the couches, easy chairs, side tables, side chairs, and so on, had been pushed toward the walls, and thirty or forty folding chairs were set up in the middle of the floor. It was a big, wide room with Chinese yellow walls and white moldings, sconces, pier-glass mirrors, a portrait of Felicia reclining on a summer chaise, and at the far end, where Felicia was standing, a pair of grand pianos. A pair of them; the two pianos were standing back to back, with the tops down and their bellies swooping out. On top of both pianos was a regular flotilla of family photographs in silver frames, the kind of pictures that stand straight up thanks to little velvet- or moiré-covered buttresses in the back, the kind that decorators in New York recommend to give a living room a homelike lived-in touch. "The million-dollar *chatchka* look," they call it. In a way it was perfect for Radical Chic. The nice part was that with Lenny it was instinctive; with Felicia, too. The whole place looked as if the inspiration had been to spend a couple of hundred thousand on the interior without looking pretentious, although that is no great sum for a thirteen-room co-op, of course . . . Imagine explaining all that to the Black Panthers. It was another delicious thought

. . . The sofas, for example, were covered in the fashionable splashy prints on a white background covering deep downy cushions, in the Billy Baldwin or Margaret Owen tradition—without it looking like Billy or Margaret had been in there fussing about with teapoys and japanned chairs. *Gemütlich* . . . Old Vienna when Grandpa was alive . . . That was the ticket . . .

The Fallen Idol: The Harlem Tragedy of Earl Manigault, from The City Game, *Pete Axthelm (1970)*

Pete Axthelm was raised in Rockville Center, Long Island, attended high school at Chaminade in Mineola, and received a scholarship to Yale University. Following graduation, Yale University Press published his senior thesis, "The Modern Confessional Novel," in 1967. But Axthelm's real loves were sportswriting and New York City, and he quickly became a columnist for the *New York Herald-Tribune.* Tragically, he succumbed to liver failure in 1991 at the age of 47.

Axthelm's book, *The City Game,* was, as he put it, "simply, the story of the city game, as it is experienced in the city that knows and loves it best." For Axthelm, basketball's "battlegrounds are strips of asphalt between tattered wire fences or crumbling buildings; its rhythms grow from the uneven thump of a ball against hard surfaces." Basketball is the game "for young athletes without cars or allowances—the game whose drama and action are intensified by its confined spaces and chaotic surroundings." As a result, Axthelm's book was not just about New York's professional team, the Knicks, and the acknowledged mecca of "hoop junkies," Madison Square Garden.

New York City had quickly become the spiritual home of the game James Naismith invented in Springfield, Massachusetts, in 1891. Basketball, Axthelm noted, had "always been something special to the kids of New York's bustling streets." And it was in the playgrounds of Brooklyn, the Bronx, and especially Harlem that some of the game's greatest legends were born. Earl Manigault, who died in May 1998, was one of the greatest of those legends of "the city game." One can still hear "the Goat's" name invoked on any given summer night on the Rucker Playground on 155th Street opposite the site of the old Polo Grounds.

In the litany of quiet misfortunes that have claimed so many young athletes in the ghetto, it may seem almost impossible to select one man and give him special importance. Yet in the stories and traditions that are recounted in the Harlem parks, one figure does emerge above the rest. Asked about the finest athletes they have seen, scores of ballplayers in a dozen parks mention Connie Hawkins and Lew Alcindor and similar celebrities. But almost without exception, they speak first of one star who didn't go on: Earl Manigault.

No official scorers tabulate the results of pickup games; there are no composite box scores to prove that Manigault ranked highest among playground athletes. But in its own way, a reputation in the parks is as definable as a scoring average in the NBA. Cut off from more formal channels of media and exposure, street ballplayers develop their own elaborate word-of-mouth system. One spectacular performance or one backward, twisting stuff shot may be the seed of an athlete's reputation. If he can repeat it a few times in a park where the competition is tough, the word goes out that he may be something special. Then there will be challenges from more established players, and a man who can withstand them may earn a "neighborhood rep." The process continues in an expanding series of confrontations, until the best athletes have emerged. Perhaps a dozen men at a given time may enjoy "citywide reps," guaranteeing them attention and respect in any playground they may visit. And of those, one or two will stand alone.

A few years ago, Earl Manigault stood among the loftiest. But his reign was brief, and in order to capture some feeling of what his stature meant in the playground world, one must turn to two athletes who enjoy similar positions today. Herman "Helicopter" Knowings, now in his late twenties, is among the most remarkable playground phenomena; he was a demigod before Manigault, and he remains one after Earl's departure. Uneducated and unable to break into pro ball, the Helicopter has managed to retain the spring in his legs and the will power to remain at the summit after many of his contemporaries have faded from the basketball scene. Joe Hammond, not yet twenty, is generally recognized as the best of the young crop. Neither finished school and vaulted into the public spotlight, but both pick up money playing in a minor league, the Eastern League—and both return home between games to continue their domination of the parks.

The Helicopter got his name for obvious reasons: when he goes up to block a shot, he seems to hover endlessly in midair above his prey, daring him to shoot—and then blocking whatever shot his hapless foe attempts. Like most memorable playground moves, it is not only effective but magnetic. As Knowings goes up, the crowd shouts, "Fly, 'copter, fly," and seems to share his heady trip. When he shoves a ball down the throat of a visiting

NBA star—as he often does in the Rucker Tournament—the Helicopter inflates the pride of a whole neighborhood.

Like Connie Hawkins, Knowings can send waves of electricity through a park with his mere presence. Standing by a court, watching a game in progress with intent eyes, the Helicopter doesn't have to ask to play. People quickly spot his dark, chiseled, ageless face and six-foot-four-inch frame, and they make room for him. Joe Hammond is less imposing. A shade over six feet, he is a skinny, sleepy-eyed kid who looks slow and tired, the way backcourt star Clinton Robinson appeared during his reign. But like Robinson, Hammond has proved himself, and now he stands as the descendant of Pablo Robertson and James Barlow and the other backcourt heroes of the streets.

The kings of playground ball are not expected to defend their titles every weekend, proving themselves again and again the way less exalted players must. But when a new athlete begins winning a large following, when the rumors spread that he is truly someone special, the call goes out: If he is a forward, get the Helicopter; if he's a guard, let's try him against Joe Hammond. A crowd will gather before the star arrives. It is time for a supreme test.

Jay Vaughn has been in such confrontations several times. He saw the Helicopter defend his reign, and he watched Joe Hammond win his own way to the top. He described the rituals:

"When I first met the Helicopter, I was only about seventeen, and I was playing with a lot of kids my age at Wagner Center. I was better than the guys I was playing with and I knew it, so I didn't feel I had anything to prove. I was playing lazy, lackadaisical. And one of the youth workers saw how cocky I was and decided to show me just how good I really was. He sent for the Helicopter.

"One day I was just shooting baskets, trying all kinds of wild shots, not thinking about fundamentals, and I saw this older dude come in. He had sneakers and shorts on and he was ready to play. I said, 'Who's this guy? He's too old for our games. Is he supposed to be good?'

" 'The coach sent for him,' somebody told me, 'He's gonna play you.'

"I said to myself, 'Well, fine, I'll try him,' and I went out there one-on-one with Herman Knowings. Well, it was a disastrous thing. I tried lay-ups, jump shots, hooks. And everything I threw up, he blocked. The word had gone out that Herman was there, and a crowd was gathering, and I said to myself, 'You got to do something. You're getting humiliated.' But the harder I tried, the more he shoved the ball down into my face. I went home and thought about that game for a long time. Like a lot of other young athletes, I had been put in my place.

"I worked out like crazy after that. I was determined to get back. After about a month, I challenged him again. I found myself jumping higher, feeling stronger, and playing better than ever before. I wasn't humiliated again. But I was beaten. Since that time, I've played against Herman many times. He took an interest in me and gave me a lot of good advice. And now, when I see he's going to block a shot, I may be able to fake and go around him and score, and people will yell, 'The pupil showed the master.'

"Then, of course, he'll usually come back and stuff one on me. . . ."

"Joe Hammond was playing in the junior division games in the youth centers when I was in the senior games," Vaughn continued. "He was three years younger than me, and sometimes after I'd played, I'd stay and watch his game. He wasn't that exceptional. Just another young boy who was gonna play ball. In fact, at that time, I didn't even know his last name.

"Then I came home from school in the summer of 1969, and one name was on everyone's lips: Joe Hammond. I thought it must have been somebody new from out of town, but people said, no, he'd been around Harlem all the time. They described him and it sounded like the young kid I'd watched around the centers, but I couldn't believe it was the same guy. Then I saw him, and it was the same Joe, and he was killing a bunch of guys his own age. He was much improved, but I still said to myself, 'He's young. He won't do much against the older brothers. They've been in business too long.'

"But then I heard, 'Joe's up at 135th Street beating the pros. . . . Joe's doing everything to those guys.' I still didn't take it too seriously. In fact, when Joe came out to Mount Morris Park for a game against a good team I was on, I said, 'Now we'll see how you do. You won't do anything today.'

"Now I believe in him. Joe Hammond left that game with seven minutes to go. He had 40 points. Like everybody had said, Joe was the one."

Many reputations have risen and fallen in the decade between the arrival of the Helicopter and of Joe Hammond. Most have now been forgotten, but a few "reps" outlive the men who earn them. Two years ago Connie Hawkins did not show up for a single game during the Rucker Tournament. When it was time to vote for the Rucker All-Star team, the coaches voted for Hawkins. "If you're going to have an all-star game in Harlem," said Bob McCullough, the tournament director, "you vote for Connie or you don't vote." (Having been elected, The Hawk did appear for the All-Star game—and won the Most Valuable Player award.) One other reputation has endured on a similar scale. Countless kids in Harlem repeat the statement: "You want to talk about basketball in this city, you've got to talk about Earl Manigault."

Manigault played at Benjamin Franklin High School in 1962 and 1963, then spent a season at Laurinburg Institute. Earl never reached college, but when he returned to Harlem he continued to dominate the playgrounds. He was the king of his own generation of ballplayers, the idol for the generation that followed. He was a six-foot-two-inch forward who could outleap men eight inches taller, and his moves had a boldness and fluidity that transfixed opponents and spectators alike. Freewheeling, unbelievably high-jumping, and innovative, he was the image of the classic playground athlete.

But he was also a very human ghetto youth, with weaknesses and doubts that left him vulnerable. Lacking education and motivation, looking toward an empty future, he found that basketball could take him only so far. Then he veered into the escape route of the streets, and became the image of the hellish side of ghetto existence. Earl is now in his mid-twenties, a dope addict, in prison.

Earl's is more than a personal story. On the playgrounds, he was a powerful magnetic figure who carried the dreams and ideals of every kid around him as the spun and twisted and sailed over all obstacles. When he fell, he carried those aspirations down with him. Call him a wasted talent, a pathetic victim, even a tragic hero: he had symbolized all that was sublime and terrible about this city game.

"You think of him on the court and you think of so many incredible things that it's hard to sort them out," said Bob Spivey, who played briefly with Earl at Franklin. "But I particularly recall one all-star game in the gym at PS 113, in about 1964. Most of the best high school players in the city were there: Charlie Scott, who went on to North Carolina; Vaughn Harper, who went to Syracuse, and a lot more. But the people who were there will hardly remember the others. Earl was the whole show.

"For a few minutes, Earl seemed to move slowly, feeling his way, getting himself ready. Then he got the ball on a fast break. Harper, who was six feet six, and Val Reed, who was six feet eight, got back quickly to defend. You wouldn't have given Earl a chance to score. Then he accelerated, changing his step suddenly. And at the foul line he went into the air. Harper and Reed went up, too, and between them, the two big men completely surrounded the rim. But Earl just kept going higher, and finally he two-hand-dunked the ball over both of them. For a split second there was complete silence, and then the crowd exploded. They were cheering so loud that they stopped the game for five minutes. Five minutes. That was Earl Manigault."

Faces light up as Harlem veterans reminisce about Manigault. Many street players won reputations with elaborate innovations and tricks. Jackie Jackson was among the first to warm up for games by picking quarters off the top of the backboard. Willie Hall, the former St. John's leader, apparently originated the custom of jumping to the top of the board and, instead of merely blocking a shot, slamming a hand with tremendous force against the board; the fixture would vibrate for several seconds after the blow, causing an easy lay-up to bounce crazily off the rim. Other noted leapers were famous for "pinning"—blocking a lay-up, then simply holding it momentarily against the backboard in a gesture of triumph. Some players seemed to hold it for seconds, suspended in air, multiplying the humiliation of the man who had tried the futile shot. Then they could slam the ball back down at the shooter or, for special emphasis, flip it into the crowd.

Earl Manigault did all of those things and more, borrowing, innovating, and forming one of the most exciting styles Harlem crowds ever watched. Occasionally, he would drive past a few defenders, dunk the ball with one hand, catch it with the other—and raise it and stuff it through the hoop a second time before returning to earth.

"I was in the eighth grade when Earl was in the eleventh," said Charley Yelverton, now a star at Fordham. "I was just another young kid at the time. Like everybody else on the streets, I played some ball. But I just did it for something to do. I wasn't that excited about it. Then there happened to be a game around my block, down at 112th Street, and a lot of the top players were in it—and Earl came down to play. Well, I had never believed things like that could go on. I had never known what basketball could be like. Everybody in the game was doing something, stuffing or blocking shots or making great passes. There's only one game I've ever seen in my life to compare to it—the Knicks' last game against the Lakers.

"But among all the stars, there was no doubt who was the greatest. Passing, shooting, going up in the air, Earl just left everybody behind. No one could turn it on like he could."

Keith Edwards, who lived with Earl during the great days of the Young Life team, agreed. "I guess he had about the most natural ability that I've ever seen. Talent for talent, inch for inch, you'd have to put him on a par with Alcindor and the other superstars. To watch him was like poetry. To play with him or against him—just to be on the same court with him—was a deep experience.

"You can't really project him against an Alcindor, though, because you could never picture Earl going to UCLA or any place like that. He was never the type to really face his responsibilities and his future. He didn't want to think ahead. There was very little discipline about the man. . . ."

And so the decline began. "I lived with the man for about two or three years," said Edwards, "from his predrug period into the beginning of his drug period. There were six of us there, and maybe some of us would have liked to help him out. But we were all just young guys finding themselves, and when Earl and another cat named Onion started to get into the drug thing, nobody really had a right, or was in a position, to say much about it. And even as he got into the drugs, he remained a beautiful person. He just had nowhere to go. . . ."

"The athlete in Harlem," said Pat Smith, "naturally becomes a big man in the neighborhood. And if he goes on to college and makes his way out of the ghetto, he can keep being a big man, a respected figure. But if he doesn't make it, if he begins to realize that he isn't going to get out, then he looks around, and maybe he isn't so big anymore. The pusher and the pimp have more clothes than they can ever get around to wearing; when they walk down the street they get respect. But the ballplayer is broke, and he knows that in a certain number of years he won't even have his reputation left. And unless he is an unusually strong person, he may be tempted to go another way. . . ."

"You like to think of the black athlete as a leader of the community," said Jay Vaughn, "but sometimes the idea of leadership can get twisted. A lot of the young dudes on the streets will encourage a big-time ballplayer to be big-time in other ways. They expect you to know all the big pushers, where to buy drugs, how to handle street life. And if they're fooling with small-time drugs, maybe they'll expect you to mess with big-time drugs. It may sound ridiculous at first, but when you're confronted with these attitudes a lot, and you're not strong enough, well, you find yourself hooked."

It didn't happen suddenly. On the weekends, people would still find Earl Manigault at the parks, and flashes of the magnetic ability were there. Young athletes would ask his advice, and he would still be helpful; even among the ones who knew he was sinking deeper into his drug habit, he remained respected and popular. But by early 1968, he seldom came to the parks, and his old friends would find him on street corners along Eighth Avenue, nodding. "He was such a fine person," said Jay Vaughn, "you saw him and you wished you could see some hope, some bright spot in his existence. But there was no good part of his life, of course. Because drugs do ruin you."

In the summer of 1968, Bob Hunter was working on a drug rehabilitation program. He looked up Earl. They became close, building a friendship that went deeper than their mutual respect on a basketball court. "Earl was an unusual type of addict," said Hunter. "He understood that he was a hard addict, and he faced it very honestly. He wanted to help me in the drug program, and he gave me a lot of hints on how to handle younger addicts. He knew different tricks that would appeal to them and win their trust. And he also knew all the tricks they would use, to deceive me into thinking they were getting cured. Earl had used the tricks himself, and he helped me see through them, and maybe we managed to save a few young kids who might have got hooked much worse.

"But it's the most frustrating thing in the world, working with addicts. It's hard to accept the fact that a man who has been burned will go back and touch fire. But they do it. I have countless friends on drugs, and I had many more who have died from drugs. And somehow it's hard to just give up on them and forget that they ever existed. Maybe you would think that only the less talented types would let themselves get hooked—but then you'd see a guy like Earl and you couldn't understand. . . . "

Some people hoped that Earl would be cured that summer. He did so much to help Hunter work with others that people felt he could help himself. Hunter was not as optimistic. "The truth is that nobody is ever going to cure Earl," he said. "the only way he'll be cured is by himself. A lot of people come off drugs only after they've been faced with an extreme crisis. For example, if they come very close to dying and somehow escape, then they might be able to stay away from the fire. But it takes something like that, most of the time."

Earl was not cured, and as the months went on the habit grew more expensive. And then he had to steal. "Earl is such a warm person," said Vaughn, "you know that he'd never go around and mug people or anything. But let's face it: most addicts, sooner or later, have to rob in order to survive." Earl broke into a store. He is now in prison. "Maybe that will be the crisis he needs," said Hunter. "Maybe, just possibly . . . But when you're talking about addicts, it's very hard to get your hopes too high."

Harold "Funny" Kitt went to Franklin three years behind Earl Manigault. When Funny finished in 1967, he was rated the best high school player in the city—largely because he had modeled himself so closely after Earl. "We all idolized Earl in those days," Kitt said. "And when you idolize somebody, you think of the good things, not the bad. As we watched Earl play ball, we had visions of him going on to different places, visiting the whole world, becoming a great star and then maybe coming back here to see us and talk to us about it all.

"But he didn't do any of those things. He just went into his own strange world, a world I hope I'll never see. I guess there were reasons. I guess there were frustrations that only Earl knew about, and I feel sorry for what happened. But when Earl went into that world, it had an effect on all of us, all the young ballplayers. I idolized the man. And he hurt me."

Beyond the hurt, though, Earl left something more. If his career was a small dramatization of the world of Harlem basketball, then he was a fitting protagonist, in his magnitude and his frailty, a hero for his time. "Earl was quiet, he was honest," said Jay Vaughn, "and he handled the pressures of being the star very well. When you're on top, everybody is out to challenge you, to make their own reps by doing something against you. One guy after another wants to take a shot, and some stars react to all that by bragging, or by being aloof from the crowd.

"Earl was different. The game I'll never forget was in the G-Dub [George Washington High] tournament one summer, when the team that Earl's group was scheduled to play didn't show. The game was forfeited, and some guys were just looking for some kind of pickup game, when one fellow on the team that forfeited came in and said, 'Where's Manigault? I want to play Manigault.'

"Well, this guy was an unknown and he really had no right to talk like that. If he really wanted to challenge a guy like Earl, he should have been out in the parks, building up a rep of his own. But he kept yelling and bragging, and Earl quietly agreed to play him one-on-one. The word went out within minutes, and immediately there was a big crowd gathered for the drama.

"Then they started playing. Earl went over the guy and dunked. Then he blocked the guy's first shot. It was obvious that the man had nothing to offer against Earl. But he was really determined to win himself a rep. So he started pushing and shoving and fouling. Earl didn't say a word. He just kept making his moves and beating the guy, and the guy kept grabbing and jostling him to try to stop him. It got to the point where it wasn't really basketball. And suddenly Earl put down the ball and said, 'I don't need this. You're the best.' Then he just walked away.

"Well, if Earl had gone on and whipped the guy 30 to 0, he couldn't have proved any more than he did. The other cat just stood there, not knowing what to say. The crowd surrounded Earl, and some of us said things about the fouling and the shoving. But he didn't say anything about it. He didn't feel any need to argue or complain. He had everyone's respect and he knew it. The role he played that day never left anyone who saw it. This was a beautiful man."

Ode to New York, Reed Whittemore (1974)

Reed Whittemore, born in 1919, taught at Carleton College and later at the University of Maryland from 1967 to 1984. He is one of only two poets to serve two terms as the Poetry Consultant for the Library of Congress, once in 1964–1965 and again in 1984–1985. His first book of poems was published in 1945, and he was the literary editor for the *New Republic* from 1969 to 1973. Whittemore has written that "poets should look out. Not in." In "Ode to New York" he playfully and sarcastically takes New York City to task for its multitude of sins.

Let me not be unfair Lord to New York that sink that sewer
Where the best the worst and the middle
Of our land and all others go in their days of hope to be made
over
Into granite careerists
Let me not be unfair to that town whose residents
Not content to subside in their own stench
Drag down the heavens let me not be unfair because I have
known
An incorruptible New Yorker (he was a saint)
Also NY has produced at least three books
Two plays
A dozen fine dresses meals shirts taxidrivers
Not to mention Jack (Steve?) Brodie
And Mayor La Guardia why should it matter.
That the rest is garbage
No let me be fair
And mention wonders like East 9th Street
Why should anybody care that NY is 2/3 of our country's ills
(And Washington 1/3, and Muncie Dallas Birmingham and LA
the rest)

When it has crooks so rich and powerful that when they drive to
town
They can park?
Let us not forget that TV is in New York and
the worst slums
the largest fortunes
the most essential inhumanity
Since Nero or maybe Attila as well as
Hospitals that admit no patient without a $300 deposit
if I were a local
I'd take the express to Rahway but let me just say
That I don't like New York much
All that corrupt stone
All those dishonest girders decadent manholes diseased
telephones
New York reminds me of when I had jaundice
New York is sick in the inner soul
Of its gut but we'll be dead of it
Before it is and so New York
You wonderful fun town
Who inspireth my animus
And leadeth two hundred million other Americans to wish they
had not
been born under the spell of free enterprise out in a
Martian restroom
New York
I know that when I speak of you I speak of me
I speak of us
I speak of selves who resolved at the age of four to
convert themselves into currency
Because at the age of four they (I, we) had already
learned
That no food clothing housing
Existed other than currency
And no faith hope charity
Other than currency
good waterproof dollars
And if there were labor that could not be turned into
currency

They (I, we) knew not to do it
And if there were thoughts that could not be turned
into currency
They (I, we) knew not to have them

So here we are in the latter day of our wisdom
Yesterday sweetness and light reached a new low
In heavy trading
Even porn is in trouble
what can be done?
In a decade a dozen of our holiest ones
Will own the island
But rats will be running the island

In a decade not a minute of a working man's day will
belong to a working man
All subway riders will pay dues to the Limousine Club

Rats will be running the island
There is no surer route to the grave than through NY
And all American routes go through NY
NY lurks in the corners of our churches paintings novels
NY infests our playing fields newspapers trade unions
There is not a square foot of American sidewalk without
the mark of a NY entrepreneur
Wherever you drive he will cut in front of you
he will get there first

Rats on the island
Ravenous rats
Bred by the banks and the stock exchange
Fed by the eighteen percenters
World that will end
But when?

Lord
you have sent us prophets
They have prattled about revolution and pocketed the
proceeds
They have made it
by an infallible law of New York

In direct proportion to the extravagance and falsehood
of their announced visions
They have built the hysteria of constant and drastic
social change into each breakfast
They have taught our children how to stop war on
Monday poverty on Tuesday racism on Wednesday
sexism on Thursday and final exams on Friday

Yet nothing changes

And wherever one drives the prophets are out in front
they get there first

Rats on the island

Oh New York let me be fair you hell town
I was born to the north of you have lived to the west of
you
I have sneaked up on you by land air and sea and been
robbed in your clip joints
I have left you hundreds of times in the dream that I
could
Leave you
but always you sit there
Sinking
my dearest my sweet
Would you buy these woids?

New York, Edward Field (1977)

Edward Field was born in Brooklyn on June 7, 1924. He attended New York University but left to go to Europe and begin a writing career. His first book of poems, *Stand up, Friend, with Me* (1963), was given the Lamont Award. He has published multiple volumes of poetry and has been awarded a Guggenheim Fellowship, the Prix de Rome, and the Shelley Memorial Award. Field has also edited poetry anthologies and wrote the narration for the documentary film *To Be Alive,* which won an Academy Award in 1965. A long-time resident of Greenwich Village, he collaborated with Neil Derrick in 1982 to write a novel, *The Villagers,* which fictionally chronicles the history of the Village from 1840 to 1975.

Field's work is often marked by a sly, playful humor, and his poem "New York" evokes the spirit of Walt Whitman both in his understanding of the eroticism of the city and in his desire to, as Whitman put it, "loaf and invite his soul."

I LIVE in a beautiful place, a city
people claim to be astonished
when you say you live there.
They talk of junkies, muggings, dirt, and noise,
missing the point completely.

I tell them where they live it is hell,
a land of frozen people.
They never think of people.

Home, I am astonished by this environment
that is also a form of nature
like those paradises of trees and grass
but this is a people paradise
where we are the creatures mostly
though thank God for dogs, cats, sparrows, and roaches.

This vertical place is no more an accident
than the Himalayas are.
The city needs all those tall buildings
to contain the tremendous energy here.
The landscape is in a state of balance.
We do God's will whether we know it or not:
Where I live the streets end in a river of sunlight.

Nowhere else in the country do people
show just what they feel—
we don't put on any act.
Look at the way New Yorkers
walk down the street. It says,
I don't care. What nerve,
to dare to live their dreams, or nightmares,
and no one bothers to look.
True, you have to be an expert to live here.
Part of the trick is not to go anywhere, lounge about,
go slowly in the midst of the rush for novelty.
Anyway, beside the eats the big event here
is the streets which are full of love—
we hug and kiss a lot. You can't say that
for anywhere else around. For some
it is the sex part they care about and get—
there's all the opportunity in the world if you want it.
For me it is different:
Out walking, my soul seeks its food.
It knows what it wants.
Instantly it recognizes its mate, our eyes meet,
and our beings exchange a vital energy,
the universe goes on Charge
and we pass by without holding.

The Brooklyn Bridge, from Sketches from Life, *Lewis Mumford (1981)*

Lewis Mumford was born in Flushing, Queens, in 1895 and studied at City College, Columbia, and the New School for Social Research. Mumford spent much of his career theorizing about the place of art, architecture, and technology in urban life. His opus *The City in History* (1961) won the National Book Award, and his architecture columns in *The New Yorker,* "Skyline," were widely praised. Mumford lived in and championed the model community Sunnyside Gardens in Queens before moving to upstate New York for the last half century of his life. For Mumford, though, the city had to be "rational" and, as a result, he was an early champion of the Regional Plan Association that sought to widen the perspective of urban planners to see more than just central cities. Mumford had numerous battles with Robert Moses (who once tried to run Fifth Avenue through the middle of Washington Square Park) but also with Jane Jacobs, whose landmark book *The Death and Life of Great American Cities* (1961) he disdainfully referred to as "Mother Jacobs' Home Remedies for Urban Cancer." Mumford's life spanned virtually the entire twentieth century, and he eventually moved upstate to a small town, Amenia, as he watched New York City turn from what he called a "Metropolis to a Necropolis."

DURING this early period of manhood (1914–1919) I began to experience the waterfront of New York, by repeated rides on ferryboats, in a fashion that has now become impossible. Everywhere the wholesale commitment to bridges and tunnels across and under the rivers and bays, for the sake of speed alone, is depriving us of this primal source of recreation, causing us to go farther in search of enlivening change—and often to fare worse.

But surely the ferryboat was one of the great inventions of the Nineteenth Century: that great turtlelike creature—plodding through waters often iridescent with scum near the ferry slips, doggedly meeting the hazards of time and weather, sometimes serving as a summer excursion boat to Staten Island, sometimes bumping and cracking through the ice floes in the surly black water, so that the salt spray would tingle in one's nostrils.

What endless variations on the simple theme of "passage" by water! Even the short trips to Jersey City from downtown New York provided a touch of uncertainty and adventure, allowing for the tide, dodging other boats and ships, all with a closeness to the sea and sky and the wide sweep of the city itself that no other form of locomotion could boast.

Ferryboats would have been worthwhile for their value as a source of recreation alone: no, I would go further, they were worth running if only to give sustenance to poets and lovers and lonely young people, from Walt Whitman to Edna St. Vincent Millay, from Alfred Stieglitz and John Sloan to myself. Ferries had uses beyond the ordinary needs for transportation, and their relative slowness was not the least part of their merit—though as to speed, it has often taken far more time to cross by motorcar from Manhattan to Brooklyn or from San Francisco to Oakland during the rush hour, amid poisonous fumes and irritating tensions, than it once did by ferry. Those who put speed above all other values are often cheated even of speed by their dedication to a single mode of mass locomotion.

No poet, hurtling by plane even as far as Cathay, has yet written a poem comparable to "Crossing Brooklyn Ferry"; no painter has come back with a picture comparable to John Sloan's "Ferryboat Ride," which, for me, in its dun colors, recalls one of the moments I liked best on the North River: a lowery sky, a smoke-hung skyline, and the turbid waters of the river. When I read Whitman's poem now, I realize the special historic advantage of belonging to a generation that is "ebbing with the ebb-tide," for I am old enough to have felt every sensation he described, to have seen every sight—except the then-bowered heights of Hoboken—with a sense of identification that even the most active imagination could hardly evoke now.

Those wonderful long ferry rides! Alas for a later generation that cannot guess how they opened the city up, or how the change of pace and place, from swift to slow, from land to water, had a specially stimulating effect upon the mind. But if I loved the ferries, I loved the bridges, too; and one after another I walked over all the bridges that linked Manhattan to Long Island, even that least rewarding one, the Queensboro. But it was the Brooklyn Bridge that I loved best, partly because of its own somber perfection of form, with its spidery lacing of cables contrasting with the great stone piers through which they were suspended: stone masonry that seemed in its harmony of granite pier, classic coping, and ogive arch to crystallize the essence of Roman, Romanesque, and Gothic architecture; while its cables stretched like a bowstring to shoot a steel arrow into our own age.

Since we lived on Brooklyn Heights between 1922 and 1925, I took every possible occasion to walk back and forth across the Brooklyn Bridge; and I knew it in all weathers and at all times of the day and night: so it is no wonder that when I came to write "Sticks and Stones" in 1924, I gave perhaps the first critical appreciation of that achievement since Montgomery Schuyler's contemporary essay, published in his "American Architecture" in 1893.

At that period, as it happened, Hart Crane and I—then personally unknown to each other—were living on Brooklyn Heights, and he, in his poet's way, was engaged in a similar enterprise: indeed, some time later, after I had moved away, he consulted me about biographic materials on the Roeblings, the builders of the Bridge. Thousands of people must have felt the same as we in our different ways had felt, ever since the Bridge was opened; but no one had freshly expressed it until the twenties. Only then did the first formal biography of John Roebling appear, to be followed a decade later by David Steinman's detailed study of the building of the Brooklyn Bridge—a book that by happy chance passed under my favorable editorial eye before my own publishers decided to go ahead with it.

So deeply did the Bridge itself capture my imagination that before I had abandoned my aim of becoming a playwright (as late as 1927), I wrote the first draft of a long play on the theme of the Bridge: a play that I recognized, even while writing it, could be produced only when done over into a motion picture. Fragments of that play still haunt me: not least a love scene, at night, high up on one of the piers of the half-finished structure, with a sense of giddy isolation heightening the passion of the lovers—and the muted whistles and hoots from the river below, in the spreading fog, underscoring with the note of the city itself their private encounter.

That scene no one will of course find in any Roebling biography, but the stuff of it I was soon to encounter, if less exaltedly, in my own life; for many of my written fantasies have turned out to be gropings, forebodings, formative anticipations of unconscious urgings that were soon to take on outward shapes, all the more because of their contrast with the sober, neatly planned, dutiful routine, so close in its more workmanlike qualities to that of an engineer, that characterizes such a large part of my workaday existence.

There was a slightly older contemporary who, as it seemed in 1915, had caught the very beat of the city, a beat that had begun to pulsate with quickening consciousness in all of us. This was Ernest Poole, who in "The Harbor," through his choice of scenes, characters, social issues, said something for my generation that no one else had yet said, though he was never—that was perhaps his tragedy!—to say it so well again. Brooklyn Heights and "The Harbor" took shape almost entirely in Poole's imagination. But he captured the contrast between the depths of Furman Street, on the level of the waterfront, rimmed by a jumble of warehouses and docks, and the top of the stone-walled escarpment, with its seemly rows of brick or serpentine houses which commanded the whole harbor. There on Furman Street in the middle of the afternoon I had already seen an aged, drunken slattern, foul with whiskey and fouler with words—exhibiting the destitution and squalor that the gardens and mansions above both actually and figuratively overlooked.

I hardly dare to look at "The Harbor" to find out how the printed pages would compare now with the sensations I had in 1915, when I first read the book. Somehow that novel seethed with my own hopeful excitement over the contemporary world of factories and steamships, of employers and labor unions, of political strife and private ambition, giving me much the same reaction I had felt earlier when reading H. G. Wells's "The New Machiavelli" or his "Tono-Bungay"—both books that influenced my youth. "The Harbor" satisfied my appetite for the concrete and the contemporary, which was a very real appetite in those quickening days. The fact that Poole saw the city in much the same way I was beginning to see it gave moral backing and political support to my own efforts.

Not that I needed much backing! We all had a sense that we were on the verge of translation into a new world, a quite magical translation, in which the best hopes of the American Revolution, the French Revolution, and the Industrial Revolution would all be simultaneously fulfilled. The First World War battered and shattered those hopes, but it took years before the messages received through our eyes or felt at our fingers' ends were effectively conveyed to our brains and could be decoded: for long those ominous messages simply did not make sense. Until well into the 1930s we could always see the bright side of the darkest cloud. We did not, while the spirit of our confident years worked in us, guess that the sun upon which we counted might soon be in eclipse.

Yes: I loved the great bridges and walked back and forth over them, year after year. But as often happens with repeated experiences, one memory stands out above all others: a twilight hour in early spring—it was March, I think—when, starting from the Brooklyn end, I faced into the west wind sweeping over the rivers from New Jersey. The ragged, slate-blue cumulus clouds that gathered over the horizon left open patches for the light of the waning sun to shine through, and finally, as I reached the middle of the Brooklyn Bridge, the sunlight spread across the sky, forming a halo around the jagged mountain of skyscrapers, with the darkened loft buildings and warehouses huddling below in the foreground. The towers, topped by the golden pinnacles of the new Woolworth Building, still caught the light even as it began to ebb away. Three-quarters of the way across the Bridge I saw the skyscrapers in the deepening darkness become slowly honeycombed with lights until, before I reached the Manhattan end, these buildings piled up in a dazzling mass against the indigo sky.

Here was my city, immense, overpowering, flooded with energy and light; there below lay the river and the harbor, catching the last flakes of gold on their waters, with the black tugs, free from their barges, plodding dockward, the ferryboats lumbering from pier to pier, the tramp steamers slowly crawling toward the sea, the Statue of Liberty erectly standing, little curls of steam coming out of boat whistles or towered chimneys, while the rumbling elevated trains and trolley cars just below me on the bridge moved in a relentless tide to carry tens of thousands homeward. And there was I, breasting the March wind, drinking in the city and the sky, both vast, yet both contained in me, transmitting through me the great mysterious will that had made them and the promise of the new day that was still to come.

The world, at that moment, opened before me, challenging me, beckoning me, demanding something of me that it would take more than a lifetime to give, but raising all my energies by its own vivid promise to a higher pitch. In that sudden revelation of power and beauty all the confusions of adolescence dropped from me, and I trod the narrow, resilient boards of the footway with a new confidence that came, not from my isolated self alone but from the collective energies I had confronted and risen to.

I cannot hope to bring back the exaltation of that moment: the wonder of it was like the wonder of an orgasm in the body of one's beloved, as if one's whole life had led up to that moment and had swiftly culminated there. And yet I have carried the sense of that occasion, along with two or three other similar moments, equally enveloping and pregnant, through my life: they remain, not as a constant presence, but as a momentary flash reminding me of heights approached and scaled, as a mountain climber might carry with him the memory of some daring ascent, never to be achieved again. Since then I have courted that moment more than once on the Brooklyn Bridge; but the exact conjunction of weather and light and mood and inner readiness has never come back. That experience remains alone: a fleeting glimpse of the utmost possibilities life may hold for man.

It's Six A.M. *Do You Know Where You Are?, Jay McInerney (1982)*

"It's Six A.M. Do You Know Where You Are?" was originally published in the *Paris Review* and became the first chapter of Jay McInerney's best-selling novel *Bright Lights, Big City* (1984). That novel chronicled the life of a young "fact checker" working at *The New Yorker* (as Truman Capote had before him) trying to make enough money to live during the day and living a life of dissipation in the nightclubs of 1980s New York City. As McInerney himself has said, he "rode the eighties very hard and drained the cup dry in New York."

McInerney spoke to a generation of yuppies in much the same way that the young F. Scott Fitzgerald had to the Jazz Age in *This Side of Paradise*, and he became something of a cult hero as part of a celebrated "Brat Pack" of young authors that included Bret Easton Ellis. McInerney left the city because "New York is such a sensory overload that the only way to survive is to block out some of the input, to become inured—to develop that famous New York shell and pretend that life here is normal. Step over bodies, as it were. But for a writer, it's death to stop noticing, to start taking things for granted. This is a weird place, and as soon as you forget that, you should go away for a while."

YOU are not the kind of guy who would be at a place like this at this time of the morning. But you are here, and you cannot say that the terrain is entirely unfamiliar, although the details are a little fuzzy. You are at a nightclub talking to a girl with a shaved head. The club is either the Bimbo Box or the Lizard Lounge. It might all come a little clearer if you could slip into the bathroom and do a little more Bolivian Marching Powder. There is a small voice inside of you insisting that this epidemic lack of clarity is the result of too much of that already, but you are not yet willing to listen to that voice. The night has already turned on that imperceptible pivot where two A.M. changes to six A.M. You know that moment has come and gone, but you are not yet willing to concede that you have crossed the line beyond which all is gratuitous damage and the palsy of unravelled nerve endings. Somewhere back there it was possible to cut your losses, but you rode past that moment on a comet trail of white powder and now you are trying to hang onto that rush. Your brain at this moment is composed of brigades of tiny Bolivian soldiers. They are tired and muddy from their long march through the night. There are holes in their boots and they are hungry. They need to be fed. They need the Bolivian Marching Powder.

Something vaguely tribal about this scene—pendulous jewrid of this bald girl because she is doing bad things to your mood.

In the bathroom there are no doors on the stalls, which makes it tough to be discreet. But clearly, you are not the only person here to take on fuel. Lots of sniffling going on. The windows in here are blacked over, and for this you are profoundly grateful.

Hup, two. Three, four. The Bolivian soldiers are back on their feet. They are off and running in formation. Some of them are dancing, and you must do the same.

Just outside the door you spot her: tall, dark, and alone, half-hiding behind a pillar at the edge of the dance floor. You approach laterally, moving your stuff like a bad spade through the slalom of a synthesized conga rhythm. She jumps when you touch her shoulder.

"Dance?"

She looks at you as if you had just suggested instrumental rape. "I do not speak English," she says, when you ask again.

"Français?"

She shakes her head. Why is she looking at you that way, like there are tarantulas nesting in your eye sockets?

"You are by any chance from Bolivia? Or Peru?"

She is looking around for help now. Remembering a recent encounter with a young heiress's bodyguard at Danceteria—or was it New Berlin?—you back off, hands raised over your head.

The Bolivian soldiers are still on their feet, but they have stopped singing their marching song. You realize that we are at a crucial juncture with regard to morale. What we need is a good pep talk from Tad Allagash, but he is not to be found. You try to imagine what he would say. *Back on the horse. Now we're* really *going to have some fun.* Something like that. You suddenly realize that he has already slipped out with some rich hose queen. He is back at her place on Fifth Ave., and they are doing some of her off-the-boat-quality drugs. They are scooping it out of tall Ming vases and snorting it off of each other's naked bodies. You hate Tad Allagash.

Go home. Cut your losses.

Stay. Go for it.

You are a republic of voices tonight. Unfortunately, the republic is Italy. All these voices are waving their arms and screaming at each other. There's an *ex cathedra* riff coming down from the Vatican: *Repent. There's still time. Your body is the temple of the Lord and you have defiled it.* It is, after all, Sunday morning, and as long as you have any brain cells left there will always be this resonant patriarchal basso echoing down the marble vaults of your churchgoing childhood to remind you that this is the Lord's day. What you need is another overpriced drink to drown it out. But a search of pockets yields only a dollar bill and change. You paid ten to get in here. Panic is gaining on you.

You spot a girl at the edge of the dance floor who looks like your last chance for earthly salvation against the creeping judgment of Sunday morning. You know for a fact that if you go out into the morning alone, without even your sunglasses, which you have forgotten (because who, after all, plans on these travesties), that the harsh, angling light will turn you to flesh and bone. Mortality will pierce you through the retina. But there she is in her pegged pants, a kind of doo-wop retro ponytail pulled off to the side, great lungs, as eligible a candidate as you could hope to find this late in the game. The sexual equivalent of fast food.

She shrugs and nods when you ask her to dance. You like the way she moves, half-tempo, the oiled ellipses of her hips and shoulders. You get a little hip and ass contact. After the second song she says she's tired. She's on the edge of bolting when you ask her if she needs a little pick-me-up.

"You've got some blow?" she says.

"Monster," you say.

She takes your arm and leads you into the Ladies'. There's another guy in the stall beside yours so it's okay. After a couple of spoons she seems to like you just fine and you are feeling very likable yourself. A couple more. This girl is all nose. When she leans forward for the spoon the front of her shirt falls open in a way you can't help noticing. You wonder if this is her way of thanking you.

Oh yes.

"I love drugs," she says, as you march towards the bar.

"It's something we have in common," you say.

"Have you ever noticed how all the good words start with D? D and L."

You try to think about this. You're not quite sure what she's driving at. The Bolivians are singing their marching song but you can't quite make out the words.

"You know? Drugs. Delight. Decadence."

"Debauchery," you say, catching the tune now.

"Dexedrine."

"Delectable. Deranged. Debilitated."

"And L. Lush and luscious."

"Languorous."

"Lazy."

"Libidinous."

"What's that?" she says.

"Horny."

"Oh," she says, and casts a long, arching look over your shoulder. Her eyes glaze in a way that reminds you precisely of the closing of a sandblasted glass shower door. You can see that the game is over, though you're not sure which rule you broke. Possibly she finds "H" words offensive. She is scanning the dance floor for a man with a compatible vocabulary. You have more: *down* and *depressed; lost* and *lonely.* It's not that you are really going to miss this girl who thinks that *decadence* and *dexedrine* are the high points of the language of the Kings James and Lear, but the touch of flesh, the sound of another human voice. . . . You know that there is a special purgatory waiting out there for you, a desperate half-sleep which is like a grease fire in the brain pan.

The girl half-waves as she disappears into the crowd. There is no sign of the other girl, the girl who would not be here. There is no sign of Tad Allagash. The Bolivians are mutinous. You can't stop the voices.

Here you are again.

All messed up and no place to go.

It is worse even than you expected, stepping out into the morning. The light is like a mother's reproach. The sidewalk sparkles cruelly. Visibility unlimited. The downtown warehouses look serene and rested in this beveled light. A cab passes uptown and you start to wave, then realize you have no money. The cab stops. You jog over and lean in the window.

"I guess I'll walk after all."

"Ass hole." He leaves rubber.

You start north, holding your hand over your eyes. There is a bum sleeping on the sidewalk, swathed in garbage bags. He lifts his head as you pass. "God bless you and forgive your sins," he says. You wait for the cadge, but that's all he says. You wish he hadn't said it.

As you turn away, what is left of your olfactory equipment sends a message to your brain. The smell of fresh bread. Somewhere they are baking bread. You see bakery trucks loading in front of a loft building on the next block. You watch as bags of rolls are carried out onto the loading dock by a man with a tattooed forearm. This man is already at work, so that regular people will have fresh bread for their morning tables. The righteous people who sleep at night and eat eggs for breakfast. It is Sunday morning and you have not eaten since . . . when? Friday night. As you approach, the smell of the bread washes over you like a gentle rain. You inhale deeply, filling your lungs with it. Tears come to your eyes, and you are filled with such a rush of tenderness and pity that you stop beside a lamppost and hang on for support.

You remember another Sunday morning in your old apartment on Cornelia Street when you woke to the smell of bread from the bakery downstairs. There was the smell of bread every morning, but this is the one you remember. You turned to see your wife sleeping beside you. Her mouth was open and her hair fell down across the pillow to your shoulder. The tanned skin of her shoulder was the color of bread fresh from the oven. Slowly, and with a growing sense of exhilaration, you remembered who you were. You were the boy and she was the girl, your college sweetheart. You weren't famous yet, but you had the rent covered, you had your favorite restaurant where the waitresses knew your name and you could bring your own bottle of wine. It all seemed to be just the way you had pictured it when you had discussed plans for marriage and New York. The apartment with the pressed tin ceiling, the claw-footed bath, the windows that didn't quite fit the frame. It seemed almost as if you had wished for that very place. You leaned against your wife's shoulder. Later you would get up quietly, taking care not to wake her, and go downstairs for croissants and the *Sunday Times,* but for a long time you lay there breathing in the mingled scents of bread, hair and skin. You were in no hurry to get up. You knew it was a moment you wanted to savor. You didn't know how soon it would be over, that within a year she would go back to Michigan to file for divorce.

You approach the man on the loading dock. He stops working and watches you. You feel that there is something wrong with the way your legs are moving.

"Bread." This is what you say to him. You meant to say something more, but this is as much as you can get out.

"What was your first clue?" he says. He is a man who has served his country, you think, a man with a family somewhere outside the city. Small children. Pets. A garden.

"Could I have some? A roll or something?"

"Get out of here."

The man is about your size, except for the belly, which you don't have. "I'll trade you my jacket," you say. It is one hundred percent raw silk from Paul Stuart. You take it off, show him the label.

"You're crazy," the man says. Then he looks back into the warehouse. He picks up a bag of hard rolls and throws them at your feet. You hand him the jacket. He checks the label, sniffs the jacket, then tries it on.

You tear the bag open and the smell of warm dough rushes over you. The first bite sticks in your throat and you almost gag. You will have to go slowly. You will have to learn everything all over again.

Boodling, Bigotry, and Cosmopolitanism: The Transformation of a Civic Culture, from Dissent, *Jim Sleeper (fall 1987)*

Jim Sleeper grew up in Springfield, Massachusetts—"the northernmost city where one could buy each day's *New York Times* in the 1950's"—and encountered the crusading liberal *New York Post* of that time through his Aunt Leah Wechsler Sleeper, a cousin of its editor James Wechsler. On graduating Yale and earning a doctorate from Harvard, Sleeper packed a rental van and moved to central Brooklyn in 1977, feeling, "unaccountably . . . that a very large part of me felt as if I had lived in it all my life."

For five years he was a journalist in poor, nonwhite Brooklyn neighborhoods, writing for local weeklies and the *Village Voice* and *Dissent.* In *The Closest of Strangers* (1990), he foretold the implosion of the city's liberalism on misguided racial policies, and, during the tumultuous 1993 mayoral campaign when Rudolph Giuliani defeated the city's first African American mayor, David Dinkins, Sleeper's thrice-weekly *Daily News* column was required reading for other journalists and politicians. "New York's irrepressible idea," he reminded *News* readers the day after Dinkins's defeat, "means knowing that . . . you can rise above anything in your past that has made you small. You can join great, trans-ethnic movements for social justice or pour your gifts of imagination into an urban experiment E. B. White called 'cosmopolitan, mighty, and unparalleled.' Becoming an American means leaving your old neighborhood and finding the world. And the City of New York is your stairway to the stars."

LIKE the mountains that labored and brought forth a mouse, the ongoing eruptions of charges against New York City officials for bribery, extortion, and racketeering over the past two years have brought forth two quips.

The first belongs to Murray Kempton, long-suffering watchman of the city's civic virtue. Remarking the frequency with which Mayor Ed Koch stood before the City Hall press corps last year saying, "I am shocked" by some revelation of corruption, Kempton discovered that the great seal of the City of New York bears no motto and proposed that whatever is Latin for "I am shocked" be promptly affixed, in backhanded tribute to the deep public apathy that has itself become an aspect of the corruption.

The second came from journalist Sidney Zion. Watching U.S. Attorney Rudolph Giuliani in titanic struggle with defense counsel Thomas Puccio at the trial of Bronx boss Stanley Friedman, Zion noted that, for the first time in anyone's memory, "all the defendants are Jewish and all the lawyers are Italian." This inversion of "natural" order was soon righted with the indictments of former Transportation Commissioner Anthony Ameruso, former Brooklyn Democratic boss Meade Esposito, and Representative Mario Biaggi; but that left undisturbed an irony in a mayoral administration that had come to power pledged to purge minority "poverty pimps" allegedly coddled by its predecessors: with the exception of indicted Representative Robert Garcia, all the major malefactors in the recent probes are white.

The racial and ethnic role reversals anticipated in Zion's quip may help explain the seemingly invincible public indifference implicit in Kempton's. New Yorkers of all races seem to sense that, on the other side of the current upheavals, the city's once-vibrant, predominantly white ethnic and proletarian political culture—progenitor of the New Deal, the 1939 World's Fair, Hollywood, the interracial Brooklyn Dodgers, municipal unions, myriad bohemias, and even the early Levittowns prototypical of the suburban American Dream—will lie dead or dying. The city is in the grip of demographic and economic sea changes, deeper than the fiscal and political cycles noted by some observers, that could make the New York of 1995 unrecognizable to keepers of the civic flame ignited by Al Smith and Fiorello H. La Guardia. If the scandals arouse little outrage, it is not only because they partake of the spirit of the times on Wall Street and in the White House, but because they are part of an old local order's melancholy, long withdrawing roar.

In its place must come a new political culture responsive to the burgeoning, unfocused vitality of aliens—the bearers of a black, Latin, and Asian cosmopolis emerging from a hundred immigrant streams deluging the city at levels unprecedented since the 1920s. That tide has been slow gathering strength partly because of its own mind-boggling diversity. After all the talk about a "majority-minority" city that became less than half white at some point during the mid-1980s, New York is only slowly coming to realize that, unlike predominantly black Atlanta or Detroit, it will never, ever have an ethnic or racial majority. A third of its 1.9 million blacks are Caribbeans whose experiences and agendas mesh imperfectly with those of native American blacks; a varied Asian population of 350,000 is expected to grow 150 percent by 1995 with revolution in Korea and the defenestration of Hong Kong; nearly a million Puerto Ricans have been joined by almost as many other Hispanics, including Dominicans, Cubans, and South Americans. This Asian and Hispanic growth seems to be holding blacks' own slower expansion to under 30 percent of the whole, while even the city's white population has been augmented in recent years by 200,000 Russian Jews, Israelis, Poles, Italians, Irish, and Greeks, to say nothing of the young professionals, managers, artists, and activists from the American heartland.

As important as the diversity of these 2.5 million newcomers is the brevity of their time in New York. Most are not English-speaking citizens, let alone registered voters. Scrambling for shelter, taxi medallions, and career training of every sort, they haven't yet constituted themselves politically. Asians make up 25 percent of the city's elite public Stuyvesant High School, but as a substitute teacher there for a few days in 1983 I couldn't make them stop studying chemistry in a class on American labor history. Recently off the boat from Hong Kong or Seoul, they seemed to have had their fill of history and to be intent on rocketing themselves out of its tragedies as scientists or computer magnates. Who could blame them? Not every young Jew who warmed a seat here before them and whose parents labored in sweatshops as do theirs was inclined to build the International Ladies' Garment Workers Union. But then, enough young Jews were indeed so inclined that one can't help wondering how the differences in culture and historical expectation now visible in the schools will shape the city's future. It is too soon to know. There may be one or two more Jewish mayors, and after that this American world city will be read only by those unafraid to look into dark young faces.

There is, for some, a certain romance to the prospect. Think of New York as a great human heart which draws into itself those immigrant bloodstreams and, after working its strange alchemy, pumps them back out again across America and the world bearing athletes, impresarios, engineers. The city has done this uncomplainingly for so much of the country for so long that one in eight Americans can trace family ties to Brooklyn alone. A question posed by the old order's decay is whether New York's great heart can keep beating. Uncertainty about the answer may be all the newcomers have in common.

Here the romance of immigration sometimes fades for liberals as much as xenophobes: it is noted that blacks resent Korean merchants, or that Russians are as racist as American "rednecks," or that many Chinese won't join unions. Racial succession in labor organizations, boardrooms, nonprofit organizations, and political offices has been erratic, at best; the ominous language of separatism is more prevalent than that of liberal pluralism, let alone proletarian solidarity. Where is the new La Guardia, himself not only Italian and Jewish but Spanish-speaking, whose passionate leadership helped fuse new New Yorkers into a polis? Where are the touchstones and training grounds for such leadership and a citizenry responsive to it?

These questions are complicated by an erosion in the status of cities themselves as foci of national cultural and political concern and as centers of locally committed wealth. What is the political meaning of a city when increasingly fluid market forces move capital and leadership cadres worldwide at whim? Since its earliest days as a Dutch-run, polyglot trading port, New York has always been a conduit for such forces and populations; but even the maintenance of a conduit would seem to require some political consensus, some ability to influence or make claims upon new configurations of technology, investment, employment, consumption, demographics, and immigration. To say nothing of a federal urban policy whose ignorance and bad faith regarding New York's mission have been appalling, the more so when compared to the resources other nations lavish on their premier cities. Who can reconstitute the New York conduit on terms America can support?

White Rage

As these questions lie unanswered in the interregnum between the old order and the new, confusion about the meaning of civic responsibility and belonging is evident in other racial role reversals, not only in the corruption dramas but also in the streets, where an impressive number of last year's rioters were white. In Howard Beach just before Christmas 1986, bat-wielding whites attacked three blacks, one of them killed as he fled into the path of an oncoming car. That horror recalled one four years earlier when whites pummeled to death a black transit worker coming off his shift. "I love you, Mom!" cried one assailant as the jury convicted him of "manslaughter-two" in that incident. None of his sobbing neighbors, who'd backed Koch in part because of his support for the death penalty, could be heard calling for a murder conviction.

Bernhard Goetz came to trial this year for gunning down four black youths who he said had menaced him on an IRT train, paralyzing one of them from the waist down for life by shooting the youth a second time after saying, "You don't look so bad, here's another." Goetz's victims were found to have police rap sheets as long as their arms, except for the one who will never walk again and whose own father was murdered years earlier while trying to wrest his taxi from a thief. The brutal strangling of young Jennifer Levin in the summer of 1986 prompted her uncle to pronounce New York "a social experiment that has failed," an observation that assumed an interesting aspect when the killer turned out to be Levin's white preppie escort, Robert Chambers.

New York's Year of White Crime continued in The Bronx, a borough half-leveled in the 1970s by tax write-off and arson-for-insurance scams perpetrated upon hapless welfare tenants by a cabal of sociopathic white real estate agents and slumlords. Hispanic entrepreneur John Mariotta became so successful a minority defense contractor, lionized by Ronald Reagan, that he sought help with his booming business from former presidential counsel James E. Jenkins, former White House communications director Lyn Nofziger, and other well-connected white professionals, some of whom fired him, took over his stock rights, and ran his company, Wedtech, into the ground along with the jobs of more than 1,000 workers.

That was child's play beside the rompings downtown of Ivan Boesky and kindred spirits, who sent tremors through the edifice of finance capital, which only recently had been extended out into the Hudson on landfill dumped there as if in arrant mockery of all the square footage and infrastructure abandoned in the Bronx and on Main Streets all over the country whose assets had been liquidated by the arbitrageurs. Meanwhile, a professor of ethics at New York University's Business School told the MacNeil-Lehrer News Hour that 80 percent of his students chose, in a simulation of corporate decision making, to fight the FDA rather than stop marketing a drug known to have killed twenty-two people. As more of the city's "elite" work force engages in the manipulation of words and symbols that consolidate corporate power, abstracted from the rewards and constraints of union and neighborhood roots, the social and political basis for La Guardia's vision of a just, integrated city dissolves.

In a purely tactical sense, public silence about corruption suggests that whites, who still dominate established politics and media, are themselves immobilized by the charges. It is hard to champion capital punishment for murderers and long sentences for boodlers when the boy next door is a candidate for death row and the avuncular clubhouse captain down the block is sweating a subpoena from the grand jury.

But that silence also reflects an embitterment, beyond words, of white ethnics suddenly marginal to civic cultures they struggled hard to make their own. Expressions of moral outrage assume a consensus that has been violated but to which one can still appeal. For whites who think such a consensus has unraveled, and who felt their claims upon it tenuous in the first place, outrage gives way to simple rage—to street violence and lawless plunder of the commonweal. The decay of white ethnic political culture reflects not just demographic change, but also the conviction of many white New Yorkers that the rules have been changed against them.

Overall, it isn't minorities they're losing ground to—Boesky and the yuppie managerial class come to mind. But try to tell that to people driven out of "the old neighborhood" by muggings and decay. The connections they make between racial change, rising crime, and their plummeting property values are empirically valid and seared into personal experience. The fact that racism itself, including the machinations of unscrupulous white brokers, helps make self-fulfilling prophecies of such fears seem beside the point to people trapped by the consequences.

To them, the real municipal scandal isn't the fixing of government contracts but the unchecked rise of street crime and social and physical disintegration among encroaching poor minorities, as well as the rigid, often naïve illogic of redistribution imposed on them by liberal jurisprudence and politicians like John Lindsay, who, they feel, preferred to spend their taxes on siting public housing in their areas rather than on police. Such impositions seem extortions of gains they've won by following the disciplines of an upward mobility that many of them were willing to share with minorities, until they began to believe that minorities preferred a "free ride" from liberals.

That these "extortions" reached their peak in the mid-1970s, just as inflation and urban disinvestment were undermining their own upward mobility, only compounded their desperation. What Jonathan Rieder, the sympathetic ethnographer of Brooklyn's white-working-class Canarsie, calls "indignation, an emotion born of the perception of injustice," lay at the heart of their transformation. Even now—and the Italian and Jewish lower-middle-class residents of places like Canarsie are furious at us for not understanding this—what distinguishes their rage from the reactionary ideologies or blood racism of the Nazis or the Klan is its focus against specific, wrenching interventions in their neighborhood turf. The perceptions of injustice fueling their indignation may not always be accurate, but neither are the values they believe to be under assault always invalid.

Since the mid-1970s, then, there has been a decay in the city's white-working-class idiom, from one that could express its grievances in tart humor, irony, and flashing insight into one of sullen, evasive rationalization for attacks on blacks. Compared to that, the transmutation of Jackie Gleason's Ralph Kramden, the garrulous, decent "Big Mouth," into Carroll O'Connor's Archie Bunker, quiver of barbed retorts, was a triumph of human spirit.

By contrast, the new silence is so eerie, so ominous that I was almost relieved to hear it broken on a Brooklyn street one recent warm summer dusk by a bloodied, hard-muscled Italian teenager who came tearing down the block and spun around to face his black pursuers from the safety of the sidewalk counter of a pizzeria where some of his buddies worked. The black youths faded back into a deepening pool of shadows down the block as the boy's white-clad pizza parlor friends stepped wordlessly into the street, brandishing bats. The veins in his neck throbbed as, finding his breath, he cried out to the blacks in a register so deep from the gut it seemed to tap a bottomless hurt more startling than his anger.

"You *muh*-tha . . . *fuck*-in' . . . *nig*-guhs. You're *all shit! Eh*-very *one*-a' yous! They otta *ship* yous *all back!*" He doubled over, gasping for air, hands on his knees, then straightened up, not satisfied. "I don' care, I tell ya da trut'. I wish *eh*-very *one*-a'yous was *dead*. You ruin *eh*-very *fuck*-in' *thing*," he moaned in a despair so deep it riveted everyone on the street. "I *spit* on ya *muh*-thas," he shrieked, "I wish you was *nev*-veh *ee*-ven *born!*"

Black Rage

What startles about the white youth's rage is its utter conviction that blacks "ruin" the social compact, as if white ethnic organized crime and "machine" corruption hadn't also diminished every benign form of citizenship by making force and fraud the never-distant arbiters of social order. However exalted La Guardia's notions of justice and community, millions of New Yorkers have always passed their lives in complex webs of complicity with enemies of liberal virtue. It wasn't only the orthodox Marxist left that considered bourgeois citizenship a sham and organized violence the reality; the harsh logic of protected group "turf," both geographically in neighborhoods and economically in industry and bureaucracies, always shaped the contours of liberal citizenship in New York.

Even so, if one measure of civility is the degree to which force and fraud are kept at bay in the calculations of daily life, then New York is a place less civilized today than it was in the 1950s and early 1960s, though not, perhaps, in earlier times. Some would argue that even La Guardia managed to construe liberal institutions not as bourgeois heavens of meaningless "rights" but, in today's parlance, as a "level playing field" where ordinary people might mobilize against greed and reactionary nationalisms. It's that sense of engagement and dialogue across racial and ethnic lines that seems to have diminished.

What the recent racial role reversals in courts and streets suggest is that, if we except the crimes committed by young males, most blacks have kept La Guardia's faith better than whites, whether it be in the courageous, sometimes heartbreaking simplicity of elderly churchgoers and civil rights marchers or the sophisticated electoral decisions of black voters who have supported worthy white incumbents against facile black challengers when it seemed to them appropriate to do so. Blacks came to New York in large numbers after the war seeking jobs, not welfare, so much so that Irving Kristol, inventor of the insidious little *mot* that a neoconservative is a liberal who's been mugged by reality, wrote in a 1958 Sunday *New York Times Magazine* essay that blacks would in the course of another generation assimilate, like all other groups, to the blessings of economic security and citizenship. One may even say that, in the immediate postwar years, white migration to suburbia wasn't so much a "flight" from minority crime and decay as a response to the lure of privately marketed, publicly subsidized greener pastures.

As the middle-class tax base slipped and jobs left New York for the Sunbelt, however, minorities—last hired, first fired—bore the brunt of a downward spiral of unemployment, shrinking tax revenues, curtailed services based on those revenues, along with increased dependency on the curtailed services. It's important to make distinctions: black women benefited more than black men from the new service economy; more whites lost jobs than blacks. Still, indicators of social distress—infant mortality, welfare dependency, truancy, alcoholism, drug addiction, crime, housing abandonment—began edging upward among blacks, both absolutely and in comparison to whites.

Nor, when all is said and done, can the role of unemployment and discrimination in deepening that suffering be overemphasized. When the full history of the agony of the South Bronx and central Brooklyn in the 1970s is written, the pathologies of "multi-problem" speculators and other, mostly white, schemers will assume greater prominence alongside the pathologies of the large welfare families who were the ultimate victims of bank redlining, blockbusting, and mortgage insurance scams. And not only the minority poor: the true Job of neighborhood racial change in New York is the black lower-middle-class family that scrimps to buy a home in a predominantly white area only to find its own arrival used by brokers as a signal to disinvest, prompting general white flight.

All of this leads to a black embitterment and to black defection from civic consensus, a defection evident since the 1968 "community control" battles in the schools not only among poor but also among middle-class blacks. Some of the latter could be found in 1984 applauding Louis Farrakhan at Madison Square Garden and in 1987 cheering Alton Maddox, Jr. at a "blacks only" rally at a public high school in the wake of the Howard Beach incident. According to Nat Hentoff, the New York Civil Liberties Union was at first confused about how to respond to the use of a public school building for a racially exclusive meeting; the progressive civic culture of the past has been routed as whites embrace varieties of privatization and so feel disarmed when blacks indulge in separatist gestures.

What models of empowered, integrated citizenship might bridge the gaps in communication and trust, avoiding both doomed black separatism and terminal white cynicism? As always, in a nation virtually tone-deaf to either side in the tragedy of urban polarization, we find ourselves grasping at straws.

A New Cosmopolitanism?

On a freshly fenced ballfield in Brooklyn's devastated Brownsville section in October 1982, gaily colored banners mark off a milling throng of 8,000 American and West Indian blacks, Hispanics, and a small minority of whites by congregations: Lutheran Church of the Risen Christ, Community Baptist, Our Lady of Consolation, R.C., and so on. Their umbrella group, East Brooklyn Churches (EBC), is breaking ground for 1,000 single family homes it's building with an ingenious package of subsidies on fifteen abandoned blocks delivered free by the city. Half the buyers—nurses, paralegals, teachers' aides, transit workers—have come from the neighboring high-rise public housing projects, bearing small nest eggs they'd dreamed of investing in their community.

The new "Nehemiah" housing, now almost completed, was named for the biblical prophet who convinced his despondent neighbors to rebuild Jersualem's battered walls. It represents a triumph of urban republican virtue across years of patient community organizing by East Brooklyn Churches. EBC representatives stunned the local political establishment by handing the Brooklyn borough president their resignations from do-nothing community boards and demanding a meeting with his shadow boss, the county Democratic party leader, to talk about city services. EBC registered 10,000 new voters, 70 percent of them black, without once using slogans about black power or anyone's time having come. It also doubled local turnout in the November 1984 presidential elections.

"Contrary to common opinion," cries the Rev. Johnny Ray Youngblood at the rally, "we are not a 'grassroots' organization. Grass roots grow in *smooth* soil. Grass roots are *shallow* roots!" His incantatory power catches his listeners, summoning their strength and spontaneous "Amens." "*Our* roots are *deep* roots!" ("Aw-right!" "Praise God!") "Our roots have fought for existence in the shattered glass of East New York and the blasted brick of Brownsville! And so we say to you, Mayor Koch, We Love New York! And we say to you, Council President Bellamy"—the crowd joining him now, on its feet, thundering, "WE LOVE NEW YORK!," shifting the emphasis gradually to "WE," as in "Listen to us: *WE* Love New York!"

The mostly white dais is stunned. The bishop of Brooklyn is blinking back tears. Here, in 1968, watching people pick their way to the elevated IRT past rows of abandoned buildings and over rubble-strewn lots prowled by wild dogs, visiting Boston Mayor Kevin White made the *Times's* Quote of the Day by sputtering that he'd just seen "the beginning of the end of our civilization." In 1975, with virtually nothing left standing but public housing, the then city-housing commissioner Roger Starr proposed "planned shrinkage" of the area—the calculated withdrawal of services and resettlement of population. Then in 1979, EBC began building a "power organization" and turned the city fathers' assumptions upside down. In hundreds of house meeting and lay leadership training sessions run by the late Saul Alinsky's Industrial Areas Foundation (IAF), EBC studied the structure of local power. It began simply, with winnable goals: new street signs, cleanups of local food stores under polite but daunting threats of boycott; crackdowns by the district attorney on local "smoke shops."

The group's growing clout caught the attention of its national parent church bodies, which together contributed almost $9 million for the Nehemiah project. The city donated the land and a $10,000 federal Community Development subsidy to write down the purchase price of each house. The state provided low-interest mortgages. But the initiative and ownership is EBC's—and its individual buyers', whose probity and discipline have made local bankers, contractors, politicians, and bureaucrats seem predatory by comparison; often it was only the bishop of Brooklyn who helped EBC embarrass or intimidate local elites into doing their civic duty.

Now, at the rally, the mayor leads the crowd in a dramatic countdown and a bulldozer roars, opening the earth for the homes. Huddled at the edge of the crowd are a couple hundred dazed-looking middle-aged whites who might have stepped out of Archie Bunker's neighborhood—and who, in fact, have come by bus from "his" area of Queens. They are members of the Queens Citizens Organization (QCO), another IAF affiliate. QCO's president Pat Ottinger takes the mike and cries, "Our trip to Brooklyn today has reinforced our belief that there is no boundary between us. We are all one neighborhood, one great city. Your struggles are our struggles! Your heartaches are our heartaches! Your victories are our victories!"

The crowd roars back its welcome. The Queens visitors loosen up, smile, wave. The elected officials, accustomed to shuttling two-faced back and forth across the color line, are visibly impressed. "Two years ago," Ottinger later confides, "you couldn't have gotten my neighbors here in a tank."

The EBC effort—doggedly interracial yet almost Jeffersonian in its community-based well-springs of virtue and power—is but a straw in the wind. There are others: replicable models of public/private sector collaboration, "learning curves" shared now by varied actors involved in neighborhood change—the lenders, developers, brokers, residents, planners, and media image makers and interpreters who for so long have worked at cross-purposes to make a wasteland of urban promise. The contradictions in their interest cannot be glossed over, yet the lesson of community organizing is that they can be negotiated. There are the beginnings of constructive racial succession in the leadership of unions like AFSCME and the ILGWU. Even the oftnoted mismatch between new white collar jobs and an unprepared populace may not be as stark as it seems, because of unanticipated economic developments and new cultural resources among immigrants.

But none of these encouraging developments, and not even all of them together, yet herald a new civic culture. What the Queens visitors to Brownsville experienced would have to happen to tens of thousands more like them to change a city the size of New York; and any viable new politics would have to acknowledge and somehow address some white ethnic grievances, if only because their anguish resonates so deeply throughout the powerful suburbs and the larger national culture upon whose solicitous regard the health of the city depends. Even those New Yorkers who've all too easily dispersed to suburbia carry within them pockets of civic loss and longing, and are slow to understand how something like the EBC rally in Brownsville can contribute to restoring their souls.

What's worth remarking about that event is that 8,000 mostly black and Hispanic poor people instructed white officials and onlookers in the rebuilding of civic consensus and a decent America. *That* kind of racial role reversal is part of the new tide that must gather strength. The city is blessed with two and a half million newcomers innocent of its recent mistake and ancient feuds, and another two million "outsiders" uninitiated into its subtler corruptions and cynicisms. Even thousands of young white Americans from the Heartland keep bypassing Manhattan for outermost Brooklyn and kindred locations to cast their fates with the urban struggle. "New York is the most fatally fascinating thing in America," wrote James Weldon Johnson at the turn of the century; "She sits like a witch at the gate of the country." She still does. An embodiment of our worst fears about ourselves, but also of our deepest strengths, New York offers abundant instruction to a nation becoming as diverse and interdependent as the city herself. Merely coming to know her better would constitute a reasonable return on the investment the nation ought to make in her future.

Auggie Wren's Christmas Story, Paul Auster (1990)

Paul Auster was born in Newark in 1947 and graduated from Columbia University in 1969. "Auggie Wren's Christmas Story" was created when Auster accepted a commission to write a Christmas story for the op-ed page of *The New York Times* for Christmas Day 1990. Director Wayne Wang saw the story and collaborated with Auster on the film adaptation, *Smoke.*

The author and art critic Robert Hughes has written that "everyone in Manhattan is from somewhere else. Auster has raised this almost into a literary principle. What you see through the lucid surface of his writing is a structure clad in mirrors, in which identities and stable pasts reflect one another and shift around; and, secondly, human actions ruled in a troubling, unpredictable way by chance and coincidence, but transcending their passivity in flashes of vision." New York City itself becomes a character in much of Auster's fiction and as one of his characters, Quinn from *City of Glass,* relates, "New York was an inexhaustible space, endless steps, and no matter how far he walked, no matter how well he came to know its neighborhoods and streets, it always left him with the feeling of being lost."

I HEARD this story from Auggie Wren. Since Auggie doesn't come off too well in it, at least not as well as he'd like to, he's asked me not to use his real name. Other than that, the whole business about the lost wallet and the blind woman and the Christmas dinner is just as he told it to me.

Auggie and I have known each other for close to eleven years now. He works behind the counter of a cigar store on Court Street in downtown Brooklyn, and since it's the only store that carries the little Dutch cigars I like to smoke, I go in there fairly often. For a long time, I didn't give much thought to Auggie Wren. He was the strange little man who wore a hooded blue sweatshirt and sold me cigars and magazines, the impish, wisecracking character who always had something funny to say about the weather or the Mets or the politicians in Washington, and that was the extent of it.

But then one day several years ago he happened to be looking through a magazine in the store, and he stumbled across a review of one of my books. He knew it was me because a photograph accompanied the review, and after that things changed between us. I was no longer just another customer to Auggie, I had become a distinguished person. Most people couldn't care less about books and writers, but it turned out that Auggie considered himself an artist. Now that he had cracked the secret of who I was, he embraced me as an ally, a confidant, a brother-in-arms. To tell the truth, I found it rather embarrassing. Then, almost inevitably, a moment came when he asked if I would be willing to look at his photographs. Given his enthusiasm and good will, there didn't seem to be any way I could turn him down.

God knows what I was expecting. At the very least, it wasn't what Auggie showed me the next day. In a small, windowless room at the back of the store, he opened a cardboard box and pulled out twelve identical black photo albums. This was his life's work, he said, and it didn't take him more than five minutes a day to do it. Every morning for the past twelve years, he had stood at the corner of Atlantic Avenue and Clinton Street at precisely seven o'clock and had taken a single color photograph of precisely the same view. The project now ran to more than four thousand photographs. Each album represented a different year, and all the pictures were laid out in sequence, from January 1 to December 31, with the dates carefully recorded under each one.

As I flipped through the albums and began to study Auggie's work, I didn't know what to think. My first impression was that it was the oddest, most bewildering thing I had ever seen. All the pictures were the same. The whole project was a numbing onslaught of repetition, the same street and the same buildings over and over again, an unrelenting delirium of redundant images. I couldn't think of anything to say to Auggie, so I continued turning pages, nodding my head in feigned appreciation. Auggie himself seemed unperturbed, watching me with a broad smile on his face, but after I'd been at it for several minutes, he suddenly interrupted me and said, "You're going too fast. You'll never get it if you don't slow down."

He was right, of course. If you don't take the time to look, you'll never manage to see anything. I picked up another album and forced myself to go more deliberately. I paid closer attention to details, took note of shifts in the weather, watched for the changing angles of light as the seasons advanced. Eventually, I was able to detect subtle differences in the traffic flow, to anticipate the rhythm of the different days (the commotion of workday mornings, the relative stillness of weekends, the contrast between Saturdays and Sundays). And then, little by little, I began to recognize the faces of the people in the background, the passersby on their way to work, the same people in the same spot every morning, living an instant of their lives in the field of Auggie's camera.

Once I got to know them, I began to study their postures, the way they carried themselves from one morning to the next, trying to discover their moods from these surface indications, as if I could imagine stories for them, as if I could penetrate the invisible dramas locked inside their bodies. I picked up another album. I was no longer bored, no longer puzzled as I had been at first. Auggie was photographing time, I realized, both natural time and human time, and he was doing it by planting himself in one tiny corner of the world and willing it to be his own, by standing guard in the space he had chosen for himself. As he watched me pore over his work, Auggie continued to smile with pleasure. Then, almost as if he had been reading my thoughts, he began to recite a line from Shakespeare. "Tomorrow and tomorrow and tomorrow," he muttered under his breath, "time creeps on its petty pace." I understood then that he knew exactly what he was doing.

That was more than two thousand pictures ago. Since that day, Auggie and I have discussed his work many times, but it was only last week that I learned how he acquired his camera and started taking pictures in the first place. That was the subject of the story he told me, and I'm still struggling to make sense of it.

Earlier that same week, a man from the *New York Times* called me and asked if I would be willing to write a short story that would appear in the paper on Christmas morning. My first impulse was to say no, but the man was very charming and persistent, and by the end of the conversation I told him I would give it a try. The moment I hung up the phone, however, I fell into a deep panic. What did I know about Christmas? I asked myself. What did I know about writing short stories on commission?

I spent the next several days in despair, warring with the ghosts of Dickens, O. Henry and other masters of the Yuletide spirit. The very phrase "Christmas story" had unpleasant associations for me, evoking dreadful outpourings of hypocritical mush and treacle. Even at their best, Christmas stories were no more than wish-fulfillment dreams, fairy tales for adults, and I'd be damned if I'd ever allowed myself to write something like that. And yet, how could anyone propose to write an unsentimental Christmas story? It was a contradiction in terms, an impossibility, an out-and-out conundrum. One might just as well try to imagine a racehorse without legs, or a sparrow without wings.

I got nowhere. On Thursday I went out for a long walk, hoping the air would clear my head. Just past noon, I stopped in at the cigar store to replenish my supply, and there was Auggie, standing behind the counter as always. He asked me how I was. Without really meaning to, I found myself unburdening my troubles to him. "A Christmas story?" he said after I had finished. "Is that all? If you buy me lunch, my friend, I'll tell you the best Christmas story you ever heard. And I guarantee that every word of it is true."

We walked down the block to Jack's, a cramped and boisterous delicatessen with good pastrami sandwiches and photographs of old Dodger teams hanging on the walls. We found a table at the back, ordered our food, and then Auggie launched into his story.

"It was the summer of '72," he said. "A kid came in one morning and started stealing things from the store. He must have been about nineteen or twenty, and I don't think I've ever seen a more pathetic shoplifter in my life. He's standing by the rack of paperbacks along the far wall and stuffing books into the pockets of his raincoat. It was crowded around the counter just then, so I didn't see him at first. But once I noticed what he was up to, I started to shout. He took off like a jackrabbit, and by the time I managed to get out from behind the counter, he was already tearing down Atlantic Avenue. I chased after him for about half a block, and then I gave up. He'd dropped something along the way, and since I didn't feel like running anymore, I bent down to see what it was.

"It turned out to be his wallet. There wasn't any money inside, but his driver's license was there along with three or four snapshots. I suppose I could have called the cops and had him arrested. I had his name and address from the license, but I felt kind of sorry for him. He was just a measly little punk, and once I looked at those pictures in his wallet, I couldn't bring myself to feel very angry at him. Robert Goodwin. That was his name. In one of the pictures, I remember, he was standing with his arm around his mother or grandmother. In another one, he was sitting there at age nine or ten dressed in a baseball uniform with a big smile on his face. I just didn't have the heart. He was probably on dope now, I figured. A poor kid from Brooklyn without much going for him, and who cared about a couple of trashy paperbacks anyway?

"So I held onto the wallet. Every once in a while I'd get a little urge to send it back to him, but I kept delaying and never did anything about it.

Then Christmas rolls around and I'm stuck with nothing to do. The boss usually invites me over to his house to spend the day, but that year he and his family were down in Florida visiting relatives. So I'm sitting in my apartment that morning feeling a little sorry for myself, and then I see Robert Goodwin's wallet lying on a shelf in the kitchen. I figure what the hell, why not do something nice for once, and I put on my coat and go out to return the wallet in person.

"The address was over in Boerum Hill, somewhere in the projects. It was freezing out that day, and I remember getting lost a few times trying to find the right building. Everything looks the same in that place, and you keep going over the same ground thinking you're somewhere else. Anyway, I finally get to the apartment I'm looking for and ring the bell. Nothing happens. I assume no one's there, but I try again just to make sure. I wait a little longer, and just when I'm about to give up, I hear someone shuffling to the door. An old woman's voice asks who's there, and I say I'm looking for Robert Goodwin. 'Is that you, Robert?' the old woman says, and then she undoes about fifteen locks and opens the door.

"She has to be at least eighty, maybe ninety years old, and the first thing I notice about her is that she's blind. 'I knew you'd come, Robert,' she says. 'I knew you wouldn't forget your Granny Ethel on Christmas.' And then she opens her arms as if she's about to hug me.

"I didn't have much time to think, you understand. I had to say something real fast, and before I knew what was happening, I could hear the words coming out of my mouth. 'That's right, Granny Ethel,' I said. 'I came back to see you on Christmas.' Don't ask me why I did it. I don't have any idea. Maybe I didn't want to disappoint her or something, I don't know. It just came out that way, and then this old woman was suddenly hugging me there in front of the door, and I was hugging her back.

"I didn't exactly say that I was her grandson. Not in so many words, at least, but that was the implication. I wasn't trying to trick her, though. It was like a game we'd both decided to play—without having to discuss the rules. I mean, that woman *knew* I wasn't her grandson Robert. She was old and dotty, but she wasn't so far gone that she couldn't tell the difference between a stranger and her own flesh and blood. But it made her happy to pretend, and since I had nothing better to do anyway, I was happy to go along with her.

"So we went into the apartment and spent the day together. The place was a real dump, I might add, but what else can you expect from a blind woman who does her own housekeeping? Every time she asked me a question about how I was, I would lie to her. I told her I'd found a good job working in a cigar store, I told her I was about to get married, I told her a hundred pretty stories, and she made like she believed every one of them. 'That's fine, Robert,' she would say, nodding her head and smiling. 'I always knew things would work out for you.'

"After a while, I started getting pretty hungry. There didn't seem to be much food in the house, so I went out to a store in the neighborhood and brought back a mess of stuff. A precooked chicken, vegetable soup, a bucket of potato salad, a chocolate cake, all kinds of things. Ethel had a couple of bottles of wine stashed in her bedroom, and so between us we managed to put together a fairly decent Christmas dinner. We both got a little tipsy from the wine, I remember, and after the meal was over we went out to sit in the living room, where the chairs were more comfortable. I had to take a pee, so I excused myself and went to the bathroom down the hall. That's where things took yet another turn. It was ditsy enough doing my little jig as Ethel's grandson, but what I did next was positively crazy, and I've never forgiven myself for it.

"I go into the bathroom, and stacked up against the wall next to the shower, I see a pile of six or seven cameras. Brand-new thirty-five-millimeter cameras, still in their boxes, top-quality merchandise. I figure this is the work of the real Robert, a storage place for one of his recent hauls. I've never taken a picture in my life, and I've certainly never stolen anything, but the moment I see those cameras sitting in the bathroom, I decide I want one of them for myself. Just like that. And without even stopping to think about it, I tuck one of the boxes under my arm and go back to the living room.

"I couldn't have been gone for more than three minutes, but in that time Granny Ethel had fallen asleep in her chair. Too much Chianti, I suppose. I went into the kitchen to wash the dishes, and she slept on through the whole racket, snoring like a baby. There didn't seem to be any point in disturbing her, so I decided to leave. I couldn't even write a note to say good-bye, seeing that she was blind and all, and so I just left. I put her grandson's wallet on the table, picked up the camera again, and walked out of the apartment. And that's the end of the story."

"Did you ever go back to see her?" I asked.

"Once," he said. "About three or four months later. I felt so bad about stealing the camera, I hadn't even used it yet. I finally made up my mind to return it, but Ethel wasn't there anymore. I don't know what happened to her, but someone else had moved into the apartment, and he couldn't tell me where she was."

"She probably died."

"Yeah, probably."

"Which means that she spent her last Christmas with you."

"I guess so. I never thought of it that way."

"It was a good deed, Auggie. It was a nice thing you did for her."

"I lied to her, and then I stole from her. I don't see how you can call that a good deed."

"You made her happy. And the camera was stolen anyway. It's not as if the person you took it from really owned it."

"Anything for art, eh Paul?"

"I wouldn't say that. But at least you've put the camera to good use."

"And now you've got your Christmas story, don't you?"

"Yes," I said. "I suppose I do."

I paused for a moment, studying Auggie as a wicked grin spread across his face. I couldn't be sure, but the look in his eyes at that moment was so mysterious, so fraught with the glow of some inner delight, that it suddenly occurred to me that he had made the whole thing up. I was about to ask him if he'd been putting me on, but then I realized he would never tell. I had been tricked into believing him, and that was the only thing that mattered. As long as there's one person to believe it, there's no story that can't be true.

"You're an ace, Auggie," I said. "Thanks for being so helpful."

"Any time," he answered, still looking at me with that maniacal light in his eyes. "After all, if you can't share your secrets with your friends, what kind of a friend are you?"

"I guess I owe you one."

"No you don't. Just put it down the way I told it to you, and you don't owe me a thing."

"Except the lunch."

"That's right. Except the lunch."

I returned Auggie's smile with a smile of my own, and then I called out to the waiter and asked for the check.

Autumn in New York, Murray Kempton (1990)

Murray Kempton was born in Baltimore in 1917 and was, for over four decades, one of the most distinctive voices in American journalism until his death in 1997. He wrote primarily for the *New York Post* and *New York Newsday* starting in 1942 and was awarded a Pulitzer Prize for commentary in 1985. He published four volumes, and *The Briar Patch* (1973) won the National Book Award. One of his early inspirations was the essayist H. L. Mencken, for whom he became a copy boy at the *Baltimore Evening Sun.* A devout New Yorker, Kempton was a common sight on the city streets, listening to his Walkman and chewing on his pipe as he pedaled his bicycle to work every day. Senator Daniel Patrick Moynihan described him as "the kindest man and the toughest reporter we have known in our time."

The events that Kempton refers to in his essay were evidence of the tangled and often violent state of race relations in the city in the late 1980s. Starting as early as 1984, when Bernhard Goetz shot four black youths on a subway in Manhattan, a failing economy, centuries of racial discrimination, and the disintegration of white ethnic neighborhoods had combined to unleash a brutal torrent of racial violence. In 1986, a gang of white youths in Howard Beach had attacked three black men, chasing one, Michael Griffith, to his death on the highway. The following year a young black girl, Tawana Brawley, claimed that she had been kidnapped and raped by six white law enforcement officials. In the spring of 1989, a white female Wall Street executive reported being assaulted and raped by a gang of a dozen black and Hispanic youths while jogging in Central Park. And in August of the same year, Yusuf Hawkins was murdered by a gang of white youths in Brooklyn's Bensonhurst neighborhood. In his 1990 newspaper column, Kempton used the murder of a homeless man, Carlos Melendez, to force the city to turn the focus onto its own tortured psyche.

THE lovelier of New York's days have a curious way of bobbing up on the mornings after the eviler of her nights.

Such was especially the case Friday on Ward's Island, where Carlos Melendez was hacked to death and eight other homeless men sent to the hospital by a costumed gang of Halloween revelers.

Ward's Island is as close an approach to Eden as the East River's landscape has to offer. There is, however, a significant difference between this and the first of all gardens. Adam and Eve were expelled from Eden to wander everywhere else, while most of its overnight lodgers have sunk into Ward's Island after wandering and been all but expelled from everywhere else.

Ward's Island's only historical importance has been as a chosen spot for quarantines. The nineteenth century used it for a potter's field, for a refuge for destitute aliens, and for the New York Asylum for the Insane, which is now called the Manhattan Psychiatric Center and would be the last public building left on the island except for sharing that dignity with the Charles H. Gay Volunteers of America men's shelter.

The streets of New York have been the reefs where a great part of a whole generation of men have been shipwrecked, and they wait to do the same for the boys who are those men's children. We might go too far if we said that the young who murdered Carlos Melendez were striking not at some Other but at a part of that Self they are in exigent risk of becoming in middle age. But how, after all, did these nine unlucky men offend this mob if not by incarnating the future that hangs like a sword over so many of its members?

W. H. Auden once reminded us that we must love one another or die. The soft beauties of Ward's Island's ruin served to start that thought on Friday, but the harshness of its reality fairly shouted the insistence that we cannot love one another and that therefore we will die.

Ward's Island is an Eden gone to weeds and sorrows, but its charms are somehow heightened by the ghosts of misfortuned lives that whisper in its breezes. Some of its functioning structures have columns and one has pediments, and their suggestion of the Old South is enlarged by the sight of wooden buildings long abandoned and now tumbled down to look like the wake of Sherman's march through Georgia.

Ward's Island's single prideful ornament is the stand of fine trees at the foot of the bridge that was the cutting floor for Wednesday's Halloween celebration. This grove's trees were planted long ago and in a wide variety of species, each identified by its own metal label and with its leaves turned Friday to its particular fall color.

A visitor walks through high grass along dirt trails and now and then meets a homeless man and shudders from old alarms more ridiculous than usual, because here is not the dangerous but the endangered. Our encounters are as those upon a rural path, and the airs around its foliage bring whatever scents we might suppose to lie where the woodbine twineth.

The intimations of the Old South have on short order become so inescapable that the imagination can barely resist hanging black bodies on these trees. These thoughts would be pleasanter if they had no place except in the imagination. But they have come too near to where we live.

The South has given up rabbling the helpless, and New York has taken over. Judge Lynch has changed his venue, and the mobs that are his enforcement squad belong to us. Howard Beach, Central Park, Bensonhurst, and now Ward's Island were each and every one a lynching bee.

It seemed probable Friday that the mob that fell upon Carlos Melendez and his fellow strayed innocents would be in police custody before the weekend was over. Predators for no gain but the trophy of their prey always get caught, because they do it for bragging rights and they can't shut up.

After a while it seems useless to try to explain things that cannot possibly be excused. It is, as an instance, often said that the lynch spirit draws its fires from fear and hatred of the Other. And yet, whenever a derelict is beaten or set afire in this city, his assailants generally turn out to be children whose own pinched existences are not far from the edge their victim has crossed and fallen over.

The police are already all but certain that Carlos Melendez was butchered by young men from the East River Houses, a project whose residents come in the main from the same class of the working poor that is the lost origin of most of the homeless. When the police complete their arrests, they are unlikely to find a single suspect who does not have a cousin or an uncle or even occasionally a father whom the world has as far wounded and brought so low as Carlos Melendez was.

Manhattan, 1976, from About This Life, *Barry Lopez (1993)*

Barry Lopez was born in 1945 in Port Chester, New York. After spending his early childhood in Southern California, he moved, with his mother, to East Thirty-fifth Street in Murray Hill at age eleven. Later, he attended St. Ignatius Loyola High School in Manhattan. Lopez is widely regarded as one of the leading writers detailing the natural landscape in our time; his monumental book *Arctic Dreams* won the National Book Award in 1986.

But just as Lopez's books often deal with imagination and desire, so too they address memory. In "Manhattan, 1976," Lopez remembers, waiting to go see his mother in the Lenox Hill Hospital, the feeling he has for New York City. Lopez writes, "I felt a great affection for the city, for its Joseph's coat of buildings, the vitality of its people, the enduring grace of its plane trees, and the layers of its history, all of it washed by a great tide of weather under maritime skies. Standing at the window I felt the insistence and the assurance of the city, and how I was woven in here through memory and affection."

The hours of coolness in the morning just before my mother died I remember for their relief. It was July and it had been warm and humid in New York City for several days, temperatures in the high eighties, the air motionless and heavy with the threat of rain.

I awoke early that morning. It was also my wife's thirtieth birthday, but our celebration would be wan. My mother was in her last days, and the lives of all of us in the family were contorted by grief and tension—and by a flaring of anger at her cancer. We were exhausted.

I felt the coolness of the air immediately when I awoke. I walked the length of the fourth-floor apartment, opened one side of a tall casement window in the living room, and looked at the sky. Cumulus clouds, moving to the southeast on a steady wind. Ten degrees cooler than yesterday's dawn, by the small tin thermometer. I leaned forward to rest my arms on the sill and began taking in details of movement in the street's pale light, the city's stirring.

In the six years I had lived in this apartment as a boy, from 1956 until 1962, I had spent cumulative months at this window. At the time, the Murray Hill section of Manhattan was mostly a neighborhood of decorous living and brownstone row houses, many of them not yet converted to apartments. East 35th Street for me, a child newly arrived from California, presented an enchanting pattern of human life. Footbeat policemen began their regular patrol at eight. The delivery of residential mail occurred around nine and was followed about ten by the emergence of women on shopping errands. Young men came and went the whole day on three-wheel grocery cart bikes, either struggling with a full load up the moderate rise of Murray Hill from Gristede's down on Third Avenue, or hurtling back the other way, driving no-hands against light traffic, cartons of empty bottles clattering explosively as the bike's solid tires nicked potholes.

In the afternoon a dozen young girls in private-school uniforms swirled in glee and posed with exaggerated emotion across the street, waiting to be taken home. By dinner time the street was almost empty of people; then, around eleven, it was briefly animated again with couples returning from the theater or some other entertainment. Until dawn, the pattern of glinting chrome and color in the two rows of curbed automobiles remained unchanged. And from night to night that pattern hardly varied.

Overlaying the street's regular, diurnal rhythm was a more chaotic pattern of events, an unpredictability I would watch with unquenchable fascination for hours at a time. (A jog in the wall of The Advertising Club of New York next door made it impossible for me to see very far to the west on 35th Street. But if I leaned out as far as I dared, I could see all the way to the East River in the other direction.) I would study the flow of vehicles below: an aggressive insinuation of yellow taxis, the casual slalom of a motorcycle through lines of stalled traffic, the obstreperous lumbering of large trucks. The sidewalks, with an occasional imposing stoop jutting out, were rarely crowded, for there were neither shops nor businesses here, and few tourists. But with Yeshiva University down at the corner of Lexington, the 34th Street Armory a block away, a Swedenborgian church midblock, and 34th Precinct police headquarters just up from Third Avenue, I still saw a fair array of dress and captivating expressions of human bearing. The tortoise pace of elderly women in drab hats paralleled the peeved ambling of a middle-aged man anxious to locate a cab. A naïf, loose-jointed in trajectory down the sidewalk, with wide-flung strides. A buttonhooking young woman, intently scanning door lintels and surreptitiously watching a building superintendent leaning sullenly against a service entrance. Two men in vested suits in conversation on the corner where, rotund and oblivious, they were a disruption, like a boulder in a creek. A boy running through red-lighted traffic with a large bouquet in his hand, held forth like a bowsprit.

All these gaits together with their kindred modulations seemed mysteriously revealing to me. Lingering couples embraced, separated with resolve, then embraced once more. People halted and turned toward each other in hilarious laughter. I watched as though I would never see such things again —screaming arguments, the other-worldly navigations of the deranged, and the haughty stride of single men dressed meticulously in evening clothes.

This pattern of traffic and people, an overlay of personality and idiosyncrasy on the day's fixed events, fed me in a wordless way. My eyes would drift up from these patterns to follow the sky over lower Manhattan, a flock of house sparrows, scudding clouds, a distant airplane approaching La Guardia or Idlewild with impossible slowness.

Another sort of animation drew me regularly to this window: weather. The sound of thunder. Or a rising hiss over the sound of automobiles that meant the streets were wet from a silent rain. The barely audible rattle of dozens of panes of glass in the window's leadwork—a freshening wind. A sudden dimming of sunshine in the living room. Whatever I was doing, these signals would pull me away. At night, in the isolating light cone of a streetlamp, I could see the slant, the density, and sometimes the exact size of raindrops. (None of this could I learn with my bare hands outstretched, in the penumbral dark under the building's cornices.) I watched rainwater course east in sheets down the calico-patched street in the wake of a storm; and cascades of snow, floating and wind-driven, as varied in their character as falls of rain, pile up in the streets. I watched the darkness between buildings burst with lightning, and I studied intently the rattle-drum of hail on car roofs.

The weather I watched from this window, no matter how wild, was always comforting. My back was to rooms secured by family life. East and west, the room shared its walls with people I imagined little different from myself. And from this window I could see a marvel as imbued with meaning for me then as a minaret—the Empire State Building. The high windows of its east wall gleamed imperially in the first rays of dawn, before the light flared down 35th Street, glinting in bits of mica in the facades of brownstones. Beneath the hammer of winter storms, the building seemed courageous and adamantine.

The morning that my mother would die I rested my forearms on the sill of the window, glad for the change of weather. I could see more of the wind, moving gray clouds, than I could feel; but I knew the walk to the subway later that morning, and the short walk up 77th Street to Lenox Hill Hospital, would be cooler.

I had been daydreaming at the window for perhaps an hour when my father came downstairs. The faint odors in the street's air—the dampness of basements, the acrid fragrance of ailanthus trees, the aromatics in roof tar—had drawn me off into a dozen memories. My father paused, speechless, at the foot of the stairs by the dining table. As determined as he was to lead a normal life around Mother's last days, he was at the beck and call of her disease almost as much as she was. With a high salute of his right hand, meant to demonstrate confidence, and an ironic grimace, he went out the door. Downstairs he would meet my brother, who worked with him, and together they would take a cab up to the hospital. My brother, three years younger, was worn out by these marathon days but uncomplaining, almost always calm. He and my father would eat breakfast together at the hospital and sit with Mother until Sandra and I arrived, then leave for work.

I wanted an undisturbed morning, the luxury of that kind of time, in which to give Sandra her birthday presents, to have a conversation not shrouded by death. I made breakfast and took it into the bedroom. While we sipped coffee I offered her what I had gotten. Among other things, a fossil trilobite, symbol of longevity. But we could not break the rind of oppression this terminal disease had created.

While Sandra showered, I dressed and returned to the window. I stood there with my hands in my pockets staring at the weathered surface of the window's wood frame, with its peeling black paint. I took in details in the pitted surface of the sandstone ledge and at its boundary, where the ledge met the color of buildings across the street. I saw the stillness of the ledge against the sluggish flow of early morning traffic and a stream of pedestrians in summer clothing below. The air above the street was a little warmer now. The wind continued to blow steadily, briskly moving cloud banks out over Brooklyn.

I felt a great affection for the city, for its tight Joseph's coat of buildings, the vitality of its people, the enduring grace of its plane trees, and the layers of its history, all of it washed by a great tide of weather under maritime skies. Standing at the window I felt the insistence and the assurance of the city, and how I was woven in here through memory and affection.

Sandra touched my shoulder. It was time we were gone, uptown. But something stayed me. I leaned out, bracing my left palm against the window's mullion. The color I saw in people's clothes was now muted. Traffic and pedestrians, the start-up of myriad businesses, had stirred the night's dust. The air was more rank with exhaust. A flock of pigeons came down the corridor of the street toward me, piebald, dove gray, white, brindled ginger, ash black—thirty or more of them. They were turning the bottom of a long parabolic arc, from which they shot up suddenly, out over Park Avenue. They reached a high, stalling apex, rolled over it, and fell off to the south, where they were cut from view by a building. A few moments later they emerged much smaller, wings pounding over brownstones below 34th Street, on a course parallel to the wind's.

I left, leaving the window open.

When Sandra and I emerged a half-hour later from the hospital elevator, my brother was waiting to meet us. I could see by the high, wistful cast of his face that she was gone.

Shot: A New York Story, Elizabeth Hardwick (1993)

Elizabeth Hardwick was born in Kentucky in 1916 but moved to New York City in 1939 and has lived in Manhattan ever since. Hardwick has written novels, essays, short stories, and literary criticism and has been a regular contributor to the *Partisan Review*, the *New Republic*, and *Harper's*. In 1949, she married one of the most brilliant poets of the time, Robert Lowell, after they had met at Yaddo, the writer's retreat in Saratoga Springs. Lowell died in a taxi en route to seek reconciliation with Hardwick in 1977. Hardwick, however, has been one of the most distinguished women of letters in America in the last half of the century, and, in 1963, she was one of the founders of the *New York Review of Books*.

Hardwick has seen New York City through good times and bad, and in her essay "New York City: Crash Course" (1991) she notes that in people who come to New York City "once here, a lingering infection seems to set in and the streets are filled with complaints and whines of the hypochondriac who will not budge, will not face a fertile pasture." But still, "here it is, that's all, the place itself, shadowy, ever promising and ever withholding, a bad mother, queen of the double bind . . . . . . Nevertheless."

SHE, Zona, went along the avenues of the East Side of Manhattan, turned up the brownstone side streets of the Seventies and the Nineties on the way to the houses of her group. Once there, she would iron shirts, untangle the vacuum, and at times would be called to put on her black uniform and pass the smoked salmon curling on squares of pumpernickel at cocktail parties. Occasionally, one of the group might see Zona racing up Madison Avenue in the late evening, passing swiftly by the windows where the dresses and scarves and jewelry stood or lay immobile in the anxious night glitter of the high-priced. Zona would, of course, be making her way home, although not one of her people was certain just where that home might be.

Somewhere in the grainy, indivisible out-there: area code 718, and what did that signify—the Bronx, Queens? She was tall, very thin; in her black coat, her thick black hair topping her black face, she seemed to be flying with the migratory certainty of some wide-winged black bird.

Her rushing movements were also noticeable about the house. She flew with the dust cloth-swish, swish, swish over the tabletops and a swipe at the windowsills; a splash here and there in the sink; a dash to recover the coat of a not quite sober cocktail guest. Yet, for all this interesting quickness of hand and foot, she was imperturbable, courteous, not given to chatter. And she was impressive; yes, impressive—that was said about Zona. A bit of the nunnery about her, black virgin from some sandy Christian village on the Ivory Coast. So you might say, in a stretch.

A decorator; a partner in an old-print shop; a flute player, female; and a retired classics professor, who liked to sit reading in a wheelchair. To him, Zona would say: Up, up, move, move, and he might spring to his feet or he might not. Such was Zona's group. She had been passed along to them by some forgotten homesteader, perhaps the now dead photographer from *Life*, who took her picture and used it in a spread on Somalia. These random dwellers did not see much of each other, but each had passed through the sponge of Manhattan, where even a more or less reclusive person like the professor had a bulky address book filled with friends, relatives, window-washers, foot doctors, whatever—a tattered memorial with so many weird scratches and revisions it might have been in Sanskrit.

It was at the decorator's apartment that the messenger first stopped. Tony's was a place on the first floor of a brownstone in the Seventies—a more or less rent-controlled arrangement, since the owner, an old lady, did not want to sell and did not want to fix anything: a standoff. Except for leaks and such matters, Tony was content to do up his own place in his own manner. And a neat number it was, if always in transition, since he bought at auction, tarted the stuff up with a bit of fabric, and sold to his clients, when he had clients. Freelance, that's what he was. A roving knight available for hire. But, even if his sofa had disappeared, Tony had his rosy walls in a six-coat glaze, and a handsome Englishy telescope that stood in a corner, a tôle chandelier done in a leaf design of faded greens and reds, and lots of things here and there. But not too many.

It was near the end of a nice autumn day when his doorbell rang. Lovely September air, and gather it while ye may, for tomorrow in New York a smoky heat could move across the two rivers and hang heavy as leather on your eyebrows. Tony, at the sound of the bell, looked through the peephole and saw before him a young black face, not very black, almost yellow. His mind rushed to accommodate the vision, and, talking to himself, even doing a little dance, he went through his inner dialogue. Ring the bell, open the door. You-have-got-to-be-kidding. This is New York, fella. . . . And so on. Nevertheless, curiosity had its power, and when a finger from the great city touched the bell once more, Tony called out in as surly and as confident a tone as he could summon, What's up?

There was a pause, and the young caller answered in a fading voice. He said: *From Zona.*

Whoa. Come again. Not in a million years could anyone make up the name of Zona and present it on Tony's doorstep under a rare blue-pink sky. Tony looked again through the opening. From Zona was wearing a tangerine-colored jacket, he noticed. Not bad. The latchkey lay near at hand, and with it in his pocket Tony stepped out on the stoop, closing the door behind him, and there they were, the two of them.

The young man shifted uneasily and it fell to Tony to proceed like a busy interpreter at court. From Zona, are you? And there was a nod. Zona? Now here's a coincidence. I had a few friends in the other night. Not many—about six, nothing special. But I could have used a little class in the presentation, you know how it is, and that made me think of Zona right away, but no answer from her. Tony took in the handsome, young, light-skinned face, with its black, black eyes and black, black oily curls. So what is your errand?

Zona passed away. That was the message from the slim youth, about fifteen in Tony's arithmetic.

Zona passed away. You mean dead?

Passed away, the young man repeated, leaving Tony to meet the challenge of whatever was in order—information, emotion? I call that down-right horrible news, he said. Such a wonderful person, a gem of a person, Zona. You sure have my sympathy, for what it's worth.

And then, as they stood on the steps, Tony now braced on the iron railing, a car alarm went off. A loud, oppressive, rhythmical whine, urging, Help, help! When at last it came to an abrupt, electronic end, Tony said: Be my witness. There's not a soul on that side of the street, not a soul when it went off and not a soul there now.

It's like the wind sets them off, the boy offered.

Very good, Tony said. Very good. They remind me of a screaming brat, spoiled, nothing wrong, just wanting attention. Something like that. Rotten, screeching Dodge or Plymouth or whatever it is.

The young man gave a hesitant smile before settling back into silence.

Well, business is business, and Tony gathered himself together and asked with true sweetness: What can I do for you, sir?

We're not able to make arrangements for Zona. The young man shifted and brought his doleful countenance up to meet Tony's eyes, with their flashing curiosity blinking bright in the pleasant sun.

Tony held fast to the railing. I want very much to do something for Zona, he said. And he found himself adding, like a parson, Zona who did so much for us.

The afternoon was retreating; schoolboys and schoolgirls, women with groceries, nurses with prams. Family life and double-parked maintenance trucks of electricians, pipe fitters, floor sanders taking off for the boroughs. Such sad news you have brought to my door. Tony said. And unfortunately I cannot meet the news as I would like. Consolation, all that. I don't have any cash around just now. . . . Maybe I could write you a check somehow or send something later.

Checks are hard to handle, the caller said, to which Tony replied with emphasis: *You are telling me.*

In truth, Tony didn't have any money. As he often expressed it: I don't have any money to speak of, and have you ever thought what a silly phrase that "to speak of" is? Tony didn't have any money. What he had were debts, piling up as they always did, month after month after month. Nothing ever seemed to place him ahead. Ahead? Not even in balance. When he got paid for a job or sold something, by the time the payment came through he owed most of it.

He borrowed from his friends, had borrowed from his sister until that source dried up in a ferocious finale. When reproached or reminded of a default, Tony was something grand to see and to hear. He attacked the lender and carried on with tremendous effrontery, often weeping in his rage. I don't need you to tell me that I owe you money. Don't you think I know that? Do I have to sit here and tell you that damned money is on my mind day and night? And then, in a change of pace, he would crumble, or appear to do so. Listen. I've been having a really rough time. Just now. This wonderful United States economy is in a god-awful mess. Right down there in the mud, as I see it. Or haven't you had reason to notice? You have no idea what borrowing is like. Tony would go on in an aggrieved tone. I hope you never have to go through it yourself, believe me. Borrowing from friends is the worst of it. Sheer hell on earth. Better Con Ed and the phone company after you every day, better than a friend out there waiting . . . With the utilities and all that, there are thousands in the same shitty hole. Those companies don't know you, wouldn't know you on the street, thank God. But with pals, it's torture on the rack.

Take it easy, Tony. Calm down. Everything will work out—and such was the end of that bit of troublesome arrears. Settled.

Autumn leaves lay in damp clumps along the curbs. Some of them still struggling to be yellow and red as they fell from faraway trees and were somehow carried into the treeless streets. Thinking of autumn leaves brought Tony's mind to the first vodka of the evening. It was time to step back through the door with its polished brass knocker in the shape of a lion's head. Time for his little bar alcove and zinc sink encased in pine, his American Back Porch period; time to get ice from the Sub-Zero, High-Tech period. It was time to relax, watch the evening news and, after that, "Hard Copy" or "A Current Affair." But the lovers didn't know *the wife was waiting!* That sort of problem.

Poor Zona, he said. I'd give the old eyeteeth to help you out. I really would, believe me. I know what you folks are going through, but things are a little tight with me at this point in time. That is, right now.

Tony was from Memphis. It had long been understood by him and his world in New York that he had a special sort of down-home, churchgoing way with black people. Perhaps he did, with his loquacity, curiosity, good humor—when he wasn't in a rage. There were, indeed, some occasions when he was more "Southern" than others.

The financial aspect of the transaction on the stoop in the East Seventies seemed to have blown away to rest elsewhere, like the leaves. This resolution, if you could call it that, left Tony free to ask: What's your name, fella?

My name is Carlos.

Carlos, is it? A bit out of the way to my ear. But then I don't know just where Zona got her name, either. And you might ask how I come to be Tony, like an Italian. Never laid eyes on one till I was your age.

That went by without interference, and Tony prepared for a retreat. Zona was a fine person, a special individual. Kind of a lady in her bearing. Of the old school, as they say. And how old was she? No time for that now. Time for the zinc-sink folly. He directed Carlos to another of Zona's group when he saw the young man looking at what appeared to be a list.

Check out Joseph, he said. But don't turn up before seven. He works. As a goodbye offering for Carlos, Tony went into his act, accent and all. Joseph's a good ole boy. And, just between us, he's got pigs at the trough, chickens scootin' round the yard, hay in the barn, and preserves in the cellar. Definitely not hungry, if you get my drift.

Carlos bowed his head and made his way down the stoop. Now, Tony wondered, just what was I going on about? Carlos, not even Southern, for God's sake. But, Southern or not, he called out to the disappearing tangerine back, God bless!

Inside, double-locked, vodka in hand, he rang up Joseph and gave a synopsis and foretold the boy's visit.

What did Zona die of? Joseph wanted to know.

Don't ask me. Just passed away.

At seven-fifteen the elevator man called Joseph's apartment and said that a young man named Zona wanted to be brought up, and Joseph said, Bring him up. It was an awful moment at the door, with the young man saying, Zona passed away.

Yes, I know. Tony rang me. It's very sad news indeed. I've known Zona for fifteen years. A long time for New York, I guess.

Joseph worked in a distinguished print shop on Madison Avenue, a shop owned by a distinguished dealer, a Jewish refugee from Germany. Joseph himself was a second-generation Jewish refugee from Germany. He had been brought up in America by his parents, who left Germany in the mid-nineteen-thirties, went first to England and then to New York. They left with some of their family money, and in New York the father became a successful accountant and the mother trained with Karen Horney and went into practice as a therapist. The parents died and did not leave Joseph penniless, even if what had seemed a lot in the nineteen-seventies didn't seem much at all now.

He had studied history and French at the University of Michigan in Ann Arbor, a happy place for him, which confirmed his parents' notion that young persons of foreign birth should experience the country outside New York. Several years after graduation, he married a Michigan girl and they came to the city, where he learned the old-print business from the Master. It was not long before the Michigan girl found life too old-print—too German and all that. For Joseph the marriage seemed mysteriously to dissolve, but his bride used the word "disintegrate" with unflattering fervor. She took some of Joseph's inheritance and left Joseph with his natural sentimentality and diffidence increased. She left him also in some way frightened, even though cheerfulness was his outward aspect and went handily with his stocky, plumpish figure.

Joseph was wearing a black suit, a shirt of blue stripes, and a black tie. Business wear, except that he was in his socks. The therapeutic walk of twenty blocks up Madison Avenue had taken its toll on his feet, as he explained to Carlos. He invited the young man into a study off the living room, where there was a large desk. Here Joseph planned to talk to Carlos and to write out a check in honor of Zona. Of course it was a difficult meeting, since Joseph lacked Tony's chattering, dominating intimacy with every cat and dog and beggar (Sorry, man, out of change) on the street.

Please be at ease. Uh, Carlos, isn't it? Be at ease, Joseph said. And he sent the young man to sink into an old leather chair. Here in this dark cubicle, with the desk taking up most of the space and books on the floor. Joseph switched on the lights dug into the ceiling. Under the not entirely friendly illumination, the face of Carlos was a warm, light brown, the color of certain packing envelopes. With his eyes a swim of black and his oily black curls, Carlos looked like a figure in a crowded painting of some vivid historical scene, a face peering over the gleaming shoulders of white bodies, a face whose presence would need to be interpreted by scholars. Joseph found himself lost in this for a moment or two but could not name the painting, if any, that he was trying to recall.

No, no, he said. This is going too fast. No hurry, no hurry. He led Carlos into the kitchen and brought forth a bottle of Pellegrino. They took their glasses and Joseph had the idea of showing Carlos around the flat. In a mournful voice, he said: Carlos, this was Zona's place.

The apartment was on the overstuffed side, like Joseph himself. It had been *done* by Tony, and that was the cause of their meeting. Tony's contributions were window drapery that rolled up in a scalloped pattern, a sofa in something that looked like tapestry and ended in a band of fringe around the bottom—those and the recessed ceiling lights. For the rest, there was a mahogany dining table, with six heavy high-backed chairs spread around the three rooms. The bedroom had a suite done in an ivory color with a lot of gilt on its various components, a dated bunch of pieces coldly reigning amidst the glossy white walls.

While the apartment was being renovated. Joseph had announced that he didn't intend to buy any large pieces, because he had his mother's things in storage. Tony rolled his eyes and said: A catastrophe lies ahead. And, not long after, he came face to face with the accumulation of objects as heavy and strong, and spread around as helplessly, as old, dull-eyed mammoths. Tony blew a smoke ring at Joseph and exclaimed: I wouldn't believe it. It's wonderful. Park Avenue Early Jewish!

He wanted everything sent off to Tepper's auction house. Estate sale, Joseph. Estate sale. Joseph was taken with a fit of sentimental stubbornness, and most of the loot remained. Sometimes, when friends came around, he would smile, wave his arm about, and say, Here you have it. Early Jewish. Of course, he had his prints, his library, his silver, some old clocks. And he had Zona, whom he seldom saw, but whose presence in his life was treasured. Her hours, once a week, with a single gentleman out of the house, unlike the freelance Tony, were whatever suited her. Sometimes Joseph was at home in the late afternoon and they collided. Rapid, graceful, and courteous, she filled him with the most pleasurable emotions. The wastebaskets were emptied, the sheets on the ivory-and-gilt bed changed, a few shirts, not his best, ironed. There was that, but even more it was the years, the alliance, the black bird herself.

He directed Carlos back to the room with the desk and, hesitating, uncertain of his ground, he said: Tell me what happened to Zona. That is, if you don't mind.

Zona was shot, Carlos said, lowering his gaze to the wrinkled kilim on the floor.

Joseph drank from the water glass. Then he put it down and pressed his plump hands together. Shot. What a miserable ending for Zona. Such a—what shall I say about her? In truth, Joseph did not have words to describe Zona. He often felt: I love Zona. But that did not appear to be an appropriate expression somehow. For love, although fearful of the details, he asked: Who shot Zona?

Carlos said: Mister Joseph, they haven't got him yet. The one who did it.

You mean on the street? Just like that?

It was with the driver. Her livery driver.

Livery driver?

The driver with the car who drove her around to her places, brought her into town in the morning and met her at their corner and drove her home. For a long time, it's been. Some years, the arrangement. Martin was his name.

Joseph said: Martin shot Zona?

Carlos looked at him with a curious, long glance, a look of impatience, as if he could not believe Joseph did not comprehend what he knew so well himself. Carefully, he said: Martin didn't shoot Zona. She always sat in front with him. They were both shot.

Joseph, near to a sob, said: You must mean a robbery or something like that.

That's what it was. A fare that came in on the car radio. Got in the back seat and that was it.

There it was. It was time for Joseph to ask. What can I do for Zona? Carlos said they were having trouble with the arrangements, and when Joseph got his pen to write a check, Carlos said, Checks are hard. We don't have any banks especially. Any that know us. So, in the end, Joseph found two hundred dollars and Carlos rose to leave. I'll take it to her sister.

Whose sister?

Zona's sister. My mother. And in the gloom he was escorted to the elevator and went down to the street, where now rain splashed and wind blew.

Joseph phoned Tony and said, Shot. And Tony said, Shot? Wouldn't you just know it?

Joseph said, There's a sister.

Whose sister?

Zona's sister. That's who we're talking about, right? The sister is the mother of Carlos. It's horrible to think of Zona gone like that. From the back seat.

Tony said. What back seat? But Joseph declined. Nothing, Tony, nothing. Just shot.

Tony said: History of this goddam city—at least a footnote to the history of these fucking times. The whole place is a firing range, up and down and across.

Joseph said: Zona's not a footnote to me. I loved Zona.

Didn't we all? came back over the wire.

The next morning, Carlos arrived at a town house on East Ninety-first Street, the house of Cynthia, the flute player. The door was ajar and noise could be heard inside—voices, a phonograph, a telephone ringing and answered. Carlos pushed the bell button and waited next to a stone urn of faltering geraniums. After a time, a young girl, about his age, called out for Granny and after a minute or two here came Cynthia in a smock. This time the opening line was: I'm Carlos. From Zona.

How nice. Come in, come in. You are welcome here.

There were boots and umbrellas in the hallway, coats hanging on pegs, newspapers stacked for recycling—quite a busy entrance, you'd have to say.

Carlos was led into the front parlor, where there was a piano, along with bookcases, two-seater sofas, and a big, lumpy armchair by the window, to which he was directed. Cynthia drew a chair very near to him, and her greenish, amiable eyes gazed into his liquid black ones and at last she said: I missed Zona this week. You know—Carlos, is it?—that I consider it very brave of Zona to set foot into my jungle. An army couldn't handle it. You can see that. I'm sure. But Zona found things to do, and I am much in her debt.

Carlos looked aside. Zona passed away, he said.

Cynthia sat up straight as a rod in her chair and looked up at the ceiling for a long time. At last she said: I wasn't prepared for this. Passed on from this life. Zona. Just like that.

Zona passed away, he repeated, and Cynthia seemed lost in contemplation, meditation of some kind. Oh, oh, passed away. I'm sorry. I'm sorry. I hope it was an easy death. An easy passage after a hard, honorable life.

Carlos said: No, Ma'am. It wasn't easy. Zona was shot.

Cynthia drew her chair nearer, brought her golden-gray head so close that Carlos tilted his black curls back a bit. Then Cynthia placed her long fingers on his hand and drew his other brown hand over her own so that they were in a clasp like that practiced in progressive churches. Shot, you say. More than the heart can bear.

Cynthia grew up in Baltimore, went to the Curtis Institute, in Philadelphia, had a three-week summer session in Paris with Rampal, and in her younger years had played for a time in the Baltimore Symphony Orchestra. Then she came with her husband and daughter to New York and bought the house on Ninety-first Street. Thirty-nine thousand it cost then, she would say. Only that. The money had come from the closing of her grandfather's Baltimore business, a handsome store where well-to-do women could buy dresses, coats and satin lingerie, cologne and face powder. Three floors in a fine downtown brick building, clerks long in service, and seamstresses with pins in their mouths while making alterations. Ours was a *select* business, she would say with an ironical lilt and the special tone of Unitarian modesty. It was very well known and much respected in the community. To be that, you had to be somewhat cool to ordinary people. You didn't want them to look at things and then go pale at the price. But the doors were welcoming to one and all on the Day After the Fourth of July Sale. A yearly excitement it was, people in line at seven in the morning.

Releasing the hand of Carlos, Cynthia said: Tell me what you and your family have been going through. She passed him a damp cookie and a cat entered the room and settled on his lap. Carlos ate the cookie and stroked the cat. Looking hard at Cynthia, he said in a tone of apology: You see, I never met any of the people Zona worked for before this happened. I don't know just what they might want to hear.

I want to hear what you can bear to tell, Cynthia said.

In a breathless rush, Carlos told about the livery car that had taken Zona back and forth to her work, about the passenger who got in from the radio call and hadn't been caught yet. And he added that his mother, Zona's sister, would have come round to the people but she was home crying herself crazy.

I will attend Zona's funeral, Cynthia said. I want to be there. For me, it would be an honor. And it occurs to me that if you wish I might play a little music. Something suitable, of course.

Carlos raised his hand to interrupt. It was time to complete his errand: We haven't been able to make the arrangements for Zona.

Cynthia said at this point: Funeral arrangements cost much more than they need to. I read a book about that—although I didn't need to be informed about the ways of such institutions.

Carlos, a diver at the tip of the board, fixed his glance on Cynthia's bright head of white hair, with the brown streaks turning golden. He said: She's been there a week while we couldn't make the arrangements. They put them in the ground, like in a field, they say.

Been where?

With the city down where they keep them. If you can't make the arrangements to transfer, they put them—

Oh, Cynthia said. You mean Potter's Field?

Carlos said: That sounds like it.

The granddaughter who had opened the door came into the room and introductions were made. As she was going out, she said to Carlos: You're cute.

This young person is in a state of bereavement, Cynthia called to the girl. And she added: Neither of my grandchildren is musical. They can't sing "Adeste Fideles" in tune. A deprivation.

Pigeons rested on the sills of the long, handsome, smeary windows still divided into the original panes and now interrupted only by a rusty air conditioner. I can't take it all in, Cynthia said. I would like to know what Zona's family needs.

What we want, Ma'am, he said, what we want is a coffin on a train, and a few of us family will go down and have her buried in Opelika.

Opelika? Where is that?

Alabama, Zona's town.

Opelika, Alabama. What a pretty name.

The ground down there's paid for, Carlos explained.

Cynthia drew a pencil from the pocket of her smock, found a pad, and began to write on it. I have probably waited too long to sell this house, she said. The prices are falling fast—the darkness deepening, as the hymn goes.

Cynthia and her chamber-music group occasionally held concerts in this house, and at one of those Joseph had brought Tony along. Tony, when the invitation came, said: I might have guessed you'd go for that, Joseph, German.

During the wine and cheese, inferior quality indeed, Tony approached Cynthia and in an excited mode informed her: You are sitting on a million bucks here—if not exactly in mint condition. He noted the panelling, the high ceilings, and the matching fireplaces of decorated marble on the first floor. Assets you have here. A million for sure, at the bottom.

Tony was floating like a sturdy little boat on the waters of the house market. A million for the property and another mil *at least* to do it up. They're terrorists, these buyers. They like to gut the place, break down walls, even move the staircase so they can put a powder room under it. Space, dear lady, that's the ticket. Space is what you have to sell.

Of course, Cynthia stayed on. The house, the space, was all she had to leave her daughter, the way things looked. She rented rooms to students, gave lessons, while lamenting that the lesson-takers were mostly girls and few strong enough for the instrument. In these rooms now she was contemplating life and death with Carlos. It was calculated that a thousand dollars was needed to rescue Zona. And there was the problem with cashing checks, and just two days before they would, down there at the city, before they would—

Please, please, Carlos. Don't speak of it. More than the heart can bear.

Cynthia's finances were more than a little murky. Her husband, when they moved to New York, had worked for a publishing group that put out *Family Days.* Perhaps he got a bit overloaded on that, and he squared the circle, so to speak, and shifted to *Liberty,* when that magazine was around. He also shifted to an ignorant girl in the mail room. Cynthia was left to provide for her daughter, who quit Barnard College in her freshman year, took up with a boy from Columbia, and went up to New Hampshire with him to pursue carpentry and to produce two daughters. Cynthia had bits of trust funds from the old Baltimore emporium, from a childless uncle, and from her father, who declined the clothing business and went into a small local bank, not very successfully. He raised his nice, musical daughter, who ended up on the flute.

At last, toward noon, with the temperamental city sun shining one minute and disappearing the next, as if turning a corner, Cynthia found a sweater and put her arm through the arm of Carlos, and the odd tandem made its way down Lexington Avenue to the Chemical Bank. Inside the bank, the odd tandem became an alarming couple; Carlos like a thief avoiding eye contact with the teller, a young Indian woman in a sari, and Cynthia, in an old gentlewoman's untidy fluster, withdrawing a thousand dollars in fifties and twenties.

They stood outside in humbling confusion until the money in two envelopes was passed into the hands of Carlos. Off in a gallop to the subway and to do the paperwork down there where they were impatiently holding the body of Zona. Alert the River Jordan Twenty-Four-Hour Funeral Service. And at last meet the train rolling down to Washington, D.C.: there a crunching change of cars, a wait, before wheeling through state after state, through West Virginia, passing the memory of the prehistoric Mound Builders and the rusting scaffolds of the anthracite-coal counties. On to the point of the Chattanooga Campaign, down to the grass and myrtle of the cemetery lying in the Alabama autumn. Journey's end.

Adios, Carlos, Au revoir, Zona, Rest in peace in Opelika.

Cynthia recounted the dire circumstances to Joseph, who said, I loved Zona. A great hole in my life, this is. It's like planting a field of seeds and none of them coming up. In a manner of speaking.

Cynthia said: Nothing for Planned Parenthood this year. But no matter, no matter.

Tony, informed, said: They love funerals.

Talk That Talk, from In the Place to Be, *Guy Trebay (1994)*

Guy Trebay was born in the Bronx and has been, for two decades, a contributor to the *Village Voice.* He has also written for *The New Yorker, Details, Harper's,* and *Esquire.* In 2000, he moved on to become a writer for *The New York Times.* Trebay has been a longtime chronicler of what he has called "the backwaters of New York City," and his articles have explored the adventures of drag queens in Greenwich Village, the life of Central Park carriage horses, and the workings of an East Village community gardener who dresses completely in purple.

Trebay has written that "the most permanent feature of New York is undoubtedly its air of self-importance, the locally prized conviction that, when you're here, you're in the place to be. It's mostly sham, of course, and bravado, but enlivened by wit and endurance and suppleness and a touch of improvisation—as if the character of New Yorkers were formed to justify New York the idea."

New York is a city of people talking, to themselves, to their gods, to dead parents (Mae Questel looming in the clouds), to errant lovers and doomful doctors, to the friends who come and go, and the enemies who park stubbornly in the mental backlot reserved for mean humors and old wounds.

New York is a city of people acting out (to use the jargon), folks talking loud to no one or to everyone at once on the IRT—thanking you for your generosity before it's offered, biting your pant leg with their maladies and tales of hard luck. New York is a city of menacing bargains struck by strangers, who ask charity in return for not mugging you or robbing you blind. New York is a city of people speaking in tongues. Some of them are talking to space aliens who control their brains from the antenna atop the World Trade Center. You've heard these people muttering in strange syllables. The aliens may have heard them, too.

Sometimes the remarks people make in New York are like small stories. These stories may be aimed and hostile—hatpin jabs by a fast-moving attacker—or yarns as windy as the ones your great uncle told, or they may have the power to charm you because they are discrete, intended for no one in particular when, in every case, no one in particular is you.

The redhead on the crosstown bus, for instance, is young and wearing Manolo Blahnik pumps. She has Melanie Griffith legs and her voice is an Ozone Park whine. The man to whom she is yammering perhaps knows her but very likely does not. She is inquiring the following: "Did you ever see that Spanish priest with the monkey? Village, 8th Street, kind of weird? He pushes this cart around and he has a live monkey with a crucifix." And her seatmate is giving her an expression that conveys how commonplace Spanish priests with monkeys are, as common as sadhus or firewalkers, saints with stigmata. See them all the time.

The redhead goes on: "Know the one? Yeah, well, I was going to work and I saw this guy, he has a little sign: 'Give the monkey 25 cents and make a wish.' I only had three dimes, so I dropped them in and I said to myself, 'Oh, God, let me go to California and be successful.' And suddenly, get this, the guy grabs my hand and puts a blue stone in it. He says, 'You're gonna leave New York. Big things are gonna happen to you. California is your destiny. By next April everything will be changed. Can you believe it?"

This happens in January on a brilliant, cold afternoon. The redhead leans back, tugs a Merit 100 from her bag, holds the cigarette as if lit, and takes an empty drag. "I jumped back," she says, "like '*Whoa!*' I made up my mind then and there. I bought a ticket and put my studio on the market. I went home and told my mother about it and you know what she tells me? She says, 'You're puttin' your future in a monkey's paw.' Can you imagine?"

Imagine what? In a city that outwits your efforts at every turn, answers questions you hadn't begun to formulate? Take this: Another day, predawn, on the fringes of clubland, a six-foot-six-inch drag queen in an Afro wig and a red satin mini is sucking back a seabreeze and explaining the technical aspects of achieving a crotchless silhouette in hotpants. "It's much as you'd imagine it, baby," he remarks in a dry, sibilant bass. "Some people get into ACE bandages and tape and do a thing with string, But for myself I just tuck it up into some tight cheater panties."

New York is a city of cheater panties and people who know how to use them, a puritan place some of whose famous prelates have been nicknamed Fanny and Joan, a city where a billboard shows a woman sipping from a bottle of brandy beneath the legend, "I could suck on this all night." New York is the city of fugitive sex on phone lines, an electronic territory of states called raunch-and-sleaze, hardcore, discipline, daddy, and spank. "I like to smack a guy around a little. You into that?" a slightly blurred voice speaks. "Sounds hot," comes a disembodied reply. "Yeah?" the first voice picks the dialogue up again, pausing: "Well, good. You can get as queer as you want with me."

As queer as you want and as crazy, as frank. As unwittingly Three Stooges strange as the dope fiend on the MTA bus outside Montefiore Hospital who croaks, "I've been four days without methadone and alcohol and it's rough cause my body don't have no *endolphins*."

"I'm ill," says the phrasebook for Japanese visitors to this city, found at a secondhand bookshop and flipped open to "Useful Words in Emergency." Who knows when a Japanese visitor may suddenly fall faint from endolphin privation?

"I've lost my"—is the second line in this found poem, followed by:

"Leave me alone."

"Lie down."

"Listen."

"Look."

"Look Out."

"Stop that now."

"Stop thief."

"Stop or I'll scream."

But somebody's already screaming, who'll hear you? The Rastafarian with fat cabled dreadlocks, for instance, standing outside Afrika House near 125th Street on Columbus Day barking, "Christopher Columbus was a liar who never discovered nothin' and died in 1506 from a bad case of *syphilis*." And the young black man just out of Rikers striding down 8th Street blaring, "Lack of pussy make a nigger brave!" And the group of teenagers who surround two men by an East Side restaurant one hot fall evening shouting, "What're you looking at, faggots," and keep it up until they become hoarse, insensate as Dennis Hopper after his ether blasts in *Blue Velvet*.

Looked at another way, the phrase could mean, "Stop, I don't believe my eyes and ears." At, for instance, the sights and sounds on the streets of Bensonhurst, Brooklyn, where loudspeakers ceaselessly play "O, Holy Night" to accompany Christmas-light fantasies that outkitsch Mad Ludwig's Neuschwanstein: at Pat and Walter Nordquist's 67th street house alone, an animated Santa and three reindeer, six choirboys, 16 toy soldiers, a two-story tinsel tree, and bay windows kitted out with movable dolls; glitter foil and lights picking out all the windows and doors, Nat Cole burbling canned cheer all over the sidewalk.

Or it could mean, "Stop, or I'll scream with laughter"—at the clusters of shocked Wagnerites who stand one June evening in the Lincoln Center plaza. Here is David Hockney with a late-model blond, and Sony Mehta furiously sucking on an unfiltered cigarette, and here are knots of leathermen representing a type that comes to seem like an endangered species: Eulenspiegel Society clichés with black vests over plaid-shirted paunches, engineer boots over jeans, the pant legs worn in or out according to some obscure sexual code.

Something has happened onstage: The soprano Brünnhilde got clocked during the twilight of the gods. "The cue was early, that's all," a balddomed leatherman explains to a small, nervous crowd. "The whole demolition started early and the platform went down and from what I could tell, she got hit on the head by a piece of Valhalla."

In New York this sort of thing happens all the time. Valhalla breaks up and pelts you in the streets. Nibelungen roam the boroughs, along with apparitions every bit as strange as Rhine maidens, speaking in wonderful heroic tongues.

On Fordham Road, a 200-pound woman clutches a Fendi bag to her bosom like Alberich's gold. Three pairs of door-knocker earrings jut from her small ears beneath a rich crop of Senegalese corkscrews. The woman peers at the window of a discount appliance shop where a bank of televisions show 18 Tina Turners strutting by gas-guzzling Plymouth automobiles. The woman cackles, tosses her head back, addresses the strangers who happen at that moment to be sharing her air. "Tina Turner is my girl! Don't have to talk. Don't have to sing. Don't have to dance, do nothing. All she has to do is get out there and walk that mad, mad walk!"

A Region at Risk: A Summary of the Third Regional Plan for the New York–New Jersey–Connecticut Metropolitan Area Regional Plan Association (1996)

The Third Regional Plan, released in 1996, followed the first two plans with its emphasis on improving transportation. The plan called for the building of a new Regional Express Rail (Rx) rail system that would link the tristate area as well as reduce automobile traffic through a system of increased "tolls and employer incentives."

The plan takes a larger overview than the previous two plans, however, by making the major focus the "three E's"—Environment, Equity, and Economy—"the objectives of the plan, the components of RPA's goal of improving quality of life." The region had experienced a serious decline in economic competitiveness, as witnessed by the loss of 770,000 jobs between 1989 and 1992, the largest job loss in any metropolitan area in the country since World War II. But the plan, unlike the previous two, embraces minority and immigrant labor pools by suggesting ways in which they could be brought into the economic mainstream through "expanding English literacy programs, legitimizing informal economic activities (home-based business and street vending zones), and seeking moderate reform of federal immigration statutes."

Besides combining "equity with economy" as a major goal, the *Third Regional Plan* also added a third "E"—Environment. The plan's "Greensward" initiative addresses the fact that "two generations of decentralized growth have drastically increased the region's urban land—by 60% in 30 years despite only a 13% increase in population." By establishing 11 regional reserves—comprising over 2.5 million acres—and reinvesting in "urban parks, public spaces, and natural reserves," the plan proposes to improve "the region's competitiveness and sustainability in a changing world," which will be judged not only by its economic development but by its "quality of life."

Introduction

As a new millennium approaches, the metropolitan region of New York, New Jersey, and Connecticut is a region at risk.

- Despite our strength in the global economy, we are facing years of slow growth and uncertainty following our worst recession in 50 years.
- Despite the billions of dollars spent every year by the public and private sectors on infrastructure, office space, and housing, the uncomfortable truth is that we have been living off the legacy of investments of previous generations.
- Despite a history of strength from diversity, a shadow of social division has fallen across the region.
- Despite strict laws and renewed public concern, we continue to pollute our air and water and checkerboard our rural areas with suburban sprawl.

The region faces a future in which it must compete in a global economy that offers new challenges and opportunities. The question posed is whether the next 25 years will represent the final chapter in a story of prosperity and momentum that dates back to the settlement of Manhattan in the 17th century. The warning is that modest growth in the next few years could mask the beginning of a long, slow, and potentially irreversible and tragic decline.

A regional perspective is the proper scale and context for analyzing and addressing these issues. Metropolitan regions are becoming the dominant economic, environmental and social actors of the next century. During the 1980s, the metropolitan regions in the U.S. that grew most rapidly all had central cities that also grew rapidly. And in areas where suburban incomes declined, central cities also experienced decline. Nearly one-third of the income earned in New York City ends up in the pockets of commuters, around $44 billion annually. More than ever, the economies, societies, and environments of all the communities in the Tri-State Metropolitan Region are intertwined, transcending arbitrary political divisions. Our cities and suburbs share a common destiny.

RPA has produced a plan to reconnect the region to its basic foundations, the "Three E's"—economy, environment, and equity—that are the basis of our quality of life. The fundamental goal of the plan is to rebuild the "Three E's" through investments and policies that integrate and build on our advantages, rather than focusing on just one of the "E's" to the detriment of the others. Currently, economic development is too often border warfare, as states within the region try to steal businesses from each other in a zero-sum game. Social issues are either ignored or placated by a vast welfare system that fails to bring people into the economic mainstream. And environmental efforts focus on short-term solutions that attack the symptoms rather than the causes of problems.

This summary outlines RPA's analysis and projections of the "Three E's." It summarizes the recommendations of *A Region at Risk*, the Third Regional Plan, and groups them into five major campaigns that integrate the "Three E's": creating a regional greensward, concentrating growth in centers, improving mobility, investing in a competitive workforce, and reforming governance. Each campaign combines the goals of economic, equity, and environmental improvements, leading the region to a more competitive, prosperous, fair, and sustainable future.

The "Three E's": Where We Are, Where We Are Headed

The "Three E's" are the objectives of the plan, the components of RPA's goal of improving quality of life.

ECONOMY

Between 1989 and 1992, this region fell into a steep and frightening recession that claimed 770,000 jobs—the largest job loss of any metropolitan area since World War II—eliminating virtually all our growth from the 1980s. Unlike previous recessions, however, all parts of the region suffered losses of similar magnitude. Immediate growth prospects for many key industries remain weak or uncertain, and recovery has been much slower than in other parts of the nation.

This recession and slow recovery must be considered in the context of a wrenching global transformation. New technologies have radically changed how goods and services are produced, marketed, and distributed, and a fiercely competitive global economy can quickly turn the fortunes of a business or a community. Low-skilled workers are particularly vulnerable to this transformation, as automation, rising skill requirements, and corporate downsizing have depressed wages and job opportunities.

But this region has enormous advantages in the emerging global economy. It is the world's most active and innovative center of global capital management, with more than 10,000 international businesses. It is an unsurpassed producer of information, with leadership in broadcasting, book publishing, and magazines and electronic media. This region is a premier designer of popular culture, through the arts, mass marketing, media, and an increasing multi-culturalism that equips us to compete directly in dozens of languages and cultures. With over 150 colleges and universities, it is one of the world's largest centers for research and academia. Finally, it is the meeting grounds for governments from around the world, with the United Nations, its affiliates, and permanent missions drawing an unparalleled diversity of people, interests, and ideas.

Over the next decade, the region is likely to experience sluggish growth as employment recovers to its pre-recession peak. Moderate growth fueled by new global markets and information technology will be countered by continued corporate downsizing and global competition. These trends will likely result in continued employment losses in manufacturing and government, but modest increases in financial, business, and personal services.

In the long term, the region has the opportunity to enjoy sustainable economic growth driven by productivity gains and increased sales to expanding global markets. But that promise could fail without new investments in infrastructure, communities, environment and the workforce. Increasingly, quality of life is the benchmark against which the region is judged in competition with other regions in the nation and world.

EQUITY

This region is one of the most diverse in human history. Residents speak more languages, offer a wider array of skills, reside across more extreme densities, and live under the broadest range of incomes in the nation. Demographic projections show that it will be even more diverse in the future. By the year 2020 a majority of the region's residents will be of African, Asian, or Hispanic heritage, largely as a result of a constant flow of immigrants from around the globe. Since 1970 the region has drawn nearly 3 million legal immigrants, almost one-fifth of the nation's total legal entries. Throughout the 1990s and beyond, immigrants and their children will account for virtually all of the region's expansion in working-age population. These new residents bring with them enormous talent and cultural diversity—New York City could never have become the world capital it is without them.

But even as we become a more diverse society, disturbing trends show us becoming a more isolated and fragmented society. Low-skilled workers face a future of declining incomes and sporadic employment, and over two million residents of the region already live in poverty. Nearly three million adults in the region are estimated to be functionally illiterate. Most new jobs will demand at least some college or post-secondary education, yet a large share of urban students never finish high school. And poverty remains much more concentrated among non-white residents, even when differences in education and skills are accounted for, demonstrating that bias and segregation remain persistent problems.

Entire communities are being left out of the region's growing prosperity, as too many people have come to accept the concept of a permanent underclass. Some people now see our diversity not as the enormous advantage it provides in the world economy, but as a hindrance. For a prosperous future, this region must do a better job of welcoming and assimilating its present immigrant population, as well as the 1.25 million new immigrants expected in the next 10 years. Isolated by physical barriers—such as a lack of housing or public transportation alternatives—that separate residences from new employment opportunities, inner-city communities have been cut off from the new employment centers in the region's suburbs. The region needs to work harder to integrate isolated and racially diverse communities into its social fabric and economic mainstream.

These communities can either be an enormous advantage, or a liability, depending on the policies put in place now, from affordable housing to education to economic development.

ENVIRONMENT

This region is a national leader in environmental protection, having enacted comprehensive and far-reaching environmental standards and having spent the money and political capital needed to make the laws work. As a result, the region has added 350,000 acres of public parkland since the 1960s, while air and water quality has improved significantly. Yet these achievements can obscure the serious nature of problems that still confront us. Most of the region does not meet federal air quality standards. More and more drinking water must now be filtered. Many urban neighborhoods lack park acreage and suburban development continues to sprawl across mountains and farmland.

In the past 30 years a new pattern of land use has swept the region, involving the construction of massive campus-style commercial and industrial facilities in sprawling residential suburbs. From 1970 to 1995, core urban counties lost more than 300,000 jobs while the outer suburban ring gained 2 million. Eighty percent of the 1.7 million housing units built since 1970 were constructed in the region's outer ring, as residents sought affordable housing, lower taxes, and escape from the problems of cities and inner suburbs. But these rings of deconcentrated suburbs consume vast areas of open land and shatter traditional patterns of community.

The spread-out pattern of homes and jobs has led people to drive more than ever. The number of vehicle miles traveled in the region grew by 60% from 1970 to 1990, creating congestion on highways and roads. Growing use of automobiles, trucks, and buses is also the key reason why the region is second only to Los Angeles in number of days that air quality fails to meet federal standards. But current toll policies are absolutely backward, rejecting the fundamental market principle of charging more for a scarce resource. Instead, tolls are discounted for commuters who use the roads during the most crowded times. Furthermore, parking is often provided for free and gasoline is now cheaper in constant dollars than it has ever been, costing less than bottled water.

At the same time, the region has abandoned urban areas, hollowing out cities that historically have been the locus for jobs and residences. By 1980 the majority of the region's residents did not live in a city. The most visible impact of this has been the conversion of forests, farms, and wetlands to urban uses and the paving of wildlife habitat and natural resources. The region lost 40% of its farmland between 1964 and 1987, and development outside urban areas continues at around 30,000 acres a year.

This challenge comes at a time of widespread dissatisfaction with environmental management by business and the public sectors. Government policies that call for polluted sites to be cleaned by their owners often impede beneficial site restoration. In 1994, more than $4.6 billion in state, federal, and local funds were allocated for water pollution control in coastal waters and $2.8 billion was spent disposing of garbage. But all of the region's landfills will reach capacity around the year 2000, and we will be spending more on pollution control and disposal in the future.

Efforts to protect the environment from further degradation will have to begin looking at the causes of problems—such as land use and transportation—to find innovative and comprehensive solutions. We can do a better job of protecting the environment and living within our means by learning to produce less waste, recycle, and rely on biological systems for natural resource management and pollution control.

The Five Campaigns

Strategies for improving the region's quality of life must reinforce all three of the cornerstone E's and demonstrate how our economy, equity, and environment are vitally linked to each other, or those strategies may, in fact, be counter-productive.

Five initiatives anchor the plan—*Greensward, Centers, Mobility, Workforce,* and *Governance.* Each campaign addresses all three E's. Together, they have been designed to re-energize the region by re-greening, reconnecting, and re-centering it. The *Greensward* safe-guards the region's green infrastructure of forests, watersheds, estuaries, and farms, and establishes green limits for future growth. *Centers* focuses the next generation of growth in the region's existing downtown employment and residential areas. *Mobility* creates a new transportation network that knits together the re-strengthened centers. *Workforce* provides groups and individuals living in these centers with the skills and connections needed to bring them into the economic mainstream. Achieving these ends will require new ways of organizing and energizing our political and civic institutions, as outlined in *Governance.* Collectively, all of these strategies underpin the region's quality of life and can guide us to sustainable growth as we enter the 21st century.

The goal of the campaigns in the Third Regional Plan is to integrate and improve the region's economy, environment, and equity, thereby improving our quality of life.

Call to Action

Regional Plan Association has prepared an ambitious plan that targets new investments necessary for sustained growth and continued prosperity in an uncertain future. The plan calls for radical changes in the status quo and bold initiative on the part of citizens. Some of the recommendations carry significant price tags, but the Tri-State Metropolitan Region cannot afford *not* to make these investments. Projections and analysis demonstrate that we are reaching the end of credible short-term solutions and must begin to look at the fundamental causes of our mounting problems. At their root, these issues are all regional and will require comprehensive approaches for meaningful improvements.

The five campaigns outlined in this document are presented in greater detail in *A Region at Risk: The Third Regional Plan for the New York–New Jersey–Connecticut Metropolitan Area.* To succeed, each campaign will need the active support and cooperation of government, business, and civic leadership. To the degree that our elected officials do not provide the necessary leadership, we must form new civic coalitions demanding change. These new "third sector" coalitions will build on one of the region's untapped strengths—its thousands of community, business, environmental, and other groups. New coalitions are already being formed that bring together competing interests and forge new ways of addressing old problems. These include coalitions between environmentalists and developers, between government and business, and between local interests and regional imperatives. By looking at the long-term and considering the interlocking goals of economy, equity and environment, we can build on our strengths and enter the next millennium strategically placed for another century of growth and prosperity. But we must act now. The region's competitiveness and sustainability in a changing world hangs in the balance.

Summary of Recommendations

Greensward

- Establish 11 regional reserves that protect public water supplies, estuaries, and farmlands and function as an urban growth boundary for the region.
- Reinvest in urban parks, public spaces, and natural resources, restoring and creating new spaces in urban neighborhoods and along waterfronts.
- Create a regional network of greenways that provide access to recreational areas.

Centers

- Strengthen the region's Central Business District by building a Crosstown light-rail system and district, expanding transit access to Lower Manhattan and the Jersey City waterfront, and revitalizing Downtown Brooklyn and Long Island City.
- Invest in 11 regional downtowns—New Haven, Bridgeport, Stamford, White Plains, Poughkeepsie, Hicksville, Mineola, Jamaica, Newark, New Brunswick, and Trenton—attracting new job growth and rebuilding communities rather than building on greenfield sites.
- Create incentives for new development and investment in transit- and pedestrian-friendly centers throughout the region, so they provide the quality of life that makes living and working in centers worthwhile.
- Support new institutions and uses in centers, such as "telematic" at-home businesses, mixed use districts, and arts and cultural institutions.

Mobility

- Build a Regional Express Rail (*Rx*) system that provides: airport access by connecting the Long Island Railroad to Grand Central Terminal,

Lower Manhattan, Kennedy Airport, and La Guardia Airport; direct access from New Jersey and Long Island to the East Side and Lower Manhattan; direct service from the Hudson Valley and Connecticut to the West Side and Lower Manhattan: through service from New Jersey to Connecticut and Long Island; and service between the boroughs in a new circumferential subway line.

- Promote congestion-busting through road-pricing and market approaches, such as tolls and employer incentives. Also finish missing links in the highway network that support existing centers or remedy notorious bottlenecks.
- Improve commercial transportation by building a freight rail trans-Hudson crossing and cutting congestion on the highway system.

Workforce

- Improve education in low-income communities by combining state financing of public education with local management reforms and teaching innovations.
- Reconnect education and the workplace with local school-to-work alliances linking schools to employers, state tax incentives to encourage continuous education for adult workers, and a tri-state council of business, labor, education, and civic leaders to coordinate workforce development initiatives.
- Bring immigrants and minorities into the mainstream economy by expanding English literacy programs, legitimizing informal economic activities, and seeking moderate reform of federal immigration statutes.
- Connect low-income communities by expanding support for community-based organizations, improving transportation links to job centers, and using new information technologies to expand job information networks.

Governance

- Coordinate governance in the region through state growth management plans, education finance reform, service sharing, and new regional coalitions:
    - An annual "G-3" governors' conference to coordinate policies and investments to promote regional competitiveness and a regional compact between the three governors to reduce border warfare economic development policies.

- A Tri-State Congressional Coalition to fight for essential federal tax and regulatory reforms and infrastructure funds.
- A Tri-State Business Council composed of all the major regional chambers of commerce and partnerships to coordinate regional promotion and advocacy and develop a regional business plan.

- Create new public institutions to finance and provide regional services, such as a Tri-State Regional Transportation Authority, a restructured Port Authority, and a Tri-State Infrastructure Bank.
- Improve public and private decision-making processes, incorporating sustainable economics in accounting and tax and regulatory systems and utilizing smart infrastructure approaches to capital investments.

One Large Garlic and Anchovy: The Search for the Perfect Slice, Michael Nadler (1997)

Mike Nadler was born on March 7, 1952, in Flushing General Hospital in Queens; he spent his childhood in Kew Gardens. His mother had come to the United States from Poland when she was a child, and his father's ancestors were also from Eastern Europe. Nadler went to high school in Syracuse and graduated from Harper College at the State University of New York in Binghamton. He has been writing about alimentary concerns since that time and has published work in both New York and his adopted New Mexico.

The confluence of cultures that has become New York has made it the center of the most diverse population in the world and, therefore, the most eclectic culinary feast. Yonah Shimmel's, Katz's Deli, and Guss's Pickles are classic Lower East Side establishments, but Nadler would claim the best knishes are in the "middle of Russian Brighton Beach at Mrs. Stahl's." Little Italy boasts Old World cannoli, Junior's in Fort Greene claims the best cheesecake, and, of course, the hot dog was invented at Nathan's in Coney Island. Newer waves of immigration have given the city ever more different foods — Chincse, Vietnamese, Korean, Turkish, Afghani, Cuban; all have made their mark on the taste buds of New Yorkers. But Mike Nadler contends that, for the true New Yorker, life is still about "the search for the perfect slice."

The Search for the Perfect Slice

EVERYBODY'S an expert on pizza these days. Used to be we'd share slice at Ray's on 1st. and 14th., or 3td. and 57th. It was *the* slice; thin, crusty, cheesy, chewy, tomatoey sweet and salty mozzarellean conglomeration in the mouth. The taste lingers on as the myriad voices of America now lay their claims to correct slice.

I've put myself in the thick of it, having endured weekend midnight pizzas at Franks on Erie Boulevard in the 'Cuse during my formative teenage years.

We found good slice on Vestal Parkway, in the Vestal Mall, at Mario's. Trips to the Big City would uncover new gems: Pugsley's in Portchester, Stromboli's just south of Union Square. Truth with a capital P. Cavernous ovens would meld crust, sauce and cheese correctly, and it happened anywhere in the five boroughs. The perfect atmosphere: salty New York sea level Italian ethnicity familiar with the generosity of oregano. "Enough!", you think. Provincialism might be a mighty barrier in realizing Spaceship Earth, but in some important matters of life, primacy, genius and ultimate expressions must be recognized. The best pizza in the world is found anywhere in the five boroughs of New York. There is something in the Catskillian water, and everything else, hand spun in preceding details, follows through to exact what Tom Verlaine cried out for—that "perfect slice."

Forget Dion's, forget Nunzio's (but wonder why pizza must be possessive): they are a far cry beyond pizza muff and little or no caesar's. I did have the uncanny fortune to experience one of the very first Domino's; on Floral Ave. and St. Charles St. in Johnson City, N. Y. They had the correct model in mind, but mass production in response to phone orders removed some vital karmic topping from what has become product rather than pizza.

Good pizza in the High Desert southwest is an anomaly, an anachronism, a virtual paradox. There is no harmonic convergence of crust, sauce and cheese. Something happens to pizza dough several thousand feet above sea level. The consequence is chewiness at the cost of crunchiness. Something is wrong with the tomatoe sauce out here; it hasn't been properly concocted with the requisite spices and dirty wooden spatula to create that pungently sharp vegefruit blend of bitter yet sweet tongue turning tomatoe taste. It is apparent that cattle in Texas or Colorado or Kansas cannot produce mozzarella cheese like their bovine cousins in the dairy farm country of upstate New York. There is something about complex nitration in the compostial epidermis of the Appalachian crust that produces superior cheese toppings.

Yes you want to shout "Chi-town has great pizza." It does; I had a deep dish in a dank pizza factory just west of Michigan Ave. years ago that encrusted my taste buds permanently. Of course, this ingestion took place a quick two hours after experiencing Wrigley Field for the first time, a Cubs vrs. Cardinals doubleheader, six and a half hours of pure pastime replete with a nod from Harry, a tip of the cap from John Tudor, and the fantastic verbiage of four blind young men who sat directly behind us in box seats we snuck into for the second game. Pizza tastes good after such realities.

It happens in those shimmering bulwarks of massive metal, consumed with intensity of heat. Sam gathered us in his Brooklyn living room and led us many blocks down Union St. We were walking east in the crisp late night. So correctly, yet so flagrantly we were passing one pizza parlor after another. The vigorous smell wafted through us as cheese oozed on the ovened discs of purity. We crossed Atlantic Ave. Our stomachs groveled, having growled long enough. We sat in naugahyde chairs around a rectangular linoleum table. Sam ordered one large garlic and anchovy. We winced. We grimaced. We gored Sam's consciousness with burning eyes. Twenty five city blocks to be surprised by such a pretentious order of alimentary superiority? Sam stoically smiled through the interminable bake. But, he was right. So correct. The pizza prevailed. Coca Cola in six ounce paper cups cannot be sweeter, truer, more righteously combined in nectared carbonation when it rinses down the perfect slice, especially one so smarmy, salty and right.

Think what you may of this elitist tome. Praise be your slice—from the Corrales Village Inn to the (other) City's North Beach to the US 280 Pizza Crust. Enjoy it; be it the Red Baron's or hermetically sealed in Tombstone. I just hope you will, one fair chilled autumn evening, find yourself on the upper West Side of the York wandering into the neon reality of Gino's or Sal's, with squat slate bottomed ovens molded from tons of steel emitting the smell of my lifetime, and slide that orange-yellow tip of that perfect slice into your mouth. Let us now ingest, and no longer digress.

The Second Inaugural Address: The Agenda for Permanent Change, Rudolph Giuliani (1998)

Rudy Giuliani was born in Brooklyn on May 28, 1944. After graduating from New York University Law School, he was an assistant U.S. attorney and then an associate attorney general of the United States. In 1989 he narrowly lost the mayoral election to David Dinkins, the first African American mayor of the city, but he defeated Dinkins in the election of 1993 to become the first Republican mayor in twenty-eight years.

Giuliani's effectiveness and impact on the city have perhaps only been surpassed by another non-Democratic mayor, and Giuliani's idol, Fiorello La Guardia. In the course of his eight-year term as mayor Giuliani oversaw the transformation of a city that was the cover story of the September 17, 1990, *Time* magazine issue entitled "The Rotting of the Big Apple" and finished the decade as the cover story of the January 1, 2000, *Time* magazine issue showing a rejuvenated Times Square at midnight.

Giuliani's message was a rebuke of the decades-old liberal assumption that crime and poverty are impersonal systematic forces that cannot be overturned. Giuliani's novel solution was to assert that the best way to help the poor is to reduce crime. The institution of a modern police program, COMPSTAT (a computerized statistical method of crime reporting that has been a model studied and adopted by cities all over the world), aided in reducing crime by 55 percent, reducing murders from an average of 2,000 a year to less than 700, and reducing felonies from an average of 8,259 a week to 3,556. His belief that the welfare rolls promote dependence led to a reduction of numbers, 655,000 people off the welfare rolls that stood at 1.17 million in 1993, a drop equivalent to the entire population of all but fifteen cities in the country. And aided by a booming economy, the city had an increase of 480,000 jobs between 1993 and 2001 after losing 320,000 jobs between 1990 and 1993.

Critics of Giuliani's tactics were outraged by the Special Street Crimes Unit shooting of Amadou Diallo and the sodomizing of Abner Louima by Brooklyn police officers, and former Mayor Ed Koch produced a book criticizing Giuliani's style entitled simply, *Giuliani: Nasty Man.* But the lasting legacy of Rudy Giuliani may well be that New York City is seen as the safest large city in America and a place where people want to live in the future.

Introduction

ONE hundred years ago to the day Manhattan, the Bronx, and Staten Island joined the City of Brooklyn and the various jurisdictions of Queens to unite our city. Today, we celebrate our centennial as a city of resurgence and a city of progress, as one city with one standard.

A city which has demonstrated the resiliency and uniqueness of the human spirit.

But four years ago, when I stood here and said "New York City is the Capital of the World," there was doubt.

There was fear.

There was the feeling that New York City's best days were behind us.

I didn't accept that.

Many of you didn't accept it either.

And over the last few years, in an exercise of human will and determination, you and I together have changed the direction of the City more than in any four year period in history.

And we should all be proud of that achievement.

New York City is now the city Americans most want to live in and visit.

Could you have believed that four years ago?

Now people say New York City is manageable and governable, and we are the undisputed Capital of the World.

A great opportunity now exists for us to make our changes last.

- Not for four or eight years but for decades—well into the 21st century.
- Not for a majority of New Yorkers, but for all New Yorkers.

All that we have done, all that we must continue to do together, is based on continuing to liberate the human spirit, understanding that liberty is a balance of freedom and responsibility, of rights and obligations.

The spirit of New York City has undergone such a great change because more and more New Yorkers today are freer and more independent.

They are able to make more choices for themselves.

Millions have been liberated from the reality and fear of crime.

Hundreds of thousands have been freed from lives of dependency on government welfare and are on the road to taking care of themselves and others.

Many students have experienced improvements in education and in so doing have acquired more control over their own lives and hope for a better future.

And many more people are now experiencing the very best social program of all—much better than dependency on government—that moral program is called a job.

The change in New York's spirit from defeatism to optimism is actually an overall reflection of the change in the lives of most New Yorkers.

When people are safer, working, off of welfare dependency, with schools improving, streets and highways cleaner, our beautiful parks maintained, hospitals better, taxes reduced, hotels, theaters and buildings going up, and new businesses opening—all of this liberates more and more people and improves their quality of life. The sum of those millions and millions of units of liberation and improvement in the lives of people is that the spirit of the City is now changed from "the best days are behind us" to "the best days are yet to come."

Now, it's our obligation to make that change in spirit permanent and to reach out and have it affect everyone, with no one left out, no one left behind.

This is our agenda for the next four years: to make permanent the changes that made people more independent, to ensure that those changes reach more and more New Yorkers—improving their quality of life—and to enable as many New Yorkers as possible to take advantage of the beauty of the City that we create together.

The Future

Today, I will briefly outline this Agenda for Permanent Change—some of the initiatives that will strengthen the City over the next 120 days, the next four years, and well into the future. In my State of the City address on January 15th and my budget address on January 29th we will discuss these initiatives and many more in greater detail.

As our City enters the 21st Century it must continue to be America's safest large city so that our quality of life continues to improve and our people are secure in the most basic civil right of all, public safety and domestic tranquillity.

There are some that would say that we have been so successful in reducing crime, let's declare victory and decrease the effort.

My approach is different.

To maintain our level of safety, improve our quality of life even more, deal fatal blows to organized crime and to end the drug trafficking we have known in the past, now is the precise time to increase our efforts, to put on more pressure, to fight even harder.

We will push very hard for significant changes in state and federal law, including:

- ending parole in New York
- expanding drug treatment programs
- increasing penalties and programs for domestic violence
- and the passage of strong national uniform gun control laws.

Police Commissioner Howard Safir, who has had an exceptional record of success, should be given the opportunity to make that success permanent. To do that, we are going to add over 1600 new police officers to our legislated target of 38,310. The NYPD will reach 40,000 officers and be at its greatest strength in history.

We will add five more drug initiatives to the four presently operating, more than doubling the resources devoted to those initiatives since my announcement of our anti-drug offensive on October 1, 1997.

This will allow the Department to bring unrelenting pressure on all drug dealers in all five boroughs and drive them out of this city. There will be no place left for them to hide.

It will also allow the Commissioner to add police officers and other resources based on the NYPD's award winning Compstat program, which is designed to deploy police where they can reduce crime and improve quality of life the most.

Together with Police Commissioner Safir, we will build on the great reductions in crime throughout the City to also break down the remaining barriers between the police and the people they serve so that all police treat our citizens with courtesy, professionalism, and respect.

At the same time we expect communities who wish and desire more respect from the police, to support the police when the police are unfairly accused or attacked by those who make a career of transferring all blame to the police.

Respect grows and flourishes when it is mutual.

CONTINUING TO IMPROVE OUR SCHOOLS

As we enter the next century, we will once again be a City whose educational system is the best in the nation.

We must build on the success already achieved by Chancellor Rudy Crew and his fine team and complete projects already underway, ranging from Project Read to Project Smart Schools, to providing greater seating capacity for students, making arts education a required part of the curriculum, and continuing to implement school-based budgeting.

This system is about children, and everything must serve their interests.

We must end principal tenure.

We must stop social promotions.

We must continually raise standards. We've learned in our City if you expect more, you get it.

We must encourage and expand public school choice, as well as charter schools—which are shaped by teachers, administrators, and parents alike.

We also have a moral obligation to the parents of this city that when they entrust their children to our public schools, their children will return home safely. That is why I believe the NYPD—the most professional law enforcement agency in the world—should have the primary supervisory role in securing the safety of our children in our public schools.

The Board of Education is responsible for the education of public school children—and the Mayor shares in this responsibility. But the Mayor's responsibility goes beyond this—the Mayor is responsible for all of the City's children. We have more than 265,000 non-public school students citywide, representing 19.8 percent of our total student population. Taken alone, this would be the fifth largest public school system in the country.

We must continue to provide as much help for them as is consistent with the limitations of the Constitution, including continued support for the School Choice Scholarship Foundation, which is providing children and parents with the opportunity to exercise more freedom, in this case in selecting the school of their choice.

We will continue to support alternatives, competition and options in an effort to challenge this entire system, public, parochial and private, to improve education.

ENCOURAGING BUSINESS GROWTH

As the City enters the 21st Century, New York must be a city of growth, an opportunity city. We need more jobs, and to accomplish that, we need more and expanding businesses.

The anti-business city has been replaced with the pro-business city because being pro-business is being pro-jobs. We must now continue and complete this transformation by implementing even more dramatic reforms as we enter the next century.

Over the last four years, we have reduced or eliminated 16 separate taxes, and returned over $1.1 billion to the private economy. Our financial plan already provides for a total of over 1.6 billion in tax relief by fiscal year 2001.

Today the tax burden on New Yorkers—the percentage of tax as a share of personal income—has been reduced to its lowest level since 1970.

These tax cuts have helped New York City register the greatest percentage private sector job growth ever.

And over the last four years, we have done something else unprecedented in City history—we've not only held the growth rate of City government spending in check, but we've kept it below the rate of inflation, all the while making record tax reductions.

All of this has helped us dramatically restructure our budget from the one we inherited from the prior administration with immediate deficits of over $2 billion, with budgets today producing record surpluses and providing the largest reserve and cushion in the city's history.

Because of this success, for the first time, tax cuts are considered an important part of our basic economic philosophy.

Having already succeeded in convincing the State to drop the sales tax on clothing purchases of $100 or less starting in late 1999, now we will urge them, in the upcoming session, to drop the tax for all clothing, including footwear.

Both Speaker Peter Vallone and the City Council deserve great credit for the leadership they have shown in dealing with the budget, taxes and the economy.

And to build further on that record, we will strive to reduce or eliminate more taxes with the focus always on creating jobs.

It will be an important part of our agenda because high taxes are still costing us jobs.

At the same time, in addition to reducing the actual amount of taxes, we will shortly announce a task force to make recommendations about restructuring our tax and regulatory system to reduce the number of both taxes and regulations that burden our businesses and deter economic growth.

In addition, we will continue to eradicate the influence of organized crime, which for too long has taken money out of the pockets of legitimate business people and put it in the hands of criminals. In addition to ensuring the success of our reform of the private carting industry, the Fulton Fish Market, and the wholesale food markets, we will propose similar reforms for the garment industry, the construction industry, and the air freight industry.

And we will advance key new economic development plans like the Broadway Initiative, which will modernize theaters and create more performance art space, as well as the development of Hudson River Park, the New York Coliseum site, and the freight rail tunnel and hub port. We will commit ourselves to keeping major city institutions like the New York Stock Exchange—the Yankees and the Mets—the institutions that help keep us the capital of the financial world and the capital of the business world.

RESPECTING THE INDIVIDUAL

As we enter the next century, we must return economic power to more New Yorkers, so that they can make choices that make sense for themselves and their families.

We have already transformed ourselves from the welfare capital of the nation to the workfare capital.

Work has once again returned to the center of New York City life.

It's always been strange to me that for years, those who supported increasing the number of people on welfare and did nothing to address the growing numbers of dependent people were described as progressive. It's true that welfare is a necessary and decent alternative for people at certain times in their lives. But by no means is welfare ever "progressive." For an individual, remaining dependent on welfare is retrogressive.

Over the last four years, we've seen a major philosophical shift take place in the City, so that we've come to understand that a truly progressive city does not invite and encourage dependency. A truly progressive city moves the maximum number of people to self-sufficiency through work as soon as possible, having the compassion also to understand that there are some people who need permanent help and providing that help more generously than anywhere else in the nation.

In the next 120 days, we will propose programs intended to make our welfare reductions permanent, to increase them, and to emphasize involvement in the workforce as a lasting answer to dependency.

People who are unemployed and seeking help from City government will no longer come to a welfare office, but rather to a job center.

Everything that we do must be oriented around the centrality and importance of work in people's lives. Work gives people self-worth; dependency robs them of it.

Never again will we repeat the mistakes of the past and let able-bodied people remain dependent for generations.

That's not helping them. That's forgetting them.

That's not compassion. That's guilt.

While government dependency is a major threat to the self-sufficiency of people, the greatest threat to our individual and collective autonomy, without question, is drug abuse. We cannot afford to shy away any longer from calling drug abuse what it is—a moral crisis for the nation. Drug abuse enslaves the mind and destroys the soul, causing people to abandon their duties, their children, their friends, their jobs, their education—everything that is worthwhile in life, everything that makes a City great.

With a comprehensive set of programs focusing on substantially intensified law enforcement, tough but fair treatment, and innovative prevention and education programs that pay special attention to our children, City government is attempting, like never before, to root out drugs from our neighborhoods and schools.

Four years from now, we want newspapers and magazines around the nation to write the same stories about drug reduction that they are now writing about quality of life, welfare reform, crime reduction, and job growth in the City.

Successfully combating drug abuse is the most important way to ensure a healthier, freer, and more independent future for our children. And if we can accomplish this, we will once again lead the way for cities around the nation, and achieve what America as a whole has not yet been able to accomplish.

Conclusion

Four years ago, we initiated a dialogue about improving the quality of life of New Yorkers—a topic that had never before realistically entered the city's discourse. Some people thought that was about achieving an end. But, at base, it has always been about something much more fundamental: enabling all New Yorkers, every day, to strive to create better lives for themselves and a better City for their children.

Quality of life is not so much a destination to be reached as a direction in which to strive. Quality of life is a continuous process. It demands an ongoing effort. We will never reach the perfect ideal but we must fight the battle anew each day. We must never lose sight of where we have been or how far we have yet to go.

What we are trying to do is give all New Yorkers the ability to choose how they want to live their lives.

Our commitment now is to reach out to all New Yorkers, both those who have experienced the liberation and improvement of the last four years and those who have not. All New Yorkers deserve to experience the self-fulfillment of a city of opportunity and have the blessings of political and economic freedom enlighten their lives.

To all New Yorkers we commit our tireless efforts to give them the opportunity to make the American dream—the New York dream—happen for them and their children.

We New Yorkers of 1998 have an additional responsibility and opportunity which derives from the great wealth, power, talent and energy we possess.

The greatest and most successful cities have always been those in which the arts have flourished and grown.

It is in the music, drama, dance, paintings, sculpture, and architecture created, and in the writings of our philosophers, theologians, poets, novelists and historians that we define ourselves for future generations—not only for future generations of New Yorkers, but of Americans and people around the world.

The most precious legacies of great cities are the great works of art they give the world.

Let history say of us that we used our great wealth and strength to support the creation of beauty and that, more than any time before us, we made the opportunity to experience beauty enter the lives of all New Yorkers, to lift them to a greater understanding of the uniqueness of their humanity.

If we can do this, and all that we have pledged today, we can fulfill the oath of ancient Athens, the "Athenian Oath of Fealty," to leave our city better than we found it. Not only for the next four years but for decades and generations to follow. Not only for most New Yorkers, but reaching out to all New Yorkers—no one left out, no one left behind.

On the day of Mayor Fiorello La Guardia's first inauguration he took this oath of Athens. I would like to take this same oath today. It reads: "We will never bring disgrace to this, our city, by any act of dishonesty or cowardice nor ever desert our suffering comrades in the ranks. We will fight for our ideals and sacred things of the city, both alone and with many. We will revere and obey the city's laws and do our best to incite a like respect in those above us who are prone to annul them and set them at naught. We will strive unceasingly to quicken the public sense of civic duty. Thus in all these ways we will transmit this city not only not less, but far greater and more beautiful than it was transmitted to us."

And now, to this noble pursuit I dedicate the next four years of my administration: to create a greater and even more beautiful city. I ask God to bless us and our great city—the Capital of the World now and forever.

Thank you.

Someplace in Queens, Ian Frazier (1998)

Ian Frazier was born in Cleveland, Ohio, and graduated from Harvard, where he wrote for the *Harvard Lampoon,* in 1973. Frazier became a staff writer at *The New Yorker* magazine, and has published books of humorous essays, *Coyote v. Acme* and *Dating Your Mom,* as well as penetrating books about American life, *Great Plains, Family,* and *On the Rez.*

Frazier's essay on Queens captures the spirit and dynamism of New York City's largest and most diverse borough. Queens is the largest borough in land mass (it is almost as large as Manhattan, the Bronx, and Staten Island put together) and the most diverse by ethnic identity (in 1990, 36 percent of the population was foreign born). Even before the English created Queens County (named for the queen of King Charles II) in 1683, the area had a reputation for embracing tolerance. John Bowne was banished by Governor Peter Stuyvesant in 1662 for holding Quaker conventicles at his Flushing home but was vindicated by the Dutch West India Company and returned to his home. Today, Queens has the most eclectic population in terms of race, ethnicity, and religion of any of the boroughs, and Jackson Heights is reputed to be the "most diverse neighborhood" in the world.

As a predominately residential borough with no clear commercial center, Queens is defined by neighborhood. These neighborhoods can often be described by the country of origin of the residents—Chinese and Koreans in Flushing, Haitians in Springfield Gardens, Jamaicans in St. Albans, Greeks in Astoria, Irish in Woodside, Colombians in Elmhurst, European Jews in Kew Gardens, Dominicans in Corona, and Guyanese in Richmond Hill. The number 7 subway, running through the northern section of the borough, has even been dubbed "The Multicultural Express."

OFF and on, I get a thing for walking in Queens. One morning, I strayed into that borough from my more usual routes in Brooklyn, and I just kept rambling. I think what drew me on was the phrase "someplace in

Queens." This phrase is often used by people who live in Manhattan to describe a Queens location. They don't say the location is simply "in Queens"; they say it is "someplace in Queens," or "in Queens someplace": "All the records are stored in a warehouse someplace in Queens," "His ex-wife lives in Queens someplace." The swooning, overwhelmed quality that the word "someplace" gives to such descriptions is no doubt a result of the fact that people who don't live in Queens see it mostly from the windows of airplanes landing there, at La Guardia or Kennedy airports. They look out at the mile after mile of apparently identical row houses coming up at them and swoon back in their seats at the unknowability of it all. When I find myself among those houses, with their weightlifting trophies or floral displays in the front windows, with their green lawns and nasturtium borders and rose bushes and sidewalks stained blotchy purple by crushed berries from the overhanging mulberry trees, and a scent of curry is in the air, and a plane roars above so close I think I could almost recognize someone at a window, I am happy to be someplace in Queens.

Queens is shaped sort of like a brain. The top, or northern border, is furrowed with bays and coves and salt marshes and creeks extending inland from the East River and Long Island Sound. To the west, its frontal lobe adjoins the roughly diagonal line running southeast that separates it from Brooklyn. At its stem is the large, solid mass of Kennedy Airport, at its east the mostly flat back part that borders Nassau County, Long Island. To the south stretches the long narrow peninsula of Rockaway Beach, which does not really fit my analogy. Queens is the largest New York City borough. It has the longest and widest avenues, the most freeways, and the most crowded subway stations. It has more ethnic groups and nationalities than any other borough; observers say that it has more ethnic diversity than any other place its size on earth. Some of its schools are the city's most overcrowded. In one Queens school district, a dozen or more new pupils enroll every week during the school year, many speaking little English. Classes meet in bathrooms and on stairways; kids use stairs as desks when they practice their spelling and teachers go home hoarse every night from trying to make themselves heard. Immigrants open stores along the avenues beneath the elevated-train tracks in Queens, the way they used to under the old Second Avenue El on the Lower East Side. Queens has more miles of elevated tracks than any borough, and the streets below them teem.

I like to walk under the elevated tracks early on summer mornings, before people are up. At six-thirty, a steeply pitched shaft of sunlight falls between each pair of dark iron pillars. On down the avenue you see the shafts of light, each tinted with haze, receding after each other into the distance. Sun here is secondary, like sun in a forest or on a reef. Some of the shadows of the El on the empty pavement are solid blocks, some are sun-and-shadow plaid. Traffic lights overhang the intersections from the El's beams and run through their cycles at this hour for no one. Security gates on all the stores are down. There's a sharp tapping as an Asian man turns a corner hitting the top of a fresh pack of cigarettes against his palm. He tears off the cellophane, throws it on the ground, opens the pack, hurries up the steps to the station. Each metallic footstep is distinct. When the noise of the train comes, it's a ringing, clattering pounding that fills this space like a rioting throng. The sound pulses as if the train were bouncing on its rails, and, in fact, if you stand in the station the floor does seem to trampoline slightly beneath your feet. Then there's the hiss of the air brakes, a moment of quiet, the two notes of the signal for the closing doors, and the racket begins again. In the world under the El, speech-drowning noise comes and goes every few minutes.

Queens specializes in neighborhoods that nonresidents have heard of but could never place on a map. Long Island City, for example, is not someplace out on Long Island but on Queens's East River side, across from midtown Manhattan. High-society families had estates there when that side of the river was New York's Gold Coast. Today, it is Con Ed property, warehouses, and movie-equipment supply places. You can buy a used police car there for a third off the book price. Astoria is near La Guardia Airport, just across the river from Rikers Island, which is in the Bronx. Sunnyside is southeast of Long Island City, and below Sunnyside is Maspeth, and below Maspeth is Ridgewood, one of the most solidly blue-collar neighborhoods in the city. Springfield Gardens, in southeast Queens, has many wood-frame houses, and that general area has the city's highest fire-fatality rate. Queens used to be the city's vegetable garden and orchard, and in certain places the old farmland still bulges through the borough's concrete lacings. In Fresh Meadows, in the east middle of the borough, a cherry tree survives that was planted in about 1790. It stands on a small triangular relic of field now strewn with Chinese-restaurant flyers and abutted by the back of a beverage store, a row of small businesses, and some row houses. This year, the tree bore a crop of cherries, just as it did when it was out in the country and Lincoln was a boy.

In Forest Hills, in the middle of the borough, flight attendants in blue uniforms with red scarves wheel suitcase caddies up its sloping sidewalks. Woodside, on the northwest border, is the city's most integrated neighborhood. St. Albans and Cambria Heights, on the east of the borough, are almost all black and middle class. In Queens, the median black household income is higher than the median white household income—$34,300 a year compared to $34,000 a year. Howard Beach is just west of Kennedy Airport. It became famous some years ago when a white mob killed a black man there. Ozone Park, just north of it, has houses in rows so snug you can hardly see the seams between them, and each house has a lawn the size of a living room rug: some of the lawns are bordered by brick fences with statuettes of elephants raising their trunks, some are thick with flowers, some with ornamental shrubs in rows. People water in the mornings there, and get down on all fours to pick pieces of detritus from the grass. In front of 107–44 110th Street, a house with gray siding and black trim and a picture window, several men came up to the owner, Joseph Scopo, as he got out of a car one night in 1993, and they shot him a number of times. He made it across the street and died near the stone-front house at 107–35. The front yard of Mr. Scopo's former house is all cement; for many years, he was the vice president of Local 6A of the Cement and Concrete Workers of New York City.

On Kissena Boulevard, in Flushing, I passed a two-story brick row house with a dentist's office on the first floor and the sign "D. D. Dong, D.M.D." By now, my feet were hurting and my legs were chafed and I was walking oddly. At the end of a sunlit alley, a pink turban leaned under the hood of a yellow cab. A yellow-and-black butterfly flew over a muffler-repair shop. A red rose grew through coils of razor wire and chain-link fence. At a juicing machine on the street, I bought an almost-cool Styrofoam cup of sugarcane juice, grassy-tasting and sweet. Then I was among the Cold War ruins of Flushing Meadow Park, site of the 1964–65 World's Fair, which is now a mostly empty expanse coexisting with about half a dozen freeways at the borough's heart. No place I know of in America looks more like Moscow than Flushing Meadow Park: the heroic, forgotten statuary, all flexed muscle and straining toes; the littered grounds buffed by feet to smooth dirt; the vast broken fountains, with their twisted pipes and puddles of olive-colored water. I leaned on the railing of a large, unexplained concrete pool thick with floating trash and watched a sparrow on a soda can do a quick logrolling number to stay on top. No matter what, I could not get out of my mind "D. D. Dong, D.M.D."

Legally, you can buy wigs made of human hair in Queens, and two-hundred-volt appliances designed to work in the outlets in foreign countries, and T-shirts that say "If you can't get enough, get a Guyanese," and extra-extra-large bulletproof vests with side panels, and pink bikini underwear with the New York Police Department shield and "New York's Hottest" printed on the front, and pepper-spray personal-defense canisters with ultraviolet identifying dye added, and twenty-ounce bottles of Laser Malt Liquor, whose slogan is "Beam me up," and a cut-rate ten-minute phone call to just about any place on earth, and a viewing of the Indian movie *Sabse Bade Khiladi,* featuring "the hottest song of 1995, 'Muqubla Muqubla.'" Illegally, if you know how, you can buy drugs in bulk, especially cocaine. Drug enforcement officers say that Queens is one of the main entry points for cocaine in the United States, and that much of the trade is engineered by Colombians in the neighborhoods of Elmhurst and Jackson Heights, a district called Little Colombia. On the Elmhurst-Jackson Heights border, at Eighty-third Street just below the Roosevelt Avenue El, is a pocket-sized park of trees and benches called Manuel de Dios Unanue Triangle. It is named for a journalist killed in Queens in 1992 by agents of a Colombian drug cartel.

Manuel de Dios Unanue was born in Cuba, graduated from the University of Puerto Rico, and worked as a newspaper reporter in New York. In 1984, he became the editor of *El Diario–La Prensa,* the city's largest Spanish-language newspaper. At *El Diario,* he was, according to various accounts, obsessive, crusading, blindly self-righteous, possessed of a brilliant news sense, delusional, uncompromising, vain. He chain-smoked. He believed that the United States should open political discussions with Castro, a view that angered anti-Communist terrorist groups, and he printed many articles about the drug trade. He received death threats with a regularity that became a joke between him and his colleagues. Once, someone painted black zebra stripes on his white car and left a note saying he would "get it."

In the eighties and the early nineties, drug money flowed into Queens. Police said that check-cashing places and travel agencies and other businesses in Elmhurst and Jackson Heights were laundering it. Steamer trunks full of submachine guns traced to a realty company on Queens Boulevard led to the discovery of apartments with stashes of drugs and money elsewhere in the city. Colombians died by violence in Queens all the time. One year, 44 of the borough's 357 homicide victims were Colombians. Pedro Méndez, a political figure who had raised money for the 1990 campaign of Colombia's new antidrug president, was shot to death near his home in Jackson Heights the night before that president's inauguration. At a pay telephone by a florist's shop on Northern Boulevard, police arrested a man named Dandeny Muñoz-Mosquera, who they said was an assassin wanted for crimes that included the murders of at least forty police officers in Colombia. Although the authorities believed he had come to Queens to kill somebody, at his arrest they could hold him only for giving a false name to a federal officer. In prison, he requested that Manuel de Dios do an interview with him.

Manuel de Dios had left *El Diario* by then, fired in 1989 for reckless reporting, according to some accounts. On his own, he wrote (and published) a book called *The Secrets of the Medellín Cartel,* an antidrug exposé. He began to publish two magazines, *Cambio XXI* and *Crimen,* in which he identified alleged drug traffickers and dealers and the local places where they did business, with big photographs. In Colombia, some people—according to federal agents, José Santacruz Londono and Gilberto Rodríguez-Orejula, of the Cali drug cartel, among others—decided to have him killed. Someone hired someone and his wife, who hired someone, who hired Wilson Alejandro Mejía Vélez, a sixteen-year-old employee of a chair factory in Staten Island. One afternoon the boy put on a hood, walked into the Mesón Asturias restaurant in Queens, and shot Manuel de Dios twice in the back of the head as he finished a beer at the bar.

The *Times, The New Yorker,* Salman Rushdie, and others decried the murder. Police said they would solve it soon, and sixteen months after the killing, on a tip from an informant, they caught the killer and some of the conspirators, not including the higher-ups in Colombia. The killer and four others stood trial, were convicted, and went to jail. The triggerboy got life without parole. Manuel de Dios's magazines ceased publication after his death. His book cannot be found in the Spanish-language bookstores in Elmhurst, or *Books in Print.* People in Elmhurst know the name of the book, and they say the name of its author in a familiar rush, but they cannot tell you where you might find a copy. Recently, the number of local drug-related murders has gone down; people say this is because the victory of one big drug cartel over another has brought stability to the trade.

The Mesón Asturias restaurant is just across Eighty-third Street from the Manuel de Dios Unanue Triangle. On a hot July afternoon, I went into the restaurant, sat down at the bar, and had a beer. The bartender, a short, trim man with dark hair, put a bowl of peanuts by me and cut some slices of chorizo sausage. We watched Spanish TV on cable and commented on a piece about the running of the bulls at Pamplona. The bartender said that an American had been killed and that you had to know how to be with the bulls. I paid for the beer and got up to leave. I asked, "Is this where the journalist was killed?"

"Oh, yes," the bartender said.

"Were you here?"

"No, I was outside."

"Did you know him?"

"Yes, he was a regular."

"He must have been a brave man," I said.

The bartender stood not facing me and not facing away. He pushed the dollar I had left for a tip across the bar, and I pushed it back at him. For a while the bartender looked off toward the dim, gated window. "Well," he said, "you never know your luck."

The oldest house in Queens—perhaps in the city—is a frame farmhouse built in 1661 by a man who later suffered banishment for letting Quakers meet there. His neighbors in the town of Flushing sent the Dutch governor a Remonstrance stating their belief in religious freedom not only for Quakers and other Christians but also for "Jews, Turks, and Egyptians." Today, the house, called the Bowne House, sits on a small patch of lawn between a four-story apartment building and a city playground. The theoretical Jews, Turks, and Egyptians are now real and living nearby, but nearest are the Koreans. Almost all the signs you see in downtown Flushing are in Korean, and the neighborhood has a Quaker meetinghouse, Korean Buddhist temples, and Korean Catholic and Protestant churches. At the end of the No. 7 Flushing subway line, pamphleteers for a city council person hand you fliers saying that the line is going to hell, while other people hand you fundamentalist Christian tracts saying that you are. Pentecostal churches in storefronts all over Queens have signs in the window advising, for example, "Do nothing you would not like to be doing when Jesus comes," in Spanish and English. A multimillion-dollar Hindu temple, the largest in the city, recently went up in Flushing. Many Hindus, Buddhists, and Sikhs have recently added small celebrations of Christmas to their traditional worship calendars. Groups of Gnostics meet in Queens, and Romanian Baptists, and followers of the guru Sri Chinmoy, who sometimes express their faith by doing enough somersaults to get into the *Guinness Book of World Records.* When summer comes, big striped tents rise on outlying vacant lots with billboards advertising tent meeting revivals led by Pastor John H. Boyd.

In Douglaston, a far Queens neighborhood that still has the feel of a town, I sat on the lawn of an Episcopal church at the crest of a hill. The ancient gravestones in the churchyard leaned, the daylilies along the driveway bloomed, and the white wooden church panted discreetly in the heat through its high open windows. In Astoria, I visited St. Irene's of Chrysovalantou Greek Orthodox Church, home of the icon of Saint Irene, which witnesses say wept on the eve of the Persian Gulf War. A short woman all in black said, "Why not? Why not?" when I asked if I could see the icon, and she led me slowly up the aisle in fragrant, dusky church light. The icon, a six-by-eight-inch painting, is in a large frame made of gold bracelets, jeweled wrist-watches, and rows of wedding rings donated by parishioners. On a wooden rail below it are inhalers left by asthma sufferers whose breath Saint Irene has restored. In Richmond Hill, I stopped in at Familiar Pharmacy, managed and co-owned by Mohammad Tayyab, who knows the Koran by heart. He is thirty-nine, has a neatly trimmed beard, and wears his baseball cap backward. He told me that, growing up in Multan, Pakistan, he memorized verses from the Koran almost every day, morning to night, from when he was six until he was twelve. The Koran is about the length of the New Testament. A person who knows the Koran by heart is called a *haviz*. Mohammad Tayyab recites the whole Koran once a year in a mosque during the fast of Ramadan, and reviews three chapters every night, to keep fresh. The stored-up energy of his knowledge causes him to radiate, like a person who has just been to a spa.

In Montefiore Cemetery, in another far part of Queens, the Grand Rebbe of the Lubavitcher Hasidim, Menachem Schneerson, lies in a coffin made of boards from his lectern. By the time of Rebbe Schneerson's death, in 1994, at the age of ninety-three, some of his followers had come to believe he was the Messiah. Tens of thousands of Lubavitchers from around the world have visited his grave, sometimes annoying the black families who own homes nearby. Neighbors complained that the Lubavitchers were singing loudly, drinking beer, trespassing, and asking to use their bathrooms. The sect has since bought a house near the grave for the convenience of visitors. I went to see the grave myself, on an anniversary of the Rebbe's death. Cars with out-of-state plates lined the boulevard by the cemetery gate; some cars had their doors open to the curb, and shoeless Lubavitchers lay asleep on the seats. Along the paths to the gravesite ran that orange-webbed plastic security fence in which we now routinely wrap important public events. Some of the Lubavitchers were pink-cheeked teens with blond sidecurls. Cops not much older leaned against the cemetery gate and smoked, thumbs hooked in their belts, cigarettes between their first two fingers.

Black-clad Lubavitchers in black hats were coming and going. In the patio behind the nearby Lubavitcher house, many were reciting prayers. Occasionally, an impassioned voice would rise like a firework, bursting higher than the others. A man about my age who pointed the way to the grave suggested that I remove my shoes before approaching it: "Remember, this is a holy place," he said. My running shoes looked as bright as a television ad on top of the pile of functional black brogans of many sizes already there. I ducked through a low door to an anteroom filled with candles. It led into an enclosure of walls maybe twelve feet high, and open to the sky. At the center of the enclosure was a knee-high wall around the grave itself. Men were standing at the graveside wall and praying, chanting, flipping expertly through small prayer books in their palms, rocking from side to side with the words. Heaped on top of the grave like raked-up leaves, spilling onto the smooth pebbles next to it, drifting into the anteroom, were hundreds or thousands of small square pieces of paper on which people had written prayers for special intercessions. There are so many hopes in the world. Just out of the line of sight past the higher wall, 747s descended slowly to Kennedy Airport like local elevators stopping at every floor. Across the street just out of earshot, long-legged girls jumped double-Dutch jump rope, superfast.

The Midnight Tour: Working the Edgar Allan Poe Beat in the Bronx, Marcus Laffey (May 15, 2000)

Marcus Laffey is the pseudonym of Ed Conlon, a Bronx-based narcotics officer in the New York Police Department. Conlon is a third-generation police officer who went to an Ivy League college, but upon graduation decided to become one of "New York's finest." In 1997 he began to publish a series of articles in *The New Yorker* under the title "Cop Diary." His essays take a close look at the life of a policeman in the Bronx and particularly at the narcotics trade. He is presently working on a nonfiction book entitled *Blue Blood.*

As has been the case with other urban services—health, sanitation, fire—New York City has been a leader and a model for other cities throughout the country in police organization. The first urban police force in the country was established in New York in 1845. Presently, New York has three policing units, the NYPD, the Transit Authority Police Department, and the Housing Authority Police Department, which were combined under a central authority during Rudy Giuliani's tenure as mayor. The combination of the three gives the city the second-highest ratio of police per residents in the country, trailing only Washington, D.C.

WHEN I went to work midnights a few months ago, it was discovered that I didn't have a nickname. You need one, to talk casually over the radio: "Stix, you getting coffee?" "Chicky, did you check the roof?" "O. V., T., G. Q., can you swing by?" Nicknames never stuck to me, for some reason, and I always thought that nicknaming yourself was like talking to yourself, something that made you look foolish if you were overheard. So Hawkeye, the Hat, Hollywood, Gee Whiz, Big E., the Count, Roller Coaster, and Fierce pitched a few:

"'Hemingway'—nah, they'd know it was you."

"'Ernest' is better."

"Or 'Clancy'—he'd be a good one to have."

"What about 'Edgar'?"

"What from?"

"Edgar Allan Poe."

"What about 'Poe'?"

As I thought about it, the fit was neat: Poe, too, in his most famous poem, had worked, weak and weary, upon a midnight dreary. He moved to New York City in 1844, the same year that legislation created the New York City Police Department. And he wrote the first detective story ever, "The Murders in the Rue Morgue," in which the killer turns out to be a demented orangutan with a straight razor. There is also a brilliant detective, an earnest sidekick, and a mood of languor and gloom—all now hallmarks of a genre that has endured for a century and a half. Poe spent his last years in the Bronx, living and working in a cottage that is midway between where I live and where I work. I am a police officer in the Bronx, where kids sometimes call the cops "po-po." And so "Poe" it was.

Midnights for Edgar Allan Poe seemed less a time than a territory, a place of woefully distant vistas, as if he were stargazing from the bottom of a well. A lot of that has to do with needing sleep, I think. Everyone on the late tour lacks sleep, and this state of worn-out wakefulness while the rest of the world is dreaming tends to stimulate thoughts that meander. Each precinct has a list of "cooping-prone locations," which are out-of-the-way places, under bridges and by rail yards and the like, where bosses are supposed to check to make sure patrol cars haven't stopped in for a nap. The list is posted in the station house, and when you're tired it reads like a recommendation, a Zagat guide for secret sleep, as if it might be saying, "St. Mary's Park, with its rolling hills and abundant trees, offers superb concealment in a pastoral setting—we give it four pillows!" On midnights, we talk about sleep the way frat boys talk about sex. Did you get any last night? How was it? Nah, nah, but this weekend, believe me, I'm gonna go all night long! Although I've asked practically everyone on the tour how long it takes for your body to adjust to an upside-down life, only three people have given precise answers, which were "Two months," "Four years," and "Never." Nevermore.

I went to midnights after my old narcotics team split up. It seemed like a good interim assignment, a way station until something better came along, and I thought I could use the free time during the day. Mostly, you drive around and check things out until a job comes over the radio. There are fewer jobs than during the other tours of duty—although the jobs tend to be more substantial—and even on weekend nights they tend to taper off after two or three in the morning. You usually have to check a few buildings, and you'd probably get into trouble if you never wrote a ticket, but you have more time to yourself than on any other tour. My uncle finished his thirty-three years as a cop working midnights in the Bronx; he would have said that he liked it because the bosses leave you alone. Still, to be back on patrol feels odd sometimes, and when I think about my past and the past of this place I wonder where I'm going. It can bring on a terminal feeling.

One night, I drove with my partner to the corner of 132nd Street and Lincoln Avenue—a cooping-prone location, though that wasn't the reason for the visit—which is a dead end at the very bottom of the Bronx, with a warehouse on one side and a parking lot on the other. Across the black shimmer of the river you can see Harlem, and the salt piles along the F.D.R. The Bronx begins here physically, and it began here historically as well; this was the site of Jonas Bronck's farmhouse. Not much is known about him: he was a Swedish sea captain who was induced to settle the area by the Dutch West India Company. A peace treaty signed at Bronck's house ended years of sporadic but bloody skirmishes between the Dutch and the Weckquasgeeks. Bronck didn't have much to do with it, but his house was the only one around. "When did he move?" my partner asked. It was a funny question, because it made me think of the Bronx as a place where people come from but not where they stay, if luck is on their side.

The Bronx was a place of slow beginnings: Bronck came here in 1639 to homestead, and at the beginning of the twentieth century there was still farmland in the South Bronx; it became citified only as the subway was built. A person alive today could have witnessed the borough's entire metropolitan career: two generations as a vibrant, blue-collar boomtown, and one as a ravaged and riotous slum. When Jimmy Carter visited Charlotte Street, in September, 1977, he saw vacant and collapsing buildings inhabited by junkies and packs of wild dogs. A week later, during a broadcast of the World Series at Yankee Stadium, there was a fire at a school a few blocks from the game. Millions watched it as Howard Cosell intoned, "The Bronx is burning." One of my uncles was a fireman here at the time, and he told me that they were busier than the London fire department during the Blitz.

My partner and I cruised up to 142nd Street between Willis and Brook Avenues, a block with a row of little houses on one side and a school on the other. I used to chase a lot of junkies down that street, when they were buying heroin with the brand name President from the projects on the corner. A hundred years ago, the Piccirilli brothers, sculptors from Pisa, had a studio here, where they carved the statue for the Lincoln Memorial, but I don't suppose the dope was named in any commemorative spirit. Four blocks up and two over, Mother Teresa's order runs a soup kitchen and a shelter next to the Church of St. Rita, a boxy old building painted robin's-egg blue. The work the order does is holy and noble, but for us there is something embarrassing about it: nuns reassigned from leper duty in Calcutta to lend us a hand. There was a picture in the *News* a few years back of Mother Teresa and Princess Diana visiting the mission together, and one of my old partners was there, standing guard, just out of the frame. A little farther out of the frame is the building where Rayvon Evans died: a little boy whose parents kept his corpse in a closet until the fluids seeped through to the floor below and the neighbors complained. No one was ever charged with the murder, because there wasn't enough left of him to determine how he died. There is a garden dedicated to Rayvon, but no sign of the Princess or the sculptors. Memory is short here, but the past is visible all around you—at least, until the present calls you back. It can take time for your eyes to adjust.

Midnights tend to magnify things, to set them in sharp relief against the empty night, like gems on a black velvet cloth. You meet lonely people who seem more solitary and sorrowful at night, such as the chubby little woman who reclined in her armchair like a pasha after attempting suicide by taking three Tylenol PMs. Or the woman with dye-drowned blond hair going green, who denied trying to hurt herself, though her boyfriend confided that she had: "She slapped herself, hard." Domestic disputes are all the more squalid and small-hearted when they take place at five in the morning—like the one between two middle-aged brothers who were at each other's throats hours before their mother's funeral. The place stank and the walls seethed with roaches. One brother had a weary and beaten dignity; he was sitting on the couch with his overcoat and an attaché case when we arrived, like a salesman who'd just lost a commission. The other brother shouted drunkenly, jerking and flailing like a dervish afflicted with some unknown neurological misfiring. They had argued because he had started drinking again.

I took the jerky one aside, to let him vent a little. His room was littered with cans of Night Train; military papers and alcohol-rehab certificates were taped to the wall. As he punched the honorable discharge to emphasize that his had been a life of accomplishment, a burst of roaches shot out from underneath. I wanted to punch his rehab diploma, to show that he still had some work to do, but I thought better of it.

My partner and I knew that we would be back if both brothers remained there, and we dreaded the idea of having to lock one of them up before the funeral, so we asked the sane brother if he wouldn't mind leaving for a while.

He agreed that it was the best thing to do; we agreed that it was deeply unfair. He used to work as a security guard, and he offered us his business card. "If there's anything I can do for you gentlemen," he said, and he went out to walk until daybreak.

If some people call because they need someone—anyone—to talk to, there are others for whom we're the last people they want to see. For them, we arrive the way the Bible says Judgment will: like a thief in the night. It felt like that when we showed up to take a woman's children away. We were escorting two caseworkers from the Administration of Children's Services who had a court order to remove the one-, two-, and three-year-old kids of a crackhead I'll call Pamela. The midnight visit was a sneak attack, as she had dodged the caseworkers the day before. We were there—not to put too fine a point on it—as hired muscle.

When we knocked, a woman answered ("Who?") and then delayed ten minutes, muttering excuses ("Hold on," and "Let me get something on," and "Who is it, again?"), before surrendering to threats to kick the door down. She was just a friend, she said, helping to clean up—probably in anticipation of such a visit. Pamela was out. Yes, there were kids in the back, but they were Pamela's sister's kids, and the sister was out, too. As we looked in on the sleeping children, another woman emerged from a back bedroom, and she was equally adamant: "But those are my kids, and I'm not Pamela, I'm her sister, Lorraine! I can show you you're making a mistake!"

We grilled both women, but they never deviated from their story, and we could find no baby pictures or prescription bottles or anything else that would tie these children to the case. So when "Lorraine" said she could prove that they were hers if we'd let her call her mother to get her I.D. we agreed, as it would clearly demonstrate whether we were professional public servants doing a difficult job or dim-witted repo men hauling off the wrong crack babies.

But she didn't call for her I.D., she called for reinforcements, and the apartment was soon flooded with angry women. We held the baby boy while Pamela managed to grab the two girls; then a neighbor took one of the girls as Pamela tried to get out with the other, making it all the way into the hall. More cops came, and one started after her, telling her to stop, but a neighbor blocked his way, howling, "Call the cops! Call the cops and have him arrested! He ain't leaving till the cops come and arrest him!"

The sergeant called for backup, and even more cops arrived, two of them running up twelve flights of stairs—but then one had to lie down in the stairwell, and the other was rushed to the hospital with chest pains. The press of angry bodies made the apartment hot, and some women yelled for everyone to calm down, and some women yelled the opposite, and as we tried to dress the crying kids some women tried to help in earnest, finding their jackets and socks, while others were still plainly angling to spirit them away.

When Pamela's last child had been taken, she swung at a cop, but then another cop grabbed her wrists, and her friends took her aside, and after a few more eruptions of screaming we got the kids out. One woman yelled, "This is why people hate the cops!" Although I thought very little of her and the rest of them—Mothers United for Narcotics and Neglect—she had a point: no one likes people who steal babies in the middle of the night. And we had just started our tour.

The midnight tour is also called the first platoon, the second being the day tour and the third being the four-to-twelve. You begin at 2315 hours and end at 0750. If you have Tuesday and Wednesday off one week, say, you have Tuesday, Wednesday, and Thursday off the next, and then Wednesday and Thursday the week after that. It takes some getting used to, because if you're working a Friday you don't come in Friday—you come in Thursday night. Another depressing thing about midnights is that when you finish work in the morning, at ten minutes to eight, you don't say, "See you tomorrow," which would seem soon enough; you say, "See you tonight." Tonight began yesterday, and tomorrow begins tonight, and the days become one rolling night.

When I first went on the job, I started out on steady four-to-twelves, Sunday to Thursday, working in a project called Morris Houses, which, with Morrisania, Butler, and Webster Houses, make up a huge complex of thirty apartment buildings called Claremont Village, in the heart of the South Bronx. On that beat, I was generally busier than I am now, when I might cover an entire precinct. I knew less local lore then, and the landmarks I navigated by were of recent relevance: the pawnshop to check after a chain snatch; the crack house where a baby overdosed; the rooftop where they fought pit bulls, sometimes throwing the loser to the street below. I still occasionally drive through this area with my partner, but even with my grasp of the neighborhood's history I'm not sure why things turned out as they did, and still less what led me here.

Morris Houses was named after Gouverneur Morris, a Revolutionary War hero, who was with Washington at Valley Forge, and later established the decimal system of United States currency, proposing the words "dollar" and "cent." His half brother Lewis was a signer of the Declaration of Independence, and tried to get the Founding Fathers to establish the nation's capital on the family estate, but the idea was more or less a nonstarter. The Morrises owned most of the South Bronx for nearly two centuries, and their name is everywhere: Morrisania, the neighborhood in the Forty-second Precinct, where my beat was; Morris Heights; Port Morris; Morris High School, which the industrialist Armand Hammer and General Colin Powell graduated from. Yet I couldn't say it means much to anyone here. The kids that Bernhard Goetz shot in 1984—four thugs who failed to recognize a subway-riding vigilante—came from Morrisania. One of them remains confined to a wheelchair, and I'd sometimes see him around; I locked up another one's sister for robbery, after a nasty girl-gang fight. I can't imagine that her mother said, upon her return from jail, "Gouverneur Morris and his half brother Lewis must be rolling in their graves!" The Morrises made this place and helped make this nation, but they might as well have knocked up some local girls and split after the shotgun wedding, leaving nothing behind but their name.

On midnights, there is a risk of drifting within yourself, trailing off on your own weird train of thought, so that when the even weirder world intrudes it is hard not to laugh. One night not long ago, it was so slow that three patrol cars showed up for a dispute between two crackheads over a lost shopping cart. To pass the time, we conducted an investigation, asking pointed questions: What color was the cart? Do you have a receipt? It was cold, and after a while one of the cops said we should leave. But I was bored enough to want to talk to the crackheads, who relished the attention. I said to the cop, "They have issues, we can help them work through them, the relationship can come out even stronger than it was before." He looked at me and said, "Hey, I'm no Dr. Zhivago—let's get out of here."

On another job, we received a call for help from an old man and his sick wife. They seemed like good people: he had an upright, military bearing, and she was a stick figure, with plum-colored bruises all over, gasping through a nebulizer, "*Ayúdame, ayúdame, ayúdame.*" We made small talk, in broken English and Spanish, while waiting for E.M.S. On a shelf, there was a photograph of a young man in a police uniform, who the old man said was his son, a cop in San Juan who died at the age of thirty-four, from cancer. The entire apartment was a Santería shrine: cigars laid across the tops of glasses of colorless liquid; open scissors on dishes of blue liquid; dried black bananas hanging over the threshold; Tarot cards, coins, and dice before a dozen statues of saints, including a huge Virgin Mary with a triple-headed angel at her feet. Suddenly, I thought, They keep the place up, but it's more *House Voo-*

dooful than *House Beautiful.* The line wouldn't leave my head, so I had to pretend to cough, and walk outside.

You get in the habit of reading these scenes for signs, whether forensic or sacramental, of sin and struggle in the fallen world. Santería shrines and offerings are often placed in the corner of a room near the entrance, and in just that corner of one apartment we found a black-handled butcher knife next to blood that had not just pooled but piled, it lay so thick on the floor: dark, sedimentary layers with a clear overlay, like varnish, which I was told came from the lungs. The woman responsible for this handiwork explained why she had tried to sacrifice her brother at the house-hold altar: "Two years ago, he broke my leg in five places. I came in tonight, he sold my couch. He killed my mother. Well, she died from him and all his nonsense." She stopped talking for a moment, and tried to shift her hands in her cuffs as E.M.S. took her brother out in a wheelchair, pale and still. "I didn't stab him," she went on. "He stabbed himself by accident, in the back, during the tussle."

Some objects tell simple stories of fierce violence, like the two-by-four, so bloody it looked as if it had been dipped in the stuff, that a woman had used to collect a fifty-dollar debt, or the rape victim's panties in the stairwell, covered with flies. Others are more subtle and tentative, like the open Bible in the apartment of a woman whose brother, just home from prison, had suffered some sort of psychotic break. "He sat there reading the Bible for a while, and then he just looked up and said he was going to kill me," she said. The Bible was open to Proverbs 1:18, which states, "These men lie in wait for their own blood, they set a trap for their own lives." Maybe he'd read only the first part of the sentence. The woman's husband had just died, and next to the Bible there was a sympathy card from someone named Vendetta.

As a cop, you look for patterns—for context and connections that tell a fuller truth than a complainant may be willing to tell. Sometimes, though, the parts belong to no whole. So it was with a pair of attempted robberies, only twenty minutes and four blocks apart. Each perp was a male Hispanic, tall, slim, and young, in dark clothes, with a razor blade, though in the second robbery the perp wore a mask and a wig. And so when we came upon a tall, slim, young male Hispanic in dark clothes with a wig, mask, and razor in his pocket, in a desolate park between the two crime scenes, I reasonably expected to have solved at least one crime. Both complainants were sure, however, that he wasn't the man responsible, and we let him go.

In such cases, the solution seems out of sight but within reach, like the winning card in three-card monte. But there are other, older mysteries, and if there is a hint of a game in what unfolds you feel more like a piece than like a player. One night, we went to a routine "aided case," an old woman with a history of heart trouble, whose breath was rapid and shallow. She moaned, "Mami!" as she sat on a red velvet couch, flanked by two teen-age girls. As the old lady left with E.M.S., my partner told me that she was raising her two granddaughters. An hour or so later, we had another aided case, a "heavy bleeder." When we went inside, a woman said, "She's in bed," and then, "It's in the tub." We checked on a teenage girl in the bedroom, who said she was fine, and then looked in the bathtub; there, nestled in the drain, was a fetus the size and color of a sprained thumb. The head was turned upward and the eyes were open and dark.

When the E.M.T.s came—the same guys we'd met on the previous job—they asked for some plastic wrap or tinfoil, and were provided with a sandwich bag to pick it up. As we helped them put the teen-age girl in the ambulance, they told us that the old lady had gone into cardiac arrest and wouldn't make it. Nothing else happened that night, and as we drove around I kept thinking that for everyone who dies another isn't necessarily born. It was late but also too early, not yet time to go home.

From the sixties through the eighties, the landscape of the Bronx was a record of public failure, high and low—from Robert Moses, who moved through the Bronx like Sherman through Georgia, evicting thousands in order to build highways, to the scavengers and predators who made ordinary life impossible for ordinary people. I've often wondered what Poe would have thought of the South Bronx at its worst—what his ghost would make of our ghost town. He wrote about loves lost to death at an early age, and set his tales in ancestral houses gone to ruin, but he might have taken to the abandoned factories and the tenements whose graffiti-covered walls had collapsed, leaving them open like doll houses. He might have said, "Don't change a thing!" Then again, such a landscape might have left little room for the imagination, or offered too much.

Since then, the landscape has changed for the better, and the record has been rewritten, often quickly and well. Of course, when something returned from the dead in Poe's world no good came of it, like the hideous beating of that telltale heart. On the other hand, the phrase "with a vengeance" does come to mind when I look at Suburban Place, one block from Charlotte Street, which is now the center of several blocks of well-tended ranch houses. There is something surreal about this development, with its fences and lawns, given both the area's past and its surroundings, which are still rough. You could look at it as a plot twist as unexpected as anything in Poe. You have to wait for it, and be accepting of surprise.

One night, we raced to the scene of "shots fired" from an elevated subway platform—a call that E.M.S. workers had put over as they were driving past. A number of passersby confirmed it, but the shooter was long gone. Four hours later, with little to do in the interim except drive around in the dark, we received another job of shots fired, from an apartment right next to the El. Inside, a lovely old couple pointed out a hole in the window, and the neat chute that the bullet had cut through a hanging basket of African violets, littering stems and leaves on the floor. "I love my plants, they're my babies," the woman said, more concerned about what had happened than about what might have happened.

The woman was a kind of grandmother to the neighborhood, and had been for more than a generation. There was a picture on the wall of her with Mayor Lindsay, who she said had let her have a house for a dollar a year to take care of local children. "Give your plants a big drink of water," I said. "And I'll play them some nice soothing music, too," she added. We saw where the bullet had hit the back wall—not far from Mayor Lindsay—but then had to dig around in the kitchen for a while before we found it, under the refrigerator. The heat and speed and impact had transformed the sleek missile into an odd-shaped glob, like a scoop of mashed potato, harmless and pointless. It was a big slug, probably from a 45, and had she been watering her plants it would have taken her head off. It frightened her, to be sure, but she had slept through its arrival and she would sleep again now that it was gone.

The bullet had taken less than a second to travel from the barrel into the couple's home, but in my mind the journey had taken four hours—from when the bullet was heard to when it was found—and I could picture it in slow motion, floating like a soap bubble on a windless night. Both perspectives seemed equally real, the explosive instant and the glacial glide, and I was glad to be able to see each of them, in the luxury of time. The old couple, I'm sure, were glad of it as well. My partner and I took the bullet with us, and morning arrived as we left.

Down and Out and Up Again: Walking Freestyle Through the Upper East Side and Sleeping Rough in Central Park, from Time Out Book of New York Walks, *Lee Stringer (2000)*

Lee Stringer is the author of *Grand Central Winter: Stories from the Street* and coauthor, with Kurt Vonnegut, of *Like Shaking Hands with God: A Conversation on Writing.* His essays have appeared in a number of publications, including *The New York Times,* the *New York Observer, Newsday,* and the *Nation.* His next book, *Sleepaway School,* is slated to be published in the fall of 2002.

Though there have always been homeless people in New York, the first institutional response was the creation of "a house of correction, workhouse and poorhouse" in 1734. However, it was customary for police to designate a station house to lodge "vagrant and disorderly persons" until Police Commissioner Theodore Roosevelt, at the insistence of one-time resident Jacob Riis, closed them in 1896. The first Municipal Lodging House was opened at 438 East Twenty-fifth Street in 1909, but the most significant change in policy came in 1981 as a result of the case of *Callahan v. Carey.* The case was settled by a consent decree that made New York City the only municipality in the country that affirmed a court-ordered right to shelter for its residents.

Through the 1960s and 1970s thousands of the mentally ill were discharged from institutions and psychiatric disorders rivaled alcoholism and drug abuse as major causes of homelessness. Increasingly, homeless people became fearful of the city's warehouse-style "munis," and numbers rose to a high of 28,737 in March 1987. At that point, the Koch administration put forth a ten-year plan to provide permanent housing. But by the summer of 2001, the number of homeless had topped 28,000 again (including a record 6,252 families with 11,594 children) and city officials were predicting significant increases in the winter.

FOR most of my 25 years in Manhattan I was no different from other veteran New Yorkers who, convinced of our great importance as we are, are known less for leisurely strolls than for frantic dashes from here to there. But over ten of those years, homeless, drug-dazed and wandering the pavement, I developed an intimate street-level relationship with this city of towers.

Of the many walks I took at that time, the most memorable (because I made it again and again) began around 100th Street, just above Yorkville—as the once sleepy but increasingly manic Upper East Side is known—on the periphery of Spanish Harlem, where on any given night any number of young gangstas-in-training would be huddled in the shadows of the projects ready to serve up my substance of choice (crack cocaine at the time).

I'd hustle around the nearest corner after copping my stuff, "slam dunk" a good chunk of my stash and, hyperenergised by the coke rush, blunder along the streets frog-eyed and crook-necked, my gaze everywhere at once, not stopping—except to lean into the odd phone booth for a surreptitious refresher blast—until I found myself 50 blocks south, at Grand Central Terminal, under the roof of which was the crawlspace I then called home.

My thought was to reconstruct a good part of this walk in the fresh light of my now cleaner, saner existence. The result is a more interior than exterior tour, one that some of you might find more suited to armchair rumination than for shoe-leather witness. All the same, it's a walk that perhaps will give new eyes to any of you contemplating a trip here, a different way of seeing the New York you will see.

I start out at 97th and Third, on the corner where a scant half-dozen years ago a sleek and modern mosque ascended on what was then a huge rubble-strewn lot. I remember considering it something of an anomaly when it first appeared, situated as it was on the brink of the projects and the dusty, low-rise tenements surrounding them, its beige, domed façade tucked into the farthest corner of the property so that what first struck your eyes was a brilliant green desert of lawn, testifying to a serenity for which Manhattan is not known.

But this day I find the place under siege, surrounded by huge mud-stained, steel-limbed, earth-altering monsters: everything is sheathed in dirty gray construction shrouds, an ugly skinless four-square cinderblock structure-in-progress now rudely intruding across the once resplendent grass. As I make the turn east at 96th Street, I spot a huge plywood sign standing sentry and announcing, to all who care, the coming of the Islamic Cultural Center School.

I stroll down to 96th; waving at the five-storey walk-up between Lexington and Third in which I once lived and that is now dwarfed by the soaring, cocoa-brown Normandy Towers directly across the street, an apartment complex that sprouted during the go-go '80s and that has no actual sister building in its namesake region. I am headed for the promenade of sorts that fronts the East River and runs, in rough parallel to the FDR Drive, right down to Manhattan's southern end. Heidelberg has its Philosopher's Mile, which snakes upward from the river into the hills and which I have seen. But for my money the ying and yang of sauntering along this promenade—quietude of the river riding one shoulder, angry snarling traffic riding the other—seldom fails to provoke the kind of internal debate upon which the best of philosophy is founded.

It's a warm day, cooled by a breeze off the river, which is never in a particular hurry, only rambles along, like a wise and weary old soul. The usual scattering of people are enjoying the sunshine: on one of the benches, a young couple, limbs entwined, their lunch things already laid bare and ravaged beside them, making a sweet dessert of each other's lips; a desk jockey flies by pumping and panting with the regularity of a pile driver, as he jogs off the consequences of a sedentary existence; sun-baked fishermen sweating into their portable coolers, rods soldiering along the guardrail. They smile back when I wish them luck and it occurs to me that one cannot be a good fisherman without embracing a bit of Zen.

North of them the Wards Island footbridge sits low above the river. Despite its ugly chalky-green hue, its profile—tall, narrow, twin towers ascending astride the apex of the arch its seemingly pencil-thin span barely makes—always strikes me as unfussy and kind of eloquent. Lonesome, too. One of New York's dozen or so movable bridges, it stands ever ready to raise its centre wing in welcome to tall ships that, alas, rarely if ever happen by.

Speaking of which, downriver a bit lies Roosevelt Island, the blur of land visible across the water that was once known as Welfare Island, back during an earlier attempt to consign the poor to oblivion in the 1920s. Even in its previous incarnation as Blackwell's Island—after the husband of Mary Manningham who had inherited it from her stepfather in 1686—this site had for the most part served as a repository for the unwanted, having hosted a prison (in which Mae West was once incarcerated for obscenity), an insane asylum (about the terrace of which Charles Dickens once waxed euphoric) and a smallpox isolation hospital.

In 1973, however, under the auspices of the Urban Development Corporation, it was transformed into a city planner's wet dream, an impossible, multi-ethnic, mixed-income haven from the ruder influences of urban existence. Even those most venerable icons of city life—trash cans and garbage trucks—were factored out, replaced by an automated conveyance system that hurtles the discards of life along underground faster than a speeding subway train.

A side trip to get a gander at this city of the future might be worth your time. The tram ride over from 59th Street—eight storeys up, dangling out over the water, heaving to and fro on the wind—is an attraction in and of itself. And the view of Manhattan's skyline—ever more majestic as it falls beneath your toes—is sure to start camera shutters winking. Climb aboard a Green Line bus when you alight (one leaves about every 15 minutes) and circle the entire 147-acre island for ten cents. You'll find five of New York's landmarks here: the 128-year-old James Renwick Jr-designed stone lighthouse still standing on its northern end (Renwick was also responsible for St Patrick's Cathedral); New York's original mental hospital, its octagonal shape considered an architectural marvel at the time; the Strecker Laboratory, built in 1892 and now home to the Russell Sage Institute of Pathology; the 200-plus-year-old wooden Blackwell House, one of New York's oldest; and the Chapel of the Good Shepherd, erected in 1888.

But back to the promenade.

Most of my former walks along here were after dark, when a more threadbare crowd was in evidence: pipe-heads scraping on their stems for that last hit of "res"; crashed-out canners tethered to their shopping carts so no one would steal them in the night; a wino or two, perhaps, making merry with themselves. Eventually, the constant honk and growl of traffic would invariably begin to rattle my hyped-up brain and set my teeth on edge and I would end up scrambling down the promenade to 90th Street where it tapers off into Carl Schurz Park.

Like pretty much everything else in New York, ownership of this 15-acre plot can be traced back to 16th-century Dutch settlers. Under entitlement to a fellow with the unfortunate name of Sybout Classen, what we now call Carl Schurz Park remained blissfully undeveloped for over a century. A subsequent owner, Jacob Walton, built a house on the property in 1770, but it was reduced to rubble during the Revolution half a dozen years later and the Continental Army—which had built a stronghold around the house against the possible invasion of Hell Gate, the strategic shipping passage there—was routed by the Brits.

Another good 100 years passed before the city bought the land, during which time Archibald Gracie built the mansion that still bears his name and that in 1932 became, after an eight-year stint housing the Museum of New York, the official Mayor's residence.

My first time ever seeing Gracie Mansion was during the early '70s when, training as a newsreel cameraman and staying at the 34th Street Y, I got swept up in a protest march bearing down Fifth Avenue. Giddy at the prospect of being part of an actual protest, revelling in the anarchy of it all, I plunged into the human tide. Someone shouted, "Let's take it to the Mayor's house," which we did, chanting thunderously all the way, then stood vigil at the Mayor's doorstep demanding he give us an audience.

As I recall, Mayor John Lindscy never came out. And I remember feeling righteous indignation over this, even though, truth be told, I was only along on a lark. I don't even remember exactly what we were protesting—something to do with Vietnam, I suppose—but I do remember the march.

It was a little after the turn of the century that the property got its present name, after Carl Schurz, an émigré from Cologne, Germany, who first made his bones here turning out the German vote for Abraham Lincoln. During the war he commandeered the 26th Regiment of the Continental Army, which earned the nickname "The Flying Dutchmen" after their controversial retreat at Mayes Hill. Inglorious as this defeat may have been, it didn't prove particularly detrimental to Schurz's upward mobility. He went on to the U.S. Senate, later became Secretary of the Interior, and later still took to journalism—perhaps the last refuge of a statesman—as editor of the *New York Tribune.*

Besides the usual addenda of municipal parks—playgrounds, basketball courts, winding blacktop trails—Carl Schurz Park offers some pleasant grassy knolls upon which the melanin-challenged can burnish in a summer tan. Or, if the heat is too much, just inside the northernmost entrance there's a kind of a cul-de-sac ringed by trees in the shade of which are a number of benches. And the seven-block, bench-lined waterfront boardwalk is a dream for midnight strolls, particularly with a full moon silvering the ripples of the river.

During the time I was hanging out there, the park had a resident contingent of nightly squatters who, sometimes and sometimes not, clashed mightily with the regular crew of upscale sexual mavericks out for a casual tryst with whatever willing tight-jeaned young man. Some people saw it as a shame that the Mayor should permit his backyard to be so littered with down-and-outs. I saw it differently. To me it was a vivid symbol of a democracy strong enough to take a punch.

Of course, all that is now finished. Thanks to the combined efforts of the City Parks Department and Carl Schurz Park Association, the site has been by and large disencumbered of the quirks of human existence. The homeless have been cleared out, the shrubbery has been trimmed back enough to put a damper on clandestine coupling, no matter what the gender, and—as I intuit from the new signage—the most pressing problem now seems to be canines who do their business in other than the designated area.

I emerge at the park's south end, 84th Street and East End Avenue, along which pre- and post-war apartment buildings loom over small, one- and two-room shops, which, in the tradition of an older Yorkville, are put to bed each day at dusk. I walk west, past brownstones mostly with tidy little stoops, upon which it is no longer the vogue, sadly, to seek the cool of the night; past a club that on weekend nights never fails to draw an anxious queue of young urban scene-makers begging a nod from the surly, black-clad bouncer stationed at the door; past 84th and Third, which I'll always think of as my corner. This is where I hawked copies of *Street News*—the preferred meal ticket of many New York down-and-outers—just about every night for years. Tourists are finding their way to this spot, drawn by the bars, clubs, restaurants, cafés and specialty shops that have proliferated over the last decade or so. From 93rd Street down to the mid-70s, along First, Second and Third Avenues, every block is littered with them—too many to survive on the locals' patronage alone.

Yet the residents, refusing to cede their turf completely to commerce, are always out in force as well. You see them "walking their dogs, chatting with their neighbours, closing the details of deals on the corner, dashing in and out of taxis, dipping in and out of the joints, zipping by on skateboards, on bicycles, on Rollerblades, laughing, singing, shouting to the sky." (I commit the cardinal sin of quoting myself here, for which I'll doubtless burn in literary hell.) It's a great opportunity to catch real New Yorkers in the act of being themselves and, in concert with the reckless cacophony raised by restless wanderers who descend after dark, it makes for a special brand of kinetic fever you don't quite get on the Upper West Side.

Of course, whenever I was "skeed up," I would find all this a bit too frenetic and cut up to Fifth Avenue for a more bucolic meander along the edge of Central Park and down what is known as Museum Mile. It's more than a mile, actually, encompassing some 20 blocks. Along it you will find about ten museums or galleries. It's quite an eclectic convening of art and culture and history, but merely a bite out of the endless move-through feast Manhattan has to offer along these lines. But these are among—if not *the*

—biggest in the world. Size definitely matters to us, whatever our pretenses to culture and civilisation. It ever remains New York's foremost crowing point.

North of where you join Fifth Avenue lies the Cooper-Hewitt National Design Museum. I've never been in but I am always impressed by it whenever I pass, impressed by the grounds, like a chunk of English countryside plopped down amidst New York's relentlessly vertical thrust. I have been in the Guggenheim. When I was in high school we had a class trip to see an exhibition of Italian sculpture. But for me it was the design of the museum itself, wherein you take an elevator to the top and work your way down the long, winding helix of a ramp, that floored me. Years later I had the notion of making an art video by climbing into a shopping cart and taping the art as it sailed by with greater and greater velocity as the cart shot down the spiral. The fact that I'm here to tell about it testifies to the fact that I never actually tried to do this.

About 20 years ago, I treated a visiting friend to the whole tourist thing and we made half a day out of roaming through the Metropolitan Museum's many rooms. We got separated at one point and looking for him I happened into this large sitting room filled with tables and chairs in which sat about three dozen people—at least I *think* they were people, because they were all silent and stony faced as statues. To this day I wonder what that was all about.

It was many years later, while "living rough," that I was reintroduced to the Metropolitan. Following a particularly exhaustive nocturnal crawl, I crashed just inside the park, on the slope that tilts down from the atrium on the north side of the Metropolitan Museum. I woke up the next day to find a groundskeeper looming over me, a crisp $20 in his hands. "Here," he said with a kindly smile, "I think you dropped this."

Another night I met a man there who, coincidentally, lived just down the block from the corner on which I sold *Street News.* Recognising me, he suggested that I might use his shower every now and again if need be—an offer of which I was happy to avail myself quite regularly. With this good karma recommending it, I chose the slope by the museum whenever sleeping outdoors, and eventually grew quite fond of the atrium, its huge glass and aluminum geodesic planes slanting skyward in a narrowing grid, lending breathtaking scale to the Egyptian artefacts visible through the lowest panes. Gaping at those crude but somehow eloquent slab stone dwellings I realised that peeking down from a 20th-floor living room is the anomaly, not stretching out for the night on the grass.

My usual walk would take me straight down Fifth Avenue to 59th Street before crossing east to Madison and on to Grand Central Terminal. Fifth Avenue may be best known as an upmarket shoppers' mecca, but, for the people who can afford to shop there, the real Fifth Avenue lies above 59th where nothing so crude and vulgar as a store or shop has ever been tolerated. Even gods of fashion such as Gucci, Versace and Tiffany wouldn't dare think of emblazoning their logos here.

During my days on the street I thought of this stretch as Doorman's Row. At night you see them peering out at the street, silhouetted in the blue-green fluorescence of artificial light, sentries at the gates of Babylon, perhaps. No matter how threadbare and ragged-edged I ever was, stumbling down the park side of the street, I could always squeeze a bit of bemused satisfaction out of the knowledge that the postcard-perfect views the rich and famous pay so dearly to behold from their bedroom windows are equally available to even the most penniless soul. Sit on one of the benches along here some balmy night, raise a bottle of cheap wine to the mammoth brownstones shouldered along the opposite side of the street and gloat over the grand bargain of it all.

It was the wealthy who first urged construction of Central Park upon city officials. And using the government's right of eminent domain—which is a nice way of saying seizure without due process—1,600 poor families were put out of their homes to make way for it (it wouldn't do for the rich to have their park on development-worthy terra firma). For its first decade or so, the park's rules and regs were openly hostile to those without means, and the panoply of public attractions that one now finds there exist chiefly due to political agitation over the years from advocates for the poor and working class.

Nowadays during summer months the park is never without something going on for the masses. The most democratic of these are, for my money, the Delacorte Theater (Shakespeare) and the free concerts (opera and orchestras on the great lawn). I would either walk along outside the park or dip in one of the six entrances between 85th and 59th—the first of these being just north of the Metropolitan Museum and the last being just above the zoo. The zoo remains one of the biggest park attractions. It was renovated and upscaled during the '80s and a very pleasant café has been added with a thought for weary adults run ragged by tireless children.

The 79th Street entrance takes you past the south end of the Metropolitan Museum to the Great Lawn, where every summer a number of free concerts are staged; and the Delacorte Theater, in which one can see Shakespeare played as nowhere else, with the rocky edge of bluff leading to Belvedere Castle as a natural backdrop.

As a homeless person I had an inside edge on grabbing the best seats for these events, having more free time and being able to arrive earlier than most. Some of us had a cottage industry as professional "waiters" for the more affluent set who couldn't be bothered idling in line for four hours to snag the first-come-first-served free tickets. Not entirely fair, I'll give you, but quite lucrative.

Enter at 72nd and you can traipse around The Mall, a long, tree-lined corridor with asphalt footpaths on either side: make your way westward, to the great band shell, the ever gurgling Bethesda Fountain and the Boat House by the lake. Summer nights I'd be lured by music and voices on the air and find my way to the Boathouse Café and the romance of cocktails and jazz served up by the shimmering moonlit lake.

More often than not, I would skim the edge of the park, go in one entrance, stop for a refresher blast on one of the benches or in one of the deserted playgrounds, then scramble down and out the next. This trip, however, I am content to stroll under the shade of the trees overhanging the sidewalk and people-watch.

By the time I reach 59th Street, that enduring hub of swank where several of New York's priciest boulevards converge on Grand Army Plaza, the sky has taken on the red-orange glow of early dusk. It is my favourite time of day, one that seldom fails to drudge up a bit of sentimentality in me. I decide to end my walk here, where eely limos ferry a luckier breed than I to the imported marble steps of the Plaza Hotel; where horse-drawn hansom cabs-to-nowhere idle, waiting upon the pleasure of the next romantic; where Asian portrait artists line the benches just inside the park, their charcoal sticks at the ready; where peals of child laughter ascend from Central Park Zoo and break on the still air. I will leave you with the last thing I see as I am jotting this down: a balloon, silver on one side, pink and blue pastel on the other, has won its freedom, has broken loose of its string, and heads merrily skyward, to whatever its next adventure.

The Synthetic Sublime, from Quarrel and Quandary, *Cynthia Ozick (2000)*

Cynthia Ozick was born in 1928 in a brownstone on East Eighty-eighth Street between First and York Avenues and grew up in the Bronx. Although she did not publish her first novel until 1966, she became one of the preeminent voices in American letters in the last half of the twentieth century. Her written work has embraced virtually every genre—novels, short stories, essays, drama, literary criticism, and translations. Anita Brookner has written that "she is as authentic a voice of New York as was Edith Wharton before her, but Ozick's New York is an affair of battered suburbs, of cavernous municipal buildings, of ancient Hebrew teachers living above Cuban grocery stores, of public libraries, wily lovers and miraculous if inconvenient apparitions."

E. B. White in his 1948 classic essay, *Here Is New York,* wrote that to "a New Yorker the city is both changeless and changing," and he ended his piece with a meditation on the threat of nuclear annihilation. Ozick's New York, seen half a century later, "disappears and then disappears again; or say that it metamorphoses between disappearances, so that every seventy-five years or so another city bursts out," but she ends with the musing that "the crowds will stream in the streets—what thoughts will they think? Will they think our outworn thoughts, or imaginings we cannot imagine?"

Regardless of the differences, both essays and New York itself exemplify what Ozick has written elsewhere: "An essay is a thing of the imagination. If there is information in an essay, it is by-the-by, and if there is an opinion in it, you need not trust it in the long run. A genuine essay has no educational, polemical or sociopolitical use; it is the movement of a free mind at play. Though written in prose, it is closer in kind to poetry than to any other form."

1.

More than any other metropolis of the Western world, New York disappears. It disappears and then it disappears again; or say that it metamorphoses between disappearances, so that every seventy-five years or so another city bursts out, as if against nature—new shapes, new pursuits, new immigrants with their unfamiliar tongues and worried uneasy bustle. In nature, the daffodil blooms, withers, vanishes, and in the spring returns—always a daffodil, always indistinguishable from its precursor. Not so New York, preternatural New York! Go to Twenty-third Street and Eighth Avenue: where is the Grand Opera House, with its statuary and carvings, its awnings and Roman-style cornices? Or reconnoiter Thirteenth Street and Broadway: who can find Wallack's Theatre, where the acclaimed Mrs. Jennings, Miss Plessy Mordaunt, and Mr. J. H. Stoddart once starred, and where, it was said, "even a mean play will be a success"? One hundred years ago, no one imagined the dissolution of these dazzling landmarks; they seemed as inevitable, and as permanent, as our Lincoln Center, with its opera and concerts and plays, and its lively streaming crowds.

In Archaeology 101 they tell a New York joke. It is the year 3000. Archaeologists are sifting through the rubble of overgrown mounds, searching for relics of the lost city that once flourished on this brambly wild site. They dig here and there without reason for excitement (beer cans, a plastic sherd or two, unbiodegradable grocery bags), until at last they uncover what appears to be a primitive concourse of some kind, along which is placed, at surprisingly even intervals, a row of barbaric-looking poles. The poles are molded of an enduring ancient alloy, and each one is topped by a head with a single glass eye and an inch of crude mouth. "Identical sacrificial cultic stands in homage to the city's divinity-king," the archaeologists conclude. What they have found are Second Avenue parking meters: the Ozymandias of the late twentieth century.

The joke may apply to other modern societies (no contemporaneous city, after all, was as modern as Nebuchadnezzar's Babylon), but New York eludes such ironies. New York will never leave town. It will never sink into a desert waste. Catapult us forward a thousand years, and we won't recognize the place; yet it is certain to be, uninterruptedly, New York, populous, evolving, faithfully inconstant, magnetic, man-made, unnatural—the synthetic sublime. If you walk along Lexington Avenue, say, it isn't easy to be reminded that Manhattan is an island, or even that it lies, like everything else, under an infinitude of sky. New York's sky is jigsawed, cut into geometric pieces glimpsed between towers or caught slantwise across a granite-and-glass ravine. There is no horizon; the lucky penthouses and fifteenth-floor apartments and offices may have long views, but the streets have almost none. At night the white glow that fizzes upward from the city—an inverted electric

Niagara—obscures the stars, and except for the Planetarium's windowless mimicry, New York is oblivious of the cosmos. It is nearly as indifferent, by and large, to its marine surround. Walt Whitman once sang of the "tall masts of Mannahatta" and of the "crested and scallop-edg'd waves," but the Staten Island ferry and the Circle Line beat on mastless, and the drumming ribbon of the West Side Highway bars us from the sound and smell of waters rushing or lapping. New York pretends that it is inland and keeps dry indoors and feels shoreless; New York water means faucets and hidden pipes and, now and then, a ceiling leak or the crisis of a burst main. Almost in spite of itself, Riverside Drive looks out on the Hudson, and can, if it likes, remember water. On Manhattan's other flank, the F.D.R. Drive swims alongside the East River like a heavy-chuffing landlubber crocodile, unmindful of the moving water nearby. And here come the bridges, the Queensboro, the Manhattan, the Williamsburg, and finally the Brooklyn, Hart Crane's fabled "harp and altar." These varied spans, squat or spidery—together with the grand George Washington to the north and west—may cry out their poetry of arch and tide and steely ingenuity; but when you ride across in car or bus they are only, again, urban roadways. The tunnels are the same, with their line of lights perpetually alert under the river's tonnage. New York domesticates whatever smacks of sea. And when the two rivers, the Hudson and the East, converge and swallow each other at the Battery's feet, it is the bays alone, the Upper and the Lower, that hurry out to meet the true deep. New York turns its back on the Atlantic. The power and the roar New York looks to are its own.

And if New York is to be misinterpreted and misunderstood, it will not be by future antiquarians, but by its present-day citizens. The Village stymies Wall Street. Chinatown is Greek to Washington Heights. Harlem and Tribeca are mutual enigmas. Neighborhoods are sealed off from one another by the border police of habit and mindset and need and purpose. And there is another border, even more rigid, and surely more disconsolate, than geography: the divide between then and now, a gash that can occur in a single lifetime. Fourth Avenue, masquerading as Park Avenue South, has lost its venerable name; Sixth Avenue—despite its rebirth, half a century ago, as Avenue of the Americas—has not. Where are the hotels of yesteryear? The Astor, the Chatham, the Savoy-Plaza? The Biltmore and its legendary clock? Where are the rows and rows of second-hand book stores that crept northward from Astor Place to Fourteenth Street? Where are Klein's and Wanamaker's and Gimbel's and Ohrbach's? Where are those urban walkers and scribes—Joseph Mitchell, Meyer Berger, Kate Simon, Alfred Kazin? Where is that cloud of gray fedoras that made men in crowds resemble dandelions gone to seed? When, and why, did New York hats give up the ghost? And who was the last to dance in the Rainbow Room?

The Russian poet Joseph Brodsky—born in Leningrad, exiled to New York, buried in Venice—used to say that he wrote to please his predecessors, not his contemporaries. Often enough New York works toward the opposite: it means to impress the here-and-now, which it autographs with an insouciant wrecking ball. Gone is the cleaner-and-dyer; gone is the shoe-repair man. In their stead, a stylish boutique and a fancy-cookie shop. To see—close at hand—how the present is displaced by a newer present, how streets long confident of their particularity can rapidly molt into streets of a startlingly unexpected character, is to be a bit of a god: what is Time, what is Change, to the gods? For New Yorkers, a millennium's worth of difference can be encompassed in six months. Downtown lofts on spooky dark blocks that once creaked under the weight and thunder and grime of industrial machinery are suddenly filled with sofas upholstered in white linen and oak bars on wheels and paintings under track lighting and polyurethaned coffee tables heaped with European magazines. Bryant Park, notorious shady hangout, blossoms into a cherished noonday amenity. Or else the deserted tenements along the Metro-North line, staring out eyeless and shamefaced at the commuters' train down from Stamford, will, overnight, have had their burnt-out hollows covered over with painted plywood—trompe l'oeil windows and flower pots pretending, Potemkin-like, and by municipal decree, that human habitation has resumed.

Yet despite New York's sleight-of-hand transmutations and fool-the-eye pranks, the lady isn't really sawed in half; she leaps up, alive and smiling. If physical excision is the city's ongoing principle, there are, anyhow, certain surprising tenacities and keepsake intuitions. Wait, for instance, for the downtown No. 104 at the bus stop on Broadway and Seventy-second Street, look across the way, and be amazed—what Renaissance palazzo is this? A tall facade with draped female sculptures on either side, arched cornices, patterned polychrome bricks: ornamental flourish vying with ornamental flourish. And then gaze down the road to your right: one vast slab after another, the uncompromising severity of straight lines, brilliantly winking windows climbing and climbing, not a curve or entablature or parapet or embrasure ruffling the sleek skin of these new residential monoliths. In sharp winter light, a dazzling juxtaposition, filigreed cheek by modernist jowl. The paradox of New York is that its disappearances contain constancies—and not only because some buildings from an earlier generation survive to prod us toward historical self-consciousness. What is most steadfast in New York has the fleet look of the mercurial: the city's persistent daring, vivacity, enchantment, experiment; the marvel of new forms fired by old passions, the rekindling of the snuffed.

The Lower East Side, those tenement-and-pushcart streets of a century ago, once the venue of synagogues and succahs and religious-goods stores and a painful density of population, and later the habitat of creeps and druggies, is now the neighborhood of choice for the great-grandchildren of earlier tenants who were only too happy to escape to the Bronx. The talismanic old Rainbow Room has shut its doors? Never mind: its drama and urgent charm have migrated south. The downtown bands and their girl singers have a different sound, but the bands are there, and the girl singers too. At the Knitting Factory and other clubs—with names like Arlene Grocery, Luna Lounge, Baby Jupiter—you may catch up with Motel Girl, a band specializing in "Las Vegas stripper noir": avant-garde jazz described as jarring, seedy, sexy, Movietone-violent, dark. Even Ratner's on Delancey, the destination of senior citizens with an appetite for potato pancakes and blintzes, has succumbed to bands and poetry readings. Many of the singers and musicians live in the old tenement flats (toilet down the hall) on Avenue B, with monthly rents as high as a thousand dollars. Broadway and Prince, where Dean & DeLuca boasts three hundred varieties of cheese, was home to a notions shop two generations ago; not far away, on Orchard Street, the Tenement Museum stands as an emblem of nostalgic consecration, ignored by its trendy neighbors. You can still buy pickles out of the barrel at Guss's, but the cutting-edge young who come down to Ludlow and Stanton for the music or the glitz rarely find those legendary greenhorn warrens of much historic interest; their turf is the East Village. The Lower East Side's current inhabitants, despite their fascination with the louche, are educated and middle-class, with mothers back on Long Island wishing their guitar-playing daughters had gone to medical school. What these seekers on A, B, and C are after—like Scott and Zelda plunging into fountains to jump-start the Jazz Age—is New York's insuperable constant: the sense of belonging to the glamorous marrow of one's own time.

Uptown's glamour drive is more domestic. On the Upper West Side, the bodegas and the little appetizing and hardware stores on Amsterdam, Columbus, and Broadway are long gone, and the great style emporia dominate, behemoths of food, cooking devices, leather accessories, "natural" cosmetics, no-color cotton sheets, Mission furniture. Zabar's, the Fairway, Barney Greengrass, Citarella, H & H Bagels—dizzyingly flooded with epicurean getters and spenders—harbor prodigalities of dimpled breads, gourmet coffees, the right kind of polenta, the right kind of rice and salsa, the right kind of coffeemaker and salad-spinner. Body Works offers soaps and lotions and oils, Godiva's chocolates are set out like jewels, Gracious Home dazes with kitchenware chic. There is something of a puzzle in all this exuberant fashionableness and household seductiveness, this bean-grinding, face-creaming, bed-making: where are the political and literary intellectuals the Upper West Side is famous for, why are the conversations about olives and fish?

Across town, the Upper East Side seems, in contrast, staid, reserved, nearly quiet. The streets are less peopled. The wind is colder. A hauteur lurks in the limestone. If the West Side is a roiling marketplace, the East Side is a marble lobby presided over by a monarchical doorman. Fifth Avenue can be tacky here and there, but Madison grows more and more burnished, New York's version of the Rue du Faubourg St. Honoré. Here march the proud shops of the élite European designers, whose names make tailors' music: Yves St. Laurent, Versace, Gucci, Valentino, Giorgio Armani, Prada, Missoni, Dolce & Gabbana. Here is the Tiffany's of greengrocers, where Mozart is played and a couple of tomatoes will cost as much as a movie ticket. Here are L'Occitane for perfumes and Bulgari for diamonds. On Park and Madison affluence reigns, and with it a certain neighborhood serenity—a privacy, a regal seclusion. (Over on Lexington and Third, the city's rush begins again.)

Posh East and extravagant West dislike each other, with the ingrained antipathy of restraint and profusion, calm and bustle; nor are they likely, except for an audacious handful of crosstown adventurers, to rub elbows in the shops. A silent cold war chills Manhattan. Its weapons are Zabar's in the West, Versace in the East. There is no hot line between them.

2.

Who lives in New York? E. B. White, mulling the question fifty years ago, imagined "a farmer arriving from Italy to set up a small grocery in a slum, or a young girl arriving from a small town in Mississippi to escape the indignity of being observed by her neighbors, or a boy arriving from the Corn Belt with a manuscript in his suitcase and a pain in his heart." This has a musty if sweetish scent for us now—eau de Jimmy Stewart, perhaps. The circumstances of the arrivals were generally not so benign; nor was their reception. In a 1922 address before the New York-based American Academy of Arts and Letters, Owen Wister, the author of *The Virginian,* said of the newcomers, "Recent arrivals pollute the original spring. . . . It would be well for us if many recent arrivals would become departures." He meant the immigrants who were just then flooding Castle Garden; but the children of those immigrants would soon be sorting out the dilemmas of welcome and unwelcome by other means.

I remember a ferocious street game that was played in the northeast Bronx long ago, in the neighborhood known as Pelham Bay. It was called "War," and it was exclusively a girls' game. With a piece of colored chalk you drew a small circle, in which you placed a pink rubber ball. Then you drew a second circle around it, concentric but far larger. This second circle you divided into as many pie-slices as there were players. Each player was assigned a pie-slice as her designated territory and wrote in it the name of a country she felt to be her own. So it went like this: Peggy Scanlon chose Ireland; Dorothy Wilson, Scotland; Hilda Weber, Germany; Carolyn Johnson, Sweden; Maria Vigiano (whose Sicilian grandmothers yearly wrapped their fig trees in winter canvas), Italy; Allegra Sadacca (of a Sephardic family recently from Turkey, a remnant of the Spanish Jews exiled by Ferdinand and Isabella in 1492), Spain; Madge Taylor (an immigrant from Iowa), America; and I (whose forebears had endured the despots of Russia for nearly a thousand years), Palestine. So much for the local demographics. Immediately after these self-defining allegiances were declared, someone would shriek "War!" and the asphalt mayhem of racing and tackling and tumbling would begin, with the pink rubber globe as prize. I don't suppose little girls anywhere in New York's boroughs nowadays play this disunited nations game; but if they do, surely the pie-slices are chalked up with preferences for Trinidad, Jamaica, Haiti, Puerto Rico, the Dominican Republic, Colombia, Mexico, Peru, Greece, Lebanon, Albania, Pakistan, India, China, and of course—for antecedents who were never willing immigrants—Africa. In New York, origins still count, and not always benevolently.

3.

The poor of New York occupy streets only blocks away from the palaces. There are cities where such matters are handled otherwise. In Paris some time ago, heading for the Louvre—a row of former royal palaces—I passed a pitiful maternal scene: a dark-eyed young woman half-reclining on the pavement, with a baby in the crook of her arm and a sad-faced little girl huddled against her. The infant's only covering was a newspaper. "Gypsies," someone explained, in a tone that dismissed concern. "By the end of the day, when she's collected her hoard of francs, her husband comes to fetch her in a white limousine." Behind this cynicism lay a social reality. The woman and her children had to be taken, however sardonically, for canny entrepreneurs, not outcasts begging for pennies. The outcasts were elsewhere. They were not in the shadow of the Louvre; they were in the suburbs. In New York lingo, "suburbs" evokes green lawns and commuters of middling affluence. But the great European cities—Paris, Stockholm—have cordoned off their needy, their indigent, their laboring classes. The habitations of the poor are out of town, away from the central brilliance, shunted off and invisible. In New York you cannot lose sight of the poor—the workfare leaf-rakers in the parks, the ragged and piebald homeless, who appear on nearly every corner, some to importune, some to harass, and the pressing mass of the tenement poor, whose eager children fill (as they always have) the public schools. The vivid, hectic, noisily dense barrio, bouncy and bedraggled, that is West 155th Street leads straight across northern Broadway to that austerely resplendent Venetian palace, designed by McKim, Mead, and White, where Owen Wister inveighed against the intruders. But New York, like the stories of O. Henry (one of its early chroniclers), is pleased to spring ironic endings—so there stands the noble Academy, far uptown's distinguished monument to Arts and Letters, surrounded now by poor immigrants, an emerald's throw from the buzz and dust of Broadway's bazaar, where rugs and pots and plastic gewgaws clutter the teeming sidewalks. In New York, proletarian and patrician are neighbors.

4.

As for the upper crust in general, it is known to run New York. This stratum of the social order was once dubbed the Four Hundred, but New York's current patriciate, however it may have multiplied, escapes being counted—though it counts as heavily as ever and remains as conscientiously invisible. Elitism of this kind is rarely political; it almost never becomes mayor. In a democratic ambiance New York's potentates and nabobs have no easy handle; no one names them, not even in tabloid mockery. Then let us call them, collectively, by what they possess: Influence. Influence is financial, corporate, loftily and discreetly legal; Influence is power and planning and money. And money is the armature on which the mammoth superstructure that is New York is sculpted: architecture and philanthropy, art galleries and libraries and foundations, zoos and conservatories and museums, concert halls and universities and houses of worship. The tallest buildings—the Chrysler, the Empire State, the risen polyhedrons of Rockefeller Center, the Twin Towers, assorted old spires—all have their ankles in money. Influence *means* money, whether in the making of it, the spending, or the giving. Influence is usually private and guarded; it may shun celebrity; it needs no public face; its precincts are often reclusive. You are not likely to follow Influence in its daily maneuvers—though you can, all week long, observe the subway riders as they patiently swarm, intent on getting in and getting out and getting there. The jerky cars grind out their wild sawing clamor; locked inside the racket, the passengers display a Buddhist self-forgetfulness. Noiseless Influence, meanwhile, is driven in smoked-glass limousines, hidden, reserved, arcane. If all the rest of the citizenry were carted off, and only Influence were left, the city would be silent. But if Influence were spirited away in some grand and ghostly yacht, a kind of Flying Dutchman, say, the men in their dinner jackets, the women in their gowns, what would happen to New York? The mysterious and mazy coursings of money would dry up. The city would come to a halt.

Old money (old for us, though it was new then) made the palaces. Here is James D. McCabe, Jr., writing in 1872 of the transport cathedral, in Second Empire style, that was the brain-child of Cornelius Vanderbilt, the railway magnate:

> One of the most imposing buildings in the city is the new Grand Central Depot, on Forty-second street and Fourth Avenue. It is constructed of red brick, with iron trimmings painted white, in imitation of marble. The south front is adorned with three and the west front with two massive pavilions. The central pavilion of each front contains an illuminated dock.... The car-shed is covered with an immense circular roof of iron and glass.... It is lighted from the roof by day, and at night large reflectors, lighted by an electrical apparatus, illuminate the vast interior.

And here again, in 1948, is E. B. White (a man who knew how to catch the beat of what he called "Manhattan's breathing"), describing his own encounter with the Depot's successor, built in 1913 on the same site:

> Grand Central has become honky-tonk, with its extradimensional advertising displays and its tendency to adopt the tactics of a travel broker. I practically lived in Grand Central Terminal at one period (it has all the conveniences and I had no other place to stay) and the great hall

> seemed to me one of the more inspiring interiors in New York, until Lastex and Coca-Cola got into the temple.

Kodak got in, too, and honky-tonk turned into logo. Like some painted colossus, Kodak's gargantuan sign, in flaming color (it was named the Colorama), presided for years over the criss-crossing rush-hour flow—a fixture of the terminal's contemporary identity. The gilded constellations on the vaulted horizon dimmed to an undifferentiated gray; no one troubled to look up at blinded Orion. A gluey grime thickened the interstices of the marble balustrades. Frankfurter wrappings and sticky paper soda cups littered the public telephones. Commuters in need of a toilet knew what to avoid and went next door to the Grand Hyatt. The temple had become a routinely seedy train station.

And then New York, the Eraser and the Renewer, with a sweep of its resuscitating will, cleansed the temple's degradation. What old money brought into being, new money, along with civic determination, has refurbished. The theme is artful mirroring: the existing grand stair engenders an answering grand stair on the opposite end of the great concourse. The gawky advertising signs are banished and the heavens scrubbed until their stars glitter. Below and behind, the secret ganglia of high-tech engineering and up-to-date lighting may snake and throb, but all across the shining hall it is Commodore Vanderbilt's ghost who walks. Grand Central has no fear of the ornamental; it revels in breadth and unstinting scale; it *intends* to inspire. The idea of the publicly palatial—unashamed lavishness—has returned.

And not only here. Follow Forty-second Street westward to Fifth Avenue and enter the most illustrious temple of all, the lion-sentried Library, where the famed third-floor Reading Room has just undergone its own rebirth—both in homage to, and in dissent from, the modern. Card catalogues have descended into the dustbin of antiquated conveniences. Electrical outlets accommodate laptops; rows of computers parade across the vast polished tables under a gilded rococo ceiling, a Beaux-Arts confection frosted with floral arabesques. Whatever the mavens may say, and however the critics may scowl, New York (in at least one of its multiple manifestations) thirsts for intimations of what the Victorians did not hesitate to invoke: Noble Beauty. New York has learned to value—though never to venerate—its old robber-baron muses, not for their pre-income-tax devourings, but for their appetite for the baronial: the Frick Collection, the Morgan Library, the Cooper-Hewitt (housed in Andrew Carnegie's sixty-four-room mansion). The vanished Pennsylvania Station, the original—razed a generation ago as an elaborate eyesore, now regretted, its bargain-basement replacement a daily discouragement—will soon rise again, in the nearby body of the superannuated General Post Office (Roman, kingly, columned). Fancy, then, a soaring apparition of the Metropolitan Museum of Art, that prototype of urban palace, and of its philosophical rival, the Museum of Modern Art, hovering over the city, scanning it for symptoms of majesty—the Met and MOMA, joined by spectral flights of the City Ballet, the serious little theaters, and Carnegie Hall, all whispering "Aspire, aspire!"

Susurrations of grandeur.

5.

But grandeur on this style is a neighborhood of the mind, and a narrow one at that. Real neighborhoods and psychological neighborhoods may, in fact, overlap—literary Greenwich Village being the most storied case in point. In the Village of the psyche, the outré is always in, and it is safely conventional to be bizarre. Writers once looked for cheap rent in these streets, after which it began to *feel* writerly to live in the Village, within walking distance of the fountain in Washington Square. The earlier luminaries who resided here are the more enshrined—Washington Irving, James Fenimore Cooper, Louisa May Alcott, Mark Twain, Edgar Allan Poe, O. Henry, Horace Greeley, Walt Whitman, Theodore Dreiser, Bret Harte, Sinclair Lewis, Sherwood Anderson, Upton Sinclair, Willa Cather; and, in a later generation, Thomas Wolfe, E. E. Cummings, Richard Wright, Djuna Barnes, Edmund Wilson, Elinor Wylie, Hart Crane, James Agee, Marianne Moore, W. H. Auden! Yet fame re-enacted can become parody as well as homage, and there was a touch of in-your-face déjà vu in the nineteen-fifties, when Allen Ginsberg, Jack Kerouac, and LeRoi Jones (afterward known as Amiri Baraka) established the then newborn East Village as a beatnik redoubt. Nowadays it would be hard to discover a writers' roster equal to those of the past, and West Village literariness hangs as a kind of tattered nimbus not over the old (mostly temporary) residences of the celebrated but over the bars, cellars, and cafés they once frequented. The Saturday night hordes that flow through Bleecker Street are mostly from New Jersey. ("The bridge-and-tunnel crowd," sniffs the East Village of the hour.)

Neighborhoods of the mind, though, are rarely so solidly placed in a single location. Of actual neighborhoods (or "sections," in moribund New Yorkese)—Soho, Little Italy, Chelsea, Gramercy Park, Murray Hill, South Street Seaport, and all the rest—only a few are as determinedly self-defined as the Village. But a courageous denizen of any of them (despite home-grown inhibitions of boundary and habit) can venture out to a collectivity of taste and imagination and familiarity unconstrained by geography. Jazz and blues and nightlife aficionados, movie buffs, gays, rap artists, boxing and wrestling zealots, singles, esoteric-restaurant habitués, Central Park joggers, marathon runners, museum addicts, lovers of music or theater or dance, lonely-hearts, shoppers, hotel weekenders, barflies, churchgoers, Talmud enthusiasts, Bronx-born Tibetan Buddhists, students of Sufism, kabbalists, theosophists, voice or ski coaches, SAT and LSAT crammers, amateur painters, union members, members of boards and trustees, Internet devotees, fans of the Yankees or the Mets or the Jets or the Knicks, believers in psychics and tea-leaves readers, streetwalkers and their pimps, antiques fanciers, art collectors, philanthropists, professors of linguistics, lexicographers, copy editors, librarians, kindergarten teachers, crossing guards, wine votaries, storefront chiropractors, Chinese or Hebrew or Arabic calligraphers—all these, and inconceivably more, can emerge from any locality to live, if only for a few hours, in a sympathetic neighborhood of affinity. Expertise and idiosyncrasy and bursting desire burn and burn in New York: a conflagration of manifold, insatiable, tumultuous will.

6.

I was born in a brownstone on East Eighty-eighth Street, between First and York Avenues—but both the latter avenue and the area have since altered their designations and their character. York was once Avenue A, and the neighborhood, populated largely by German immigrants, was called Yorkville. It was in Yorkville before my birth that my infant brother was kidnapped by a madwoman. The story as it was told to me is set in a certain year, but not in any special weather; it seems to me that it must have been summer. I see my mother, hot, sleeveless, breathless, frantic, running through the night streets of Yorkville to find the kidnapper and snatch her baby back. He had been sleeping in his wicker carriage in a nook among rows of brown bottles and drawers filled with maple-flavored rock candy on strings, not four yards from where my young father in his pharmacist's jacket, a fountain pen always in its pocket, stood tending to his mortar and pestle, working up a medicinal paste. Into my parents' drug store the madwoman flew, seizing baby and carriage and all, and out into the dark she fled, only to be discovered some hours later in nearby Carl Schurz Park, disheveled and undone by furious infantile howls, and grateful to relinquish the captive screamer.

In my half-dreaming re-creation of this long-ago scene—the stolen child, the fleeing madwoman—why must it be summer-time? I think I know why. New York in summer is another sort of city; in mood and weight it has nothing in common with wintry New York. A New York summer is frenetic, syncopated, blistered, frayed, dusty. There is a desperation in its heat, and a sense of letdown, despite relief, in its air-conditioned indoors. Melting squads of tourists, in shorts and open shirts or halters, sweat pooling under their camera straps, their heads swiveling from one gaudy carnival sight to the next, push through Times Square in anxious quick-march. Smells of perspiring hot dogs under venders' grease-lined umbrellas mingle with the exhaust fumes of heaving buses. There is nothing relaxed about the summer city. New York's noise is louder, New York's toughness is brasher, New York's velocity is speedier. Everything—stores, offices, schedules, vacations, traffic—demands full steam ahead; no one can say that the livin' is easy. New York in July is out of synch, not quite itself, hoping for ransom, kidnapped by midsummer frolicking: picnickers awaiting free twilight performances of Shakespeare in Central Park; street parades of night-time swelterers along Museum Mile, where tappers and clappers gather before the Jewish Museum to salute the tootling klezmer players; breakdancers down from Harlem, twelve-year-olds effortless and expert and little and lithe, who spin on their heels across from the hive of Madison Square Garden. In the American heartland in summer, babies fall down wells and pipes, and that is news. In New York—fidgety, frittering, frenzied, boiling New York—summer itself is news.

The true city is the winter city. The woolly enchantment of a population swaddled and muffled, women and men in long coats, eccentric boots, winding scarves; steam sculptures forming out of human breath; hushed streets; tiny white electric points on skeletal trees! The icy air like a scratch across a sheet of silver, the smoky chestnut carts, the foggy odor of hot coffee when you open a door, a bakery's sweet mist swirling through its transom, a glimpse of rosy-nosed skaters in the well of the Rockefeller stelae, the rescuing warmth of public lobbies—New York in January is a city of grateful small shocks. And just as in an antiquated English novel of manners, New York has its "season"—lectures, readings, rallies, dinner parties, chamber music in someone's living room. While in summer you cannot rely on the taxis to turn on their air-conditioning, in winter each yellow capsule is a hot little bullet; the driver in his turban remembers his subcontinental home. There is no dusk like a New York winter dusk: the blurry gray of early evening, when the lone walker, ferried between day and night, jostled by strangers in packs, feels most desolate, and when the privacy of burrowing into a coat collar brings on a nameless loss. At such a moment the forest of flowering lights (a brilliance suddenly apprehended) makes its cheering claim: that here, right *here,* is importance, achievement, delight in the work of the world; that here, right here, is the hope of connection, and life in its fulfillment. In a gregarious New York winter, especially in restaurants at eight o'clock, you will hear jokes, stories with amazing climaxes, futures plotted out, jealousies retailed, gossip above all: who's up, who's down, what's in, what's out. Central heating never abolished the theory and practice of the fireside.

7.

What Manhattan talks about, obliquely or openly—what it thinks about, whatever the season—is ambition. Europeans always make much of this: how *hard* New Yorkers work, the long days, the paltry vacations, the single-minded avarice for status, the obsessiveness, the terrible drive. What? No *dolce far niente?* But only an outsider would remark on the city's striving; for New Yorkers it is ingrained, taken for granted, valued. Unlike Bartleby, downtown's most distinctive imaginary inhabitant, New York never prefers not to. New York prefers and prefers and prefers—it prefers power and scope to tranquility and intimacy, it prefers struggle and steel to acquiescence and cushions. New York is where you go to seize the day, to leave your mark, to live within the nerve of your generation. Some might say that there is nothing new in this—why else did Willa Cather begin in Red Cloud, Nebraska, and end on Bank Street? Why else did Jackson Pollock, born in Cody, Wyoming, land in New York?

Yet there is a difference. New York ambition has changed its face. Fifty years ago, when postal clerks and bank tellers wearing vests were what was still called "family men," the hankering young were on the lowest rung of any hierarchy. Their patience was commanded; their deference was expected. It was understood that power and position were the sovereign right of middle age, and that a twenty-three-year-old would have to wait and wait. Opportunity and recognition were light-years away. A few—writers mostly—broke out early: Mary McCarthy at twenty-two, Norman Mailer at twenty-five, Philip Roth and John Updike at twenty-six. Leonard Bernstein and Bobby Fischer were youthful stars. Still, these were all prodigies and exceptions. In the run-of-the-mill world of getting ahead, the young were at the bottom, and stayed there until judged—by their elders at the top—to be sufficiently ripe. The Information Age, with its ear to the ground, reverses all that. The old ways are undone. A twenty-something young woman in publishing keeps a television set on in her office all day, monitoring possible acquisitions: what sells, who's cool. The auditory and the visual, in whatever mode, belong almost exclusively to the newest generation. Everywhere in New York the knowledgeable young are in charge of the sound, the image, the latest word; ambition need no longer stand in line and wait its graying turn. (Fifty-somethings, their passion still unspent, and recalling the slower passage of long ago, may be a little wistful.)

In a city always relinquishing, always replacing, always on the wing, mores close down and expectations alter; milestones fade away; landmarks vanish. In its shifting primordial constancy, New York is faithful to loss and faithful to change. After the hullabaloo over the demise of Books & Company on Madison and Shakespeare & Company on upper Broadway, some still mourn those small principalities of letters. But does anyone born since the Second World War miss the intellectual newsstand next to the Chock Full O' Nuts across from Washington Square, or the Forty-second Street Automat, where you could linger over your teacup and read your paper all afternoon?

Now and then, heartstruck, I pass the crenellated quasi-Gothic building that once housed my high school, where latecomers, myself among them, would tremble before its great arched doorway, fearing reprimand; but the reprimanders are all dead. My Latin teacher is dead. My German teacher is dead. My biology teacher is dead. It is only the city itself that lives on, half-amnesiac, hardly ever glancing back, re-inventing its fabric, insisting on being noticed for what it is now. There is no grief for what precedes the common memory, and ultimately the fickle urban tide, as immutable as the Nile, accommodates every disappearance.

8.

In May of 1860, when Frederick Law Olmsted's Central Park was just in the making, a forty-year-old Wall Street lawyer named George Templeton Strong recorded in his diary his own preference:

> The park below the reservoir begins to look intelligible. Unfinished still, and in process of manufacture, but shewing the outline now of what it is to be. Many points are already beautiful. What will they be when their trees are grown and I'm dead and forgotten?
>
> One thinks sometimes that one would like re-juvenescence, or a

> new birth. One would prefer, if he could, to annihilate his past and commence life, say in this A.D. 1860, and so enjoy longer acquaintance with this era of special development and material progress, watch the splendid march of science on earth, share the benefits of the steam engine and the electric telegraph, and grow up with this park—which is to be so great a fact for the young men and maidens of New York in 1880, if all goes well and we do not decompose into anarchy meanwhile. . . . Central Park and Astor Library and a developed Columbia University promise to make the city twenty years hence a real center of culture and civilization, furnishing privileges to youth far beyond what it gave me in my boyhood.

A century and a half on, Strong's "era of special development and material progress" may seem quaint to us, for whom fax and e-mail and jets and microwaves are everyday devices, and whose moonwalkers are already old men. By now the park below the reservoir, the library on Fifth Avenue, and the university on Morningside Heights are seasoned inheritances—established components of the city's culture and civilization. But even standing as we do on the lip of the new millennium, who can resist falling into George Templeton Strong's wishful dream of a new birth and a longer acquaintance? His New York of steam engine and telegraph, as ephemeral as the May clouds of 1860, has ceased to be. Our New York, too, will disappear, and a renewed and clarified city will lift out of the breathing breast of the one we know. New York, Enemy of the Merely Picturesque, Headquarters of Misery and Marvel, Eraser and Renewer, Brain and Capital of the Continent!

The immigrants will come—what language will they speak? The towers will climb to the sky—what shapes will they have? The crowds will stream in the streets—what thoughts will they think? Will they think our outworn thoughts, or imaginings we cannot imagine?

New York: Science Fiction, Junot Diaz (2000)

Junot Diaz was born in Santo Domingo, Dominican Republic, in 1968 and came to the United States in 1975 at the age of seven. He graduated from Rutgers University, received an M.F.A. from Cornell University, and presently is on the faculty at Syracuse University. In 1999, *The New Yorker* magazine named Diaz one of the best twenty fiction writers in America, and he was recently awarded a Guggenheim Fellowship.

The story of the Dominican immigration to New York City in the last quarter century must be seen through the lens of U.S. involvement with the Caribbean island. The first surge of immigration occurred after the assassination of dictator Rafael Trujillo in 1961, the defeat of a popular revolt in 1965, and the invasion of the island by U.S. troops in that year. Also in 1965, Congress passed the Family Reunification Act, which allowed family members to reunite with relatives already living in the States. Coupled with failed U.S. attempts to "modernize" the Dominican economy that led to wild inflation and massive unemployment, immigration figures have risen steadily in the last three decades (and by fully 50 percent in the last decade) to where, according to the 2000 census, there are more than half a million Dominicans living legally in New York City, and potentially scores of thousands more living illegally.

The "Puerto Rican Obituary" that Diaz refers to in his piece is a reference to a poem by Puerto Rican Pedro Pietri that was first published in *Palente: Young Lords Party* in 1971. The poem vividly describes the failure of recent immigrants to attain the American dream and chastises them for giving up their cultural roots in the process. The reference is representative, however, of the effect that Dominicans have had on other Latino groups, especially Puerto Ricans. Dominicans and Puerto Ricans have come in close contact with one another in Harlem and Washington Heights, and at least one Boricua activist has remarked that Puerto Ricans have become "more" Puerto Rican because of their contact with Dominicans.

Diaz's first childhood view of a city that "looked like science fiction" is a startling and appropriate contrast to the sighting of one of the first explorers to see Manhattan 366 years before—Henry Hudson.

My father was first; he reached Nueva York at the start of the Seventies, in the Years of the Puerto Rican Obituary. This was the decade of "benign neglect" and "planned shrinkage," when New York City—specifically the poor colored neighborhoods in which my father was attempting to live—was being burned to the ground by the "cost-effective" policies of Roger Starr and his Rand Corporation cronies.

He had the "usual" Caribbean immigrant experience: he worked crap jobs, he slept in unheated buildings, he starved his ass off. All around him buildings exploded into fire. Fortunately he wasn't in them, but it didn't help his sleep any knowing that a family of seven had been roasted to death the week before. The stench of the smoke, of those destroyed lives, seeped into his dreams.

Who's surprised that after five unhappy years in Nueva York my father decided that he'd had enough? Right before he brought the rest of us over from Santo Domingo my father abandoned New York City, where he had friends, where he had a life, and relocated to New Jersey, where he knew no one. He said it was for our sake—we didn't hear about this move until after we arrived—but I think it was also for his peace of mind. He settled in a Section 8 apartment complex that was bounded on one side by Old Bridge (where Vitamin C is from) and on the other by Sayreville (BonJoviLand). This is where me and my siblings lived when we reached the States, where I spent my Ghetto-American childhood, marooned in the middle of suburbs white as a gringo's ass.

New York went from the Oz I dreamed about in the Dominican Republic to the distant sight of the Verrazano Bridge (visible from the entrance of my development). Transformed from the City of Everything to the ruined boroughs we visited on weekends. A future that had been promised but never arrived.

Eventually I would move to Nueva York, at twenty-six gaining the life I always thought should have been mine to begin with. I didn't arrive in the Years of the Puerto Rican Obituary; it was, by then, the Years of the Nightstick. I had the "usual" Caribbean college-graduate New York experience. I worked temp jobs, I lived in an unwinterized apartment in Brooklyn, I smoked cheap hydro and was too broke for anything but activism. Nothing burned, thank God, not even bread. Often I found myself in Washington

Heights, the Capital of the Dominican Diaspora, visiting friends, visiting relatives; sometimes I would stand on the street corners with my writer's notebook, trying to imagine what-could-have-been.

Certain nights, when I was restless and nothing was working out, I'd take the D over the Manhattan Bridge. As the train left the tunnel and began to cross the East River I'd step between the cars. This, for some reason, made me happy. It wasn't really dangerous and the view it afforded of New York was beyond words. A city ablaze, suspended between blacksky and river. Our first night in the States my old man wanted us to see a similar city, on our drive from JFK. I remember our silence, the cold of the windows against our faces. The city looked like science fiction. Like an incubator for stars, where suns are made. This was before we realized that we were actually bound for New Jersey, when we thought one of those lights was going to be our home.

The Resilient City, John P. Avlon (2001)

For over a quarter century, the Twin Towers helped define New York City to the world and to itself. The World Trade Center crowned the skyline, providing a visual backdrop to the Statue of Liberty and streets throughout the city. It was used by New Yorkers to determine their sense of direction—whenever the towers loomed, there was due south—and it also lent credence to New York's claim to be the Capital of the World. The Twin Towers were born amid controversy in 1966, when David Rockefeller—then president of Chase Manhattan Bank—called his brother Nelson—then governor of the state of New York—and proposed a building scheme that would revive Lower Manhattan.

Ironically, the construction of this symbol of free trade was presided over by a government entity, the Port Authority of New York and New Jersey. When prospective architects protested that it was impossible to build a 110-story building, new architects were found. When they were completed in 1973 at a cost of nearly $1.5 billion, the Twin Towers contained 43,600 windows, 23,000 fluorescent lights, and 194 elevators, and weighed 1.5 million tons. The buildings succeeded in beginning the commercial, cultural, and residential revival of Lower Manhattan. But they remained oddly unappreciated for such iconic structures—unloved in comparison to the Chrysler or Empire State buildings—until one February afternoon in 1993, when they became the target of their first terrorist attack. Six people were killed and thousands were injured when a van full of explosives was detonated in the basement garage; it was the first large-scale terrorist attack on American soil. Then on September 11, 2001, two hijacked airplanes were crashed into the Twin Towers, leveling the buildings within hours and unleashing a scene of previously unimaginable devastation. The destruction of what had been billed as "the first buildings of the twenty-first century" became a dark symbol of the beginning of the new century, as much as the fall of the Berlin Wall had been a hopeful symbol of the passing of the twentieth.

John P. Avlon was born in New York City the same year the Twin Towers were completed. Twenty-eight years later he was three blocks away, in City Hall, when they were destroyed. Avlon—known to his friends as "Fipp"—attended Yale University and worked as a musician and editor of an Internet newspaper before serving as Chief Speechwriter and Deputy Communications Director to Mayor Rudolph W. Giuliani. In the aftermath of the attacks, he was responsible for writing or editing the eulogies for each of the more than four hundred firefighters, police officers, and other rescue workers killed on September 11.

On September 11, 2001, New York City experienced its day of infamy. The worst terrorist attack in human history claimed more lives than Pearl Harbor and destroyed the Twin Towers that had defined our city's skyline since 1973. The buildings' architect—a second-generation Japanese-American named Minoru Yamasaki—had intended the trade center to serve as a symbol of world peace, saying "World trade means world peace . . . the World Trade Center should become a representation of man's belief in humanity, his need for individual dignity, his beliefs in the cooperation of men, and through cooperation, his ability to find greatness."

THREE hundred and forty-one New York City firefighters. Twenty-three New York City police officers. Thirty-seven Port Authority police officers. Three court officers. Two EMS workers. Thousands of innocent civilians. Numbers alone, of course, cannot do them justice.

A whole portrait of America was taken from us in an instant: individuals of every race, religion, and ethnicity; fathers and mothers, children and newlyweds, brothers, sisters, and best friends. Amid our grief we now see that New York had been distracted by flash and wit and cash for too long. The heroic actions of those we lost reawakened us to the essential importance of personal courage. Overnight, and somewhat to our surprise, New York has been embraced as the nation's symbol of resilience, the indomitable heart of America.

On my desk at City Hall is a list of every firefighter, police officer, and uniformed service member who died in the line of duty on that day. Their names fill forty-seven pages. As Mayor Giuliani's speechwriter, it has been my responsibility to write or edit each of their eulogies. The New York City Fire Department had lost 778 men from its founding in 1865 until September 10, 2001. In the course of one morning, it lost nearly half that historic total.

Nothing had prepared the city or the department for this volume of loss. And so it fell to four of us in our small office to do the best we could to do them justice, to say thank you, to provide some measure of comfort to their families on behalf of their city.

It should not be forgotten that September 11th began as a beautiful blue-sky day. Primary elections were being held throughout the city, and as people were lining up to vote at polling places or dropping their children off at school, suddenly they stopped and turned their heads toward a rumble in the sky. It was 8:46 A.M. The pilot of the first hijacked airplane, Mohammed Atta, was flying American Airlines flight 11 low and loud down the length of Manhattan with the lives of 92 passengers in his hands, above stores, churches, and finally past the Washington Square Arch as he aimed for the heart of the Twin Towers.

The first plane flew by my window. I was sleeping late after a long weekend of work, when my girlfriend heard the roar of its engines approaching. She shook me and we both saw its silver underbelly pass by the window of my fifth-floor walk-up in Greenwich Village. We assumed it was going to crash, but the plane seemed strangely in control to be flying so low. We waited for impact, heard a faint sound, and then saw the beginning of the black smoke curl above the trees, beyond the church steeple of Our Lady of Pompeii. Then the first sirens of that long day sounded in the distance. I recalled that a plane had once crashed into the Empire State Building in 1945. Despite the cloudless sky, I tried to convince myself that this also could have been an accident.

At 9:03, the second plane banked sickly toward the south tower as the world watched on television. An orange blossom of flame exploded on our screens as a new reality dawned. As I left the apartment for City Hall, fire companies from around the city were already racing to join those who had already arrived at what would become ground zero.

On the streets people stood frozen in mid-commute, gathered at street corners, talking to strangers or on their cell phones, gazing at the blazing scars cut into the sides of the Twin Towers. I passed a kindergarten playground opposite a firehouse where children were still playing as their teachers looked over their shoulders at the buildings burning in the distance. The steel seemed to have melted around the impact zone and it reflected the sunlight, giving the edges a quicksilver sheen, like an overwrought special effect. Despite the horror of the scene there was an assumption that the worst had already occurred; few people thought that the towers would actually come down. After all, they had been bombed before in 1993, and though six people had died and thousands were injured, the Twin Towers still stood.

Subways were shut down and taxis proved impossible to find, so I made my way down Broadway against a sea of people evacuating uptown. Black smoke now filled the sky, evident from anywhere on the island. I expected to see mass panic, but instead the exodus was relatively calm and orderly. It was the response of a civil society to a massive attack.

Friends and colleagues were standing on the steps of City Hall, staring up at the towers burning less than three blocks away. Inside the hall there was concern and controlled panic—grim glances passed between co-workers who knew that the situation went well beyond words. We wondered whether sites like Times Square and the United Nations would be targeted next. Reporters were calling the press office for comment. I looked at a newspaper someone had thrown across the desk and committed the date to memory. Its contents were instantly irrelevant, news from another century. Three blocks away, people were throwing themselves from upper floors of the World Trade Center. One observer recalled them hitting the ground "like melons," as the music piped into the plaza played "How Deep Is Your Love?"

Firefighters in full bunker gear were rushing up the stairs of the trade center as workers tried to get down to safety. This was the image that survivors would repeat over and over, "as we were going down, as they were going up."

In City Hall, we received word that the mayor was getting ready to do a press conference on a street one block from the burning buildings. The purpose was not only to get information out to the general public but also to get information up to those who were still trapped above the flames in the Twin Towers. They were calling out to family and friends, asking if there was anything that could be done, and in some cases, saying good-bye.

At 10:05 the south tower shuddered and collapsed; twenty-three minutes later the north tower fell as well. It was an avalanche in lower Manhattan, reaching 2.4 on the Richter scale. The rumble of the buildings coming down was like a thousand jets taking off at once. Below the roar you could almost hear the collective sigh of human life, the disbelief, horror, and resignation as the steel finally buckled and 110 stories imploded, floor upon floor.

A gray cloud of debris rolled violently toward us across City Hall Park, an unforgiving wall of pulverized concrete against the still briefly blue sky. Then it hit City Hall, and everything became dark as night and quiet, except for the patter of debris hitting the roof of the old stone building. For a moment, we thought that we might all die, if not from the building collapse itself then from some biological agent swirling around in the air. Base alloys of emotion bubbled up to the surface. Tough women with children at home curled up in the rotunda at the foot of the grand staircase. Some men grew silent, scared. Others shouted conflicting orders. After several minutes, the dust cleared enough to let some light through, and we could see that Lower Manhattan had been transformed into a gray wasteland of ash and smoke pierced by sirens.

It seemed that every New Yorker knew someone in the towers. In City Hall, we worked alongside the uniformed services every day: they were friends and, in some cases, family. Captain Terence S. Hatton was the leader of Rescue One, the city's elite rescue unit. He and the mayor's executive assistant Beth had been married four years before in a ceremony at Gracie Mansion. His photograph on her desk—face covered in soot after fighting a fire—was a constant reminder of who we really worked for and what real courage looked like. Terry Hatton could have been anything he wanted to be. He was six-foot four, with the inner dignity of a young Gary Cooper. He could have been a movie star. But if he had been a movie star, his job would have been playing people like Terry Hatton—impossibly courageous and down to earth, possessing both integrity and intelligence. Like his father before him, Terry Hatton loved being a New York City firefighter. He had been decorated for bravery nineteen times in his twenty-one-year career. In August 2001, Terry had rescued eight people perilously stuck in an elevator shaft near the 80th floor of the World Trade Center. Rescue units were among the first responders, and on the 11th of September they were presumably the highest up the towers, racing to put out the fires and save the people who were stranded. Rescue One lost ten of its men that day.

We lost so many of the best of New York's Bravest, including sixty off-duty firefighters who rushed to the towers when they heard of the attack. The legendary Captain Paddy Brown was by some accounts the most decorated firefighter in the nation. He'd served two tours as a Marine in Vietnam, come back home to Queens and devoted his life to fighting fires and saving lives; lately, he'd taken up yoga and teaching blind people martial arts. We lost Father Mychal Judge, the beloved Department Chaplain who shepherded families through the tragedies ranging from fires to the crash of TWA Flight 800 off the coast of Long Island. We lost Chief of Special Operations Ray Downey, a 40-year veteran who led the recovery mission after the first bombing of the World Trade Center, and then FEMA's rescue effort after the attack at Oklahoma City. In return for his heroics and battlefield expertise, Ray Downey had been appointed to serve on the president's antiterrorism task force. His sons, also in the FDNY, would spend the better part of the next month digging through ground zero, looking for their father.

In the hours and days immediately following the attack, New York City was transformed into something like Battle of Britain-era London, with whole sections of the city evacuated and a military presence on street corners. The acrid smell of smoke and ash hung in the air, and people walked around shell-shocked—a mixture of adrenaline and despair—as they waited for what many assumed was the inevitable next attack.

Four hours after he had almost been killed in the collapse of the south tower, Mayor Giuliani appeared in front of reporters at the Police Academy on East 20th Street. He was asked how many people had been killed. "More than any of us can bear," he said simply. He spoke without notes and inspired confidence in a hurt world because of his directness, honesty, and compassion. That evening he returned to ground zero to supervise the recovery effort and strode around the wreckage of the city he loved like a latter-day Churchill. In his morning and evening executive staff meetings away from the cameras, the mayor transformed himself into a wartime leader, decisively organizing massive amounts of information and directing the recovery effort. The mayor was now spontaneously applauded when he walked down the street. His tireless courage inspired us to rise above the devastation. Working around the clock, we met whatever challenges we faced—after all, the extraordinary is ordinary to the people experiencing it. The city's emergency command center had been destroyed in the attack, but seventy-two hours later, a new command center was fully operational within a pier near 52nd Street by the Hudson River. Outside the mayor's office in the new command center we pinned a Revolutionary War-era flag to the wall bearing the phrase, "Don't Tread On Me."

The morning after the attack, I returned to City Hall. The FDR Drive was closed to all traffic except emergency vehicles, and we drove down it with lights and sirens flashing. The beauty of the blue-sky day ignored what had occurred 24 hours before. The absence of the Twin Towers in the skyline was jarring, as was the sight of tanks and humvees posted along Park Row. Crushed police cars were lined up along the side of the road. On storefront windows, messages had been written into the dust on the glass: "Rest in peace to all the people who died today 9/11/01." City Hall was dark and empty except for a few guards. In the mayor's office, the portrait of Fiorello La Guardia stared intensely into the tomblike silence. Outside, somebody had taken care to lower the flags to half-mast.

I wandered down to St. Paul's Chapel off the southern tip of City Hall

Park, passing rescue workers trudging back from the smoking skeletal wreckage of ground zero, discouraged to their bones that so few survivors had been found. When St. Paul's had been built in 1766, the land around it was considered countryside. George Washington had walked there to pray after he was inaugurated the first President of the United States. Since 1973, St. Paul's had stood across the street from the World Trade Center. Now in the chapel's graveyard, trees were torn out at their roots, two-hundred-year-old tombstones were cracked or knocked over entirely, ripped sections of Venetian blinds rattled amid branches, and a six-inch-thick blanket of papers, debris, and ash coated the ground. Upon closer inspection these were pieces of bills, bank statements, old photographs, and company ledgers from people who had worked in the World Trade Center. What once seemed important was brutally exposed as irrelevant. Outside the gates of the graveyard, on the edge of ground zero, an advertisement for *Investor's Business Daily* above a subway entrance was still intact: it read: "choose success." One minor miracle was apparent amid the devastation—St. Paul's Chapel had escaped the towers' collapse without a single broken window.

As city government mobilized to overcome the effects of the attack, the speechwriting department began to plan for the inevitable memorial services. Remote historic figures such as Churchill and Roosevelt gained new relevance with their themes of courage, defiance, and freedom from fear. A biblical quote, John 15:13—"Greater love hath no man than this, that a man lay down his life for his friends"—resonated because hundreds had laid down their lives for thousands of strangers. But for us, the greatest inspiration by far came from the deep grief of ordinary New Yorkers: makeshift memorials of notes and melting candles in parks outside firehouses; the American flags that hung from almost every apartment building; the steadfast souls who stood along the West Side Highway every hour of the day and night for more than a month, holding handwritten signs and cheering the rescue workers on their way to and from ground zero. This was the spirit of a resilient city—outraged, engaged, and unified. Slowly the eulogies began to take shape, common themes woven through the contours of their extraordinary individual lives.

On September 15th, four days after the attack, the first funeral was held. It was for Father Mychal Judge, the beloved Fire Department Chaplain who had been killed by debris as he administered last rites to a fallen firefighter. Three months later to the day, we laid to rest Chief Ray Downey. In between, there were more than four hundred other heroes of the uniformed services and thousands of civilians from eighty-three different nations. Their stories were told again and again in an attempt to assimilate the tragedy, to comprehend the incomprehensible. There was the middle-aged woman from Kazakhstan who had reported early for her first day of work in America, and the young bond trader who was killed on her one-month wedding anniversary. Firefighter John Chipura had survived the 1983 terrorist attacks on the Marine barracks in Beirut that killed 241 of his colleagues and then served seven years as a member of the NYPD before joining the Fire Department. John O'Neil spent a career serving as a counterterrorism expert for the FBI and leading the search for Osama bin Laden after the Al Qaeda attack on the *USS Cole*, before taking a job as director of security for the World Trade Center in August 2001. Henry Thompson was a court officer who commandeered a van and raced to the towers with two of his co-workers. Chief of the Department Pete Ganci had ordered his men to move the FDNY command post away from the trade center and then walked toward the burning buildings minutes before their collapse. Glenn Winuk was a respected lawyer who also served as the commissioner of the volunteer fire department in his hometown of Jericho, New York; after the attack he helped evacuate coworkers from his law firm and then headed toward the towers to help the rescue effort. Captain Timothy Stackpole was a father of five who had recently returned to the job after recuperating from burns over 90 percent of his body that he sustained in a fire that killed two of his friends. Police Officer Moira Smith had been among the first to report that a plane had smashed into the towers, and hours later this mother of a two-year-old and wife of a police officer became the first female NYPD officer killed in the line of duty. The legendary seventy-one-year-old First Deputy Fire Commissioner Bill Feehan, who had held every position in the department, became the oldest New York City firefighter in history to die in the line of duty. Firefighting and police work tend to be family traditions in the city of New York, and the attack affected some families and communities disproportionately: the brothers Joseph and John Vigiano; brothers Thomas and Peter Langone; brothers Timothy and Thomas Haskell; cousins Manuel and Dennis Mojica; and the father and son Joseph Angelini, Sr. and Joseph Angelini, Jr.—all died together on September 11th. This was more than just the fraternal bond between firefighters and police officers; this was family.

Their services have been held in small chapels, ornate synagogues, simple firehouses, and grand cathedrals. More than a dozen have been held at St. Patrick's Cathedral on Fifth Avenue. It is there that you get the fullest sense of the majesty and tragedy of this city transformed.

Thousands of firefighters in their dress blue uniforms line the street. Hundreds of friends, admirers, and fellow citizens crowd the steps of the cathedral. Two fire trucks are parked side by side, with their ladders raised and extended as a large American flag hung between them waves in the breeze. Everyone falls silent as the black limousines carrying the family arrive. Then the faint sound of bagpipes and drum rolls grows louder as the Emerald Society pipe band marches closer, announcing the approach of an engine truck rolling mournfully slow with a flag-covered coffin and flowers placed on top. When the truck reaches the door of the cathedral it slows to a halt, and simultaneously a thousand firefighters snap into a salute that is held until the coffin and family are led inside. During the service, prayers are read; family and friends offer eulogies, followed by the mayor or surrogates such as Fire Commissioner Tommy Von Essen and Police Commissioner Bernard Kerik. After the final blessing is given, the coffin is carried out by brothers from his fire company and lifted onto the waiting truck, on the back of which is written "we will never forget." The salute is held again as the engine disappears down Fifth Avenue, preceded by the bagpipes playing "Amazing Grace," "America the Beautiful," "Battle Hymn of the Republic," and "Going Home."

One unseasonably warm night in early December I went walking down from my office toward ground zero. I walked without a coat, wanting to take a break and refocus my mind. We had written nearly four hundred eulogies for the mayor and his surrogates to deliver over the past three months, as many as forty-five in a single weekend, with the mayor attending up to nine wakes and memorials in the course of each of his marathon 18-hour days. The relentless pace required us to impose a certain degree of emotional distance to get the job done. But now the feelings of heartache increased as the workload diminished.

Rescue workers had been laboring at ground zero every hour since the disaster. At night the site was lit by spotlights, like a movie set. Fires had burned there for eighty days, rekindling when a lower level of the underground fire was exposed to the oxygen in the air. Now tourists and well-wishers on pilgrimage sought out the site, standing at great distances, taking pictures of the hulking wreckage and skeletal spires looming over the fences. There were flowers left against every gate and poetry scribbled out on paper taped to the lampposts. The missing-person posters that had appeared around the city in the days after the attacks had given way to heart-wrenching good-byes, handwritten cards with photographs promising them that we would never forget. Family members still gathered at the platform set up on the edge of the site and gazed at their loved ones' last resting place with haunted eyes. The largest mass grave in America existed uneasily as both hallowed ground and deconstruction site. The scope of the destruction, the size of the wound cut into the heart of our city, remained humbling and retained its ability to inspire calm outrage, cold purposefulness.

On my way back from ground zero, I stopped by St. Paul's Chapel. It now served as a shrine of sorts, its metal gates covered with posters and canvas tarps upon which people wrote notes urging faith, expressing sadness, and calling for courage. Inside, the chapel had been transformed into a sanctuary for rescue workers with beds, food, clothing, and massage tables, and occasionally a string quartet to help soothe their souls. The pew where George Washington had prayed now served as a nurse's station, full of bandages and medications. The sheer functionality of this sacred space was heartening—democracy and theology effortlessly intertwined. Most startling and beautiful was this: along all the walls of the church, posted on pillars and taped in pews, were letters and cards written by children from across the United States, covered with brightly colored drawings of eagles, firemen, the towers under attack, and American flags. They bore messages of hope, faith, and gratitude: "Thank you . . . you are my heroes . . . I am sorry the people died . . . thank you for saving the people . . . I love the city . . . God Bless America." These notes sustained the spirits of the men who each day would sift through the debris, finding body parts that, as often as not, would disintegrate at the touch. Their actions and those cards were powerful examples of why our city and nation would triumph over terror: in ways both large and small, we had met the worst of humanity with the best of humanity.

After leaving St. Paul's Chapel that silent New York night I walked down Broadway, past Wall Street and Trinity Church, past Bowling Green and into Battery Park. I stared out into the dark waters of New York Harbor for a time and then looked up and was almost surprised by the sight of the Statue of Liberty and Ellis Island still standing serenely in our harbor. And then, for a moment, I saw the city through history's eyes. I remembered that this was the same body of water into which Henry Hudson had sailed the *Half Moon* in 1609. He could not have imagined the wilderness he saw becoming home to 8 million people from all over the world. He could not have imagined that buildings taller than mountains would one day crowd the island. In less than four hundred years our city has grown more than other cities have in a millennium, fueled by the energy, resilience, and innovations of each successive generation. Our great symbol of world trade is now gone—what was intended by its architect to be a symbol of world peace was destroyed in a vicious, unprovoked act of war. But what was really attacked on

September 11th was the idea of New York City and America itself—a beacon of freedom, diversity, and equal opportunity. That spirit is intact and undaunted. In fact, our devotion to those ideals has only been strengthened by the selfless heroism we have seen. We now recognize that we are all part of a larger narrative, and while our city may never be the same, we will be better and stronger as a result of all we have experienced. Much has been taken from us, but much remains; and even in the dark, a great deal of light still shines upon the city of New York.

SOURCES AND ACKNOWLEDGMENTS

"Account of Henry Hudson's Voyage in 1609" from *History of the City of New York from its Earliest Settlement to the Present Time,* edited by Mary L. Booth (1860)

"Letter of the Eight Men" from *Historic New York, Being the first series of the Half Moon Papers,* edited by Maud Wilder Goodwin, Alice Carington Royce, and Ruth Putnam (1898)

"The Representation of New Netherland, 1650" from the collections of the New-York Historical Society

"Description of the Towne of Mannadens" from *Narratives of New Netherland,* edited by J. Franklin Jameson (New York: Scribner's & Sons, 1909)

"Leisler's Rebellion: Benjamin Blagge's Memorial" from *The Documentary History of the State of New York*

"State of the Province of New York" from the collections of the New-York Historical Society

"Hessian Views of the City" from *Letters from America, 1776–1779,* edited by Ray W. Pettengill (Port Washington, NY, 1964)

"Letter, March 1, 1833" by John Pintard from the collections of the New-York Historical Society

"Selected Writings of African Americans in Brooklyn," edited by Ann Meyerson and the Brooklyn Historical Society from their exhibition *Brooklyn Works: 400 Years of Making a Living in Brooklyn* (2002). Reprinted by permission of the Brooklyn Historical Society.

"The Workingman's View of his Situation" from *The Testimony of the Senate Committee on the Relations between Labor and Capital* (1883)

"Sanitary Conditions in New York" from *Street Cleaning* by George Waring (1897)

"New York, A.D. 1997: A Prophecy" from *Life of Col. George E. Waring Jr.: The Greatest Apostle of Cleanliness* as told by Dr. Albert Shaw (New York, 1899)

"Brooklyn Could Have Been a Contender" by John Tierney. Copyright © 1998. Reprinted by permission of the author.

"Built Like a Bonfire: The *General Slocum* Disaster, June 15, 1904" by Ed O'Donnell. © 2001. Reprinted by permission of the author.

"The City of My Dreams" and "The City Awakes" from *The Color of a Great City* by Theodore Dreiser. Reprinted by permission of Harold J. Dies, Trustee, The Dreiser Estate.

"Ferryslip" and "Steamroller" from *Manhattan Transfer* by John Dos Passos. Copyright © 1925 renewed by John Dos Passos 1953. Reprinted by permission of Lucy Dos Passos Coggin.

"Arrangement in Black and White," copyright 1927, renewed 1955 by Dorothy Parker. Originally appeared in *The New Yorker Magazine,* from *The Portable Dorothy Parker* by Dorothy Parker. Used by permission of Viking Penguin, a division of Penguin Putnam, Inc.

"General Retrospect and Summary" from *The Graphic Regional Plan of 1929.* Reprinted by permission of the Regional Plan Association.

"The Web and the Rock" by Thomas Wolfe copyright © 1939 by Maxwell Perkins as Executor, Estate of Thomas Wolfe. Reprinted by permission of Eugene Winick, Administrator C.T.A.

"Only the Dead Know Brooklyn" by Thomas Wolfe copyright © 1935 by Charles Scribner's Sons. Reprinted by permission of Eugene Winick, Administrator C.T.A.

"Harlem Runs Wild" by Claude McKay. Reprinted with permission from the April 3, 1935, issue of *The Nation.*

"New York" by Marianne Moore. Reprinted with the permission of Simon and Schuster from *The Collected Poems of Marianne Moore.* Copyright 1935 by Marianne Moore; copyright renewed © 1963 by Marianne Moore and T. S. Eliot.

"The Man-Moth" from *The Complete Poems 1927–1977* by Elizabeth Bishop. Copyright © 1979, 1983 by Alice Helen Methfessel. Reprinted by permission of Farrar, Straus and Giroux, LLC.

Selection from *Going to the Territory* by Ralph Ellison. Copyright © 1986 by Ralph Ellison. Reprinted by permission of Random House, Inc.

"The Fourteenth Ward" from *Black Spring* by Henry Miller. Copyright © 1963 by Henry Miller. Used by permission of Grove/Atlantic, Inc.

"My Lost City" by F. Scott Fitzgerald, from *The Crack-Up*, copyright © 1945 by New Directions Publishing Corp. Reprinted by permission of New Directions Publishing Corp.

Excerpt from *When the Cathedrals Were White,* copyright 1947 by Harcourt, Inc., and renewed 1975 by Francis E. Hyslop Jr., reprinted by permission of the publisher.

"Apology for Breathing" from *Back Where I Came From* by A. J. Liebling. Copyright © 1938 by A. J. Liebling. Copyright renewed 1966 by Jean Stafford Liebling. Reprinted by permission of North Point Press, a division of Farrar, Straus and Giroux, LLC.

Excerpt from "The Mohawks in High Steel" from *Up in the Old Hotel* by Joseph Mitchell, copyright 1992 by Joseph Mitchell. Used by permission of Pantheon Books, a division of Random House, Inc.

"In Dreams Begin Responsibilities" by Delmore Schwartz, from *In Dreams Begin Responsibilities,* copyright © 1961 by Delmore Schwartz. Reprinted by permission of New Directions Publishing Corp.

"Ten Misconceptions of New York" by Fiorello La Guardia from the New York City Archives (1939)

"The Eighty Yard Run" reprinted with permission © 1942 Irwin Shaw. "The Eighty Yard Run" appears in *Short Stories of Five Decades,* published by the University of Chicago Press.

"The Making of a New Yorker" by John Steinbeck. Copyright © 1943 John Steinbeck. Reprinted by permission of McIntosh and Otis, Inc.

"Voice" by Woody Guthrie ca. 1945 appears courtesy of the Woody Guthrie Foundation and Archives.

Excerpt from "The Block and Beyond" in *A Walker in the City,* copyright 1951 and renewed 1979 by Alfred Kazin, reprinted by permission of Harcourt, Inc.

"A Place (Any Place) to Transcend All Places" by William Carlos Williams, from *Collected Poems 1939–1962, Volume II,* copyright © 1948 by William Carlos Williams. Reprinted by permission of New Directions Publishing Corp.

"Here Is New York" by E. B. White. Copyright © 1949 by E. B. White. Reprinted by permission of International Creative Management, Inc.

"Harlem" from *Collected Poems* by Langston Hughes. Copyright © 1994 by the Estate of Langston Hughes. Reprinted by permission of Alfred A. Knopf, a division of Random House, Inc.

"When the Negro Was in Vogue" from *The Big Sea* by Langston Hughes. Copyright © 1940 by Langston Hughes. Copyright renewed 1968 by Arna Bontemps and George Houston Bass. Reprinted by permission of Hill and Wang, a division of Farrar, Straus and Giroux, LLC.

"The King of Harlem" by Frederico Garcia Lorca, translated by Stephen Spender and J. L. Gili, from *The Selected Poems of Frederico Garcia Lorca,* copyright © 1955 by New Directions Publishing Corp. Reprinted by permission of New Directions Publishing Corp.

"Angel Levine" from *The Stories of Bernard Malamud* by Bernard Malamud. Copyright © 1983 by Bernard Malamud. Reprinted by permission of Farrar, Straus and Giroux, LLC.

"The Day Lady Died" from *Lunch Poems* by Frank O'Hara. Copyright 1964 by Frank O'Hara. Reprinted by permission of *City Lights Books.*

"Fifth Avenue Uptown: A Letter from Harlem" © 1961 by James Baldwin originally appeared in *Esquire.* Copyright renewed. Collected in *Nobody Knows My Name,* published by Vintage Books. Reprinted by arrangement with the James Baldwin Estate.

"New York Scenes" from *Lonesome Traveller* by Jack Kerouac reprinted by permission of Sterling Lord Literistic, Inc. Copyright 1988 by Estate of Jan Kerouac.

Excerpt from *POPism: The Warhol '60's,* copyright © 1980 by Andy Warhol, reprinted by permission of Harcourt, Inc.

"The Balloon" by Donald Barthelme copyright © 1981 Donald Barthelme, reprinted with the permission of The Wylie Agency, Inc.

"Introduction and Summary" from *The Second Regional Plan.* Reprinted with the permission of the Regional Plan Association.

"Goodbye to All That" from *Slouching Towards Bethlehem* by Joan Didion. Copyright © 1966, 1968, renewed 1996 by Joan Didion. Reprinted by permission of Farrar, Straus and Giroux, LLC.

"The Yankees" by Bruce Catton from *New York, N.Y.* Copyright © 1968 by American Heritage Publishing Co. Published by American Heritage Publishing Co., Inc.

"Bedford-Stuyvesant: Giving a Damn About Hell" from *Robert Kennedy: A Memoir* © 1988 by Jack Newfield. Reprinted with the permission of the author.

Excerpt from "Radical Chic" from *Radical Chic and Mau-Mauing the Flak Catchers* by Tom Wolfe. Copyright © 1970 by Tom Wolfe. Reprinted by permission of Farrar, Straus and Giroux, LLC.

"The Fallen Idol: The Harlem Tragedy of Earl Manigault" from *The City Game* by Pete Axthelm. Reprinted by permission of Sterling Lord Literistic, Inc. Copyright by Robert T. Abbott.

"Ode to New York" from *The Past, the Future, the Present* by Reed Whittemore. Reprinted with the permission of the author.

"New York" by Edward Field was published in the *New and Selected Poems* by The Sheep Meadow Press. Reprinted with the permission of the author.

"The Brooklyn Bridge" from *Sketches from Life* by Lewis Mumford, copyright © 1982 by Lewis Mumford. Used by permission of Doubleday, a division of Random House, Inc.

"It's Six A.M. Do You Know Where You Are?" reprinted by permission of International Creative Management, Inc. Copyright © 1982 by Jay McInerney.

"Boodling, Bigotry, and Cosmopolitanism" by Jim Sleeper reprinted with the permission of the author. This essay was first published in "In Search of New York," a special issue of *Dissent* magazine edited by Jim Sleeper and republished in 1989 by Transaction Publishers, New Brunswick, N.J.

"Auggie Wren's Christmas Story" by Paul Auster reprinted with the permission of the author. Copyright © Paul Auster; first appeared in *The New York Times* December 25, 1990.

"Autumn in New York" from *Rebellions, Perversities and Main Events* by Murray Kempton, copyright © 1994 by Murray Kempton. Used by permission of Times Books, a division of Random House, Inc.

"Manhattan, 1976" from *About This Life* by Barry Lopez. Copyright © 1998 by Barry Lopez. Reprinted by permission of Alfred A. Knopf, a division of Random House, Inc.

"Shot: A New York Story" by Elizabeth Hardwick reprinted with the permission of the author. This story first published in *The New Yorker.*

"Talk That Talk" excerpted and reprinted from *In the Place to Be: Guy Trebay's New York* by Guy Trebay, by permission of Temple University Press. © 1994 by Guy Trebay. All Rights Reserved.

"A Region at Risk" from *The Third Regional Plan* reprinted with the permission of the Regional Plan Association.

"One Large Garlic and Anchovy: The Search for the Perfect Slice" by Michael Nadler reprinted with the permission of the author.

"The Agenda for Permanent Change: The Second Inaugural Address 1/1/98" by Rudolph Giuliani appears with the permission of the author.

"Someplace in Queens" by Ian Frazier appears with the permission of the author. The essay first appeared in *The New Yorker.*

"The Midnight Tour" by Marcus Laffey appears with the permission of the author. The essay first appeared in *The New Yorker.* Marcus Laffey is the pseudonym of an officer in the NYPD. His book *Blue Blood* is due to be published by Riverhead Books.

"Down and Out and Up Again" by Lee Stringer appears with the permission of the author. This walk is one of 23 walks in the *Time Out Book of New York Walks,* published by Penguin Putnam.

"The Synthetic Sublime" by Cynthia Ozick from *Quarrel & Quandary* by Cynthia Ozick, copyright © 2000 by Cynthia Ozick. Used by permission of Alfred A. Knopf, a division of Random House, Inc.

"New York: Science Fiction" by Junot Diaz appears with the permission of the author.

"The Resilient City" by John P. Avlon appears with the permission of the author.

INDEX